c.1

Contemporary literary
criticism.

Contemporary
Literary Criticism

Yearbook 1989

Guide to Gale Literary Criticism Series

When you need to review criticism of literary works, these are the Gale series to use:

If the author's death date is:	You should turn to:
After Dec. 31, 1959 (or author is still living)	***CONTEMPORARY LITERARY CRITICISM*** for example: Jorge Luis Borges, Anthony Burgess, William Faulkner, Mary Gordon, Ernest Hemingway, Iris Murdoch
1900 through 1959	***TWENTIETH-CENTURY LITERARY CRITICISM*** for example: Willa Cather, F. Scott Fitzgerald, Henry James, Mark Twain, Virginia Woolf
1800 through 1899	***NINETEENTH-CENTURY LITERATURE CRITICISM*** for example: Fedor Dostoevski, Nathaniel Hawthorne, George Sand, William Wordsworth
1400 through 1799	***LITERATURE CRITICISM FROM 1400 TO 1800 (excluding Shakespeare)*** for example: Anne Bradstreet, Daniel Defoe, Alexander Pope, François Rabelais, Jonathan Swift, Phillis Wheatley ***SHAKESPEAREAN CRITICISM*** Shakespeare's plays and poetry
Antiquity through 1399	***CLASSICAL AND MEDIEVAL LITERATURE CRITICISM*** for example: Dante, Homer, Plato, Sophocles, Vergil, the Beowulf Poet

---

Gale also publishes related criticism series:

CHILDREN'S LITERATURE REVIEW

This series covers authors of all eras who have written for the preschool through high school audience.

SHORT STORY CRITICISM

This series covers the major short fiction writers of all nationalities and periods of literary history.

ISSN 0091-3421

Volume 59

Contemporary Literary Criticism

Yearbook 1989

The Year in Fiction, Poetry, Drama,
and World Literature and the Year's
New Authors, Prizewinners, Obituaries,
and Outstanding Literary Events

Roger Matuz
EDITOR

Cathy Falk
Mary K. Gillis
Sean R. Pollock
David Segal
Bridget Travers
Robyn V. Young
ASSOCIATE EDITORS

 *Gale Research Inc.* • DETROIT • NEW YORK
WASHINGTON, D.C. • CHICAGO • LONDON

STAFF

Roger Matuz, *Editor*

Cathy Falk, Mary K. Gillis, Sean R. Pollock, David Segal,
Bridget Travers, Robyn V. Young, *Associate Editors*

Susanne Skubik. Allyson J. Wylie, Shannon J. Young, *Assistant Editors*

Jeanne A. Gough, *Production & Permissions Manager*
Linda M. Pugliese, *Production Supervisor*
Jennifer Gale, David G. Oblender, Suzanne Powers, Maureen A. Puhl, Linda M. Ross, *Editorial Associates*
Donna Craft, *Editorial Assistant*

Victoria B. Cariappa, *Editorial Research Manager*
H. Nelson Fields, Judy L. Gale, Maureen Richards, *Editorial Associates*
Paula Cutcher, Alan Hedblad, Jill M. Ohorodnik, *Editorial Assistants*

Sandra C. Davis, *Permissions Supervisor (Text)*
Josephine M. Keene, Kimberly F. Smilay, *Permissions Associates*
Maria L. Franklin, Michele Lonoconus, Camille P. Robinson,
Shalice Shah, Denise M. Singleton, Rebecca A. Stanko, *Permissions Assistants*

Patricia A. Seefelt, *Permissions Supervisor (Pictures)*
Margaret A. Chamberlain, *Permissions Associate*
Pamela A. Hayes, Lillian Quickley, *Permissions Assistants*

Mary Beth Trimper, *Production Manager*
Marilyn Jackman, *External Production Assistant*

Art Chartow, *Art Director*
C. J. Jonik, *Keyliner*

Laura Bryant, *Production Supervisor*
Louise Gagné, *Internal Production Associate*

The paper used in this publication meets the minimum requirements
of American National Standard for Information Sciences—Permanence
Paper for Printed Library Materials, ANSI Z39.48-1984.

Copyright © 1990
Gale Research Inc.
835 Penobscot Bldg.
Detroit, MI 48226-4094

Library of Congress Catalog Card Number 76-38938
ISBN 0-8103-4433-5
ISSN 0091-3421

Printed in the United States of America

Published simultaneously in the United Kingdom
by Gale Research International Limited
(An affiliated company of Gale Research Inc.)

Contents

Preface vii

Acknowledgments xi

Authors Forthcoming in *CLC* xvii

Preface

Scope

Contemporary Literary Criticism Yearbook is part of the ongoing *Contemporary Literary Criticism (CLC)* series. *CLC* provides a comprehensive survey of modern literature by presenting excerpted criticism on the works of novelists, poets, playwrights, short story writers, scriptwriters, and other creative writers now living or who died after December 31, 1959. A strong emphasis is placed on including criticism of works by established authors who frequently appear on syllabuses of high school and college literature courses.

To complement this broad coverage, the *Yearbook* focuses more specifically on a given year's literary activities and highlights a larger number of currently noteworthy authors than is possible in standard *CLC* volumes. *CLC Yearbook* provides students, teachers, librarians, researchers, and general readers with information and commentary on the outstanding literary works and events of a given year.

Highlights of *CLC*, Volume 59: *Yearbook 1989* include:

☞ Extensive coverage of the unprecedented international controversy surrounding Salman Rushdie's novel, *The Satanic Verses*, with viewpoints representing diverse factions in this intense debate.

☞ Reprinted criticism spanning the entire career of 1989 Nobel laureate Camilo José Cela.

☞ Critical commentary, from the earliest reviews to recent essays, to commemorate the fiftieth anniversary of the publication of John Steinbeck's novel, *The Grapes of Wrath*.

☞ Numerous reviews of such popular and critically acclaimed works as Amy Tan's *The Joy Luck Club*, Anne Tyler's *Breathing Lessons*, and Wendy Wasserstein's *The Heidi Chronicles*.

Format

CLC, Volume 59, *Yearbook 1989*, which includes excerpted criticism on more than forty authors and comprehensive coverage of four of the year's significant literary events, is divided into five sections—"The Year in Review," "New Authors," "Prizewinners," "In Memoriam," and "Topics in Literature: 1989."

● **The Year in Review**—This section consists of specially commissioned essays by prominent writers who survey the year's works in their respective fields. Wendy Lesser discusses "The Year in Fiction," Sidney Burris "The Year in Poetry," Robert Cohen "The Year in Drama," and William Riggan "The Year in World Literature." For introductions to the essayists, please see Notes on Contributors, page 30.

● **New Authors**—*CLC Yearbook 1989* introduces fourteen writers who published their first book during 1989. Authors were selected for inclusion if their work was reviewed in several prominent literary periodicals.

● **Prizewinners**—This section commences with a list of literary prizes and honors announced in 1989, citing the award, award criteria, the recipient, and title of the prizewinning work. Following the listing of prizewinners is a presentation of thirteen entries on individual award winners, representing a mixture of genres and nationalities as well as established prizes and those more recently introduced.

● **In Memoriam**—This section consists of reminiscences, tributes, retrospective articles, and obituary notices on eight authors who died in 1989. In addition, a five-page Obituary section provides information on sixteen other recently deceased literary figures.

● **Topics in Literature**—This section focuses on literary issues and events of wide public interest, as evidenced in extensive multimedia coverage. The entry on the *Satanic Verses* controversy broadens coverage of this topic provided in *Contemporary Literary Criticism*, Volume 55, *Yearbook 1988*; combined, the two entries offer over 90,000 words and comments by over two hundred political leaders, authors, and religious figures. In "*Glasnost* and Soviet Literature," commentators explore how writers have influenced and have been affected by the massive cultural, political, and social changes occurring in the Soviet Union. Also featured in this section are four teenaged playwrights whose works were performed as part of the Young Playwrights Festival, an annual event open to American youths.

Features

With the exception of the four essays in "The Year in Review" section, which are written specifically for this publication, the *Yearbook* consists of excerpted criticism. There are approximately four hundred individual excerpts in *CLC Yearbook 1989*, drawn from literary reviews, general magazines, newspapers, books, and scholarly journals. *Yearbook* entries variously contain the following items:

- An **author heading** in the "New Authors" and "Prizewinners" sections cites the name under which an author publishes and the title of the work covered in the entry; the "In Memoriam" section includes the author's name and birth and death dates. The author's full name, pseudonyms (if any) under which the author has published, nationality, and principal genres in which the author writes are listed on the first line of the author entry.

- The **subject heading** defines the theme of each entry in "The Year in Review" and "Topics in Literature" sections.

- A brief biographical and critical introduction to the author and his or her work precedes excerpted criticism in the "New Authors" and "Prizewinners" sections; the subjects, authors, and works in the "Topics in Literature" section are introduced in a similar manner.

- A listing of **principal works** is included for all entries in the "Prizewinners" section.

- **Cross-references** have been included in all sections, except "The Year in Review," to direct readers to other useful sources published by Gale Research: *Short Story Criticism* and *Children's Literature Review*, which provide excerpts of criticism on the works of short story writers and authors of children's books, respectively; *Contemporary Authors*, which includes detailed biographical and bibliographical sketches on more than 95,000 authors; *Something about the Author*, which contains heavily illustrated biographical sketches of writers and illustrators who create books for children and young adults; *Dictionary of Literary Biography*, which provides original evaluations and detailed biographies of authors important to literary history; and *Contemporary Authors Autobiography Series* and *Something about the Author Autobiography Series*, which present autobiographical essays by prominent writers of adult literature and those of interest to young readers, respectively. Previous volumes of *CLC* in which the author has been featured are also listed.

- A **portrait** of the author is included in the "New Authors," "Prizewinners," "In Memoriam," and "Topics in Literature" sections, and **an excerpt from the author's work**, if available, provides readers with a sampling of the writer's style and thematic approach in the "New Authors," "Prizewinners," and "Topics in Literature" sections.

- The **excerpted criticism**, included in all entries except those in the "Year in Review" section, represents essays selected by editors to reflect the spectrum of opinion about a specific work or about the author's writing in general. The excerpts are arranged chronologically, adding a useful perspective to the entry. All titles by the author are printed in boldface type, enabling the reader to easily identify the work being discussed.

- A complete **bibliographical citation**, designed to help the user find the original essay or book, follows each excerpt.

Additional Features

- A list of **Authors Forthcoming in *CLC*** previews the authors to be researched for future volumes.

- An **Acknowledgments** section lists the copyright holders who have granted permission to reprint material in this volume of *CLC*. It does not, however, list every book or periodical reprinted or consulted during the preparation of the volume.

- A **Cumulative Author Index** lists all the authors who have appeared in *CLC, Twentieth-Century Literary Criticism, Nineteenth-Century Literature Criticism, Literature Criticism from 1400 to 1800, Classical and Medieval Literature Criticism,* and *Short Story Criticism,* with cross-references to these Gale series: *Children's Literature Review, Contemporary Authors, Contemporary Authors Autobiography Series, Contemporary Authors Bibliographical Series, Dictionary of Literary Biography, Something about the Author, Something about the Author Autobiography Series, Yesterday's Authors of Books for Children,* and *Authors & Artists for Young Adults.* Readers will welcome this cumulated author index as a useful tool for locating an author within the various series. The index, which lists birth and death dates when available, will be particularly valuable for those authors who are identified with a certain period but whose death date causes them to be placed in another, or for those authors whose careers span two periods. For example, Ernest Hemingway is found in *CLC,* yet a writer often associated with him, F. Scott Fitzgerald, is found in *Twentieth-Century Literary Criticism.*

- A **Cumulative Nationality Index** alphabetically lists all authors featured in *CLC* by nationality, followed by numbers corresponding to the volumes in which the writers appear.

- A **Title Index** alphabetically lists all titles reviewed in the current volume of *CLC.* Listings are followed by the author's name and the corresponding page numbers where the titles are discussed. English translations of foreign titles and variations of titles are cross-referenced to the title under which a work was originally published. Titles of novels, novellas, dramas, films, record albums, and poetry, short story, and essay collections are printed in italics, while all individual poems, short stories, essays, and songs are printed in roman type within quotation marks; when published separately (e.g., T.S. Eliot's poem *The Waste Land*), the title will also be printed in italics.

- In response to numerous suggestions from librarians, Gale has also produced a **special paperbound edition** of the *CLC* title index. This annual cumulation, which alphabetically lists all titles reviewed in the series, is available to all customers and will be published with the first volume of *CLC* issued in each calendar year. Additional copies of the index are available upon request. Librarians and patrons will welcome this separate index: it saves shelf space, is easy to use, and is disposable upon receipt of the following year's cumulation.

A Note to the Reader

When writing papers, students who quote directly from any volume in the Literary Criticism Series may use the following general forms to footnote reprinted criticism. The first example pertains to material drawn from periodicals, the second to material reprinted from books:

[1]Anne Tyler, "Manic Monologue," *The New Republic* 200 (April 17, 1989), 44-6; excerpted and reprinted in *Contemporary Literary Criticism,* Vol. 58, ed. Roger Matuz (Detroit: Gale Research, 1990), p. 325.

[2]Patrick Reilly, *The Literature of Guilt: From 'Gulliver' to Golding* (University of Iowa Press, 1988); excerpted and reprinted in *Contemporary Literary Criticism,* Vol. 58, ed. Roger Matuz (Detroit: Gale Research, 1990), pp. 206-12.

Suggestions Are Welcome

The editors welcome the comments and suggestions of readers to expand the coverage and enhance the usefulness of the series. Please feel free to contact us by letter or by calling our toll-free number: 1-800-347-GALE.

Acknowledgments

The editors wish to thank the copyright holders of the excerpted criticism included in this volume, the permissions managers of many book and magazine publishing companies for assisting us in securing reprint rights, and Anthony Bogucki for assistance with copyright research. We are also grateful to the staffs of the Detroit Public Library, the Library of Congress, the University of Detroit Library, Wayne State University Purdy/Kresge Library Complex, and the University of Michigan Libraries for making their resources available to us. Following is a list of the copyright holders who have granted us permission to reprint material in this volume of *CLC*. Every effort has been made to trace copyright, but if omissions have been made, please let us know.

COPYRIGHTED EXCERPTS IN *CLC*, VOLUME 59, WERE REPRINTED FROM THE FOLLOWING PERIODICALS:

America, v. 160, June 17-24, 1989 for a review of "The One Day" by Daniel Mark Epstein. © 1989. All rights reserved. Reprinted by permission of the author.—*The American Book Review,* v. 11, March-April, 1989; v. 11, November-December, 1989. © 1989 by *The American Book Review.* All reprinted by permission of the publisher.—*American Literature,* v. 54, October, 1982. Copyright © 1982 Duke University Press, Durham, NC. Reprinted with permission of the publisher.—*The American Poetry Review,* v. 18, January-February, 1989 for an interview with Liam Rector by Donald Hall; v. 18, May-June, 1989 for "The Journey to Celebration in McGrath's Poetry" by Dale Jacobson. Copyright © 1989 by World Poetry, Inc. Reprinted by permission of the respective authors.—*The American Spectator,* v. 22, October, 1989. Copyright © *The American Spectator.* 1989. Reprinted by permission of the publisher.— *The Antigonish Review,* n. 73, Spring, 1988 for a review of "Nights Below Station Street" by Sheldon Currie. Copyright 1988 by the author. Reprinted by permission of the publisher and the author.—*The Antioch Review,* v. 46, Spring, 1988; v. 47, Summer, 1989. Copyright © 1988, 1989 by the Antioch Review Inc. Reprinted by permission of the Editors.—*Atlantic Monthly,* v. 178, August, 1946 for "American Novelists in French Eyes" by Jean-Paul Sartre. Copyright 1946, renewed 1974 by The Atlantic Monthly Company, Boston, MA.—*Audubon,* v. 91, July, 1989. Copyright © 1989 by the National Audubon Society. Reprinted by permission of the publisher.—*Barron's,* v. LXIX, May 15, 1989. Copyright © Dow Jones & Company, Inc. 1989. Reprinted by permission of the publisher.—*Black American Literature Forum,* v. 23, Spring, 1989 for "Sterling Brown Ain't Dead Nothing. . . .He Ain't Even Passed" by John F. Callahan. Copyright © 1989 John F. Callahan. Reprinted by permission of Indiana State University and the author./ v. 23, Spring, 1989 for "The New Negro Poet and the Nachal Man: Sterling Brown's Folk Odyssey" by John S. Wright. Copyright © 1989 Indiana State University. Reprinted by permission of Indiana State University and the author.—*The Bloomsbury Review,* v. 8, May-June, 1988 for an interview with James Salter by Robert Burke; v. 8, May-June, 1988 for "Life in Mid-Life" by Robert Burke. Copyright © by Owaissa Communications Company, Inc. 1988.—*Booklist,* v. 85, November 15, 1988. Copyright © 1988 by the American Library Association. Reprinted by permission of the publisher.—*Book World—Chicago Tribune,* May 28, 1989. Contents copyright © 1989 by the *Chicago Tribune.* Reprinted by courtesy of the *Chicago Tribune.—Book World—The Washington Post,* August 28, 1988; November 13, 1988; December 18, 1988; March 5, 1989; April 16, 1989; May 7, 1989; June 4, 1989; June 25, 1989; September 3, 1989. © 1988, 1989 *The Washington Post.* All reprinted by permission of the publisher.—*Books,* London, n. 19, October, 1988; n. 2, May, 1989. © Gradegate Ltd. 1988, 1989. Both reprinted by permission of the publisher.—*Books in Canada,* v. 17, May, 1988 for "Forrest and Town" by David Homel; v. 17, May, 1988 for "Violent River" by Douglas Glover. Both reprinted by permission of the respective authors.—*Boston Review,* v. XIII, October, 1988 for a review of "The One Day" by Stephen Sandy; v. XIV, December, 1989 for "They Had Been Wanting to Sing for Some Time" by Sonya Michel. Copyright © 1988, 1989 by the Boston Critic, Inc. Both reprinted by permission of the respective authors.—*Chicago Tribune,* December 27, 1989. © copyrighted 1989, Chicago Tribune Company. All rights reserved. Used with permission by the publisher.—*Chicago Tribune—Books,* August 28, 1988 for " 'Breathing Lessons': Anne Tyler's Tender Ode to Married Life' " by Hilma Wolitzer; November 20, 1988 for "A Fierce, Manic Wit Fuels Fay Weldon's Vivid, Rural Satire" by Melissa Pritchard; February 26, 1989 for "A Poet's Voyage to Mississippi" by James Idema; March 12, 1989 for "Mother's and Daughters" by Michael Dorris; April 23, 1989 for "The Lost Father" by Constance Markey; June 18, 1989 for "The Power of Winning" by Frederick Busch; June 25, 1989 for "Growing Up with a Father Who Was Truly Monstrous" by Maude McDaniel; July 2, 1989 for "Winter Losses" by William O'Rourke; July 16, 1989 for "First Novels Show Promise Beneath Stylistic Posturing" by David R. Slavitt; July 23, 1989 for "A Japanese Girl Wistfully Drifts Across America" by Gretel Ehrlich. © copyrighted 1988, 1989, Chicago Tribune Company. All rights reserved. All used with permission by the respective authors./ October 1, 1989. © copyrighted 1989, Chicago Tribune Company. All rights reserved. Used with permission.—*The Christian Century,* v. 106, April 5, 1989. Copyright 1989 Christian Century Foundation. Reprinted by permission from *The Christian Century.*— *The Christian Science Monitor,* April 27, 1989 for "Comedy About Aristocratic Irish Family's Hard Time Gets Admirable Staging" by John Beaufort; August 4, 1989 for "Mysteries: Modern Morality Plays" by B.J. Rahn. © 1989 The Christian Science Publishing Society. All rights reserved.

Authors Forthcoming in *CLC*

To Be Included in Volume 60

Douglas Adams (English novelist)—In his popular series of satirical novels beginning with *The Hitchhiker's Guide to the Galaxy,* Adams uses the devices of science fiction to lampoon modern culture. Adams blends slapstick and fantasy in his recent novels, *Dirk Gently's Holistic Detective Agency* and *The Long Dark Tea Time of the Soul,* to portray the unusual adventures of a private investigator.

Erskine Caldwell (American novelist and short story writer)—The author of such controversial Depression-era novels as *Tobacco Road* and *God's Little Acre,* Caldwell blended realism and comic pathos in his work to portray the desperate existence of poor Southerners.

Annie Dillard (American essayist and poet)—Dillard is best known for *Pilgrim at Tinker Creek,* her Pulitzer Prize-winning meditation on nature that critics have compared to Henry David Thoreau's *Walden.* She has also earned praise for her works of literary criticism, poetry, and autobiography.

Umberto Eco (Italian novelist and semiotician)—Acclaimed for his international best-seller *The Name of the Rose,* Eco has generated widespread interest with his recent mystery novel, *Foucault's Pendulum.* Spanning several centuries and exploring the nature of language and words, this work combines intrigue, autobiography, political commentary, and esoteric motifs.

Carlos Fuentes (Mexican novelist and essayist)—In his internationally acclaimed works, Fuentes often employs myth, legend, and history to examine Mexico's past and contemporary social and cultural issues. This entry will focus on his recent novel, *Christopher Unborn,* and *Myself with Others: Selected Essays.*

Shirley Jackson (American novelist and short story writer)—A prolific author, Jackson is generally known for such Gothic horror tales as "The Lottery" and *The Haunting of Hill House.* In lucid prose juxtaposing humor with intense psychological states and an atmosphere of foreboding, Jackson explores the dark side of human nature.

Harper Lee (American novelist)—Lee's Pulitzer Prize-winning novel *To Kill a Mockingbird,* which examines racial attitudes in the Deep South through the experiences of a young girl in a small Alabama town, will be the focus of this entry.

Anaïs Nin (French-born American diarist, novelist, and short story writer)—Nin is best known for the erotic pieces she wrote during the 1930s and 1940s and for her numerous books containing excerpts from her diaries. This entry will emphasize recent analyses of her work.

Molly Peacock (American poet)—In such collections as *Raw Heaven* and *Take Heart,* Peacock uses humor, unusual rhyme schemes, and contemplative tones to examine family bonds, love, and sexuality.

Kurt Vonnegut (American novelist and short story writer)—Widely regarded as a masterful contemporary writer, Vonnegut uses satire, irony, and iconoclastic humor to explore social values and the meaning of life. This entry will focus on *Slaughterhouse-Five; or, The Children's Crusade,* Vonnegut's absurdist novel about his experiences as a prisoner of war during the firebombing of Dresden, Germany, in World War II.

Nicholson Baker (American novelist)—Baker has received critical praise for his debut novel, *The Mezzanine,* a contemplative, detail-oriented work in which an escalator ride inspires revelations on the unexamined, seemingly trivial aspects of daily life.

Malcolm Bradbury (English novelist and critic)—A prolific author, Bradbury writes satirical novels about British and American university life in which he examines themes of social dislocation and liberalism.

Gillian Clarke (Welsh poet)—Considered an important new voice in contemporary Welsh poetry, Clarke utilizes traditional Celtic metrics that resonate throughout her primarily meditative verse. Clarke often employs these subtle sound and rhythmic patterns to explore the nature of female experience.

Maria Irene Fornés (Cuban-born American dramatist)—Winner of six Obie awards, Fornés is a leading off-Broadway dramatist. Although unconventional, her humorous, intelligent plays reflect such traditional concerns as human relationships and social and political corruption.

Larry Gelbart (American scriptwriter and dramatist)—Chief writer for the first five years of the television series "M*A*S*H," Gelbart has recently garnered praise for his comic plays *Mastergate*, a satire on the Iran-Contra scandal, and *City of Angels*, a parody of 1940s detective films.

Ernest Hemingway (American novelist and short story writer)—Recognized as one of the preeminent American authors of the twentieth century, Hemingway wrote powerful, terse narratives of disillusionment, personal loss, and stoic resolve in the face of an apparently meaningless world. Critical commentary in Hemingway's entry will focus upon his acclaimed novel, *The Sun Also Rises*.

Zora Neale Hurston (American novelist and short story writer)—Regarded as an important writer of the Harlem Renaissance, Hurston is respected for works that provide insights into black culture and the human condition. Hurston's entry will focus on her novel *Their Eyes Were Watching God*, which is enjoying renewed popularity through Women's Studies courses.

Jack Kerouac (American novelist)—Kerouac was a key figure in the artistic and cultural phenomenon known as the Beat Movement. This entry will focus on his novel *On the Road*, considered a quintessential work of Beat literature for its experimental form and its portrayal of a rebellious, hedonistic lifestyle.

Stephen King (American novelist and short story writer)—King is a prolific and popular author of horror fiction. Nonsupernatural in emphasis, King's recent novels include *Misery*, in which a bestselling writer is held captive by a psychotic nurse, and *The Dark Half*, about a pseudonymous author attempting to shed his persona who finds that his submerged alter-ego seeks revenge.

George F. Walker (Canadian dramatist)—Closely associated with the Factory Theater, a group that promotes alternative drama in Toronto, Walker writes social satires in which he employs black humor and a variety of unconventional theatrical devices. His recent play, *Nothing Sacred*, for which Walker received his second Governor General's Award, was popular in regional theaters in the United States and Canada.

The Year in Review

The Year in Fiction

by Wendy Lesser

1989 was, above all, the year of *The Satanic Verses.* Salman Rushdie's novel had been published in England in 1988, and had already met with a difficult reception there, including bookburning and rioting in the Muslim communities of Bradford and elsewhere. But it was not until the book came out in America in February, 1989 that the Ayatollah Khomeini demanded Rushdie's death and set a price on his head. Only in 1989 did readers see the amazing and terrifying spectacle of a threatened novelist appearing as front-page news day after day.

All of this has, in one way, nothing at all to do with the book, which Rushdie wrote as a work of art, and which only created such a noticeable disturbance because of the proclamation of a tyrant. And yet in another way it has everything to do with the novel, which is Rushdie's most personal book to date and, I think, his best. To someone reading *The Satanic Verses* during the uproar that surrounded it, as I was, it became clear that Rushdie had foreseen—fictionally, if not in his waking, normal life—exactly the effect this book would have. The book itself is *about* blasphemy, *about* the martyrdom of truth-tellers, *about* the conflicts between Eastern and Western, religious and secular, ancient and modern modes of thought. It is also very much about Rushdie's own situation as an Anglo-Indian, Muslim-raised British citizen. At least two of the book's characters, Gibreel Farishta and Saladin Chamcha, are avatars of Salman Rushdie himself; more minor characters, as well, share some of his characteristics. All of these people are treated with irony and distance, but also with affection, so that in the end Rushdie's own arrogance and ambition are criticized and tamed. The book is written in the most beautiful, lush English to be seen in fiction since Dickens, and it has some of Dickens's amazing vitality—as if the sentences were sinuous, powerful, flying dragons on which the author rides, only barely managing to keep his seat. But in the end each sentence lands safely (unlike the London-bound airplane carrying Farishta and Chamcha, which crashes at the beginning of the novel), and the reader heaves a gasp of admiration and delight that Rushdie has brought off the flight. The same could be said of the whole book, which will long endure as Rushdie's masterpiece, far outlasting the outcry that accompanied its publication.

Another great British achievement of the year is, like Rushdie's, not entirely British. Kazuo Ishiguro's third novel, *The Remains of the Day,* won the Booker Prize, and deservedly so. It is the first-person tale of Stevens, an English butler, told in restrained, dignified, humorless prose; the novel is set in the late 1950s, but mainly concerns the butler's memories of the service he rendered to his master, Lord Darlington, during the period immediately preceding the Second World War. What gradually emerges from Stevens's roundabout musings is that Darlington was a German sympathizer, a proponent of appeasement and perhaps even a traitor—a characterization which Stevens, with his emphasis on household detail and overriding loyalty, refuses to accept. He is thus the ultimate unreliable narrator, and though he is our only source of information, we come to know much more than he does—about his family relations and even his love life (or lack thereof) as well as about his history of service. Although he was raised in England, Ishiguro is of Japanese birth and ancestry, and his previous novels focus wholly or partly on the Japanese experience of World War II and its aftermath. What is wonderful about this novel is the way it takes essentially Japanese concerns—not only the interest in war-mongering and war-guilt, but also the emphasis on dignity, face-saving, covering over unpleasant truths, and preserving old rituals—and translates them perfectly into the concerns of an English butler. The prose, though beautifully restrained, is not entirely English; one catches lapses of grammar or custom here and there. But so does one with Conrad, another great British acquisition. And it doesn't really matter if Stevens sounds like a "real" English butler. The truths rendered by *The Remains of the Day* are larger than those of verisimilitude. They have to do with Ishiguro's ability to both depict and create feeling with enormous delicacy, to make us perceive a character simultaneously from the inside and the outside, with a little bit of amused distance but with a great deal of empathy as well.

Whereas Ishiguro is truly a master of delicate irony, Anita Brookner often only appears to be: her effects are frequently rather heavy-handed, her tortoise-losing-to-hare plots somewhat redundant. But *The Latecomers* is her best novel to date—in part, perhaps, because instead of giving us yet one more time the frustrated romantic yearnings of an overdressed woman, it focuses instead on the less specific longings of an exiled Jewish businessman in London. Fibich, compared to his jolly (also Jewish, also immigrant) business partner and best friend, is a pale, thin, passive creature, not obviously worthy of our sympathy. But the way this novel is presented (with less dialogue and event than in Brookner's other works, and with more summarized history, more flashback, more interior musing) favors the passive types like Fibich. It is he, finally, who suits the novel's tone best, and it is he who earns its moments of realization and recognition when he decides to revisit his homeland toward the end. Although Brookner focuses lovingly on the furnishings of the business partners' various apartments and the clothes their wives wear, such details are less essential to this book than to her earlier ones. *The Latecomers* is, for once, a novel more about substance and memory than about style and event.

Kingsley Amis can't publish a great book every year, and *The Old Devils* (which came out a few years ago) was so good that it may take him a few years to work up to that level again. But this year's *Difficulties with Girls* is a far better comic novel than most reviewers suggested. It is not *Lucky Jim—*

but then what else is? In **Difficulties with Girls,** Amis revisits the characters he introduced in *Take a Girl like You,* this time transplanted to a London life of publishing careers and furtive adulteries. The plot is thin, and the wife's pregnancy at the end (necessary to bring home the wandering husband) is a hackneyed and unsatisfying conclusion, but sentence by sentence this novel contains some of Amis's best humor. Amis is, of course, the master of the bad-tempered send-up, and I especially loved the publishing party near the beginning of the book; the hateful modern poets were priceless. The weird character who for no apparent reason fears he may be homosexual is also quite good and gets to play a scene of Amis's incomparable physical humor. Kingsley Amis has taken a lot of flack for being nasty about women, Americans, and homosexuals; in this novel he goes for all three (sometimes in combination, as when the main character keeps asking a particularly obnoxious woman, "Are you *sure* you're not American?"). But there is a certain kind of humor that cannot exist without such nastiness, and in Amis it's never exclusively at the expense of the victims. The perpetrators of this bitter laughter are often his most hateful characters, and acknowledgedly so.

No matter how grumpy Kingsley Amis is, one derives pleasure from his irritation. The same cannot be said for his son Martin, who published **London Fields** in England this year (it comes out in America in 1990) to critical acclaim and enormous sales. I am not a great Martin Amis fan, in part because I keep comparing him unfairly to his father. But it does seem to me that if you compare him to someone else—say, Salman Rushdie, to whom critics often link him as one of the great new "wild," "untrammeled" English writers—you can see his serious shortcomings. If Rushdie's sentences are flying dragons on which he rides, Martin Amis's are poor, beaten slaves who have been whipped unmercifully from beginning to end. There's no sense of joy, of revelry, of release in his writing; there's only "play" in the tedious, academic sense of punning and self-referentiality. Every recent Amis novel has allusions to the author (*Money* actually has a character named Martin Amis, as well as one with the last name Self), and this one has a walk-on part in the form of the successful, famous, lady-killing British writer Mark Asprey. But the main characters here are a deadly quadrangle: the narrator (one Samson Young, an American Jew in London), a lower-class lout named Keith Talent, an upper-class prig named Guy Clinch, and a smart, slutty *femme fatale* named Nicola Six (alternately pronounced "sex" and "cease"). Psychic Nicola foresees her own death by murder, and the problem of the novel is to figure out which one of the other guys (no pun intended) is going to do it. Along the way we get lots of complaints about the decline of modern England and the after-effects of a nuclear holocaust, as well as some passing remarks about child abuse, pub-cruising, burglary, and the generally unattractive habits of poor people. This book is offensive in the least literary way—it's just nasty, without the vibrant, self-mocking, language-loving pay-offs we get from Amis *pere.* And the fact that the narrator ends up being the murderer should suggest to Amis *fils* his own biggest problem: with his overweening reliance on authorial control, he's in danger of killing off all of his characters.

Martin Amis's novel at least filled me with distaste; far worse is Margaret Drabble's latest book, which leaves one with no feeling at all. **Natural Curiosity** is a trumped-up sequel to her more successful *Radiant Way,* following the same three female friends, plus assorted acquaintances and relatives,

through the next half-decade of their lives. Perhaps because she expects us to have read the first volume, Drabble doesn't bother to flesh out her characters at all. They get, at most, a sentence of stereotypical classification (sometimes repeated later in the novel, in case we've forgotten who they are), and then we're off and running into the story. Wildly melodramatic, the plot includes the homelife of an axe-murderer, the sudden death of a poet laureate, the suicide of a small-time businessman, and the resultant Parisian spree of his sprung-loose widow. *The Radiant Way* begins with a big party, and this book ends with one: it's Drabble's way of getting all the characters together onstage at once so we can see the lines of relationship crossing and tangling. But an author owes us more than a serve-yourself bash, and in this case Drabble gives us little else. Like Martin Amis, but far more perfunctorily, she tries to comment trenchantly on the state of Thatcherite England. But such commentary may not be as easy as modern British novelists apparently think it is. Only history that's had time to age a little, as in **The Remains of the Day** or *The Latecomers,* can be absorbed comfortably into the texture of fiction. It takes a visionary master like Salman Rushdie to chronicle contemporary events even before they happen.

Sometimes one conveys the present best by duplicating the past. David Lodge's highly enjoyable new novel, **Nice Work,** is a rewrite of the British nineteenth-century "industrial novel," along the lines of Elizabeth Gaskell's *North and South* or Dickens's *Hard Times.* Such texts, in fact, appear on the reading list of a character in **Nice Work,** the young academic Robyn Penrose, who doesn't believe in literary characters and yet is one herself. Her unexpected partner in this industrial romance is a local businessman in the northern factory town that houses her university (the Rummidge of Lodge's previous satires). The two of them fall in love, and, through a series of *deux ex machina* Victorian devices, get rewarded with a happy ending. All this sounds very artificial, no doubt, but in Lodge's hands it can be both moving and fun. And the book, in passing, manages to illuminate not only the current state of literary studies but also the current landscape of British industry. An economist friend of mine, who enjoyed the novel as much as I did, commented that the descriptions of factories could only have come from either England or America, where industrial design is still, in most respects, in the nineteenth century. So the mock-Victorian form of the novel turns out to be distinctly suited to its subject.

John le Carré, whose best work (among living British writers) is inferior only to that of Graham Greene, gave us a half-hearted but well-intentioned effort this year in the form of **The Russia House.** Good le Carré, like *The Spy Who Came In from the Cold* or the Smiley series or *The Perfect Spy,* depends upon the sense of the intimate enemy, the betraying forces with which one must nonetheless ally oneself. Unfortunately, history has overtaken this interesting idea, and at this point even nonliterate heads of state realize that our best allies may now be our former Cold War enemies. The miraculous political events of 1989, a year which—in Eastern Europe, at least—has turned out to be a sort of 1848 revisited, have reduced le Carré's notions to something between meaninglessness and cliché. Written to celebrate (though mordantly, as one might expect of a le Carré celebration) the arrival of glasnost, **The Russia House** was dated before it even came out. Despite an interesting female character and some nicely detailed Russian settings, this is definitely minor le Carré.

Paul Theroux, at this point in his transatlantic career, falls somewhere between being an English and an American novelist, and his 1989 book *My Secret History* is very much a conglomerate venture. Not only does it lead its autobiographically-based central character, Andre Parent, from a childhood near Boston to a Peace Corps youth in Africa to married adulthood in England, it also amalgamates the two forms—novelistic fiction and nonfiction travel writing—for which Theroux has previously been known. But here, instead of the simulated objectivity of Theroux's travel books (which are really frank expressions of his subjective feelings), we get the "secret history," the private life that was dictating the public perceptions in each location. And instead of the gauze of distance that fiction usually draws over the characters, we get the author's own secrets, himself as a creature exposed and criticized. Parent has many character flaws (of which his author is fully and no doubt guiltily aware), but the main one is his obsessive womanizing. It is one of this novel's chief virtues that it manages to give Parent something like a fair comeuppance without seeming either aesthetically rigged or unpleasantly moralistic. *My Secret History* is not quite Theroux at his best (for that one has to look back to *The Family Arsenal*), but it is still very good indeed.

A pleasant surprise to those who haven't particularly admired E. L. Doctorow's historical pastiches came this year

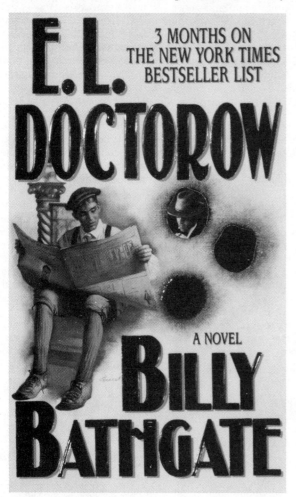

Cover of Billy Bathgate, *by E.L. Doctorow. Cover art by Ron Lesser.*

in the form of *Billy Bathgate,* his latest contribution to the genre he virtually invented. What works in this book's favor is that its historical figure, the gangster Dutch Schultz, might just as well have been invented: it doesn't matter to the plot, really, that he actually existed. This novel is true to the lived detail of the life of its time—to the ghetto life of 1930s New York, to the races at Saratoga, and to the ritualized power plays of the hoods surrounding a character like Dutch Schultz. The eponymous narrator is a Bronx boy who, during one summer, gets drawn into Schultz's gang and is eventually present at his death. *Billy Bathgate* includes a tour de force scene of a doomed gangster having his feet set in cement, a wonderfully choreographed getaway for an endangered lady, a quite touching relationship between the teenage narrator and his beloved crazy mother (they enjoy eating at Schrafft's together), and the most remarkable accountant ever to hit fiction—one Abba Dabba Berman, a man who trusts only numbers. He alone would make the book worth reading, but he doesn't need to stand on his own: Doctorow's oceanic sentences and complexly pieced-together plot fully support him and the other characters and make this by far Doctorow's best novel to date.

Another very satisfying accomplishment is Russell Banks's *Affliction.* I had very mixed feelings about Banks's previous novel, *Continental Drift,* which welded together the story of a New England working-class man (very well portrayed) and the story of a Haitian refugee woman (very badly portrayed). In *Affliction,* it's as if he had developed only the good parts of *Continental Drift,* cutting out the pompously overblown authorial pronouncements and the condescendingly presented characters, and ending up with only a core of absolute truth from which to generate a whole story. This novel about a rather ordinary man's inexplicable but carefully detailed violence is both intense and restrained. It builds unbearably toward its climax (which, perhaps predictably, is its least satisfying moment) and insists we submit to its emotional pull. Interestingly, the novel is told from the view of the primary character's rather prissy, uninvolved brother—a device that some critics found objectionable but which I consider one of the book's central virtues. For *Affliction* turns out, in part, to be about the effort to reach inside minds unlike one's own, its violence viewed as something we displace onto a few people so we don't all have to commit it. The novel is also about the emotional, imaginative power of violence and the potential emotional coldness inherent in its renunciation—for the narrating brother too becomes a character and is finally as despicable (in his own way) as the man he sets out to describe.

Another man-in-violent-conflict-with-the-world novel is John Casey's *Spartina,* which won both the National Book Award and the Pulitzer Prize this year. The chronicle of Dick Pierce, a Block Island fisherman whose family has come down in the world and who longs for nothing so much as to build and then captain his own fishing boat, *Spartina* is often just that—a chronicle. Although competently written on the sentence level and filled with accurate detail about fishing and sailing, the novel has almost no narrative momentum. There are a few adulterous love affairs and an illegitimate baby to spice things up, but even they sink into the general rhythm of the oceanside daily life. This is what, in a less gender-charged time, I might casually have described as a "man's novel"—or more accurately a boys' adventure story, where the thrill of the book comes mainly from the way the protagonist challenges himself and proves himself against nature. It left me cold but respectful of Casey's skill.

A surprise hit of the year, and a big financial winner for its first-time-out author, was Amy Tan's *Joy Luck Club.* Despite its bestseller status, this is a good book. It does for Chinese-Americans what the first wave of Jewish-American writing—Malamud, Bellow, Henry Roth—did for their population. That is, it creates a version of written English that partakes of the "home" language (in this case, Chinese) and at the same time comes across as vibrantly American. Amy Tan's tale of four mothers from the old country and their four very Americanized daughters rings true to the little I know about the San Francisco Chinese community. The mother sections (many of them fantastical or historical sequences set in China) have a slight echo of Maxine Hong Kingston, but the daughter sequences feel totally original, especially in the way they convey the absolutely uncompromising harshness of the Chinese mothers. There is a tone here I've not found in any other writing, a relationship to feeling that is tougher and more hard-edged than what one usually finds in "ethnic" family tales. Tan's writing already has a polish that makes one a bit suspicious, as if learning to do things well has been too easy for her, but if she refuses to rest on her laurels and instead continues learning, she will produce a series of admirable books.

Another very appealing first novel is Jane Vandenburgh's *Failure to Zigzag.* Unlike Tan's, this book received no major prizes and earned no great sums of money. But it is one of those rare items in fiction—a family saga which is simultaneously horrifying and hilarious. The novel tells the story of Charlotte, a Southern California adolescent; Katrinka, her schizophrenic and frequently hospitalized mother; and her even crazier (but still functional, and therefore not hospital-

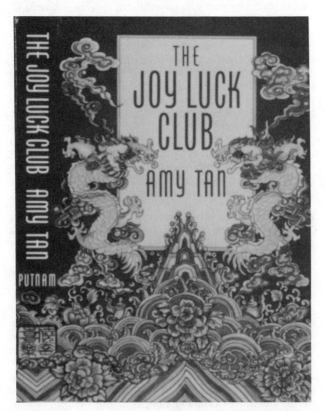

Dust jacket of The Joy Luck Club, *by Amy Tan. Copyright © 1989 by Amy Tan. Jacket illustration © 1989 Gretchen Schields.*

ized) grandparents. Katrinka is a marvelous character, destructive but entertaining, with an outrageous, pertinent remark to meet every situation and a talent for ventriloquism (obtained, we gather, through her experiences with imaginary voices in her head) that she occasionally uses to support herself in sideshows. The story of what happened to Charlotte's father—whether he was a war hero, as the family claims, or died under more suspicious circumstances—is the suspenseful thread that keeps the novel moving, but its real power lies in the depictions of family relationships. The book reminded me a little of Christina Stead's *The Man Who Loved Children,* another neglected classic which suggested the way craziness and normality can mingle in all families.

Family relationships and special kinds of craziness—though at a far less extreme level than in *Failure to Zigzag*—are also among the themes of Brad Leithauser's second novel, *Hence.* Better known as a poet and book critic than as a novelist, Leithauser has the kind of cleverness and eye for specifics that one would expect of a writer of his diverse accomplishments. *Hence* is, in part, the story of a young chess prodigy trying to beat an MIT-programmed computer during a period of history shortly in advance of our own (a few years "hence," that is). Like *Affliction, Hence* is narrated by the cold-fish brother of the overheated protaganist. But Leithauser makes much more of a big deal out of this narrative ploy than Banks does—in fact, his novel ends up switching narrators on us in midstream, mixing up the issue of author and narrator and emphasizing its role as a printed artifact, a published book. All this is actually quite amusing, although in less skilled hands it could easily be irritating. While the ending of the novel doesn't, for me, live up to its beginning, *Hence* is still among Leithauser's most accomplished productions to date.

Families are also important in the story collection *Total Immersion,* the first work by twenty-one-year-old Allegra Goodman. This book deserves note not only because of the author's youth, but also because of her even more surprising skill: many of the stories here seem the work of a middle-aged master. What ties them together is, for the most part, their Jewishness: they track the oddly unassimilated lives of Jewish characters in Hawaii, in California, on the East Coast, and in England. (There is, however, also one tale about an Asian girl in Hawaii.) Some of the characters traipse through various stories, so that the book as a whole almost has the feel of an embryonic novel. What is unusual here is Goodman's capacity for getting inside the minds of people totally unlike herself: the crazy woman, for instance, is done as sympathetically as the young husband or the aging grandmother. The prose is precise and unusual: Yiddish, Hebrew, and Hawaiian words sprinkle the text as if we are meant to understand them, and therefore we do. Like Tan's work, *Total Immersion* breaks new ground for a cultural sub-community—in this case, the Jews of Hawaii.

The Jews of the rest of America once again see themselves reflected in Saul Bellow's *The Bellarosa Connection.* This novella (it's only 102 pages) is not vintage Bellow, but even Bellow at his most half-hearted is worth reading. The present tale, told by a mnemonist, recounts the life of a relative who was saved from the Nazis by Billy Rose's network in Italy (hence the misheard words of the title). Bellow refrains from overworking the connections between memory and the Holocaust, but the device itself is already a little clichéd, and what is best about this story is the fat, intelligent wife of the man

Dust jacket of Failure to Zigzag, *by Jane Vandenburgh. Jacket illustration by Claire McQueeney. Jacket design by David Bullen.*

who was saved—she evokes some of Bellow's best and most characteristic writing. Like Goodman's collection, this book is in part about assimilation and non-assimilation, for the narrator has become the closest thing possible to a WASP, and his immigrant relatives therefore embarrass him. The book feels the wrong length to me: it had the potential to become a full-length novel if it were fleshed out, but with this amount of material it probably should have rested satisfied with being a short story.

Novellas were big this year, though. Two of the best are contained in Jane Smiley's collection, **Ordinary Love and Good Will.** Smiley has already shown herself to be a master of the mid-length form in *The Age of Grief,* and these two should further her reputation. The first, **Ordinary Love,** is the story of a woman who left her husband and five children when she had a brief love affair and is now trying to pull the family back together after twenty years. This is the weaker of the two novellas in that it depends for its emotion on a kind of pathos of regret. Can she ever rectify the wrong she did her children? How responsible do they hold her for their subsequent sufferings as children and adults? Did she have a choice in shaping her life? Such questions hover in the background of the story, interfering with the marvelously rendered detail of daily family life at which Smiley so excels. But the second

novella, **Good Will,** not only has a tense power of its own but reflects back over the first story, improving it in retrospect. **Good Will** describes the extremely circumscribed, carefully wrought life of a back-to-the-earth farmer who utterly dominates his wife and child. The domination is well-intentioned (as the book's title suggests) in that he's aiming to raise a family in a pure, moral setting and admittedly has to fight the rest of the environment to do it. But the result is nonetheless disastrous, and the man is nonetheless a petty tyrant. What is so wonderful about **Good Will** is the way it takes us inside the main character's good intentions and makes us appreciate the texture of the life he's made, even as it allows us to condemn him for his blind self-centeredness. And in showing how one central character can be sympathetic and yet blindly selfish, the novella makes us—made me, at any rate—realize that **Ordinary Love** could well be about the same kind of love: a love that only wants the best for others and yet insists on defining that "best" according to its own terms. Both novellas, in very different ways, explore the extreme selfishness that can lie at the root of the most intense parental feeling.

Another novella appears in Cynthia Ozick's brief collection **The Shawl,** which actually consists of a story called **"The Shawl"** and a novella called **Rosa.** The book's title suggests that the story is the primary achievement (and the previous attention it has received, including a first-place O. Henry Prize, would support that notion). But to my mind the novella is the better work. It follows the fate of Rosa—the woman whose baby, Magda, was thrown against an electric fence by a Nazi concentration camp guard in **"The Shawl"**—into her late middle age in Florida, where she has gone to retire. Where **"The Shawl"** is Holocaust literature at its most overheated, **Rosa** has a healthy dose of humor mixed in with its pathos, and Rosa herself is both pitiable and dislikable, incisive and insane. The main problem is that the two works, while obviously connected in terms of content, have a very bad ricochet effect on each other when they appear together in the same volume. **Rosa** tells us things about the characters in **"The Shawl"** (that Magda's father may have been a Nazi; that Stella is only Rosa's niece, not her older daughter; that the two other characters will survive the baby's death, even if unhappily) which we'd rather not know and which make the story less stark. And **"The Shawl"** keeps seeping into **Rosa,** grabbing up otherwise innocuous words like "electric" and filling them with horrendous connotations, while making us feel guilty for finding anything humorous in Rosa's craziness. The story limits what we can get from the novella. For instance, the fact that we've just read **"The Shawl"** means that we know from the start of **Rosa** that Magda is dead; without the story, the novella would allow us, at least for a time, to share some of Rosa's crazy belief in her daughter's adult existence. Most disturbingly, the background given for Rosa in **"The Shawl"** and the life she leads in Miami are simply incommensurable—just as are the Holocaust and the normal world that came after it. But history can get away with what fiction can't, because we *have* to accept it. And that, in a way, appears to be the overall lesson of 1989: history, to be believed, must be toned down for its appearances in fiction.

The Year in Poetry

by Sidney Burris

In his essay, "The Metaphysical Poets," T. S. Eliot recognized the peril of disagreeing with Samuel Johnson—"a dangerous person to disagree with," were Eliot's cautionary words—and even though Eliot's caveat issued from his high regard for the Johnsonian canon of taste, it was just this ponderous canonicity that Eliot was assailing. The most memorable literary squabbles often boil down to the matter of taste, and there, scorched in the pot, the matter remains until one critic mounts the inevitable offensive and accuses the other of having no taste at all. Where disputation fails, denial succeeds.

The subject of taste found its way back into the headlines again in 1989, and no survey of the year's work would be complete without mentioning the proliferating notoriety of Helen Vendler, who by all accounts is one of several preeminent critics of contemporary American poetry. For her detractors, of course, her preeminence is precisely their problem. *The American Poetry Review, The Kenyon Review,* and *The Hudson Review* published interviews or essays by various poets who attempted either to reveal her latent incompetence or to topple what was characterized as her suffocating power in the literary world. Because much of the invective was directed toward her taste in poetry without offering a definition of taste, or simply toward her accomplished professional standing, much of it was difficult to countenance. One poet suggested that she ought to write more disapproving reviews—the lion's share of her reviewing is given to praise—so that her audience might see the veiled half of her mind, the half that quarrels. And another claimed that her own inability to write poetry had crippled her critical perceptions.

These are curious charges. Seldom have so many poets become so enthralled with a single reviewer, and seldom have so many diagnoses of an illness been so barren of a remedy. Certainly the notion of taste, with its silent agenda of privilege and ascendancy, has come under fire recently, and as the academic canon is being restructured and broadened, new categories of organization are being developed. Along with these new categories have come new confusions; the quiet criteria of excellence that once accredited works by a largely white male authorship have been superseded by strenuously revisionary standards that are not only intended to widen the gates of canonical admission, but also to question the very assumptions of canonicity. Reviewers of contemporary poetry, then, are situated in a particularly precipitous position: working above the groundswell that attends any campaign to install one of the new literatures, reviewers, particularly in the choices they make, might well seem to have canonical impact whereas in the past their choices seemed *only* choices, *only* preferences being exercised within the unassailable boundaries of The Great Tradition. But, such authoritarian assumptions are no longer tenable, and single opinions no longer hold quite the same sway they might once have held. "No po-

etry," as Vendler replied recently in *The Harvard Magazine* (March-April 1990), "is going to be killed by a bad review from me." An understandable anxiety, however, has visited those writers who are skeptical about this and whom Vendler believes worthy of omission—an unenviable conjunction, for all those concerned, of skepticism and belief.

Younger American Poets

Luckily, many of our best young poets have gone about the business of setting their own standards with their own precise abandon. Foremost among them this year are three, Michael Ryan, Rita Dove, and Wyatt Prunty. Ryan's *God Hunger* (Viking), particularly in the two poems **"The Gladiator"** and **"Spider Plant,"** continues to mine the erotic vein discovered in his two earlier collections, *Threats Instead of Trees* and *In Winter,* but now there are other, newer additions to his field of subjects. Ryan has begun to write a poetry of wry, social observation, unafraid of clarity and adept at the now obscure art of phrase-making. The first stanza of **"Meeting Cheever"** is exemplary in its efficient portrayal of the traveled story-writer: "Above a half pizza and double gin, / his proffered hand trembled in the dark / as if, polished and slapped with cologne, / he had ridden a jackhammer from New York. . . ." This crisp character portrayal is buoyed by Ryan's developing ability to manage the narrative line, and this ability is lustily exhibited in the long poem of the collection, **"The Burglary,"** where he details the results of a break-in that occurred while he was in residence at Yaddo, the artist's colony in New York state. Throughout the more than 250 lines of this poem, Ryan manages to remain laconic, a stylistic feat in itself, and the extreme social disjunctions that order the vignettes of the poem—in one, the poet attends a party thrown by a dentist—render **"The Burglary"** a work of comedy in the old, high sense. Few poets are successfully attempting such heady projects these days, but in a poem like this Ryan is impressively reclaiming several structural components for poetry that have strayed into the realm of prose fiction.

Dove's Pulitzer Prize in 1987 catapulted an already admired poet to even higher stations, and **Grace Notes** (Norton), her newest collection, will do nothing to tarnish her reputation. Coming only two years after the award-winning volume **Thomas and Beulah,** these poems do not mark a cataclysmic development in Dove's career. In one sense, many of these lyrics might justly be characterized as exercises in what Dove does well—molding the quietly intelligent utterance as she conforms her lines to an inner music that seems at once illusive and bold. Her singular talent lies in her ability to discover the one phrase that encapsulates her intentions with daunting efficiency; and the encapsulating phrase is never simply accurate. In fact, its inspired inaccuracy often provides us with the immediate, disjointed perspective that often attends the sudden liberation felt when reading the best lyric poetry, as in the third line of this stanza from **"The Other Side of the House"**: "From the beautiful lawnmower / float curls of evaporated gasoline; / the hinged ax of the butterfly pauses." Dove's talent quickly earned the label "mature," and in this collection she has continued to find the subject matters that inspire her accomplished verse.

Prunty's third book of poems, **Balance as Belief** (Johns Hopkins), earns the label "meditative," and does so with an ease and grace rare in contemporary verse. His poems are unafraid of the propositional beginning—the surest sign of an imminent meditation—because he is a poet constitutionally drawn to thinking, not poeticizing, in measured lines. "Some roads never pass beneath you," begins one poem, and "How can we own a thing that travels / Constantly . . . ?" begins another, as if Zeno were priming his audience for another paradox. But that is Prunty's invigorating sleight-of-hand at work, invigorating because his strongest gift never deserts him. Amidst the conceived argument of the poem, within its rational framework, the inconceivable detail comes to him, fleshes out his idea, and does so with an enviable efficiency and precision. **"The Bed,"** for example, concerns the succession of beds that pass through any couple's life, and Prunty's description of the one that helped this particular couple begin their family is typical of his casual subtlety: "It sagged and angled gravity / And rolled the two of them together, / Peacefully fallen in their sleep / Where curling the same way every night / They shared his snoring, her chilly feet." Prunty's readers will go far afield in his hands, but never astray; **Balance as Belief** is a successfully ambitious collection of lyrics distinguished both by its stylistic achievement and its conceptual sophistication.

One of Dove's poems—**"Poem in Which I Refuse Contemplation"**—had taken place in Germany following a six-hour drive from Paris, and Elizabeth Spires's new collection, **Annonciade** (Penguin), continues a developing theme in American poetry that has so far found its fullest exposition in the poetry written by Elizabeth Bishop in Brazil, Robert Lowell in England and Ireland, and James Merrill in Greece. America is on the verge of developing a travel literature in the great tradition of the English sojourners who believed their travels were fraught with ambassadorial implication. With the Ugly American as a nagging predecessor, many of our writers have avoided the persona of the ambassador, although a sizable portion of the work in this vein has assumed what seems to be cathartically political overtones—Carolyn Forché's work comes to mind. In Spires's new work, England and France figure heavily, particularly in the first section of the book, but these countries supply her with opportunities for isolating those moments in which the observer, the American I/eye, is forced back on itself by the observed, in this case, by Josephine, a great Indian hornbill in the London zoo: "I look her straight in the eye. / Her pupils dilate and contract, cagily taking me in / as I take her in, an old cross-eyed dowager." There is much to be said here about inheritance and denial, and throughout this fine collection Spires is alert to the many ways in which an individual identity ultimately issues, through assimilation and rejection, from its own cultural milieu.

The most likely and unjust criticism to visit Molly Peacock's newest collection, **Take Heart** (Random House), will be technical in nature—the formality of her verse, especially the clanging rhymes, will repel those of the fragile opinion that

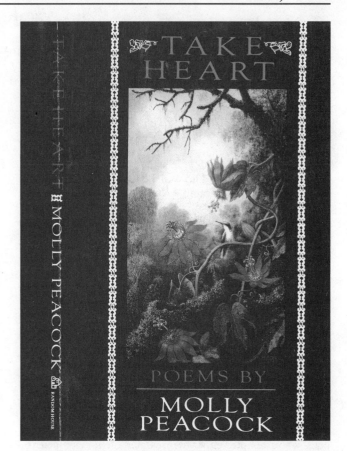

Dust jacket of Take Heart, *by Molly Peacock. Jacket design by Susan Shapiro. Jacket painting: "Hummingbird and Passion Flowers," by Martin Johnson Heade.*

such a technique was happily abandoned with the advent of free verse in the early twentieth century. But Peacock has a deep and idiosyncratic intelligence that continually impresses with its austere commitment to precise, original expression. Here are the first two stanzas of **"Joy"**: "Joy seeps. It's not / the hot sporadic light / that siblings fight / for, or the shot // the deprived demand, / the hot want of Big Love. / It doesn't glove / a feeling hand. . . ." Peacock's passion for the terse perspective tersely rendered—even in her longer lines, it is evident—has already stamped her verse with the sort of distinctive verbal patterning that we associate with the founding of an authentic voice.

Jim Elledge's **Various Envies** (Copper Beech)—the title is from Auden's "In Praise of Limestone"—exhibits a similarly incisive talent for continually envisioning the smallest detail in its largest most illuminating context, and this is a project that, in less capable hands, often descends to vapid moralizing. But Elledge is too good of a conductor to lose the proper tonality, as the opening lines of **"Homage"** demonstrate: "The second Big Ben tolls its / twelfth and big and little hands / clasp, drawing the 20th century / through its 360th degree / into the 21st. . . ." Here is a poetry of supple understatement, refreshingly content to speak simply and clearly. Copper Beech also published another first collection, **Country Airport,** by Peter Schmitt, and although Schmitt shares Elledge's commitment to a kind of native clarity, he more readily embraces the colloquial rhythm than Elledge does, and he is more willing to sharpen its provincial sound by marshalling it into an etched, slant-rhyming stanza. **"Harbinger,"** for example, begins: "The man in jeans and a workshirt / dragging the heavy wooden cross / I have seen now all over town— / does he carry it on the bus?" Much discussion has attended the recent renovation of traditional form in contemporary poetry—it is called the New Formalism—and both Elledge and Schmitt seem already capable of insuring that it does not fall prey to the mitigating nostalgia that often cripples such historically oriented refurbishings.

Amidst all the clamor for the rejuvenation of traditional form, Marie Boruch's new collection, **Descendant** (Wesleyan), will make certain that the painstaking art of free verse is carefully nourished. Boruch is consistently drawn to landscapes that, once described by her, seem to share a preternatural sympathy with the rambling lines that have created them; over and over again, it seems that her verse would be actually confined by traditional stanza schemes and patterns of rhyme, and this is an illusion essential to her chosen method. The first four lines of **"Trucks in Rain"** provide a good example of the kinds of liberty she enjoys in her descriptive passages: "Against the sky's rough milk, hills are only color. / And the tarpaulin is a wayward thing / thrown back by wind: glimpse / of wood cut clean, stacked, now stained black." No need here to mention the truck; for Boruch the truck is the least important element of the passage because its presence would overshadow its more striking attributes—the tarpaulin, for example, "a wayward thing". Boruch's is a refining imagination, and her refinements depend upon the various formal and conceptual liberties that distinguish her free verse. David Mura's first collection, **After We Lost our**

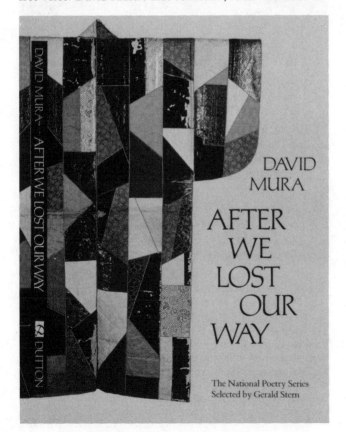

Dust jacket of After We Lost Our Way, *by David Mura. Jacket design © Earl Tidwell.*

Way (Dutton), was one of five winners of The National Poetry Series for 1989, and this young poet already shows a formidable ability to manage skillfully the high seriousness that naturally attends his subject matters as well as the fluidity of expression that even more naturally attends those poems less ambitiously conceived. Mura, a third generation Japanese-American, confronts his tradition with an honest lyricism, one that is capable of achieving a tragic dimension within the lyric's essentially aesthetic framework, and this is nowhere more evident than in the beginning of the second section of **"Suite for Grandfather & Grandmother Uyemura: Relocation"**: "Two decades pass, his greenhouse hisses / with his orchids like petulant courtesans, / the eucalyptus rattles out back in the moonlight. / He's gone to Jap Town, Cuban cigar jammed // in his jaw."

ALSO RECOMMENDED: D. W. Fenza, **The Interlude** (Galileo); Kimiko Hahn, **Air Pocket** (Hanging Loose Press); Stefanie Marlis, **Slow Joy** (Wisconsin); Jim Peterson **The Man Who Grew Silent** (The Bench Press).

Contemporaries

For years now, New Directions has been publishing Denise Levertov's work, and she has properly become one of that press's most valuable commodities. In 1989, her **Door in the Hive** marks her sixteenth New Directions title, and the libretto included here, **"El Salvador: Requiem and Invocation,"** although it is not the strongest offering of the book, sets the governing tone for the volume. Asked by the composer Newell Hendricks to provide the text for him in composing an oratorio, Levertov suggested El Salvador as a theme, one to be developed by focusing specifically on the murder of Archbishop Romero and the three American nuns and lay sister. All libretti need their music, and it is perhaps presumptuous to ask the general reader to imagine it, as it ought to be, fully accompanied by the score. Still, a clear and plaintive outcry survives several readings of it—Levertov skillfully uses excerpts from actual letters written by the four sisters—and the piece, resonating at a level beyond outrage, approaches the condition of forgiveness. The book is unalterably deepened by its inclusion, and the single lyrics that surround it—concerning paintings, woodcuts, parables, and landscapes—assume by contrast the luxury of indulgence that ultimately provides the context for most artistic creation. **A Door in the Hive** is a most distinctive addition to a prolific career.

Paul Zimmer's **The Great Bird of Love** (Illinois) was selected by William Stafford as one of the winners of The National Poetry Series, and the poems included under that title are as distinctive as any that appeared during the year. They are also difficult to describe, and in many cases it is unfair to quote snippets from them because Zimmer's tone—seriously playful, I think, gets it right—depends more extensively on a gradual contextual development than most poetry currently being written. The title poem ends the book, and that alone is odd, but by that time the opening lines of **"The Great Bird of Love"** seem perfectly natural, organically conceived, and simply well done: "I want to become a great night bird / Called The Zimmer, grow intricate gears / And tendons, brace my wings on updrafts . . . / To fly above the troubles of the land." Excerpted they seem somewhat self-indulgent. They are not. An allegorical patina gleams here, but there are no characters called Everyman; instead, we get Zimmer, and he appears throughout the collection, providing an effective solution to the over-abundance of the first-person pronoun in contemporary poetry, yet still—it is, after all, the poet's name—reaping the benefits of the first-person intimacy. Adroitness has always been one of Zimmer's talents, one which reduces the work of lesser poets to mere intellectual exercises. Not so with *The Great Bird of Love.* Zimmer has produced another valued collection.

Eamonn Grennan is Irish, but teaches in America. His work has been known for some years through its publication in various journals, and North Point has now published his first American trade edition. *What Light There Is & Other Poems* gathers together work previously appearing in *Wildly for Days* and combines these poems with Grennan's more recent verse. The overall effect is one of sure, but subtle development. Grennan is not a poet of extravagant subject matters; here is the beginning of **"Winter Morning, Twelve Noon,"** a title that could only be called opportunistic for a poet such as Grennan: "Light snags in January branches. On the sunstark / living-room wall two starlings are a writhing / smear of shadow. . . ." Later it begins to snow, "a slow / featherdown drift," and the poet recalls that in Sweden they wait "impatient for the first big snow / to brighten their all-day dusk." To end the poem, Grennan imagines these Swedes standing "bareheaded . . . in happy groups," but in an essential, unparalleled way, Grennan's poems, moving line by line with such descriptive grace and satisfaction, are continually ending, continually capable of resting on what has preceded. Grennan has, above all, both a remarkable eye and the fluency of tongue to convince us of his vision.

June Jordan's *Naming Our Destiny: New and Selected Poems* (Thunder Mouth Press) comprises over three decades of work, three decades that reflect one of the strongest strains of activist poetry in the late twentieth century. From the beginning, which was 1958 for Jordan, she has fashioned a robustly responsive literature—"New energies of darkness we / disturbed a continent / like seeds," she writes in the early **"Who Look at Me"**—and she has continued throughout her career, as this volume testifies, to fashion a poetry of political commitment and rhetorical consistency. Maxine Scates's *Toluca Street* (Pittsburgh) won the Agnes Lynch Starret Poetry Prize for 1988. In many ways, this volume is Scates's *Portrait of the Artist.* But the region recovered—the blue-collar neighborhoods of Los Angeles—adds a new landscape to American poetry, particularly in the eloquently prosaic tone that Scates manages to invoke as she goes about her business of writing poetry, line by line. The beginning of **"Easter, 1984"** is characteristic of the good work found throughout much of this volume: "I spent last night halfway to heaven / on a rooftop gothic with crosses."

Stephen Dunn's new volume, *Between Angels* (Norton), continues the distinctive experiment with form that, to my mind, has become over the past decade or so one of his most alluring calling cards. "How to fashion a verse," he seems to have asked himself, "that will house my austere meditational impulse yet indulge my love of informality, of conversation and suburban observation?" He has made his mark with the three-line stanza, in all shapes and sizes, and it is the stanza used most frequently in this collection. But there is a new and natural note of acceptance in this volume, a note that he has tried to sound in previous collections. The title poem contains several lines that must have very much satisfied Dunn because they are lines that he has struggled to create earlier, but not with such casual success: "Oh, everything's true / at different times // in the capacious day / just as I don't forget

/ and always forget // half the people in the world / are dispossessed." Dunn is one of the few poets working now who so successfully combines abstract meditation and colloquial rhythms; his verse is a compendium of techniques designed to maintain this difficult and impressive balance. Robert Hass's *Human Wishes* (Ecco) treads similar grounds but does so with segments of prose poems and a longer line that strives for a kind of random inclusiveness. A poem by Hass might begin anywhere, and surely this is an intentional effect; **"Tahoe in August"** begins: "What summer proposes is simply happiness: / heat early in the morning, jays / raucous in the pines. Frank and Ellen have a tennis game / at nine, Bill and Cheryl sleep on the deck to watch a shower of summer stars. . . ." This is not mundane, although it is not charged with energy. Hass's most memorable work has always insisted on the grand inevitability of day-to-day life, particularly the day-to-day life overlaid by a pensive self-consciousness, and there is much of this here in his third volume.

Dust jacket of Human Wishes, *by Robert Hass. Jacket design by Beth Tondreau Design/Jane Treuhaft. Jacket illustration: "The Open Window," by Pierre Bonnard, 1921.*

The title of Carol Muske's new volume, *Applause* (Pittsburgh), is taken from a photographic exhibit by Holly Wright, and the individual poems that constitute the collection are arranged like neatly captured scenes-from-a-life. **"Intensive Care"** begins: "Then, at 3 a.m., I see her bend / over the stricken infant, her face / that face reproduced for us so many times // in art, as a historical moral: / *whose love endureth even death, / whose beauty is forebearance.*" Muske's poems typically embroider such extreme moments with grace and understanding, and this is a collection brimming with both of these qualities. Norman Dubie is back, and his devoted readers—I count myself among them—will find much to applaud in *Groom Falconer* (Norton). As always, Dubie's encyclopedic range of subject matters is here, as well as his restless attention to a rich gallery of historical figures. Still, who could have predicted **"The Apocrypha of Jacques Derrida"**? His mastery of the monologue continues unabated, his sense of narrative remains unchallenged for its uniqueness, and his humor, his sense of comic disjunction, has sharpened its focus in this fine collection.

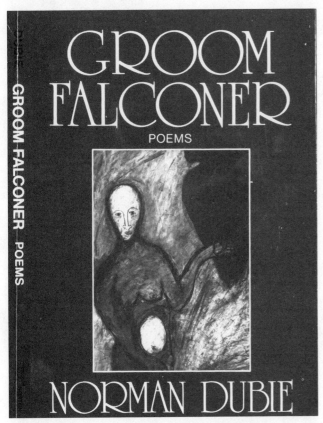

Dust jacket of Groom Falconer, *by Norman Dubie. Jacket design by Jay J. Smith. Jacket painting: "The Falcon," by Michael P. Berman.*

I should mention too that New Directions and Louisiana State University reissued important collections that had gone out of print. Delmore Schwartz's **Last & Lost Poems** (New Directions), with its succinct and helpful introduction by Robert Phillips, originally appeared in 1979. At that time it was widely admired, and this time around, 16 recently discovered poems have been added to Schwartz's distinctive canon, making this volume essential to any assessment of one of America's most famous, most infamous, and most puzzling poets. And who else but LSU should bring out Allen Tate's **Collected Poems**? Published by arrangement with Farrar, Straus, and Giroux, this volume will be of little interest to those who own its New York incarnation, but the Spartan simplicity of the new cover design would most certainly have pleased the last Augustan, and it insures that Tate's work remains readily available for critics and students alike.

ALSO RECOMMENDED: Edgar Bowers, **For Louis Pasteur** (Princeton); Raymond Carver, *A New Path to the Wa-* terfall (Atlantic Monthly) Charles Causley, **Secret Destinations** (Godine); Fred Chappel, **First and Last Words** (LSU); Leo Connellan, **New and Collected Poems** (Paragon House); Wesley McNair, **The Town of No** (Godine); James Laughlin, **The Bird of Endless Time** (Copper Canyon); Thomas Lux, **Sunday** (Carnegie-Mellon); Alicia Ostriker, **Green Age** (Pittsburgh); Robert Pack, **Before It Vanishes** (Godine); David Slavitt, **Equinox** (LSU); Ira Sadoff, **Emotional Traffic** (Godine); Baron Wormser, **Atoms, Soul Music and Other Poems** (Paris Review); John Yau, **Radiant Silhouette** (Black Sparrow).

International

Douglas Dunn is easily one of the most decorated Scottish poets of the twentieth century, and his **New and Selected Poems: 1966-1988** (Ecco) provides American readers with a handsomely efficient means of familiarizing themselves with a distinguished career in English letters. *Elegies,* the series of love poems to his wife, will most likely become the showcase section of this volume because they represent in lyric form that rare combination of personal affection and deep individual sorrow—his wife is dying of cancer. It is a difficult mixture to manage because poetry of this sort often descends to the maudlin or sentimental, but Dunn avoids these extremes at every turn. Here is the way Dunn ends **"Second Opinion,"** a poem that chronicles the act of sanctioned desperation that informs the search for another opinion: "Professional anxiety— / His hand on my shoulder / Showing me to the door, a scent of soap, / Medical fingers, and his wedding ring." Dunn's intervention in this scene is minimal and unnecessary because he has the inestimable talent that allows him to choose the articulate detail.

Bloodaxe Books, the English publishing house located at Newcastle-upon-Tyne and distributed in this country by Dufour Editions, carries an impressive poetry list, and two of their publications for 1989 deserve special mention. First, Jack Clemo's **Selected Poems** represents a culling from over three and a half decades of steady, prolific composition. His verse reads like a gnarled conversation, muscular with easy rhythms, but punctuated by carefully planned reverses in accent and idea—the various arrangements that separate poetry from conversation. In **"Palazzo Rezzonico,"** he attempts, yet once more, a description of Venice, certainly one of the most storied cities in the literature, and it is typical of Clemo's fine ability to meld the personal and political: "Canal-veined city: its golden heart now beats / Congruous to my new destiny, / Naming the broad sea, / the split channels / Unstained by fevers of cramped history." Deborah Randall's **The Sin Eater** was chosen as a Poetry Book Society Recommendation—an English equivalent to our Book-of-the-Month-Club, except only for poetry—and that alone brings distinction to the volume. American readers will most likely find the lyrics collected here eccentric, fetching, and teasing. They are often obscure. But Randall has an extraordinary ability to find unlikely subject matters that yield surprising, well-expressed insights. Here are three lines from **"Holding,"** which must be accompanied by the note, taken from the text, that "Holding Therapy was developed in America and is a controversial self-help method for the autistic child and his family": "Child give me mercy as you become mirage then / simmer into tears, the hours I have known tears boil and beg / and after, the empty room of you and I." Randall is dealing here with an inexplicable subject, and her verse succeeds admirably in finding the words that reflect the penitence and patience that accompany such an extreme experience.

The University of Pittsburgh Press several years ago published a translation of the Salvadoran poet Claribel Alegría entitled *Flowers from the Volcano,* and this year they are issuing another volume, **Woman of the River,** translated by D. J. Flakoll. Although Alegría was born in Nicaragua, she considers herself Salvadoran, having grown up in Santa Ana, El Salvador, and she obviously has spent a good deal of that time writing—she has published more than twenty books in Spanish. Like many of the poets from Central and South America, she naturally addresses the political subject, and as a result her poems reflect a penetrating awareness of the seamless continuum that exists between the individual and the state— the first condition of an authentic poetry of social awareness. Her poems are at once accessible and complex, and Pittsburgh is to be applauded for adding her voice to the many fine voices from Central and South America currently being heard by Americans for the first time.

The Year in Drama

by Robert Cohen

The big news on Broadway in 1989 was clearly the return of the American musical; not one but two original and often stunning shows arrived right on top of each other at year's end: Tommy Tune's *Grand Hotel,* shortly followed by the Lee Gelbart/Cy Coleman/David Zippel *City of Angels.* Musicals are a big business in America (The Broadway Theatre housing *Les Miserables* had more ticket income last year than the New York Giants and Mets combined), and all American theatre has been somewhat under a cloud over the past few years, as its biggest commercial hits were foreign-born. No longer.

City of Angels is a meta-spoof, a spoof within a spoof. It's a send-up of Hollywood detective films of the 1940s, surrounded by a send-up of Hollywood film-*making* of that era. It's a masterpiece of witty construction: a deconstructed musical, in which the film and the filmmaking are portrayed side-by-side, often simultaneously. At the left, "Stine" pecks away at his typewriter; at the right, Stine's filmic creation—detective "Stone"—solves a missing persons case. Stine manipulates Stone like a ventriloquist operates his puppet; when Stine rewrites his script, Stone and his co-characters simply "rewind" themselves and start over. In one of *City*'s most clever strokes, the film characters are dressed strictly in black and white; watching these monochromatic, celluloid shadows walk and speak backwards, sucking their words back into their mouths with professional aplomb, contributes much of the opening hilarity.

This is also a musical *comedy* in a welcomely old-fashioned sense. It's happily centered in its book (by Larry Gelbart), which begins with a terrific idea, and delivers both an engaging story and a spoken text filled with clever and pungent satire. *City of Angels* is moment-to-moment funny, its musical numbers are tightly integrated with its action, and occasionally it's even suspenseful. Emphasis is on comedy and cleverness. The jokes are genuine; we don't feel like we're simply programmed to laugh as in, say, *Legs Diamond* or *The Mystery of Edwin Drood.* The lyrics are tremendously clever and inventive as well: David Zippel, in his Broadway debut, has come up with some terrific multi-syllable rhymes, bright rhythm breaks, slangy juxtapositions, and apt aphoristic refrains. He's exactly one step ahead of us, not so far as to leave us in the dust (as Stephen Sondheim often is), but just a beat faster; he tantalizes and dazzles at the same time. Cy Coleman's tunes are fetching, and they develop a good momentum: the harmonics are as deconstructed as the story, and both the first and final acts end in big, eminently satisfying blasts of unison singing by the bifurcated male lead(s), Stine and Stone, rhapsodizing together on the theme of "You're nothing without me."

I've given away just enough of the plot. I can also tell you that James Naughton is a sexy powerhouse as Stone, the alter ego filmstar-cop, and Gregg Edelman is wittily articulate as

Playbill for City of Angels.

Stine, the struggling-novelist-turned-sellout-scenarist. Also pivotal and perfect is their rampaging director, played by René Auberjonois in one of his trickiest character turns ever. The whole thing is delightful, if slight, and you even get a bitter taste of the moviemaking business—which, as the recent Art Buchwald-Paramount Pictures case makes clear, has not changed all that much in the past several decades.

The other big musical of the year was *Grand Hotel,* which everyone wants to say is "by" Tommy Tune. It's not by Tune at all, if you mean written or produced by: the book is credited to Luther Davis based on the film by Vicki Baum; most of the songs were written by Robert Wright and George Forrest for an earlier version which never made it to Broadway, with new, additional music and lyrics by Maury Yeston. Perhaps because of the play's long developmental period, its producers' names are stacked above the title in what resemble boxcars from a train wreck—each in its own orthographic presentation—and you would have to be a performing arts historian to break down the exact contributions of each creative participant. But Tommy Tune directed and choreographed the whole; his hand seems to be everywhere on the piece, and a very sure and integrating hand it is.

Grand Hotel might be described as a period dance with words: sashaying ambience is all. It is 1928, at the Grand Hotel in Berlin, and the orchestra sits high above the stage on its plexiglass floor; beneath, through the ever-revolving glass door—the production's theme prop—come the Baron, the countess, the gigolo, the Jew, the courtesan, the detective, the ballerina, the typist, the bellboys, the scullery workers, and the telephone operators, all playing their wan stories against the romantic strains of Weimar decadence and interregnum angst. Society Rampant: between the Kaiser and Hitler, between the waltz, the tango, the Charleston, and the goose-step.

I loved this piece, but perversely, I suspect; the audience was cool and most of the critics reserved. But how can you not love (since you don't have to *be*) an entire cast of cigarette smokers, puffing their way through a myriad of delicious flirtations, despairing duets, the "Dance of Love and Death," and "The Grand Waltz of Life?" There's a story here of a defunct Baron, the blond who loves him, the Jew who adores *her,* the hotel manager who persecutes *him,* and the wry Doctor who detests them all; but more significant than any story are the ever-present curls of cigarette smoke, gliding around glass pillars and snaking up to the upstairs orchestra; the prison-like bars that surround and intensify the action, cruelly penning the blithe aristocrats into their dying high society; the ever-inflating Weimar deutsche marks, passed hand to hand in grossly blatant, over-the-counter blackmailings; and, of course, the ubiquitous bellboys. Ask not for whom their bells will toll; this is a play to sit back and absorb, to enjoy purely because of its glittery surfaces, its exacting professionalism, and then to let its deeper resonances strike where they will. Or where Tommy Tune will; he is clearly a master of unconscious penetration. Those of us with deep roots in the life of this century will not be untouched or unmoved.

Last year, *Coastal Disturbances* tried to make a summer vacation romance into some sort of cosmic deliverance; this year it was Willy Russell's *Shirley Valentine. Shirley* is written, however, with an English accent: its eponymous heroine, the only character in the play, is a forty-two-year-old Liverpudlian housewife bored with the routines of English domesticity (marriage is a "time bomb" she says) who, having been invited by a girlfriend to vacation in Corfu, takes up with a waiter from the local fish taverna, and—sending the girlfriend and her luggage back to Liverpool—stays on in her Aegean idyll. "Most of us die long before we're dead," she tells us. "I'[ve] fallen in love with the idea of living."

There's a whole world of Romantic literary history behind this notion, of course. Keats, Byron, and Shelley lived and died in and around these same Mediterranean waters, escaping the dreariness of English weather and pre-Victorian morality, and *Equus*'s Dr. Dysart is only the most recent of English dramatic characters seeking a fuller life by voyaging out of the London fog and into the Hellenic sunshine. What makes *Shirley Valentine* an important and individual work is its post-feminist slant. Shirley claims not to be a feminist at all (it's a feminist friend who invites her to Greece—and then abandons her for a four-night-long dinner date upon arrival), but Shirley is not going to be "St. Joan of the kitchen" either, nor does she plan to end her life talking to her apartment walls. She's heard about modern women and their pursuits of pleasure (" 'clitoris kids,' I call 'em") and she's bravely seeking her piece of the new action. She has fond dreams—of drinking wine on the beach "in the country where it's made"—and she has even fonder memories—of being "Shirley Valentine" rather than "Mrs." somebody, or "Mom." Shirley misses her youthful potential with its unlimited vistas: "the excitement of not knowing" what lay in store. "What happened, wall?" she asks. "Where did Shirley Valentine go?"

Shirley Valentine is a charming play. It's entertaining, there's a reasonably suspenseful narrative story, and it holds our attention—all remarkable achievements for a two-hour-plus one-person play. But it's ontologically simplistic and sentimental: it suggests that we have a pure, recoverable, *innate* identity, wholly apart from our political and familial roles, and as appealing a notion as this may be (it pretty much carries the audience during *Shirley*'s stage time), it glosses over hard social facts that we have to remember after the curtain comes down. Growing up is a matter of reconciling ourselves with the outside world, not separating from it (which comes eventually in any event), and Shirley's fantasy solution—or escape—would, in fact, strip her identity, not reforge it. What she imagines as identity ("Who is *me?*" she asks) is mainly an unleashed nostalgia for youth, potential, ambiguity, and sensuality. We all have these yearnings, and a summer in Corfu is a satisfying tonic that slakes our thirst for the absolute. But it is ultimately recreation, not ontology, and we shouldn't mistake it for the cosmic nirvana that Russell seems to be proposing.

Shirley's preachiness (a danger for any one-person show) finally becomes tedious: she is no longer discovering from her experience, she is just lecturing the audience. This may be the time to request a playwriting moratorium on the phrase: "The point is. . . ." The point here is that there is no point: waiting on tables in Corfu is not, in the eyes of eternity, superior to waiting on Harry in Liverpool, and come the inevitable winter of her discontent, I'm afraid, Shirley will be back in Liverpool as fast as British Airways can carry her. This is a Hallmark Valentine, self-addressed.

Shirley wasn't the only one-person show in New York this year, nor even at the Booth Theatre. December brought *Tru,* a solo spiel about, and largely by, Truman Capote, the late, briefly-celebrated novelist, essayist, TV wag, and occasional Broadway author (Capote wrote the story and book for the wonderful Harold Arlen musical *House of Flowers*). Capote's words are here arranged, with a few linking lines presumably thrown in, by Jay Presson Allen; the role was performed—to a veritable T-R-U—by Robert Morse in one of the most captivating stage appearances of the year.

A one-man play is not necessarily about a man alone, but *Tru* is a vivid portrayal of loneliness. Tru's apartment, brilliantly designed by David Mitchell, grandly overlooks—through giant wall-windows that comprise the entire rear of the set— most of midtown East Manhattan at night, foregrounded by the brightly lit United Nations tower. It is against this opulence of nighttime activity—all humanity at play—that we

Playbill for Tru.

confront our Tru, shuffling about, alone in his room, in what must be the ugliest costume ever conceived for Broadway (a formless brown cardigan sweater, baggy off-off-white chinos, tan camp slippers without soles) dwarfed by a sparkling Manhattan and a luminous UN. Tru wheezes out his life's story, his hopes, his complaints, his sadness, his despair, against a constant reminder that the rest of humanity has far better things to do—and plenty of folks to do them with.

And the despair is profound. It's not a lack of pride, nor a late regret at skirting the norms. "I've never had any problem with being homothekthual," Tru reminds us brightly, tossing his head with wonderful Capotian aplomb, and laughing himself into a frenzy of self-amusement. "I was always a sort of two-headed calf," he tells us, by way of explanation, and we do certainly laugh—after all, we're first-timers in his brilliant company, and first-timers find him charming indeed. Nor is it a lack of communication: the phone is always ringing, and there are flowers by wire and a man to trim the tree (between acts). But we soon come to realize that Tru's just tired everybody out. Although he gave the "party of the decade" a few years ago, he's on the "B" list now; his clever witticisms now appear offensive (if not libelous), and his gamy boyishness, in light of his pot belly and puffy, blotchy cheeks, now seems ab-

surd. There's a "universal party" somewhere out there, Tru knows, but he's no longer invited.

It's a good, wrenching play, filled with contrasts. I especially favored Tru's wry musing over his own answering machine; hearing the gaiety of his own pre-recorded message against the growing despair of the present moment was sort of a Tru's Last Cassette. When Morse dons Capote's famous black brimmed hat to go off into the night, we know it's a darker night he's headed for, and we wonder if we should have known at the time. *Tru* carries a pun in the title and in the man himself. (Capote took the nickname because "somehow I liked it," he tells us here.) Unlike **Shirley Valentine, Tru** is about a true person, true in both the sense of real and true to himself. Perhaps you have to know a little—and be prepared to feel a little—about Capote and his times to get the full value from this fairly quiet, superficially uneventful drama; the play doesn't stand wholly on its own. But in Morse's masterful rendition, this work reaches deep and movingly into a human soul.

Jerry Sterner's **Other People's Money** ("OPM," it is called, "the ultimate seduction") isn't a one-person play, but maybe it should have been. Sterner has created an extraordinary character, Lawrence Garfinkle, or "Larry the Liquidator," as he is known on the street (Wall Street), and as performed by Kevin Conway, the role is utterly unforgettable. The play and characters surrounding Garfinkle are substantially less remarkable, however, so that the play, while sustaining throughout, is only incompletely successful.

Garfinkle is a short, waddling, corporate buy-out man. He gobbles up companies like donuts—and is addicted to both. This time he's scouted up a small, venerable Rhode Island wire and cable factory, family-run and community-spirited. The company is worth more dead than alive, so Garfinkle's buying it to sell the parts. What we have here seems to be Ivan Boesky against Norman Rockwell, with Boesky having all the good lines.

Somewhat clumsily, the play provides us a basic lexicon for modern finance. We hear enough about junk bonds, greenmail, golden parachutes, poison pills, and white knights to know what's going on. We're informed, but not terribly enlightened; this would all be *Weekly Reader* stuff ("How Corporate Takeovers Work") except for Garfinkle (it's hard to know here how much of the brilliance of the character is author Sterner's, how much is actor Conway's), for whom capitalism is sensuality and greed is carnal. Vilely entertaining, Garfinkle brooks no fools, wastes no time, pulls no punches. He bullies, he charms, he deals: he gives people what they want by giving them a taste of their proper desserts. And he relishes every moment of it. "I'm your only friend," he tells the stockholders, and, in this bottomlined capitalist society, he's about right; he's a modern-day Andrew Undershaft. Garfinkle gets the company; he even gets the girl brought in to save the company. He's a delight to watch—from the safety of our seats in the audience—but Sterner doesn't seem to know what to do with him; Sterner's sympathies are still on the other side. So the author withholds Garfinkle's best arguments; Larry the Liquidator actually has a better moral case than he delivers. And the failing wire company is made to seem higher-sounding than the circumstances provide; the play's structure puts the little guy on top (the play's narrator, who submits to Garfinkle during the takeover, concludes that Garfinkle is evil in the play's denouement) and keeps Garfinkle from soaring. One gets the feeling that Sterner started out writing about a wonderful old company being taken over by the devil and then, despite himself, fell in love with the devil while writing. It's a confused play with one hell of a character.

A Few Good Men is also a confused play, although it seems absolutely straightforward at first glance. Set for the most part in Guantanamo Bay, Cuba, it purports to tell a story of discipline and racism in the Marine Corps, and to expose—as well as to celebrate—the military mind. The issue is clear enough: a Hispanic Marine seeking reassignment is dead, owing to a too-hasty, too-rigorous enforcement of an informal "Code Red" disciplinary system existing at the U.S. base. His two assailants, on trial by court martial, have acted under orders; loyally, they have pleaded guilty and are prepared to serve their terms, and the efforts of the hero-attorneys, played by Tom Hulce, Megan Gallagher, and Mark Nelson, are to get the higher-ups who created this awful system. But is it so awful? It takes a fierce discipline to run an army, the counter-argument goes; these are the men (and in this play they're all men) who, after all, "stand on a wall" twenty-four hours a day, protecting the rest of us from intrusion and attack. The "code reds," we are given to understand, though not in any operating manuals, are the substructures of military order. Or are they? Maybe they're more for bonding and morale-building than discipline—a fraternity hazing run rampant? Maybe they're mainly for fun: there's not, after all, a lot to do on an isolated naval base on Cuban shores. The wall these men stand on also walls them in—these guys are safeguarding their own imprisonment.

Virtually every reviewer with any memory compared this play to Herman Wouk's *The Caine Mutiny Courtmartial,* and such juxtaposition is unavoidable: in many ways it's the same argument all over again. But *Few* is a far clumsier work. Though author Aaron Sorkin throws in some refreshing humor, a contemporary ethnic mix, and a lady attorney (she proves incompetent in a purely "feminine" way—being only a "paper lawyer" and unable to master the rough and tumble of the courtroom), the play stumbles more than it moves cogently or dramatically through its issues. Part of the problem is an arbitrariness in the quarrels of the defense attorneys, who seem to be debating and joke-telling just to extend the play to full-length duration. A greater problem is with basic plot mechanics. Since the killers have already pleaded guilty, the only decision driving the play (which is, after all, a courtroom drama) is just *how* guilty the boys are. Such matters of degree, however, provide little in the way of audience suspense or involvement. Fairly complex issues of precise motivation and intent, then, are left complex and unresolved (there being no blanket verdict by the judge—or author), but since the characters are not drawn with any particular specificity or depth, the motivational complexity results only in a final murkiness, not in a revelation of a human condition. Thus, *A Few Good Men* has neither a melodramatic punch nor a Chekhovian texture and remains well beneath the Wouk work, which had quite a bit more of both. Don Scardino's staging and Ben Edwards's too-simple setting are also clumsy, with the defendants seated awkwardly on some architecturally meaningless steps and the judge speaking to the very back of the witnesses' heads. Bravura performances by some close-to-skinhead Marine extremists were, in my opinion, more bravura than performance (lots of tired histrionics by the time I saw it), keeping the play on the level of a generally worthy but occasionally tiresome school production.

Playbill for Lend Me a Tenor.

Ken Ludwig's *Lend Me a Tenor* certainly proves that American farce is far from dead. This is a classic effort and unquestionably the most successful farce this side of the Atlantic in the current decade. Farce, of course, refers to a wholly manipulated comic structure, the devices of which bear only a semiotic rapport with observable reality. Classic farce elements—a half-dozen slammable doors, identical costumes leading to mistaken identities, hidings in closets, removals of suspected corpses, sustained shouting episodes immediately followed by sustained minutes of silent shocked stillness—abound here, sturdily propelled by a maniacally driving, always-silly plot. Philip Bosco, winner of the Tony Award for best actor, plays a furiously energetic opera impresario in Cleveland whose Italian tenor arrives late and drunk for the evening performance. Bosco's assistant, played wondrously by Victor Garber (who gives, by far, the better performance in my opinion), and various opera hangers-on provide the cogs that turn and are turned by Ludwig's wheel, which rotates surely, consistently, and ever forward. The mechanics are in good order here, and the high-voltage performances (Bosco can be heard across the street) make even routine credibility unnecessary: we can even accept that the Cleveland audience could mistake the impresario's assistant for a world-famous Italian tenor in the title role of *Otello.* (The play is set in 1934, for no other reason, it seems to me, than to appease the current residents of Cleveland.) The play makes no other demands on us, so neither should we on it; it shamelessly delivers its laughs, some of which come right out of Plautus and earlier wits, and it concludes with the niftiest curtain call in memory. It works and it hums. Jerry Zaks staged the play and emerges the star.

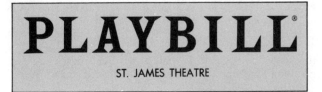

Largely New York is 1989's amazing curiosity: a seventy-minute wordless "play" by Bill Irwin, who also directs and stars. It is probably the most enchanting seventy minutes in town, although it's not entirely clear what, if anything, it adds up to. Irwin is a product of America's experimental and regional theaters. He was one of the founding members of Herbert Blau's "Kraken" company and an original member of the Pickle Family Circus in San Francisco. Here he is "the postmodern hoofer," trying to practice a soft shoe version of "Tea for Two" but lured from his labors by more contemporary competitors: two "poppers" (which must be a newer term for what we used to call "break dancers"), a Merce Cunningham-type solo ballerina, an avant-garde videographer, and a veritable army of academics. Nobody in this crowd talks; they dance, they videotape, and they tumble into the orchestra pit. In a theater season limp on ideas, critics have scoured the work for meanings (*The New Yorker*'s capsule review reminds us weekly of its critic's notion that the piece has

"the best 'book' on Broadway") but one shouldn't jump to the idea that this work is dramatic. Rather, it is essentially an extended circus mime that often brilliantly contrasts what seemed the sophisticated entertainment of past decades with the more explosive, corrosive, and technological aesthetics of today. What is wonderful about this act is its ecumenicism: *everything* is enjoyable, and art, in Irwin's vision, is non-sectarian, nonexclusive, and free for all. And *a* free-for-all. Such lampooning as exists is reserved for the academics, and even they end up joyfully trampolining in and out of the orchestra pit. The highlight of **Largely New York** is clearly some astonishing street dancing, particularly of the two inspired "poppers," and Irwin's own unquenchable agreeability. There is also some absolutely inspired miming with a video interface—and inner face—that leaves one gasping both in amazement and hilarity. An international tour is in the offing, and I suspect **Largely New York** will be playing somewhere or other off and on for the rest of the millennium.

Also on the curiosity front was Steven Berkoff's **Metamorphosis**, adapted from the Franz Kafka novella and resurrected more than revived on Broadway twenty years after its 1969 London premiere. Other than a change in cast, the production (staged by the author) is virtually identical to the original, but the casting—of ballet star Mikhail Baryshnikov, making his stage debut in the role of Gregor—was the curiosity and the obvious reason for this New York presentation. When Baryshnikov had duties elsewhere, the production closed, re-opening upon his return.

Baryshnikov, perhaps surprisingly, was very good, both as a mime, portraying Franz Kafka's famous insect, and as a speaking actor, his Russian accent actually helping to estrange him from the bourgeois family to which he disbelongs. The agony of the outcast came clearly from within—or are we merely here indulging in vicarious reflections of the Russian ballet dancer's well-publicized life in exile? New York critics have never favored Berkoff's stylistic grotesqueries and didn't here: the wantonly choreographed strutting and shouting of Gregor's family—capitalist pigs in Berkoff's hyper-Marxist cartooning—came in for a press pounding. There is, to be sure, far more shading and detailing in the Kafka text than Berkoff permits in this adaptation, but "metamorphosis" of Baryshnikov-Gregor, from dapper mittel-European "commercial traveler in the cloth trade" to dead beetle on the family floor, was carefully and creatively delineated in discrete, meaningful stages and was, for most observers, including myself, affective and moving.

Terence McNally's **The Lisbon Traviata** is an exciting two hours of theater, no matter how you look at it, and you can look at it any number of ways. There's a hysterically funny first act about a pair of gay opera buffs, devotees of Maria Callas, one of whom is *in farcical extremis* over news of a previously unknown recording of the diva's "Traviata" in Lisbon. And there's a brutally insipid second act, as one of the buffs returns home to break up with (or to be broken up by) his longtime lover. But then grand opera is, as often as not, brutally insipid—McNally's play, which begins about opera, ends (soap) operatically. I am given to understand that in the original off-Broadway production a murder concludes the piece, and it is easy to guess who kills whom; the current ending is sadder but wiser, and presumably truer to (most) life, but one never knows. The play makes one of the fiercest arguments against the possibility of combining open promiscuity with emotional fidelity that I've ever seen.

Success in the second half of **Lisbon** would have to come from extraordinary performances in the two leads, and both the actors, including Anthony Heald, who had won extraordinary reviews as Stephen (the principal part in both acts), were not performing on the night I saw it, about a week before closing, and their replacements were inadequate, at best. It has become occasionally customary (perhaps even fashionable, among their peers) for leading actors to desert a show in its waning weeks, seeking, no doubt, fresh employment elsewhere, but this practice is likely to have a horrendous effect on the theater, and both critics and audiences should protest vigorously. It is, of course, possible that the two actors (they constituted fully half of the cast) were indeed ill on the night I visited the theater, but it's also possible that they weren't; in any evènt, without the passionate authority of confident performers in the second act—matching (it can hardly be topped) the splendor of Nathan Lane's "Mandy" in the first (Mandy is the most expressive of the two Callas-ites), **The Lisbon Traviata** peters out.

Larry Gelbart's brilliantly satirical **Mastergate** also had peter-out problems, which is too bad, because the script *reads* as funny as anything in this season—perhaps any in recent memory. But satire "is what dies on Saturday night," as George Kaufman is supposed to have said, and **Mastergate** closed, if not quite at week's end, after a short-to-medium Broadway run. Kaufman was right this time: most of the energy of **Mastergate** is exhausted somewhere shortly after the halfway point, but the verbal dexterity is both pointed and, much of the time, breathtakingly funny.

Like **City of Angels** (which Gelbart also wrote—this was a great year for him), **Mastergate** is a Hollywood satire, but this time the theme is military politics and involves an army docu-drama called "Tet! The Movie" that is somehow designed to serve as the depository for funds laundered out of a failed Irangate scandal now being investigated by Congress. The language is contemporary double-talk:

> REPRESENTATIVE SELLERS: Did the President know of the Masterplan plan?
>
> MAJOR MANLEY BATTLE: I was told he didn't know.
>
> SELLERS: By whom?
>
> BATTLE: By the same people who told *him* he didn't know.
>
> SELLERS: And they would be who, would you know?
>
> BATTLE: Key members of his staff; those players who keep track of what he knows, what he knew, and what he never will. The people who have the President's memory at their fingertips.
>
> SELLERS: The President, then, to the best of your knowledge, had absolutely none of his own.
>
> BATTLE: He may have had knowledge of it, without knowing he did.
>
> SELLERS: The President can't be expected to know everything he knows, is that what you're saying?
>
> BATTLE: It's hard enough for him to remember all that he doesn't.

Gelbart races us, in prolix abandon, around the Pentagon, the

Halls of Congress, and the hills of Hollywood—with detours to San Elvador and the Republic of Ambigua, the latter recently taken over by a "Dr. Overtaga, a former podiatrist and his band of foot soldiers"—illuminating the way with some gaggingly clever government-speak ("the Director of the CIA told you in an ICU that you would no longer be answerable to the IRS?" "No one else was in a position not to know as much as the President didn't"), lawyer-speak ("the crux of your thrust," "the gist of his drift," "his compliance was of the non-variety"), and post-hip modernism ("gung-holier than thou," "land considered to be highly condominiable," and "you can't swing a dead cat over your head without hitting some South, Central or Sub-American country that isn't revolting in some way or other"). It's terrific, for a while.

Of course, it's obvious that Gelbart has nowhere, finally, to go with all this, so the racing grows a bit tedious somewhere before the play's surrealistic (and not quite satisfactory) close. But not before leaving some indelible pictures of America in confusion. The production, which I saw in its American Repertory Theatre premiere in Cambridge, is also a visual delight, with a cast of mannequin-supers filling up the galleries, and with TV cameras, newscasters, and monitors creating a media surround. All in all, **Mastergate** is wittily and wryly unforgettable.

"We have no idea what that's about and never will," Tom Stoppard explains (?) in the published version of his often impenetrable **Hapgood,** and the author's candid remark, which technically concerns a single episode, may pretty much stand for the whole play. **Hapgood** is alternately about espionage and particle physics and about double and triple agents wrestling with Heisenberg's Principle of Uncertainty, and Stoppard makes clear at every turn that he is intellectually up to the task: this is a play virtually exploding with scientific observation and apt political parallels. "Compared with the electron, everything is banal," says Kerner, a Russian particle physicist, whose research is finding potential military applications for anti-particles. For years Kerner has been a British double agent who British intelligence officers fear may have turned triple and who himself worries that he has turned quadruple or quintuple. He is like an electron in a post-Heisenbergian atom, turning and returning at the same time, simultaneously; leaping through inner space and time by discrete quanta; existing in two places at once—or in neither. Particle indeterminacy is not mere theory, either, but leads to probability applications in knocking foreign-launched ICBMs out of the sky with X-ray lasers and precise bolts of colliding anti-matter. Kerner's physical world is also a political world, a killing field where the fission and fusion of multiple intellectual allegiances is a matter of course (and survival). "Quantum mechanics made everything random," Kerner explains. "You think you have seen to the bottom of things, but there is no bottom."

There is no plot, either—certainly no plot the audience can follow (or perhaps there is just too *much* plot—like the million tinfoil decoys, "reflectors," Stoppard calls them, that go off with the ICBMs), and reading the text afterward doesn't add much in the way of comprehensibility. Superficially, **Hapgood** is a spy thriller; the action begins with a quick series of comings and goings in a London shower room, with various briefcases left and picked up in various cubicles, mostly by persons apparently in disguise (although, since we don't know them yet, we don't know who they're supposed to be disguised *as*), and much of what follows is the uncovering and recovering of these disguises, often by intelligence officers themselves in and out of disguise—even to each other. There are a host of typical whodunit props, often taking a metaphysical turn: hidden microphones that may or may not be alive, computer disks that may or may not contain texts, photographs of photographs (that turn out to be photographs of photographs of photographs), various sets of real and imaginary twins, and an "interscene" in which one character makes a "quantum jump" (you only get to know this in the published stage directions) to become, while standing still, a totally different person. "We're all doubles," says the double/triple/quadruple/quintuple Kerner as he heads back to Kaliningrad. That's not much help. "Objective reality is for zoologists," he says with a sneer.

Hapgood is best when it's a thinly dramatized lecture on contemporary science and politics, and Stoppard brilliantly limns the irony of the defector ("I don't even know if I was a genuine defector," Kerner says, "I wasn't seeking asylum, I was seeking an IBM one-nine-five"). One is not oblivious, either, to Stoppard's Czech beginnings. Yet the play's personal matters, which involve equally urgent intrigues of love, children, and career, are simply overwhelmed by the lecture. We need at least the *illusion* of an objective reality if we are to care and feel—and if we don't care and feel, then there's little of interest in what is, science and politics apart, a soap opera. The title character, a lady who plays chess without a board and roots her son's team to victory at the soccer field— all while running the British intelligence office—is supposed to hold the play together, but the character is unrealized. Judy Davis, in this role, and Roger Rees, as Kerner, were verbally scintillating in the United States premiere in Los Angeles, but intellectual excitement isn't enough here. *Hapgood* provides, in the main, deeply frustrating theater.

The same might be said for Nick Dear's *The Art of Success,* also an English transplant, which enjoyed some strong attention in its Manhattan Theatre Club run. Putatively the story of William Hogarth, the eighteenth-century engraver ("The Rake's Progress" is part of the story here), *Art of Success* is about the two nouns of its title: art and success, particularly in the real-world admixture of rampant carnality, prostitution both political and conventional, and deep criminality (murder, dismemberment, and, worst of all in some quarters, artistic piracy). If that weren't enough, there's a dream world as well here, side by side with the real one, and a cast of characters that includes Harry (Henry) Fielding, Robert Walpole, and Queen Caroline, along with some other whores, drunks, and murderesses, all slipping from one world to the other and back again. There's too much turning to keep track of what goes on here, so the future becomes the still point. "You have to win through to posterity, William, or you are worth nothing," Walpole tells Hogarth. "You have to exist in the future, and for that you have to function in the present."

So, does the future lie in art or in success? Almost mundanely, the play devotes more than a measure of time to the emerging English Copyright Law and the protection it might give visual artists like Hogarth versus playwrights like Fielding or novelists like the Fielding that will come to be. There are comparable discussions of the infamous Licensing Act and the political censorship of theatrical, i.e., public art versus the more private, one-on-one forms of aesthetic (and satiric) communication. And so, alternating with lots of lively, graphic sexuality and quite novel (I will spare descriptions) under-the-skirt skirmishes, we are asked to attend attentively to fragments of eighteenth-century literary debates virtually lifted from the Encyclopedia Brittanica. There's some wonderful inventiveness here, both intellectual and stylistic, but too much for one evening (Dear has apparently condensed ten years of history, 1727-1737, into a single night), and the final impact is mainly of an author (Dear) trying to make a big splash rather than an engraver and his tormented compatriots wrestling with the big ones.

The South Coast Repertory Theatre in Orange County, California, has enjoyed remarkable success in producing new plays over the years (the company won the regional Tony Award, largely for its success in new play productions, in 1988), but it still awaits its first "breakthrough" national hit to compare with *The Great White Hope* (from Washington's Arena Stage), *Fences* (Yale Rep), *Glengarry Glen Ross* (Chicago's Goodman Theater), *Children of a Lesser God* (Mark Taper Forum), or Beth Henley's *Crimes of the Heart* (Actor's Theater of Louisville). Perhaps thinking of this latter play, which won the 1979 Pulitzer Prize after its Broadway opening, SCR commissioned a new play from Ms. Henley, which, entitled *Abundance,* opened a decade later; it is not, however, a breakthrough, either for SCR or Ms. Henley. While Henley's gift for striking oddities remains abundant, as the title suggests (that's *all* the title suggests), this rambling tale of two married couples, spread out across twenty-five years in the Wyoming Territories of the last century, contains little plot and less fascination. The couples, who are mismatched to start with, grow further and further apart; the characters, who mostly range from insipid to obnoxious as we meet them, simply worsen with age. There's doubtless the idea of a play here, but for the most part all we are given is the idea of idealism defeated and of romance denied. This is schematic formula writing; neither intelligence, vision, humor, nor passion animate these four stolid people, and the play is moved along solely by fits of random violence and theatrical novelties— shooting an ox, tossing about a glass eye, playfully pistoling a woman's feet, wolves digging up and eating a baby's corpse, a scalped wife ("that's all I have left of her," says the bewildered husband, wanly referring to the scalp), a pet prairie dog, and various and sundry dismemberments by the farm machinery. This is Beth Henley trying to write her Sam Shepard play (this is becoming a national passion), and her whimsical tone is at odds with the Shepardian abstract nastiness. At the play's end, we are only too happy to be rid of these dismal characters, of whom only the two women even the playwright seems to admire—mainly, it seems, because they whistle. *Abundance* is an incompetent play by a Pulitzer Prize-winning playwright and was indifferently produced by a Tony Award-winning theater. In dramatic art, there are no guarantees.

Les miserables, Les liaisons dangereuses, The Phantom of the Opera—several top-of-the-line plays of recent seasons have been adapted from one- and two-hundred-year-old European novels. *Nothing Sacred,* which Canadian playwright George F. Walker spun out of Ivan Turgenev's *Fathers and Sons,* is up there with the best of them.

Nothing Sacred, which I saw in a glorious production directed by Robert Woodruff at San Francisco's American Conservatory Theatre, has been something of a regional theater phenomenon. The play opened in Toronto in 1988 and will be seen in dozens of North American theaters this year—before any New York or London premiere has even been set. There is no wonder about its success: *Nothing Sacred* is a beautifully constructed play that manages to be radical and comforting at the same time, a Brechtian Chekhov and a highly entertaining comedy as well. *Sacred*'s topics are the usual nineteenth-century Russian tea-time conversation pieces: What is Love? What is Russia? What is the World? But Walker's panorama soon narrows to the sharply specific.

Events center on Yevgeny Bazarov, a brilliant, rude, audacious, and charismatic young medical student and pre-revolutionary leader. Lacking a program, Bazarov has become a nihilist seeking (and attracting) acolytes—one of whom, his fellow student Arkady, has brought Bazarov to his home for summer vacation. Broken two-hundred-year-old plates and shifting romantic and social allegiances soon follow. "I would simply like to know what you are planning to do after you have torn everything down," Arkady's uncle asks Bazarov. "I'll do nothing," replies the nihilist. "The tearing down is sufficient. In fact an entire life's work. The next generation can do the building."

A naive young student (Scott Freeman, right) admires the brazen approach to life taken by two revolutionaries (Christopher McCann and Fredi Olster) in a scene from Nothing Sacred, *George F. Walker's freewheeling play based on the classic Russian novel* Fathers and Sons.

There is wonderful talk in this play, but what sets **Nothing Sacred** apart from most of its contemporaries is its series of striking and well-realized incidents and characters, mostly taken from Turgenev, that integrate elastically into a coherent and compelling story. Walker's trenchant observations (about class, education, sexual allegiance) and his elegant dramaturgical twists and bon mots are fully supported by characters we care about and situations that oblige our attention. His final scene—I won't describe it—is deeply moving yet punctuated with an astounding hilarity. The Woodruff

production, with European-style scenery (a gigantic Chinese-red threshing machine, its interstices wired with yard-long florescent bulbs, covered the stage, blanketing a few sleeping peasants; a bile-green wall, in front of which aristocrats drink bright green champagne, served as the backdrop), threw everything into the broadest Brechtian ("we could have done this differently") perspective, making the mind work through Walker's conundrums and complexities. This is a play, and, perhaps, a production that should be widely seen in the coming years.

Except for its unfortunate title, Keith Reddin's **Nebraska** is a well-crafted and affecting play, and its summer premiere at the La Jolla Playhouse was reasonably auspicious. Like Reddin's **Rum and Coke, Nebraska** is set in a military environment, but unlike the earlier, largely political and satirical work, **Nebraska** is centered on human relationships—particularly marriage, friendship, and betrayal—and the nervous interplay among six otherwise isolated souls working and living in and around a nuclear missile silo under our mid-American plains. **Nebraska** is a tough play about good people, ordinary in their tastes and aspirations, demoralized by forces just beyond their range.

In his silo, young Lieutenant Dean Swift well understands that fail-safe procedures rule all down there: two keys, two lieutenants, and a set of enabling codes stand sturdily between civilization and its missile-borne annihilation. But above ground there is no fail-safe: there, Swift finds, "the word is 'random.'" Swift's dog dies. His marriage is falling apart—his wife can't seem to pass her driving test, she thinks of his career as just "work," and he starts to have eyes for other women, including his base commander's wife. That feeling—as are few others in the play—is reciprocated, if briefly. But most communication in the play is aborted. There are no children. Awkward silences prevail in nearly every scene. A failed barbecue party is the centerpiece of the second act, along with broken glasses of a marital spat. Inevitably, the randomness of life above ground percolates down into the silo. Fail-safe starts to come apart at the seams, putting the whole country at risk. This is a play about the peacetime army, supervising hot war weapons as they silently obsolesce in their post-cold war abandonment. But Reddin reminds us that they're still there and they're still armed and they're ready to fly, even if forgotten. They're managed by a dying breed—dying, in part, because the job is killing them, and maybe also because *we're* killing them. Obloquy—the misery of anonymous life on a military post, in Heidelberg, in Nebraska—is the subtheme.

Reddin's craftsmanship is sharp, his dialogue witty and precisely pointed, his silences deeply meaningful. My only quibble is with his title. Reddin's play is about a state of mind, not a state of the union, and Nebraska has nothing to do with what he's saying. In the 1940s, playwrights blamed everything on Mom, in the 1950s on Dad, in the 1960s and 1970s on "Amerika," and in the 1980s, it seems, on the midwest. Perhaps it's our new breed of bi-coastal playwrights, or perhaps its simply because there is no professional regional theater in Nebraska to offend. In any event, Nebraskans will be disappointed in this play; it's certainly not going to prove their *Oklahoma!* And they're certainly not to blame for Swift's dilemma, or his adultery, or his boss's suicide, or his dog's death. Reddin should rethink his title.

One must conclude this review of the year in drama with the sad note that the last days of the year brought the death of

Samuel Beckett, who, more than any playwright of the last half-century, showed us how funny profundity can be and how various the dramatic potential. Beckett liberated theater from its most noxious conventions and renewed creativity in every aspect of the medium. His influence is felt everywhere in the theater and can be traced in most if not all of the plays discussed above.

The Year in World Literature

by William Riggan

A handful of literary figures abroad made big headlines in 1989 not for their writing talent but for their political skills and courage. Václav Havel became president of Czechoslovakia after leading the principal opposition group's ouster of the old regime; Mario Vargas Llosa became the odds-on favorite to capture Peru's presidency; Ana Blandiana and Mihai Eminescu played prominent roles in the overthrow of Romania's hated ruler Nicolae Ceausescu and in setting up a new transition government in that beleaguered nation; Wang Meng resigned as China's minister of culture in the wake of his government's brutal suppression of prodemocracy demonstrators; Valentin Rasputin was one of many new-breed citizen politicians elected to the Soviet Union's revamped legislative assembly, stressing environmental issues (he represents a threatened area of eastern Siberia) and a surprisingly conservative stance toward certain non-Russian minorities; Vasil Bykau spearheaded a much-publicized Soviet investigative commission which uncovered irrefutable evidence of large-scale civilian massacres in Belorussia by the Red Army during and immediately following World War II; and, of course, Salman Rushdie had to go into hiding as a result of the Ayatollah Khomeini's death edict for the perceived blasphemies of **The Satanic Verses,** published in late 1988. In comparison with such events, "merely literary" news from 1989 paled somewhat, as life overtook and usually surpassed art in many separate corners of the globe. Still, a profusion of important new works did appear, most notably in the Hispanic world and in Asia.

The most eagerly anticipated and, in many ways, most controversial single literary publication outside the Anglo-American orbit in 1989 was undoubtedly Gabriel García Márquez's big new novel, **El general en su laberinto** (*The General in His Labyrinth*), an earthy, imaginative, and largely affectionate portrait of the perplexing final months in the life of Latin America's revered hero, Simón Bolívar, that manages both to demythify the "Liberator" and add to the myths surrounding his life and person. Having already occasioned heated discussion throughout the Hispanic world both for its refusal to overlook the general's many human failings and for its clearly pro-Bolívar political stance, and offering a virtuosic mix of tragedy, epic, and magical realism in portraying its protagonist's ultimate failure to realize his Utopian dream of Latin American unity, the novel is sure to provoke worldwide commentary as it begins appearing in translations abroad in 1990.

Even without García Márquez's blockbuster, the year would have been a respectable one in Latin America. **Divertimento,** a very early (1949) unpublished short novel by the late Julio Cortázar, was rescued from oblivion and clearly revealed the formal experimentalism and playful narrative style that were to characterize the Argentine author's later novelistic writing. Fellow Argentine Manuel Puig, famed for such film-

Cover of Cae La Noche Tropical, *by Manuel Puig.*

based novels as *Kiss of the Spider Woman* and *Betrayed by Rita Hayworth,* returned to novel writing after a six-year silence with **Cae la noche tropical** (*Tropic Nightfall*), a sad and moving account of two sisters fading quietly into the lonely twilight of their lives, commenting all the while on their misfortune, insomnia, and drab existence. **Son of Man,** by Augusto Roa Bastos, which recounts his native Paraguay's savage twenty-year war with Bolivia from 1912 to 1932 and the repressive conditions there both before and after the conflict, reached a wider audience in 1989 via its first U.S. publication. The novelist and playwright Luis Rafael Sánchez presented **La importancia de llamarse Daniel Santos** (*The Importance of Being Called Daniel Santos*), a self-proclaimed "Puerto Rican contribution to the formation of the world of popular myth applicable to all of Latin America," as embodied in the story of a celebrated *bolero* singer. The Nicaraguan poet and longtime minister of culture Ernesto Cardenal evoked his nation's pre-Columbian past in the collection *Los ovnis de oro* (*The Golden UFO's*), subtitled "Poemas indios" (Indian Poems). *Cristóforo nonato,* by Mexico's premier novelist, Carlos Fuentes, made its debut in Spanish early in the year and in English (as *Christopher Unborn*) at year's end, getting the jump on quintocentennial celebrations of Columbus's voyage of discovery with the prolix carnivalesque narrative of a fetus as it gestates toward cataclysmic birth in the horribly overcrowded "Makesicko City" megalopolis of 1992. The original's wild wordplay and outrageous linguistic fun unfortunately suffer considerable diminution in English but still leave much to fascinate, amuse, and shock the reader. Fuentes's countryman Fernando del Paso hit the Spanish American bestseller list with *Novedades del imperio* (*News from the Empire*), a historical novel about the Emperor Maximilian and Empress Carlotta. The English-speaking world was finally introduced to this writer via the appearance of *Palinuro of Mexico,* a Joycean-Rabelaisian-Borgesian extravaganza centered on a twenty-year-old medical student whose experiences are emblematic of the nation's idealistic youth who were slain in the Zócalo tragedy of October 1968.

From Spain proper, home of the 1989 Nobel laureate Camilo José Cela, the year's most noteworthy new works were *Las virtudes del pájaro solitario* (*The Virtues of the Solitary Bird*), Juan Goytisolo's lyric account of the life and vision of Saint John of the Cross, and *En la penumbra* (*In the Shadow*), Juan Benet's best-seller, which uses an ably told domestic story to fashion a metaphor of the writer's world of words and verbal passion.

The year in Asian literature witnessed a profusion of riches. From China, so much in the news for the events of June 4th in Beijing and Shanghai, several younger writers made their "debuts" in the West. *The August Sleepwalker* introduced the remarkable underground verse of Bei Dao, one of the most gifted poets to emerge from the last decade's upheavals. *Bolshevik Satire,* by Wang Meng, the erstwhile minister of culture, was the first Chinese modernist novel to appear in English translation. This work follows the life of a committed young party member who is branded as a rightist and exiled to manual labor in the countryside. The stories in Can Xue's *Dialogues in Paradise* combine naturalistic detail and nightmarish fantasy in a manner that may recall several of Latin America's magic realists. Liu Zongren's *6 Tanyin Alley* hews to a more strictly realistic autobiographical line in its account of daily life in a rundown Beijing neighborhood. Written directly in English (the author is a journalist and translator for one of China's largest official English-language magazines), this novel is not the long-awaited epic of the Cultural Revolution years, but it does provide at least a glimpse of what that period must have been like for untold numbers of Chinese. Wang Anyi chronicles rural, agrarian life in the 1960s and 1970s in the novels *Baotown* and *The Flow,* the latter filtered through the consciousness of a middle-class, middle-aged woman much like the author herself. The late Ding Ling, often termed China's finest woman writer of the century, was honored posthumously with a volume of selected writings in translation entitled *I Myself Am a Woman.* The novel *Heavy Wings* by Zhang Jie, a woman writer of a later generation, tracks several families and individuals as they adjust to a changing China in the early days of Deng Xiaoping's reform era following Mao's death.

Cover of La Importancia de Llamarse Daniel Santos, *by Luis Raphael Sanchez. Cover art by Visual Design.*

Japan's literary *éminence grise,* Yasushi Inoue, saw two works released to the West: the powerful prizewinning novelette *The Hunting Gun,* relating in *Rashomon* fashion the story of a tragic love triangle in the immediate postwar period, and *The Counterfeiter,* a collection of three short stories, of which the title work centers on the biographer of a printer whose works are imitated by a forger. The Catholic novelist Shūsaku Endō accomplished a similar double with the short story collection *Foreign Studies,* two selections of which are presumably based on the author's own studies in France during the 1950s, and the three-act play *The Golden Country,* about Christianity's slow progress in seventeenth-century Japan. The younger novelist Takeshi Kaikō, who passed away unexpectedly near year's end, showed a more modern, anguished sensibility in the stories of *Five Thousand Runaways.* Many of these stories are set in Vietnam and the South China Sea and feature a variety of fascinating, obsessive characters. *Acts of Worship* gave Western readers a first look at seven superbly crafted stories by the late Yukio Mishima on such themes as sexual awakening, the rejection of Western civilization, and, in the long title story, the protracted and ever so discreet development of the relationship between a brilliant, revered professor and his widowed, devoted housekeeper into something very like the beginnings of love. The title novella in Fumiko Kometani's *Passover,* which won her the coveted Akutagawa Prize upon publication in Japanese in 1986, presented a darker side of the Japanese character in its angry, anti-Western, and antireligious (some say anti-Semitic) depiction of the troubled, vitriolic marriage between a Japanese woman and an American Jew.

From elsewhere in East Asia came several unexpected treats as well. The short stories of Korea's most distinguished living prose writer, Hwang Sun-Won, appeared for the first time in English translation under the title *The Book of Masks.* His much-lauded and often controversial young countryman, Yun Heung-gil, debuted in the West with *The House of Twilight,* a volume of short fiction set during and after the bloody civil war. Singapore's best-known author, Catherine Lim, published *Or Else, the Lightning God,* her second short-story collection on that city-state's fast-paced contemporary scene. And Pramoedya Ananta Toer, whose persecution and incarceration by Indonesian authorities have only added to his international literary renown, saw the publication abroad of *The Fugitive,* a novel set in August 1945 as the Japanese occupation was ending and the fight for Indonesian independence was beginning.

Mistaken Identity, the new novel by Nayantara Sahgal, who is considered by many India's finest woman novelist (she is also closely related to the Gandhi family), explores through the revealing prison narrative of the minor raja Bhushan Singh the social and political upheavals that marked the end of the British raj. Anita Desai, perhaps even better known abroad than Sahgal, published the novel *Baumgartner's Bombay,* which tracks the peripatetic experiences of a shy, quintessential outsider from Nazi Germany to post-Partition India. Several superb recent Hindi tales by Premchand were at last made accessible to the English-reading public in *Deliverance and Other Stories.* Bharati Mukherjee, herself a resident of Canada for several years, wrote of refugees, transients, immigrants, and cultural dislocation in *The Middleman and Other Stories* and in her third novel, *Jasmine,* an expanded version of one of the *Middleman* tales about a young Indian widow's peripatetic experiences in America. And finally, Bhisnam Sahni's bestselling Hindi novel *Tamas* (*Shame*) likewise appeared in English translation, bringing to a world-wide audience its devastating fictional account of events leading up to the murderous 1947 Partition riots in the Punjab. The acclaimed film version of the novel now playing in India has only added to the impact of Sahni's powerful work, and both have met with considerable disapproval for reopening old wounds and rekindling the hatred and violence of that traumatic time four decades ago.

From Africa in 1989 came a very respectable set of works by established authors and newcomers alike. The Nigerian Nobel laureate Wole Soyinka issued a collection of recent essays entitled *Art, Dialogue, and Outrage* as well as *Ìsarà,* something of a "prequel" to his acclaimed autobiography *Aké* of several years back. *Ìsarà* is a moving tribute to and elegy for his father, "Essay," that captures much of the tension, ambiguity, and mutual dependency between British colonialists and Africans that marked the first several decades of this century. The 1987 Gikuyu novel *Matagari* by Kenya's Ngugi wa Thiong'o made its first appearance in English. This work tells the story of a legendary rebel figure who reemerges from the forest seeking "truth and justice" as well as family and home in the exploitative, capitalist Kenya of the 1980s. At once roguishly satiric and earnestly polemical, the novel follows its superhero through a series of near-miraculous

Cover of Tamas, *by Bhisham Sahni.*

scrapes and escapes to a final realization that arms and not words alone will be necessary to achieve his true liberation. *To Every Birth Its Blood,* the first novelistic effort by the noted South African poet Mongane Serote—at last made available following its banning upon its scheduled debut in 1981—movingly evokes the 1976 Soweto riots and their aftermath. Serote's compatriot, the poet-painter Breyten Breytenbach, added to his list of recent prose works with the futuristic political novel *Memory of Snow and Dust. The Family,* by Nigeria's Buchi Emecheta, charts the sad fate of a dysfunctional immigrant Jamaican family in London through the eyes of the young daughter. Two newer writers to watch are Nigeria's Ben Okri and Zimbabwe's Charles Munyoshi, who made considerable impact with the story collections *Stars of the New Curfew* and *The Setting Sun and the Rolling World,* respectively. From Francophone Africa came *Before the Birth of the Moon* by Zaïre's V. Y. Mudimbé and *Le sommeil d'Ève* (*Eve's Sleep*) by Algeria's Mohammed Dib. The superb Caribbean poet-playwright Derek Walcott produced a book-length narrative poem entitled *Omeros,* which recasts Homer's *Odyssey* from the standpoint of the Antillean-African experience. And in the stories of *Higher Ground,* Caryl Phillips of St. Kitts proved that the success of his *Frangipani House* three years ago was no fluke. The power and control of such pieces as the novella-length **"Cargo Rap,"** the opening **"Heartland"** sequence, and the title story are stun-

27

ning and mark Phillips as a major new talent in Anglophone writing.

The most notable titles to reach the West from the Middle East in 1989 included three new novels by major Israeli writers. In *For Every Sin,* Aharon Appelfeld again explores the breakdown of the communal spirit shared by Holocaust survivors. To many readers, this theme is adumbrated more successfully in his previous book, *The Immortal Bartfuss;* in *For Every Sin,* the focus is on the dazed, postapocalyptic, *Painted Bird*-like wanderings of a newly liberated survivor of "Camp Number 8" and his efforts to return home in body and spirit and begin to overcome the misery, pain, and dehumanizing horrors he has experienced. David Grossman's *See Under: Love* is a challenging and intricately constructed work. This tale of a Holocaust survivor interweaves "borrowed" Hebrew adventure stories and an account of the Polish writer Bruno Schulz's death at the hands of the Nazis in 1942 with a Vergilian first-person narrative by an "eternal" indestructible Jew who lived to tell of the death camp experience. In *His Daughter,* Yoram Kaniuk follows a retired *sabra* general on a desperate and dangerous search for his soldier daughter. A hopelessness bordering on nihilism permeates the book, which is ultimately, in the words of one critic, "a condemnation of the Zionist ideal of the sabra, the 'Jewish Aryan,' utterly self-sufficient, who knows he must fight to defend his people." Also appearing in 1989 was *Shira,* the first English edition of 1966 Nobel recipient S. Y. Agnon's posthumous (and unfinished) 1971 novel about Jewish residents of Palestine under the British Mandate in the 1930s.

From the Arab world came *Leo Africanus,* a historical novel by the Francophone Lebanese author Amin Maalouf that chronicles the first forty years in the life of the fifteenth-century Andalusian Arab adventurer and scholar whose life brought him in contact with pirates and popes, vagabonds and kings, peasants and scientists, poets and philosophers. *The Circling Song* became the third novel by Egyptian woman physician Naawal El Saadawi to appear in English translation since 1980. This work tells a terrifying tale of urban corruption and dark brutality as it traces the efforts of twins Hamida and Hamido to relocate each other after years of separation. The story collection *Playhouse* marked the successful English debut of Simin Saneshvar, Iran's bestselling woman writer and widow of the revered Jalal Al-e Ahmad. And *The Prizegiving,* a thinly disguised autobiographical novel, marked a similar debut for Turkey's Aysel Özakin. The plot of this work suffers somewhat from frequently heavy-handed antimale rhetoric but shows considerable skill when not simply decrying the protagonist's mistreatment by a string of worthless men and patronizing philistines in Ankara's literary circles.

Russian writers enjoyed a reasonably good year, particularly in Western translations. Tatyana Tolstaya made perhaps the biggest splash, revealing an exuberant and canny talent eminently worthy of her famous surname in her short story collection *On the Golden Porch.* Vladimir Soloukhin's *Scenes from Russian Life* presents eight autobiographical stories on such themes as illness, intervillage hostilities, abortion, and the pristine beauties of nature. Vassily Aksyonov, arguably one of the best-known Russian émigré authors after Solzhenitsyn and Brodsky, enjoyed the English publication of two recent novels: the jazz-influenced satire *Our Golden Ironburg* and the more ambitious but equally wicked *Say Cheese!,* which skewers Soviet intellectual and artistic life. *Siberia on*

Fire gathers several newer stories and essays by the noted (and only recently "rehabilitated") village prose writer Valentin Rasputin which confirm that his pre-*glasnost* decade of forced silence in no way diminished the originality and prowess displayed in such masterworks as the 1976 novella *Farewell to Matyora.* In Russian, the highlight of the year—aside from all the *glasnost*-induced first Soviet releases of innumerable long-banned writers—was Vladimir Vysotsky's three-volume *Sobranye stikhov i pesen* (*Collected Poems and Songs*), the most complete and authoritative edition yet published of the late underground bard's acclaimed lyric and satiric work.

East European literature was of course greatly overshadowed in 1989 by the year's epochal sociopolitical changes. Still, a few events and works bear noting. *Temptation,* the dissident dramatist Václav Havel's Faust play, emerged from the Czech underground and premiered to great acclaim in New York and Los Angeles several months before his leadership of the opposition group Civic Forum thrust him into the national and international spotlight and brought him the presidency of Czechoslovakia. *Life with a Star,* the first Western translation of Czech author Jiří Weil's posthumously published 1964 masterpiece, added a remarkably original and understated novel to the evergrowing catalogue of Holocaust literature. Two of Hungary's finest twentieth-century poets were honored by abundant new English editions of their work: the nimble and versatile Sándor Weöres, with *Eternal Moment,* and the hauntingly intense János Pilinszky, with *The Desert of Love. Rondo,* by accomplished Polish novelist and wartime survivor Kazimierz Brandys, is a virtuosic and devilishly complex, madly digressive first-person reminiscence of a Polish underground organization called Rondo that also manages to bring in a host of other themes both large and small due to the narrator's (and the author's) proclivities toward prolixity and encyclopedic inclusiveness. The second and final volume of iconoclastic Polish novelist Witold Gombrowicz's revealing and influential *Diary,* covering his return from Latin American exile and his final years in Italy and France, was issued in translation in September. Ismail Kadare, Albania's lone international literary standard-bearer, saw two more of his recent novels released in French: the epic thriller *Dossier H,* and the historical novel *Le concert* (*The Concert*), which treats events leading up to the break in Albanian-Chinese relations.

German letters made a very respectable showing in 1989, led by three superb women writers. The twenty-six stories collected in Gabriele Wohmann's *Kassensturz* (*Audit*) depict a like number of unhappy families and individuals whose lives are foundering not through tragic occurrences but from the sheer banality and tedium of their everyday existence in modern West Germany. Christa Wolf's *Sommerstück* (*Summer Story*), in contrast, finds an antidote to such present-day ennui in the memory of a glorious summer spent with companions exploring the back country of East Germany and learning most of all the value of genuine friendship. Friederike Mayröcker's *Gesammelte Prosa, 1949-1975* (*Collected Prose, 1949-1975*) gathered a quarter-century of the Austrian poet's offbeat and often startling short fiction, sketches, impressions, and stylistic experiments. Her compatriot, Peter Handke, weighed in with the novella *Versuch über die Müdigkeit* (*Experiment in Fatigue*) and the full-length drama *Das Spiel von Fragen* (*The Question Game*), an intricate and somewhat Stoppardian "play" on words, Socratic inquiry, role-playing, and the very nature of verbal art. Also of note were the West German author Hermann Lenz's short novel *Jung und alt* (*Young and Old*), the late Thomas Bernhard's fragmented lyric novelette *In der Höhe* (*On High*), Hans Magnus Enzensberger's miscellany of poems, dialogues, and essays entitled *Der Fliegende Robert* (*The Flying Robert*), the East German Stefan Heym's fascinating memoirs collected in *Nachruf* (*Posthumous Fame*), and the 1946-1948 installment of Thomas Mann's voluminous diaries.

French letters endured a lackluster year. Rising above the pack, although deriving quite literally from another era, were the third and final installment of Albert Camus's sensitive, anguished *Cahiers* (*Notebooks*), covering the years 1951-1959; the octogenarian Julien Green's leisurely historical novel, *Les étoiles du sud* (*Stars of the South*); and the nonagenarian post-novelist Aragon's volume of often scandalous confessions, *Pour expliquer ce que j'étais* (*To Explain What I Was*). Claude Simon led the way among the moderns with *L'acacia* (*The Acacia Tree*), his first major work since garnering the Nobel Prize in 1985. This complex novel evokes French military disasters in 1914 and 1940 and the Belle Epoque and the interwar years through a successful, even magisterial revival of many *nouveau roman* aspirations and techniques. The octogenarian Nathalie Sarraute, unlike coevals such as Green and Aragon, continued her half-century of quiet narrative experimentation with *Tu ne t'aimes pas* (*You Don't Love Yourself*), surely the only first-person-*plural* novel any reader will have seen in recent years, if ever. *Une chambre dan les bois* (*A Room in the Forest*) by Patrick Drevet and *Vous qui passez dans l'ombre* (*You Who Walk in the Shadow*) by Jean-Baptiste Niel were widely praised as the best and most original novels of the *rentrée*, the early-autumn postvacation season that is traditionally one of the most important periods of the French literary year. In *L'oublié* (*The Forgotten*), Elie Wiesel produced yet another moving novel of memory and forgetfulness, of personal and communal history, and of familial heritage and national commitment, as an aging survivor of the war attempts to pass on the memories of his experiences to his indifferent new-age son before they fade forever from his grasp.

Translations served to disseminate worldwide the work of four first-rate Brazilian authors in 1989. *Soulstorm* offered the late prose writer Clarice Lispector's short stories; *This Earth, That Sky* introduced the supple, versatile poetry of the late Manuel Bandeira; *The Republic of Dreams* displayed Nélida Piñon's novelistic craft in all its elegance and intricacy; and *An Invincible Memory* revealed João Ubaldo Ribeiro as a worthy successor to Jorge Amado in composing vast panoramic epics filled with scintillating characters, diverse

Dust jacket of An Invincible Memory, *by João Ubaldo Ribeiro. Jacket design © 1989 by William Graef. Jacket illustration © 1989 by Greg Ragland.*

prose styles, and highly diverting actions. Amado himself brought out yet another rollicking and colorful historical novel, *O sumiço do santo* (*The Saint's Disappearance*). In a final note on Romance literature, a large selection from the work of the outstanding Romanian poet and prominent National Salvation Front member Ana Blandiana became available late in the year (prior to the stunning overthrow of Ceausescu in December) with the publication of *The Hour of Sand.* Culled from twenty years of steady production and revealing a romantic, mystical, nature- and folklore-tinged verse marked as well by personal vulnerability and a singleminded obsession with purity in an astonishingly corrupt time and place, Blandiana's work, like Havel's, can stand up to the heat of public scrutiny that her sudden international prominence may occasion.

Notes on Contributors

Wendy Lesser is the editor and publisher of *The Threepenny Review,* which she founded in 1980. She is the author of *The Life Below the Ground: A Study of the Subterranean in Literature and History* and the forthcoming *His Other Half: Men Looking at Women Through Art.* She is a board member of the National Book Critics Circle, and her reviews and essays have appeared in the *New York Times Book Review,* the *Hudson Review,* the *Washington Post,* and elsewhere. She holds a Ph.D in English from the University of California, Berkeley, an M.A. from King's College, Cambridge, and a B.A. from Harvard.

Sidney Burris has published a collection of poetry, *A Day at the Races,* and a critical study, *The Poetry of Resistance: Seamus Heaney and the Pastoral Tradition.* His most recent essays have appeared in *The Southern Review* and *Contemporary Literature,* and he wrote three articles for the forthcoming revised edition of *The Princeton Encyclopedia of Poetry and Poetics.* Burris is Assistant Professor of English at the University of Arkansas.

Robert Cohen has written several theater texts and treatises, including *Theatre, Giraudoux: Three Faces of Destiny, Acting Power, Acting One, Acting Professionally, Creative Play Direction,* and the forthcoming *Acting in Shakespeare,* as well as essays for various academic and theater journals. Cohen has directed drama, lectured on theater at many schools and universities, and he has staged plays at the Colorado Shakespeare Festival, the Utah Shakespeare Festival, and the Focused Research Program in Medieval Drama at the University of California, Irvine, where he is Chair and Professor of Drama. Cohen earned his doctrate in Fine Arts from Yale University.

William Riggan is Associate Editor of *World Literature Today* at the University of Oklahoma, with responsibilities for coverage of Third World, Slavic, Anglo-American, and smaller European literatures. He holds a doctorate in comparative literature from Indiana University, is the author of *Picaros, Madmen, Naïfs, and Clowns: The Unreliable First-Person Narrator,* has written extensively on the history and selections of both the Nobel Prize in Literature and the Neustadt International Prize in Literature, and regularly reviews new foreign fiction and poetry for several journals and newspapers.

New Authors

Edward Allen
Straight Through the Night

Allen is an American novelist, born in 1948.

Straight Through the Night details the travails of Chuck Deckle as he passes from job to job and drives around the New York City area in his delapidated car. In an animated prose style, Allen provides witty, ironic commentary on urban America of the 1979-1980 period, emphasizing the sluggish economy and the Iran hostage crisis, and employs working-class vernacular to portray the struggles of a disaffected, intelligent man attempting to fulfill proletarian values. Deckle's present miseries are underscored in his reminiscences about his privledged upbringing, his experiences in prep school and college, and a violent act he committed during a student protest that injured a counter demonstrator. The gritty realism of Deckle's lifestyle is accentuated in passages that describe his work in the meat industry, where he is involved in slaughtering animals as well as processing, packing, selling, and distributing meat. While some critics found Deckle incapable of arousing sympathy, particularly as he descends into bigotry, Allen won praise for his counterpointing of brutish realism and lyrical descriptions. Merle Rubin commented: "*Straight Through the Night* is an exhilerating ride through a darkling landscape. The sheer exuberance of its style . . . transfers a depressing subject into one that is richly sad: funny, poignant, frightened and curiously cheerful, even on the brink of tears."

PUBLISHERS WEEKLY

Self-consciously resonant with the heaven-storming lyricism of Thomas Wolfe, [*Straight Through the Night*] offers a graphic guided tour of the meat-packing and -selling industry from the down-and-out perspective of an ex-preppie, ex-student activist. Narrator Chuck Deckle, whose world view includes T.S. Eliot, Handel, *Pink Floyd* and various TV shows, is not really cut out to be a butcher. As we follow him on a string of jobs from lower Manhattan through Harlem and from Rockland and Westchester counties to a kosher plant in Hoboken, N.J., he reminisces about his girlfriends and boyhood, waxes lyrical on the sounds, sights and smells of New York, and sounds off on the sorry state of America. His slow descent into anti-Semitism is ugly. Allen, a former butcher and meat salesman who is also a poet and teacher at Ohio University, Athens, has a good ear for raunchy working-class vernacular, but he squanders his obvious literary talents on endless self-rumination, leaving little room for full-bodied characters to emerge.

A review of "Straight Through the Night," in Publishers Weekly, *Vol. 234, No. 22, November 25, 1988, p. 55.*

RICHARD EDER

Chuck Deckle is the baby who fell out of the tub while trying to throw out the bathwater. He comes from a moderately privileged family, went to Hotchkiss and an ultra-progressive college, experimented with group living on a farm or two and marched for various leftish causes.

It was a comfortable inauthenticity, a subsidized playpen for the privileged young. And in a few years, by rights, he would have drifted with his playmates into an even more comfortable inauthenticity on the other side: a job in advertising or law or banking, a yuppie life style.

Instead, he short-circuited. On one of the marches, he had punched an elderly counter-demonstrator who was carrying an American flag; the man's false teeth had popped out. Suddenly, seeing the old man's empty pink gums—by color association, the sight made him temporarily impotent—Charles had a conversion.

He dropped out. But it wasn't the conventional romantic Bohemian dropout. It was a dropout to an equally romantic, entirely artificial dream of a Middle America; shopping malls, close-in suburbs, industrial pollution and Archie Bunker opinions.

Straight Through the Night is a novel about Deckle's quixotic and utterly loony pilgrimage in search of the American norm. He will become, he concedes, the person pictured in beer ads and television sitcoms, the conservative backlasher constructed by opinion polls, the bluff, lower-middle-class chauvinist that East Coast journalists continually surprise themselves by discovering.

Edward Allen's novel is a disconcerting mix of wit, powerful irony and fearsome overwriting. Deckle's quest, increasingly nightmarish, is clouded by confusion. Sometimes he seems to be the author's alter ego, sometimes his butt. He is by turns a touching flesh-and-blood figure and a zany caricature.

Dizzy with talent, the book continually loses its bearings, starts anew and goes off on tangents. It is a work of brilliant parts—blazing black satire, a tender realism and an exalted rhetorical grandiloquence—whose transitions and relations to each other are muddy and imprecise.

Chuck, renouncing the connections and advantages that his upbringing might have brought him, falls vertiginously through the air. When the book begins, he has taken on and been fired from several jobs as a meat cutter. He is hopelessly slow with his hands. . . .

Nevertheless, he persists. As the story proceeds, he will work in two small packing houses, a slaughterhouse and a kosher butcher's. Meat is bedrock, somehow; it is authenticity. And when the least sulfurous of his short-tempered bosses demands to know what he's doing in the business, he modestly replies: "Trying to improve, I guess."

It is absurd, of course. As he describes himself, "I am a moderate Republican intellectual." He is hopelessly out of place; for example, he remarks of his fellow workers: "I have known lost souls in the meat business with their faces so buried in the New York Post that they forget that the Dreyfuss Fund exists."

That is comic caricature, but comedy is only one level of this many-leveled novel. To work in meat is the centerpiece of poor Chuck's fantasy about the American norm. He is happiest among the ghastly scenes and the rough camaraderie of the slaughterhouse. (p. 3)

He is consciously trying to fashion himself into a postmodern yahoo.

He has a brief affair with an overweight nurse, who leaves him as soon as she gets thinner. He dreams of taking her for walks in the fetid New Jersey marshes. He insists that their refineries and industrial stink are beautiful. They make malls possible, and fast-food outlets. . . .

Chuck's loonyness grows darker and darker. He works for a crooked New Jersey meatpacker who puts him on a killing schedule of 16-hour days, picking up meat and delivering it. From there, he goes to work for two kosher butchers, refugees from the death camps in Europe.

They are maniacal bigots. They scream at Charles continually; their grotesque vindictiveness is fueled partly by his inefficiency but mostly by his condition as a WASP. They see in him a potential conductor of pogroms.

And, by the time they fire him, the deranged Chuck has begun to sneak into the supermarket and draw swastikas on the gefilte fish jars. Clinging to wisps of gentility, he takes pride in not drawing them backward, as less-educated bigots do. And he wears a cutout Izod crocodile pinned to his collar; it is his WASPy amulet against his employers' own cabalistic mysticisms. When he walks out, he screams anti-Semitic epithets.

Straight Through the Night is a brilliant, self-destructive civil war; sometimes it is simply a mess.

The author is capable of grotesque wit and quiet irony. He is capable of an absorbing realism; many of the passages on the meat business are fascinating. There is some genuinely beautiful writing; the evocation of Manhattan's meat district at 4 in the morning is haunting. And there are long, unbearably overcharged passages reminiscent of the purpler writings of the late Thomas Wolfe.

The book's principal, unsurmountable defect, though, is Allen's inability to define what he wants Chuck Deckle to be and to represent. At times, we see him in a vein of sympathetic portraiture, a man of an odd idealism struggling, failing and disintegrating.

At other times—most of the time, perhaps—he is a figure of wild parody. What he is parodying is never really clear. Is it the pretensions of both liberal vision and the conservative vision? Is it the folly of being sucked into any of the political or cultural fantasies retailed in our public discourse?

I think Allen wants to signify all of these things, because he has all of them to say and they're all worth saying. But he can't have them all. He has written an impressive book that he does not yet—it is his first—quite know how to write. (p. 6)

Richard Eder, "The Mad Joy of Butcher Shop Chic," in Los Angeles Times Book Review, January 15, 1989, pp. 3, 6.

ELIZABETH BENEDICT

Fiction about the lives of working-class men and women on the job is something of an endangered species these days. Still, several recent examples—among them John Sayles' short-story collection *At the Anarchists' Convention,* Michael Ondaatje's novel *In the Skin of a Lion* and Robert Ward's novel *Red Baker*—offer a vision of blue-collar workers that is compassionate, even affectionate, without being sentimental.

Edward Allen's first novel, *Straight Through the Night,* is a proletarian novel with an upper-class twist. There may be no other piece of fiction, however, that describes the workings and workers of the modern meat industry with such precision, detail and drama. From the "kill floor" to the shaping of hamburger patties in the local kosher butcher shop, Mr. Allen's narrator, Chuck Deckle, is an unlikely member of the working class. He's a second-generation Hotchkiss graduate, the son of a Prudential Insurance Company executive, a Protestant, as he often reminds us, who spent his teen-age summers on Martha's Vineyard and dropped out of college after three years. Like Chuck himself, even his old Volkswagen, whose frame is bent out of shape, "doesn't go where it's pointed."

How, at the age of 30, does Chuck find himself in the meat business with a résumé that shows so many short-term jobs that it reads like a criminal's rap sheet? Though Mr. Allen tries to answer that question—to come to terms with who Chuck is—he doesn't quite succeed in the course of his ambitious, disturbing and sometimes beautifully written novel.

Chuck's story begins by the light of Venus, on "a warm, moonless December morning." It's 1979. Jimmy Carter is President. Iranians are holding 48 American hostages and Chuck is on his way from Rockland County to a new job—the first of five he'll hold during the year the novel takes place—at the Denny Meat Packing Company on West 13th Street. "During the months I drove in the dark to Manhattan," he tells us, in the seductive first paragraph, "I came to think of the planet Venus as my secret morning companion, silent, untouchable, demanding nothing."

At first, Chuck strikes us as an appealing eccentric, a loner, a latter-day hippie who admits to us that he has performance anxiety in bed. He used to live on a commune and march against the Vietnam War, and now he rather enjoys the cultural differences between himself and the men he works with. For the first 100 pages, his intoxication with the night is intriguing.

At its best, Mr. Allen's prose is exuberant, precise, mournfully romantic, an almost touching counterpoint to the grisly world of butcher shops, meat-packing plants and slaughterhouses where Chuck puts in his time. He describes the kaleidoscopic lights of nighttime thruways, the rank odors of truck exhausts and abattoirs and the cacophony of sounds on city streets with the precision of a surveyor and the soul of a Beat poet. . . .

But once Mr. Allen establishes the atmosphere, and once we realize that Chuck's performance anxiety extends to every facet of his life, that he has no friends, that he can't hold a job, that his fondness for children's television shows is not just a fleeting affectation and that he manages to infuriate just about everyone he knows, it dawns on us that all of these complicated lights, sounds and smells are his substitutes for relationships with people.

He's not unaware of his failings—he compares himself to Jimmy Carter—and halfway through the book he says, "All I had to do was fix my gaze on the land around me, on the textures and the undulations and the haze of bright smoke in the shape of the night; if I looked at such things, then other things would fail to hurt." But this bit of self-knowledge doesn't sink in. As soon as he states it, he's off, never to return to it, on a rant about how he loves dirty rivers.

Mr. Allen has a gift for describing the physical, even the industrial, world. But when the subject is Chuck and how he ended up so far from where he was pointed, Mr. Allen's prose, and Chuck's logic, go into a tailspin. . . .

By the end, Chuck has become a cauldron of racist, anti-Semitic rage. Perhaps mirroring the xenophobia that was popular during the hostage crisis—which plays out in the background of the novel—Chuck blithely admits bigotry toward the elderly and the infirm (whom he calls "whiteheads" and "crutch-monkeys") and scorn for nearly everyone else, including the people he grew up with in "Protestant-land." To express his rage against his last boss, a kosher butcher, he repeatedly paints swastikas on jars of gefilte fish in supermarkets. By the time he says to the man, "It's bastards like you

that turn people into Nazis," we wonder whether the author or the character is speaking. And since neither the author nor the character ever seems to acknowledge the impact of the insults, why are we listening?

While **Straight Through the Night** makes no claims to being what Holden Caulfield might call "Chuck Deckle's goddam autobiography," the absence of information about Chuck's family—except for passing references to the schools, country clubs and stores they patronized—is curious. When his father visits on the Fourth of July, the scene lasts slightly more than a page and consists of one paragraph of banal dialogue and detailed descriptions of the firecrackers going off around them. When Chuck goes home for his uncle's memorial service, Mr. Allen spends eight pages describing the journey there—that is, the sights and sounds that whiz by—a paragraph on the service, and a page on Chuck's meeting with his uncle's executor. . . .

It's as if he's telling us that being raised by well-off WASP's is explanation enough for anyone's maladjusted behavior.

Over the long haul of the novel, Chuck seems not to learn anything about himself; after he apologizes, in the closing pages, for his anti-Semitic behavior, he lapses instantaneously into an interior monologue that suggests delusions of grandeur. Does Mr. Allen mean for us to accept Chuck as a sympathetic character in a psychological novel, or perhaps as an analogue of the United States during the hostage crisis—a once powerful nation held hostage by uncontrollable outside forces? It's never clear.

Edward Allen is a talented writer. One hopes that next time out his characters will not be so afraid to examine the complexities of their inner lives, which can be every bit as luminous as "the searchlights of a thousand grand openings of a thousand shopping centers, fading out opposite Yonkers."

> Elizabeth Benedict, "From Martha's Vineyard to the Kill Floor," in The New York Times Book Review, February 12, 1989, p. 11.

MERLE RUBIN

The polluted marshlands of industrial New Jersey and the unlovely world of the meat business, from slaughterhouse to butcher shop, are the seemingly unpromising materials from which Edward Allen has fashioned a novel that not only captures such signs of the times as failure, downward mobility and the large-scale disappointments of the generation that came of age in the 1960s, but also has the excitement of an authentic work of art.

The narrator-hero of **Straight Through the Night** is the product of a leafy, suburban childhood. Through a series of "accidents" he can't quite understand—a combination of bad luck and bad decisions—he has become part of the meat trade. Despite the aptness of his name—Charles ("Chuck") Deckle—he is not even a good butcher: he can't seem to get the hang of cutting meat. A self-described "WASP diaspora of one," he valiantly clings to his sense of identity in a world where identity is defined by one's profession, status and income.

"Let it be known," he states in a characteristic peroration, "that I remained a gentleman and an intellectual and a professional and a Protestant, late of Hotchkiss '69, ex Quinnipiac '72, visitor by Volkswagen to all forty-eight contiguous states, spiritual adventurer, moderate Republican, watcher of the moon . . . " His irony mocks, but does not cancel out, the defiant, silly pathos of the assertion. Engagingly idiosyncratic, yet achingly typical, Chuck may well be the Holden Caulfield of the "almost grown," "thirtysomething" set.

Chuck struggles—with some success—to find a kind of beauty in the meat trade, which furnishes some remarkably lyrical passages in his narrative. Worse than the external squalor, however, the erstwhile gentleman and intellectual is besieged from within. Under the strain of working for an exceptionally rebarbative kosher butcher, Chuck finds himself, to his horror, scrawling swastikas on jars of gefilte fish.

Everything about this book rings true: Chuck's pretentiousness and sincerity; the genuine nostalgia he feels for his lost suburban Eden and the note of self-mockery that creeps into his paeans to swimming pools, shopping malls and the Mickey Mouse Club. As its title suggests, **Straight Through the Night** is an exhilarating ride through a darkling landscape. The sheer exuberance of its style—and by style I mean not only the diction, rhythm and flow of sentences and paragraphs, but also the voice that emerges through the technique—transforms a depressing subject into one that is richly sad: funny, poignant, frightening and curiously cheerful, even on the brink of tears.

> *Merle Rubin, in a review of "Straight Through the Night," in* Book World—The Washington Post, *March 5, 1989, p. 6.*

JEFF DANZIGER

"On worn tires, you feel close to the ground, and there is a jangling, wounded kind of weariness, that only people who did not finish college can feel."

Books about young men meeting life head-on are a particular American type and you can have them. But this is an exception. **Straight Through the Night** is enjoyable and riveting at the same time, smoothly written but flawed and asymmetrical as any really original creation must be.

Charles Deckle, prep school product, doesn't finish college. He finds himself working for his living in New York in the meat cutting district in lower Manhattan, where the restaurant owners buy. . . .

He's on his own in a rough world that he never knew existed, which might as well be another planet. How he fares, sometimes successfully, sometimes not, is the heart of the book. He is working, *real work,* for the first time in his life, a life that now mercilessly depends on work. His co-workers and bosses are all from the great uneducated, and for Charles Deckle, unknown, blue-collar class.

They cut meat; they debone it; they slaughter and skin animals; they do the violent bloodstained things that an education can prevent you from ever having to think about. Sometimes he sees his co-workers as noble laborers, providing sustenance for the race; other times, he sees them as animals cutting up other animals in a grim commercial *danse macabre.* He has additional experiences, but it is his work that runs his life, and that's a measure of the accuracy of this book.

This is Edward Allen's first novel, and you can't help being impressed with his gift for description and prodigious detail, and intrigued by the humor he discovers in his unlikely hero. He sees the dignity of the hard labor that Deckle and his co-

workers are sentenced to and he's fascinated by the interplay of meat and men and money. He writes like a painter; he drafts the sweeping background and then points up the detail to which he wants to lead your eye. Underneath is Charles Deckle's emerging character, forced suddenly from years in protective prep schools and universities, into the workaday world, a world where there are no credentials to get you through when you can't perform.

Straight Through the Night reminded me more of *Down and Out in Paris and London* than anything I've read in a long time. It's like a passionate Americanization of that marvelous George Orwell book. As with Orwell, the author explains by taking you with him to the job, with him in the delivery truck, with him in his beat-up car, with him to his tiny apartment, which is all he can afford.

Charles Deckle reaches the end of the book an informed innocent, sadder but wiser about the way huge numbers of his fellowmen spend their days. His experience also says some subtle things about education in this country: that it hides more of life than it reveals, and that it provides more opportunity to avoid than to accomplish. These are things well-educated people can spend their entire lives and never know.

> *Jeff Danziger, "A Preppy's Meat-Plant Education," in* The Christian Science Monitor, *April 24, 1989, p. 13.*

BRIAN MORTON

[In **Straight Through the Night,** college] dropout Chuck Deckle inhabits the curious calm that comes from keeping half his education and intellect in cold store, specifically the cold store of a New York City meat market, where he works as a butcher among guys who speak monolingual Fuckinese and think Jimmy Carter is a pussy. For comfort, Chuck can always defrost a little learning. Watching *The Partridge Family* on afternoon television, he draws a wan sexual glow from Laurie's wax-sculpture face—with the added fillip that he is "perhaps the only person in the whole 14th Street Market who knew what a philtrum was". Things are going badly for the market, as for America. "Gonna be a *wasteland,* my friend, gonna be *unreal,* and I just hope you're freakin' prepared!" says a meat man who has never heard of Thomas Stearns Eliot. Chuck, of course, has, and indulges a few allusions about his Unreal City.

In the depths of the cold store, Chuck is becoming a virtuoso of decay, learning to disguise and pass off spoilt meat. Edward Allen brilliantly camouflages a cold anatomization of America's decline in the pre-Reagan years, a crisis of political ideas and methods that have passed their sell-by date. Out in the Gulf, American carcases are being loaded into body bags in the aftermath of Carter's botched attempt at freeing the Tehran hostages. The torchlight is increasingly red on sweaty faces, on 14th Street as in Iran.

There is, though, a subplot that binds the theme of food to a more optimistic but no less critical path. Chuck falls for Jill, a luxuriantly fat nurse, who, though not at all bulimic and with a perfectly accurate body image, thinks nothing of throwing up dinner to make room for one more dessert. Jill's fat is not a feminist issue, but America's is a political one: a flabby, food-growing President, and a TV-dinner culture. The United States has been burning carbs and carburettors for so long and to so little purpose that the threat of shortage—oil, food—is at once a national disaster and a jaw-wiring solution.

Not that Allen's first novel is a polemic. It is a hilarious and touching vision, almost as if Upton Sinclair's *The Jungle* had been rewritten by Nabokov or the early Pynchon. It's also a spoof on a particular brand of literary apprenticeship: "Edward Allen has held all the prerequisite author jobs, bartender, truck driver, ranch hand, dishwasher, butcher, meat salesman", announces the dust-jacket. Where others have indulged in "real life" fantasies, however, Allen doesn't pretend to be illiterate; he is not a college dropout. He knows that *The Waste Land* corresponded at some points to a real city, and that its vision is no less valid than the view from the cutting-room floor.

Brian Morton, "Beyond the Sell-by Date," in The Times Literary Supplement, No. 4497, June 9, 1989, p. 634.

GEORGE PACKER

[*Straight Through the Night*] has a viewpoint probably unique in contemporary American fiction: that of a son of the Protestant upper middle class who sinks down toward the ethnic working class and begins to spew hatreds that his people have always been too respectable to utter. It is also that rare thing, a novel about labor, and it describes the dreary meanness, the idiocy and rage, of work in the meat business with utterly persuasive detail. It has humor, intellect, and long passages of celebratory or elegiac lyricism. *Straight Through the Night* isn't a great first novel; some of it is self-indulgent, and as a whole it lacks one crucial element, a story. But Edward Allen's subject is new and important and his talent genuine.

He writes in the American grain of Whitman, Miller, Wolfe, Kerouac: a poet of dirty rivers. A rainstorm in Manhattan sends his narrator, Chuck Deckle, whirling into thoughts like these as quickly as it sends everyone else running under an awning:

> There are some people whom the rain makes happy, and there is a theory about negative and positive ions in the synapses, an electrochemical explanation for the wild looming excitement that children feel just before the lightning starts. There are some people whom the rain makes angry, old men who have forgotten their umbrellas, old men with lopsided black loafers, men with white hair stained from cigarette smoke into a kind of yellow that, like the yellow of taxis, gains intensity on a rainy day. Such men invariably spend their entire lives in the meat business.

Sentences like the last are what keep this prose from slogging deep into sentimentality or preciosity.

An obscure mix of aimlessness, bad luck, and mild lunacy has

expelled Deckle from his native land of moderate Republicanism and Vineyard summers; his ache to get back to the club tennis court makes him an atypical romantic hero. He's too old, too smart, too weak to feel his blue collar as anything but a garrote. But he's also a fuckup, as his bosses would say, and he can't get away from meat, which appears so often, so variously, that it comes to stand for something like the raw implacability of work and life. After *Straight Through the Night* you may never feel the same about a cheeseburger again. The meat-packing scenes, and Deckle's hapless descent from bad job to worse—the predawn shifts, the calves hoisted over the kill floor, the pale hands cutting veal portions, the smell of the delivery van in July, the profanity of men under monotonous but unbearable pressure—ground the writing and give the novel what narrative it has.

Deckle's viewpoint is aesthetic, not moral. Light, as a counterpoint to meat, is this exuberant and life-fearing man's only positive good. His odes to the night sky and Route 59 preoccupy him to the near exclusion of social or psychological insight. Allen's beautiful writing is beautiful on the subject of, say, waiting for a train to a family funeral, which is then barely described. Lyrical inwardness poses dangers over the course of a whole novel: it flattens the world into a single sensibility, with cars and characters floating in and out; it deadens narrative drive. Though the book is never uninteresting, it is interesting in the same way again and again.

When the novel finally turns into a story—a fascinating, grim one—it is in spite of Allen's best effort to keep it clean of moral vision. . . . Though Allen never condones Deckle's hatred, the unironic first-person narrative prevents any larger understanding of the bigotry or the regret.

When Deckle's rage defeats his conscience, the intensity of the final humiliation is shattering. For all the vagueness about how he got here and why he's stuck, the portrait of a sensitive man turning into a spitting bigot commands belief. An easy liberalism pervades most contemporary fiction, based on good intentions, bad conscience, and money. Take away that cushion, and the highmindedness is hard to maintain. In the world of *Straight Through the Night,* recession ends jobs and butchers take the Iran hostage crisis as a daily personal insult. The year is 1980, but the nastiness and fear, the sense of everything out of control and oneself sinking, have at least as much to do with 1989. Deckle, an outsider in this world, condemned to the meat business for unspecified sins, comes close enough to get the smell on him and tell us what it is like. "Work is supposed to hurt. Days are furrows of poisoned earth to be struggled through. Any man who doesn't hate his job is doing it wrong. Any man who can smile at his own thoughts is a hophead."

George Packer, "The Meat Beat," in The Village Voice, Vol. XXXIIII, No. 31, August 1, 1989, p. 58.

Jerome Badanes
The Final Opus of Leon Solomon

Born in 1937, Badanes is an American novelist and film-maker.

The Final Opus of Leon Solomon takes the form of a lengthy suicide note by the title character, a Judaica scholar and survivor of the Auschwitz concentration camps. Solomon has recently been banished from libraries for having stolen ancient manuscripts. This occurrence and the loss of the love of his wife and son lead him to a run-down hotel near Harlem, New York, determined to kill himself. During the three days he has allowed himself to write this farewell note, Solomon recalls his incarceration in Auschwitz as a young man, his marriage to Inge, a fellow concentration camp survivor, and their subsequent emigration to the United States where he became a preeminent Jewish historian. Solomon's marriage is destroyed by infidelity, both his own and his wife's, and by his increasing contempt for his wife's German ancestry. Details of his sexual fantasies frequently interrupt these memoirs; the objects of his desire include his sister, the daughter of an SS officer, and Fulani, a pro-P.L.O. radio talk-show hostess. Although some critics found Solomon's sexual exploits an unnecessary diversion from his investigation of the moral dilemmas facing Jews in the twentieth century, most were pleased by the frequently humorous observations made by this complex and charismatic protagonist. Nancy Schwerner commented: "This first novel is an accomplished and important piece of writing. Badanes . . . has created a haunting character in Solomon, at once enormously touching and richly comic."

EDITH MILTON

Though *The Final Opus of Leon Solomon* is Jerome Badanes's first novel it is a masterly piece of fiction. Its setting is today's New York, but since the narrative is in the form of a memoir in the process of being written by the protagonist, Leon Solomon, a large part of the novel focuses on the past. Leon is spending his last hours of life in a sleazy midtown hotel room, planning to kill himself at the end of his third day there; as the book opens we are already well along in Day Two.

It is clear from the beginning that for Leon Solomon—friendless, divorced, growing old, in trouble with the law, alienated from his son—life has become untenable. It is also clear that the crisis of his self-disgust originated long before the specific event that has precipitated his decision to commit suicide: it is now public knowledge that he has cut, stolen and sold pages from antique texts in the Judaica collection of the New York Public Library, and that he is therefore banned forever from all libraries and from his life's work as a histori-

an. As he dredges through his memories and writes down random recollections of his childhood in Vilna, his years in Auschwitz, his difficult marriage, his solitary exile in two rooms at the edge of Harlem, the surface images which first come to his mind entangle themselves more and more with an ambiguous, emotionally charged chaos underneath. It begins to seem possible, for instance, that the theft of ancient documents may have complex causes, may be a dramatization of his own subversive idea of Jewishness.

With its opening sentence the book conjures with paradox:

> There is a metaphysical law, and you can depend on metaphysical laws, that unity is a figment of the imagination. As soon as a unity is slowly, bloodily forged it has already started breaking down—and right in the bitter heart of the breaking down a new unity is already being dreamed up in the darkness.

This sense that wholeness is illusory informs the novel, admitting the possibility that by desecrating manuscripts Leon is re-enacting the fragmentation and interruptions of Jewish history; there is even a suggestion that his projected suicide is a species of resurrection. Indeed, convolution, paradox and contradiction are the heart of this book. For Leon, the world has turned upside down, and the precepts of conventional morality do not even touch on reality. His deepest sin, as he sees it, and as we come to believe, is his failure to kill his sister, Malka, before her appalling public death, tied up and beaten with other Jews in a Warsaw park. His second sin is his conventional obedience to incest taboos. And he recalls Auschwitz, about which the novel keeps its decent silence except for one memorable, grotesquely humorous episode, less as an embodiment of human evil than as a community of suffering, the poignant alternative to his present death by isolation. In a world so confused, moral life has become impossible. . . .

But though its moral ambiguities sound depths that few contemporary novels even aim for, *The Final Opus* is pointedly a story of our day: most evidently, perhaps, in the fact that sexuality is ubiquitous and, like the rest of the world, has been distorted and made perverse. In a scene in which the young Leon is simultaneously humiliated and seduced, the helpless victim of an inventive anti-Semitism, it becomes clear that in the world he lived in and lives in, desire, degradation and shame have often been inextricable.

Indeed, Leon's love life in general is nothing if not contradictory. His ex-wife is a German Jew whom he now hates for her Germanness. He projects most of his affections as well as his lubricious and deviant fantasies upon Fulani, a young black woman whom he hardly knows, who stars on an anti-Semitic, pro-P.L.O. radio phone-in show. He himself phones in regularly, posing as a professor, an authority on Emile Durkheim's sociological theories of anomie, which, of course, in a sense, he is. Meanwhile, his affair with Kristin, the daughter of an SS officer, out to atone on Leon's aging body her guilt for her father's crimes, is fraught with all the inherent contradictions of sadomasochism. Their contortions are graphically described, and their relationship manages to be both funny—one of Kristin's compulsions being a Germanic passion for doing laundry—and also sad: for instance, when she, too, phones into Fulani's show and adopts the persona of a Holocaust survivor.

But for all its darkness, this is a novel filled with illumination: "A light is one thing," Leon writes of the surprising brilliance of his hotel room. "A light reflected by a mirror is another thing. But a light that comes in my window and bounces from a mirror to a mirror to my eyes, that is unusual." That image sums up the unexpected refractions of light that clarify the darkness of this world; deep humor balances the sharpness of the novel's ironies, and the remnants of childhood affections and playfulness—embodied in Leon's single memento, the little toy mouse in which he and Malka passed messages to each other as children—are still preserved under the grim distractions of the present.

The book ends enigmatically. Leon, having already spent his three days harrowing the hell of his own past, sits, like some self-convicted Eichmann, in a glass phone booth in the hotel lobby, making calls that never quite get through. And just when the last quarter of his last $300 has been spent and his ties to existence are ready to dissolve, an unasked-for instant of pure joy and total ordinariness smites him from the past. It is, in context, rebirth of a sort, a retrograde resurrection possibly of no use to anyone; but like much of *The Final Opus of Leon Solomon* it suggests that the most unhappy life in the most unjust world is luminous with complexities. . . .

[Badanes] has endowed his book with the uncanny authority of an eyewitness account. In fact, *The Final Opus of Leon Solomon* is a powerful transformation of a man's disintegration into that "new unity . . . being dreamed up in the darkness" with which its narrator's testimony begins. Its insights into the incongruities of recent history and its understanding of the paradoxical morality of our time go far beyond the conventions we have established for these matters, and they are deeply compelling.

Edith Milton, "When Moral Life Is Impossible," in
The New York Times Book Review, *February 12, 1989, p. 3.*

SUSAN SLOCUM HINERFELD

The Final Opus of Leon Solomon will anger some people and make others cry. It is the diary of a suicide, a survivor of the Holocaust who does not, in the end, survive.

The Holocaust was, is, and will forever be an issue of politics, literary politics included. An Old Guard, proprietary and protective, stands anxious to authenticate accounts. They have not always been kind, especially not to writers of Holocaust fiction, whom they have savaged in print. Fiction on this subject is to them a travesty or heresy. Reality, they believe, is terrible enough.

What will the Old Guard make of this fiction, the often-outrageous story of a sensualist, a historian whose theory of the vitality of history involves excising pages from ancient texts in the Judaica Room of the New York Public Library and selling them—at $65 a clip—to Harvard? . . .

How did he become a historian? "Once I asked my father if he knew someone who would live forever," Leon writes with his Mont Blanc pen ("three times rebuilt in a factory in New Jersey") on one of five yellow pads he has taken from his office at the Jewish History Institute to the Hotel America on Lexington Avenue, where he will die.

"The Jewish people will live forever," his father answers. "At that moment," Leon writes, "he planted in me a kernel which would turn me into a historian."

History is life. In Auschwitz, Leon undertakes the solemn duty to remember those who are about to die; to remember "that they once were." "[M]emorizing the faces of the others was keeping me alive." In postwar Paris, "Only . . . retrieving the archives from all the corners of the world . . . only this saved me." . . .

Caught in the Judaica Room, cutting pages with a razor, Leon will be banned from libraries. It is a sentence of death. . . .

Although a writer and his fictional character are not congruent, though here even their first languages are different, still the ideas on the yellow pad seem those of both character and author.

What is the difference between reality and memory? What is the difference between reality and reconstruction? These are the central questions both within the novel and about it.

First among answers is that "[i]t is not possible to fully recover what is lost." Another, not quite articulated (but then Leon is not always articulate), is that "only the memory holds actual bits and pieces of what is gone."

A principal and spectacular image of the text is of Leon's colleagues at the Jewish History Institute walking backwards, "just like a movie in reverse," "toward our lost world. . . ."

Oblivion is right behind them. "When you walk backwards toward the past, you see nothing but the illusion of a future always receding." It is necessary to look often over your shoulder, ready "to make a lightning raid into its blackness to rescue a single image . . . " "to . . . surprise the blinding darkness. . . ."

On the other hand.

This is a sensational book. Leon is an intellectual who lives through his senses. He cannot control them; cannot, for instance, extinguish desire. His acute sense-memory is like a door to the past. When the door opens, Leon and the narrative travel through time and space.

This book is also the story (explicitly, as they say) of Leon's sensual and sexual adventures; of the significance of the perfume, Joie de Patou; of his tender and incestuous bond with his sister Malkele; of his rape on the train taking him to his father's funeral; of his three-night stand with Kristin, the blonde and six-foot-tall obsessive daughter of a German officer, who comes to him dressed in white, and scrubs his apartment ("the toilet water was now blue like her eyes"); of Inge, his wife, to whom he sends lewd messages typed on his Royal ("my American typewriter") (as opposed to his Yiddish one) and enclosed in "official" envelopes of the Institute.

Here, too, is the story of Leon's own obsession with Fulani (real name: Ruth), daughter of the Institute's black janitor, hostess of a late-night pro-PLO call-in radio show, and his infatuation with the "nearly unendurable" smell at the neck of her coat, where her body odor mingles with Patchouli.

Why such confessions here? Because

> A man's private fantasies . . . end forever, and as though they never existed, when the man dies—unless he confesses them to another. Or writes them down. If he does write them down . . . they become a part—an essential part—of the historical record.

The Holocaust will soon no longer be a living memory. Those who survived it will have died of life. When they are gone, how will we know what it meant? Reality will no longer be terrible enough. Perhaps it has never been.

Photographs and documents make up the exhibits in the glass cases in the lobby of the Institute—Resistance among the Jews of Vilna, for instance—sepia and as dry as the dust of bones. If Badanes is right, and "It is not possible to fully recover what was lost," then no historic reconstruction can equal the "bits and pieces" of memory. . . .

At times in their history, the Jews have refrained from depicting the human face, believing that God alone can create a man. Perhaps that accounts for the Old Guard's distrust of fiction. Is the creation of character profane? Is fiction occult? Is a character too like a golem, the artificial man of myth?

Might we not think instead of talent as God-given or otherwise inspired, and of fiction as a medium that can bear witness?

Susan Slocum Hinerfeld, "The Passions of a Survi-
vor," *in* Los Angeles Times Book Review, *March 5, 1989, p. 8.*

An excerpt from *The Final Opus of Leon Solomon*

Do I debase myself? Very well, I debase myself. But keep in mind that our main work now, and I've known this since 1944, much earlier than the others, is to find—to touch up William James a drop—the spiritual equivalent of vengeance. Remember that vengeance gives us a purpose, a sense of mission, a thing worth dying for—and a concentration on another, on every smallest detail of his person, each mole as it were; and a passion to research, to spy out his most private history. The pictures we paint in our brains of his excruciating torture are liberating and in that way spiritually uplifting. You might say that this devotion to vengeance brings us closer to God. Certainly it is one of the few available techniques for living through hell. I knew as early as 1944, when we began to perpetrate acts of resistance in Auschwitz, and the taste became quickly insatiable, that this thirst for vengeance might well turn us into Christians.

On the other hand, a concentration on the other Jews in Auschwitz nearly unhinged me. Only the task of retrieving the archives from all the corners of the world immediately after the war ended—before they fell into the hands of collectors, professionals who knew the value of their possessions—only this saved me, because it forced the beings who gnawed ceaselessly at my soul, as they say, to slow their carnage, temporarily, and to become my conspirators in this common work. Sometimes dangerous work, undercover work.

In the midst of the night, half a lunatic from hunger, from the cold, the bright bulb on the ceiling always burning, casting dim yellow light over the barracks, I would begin to study the others. I developed the power to bring them into sharp focus. The almost uniform shapes of the bodies, one man next to the other, most on their backs on the hard wooden shelves arranged like a warehouse or an oversized archive. The moans, the groans, the breathing, the in, the out, at differing tempos, the various styles of snoring—some snores were sudden short gasps, others were punctuated with a popping noise, still others ended with a click, and behind them always was the long, steady snoring keeping time, as it were. Take these together with the almost inaudible but never-ending whimpers and I was listening to an orchestra of drunken musicians tuning up for a midnight concert.

THE NEW YORKER

In the grimy midtown hotel where the Holocaust survivor and brilliant Jewish historian Leon Solomon plans to do himself in, he scribbles on one of the legal pads he brought with him to prolong his life and record his history, "Should I cover these mirrors with the sheets? That was my first thought when I checked in here yesterday, how come I didn't do it?" Immediately, the reader [of *The Final Opus of Leon Solomon*] begins to cling to the hope that this man, who is still healthy and astute, who has such a rascally zest for the life he wants to quit, will write himself out of the desire to die. And what writing! He confesses (in Yiddish, we are supposed to imagine) that he has just been arrested for snipping pages from a manuscript at the public library and selling them to a colleague at Harvard; that he is estranged from his only son and from the wife he still loves . . . and that his greatest passion remains an unconsummated yearning for his sister, whom he saw beaten to death by Nazis. At one point, he mentions that he had an idea for an article that he never wrote called "Nostalgia for Auschwitz." Then, in a devastating parenthetical note, he adds, "Perhaps I am writing it now."

A review of "The Final Opus of Leon Solomon," in
The New Yorker, *Vol. LXV, No. 7, April 3, 1989,
p. 115.*

PHILIP GOUREVITCH

Primarily memoir, ***The Final Opus of Leon Solomon*** avoids straight chronology, creating instead a carefully ordered collage of memory, commentary, and immediate drama that insistently evokes the past's anxious grip upon the present.

Solomon tells in sharp detail of his Vilna childhood, his passionate, incestuous love for his sister, her brutal murder by the Gestapo in Warsaw, his survival of Auschwitz, and his postwar life as a vengeful historian, archive thief, and estranged husband and father prone to abusive sexual exploits and fantasies. Auschwitz is the keystone of Solomon's consciousness—the origin of his identity and the source, it seems, of his present as much as his past. The lovely passages remembering prewar Vilna are as permeated by Solomon's encounter with Nazism as is his postwar career. Solomon's sense of displacement in contemporary America is finely evoked in a dark, sober voice that has all the authority of witness. There is less irony than one would like when Solomon mentions his idea for an article he never wrote—"Nostalgia for Auschwitz"—and declares, in parentheses, "Perhaps I am writing it now."

This perverse notion, nostalgia for Auschwitz, deftly reveals Solomon's condition: his violation is so absolutely his identity that he finds in it not only motivating anger but also pride and pleasure. And often the narrative uncovers the unlovely tangles of contemporary Jewry's love-hate relationship with Jewish nationalism. . . . Solomon's character functions as both a radical justification and a critique of the moral ambiguities that burden Jews today. If the need to remember the Holocaust is inarguable, Badanes seems to ask, must we cherish that memory?

It is a timely and excellent question, and one his historian antihero seems equipped to wrestle with. But unfortunately Badanes shies away from the political issues, instead devoting most of the book to graphic details of Solomon's sex life. A virgin before the war, Solomon learns the erotic extremes of sweetness and violation in his unfulfilled passion for his murdered sister and his rape by a Jewish whore and two SS men on a train. After liberation Solomon marries, has an affair with his sister's best friend, then watches his marriage collapse because of his wife's blatant involvement with his sister's ex-suitor. Alone and spiteful, Solomon develops a masturbatory fantasy about one Fulani, the black radio host of a pro-PLO talk show on WBAI; he dreams that "the conviction that pulled her to the exotic name 'Fulani' " will "draw her also to the numbers on my wrist." Later he has his last tango with a young German neighbor named Kristin Diet-

rich, the daughter of an SS officer, with whom he entertains the delusion of an elaborate erotic economy of reparations.

Unfortunately, the constant braiding of Nazism and sex reduces both to exotic melodrama, rather than propelling the vision of a morally undermined postwar world that Badanes seems to be after. By creating a historian who expresses so much of his Auschwitz inheritance as erotic malaise, Badanes paints over many gray areas with a generic black.

The climactic exploitation scene, when Kristin calls in to Fulani pretending to be Solomon's sister telling her own story, may serve the author's yen for theater, but it does not serve our understanding of Solomon's character and concerns. Like Solomon's theft of documents, which is never explained, it is a plot hook that burdens without illuminating. The novel's quieter moments are its most compelling, as when a colleague's secretary explains that she quit her children-of-survivors group because she found it "too self-congratulatory"; or when Solomon describes his failure to poison his crippled sister before the Gestapo got her as an eternal sin. This is powerful stuff, written with passionate restraint and eloquence, and so it is doubly maddening that Badanes could not let Solomon explore it more directly, and with his pants on.

Philip Gourevitch, "Death Kit," in The Village
Voice, *Vol. XXXIV, No. 17, April 25, 1989, p. 53.*

DOROTHY H. ROCHMIS

Reading [***The Final Opus of Leon Solomon***] is a gut-wrenching and mesmerizing experience. One doesn't want to turn the pages, yet is impelled to do so because of the unrelenting rhythm of its protagonist's heartbeat. This first novel by Jerome Badanes is set in today's New York and yesterday's Holocaust. Leon Solomon writes in first person as a historian, Auschwitz survivor, lover, hero, thief and doomed Jew.

The story begins as he checks into a seedy midtown Manhattan hotel. He has come here to commit suicide and has the necessary baggage to do so—the required amount of phenobarbitol and a bottle of bourbon, plus a store of debilitating, shattering and consuming memories, the most recent and plaguing of which is his theft of documents from the Judaica collection of the New York Public Library. The result of this act is the permanent banishment from all libraries and thus the end of his life's work, since he is a historian and dependent on the archives in libraries. "I have devoted more than forty years to the historical enterprise, as they say, more than forty years to bring life again—posthumously—to our slaughtered people," he writes in an ongoing ledger, some six yellow legal-sized pads that he fills compulsively.

By writing on these pads, Solomon delays the taking of his life. He writes about his boyhood in prewar Poland, about the loss of his adored sister, Malkele, of his internment in Auschwitz, his estrangement from his German-Jewish wife and his American-born son. He writes, too, of his erotic preoccupation with a black talk-show hostess on the radio, and of his passionate affair with a daughter of a former SS officer. . . .

This is a book you have to force yourself to read and once you do, you will never forget.

Dorothy H. Rochmis, in a review of "The Final Opus

of Leon Solomon," in West Coast Review of Books, *Vol. 14, No. 5, May-June, 1989, p. 29.*

NANCY SCHWERNER

[*The Final Opus of Leon Solomon*] takes the form of a 272-page suicide note. Solomon's previous works have all been in the field of Jewish history, and his final opus is no exception. As he sits in the desolate Times Square hotel in which he has chosen to die, the historian in him will not easily allow him to make an end without a full explanation and analysis.

Having survived Auschwitz, he has become a historian of the Holocaust, and lately a thief. He has seen his family and his world destroyed and witnessed the torture, humiliation, and death of his sister. He has married a fellow death-camp survivor and immigrated to America to continue his work at New York's Institute of Jewish History. Finally, however, he is unable to create a whole life for himself; nothing in his life seems to last or to remain whole. Solomon's marriage, his relationship with his son, his scholarly reputation and career all decay, and not without some help from Leon himself. His life experience has not taught him to be safe; he has learned to live—can feel alive—only with danger. He fails to struggle to save his marriage or to maintain a relationship with his son. . . .

This first novel is an accomplished and important piece of writing. Badanes . . . has created a haunting character in Solomon, at once enormously touching and richly comic.

Nancy Schwerner, in a review of "The Final Opus of Leon Solomon," in The Antioch Review, *Vol. 47, No. 3, Summer, 1989, p. 367.*

April Bernard
Blackbird Bye Bye

Bernard is an American poet and journalist.

In *Blackbird Bye Bye,* Bernard captures a wide variety of contemporary experience using humor, invective, and irony. Divided into three sections and echoing the styles of T. S. Eliot, the King James Bible, and Emily Dickinson, among others, *Blackbird Bye Bye* has been commended for its diverse and unusual subject matter. For example, this volume contains two poem sequences, one depicting a bank robbery, and one updating the Stations of the Cross. In other pieces, Bernard addresses political and social inequities with biting colloquialisms and sharp imagery. Her love poems, spiced with humor, illuminate dull and humiliating aspects of dating in late twentieth-century America. Critics also applaud Bernard's unflinching portrayal of contemporary experience, although some express disappointment in her failure to propose solutions to the problems she addresses. Helen Vendler remarked: "[Bernard] is rather improbably described on her book jacket as 'also a playwright, journalist and screenwriter . . . at work on a book about hurricanes and a novel.' She may end up outside poetry altogether; or she may find a way to carry on as a poet in her best vein, which is socially observant, often satiric, self-critical, and dashing." *Blackbird Bye Bye* won the prestigious Walt Whitman Award presented by the Academy of American Poets.

PUBLISHERS WEEKLY

By turns dazzling and perplexing, [*Blackbird Bye Bye*], the 1988 Walt Whitman Award winner, often juxtaposes diverse themes, images, characters and tones of voice. The works are most successful when set within a frame or structure—as in the poem interpreting the 14 stations of the cross in imagery evoking car commercials and cab drivers, combining popular culture, cliché and black humor to mock and, perversely, affirm the concept of faith. But other fragmented poems do not offer readers a foothold as they remain deliberately obscure. This tendency is all the more frustrating because Bernard's potent language, dense with allusion, forms some passages that are breathtaking: "Cow herd and vine: what we eat once prowled the earth, / ravening like the opened faces there, / upon whose weedy bones the lion sucks."

A review of "Blackbird Bye Bye," in Publishers Weekly, *Vol. 235, No. 8, February 24, 1989, p. 227.*

JOHN ASH

April Bernard has said that she writes "poems that are like the things you want to scream at a dinner party," and there is absolutely no polite literary table-talk or background music in *Blackbird Bye Bye,* which has won the Walt Whitman Award for a first book of poetry. Hers is a world in which the veneer of civilized manners has worn so thin it threatens to crack beyond repair:

> It was during the salad course,
> and the fifth bottle of wine,
> when a shot was fired, and the power failed,
> that we realized we had not dressed for this.

Her anger and mordant wit are directed against a "sham democracy" that has reduced the idea of freedom to "a colossus wrenched from rock and metal, / a plaza spread open like a flat concrete flower." Her determination to puncture the complacency of the "you who" has "come prepared with green glasses and visor" to observe the plight of the disadvantaged has little to do with any desire to *epater la bourgeoisie.* She implies that we are all unwitting oppressors, including those of us who recognize the need for "revolution but settle for bad manners," and that however eloquent our speech may be, it is not appropriately dressed—or undressed—for the intractable subject in hand:

> How the unschooled legions of the dead guffaw at the
>   spectacle
> of us making the connections; they laugh themselves sick.

In her long and ambitious title poem Bernard opts for a style that takes us all the way back from Ginsberg, via Eliot and Whitman, to the King James Bible. Her lines are long and psalmic; her language is modern and ancient, her tone at once oblique and direct as folk wisdom. She holds to the unfashionable belief that poetry can change people's thinking, and that it is the reader who must finally speak if anything is to be put right:

> Oh, you who say nothing and remember everything . . .
> You who have stood through all this fire and snow
> and taken this beating . . .
> Speak back, say something else
> of these bad times to me.

> John Ash, "The Shock of the New," in Book
> World—The Washington Post, May 7, 1989, p. 10.

HELEN VENDLER

April Bernard's style when it sins, sins by derivativeness. [In **Blackbird Bye Bye,** one] listens to her but hears, for instance, John Ashbery:

> Almost no one in them.
> If it looks like it flies two continents
>   it must be the right kind of thing.
> It is encapsulating it for the sake of
>   whatever sake.
> I'm a lumper rather than a splitter.

And she should not, unless she wanted to induce a backlash of admiration for Dickinson, have published her Dickinson poems:

> If there were just one Answer
> to every Question posed,
> If every thorn along the way
> bloomed—sudden—into Rose—

> If blood be wet, and roses red,
> and you—my Valentine—
> Then does my heart await in me
> as rubies—the Pick—in mines?

Dickinson would have winced at the grammar and rhythm of the closing lines. In the twelve-page title poem of [**Blackbird Bye Bye**], mercifully printed last, the echoes of *The Waste Land* are rawly unassimilated:

> Now that you walk with fear beside
>   you like a baby brother, . . .
> Now that you drag your father's
>   ghost from the wickiup, . . .
> Now you cry, and their hearts break
>   no more.
>   • • •
> Oh, you who say nothing and
>   remember everything . . .
> You who have stood through fire
>   and snow and taken this beating . . .
> Speak back, say something else
>   of these bad times to me.

The final two ellipses are, alas, Bernard's own.

But there is more to April Bernard than these leftovers from the past. She is rather improbably described on her book jacket as "also a playwright, journalist and screenwriter . . . at work on a book about hurricanes and a novel." She may end up outside poetry altogether; or she may find a way to carry on as a poet in her best vein, which is socially observant, often satiric, self-critical, and dashing. I reprint in full her poem **"Gases"** on successive unsatisfactory dates with various men; it despairs of encountering anyone who can be known and trusted, anyone who is not a threat or a trap:

> The cough like oysters in the throat,
>   the light from the lamp oyster-white
> "My business is to discover what
>   makes for the intellectual impulse"
> Dear God and all that time with me
>   here thinking you were an ordinary
>   guy

> She had eaten lunch with the fourth
>   unsung hero of our generation this
>   week'
> An understandable fatigue was the
>   result
> When the water is brown the only
>   civilized thing is to make tea

> Since the biographer will be here any
>   minute you'd better tidy up
> Things said with the ring of truth
>   rarely have it
> Get all the best people and mistrust
>   them.

> The meaning of consecutive and sus-
>   tained has made a sustained dis-
>   appearance
> Every office has a trapdoor slightly
>   to one side of where you're standing
> The hand on the throat like a fever,
>   like an airgun, like a fork

A shrewd glance at worldly invitations animates **"Nevertheless"**:

> They are ready to build edifices around me.
> Or, they are ready to take me into their arms.
> Because I am an embraceable you.
> This set of friends, that sort of music,
>   someone else's grasp of the higher things.
> If it gets dull—then,
> replace me, you replaceable you.

"Nevertheless" is the last poem in a sequence called "Prayers and Sermons for the Stations of the Cross," and corresponds to the rubric "He is laid in the tomb." I find the connection useless in this instance, suggestive in some others; but for a sequence on the Stations, it's hard to compete with Claudel, who did it so well as to discourage others. Here is Bernard's **"first fall,"** a rape poem from the same sequence:

> Learning to walk is learning to fall.
> There's a lot of cute songs about things like that.
> Fox went out on a chilly night, just down to the corner
> for cigarettes. Goose drove into his jaws
> on teetering wheels, but I guess
> that's an old story.
> The farmer's daughter who didn't come home
> though they threw open the window to look
> when fox grabbed grey goose via neck.
> He didn't mind the quack quack quack
> and the legs all dangling, down-o.

American demotic—"just down to the corner for cigarettes" or "There's a lot of cute songs about things like that"—is still making its way into lyric. Bernard is rather too enamored of it (she thinks she can make a lyric sequence out of a bank heist) but she has an ear for it, and should keep on making use of it. She has antennae for the censored, the dramatic, and the indicative detail, especially when she writes with female props:

> The difficulties, in passion,
> are not news: the knot at the throat,
> the lipstick that smears, the skirt
> which induced such provocative hobbling
> yet will not rise above the thighs.

The language here, so far from her Eliotic languishings in **"Blackbird Bye Bye,"** is brisk, artfully paced, and wry. The piece I have just been quoting is from an *ars poetica* entitled **"Come As You Are"** that tries to find a language about dressing that will be appropriate for "The Way We Live Now" (the Trollopian title of the two-part poem of which **"Come As You Are"** is the first part). Bernard's witty pieces of advice to herself on how to write show she knows what does not work ("the aria will not soar / if the diva is sitting down"; "we do not advocate nudity, exactly"). More promisingly, she dismisses her own dangerous affection for the role of the hard-boiled movie moll: "nor / the slattern in the unbelted kimino / swigging beer from a bottle by the electric fan." She does not answer her own problem, but she puts it well, and honestly, and funnily. (pp. 26-7)

> *Helen Vendler, "Four Prized Poets," in* The New York Review of Books, *Vol. XXXVI, No. 13, August 17, 1989, pp. 26-30.*

An excerpt from "Blackbird Bye Bye"

Early training—
to appease the gravitational pull, to anticipate—
to give not take, bend not break. Always
keep your name out of the papers;
never smoke in the street.
To squeeze your breast till it's pouring out all over
   the place,
giving until it chokes them, until they want no
   more.

Hence some perfectly nice girl
running around in a pink shortie screaming, "Cunt,
   cunt, cunt!"
Hence the shaking of the heads of the dearly beloved.
Spare us the therapeutic realignment
into the personal. Softly padding,
all the neighborhood cats follow the girl with the
   bottles.

Somewhere on the Rio Pisco an ill-tempered itch.
Lips lock on the same puerile
"send me photographs and souvenirs."
Mister Christian lends a hand
to those on the mudbank, then slides into the dark
   water
where pink dolphins on this occasion breach.

You, old bat, beating the air that closes around me
   like a halo,
seek the forgiveness of the hungry,
which I must grant.

David Shapiro has referred to April Bernard as having "a bitter intelligence" and that phrase seems very apt in describing [**Blackbird Bye Bye**], the Walt Whitman Award Winner for 1988. The perceptions here are skeptical, distrustful, the reasonable products of a modern world closely observed and well-learned.

> "You're a young man, you can still learn. Pay attention
>   to this.
> You can steal in this country, you can rape and murder,
> you can bribe public officials, you can pollute the morals
>   of the young,
> you can burn your place of business down for the insur-
>   ance money,
> you can do almost anything you want,
> and if you just act with a little caution and common sense
> you'll never be indicted. But if you don't pay your income
>   tax, Grofield,
> you will go to jail."

In this world, there are few survival tools, honesty and wit being two of them abundantly evident in Bernard's poems.

> We seek a slogan, and find only the old ones.
> We need revolution, but settle
> for bad manners.

This book is not pleasant, but it is real. It is not an "easy read," but it is worthwhile. It is challenging, frightening, relevant. It brings up questions that have probably been asked in all times, in all cultures, but that seem particularly applicable today.

> *A review of "Blackbird Bye Bye," in* Kliatt Young Adult Paperback Book Guide, *Vol. XXIII, No. 6, September, 1989, p. 25.*

ALFRED CORN

Even though [**Blackbird Bye Bye**] comes with a publicity package that includes a photocopy of a plug for the author in *Interview* magazine (she seems to be ensconced in some downtown café or other) and a bio note telling us that she is at work on a novel titled *Pirate Jenny* and a study of hurricanes, I'm going to take this book seriously. It is Amy Clampitt's choice for the 1988 Walt Whitman Award (for a first book) sponsored by the Academy of American Poets. To prepare us for the reading Amy Clampitt quotes Williams on *Howl:* "Hold back the edges of your gowns, ladies, we are going through hell." A new *Une Saison en enfer,* then? Yes, but not right away. The opening poem concludes quite placidly:

> Come autumn, the leaves slide off in sheaves—
> letters unwritten and unread,
> but red, and yellow, and received.
>
> **"Landscape Poetry Is a Dead Letter"**

In fact the opening section of eight poems is largely indistinguishable from competent writing-school verse written by Everystudent, with of course an obligatory *hommage* to Ashbery in **"Vaucanson's Duck"**:

> The make of you: what year did you return,
> beloved Wall, reckless with sense. Paste ranunculus, O
>   best
> beloved of no-one, only me.

In this Midsummer Night's Dream playlet, if Wall appears

Lion cannot be far behind, and probably Moonshine as well. Part II of the book qualifies, I suppose, though the roars are mild enough and the scenes are all set in broad daylight. These fourteen poems are called, collectively, "Prayers and Sermons for the Stations of the Cross," referring of course to a late-medieval series of devotions not much favored nowadays by those concerned with the living God. That's not to say it would be impossible to do something with them in contemporary poetry, but this sequence hasn't managed it. For example, the second station, "He takes up his cross," is rendered [in a poem called **"Car Talk"**]:

> She'd been talking about it a while;
> I could feel an analogy coming on.
> "It's like, you're in a car, speeding
> through an obstacle course, but you can see yourself too,
> like in the ads,
> and you're the dummies that go through the windshield
> and the head that rolls off to the side with no eyes." . . .

The sequence ends with a two-line **"Coda"**: "He told them the parable of the mustard seed. / I remain unpersuaded." Surely free-thinking deserves better poetic expression than this.

Every generation hopes that something brilliant and lasting will emerge from its own particular Bohemia. We've seen them appear, flash, and fade since the Teens of the century—Max Bodenheim, Edna Millay, e.e. cummings, Kenneth Patchen, Ferlinghetti, Ted Berrigan, others. The third and fourth parts of this book will have been April Bernard's own harrowing of that perilous underground, which owes something to Dante and Rimbaud, no doubt, but still more to MTV. Titles like **"Your Own Private Thermidor"** (not to be confused with a case for cigar storage; *thermidor* was July-August in the French Revolutionary calendar) and **"The Poverty of Poverty"** give an idea of the tone and scope. There are three longish sequences, one called **"The Score,"** a brash recounting of some sort of Chandler-styled caper I am unable to decipher or care about; **"The Way We Live Now,"** which includes this profundity: "We need revolution, but settle / for bad manners"; and **"Blackbird Bye Bye,"** much less entertaining than the Dixon and Henderson song it borrows its title from. Yes, there are glints of sincerity and originality here and there; yes, we can see some effort to create a language at once contemporary and durable. But I can't help wondering why a person who has intelligence, learning, and talent settled for a book where the dilemmas of the 1980's seem more relished for their potential as hot copy to be handled by a cool hand than taken up for investigation and challenge. (pp. 283-85)

Alfred Corn, "The Calm at the Center of the Storm," in Poetry, *Vol. CLV, No. 4, January, 1990, pp. 283-96.*

Carey Cameron
Daddy Boy

Cameron is an American novelist, born in 1952.

Daddy Boy is a humorous, first-person chronicle by Robin Drayton, the youngest daughter of the title character, a flamboyant Texas oil tycoon. Along with her three siblings, Robin is shuttled back and forth between the homes of her parents after their divorce, and the narrative comprises her naïve observations of her father's parties, friends, and decadent lifestyle in California during the 1960s. Robin was born without a muscle in one eyelid, preventing that eye from opening completely and making her an object of ridicule. Despite his generosity in financing unnecessary cosmetic surgery for his girlfriends, Daddy Boy refuses an operation for his daughter. The central metaphor of *Daddy Boy* is sight, for after Robin does have surgery she trusts her own perceptions for the first time and begins to mature. Commentators applauded Cameron's evocative narrative voice, which renders Robin's pain and confusion without self-pity. Karen Cochran wrote: "The narrative voice, a rich combination of lyricism and light-heartedness, couples the perspective of a young girl's innocent observations with a wry adult irony, so that we never mistake a character's naïveté for the author's. Carey Cameron succeeds in thoroughly entertaining with a style that neither overdramatizes nor dismisses the sadness at the heart of this memorable first novel."

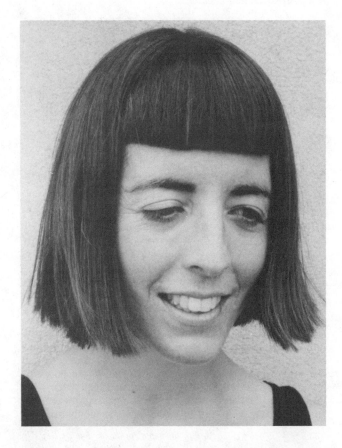

ARDEN KASS

On its surface, *Daddy Boy* is a zippy, funny novel about growing up in California in the wild and crazy 1960s. One easily accessible level below its surface, it's a novel about vision—first about physically gaining the ability to see, and then, the ability to see who and what one's parents are. In her first novel, Carey Cameron covers a great deal of personal, psychological ground with a light touch that never leaves us feeling "instructed."

The novel unfolds in a funky, disjointed first person sprinkled with stream-of-consciousness riffs. Scenes switch cinematically, appropriately mimicking the rhythm of life for four children who are shuttled back and forth between their divorced parents' homes on a weekly basis. . . .

Cornelius "Daddy-boy" Drayton, the father of "Robin-girl" (Daddy-boy's lingo) and her three older siblings, is a zillionaire tycoon who made his first oilstrike with a five-dollar investment, and never tires of telling his own story. A living caricature of himself, and of every cartoon about a Texas oilman gone overboard with money, power and women, he surrounds himself with an endless swarm of sycophants—"beautiful showgirls, nothing but beautiful showgirls," hack

actors and gossip columnists—creating a studio audience to laugh and clap on cue at his anecdotes and boozy hijinks. Weekends, Robin observes the goings-on at his mansion, which may include parades of six white Cadillac limousines to Trader Vic's, where every woman at the table is sporting fresh bandages from plastic surgery, courtesy of Daddy Boy.

During the week she lives with Mother, an ex-model and B-movie starlet who had been Daddy Boy's fourth wife. Mother hasn't the time to pay much attention to her children's emotional needs. She's too busy caring for her lover Peter, who has bleeding ulcers, for her senile mother and "poor, but well-born" cousins from Virginia, and for every amputee or black person she can befriend in the supermarket.

Robin, who was born with one eye nearly closed as a result of a missing muscle in her eyelid, becomes a pawn in her parents' games with each other. Daddy Boy hands out nose jobs and tummy tucks to prospective girlfriends, but he won't allow anyone to operate on his beloved baby daughter's eye. . . .

Essentially, what Robin can or can't see about Mother and Daddy-Boy and her brothers and sisters becomes the metaphor for the book. When Mother sneaks her off to New York and has her eye operated on, the surgeon opens it too wide, so that Robin can't help but see everything about her "amazing" father and her "wonderful" mother, whether she wants to or not.

Daddy Boy is fun to read, for its dead-on depiction of Hollywood grossness, for its wicked characterizations and for its powerful emotional insights.

Arden Kass, "Big Bad Dad," in Philadelphia City Paper, June 16-23, 1989, p.13.

WILLIAM J. HARDING

[*Daddy Boy*] is a restrained, modestly engaging account of growing up rich and spoiled in Hollywood in the early 1960's. Ten-year-old Robin, the narrator, is the youngest of four children. Her father, Daddy Boy, is her main subject. He's a wealthy, hard-drinking Texas playboy who made his money in oil. As the title implies, Daddy Boy is far from a responsible grown-up. He's eccentric and domineering, a handsome, seductive bully. And he refuses to accept the fact that Robin, his youngest and favorite child, was born with a minor physical defect. This condition, which invites the ridicule of her peers, is left untreated for a decade—until Robin's mother (the fourth of Daddy Boy's divorced wives) dramatically whisks her off to a New York hospital for corrective surgery. At first, as you read the novel you wonder if this is a *roman à clef.* However, it soon becomes apparent it's not that kind of book. Rather, it's an impressionistic account of the child as survivor. Ms. Cameron avoids self-pity and melodrama, managing to combine a child's awe with an adult's wariness. Her writing is vivid and lively, but perhaps a little too smooth. As the story proceeds, crazy, disturbing things occur, but they are not judged. Yes, this is outrageous and sometimes appalling and sometimes sad, Ms. Cameron seems to be saying, but it's not without excitement, and even some satisfactions. So *Daddy Boy* emerges as a portrait rather than an exposé. It's slight, but it has its own special charms.

William J. Harding, in a review of "Daddy Boy," in The New York Times Book Review, June 18, 1989, p. 20.

MARY ANN McKINLEY

Carey Cameron's first novel, *Daddy Boy,* is as eccentric as the characters who inhabit it. At once savagely bitter and funny, it proceeds in vivid vignettes from the perspective of the family's youngest child, Robin, who was born with one eye closed. And closed it remains until she is nearly grown.

Although Daddy Boy is fond of paying for his showgirl friends' face lifts, boob jobs, tummy tucks, new noses, braces, you name it, he refuses to acknowledge that his daughter needs corrective surgery.

To Robin, that's an especially enormous travesty because, following Mommy Girl, he has a stream of hot and cold running showgirl maids, girlfriends and wives. All have heads swathed in white gauze or mouths aglow with silver wire at one time or another.

However, having only one functioning eye does not keep Robin Girl from seeing plenty. She is compensatorily obsessed with seeing. She goes so far as to climb through the air ducts in her father's mansion so she can observe Daddy Boy. And what sort of thing does she spy with her one good eye?

> Daddy is kissing another woman now. All the other women are crowding around him . . . 'Cute,' one woman says. Daddy lets go of the woman he has been kissing, turns to the woman who has just said 'cute' and starts kissing her. Then another woman. . . .

Daddy Boy's observed life is one endless party. But Robin and her siblings go to their father's only on weekends. Weekdays they live with their mother.

She, freed from her terrible Texan, reverts to her Virginia ways, marries an East Coast painter and begins to take in ne'er-do-well relatives and strangers by the dozen.

Robin sees her, too:

> Mother has people she meets in the supermarket over for dinner. Some are missing arms or legs. Others are black. She follows them down the aisles while Butch and I beside her whisper, 'Don't please don't please don't please don't.'

The absurd contrast between her father's Beverly Hills gilt and glitter and her mother's Eastern genteel liberalism works on Robin, and in so doing becomes the heart of the novel.

The child's awakening to the preposterousness of both parents is as refreshing as the Trader Vic's fruit punch the children drink every Saturday night: "one . . . after another without raising our heads: The waiters just keep them coming." Carey Cameron just keeps the childhood images coming, too, so the reader knows before she does that the girl never really loved her father.

Daddy Boy is a short book, but one as carefully crafted as fine poetry. It is original, and it is funny.

Mary Ann McKinley, " 'Daddy Boy' Full of Eccentricity, Savage Humor," in The Kansas City Star, June 19, 1989, p. 3C.

MAUDE McDANIEL

Written throughout from the viewpoint of his youngest, favorite child, Robin, *Daddy Boy* never quite makes it clear whether Daddy is mentally unbalanced or just naturally revolting. A Texas oil baron who worked his way to the top, he is a repulsive meld of gross sexual, racist and personal habits. Toadied to by sycophants and a rapid turnover of mistresses and "live-in maids," he seems compelled to "make love . . . to every woman he meets . . . like drilling holes in the ground, or something." His awfulness somehow seems encapsulated in his custom of referring to everyone, including himself, as "boy" or "girl": Daddy Boy, Midge Girl, Corny Boy, etc.

Standing self-consciously against his values is his divorced wife, Elizabeth, Robin's mother, once a beautiful if inept starlet, now married to an artist. A card-carrying nice person, liberal Elizabeth invites every unfortunate she can find home to lunch and follows blacks out of the supermarket saying, "It's so nice to have you in the neighborhood!"

Also complicating Robin's life are a sister and two brothers who tease her sadistically because of her drooping eyelid. Daddy Boy will not allow it to be operated on (to keep her under his control, speculates the housekeeper), although he eagerly finances cosmetic surgery for his other women.

Torn between her parents' clashing lifestyles, Robin can't help but turn out a little neurotic as she grows into adolescence. Her siblings are even worse off: the boys succumb to all the worst influences of the '60s, and her sister cannot stay married. Eventually, Robin's eyelid gets fixed and they all come together at Daddy's funeral, but damage has been done.

Daddy Boy has some writing-school virtues and faults, like the fairly successful ploy of dividing each chapter into blocks ranging from a single sentence to several pages, and the un-

---

An excerpt from *Daddy Boy*

We watch the party from the balcony overlooking the living room, dangling our feet, with dustmop bedroom slippers on them, through the balustrades. Some of the people look up and smile at us and wave and nudge other people who also look up and wave. Some of the people who wave then break away from the crowd and climb the stairs to see us. As they climb the stairs, I pray that they won't be famous, because famous people make my heart beat fast and make me feel as if I have to go to the bathroom and make the word *famous, famous, famous* resound in my head, until I almost say, "You're famous," right to their faces.

They sit down between us, putting their legs through the balustrades. The women have to hitch up their tight skirts all the way above their stockings to put their legs through. They shout at their friends below and throw balled-up napkins at them ("Check her pits when she raises her arms," Butch says about the women. "Check 'em now, check 'em") when they won't look up. Then they turn to us and ask us what our "impressions" are of such-and-such. They pull the corners of their mouths down, trying not to smile when they ask us that. I squirm and say, "I don't know. . . ." and Jennifer looks at the ceiling and says, "Um, I think, um, I think. . . ." and without waiting for her to finish, they say, "Your dad's amazing, you know? He really is. You must never forget that."

I searched the crowd for Daddy until I found him, in the middle of a group of women, making big circles with his right arm in the air above his head. He was showing them how to lasso a dogie, I knew, and explaining to them that a dogie was not a dog but a calf, a veal.

"Amazing," I thought, "amazing." It was amazing how I could have a father who was amazing and spend whole days not thinking about it. Then, when someone said Daddy was amazing, or when I remembered on my own that people thought so, it was as if a big bubble burst, covering Daddy and everyone around Daddy with sparkling dust, like the kind of dust that poofed out of Tinkerbell's wand as she flashed around the Fantasyland castle at the beginning of the "Walt Disney Show" at eight o'clock on Sunday nights.

---

successful and grating one of alternating those blocks between past and present tenses for no apparent reason. Also, what may conceivably hold a child's attention soon wears thin for adult readers ("Midge's ten red toes then became like heads in a theater, watching. Then the toes stopped being bright red and started being fierce red. . . .").

Sensitive and occasionally ironic, to me this book did not seem hilarious, lyrical or rocking with laughter, as touted on the dust cover. Still, one reader's fun may be another reader's pain.

Real coming-of-age is not just finding yourself, but also re-finding your parents and their place in your life. Haphazardly, *Daddy Boy* finally achieves its purpose: to compose a perverse paean to parents and their enduring effect upon the children who become their "crazy, built-up jigsaw monument[s]."

Maude McDaniel, "Growing Up with a Father Who Was Truly Monstrous," in Chicago Tribune— Books, *June 25, 1989, p. 6.*

KAREN COCHRAN

Daddy Boy is the story of how Robin D. grows up as the youngest of four children caught between overbearing, fanatical parents. Her father, an oil magnate whom she and her siblings Jennifer, Butch, and Sonny visit on weekends, is a man obsessed with controlling everyone in his entourage—especially women. He surrounds himself with servants or girlfriends (or both) who cater to his constant demand for attention and willingly submit to unnecessary cosmetic surgery and orthodontia at his behest. "And when they start assuming they're going to spend the rest of their life with him, he just says 'why don't you take a little tuck?' again! . . . until they either get fed up or start looking like goddamned Incas." All women are "showgirls" to Daddy Boy, and he hasn't met a showgirl he couldn't improve, except for his favorite daughter, Robin, born with a drooping eyelid that seriously impairs her vision. In a preposterous effort to control his daughter's appearance and thereby her destiny, Daddy Boy refuses to have Robin's eye operated on, even going to the trouble of hiring private detectives to follow the child's movements when she is staying with her mother.

But while Cornelius "Daddy Boy" D. is certainly the most flagrant character in the book, he is not always its most interesting personality. Equal time is given to Robin's mother, Elizabeth, an ex-actress proud of having descended from poor but, "well-bred" Southern stock. She struggles to be as selfless as Cornelius is selfish and cannot control her passion for taking in people she feels sorry for—strangers she pays more attention to than her own children.

> . . . Mother invites them over for dinner, then calls up other blacks or amputees she has met at other times in the supermarket and invites them over for dinner, too. Sometimes she forgets whether the person she has invited is black or has had something amputated, so that a black often finds himself shaking a stump instead of a hand or an amputee often finds himself stumping into a party of beaming blacks.

Though Elizabeth is as inept at charity work as she is at parenting, she nevertheless manages to sneak her daughter off to New York for eye surgery. But when Elizabeth visits Robin in the children's ward, she is ashamed that her daughter's affliction is "so minor" compared to those of the other children: "eyes that were going to be removed," "eyes that jiggled or eyes that blinked all the time." Elizabeth feels for all the infirm children in the ward, but hasn't remembered to pack her daughter's underwear, so that Robin leaves the hospital wearing rolled-up pajama bottoms under her dress. (pp. 6-7)

To Cameron's credit, Robin never feels sorry for herself. She treats her disfigurement lightly; her drooping eyelid is neither a blessing nor a tragedy, neither "an emblem of the Lord's favor" nor cause for an eternally wounded self-image. Though her brother Butch, a hilariously drawn pubescent obsessed with the subject of armpit hair, frequently torments Robin with long, highly inventive stories about her "gross" body, these scenes aren't there to elicit our sympathy. Rather, they provide occasions for Cameron's comic insight into the hormonal dynamics of adolescence.

[**Daddy Boy**] is not so much, as Robin claims, "a crazy built-up jigsaw monument to Daddy" as a realistic portrayal of a young girl's anomalous, surefooted passage into maturity despite the maelstrom she grows up in. The consistent humor with which Cameron treats the idiosyncrasies of Cornelius and Elizabeth drives the prose and keeps the story from veering toward self-indulgent, Parent Dearest waters. The narrative voice, a rich combination of lyricism and lightheartedness, couples the perspective of a young girl's innocent observations with a wry adult irony, so that we never mistake a character's naïveté for the author's. Carey Cameron succeeds in thoroughly entertaining with a style that neither overdramatizes nor dismisses the sadness at the heart of this memorable first novel about learning to be "just as free as you please." (p. 7)

Karen Cochran, in a review of "Daddy Boy," in VLS, No. 76, July, 1989, pp. 6-7.

AMY KRAUSS

Carey Cameron has succeeded in turning out a truly hilarious and compelling first novel. [In **Daddy Boy**] Cameron has captured perfectly the utter innocence of a 10-year-old girl growing up in the 1960s.

Robin, the narrator of the story, is a girl caught between her constantly fighting divorced parents. Robin's father is an ultra-wealthy oil baron who throws huge Hollywood parties just for fun and enjoys indulging his little "Robin Girl" and all of the beautiful "showgirls" that turn into live-in "maids."

Her mother, on the other hand, is a ravishing former cover-girl and movie starlet who married and gave up her career at its peak. Her mother now looks for down-and-outers with a physical or mental abnormality who can benefit from her smile and companionship, much to Robin and her siblings' embarrassment.

Much of **Daddy Boy** is a pre-adolescent interpretation of adult situations and her perceptions of everyday things that occurred in the Hollywood of the '60s. It's occasionally difficult, however, for the reader to figure out what Robin is really seeing and experiencing.

On the other hand, reading how young Robin reacts to the very idea of her father having sex with a girlfriend ("They don't really do that!") is both hilarious and touching. At one point, Robin even stops to ponder her own existence: "The amazing part was, not so much that Daddy was amazing, but that of all the souls that God sent down to be the children that Daddy made, God had to send down us. The really amazing part was that I was in me."

While it may take some time to get used to the style, Cameron awakens a certain child-like thinking in the reader. The reader may find himself thinking about things he hadn't thought of in years in the simple and innocent way of a child, completely void of any adult interpretation. . . .

At the beginning of the book we get stories of her older siblings' teasing Robin, the youngest and Daddy's girl. There are all the typical names that one is called by an older brother ("turd face," "butt breath") and the reader can't help but chuckle at the memory of saying or having those things said to them as they're pinned to the ground.

Daddy Boy is an excellent first effort for this author. As the reader sees young, confused Robin grow up into an older, still confused high school sophomore, the reader will have felt like he grew up again. The author's attempt to portray a 10 year old's innocence in this anything but innocent world is unbelievably successful, no doubt because of her ability to write as a 10 year old privately thinks inside her head.

Amy Krauss, "First Novel Scores a Perfect 10," in The Grand Rapids Press, July 9, 1989, p. B11.

SHARON LLOYD STRATTON

Set in a tapestry of Hollywood glitz, Texas oil and Virginia tradition, [**Daddy Boy**] examines what happens in one offbeat family when values collide.

Robin Drayton is the amazingly normal youngest child of a mismatched set of parents whose marriage was made in Hollywood rather than in heaven. Robin is the narrator of Ms. Cameron's novel.

The centerpiece of the novel is Robin's Daddy, a colorful, original character whom the reader will love to hate. Daddy Boy is a self-made man who loves to tell his rags-to-riches story of scoring big in Texas oil. . . .

Daddy Boy is a jetsetter, yet the essence of poverty and ignorance clings to him like the stale odor of fried onions. Robin recalls that Daddy "hadn't always been rich, though, and hadn't always had lots of showgirls to go out with, one after the other. Daddy had lived in flimsy houses, where screen doors had kept banging in a constant wind."

The memory of humble beginnings makes Daddy a desperate, driven man, a man with an insatiable desire to be worshiped. Does a newly hired maid have buck teeth? Daddy will pay for her orthodontia. "You've got to shave down those nostrils, Judy Girl!" Daddy Boy pays for her nose job.

Daddy pays for the repair of defects on half the women in Southern California, but it is the defect closest to his heart that he cannot bear to fix. Robin was born with no muscle attached to one eyelid, a condition that causes one of her eyes to droop in a perpetual wink. He fears that if Robin receives the surgery necessary to repair her eye, she will turn into a copy of her beautiful mother and leave her Daddy Boy.

Robin's mother is a dazzling former cover girl who married Daddy at the height of her modeling career. Mother was reared in Virginia in conditions she prefers to think of as gen-teel poverty. Comfortably well-off from her modeling income, Mother's household now includes her hilariously senile mother and a host of relatives who waltz into her life looking for a handout.

Like Daddy Boy, Mother needs to be worshiped, and, unfortunately, the love of her children is not enough. She constantly picks up stray people—in the grocery store, on the way home from a hospital stay—and brings them home. Her children, much to their embarrassment, are forced to share her with the handicapped, the injured, the displaced and the homeless.

Robin grows up, shuttled between these two households, hearing the world tell her that her parents are wonderful and that she is a lucky child. Her story is not tragic, for she is a survivor, although the rebellions of her sister and brothers do lend a bitter element to the book.

At length, there is an end to Daddy Boy, and Robin finally begins to sort out her feelings for the confusing man who has shaped her life.

Carey Cameron has crafted a fine first novel, strengthened by insightful characterization and wise, bitter humor.

Daddy Boy is an intelligent summer refreshment.

> *Sharon Lloyd Stratton, "Original Characters and Wise, Bitter Wit Color Fine First Novel," in* Richmond Times-Dispatch, *July 16, 1989, p. G-5.*

CAREY CAMERON [IN CORRESPONDENCE WITH *CLC YEARBOOK*]

[*CLC*]: *Comment on the process of writing* **Daddy Boy,** *including its inspiration and any obstacles you may have overcome.*

[Cameron]: You could say that **Daddy Boy** was written over a period of 17 years, for I have been writing on the same subject for that long, with long goof-off periods lasting as long as 2 years, though it didn't start to take shape as a novel until about 10 years ago. . . . My greatest obstacle to completing **Daddy Boy,** however, was not editors not buying my book but my own willingness to give top priority to the slightest distraction because of a lack of conviction in myself as a writer.

Relate the terms of any background research you conducted.

Background research consisted of being foolish, making mistakes, being humiliated and observing the same happen to others.

What audience are you hoping to reach?

The most uptight.

Please describe any works-in-progress.

I am presently at work on a series of short stories. I don't know if I am capable of writing short stories but we'll see.

Bryce Courtenay
The Power of One

Born in South Africa in 1933, Courtenay is an advertising executive and novelist currently residing in Australia.

Set in South Africa during and immediately following World War II, *The Power of One* revolves around the adventures of Peekay, a precocious boy of English descent struggling to overcome the prejudices of Afrikaners, who are gaining political and social dominance. Peekay is sent to boarding school at the age of six where he becomes the victim of his sadistic Afrikaner schoolmates. On a train ride home, however, Peekay meets Hoppie, a former boxing coach who instills in him the desire to become a fighter. Through the guidance of Hoppie and other mentors, including Inkosi-Inkosikazi, a Zulu medicine man, Geel Piet, a mulatto boxer, and Doc, a German naturalist imprisoned as a war criminal, Peekay ultimately discovers "the power of one," the magical strength of the inner self to prevail against the intolerance of others. While some reviewers faulted Courtenay's portrayal of South Africa's tumultuous history as simplistic, others agreed with David Keymer that *The Power of One* "is a near-perfect popular novel, grand in theme, rich in narrative vigor, resolutely old-fashioned in form but not in sentiment. It stands comparison with the works of such master African storytellers as John Buchan and Laurens van der Post. Readers will remember it."

DON G. CAMPBELL

[The] first novel by mature Australian advertising executive, Bryce Courtenay [*The Power of One*], is one of those maddening, epic, novels that defy easy explanation because it would seem to sprawl, but somehow doesn't; that seems to lack a central point, but most certainly has one; that seems to have a protagonist of limited appeal, but who, instead, is riveting. *The Power of One* covers the adventures of Peekay, a boy of British descent from age 5 through 17, and his upbringing in South Africa during, and immediately following, World War II when English influence was passing into Afrikaner hands and the grim seeds of today's Apartheid were beginning to flower. Here is a boy who should be insufferable—he's bright-bordering-on-brilliant, multitalented and born with a charisma that cuts through social and racial lines like a knife. His ambition, almost from the first page: to become the welter weight champion of the world. Oh, a boxing story? Perhaps, in about the same way that *The Old Man and the Sea* was a fishing story. The influences on Peekay's character—known as "Tadpole Angel" to the thousands of bush Africans who fall under his almost mystic spell—range all the way from, of all things, a scraggly chicken known as Granpa Chook, to an illiterate, gnarled Kaffir, Geel Piet, his first

trainer, to Doc, an aging German naturalist who becomes his mentor. Told against the background of the growing racial tensions in South Africa and the constant English-Boer frictions, *The Power of One* is a totally engrossing story of the metamorphosis of a most remarkable young man and the almost spiritual influence he has on others. No goody-goody, Peekay has both humor and a refreshingly earthy touch, and his adventures, at times, are hair-raising in their suspense.

Don G. Campbell, "Storytellers: New in June," in Los Angeles Times Book Review, *May 21, 1989, p. 10.*

PETER TONGE

[*The Power of One* is] a compelling tale of a young boy's refusal to be demoralized by fearful racial torment; of the discovery that loyalty, strength, and courage can be fused into the "power of one" so that nothing worthy of achievement lies beyond his grasp.

The work is an epic, flowing from the imagination of a talented new writer. But in part, the experiences of the young hero, Peekay, are those of Courtenay himself.

A leading figure in the Australian advertising industry, the author was born and raised in South Africa. Like his fictional hero, Courtenay would have experienced the divisions the turbulent war years produced, including the rise of Hitlerism among a segment of Afrikaners, who saw in the Nazi leader a savior who would rid them of the English yoke. Later he would have watched the changing of the guard as English political dominance passed into Afrikaner hands. Also like his hero, Courtenay spent a year in the copper mines of Northern Rhodesia, now Zambia, before going on to Oxford University.

Perhaps because of the great bond between the little boy and his Zulu nanny during his early years, Peekay effortlessly sees the absurdities of a system based solely on white privilege, not from any high sense of moral purpose, but because he is naturally drawn to people for *what* rather than *who* they are.

Peekay's friends and mentors are drawn from Afrikaners as well as English-speakers. They also include the twins, Dum and Dee, from the Shona tribe; his beloved Doc, the German professor of music; and Morrie, who in his own words, is "the token Jew" at the exclusive boarding school they attend in Johannesburg. Then there is Geel Piet, the mixed-race lag (prisoner) at the Barberton jail, who showed him how dancing feet and a moving head could make a small man the equal of a more powerful one in the boxing ring.

Significantly, too, Peekay is able to impersonalize the brutality he witnessed as an outsider at the Barberton jail: "We saw," he says of himself and Doc, incarcerated as an enemy alien for the duration of the war, "the brutality around us, not as a matter of taking an emotional side or of good versus evil, but the nature of evil itself."

The pace never falters as the author's well-chosen words parade a steady flow of clearly drawn images: from a wizened witch doctor's kindly rapport with a troubled little white boy as they squat facing each other over a circle drawn in the sand, to the frozen moment when a deadly mamba's swaying head and flicking tongue come to within inches of the now young man's face, and on to a fight scene in the copper mines of central Africa, where skills nurtured from childhood triumph over brute force and bestiality and a personal hatred is finally dissipated.

Consider the way the author introduces the reader to the five-year-old's arrival at boarding school:

> Then began a time of yellow wedges of pumpkin,
> burnt black and bitter at the edges; mashed potato
> with glassy lumps; meat aproned with grissle and
> grey gravy; diced carrots; warm, wet, flatulent cab-
> bage; beds that wet themselves in the morning; and
> an entirely new sensation called loneliness.

A reader can only ache for the little boy at this stage. But though periods of trial, even humiliation, follow, they all build the character, determination, and muscle needed for ultimate triumph and a clear road to Oxford.

While the day-to-day events in the book accurately represent the South Africa of the time, the work remains a fictional exaggeration that includes a touch of African mysticism. It is too much to expect that so many highly charged events

would enter the life of one child, and readers may question the sustained quality of the conversations between Peekay and Morrie at high school, brilliant students though they are. But, that aside, this is a cracking tale, as inspiring as it is entertaining.

A steady stream of South Africans, frustrated by a government unwilling to reform its race practices, has emigrated to other parts of the English-speaking world in recent decades. Some have gone to England, a few to the United States, and many more to Canada. But a majority have been drawn to Australia and New Zealand. Courtenay is among the latter group, and in this instance Australia's gain is a significant loss to South Africa's literary community.

> *Peter Tonge, "South African Crucible for Courage,"*
> *in* The Christian Science Monitor, *June 1, 1989, p.*
> *13.*

ANNA MURDOCH

Conjure it up: a soft purple African evening, the peace and beauty of the northern Transvaal, a white moon, soft, warm dust under the bare feet, and a small English boy is being tortured by his Boer schoolmates under a jacaranda tree. After gross indecencies and cruelty, the boy survives but his pet, his only companion and friend, dies. From that moment on the boy discovers a way to survive, "the power of one," and begins an odyssey towards his ultimate triumph over his tormentors.

Bryce Courtenay has written a marvelous first novel [*The Power of One*], the story of a boy's early years in South Africa. Through the eyes of Peekay, a precocious but sensitive *"verdomde rooinek"* (damned English) boy, Courtenay transports us to the South Africa of the late 1930s. The Afrikaners supported Hitler and hated the *"rooineks,"* hated the *"kaffirs"* (the blacks), hated the *"charahs"* (the Indians) and anyone else they perceived as different from themselves.

Peekay learns to survive by adopting camouflage; he will be clever, but he will not show it; he will be strong, but he will act afraid; he will never cry.

Peekay dreams of becoming the welterweight champion of the world (Courtenay himself was an amateur boxer as a child and a young adult), and some of Courtenay's best writing describes the training and the fights. . . .

Courtenay's powers of observation are similarly exploited when he describes Peekay working in the copper mines of Northern Rhodesia, or exploring the dark *"kloofs"* behind his home. "These green, moist gullies of tree fern and tall old yellowwood trees, their branches draped with beard lichen and the vines of wild grape, made a cool, dark contrast to the barren, sunbaked hills of aloe, thorn scrub, rock and coarse grass."

There are times when Courtenay's writing can seem a little mawkish, displaying a Dickensian preference for caricature, for example the portrayal of Peekay's Jewish friend, Morrie Levy, as an over-smart, guilt-ridden, money-making outsider. And sometimes the dialogue sounds stilted or the childish crudities of language sound false to the ear, but the author quickly recovers with some real stuff so you forgive him for it.

It is the people of the sun-baked plains of Africa who tug at the heart strings in this book. There is Peekay's Zulu wet nurse, who calls in the great Inkosi-Inkosikazi, the best medicine man in Africa, to solve the problem of Peekay's "night water." It is Inkosi-Inkosikazi, with his fly-switch and his mismatched suit, who first teaches Peekay to use the magic strength of his inner self. There is Hoppie, the train conductor-cum-boxer who befriends Peekay at a critical time and from whom he learns the lesson that Little can defeat Big.

There is Doc, the German music teacher, the most important person in Peekay's life, who is imprisoned as an alien when England declares war on Germany. There is Geel Piet (Yellow Peter) "who had no tribe, whose blood was the mixture of all the people of Southern Africa . . . the result of three hundred years of torture, treachery, racism, and slaughter in the name of one color or another."

There is also the mystery of the Tadpole Angel, the songs of

the black tribes, the Zulus, the Swazis, the Ndebele, the Sotho and the Shangaans, the tragi-comic faith of Peekay's mother—Courtenay draws them all with a fierce and violent love. When we leave Peekay, now aged 17, we have been with him through his torment, we too have heard the music. "The voice music is not the keening of despair but the expression of a certainty that Africa will live and the spirit will survive brutality."

Read the book and judge for yourself.

Anna Murdoch, "A White Son of Africa," in Book World—The Washington Post, June 4, 1989, p. 6.

FREDERICK BUSCH

[*The Power of One*] is going to be a big-seller, maybe a best-seller, and it isn't a wonderful book.

It will, inevitably, be compared to *David Copperfield*—this saga of the travails and ultimate triumphs of a Dickensian waif, abandoned (though not for that long) and tested by the rigors of a harsh land (South Africa) in a difficult time (the years leading up to, and following, World War II). And we will feel sorry for Peekay, sent from the warmth of his Zulu nanny and his English-ancestry family (despised by the Boers) to a boarding school filled with louts who torture the boy and his pet Zulu chicken, and who practice every sort of bigotry imaginable.

Peekay is small, frightened, lonely. He is a friend to the black Africans and is always beloved of them. He speaks their language (and several others). Bright, quick to learn, and eventually quite tough, he triumphs. One can say much the same about David Copperfield.

But the Dickens novel is about a boy's education in the realest sense: he learns about the values required of a decent, sensitive and selfless man. A first-person novel (like Courtenay's), it is narrated by David the Elder—the grown man who judges himself in terms of the problem he poses with his first sentence. Dickens has him write, "Whether I shall turn out to be the hero of my own life, or whether that station will be held by anybody else, these pages must show." Courtenay's narrator-protagonist has no such doubt.

Leaving his beloved home, exiled (with his chicken) to the brutal school, Peekay is oppressed by a boy called The Judge, who becomes a Nazi and on whom Peekay finally exacts revenge. While *David Copperfield* ends with an eye for heaven, a hymn for love and a sense of manhood achieved, Courtenay's novel ends with grim justice, Peekay's achievement of peace and an echo of a Zulu shaman's spell.

The fusion of black and white here is happy and praiseworthy. The character of Peekay, however, is not, for throughout the book Courtenay celebrates a hard pragmatism. It is that quality—not the moving plight of the waif, the chanting of black Africans, the music and science of Doc, who becomes the boy's surrogate father, and not the generosities of the many adults who help the boy along—that the novel is really about.

Peekay is taught, when small, to box. He learns from several men that this is his hope for survival. Vulnerable, he learns to avoid punishment and to dish it out. The boxing scenes (there are many) are well written, and boxing dominates the novel's action. It's what the book gives the most of—contest and victory.

An excerpt from *The Power of One*

Doc rose and took a bow and nodded for me to return to my seat next to Mrs. Boxall. Then he removed several sheets of music from inside his piano stool and fixed them carefully to the music rack. He turned to the audience and cleared his throat.

"Ladies and gentlemen. Tonight I would like to dedicate this next piece of music, which I have played once only before, to a friend, a very good friend. I have named this music by his name, and it is for him. I give you 'Requiem for Geel Piet'!"

Without further ado Doc sat down at the Steinway and commenced to play the "Concerto of the Great Southland," which he had now renamed. The melodies of the tribal songs seemed to take over the hall as the Ndebele song followed the Sotho with its more strident rhythm. Doc's right hand taking the part of the solo high-pitched voice and the left chasing it as the singers themselves had done. The Swazi melody followed and then the Shangaan, each separated by the haunting refrain that carried a hint of each, yet acted to lead away from the one and into the other. Finally came the victory song of the great Shaka, and the Steinway seemed to build the drama of the magnificent Zulu *impi,* the chords crashing as they marched into battle. The requiem closed with a muted and very beautiful compilation of the songs of the tribes. The music seemed to swell as all around us from the cells beyond the hall the voices came as the tribes completed the requiem. Geel Piet, who had had no tribe, whose blood was the mixture of all the people of Southern Africa—the white tribe, the Bushman, the Hottentot, the Cape Malay, and the black tribal blood of Africa itself—was celebrated in death by all the tribes. He was the new man of Southern Africa, the result of three hundred years of torture, treachery, racism, and slaughter in the name of one color or another.

There was a special kind of silence as the performance ended. To our own was joined the silence of the listeners beyond the hall. We had all been a part of the lament for Africa. "Requiem for Geel Piet" was a lament for all of us, the tears shed for South Africa itself.

Written in a serviceable, inelegant prose, the novel often slips into anachronisms (someone's "cover is blown"); they are caused by the inability of the narrative persona to keep the voice of the book rooted in either the elder Peekay, telling the story, or the voice of the child he once was. The point of view bounces between these states; at one point, the narrator, lisping childishly, says, "Obviously being a Jew was a very profitable business. Maybe I would be one when I grew up." At another moment, not that many years along, he reports, "We were the cultural meat in a popular sandwich otherwise liberally filled with amateur vaudeville acts."

Such novelistic amateurism gives way entirely at times, and the narrator sounds like a successful advertising man writing his memoirs: "All my life I had let others provide for me, and while I loved the people who had nurtured and built me intellectually, I felt that emotionally it was time to look after myself."

Because he's not a good novelist but has an exciting story to tell, Courtenay is himself seduced by parts of it. A train ride not essential to the story takes a long chapter; the sequence in which Peekay works in the copper mines to make money for college—worth a novel, or much of one—seems briefer than that train ride. And the author's prejudices in what seems to be a "liberal" book—full of speaking, dreaming and socializing in equality with oppressed Zulus—begin to emerge.

The earlier remark about Jews is important, for it is not only an unsophisticated boy who makes such comments. A Jewish boy named Morrie conveniently discusses himself and the Jews soon after making Peekay's acquaintance. The Holocaust and its victims are dismissed by pre-adolescent Peekay: "We have to conclude that the Jews failed to defeat Hitler, failed to defeat the system, and as a consequence paid a terrible price." Morrie grins and acquiesces.

At last we learn what *The Power of One* is about—not black and white together, not dear Doc and his love of the African land and not the strength of love, given to Peekay so unstintingly by so many. It is about using "the system," whether in boarding school, prison camp or copper mine. . . .

That's why this book may be popular. Never mind its ill-managed point of view (Peekay manages to narrate a rescue operation during which he lies unconscious, buried under tons of mineshaft rock). Never mind its warm, gladdening moments, as when Doc, in prison camp, plays his "Concerto of the Great Southland" and hundreds of black African prisoners, led by Peekay, sing in harmony.

Instead the novel is a hymn to Courtenay's belief that "survival is a matter of actively making the system work for you rather than attempting to survive it." The Jews, according to his logic, died in hell on earth. . . . because they failed to master the system, while Peekay has succeeded. This social Darwinism is breathtakingly heartless, stupid and smug.

Acquiring power and retaining it, "using the human resources around me," is the subject of *The Power of One* and the reason for its probable success. Peekay is the sort of world-conquering, self-made and self-satisfied Victorian whom Dickens often satirized; he is the sort who cannot understand—and whom Dickens saw as blighting his own age with this incomprehension—why the poor, the ill, and the victimized are not more like he. And while Dickens loved

cash and victory more than most, I would not confuse Bryce Courtenay with The Inimitable. Think, rather, of Ayn Rand.

Frederick Busch, "The Power of Winning," in Chicago Tribune—Books, *June 18, 1989, p. 6.*

CHRISTOPHER LEHMANN-HAUPT

If a shrewdly programmed computer were to design the ultimate international best seller, it couldn't do much better than this first novel by Bryce Courtenay, an advertising man from Sydney, Australia.

On almost any scale of measurement, *The Power of One* has everything: suspense, the exotic, violence; snakes, bats and Nazis; mysticism, psychology and magic; schoolboy adventures, drama in the boxing ring and disasters in a copper mine. . . .

In fact, the only thing missing in *The Power of One* is sex. And this lack can't be attributed to any modesty on the author's part. It's just that Mr. Courtenay's hero hasn't time for sex. He's too busy growing up and triumphing over the incredible odds against him.

Any summary of *The Power of One* is bound to make it sound unbelievable. Its 5-year-old hero, a South African boy of English descent known simply as Peekay, seems a little on the young side to be torn away from his Zulu nanny and sent to a boarding school where he is brutally persecuted by the older Afrikaners for the role of his presumed ancestors in the Boer War.

There's a comic-book quality to the way Peekay's scrawny pet chicken, Granpa Chook, tries to protect his master and to the violence with which Granpa Chook is killed by the Afrikaner known as the Judge, who has tattooed his arm with a swastika in anticipation of Adolf Hitler's arrival in South Africa.

And the prose can be irritatingly cute and sentimental. . . .

Still, Peekay's story races along. His family gets him released from the terrible school. On the train going home he meets a boxer who inspires him to become the welterweight champion of the world. At home, he is befriended by a botanist and musician named Karl von Vollensteen whom Peekay calls Doc and who tells Peekay to stand on one leg and say: "No matter what has happened bad, today I'm finished being sad. Absoloodle!"

When World War II begins and Doc gets arrested for being a German alien, Peekay is allowed to pay regular visits to the prison, where he discovers a boxing team and a half-caste inmate named Geel Piet who is willing to train him in exchange for certain favors.

Despite your better instincts you get involved in *The Power of One.* You accept Mr. Courtenay as a natural if somewhat naïve storyteller, and the incredibility of it all begins to dissolve. What did the trick for this reader happened to be Doc's speech to Peekay's born-again Christian mother on the subject of the cactus. "God and I have no quarrels, madame," Doc says.

> The Almighty conceived the cactus plant. If God would choose a plant to represent him, I think he would choose of all plants the cactus. The cactus has all the blessings he tried, but mostly failed, to

give to man. . . . It is the plant of patience and solitude, love and madness, ugliness and beauty,
toughness and gentleness. Of all plants, surely God
made the cactus in his own image? It has my enduring respect and is my passion.

But for other readers the hook may be the moment when
Peekay, as a 6-year-old, boxes his first three rounds and wins.
Or when his coach, Geel Piet, is secretly beaten to death by
a racist prison administrator. Or when Peekay first discovers
the Power of One, "that in each of us there burns a flame of
independence that must never be allowed to go out."

Or when Doc von Vollensteen gives a piano concert for the
prisoners and plays for them his newly composed "Concerto
for the Great Southland," which incorporates the melodies
of the inmates' various tribal songs:

> Never had a composer's work had a stranger debut
> and never a greater one. Eventually the composi-
> tion would be played by philharmonic and sympho-
> ny orchestras around the world, accompanied by
> some of the world's most famous choirs, but it
> would never sound better than it did under the Af-
> rican moon in the prison yard when 350 black in-
> mates lost themselves in their pride and love for
> their tribal lands.

According to the novel's concluding biographical note, Mr.
Courtenay was born in South Africa, was educated there and
in England and, in 1958, immigrated to Australia, where he
went into the advertising business. If the old cliché is true
that copywriters are frustrated novelists, then Mr. Courtenay
should be "finished being sad," as Doc von Vollensteen
would say.

Absoloodle!

Christopher Lehmann-Haupt, "Everything but Sex
(Lack of Time)," in The New York Times, June 19,
1989, p. C13.

MARQ DE VILLIERS

Anyone who reads Bryce Courtenay's powerful novel will
have a deepened but flawed understanding of the tragic
events in South Africa.

The Power of One is an attempt to come to terms with the
cauldron of emotions that is contemporary South Africa. The
author tries to make sense of the seething cross-currents of
rage and love, racism and generosity, tragedy and courage
that keep human relationships at a level of intensity found in
few other places on earth. In this he fails. What Courtenay
does do is perpetuate a particular set of prejudices and wish-
fulfilments that are current mostly among outsiders. Courtenay is not an outsider in the traditional sense (he has lived
most of his life in South Africa), but he brings to his understanding of the country his own set of prejudices, which are
every bit as primitive as those of the British jingoes of the
Boer War or the Afrikaner-run National Party that governs
the country today.

This having been said, there is much to admire in *The Power
of One.* The story is straightforward and epiphanic. It concerns a boy named Peekay, who lives with his English-
speaking family in a small town in northern Transvaal. As
the novel opens Peekay is 5 and the Second World War has
just been declared. The boy's family consists of a mother who

has just had a nervous breakdown, a chuckle-headed grandfather, and Nanny, a large, warm Zulu woman. . . . The
mother's illness forces the family to send Peekay to a boarding school attended by Afrikaners—thick-headed Afrikaners
at that, violent, brutal, and uncouth.

The Power of One takes Peekay through one decade and several epiphanies. At school he is beaten, tortured, and bullied
for being a *rooinek,* an Englishman. The first epiphany comes
with his crucial encounter with an African witch-doctor, who
cures him of bed-wetting and arms him with a mantra against
future harm. The next occurs when, on his way home, he
meets a saintly train conductor who teaches him to box;
Peekay determines to become the "welterweight champion of
the world." At home with his family (now inexplicably nan-
nyless) he has a third important meeting—with an equally
saintly German music teacher who lectures him in comic English about sanity and balance. Then, while at a posh Johannesburg school, Peekay learns to fend for himself.

Finally, when Peekay is working in the mines in Northern
Rhodesia (now Zambia), he has his final epiphany—a confrontation with a dumb ox of an Afrikaner with a swastika
tattooed on his left arm. Our hero, now a superb boxer, beats
the bejesus out of the ox and uses a knife to carve the Union
Jack over the swastika. This is the limit of the novel's political
understanding: beat the Nazi brutes by reimposing the "British Empiah."

Courtenay's views of the people who make up this most complicated of countries are simplistic, if not simple-minded.
Very few blacks appear in the foreground except for Nanny,
the witch-doctor (dismissed by white adults as a stinking
primitive but actually a man of great natural wisdom), a convict called Geel Piet, whose main function in the book is to
be sadistically murdered by yet another Afrikaner brute, and
a Zulu chieftain whose role is to embody tradition. Otherwise, the blacks are simply there as background noise, a romanticized, dispossessed people with a mystical attachment
to their land and a huge capacity for surviving oppression
with good humour.

The English-speaking South Africans are about as real. With
the exception of a few caricatures . . . , they are mostly benign nonentities.

And the Afrikaners? They are uniformly repulsive, ill-
formed, brutal, and racist. They are Nazi sympathizers who
kill blacks without compunction.

Political stereotyping aside, *The Power of One* is in many
ways a very good book, written in an accessible, compelling
style. It reminds me strongly of John Irving's *A Prayer for
Owen Meany.* In both, the politics, larded in gratuitously, are
banal. Both are written in a naturalistic style that is covertly
allegorical. And both are wonderfully readable.

In *The Power of One* it's not the story that compels so much
as Courtenay's eye for detail and his fascination with the arcane details of boxing, cactuses, and tribal melodies. There
are many real insights into South Africa, and Courtenay's descriptions of small-town life ring true. (Some characters seem
so real I almost remembered having met them myself while
growing up in South Africa.) And, on those rare occasions
when he transcends ethnic stereotyping, Courtenay displays
a feel for the underlying racism of white South Africans that
is painfully accurate.

Marq de Villiers, "The Power of Prejudice Colours First Novel," in Quill and Quire, Vol. 55, No. 7, July, 1989, p. 46.

EDNA STUMPF

[*The Power of One*] is a brash and burly first novel from Bryce Courtenay, one of Australia's premier advertising men, a gentleman who writes as if he's well schooled in the popular reading tastes of the American public. His venue, however, is the South Africa of World War II and the years shortly thereafter, the era when that melting-pot colony was in the process of becoming a racist rampart. Mr. Courtenay's hero is Peekay, a tormented schoolboy from an English-speaking family. . . . Young Peekay, who narrates the story, controls his fear of assorted Boer bullies and dreams of becoming the world welterweight boxing champion, an ambition that survives upward of 500 pages and his passage into early adulthood. Over the years, Peekay rejects the influence of his fundamentalist mother but accepts lessons in life from a scholarly German musician and horticulturist known as Doc and a sterling Jewish fellow whom he meets when he's sent to boarding school in Johannesburg. Throughout his adventures, Peekay is suspiciously lucky—until he is almost killed in a mining accident. In the end, though, he lives to wreak vengeance on his principal childhood tormentor and to advance triumphantly, one suspects, into the sequels that are likely to follow. *The Power of One* is a wish-fulfillment fantasy, a masculine psychodrama of success through self-discipline and male bonding. On the other hand, Mr. Courtenay's uneconomical but bouncy prose often offers fine bursts of Mark Twainish wit. And so, despite its sometimes packaged aura, *The Power of One* turns out to be an appealing book, a product that deserves a market share of readers. (pp. 12-13)

Edna Stumpf, in a review of "The Power of One," in The New York Times Book Review, July 2, 1989, pp. 12-13.

BRYCE COURTENAY [IN CORRESPONDENCE WITH *CLC YEARBOOK*]

[*CLC*]: *Comment on the process of writing* **The Power of One** *including the inspiration and any obstacles you may have overcome.*

[Courtenay]: *The Power of One* was written without an outline in precisely a year in my spare time. I regarded it as a practice book and it didn't occur to me it might be published. I reasoned that I would need to write five books before I had any chance of finding a publisher. I decided to write these, one each year, so that upon my retirement as creative director of an advertising agency I could attempt to become a writer of published fiction. Thus I divided a ninety hour working week equally between work and writing. I wrote every day, with the major part of my fiction writing (30 hours) taking place over the weekend. At the end of the year I had, in effect, 365 bits of narrative glued together in what proved to be a five hundred page novel. In case I appear to make all this sound easy, it was the most difficult thing I have ever done. It was also the most satisfying. The second of the five practise books is underway, the routine is identical, though hopefully the next book will gain from the experience of having written the first.

Does the work reflect your personal experiences?

The structural heart of the book is based on both personal experience and observation, it's difficult to know how else one might begin to write a novel of this kind. Things experienced and observed are the soup bones and the scrag ends with which one starts the broth, the soup is given its final character from the vegetables, herbs and spices tossed willy-nilly into it. If the soup tastes well the autobiographical component is not the reason, the added ingredients must take the major credit. In essence *The Power of One* is a work of fiction.

Relate the terms of any background research you conducted.

Apart from spelling and place names and a small amount of translation from Afrikaans and Zulu, the book required no research other than the kind at which copy editors are skilled.

What motivates you to write, and/or what do you hope to accomplish through writing?

I am not yet a writer in the sense that I can dispassionately discuss writing as a craft or vocation. I would like to think of myself as a storyteller. Stories are important to me. In all of us there is a deep atavistic need for stories. "Once upon a time" are four of the most magic words in our language.

If the story *must* carry a message then the message should be secondary. The reader does the writer a favour by allowing this added indulgence, therefore it should never be intrusive. I see my task essentially as the telling of a story, it must be the principle delight for the reader.

Ideally, my narrative hand should be invisible, form does not take precedence over function. The writer should not be observed working his wily way through the prose, whereas the reader should find him or herself everywhere in it. Trying to do this task successfully threatens to preoccupy the remainder of my life.

What audience are you trying to reach?

When stories began they were for everyone. The family or the tribe gathered around the fire and they listened spellbound as the teller of tales fired their imaginations. . . . Stories are for people and they come in all shapes, sizes, ages and backgrounds with only one set of common emotions. We all share the same loves and hates, joys and anxieties. We are, in the end, the same person.

Whom do you consider your primary literary influences, and why?

At age twelve Mickey Spillane gave me great pleasure, at fifty-five I derive the same intensive joy from Saul Bellow and M. Tournier. In between there has been Faulkner, Hemingway, Steinbeck, Williams, Maughm, Green, Heller, Stedman, Parker, Grass, Nabokov, Vidal and a host of equally brilliant writers who reached out and touched me. I don't want to write like any of them but each, in his or her way, has left me gasping with admiration and filled me with pleasure. Alas, in the end, as a writer, you can only be yourself.

Please describe any works-in-progress.

I am writing a love story set in Africa. At the moment I am finding it impossibly difficult. There have been so many love stories, how shall I write a new one? It is to be called *The Tadpole Angel*. . . . [It] is the story of a white man who makes the terrible mistake of falling deeply in love with a Col-

oured woman in the South Africa of the fifties and sixties.
What a mess! If I can write well the love will win and the hate
will lose but there will be a price, a terrible price, because
there always is in South Africa.

David B. Feinberg
Eighty-Sixed

Feinberg is an American novelist and short story writer, born in 1956.

Eighty-Sixed chronicles through protagonist B. J. Rosenthal's first-person narration the impact of Acquired Immune Deficiency Syndrome (AIDS) on New York's gay community. The first half of the novel, "1980: Ancient History," comically details B. J.'s first year in New York as a carefree college student experiencing the city's hedonistic homosexual subculture. The book's second section, "1986: Learning How to Cry," poignantly recounts B. J.'s increasing anxiety, despair, and sense of responsibility as his friends and former lovers succumb to AIDS. Although some critics found the novel's minor characters underdeveloped and B. J.'s recurrent wisecracking irritating, others praised Feinberg's portrayal of homosexuals and his unsentimental treatment of a somber subject. Comparing *Eighty-Sixed* to Edmund White's *The Beautiful Room Is Empty,* Ben David observed: "[These novels] are honest, unapologetic stories and seem to represent a positive step forward in gay literature. These books are neither defensive glorifications of the gay urban life-style nor masochistic laments about the sickness of gay life."

PUBLISHERS WEEKLY

[*Eighty-Sixed*] records the changes in gay lifestyles precipitated by the AIDS epidemic between 1980 ("Ancient History") and 1986 ("Learning How to Cry"). The novel's greatest asset is also its chief flaw: diary-like monthly reports describe the narrator's romantic and sexual experiences with bracing immediacy, but finally the novel reads less like fully imagined fiction than a heavily detailed but uninspired newspaper account. The narrator doggedly recounts his faltering attempts to come to terms with the spectre of death in his friends' lives and his own, but Feinberg relates events without enabling the reader to feel or understand the tragedy he gradually unfolds. . . . Readers will be saddened as a friend of the narrator's dies in the second half of the narrative, but the limited emotional impact of the scenes—and the novel itself—derives from the fact that it is about AIDS and death, rather than from the author's ability to shape experience and manipulate our sympathies.

A review of "Eighty-Sixed," in Publishers Weekly, *Vol. 234, No. 19, November 4, 1988, p. 73.*

CATHERINE TEXIER

The title of David B. Feinberg's first novel, *Eighty-sixed,* refers to the gay community, wiped out by AIDS. It is hard to find a more topical subject, and novels concerned with the AIDS crisis have started to come out more and more frequently in the last couple of years. As an addition to the genre, Mr. Feinberg's novel stands out for its frankness, ferocious wit and total lack of sentimentality or self-pity.

In a structure calling to mind those "before and after" photographs advertising a cure for baldness, a nose job or a miracle diet (although in this case the "after" photo looks much worse than the "before"), *Eighty-sixed* contrasts the heyday of the hip and loose gay life style at the beginning of this decade and the anxiety and sense of doom permeating a community half destroyed by AIDS just a few years later.

"1980: Ancient History," the "before" section of the diptych, is a hilarious account of gay life in the fast lane at its peak, back in the times when being a homosexual man meant, for many, being promiscuous and trashy, exploring the limit of one's unleashed libido while giving a collective slap to the face of straight, puritanical America. B. J. Rosenthal, a 23-year-old college student recently moved to New York City from Rochester, lives the life of the perfect clone, the self-deprecating term used to define the typical Christopher Street homosexual: trimmed mustache, steely pecs, skintight Levi 501 blue jeans and an endless supply of one-night stands. As he puts it: "I was only expending ninety-five percent of my waking hours thinking about sex."

B. J.'s hunt for the perfect boyfriend—or, failing that, his hundredth trick—takes us on an extensive tour of the then thriving gay hangouts, from the Lower West Side dives to Central Park's "Gay Acres" via Christopher Street and the St. Marks Baths, with a side trip to Jones Beach in the dead of August. This makes for great sociohistory. Mr. Feinberg, who lives in New York, has a perfect ear. The deadpan dialogues, the constant sexual innuendoes, the sick jokes, the horrific puns, the hysterical shriek of the "queen" in heat—it is all there, and it is wickedly funny. At times, *Eighty-sixed* reads like a Miss Manners guide to excruciatingly correct behavior for the urban clone, a self-help manual, an encyclopedia of proper gay conduct. . . . B. J. does not describe the hard-core sadomasochistic scene; otherwise, he does not spare us any detail, graphic or otherwise. The only shadows in his world, other than being turned down by a gorgeous stud, are the temporary nuisances of venereal disease and being eighty-sixed from a hot club.

Eighty-sixed, of course, takes on a new and foreboding meaning as word of AIDS spreads daily in the pages of the newspapers and former lovers fall like dominoes to the disease. "1986: Learning How to Cry," the second section, gives Mr. Feinberg's novel poignancy and frightening emotional resonance as B. J., like a good trooper, keeps the sarcasm going and the biceps pumping in the midst of the killing fields.

B. J. has become a low-echelon manager at Amalgamated Bank and is now obsessed with purple bruises and lymph nodes, night sweats and T-4 cell counts, as well as bulging pecs and crotches. AIDS has hit: "By the time you read these words I may in all likelihood be dead." Richard, an ex-lover, is diagnosed with AIDS-related complex; Bob, an ex-trick, is in a hospital with Pneumocystis carinii pneumonia; and B. J. starts therapy to help him deal with his anxiety about AIDS. The proximity of death gradually overwhelms him. . . . *Eighty-sixed* works best as the scorched voice of New York City gay culture, of its repertory, its codes, its excesses and its curse. The minor characters . . . tend to have the same witty, ironical tone, providing an endless stream of clever repartee and acting as a sounding board for B. J. rather than being developed into full-fledged characters. What carries the novel is B. J.'s brave, unrelenting voice, totally authentic and becoming ever more poignant as it refuses to break down. Sarcasm is both the weapon and the shield that keeps B. J. from falling apart, whether at his mother's Thanksgiving dinner, poised above the matzoh ball soup between his batty grandma and his jock of a brother-in-law, or when he visits dying Bob at the hospital. B. J.'s therapist is always urging him to cry. But it is the bottled-up pain, the fear that "if I ever let go, even for a moment, I'll fall to pieces," that makes *Eighty-sixed* such a harrowing first-person account of gay life in the age of AIDS.

> Catherine Texier, "*When Sex Was All That Mattered,*" *in* The New York Times Book Review, *February 26, 1989, p. 9.*

DANIEL CURZON

For those who don't know, *eighty-sixed* ordinarily means expelled from a bar. In David B. Feinberg's [*Eighty-Sixed*], it refers to those who are being expelled from life by AIDS. The book seems to have been written to show that a superficial, snotty man can remain true to himself throughout the AIDS crisis by continuing to be superficial and snotty.

He seems to believe that he has been changed by the illness and deaths of his former tricks, but, no, he's unpleasant throughout. If this book was written to make readers think a lot of vacuous gay men have gotten AIDS so good riddance, then it succeeds admirably.

Narrator B. J. Rosenthal tells about his many tricks, all of whom somehow are never good enough for the acid-tongued main character. If he's sexually attracted to one, you can be sure he'll bad-mouth this character later when the man puts on a pound or two. There is little or no plot as these various tricks parade before the reader, and thus all that holds the reader's interest is the personality of the storyteller, but the man is so repellent that the only possible response is, "Why am I stuck in this book with this awful human being?"

The book is advertised as a black comedy about AIDS. If only it were! Instead, it's full of tired and sophomoric jokes. It's set in New York City and presumably should be sophisticated and ahead of the rest of us. But there is nothing about anything in this book, including AIDS and gay humor, that hasn't been done better somewhere else. . . .

The real problem is that this is an amateur first novel that commits most of the sins of the first novel. It should not be told in the first person, because the author doesn't have enough control over the persona.

The "hero" goes on and on, telling everything from his bowel movements to his grandmother's eating habits to his difficulty of firing an employee, with absolutely no sense that all this needs to be processed and re-shaped and made meaningful to other people. . . . A certain glibness of language is not enough.

The novel makes another fundamental error too: not fully describing the different characters or distinguishing them. When they return to the story later, presumably for our concern and sympathy, they are merely names . . . Feinberg shows little skill at making us believe in his characters. . . .

Eighty-Sixed is a rare thing among published novels. Except for fleeting moments here and there near the very end, the reader grows more and more removed from the characters as the book progresses and wants only to get away from them.

> Daniel Curzon, "*Bounced from the Bar of Life,*" *in* Los Angeles Times Book Review, *March 5, 1989, p. 6.*

BEN DAVIS

This first novel [*Eighty-Sixed*] about a young Jewish gay male in New York City has strong similarities to another recent novel, Edmund White's *The Beautiful Room Is Empty.* Both books share a similar theme—the painful maturation of a middle-class, college-educated gay man who has migrated to the big city.

They both also treat the theme similarly. They are honest, un-

An excerpt from *Eighty-Sixed*

At three o'clock I decide that I am dying. Five years ago I could have attributed my sore throat to strep, clap, or sheer stretching in the act of fellatio, but now I know that it is candidiasis, a.k.a. thrush, a.k.a. a logical precursor to AIDS, which means that I will be dead before the year is out. I am at work, shuffling papers and solving crises with mild-mannered telephone calls and drop-dead memos. Suddenly, it all seems existentially absurd, even more meaningless than yesterday.

At four o'clock I begin to make plans for disposing of my worldly goods. I'll give the lease to my rent-stabilized apartment to my friend Philip, who gave me herpes years ago. I figure that will really make him feel guilty, and at least I'll be remembered this way. The books and magazines will go to the hospital across the street with the AIDS unit. I hope the nuns don't mind the pictorials from Power Tool. *There are no plants, because I refuse to allow any other living organisms in my apartment—OK, Jessica can get the cockroaches. Dennis can take what's left of the Dewar's. I'll give Gordon the unreadable novel I wrote in college. I can already hear him smirking to his lover, Jonathan, "It's a tour de force." The nude photos of me can go back to the photographer so he can sell a limited-edition printing of maybe twenty million poster-sized beefcakes, proceeds to be donated to the AIDS foundation of his choice. The swimsuit of most recent vintage goes back to the salesperson who drooled when I tried it on, the gym apparel to my sleazy health-club. I'd like to be burned or buried in the Fortunoff watch. . . .*

At five o'clock my throat burns like a flame as I take the subway to my doctor. I take a seat. My senses seem hypersensitive, acute. I notice every detail. A woman sitting next to me is picking her cuticles, then shaking her floor-length, fake-fur coat. The train is stuck. I move down the car. I can't take it. I am dying. I sit again. The woman across from me makes loud popping noises as if she is cracking her knuckles. I look closely and see it is her gum she is snapping. Why are these sounds so magnified? Why is everything so loud and horrible? An attractive man stands by the door, glasses and a brown mustache, reading Barbara Pym. I decide I am entitled to one last cruise. I am going to die. I might as well look.

At six o'clock the doctor says, "Yes, your tonsils are inflamed. You appear to have a sore throat." He recommends lozenges. I'm ready for a prescription. "You can try Sucrets or Luden's cough drops. You can find them at any drugstore."

My voice is a whisper. I can barely say it. "It's not . . . it's not thrush or anything?"

He looks at me, puzzled, then sighs. He looks at me calmly. He thinks about his house in Maine. He says quietly, reassuringly, "Oh, no. Thrush typically produces white spots on the palate. You have nothing to worry about. It's quite painful. You would know it if you got it."

At 6:12 .. I leave the doctor's office with a new lease on life. But for how long?

apologetic stories and seem to represent a positive step forward in gay literature. These books are neither defensive glorifications of the gay urban life-style nor masochistic laments about the sickness of gay life."

Part I, "1980: Ancient History," is problematic. Its length, which is equal to that of the second part, is not justified by its function, which is essentially to serve as a prologue to the latter. Episodic in structure, Part I sketches in B. J.'s first year in the city. . . .

Holding this part together is the relentlessly hip first-person voice of B. J., who is telling his story. Frankly, the voice is tedious and irritating initially. An inveterate wisecracker, B. J. uses humor to ward off intimacy, even though the year 1980 was dominated by his self-defeating search for a boyfriend. Only as the story progresses does the adolescent, cynical voice begin to mellow and become appealing. Through the author's relentless honesty and close attention to detail, the humanity of the character begins to emerge. B. J. is not noble or sympathetic. He chases unattainable muscle men and irresponsible eighteen-year-olds; he has an affair with an unstable ex-alcoholic. But he is likable and recognizable.

The novel blooms with the second part, "1986: Learning How to Cry." B. J. begins to grow up as the epidemic of AIDS hits the gay community in New York City and forces him to confront difficult feelings in different areas of his life and to take responsibility for these issues.

Part II is handled beautifully and intelligently. B. J. is reluctantly drawn into helping to care for a former trick, Bob Broome, who has fallen ill with AIDS. But the author has made Broome someone to whom B. J. was never close, and whom he has always thought of as a bore. B. J. doesn't change his mind as he becomes involved in caring for him. The conflicts among his basic indifference to Broome, his feeling of responsibility for this dying person alone in the city, and his confrontation with his feelings and fears concerning death make his emotional struggles more vivid and honest, and less sentimental, than if Broome had been close to him. His situation also personalizes the experiences of the gay community as it draws together to deal with the epidemic. B. J.'s voice, while retaining its humor, deepens and becomes memorable. So does the book.

Ben Davis, in a review of "Eighty-Sixed," in Wilson Library Bulletin, *Vol. 63, No. 8, April, 1989, p. 114.*

DAVID B. FEINBERG [IN CORRESPONDENCE WITH *CLC YEARBOOK*]

[CLC]: *Comment on the process of writing* **Eighty-Sixed**, *including the inspiration and any obstacles you may have overcome.*

[Feinberg]: I started with a few chapter interludes, "Egg Paranoia" and "How to Have Safe Sex in the Age of Anxiety." Then I came up with the idea of writing about gay life in New York City, before AIDS and during AIDS. I eventually came up with the structure of two parts, twelve chapters per part, with interludes separating the chapters. In a way, the structure was an involute, framed around the original interludes. As I was writing, Glenn Person (to whom the book is dedicated) was diagnosed with AIDS. He died as I was finishing the first draft, ten months later. He was in my writing group which met irregularly. I still miss him.

What motivates you to write, and/or, what do you hope to accomplish through your writing?

I want to communicate my experiences to share them with others. I want people throughout the country to understand how devastating the AIDS crisis is.

Whom do you consider your primary literary influences, and why?

Philip Roth for his Jewish, sex-obsessed humor, and Woody Allen for his mixture of somber topics with deadpan irony. Fran Lebowitz for her icy sarcasm.

Cynthia Kadohata
The Floating World

Kadohata is an American novelist of Japanese ancestry.

The Floating World offers a view of America in the 1950s through the eyes of Olivia Osaka, a precocious Japanese-American girl travelling through the Southwestern United States with her family. Olivia is witness to her parents' quietly unhappy marriage and is the reluctant confidante of Obasan, her superstitious, forceful grandmother. From Obasan's stories and, after her death, her diary, which illuminate aspects of the family's experiences that are uniquely Japanese, Olivia learns about her spiritual inheritance. Her increasingly mature revelations concerning the world and people around her converge into brief, image-laden episodes that chronicle years on the road, settling in a small Arkansas town during her teenage years, and moving back to California as a young woman to attend college. Ralph Sassone remarked: "Cynthia Kadohata's assured mix of direct and metaphorical prose, of lyrical writing about enduring natural phenomena and delicate humor about ephemeral relations, separates *The Floating World* from less poised (and whinier) bildungsromans by her contemporaries. She attends to people's strengths and weaknesses without a trace of adolescent self-pity."

SUSANNA MOORE

What is a child, a small Japanese girl child, to make of a grandmother who insists her son-in-law quickly turn off a road she senses is full of malevolence? A stepfather named Charlie-O, a migrant farm worker and body-and-fender man with bad luck, who married her mother when she was eight months pregnant with another man's child? . . .

What she makes of it in this melancholy and lovely first novel [*The Floating World,*] by Cynthia Kadohata is a picaresque, sometimes fantastical sojourning; a pilgrim's progress.

The Osaka family—Charlie-O; Laura, the mother; a grandmother Oba-san; Olivia, the 12-year-old narrator; and her three small brothers—leave the Pacific Northwest for Arkansas, where Charlie-O has a chance to start over with a job in a garage. While Olivia is always sad to leave her temporary home in Washington (or California or Wyoming), she also loves the life of the road. Her parents, broke and worried and gently dissatisfied in their marriage, have little privacy in the dreary motels where the family sleeps in one room or during the long, warm days inside the car.

Olivia listens to them—when they quarrel quietly, when they make love at night after the children are asleep, when the old lover of her mother's unexpectedly comes to call. The grandmother, Oba-san, dies in a motel in California. Olivia's mother gives her Oba-san's diaries, which are ill-tempered and frank, but oddly illuminating to the child. The family settles down in the small town of Gibson. Charlie-O's business is a success; the children go to school, make friends, barbecue in the humid, fragrant summer nights. Olivia grows up. She falls in love and works in a hatchery inoculating baby chicks. She leaves home for college in California. Her natural father dies and she is asked by his widow to take over the maintenance of his vending machine route throughout the Southwest. (p. 5)

The title, *The Floating World,* is a reference to a genre of Japanese fiction popular in the 17th century: the *ukiyo*—the floating world of pleasure; of courtesans and newly prosperous shopkeepers. In earlier usage, *ukiyo* reflected the Buddhist belief in the poignant, but seemly, impermanence of life and it is of this older style that *The Floating World* is most reminiscent. It is a book of piquant, sometimes randomly organized episodes, linked by theme and characters. Kadohata also writes in the style of Japanese colloquial poetry, *haikai,* in which images—delicate, fragmentary and fleeting—float by. Watching the Osaka family as it travels by car across

America is not unlike viewing the slow, horizontal unfolding of a picture-scroll. On a journey that invites a kind of macadam-realism, Kadohata has composed a meandering, anecdotal daydream:

> The trees bending over the road made it seem as if a long cave lay before us. As we moved down the street we had to close the windows or the cicadas would jump into the car. Instead they hit the windshield like tiny demons and went skidding to the side. It was stifling in the car. The only noise was the motor and the tiny taps and thumps of the cicadas hitting the glass.

Because Kadohata does not adhere to the classical strictures of fiction, her subject, as well as her reader, might have been better served had she chosen the memoir form rather than that of the novel. There is an unrelenting tone of sensitive isolation. Even the astonishing scene when Olivia finds her grandmother dying on the floor of a motel bathroom and is asked by the woman to summon her daughter, Laura, a request the child calmly ignores as she goes back to bed, is described with cool, slightly congratulatory, self-knowledge. The child's willingness to accept responsibility, her serene pleasure in the perverse moral courage it requires to deny the dying woman, is written in a flat and matter-of-fact tone. Because everything is given almost equal weight—the grandmother's death, a lost child, a slumber party—the reader is curiously unnerved even when the writer seems not to be.

Kadohata has written a book that is a child's view of the floating world, a view that is perceptive, unsentimental and intelligent. Just as a child in its solipsistic, porous way assumes that everything it perceives is, in fact, real, so too does the narrator, Olivia, suffer no doubt that it is her view, her understanding, that constitutes truth. This accurate rendering of that altered state experienced by the precocious child is dry and unsentimental, and it is oddly reassuring.

The melancholic inheritance that children possessed of vivid sympathy receive from well-intentioned parents who are themselves lost in consideration—consideration of the other, of the past, of their own overwhelming and subtle legacies of dread and doubt and regret—is passed on to the reader. And while he may not be driving to Arkansas to look for work, it both saddens and eases his way. (pp. 5, 7)

> *Susanna Moore, "On the Road with Charlie-O," in* Book World—The Washington Post, *June 25, 1989, pp. 5, 7.*

MICHIKO KAKUTANI

For Olivia, the narrator of Cynthia Kadohata's lucid first novel, "the floating world" (or "ukiyo," in Japanese) refers to the transient life on the road that she and her immigrant family have grown accustomed to as they traverse the country during the 1950's, looking for work. It also refers to the impermanence of childhood, the ebb and flow of memories and experiences that make up our disappearing past.

"The floating world was the gas station attendants, restaurants and jobs we depended on, the motel towns floating in the middle of fields and mountains," Olivia observes.

> In old Japan, ukiyo meant the districts full of brothels, teahouses and public baths, but it also referred to change and the pleasures and loneliness change brings. For a long time, I never exactly

thought of us as part of any of that, though. We were stable, traveling through an unstable world while my father looked for jobs . . .

While the frequent moves seem to galvanize the restlessness and dissatisfaction that Olivia's parents feel in their marriage, Olivia, herself, savors the anonymity conferred by a life on the road. She loves watching the countryside slip past her through the windows of the car, and she carefully hoards images of people and places glimpsed on the way: "a pet camel in someone's backyard, or a set of elderly men triplets, dressed the same way down to their canes," a small town, lit up in neon, in the emptiness of the desert, a motel with a pink vacancy sign and almond trees in the backyard.

Because of the immediacy of Olivia's descriptions, because of the intimate, confessional tone of her voice, because of the lack of authorial distance between her and Ms. Kadohata, the reader is inclined to think of *The Floating World* in terms of a memoir rather than as a novel. One is reminded of Cyra McFadden's bittersweet portrait of her parents' days on the rodeo circuit (*Rain or Shine*) and Tobias Wolff's tender, darkly colored account of growing up in Florida and the Far West (*This Boy's Life: A Memoir*). Like those works, *The Floating World* shows us the effects on a child of a rootless, peripatetic life, and like those works, it gives us an indelible portrait of a family in disarray. In addition, it leaves us with a sense of what it means to grow up as part of an immigrant family, what it means to belong to America and yet to stand apart.

Writing in beautiful, clean yet lyrical prose, Ms. Kadohata creates an emotionally precise picture of each member of Olivia's family: her tyrannical grandmother, who bullies and abuses the rest of the family only to regale them with a wonderful story about old Japan (in which towns are invaded by fireflies, and strange clouds herald good fortune); her sad, pensive mother, who married not for love but for honor, and her cheerful but ineffectual stepfather, who increasingly seeks refuge from his problems in compulsive card-playing.

From a fearful curiosity about the tension between her parents, Olivia will move toward a regretful understanding of their imperfect liaison. She will attempt to come to terms with her real father—a married man with whom her mother once had an affair—and she will learn, from these emotional transactions, to see the world as a place of receding horizons, a place in which everything is subject to change.

By the time Olivia is 16, her family has moved to a small town in Arkansas named Gibson, where her father plans to buy into a partnership in a garage. It becomes their first real home. There in Gibson, most of the Japanese work as "chicken sexers"—a bizarre occupation involving the identification of male chicks, which are then drowned, since they are useless for egg production—and Olivia, too, soon gets a job at the hatchery. She falls in love with a fellow worker named Tan, and she is initiated into his family's problems as well. . . .

In time, of course, Olivia—like so many small-town heroines—does leave Gibson for the "real world" beyond. She will move to Los Angeles, get a new job and a new boyfriend, and she will try to live up to her "obligation"—to "have a happier life than my parents had."

In telling Olivia's story, Ms. Kadohata does not shirk from examining all the sad, painful details of her family's thwarted lives, but she does so with tenderness, compassion and wit. She describes Olivia's mother comparing her own father's death to the discovery of a wooden rose—something rumored to be possible, but inconceivable all the same. She describes the shame and protectiveness that Olivia and her brothers feel as they watch their father lose all his money in a poker game. And she describes the epiphany Olivia experiences as she places a bouquet of red plastic flowers on her grandmother's grave—a "flash of color in the gray cemetery" that seems to distill her grandmother's entire life.

Such moments not only help to capture the emotional reality of these people's lives in a delicate net of images and words, but they also attest to Ms. Kadohata's authority as a writer. *The Floating World* marks the debut of a luminous new voice in fiction.

> Michiko Kakutani, *"Growing Up Rootless in an Immigrant Family,"* in The New York Times, *June 30, 1989, p. C27.*

GRACE EDWARDS-YEARWOOD

The Floating World, Cynthia Kadohata's first novel, centers around the Osaka family, part of a migratory wave of Japanese-Americans traveling through the Pacific Northwest searching for work in the early 1950s.

Twelve-year-old Olivia, through whom this remarkable story is told, listens as her grandmother, Obasan, laments," my memories are a string of pearls and rocks." Obasan, who has outlived three husbands and seven lovers and who scandalized society as a young woman by smoking cigars when women were not even permitted to smoke cigarettes, complains to everyone who will listen but mainly to Olivia, "because she is the oldest (of the children). . . ."

Olivia's family is in constant motion, saying goodby, packing, unpacking, looking ahead and wondering what the next stop will bring. Though they are on the move, she feels secure within the cocoon-like closeness of her family. "*We* were stable traveling through an unstable world while my father looked for jobs."

Traveling however, in the narrow confines of the family auto and sharing one motel room, the girl becomes a reluctant witness to the dynamics of her parents' unhappy relationship.

Charles Osaka, whom everyone calls Charlie-O, had married Olivia's mother when she was seven months pregnant by another man. Just as the family seems unconnected to their temporary surroundings, Olivia's mother, well mannered and refined, appears to float in a private world of disappointment, unconnected to Charlie-O's love for her.

> "What do you want?" said Charlie-O very quietly.
> "I don't want anything," my mother said.
> "You don't understand—I want you to want something."
> "I just don't want you to be mad," my mother said to the window. A small steam circle formed on the glass where she was talking. I felt very old suddenly, because I knew she'd only said that for him. What she'd said first was closer to the truth: She didn't want anything he could give her.

So the family remains in motion, in pursuit of equally elusive emotional and financial fulfillment. . . .

Throughout their travels, Olivia, her mother, and her stepfather remain caught up in this heartbreaking tug-of-love.

Before settling in Arkansas where Charlie-O buys into a garage business, their search takes them through Oregon, Washington, Wyoming and California. They travel lightly, taking care not to offend as they traverse a post-World War II landscape pockmarked by memories of midnight arrests and mass internments.

They act politely, smiling at strangers:

> "Smile at them," my grandmother would say. "*Hakujin* (white people) don't know when a smile is an insult." She always said her experience showed that if you hated white people, they would just hate you back, and nothing would change in the world; and if you didn't hate them after the way they treated you, you would end up hating yourself, and nothing would change that way either. So it was no good not to hate them. So nothing changed.

As the family moves, Kadohata skillfully draws us into Olivia's world by allowing us to see through her eyes "a pet camel in someone's back yard, or a set of elderly triplets dressed the same way down to their canes."

We see the dimensions of small towns when she says, "I like the downtowns best, the way the neon and shadows cut into each other when the streets are empty."

And the landscape assumes a surreal aspect ". . . when cars went by, far away, the beams were so bright they seemed to be ropes of light pulling the cars behind. . . ."

On the road, Olivia learns how her great-grandparents in Hawaii were forced by the local schoolboard to give their children American names so that "today, their original names are just shadows following them."

Olivia's coming of age is convincingly detailed and her adolescent dreams are rendered with such tenderness that her sexual awakening only seems to enhance her innocence.

Kadohata's prose also renders scenes of horror and loss: Olivia, now a young woman living in California with her boyfriend, notices

> . . . there was an influx of Chinese refugees from Vietnam and Cambodia around the time Andy and I moved, and the children all played outside until bedtime. Our first year there, a mass murderer was loose in Los Angeles, and the children stopped playing outside for a while. The murderer had strangled someone across the street and his presence hung like fine dust over the rows of stucco apartments and rooming houses in the neighborhood. . . .

At the beach with a party of friends, she observes

> . . . a boat apparently stuck on a sandbar, sat near shore. Several times during the afternoon someone swam out to explore . . . so I swam out to the boat. I could smell it as I neared, a moldy, old, sad smell. On deck, the floor was damp and blackened, the steering wheel corroded. A plastic flag whipped in the wind. For a moment I stared at the flag, the only moving thing except for myself on board. I gasped when I saw a pair of children's shoes hanging from a nail—I thought they were feet hanging down. Inside the shoes I found a damp pair of socks wrapped around two quarters, a nickel, a penny.

The boat jolted with each wave. The shoes had an eeriness about them, and it didn't surprise me that none of the afternoon's explorers had taken the money. I got the feeling the shoes' owner had passed away; and out of respect for him or her, I rewrapped the coins and replaced them. There was something about the care with which the socks were wrapped that indicated a conscientious, serious child; also, something about the 56 cents touched me, for at one time I believed that pennies could buy a great deal and so deserved to be wrapped carefully. . . .

Kadohata writes compellingly of Olivia's coming of age, her determination to grow beyond her parents' dreams; and break free, or at least outdistance, the yoke of guilt bequeathed by Obasan's death. We feel the poignancy of Charlie-O's fumbling search for a meaning to his personal chaos, his need for a moral order to still the shifting sand beneath his feet. And filtering through these small personal struggles looms the larger one of a people trying to find a workable niche in an alien, sometimes hostile, environment.

As Obasan notes, memory is indeed a string of pearls and rocks, but Kadohata's imagery makes the pearls shine and the rocks glow.

Grace Edwards-Yearwood, *"Growing Up Japanese-American," in* Los Angeles Times Book Review, *July 16, 1989, p. 12.*

GRETEL EHRLICH

The Floating World is a first-person fictional account of a young Japanese-American girl growing up in post-World War II America. The title is borrowed from the Japanese *ukiyo,* a word whose two roots are *uki* (sadness or grief) and *yo* (world). At one time *ukiyo* referred to the world of prostitutes, as depicted in Utamaro's woodblock prints. But a pun on the word spun it into motion, connoting the sadness that comes from knowing that our sense of solidity and permanence is a dream.

Wise beyond her years, Olivia, Cynthia Kadohata's 12-year-old narrator, describes life on the road with her family: Charlie-O, her gregarious but unprosperous stepfather; her wistful, cultivated mother; her three brothers; and Obasan, her incorrigible, despotic grandmother. . . .

From Northern California, through Los Angeles, across the southern states to Arkansas they go, but not merrily. Kadohata is no Kerouac; and it is not free-spiritedness that drives them but post-war racial prejudice, insolvency and marital strife, as if movement itself could brush off such burdens. It does not. But a life on the road affects the way Olivia sees and thinks and feels, and Kadohata beautifully captures this world in flux with sharp, lyrical language.

"My earliest memories were of pictures from the car window—telephone wires illuminated by streetlamps, factories outlined against a still, sunless sky—pictures of one world fading as another took its place," Olivia says. The landscape is decidedly '50s America, but one cannot help thinking of the way Japanese literature—especially the *nikki no michi* (poetic diaries)—used the journey to hint at life's transience.

Olivia's external journey to Arkansas and settlement there is an inward journey as well—toward comprehension of how the pieces of family history and geography-as-destiny fit together and why they come apart. . . .

Charlie-O (for Osaka), takes up gambling; and through Olivia's eyes we watch his growing emotional and financial impoverishment. As the oldest, she is responsible for her young brothers and is somehow the guardian of her grandmother, as Obasan herself has been asked to look after Olivia. And through the long journey they go, like enemies handcuffed together. To Olivia, to the world, Obasan shouts obscenities, boxes ears, inflicts all kinds of small cruelties. Then she cast a spell with her stories. "My grandmother owned a valise in which she carried all her possessions, but the stories she told were also her possessions. . . . She would run after me, shouting her facts: 'I had a white dog! I broke my leg three times! My first husband and I had sex in a public bathroom!' " After Obasan's death, it is her grandmother's diaries that sow restlessness in Olivia's soul.

She and her family settle down in Gibson, a small Arkansas town, and it is there that Olivia comes of age. At 16 she takes a job at the hatchery where most of the Japanese in town work as chicken sexers. She meets Tan—Tanazaki—who becomes her first lover. As Olivia's interests move from family to the outside world, the landscape changes: "Everything around me seemed very sexual to me: the slope of the hills, the way the humid Arkansas air felt just slightly heavy."

But Gibson is only a temporary refuge. After high school Olivia leaves, returning to Los Angeles. All through the book we have seen the world through this child's uncorrupted, unflinching eyes. Starting out on her own, though, she seems to lose her penetrating vision and gives herself up to ignorance: "After I left Gibson, I lived a disorderly life, not from any spirit of rebellion . . . but simply because I didn't yet realize

---

An excerpt from *The Floating World*

We were in bad spirits later. From around three to five was usually the worst time. We were often hot, and tired of driving. All six of us were in a terrible mood at once that day. We stopped at a crossing because a train was coming. But it moved so slowly! My father, usually the most good-natured, pounded the steering wheel with impatience. As the engine passed us, my brothers and I leaned out the windows, waving and shouting "Hi" to the three men in the engine. "Say Hi back," screamed Ben. "What's wrong? Are you guys deaf ? I hate you. *Say Hi.*" The engine passed, and then the whole train halted.

"Oh, now what. We're going to be here all day," said my father.

The train backed up. Three men sitting in the engine pondered us. "Uh-oh," said Ben. "Duck—they're going to shoot." Peter ducked. The men smiled and waved. One of them yelled "Cute kids" to my mom. Then the train moved forward. My brothers and I were amazed—we had stopped a whole train. After that, we were all in better spirits. My brothers and I behaved for the rest of the afternoon. The noise inside the car was soothing and constant, like the breath of the sea in a shell.

We passed in and out of alertness while we traveled.

---

there were other ways of living."

These last chapters do not live up to the preceding riches. The material is there, but Kadohata does not use it fully. One longs for excerpts from Obasan's diary, constantly referred to but quoted from infrequently. And the irony of the L. A. boyfriend whose livelihood is wrecking cars—as if to stop the journey of life—is an irony unused.

"Watch out for life, it's harder than it looks," admonished Obasan. At the end of [**The Floating World**], Olivia is alone in the world; her driving passion to know has, as she predicted, "faded into a soft craving, a sort of ache, until finally I felt used and exhausted." Instead of pursuing knowledge, she is pursued herself by the old ghosts—Obasan's and Jack's (her biological father)—and ends up on the road again, as though the highway were the only suitable place in America for the outsiders it makes of its own citizens.

> *Gretel Ehrlich, "A Japanese Girl Wistfully Drifts across America," in* Chicago Tribune—Books, *July 23, 1989, p. 6.*

DIANA O'HEHIR

What was it like to be Japanese-American, 12 years old, traveling across the country in the 1950's? At first, the reader of Cynthia Kadohata's [**The Floating World**] may be puzzled about how she proposes to answer this question. Ms. Kadohata's narrator, Olivia, and her rootless family put miles of motels, fruit stands, bus stations, town squares and dusty arguments behind them, all in an apparently standard American search for a better life. "With the light off," Olivia says, as their car hurtles east toward Arkansas, "the tension seemed to escape through the cracks between the windows and doors, easing out into the dark. I imagined it on the roadside now, waiting. I fell asleep, and when I woke again the Ozarks were swelling on the horizon." . . .

The "gray, whale-shaped" car contains Olivia, her parents, [her] three brothers and a grandmother. And it's through this last character that the narrator and the reader find a link with a Japanese past. For Olivia, Obasan (the most formal address for Japanese grandmothers) is a strong figure, a figure of love and hate against whom she pits herself; she's a unifying force for experience, a violent maternal power, directing, tale-telling, punishing, cigar-smoking, a foil for the young girl's resentments. Dead by page 29, she is the character who has most acknowledged the superstitions that grip these travelers. (" 'Too much magic on the road,' Obasan always said.") Her death supplies a reservoir of energizing guilt.

The Floating World is about families, coming of age, guilt, memory and, especially, this magic. Ultimately it is also about being Japanese-American in the United States of the 1950's, but this latter theme is so subtly presented that the reader tends to lose sight of it for long periods of time.

The novel occurs in a loosely strung series of delicate, perceptively rendered episodes that move through Olivia's adventures on the cross-country drive, her teen-age years in a small Arkansas town, her job in a chicken hatchery and her later life on her own, in a Los Angeles apartment building filled with starstruck neighbors. Concealed but always incipiently present is the dead grandmother's threatening, magic world: "He was tapping something," Olivia says of her California boyfriend, Andy Chin. "It reminded me of my grandmother's

arthritic clicking knee. The next day Andy told me that I'd fallen asleep and shouted, "Stop hitting me, you witch!' "

Ms. Kadohata's narrative tone is straightforward and direct, and Olivia's personality emerges in similarly economical glimpses. Her aim and the book's seem to be one: to present the world affectionately and without embroidery. To notice what's there. To see it as clearly as you can.

The indications that Olivia's family is Japanese—and is treated in a special way because of this—are very delicately handled. The father owns a garage, but most of his friends are chicken sexers, workers who separate male from female chicks—certainly an unusual job, but is it a skilled trade or a demeaning one, or both? When the father and his friends are arrested as members of a betting ring, the chief of police in the small Arkansas town says cheerfully, "One year we arrested the mayor, this year we decided to arrest a bunch of Japs." But no motels or restaurants refuse to accommodate the family or offer them slow service; their friends are Japanese, but their neighbors aren't. So it comes as something of a surprise when a grown-up Olivia, about to leave Arkansas, says:

> My parents had taught me many things they hadn't meant to teach me and I hadn't meant to learn. One of these things was fear: their first big fear, during the war; and when my father was arrested; . . . concern that I would be all right in the future; and a hundred other interwoven fears. That was what I wanted to leave.

Ultimately it is the grandmother, her stories of the past, her pinching, her persistence, her identification of the American version of the transient life of old Tokyo from which the book takes its title ("*We* were stable, traveling through an unstable world."), her pinpointing of the magic in even the most ordinary scene, that shape [**The Floating World**] and supply its energy.

> *Diana O'Hehir, "On the Road with Grandmother's Magic," in* The New York Times Book Review, *July 23, 1989, p. 16.*

RALPH SASSONE

Ever since Huck went down the Mississippi and Holden Caulfield ditched the crowd at Pencey Prep, American coming-of-age novelists have delighted at youngsters in flight from authority. But in fine recent fiction like [Marilynne Robinson's] *Housekeeping,* [Mona Simpson's] *Anywhere but Here,* and Cynthia Kadohata's **The Floating World,** there's a new twist: it's restless adults who set out on a peripatetic course, taking their sage pubescents along for the ride.

Kadohata's accomplished debut is narrated by a Japanese-American girl named Olivia, who travels with her mother, stepfather, three younger brothers, and greatly feared grandmother across several western states during the '50s and '60s. They migrate in a "gray, whale-shaped car" from which Olivia observes "telephone wires illuminated by streetlamps, factories outlined against a still, sunless sky—pictures of one world fading as another took its place." What's mostly an economic choice (it's hard for Japanese to find steady jobs in postwar America) has its therapeutic side as well: Olivia's mom and stepdad use the shifting venues to distract them from their disappointing marriage. For the entire brood, the floating world is "the gas station attendants, restaurants, . . .

the motel towns floating in the middle of fields and mountains. In old Japan [it] meant districts full of brothels, teahouses, and public baths, but it also referred to change and the pleasures and loneliness change brings."

Kadohata delineates these pleasures and pains episodically, somewhat fleetingly, even after Olivia's family settles down in Arkansas. Minor characters amble in and out of the novel like sightseers at a particularly alluring roadstop. One vivid scene follows another, like a traveler's snapshots, with no obvious narrative arrangement. But it's a measure of Kadohata's control that this picaresque book never once meanders; Olivia's progress is as fluid as a nonstop trip through a terrain at once ordinary and exotic. Farmlands in Nebraska, chicken hatcheries in Missouri, westward-moving buses, lakeside slumber parties, Japanese gambling circles—all funnel into the memoir of an imaginative girl whose family drifts between towns and alliances, but remains solidly anchored in her memories.

And with reason. In the midst of providing dispatches from the transient life, Kadohata conjures up wonderful characterizations of Olivia's kin—particularly her stepfather, Charlie-O, and her maternal grandmother, Obasan. The old woman is unforgettable: a thrice-married, cigar-smoking matriarch with several lovers in her past, given to criticizing Olivia and boxing her ears, but also vulnerable and ready to defend the girl to the death. Olivia is the one to whom Obasan confides her secrets before dying early in the book ("She would run after me, shouting her facts: I had a white dog! I broke my leg three times! My first husband and I had sex in a public bathroom!"); the elder's love of storytelling permeates the novel. So does the profound decency of Charlie-O, a kindly auto mechanic who gambles to compensate for an unlucky life. He is a man who doesn't sour, in spite of unemployment, discrimination, and cuckolding. . . .

Cynthia Kadohata's assured mix of direct and metaphorical prose, of lyrical writing about enduring natural phenomena and delicate humor about ephemeral relations, separates *The Floating World* from less poised (and whinier) bildungsromans by her contemporaries. She attends to people's strengths and weaknesses without a trace of adolescent self-pity. At novel's end, the resilient Olivia announces that it's "high time" to leave yet another stopping point in her travels, but few readers are likely to agree with her. Kadohata's narrator has the kind of sweet, solid authority one doesn't want to escape for an instant.

> Ralph Sassone, "The Wander Years," in The Village Voice, *Vol. XXXIII, No. 38, September 19, 1989, p. 55.*

JOHN SPURLING

Cynthia Kadohata's *The Floating World* is a subversive, inside-out novel. Several of the self-contained chapters have appeared as separate stories in various American magazines, including the *New Yorker,* and the whole thing has that veneer of polished artlessness, of lightly touched-up ordinary folks' autobiography which is appropriate to the commonplace North American subject-matter: coming-of-age, family life in suburbia, travelling towards something better.

Yet these are not quite ordinary folk: they are Japanese in the aftermath of the Second World War who, although they have been living in the US for nearly three generations and have

American first-names, remain nomadic and distinctly Japanese.

They drive *en famille* across the States—significantly from west to east, in the opposite direction to the pioneers—staying at motels, doing what manual work they can find (as chicken-sexers, farm-workers and motor-mechanics), but belonging always to an exclusively Japanese community. The young narrator's sense of her roots is mainly inculcated by her domineering grandmother:

> We were travelling then in what she called *ukiyo,* the floating world. The floating world was the gas-station attendants, restaurants, and jobs we depended on, the motel towns floating in the middle of fields and mountains . . . *We* were stable, travelling through an unstable world . . .

The narrator dislikes her grandmother—indeed guiltily leaves her to die on the floor of a motel bathroom without fetching help—and at the end of the book is beginning to break free of the Japanese community, at least to the extent of living with a young Chinese criminal in Los Angeles.

Nevertheless, just as the Indian narrator in V. S. Naipaul's *The Enigma of Arrival* politely demonstrates that the outwardly solid and traditional world of Wiltshire where he has settled is really just as rootless and alien as himself, so Kadohata subtly undermines the whole North American ethos, the myth of the solid, ordinary folk at home in their land. Are these Japanese any more or any less stable than all the other uprooted peoples who call themselves Americans and give themselves names like Walker Roy and Olivia Ann? The land is one thing, the people coming and going are quite another, their legitimacy as fragile and ephemeral as their jobs, their vehicles and their settlements.

> John Spurling, "East, West, Which Is Best?" in The Observer, *October 1, 1989, p. 49.*

CAROLINE ONG

[*The Floating World*] looks back on a girlhood spent wandering up and down the Pacific Northwestern coast of America, growing up in an exiled cultural group, a tiny community of Japanese-American farm-workers always on the move, looking for chicken farms to work. In the early 1950s, when white Americans and Japanese Americans still painfully remembered the Japanese atrocities of the Second World War and the forceful internment of all orientals of Japanese descent, Olivia (the central character) and her family are forced to live the itinerant life of the migrant worker, because they are always treated with distrust and fear wherever they try to settle. The novel's title comes from an old Japanese word, *ukiyo,* meaning "the floating world". Olivia's grandmother explains, "[it] was the gas station attendants, restaurants, and jobs that we depended upon, the motel towns floating in the middle of fields and mountains". But the irony in the phrase is most apparent when Olivia and her family put down roots in a town—Gibson, Arkansas—that offers as marginalized and exiled an existence as life on the road once did.

Olivia's stories are the naive observations of a curious but perceptively mature teenager, struggling to understand the peculiar customs and behaviour of the adults; and we are privy to her closest friendships, her deep resentment against her grandmother's strict upbringing, her first sexual awakening, her secret pleasures and thoughts.

Kadohata's reminiscences ramble through time, people and events. Yet [**The Floating World**] is haunting because of its very simplicity and starkness, its sketchy descriptions fleshing out raw emotions and painful truths.

Caroline Ong, "Roots Relations," in The Times Literary Supplement, No. 4526, December 29-January 4, 1990, p. 1447.

James Kaplan
Pearl's Progress

Kaplan is an American novelist.

Set in a small college town in rural Mississippi, *Pearl's Progress* is a satire of academic life. Philip Pearl, a Jewish poet from Manhattan, haphazardly becomes the newest member of the English faculty at Pickett State University. The first half of the book chronicles Pearl's arrival in Pickett, his humorous incomprehension of Southern customs and accents, and his homesickness for New York. The plot hinges on the outcome of Pearl's various romantic interests and his humorous attempts to identify a mysterious assailant. While some commentators suggested that Kaplan failed to fully exploit the opportunities for comedy provided by his bewildered protagonist, most applauded his prose style, which alternates outrageous puns with passages of nostalgic lyricism. James Marcus wrote: "*Pearl's Progress* succeeds as a deft and witty endorsement for the shock of the new. As Pearl progresses through one new territory after another—romantic as well as cultural—he persuades the reader to share both his excitement and his discomfort: no mean feat, for a series of experiences he's earlier compared to 'losing your virginity over and over.'"

PUBLISHERS WEEKLY

By turns hilarious and melancholy, [*Pearl's Progress*] is the epitome of a first novel: its flaws are balanced by an appealing promise. Philip Pearl is a young Jewish poet from New York who ends up, almost by accident, teaching in the English department of a small university in the heart of Mississippi. Kaplan mines rich material from this vein, starting with Pearl's initial encounter with a motel desk clerk who says nothing is available "poo-sod." ("Poo-sod?" "Yessir? By the poo?") Pearl finds himself wading into the intrigues of the department and various romantic tangles, all of it drenched in the mysterious and opaque quality of the Deep South as it seems to outsiders. The book's plotting is somewhat confused—the story builds and then collapses without sufficient explanation. But then, little that Pearl encounters can be quite explained. Kaplan's writing is crisp, authentic and brimming with originality and wit.

A review of "Pearl's Progress," in Publishers Weekly, *Vol. 234, No. 23, December 2, 1988, p. 45.*

DAVID GATES

It's unlikely that James Kaplan is *really* daring reviewers to trash his delightful *Pearl's Progress*. But it's equally unlikely that so knowing a first novelist isn't aware that one simply doesn't: (A) flaunt oneself with epigraphs from both T. S. Eliot and David Byrne; (B) make one's hero a self-doubting poet; (C) plop said poet down to teach college in exotic Mississippi, especially if he's a Jewish New Yorker; and (D) populate said Mississippi with white girls who talk in questions ("My name's Tammy?") and black men playing bottleneck guitar on front porches. Kaplan's other offenses include trotting out a major character who'd been neatly disposed of simply for a curtain call, and scheduling portentous reappearances of minor characters with no significant payoff. . . .

But Kaplan should be granted a full pardon for this literary crime spree on the ground of sheer good writing. His Tammys, familiar as they are, appear to be living creatures, not caricatures, and images of his front porches and grizzled guitarists persist in the memory after the book is closed. He gets these effects (how else?) by minute observation and exact expression: a chronically brisk professor answering the phone by saying "Yellow," a vomiting drunk making a noise "like cloth tearing." And though the plotting isn't up to Nabokov's standards, the punning is. As Pearl undresses for a tennis game with the father of his inamorata, the older man averts his eyes to avoid seeing "what might be pending for his daughter." As Kaplan describes it, even a mall parking lot becomes rare and strange as windshields reflect "a thousand miniature suns." And he shows Pearl's feelings of frustration and impotence at getting nowhere with the bored, beautiful Francesca in a simple, almost painful metaphor: "He was pushing a string."

Kaplan's best trick is breathing life into the stock figure of Pearl. He's your standard Stephen Dedalus / Woody Allen composite, lines from Wordsworth and Stevens bobbing up unattributed in his stream of consciousness, along with worries that he's not crazy enough to be a genius. Poor, of course. And, of course, so lovelorn that he resents beautiful women for their power over him. Once he stares at Francesca and "the longer he looked at her . . . the stranger her face seemed—like a word repeated to absurdity. The proportions were wrong: the eyes too big, the moles too numerous. He savored the moment." We believe in Pearl because what we see through his eyes is so believable—and because his anxieties are ours.

David Gates, "Stylish Tales of Castaways," in Newsweek, *Vol. CXIII, No. 8, February 20, 1989, p. 64.*

JAMES IDEMA

Consider the situation in which the hero finds himself at the start of this occasionally funny first novel [*Pearl's Progress*].

A 31-year-old Jewish Manhattanite, a poet with a master's degree in English, Philip Pearl has emerged from a year or so of self-imposed exile in upstate New York to take a teaching job at a small university in Mississippi. The reasons for Pearl's exile are vague, but he's emerged because he needs a job—desperately, he makes it clear at the start, otherwise why would he have accepted an assistant professorship at Pickett State.

Even the condescension evidenced in the opening pages—what's a guy like me doing in a place like this?—suggests how it might develop: Sensitive young urban intellectual gets his comeuppance when the hicksville he lands in turns out to be full of challenging discoveries. A new literary flowering, perhaps, in the land of Faulkner. Or it might take a more somber turn: Liberal Jew from up North discovers that the old anti-civil rights feelings still run deep in the deep South.

But neither of these scenarios is the way Pearl progresses. His modest discoveries include the facts that Mississippi in August is beastly hot, the small-town landscape is "homely, sleepy and spread-out," the pace of life is not generally lively and the people talk funny. The author makes a stab at getting the native dialect on the page, but it never rings quite true nor is it consistent. . . .

There are passages where the young professor's experiences are affectingly described. Anyone who has ever taught will appreciate how that dreaded rite of passage, the first day, is handled. . . .

And there are two or three characters who stand out. A colleague named Untershrecker, for example, wants Pearl to help him peddle a book of Shakespearean insults.

But for the most part the people in *Pearl's Progress* are pas-

sive types. Even the hero's pursuit of a ravishing coed lacks spirit. Those who work at the university share in a general scorn for the institution, and the students are mostly bored and unpromising. As the year draws to a close, Pearl ponders whether to stay on at this dreary place or flee for home. His decision won't surprise anyone.

James Idema, "A Poet's Voyage to Mississippi," in Chicago Tribune—Books, *February 26, 1989, p. 6.*

JAMES MARCUS

In James Kaplan's first novel, a poet named Philip Pearl accepts a university teaching job in the tiny hamlet of Pickett, Miss. For this bred-in-the-bone Manhattanite, "progress" consists largely of a bumpy and somewhat bemused adjustment to life in the Magnolia State. At first, Pearl's point-by-point comparison of the two regions provides the novel with its comic mainspring. But as Pearl's attachment to Pickett grows, this regional comedy softens. Indeed, by the time *Pearl's Progress* concludes, Mr. Kaplan's portrait of small-town Mississippi has acquired a fine patina of lyricism. . . . In the meantime, the transplanted Pearl threads his way through a cultural obstacle course: country music, the Little Big Mall, a Faulkner-obsessed colleague reminiscing about "ol' Mr. Bill" and a plateful of inedible fried catfish. Mr. Kaplan is hardly the first writer to attempt such an anthropology of the New South, but his perceptions seem remarkably fresh. In fact, his gift for sidestepping clichés fails him only

---

An excerpt from *Pearl's Progress*

[Pearl] walked back and forth between the Volvo and Dawn's studio, carrying everything he owned—suitcases, boxes, sports jackets on hangers. The heat was unbelievable. As was the amount of stuff he'd brought. Whatever had possessed him to think he would need his Brooks Brothers trench-coat here? He gritted his teeth and cursed as he balanced boxes under his chin. He passionately hated moving. Why couldn't he just have stayed put? His shirt and pants were soaked through, a lost cause. The Margaritaville song played over and over again in his head, unbidden, idiotically, as he tripped up Juniper's porch steps.

But soon he was bearing in the last few things—a few ties, a bottle of Scotch. (He never wore ties; he never drank Scotch.) In a square of sunlight on the porch, he suddenly stopped short. He stared at this square of light. Hadn't he dreamed up Juniper's house once, long ago, in a night of indigestion? The conviction seemed both undeniable and unbelievable. It then gave way to a wave of intense home-those shacks along the road in Alabama. Whatever it was, the sensation kept flowing through him, a sweet sharp pain in the center of his chest. He would, he knew, remember this instant forever, in minutest detail: the webwork of cracks in the gray paint on the floor, the broken screen, the bobbing wasp, the smell of hot pines, the dots of white sunlight diffracting in the slowly waving branches, the sough of wind. Time was a trifle, a joke. He felt close to tears. Perhaps he was overtired. Somewhere, a car horn honked—a car horn here and now. Wednesday morning was approaching at the speed of light.

once, when Pearl encounters an ancient black man on the porch of a shotgun shack, busying himself with gnomic utterances and a battered guitar. Otherwise, *Pearl's Progress* succeeds as a deft and witty endorsement for the shock of the new. As Pearl progresses through one new territory after another—romantic as well as cultural—he persuades the reader to share both his excitement and his discomfort: no mean feat, for a series of experiences he's earlier compared to "losing your virginity over and over."

James Marcus, in a review of "Pearl's Progress," in The New York Times Book Review, *April 23, 1989,* p. 20.

BILL MARX

[Tales] of academe usually whittle the ivory tower down to size; their learned protagonists are transformed into figures of fun who trip over their lesson plans as well as their undies. In England, the genre has been mastered by Malcolm Bradbury and David Lodge, whose sophisticated farces fuse slamming doors, kinky cuddling, class warfare, and literary chit-chat. On these shores certain campus novels (like [Bernard] Malamud's *A New Life*) tend toward therapeutic confession: the undersexed professor's quest for success and sensuality amid departmental cocktail parties and listless classes becomes a chronicle of self-discovery. Thus in James Kaplan's first novel, *Pearl's Progress,* the arrival of a nebbishy Jewish teacher in a hick Mississippi university doesn't kick off a wild culture clash between cracker and matzoh but a soothing (sometimes too damn soothing) study of a modern Prufrock.

Kaplan's straitlaced approach makes this otherwise enjoyable book somewhat irritating. He continually frustrates conventional expectations of lusty buffoonery and classroom mayhem; as a result *Pearl's Progress* threatens to become a comic travelogue that rolls by so smoothly you forget to laugh. Described as a "Jew, mooner, fugitive from a farm," Philip Pearl is plucked out of Manhattan for a year's stint at Pickett State University. His one published book of anemic poetry, *Oedipus at Secaucus,* makes the good old profs peg him as an exotic intellectual. For this rookie teacher, the warm Southern hospitality offers a shot at spiritual renewal: "If . . . he had come to the end of his rope, why not (as in a rope trick) simply leave the rope behind?" And the steamy climate, Technicolor vistas, catfish dinners, and Southern belles do indeed blot out his memories of concrete canyons. Pearl's extracurricular interests include Francesca, a knockout who has his envious colleagues drooling in the schoolyard ("Other women looked beautiful from certain angles . . . Francesca was clinical beauty, the *Ding-an-sich*"), and the neurotic tough dame Jewel, whose used-car salesman lover packs a pistol and likes kicking down the apartment doors of Yankee rivals.

Given the collisions with plastered big-league writers, academic bores, eccentrics, and rednecks that Kaplan puts his protagonist through, Pearl's detour to Dixie could easily have become a vaudevillian shake and bake. But Kaplan never pushes the phlegmatic tale into Southern-fried farce. Francesca ends up saying she just wants to be friends and drops out of the book; Jewel leaves town, her homicidal boyfriend crumpling into unmacho despair; a famous writer's sexual come-on is easily fended off; and Pearl isn't even around to see his own door get kicked in. Instead of the usual horny,

opportunistic prof who finds youth contagious, Pearl is "in it for the long haul, belted in by moderation in all things. The Moderate Poet. This, of course, was part of the problem." He's right: because Kaplan refuses to nudge Pearl into any shenanigans, his character ends up spending a lot of time languishing in the hot sun or driving down country roads, meditating on Mississippi's landscape and inhabitants, the homogenization of Southern culture, and the possibility of settling down in this polluted backwater.

Luckily, Kaplan compensates for the missed yuks with quirky insights, detailing, for instance, the character's incredulity at the strangeness and familiarity of the kudzu-choked unknown:

> There was more to it than homesickness: the hot sweet dusk air shooting in the windows seemed redolent of a lost age, a time and place that Pearl, Manhattanite, had never known yet seemed to know deeply . . . This was a past he recognized from the movies—but an actual breath of it, a *revenant.*

Kaplan's lulling prose has an easy cadence and creamy tone, its calm surface occasionally swelling into deadpan grandeur. . . . It may seem grudging to demand more. But Pearl drifts antiseptically through Pickett State like one of Kaplan's favorite images, a spaceship, and the restless reader yearns to see him ejected from his author's overprotective shell, if only for a raucous tumble in freefall.

Bill Marx, "It's Academic," in The Village Voice, *Vol. XXXIII, No. 20, May 16, 1989, p. 60.*

CHARLOTTE FOX ZABUSKY

When *Pearl's Progress* opens, our hero, Phil Pearl, a thirty-two-year-old New York Jew of average looks and abilities, is on his way to a new job, teaching English at Pickett State, a small college in rural Mississippi. We know very little about Pearl, except that he has just spent a year of solitude on a farm in upstate New York, he has never taught, and he has landed this job on the basis of two published poems in *The New Yorker.* Somewhat anxious about teaching for the first time, he is grateful for this opportunity to gain, at last, a toe-hold on a real life.

Pearl's myopic New York eyes find Pickett an alien landscape peopled by exotic creatures. The students, untouched by inner city problems, seem to have sprung from some forties musical, polite, clean-cut, and innocent. His colleagues in the English Department are a colorful bunch, some of them bordering on weird. Guitar-strumming Ted Juniper, for example, who invites Phil, the very moment they meet, to move in with him rent-free. Or the enigmatic Wunsch, who was instrumental in bringing Phil to Pickett but now seems less interested in him. Then there is the unconventional Raffi family: father Joe a music professor who collects cars; mother Helen who takes Phil in as one of the family as soon as she hears his voice on the telephone; daughter Francesca, the town beauty, who, poker-faced but pleasant, allows Phil to court her. (pp. 116-17)

As the novel moves to a climax, the momentum of action overtakes the leisurely pace of reflection, and reality falls apart. Perplexed by veiled warnings from several colleagues and finding himself suddenly the object of an unknown assailant, the mild Pearl turns amateur detective, obsessed with finding his tormentor and fearless in pursuing the slightest of clues. Driving his Volvo to the ends of the earth, it seems to him, Phil finally solves his mystery, the reader cheering him on through every tongue-in-cheek red herring, one with a hint of the supernatural, too-convenient coincidence, and a scene of unconvincing suspense and danger. All ends well, virtue rewarded and evil punished, with plenty of good laughs along the way. (p. 117)

> *Charlotte Fox Zabusky, in a review of "Pearl's Progress," in* Wilson Library Bulletin, *Vol. 63, No. 10, June, 1989, pp. 116-17.*

Timothy O'Grady
Motherland

O'Grady is an American-born Irish novelist, editor, and film-maker, born in 1951.

In *Motherland,* an unnamed, middle-aged narrator with a strong Oedipal fixation and limited intellectual capacity explores eight-hundred years of Irish history while discovering his own family's past. In the novel's opening, the narrator's mother disappears from her flat, leaving behind a chronicle of the Synnot family dating from the twelfth century. The narrator is joined in his search for his mother by an old man who teaches him how to read this book and who eventually reveals himself to be the narrator's grandfather. Their physical and metaphorical journey reminded critics of Dante's passage through Hell in his *Inferno.* The narrator's clairvoyance and O'Grady's inclusion of medieval fables, visions, and rituals lend *Motherland* qualities of magical realism. Critics admired O'Grady's control of extensive and arcane detail and his ability to filter a vivid and provocative story through the perspective of his limited narrator. Susannah Herbert remarked: "Like the writers he admires, Gabriel García Márquez and Toni Morrison, O'Grady's art is firmly rooted in a sense of identity explored through the continuities of the narrated past and its imaginative legacy. Exuberant, erudite, his voice deserves to last."

SUSANNAH HERBERT

The Irish writer as exile is a figure long sanctified by literary tradition, but Timothy O'Grady puts a twist on the cliché by reversing the terms. Born and educated in Chicago, he was a foreigner in his own nation on arrival in Ireland in the early Seventies. The curious experience of transition—from the intellectually rarefied heights of campus life, to a deserted island off Donegal—seems to have shaped the quickened perceptions and stranger's perspective that characterise his extraordinary first novel, *Motherland. . . .*

Like the book's narrator, O'Grady says he had to come to terms with himself in relation to the country and its past, but there the resemblance stops. His nameless hero is a semi-monstrous middle-aged infant with clairvoyant powers, who travels through Ireland on a search for his mother which widens to include a quest for the missing pages of his family's annals. The journey is an emotional excavation of Ireland's history, juxtaposing the twelfth and twentieth centuries in a weird mosaic of fables, visions and rituals.

Like his compatriots Seamus Heaney and Brian Friel, O'Grady uses historical displacement to approach a political situation whose excesses have been reduced to banality by the media. His manipulation of the past is not merely a device,

however; it stems from personal experience of the continuity of controversy. After arriving from America, he became involved in a project to film a documentary on the life of Michael Collins, the guerrilla leader who died in 1922. The film, consisting mainly of interviews with Collins's contemporaries, was banned for political reasons, but in 1982, O'Grady and the film's producer, Kenneth Griffith, resurrected some of the material gathered and wrote *Curious Journey: an Oral History of Ireland's Unfinished Revolution.*

The research for this book convinced O'Grady that Irish history was locked in a state of suspension 'where time had collapsed, there was no historical movement, the same issue had been the overriding issue for 800 years'. This recognition eased the translation from political deadlock into artistic expression. . . . O'Grady's work draws upon an oral tradition of stories transmitted down the generations, a tradition which licenses the novelist to be as fantastical or fabulous as he pleases, without incurring charges of escapism. . . .

Like the writers he admires, Gabriel Garcia Marquez and Toni Morrison, O'Grady's art is firmly rooted in a sense of identity explored through the continuities of the narrated past and its imaginative legacy. Exuberant, erudite, his voice deserves to last.

Susannah Herbert, in a review of "Motherland," in Harpers and Queen, January, 1989, p. 32.

DAVID SELF

Motherland gives every indication of being thoroughly pretentious. Everything seems to be laden with, well, *significance*. It's about Ireland, you see. The Irish problem, the Irish nation, the Irish family:

> We have had inflicted on us a wound which has never healed and for which no retribution has yet been exacted. It has passed on from age to age. We have fought and subverted, wandered in dimness, been made vagrants and dreamed of ideal cities . . .

There is indeed a lot of wandering and dreaming in this novel, much of it in dimness. The narrator is on a quest for his errant mother, helped mainly by a handwritten, beautifully bound history of his ancestors which he must decode. (See what I mean about significance?) This tome begins with two brothers enlisting in Bristol to go and fight in Ireland to help the improbably named King Dermot MacMurrough (circa 1169) and ends with anti-terrorist soldiers being exploded in Border country.

It could all be just too much except that what I hope is intentional humour keeps breaking through the story. It is not just the way the web-fingered narrator is described by a charitable relative, "You are slovenly and fat and you have the mental discipline of a slug." It is more in the way the narrator and his guardian are accompanied on their historic journey by a monkey, a poodle, plenty of claret and a total unconcern for all things practical. (p. 50)

David Self, "Empire Made," in Punch, February 24, 1989, pp. 48, 50.

D. J. TAYLOR

The opening chapter of *Motherland,* Timothy O'Grady's first novel, pulls together a string of arresting images. A middle-aged man returns to his mother's flat in Dublin to find her gone. Inventorying the weird chaos of her absence—an abandoned monkey, an ancient vellum folio, the mirror's lipsticked scrawl—reflecting on the odd chronology of their life together, he isolates the book's theme in a single sentence: "I yearned painfully for her presence . . . I knew too that I could have no other purpose except to bring her home."

This stage-setting, conveyed in the self-absorbed, half-mad tones of the modernist anti-hero, is densely allusive. For a moment, all of Ireland and its ghosts seem to be beckoning, the snow looks set to fall again out over the mutinous Shannon, the shadows of the past are reassembling. Unfortunately, what follows cannot sustain this heady initial impetus. As the narrator traces his rare folio, the history of a family of 12th century Anglo-Norman settlers named Synnott, back to the old man who guided it into his mother's hands, the reader grows ever more aware of ambitious aims falling strangely short of fulfilment.

Motherland, following the well-trodden route of the mystery quest novel, is a labyrinth of hints and allusions. There are the unnamed hero's uncannily resonant visions; a matter of seeing your own past take shape around you. There are the ghostly parallels—a trawl through Synnott family history reveals that the first scion to be born in Ireland had the same webbed hands as the narrator. Finally, there is the determinist strategy of the old man, a Synnott himself, who "had placed his ancestors' secrets into my mother's hands and thence into mine with the deftness of a conjuror". . . . The eventual unmasking of his maternal grandfather is only the first in a series of implausible revelations.

Characteristically, mystery quests begin at the mildest provocation. Here it is enough for grandfather to reveal that the history of the Synnotts is missing a vital section. Yet, as they journey in search of it, on through a futuristic Ireland wrecked by riot and errant soldiery, the pages are a hook on which to hang much resolute exposition. There is a great deal along the way about the Irish past, most of it flagged by narrative giveaways. "We have in this country an unresolved and blood-stained history," grandfather declaims at one stage; a hint to the reader of lurking intent, of something unnecessarily schematised and worked-out. . . .

An excerpt from *Motherland*

From what my mother has told me—and she has told me very little as it was an unhappy time for her—we passed the first three years of my life in a small flat in Herbert Place overlooking the canal. I do not know if my father ever lived with us there. I never knew him, and cannot be certain how well my mother knew him either, although I gather, at least, that they were married. She spoke of him only when pressed to the limit of her endurance by my childish questioning, and when she did the version of their life together and his whereabouts which she put to me usually differed wildly from all previous ones. When I was very young she seemed to try to appeal to my imagination with these stories, but as I grew older I believe she only tried to please herself. For some time in my early childhood I believed that my father was the statue of Saint Dominic that resided in the chapel that we used to attend. On Saturday afternoons when my mother went to confession, or on Sundays after Mass, I used, in consequence, go alone to the altar of Saint Dominic and whisper things to him. I told him that my mother was sad because he did not live with us, that I had memorised a new rhyme or that I was learning to count, and on one occasion I supplied for him a list of what I wanted for Christmas. That his plaster visage, with its sallow complexion, its gaudily painted features and oddly unfocussed eyes was immobile and mute did not, for some time, deter me from speaking to him. It was not until years later, when I could distinguish between statues and living people, that I discovered that far from the handsome, kindly image presented by the ecclesiastical sculptors, Dominic was a hard-hearted and rather grim Castilian, whose order became the great enthusiasts of the Inquisition and whose only departure from strict orthodoxy was to confess to one Jordan of Saxony that he preferred the company of young women to old ones.

To dwell on *Motherland*'s obvious contrivance—even the missing parts of the book were invented by grandfather as an excuse for company—is to ignore O'Grady's neat, solipsistic narrative voice and the display of a great deal of slightly unfocused talent. This is a flawed novel, its occasional felicities never entirely balanced by an impression of what it is trying to achieve. The recapitulation of Synnott history is plain tedious and at the end, when the narrator discovers his mother and one or two salient facts about his family, there is no sense that personal and national history have somehow come together. Above all, *Motherland* suffers from a mighty intentness, a lack of the self-deprecating qualities that enliven novels built on the power of myth and artifice. While O'Grady's promise is unquestionable, much of this reads like an exercise—an artful and tricksy exercise, but an exercise nonetheless.

D. J. Taylor, "Ancestral Secrets," in The Sunday Times, *London, March 12, 1989, p. G6.*

PHILIP HORNE

Pythagoras, spokesman for the doctrine of metempsychosis, of the fusion of identities across history, is the abiding spirit of Timothy O'Grady's extraordinary first novel, *Motherland.* It may suggest the scope and texture of this risky, ambitious, consciously Irish work, which broadens and concentrates its protagonist's mind by having him travel about in Ireland and back in time, to quote the hero's mentor speculating on why the 12th-century Norman Bertrand de Paor, the novel's prime authority figure, so admired Pythagoras:

> I believe it was because Pythagoras was both a logician and a mystic. He discovered the rule of right-angled triangles and at the same time two of the principal tenets of his society were abstention from beans and the injunction not to sit on a quart measure. Can you credit that? How did he reconcile these things? . . . He thought with his whole being. He was a repository of reason and unreason, unlike others who came after him who regarded the two as exclusive.

There would be no point in denying the presence of a healthy leavening of blarney in this passionately articulate novel, which takes certain surreal premises as real in order to conduct its mythic discussion of Irish histories. To grant these premises for the duration of a reading is in this case, as it is not in much 'playful' fiction, to be carried with great momentum into an unfamiliar but internally consistent world, where serious, intelligent fantasy is the medium for an all-encompassing attempt at wisdom and reconciliation in the face of centuries of slaughter and waste.

Pythagoras appears here as reconciling opposites and inspiring the Norman wisdom of Bertrand. The myth of origin which O'Grady proposes, registered in the huge family book which the bloated 42-year-old mother's boy of a narrator struggles to decipher and interpret, is itself a myth of racial reconciliation reaching back beyond the usual records of animosity and atrocity. Like Kipling in *Puck of Pook's Hill,* bringing home to modern children the origins of the English race in alliance and friendship between the Saxon Hugh and the Norman invader Sir Richard, O'Grady, whose political opinions are mostly unlike Kipling's, brings home to his infantile though middle-aged detective-clairvoyant hero the origin of his Irish family in a vision of the lyrical coupling of the Norman Hervey Synnott with the Celtic Emer MacDiarmuid, an act of union which practically embodies the tragically doomed scheme of Bertrand. Bertrand's experiment, a mixed-race commune, 'is essentially an attempt to strike a harmonious balance between the characteristics of our race and those of our hosts, which I perceive at present to be diametrically opposed'. He foresees the terrible consequences of failure in the long Irish future: 'these sets of opposites will become so prominent that the way in which they are handled by their representatives will determine how life is to be lived here for many centuries to come.' They have in the event been handled with disastrous crudity, and O'Grady, who is now based in London after living in Chicago and Dublin, sympathetically investigates in Bertrand's eloquent exposition the Pythogorean perception that if 'you can truly *see,* you will comprehend that that which is your opposite is in possession of something which you lack, which may in fact be your complement.'

Motherland's epigraph is from the second canto of the *Inferno,* where Dante follows Virgil on 'that savage path', and the quest of the fat, childish narrator, 'a journey without a known endpoint or even a method by which to plot a course', is also undertaken in the company of a guiding authority, a wise but embittered mentor who seems to be a modern equivalent of Bertrand. The reference to Dante and his encounter with Virgil may appropriately recall T. S. Eliot's meeting with the 'familiar compound ghost' in 'Little Gidding'; or more recently, and Irishly, we may think of the admonitions received from the ghost of William Carleton in *Station Island* (1984) by Seamus Heaney, a translator of Dante:

> you have to try to make sense of what comes.
> Remember everything and keep your head.

The attempt to make sense, and unity, out of a chaotic and divided history, is the heroic striving of O'Grady's fine book. If the blend of history and mysticism recalls Eliot, there would also be a parallel with Kipling's *Kim,* where the aged lama shows the young Irish Kim (short for Kimball O'Hara) 'the Way', a meditative route to truth, while on an unmethodical pilgrimage through a tumultuous nation seeking the site of a long-past event. Both novels end with a reconciling vision and a new freedom, the completion of a rite of passage; in the case of *Motherland,* there is a moving discovery of twinship and complementarity between North and South, the emotionally satisfying resolution of one of the mysteries the narrator has needed to understand. The claims of family are touchingly met and properly transcended.

Motherland is a bewilderingly complex work, demanding but generous in return. It is far from certain that its surreal abundance of weird detail is *all* essential to the necessary complexity of a rendering of O'Grady's complex concerns: but everything is made interesting, and the plotting of its bizarre action is a triumphant correlative of the ornate design on the cover of the Synnott family book: 'ingeniously intricate, wayward and explosive, so that each individual tooled line pursued its course through astonishing convolutions to its own unpredictable end.' (p. 11)

Philip Horne, "Dark Strangers, Gorgeous Slums," in London Review of Books, *Vol. 11, No. 6, March 16, 1989, pp. 10-12.*

GERALD MANGAN

"You are slovenly and fat and you have the mental disposition of a slug." The unattractive but intriguing narrator of Timothy O'Grady's [*Motherland*], who meekly acknowledges the accuracy of this description of himself, is a forty-three-year-old virgin with webs between his fingers, no visible occupation and an unhealthy devotion to an erratic mother. In a powerful opening chapter, where he returns to their Dublin flat after several weeks of sulking, the disappearance of his mother is dramatically advertised by the emaciation of their pet monkey, the corpse of their tortoise, and a "jungle atmosphere" where house-plants luxuriate in steam from a bath-tap. Guilt and apprehension mount as he rummages through her customary disorder for clues; and the mystery provides the motive as *Motherland* develops into a highly charged and often haunting symbolic quest.

Memories of a solitary childhood lead initially through settings well marked by Irish Gothic, as he recalls the decaying manor house where his once-placid mother served as cook and comforter to a kindly judge. Her fits of mental and physical wandering, which increase after the death of this father-substitute, have usually landed her somewhere in Ulster; but the only major clue on this occasion is the sumptuously bound and polyglot chronicle of a family called Synnott, which leads him ultimately to its former owner, a white-maned but sprightly *savant* by the name of Declan Synnott. Having agreed to assist in the search, Declan finally reveals himself as the real father of the missing mother.

Declan's well-formed Socratic speeches to his bemused grandson are not the only literary device that points back to Flann O'Brien; but the more patent improbabilities are acceptable as part of the framework for a dramatized meditation on Ireland's "unresolved and blood-stained history". The chronicle-within-the-novel is a series of first-hand accounts, supposedly paraphrased and elaborated by the narrator's powers of clairvoyance, which trace the family's violent fortunes from their medieval origins as an artisan commune under an enlightened Norman baron. Declan's nationalist interpretation of this ancestry, delivered in instalments as the pair set out through a luridly shabby townscape, underlines its cultural degeneration. . . .

O'Grady weaves a dense network of parallels between the two stories, which enables the "guide and mentor" to persuade his acolyte that past and present are mutually reflective. The farcical Voltairean odyssey they embark on, trailing the monkey through a land of mendicants and pious frauds, is ostensibly a search for a missing fragment of the text as well as a lost mother and daughter. But the buried truths it brings to light include the real facts of their respective lives; and a metaphor of the Irish condition comes gradually into focus as the sluggish but deeply intuitive "middle-aged infant" responds to the urgent lessons of history. [*Motherland* 's] submerged symbols form a root-system that is often too rarefied to grasp, but they are more original than the historical anger behind them. They serve an ambitious fable of reconciliation and rebirth, whose overtones are inevitably political.

Gerald Mangan, "Violent Fortunes," in The Times Literary Supplement, No. 4486, March 24-30, 1989, p. 300.

JOANNA PORTER

Central to Timothy O'Grady's marvellous *Motherland* is the deciphering of an ancient history. The task is awesome: the Synnott chronicle is written mostly by hand and in a number of languages, having a time-span of some seven centuries. The hapless narrator gains much inspiration from the 'strange and evocative uniqueness' of the words on the page; he is also aided by special if generally dormant visionary powers and a mentor who plays Virgil to his Dante. . . .

Simultaneously, this 'foolish, blundering whale' of a hero is seeking his adored but wayward mother. His attempt to make sense of her disappearance becomes inextricably linked with the chronicle when he discovers that he too, through the maternal line, is a Synnott. This is revealed by his grandfather, who in the aforementioned Virgilian role proves doggedly if impatiently devoted to his grandson's personal and prophetic development. Together they embark on a quest of Wandering Aeneas proportions and establish in its course a relationship which is a joy for the reader to share.

This 'middle-aged infant' is initially reluctant to grapple with interrelations of past and present. It is grandfather who insists that he apply his sluggish mind to the intricate patterns revealed in such correspondences, guiding him away from the obsessive 'twoness' of an exclusive mother-son relationship and so enabling him to find his place at the end of a remarkable family line and within his motherland of Ireland. It is, he explains, like 'a fairground wheel with the same faces coming round again and again'.

Appropriately, then, [*Motherland*'s] end mirrors its start. It begins in Dublin where a distraught son's search for his mother prompts a mystical journey; it ends in Derry where that same man, much changed, encounters another son mourning another mother. 'Serene and unafraid', he can now link both sons and both mothers, all of whom he had seen, but not comprehended, in an earlier dream. In a synchronous vision, he experiences the fearful beauty of a 'mind moving in harmonious consort'. At last the fairground wheel ceases: the chronicle is completed and with it a remarkable first novel.

Joanna Porter, "Two and Two Together," in The Listener, Vol. 121, No. 3117, June 8, 1989, p. 25.

TIMOTHY O'GRADY [IN CORRESPONDENCE WITH CLC YEARBOOK]

[*CLC*]: *Comment on the process of writing* **Motherland**, *including the inspiration and any obstacles you may have overcome.*

[O'Grady]: I wrote **Motherland** over a period of four and a half years, having begun to think about it perhaps six years before I began to write. It derived from two distinct ideas which I did not for a long time think were connected. One was the idea of a woman wandering around Ireland driven by a force she did not comprehend but originating somehow from a book of ancient manuscripts. I wanted to write about the presence of history in the lives of Irish people and this was a way to do this. The other idea had to do with a pedagogic relationship between an old man and a younger man. The latter beginning from a position of naïvete and psychological ruin and struggling through the course of a journey towards physical, intellectual, psychological, spiritual and political liberation. It was not until I came upon the figure of the narrator and his manner of speaking that I was able to begin writing.

Relate the terms of any background research you conducted.

There are many aspects of the book which required me to do research. The most extensive specific reading I did involved the history of the Normans in Ireland in the 12th century. Three books were particularly important to me: *The Irish* by Sean O'Faolain, *The History of Western Philosophy* by Bertrand Russell and *The History and Topography of Ireland* by Giraldus Combrensis.

Whom do you consider your primary literary influences, and why?

I have been particularly struck by Gogol for his wildness, Chekhov for his objective sympathy, Dostoevsky for the scale of his themes, Bob Dylan for his lyrical intensity, John Berger for his honesty and Gabriel García Márquez for revealing the endless possibilities of literature at a time when I had been persuaded in a rather academic way that we had reached the end of the line.

Mark Probst
Winter Losses

Probst is an American novelist, born in 1925.

Winter Losses probes the character of Philip Kreg, a middle-aged Manhattan lawyer engrossed in his work, whose well-ordered, solitary lifestyle is upset by the machinations of crime and high finance. As a dedicated legal counsel for a firm and foundation begun by a man he deeply admired, Kreg must fend off a hostile takeover bid. At the same time, his son asks for his help after having run off with a large sum of money he collected for an organized crime group. The novel details Kreg's negotiations on these two fronts as well as his emotionally empty life, which is dominated by work. In a review of *Winter Losses,* Cheri Fein observed: "[Few] writers have revealed [the battle for financial power] and its players as three-dimensionally as Probst does in his insightful, keenly observed first novel. . . . And few, if any, have so convincingly linked the two seemingly unconnected high-stakes games—one legal, one not—that two very different kinds of business people play."

PUBLISHERS WEEKLY

This first novel [**Winter Losses**], by a stockbroker and former assistant district attorney, has a distinctly odd flavor, as if a post-modern version of a Louis Auchincloss novel had been infused with a dash of Elmore Leonard. Its protagonist is Philip Kreg, a Manhattan lawyer much involved in corporate affairs. He is a dour, unyielding man declining into solitude after the departure of an alcoholic wife; but when his grown son, Adam, a flashy ne'er-do-well, becomes involved with California and Florida gangsters, he allows his life to be turned inside out in the effort to rescue him from terrible danger. Probst writes in a highly sophisticated, allusive style that catches mood brilliantly but does not always clarify the progress of events. The time frame is sometimes unclear and there are too many characters in Kreg's life who are insufficiently differentiated, or whose roles seem superfluous. But Probst knows his lawyers and corporate chiefs, and his glitzy crime scenes, described through Adam's eyes, have a fine malevolence. The denouement, while perhaps inevitable, seems rather perfunctory and the muted ending is flat. But there's no doubt about Probst's original voice, and his ability to evoke middle-aged *angst.* (pp. 451-52)

A review of "Winter Losses," in Publishers Weekly, *Vol. 235, No. 4, January 27, 1989, pp. 451-52.*

ALBERT E. WILHELM

Philip Kreg is a highly respected Manhattan lawyer whose livelihood and integrity are threatened by a hostile corporate takeover. His son Adam steals from the West Coast gangsters who employ him. In this counterpoint of geography and generations, Probst provides a contrast between keen moral sensibility and total lack of conscience. The parallel stories merge when Philip tries unsuccessfully to shield Adam from mob retribution. Only after losing his son, his position in the law firm, and most of his fortune does Philip begin to gain a sense of himself. [**Winter Losses**] offers a touching picture of a father's tragedy as well as a convincing portrayal of the machinations of big business and big-time crime, but at times the exposition is rather tedious.

Albert E. Wilhelm, in a review of "Winter Losses," in Library Journal, *Vol. 114, No. 3, February 15, 1989, p. 178.*

CHERI FEIN

Much has been written, in both fiction and nonfiction, about the carnivores of business—those men whose highest priority is the accumulation of power. But few writers have revealed that world and its players as three-dimensionally as Mark Probst does in his insightful, keenly observed first novel, *Winter Losses.* And few, if any, have so convincingly linked the two seemingly unconnected high-stakes games—one legal, one not—that two very different kinds of business people play.

The central character in *Winter Losses* is Philip Kreg, an overweight, mid-50's, long divorced, successful New York attorney who earlier in his career wrote a number of respected books on constitutional law. "A man of somewhat abrasive manner or anyway not ingratiating," Kreg is an intractable loner "with something of a tendency to melancholy" and most definitely a tendency to embrace guilt as a motivating force.

Many of Kreg's more melancholy moments are spent reflecting on a man named Brandt, a dead but fondly remembered client whose company, Brandt Systems, Kreg still represents. Kreg also administers a foundation Brandt set up. Together, these two activities take up the majority of Kreg's professional time. Now Brandt Systems is being threatened by a takeover attempt, a potentially dangerous situation that preoccupies Kreg.

Meanwhile, in Los Angeles and then in Miami, Kreg's grown son, Adam, is getting himself into a heap of trouble. Never exactly a stellar offspring, Adam has become involved with "a real-estate group that operated for its own account, private investors with also an affiliated import-export business." Translation: an organized crime-related gang reminiscent of "Miami Vice" that exchanges arms and other such products for leather attaché cases full of cash. Adam is merely a gofer—that is, until he impulsively bops a customer with an ashtray and takes off with a million dollars. Once Adam surfaces, he commissions his father to negotiate the return of the money and insure his safety.

The outcome of the two negotiations—the one for Brandt Systems, the other for his son—completely shatters Kreg's neatly constructed life.

Interesting as Mr. Probst's story is for its behind-the-scenes look at the machinations of business and at those who flip the switches, it serves more as a backdrop for the complex character of Philip Kreg. . . .

Kreg is observant in surprising ways. Who would think someone like him would notice that a woman's Peter Pan collar didn't suit the shape of her face? He is a cultured man who knows music, art and wine, who has integrated his knowledge into his life, in the same way he's integrated his wealth and, later, the loss of that wealth. In any conversation, Kreg is aware of the undertone, the meaning behind what is being said and what isn't. In other words, he is very smart, as are all the characters in this book.

What a relief it is to read intelligent dialogue, written in a clever shorthand that assumes an intelligent reader. How fascinating it is to be in the company of men (and the majority of characters in this book are men) who, while not particularly concerned with concepts like happiness, do not become cardboard cutouts as they pursue their goals. In fact, the writing in *Winter Losses* is so solid that it's hard to believe this is a first novel.

If there is a weak link, it is Adam. As if he interests Mr. Probst less than do Kreg and certain other characters, Adam appears rather late in the story and remains merely a callow, selfish troublemaker who serves little more purpose than to advance the story. The scenes between Kreg and Adam go flat in a way that other scenes do not.

Flat perhaps, but never soft. There isn't a soft spot in this story. Mr. Probst, himself an attorney and financial consultant, has written a book that's as tough and tight as any business negotiation.

Cheri Fein, "How Not to Make Your First Million," in The New York Times Book Review, *April 23, 1989, p. 19.*

DIANA HENRIQUES

Some authors introduce their readers to the financial world the way an amused parent shows his children the monkey house at the zoo. This is how some strange and clever animals live, they say, but it has nothing to do with you. [In *Winter Losses* Mark Probst] doesn't just take readers inside the deals; he takes us inside the hearts of the people who make those deals, revealing their dryeyed heartbreak, their impotent anger and their dignified defeats.

His protagonist is lawyer Phillip Kreg, a superficially successful man who isn't easy to like. Righteous and remote, emotionally mute, he seems to repel a reader's sympathy as automatically as he rejects the proffered assistance of his few close friends. As the novel opens, Kreg has just learned two things: His grown son Adam is in trouble with his boss, a politely ominous arms merchant. And Brandt Systems, the company on which much of Kreg's legal practice relies, is "in play," fixed in the sights of a graceful raider who cannot succeed without the shares Kreg controls through the foundation he chairs.

Unlike the cheap heroics attributed to such battles in their non-fiction state, the campaign for Brandt Systems is replete with petty indignities and ironies. Lawyers huddling at fancy bars are distracted by the afternoon dalliances at the next table. Unintended insults erupt from the sweaty and uninspiring management team. And all the while, the participants have other, profoundly more important, things on their minds.

Kreg is thoroughly uneasy in this arena. But he stumbles forward, trying not to trip on his own moral shoelaces. In the process, he earns our grudging respect—until Adam's trouble suddenly becomes overtly menacing. And then, slowly and implacably, Probst starts to sketch the cataclysm that can occur when people try to live their private lives by the rules of the public game they play on Wall Street.

A father negotiates for his son's safety just as for his client's independence, foolishly believing that all the victims of a selfish life can be gathered around the bargaining table. A son betrays himself, just as a raider might, through a cocky inattention to the interests of others. But this time, the consequences are tallied in terms far more serious than percentages of ownership. No one files a Schedule 13D for control of a human heart.

Probst, who has done a stint as a New York district attorney in addition to working for years on Wall Street, effortlessly weaves into the fabric of Phillip Kreg's life the subterranean businessmen who threaten Adam. This is accomplished almost before we can appreciate what that melding signifies: the coziness of money-movers and moneymakers on both sides of the law, where details of life and dress and breeding distinguish but do not divide them.

But by the novel's emotionally devastating conclusion, the Wall Street gaming table is, at last, almost irrelevant. It is simply the scene of the disasters that befall Kreg, tragedies that could have as easily occurred on a farm or in a platoon or at a family-owned store on the edge of the prairie. A man struggles to do the honorable thing in a world where such exertions are greeted with amused exasperation, where power is not and never will be a vaccine against the loss of love.

If you want to know the play-by-play by which Wall Street deals are made, read non-fiction. If you want to know how life looks and feels to the people who are caught up in such affairs—people who are awkwardly nursing aching knees, broken hearts, bruised children and too many glasses of scotch—read this granite-hard but beautifully sculpted novel.

Diana Henriques, in a review of "Winter Losses," in Barron's, *Vol. LXIX, No. 20, May 15, 1989, p. 114.*

WILLIAM O'ROURKE

These two accomplished, satisfying novels concern the contemporary half-family: a single parent and a child. Countering statistics, though, both parents are male: a widower in Richard Bausch's *Mr. Field's Daughter,* a divorced father in Mark Probst's *Winter Losses.* And both children bring menace and mayhem into their fathers' lives. (p. 3)

The father of Mark Probst's *Winter Losses* is Philip Kreg, a partner in a Manhattan law firm, an expert on constitutional law and director of a grant-dispensing foundation. And most of the action of the book is woven into the fabric of big-city deal making.

Kreg's son, Adam, shows up with an attache case containing a million dollars he has stolen from his unsavory and now very angry employers, a pack of international arms and drug merchants. Kreg spends a million dollars of his own money in an attempt to save his son.

Getting the money is never an issue; the characters of *Winter Losses* all have highly developed cash aesthetics. They are mostly in fear of the second rate: "He looked at his left wrist (a wafer Patek with a gold mesh strap")". Good taste is the only thing available to justify their wealth.

Probst certainly knows something of the world, and he is definitely making sharp social comments. The illegal enterprises of Kreg's son are meant to mirror the legal activities of Kreg. Business is business, and both sides meet in the gray world of overlapping profit taking. But Philip Kreg is the kind of man you would want to have on your side.

Both *Winter Losses* and *Mr. Field's Daughter* demonstrate that social and economic boundaries once thought to be insurmountable may no longer act as barriers at all. One person's shattered life is quite likely to infect someone—anyone—else's; all people are contagious now.

One thing these novels may not share, though, is the same set of readers, which would be a shame. Those attracted by the trappings of the glamorous, big-city novel might find much to like (and be excited by) in *Mr. Field's Daughter.* And those who look only to such overtly literary writers as Richard Bausch might profit from an encounter with the less polished, though more directly engaged, world of Mark Probst's *Winter Losses.* (pp. 3, 7)

William O'Rourke, in a review of "Winter Losses," in Chicago Tribune—Books, *July 2, 1989, pp. 3, 7.*

MARK PROBST [IN CORRESPONDENCE WITH *CLC YEARBOOK*]

[*CLC Yearbook*]: *Comment on the process of writing* Winter Losses, *including the inspiration and any obstacles you may have overcome.*

[Probst]: *Winter Losses* is my first published work, began when I was almost sixty. The book was written over a period of about three and one-half years in such a time as was available after satisfying the requirements of a full time job. It was necessary to learn even such basic skills as typing and later the use of a word processor.

I began with only a sense of where the book would go. Plotting is important to me but comes later as the book takes shape. . . .

I'm not easy with the word "inspiration", but no question the concentration and intense application required for literary composition does seem to call up deeper resources than you might think you possessed. There's a release of the imagination and clearly some call on the unconscious.

Does this work reflect your personal experiences?

Psycho-historians would answer yes for me and every other writer. My fiction, though, is a fiction. The major settings are settings with which I am familiar, except that I haven't dealt in illegal arms or drugs, nor have I laundered money. But a fair bit of information on most kinds of criminal activities is available through the newspapers. I was once an assistant district attorney for New York County, which also helped on background.

What audience are you hoping to reach?

As wide as possible. The work seems to me open and simply told—no barriers.

Whom do you consider your primary literary influences, and why?

To answer why, I'd have to write a treatise on aesthetics and psychology, which I'm not capable of. But here are a few names: Shakespeare, Joyce, Auden, Ford Maddox Ford, Anthony Powell, Wallace Stevens, Babel, Hemingway, Faulkner

Jean Giono, Uwe Johnson. Some of these are not major figures, but all touch me strongly. There's also the reading of childhood and adolescence: Robin Hood, Thomas Wolfe, etc.

John Burnham Schwartz
Bicycle Days

Schwartz is an American novelist, born in 1965.

In *Bicycle Days,* Alec Stern, a recent Yale graduate, fulfills his childhood dream by taking a job with a computer firm in Tokyo and moving in with a Japanese family. In brief, detailed chapters, Schwartz depicts Alec's comic disorientation upon arrival and his gradual acclimatization to Japanese manners, language, and customs. As Alec becomes attached to his host-family, especially to the mother, unpleasant memories of his own family, which was broken by a bitter divorce, are temporarily repressed. The arrival of his older brother and the disintegration of Alec's relationship with an older woman are the emotional crises at the center of *Bicycle Days,* convincing Alec that he must return to the United States and come to terms with his past. Critics responded positively to Schwartz's lightly comic touch, his eye for poetic detail, and his assured manner of storytelling. Michiko Kakutani remarked: "It's a familiar enough story, of course—the classic tale of a young man's coming of age, but as handled by Mr. Schwartz, it has freshness and energy, and it announces the debut of a bright new voice in fiction."

KELLI PRYOR

Schwartz, 23, has just published a coming-of-age novel that sports wisdom and wit. ***Bicycle Days***—about a young Yale grad working in Tokyo who's grappling with his New York childhood—has the compassion of Richard Ford's short stories, the endearing self-questioning of early Jay McInerney, and as much insight into another culture as Mark Salzman's nonfiction tome, *Iron & Silk.* It's a book that is bound to win Schwartz . . . attention—especially since the back jacket cover is a windblown portrait showing off his thick sheaf of hair, intense eyes, and open face.

Schwartz never intended to write ***Bicycle Days.*** Two years ago, just before graduating from Harvard, he accepted a job as a banker with First Boston. Then he set about completing his thesis—100 pages about working at a computer company in Japan in the summer of 1986. "It stirred up emotions in me that weren't going away," he says.

Family friends suggested he polish it and send it to ICM agent Binky Urban. Naïvely brash, he shipped it off to her immediately, and she was so encouraging that he deferred his banker's job for a year, retreating to Nantucket, where he wrote the first of four drafts. When he came off the island, Urban quickly sold the manuscript to Summit Books.

"I turned down the bank forever," says Schwartz. . . . "Writing the book is the most interesting thing I've done in terms of discovering myself and my life. I realized I felt very

strongly about family and memory and the journeys one makes in various ways, both actually and imaginatively."

Schwartz also had a change of heart about Japan. "It was the kind of love you have for that girl in the magazine whom you've never talked to. Then you talk to her, and maybe she is as wonderful as you thought, or maybe she's not. But she's a real person. And Japan for me was very real.

"I was treated as a white male from Harvard, and I stress *white male from Harvard.* Because of that, I was treated like royalty." He notes that he wasn't blind to the rampant racism and sexism around him: "God help you if you're a woman . . . or from Southeast Asia."

Disillusioned with Japan, he's found a new love—writing. "The idea of starting a novel makes me feel something akin to vertigo," he says. Although he's working on a screenplay and fretting about reviews for ***Bicycle Days,*** Schwartz wants more: "I don't have enough experience. I am hungry for the kind of life that creates larger books. I am so much more ambitious than my experience. I have to live a little more."

Kelli Pryor, " 'Am I Somebody?' " in New York Magazine, Vol. 22, No. 17, April 24, 1989, p. 32.

MICHIKO KAKUTANI

In the days of Henry James and Ernest Hemingway, Europe was the place young Americans went to test their innocence and to lose their youthful illusions. . . . Nowadays, Japan seems to have replaced Europe—not only as an economic power, but also as an esthetic pit stop, visited by the young heros of American Bildungsromans.

In Brad Leithauser's lovely first novel, *Equal Distance,* a 22-year-old innocent named Danny Ott takes a year off from his law studies to visit Kyoto, where he hangs out with other expatriates and tries to sort out his hopes and fears. In Jay McInerney's second novel, *Ransom,* a young man named Ransom travels to Japan, "looking for freedom in the homeland of fatalism, looking for he didn't know what—but something more vital than the pallid choice of career." And now in *Bicycle Days,* John Burnham Schwartz's delicately modulated first novel, a recent Yale graduate named Alec takes a job in Tokyo, in an effort to erase his familial past and begin a new life of his own, tabula rasa.

Set down in quick-moving cinematic takes, *Bicycle Days* begins as a sprightly comic novel, reminiscent of *A Good Man in Africa* by William Boyd or one of Kingsley Amis's gentler comedies of manners. Alec's efforts to find his way to work on the crowded Tokyo subway; his lame attempts to hold up his end of the conversation in a business meeting; his embarrassment at the hands of a zealous barber, intent on giving him a Japanese crewcut—each of these scenes is wittily executed, revealing Alec's good-natured naïveté and the huge gap between American and Japanese cultures, as yet unbridged by technology and money.

Most disconcerting of all, Alec finds, is the different attitude that obtains toward women. A business colleague tells him that at 33, she's considered over the hill, a slice of leftover "Christmas cake," spurned by eligible men. His surrogate mother tells him that he should have no problem finding a girlfriend, but he must be careful to find someone from a respectable family. And a male friend gives him some perplexing advice about dating Japanese women.

"First date, second date, third date, on each one she expects that you act a certain way, that you do and say certain things," the friend explains. Once a woman has been found, he continues,

> you must walk up to her slowly and compliment her. Not like a big movie star, but quietly. I would say that quiet confidence is very important. So, you compliment her beauty and her clothes, everything, and you make her laugh. And then you suggest dancing. Before you leave, you tell her that if you do not see her again, you will become very ill, you will be hospitalized. When she hears that, she will give you her phone number. That is the first meeting.

After several depressing visits to various bars and nightclubs, and a short-lived fling with a professional hostess, Alec does find a Japanese girlfriend—Kiyoko, the co-worker who told him she was too old; and he also becomes increasingly immersed in the day-to-day life of his friends and associates. In fact, as an outsider observer, Alec—like Nick Carraway in *The Great Gatsby*—finds himself privy to the secret hopes and griefs of everyone around him. He learns that his surrogate mother and father virtually never speak to each other; that his American boss, Joe Boon, lives a solitary, work-obsessed life since his wife and daughter left him to return to the States; that Kiyoko finds it difficult to reconcile her traditional upbringing in the provinces with the hectic demands of contemporary Tokyo life. . . .

[Schwartz] has managed to achieve remarkable perspective on his material, describing Alec's adventures with sympathy and wry humor. His cameos of Alec's acquaintances are funny and pointed, without ever turning into clichés; and his descriptions of Tokyo demonstrate a highly observant eye. We are made to see a city torn between rampant consumerism and ancient beliefs, a city reeling from American culture shock (the children in Alec's surrogate family talk incessantly about Michael Jackson and Hulk Hogan) and yet deeply committed to traditional ideas—about women, about business, about families.

It is in the second portion of the book, however, when Mr. Schwartz begins to focus more closely on Alec's inner life, that *Bicycle Days* begins to grow into something more than a lightly comic novel, taking on an emotional density that both surprises and moves the reader. When his older brother, Mark, arrives for a visit, Alec is abruptly reminded of what he'd tried to leave behind in coming to Japan—his parents' divorce, his difficulties dealing with his own feelings of loss and fragmentation, his conflicted memories of familial love and disintegration—and he's slowly forced to try to come to terms with time present and time past.

It's a familiar enough story, of course—the classic tale of a young man's coming of age, but as handled by Mr. Schwartz, it has freshness and energy, and it announces the debut of a bright new voice in fiction.

Michiko Kakutani, "Sorting It Out in Tokyo, This Generation's Paris," in The New York Times, *May 9, 1989, p. C18.*

PEGGY PAYNE

There is a quality in [*Bicycle Days*] that brings to mind the Japanese idea of *shibumi:* the simplicity of a single flower, carefully chosen, standing in a tall glass vase, placed to catch the light.

The best of *Bicycle Days* is a series of small, finely drawn pictures of contemporary life in Japan, as seen through the eyes of a very young businessman with a summer job in the Tokyo office of a multinational corporation. The same care is given to the flashback renderings of his childhood in New York. There are moments brought to life by the telling details that are luminous: they linger after the story is finished.

And yet these moments are bound to one another in a narrative that, as a whole, does not begin to live up to their standards.

The impression that remains, along with the haunting evocations of Japan and of family life, is that John Burnham Schwartz is a writer of significant potential who has made a tentative, faltering beginning in this novel. . . .

Bicycle Days is the story of Alec Stern, newly graduated

from Yale, who goes to Japan to live with a Japanese family, work for Compucom Inc. and try to escape from his own life.

The pictures of life in Japan are created largely by careful observations of behavior. When Alec arrives for his first day of work in Tokyo he passes through the building's sleek metal doors and is greeted by a security guard who bows from the waist and says good morning. The guard "repeated the gesture automatically for every person who came in. His voice never changed tone, he never bowed lower or higher than he had the time before."

An excerpt from *Bicycle Days*

He began to daydream, sometimes for hours at a time. He became good at it. He went places and did things and never told anyone about any of it. Often he was a famous child actor or a tennis star. Or both. He owned a motorcycle and rode it across the country. He stopped in places where he had never been before, but where everyone seemed to know him. And then he rode off again. He never needed anything else; he took it all with him wherever he went.

One afternoon, he went with his class on a trip to a children's museum, where a traditional Japanese house had been built. He saw plastic figures dressed in stiff robes sitting around a low table. There was no other furniture, and he thought it must be strange to live in an empty house. And the floor wasn't really a floor at all, but large woven mats placed together with no space in between. The teacher told him that the mats were called *tatami*, and that Japanese people never wore their shoes inside the house. When Alec took off his shoes, he felt the reed floor tickle his feet; it moved when he did, as though it were alive in some way. And it smelled good, like running barefoot in the country.

The house was all clean emptiness and he felt close to it, as if he knew it. The wood was what he thought wood should look like, it wasn't painted or stained. There weren't any pictures, only tall, beautiful flowers in a bowl with white pebbles. The flowers sat on a shelf in one corner of the room where the table was.

When he got home that day, Alec told his mother he didn't want to wear shoes inside the house anymore. But she didn't ask him any questions this time about what he had seen and done and felt. She just smiled absently and touched his hair.

She never asked him about Japan, so he never told her how often he thought about it. Never told her that the motorcycle dreams were all gone now, that he was no longer a famous child actor or a tennis player. He never mentioned how a family had grown out of the picture of the house he had seen. It was his family—a second family—and they lived in Japan, which was his, too, because it looked just the way he thought it should, all wood and reed and tall, beautiful flowers. He had a sister in his new family, and they played cards together. His Japanese parents stayed home most of the time, as though neither of them had a job at all. And no one ever mentioned how different he looked from everyone else. Not a single word about it.

Upstairs, Alec next faces the receptionist, a shy young Japanese woman, also on her first day at work, who hides behind her hand. He asks her name.

> Her face turned red, the hand went up again, curved and feminine. "Keiko."

> He put his own hand forward, holding it just above the desk. "I am Alec. Nice to meet you." As he said it, he realized that the literal translation from the Japanese was something like "Please look after me." . . .

Though Alec enjoys a couple of romances during his summer, he receives the welcome he wants from the vividly portrayed Mrs. Hasegawa, whose family he lives with. "Full-waisted, low-set, with fleshy fingers and ears, fleshy nose and a wide mouth, she was the sort of woman from the provinces who might be found one evening dragging an uncooperative bull into its stall by the horns or wading through the murky waters of a rice field." Mrs. Hasegawa takes him shopping, tells him to eat more shrimp, tells him that girls of "good family" are right for him, sits up late with him talking and drinking Scotch. . . .

Poignant scenes unfold, again and again. Yet they are often marred, particularly at the conclusions, by several persistent problems. The most troublesome is a tendency to wrap up chapters, and the novel itself, with a sentimental twist or a self-consciously poetic image: "the moon rising over a wood full of hand-carved hearts, a tunnel of hearts, leading him up to the white gravel path and home." The author also spoils some vivid images by going on to explain them. And there are passages in which the main character arrives at conclusions that are too neat and easy, that descend into platitude: "Maybe waiting is harder when you don't know what you're waiting for." The effect is to rob the narrative of an overall power; contrivances and neatness make this a story that, in spite of some of its grittier episodes, still seems somehow euphemistic.

Even so, Mr. Schwartz has written a book with some memorable moments and some very deft sketches—a fish market, a funeral, a live sex show, a dinner with Japanese businessmen, a department store, the crowds that are polite and quiet even when pouring out of the subway. Although *Bicycle Days* does not work as a fully satisfying narrative, many passages linger in the mind of the reader and yield continuing pleasure.

*Peggy Payne, " 'I Am Alec. Please Look After Me',"
in The New York Times Book Review, July 9,
1989, p. 11.*

DAVID R. SLAVITT

[John Burnham Schwartz is] a minimalist, with only a couple of chapters [in *Bicycle Days*] that go beyond four or five pages. Each flashcard chapter points toward the tag-line of its title, and we get a series of fast takes about a young man finding himself as, fresh out of Yale, he works at his first job in exotic Japan. What makes this funny is that almost any job would be exotic. For Alec Stern, all grown-ups are foreigners.

Those quick scenes are fairly efficient and easy to take, but they don't add up to as much about Japan as Bruce Jay Friedman's *Tokyo Woes,* which was funnier and sharper. But Schwartz's point is rather different. He is interested in showing us Alec's flight from awkward family life back home and his consequent longing for a place to feel at home. This rather less exotic subject insinuates itself with an accuracy and an honesty that lets us feel the young man's pain.

He leaves Tokyo to spend some time in the rural village where, among the simple routines of his hosts' lives,

> he started to remember things he thought he had forgotten long ago. They came to him as they had from his first day in Japan, as images and scenes, each one belonging to something larger and unidentifiable. It was as if he had lost control somehow, as if his memory did as it pleased, mocking him by playing his childhood back to him in bits and pieces. He watched them as he would someone else's home movies, and felt the foreignness of his own life.

The promotional material the publishers sent along with review copies compares Schwartz to "the endearing self-questioning of early Jay McInerney." McInerney has three books out, so I guess it is actually possible to talk of "early" and "late." And there is a kind of relationship between his work and the impressionist, almost pointillist strategy Schwartz mostly relies on. But it is limited and limiting.

> *David R. Slavitt, "First Novels Show Promise Beneath Stylistic Posturing," in* Chicago Tribune—Books, *July 16, 1989, p. 5.*

DAVID NICHOLSON

Bicycle Days, by John Burnham Schwartz, is a coming-of-age novel with a twist—it takes place in Japan, where the troubled hero, Alec Stern, has gone to work for a summer for a computer firm. The book opens with Alec, disoriented after a long plane ride and a bus trip from the airport, standing on a street corner trying to make sense of the city. "I knew it would be different," Alec tells a Japanese coworker, Nobi. "But it's . . . I don't know. It's just really different."

That difference is just what Alec has been seeking, however. As a child, he had fantasized about a

> family—a second family—and they lived in Japan . . . He had a sister in his new family, and they played cards together. His Japanese parents stayed home most of the time, as though neither of them had a job at all.

Gradually Alec—fluent in the language and competent in his work—comes to enjoy living in Japan. . . . After a disastrous beginning, he embarks on an affair with a co-worker, Kiyoko. He visits Kiyoko's grandparents, and is scolded by her grandfather for his ineptitude at fishing and woodcutting because "you do not think. You expect too many things." And Alec finds acceptance from the family he lives with—at the mother's request he calls her "Mother."

The search for family is what this novel is really about. Alec's parents were divorced when he was in high school, and he is still trying to come to terms with it. During the course of the novel, he does, and decides to return home. The trouble is that Alec's insights about himself are, for the most part, unconvincing. We've also read other books about Japan, and *Bicycle Days* adds little to what appears to be a growing body of literature about young Americans in Japan.

> *David Nicholson, "Terms of Endearment," in* Book World—The Washington Post, *September 3, 1989, p. 10.*

YUMIKO MIYANO AND YOICHI CLARK SHIMATSU

The trauma of the Russo-Japanese War irrevocably bifurcated the Western depiction of Japan into two opposing images. One frame encloses the "traditional" country of innocent sensuality, demure manner and aesthetic refinement. The other holds the "modern" nation, brimming with arrogance, brutal chauvinism and robot-like discipline. Applying the terminologies of psychological repression and "exoticism," the West unconsciously associated gender with each segment. The former values were identified with the feminine sphere of the household, the rural village, and the geisha quarter, the latter with the masculine world of the factory, the military and the political machine. (pp. 25-6)

The cultural theory of a feminized Japan has found expression in a whole genre of post-war American novels and films that portray the international relationship through biracial love affairs. Such romantic entanglement has by now become an all-too-familiar cliché, colored by the colonial overtones of the American as dominant male and the Japanese as exotic female.

Bicycle Days by John Burnham Schwartz is a coming-of-age novel from this mold. Yale graduate Alec Stern seeks to suppress his childhood memories of nightly arguments and outbursts of violence between his parents. Lacking wholeness, his family is like a picture "being broken down into unrecognizable pieces," a process that has culminated in the divorce of his father, a self-made businessman, from his remote, intellectual mother.

The rejected son's flight to Japan is an allegory of forgetting, of erasing the past. Transplanted to a Tokyo computer company, Stern discovers a sense of belonging he had never known in the anonymity of America. Soon, he finds himself reconstructing the broken relationships of his childhood and realizing the unconscious longing of his Oedipal search in two older women—Mrs. Hasegawa, the nurturing maternal figure of his host family, and Kiyoko, a reticent, introverted lover.

In the mountainous North, he meets Kiyoko's grandfather, a nearly mythic figure of intact manhood. The old man's death sets off a chain of events leading to a moment of remembrance; Alec's violent act of erasure is overcome through healing memories of the "bicycle days" of his childhood, idyllic moments with his mother.

As Alec's memory returns, however, "Japan" vanishes like a projection on a blank wall. The Japanese become merely the tolerant, wise and accepting background shadows for a self-infatuated psychodrama, and [*Bicycle Days*] comes to share the affliction of the West, never to see except into the mirrors of its own self. (pp. 26-7)

> *Yumiko Miyano and Yoichi Clark Shimatsu, "The Occidental Tourist," in* San Francisco Review of Books, *Fall, 1989, pp. 24-7.*

ALEX HEARD

USA Today recently published a feature on a horde of very young Ivy League writers—all but one are 26 or under—who will soon be in our faces: among others, John Burnham Schwartz (in our faces already; author of *Bicycle Days,* the story of a young man coming of age in Japan), Jonathan Ames (coming soon; author of *I Pass Like Night,* the tale of a young man from the suburbs coming of age on New York's angsty streets), Marti Leimbach (*Dying Young,* about a young man coming of age while dying), Eric Swanson (*The Greenhouse Effect,* a tale of a young man coming of age while trying to make it as an actor in New York), and David Lipsky (*Three Thousand Dollars,* a book of short stories, most of them satirical looks at young men coming of age haphazardly in prep school and the Ivy League). (p. 27)

Most of these writers are going to disappear from sight faster than a burger placed in front of Wimpy, and it's interesting, in a morbid way, to watch what the publishers do to achieve maximum hype-istic frenzy while they last. At present only two of the novels are available for serious study (*Bicycle Days* and *I Pass Like Night*) and only *Bicycle Days* has gone through the entire hype cycle. Successfully, too. This past summer, as you probably noticed unless you were in Auckland, was the Season of Schwartz. In terms of setting the pace for peers who will follow, [Schwartz is] shaping up to be the [Jay] McInerney of his Generation, and the marketing of this talented, brooding youth featured a few interesting twists that I feel sure we'll see again.

First, predictably, was vociferous *Disassociation from the Original Brat Pack.* Brat Pack I never marched in lockstep—there were grim writers (Ellis, for example) and gentle writers (Leavitt)—but the official line, as pushed this summer by Schwartz's handlers, is that most all of them were sour-faced nihilist snots. "[Schwartz] radiates none of the I've-seen-it-all, tried-it-all, smoked-it-all and drunk-it-all qualities that characterize many of his comrades in the burgeoning literary Brat Pack of *auteurs* under the age of 30," the *Los Angeles Times's* Elizabeth Mehren gushed. "He seems eager, not bored or blasé. Like Ethan Canin, a best seller by age 27 and an inspiration of sorts to John Burnham Schwartz, he writes with hope. . . . Not one character takes drugs or undergoes a crisis of gender identification, the staples of what his editor, Ileene Smith, calls 'all those fashionable and extremely irritating books' by young writers who seem to take negativity pills along with their morning coffee. 'I'm a positive person, I guess,' Schwartz [says]. 'I really enjoy people. I like to laugh, and I like to laugh at myself. As much as I can, I do.' "

And unlike BP I writers, Schwartz is not a self-obsessed navel gazer. "Lest he be accused of creating an autobiographical character," the *L. A. Times* said, "Schwartz . . . disguises Alec by making him a student at Yale." Schwartz went to Harvard. Nor is he a permaBrat: "Lately he has been reading Plato. 'Why not?' he said. 'I want to find out what fits where. I would like to have a world view that is larger than the one I have.' " (pp. 27, 29)

For Schwartz, who was at once young, well-off, and well-connected—he prepped at Choate, went to college at Harvard, and had a job lined up at First Boston upon graduation—the trick was to prove that these things were in fact *obstacles* that stood between a young man and his art. "I realized that I'd been on a track all my life," he told *New York* [see excerpt above], "from Choate to Harvard, and whole parts of my life had gotten submerged." But with help from the Muse he punched his way out of the pinstriped suit. According to the *L. A. Times* piece, at age 19 John, returning from a trip to Maui with his mother and stepfather (the poet W. S. Merwin), impulsively scribbled a short story on an air sickness bag, titled, "A Sensitive Man of the 80s." At Harvard he majored in East Asian studies and took economics classes—all in preparation for the philistine career in back-

ing. But the flames did not die, and after graduation, in a Kerouacian "three-week nonstop, no-sleep frenzy at his word processor," he wrote a novel—based on his experiences working for TRW two summers in Japan—as his thesis. . . . John retreated to Nantucket, where he further paid his dues spending a hellish year in a vacation cottage rewriting the book four times.

Finally, keep an eye on the all-important angling for *Off-the-Book-Page Coverage.* Tama Janowitz pioneered this, but her techniques—the three-foot-high fright wig, Amaretto ads, and crashing into the Four Seasons to hand out leaflets touting her book—are out. This time, diffident, rabbity shyness will be in, and if the author happens to be pretty, his or her publicists will make sure the dust-flap photo gets blown up extra-large. Schwartz's boyish good looks have not gone unnoticed. "[The] backjacket cover is a windblown portrait showing off his thick sheaf of hair, intense eyes, and open face," sighed *New York.* . . .

Thoughtful reviewers will notice that I philistinishly haven't said a word about . . . the work. Can John Burnham Schwartz write? Oh, I suppose. But he's not nearly as good as the hypesters would have you believe, and if we follow the Leimbach Dictum that age shouldn't be factored into considerations of literary merit, [*Bicycle Days*] falls short of half-assed. The hero, Alec, arrives in Tokyo after graduating—*from Yale*—and meets the host family with whom he will stay during his trial year at an American firm, Compucom, Inc. Lying on his futon the first night in this alien land, he thinks back to the first time he was sent off to summer camp. "He had not wanted to go away then," we read in Chapter Two. "He had cried and screamed at his parents. It hadn't been his decision—not the way it had been later, when he went away to school . . . " Yes, this boy is mad at his family. And I'm sorry, but that's when I began to miss the old McInerney/Ellis sex-and-drug romps through nightclubs. As it turns out, the dramatic nut here is that Mom and Dad—no, they didn't die; that was the staple of BP I writers—they . . . get divorced when Alec is 15. In a purely non-autobiographical coincidence, the exact same thing happened to Schwartz when he was at Choate. In response, he told the *L.A. Times,* at Harvard "he staged a 'tumultuous' freshman year with mandatory complements of sex, drugs and rock 'n' roll." Unfortunately this is the kinder-gentlerized version, so we don't get that.

What we do get, in the novel's first half, are whimsical, occasionally funny and sharp sketches of Tokyo life that keep the novel on autopilot until Schwartz has to return to Alec's divorce-caused angst. Reviewers have lauded the book for its sparkling, original insights into Japanese culture, but I just don't know. Among the things we learn are: Japanese are chauvinistic; Tokyo is crowded and it costs a lot to play golf there; Japanese women don't respond to come-ons by foreigners; the Japanese don't like Koreans; Japanese businessmen are proud, mysterious, and do gross things to Filipino prostitutes; many Japanese youth are attracted to Western ways; many Japanese slurp when they eat; Japanese think Americans are big and hairy; tea ceremony teaches the art of patience; and Americans are better at baseball. (I've never been to Japan, but I knew all these things from reading *Junior Scholastic.*)

A few of the characters are interesting—I of course especially liked the Korean, Park, who takes Alec to a club where Japanese businessmen play Rock, Paper, and Scissors to see who gets to strip naked and go onstage to receive manual dexterity demonstrations from prostitutes. But some of them—well, if they aren't stereotypes, then I'm staying clear of Japan. Especially Northern Japan, where Alec spends a weekend learning the ways of the Pat-Morita-in-the-*Karate-Kid*-like grandparents of the Japanese woman he loves. Grandfather takes Alec fishing, but Alec, he too impatient and scare fish away while Grandfather, he patient and fill up creel with trout. Inside the house, as Alec chops an onion with Zen carefulness, Grandmother explains that simple acts have *much* meaning. "With Grandfather, you can practice fishing and chopping wood. . . . And with Grandmother, you can practice cooking. . . . In Yamadera, these are the important things, Alec. In Tokyo, in the cities, these things are no longer important."

Fortunately, Alec scurries back to Tokyo and, with a penumbra of wisdom now radiating from his being, succeeds in bedding his true love, Kiyoko, the granddaughter of the wise old pair. (True to her genes, she bores us first: "Tea ceremony is about beauty and waiting," she tells Alec. "And there can be great pleasure in waiting. Tonight, I would like to do that for you, Alec. To make you wait and give you pleasure.") But

by now unhappiness is at hand: a major source of Alec's angst, his older brother Mark, has shown up in Tokyo to berate him about not keeping in touch with the family. . . . They argue, in the process stomping the old theater injunction "Show Me, Don't Tell Me" flatter than a Kansas roadkill. Alec says he had run away to escape the old pains and ties. Mark yells:

> I guess it's my fault for thinking that family still meant something to you. And my fault for thinking you'd be there for me when I needed you. But life's too short to waste time thinking about family, isn't it? And you're too goddamn selfish. Just be careful you don't get the same treatment if you ever try to come back home.

After this Alec steals a bike, gets jailed, yells at his boss, brattily ignores Kiyoko until she breaks up with him, Grandfather dies—making Alec feel quasi-filial loss—and eventually he does the right thing: he quits his job and goes home to family. (p. 29)

Alex Heard, "Brat Pack II," in The American Spectator, *Vol. 22, No. 10, October, 1989, pp. 27-9.*

Amy Tan
The Joy Luck Club

Tan is an American novelist of Chinese descent, born in 1952.

Through sixteen interconnected stories told by four immigrants from China and their four American-born daughters, *The Joy Luck Club* illuminates the nature of mother-daughter relationships in both cultures. The theme of Tan's novel is the impact of past generations on the present, and the structure, in which the daughters' eight stories are enveloped by those of the mothers, implies that the older generation may hold a key to resolving the problems of the young. Critics praised Tan's striking metaphors, her wry wit, and her avoidance of sentimentality. The diverse voices related in *The Joy Luck Club* demonstrate Tan's ability to capture both the fractured English of Chinese immigrants and the abrupt, colloquial English of their Americanized daughters. Michael Dorris commented: "*The Joy Luck Club* is that rare, mesmerizing novel one always seeks but seldom finds. Tracing the poignant destinies of two generations of tough, intelligent women, each gorgeously written page welcomes the reader and leads to an enlightenment that, like all wisdom, sometimes brings pleasure and sometimes sadness."

SUSAN DOOLEY

"I thought up Joy Luck on a summer night that was so hot even the moths fainted to the ground, their wings were so heavy with the damp heat," Jing-mei's mother tells her, remembering the town of Kweilin in China where she waited with other refugees for the approach of the Japanese army.

> I sat in the dark corners of my house with a baby under each arm, waiting with nervous feet. When the sirens cried out to warn us of bombers, my neighbors and I jumped to our feet and scurried to the deep caves to hide like wild animals. But you can't stay in the dark for so long. Something inside of you starts to fade and you become like a starving person, crazy-hungry for light.

And crazy-hungry for a life with a bit of joy in it, and a bit of luck. And so Jing-mei's mother invites four other women to join her in the Joy Luck Club. Each week they gamble at mah-jongg; they tell outrageous stories and laugh and feast on the food they have saved. . . .

Years later in San Francisco, the club goes on, but now Jing-mei's mother is dead and she has been asked by the Joy Luck aunties to sit in her mother's place. She moves uneasily into the East position, remembering how once, in anger, her mother had said, "You don't even know little percent of me!"

And Jing-mei knows she does not. Amy Tan's brilliant novel flits in and out of many realities but all of them contain mothers and daughters. In America something has gone wrong. These women from China find trying to talk to their daughters like trying to plug a foreign appliance into an American outlet. The current won't work. Impulses collide and nothing flows through the wires except anger and exasperation. When one daughter remarks, "I'm my own person," the mother thinks, "How can she be her own person? When did I give her up?"

Tan has written a novel without a central plot but with characters and events that are as powerful as myth, and which often entangle it. The stories of the aunties are interspersed with events involving the daughters, so that China and America come together in fantastic and unconnected succession. Ying-ying recalls how, when her first husband left her years ago in China,

> I opened wide my bedroom windows, even on cold nights, to blow his spirit and heart back my way.
>
> What I did not know is that the north wind is the coldest. It penetrates the heart and takes the

warmth away. The wind gathered such force that it blew my husband past my bedroom and out the back door. I found out from my youngest aunt that he had left me to live with an opera singer.

It is these older women transported from China who know "How to obey parents and listen to your mother's mind. How not to show your own thoughts, to put your feelings behind your face so you can take advantage of hidden opportunities. Why easy things are not worth pursuing. How to know your own worth and polish it, never flashing it around like a cheap ring. Why Chinese thinking is best." And it is these women ejected from their culture who are the strength of the story, as though knowledge and certainty had been layered onto each of them over centuries.

The reader is not always sure who is speaking, or which daughter belongs to which mother, but each story is a fascinating vignette, and together they weave the reader through a world where the Moon Lady can grant any wish, where a child, promised in marriage at two and delivered at 12, can, with cunning, free herself; where a rich man's concubine secures her daughter's future by killing herself and where a woman can live on, knowing she has lost her entire life.

Susan Dooley, "Mah-Jongg and the Ladies of the Club," in Book World—The Washington Post, March 5, 1989, p. 7.

MICHAEL DORRIS

The Joy Luck Club is that rare, mesmerizing novel one always seeks but seldom finds. Tracing the poignant destinies of two generations of tough, intelligent women, each gorgeously written page welcomes the reader and leads to an enlightenment that, like all true wisdom, sometimes brings pleasure and sometimes sadness.

The book's four aging mothers, born in a pre-World War II China just embarked on a major cultural transition, are migrants who interpret life through the vivid eyes of their youth, through the experience and example of their own mothers. Their four daughters, first-generation Californians, stand at the midpoint of a seesaw. If they inch in one direction, they are traditional Chinese; if they inch in the other, they are Americans. Theirs is an ongoing quest for balance between the past and the future.

To tell this complex story, Amy Tan, a writer of dazzing talent, has created an intricate tapestry of a book—one tale woven into the other, a panorama of distinctive voices that call out to each other over time.

Tan's characters, regardless of their cultural orientation or age, speak with authority and authenticity. The details of their lives, unfamiliar to most American readers, are rendered with such conviction that almost immediately their rules seem to become the adages and admonitions with which we ourselves grew up. . . .

The book opens and closes with the voice of Jing-mei "June" Woo, whose mother, Suyuan, had decades before, in a war-torn refugee center in interior China, initiated the Joy Luck Club.

"My idea," Suyuan confides, "was to have a gathering of four women, one for each corner of my mah-jongg table." She invited An-mei Hsu, Lindo Jong, and Ying-Ying, who was later

to marry an American named St. Clair, to join her. They were a disparate group, uprooted from different regions and economic strata, but had in common their youth and their "wishful faces," their anxiety and their loneliness. Each week one of the women hosted a party, served special though simple delicacies and defined the depression their precarious circumstances might dictate. . . .

The Club, and the friendships it reflects, endured. It expanded to include the women's spouses; it became the clearing house for news about their children. Eventually all money won or lost was shared in common, an emergency bank on which any member could draw. Joy Luck remained their stable center despite the turbulence of immigration and social change; and when Suyuan dies, June is invited to take her mother's place ("on the East, where things begin") at the mah-jongg table.

It seems at first an uncomfortable and artificial wedding of generations grown apart, until, at the conclusion of the first evening's session, the existence of June's two half-sisters— lost as infants and believed dead—is revealed. June is instructed to go to Shanghai, meet her siblings and answer their inevitable questions.

" 'See my sisters and tell them about my mother?' June says, nodding. 'What will I say? What can I tell them about my mother? I don't know anything. She was my mother.' " (p. 1)

" 'Tell them stories she told you . . . what you know about her mind that has become your mind,' says Auntie Ying."

There follows a litany of specific suggestions of what to convey: Suyuan's kindness, her intelligence, her hopes, the good food she knew how to cook. Finally June understands.

> They are frightened. In me, they see their own daughters, just as ignorant, just as unmindful of all the truths and hopes they have brought to America. They see daughters who grow impatient when their mothers talk in Chinese, who think they are stupid when they explain things in fractured English. They see that joy and luck do not mean the same to their daughters, that to these closed American-born minds "joy luck" is not a word, it does not exist. They see daughters who will bear grandchildren grown without any connecting hope passed from generation to generation.

"I will tell them everything," June says simply, and the aunties look at her with "doubtful faces."

They need not have worried. Not only does June fulfill her promise, but also, before she deplanes at the Shanghai airport, eight lives have been meticulously revealed. In exquisite passages, each of the senior women reflects on the formative events in her past; then, in counterpoint, each of their daughters—June, Rose, Waverly and Lena—examines her own path to maturity.

It is a large cast for a first novelist to direct, and *The Joy Luck Club* is an ambitious book. But Tan performs the miracle of making every character, even the minor and disagreeable ones, ultimately sympathetic. We understand their obsessions, the sources of their weaknesses and strengths, the quiet love or desperate fear that underpins their sacrifices. Elements of Chinese-American culture that have often been distorted or ignorantly stereotyped are here illuminated, burnished, made fresh.

Literature is writing that makes a difference, that alters the way we understand the world and ourselves. By that standard, *The Joy Luck Club* is the real thing. Without a hint of polemic, it leaves the reader changed, more aware of subtleties, anxious to explore the confusions of any parent's motivation, any child's rebellion. Tan succeeds not only in her careful language, not only in the vista she opens before us, but also in the heart with which she invests this generous book. *The Joy Luck Club* is well-named; it is a pure joy to read. (p. 11)

> *Michael Dorris, "Mothers and Daughters," in* Chicago Tribune—Books, *March 12, 1989, pp. 1, 11.*

CAROLYN SEE

The only negative thing I could ever say about this book is that I'll never again be able to read it for the first time. *The Joy Luck Club* is so powerful, so full of magic, that by the end of the second paragraph, your heart catches; by the end of the first page, tears blur your vision, and one-third of the way down on Page 26, you know you won't be doing anything of importance until you have finished this novel.

The main narrative here is taken up by Jing-mei Woo, a first-generation American-Chinese woman whose whole tone is tuned to the fact that she is, essentially, lost. She's swimming upstream in American culture, doing the best she can, but she's gone through several jobs, she's gotten into the habit of settling for less than she should, and her own Chinese mother appears to be bitterly disappointed in her. Then, her mother dies, and Jing-mei is asked by three old family friends to take her mother's place at their mah-jongg table, at a social club they've been carrying on in San Francisco for the last 40 years. . . .

[The] original Joy Luck Club was started in Chungking during the last of World War II by Jing-mei's mother when she was a young widow, literally setting herself and her friends the task of creating joy and luck out of unimaginable catastrophe:

> What was worse, we asked among ourselves, to sit and wait for our own deaths with proper somber faces? or to choose our own happiness? . . . We decided to hold parties and pretend each week had become the new year. Each week we could forget past wrongs done to us. We weren't allowed to think a bad thought. We feasted, we laughed, we played games, lost and won, we told the best stories. And each week, we could hope to be lucky.

(p. 1)

The four women who have consoled themselves in America for 40 years with friendship, mah-jongg and stories, have already lived lives that are, again, unimaginable. On top of all their other terrors and adversities, their pasts have been *lost;* as if these horrors have taken place not just in another country but on another planet. Their deepest wish is to pass their knowledge, their tales, on to their children, especially to their daughters, but those young women are undergoing a slow death of their own; drowning in American culture at the same time they starve for a past they can never fully understand.

The author leavens this *Angst* with Marx brothers humor, making you laugh, literally, even as you cry. What can you *do* with a Chinese couple who name their four boys Matthew,

Mark, Luke *and* Bing? What can you tell a mother who thinks she's getting "so-so security" from the government, or (as Jing-mei remembers her own mother deep in indignation about an irate neighbor who believes that she's killed his cat) ". . . That man, he raise his hand like this, show me his ugly fist and call me worst Fukien landlady. I not from Fukien. Hunh! He know nothing!"

But the misunderstandings don't come merely from vagaries of language. *The Joy Luck Club* is about the way the past distances itself from the present as speedily as a disappearing star on a "Star Trek" rerun. It's gone, gone, and yet the past holds the only keys to meaning in every life examined here. On her first night at the mah-jongg table, her mother's friends revealed to Jing-mei that she has two half-sisters still in China, and that the Joy Luck ladies have saved money so that she, Jing-mei, can go home to tell them about their mother. "What can I tell them about my mother?" Jing-mei blurts. "I don't know anything . . . ." But the book is dedicated by the author: *"To my mother and the memory of her mother. You asked me once what I would remember. This, and much more."* What results from this stunningly devotional tour de force is an entrance into eight separate lives: four women whose "real" life occurred in China, in another world, in another *mind;* and four of their daughters, themselves grown women now. To say they are all products of conflicting value systems is heavy-handed inaccuracy, wimpy paraphrase.

Here, for instance, is Eurasian Lena St. Clair, Ying-ying's daughter, translating her mother's Chinese to her Caucasian father, after Ying-ying has given birth to her stillborn baby brother: Lena's mother cries out ". . . Then this baby, maybe he heard us, his large head seemed to fill with hot air and rise up from the table. The head turned to one side. . . . It looked right through me. I knew he could see everything inside me. How I had given no thought to killing my other son!" Lena translates to her sad, ignorant father: ". . . She thinks we must all think very hard about having another baby. . . . And she thinks we should leave now and go have dinner."

And, 15 or so years later, it seems inevitable that Lena should end up with a Hungarian "rice husband" (so named for all those Chinese "rice Christians" who hung around missionaries in China simply so they could get a square meal). In the name of feminism and right thinking, this husband is taking Lena for every cent she's got, but she's so demoralized, so "out of balance" in the Chinese sense, that she can't do a thing about it.

If, so far, I haven't done justice to this book, that's because you can't turn a poem into prose, or explain magic, without destroying the magic, destroying the poem. One can only mention scraps: The four mothers come from different parts of (and times in) China, so for instance, the author allows us to see one peasant mother, Lindo Jong, who remembers she was *not* worthless: "I looked and smelled like a precious bun cake, sweet with a good clean color." Lindo, betrothed at 2, wangles her way out of a horrible marriage with courage and wit. But another mah-jongg lady, An-mei, has watched her own mother lose her honor and "face" by becoming third concubine to a hideous merchant in Tiensing. An-mei's mother times her suicide in such a way that her ghost can come back to haunt the house on New Year's Day, thus insuring a good future for her child, who, in turn, comes to America, has a daughter, Rose, who somehow rustles up the courage to defy an American husband who's trying to swindle her. . . .

But the stories of the four mothers, the four daughters, are not really the point here. *The Joy Luck Club* is dazzling because of the *worlds* it gives us: When Lindo, old now, says, "Feel my bracelets. They must be 24 carats, pure inside and out," if you have any sense at all, you let yourself be led down a garden path into a whole other place; where a little girl in San Francisco becomes chess champion at age 6 by using her mother's "invisible strength," where a woman who comes from the richest family in Wushi (with boxes of jade in every room holding just the right amount of cigarettes) is given the name of Betty by her dopey American husband, who doesn't know she's already "dead," a "ghost. . . ." (pp. 1, 11)

The Joy Luck Club has the disconcerting effect of making you look at everyone in your own life with the—however fleeting—knowledge that they are locked in the spaceships of their own amazing stories. Only magicians of language like Amy Tan hold the imaginative keys to the isolating capsules. Which is why we have novels and novelists in the first place. (p. 11)

> Carolyn See, "Drowning in America, Starving for China," in Los Angeles Times Book Review, March 12, 1989, pp. 1, 11.

An excerpt from *The Joy Luck Club*

My mother named me after the street that we lived on: Waverly Place Jong, my official name for important American documents. But my family called me Meimei, "Little Sister." I was the youngest, the only daughter. Each morning before school, my mother would twist and yank on my thick black hair until she had formed two tightly wound pigtails. One day, as she struggled to weave a hard-toothed comb through my disobedient hair, I had a sly thought.

I asked her, "Ma, what is Chinese torture?" My mother shook her head. A bobby pin was wedged between her lips. She wetted her palm and smoothed the hair above my ear, then pushed the pin in so that it nicked sharply against my scalp.

"Who say this word?" she asked without a trace of knowing how wicked I was being. I shrugged my shoulders and said, "Some boy in my class said Chinese people do Chinese torture."

"Chinese people do many things," she said simply. "Chinese people do business, do medicine, do painting. Not lazy like American people. We do torture. Best torture."

ORVILLE SCHELL

[It is out of the] experience of being caught between countries and cultures that writers such as Maxine Hong Kingston and now Amy Tan have begun to create what is, in effect, a new genre of American fiction.

Born in Oakland, Calif., in 1952 to a father educated as an engineer in Beijing and a mother raised in a well-to-do Shanghai family, Amy Tan grew up in an American world that was utterly remote from the childhood world of her parents. In *The Joy Luck Club,* her first novel, short-story-like vignettes alternate back and forth between the lives of four Chinese women in pre-1949 China and the lives of their American-born daughters in California. The book is a meditation on the divided nature of this emigrant life.

The members of the Joy Luck Club are four aging "aunties" who gather regularly in San Francisco to play mah-jongg, eat Chinese food and gossip about their children. When one of the women dies, her daughter, Jing-mei (June) Woo, is drafted to sit in for her at the game. But she feels uncomfortably out of place in this unassimilated environment among older women who still wear "funny Chinese dresses with stiff stand-up collars and blooming branches of embroidered silk sewn over their breasts," and who meet in one another's houses, where "too many once fragrant smells" from Chinese cooking have been "compressed onto a thin layer of invisible grease." The all-too-Chinese ritual of the Joy Luck Club has always impressed her as little more than a "shameful Chinese custom, like the secret gathering of the Ku Klux Klan or the tom-tom dances of TV Indians preparing for war."

She is made uncomfortable by the older generation's insistence on maintaining old customs and parochial habits, which she views as an impediment to breaking loose from her parents' cultural gravity. What she yearns for is to lead an independent, modern and American life free of the burden of her parents' Chineseness and the overweening hopes for their children that they can't even "begin to express in their fragile English."

"At first my mother tried to cultivate some hidden genius in me," recalls June.

> She did housework for an old retired piano teacher down the hall who gave me lessons and free use of a piano to practice on in exchange. When I failed to become a concert pianist, or even an accompanist for the church youth choir, she finally explained that I was late-blooming, like Einstein, who everyone thought was retarded until he discovered a bomb.

What she fears most of all is being dragged under by all that the Joy Luck Club symbolizes and transformed

> like a werewolf, a mutant tag of DNA suddenly triggered, replicating itself insidiously into a *syndrome,* a cluster of telltale Chinese behaviors, all those things my mother did to embarrass me—haggling with store owners, pecking her mouth with a toothpick in public, being color-blind to the fact that lemon yellow and pale pink are not good combinations for winter clothes.

Part of June's struggle is to distance herself from the kind of helpless obedience that she recognizes in traditional Chinese women, and that she fears is manifesting itself in passivity in her own American life. "I was raised the Chinese way: I was taught to desire nothing, to swallow other people's misery, to eat my own bitterness," says June's mother, spelling out the dangerously congenital nature of this Chinese female submissiveness.

> And even though I taught my daughter the opposite, still she came out the same way! Maybe it is because she was born to me and she was born a girl. And I was born to my mother and I was born a girl.

All of us are like stairs, one step after another,
going up and down, but all going the same way.

With a weary fatalism that speaks for June as well, her sister
Lena confesses her propensity for "surrendering everything"
to her American husband "without caring what I got in return."

However, after the death of June's mother a mixture of grief,
guilt and curiosity, coupled with the relentless goading of the
aunties of the Joy Luck Club, conspire to draw her into the
very world from which she had so assiduously sought to distance herself. As the aunties talk over their mah-jongg game,
even scolding June at one point for her evident lack of interest
in her parents—"Not know your own mother?" asks one of
them. "How can you say? Your mother is in your bones!"—
June begins to see her mother's generation in a different light.
Rather than viewing the aunties as expressionless aliens from
an opaque and distant land who hound and embarrass their
children, bit by bit she begins to understand the real dimensions of the "unspeakable tragedies they had left behind in
China," and to sense how vulnerable they actually are in
America. Slowly she begins to comprehend how, after all
they have endured, they might well be anxious and concerned
lest all cultural continuity between their pasts and their children's futures be lost.

"Because I remained quiet for so long now my daughter does
not hear me," laments one auntie. "She sits by her fancy
swimming pool and hears only her Sony Walkman, her cord-
less phone, her big, important husband asking her why they
have charcoal and no lighter fluid." It comes as a revelation
to June that

> they are frightened. In me, they see their own
> daughters, just as ignorant, just as unmindful of all
> the truths and hopes they have brought to America.
> They see daughters who grow impatient when their
> mothers talk in Chinese, who think they are stupid
> when they explain things in fractured English.
> They see that joy and luck do not mean the same
> to their daughters, that to these closed American-
> born minds 'joy luck' is not a word, it does not
> exist. They see daughters who will bear grandchil-
> dren born without any connecting hope passed
> from generation to generation.

When the aunties finally inform June that the two half sisters
her mother had been forced to abandon during the war miraculously survived and are now living in Shanghai, she is finally jolted into feeling the ways in which her mother is, in
fact, still "in her bones." But it is not until she actually leaves
with her aging father for a pilgrimage to China and a rendezvous with these half sisters that the reader feels the intensity
of heat building up, heat we know will finally fuse her to her
hitherto elusive ancestral home. And when at last she steps
off the plane to embrace these errant relatives who have
grown up on the other side of the divide that once separated
China from the United States so absolutely, we feel as if a
deep wound in the Chinese-American experience is finally
being sutured back together again:

> "Mama, Mama," we all murmur, as if she is among
> us.
> My sisters look at me proudly. . . . And now I
> also see what part of me is Chinese. It is so obvious.
> It is my family. It is in our blood. After all these
> years, it can finally be let go.
>
> (pp. 3, 28)

As Amy Tan tells us of her own homecoming on the jacket
of *The Joy Luck Club,* it was just as her mother had told her
it would be: "As soon as my feet touched China, I became
Chinese."

Woven into the narrative of the lives of June and her mother
are the stories of the three other Joy Luck aunties and their
California-born daughters. Moving back and forth across the
divide between the two generations, the two continents and
the two cultures, we find ourselves transported across the Pacific Ocean from the upwardly mobile, design-conscious, di-
vorce-prone and Americanized world of the daughters in San
Francisco to the world of China in the 20's and 30's, which
seems more fantastic and dreamlike than real.

We come to see how the idea of China—nourished in America by nothing more than the memories of this vanished reality—has slowly metamorphosed in the minds of the aunties
until their imaginations have so overtaken actual memory
that revery is all that is left to keep them in contact with the
past. When we are suddenly jerked by these sequences from
the comforting familiarity of the United States into a scared
child's memory of a dying grandmother in remote Ningbo,
to remembrances of an arranged marriage with a murderous
ending in Shansi or to recollections of a distraught woman
abandoning her babies during wartime in Guizhou, we may
readily feel bewildered and lost. Such abrupt transitions in
time and space make it difficult to know who is who and what
the complex web of generational Joy Luck Club relationships
actually is.

But these *recherches* to old China are so beautifully written
that one should just allow oneself to be borne along as if in
a dream. In fact, as the story progresses, the reader begins to
appreciate just how these disjunctions work for, rather than
against, the novel. While we as readers grope to know whose
mother or grandmother is getting married in an unfamiliar
ceremony, or why a concubine is committing suicide, we are
ironically being reminded not just of the nightmarishness of
being a woman in traditional China, but of the enormity of
the confusing mental journey Chinese emigrants had to
make. And, most ironic, we are also reminded by these literary disjunctions that it is precisely this mental chasm that
members of the younger generation must now recross in reverse in order to resolve themselves as whole Chinese-
Americans; in *The Joy Luck Club* we get a suggestion of the
attendant confusion they must expect to endure in order to
get to the other side.

In the hands of a less talented writer such thematic material
might easily have become overly didactic, and the characters
might have seemed like cutouts from a Chinese-American
knockoff of "Roots." But in the hands of Amy Tan, who has
a wonderful eye for what is telling, a fine ear for dialogue, a
deep empathy for her subject matter and a guilelessly
straightforward way of writing, they sing with a rare fidelity
and beauty. She has written a jewel of a book. (p. 28)

> *Orville Schell, in " 'Your Mother Is in Your Bones',"*
> *in* The New York Times Book Review, *March 19,*
> *1989, pp. 3, 28.*

RHODA KOENIG

Snappy as a fortune cookie and much more nutritious, *The
Joy Luck Club* is a jolly treatment of familiar conflicts (between mothers and daughters, immigrants and natives) in a

new guise. The club's four mah-jongg-playing ladies are Chinese, but their daughters (three of whom have Chinese fathers) are American. Or so *they* say. Even after 40 years in San Francisco, certain behavior patterns do not unravel. When a girlfriend advises Waverly Place Jong to tell her mother "to stop ruining your life. Tell her to shut up," she replies, "Well, I don't know if it's explicitly stated in the law, but you can't *ever* tell a Chinese mother to shut up. You could be charged as an accessory to your own murder."

Murder is in the air, though, and not as a joke, when Jing-Mei Woo's mother, a refugee in Kweilin from the Japanese invasion of 1949, sees "arms and legs hanging from telephone wires and starving dogs running down the streets with half-chewed hands dangling from their jaws." To keep her spirits up, Suyuan Woo forms a club presided over by a different mah-jongg player each week. "The hostess had to serve special *dyansyin* foods to bring good fortune of all kinds—dumplings shaped like silver money ingots, long rice noodles for long life, boiled peanuts for conceiving sons, and of course, many good-luck oranges for a plentiful, sweet life." Oranges and noodles, however, prove fragile magic against the Japanese. Suyuan flees with a baby in a sling over each shoulder and bags of food and clothes in her hands. After days on the road, exhausted and bleeding, she is forced to abandon everything. "What do you mean by 'everything'?" her daughter asks in horror. "Your father is not my first husband," Suyuan explains. "You are not those babies."

While the men in *The Joy Luck Club* are mostly tyrants or simpletons, Amy Tan's women don't wallow in anger or self-pity, not even in the prison of prewar China. Betrothed at two, Lindo Jong becomes an interloper in her own family ("My mother would say to me when the rice bowl went up to my face too many times, 'Look how much Huang Taitai's daughter can eat' ") and is sent to live with her future in-laws at twelve, to learn housework and obedience ("I saw Tyan-yu at the evening meal. . . . I knew what kind of husband he would be, because he made special efforts to make me cry"). At sixteen, on her wedding day, Lindo considers throwing herself into the river but decides, "I would always remember my parents' wishes, but I would never forget myself." How Lindo gets out of her hateful marriage is a delightful combination of feminism and fairy tale: Using superstition for her own ends, she terrorizes her mother-in-law until she is pelted with money and begged to go. And every year, "On the day of the Festival of Pure Brightness, I take off all my bracelets. I remember the day when I finally knew a genuine thought and could follow where it went."

Able to choose their own mates, the Joy Luck daughters do worse than the mothers who had to obey their parents or the immigration service. Lena St. Clair marries a man who believes in dividing the cost of each common expense, though at first he is swept away by passion: "When we got married at city hall, he insisted on paying the fee." Thereafter, he tallies up the dollars and cents with a neatness that writes Lena out of the marital equation. Her mother visits and says, "She become so thin now you cannot see her. She like a ghost, disappear." The thick husband believes she's talking about a diet. But the daughters' Chinese backbone eventually serves them better than their American education. They stand up to husbands and even mothers, learning that cringing is not a form of respect.

The Joy Luck Club is lively and bright but not terribly deep. The stories resolve themselves too neatly and cozily, and are often burdened with symbols (a spindly-legged table or a weed-choked garden for an unhappy marriage) that flatten them out. One cannot help being charmed, however, by the sharpness of observation, the mixture of familiarity and strangeness, and, finally, the universality of Tan's themes: I was amused by how Jewish the Chinese mothers sound, with their honey-voiced, dragon-hearted competitiveness over children and food, their insistence that they are not criticizing, merely remarking. Working on a fortune-cookie assembly line, Lindo thinks the messages are ridiculous (a colleague translates "Money is the root of all evil. Look around you and dig deep" as "Money is a bad influence. You become restless and rob graves") but realizes how she can use even such nonsense to win a husband. At such moments, *The Joy Luck Club* becomes a happy illustration of its own subject, a combination of Chinese subtlety and American ingenuity. (p. 82)

Rhoda Koenig, "Heirloom China," in *New York Magazine*, Vol. 22, No. 12, March 20, 1989, pp. 82-3.

DAVID GATES

"A little knowledge withheld is a great advantage one should store for future use," says Waverly Jong, a chess prodigy whose emigrant parents named her after their street in San Francisco's Chinatown. "[Chess] is a game of secrets in which one must show and never tell." Amy Tan is to be commended for not obtruding a poet (or painter or architect) into her elegant first novel—just a chess player who talks like [short story writer and editor] Gordon Lish. And Tan takes the advice she's put in her character's mouth. No need to tell us that Husband X is uptight: just show him in his garden, kneeling on a rubber pad. . . . Tan is so cagey it takes a while to discern that fetching little Waverly, who posed for the press with "the delicate points of my elbows poised lightly on the table," has become a disagreeable young woman.

Waverly is just one of eight main characters—four Chinese-born mothers and their American-born daughters—in *The Joy Luck Club.* The "club" is the mothers' weekly mah-jongg game; when one of them dies, her daughter Jing-Mei Woo (Westernized to "June") takes her place. Tan lets each woman tell her own story; at the center of every tale is the ferocious love between mother and daughter. ("How can she be her own person?" one mother asks rhetorically. "When did I give her up?") On the periphery are some of the most worthless men this side of *The Color Purple*. Such an ambitious narrative scheme would be a handful for any writer; inevitably the voices sound alike, and the ill-chosen menfolk seem interchangeable. So do the mothers' awful life stories. (p. 68)

But Tan is so gifted that none of this matters much. Her eye ranges from the exotic (mountain peaks like "giant fried fish heads") to the homely (bunk beds with "scuffed, splintery ladders"); she suggests unwritten scenes with a single detail, as in Waverly's reminiscence of her ex-husband with "one hundred forty-six straight black hairs on his chest." Her best device is what Vladimir Nabokov, another chess-obsessed novelist, once characterized as a "knight's move": an oblique change of direction at the end of a passage that suddenly throws everything before it into ironic context. (He was discussing Jane Austen.) Waverly first plays chess on her brother's set, a hand-me-down from a condescending church lady. "When we got home, my mother told Vincent to throw the chess set away. 'She not want it. We not want it,' she said, tossing her head stiffly to the side with a tight, proud smile." A merely sentimental writer would stop here; Tan goes on. "My brothers had deaf ears. They were already lining up the chess pieces and reading from the dog-eared instruction book." This is *The Joy Luck Club* at its best: showing the tragi-comic conflicts of cultures and of generations, and never telling a word. (pp. 68-9)

David Gates, "A Game of Show Not Tell," in Newsweek, *Vol. CXIII, No. 16, April 17, 1989, pp. 68-9.*

DOROTHY WANG

When *The Joy Luck Club* was sold to Putnam in 1987, Amy Tan thought it was "all a token minority thing. I thought they had to fill a quota since there weren't many Chinese-Americans writing." But her insights into the complexities of being a hyphenated American, connected by blood and bonds to another culture and country, have found a much wider audience than Tan had ever imagined. . . .

While growing up in California, Tan, 37, dreamed of getting plastic surgery to Westernize her features. "There was shame and self-hate," she recalls. "There is this myth that America is a melting pot, but what happens in assimilation is that we end up deliberately choosing the American things—hot dogs and apple pie—and ignoring the Chinese offerings." It wasn't until she moved to Europe at the age of 15, with her mother and younger brother, that Tan began the slow and painful process of accepting her dual status. . . . But she was 35 before she was "finally able to say, 'I'm both Chinese and American.' " That was the year she went to China for the first time and—like Jing-Mei in her novel—met her half sisters from her mother's first marriage. "Suddenly some piece fit in the right place and something became whole."

Born in Oakland, shortly after her parents emigrated from China, Tan won a writing contest at age eight. She cites Bible stories, told by her late father, a Baptist minister, and "tons of fairy tales, both Grimm and Chinese," as influences. But in 1985 she read the novel that changed her life: Louise Erdrich's *Love Medicine,* a set of interwoven stories told by different generations of a Native American family. Captivated by Erdrich's images and voice, Tan began writing stories when she wasn't freelancing as a business writer. . . .

She's now working on a new novel, and while she doesn't feel she can write only about Chinese-Americans, she still feels drawn to such material "because of who I am. There are no stories in me about bright lights, big city."

And how does her mother, who had wanted her to be a neurosurgeon—and a concert pianist on the side—feel about her daughter's success? "She's busy going to bookstores to see if they have the book. If they don't, she scolds them," Tan laughs. "And she's been hinting my next book should *really* be about her life—the 'true story.' "

Dorothy Wang, in a review of "The Joy Luck Club," in Newsweek, *Vol. CXIII, No. 16, April 17, 1989, p. 69.*

VALERIE MINER

The Joy Luck Club is a segmented novel eloquently blending the voices of four Chinese immigrants and their daughters. The mothers become friends, meeting regularly in what they call "the Joy Luck Club" to play mah-jongg, buy stocks and gossip. The novel is narrated horizontally as well as vertically; friendships and rivalries develop among the daughters as well as among the mothers:

> Auntie Lin and my mother were both best friends and arch-enemies who spent a lifetime comparing their children. I was one month older than Waverly Jong, Auntie Lin's prized daughter. From the time we were babies, our mothers compared the creases in our belly buttons, how shapely our earlobes were, how fast we healed when we scraped our knees, how thick and dark our hair was, how many shoes we wore out in one year, and later, how smart Waverly was at playing chess, how many trophies she had won last month, how many newspapers had printed her name, how many cities she had visited.

Tan's book is organized into four chapters—the first relating the separate lives of the mothers; the next two focusing on the daughters' stories; the last returning to the mothers. Tan is a deft, vivacious conductor, evoking spirited individuality as well as harmony.

The mothers bequeath dramas of loss, courage and survival. An-mei Hsu watches her own mother, a concubine, commit suicide. Lindo Jong runs away from a suffocating marriage and emigrates to the U.S. under the pretext of being a theology student. Suyuan Woo escapes the Japanese invasion of Kweilin with two babies on her back. Ying-ying St. Clair is abandoned by a rich husband, goes to live with poor relatives for ten years, then meets a white American visiting China and settles with him in California.

The daughters' journeys—less epically proportioned—also reveal strength and grace. Each of these children of the 1950s has achieved some American success and each has remained close to her difficult mother. We meet Jing-mei Woo at the beginning of the novel, several months after her mother, Suyuan, has died. The three other members of the Joy Luck Club have decided to send Jing-mei to China to find her lost half sisters. Rose Hsu Jordan reflects about the day her brother was drowned; she is coping with a divorce and consulting (foolishly, her mother thinks) a psychiatrist. Waverly Jong, under ambitious maternal management, becomes a chess champion and tax attorney. Lena St. Clair, an architect, is weathering a troubled marriage, living (against her mother's objections) in a refurbished barn.

Throughout *The Joy Luck Club,* Tan tests the distance between expectation and reality. Jing-mei Woo explains, "America was where all my mother's hopes lay. She had come here in 1949 after losing everything in China: her mother and father, her family home, her first husband, and two daughters, twin baby girls. But she never looked back with regret. There were so many ways for things to get better." But she goes on:

> In the years that followed, I failed her so many times, each time asserting my own will, my right to fall short of expectations. I didn't get straight A's. I didn't become class president. I didn't get into Stanford. I dropped out of college. . . . For unlike my mother, I did not believe I could be anything I wanted to be. I could only be me.

Each of these first-generation daughters is a guardian angel, helping her mother negotiate the baffling San Francisco culture. And the mothers remain loyal to their often-disappointing daughters. The women in each family are held together by pride, embarrassment and longing. They are, indeed, the loves of one another's lives.

Tan has a remarkable ear for dialogue and dialect, representing the choppy English of the mothers and the sloppy California vernacular of the daughters with sensitive authenticity. These stories are intricately seamed with the provocative questions about language that emerge from bilingual and trilingual homes. In families where verbal exchanges can prove problematic, one sometimes turns to other kinds of oral communication: Tan's cooking scenes are drawn with subtle intensity.

> My father hasn't eaten well since my mother died. So I am here, in the kitchen, to cook him dinner. I'm slicing tofu. I've decided to make him a spicy bean-curd dish. My mother used to tell me how hot things restore the spirit and health. But I'm making this mostly because I know my father loves the dish and I know how to cook it. I like the smell of it: ginger, scallions and a red chili sauce that tickles my nose the minute I open the jar.

The segmented structure of *The Joy Luck Club* encourages readers to think simultaneously in different directions. There are some flaws. Several characters, particularly Rose Hsu Jordan and Ying-ying St. Clair, could be more fully developed. Occasionally a device used for narrative effect—such as when Jing-mei Woo asks in the last chapter, at age 36, what her Chinese name means—defies credibility. Generally, however, *The Joy Luck Club* is a stunningly auspicious debut. Tan is a gifted storyteller who reaches across cultures and generations: "Then you must teach my daughter this same lesson. How to lose your innocence but not your hope." (pp. 566-68)

> *Valerie Miner, "The Daughters' Journeys," in* The Nation, *New York, Vol. 248, No. 16, April 24, 1989, pp. 566-69.*

DENISE CHONG

In the Chinese game of mah-jongg, the prevailing wind for each hand but the first is determined by a throw of the dice. The game starts, always, with the east wind. And that's also where Amy Tan's first work of fiction, *The Joy Luck Club,* begins. In its opening chapters, a Far Easterly wind blows from China, as four women recount haunting tales, interwoven with Chinese myths, of their childhoods in a China of decades ago. But the wind at this fictional mah-jongg table shifts when the women's daughters tell of their childhoods and marriages in modern-day North America. This East meeting West across continents and across generations turns past and present relationships topsy-turvy.

The story opens nearly 40 years after four Chinese women first began meeting, in 1949 in their adopted city of San Francisco, to play mah-jongg, eat dim sum, and talk. Calling themselves the Joy Luck Club, they meet every week until the club founder dies and the remaining three invite her daughter to take her place at the eastern side of the table. Tan's book seems to be constructed like a mah-jongg game itself: with each round one of the four is "the boss," the one who rolls the dice and counts out where to break an opening in the wall of mah-jongg tiles.

The original four women have four daughters, and all eight take turns telling their stories to the reader. First to speak are the mothers, who recall mysteries of their childhoods: arranged marriages, bride suicides, concubines, floods, and war. Then it's the daughters' turn—one of them part Chinese, part English and Irish—to ponder the cross-cultural confusion of their childhoods and the contemporary crises in their faltering careers and marriages to Caucasian husbands. Some of the incidents the daughters relate have haunted their lives. There are the hopes carried across oceans and generations that are dashed, as with Lindo Jong's daughter, Waverly, whose talent as a child chess prodigy was wasted. There's An-Mei Su's daughter, Rose, who witnesses the accidental drowning of a younger sibling, her responsibility by virtue of her Chinese upbringing, then later sees herself taking no responsibility in her marriage. But the last word goes to their mothers. They speak of truths learned that could heal embarrassments and wounds in their daughters' lives.

Though the book makes references to San Francisco and cities in China, mostly near Shanghai, the true landscape of *The Joy Luck Club* is one of emotions. The emotional journey through these characters' lives is all the more powerful because Tan has imbued them with the outward inscrutability expected of an Oriental upbringing. . . . But for the reader, each confesses all. Knowingly or not, they confront ghosts from Chinese myths and superstitions, from secrets never told of life in China, from childhood scenes that festered till they became adult self-doubts. Each begins to sort out what to keep of values Chinese or American—the flaw, says one of the daughters, is "too many choices," making it easy to pick the wrong one. Each wonders what to pass from mother to daughter, from woman to woman.

These moving and powerful stories share the irony, pain, and sorrow of the imperfect ways in which mothers and daughters love each other. Tan's vision is courageous and insightful. Says one daughter, June, of her mother Suyuan Woo: "I could sense her anger rising to its breaking point. I wanted to see it spill over." Tan's wit makes the reader see differently: the famous misty hills of Guilin in China, long immortalized in Chinese scroll painting, are seen by one of her characters as peaks of "giant fried fish heads trying to jump out of a vat of oil." Her wit adds honesty: "My daughter doesn't know that Saint [her father] had to wait patiently for four years like a dog in front of a butcher shop."

A mah-jongg game ends when one player has a complete hand, leaving the other three hands incomplete. The daughter who has taken her mother's place learns that her mother has died before the news can reach her that two other daughters are still alive in China—and she visits them in her mother's stead. But for the other characters, not all the wounds laid bare in *The Joy Luck Club* are healed. One mother wonders if mothers and daughters are blessed, and doomed, to be "like stairs, one step after another, going up and down, but all going the same way." Another cannot say whether her Chinese or American face is better: "If you show one, you must always sacrifice the other." Those voices may be telling of the author's voyages into her own past.

> *Denise Chong, "Emotional Journeys through East and West," in* Quill and Quire, *Vol. 55, No. 5, May, 1989, p. 23.*

CAROLE ANGIER

The Joy Luck Club is a huge hit in America . . . US paper-back rights sold for one and a quarter million dollars. It's good, but not *that* good: what it is is ethnic, and about mothers and daughters. I can just see the jubilation when this perfect combination of flavours-of-the-American-month arrived on the publishers' desk. By contrast the English reaction to ideological correctness has always been deep suspicion. If *The Joy Luck Club* is successful [in England] I hope it will be for its intrinsic qualities, and in proportion to them.

It has many. The oriental artist starts with an advantage: a culture of indirection and artifice; the knowledge that successful stories (all successful communication) must be cunningly crafted. *The Joy Luck Club* is *very* cunningly crafted—thus disproving one of its own themes, that American children lose Chinese values. It has four mother-daughter pairs, four parts of four chapters each, four corners of the mah-jongg table at which the women of the Joy Luck Club tell their stories. . . .

This is very clever. The Chinese stories can't help but be fascinating, and so we are caught and held to the end. They're also cleverly planned to cover every sort of Chinese woman's character and experience: strong and weak, rich and poor, wife and concubine. Lindo Jong is poor but strong: married off to a mean spoiled boy, she plots and achieves her freedom. Ying Ying St Clair is rich but broken, having lost her *chi,* her spirit, when her cruel husband left her. An-Mei Hsu is weak but resilient, brought up in a rich house but without respect, the daughter of a concubine. Suyuan Woo is strong again but poor, forever haunted by having had to abandon her baby daughters as she fled from the Japanese.

In parts two and three we see what happens to these women in America, through the eyes and fates of their daughters. Some of this is realistic and amusing: the daughters' embarrassment over the mothers' unAmerican ways, the mothers' fierce competition over the daughters. All of it is interesting: Chinese customs, ideas and superstitions; the contrast between Chinese suffering and strength, American ease and unhappiness. "I wanted my children to have the best combination," Lindo says, "American circumstances and Chinese character. How could I know these two things do not mix?"

But some of it, I feel, Amy Tan's teacher, writers' group and editors should have cautioned her against. *The Joy Luck Club* is *over*-schematic. We move too often from one corner of the table to another to remember or care enough about each. And at the same time it is over-significant. In the end it gives you indigestion, as if you've eaten too many Chinese fortune cookies, or read too many American Mother's Day cards. . . .

Finally, in all this craft and care there is a central imbalance. Most of the stories come out of Amy Tan's own family; out of her life, her mother's and grandmother's. Suyuan Woo's Joy Luck Club is real; so are her twin daughters left by the roadside in 1949. Even if I hadn't learned this from the publicity handout I would have felt it from Jing-Mei Woo's role as our central storyteller, and from the special drive and passion of Suyuan's story. But Amy Tan gives half her mother's story to An-Mei, so that we learn less of Suyuan's story than of the other mothers'; and she tells us less of Jing-Mei's grown-up life than of the other daughters'.

That is (I think after reading this novel) very Chinese. But it left a gap in a book otherwise as strictly balanced as an equation. . . . Amy Tan's first novel would have been better if it had been about her mother and grandmother; then she could have left the others for her second and third. And they would have been better still. As it is, I hope her too early and too easy—her too American—success won't have spoilt her altogether. I bet her mother has a Chinese proverb about *that.*

Carole Angier, "Chinese Customs," in New Statesman & Society, *Vol. 2, No. 56, June 30, 1989, p. 35.*

NANCY WILLARD

The Joy Luck Club is a splendid first novel. It tells of four Chinese women who meet in San Francisco to play mah-jongg, invest in stocks, eat *dim sum* and chatter about their children. When one of the women dies, her daughter, June Woo, sits in for her at the game.

Through interwoven stories in the different women's voices, Amy Tan presents the lives of the four Chinese mothers and their four Chinese-American daughters. June Woo speaks for them all when she observes that mother and daughter speak two different languages: "I spoke to her in English, she answered back in Chinese." The difference runs deeper than language, however. "My mother and I never really understood one another," she explains. "We translated each other's meanings, and I seemed to hear less than what was said, while my mother heard more."

In the opening chapter, June discovers that she has two sisters in China, the twin baby girls her mother was forced to abandon during the Japanese invasion. The members of the Joy Luck club have collected enough money to send her to China, so that she can tell the sisters about their mother. "Tell them stories she told you, lessons she taught, what you know about her mind that has become your mind." She finds that her mother's stories taught her most when they seemed not to be teaching at all, "casting long shadows into her life, and eventually into mine."

Through the mothers' stories runs a common thread: the fate of the woman who has been taught to efface herself in the name of obedience but knows there is something better. "[A] girl should stand still," Ying-Ying St. Clair recalls being told. "If you are still for a very long time, a dragonfly will no longer see you. Then it will come to you and hide in the comfort of the shadow." Lindo Jong, whose disastrous marriage is arranged when she is two, promises herself on the way to the wedding that she will both remember her parents' wishes and keep a sense of who she is. "I had genuine thoughts inside that no one . . . could ever take away from me." Her marriage is a life of menial service without love, to which she nearly succumbs. "It's like those ladies you see on American TV these days, the ones who are so happy they have washed out a stain so the clothes look better than new."

For their American daughters, the mothers want nothing less than perfection. They believe that anything is possible for a daughter if the mother wills it. And so the mothers visit on their daughters the sin of demanding perfect obedience. They criticize, manage, manipulate. There are only two kinds of daughters, June's mother tells her. "Those who are obedient and those who follow their own mind! Only one kind of daughter can live in this house. Obedient daughter!" In a free society, the daughters are not free to fall short of their mothers' expectations. And so even the most successful daughters are haunted by a sense of failure, and even the most determined mothers are dismayed to find their daughters repeating their own weaknesses. . . .

Nowhere is the painful bond between mother and daughter put so well as in the passages in which Waverly Jong recalls her childhood as a chess prodigy.

> My mother was doing it again, making me see black where I once saw white. In her hands, I always became the pawn. I could only run away. And she was the queen, able to move in all directions, relentless in her pursuit, always able to find my weakest spots . . . But in the brief instant that I had peered over the barriers I could finally see what was really there: an old woman, a wok for her armor, a knitting needle for her sword, getting a little crabby as she waited for her daughter to invite her in.

Amy Tan's special accomplishment in this novel is not her ability to show us how mothers and daughters hurt each other, but how they love and ultimately forgive each other. If the book has a plot, it is her characters' slow progress from confusion to understanding. She gives us no easy revelations, only fragile moments of insight and longing. A crushing remark can destroy them. But these moments, as Amy Tan writes them, illuminate that complex relationship for all of us.

"I will gather together my past and look," says Ying-ying St. Clair.

> I will see a thing that has already happened. The pain that cut my spirit loose . . . I will use this sharp pain to penetrate my daughter's tough skin and cut her tiger spirit loose. She will fight me, because this is the nature of two tigers. But I will win and give her my spirit, because this is the way a mother loves her daughter.

> *Nancy Willard, "Tiger Spirits," in The Women's Review of Books, Vol. VI, Nos. 10-11, July, 1989, p. 12.*

CHARLOTTE PAINTER

The liberating influence of Maxine Hong Kingston appears in an absorbingly beautiful first book by Amy Tan, **The Joy Luck Club.** The members of a mah-jongg club tell their stories, many of which have mythic qualities. These borrowings from family tales and cultural legend are linked together with a common denominator, the universal mother-daughter bond. Perhaps in no other immigrant culture is that bond more strongly felt than in the Chinese, where it becomes double-knotted with the unrealistic expectations of what the "gold mountain" country might offer a new generation. The mothers in these stories expect more of their daughters than they can ever realize, their ambitions for them are lavish beyond all hope, the judgment they bring to bear extreme and punishing to both themselves and their children. The consequence is almost always an alienation filled with an estranged, anguished love.

When the founder of the mah-jongg club dies, the other three members, all immigrants now grown old, invite her daughter of thirty-five to take her place. Tan's humorous account of their party, which has evolved beyond the mere-mah-jongg game into dining and playing the stock market together, sets the book's complex structure, starting with the daughter's

voice, then moving to her dead mother's. Their stories turn upon the generosity of the three older women. In an attachment to the past, they make a gesture that extends toward the future: they give the daughter a ticket to China to meet her mother's other legendary daughters, twin babies abandoned on the roadside during the Japanese invasion of China, and rediscovered only after the mother's death. They want her to fulfill the mother's "long cherished wish" to find those children, and more, to tell the twins about their mother. "Tell them stories she told you, lessons she taught, what you know about her mind that has become your mind."

The process of becoming one's mother, however one resists, while the struggle to become oneself goes on, obsesses Tan and makes this a powerful, deeply felt book. She expresses this legacy in one of the early stories, adapted from a famous legend of Buddha feeding his own flesh to a hungry lioness and her starving cubs:

> . . . my mother cut a piece of meat from her arm. Tears poured from her face and blood spilled to the floor. My mother took her flesh and put it in the soup. She cooked magic in the ancient tradition to try to cure her [own] mother. . . .

A belief in magic and Feng Shui, ghosts, ancestors and tradition pervades the lives of the older women, while the daughters try to lead their contemporary lives as lawyers and architects with lovers and husbands, each coming to experience the fierce grief of their mother's attachment to them.

Stories of the four older women alternate in several rounds with the daughters' stories. They are for the most part skillfully crafted, but the book holds technical difficulties Tan has not overcome. The voices, in unrelieved first person, resemble one another too closely. "Who's speaking now, whose mother, whose daughter?" one must constantly wonder. I wish Tan had taken charge with an authorial voice, given that the book's theme, the author's overriding obsession, is so constant throughout. The reader can best enjoy the singular strength in this writing by surrendering to Tan's preoccupation, appreciating her startling perceptions, and enjoying the book as a composite depiction of maternal passion as it moves between youth and age. One mother looking in a beauty parlor mirror before her daughter's wedding says: "I see my reflection. I cannot see my faults, but I know they are there. I gave my daughter these faults. . . . Her character, it came from my circumstances." It might be any mother in the book speaking, or any mother anywhere with the insight to see.

The two stories that begin and end the book, in which the mystery of the abandoned twins is elaborated, are worth the whole volume. The narrator, remembering her dead mother, sees her sister for the first time as she gets off the plane, and says:

> And then I see her. Her short hair. Her small body. And that same look on her face. She has the back of her hand pressed hard against her mouth. . . . And I know it's not my mother, yet it is the same look she had when I was five and had disappeared all afternoon, for such a long time she was convinced I was dead. . . . And when I appeared, sleepy-eyed, crawling from underneath my bed, she wept and laughed, biting the back of her hand to make sure it was true.

Throughout these stories Amy Tan explores a wealth of fresh material, which suggests she could write with an equally strong passion on the complete range of the Chinese American experience. There's enough life in this book for at least four novels. Let's hope Tan's imagination is an inexhaustible wellspring, and that more will be forthcoming. (pp. 16-17)

Charlotte Painter, "In Search of a Voice," in San Francisco Review of Books, *Summer, 1989, pp. 15-17.*

Jane Vandenburgh
Failure to Zigzag

Vandenburgh is an American novelist and short story writer.

In *Failure to Zigzag,* the adolescent protagonist, Charlotte, attempts to maintain her sanity despite the madness in both her environment and family history. Charlotte's mother, Katrinka, is an alcoholic schizophrenic who works as a ventriloquist in the local carnival between stays in a mental hospital. Winnie and Lionel, Charlotte's grandparents, who are raising their granddaughter in the same manner as they raised Katrinka, suffer from a variety of obsessive/compulsive behaviors that provide some of the novel's most humorous incidents. Charlotte has been told that her father died during World War II after his ship failed to employ a zigzag-maneuver to escape enemy fire. In turn, Vandenburgh depicts Charlotte's adolescence as a continuing struggle to avoid provoking her grandparents' and her mother's eccentric, and at times, outrageous behavior. Critics admired Vandenburgh's ability to portray the humorous as well as tragic aspects of Charlotte's circumstances. Laura Shapiro remarked: "Craziness and poignancy make risky turf for a novelist—they so easily end up looking picturesque—but Vandenburgh's prose is bright and honest; and it triumphs. *Failure to Zigzag* introduces a writer of great daring and skill to match."

LAURA SHAPIRO

Charlotte, the teenage narrator of Jane Vandenburgh's splendid first novel, [*Failure to Zigzag,*] is trying hard not to grow up crazy. Her mother, Katrinka, is a mental patient virtually by profession: the carnival banner announcing her ventriloquism act reads "Katrinka L. W. Ainsworth, M.P." Meanwhile Charlotte's grandmother Winnie, who is raising her, breaks into screaming frenzies and throws turpentine, or frozen turkey, when life demands too much. "Charlotte thought of insanity as a thing in motion, like the nude in one of Winnie's artbooks," writes Vandenburgh. . . . Perhaps the most vivid of Vandenburgh's achievements is the seamless depiction of a madness at once funny and horrifying.

Charlotte's father died in a naval disaster after his ship was torpedoed by the Japanese, or so Charlotte was told; her search for the truth of his life and death has become an obsession. "Failure to zigzag" was the crime for which the ship's captain was court-martialed, and Charlotte is fearful of the same charge—failure to avoid destruction.

Vandenburgh's deeper subject is the underbrush of Charlotte's imagination, in which clashing emotions eventually find their own peaceable kingdom. Craziness and poignancy make risky turf for a novelist—they so easily end up looking picturesque—but Vandenburgh's prose is bright and honest; and it triumphs. *Failure to Zigzag* introduces a writer of great daring and skill to match.

Laura Shapiro, "In Search of a Peaceable Kingdom," in Newsweek, *Vol. CXIII, No. 14, April 3, 1989, p. 72.*

MARGOT MIFFLIN

Failure to zigzag, in the eyes of Charlotte, the teen-age heroine of Jane Vandenburgh's first novel, is failure to dupe the enemy; it's the mistake that resulted in the sinking of the U.S.S. Indianapolis in 1945, which, she's been told, caused her father's death before she was born. And in a larger sense, it's also her own greatest fear. Born to Katrinka, a mentally scrambled alcoholic, Charlotte is forced to tiptoe around the psychological land mines that can set her mother off at any given moment. . . . Charlotte is willing to tread dangerous turf—zigzagging when necessary—in her effort to extract a true version of her family history from the propriety-stricken grandparents who raised her and from Katrinka, who bounces between a mental institution and the traveling carnival in which she is a ventriloquist. Almost against her will, Charlotte appreciates the truth and humor in Katrinka's cutting condemnations of the normal world; even the imaginary, schizophrenia-induced characters who speak through her are mordantly funny. Likewise, Katrinka is sane enough to know that she's insane, a pathetic excuse for a mother, a woman whose efforts to conform are disastrous and whose inadequacies have wrestled her daughter into premature adulthood. In *Failure to Zigzag,* Charlotte and Katrinka are each other's best loves and heaviest burdens, and Jane Vandenburgh's depiction of their jagged, tangled lives, though slow moving at first, is superb.

> *Margot Mifflin, in a review of "Failure to Zigzag," in* The New York Times Book Review, *April 16, 1989, p. 21.*

RAYMOND SOKOLOV

Just as I was beginning to understand what my betters meant by literary minimalists, I have been hearing that the movement is petering out. This may or may not be true, but the concept has a paradoxical savor to it, since minimalism was so minimally energetic that one wonders how the literary trend spotters who first noticed it can now tell that it is slowing down.

Minimal pace, minimal emotional temperature, minimal characterization, minimal plot—all ended up reminding me of an empty toothpaste tube, nothing left but the brand name. And the minimalists did (or do—none has actually died except for Raymond Carver) depend heavily on brand names and the careful identification of characters' possessions to develop the fictional atmosphere of their works. There were basically two minimalist milieus; each of them definable automotively: the Volvo-driving yuppie world that produced Ann Beattie's wayward children and the pickup-driving, hillbilly lower depths of Bobbie Ann Mason.

If this is not the literary future you want, some real hope lies at hand in the form of Jane Vandenburgh's first novel, *Failure to Zigzag.*

Here is a book one is tempted to call maximalist, because it marches right into a mess of strong feelings in its story of three generations of a fallen-genteel Southern California family. It offers us rich portraits of four people, outstandingly that of Katrinka Ainsworth, bravely humorous, schizophrenic, ventriloquist and mom to the teen-age Charlotte.

The action takes place at many times in real history, ranging from Katrinka's college days as a campus bohemian at Berkeley in the '40s to Charlotte's high school years in the early '60s. This is done through flashbacks and chapters of Charlotte's childhood memories and also with Katrinka's extremely untrustworthy accounts of times before Charlotte was born. And at the center of these family "histories" and legends is the piecemeal story of how Charlotte's father died. This does eventually come into focus, along with much else, as Charlotte's own sense of things matures and when Katrinka surrenders the truth to her.

In a narrow sense, this process of Charlotte's coming of age and coming to terms with her family history of multiple insanity is what happens in *Failure to Zigzag.* And it is impossible not to speculate that it is autobiographically inspired. Ms. Vandenburgh lives in California and looks, in her jacket photo, to be the right age to have been Charlotte (otherwise, we are told only that her stories have appeared in *Redbook* and *Nimrod* and that she won a fiction prize in 1981). So there is no firm reason to connect her with her story except that it is so vividly set forth. Katrinka is a mother, it is one's indefensible reflex to observe, whom no one could have invented.

We meet her with Charlotte in a soda fountain in 1960. Charlotte is trying to talk her mother out of a paranoid fantasy while they eat ice cream and Katrinka "sharpened the ash of her cigarette on the rim of the little plate where her rainbow sherbet sat in a steel goblet, untouched, melting." Katrinka, it seems, has been claiming that psychiatrists have been following her in threesomes.

> "Why threes, Mom?" Charlotte asks. . . . "Why would they want to be so noticeable, Mom? . . .
>
> Katrinka put the cigarette out with a hiss in the puddle that had formed beneath the sweating goblet. "That, sweetie, is just my point," she said, taking another cigarette out of the pack. "They want me to notice them, obviously. They want me to notice them and to fall in love with them." She lit the cigarette, then squinted at Charlotte through the smoke. "But," she exhaled, "I prefer not to get involved."

Charlotte objects. The story doesn't make any sense.

> "Well, really!" Katrinka was still poised with one eye squeezed shut. "What is it that you want me to tell you? That the psychiatrists of the state of California are following me in cars in sets of threes because they are trying to drive me crazy? Do you realize, Charlotte, that every other mental patient on Ward G-1 in the state hospital at Camarillo thinks the doctors are conspiring to drive her crazy?"
>
> "But not you, right?" Charlotte asked.
>
> Katrinka tipped her chin up. "I am," she announced, "much more original than that."

This is the tone of the book, every line set up as carefully for humorous effect as a stand-up comic's routine and yet every line a cover for unspeakable wretchedness. Katrinka is an awful mother. She brings her daughter up in squalor. She cooks the most horrible concoctions. But I doubt anyone will have trouble understanding why Charlotte is deeply drawn to her mother. Ms. Vandenburgh sees astonishingly far into this complicated pair.

Recently, I saw an angry letter from the head of an organization that defends the insane. How could anyone admire a film *(The Dream Team)* that told an uplifting and amusing story about the lives of mental patients? he asked. In his view, insanity was one monochromatic grimness, pathetic and sad and that was that. *Failure to Zigzag* is far from slapstick, but it never reduces its characters to one-dimensional mental "cases." This is a sad book cast in the rhetoric of comedy. It could easily be a powerful film. It is already an important novel.

> *Raymond Sokolov, "A Crazy, 'Maximalist' Tale," in* The Wall Street Journal, *May 9, 1989, p. A20.*

An excerpt from *Failure to Zigzag*

"Put that away," Katrinka said, waving one imperious hand. "I'm the mother around here and this is my treat." She said this grimly, out of the side of her mouth like a gun moll. She was busy now stacking the coins in a new way: quarters with quarters, dimes with dimes.

"Mom, really!" Charlotte said.

"Really really," Katrinka retorted, going on then in ventriloquy: "Now, I will be the judge of all this and all that, of who is and is not the mother around here, and of all things Nellie-ish and Tweedyish and all things monetary!" This voice was deep, male, authoritarian. It was Ogamer, Katrinka's old man character. She hadn't brought the dummies into the soda fountain that day, but the voices were with her always, except for when she could be persuaded to take her medication.

"All right!" Charlotte said. She did want the dollars, which still looked new. She liked the heft of them and the soft, deep shine that made them seem more valuable than paper dollars. Still, taking money from her mother, who was so poor she sometimes got public assistance, made Charlotte's skin crawl. Her whole epidermis, including her scalp, seemed to lift, to move. The skin was itself an organ, she knew, the one designed for the specific purpose of differentiation, to keep the self of a person in from the outside world. Was it scientifically possible, she wondered, for a human being to molt like a crab or snake?

"Anyway that Jew bastard Sugarman has given me my job back at his lousy crappy flea circus, so you don't have to worry about me on the subject of mun-mun."

"All right!" Charlotte said again, her flesh still crawling. She looked at the underside of either arm, where her skin felt like it was about to break out in hives.

Looking up from this self-appraisal, she noticed her mother's thin fingers gathering the coins. Katrinka's money was terrible to look at. It was clotted with some dark gunk into which were stuck the shreds of tobacco that always collected in the recesses of her pocketbook. Charlotte inclined her head, observing her own hands, which lay poised in her lap with the fingers curled and the palms turned upward. At times like this her hands tended to ache, pulsing in the center. She was always surprised that the act of leave-taking could cause such a physical and specifically martyrish pain.

"Oh, Lord God! *Now* what have I done?" Katrinka cried out, but Charlotte's mouth, gasping, gaping open, watering, couldn't speak to reassure her. She couldn't speak nor raise her aching hands, nor do anything at all aside from moving her heavy head slowly from side to side. As she cried, Charlotte kept her eyes tightly shut. She did this to try to keep her tears in, to keep her soul in, and to save herself from the sight of these, her gifts: her mother and her mother's dirty money.

ELAINE S. APTHORP

[Charlotte, the heroine of *Failure to Zigzag*,] is immersed in a swirling mysterious strangeness, negotiating unhappily between the wild dark foliage of childhood/mother and the cold bright prospect of adulthood alone in mainstream America.

Failure to Zigzag concerns an Anglo-American family in California, but the young girl Charlotte is, if possible, even more alienated and culturally at sea than Marisol [the protagonist of *The Line of the Sun* by Judith Orliz Cofer]. Her schizophrenic mother's teachings are hopelessly tangled in madness and her grandparents, Lionel and Winnie, are crazier in their separate ways than her mother. It is implied that Lionel was broken mentally as well as professionally by the Depression, that he abused his daughter sexually, and that he has wandered towards this course with his granddaughters.

Charlotte is recognizable as Lionel's and Winnie's granddaughter

> because of the kinds of things they made her wear . . . Other kids in Charlotte's school who had dead parents or other similar tragedies all wore the same sorts of crappy things. Even if they did dress in a more normal, teenaged way, Charlotte could pick them out by their dour, shadowed, defiant faces, or by the scared look that made their eyes jump, as if they expected to be criticized momentarily. Having no parents, she had decided, was like coming to school every day as an immigrant from a foreign country.

At sea in a family culture her public schooling renders her unable to interpret, or stranded in a world empty and drab, where the deep-layered family culture, her emotional center, is invisible and unacknowledged, Charlotte's alone either way—included only as she chooses, and clings with fitful loyalty to, a dark alliance with the outcast schizophrenic mother. Like Marisol, who chooses to claim the wild uncle Guzmán as her spiritual parent, her chosen allegiance is a symbolic affirmation of the values she chooses to live by, regardless of the opinions of those around her. Though aliens both within and outside their own family culture, Charlotte and Marisol learn there—within the family heritage that, wielded by others, threatens to submerge them—the skills needed to negotiate their aloneness in the larger world. Separation frees them of the fear that they will be submerged by the mother's will and the culture's expectations. Each creates her own acceptance through compassionate understanding and imaginative selection, choosing at will the characteristics of their parents that are healing, rejecting those that damage. And each is able to sing her own song when she has sung her mother's.

Charlotte grows up almost exactly as her mother did, "in the dusty same house, being raised by the same people who raised her mother and in the same lousy way," charted for a third generation of insanity. The question haunting her is whether it is possible for her to avoid her mother's fate, to break the cycle and emerge into the clear, bracing light of sanity and uncorrupted love, to achieve the normalcy she wistfully admires in other teenagers. But she is haunted by the tale her grandparents told her to explain her father's death—the sinking of the *Indianapolis* at the end of World War Two, in which, they tell her, her father drowned. She fantasizes intensely about that awful three-day disaster at sea, the lonely, hopeless sailors drowning each other and themselves, one by one, as they bobbed alone in the sea a thousand miles from oblivious aid: the *Indianapolis* disaster—caused, it was alleged, by the ship's "failure to zigzag" in its course to keep out of moonlight that made it a visible target for submarines—becomes a symbol of Charlotte's own fear that she is doomed to sink in the elements of her environment.

The incident casts its thick shadows on Charlotte's waking thoughts, signifying for her her own helpless vulnerability, and the wretched loneliness that causes human beings like Lionel and Winnie to drag down with them all that they touch, like the abandoned sailors who, driven mad by exposure and despair, "tried on the first day to help one another . . . lost heart on the second day and began to kill themselves, and on the third day began to kill one another." The narrative abounds in imagery of that cold open sea, summoned whenever Charlotte is threatened by the intensity and ambivalence of her own feelings: in the heat of sexual arousal, the "voice broke up, wrecked by the swells of feeling"; desperate to turn off her awareness of Katrinka during one of her mother's mad monologues, Charlotte

> put her head down and rested the skin of her cheek right on the sticky tabletop. Sleep swam up. It was a yawning cavern, black and noisy as a sea cave, where the waves crashed, sucked at her, pulled her outward toward an ocean filled with bodies . . .

But "Charlotte herself was weightless—it was the twin stones of her two dark parents who'd always made her sink." They had all been doomed, it seems to Charlotte, because "they had all failed to zigzag," and have been held responsible for their suffering just as Charlotte bitterly imagines raped young girls are responsible for their violation—having failed to zigzag, when no such precautions would've saved them.

The novel is strongest in the earlier sections, when Charlotte is neck deep in her childhood perplexity, the fantastic boredom of her only-childhood alone in the house with the endless monologues of her grandparents, a boredom haunting and fascinating when conveyed, as Vandenburgh conveys it, with the intense particularity and emotional resonance of a child's impressions. She describes an object of interminable childhood study, her grandfather's feet:

> His toes were long and expressive of emotions, wriggling in satisfaction at the good parts of a story, or curling in on themselves in an attitude of supplication as the time drew near to lunch. The pads of his feet were rosy, and rosy, too, were the balls and heel . . . Back when Charlotte had still loved her grandfather, she'd enjoyed her detailed examination of these well-tended feet, which did seem like twin characters to her, other members of the family.

The neurotic Lionel and Winnie are wonderfully realized characters. The reader is borne into Charlotte's life with them through a supple narrative voice which slips easily into the cadence and idiom of the grandparents. Lionel's pronouncements are rendered in a grave, self-satisfied abstraction ("Lionel believed his long and shapely feet were a sign of his good breeding . . . It was possible, he said, to tell much about a person from his feet and the state of his shoeleather . . . Lionel did not himself wear shoes in the house since he felt it was the right of his feet to be allowed to breathe"), while Winnie's hysterical bitterness and sexual paranoia are rendered in logical gaps and wild shifts in subject, sudden italics and exclamation points:

> *I have not had a vacation in forty years!* Winnie was screaming. Charlotte was going to Marlborough! she was going as a *boarder!* she was going there to learn to act like less of a slut and whore! Winnie knew all about Charlotte's little secrets, Winnie was going on, all about the sorts of things she

wrapped up in brown paper lunch sacks and carried out to the fire to burn! She knew about Charlotte's filthy things and secret things and the wrapped-up halves of liverwurst sandwiches and other pieces of perfectly decent food! Everything that had ever happened to her was Charlotte's *own damned fault!*

Her life with them is as bitterly hilarious as Katrinka's ironic dialogues with the exacting voices in her head, which are Winnie's and Lionel's voices after all, for "Lionel and Winnie did not so much converse as each deliver the same monologue over and over. The major difference between them and Katrinka, Charlotte had decided, was that when they talked to themselves someone else was usually in the room."

The richest sections of the novel describe Charlotte's long wait for union with her mother. Scenes in which Charlotte visits Katrinka during her hospitalizations evoke the ambivalence of her love for a mother who can never take care of herself, much less her daughter:

> They held hands, though Charlotte could hardly bear to do so, so aware was she of the delicacy of the bones of her mother's fingers. She had understood this fragility since birth, it seemed. She understood it: she had not forgiven her. She held her mother's fingers lightly in her own, in order not to harm them, but the knowledge that they would be so simply crushed made her want to squeeze them harder. She could kill her mother, she'd always known, using nothing more than the strength of her love. . . .

[The] imaginative waiting is more powerful than the climactic passages toward the end, when the hoped-for reunions take place and the bonding's anguished incompleteness leaves each with the consolidated burden of adulthood. . . .

[The] natural negotiation between self and world is experienced as the struggle to become the center of one's own life. As Nancy Chodorow has suggested in *The Reproduction of Mothering,* this struggle is especially painful for the female child. She, no less than her brothers, demands that mother center her existence in her children's needs. As the young girl discovers her own femaleness (her likeness to the mother), she internalizes society's demand that she center her life in the fulfillment of others and holds herself responsible for the demands made of her (and, indeed, for *everything* that happens around her). The . . . young girls of these novels discover themselves in a slow process of differentiation from and reconciliation with the mother/femaleness, and with the cultures in which they are embedded by birth.

The process of maturation . . . involves developing enough detachment to perceive that the unresponsiveness of the mother is an effect of her own suffering, and of the distortions and stunting of character which that suffering has caused, not a response to her child's acts or failures to act, her qualities or lack of qualities. Each author invites the reader to experience both the particularity of her character's struggle and its largeness and resonance for the struggle of all. The particularity of alienated, neurotic Anglo-Americans in California . . . [as depicted in **Failure to Zigzag,**] opens the larger problem of family culture in tension with surrounding society, the question of when—if ever—the givenness of one's circumstances leaves off and one's individual choices begin. (p. 32)

Elaine S. Apthorp, "Coming of Age in America," in

The Women's Review of Books, *Vol. VI, Nos. 10-11, July, 1989, pp. 31-2.*

HELEN DUDAR

A first novel, *Failure to Zigzag* was published this spring [1989] to the sort of reviews that could not have been improved by hired blurb-writers. ("Superb," the *New York Times* [see excerpt above]; "An important novel," The *Wall Street Journal* [see excerpt above]). But before the manuscript fell into the hands of North Point—and sat there unread for six months—fully 23 fairly high-powered New York practitioners of agentry declined the chance to draw the standard 10% or 15% cut of its earnings. . . .

Failure to Zigzag sat on the slush pile in the office of Kate Moses for six months before she found a moment to pick it up. As Jack Shoemaker, the editor in chief [at North Point], would later tell it, his office adjoins hers, and for three days the sound from next door was laughter. Then Mr. Shoemaker read the manuscript and on May 13, 1987, phoned to say he was buying it. Ms. Vandenburgh, who was in bed nursing a severe virus infection, got up and drank champagne with her husband. After that, a lot of time and energy went into guiding a grateful author through serious revisions. When she asked for changes in the proofs, they were granted, and nobody even mentioned that, as she well knew, they would cost the company several thousand dollars.

Everything since has been gravy. The book is in its second printing. Avon has outbid four other houses for the paperback rights. Three film makers want the novel. The *Zigzag* reprint will appear next spring when Ms. Vandenburgh's second novel is published. It was written during those bad days before she found a publisher for her first novel. This second book, produced at her word processor as a form of revenge, is called *The Physics of Sunset.* It's about a Berkeley architect whose marriage is falling apart. Ms. Vandenburgh also is finishing up a third volume of fiction, a collection of related short pieces more overtly autobiographical than the two novels. . . .

[*Failure to Zigzag*] deals with a number of things, including the oppressive condition of childhood. Her protagonist, Charlotte, sometimes lives with her grandparents, Lionel and Winnie, who are textbook models of California-style self-absorption, and sometimes with her mother, Katrinka, an alcoholic schizophrenic ventriloquist who works carnivals. Katrinka hears voices and uses them to animate her dummies. Is there a better way to describe the art of writing fiction?

The book is set in Southern California where Ms. Vandenburgh grew up, the only girl among seven boys. Her father was a Lockheed executive, her mother a frustrated writer. She says that one of her brothers identified Katrinka as a portrait of "his" mother, but that's not quite what she intended. Having listened for years to the complaints of her woman friends and remembering her own rages, she merely set out to create the Great American Awful Mom at her most extreme—"the mother out of hell," as she puts it. The novel would be unbearable were it not for the grace of the writing and the fact that it is desperately funny.

It would also be less successful, less engaging if its author did not suffer a useful failing. "The fact is, I can't tell the truth," she said, dimpling up. "The truth is boring. That's the reason I'm a fiction writer. I start writing and I think, 'Well, let's put that in.' I jazz it up. And when I do, it's better."

Helen Dudar, "Jane Vandenburgh, Literary Self-Help Success Story," in The Wall Street Journal, *July 11, 1989, p. A18.*

Robert McLiam Wilson

Ripley Bogle

Wilson is an Irish novelist, born in 1964.

Ripley Bogle is an exuberant, first-person account of four days in the life of a twenty-one-year-old homeless man. Each chapter encompasses a day and begins with a vivid description of Bogle's surroundings. Bogle intersperses extended reminiscences of his past with detailed reports on his physical and mental state as he wanders around London looking for food, cigarettes, and alcohol. In exaggeratedly baroque language, Bogle recounts his impoverished, brutal childhood in a violent district of Belfast, Northern Ireland, his eviction from home at a young age, his brief career as a student at Cambridge University, and his return to vagrancy. Some critics found Wilson's swaggering, intensely self-conscious, and ultimately insane, narrator unsympathetic. Many others, however, applauded Wilson's unflagging verbal energy and wit, and his linguistic daring has been compared to that of James Joyce and Martin Amis. Peter Reading commented: "This ebullient, grotesque début is at times rather irritatingly affected in its unashamed eclecticism. . . . But the prevalent quality is haunting and horrific, an updated Thomsonian portrayal of nocturnal dreadfulness in the metropolis."

JANE DORRELL

Believe it or not, *Ripley Bogle* gets under your skin. We meet Robert Wilson's foul-mouthed young tramp when he is 'doing hand-to-hand with hypothermia' on a bench in St James's Park. He is, he tells us, 'better educated, better looking and a nicer person than the Queen . . . and yet I'm still starving to death in her front garden'. From a Thursday to Sunday in June we accompany this arrogant, articulate, self-styled 'Prince of the Pavements' as he strides around London keeping cold and hunger at bay while regaling us with the story of his birth (his recollection of which is all too vivid), his childhood in Belfast, his scholarship to Cambridge and the disasters of his career as an undergraduate which led to his present plight. The narrative, a compelling mix of the vernacular (to put it politely) and Joycean invention, such as 'youthjuiced', 'nighttwinkle city', and a 'pavement carpeted with the muckyslippyslurrysludge of a boytrodden rainy schoolday' leaps every so often into startling and shocking life. There is a tarring-and-feathering which leads directly to his father's death; his betrayal of a school-friend to the IRA; his confrontation with a murderous tramp by the Serpentine which looks as though it might lead to his own early end as Ripley is not into anything so mundane as getting stitches put into a knife wound. But it is not all cold and black. The Cambridge scenes are very funny, especially the May Week Ball as seen through Ripley's jaundiced eye and his interview with

the elderly don who has seen it all before and who outcools this particular rebel hands down, much to his chagrin. When our four days are up, this ancient mariner has us in thrall. [*Ripley Bogle*] is both comic, and, in the true sense of the word, awful.

Jane Dorrell, in a review of "Ripley Bogle," in Books, London, No. 2, May, 1989, p. 18.

JEREMY LEWIS

Written in a kind of punk prose that combines familiar echoes of Joyce and Donleavy (including composite words like "herdhappy", "river-dribble" or—for the roar as closing time draws near—"pubbub") with more than a dash of Nigel Molesworth, Robert McLiam Wilson's entertaining if overblown first novel, [*Ripley Bogle*], is remarkable for the boisterous comicality of the writing, and for its exact and often unwholesome renderings of, in particular, Irish patterns of speech ("Here, fellas, hold the fort now. I'm going down to the latrines for a slurp. Defecation's the name of the game").

Descended from "the usual cast list of subhuman Gaelic scumbuckets" and brought up on the Falls Road in Belfast, Ripley Bogle is a 21 year old tramp, now practising in London after an uneasy spell as a Cambridge undergraduate. The action of the novel is set over four days in June, during the course of which Ripley stumps about the city, from Bloomsbury to Putney and from Kilburn to Kensington, suffering all the while from cold, heat, a chronic shortage of fags and "dosh", vividly evoked intestinal and digestive complaints and a suppurating knife wound incurred during a fight with a fellow down-and-out; and as he moves from place to place,

Wilson, Robert McLiam describing—at too great a length—the life he leads and the tramp's eye view of London, he relives, rather more successfully, scenes from his turbulent, monster-haunted youth.

Despite his present circumstances and his unfortunate beginnings—mum, "a real old rolling fatbag", was on the game, while dad "once tried to disembowel me with a broken Bass bottle", had a drink problem, and ended his days being gunned down by the IRA—Ripley was a precocious, clever child, mastering the Great Victorians at an early age and driving Mr Sansom the science master apoplectic with rage after carrying the day in a Molesworth-like dispute over whether or not copper is a mineral.

Murkier elements in Ripley's past include—or do they?—the betrayal of his best friend to the IRA and impregnation of Deirdre, a Protestant—for which he is expelled from the family home, taking with him *Hard Times,* a pair of grubby underpants and a lump of Ulster Cheddar. . . .

It has to be said that Ripley the "dribblestained" tramp is something of a windbag, altogether more tedious—and less persuasive—than Ripley the demon schoolboy or Ripley the sardonic undergrad: one begins to weary of the state of his innards, and his editor might usefully have removed adverbs of the kind that are hard put to earn their keep in speech, let alone in print ("incredibly", "indescribably").

That said, by far and away the best scene in the book [*Ripley Bogle*]—indeed a masterpiece of comic writing—is set in a Kilburn pub, where Bogle overindulges and finds himself swept away in a kind of comic nightmare not far removed from the Nighttown scene in *Ulysses:* a far—and welcome—cry from the anaemic niceties of all too many modern novels.

Jeremy Lewis, "Tramp's Eye View," in New Statesman & Society, *Vol. 2, No. 51, May 26, 1989, p. 37.*

MICHAEL DIBDIN

This tramp approaches you. He wants to tell you his life story. He, and it, are called *Ripley Bogle.* Born in a Belfast slum, he has hauled himself up by his own bootlaces to obtain a Cambridge scholarship, only to be sent down as an irredeemable yob.

Robert McLiam Wilson relates these experiences in the form of epiphanic anecdotes embedded in an account of Bogle's present life tramping about London. The glimpses of growing up in Troubled Ulster are quite interesting but you can't wait to get away, because—for all his eagerness to please and impress—he has that familiar, sickly-sweet odour of the rhetoric of excess. Yep, he's been at the Martin Amis: triple restatements, mordant litotes, personification of diseases and moods, chirpy nonce-words, idioms run ragged, elided nouns—all the tell-tale signs are there. And that's not all. He's got gobs of Joyce all over him, he's flashing his Dylan Thomas and Rogeting himself fit to bust. Pity, really. He seems quite a decent bloke and might be worth knowing if only he cleaned himself up and stayed off the books.

Michael Dibdin, "Bombs in the Heart," in The Observer, *May 28, 1989, p. 46.*

An excerpt from *Ripley Bogle*

I don't quite know why I bother with all this balls-aching fire and semi-satire. It doesn't really suit me and I'm not terribly good at it. I *was* very good at being cruel and offensive when I was younger. I had a flair for spite and blind condemnation. It all seemed such a good idea then, such a useful weapon and tool. Now, it seems feeble. A demi-truth—the hard half of nothing.

History seems to have come to something of a stop for me. I opted out. I stepped off and bedded down in the crisp comfort of my own failure and decline. I just capitulated to the world and slipped away as silently and unobtrusively as I could manage. Here I am and happy to be so. I haven't been indoors at all this year. Terrible, isn't it? My muscles and sinews wither from abuse and overtime. My flesh is paling to grey with warmthlessness. I'm much more than a simple tramp. I'm a claustrophobic, a hermit, a prophet, a loser, a cipher! Bejabbers, I'm a symbol of the age! Big deal, suits me well enough.

Now, I *used* to be a success of sorts. I used to be a wiseman, a moneyed, fêted, soughtafter man. Now I'm nothing. Nobody knows me and I barely exist. I'm going the way of all flesh, i.e. fading into reality. The day before yesterday's man.

Happily though, I have at least given up lying, carping and griping. I'm keeping an eye on my invective. I've declined the gage of youth and endeavour. I've backed out of that modern, worldly brawl. It seemed only such a waste of time and I have a lot on my mind these days. I have a kind of purpose now, you see. (Portents, mystery, strange apparitions!) I'm on a quest, you might say. It sounds absurd, I know, but what can a poor boy do? Here in my poverty and my shame, amongst the debris of my aspirations and the rubble of my talents. I have a kind of purpose.

This is for what my story is. This is the sly map from which I shall exhume my goal, my task and treasure. This is where we are all going. You, me and my story (such as it is). That quest. My search for final, fundamental goodness in the world.

There were and are such things as truth, honour, wisdom and beauty to be had. It is just that they are difficult to find. They are furtive and wary of the clamp of recognition, of that proof and loss of faith. They are succubi among the contented evils of nowadays. But that is what I want. That's my base requirement. What other should there be? The evidence and residue of goodness in this one world.

(More, more, pile it on.)

JOANNA PORTER

Like Beckett's Estragon and Vladimir, Ripley Bogle is a literary tramp with time on his hands, and in the tradition of his forebears he attempts to solve the problem with words, words, words. He has a painfully extensive vocabulary which he attributes to having read Dickens and Thackeray at age five. 'Perhaps,' he muses, 'that's why my style is so florid, so rotund, so fucking courtly.' Whatever happened to W. H. Davies?

Bogle is a self-proclaimed man of rare talents, fostered by a 'leprous and deadly' childhood in Belfast—or Belfastard, as he prefers. We learn of his education at a string of Catholic schools from which this 'colon-busting prodigy' is systematically expelled, on one occasion for allegedly positing obscene liaisons between spiral staircases and pots of jam. Yet despite the inauspicious start, not to mention the turmoil of a puberty accomplished in one week (hence nickname 'zoompubes') he manages to gain a place at Cambridge to read English. Bogle sends up university and is finally sent down, ending in 'tramp city' London. Adrift amidst its 'faecal matter, cess, garbage, scum, detritus, slime, sick and general track and turds', he ruminates upon his bowels, 'autonomic snot and catarrh' and chances of getting cancer, inventing past love affairs and lengthily recounting various 'sorties into the world of the homeless'.

Ripley Bogle is commanding when describing vile, vivid terrorist atrocities but has an awful weakness for the never-use-one-word-when-three-will-do anecdote. He is exhausting and unrewarding company and also—it transpires—seriously deranged; the depravities he committed in Ireland are only fully confessed at the end of the novel, obliging us to reappraise events which when first described showed him as victim rather than victimiser. This interesting narrative device will of course be wasted on readers lacking the stamina to see Bogle through to his bitter end. This onerous book left me with the feeling of having been cornered in some sub-Joycean bar by an articulate liar for an entire evening.

Joanna Porter, "A Gentleman of the Road," in The Listener, *Vol. 121, No. 3117, June 8, 1989, p. 27.*

ZACHARY LEADER

Robert McLiam Wilson was born in 1964, which means that ***Ripley Bogle,*** his first novel, was written in his early twenties. The novel's qualities are those of immodest youth: it is ambitious, energetic, self absorbed, bursting with hormonal vehemence and self-consciousness. Structure and sequence (or plot) are not its strong points. The good bits are bits, hit you straight on, and mostly have to do with the narrator-protagonist, his wishes, delusions, comical pretensions and embarrassments. No one else gets much of a look-in, and those who do—parents briefly, a school friend, first loves, a mentor—are perfunctorily, instrumentally rendered: they matter because of the way Ripley reacts to them. All this is quite openly, cheerfully admitted on the narrator's part, and is meant to be indulged. Whether it will be, though, depends upon one's tolerance for the narrative voice, a voice which is startlingly familiar. Here is a representative passage:

> It suddenly comes to me that I am hungry. Well, perhaps 'hungry' is not quite the right word. Bowelwitheringly fucking ravenous might well be a more just and measured phrase to describe what I

am currently experiencing. All right, so I'm a young man and, no doubt, prone to the overstatement of youth but this is the real thing.

The voice here is like that of Martin Amis, whose mark is all over this novel, not just in the muscular, shouldering prose style—the style of John Self—but in Ripley's rich tangle of adolescent preoccupations, his Charles Highway-like obsession with bodily products ('matutinal lungbung' in particular), with his own appearance ('My tasty eyes . . . Much is the womanly bullshit that has been spouted about my eyes'), with 'knowing' ('My word,' Ripley announces at one point, 'isn't all this relentless self-awareness bracing?'). If you don't like or approve of this sort of thing—some people simply haven't the stomach for it—you won't get on with the novel at all. If you do, you'll still have trouble, since you'll be forced into diminishing comparisons. These Wilson has himself courted—with typical heedlessness—but he ought not to be sunk by them completely. ***Ripley Bogle*** isn't as good a novel as [Martin Amis's] *The Rachel Papers,* let alone *Money,* but its author has talent and nerve.

Like his creator, Ripley was born in West Belfast, though the novel opens in London on the eve of his 22nd birthday. Ripley lucks and talents his way out of childhood squalor and neglect, winning a place at Cambridge. There, after much posturing, he is sent down and then dumped by his girlfriend, ending up adrift in London—a cool and stylist (if rather thinly motivated) tramp. Ripley's history of rise and fall alternates with lengthy descriptive passages detailing the life of the London streets. Each chapter begins in a different borough or district, elaborately pictured, and then moves on either to Ripley's recollections or extended tramp anecdotes—a pub brawl, a stabbing, soup-kitchen charity. Some of the tramp-lore (how to keep warm, where to kip, which is the tramp's best season) is authentic-sounding; of the memories, the most successful are those that have to do with Belfast and the troubles, for these show that Wilson can frighten—even move—as well as dazzle and disarm. Two scenes of sectarian violence are especially gripping, and quite unlike the rest of the novel, in that they take Ripley outside himself. Such moments, together with the style's sure rhythms and vivid particulars, suggest that Wilson is a writer worth watching—for all the present novel's indebtedness and clamouring, bumptious self-regard.

Zachary Leader, "Down and Out in London and Amis," in London Review of Books, *Vol. 11, No. 12, June 22, 1989, p. 15.*

PETER READING

Ripley Bogle, Robert McLiam Wilson's first novel, is written in a style that looks like a mixture of Flann O'Brien, Martin Amis and J. D. Salinger. The titular hero, a young Belfast-born down-and-out, homeless in London, is the narrator. Four days of exuberant squalor, violence, hunger and drunkenness are lovingly charted, while, in a series of autobiographical flashbacks, Bogle's career is traced, from his unpromising birth and Ulster childhood, through his adolescent amatory vagaries, to his Cambridge entrance (and exit) and subsequent decline to feculent vagrancy. . . . The O'Brien influence is an attractive, fanciful gusto which carries the reader compulsively along—a manic energy (but without O'Brien's inventive craziness) reaching its climax in a dipso fantasy-choreography for ghoul, ghost and ghastly Irish piss-head in a Hibernian exiles' London boozer.

The medium [in **Ripley Bogle**] is most of the message. Apart from a bit of thought-provoking documentary on homeless-ness and some reflections on the "Troubles", nothing much happens or is achieved. Wilson's stance, towards, for exam-ple, the sectarian inanities of his internecine countrymen is common-sensed and humanitarian. There's an affectingly compassionate account of an old dosser's demise, and some casual, raunchy wisdom—"combining the act and fact of ten-derness and rutting is a difficult task, achieved only through great study and application".

This ebullient, grotesque début is at times rather irritatingly affected in its unashamed eclecticism (for example, there's a sustained, pointless, sub-Joycean glueing together of words—"brightstoned", "scantleaved", "trampnights", "mattblack", "toesharp", "blackandbrown", "betterthangood"). But the prevalent quality is haunting and horrific, an updated Thom-sonian portrayal of nocturnal dreadfulness in the metropolis: "The night is disfigured and obscene. Noise. Darkness. Hell. Everywhere you go, people are shouting, laughing, scream-ing, weeping without restraint. The faces you see are dead-ened and blank, murdered by drink and feeble lust."

Peter Reading, "Dosserology," in The Times Liter-ary Supplement, *No. 4503, July 21-27, 1989, p. 804.*

Prizewinners

Literary Prizes and Honors

Announced in 1989

•Academy of American Poets Awards•

Fellowship of the Academy of American Poets

Awarded annually to recognize distinguished achievement by an American poet.

Richard Howard

The Lamont Poetry Selection

Established in 1952 to reward and encourage promising writers by supporting the publication of an American poet's second book.

Minnie Bruce Pratt
Crime against Nature

Peter I. B. Lavan Younger Poets Award

Established in 1983 to annually recognize three accomplished American poets under the age of forty.

Melissa Green
Jeffrey Harrison
William Logan

Walt Whitman Award

Secures the publication of the first book of a living American poet.

Martha Hollander
The Game of Statues

•American Academy and Institute of Arts and Letters Awards•

Academy-Institute Awards

Given annually to encourage creative achievement in art, music, and literature.

Awards in Literature
Richard Ford, Martin Greenberg
Ron Hansen, Herbert Morris
Gregory Rabassa, David R. Slavitt
Arturo Vivante, Joy Williams

Witter Bynner Foundation Prize for Poetry

Established in 1979 and awarded annually to recognize an outstanding younger poet.

Mary Jo Salter

Sue Kaufman Prize for First Fiction

Awarded annually to the best first fiction published during the preceding year.

Gary Krist
The Garden State

Rome Fellowship in Literature

Established in 1951 to recognize young writers of promise, a year's residence at the American Academy in Rome is awarded annually.

Bob Shacochis

Richard and Hilda Rosenthal Foundation Award

Awards given annually for accomplishment in art and literature. The literature award recognizes a work of fiction published in the preceding year which, while not a "commercial success," is considered a literary achievement.

James Robison
The Illustrator

Jean Stein Award

An award is presented annually to recognize a writer of either fiction, nonfiction, or poetry, in alternating years.

Rodney Jones
(poetry)

Morton Dauwen Zabel Award

Presented in alternating years to poets, fiction writers, and critics, to encourage progressive, original, and experimental tendencies in American literature.

C. K. Williams
(poet)

•James Tait Black Memorial Book Prize•

Sponsored by the University of Edinburgh and awarded annually for the best work of fiction and the best biography published during the previous year.

Piers Paul Read
A Season in the Mist
(fiction)

•Bollingen Prize in Poetry•

Administered by Yale University Library, this prize is awarded biennially to recognize the best collection by one or more living American poets.

Edgar Bowers
For Louis Pasteur

•Booker Prize for Fiction•

Britain's major literary prize is awarded annually in recognition of a full-length novel.

Kazuo Ishiguro
The Remains of the Day
(see entry below)

•Georg Büchner Prize•

Awarded annually by the German Academy of Language and Poetry to recognize writers whose works further the cultural heritage of Germany.

Botho Strauss

•Commonwealth Writers Prize•

Awarded annually to promote new Commonwealth fiction of merit outside the author's country of origin.

Marina Warner
The Lost Father
(see entry below)

•Goncourt Prize•

Awarded annually in France by the Academie Goncourt to recognize a prose work published during the preceding year.

Jean Vautrin
Un grand pas vers le Bon Dieu

•Governor General's Literary Awards•

To honor writing that achieves literary excellence without sacrificing popular appeal, awards are given annually in the categories of prose fiction, prose nonfiction, poetry, and drama. Officially known as the Canadian Authors Association (CAA) Literary Awards.

Erin Mouré
Furious
(poetry)

David Adams Richards
Nights below Station Street
(fiction)
(see entry below)

George F. Walker
Nothing Sacred
(drama)
(see *CLC,* Vol. 61)

•Drue Heinz Literature Prize•

Established in 1980 to recognize and encourage the writing of short fiction, this annual award is given by the University of Pittsburgh Press.

Maya Sonenberg
Cartographies

•Hugo Awards•

Established in 1953 to recognize notable science fiction works in several categories.

C. J. Cherryh
Cyteen
(novel)

Connie Willis
The Last of the Winnebagos
(novella)

George Alec Effinger
Schrödinger's Kitten
(novelette)

Mike Resnick
"Kirinyaga"
(short story)

•Ruth Lilly Poetry Prize•

Awarded annually to an outstanding American poet.

Mona Van Duyn

•Lenore Marshall/*Nation* Poetry Prize•

Established in 1974 to honor the author of the year's outstanding collection of poems published in the United States.

Thomas McGrath
Selected Poems: 1938-1988
(see entry below)

•Los Angeles Times Book Awards•

Awards are given to authors in various categories to honor outstanding technique and vision.

Fay Weldon
The Heart of the Country
(fiction)
(see entry below)

Donald Hall
The One Day: A Poem in Three Parts
(poetry)
(see entry below)

•National Book Awards•

Established in 1950 to honor and promote American books of literary distinction in the categories of fiction and nonfiction.

John Casey
Spartina
(fiction)
(see entry below)

•National Book Critics Circle Awards•

Founded in 1974, this American award recognizes superior literary quality in several categories.

Bharati Mukherjee
The Middleman and Other Stories
(fiction)
(see *CLC,* Vol. 53)

Donald Hall
The One Day: A Poem in Three Parts
(poetry)
(see entry below)

•Nebula Awards•

Established in 1965 to honor significant works in several categories of science fiction published in the United States.

Lois McMaster Bujold
Falling Free
(novel)

Connie Willis
The Last of the Winnebagos
(novella)

George Alec Effinger
Schrödinger's Kitten
(novelette)

James Morrow
"Bible Stories for Adults, No. 17: The Deluge"
(short story)

Ray Bradbury
(grand master award)

•New York Drama Critics Circle Award•

Awards are presented annually in several categories to encourage excellence in playwriting.

Wendy Wasserstein
The Heidi Chronicles
(best play)
(see entry below)

Brian Friel
Aristocrats
(best foreign play)
(see entry below)

•Nobel Prize in Literature•

Awarded annually to recognize the most distinguished body of literary work of an idealistic nature.

Camilo José Cela
(see entry below)

•Obie Award•

Awards in various categories are given annually to recognize excellence in off-Broadway and off-off-Broadway theater productions.

No award given for playwriting in 1989.

•PEN American Center Awards•

Ernest Hemingway Foundation Award

Awarded annually to encourage the publication of first fiction by young American authors.

Jane Hamilton
The Book of Ruth

Faulkner Award for Fiction

Annually recognizes the most distinguished book-length work of fiction by an American writer published during the calendar year.

James Salter
Dusk and Other Stories
(see entry below)

•Edgar Allan Poe Awards•

Mystery Writers of America awards these prizes annually in recognition of outstanding contributions in mystery, crime, and suspense writing.

Hillary Waugh
(grand master)

Joan Kahn
(lifetime achievement)

Stuart M. Kaminsky
A Cold Red Sunrise
(best novel)
(see entry below)

•Pulitzer Prizes•

Awarded in recognition of outstanding accomplishments by American authors in various categories within the fields of journalism, literature, music, and drama. Literary awards usually recognize excellence in works that concern American life.

Anne Tyler
Breathing Lessons
(fiction)
(see entry below)

Richard Wilbur
New and Collected Poems
(poetry)
(see *CLC,* Vol. 53)

Wendy Wasserstein
The Heidi Chronicles
(drama)
(see entry below)

•Rea Award•

Presented annually to recognize outstanding achievement in the short story genre.

Tobias Wolff

•Tony Awards•

Officially entitled the American Theatre Wing's Antoinette Perry Awards, this award is presented in recognition of outstanding achievement in the Broadway theater.

Wendy Wasserstein
The Heidi Chronicles
(best play)
(see entry below)

•United States Poet Laureate•

Created in 1986 by an act of Congress to honor the career achievement of an American poet.

Howard Nemerov
(second term)

•Whitbread Literary Awards•

Awarded annually in several categories to encourage and promote English literature.

Paul Sayer
The Comforts of Madness
(novel)

John Casey
Spartina

Award: National Book Award: Fiction

An American novelist, short story writer, critic, and nonfiction writer, John Dudley Casey was born in 1939.

Spartina focuses on Dick Pierce, a brooding, quick-tempered, individualistic fisherman who lives off the coast of Rhode Island. At odds with the local fish-and-game laws as well as his wealthy neighbors, Pierce plans to build a fishing vessel in order to live a self-sufficient existence and provide for his family. Unable to secure a bank loan and refusing to ask acquaintances for financial help to complete his project, Pierce becomes moody, gets involved with a smuggler, and pursues an adulterous affair. These events, among others, including his attempt to navigate his newly-completed ship through a fierce hurricane, force Pierce to reexamine his priorities. While grounding *Spartina* in realism, Casey vividly evokes metaphorical and symbolic associations in the natural environment, through which Pierce finds greater understanding of his life. For example, Pierce names his boat "Spartina" after the sturdy marsh grass that thrives in saltwater, and this extended metaphor applies to his own life as well. Susan Kenney noted: "It is [Casey's] fearless romantic insistence on lyric, even mythic symbolism, coupled with the relentless salt-smack clarity of realistic detail, that makes *Spartina* just possibly the best American novel about going fishing since *The Old Man and the Sea,* maybe even *Moby-Dick.*"

(See also *Contemporary Authors,* Vols. 69-72 and *Contemporary Authors New Revision Series,* Vol. 23.)

PRINCIPAL WORKS

An American Romance   (novel) 1977
Testimony and Demeanor (short fiction) 1979
Spartina (novel) 1989

LARRY KART

Long before his remarkably rich first novel, **An American Romance,** was published in 1977, John Casey must have decided that he wanted it all: a realism that would leave out nothing of importance and would place each element in its true and proper relation to everything else.

Stated that baldly, Casey's presumed plan probably sounds a bit absurd. But if there is one thing that makes his long-awaited second novel, **Spartina,** a better, wiser book than its more obviously brilliant predecessor, it is that Casey's realism now includes the reasons a writer of fiction sets up his tabletop landscapes in the first place. Indeed, the nature of the game is almost given away by the novel's most manipula-

tive character—who insists, in a fit of comic rage, that "we ought to be able to do anything. I mean, compared with plants and animals, we can see the whole world."

Well, no, says **Spartina,** we can't see that much. Nor are we able to do anything, as in "do anything we want to do." But there are times, given to us or earned, when we can see and do a great deal—either for good or for ill. And **Spartina** is the tale of a man whose time, in that sense, has come.

Dick Pierce is 43, married and the father of two teenaged sons. He has always lived off the coast of Rhode Island, on an island that once belonged to his family but that has been sold off in bits and pieces over the years. A natural sailor, Dick has spent most of his life in boats. And in a shed in his backyard he is building a handsome 54-foot diesel-powered fishing vessel that he plans to name "Spartina," after the local salt grass, and that he hopes will make him a self-sufficient harvester of lobster, crab and swordfish—when and if he can get his hands on the $10,000 he needs to complete her.

But, financially and otherwise, Dick seems trapped. Unable

to get a loan from the bank, too stiff-necked to ask for, or to accept, help from those who might be willing to give it to him, he is an elaborately bitter, willfully glum man, in the mold of his late father—whose final display of "swamp Yankee" rectitude ("he probably held the record at South County Hospital for biggest bill ever paid by an uninsured patient") left his son with "next-to-nothing."

If most of that distress seems anchored to the personal, Casey's realism demands that Dick also be precisely placed in his social context. On one side of him—"a bad influence" but a sort of "channel marker"—lies Larry Parker, a slick, slippery customer with a perpetually light touch. Parker calls him "Dickey-bird," is not above some minor-league cocaine smuggling and says that "he'd never get Dick into anything he himself wouldn't do," which "didn't strike Dick as much of an assurance."

On the other side lie several different kinds of rich folk: Miss Perry, an aged Yankee aristocrat who takes a proprietary interest in Dick's sons, Charlie and Tom; Joxer Goode, "a single-sculler in college" who is now "out to make his million" from a crab-processing plant; Elsie Buttrick, a former tomboy who now works as "a sort of superpowered game-and-fish warden" for the Rhode Island Natural Resources Department; and Schuyler and Marie Van der Hoevel, new-rich types who have bought a summer home on what used to be Pierce-owned land and are harbingers of a future resort development.

One way to look at Dick is that he is, in Parker's words, a dedicated "nonplayer"—someone who spends "a lot of time dividing up the world into the idle rich and the true-blue salts . . . the worthy and the unworthy." Or as Dick himself puts it much later on: "Where would he be . . . without hard lines? What would he be without the hard things he was right about?"

As Parker seems to know, that insistence on "hard lines" conceals a passive, yielding strain in Dick's nature, a need to absorb whatever blows he thinks fate might have in store for him. Yet that trait is linked to what makes Dick such a good sailor and fisherman—his ability to sense and, when appropriate, give way to the flow of the natural world. And it also is what lets him lunge ahead into the events that set the novel whirling: a dangerous drug run with Parker and an emotionally turbulent love affair with Elsie Buttrick.

Such a terrific set-piece that it almost stands by itself, the drug run has the quicken-the-pulse pleasures of good genre fiction and something else besides—a whiff of genuine moral terror. (pp. 1, 6)

But the notion that the boundaries of the self are fluid also has its erotic side, which runs all the affair with Elsie. . . .

It wouldn't do to give away too much of the plot of a novel that puts so much care into the placement of what happens next. (Note the very slow emergence into the book of Dick's wife, May.) Indeed, Casey is a realist here, too. Having conjured up beings who deserve to be called human, he also has conjured up a fitting flow of fate for them, one that feels neither more nor less harsh than the flow of our own experience deems to be just. And what does the all-encompassing realism that John Casey has achieved in **Spartina** tell us about the shape of his somewhat enigmatic career—which made a steep initial ascent with **An American Romance**, leveled off with the four longish short stories collected in **Testimony and Demeanor** (1979) and then virtually vanished from the scope?

First, some facts. The 50-year-old Casey, who was born in Worcester, Mass., and teaches English literature at the University of Virginia, has been working for some time on two novels (**Spartina** is the first to emerge) and a collection of nine short stories—the whole forming what he calls his "Rhode Island trilogy." This will range back and forth through time and leave room for more than one appearance by some characters, although each book is designed to stand by itself.

How the rest of the trilogy will alter our view of **Spartina,** only time will tell. But looking back at Casey's previous books, the origins of his superb new novel seem clear. (p. 6)

Larry Kart, "When a Life's Afloat," in Book World—Chicago Tribune, *May 28, 1989, pp. 1, 6.*

ANNE TYLER

Has it really been 11 years since the publication of John Casey's first novel? It's hard to believe. **An American Romance**—his saga of a young couple careening across America together—still seems very distinct and vivid. It was one of those books that hang around long after the reader has finished. There were any number of reasons: the sweep of its plot, to name one, and a powerful writing style. Most memorable of all, though, was its hero. He managed to be both virtuous and likable—the kind of man who always puts his tools away when he's through with them.

The hero of [**Spartina**] would certainly take proper care of his tools, too. Dick Pierce is a Rhode Island waterman, involved for much of this book in constructing a 50-foot wooden boat with his own hands. And he has other good qualities: he's kind, industrious and a wonderful father. But to call him virtuous would no doubt make some of his neighbors snort— and perhaps his wife as well.

The main trouble is, he's hot-tempered. This is not a little passing irritability we're talking about; it's a rip-roaring fury. . . .

This is unfortunate for Dick, but it's a boon to the reader. Haven't you always wondered what goes on inside those tough, gruff, flinty workmen who husband their words like precious metal? John Casey will tell you. He shows events as Dick sees them, using Dick's internal voice, and he never makes the mistake of assuming that a relatively uneducated man is incapable of intelligent thought. In fact, if anything, he errs in the opposite direction. Dick experiences a number of epiphanies during the course of the book, and they're surprisingly lengthy and poetic. But for the most part, the view we're given of his interior feels exactly right. It's gentler than his brusque exterior would suggest but still crisply sensible. And he can sling a handy metaphor without appearing to strain for it. (p. 3)

At the outset, the plot of **Spartina** seems almost disappointingly simple. Will Dick finish his boat, or won't he? Will his poaching in the bird sanctuary, his involvement with the local drug-runner and his plain hard work earn him enough money? But then the story develops more layers. Dick has a love affair he never intended; he finishes his boat but a monster hurricane arrives; he deals heroically with the hurricane but is forced to confess his love affair to his wife—and therefore to reflect upon all that his present life means to him.

A friend tells Dick that his real problem is "class rage." That's certainly an underlying theme here. . . . At one point, he watches a documentary that a trendy moviemaker has filmed of him and his townsmen. "Rhode Island, poor cousin to Massachusetts," the film's narrator informs the audience. "Lowest education level of any state outside the Deep South . . . If Rhode Island were a country, it would be part of the Third World." The movie, which recapitulates the novel's events from a great, enormous distance, startles the readers as much as it does Dick. We've been so much *with* him—pulling for him to finish his boat, to haul in more swordfish—we never thought to view him as some disadvantaged poor soul. We really have, it seems, been looking out at the world through this man's eyes.

Spartina is a genus of marsh grasses that thrive in salty water. It's also the name of Dick Pierce's boat, and it might as well be his own name too. His story may not stay with us quite as long as **An American Romance;** its scope is not so broad. But Dick himself will, most certainly. He is feisty, tough and enduring, the knotty center of a highly engaging book. (pp. 3-4)

Anne Tyler, "John Casey's Yankee Waterman," in Book World—The Washington Post, *June 4, 1989, pp. 3-4.*

SUSAN KENNEY

Spartina is the name of a kind of marsh grass, and it provides the major theme [of **Spartina**] as well as the most pervasive symbol for this tale of a man and his boat, the sea and the voyage toward self-discovery:

> Under the spartina there was black earth richer than any farmland, but useless to farmers on account of the salt. Only the spartinas thrived in the salt flood, shut themselves against the salt but drank the water. Smart grass. If he ever got his big boat built he might just call her *Spartina,* though he ought to call her after his wife.

Maritime novels are by definition romance. Float a grumpy, obsessed, alienated man alone in a boat on the open ocean, bring on a big fish, better yet a hurricane (or both), and the result, as Melville, Conrad, and Hemingway recognized, is archetypal big time. Add some clam poaching, drug running, a steamy extra-marital love affair featuring a definitively erotic episode of impromptu mud-wrestling, and you have an American romance with a difference, but romance all the same.

This is not to say that Mr. Casey's story isn't grounded in realism. The details of his fictional world are rendered closely and comprehensively, and we see his characters in all their complexity of motive, in relation to nature, to each other and to their individual pasts. But there is something so obsessive yet deeply unaware, even resistant, about his main character's struggle to come to terms with himself, his life, his loves, his place in time and in the universe, that it can only be expressed in symbolic, even mythic terms. All he knows is that he wants to get his big boat built and launched, preferably on his own hook, but by crook if he has to. Nature, both human and elemental, takes it from there.

Dick Pierce is a brooding, embittered man, an unreconstructed, self-proclaimed "swamp Yankee" who has spent his whole life scratching a living as a fisherman in the narrow square of the Rhode Island seacoast west of Narragansett Bay known locally as South County. Landowners since colonial times, the Pierce family has come down in the world, selling off their land on Sawtooth Point and up Pierce Creek little by little, a lot here, several acres there. . . .

[Dick's] dream is to have a big fishing boat of his own, so he can go out and net crabs, catch swordfish, haul lobster and finally make a difference in the lives of his wife May and their two sons. The boat he names Spartina-May out of a sense of duty to his wife, but continues to think of simply as Spartina, lies encased in a ramshackle plastic tent in his yard, awaiting more funds so Dick can finish her. As his wife May describes it, the boat is a "black hole," sucking in not just money but Dick's life energy and attention. No bank will give him a loan, partly because he is a bad risk, but also because he is so notoriously bad-tempered.

More than his incredibly forgiving and loyal wife May or even Elsie, the young, well-educated, fully emancipated woman he has an affair with, Spartina is the great, pure, liberating love of his life. Dick may consider himself the scriptural salt of the earth, but this very saltiness or earthiness, his deep resentment of his lot in life, his frustrated dreams, are what make him bitter, unable, like the marsh grass he so admires, to take up what is sweet in life. It is the Spartina that provides the means for him to transcend the limitations both of his existence and his apprehension of it.

Through a complex series of negotiations with the people around him—the old rich folks up on the point, Miss Perry and Elsie Buttrick, the Fish and Wildlife officer and longtime neighbor who becomes his mistress—Pierce manages to float a loan that allows him to finish Spartina. Other characters help too in various ways—the crab-processing plant owner Joxer Goode and his friend the real estate developer and documentary film maker Schuyler van der Hoevel, the ne'er-do-well drug runner Captain Parker—and Pierce's boat is launched just before the big hurricane hits.

Inevitably, as one would expect, it is Dick's riding out of the hurricane in Spartina that functions as the most dramatic agent of self-revelation. . . .

But this mythic means of self-discovery is not the ultimate one. That takes place on a more realistically human scale, and it lies in his accepting and working out of the complex relationships among Elsie, pregnant with his child; his wife, May; his sons, Charlie and Tom; his dead father; his own bitter existence both in and out of time. Where earlier he was frightened to the point of panic by his contemplation of the endless, dissolving, inhuman cycles of the sea and the sky, finally, unexpectedly confronting the heavily pregnant Elsie, at last he understands and accepts responsibility for his own fate:

> [Let Elsie] be herself the way the salt marsh was the salt marsh for all that it flowed in and out. His mind swelled that thought—the way the sea was the sea for all the winds across her, for all the pull of the moon and the sun, for all the spinning of the earth under her, for all that sent her rocking from one edge to the other, sliding up sounds and bays, eating at shores, slithering into salt creeks and marshes. . . . He saw the marsh, the salt pond at high water, brimming up into the spartina."

It is this fearless romantic insistence on lyric, even mythic symbolism, coupled with the relentless salt-smack clarity of realistic detail, that makes *Spartina* just possibly the best American novel about going fishing since *The Old Man and the Sea,* maybe even *Moby-Dick.*

Susan Kenney, "Man Meets Boat Meets Hurricane," in The New York Times Book Review, *June 25, 1989, p. 7.*

An excerpt from *Spartina*

Parker had always scared Dick a little. Parker would do anything, that was part of it. And Parker seemed to know things about Dick that Dick didn't. Parker said he'd never get Dick into anything that he himself wouldn't do. That didn't strike Dick as much of an assurance.

Dick had gone off on some wild-ass rides with Parker. One time a few years back, Parker got hold of a motor yacht that the owner wanted moved from Newport to the Caribbean. The owner gave Parker a credit card for fuel, berthing fees and food, and two plane tickets back to Boston. The guys at the Neptune who knew Dick and Parker were surprised the two of them got along. But with just the two of them running the fifty-foot yacht, they didn't see much of each other the first week. After four hours on, one of them would wake the other up, say a word about the weather, and that was it. Each had a cabin of his own the couple of times they tied up at night. Parker was eager to get south, so they usually ran all night. With the owner's credit card on board, fuel economy was not a big item, so they ran as fast as the seas would allow.

Dick had loved the trip south. The boat was good, even in a half-gale. He liked getting a look at Chesapeake Bay, Cape Hatteras, the islands off Georgia. It was there Parker took him on a side trip in the dinghy. They went up a salt creek that cut into Ossabaw Island. "Lookee there," Parker said, "I'll bet it's the first time you saw one wasn't on a shirt." Dick looked. He saw the eyes blink first and then took in the body floating in the muddy water. He'd always liked Parker for taking the time to show him an alligator.

Parker got less amiable when he started looking for fun in the islands. He railed at Dick for turning in early, for getting cold feet at padding the expenses. Parker thought Dick was having a case of social nerves, that Dick was intimidated by the fancy bar life. Dick had to admit he was thrown some by the accents of the West Indians, the English, let alone the foreigners. Parker got into the act, even dressed the part. A pale sweater woven so loose you could just about see through it, no shirt. Cream-colored topsiders, no socks. But Dick could tell him apart from the carriage trade. Parker leaned forward, his eyes moved fast, and his mouth, with his bad teeth and gray fillings, was held in small and tight, even when he was having a good time. Parker did have a good time. Dick saw that, envied him his nerve, and admired it.

PAUL GRAY

Stories about seafaring inevitably carry a ballast of symbolism. Shimmering significance goes with the territory: people casting off in the little world of a ship, adrift on a journey at the mercies of the elements and fate. In his second novel [*Spartina*]—twelve years after his critically praised *An American Romance*—John Casey makes it plain on the opening page that some large issues are going to be entertained. He introduces his hero, Dick Pierce, in a skiff, floating among the creeks and inlets of coastal Rhode Island. In paragraph two, Pierce ponders the marsh grass around him and has an insight: "Only the spartinas thrived in the salt flood, shut themselves against the salt but drank the water. Smart grass. If he ever got his big boat built he might just call her *Spartina,* though he ought to call her after his wife."

These sentences foreshadow nearly everything to come in *Spartina,* although just how cleverly Casey tips his hand does not become clear until much later. (p. 84)

Pierce's bitterness over his lot in life helps make him its prisoner. His quick temper has got him fired from jobs that might have enabled him to buy his boat and independence. Banks will not lend him money. He has no telephone at home because he ripped it out of the wall during a fit of anger. He poaches clams at a neighboring bird sanctuary, more out of orneriness than hope of profit. And, to complicate his existence still further, he has fallen into a love affair with Elsie Buttrick, the local game and fish warden.

It would seem difficult to root for the success of such an unpleasant character, but Casey artfully provides good reasons for doing so. Pierce's "swamp Yankee" pride is based on a fierce, if sometimes obnoxious, integrity. He does not ask for anything except the chance to make a decent living at what he knows best. The world needs seafood, and Pierce has learned through long experience how to find and catch it. He is, in fact, an archetypal figure in American literature, the little guy at odds with big institutions, battling the triumph of newfangled shoddiness over old traditions. In addition, he possesses enough self-awareness to recognize and regret his bursts of bad behavior. . . .

[There are] some spirited narrative interludes: vivid scenes of hunting and "sticking" swordfish on the high seas, a sexual encounter that turns into an extended bout of mud wrestling, a hair-raising attempt to outsail a major hurricane.

Beneath this busy, engrossing surface, though, Casey traces deep moral currents. Pierce must try to free his soul from the hoard of resentments it has accumulated. If the spartina grass can filter out the salt and be nourished by the water, perhaps Pierce can accept what he has been given and forget about what he has lost. This matter remains in doubt almost to the end of the book. The resolution is worth waiting for, and so are the pleasures along the way. Here is old-fashioned, full-bodied fiction with a vengeance: remarkable characters meet and clash on fields of social class, money and sex. They do not make novels like this very much anymore; John Casey deserves gratitude for being stubborn and talented enough to do so and succeed. (p. 85)

Paul Gray, "Deep Currents," in Time, *New York, Vol. 134, No. 3, July 17, 1989, p. 84-5.*

DAN BYRNE

Dick Pierce [the protagonist of *Spartina*] is a Rhode Island lobsterman who lives near a salt marsh in which a grass called spartina grows. Spartina is tenacious stuff that survives by separating the water from the salt.

Dick's roots are in the salt marsh. A creek there is named Pierce Creek after his family. At one time, Pierces owned all of Sawtooth Island, but his forbears sold it off piecemeal. Houses of the rich are scattered around the island and a resort development is planned.

The rich, or the people he perceives as rich, and what they are doing on Sawtooth Island keep Dick more or less in a state of rage.

He has a temper and a sharp tongue. He's hard on his two boys and curt with his wife, May. He earns a tenuous living by hiring out as a hand on fishing boats. As a fisherman, he is superb. He is also a craftsman, and it is this talent that he is using to build a fishing boat.

Dick needs his own boat, his own livelihood, because his sullen anger has left him all but unemployable. . . .

Elsie Buttrick arrives on the scene. Dick and Elsie have known each other from the time she was a young (rich) girl. They get involved after she returns from college (Brown and Yale Forestry School) and becomes an officer with the state Natural Resources Department.

Soon they are making love a lot and talking a lot more. A new Dick emerges. A boor until now, he shows a depth and sensitivity that we never had a hint of before.

A character in the book tells Elsie and Dick about her father who has just died. She speaks lovingly of the man and his life. Dick recalls later that the daughter "had sifted her old man like flour through her fingers."

A felicitous phrase, but not one you would expect from the man who away from Elsie snarls obscenities at just about everyone he comes across.

Elsie, after Dick, is the book's most fully realized character. She's fun, bright, carefree, self-aware. It isn't easy to understand what she sees in Dick. But that's not the flaw. It's what Dick becomes when he is with her—sensitive, more self-aware, introspective, hardly the embittered salt-marsh fisherman. It's hard to understand how the two personalities coexist.

The novel bogs down in tedium of their incessant conversation, although much of it is fresh and inventive. At one point, annoyed with Dick's obsessive distaste for the haves, Elsie tells him, "I'm not rich, I'm privileged." It's a distinction that Dick doesn't care to make.

With Elsie's help in arranging the financing, Dick completes his boat and calls it Spartina, tacking on his wife's name, May, as a concession to local convention.

May calls it the boat that rage built. Dick, however, drains some of the rage out of the stout wooden hull and himself by surviving alone aboard it as it weathers a savage hurricane.

The hurricane is the turning point in the book. Elsie is happy to be pregnant by Dick and fully prepared to let him return to May while she looks forward to single-motherhood.

May reacts woodenly and inexplicably when Dick tells her. The author never did explain her to us. May is just vaguely pathetic and there. . . .

Casey is a careful writer. Nothing is contrived. The novel has a sense of place and most of his characters are carefully conceived and drawn. For me, the problem with the novel is Dick. Present on every page raging or ruminating, he is quite a problem indeed. As the salt marsh fisherman he's real. As Elsie's lover, he thinks and talks too much. And too well.

Dan Byrne, "The Boat That Rage Built," in Los Angeles Times Book Review, *July 23, 1989, p. 13.*

Camilo José Cela

Nobel Prize in Literature

A Spanish novelist, poet, dramatist, travel writer, and nonfiction writer, Cela was born in 1916.

Considered the most important prose writer of contemporary Spain, Cela is best known for his stylistically diverse works of fiction that chronicle the political, social, and psychological legacy of the Spanish Civil War. His early novels, *La familia de Pascual Duarte* (*The Family of Pascual Duarte*) and *La colmena* (*The Hive*), secured his reputation as a compassionate yet severe annalist of a Spanish underclass debased by social injustice and personal deficiencies. Cela is also credited with broadening the range of the Spanish language through his meticulous reproduction of working-class speech and his continuous experimentation with revolutionary modes of expression. Despite Cela's early affiliation with the Falange, the official political party of fascist Spain, the regime of Generalissimo Francisco Franco frequently banned his provocative works and attacked his literary periodical, *Papeles de Son Armadans,* for publishing the works of authors condemned by the dictatorship. Several critics who considered Cela's later work derivative of his earlier fiction objected to the choice of Cela for the Nobel Prize. Nevertheless, most commentators concurred with the Nobel Committee, which lauded Cela "for a rich and intensive prose, which with restrained compassion forms a challenging vision of man's vulnerability."

In Cela's first novel, *The Family of Pascual Duarte,* the title character composes his memoirs while awaiting his execution for murder. A victim as well as a criminal, Pascual describes his squalid upbringing by an abusive, bitter mother whose other children turned to prostitution or proved mentally incompetent. Pascual also recounts his descent into violence, beginning with the killing of animals and culminating in the murder of his mother. At the novel's end, when faced with the death penalty for yet another homicide, Pascual refuses to blame society for his downfall and instead attributes his actions to fate and his own innate sinfulness. Cela's grotesque portrayal of the vulgar, repulsive aspects of Spanish society in *The Family of Pascual Duarte* initiated a literary trend in Spain later termed *tremendismo.* Often compared to the existentialism of Albert Camus and Jean-Paul Sartre, *tremendismo* graphically depicts the perversion of morality by oppressive social forces. Cela, however, eschews this mode of expression in his following novels, *Pabellón de reposo* (*Rest Home*), which examines the private anguish of tuberculosis patients confined to a sanatorium, and *Nuevas andanzas y desventuras de Lazarillo de Tormes,* which modernizes the sixteenth-century picaresque narrative *Lazarillo de Tormes.* While these novels did not garner the widespread critical attention of *The Family of Pascual Duarte,* both are regarded as perceptive explorations of contemporary Spanish society.

Cela's subsequent novel, *The Hive,* is generally considered his greatest work. Set in working-class Madrid immediately fol-

lowing World War II, *The Hive* chronicles three days in the lives of approximately three hundred people who frequent a seedy café. Devoid of traditional plot structure or character development, the novel intricately combines the sordid experiences of maids, beggars, bakers, prostitutes, and poets to achieve a panoramic yet intimate portrait of a society reduced to avarice and vice through poverty and oppression. Frequently comparing *The Hive* to John dos Passos's *Manhattan Transfer,* critics lauded Cela's innovative use of cinematic techniques as well as his multifaceted presentation of Madrid and its inhabitants. Robert Kirsner commented that in *The Hive,* "Cela's literary persons have a durable intimate existence which is tangibly artistic. Their lives are worth creating and experiencing not because they may be imaginary 'case studies,' but because they enclose within their personal exterior an agonizing existence which is essentially that of Spain—and possibly of all humanity."

While Cela's later novels have not achieved the international renown of *The Family of Pascual Duarte* and *The Hive,* several are recognized as inventive explorations of the novelistic form. *Mrs. Caldwell habla con su hijo* (*Mrs. Caldwell Speaks to Her Son*) contains over two hundred short, unrelated chapters constructed around the rambling letters of an elderly Englishwoman to her dead son that reveal her incestuous love for him. In *Historias de Venezuela: La catira,* an ironic re-evaluation of the romantic novel, Cela narrates the adventures of an independent woman on the Venezuelan frontier. The circular novel *Tobogán de hambrientos* is comprised of two hundred separate vignettes numbered in ascending then descending order as the narrative's action returns to the opening events. In *San Camilo, 1936: Visperas, festividas y octava de San Camilo del año 1936 en Madrid,* Cela utilizes a stream-of-consciousness narrative style to examine the events leading up to the Spanish Civil War through the perspective of a young student. Often compared to *The Hive,* this elaborate study of Madrid's poor is generally regarded as Cela's most successful work since that novel.

In addition to his many works of fiction, Cela is also well known for his travel sketches that recount his *vagabundajes,* or vagabond journeys, by foot through the Iberian Peninsula. Cela's first such work, *Viaje a la Alcarria* (*Journey to the Alcarria*), garnered critical accolades for its atypical approach to the travel genre. Paul Ilie observed that Cela's *vagabundajes,* "as real acts in the author's life, become a symbolic expression of an intellectual position. As a literary form [the *vagabundaje*] has the dual purpose of gaining a direct and intuitive understanding of the nature of the Spanish personality, and of presenting a cultural anatomy of the nation's most fundamental social stratum: its provincial life." Cela's other well regarded travelogues include *De Miño al Bidasoa,* an account of his journey from his native province of Galicia to the Basque region; *Judíos, moros y cristanos,* which examines the diverse cultures of southern Spain; and *Viaje al Pirineo de Lérida,* a description of the mountainous Pyrenes region at the Spanish-French border. Cela gained further notice for his nonfiction works that combine his commentary with photographs or drawings by other artists, the best known of which are *Gavilla de fábulas sin amor,* a collaborative effort produced with Pablo Picasso, and *Izas, rabizas y colipoterras,* which depicts the desperate existence of Barcelona prostitutes. Cela also published several dictionaries of vulgar sexual terms, including *Diccionario secreto* and *Enciclopedia de erotismo,* that oppose the moralistic concerns of traditional Spanish society.

(See also *CLC,* Vols. 4, 13; *Contemporary Authors,* Vols. 21-24, rev. ed.; *Contemporary Authors New Revision Series,* Vol. 21; and *Contemporary Authors Autobiography Series,* Vol. 10.)

PRINCIPAL WORKS

NOVELS

La Familia de Pascual Duarte   1942
   [*The Family of Pascual Duarte,*   1964]
Pabellón de reposo   1943
   [*Rest Home,*   1961]
Nuevas andanzas y desventuras de Lazarillo de Tormes   1944
La colmena   1951
   [*The Hive,*   1953]
Mrs. Caldwell habla con su hijo   1953
   [*Mrs. Caldwell Speaks to her Son,*   1968]
Historias de Venezuela: La Catira   1955
Los viejos amigos   2 vols.   1960-61

Tobogán de hambrientos   1962
San Camilo, 1936: Visperas, festividy y octava de San Camilo del año 1936 en Madrid   1969
Oficio de tineblas 5; o, novela de tesis escrita para ser cantada por un coro de enfermos   1973
Mazurca para dos muertos   1983
Cristo versus Arizona   1988

SHORT FICTION COLLECTIONS

*Esas nubes que pasan   1945
*El Bonito crimen del carabinero y otras invenciones   1947
*Baraja de invenciones   1953
El molino de viento, y otras novelas cortas   1956
Cajón de sastre   1957
Historias de España: Los ciegos, Los tontos   1957
Gavilla de fábulas sin amor   [illustrated by Pablo Picasso]   1962
Las Compañías convenientes, y otros fingimientos y cegueras   1963
Izas, rabizas y colipoterras   1964
‡*El ciudadano Iscariote Reclús*   1965
‡*La familia del héroe; o, Discurso histórico de los últimos restos; ejercicios para una sola mano*   1965
Cuentos para leer después del baño   1974
El espejo y otros cuentos   1981

TRAVEL BOOKS

Viaje a la Alcarria   1948
   [*Journey to the Alcarria,*   1964]
Del Miño al Bidasoa   1952
Judíos, moros y cristianos   1956
Primer viaje andaluz   1959
Páginas de geografía errabunda   1965
Viaje al Pirineo de Lérida   1965
Madrid   1966
‡*Viaje a U.S.A.*   1967
La Mancha en el corazón y en los ojos   1971
Balada del vagabundo sin suerte y otros papeles volanderos   1973
Nuevo viaje a la Alcarria   3 Vols.   1986

OTHER

Mesa revuelta   1945
Mis páginas perferidas   (selections from earlier works of fiction and nonfiction)   1956
El Gallego y su caudrilla, y ortros amuntes carpetovetonicos   (nonfiction)   1949
La cucaña—memorias   (memoirs)   1959
Pisando la dudosa luz del día: Poems de una adolescencia cruel   (poetry)   1960
Garito de hospicianos; o, Guirigay de imposturas y bambollas   (articles)   1963
Diccionario secreto   2 Vols.   (nonfiction)   1968-70
Los sueños vanos, los ágeles curiosos   (nonfiction)   1979
Enciclopedia de erotismo   (nonfiction)   1977
Obra Completa   (complete works)   1962-83
El juego de los tres madroños   (nonfiction)   1983
El anso de Burdidán   (articles)   1986

*These works were also published as *Nuevo retablo de don Cristobita: Invenciones, figuraciones y alucinaciones* in 1957.

‡These works were also published as *A la pata de palo* 4 Vols. 1965-1967 and as *El tacata oxidado: Florilegio de carpetoventonismos y otras lindezas* in 1973.

ANGEL FLORES

With the publication of [Cela's] first novel, *La Familia de Pascual Duarte,* some ten years ago, he was acclaimed Spain's No. 1 novelist. He followed up this dramatic debut with a couple of short novels, a volume of short stories and another of poems, all adding but little to his reputation. More recently, however, with his novel, *La Colmena* . . . Cela's name appears again at the forefront of contemporary Spanish letters.

Availing himself of the expressionist technique (simultaneity, photomontage, etc.), Cela spreads out his novel to cover the life of a city rather than that of one individual or a family. At first he centers his attention on the human or subhuman patrons of Dona Rosa's cheap cafe with its depraved circle of prostitutes, pimps and small speculators, and later he expands it to include brothels, tenements, streets and, afterwards, even more extensive areas. Therefore, no main plot exists. The novel is, rather, a web of sordid episodes in the lives of unimportant people, the dregs of society. A lover of crude realism, of the slice-of-life variety, Cela's eye is clinical and miry. In this respect and on his sexual insistence he is reminiscent of the Céline of *Journey to the End of the Night,* or, to think in Spanish terms, of the novel of roguery, especially of Quevedo's work. His is a Quevedan vitriolic moralism, a ferocious wrath against hypocrisy and conformism. But the extremes of anguish make one wonder whether he means that society perverts man or whether man is perverted *ad ovum.*

As the narrative proliferates, the reader is taxed with having to follow up at one and the same time the case histories of dozens of *dramatis personae* (there are 160 characters in the novel), and since one case seems to be as important as the next, the reader is forced to memorize each subplot in order to understand the ensuing reversals of circumstance. At first the process appears bewildering, but after the first hundred pages each plot falls in place, the reader then enjoying the fruits of his efforts and patience. "Enjoying" is a paradoxical word in connection with this experience, for there is nothing gay or joyful in this novel except through the toughest sort of catharsis. *The Hive* is a sad and bitter book totally devoid of the *joie de vivre* or even the slightest trace of hope for the future of man. To Cela most men are cads and most women tarts. This gloomy outlook may be merely a passing phase (youthful bravado) of this gifted writer—of his talent and deep insights there can be no doubt—which like Péres de Alaya's (a writer he resembles and whom he admires) may be overcome as his philosophy mellows. This attitude of his cannot be summarily explained in terms of the Franco regime, of which he is a part, for Zunzunegui, to mention another gifted young novelist of Spain, has shown that humor is possible under any circumstance. The genius of Spain is unquenchable.

Angel Flores, "One Relentless Slice of Spanish Life," in New York Herald Tribune Book Review, *September 27, 1953, p. 6.*

ROBERT H. BOYLE

The publication of *The Hive* introduces to American readers Camilo José Cela, generally regarded by Spanish critics as the finest novelist writing in their country today. And while some Americans may unthinkingly attribute Cela's high place in Spanish letters to the absence of competition, one reading of *The Hive* should convince them otherwise—he is one of the most gifted and powerful writers in contemporary Europe.

Cela came into prominence in 1942 with the appearance of his first novel, *La familia de Pascual Duarte.* He was then twenty-six years old. *Pascual Duarte*—the "autobiography" of an Estremenian peasant who butchers a dog, a horse, his wife's lover, and finally his own mother—instantly was hailed as a work of major importance. It was, in brief, both a *succès de scandale* and a *tour de force.*

Cela repeated but refined his naturalistic technique in his next novel, *Pabellón de reposo,* a work—in letter form—about the sufferings of consumptives. Like *Pascual Duarte,* it shocked both the critics and the public. A recent issue of *Books Abroad* reports *Pabellón* was so realistically convincing Cela received a letter from a doctor imploring him to halt serialization on the grounds the novel had impeded the progress of his tubercular patients. . . .

Cela's next work, *Nuevas aventuras de Lazarillo de Tormes,* gave everyone a bit of respite. The publication of this picaresque novel encouraged the hope Cela had abandoned his role as a chronicler of human degradation.

But then *The Hive* appeared to end any such hope. (p. 146)

The Hive is not, properly speaking, a novel. It has no beginning, middle, or end—it does not *resolve* a moral problem. It is, in Cela's words, a "slice of life," and his artistic conscience could not allow him to write otherwise.

It is a collection of sketches, or snapshots, of the patrons of a café located in a shabby section of Madrid. But then one may say that if these sketches are snapshots, Cela employs a wide-angle lens since the reader is also presented with glimpses of the patrons' acquaintances and families. The sketches are interconnected, and while the reader gains additional insight into the more than one hundred and fifty characters by this method, it is certainly an indication of Cela's poetic vigor that almost all the sketches can stand alone without the support of one another.

Surely there are few novels which possess the despair and bitterness which Cela displays in *The Hive.* One almost believes Cela is not an author, but a grotesque version of a butterfly collector. The book often portrays the characters involved much as a neatly mounted collection under glass displays the various types of butterfly. Here are Cela's characters, pinned and isolated, exposed in all shades and varieties to the reader's eye. They may beat their wings or wiggle on the hook, but they are unable to escape either from Cela or from life.

Consider Dona Rosa, the proprietress of the café, whose

> . . . face is covered with blotches; it always looks as if she were changing her skin like a lizard. When she is deep in thought, she forgets herself and picks strips off her face, sometimes as long as paper streamers. . . .

(pp. 146-47)

No doubt *The Hive* will be both condemned and deplored for its recital of the ugly. Gerald Brenan said the note of hunger runs through the Spanish novel, and *The Hive* is no exception. Everyone in it is wracked by either a physical or spiritual hunger, and one is led to conclude that Cela—a veteran of the Civil War and a member of the Falange—has written it in expiation for the loss of human dignity which he depicts. But even in its most brutal moments, and there are many, **The Hive** is desperately optimistic.

Perhaps that desperation is best expressed by Cela when he writes

> . . . the heart of the café has an uneven beat, like a sick man's, and the air seems to get thicker and greyer, though now and then a cooler breath pierces it like a flash; no one knows where it comes from, but it is a breath of hope that opens, for a few seconds, a little window in each shuttered spirit.

(p. 147)

Robert H. Boyle, "Desperate Hope," in The Commonweal, *Vol. LIX, No. 6, November 13, 1953, pp. 146-47.*

DAVID M. FELDMAN

La familia de Pascual Duarte occupies an important place in both the history of contemporary Spanish literature and the career of its author: Camilo José Cela. Although certain critics tend to place *La colmena* on a higher level of technical and artistic achievement, **Pascual Duarte,** Cela's first novel, serves as an effective vehicle for the expression of his central philosophy: a firm faith in man's ability to survive.

Cela is the product of one of Spain's most depressing eras. He was born in 1916 under the rapidly disintegrating monarchy of Alfonso XIII, spent his youth under the dictatorship of General Primo de Rivera, fought on the side of the Falangists in the Civil War of 1936, and began to express himself in his writings in the days of an oppressive dictatorship within Spain and in the days in which the furies of World War II engulfed the major nations of the world. Casting aside the then popular "generational" type of novel and the literary search for the "tradición española," Cela sought his inspiration in the pessimism of the bitter immediate realities of life in his country in his time.

Because of the economic, political, and spiritual depression of Spain as a nation, made more manifest by the disastrous war with the United States which cost Spain her overseas empire, the search for some explanation for that depression became more intense. . . . [As a result, several Spanish intellectuals became interested in] the existentialist movement which was to influence Cela so deeply. Like many of his contemporaries, Cela has admitted his predilection for the works of Malraux, Camus, and Sartre, and has built much of the philosophical structure of his works on existentialist principles. To this basis, Cela adds his own personal conviction that man—responsible for his own acts and thoughts—is capable of the fulfillment of that responsibility.

The novel *La familia de Pascual Duarte* is a work which, on the surface, presents the autobiography of a man who, seemingly driven by circumstances to a series of senseless killings of men and animals, is garrotted in prison for the murder of a wealthy landowner of his town. Though the novel has been the subject of much critical discussion, the most perceptive is that of the late Dr. Gregorio Marañón who establishes the important point that Pascual Duarte is basically a good man. Yet he arrives at the conclusion that it is "essential human weakness" that makes Duarte the victim of external forces he is unable to control. This takes issue with a fundamental existentialist principle: that there are no accidents of fate, simple

human error. If this novel is, as may be suggested, predicated to a great extent on existentialist principles, then another conclusion must be reached.

The idea of his being driven by an inexorable destiny is developed by Pascual Duarte himself, in a search for an explanation of his personal misfortune. He speaks of men who are destined to walk the "road of flowers" and of others who must strike out along the "dusty road that leads to nowhere." He is a simple and uneducated man, and this explanation helps him to excuse himself for much of what he has done. Yet in the same chapter he declares that he has written his memoirs that "others might learn what I have learned too late." The very assumption that one may learn from his example how to avoid similar error is eloquent testimony against the validity of the idea of predestination and, although Duarte is not sufficiently sophisticated to perceive the contradiction, it is nonetheless there.

The interpretation of the novel as an affirmation of the power of external forces is predicated upon the series of deaths that occur at Duarte's hand. One can see the possibility that once placed in proper chronological order—a task which is complicated by Cela's technique of rupturing the chronological order for narrative emphasis—these deaths are explicable as natural events, with causes understandable—if not justifiable—within the given circumstances. Of the five victims, it is essential to note, only one was murdered.

The first victim is a horse, the mare that threw Duarte's first wife, Lola, causing her to abort, while Duarte had tarried in a tavern with friends. . . . Seeking to assign guilt to something, he chose the horse, killing it in the same deliberate manner and in the same awareness in which he believes the horse had injured his wife and killed his yet unborn child.

The second victim is his dog, "Chispa." While still in depression from Lola's abortion, Pascual watched the dog give birth to three stillborn puppies, which she subsequently buried in a hole she had dug. As the dog later sat before him, he believed that what he had witnessed was a transformation of Lola's abortion. The dog's eyes, seeming to accuse him for the death of her offspring, bored deeply into him. Taking his gun, with feelings of overwhelming guilt, he shot the dog, intending to obliterate the accusation she seemed to be making.

The third victim, a drifter known as "El Estirao," was the sometime lover of Pascual's sister—seriously ill with syphilis—and, during Pascual's absence in La Coruña, his wife's lover. In their first encounter, Pascual was able to endure "Estirao's" taunts and provocations. In the second, however, he challenged him to a fight in which Pascual killed him. Again, this was not murder, so Pascual was sentenced to a short jail term.

The fourth victim, and the only one to be murdered, is Pascual's mother. She was, by this time, an embittered widow, subsequently deserted by her lover and abandoned by her children, of whom one—an idiot—had died a tragic death. . . . Pascual resisted the growing desire to kill his mother by fleeing to La Coruña. There, he learned that one cannot flee from what is within one's own soul and returned home only to find conditions worsened. The process was slow but, almost against his own will, the decision to murder his mother was made. Standing over her sleeping body, knife in hand, he hesitated. A creaking floorboard awakened his mother who, frightened, bit him and fought with him. In that moment, he drove the blade into her.

It is with this murder that some critics determine that the novel ends. Yet there is a fifth victim: don Jesús González de la Riva. Although Cela, whose essentially poetic technique leads him to provide few details and to leave much to the reader's imagination, says little about don Jesús' death, it is the most significant event in the novel. (pp. 656-58)

It is possible that Duarte was released from prison, to which he had been sentenced for the murder of his mother, in the general amnesty in the early days of the Civil War. Probably returning to his home town, there he would have witnessed the brutality of the revolution as it swept through (for Badajoz was a major corridor). It was at that time that don Jesús, a man known for his kindness, generosity, and devotion, was killed. We are told that he died at Duarte's hand, but that in dying he smiled at Duarte, calling him Pascualillo. Two explanations are possible. One is that Duarte killed don Jesús as a part of a revolutionary action in which the wealthy landowner would have represented to the revolutionaries one of their greatest enemies. This would imply, however, that Duarte was a highly socially conscious and politically aware individual, something not supported by the text. The second possible explanation is that Duarte, finding don Jesús dying as the result of torture by the revolutionaries, at don Jesus' request administered the final *coup*. This view finds additional support in Cela's choice of the word *rematar,* that is, to kill someone already in the throes of death. Yet is is for the death of don Jesús that Duarte is executed.

What don Jesús represents, as I see it, is that group of principles which mankind, throughout its existence, has come to respect because only life in accordance with them permits all to survive, rather than but a few at the expense of the lives and freedom of others. It is more than pure coincidence that he is named Jesús. His death is significant because of the relationship of the two forces that killed him. The real agents of destruction, which left him in the "throes of death," were those of the revolution. This an exceedingly biting commentary by Cela on the morality of that movement, especially considering that Cela himself fought on the Falangist side. The actual agent of his death was Pascual Duarte, yet he was innocent of murder.

It is clear, then, that the deaths worked by Duarte in this novel are neither the acts of a psychopath nor those of a man driven by inexorable "fate." (p. 658)

Cela insists that man must be struck by the awesome fact of his complete responsibility for what he is, thinks, and does. Only in such awareness can he avoid destruction. Yet precisely in this regard is Cela's optimism to be noted. He believes that man, once aware of his responsibility, is capable of its fulfillment. Thus can Pascual Duarte assert that, had he only pondered what he was about to do, his course of action would have been far different. Even though Duarte killed his own mother, he lived. It was when he killed don Jesús, even in the context of the revolution, even when it was not murder, he was executed. Not even church nor state, being agents of man, can prevent man's destruction when he does not assume responsibility for himself, and the letters Cela carefully includes at the novel's end are indicative of Cela's convictions in this regard. Indeed, the choice is man's as to whether or not he will accept and nourish the values which his history has developed and passed on to him. But when he destroys them, as Duarte destroyed don Jesús, whether that destruction be in keeping with that vague precedent called the "spirit of the age," or not, he dies. Be he a Spanish Falangist, a German Hitlerite, or Pascual Duarte, the result is destruction. This, I suggest, is the lesson of Pascual Duarte, and Cela's thesis. (pp. 658-59)

David M. Feldman, "Camilo José Cela and 'La familia de Pascual Duarte'," in Hispania, *Vol. XLIV, No. 4, December, 1961, pp. 656-59.*

PAUL ILIE

In one of Camilo José Cela's autobiographical moments he wrote of himself:

> I was born in Iria-Flavia, a tiny village in the province of La Coruña [Galicia], on May 11, 1916, of a Spanish father, an English mother, and an Italian grandmother. I've done nothing of any use in my life, or at least nothing that would be recognized as such, and I've traveled more or less to the same places that every other Spaniard has. Writing is the only activity that distracts me and makes me forget the very unfunny drama of every-day existence.

This capsule confession reveals many things about Cela's ironic, offhand manner, his dry, detached style, and his attitudes toward literature, his country, and the meaning of life in the post-war era. All of these issues are pertinent to the aims of Cela's work in general . . . Above all, their treatment in [*Journey to the Alcarria*] is a major statement about the nature of both contemporary Spanish life and the condition of all men in the modern world.

Cela belongs to the generation of Spaniards whose first significant cultural experience was the Civil War. As a historical event, the war sharpened and darkened the intellectual perspective of this generation of 1936, whose outlook was to grow skeptical, bitter, and confused. And as a trauma of the collective psyche, the war dulled the nation's nerve centers, along with the individual fibers that were their human constituents. The result in literature was an emotional listlessness that clung wearily to an equally drab traditionalism. . . . This, of course, is understandable, for the tenor of the age has been one of caution and isolation. The political scene required silence, harmony was society's watchword, and withdrawn recuperation was by necessity, not choice, the highest national value. More important than immediate entry into the European literary community was the re-establishment of Spain's cultural identity, and the healing of deep spiritual wounds.

Out of the moral numbness of the war's aftermath came the bold, disruptive voice of Cela to jolt Spain from her much-desired tranquillity. He wrote with precision, authority, and ruthlessness. His cold objectivity toward pain spoke volumes. And yet his acrid tone permitted a faint touch of tenderness. In all of this, Cela was not only the unrelenting goad of his country's tired body, but the conscience of its divided soul, and he described without self-pity or remorse the physical and moral condition of his fellow men. He burst forth upon the intellectual scene in 1942 with his shocking first novel, *The Family of Pascual Duarte,* which described the passions and crimes of an inarticulate and otherwise naïve man. This tale of violence and primitivism, so clearly a symbolic product of the brutality underlying Spain's fratricidal history, gave Cela instantaneous title to the literary leadership of his generation. He still holds this position, not because, as he once said cynically, the competition was so easy, but because of his audacious originality and his superb prose style. He is today, after twenty-five years and as many books, Spain's foremost writer. . . . (pp. vii-viii)

Cela's work falls into two categories, fiction and travel sketches. Both groups are characterized by the same sophistication, technical brilliance, and overt or subtle stylization. The novels are unique, revealing little continuity among them of either theme or form, and showing even less artistic progress or emergence of an individual technique. On the contrary, they are all distinct from each other and full-grown, with no two alike in anything except their excellence. Cela has tried, as none of his contemporaries have, to experiment with a different novelistic theory in each successive narrative. As a result he achieved a disturbing esthetic of violence in *The Family of Pascual Duarte,* a state of pure contemplation in *Rest Home,* and a structural fragmentation in *The Hive.* Other novels indicate still other forms: surrealism, linguistic innovation, the picaresque, but in all of them it is the formal problem which eventually expresses the author's intellectual position. That is, instead of providing an ideological content for the subject matter of the novel itself, Cela allows certain inferences to be drawn from the structural form and technique. Thus, the removal of all action in *Rest Home,* and the conversion of its chapter sequences into a tableau of interior monologues, suggest that solitude is the basic form of existence, and that social and historical man has lost his significance in a world of incommunicability. Similarly, the treatment of gratuitous violence and primitive mentality in *The Family of Pascual Duarte* indicates the incapacity of modern man to make others understand his sense of impotence and absurdity.

The Hive is one of the best Spanish novels of the century, and probably the most spectacular. Banned in Spain because of its devastating social critique, it gained unanimous acclaim in the Hispanic world for its technical accomplishment, verbal perfection, and richly drawn characterization. It is similar in construction to Dos Passos' *Manhattan Transfer,* and traces the "uncertain paths" of a number of lives that crisscross or touch each other tangentially within a three-day period which is cut up, as a film strip might be, and restructured without regard to chronological time. Thus the disintegration of temporal order parallels the purposeless drift of the characters. The real protagonist of the novel, however, is the city of Madrid, dirty, vice-ridden, and throbbing with vitality. Her inhabitants, living in the impoverished misery and moral bankruptcy that followed the war, reveal nevertheless the vital impulses and frailties that are universally recognized as the common human denominator. Thus the novel's pathos consists first of the visible waste of men's lives desensitized by poverty and spiritual anguish, and second, of the silent and desperate hopelessness found in the characters' action and even inaction. As a pitiless incision into the tissue of Madrid society, *The Hive*'s realism is immediate and graphic. Its language is racy, poetic, and incredibly faithful to colloquial speech, while its personages are memorably individualistic even as they are typical of middle- and lower-class life.

I have dwelt this long on the first category of Cela's literary work because if *The Hive* is the crowning point of his novels, the *Journey to the Alcarria* is its jeweled counterpart among the travel sketches. In both works the sociological relevance is the same, the linguistic fidelity equally dazzling, and the philosophical undertones similar, but of different intensity. The *Journey to the Alcarria* . . . is probably the best of Cela's *vagabundajes.* It is also the first of a number of excursions into various regions of the peninsula which, as real acts in the author's life, become a symbolic expression of an intellectual position. As a literary form it has the dual purpose of gaining a direct and intuitive understanding of the nature of the Spanish personality, and of presenting a cultural anatomy of the nation's most fundamental social stratum: its provincial life. (pp. viii-x)

The *vagabundaje,* which is Cela's term for a book of travels named after its central figure, is actually a picaresque narrative made subjective and lyrical by the vagabond's consciousness of the landscape. Whether Cela journeys to the Alcarria, Andalusia, or Galicia, the technique is the same. The autobiographical form of the picaresque becomes a fictionalized biography in the third person; the peripatetic compulsiveness of the wanderer continues; and the constant preoccupation with food and lodging claims first attention. But in the process a great change occurs. The structure of life is reduced to its basic simplicity. People are met and engaged freely, with purity of intention. And a certain direct knowledge of individuals and their customs is acquired. Hence the value of the journey with respect to glimpsing the essence of human experience, while also providing an insight into the life sources of Spanish civilization.

Cela sets out to accomplish so much, and finally does, that it is almost as if he has a theory of the travel sketchbook. He himself is the vagabond, an urban resident, an intellectual, and a Spaniard in search of self-identity. In the wake of a disastrous civil war, the problem of who the Spaniard is and what his national values stand for has become a critical and urgent concern. There have been many images of Spain, all accurate in part, yet none satisfactorily illuminating her complete face. But in the contemporary period it is impossible to deduce anything from life in the great cities, which are in the midst of social upheaval due to population shifts and economic changes. The writer must go to the rural areas, where there is not only stability but a carefully preserved character as old as tradition itself. (pp. xi-xii)

The result of this quest for Spain's identity is a kind of rough literary vignette which Cela has called a bittersweet etching. It either describes with irony and stylized exaggeration an interesting person encountered during a trip, or else consists of an invented composite of a few real or probable "types." In many cases these people are Castilians, traditionally considered both the political unifiers of the land and the group that most firmly impressed its personality upon the national climate. Cela's main object is to capture the human drama, but in the process of travel other advantages also accrue. His conversations turn up bits of local history and folklore, and his descriptions subtly introduce sociological details worthy of more formal studies. In addition, we see the contrast between the external and transitory history of society and what Unamuno called the intrahistorical life of the people, the profound and unchanging emotional experience of humanity that triumphs over all events.

But in addition to this cultural purpose, Cela has a private one that is open to interpretation. His rejection of metropolitan life for a more simple form suggests a dissatisfaction with the growing artificiality and complexity of technological civilization. The cities are corrupt, spontaneity is replaced by more self-conscious styles of living, and the loss of contact with nature is no less tragic than the increasingly impersonal forms of communication among men. Modern man has in fact become isolated, and this solitude is represented in the figure of the vagabond, who escapes from the empty routines of the city, but who is condemned to a rootless existence, moving from town to town. Furthermore, his vagabond rôle is a kind of activist anti-intellectualism. Sensing his position as an outsider in society, the intellectual attributes his alienation to an oversensitive awareness of himself in relation to the values of the group. He reacts against this contemplative state by engaging physically in the most tiring of activities: rugged travel. He enshrines country simplicity not only because it is innocent of the fruitless rituals of the mind, but because its own actions are so fatiguing that they consume all of the traveler's energies, allowing him to forget his loneliness. These physical acts, of course, are themselves converted into ritual by the vagabond Cela, who, after all, is really a writer. But the esteem in which he holds them is significant proof of the judgment he has made. Nevertheless, his renunciation of intellectualist values cannot really convert him into an ingenuous rustic. And so the literary genre of the *vagabundaje* which he has perfected becomes an act of artifice in the face of its own artlessness. (pp. xii-xiii)

[Cela has said of **Journey to the Alcarria**] that it was an orthodox book of travels, conceived according to the old and venerable laws of narration: truth, simplicity, and the gratifying vision of the unforeseen. The fact that he wrote it in the third person does not diminish its biographical origin, but since the narrator is so subordinated to the material that he is recording and reflecting, the question of veracity is unimportant. In Cela's definition of the travel-sketch genre, the itinerant writer must react with genuine and simple surprise to what he sees, and jot it down without inventive alteration. There is no room for the novelesque, the discursive, or even the interpretative. Everything that is not straightforward becomes pedantic in a world whose mental dimension is neither analytical nor imaginative. (pp. xiii-xiv)

But if the travel sketchbook has its own precepts, there are also certain requirements for the traveler himself. He must not have a preformed idea of the direction of his excursion, except, of course, for the general outline. . . . Furthermore, he rids himself of evil thoughts on leaving the city, and encounters other men without ulterior motives. But above all, he accepts the world as it is offered to him, good and evil, for "all things are to be found in the vineyard of the Lord."

Nevertheless, Cela's disposition runs strongly to pessimism. If he reaches a strange village in the evening, he prefers to leave its inspection for the next day, in the belief that "the morning light is preferable and more propitious for this matter of wandering through a town." In fact, "it even seems that in the mornings people look more favorably on a stranger," whereas "at night people are tired and the darkness makes them fearful, mistrustful, and guarded." This says much about human psychology, but it is also indicative of the author's own attitude toward social relationships. He is a sentimentalist, but also a melancholic. . . . He suppresses bits of romantic verse that come to mind, his farewells become "laden with unrecognized sorrow," and he resists the "dangerous drowsiness" that overcomes him when he is "entirely too comfortable." Part of his vagabond philosophy consists of a promise not to sleep in the same place two nights in a row, and since "roads are made for walking on . . . it gets to be a bad habit to sit by the roadside talking to people."

It is to our advantage that Cela is so restless, for otherwise his pensiveness might have restricted the wealth of detail that is offered in the book. Yet it is important to recognize that the dozens of motifs about the Alcarria that are found here have been chosen from an infinity of possibilities, motifs determined by Cela's own psychological framework. The reality which emerges, therefore, does exist in fact, but its objectivity is impaired by virtue of being selective. For example, many of Cela's favorite, and sometimes obsessive, themes appear in these pages: the child, the village idiot, the beggar, and other "types" such as the old wanderer and the peddler. In some cases the scenes are presented in cheerful terms, but more frequently the people are described pessimistically as longsuffering individuals who are leading lives of quiet desperation. (pp. xiv-xv)

The affinity between the intellectual outsider and these social pariahs is clear enough, but Cela's presentation of such themes is less apparent. **The Journey to the Alcarria** is deceptively easy to read, and its observations are so casual that incidents can slip by unnoticed because they are always supplanted by fresh detail. The tiny tragedies of each day seem minimal for the sophisticated reader, but they are the only events of importance that occur in the Alcarria. . . . Even more disturbing is Cela's manner of expressing the sorrow of existence. He tells of several young bar girls who "already seem to have in their eyes that special patient sorrow that one sees in hired animals, dragged hither and yon by bad luck and evil intentions." There is one child who looks "as timid as a whipped dog." . . . In these and many other details, the weariness and futility of existence are evoked in a less than human, sometimes primitive, undertone.

Part of Cela's artistry belongs to the Goyesque tradition, not just in that certain deformed types catch his attention, but also in his use of the ugly as an esthetic category. Such descriptions are more than intense realism, for cases like the sheep-shearing scene, or the fly-plagued, bleeding donkey, or the references to garbage are graphic parallels in the concrete physical world to the spiritual despondency of the people. Perhaps in the most significant area of Cela's accomplishment—his style—is this dual effect best realized. His imagery above all, the similes and metaphors which pierce the delicate prose texture, combines sympathy and horror in an uneasy symphony of pathos. In speaking of Madrid, he says that the city's "inhabitants are still asleep and its pulse, like an invalid's, beats quietly as if ashamed of being heard." At dawn in the capital "the street doors of the houses are still closed, like stingy purses," whereas at a similar hour the traveler lets his imagination wander freely so that "it flutters like a slow, dying butterfly." (pp. xvi-xvii)

These examples, along with the muted sorrow pervading the book, are engrained in the fabric of the prose and contribute to the general mood of the journey. Nevertheless, the great sweeps of Cela's brush contrast strongly with the dark lines of his detail. His skillful use of innuendo and understatement, which leave much of what is unspoken to the reader's imagination, has a counterpart in the distinct atmosphere of buoyancy that emerges. . . . This is partly because of the lightness of the style, but due also to the sense of space and daylight that is imparted by the setting. Very little occurs at night, and still less within four walls. Cela dispenses with the nocturnal element in the re-creation of typical scenes, landscapes, or village topography, and stresses amplitude. (p. xvii)

One major aspect of the *vagabundaje* is the landscape itself, and no statement about it can replace a reading of the entire text. There is a poetic purity to be found in the magic naming of the thistles and sprigs, in following the minute movements of insect life, and in tracing the scents and sounds of a countryside trembling with sensation. The beauty of these descriptions is beyond praise, for it is essentially artless, and the scenes, stripped of adornment, leap forward unexpectedly from the tedium of travel and the emptiness of conversation. In such circumstances it is possible for Cela to affirm an absolute happiness, in which "his imagination was flooded with a swarm of golden thoughts" and an inner peace steals over his heart.

Finally, and most far-reaching, are the two contributions made by Cela to contemporary Spanish literature. One is a general feature: the image of Spain that takes form clearly and faithfully, both in its sociological relevance and in its vision of a lost grandeur and a newly found dignity. The Alcarria is still backward compared to Madrid; its values are conservative, its community structure monolithic, and its living

---

An excerpt from *The Hive*

Doña Rosa is certainly not what one would call sensitive. "And it's no news to you what I'm telling you. If I want wasters around I've got quite enough with that no-good, my brother-in-law! You're very green still, d'you hear me? Very green. A fine thing that would be! Whenever have you seen a fellow without education or morals coming to this place, puffing and blowing and stamping about as if he was a real gent? What's more, I'll take an oath that it won't happen while I've got eyes in my head."

Doña Rosa has drops of sweat on her brow and her hairy upper lip.

"And you there, you booby, slinking off to get the evening paper! There's no respect or decency in this place, that's all there is to it. One day I'm going to give you a proper thrashing if my monkey's up. Has one ever seen such a thing?"

Doña Rosa pins her small rat's eyes on Pepe, the old waiter who came to town from the Galician village of Mondoñedo forty or forty-five years ago. Behind her thick lenses, Doña Rosa's eyes resemble the startled eyes of a stuffed bird.

"What are you looking at? What are you looking at like that, you fool? You're just the same as you were on the day you came here. Not even God Almighty Himself could make you people lose your farmyard smell. Come on, wake up, and let's have no more trouble. If you'd more guts, I'd have slung you out in the street long ago. D'you hear? I'll be beggared!"

Doña Rosa pats her belly and changes her mode of address.

"Now come, come, man . . . everybody to his job. You know, we mustn't lose our sense of proportion, hells bells, or the respect, d'you get me, or the respect!"

Doña Rosa lifts her chin and takes a deep breath. The little hairs of her mustache quiver as though in challenge, jauntily and yet ceremoniously, like the black little horns of a courting cricket.

---

standards very low. During his reportorial moments Cela offers many examples to confirm this, and yet they all somehow recede before the more affirmative image of historical Spain. Here too the view is pessimistic, but with the pride of discovering a still visible cultural heritage that is worthy of a modern metamorphosis. (pp. xviii-xix)

This first contribution, however, would not be possible were it not for the greatness of Cela's style. It is his verbal brilliance which has given him much of his fame, and his use of language has indeed invigorated modern Spanish prose. . . . Cela's style is not only so colloquial that it resists translation, its very transparency is contrary to the texture and rhythm of English prose. . . . [To successfully translate his works] is most difficult, for Cela can combine in one expression not only an entire folkway, but a personal lyricism and a sly irony as well. His prose is fluid and deceptively simplistic. It is sometimes tart and frequently wistful. Never does it lack the ingenious juxtaposition of colloquial, non-abstract vocabulary alongside of metaphorical innovation. And yet whether in the humor, snatches of song, slang phrases, or nicknames, the purity and poise of its linguistic dignity is constant. From the land comes Cela's language, and from the people, his book. (p. xix)

Paul Ilie, in an introduction to Journey to the Alcarria *by Camilo José Cela, translated by Frances M. López-Morillas, The University of Wisconsin Press, 1964, pp. vii-xix.*

ROBERT KIRSNER

The vision of Spain expressed in the novels of Camilo José Cela constitutes a key to the interpretation of characters and situations. Cela's relationship to Spain is not merely that of an author toward his *patria;* it is not only a socio-political reaction on the part of the author; Cela lives Spain in its totality, as Galdós and Baroja before him, and he dramatizes his own personal feelings toward his country in terms of novelistic creation. Throughout his novels the consciousness of Spain is a motivating force in his creative process. (p. 16)

In terms of characters and situations the novels of Cela reflect the author's artistic vision of Spain. This is not a matter of cause and effect, nor juxtaposition, but rather of compenetration. Notwithstanding the literary uniqueness of the novelistic persons, they are all permeated with Hispanic values and they are definitely related to their particular environment. Be it in a negative or positive form, or perhaps submerged in a feeling of ambivalence, the characters in their inner reality take a position towards the locale that surrounds them. Whether they conquer or are conquered by their earth, the earth that is Spain flows into them and they become an integral part of Spain. That is to say, the author is not merely viewing his characters' attitude toward Spain; he is permitting them to live out their lives according to their own possibilities and aspirations. Thus, the characters embrace within their own make-up the author's vision of Spain.

The vision of Spain evolves as the development of characters unfolds. Their lives are as beautiful or as ugly as their habitat. Their possibilities are as vast or as narrow as their terrain. Their lives are as fertile or as sterile as their earth. The development of characters is integrated with the description of their environment. Yet, the persons in Cela's novels are not mere symbols. Even when viewed as abstract representations, they do not stand apart, detached from their locale. Whatever allegorical significance they may have is related to the world they inhabit. Nor are Cela's literary figures conceived as products of results of historical and geographical situations. To be sure, they are in harmony with their circumstances, but they and their circumstances are irreducible. Cela's characters live in the image of their creator's vision of Spain, but they live as artistic entities, experiencing and becoming integrated with the world around them. Their ultimate reality rests on their own novelistic experience of their circumstances.

Inasmuch as the role of Spain as a literary object is inexorably related to the creation of personages, a study of the novelistic technique is deemed essential in determining the author's vision of his *patria* and the part that this vision plays in the creative process of the novelist. There is reason to believe, as we shall see in due course, that Cela's image of Spain profoundly affects the lives he creates in his novels. More than mere "influence," it becomes the inciting force which propels his imagery and which in itself constitutes the symphonic theme of his works.

Although no author, or no other person for that matter, is completely free and emancipated from his heritage, Cela represents an explosive literary nascence, which virtually breaks with tradition. The art of Cela recognizes "stepfathers" rather than "fathers." However much it may resemble literary antecedents, it is essentially unique in its inner structure.

Cela is not, of course, the first Spanish author who confronts himself with Spain as a literary theme. Nor is there reason to believe that he will be the last. Nonetheless, any comparison that might be made between the works of Cela with those of his immediate thematic predecessors, Baroja, Galdós, and Larra would serve primarily to add to our archaeological knowledge of Spanish literary history. (pp. 16-18)

Quite naturally, one might find in the novels of Cela qualities which may be reminiscent of the acrimony of Larra, the irony of Galdós, and the despair of Baroja. Unquestionably, there are similar notes. Cela, too, borrows from the same scale of human feeling. Yet the composition of his creations reveals a totally distinct blend. Neither the fabric nor the effect of Cela's novels follows the pattern of other writers. The art of Cela is consciously unlike that of his predecessors, who retain a sense of traditional artistic symmetry even in their opposition to existing values. In fact, their critical attitude binds them to their past. Cela, on the contrary, is intent on destroying the past. His sense of reality arises out of the attempted obliteration of history. Man gains life as he destroys. And thus, Pascual Duarte, his first novelistic protagonist, comes into being. There is no longer the concept of accepted images. Life is neither a circle nor a square, but rather the elimination of symbols. From destruction, creation. (p. 18)

[For Cela], chaos is the beginning of life. But out of darkness does not come light, but more mystery. And out of chaos, confusion. Reality consists of experiencing life as a disparate agony, a suffering which has no more rhyme or reason than just being.

It would be sheer conjecture, and perhaps an oversimplification of historical circumstances, to attribute Cela's position toward Spain—and life—to the advent and aftermath of the Spanish Civil War (1936-1939). Yet, like any other intense experience of life and death, this War in which Cela was an active participant must have affected him deeply, so deeply in fact that there is a conscious effort on his part to cast it into

oblivion. What is left unsaid is often more stylistically significant than that which is explicitly stated. There are hardly any references to the Civil War in Cela's compositions. Yet, his writings deal primarily with the conflict of man against man, and more precisely with man against himself. The struggle is the thing. And the more insoluble the conflict, the more beautiful the struggle. Beauty here would be synonymous with *disparity* for Cela thrives on incongruity. The characters he creates are as discordant as the world around him. The discordance, however, does not become orderly. It is discrepant, inconsistent. If there is any harmony in his themes and characters, it is precisely the variation of dissonance, the fluidity of asymmetry. There is a pattern of harrowing, impossible situations but not a sameness in the topic or the setting. Thus, the aggregate works of Cela are in themselves heterogeneous, unrelated in subject matter. This distinct external dissimilarity, as well as their inner thematic unity, binds them and characterizes them as belonging to the same grotesque sphere.

In his treatment of Spain as a literary theme as in his forging of characters, Cela's artistic imagery appears to be distorted. One perceives a deliberate intent on the part of the novelist to present a vision of life which is in conflict with tradition. Thus, Spain as well as the novelistic characters, is fashioned in this form of self-contradiction. Indeed, the characters and Spain are seen in a perspective of *Gestalt*. Man and his habitat, man and his circumstances, are irreducible in the novels of Camilo José Cela. Together, in their literary image, they constitute Cela's vision of Spain, his inner experience of Spanish life.

The first novel of Camilo José Cela, *La familia de Pascual Duarte* (1942), marks an explosive breach with tradition. It forms a line of demarcation with the Spanish novel of the past. More than the beginning of a new movement, this novel signifies a new form of art. Far more reaching in its impact than the frivolous *nivola* of Unamuno, *La Familia de Pascual Duarte* shocks and stuns the reader with its seemingly senseless brutality. Here we have barbarity which spares no one, not even the giver of life. Moreover, monstrosity does not detract from reality; on the contrary, we are repelled because we can and do project ourselves in this abhorrent situation. Our inner concealed feelings—not to say suppressed or subconscious—are reached, and we react with hostility. When the reader regains his composure, he is likely to want to dismiss the book as "just too hideous," but it is too late; the impression of disproportionate horror has already been made. The author has succeeded in transmitting to us his positive vision of an incongruous Spanish life which is experienced in terms of violence and destructiveness.

Even though one can rationally attest to the senselessness of the action, the situation, and the style, the protestation will not remove the imprint of verisimilitude. To be sure, whatever disparity the plot may have, whatever inconsistencies there may be between the protagonist, the supposed narrator of the story, and the language he employs, they only serve to accentuate the reality of incongruity. *La Familia de Pascual Duarte* is deliberately disproportionate, intentionally cruel. In effect, it is logical in its structure.

In this novel Spain is presented as a sanguinary image. Blood is the unifying motif of the work. In life as in death, in love as in hate, the characters come alive through the appearance of the word *la sangre*. More than any other word or phrase, *blood* gives life to the literary figures and their circumstances.

At the very beginning of the account, the characterization of Pascual suggests an ordinary picaresque-type "hero" until he bursts forth with his passion for blood. (pp. 19-22)

Although externally fully formed as a man, Pascual has no life as the book begins; at the end, as he is about to lose his physical identity as a man and disappear from view, his evanescence is pregnant with reality. He can now breathe life. He has overcome its mysteries. Death frees him from all bonds of society and more significantly from himself.

In the novels of Cela little space is devoted to the description of environmental conditions *per se;* the reader acquires a vision of Spain primarily through the behavior of characters. Spain is its people. More than mere symbols—an interesting case might be made for Pascual Duarte's being an allegory of Spain—the literary persons are totally integrated with their habitat. However "universal" they may be, like La Celestina, Lazarillo, or Fortunata, they are singularly Hispanic in their structure. Only in the *particular* realm of that which is Spain can we understand the actions and motivations of all characters in **La Familia de Pascual Duarte.** Even their physical situation is singularly identifiable with Spain of the post-Civil War period. Not only is the book, then, restricted to a locale but also to a period. The characters are irreducible from the time as well as the space that surrounds them. It would be an anachronism to transfer them to another era, an anatopism to place them in another land. Circumstances of time and place counterpoise the reality of the characters. Removed from their specific situations, they would be no more than caricatures, or at best, vacuous symbols.

Unlike the Spain of Quevedo, Cela's Spain is not evil or inverse; unlike the defective Spain of Larra and Baroja, Cela's Spain is not viewed in judgment. Indeed, the most frighteningly impressive aspect of Cela's attitude toward his country is that it lacks moral perspective. Spain is recreated in its dynamic being. There are instances of goodness and many more of evil, but always in the course of expressive being. Good and evil are but fleeting moments of contemplation. Lives are lived, in the last analysis, in compatibility with their inner possibilities; they are not motivated by external social forces. Cela's characters are not plaintive; neither are they acquiescent. Their seemingly asymmetrical actions, anarchichal from a collective point of view, follow an irregular pattern that is singularly their own.

The characters in **La Familia de Pascual Duarte,** even those who seem incited only by evil, are capable of experiencing moments of goodness, which are equated with beauty. (pp. 25-7)

Unlike la Celestina or Tirso's Don Juan, Pascual is not the incarnation of evil or frivolity. Just as he is about to seem proportionately wicked in our eyes, his figure undergoes permutation. If only Pascual were completely devoid of sympathy, the book would not be so horrendous!

Another significant trait that accentuates the incongrous nature of Pascual's personality and that prevents him from becoming a picaresque protagonist is that at times he displays a profound sense of honor. Not always, but occasionally, when he *feels* affronted. There are moments, then, when he appears almost as a *pundonoroso* 17th century hero. (p. 27)

[However, the] pity he inspires is interwoven with horror. Horror and pity, with very little exaltation, are also contained in the limited descriptions of environment. As time, space, too, is presented personalitiscally. It is significant only as it relates to the characters' inner lives, for in **La Familia de Pascual Duarte** there is hardly any probing into external or physical reality. (p. 28)

In effect, there is a parallel in the meagerness of outer descriptions of people and the outer descriptions of the land. In both instances, we are impressed by this lack. Basically, the author seems to dismiss the *milieu* as he does the particular setting of a house. . . . But even when he does describe the abode, it is inexorably related to the people who dwell in it. . . . The personality of the protagonist invariably permeates the depiction of the locale. (pp. 28-9)

The relationship between characters and environment is not one of cause and effect as it is in naturalistic novels. The rapport here rests on compenetration. The literary persons are in sympathy with their time and space. It is a configurative presentation which is seen through the events of human existence. When the characters express anguish, for example, they are expressing an anguish that is theirs in their intimate totality, in their time and in their space.

If the lack of moral values in the lives of the characters is frightening, more disturbing still is the absence of judgment or evaluation in the recreation of contemporary Spanish society. There are no panegyrics and there are no vilifications. Provincial life in Spain here lacks the censure of the naturalist and the admiration of the romanticist. **La Familia de Pascual Duarte** neither extols nor condemns reason or emotion. In fact, nothing is reprehensible; nothing is eulogized. Life is experienced with intensity, often cruelly, but with no directive from good or evil. The feeling for life seems completely devoid of abstractions, it is profoundly personal. At times it may coincide with the reader's pre-conceived ideals; more frequently it is a dramatic departure—at least, from the *conscious*. In any case it does not seem patterned in the literary tradition of sympathy and antipathy. The book, then, is likely to produce a state of incompatibility and possibly complete rejection, on the part of the reader, who is trained to cope with good and evil but not with their virtual absence. (p. 29)

Perhaps if the absence of moral values were complete and perfect, the book could be easily classified as amoral. What accentuates the incongruous nature of this novel is precisely the privation of consistency. It does not follow a straight line nor is it a circular one in the sense that it ends where it begins.

As we have seen, there are glimmers or at least flickers of goodness; there are expressions, however feeble, of personal and social guilt. But they do not survive. They serve to infuse the vacuum of life with foreign matter, as it were, to keep it from being a perfect vacuum. We cannot say that "nada es nada," *nada es*. We are not at all sure what [nothingness] may be, it may not fit any rational or emotional pattern, but it *is*.

The existentialist proclaims "L'homme est néant" and thus describes a perfect vacuum, a nothingness which is absolute. In the novel of Cela not even *nothing* can complement the verb *to be*. Man is *not* nothing even if neither is he something. In effect, the verb need not link man to anything; it is self sufficient in just *being*. The essence of life is not reduced to an idea; it can only continue to be essential if it is experienced as life.

Américo Castro's profound analysis of the Hispanic *vivir desviviéndose* might help us to understand the essence of life in **La Familia de Pascual Duarte.** But here it is a *vivir* without direction, certainly without ideals; it is primarily a naked *vivir,* destructive without an end. Yet, for all its negation of social ideals, life emerges as a positive force worth living. It is not reduced to a symmetrical "existentialistic" symbol. (p. 30)

Pascual is not the only one whose life seems without purpose. Society in general appears aimless, not intent on being cruel, but yet unconcerned with kindness. It may not defend, but it certainly does not oppose the circumstances which surround it. If it has no paradigms of virtue, it also lacks symbols of sin. Human heights have no zenith and depths are without a nadir. In a sense, it is an attitude which is far more difficult to combat. In any case, it is more incomprehensible in rational terms, especially since there are instances of apparent human and literary conformity.

If the virtual absence of ethical values serves as a departure from tradition, the occasional inclusion of a literary technique, reminiscent of Cervantes and Galdós, adds to the irregular pattern of *La Familia de Pascual Duarte.* There are in this work, for example, instances of irony which recall the compassionate critical humor of *Don Quijote* and *Fortunata y Jacinta.* There are moments when the author's tears are filled with laughter. It is interesting that Pascual, as he recounts the story of his life while awaiting execution, should display a sense of humor about the foibles of humanity. There is much acrimony in the observations of the protagonist, but there is also an element of naive wonderment that makes the reader smile. (pp. 30-1)

At times one has the fleeting impression that he is faced with Cervantian situations of simultaneous laughter and tears. Thus we laugh at deplorable conditions that we recognize as a truth of human behavior. (p. 32)

In *La Familia de Pascual Duarte* all characters live according to their individual agonizing possibilities. In this *family,* which is in a broader sense Spain, there is an ensemble of discordant human voices which constitute an aggregation of solos rather than a chorale. The soloists are not melodious; they are not following any pre-conceived notion of harmony, not even of a contrapuntal nature. The performance is made more dissonant by unexpected displays of rhythmic sounds. If it is not completely symmetrical, neither is it entirely lacking in proportion. It cannot be encompassed by positives or negatives. The only proof of its existence is that the symphony consumes itself. (p. 34)

La Colmena (1951) represents the highest point of Cela's literary career. Possibly, not since the appearance of Benito Pérez Galdós' *Fortunata y Jacinta* (1886-1887) has there been such a dramatic recreation of Hispanic life in novel form. *La Colmena,* in its consideration of merely three days of human existence in Madrid, penetrates the inner core of centuries of Spanish civilization. Its external preoccupation is with the ephemeral, Madrid in the early nineteen forties; in its inner structure it reveals the meaning of a way of life which is, for better or for worse, singularly and irreducibly Spanish. The fragmentary presentation intones the theme of disintegration, "el vivir desviviéndose [to live dying for something]." Yet, however difficult, however destructive, however incongruous, the emphasis is on *vivir* [to live].

The ominous physical reality of hunger pervades the scene. It serves as a motivating force for external behavior. It is horrible. It is real. But hunger is fundamentally the literary pretext in *La Colmena.* The inner experiences of the characters, their immanent conflicts, transcend material contemplation. In spite of their similarities with contemporary counterparts of flesh and blood, Cela's literary persons have a durable intimate existence which is tangibly artistic. Their lives are worth creating and experiencing not because they may be imaginary "case studies," but because they enclose within their personal exterior an agonizing existence which is essentially that of Spain—and possibly of all humanity. Quite naturally, the inner meaning of their lives was not perceived by the censors, who, in their paleolithic role, forbade the publication of this book in Spain.

That *La Colmena* should inspire shame in its portrayal of living history is entirely comprehensible. No nation views its penury with pride. Nor does Cela manifest satisfaction with the Hell of hunger that was Spain after the Civil War. On the contrary, he cries with grief. As he creates, he feels the torture of his people, the anguish of Spain. Nonetheless, Cela's vision is not peripheral; he sees beyond matter, and beyond the circumstantial state of man. He avails himself of transitory material truth to penetrate the intra-historical significance of Spanish life. The outer reality of *La Colmena,* the plight of Spain in the early nineteen forties, so shocking to the pride of censors, is a mutable circumstance. . . . What remains constant is the artistic expression of a way of life which is integrally Spanish.

If hunger were viewed as causation in a behavioristic fashion, *La Colmena* would become a psycho-economic treatise on human conduct. And if it is that, too, it is also much more. The author is conscious of the havoc that hunger causes. But hunger is often a disguise, an apology for human actions, and Cela is intent on "unmasking life." The depiction of social conditions in itself is not conducive to an appreciation of Cela's unmasked image of Spain. Beyond the external circumstances, which constitute the scenery of their lives, their orbit, stand the characters in their unshrouded reality. In their reaction to hunger, and other prevailing conditions, in their suffering they reveal themselves. And as they lay bare their souls, they disclose their creator's conception of the world which they and he share—Spain.

In spite of the persistent horror of hunger which permeates the existence of the characters, *La Colmena* expresses a vision of Spain which is intimately sympathetic. In a fragmentary fashion, sympathy prevails in the creation of characters. Although externally it may be unbelievably appalling to the well-fed Anglo-Saxon world, and definitely unpalatable to the Spaniards who do not wish to be reminded of the circumstances of the nineteen forties, the recreation of life in Madrid is motivated by love. It is not a unidimensional feeling which can be translated in terms of *approval* or *admiration.* By no means. Especially on the part of Cela it is a complex attitude which is fundamentally disproportionate in its rhapsodical content. It is filled with grief and despair; it has no purpose other than to embrace the agony of living; it is incongruous, self-contradictory; it is "a voice in the desert." Often it is ambivalent, adulterated (or perhaps so it is purified) with hatred, but it is love, the love for Spanish life which guides the pen of Cela in *La Colmena.* The author struggles with the external prevailing structure of his civilization, but he surrenders to its inner foundation. For all his avowed intention to narrate "a slice of life without charity," his pen gains independence and intuitively it becomes profoundly charitable.

Although superficially *La Colmena* presents a panorama of human abjection with overtones of opprobrium, there is not a single character, of the more than three hundred who appear in this work, who evokes unmixed horror. Even the most cruelly repulsive ones, such as the sodomists, also inspire pity. The formula is not always rationally discernible; nor is it invariable. The blend is often crude. Nonetheless, its effect is perspicuous. Whereas in the three earlier novels *rejection* was the catalytic agent which established the rapport between the reader and the characters, here the bond is magnetic attraction. Logically, one may maintain the position of revulsion; artistically, one is charmed, as if by enchantment, into a state of compenetration. The bond of sympathy that exists between the author and his literary persons flows into the reader and radiates magic participation. (pp. 57-60)

La Colmena centers its attention on one *café*. Here is focused the languishing existence of human lives whose destinies are interwoven by hunger. The habitués, many of whom are extra-social, constitute a gallery of distinctive individuals who appear to be no more than a mass of humanity when viewed panoramically. Their uniqueness, their anchoritic existence, is revealed as the book progresses and the characters are examined microscopically not only in relation to the other characters but also in relation to themselves. Thus, the *café* of doña Rosa reaches out with its tentacles and penetrates into the inner recesses of hundreds of literary persons, who are directly or indirectly bound to this establishment. Sometimes the chain that shackles the people to their places in the *café* seems unanchored, but their purposeless life knows no other course. In the world of *Fortunata y Jacinta* man was in conflict with his destiny; in the world of *La Colmena* he hasn't even discovered what his destiny is.

La Colmena is in a sense, the sub-title of the book which is denominated as the beginning of a series, *Caminos inciertos.* In this beehive of humanity there is no gathering of honey. The convocation of drifting lives has no organization; there are no certain roads. Some of the inhabitants pretend to be searching for identity; the majority doesn't even bother. Their motions are habitual as though they were mechanically operated. Thus, they all appear to be playing their roles in life fatalistically with the complete submission to the historical circumstances of their time. This is the phantasmagoria of *La Colmena,* its stage effect.

A more penetrating perspective of the scene, an examination of the individual characters in their intimate surroundings, reveals underneath the aimlessness of their lives a world of personal agonizing frustration. Indeed, the conflict is not well-defined; sometimes it is merely the struggle of living, but it is experienced with fierce intensity. As they strive to express themselves, not quite knowing how or why, they suffer in their uncertainty. In their nebulous ties with historical values, especially the Hispanic sense of honor, they manifest a disproportionate existence which does not seem to fit any ideal pattern. They are not prepared to confront ancient images iconoclastically; nor can they afford the luxury of revering them. While the cruel reality of an empty stomach does not completely reduce them to animals, it does in part divest them of the halo of civilization. This is their struggle, to maintain an aura of civilization while physically being reduced to animalism.

The battle is patrimonially instinctive. There is a vestige of intuitive historicity. In spite of their material vicissitudes, the characters feel the need to preserve their personal dignity. Even Elvirita, the prostitute, has her pride! Often the facade of civilization has its pitiably ludicrous moments, but for all

its misdirection and senseless incongruity, it is expressed sympathetically. The most horribly ridiculous situations do not detract from the compassion that the characters inspire. Horror does not efface pity; on the contrary, in this novel the brutal reality of the physical world lends force to the understanding of equivocal lives which have "uncertain roads."

The descriptive fragmentation of individual existences does not break the spell of sympathy. As the account of one life evaporates, there is no vacuum; it flows into the narration of another. There is an arabesque continuity with no definite beginning and certainly no end. If there is no one protagonist, neither is there an antagonist, unless both be contained within the persons as in marriage. The stories proceed in all directions; some lives are recaptured, others evanesce. The thread of the narration is as irregular as the histories it retells. Incidents which at first are easily forgotten as they are replaced by others return to haunt us. Often what appeared to be insignificant is revealed with its profound fire of human hatred and love. Sometimes apparent irrelevances remain suppressed along with what seemed to be great events. The sensation is erratic. One cannot discriminate in his remembrances or his forgetfulness. The vision is overwhelming; it defies the reader's acumen. One's judgment is crushed. There only remains the impression of pity transcending horror.

The moribund atmosphere of Madrid exorcises specters of human depravation but they are transitory impressions. Impossible dreams and hopeless illusions, on the other hand, survive the tide of evanescence. Their evocative despair creates a sensation of greater reality than all the physical acts. The particular events are soon forgotten, perhaps the particular illusions, too. What endures is the grievous image of the hopeless dreams, the truth of their impossible aspirations.

In the picaresque setting of Cela's *Nuevas Andanzas y Desventuras de Lazarillo de Tormes* there were no dreams, only nightmares. In *La Colmena* man may not know what his longing should be, but often he yearns for another sphere of identity. Thus, the young bootblack happily seeks to affiliate himself with don Leonardo, a man of fine appearance, who has robbed the boy of his savings. The reality of his dream surpasses material catastrophies. The association with what he considers another social class is worth the sacrifice of his wealth, accrued in self-abnegation. Dreams are the stuff that men are made of in this novel. The myth of the *señor* persists. . . . (pp. 60-2)

In the assemblage of heterogenous personages there are those who dream very little. These are the practical people who thrive on the hunger of others. They are "realistic" in their adjustment to social conditions. Their success has the universal quality of cruelty expressed through self-preservation. The reality of these characters rests on the "true to life" fabric of ephemerality. They constitute the background of apathetic familiarity. Their banal identity, tangibly recognizable, is cast into oblivion. They are neither hated nor loved. In the process of artistic disintegration they disappear, leaving in their wake no imaginative sphere to perpetuate their existence. Their literary fate is their punishment, the author's revenge on his society.

The ordinary displays of cruelty on the part of doña Rosa are innocuously archaeological in substance. They interrupt but they do not affect the uncertain course of human lives. Along with other thriving business magnates like the uncouth don Mario de la Vega, the wealthy printer, and doña Ramona

Bragado, the usurious procuress, doña Rosa forms part of the dramatic chorus. They are all crude representations of the realm of human experience. They appear to be photographed rather than painted. They are the "facts" of the Spanish way of life, the stage for the tragedy. Without them there is no theatre. They may be facsimiles, but they are indispensable for the performance.

Although outwardly at the beginning all characters seem to be stage props, carbon copies of life, as the narration ensues introspectively beyond the scenography of the novel there is revealed before us a host of undecipherable lives struggling to exist outside of their circumscribed social limits. The vision lacks the perspective of proportion. It is fragmentary, at times virtually undeveloped, embryonic in its form. But it is sustained by sympathy and by means of this pillar it lives. In *La Colmena* the story is not completed. The events are left as if in suspended animation; so is the development of characters. What remains is the substance that links the author and the reader to the unfinished novelistic symphony—vital sympathy.

La Colmena lacks the historical continuity of the genre to be considered a traditional novel. Its disproportionate form reflects the incongruity of its content, its schism with the past. The era which Cela is recreating represents a radical departure from chronological order. Ontologically the epoch is the deformed product of chaos, an abortion of history. . . . The meaning of life is no longer contained in explicit ideals. And yet, man continues to dream admist the rubbles of human decay. This in essence is the novel of *La Colmena.* But it is more. As it captures the reality of illusions, it penetrates within the foundation of the Spanish way of life, with its contradictory irrational beauty. In its fragmentary analysis of contemporary chaotic life, Cela presents a living history of a people whose agonizing personal existence surmounts physical calamities. The real continuity of the novel rests on the projection of human lives who constitute the chain of actual history. Before one man's story is extinguished, another has begun.

The effect of this novel is a logical consequence of the deliberate novelistic technique. There is a sensation of overwhelming anonymity in the never ending incomplete personal images. The intent of the artist, to create explosive fragments of related partial lives is achieved. The approach is itself a reflection of the author's conscious experience of his society. There predominates in his art a perspective of life propelled by aimless distortive obliteration. But in the inexorable course of becoming ashes and dust life is illumined and we are infected with its vitality rather than its imperfect finality.

Immured in an abyss of degradation, gnawed by famine, human existence fulminates in uncomfortable ascendancy. The movement from the mire of despair lacks cohesion. It defies the logical confinement of patterns. It asserts itself in unpredictable moments. Sometimes it perishes in descent, as it is absorbed by the composition of its incarceration. In any case, in its rise or in its fall, the evanescent fulfillment of life is alluring in the atmosphere of eventual overwhelming destruction. The integration of man and his circumstances surpasses consideration of cause and effect. Within this valley of attrition man maps his own course of submission or resistance, adjustment or opposition. In action or inaction, in self-determination or in apathy, the path of one life affects the passage of another. The journey is trajectory as human lives traverse one another.

The kindling quality of individual experiences, the ability that unknowingly one life has to incite the fire of apparent unrelated human existence, evokes wonderment and admiration. The interactive juxtaposition of atomic experiences is neither fortuitous nor romantically coincidental. It is the collection of distinct entities that constitute the whole, and at no time is the whole more significant than any of its parts. The most socially unworthy resident of Madrid may spark a chain reaction of events that could affect the total composition of mankind in that city. The vision is personalistic. The strength of life, consciously or unconsciously, lies within the person himself. He may be victimized by the conditions that surround his birth, but he is not wrested of his innate endowment to affirm himself and exert vital influence in vanquishment as in triumph, in degradation as in exaltation. This is the living truth of *La Colmena.* In its perpetual driftway, life is vitally radiating.

Distilled in a shapeless moment of history, traditional Hispanic values are anomalously contained in the experiences of *La Colmena.* The myth of the *señor,* the concept of honor, the reverence of masculinity are expressed in varying degrees. As clothing of appearance seldom do they fit. In most cases they are worn in a pattern of horror and humor, but sporadically, as if by accident, there is an occasional semblance of harmony. In the crumbling cave that is Madrid not all succumb insensibly to the lava around them. In some cases, and these are the literary persons by whom we are most affected, human dignity prevails. (pp. 63-5)

For the most part, the characters of *La Colmena,* especially the men, are sympathetically passive. They are often unaware of their radiating vigor. It is among the women that we find the most novelistically impressive protagonists. The virility of men is expressed primarily as a socially outmoded role, the fulfillment of femininity is asserted willfully, sometimes submissively, but occasionally defiantly. Thus, when don Roque and Julita, father and daughter, recognize each other in the stairway of Celia's house, a rendezvous for lovers, it is the daughter who is the tragic character, the one who has brought about her fate. The father is the pathetic one. Immersed in his male role, his presence in this house is predetermined. Julita, on the contrary, is the socially unexpected visitor. Of course, they are both surprised to see each other, momentarily stunned. In due time, however, it will be Julita's life which will be affected by her determination to be extra-social; her father will continue to play his role with little feeling other than paternal sorrow for his daughter.

In the turmoil of Madrid life, there is a curious clarity about the structure of domesticity. The external semblance of masculine rule is unmasked. The female is the dominant creature. This is quite clear in the case of the baker, el señor Ramón, who is ensnared in the disguise of legendary tradition. He must pretend to be the master of his household. . . . By means of irony, with profound sympathy for the halucinatory male ego, the novelist brings down myths to the realm of human experience. The reader smiles with feeling at *el señor* Ramón and if he is a male also at himself. There is no acrimony in this penetrating perspective of Hispanic values. The vision does not imply judgment, other than understanding for the vacuum of social beliefs. The baker's illusory role gives him a dimension of sympathy which the non-dreamers lack. By his delusions *el señor* Ramón establishes a core of identity with the flesh and blood reader. (pp. 66-8)

In his recreation of Madrid life Cela penetrates the most recondite recesses of intimate existence. In the tradition of Galdós, whose vision of a honeymoon was masterfully described in the early pages of *Fortunata y Jacinta,* Cela delicately depicts the nuptial bliss of *los* González, parents of five children. Not all interesting characters in **La Colmena** are extra-social. . . . Don Roberto González is a kind man, but he is not absolute in his virtues. Often his common sense guides his life. Don Roberto González expresses the inadequacy of abstract values when the values conflict with self-interest. Don Roberto González reminds us of ourselves.

Remarkably free of concupiscence, **La Colmena** explores the nether regions of Madrid as well as bourgeois life. In the revolving existence of the Spanish capital there is a common denominator of intermingling experiences which relate all classes of society to a mutual chain of events. The *café* is the primary focal point, the axis. Its relentless rotation is diffusive. It creates lesser zones of convergence, the home, the business establishment, the brothel. In all cases, the recreation of life is sympathetic. Human experiences are as tenderly depicted free of conventional moral judgment in one place as in another. In all instances the emphasis is on the person, not on his type of dwelling. Regardless of his profession or social standing a character may be possessed of lust or he may be virtuous, or both. Perhaps the salient aspect of this humane attitude is the unexpected expression of goodness on the part of the extra-social people in this novel. But there is no generic classification of virtue and sin. They are not qualities that are identifiable with a given class or position; nor do they have fixed residence in their one person. There is no constancy about them. They are migratory in nature. Doña Ramona Bragado, an amateur procuress, who operates within a semblance of respectability, appears as a cruel merchant of despair in the moments that we see her. Doña Jesusa, the professional *Celestina,* on the other hand, reveals herself as a kind person, quite uncommercial in nature in the photographic glimpse we have of her. Similarly, Pura, whose name seems to belie her profession, in unison with Martín Marco reaches unpredictable novelistic heights in transcending her assigned role. . . . Free of lasciviousness and free of sentimentality the house of iniquity is just another junction for the expression of human lives. Momentarily it may sow seeds of grace. Doña Jesusa and Pura will no doubt revert to a mercenary position, proper of their vocation, but there will be unforeseen deviations. Their lives are not orderly; they do not fit social patterns of codification other than in their external figure.

Just as the citadel of peccancy may permit within its ugly walls the presence of virtue, so the expression of charity may enclose within its format a malevolent proclivity for sin. (pp. 68-70)

The derision of "applied" charity reaches out beyond the confines of the space and time of **La Colmena.** The critical references to the particular setting of the novel are usually more subtle. Mostly they are contained in the living experiences of the characters though there are dramatic incarnations of implied lamentations. The six years old child who screams a song in a shrieking voice, hoping to receive alms in his attempt to survive, represents the chorus of despair. Reappearing throughout the narration, his hunger is pathetically symbolical. A more penetrating display of pathos is contained in the experiences of doña Celia's grand nephews, who eagerly await the arrival of couples because their illicit presence means a hot meal the following day. . . .

La Colmena manifests only incidentally an anti-government attitude. The prevailing regime is dismissed scornfully as unworthy of much attention. (p. 71)

By far, more agonizing to the author than the amenities of governmental regimentation is the animalistic attitude of the people who surrender in spirit and are amalgamated into a state of being a flattering flock. They are sycophants. They will do anything in order to ingratiate themselves with the powerful. . . . Sapped of their will to be, these are the people to whom there are generic references, but whose lives are not dramatized in **La Colmena.** Their effect is that of the whole. The particular individuals who have stature in this novel may eventually be crushed and assimilated into the mass of inertia, but during their literary tenure, they are social outcasts, if not in relentless opposition, at least squirming to escape social enclosure.

Cela's attitude toward the established political rule, peripherally scornful, is basically mild. The regime is exiled into an area of insignificance. That, of course, is a greater punitive act than mere scorn. In positive terms, if **La Colmena** is an indictment at all, it is a vehement protestation against the social order of Spanish history, the caste system, the sense of honor, the concept of *el señor,* the emphasis on appearance and many other aspects of historical values which no longer fit the pattern of contemporary life. However, the element of revolt is a by-product. It is inferred by the reader as he witnesses the disproportionate lives of the people who seek to live in harmony with a past that is only weakly related to the present. The ties of history hang precariously.

In the last analysis, disapprobation is but the shadow of the lives that are illumined in this novel. Even in the creation of the most unexemplary people there is more sympathy than condemnation. Humor, grotesque though it may be, replaces traditional contempt. (pp. 72-3)

Principally, **La Colmena** presents its characters in a plane of ambivalent irony, supported by a greater proportion of pity than horror. Discrepant situations suggest a laughter that is merciful rather than mordant. The realm of the ideal is at times related to the sphere of experience coarsely but compassionately. (p. 74)

In gravity as in comedy, benign irony rather than virulence sets the mood of defiance in **La Colmena.** Solemnity, like hilarity, seldom has only one plane of vision. The author is able to laugh—even if it is with tears—at the inconsistencies of the Spanish people, even at their cruelty. The equivocal sense of morality is not censured; it is ridiculed. (p. 73)

There are countless references to the harsh structure of Spanish social order, but in most cases the persecutors appear more ridiculous than their victims, and possibly more pitiable. We feel sorry for the washerwomen of the brothels. They have descended to their lowly station after being cast from one house of prostitution to another. They now lack professional status and can afford the luxury of virtue in their physical degradation. Some of these women, like Dorita, were originally forced into nefariousness by seduction. In Dorita's particular case the culprit was a seminarist who was to attain the high office of canon of the cathedral of León. His name, Cojoncio Alba, destroys his literary personality more effectively than could diatribes or retribution. Within the foundation of social respectability, the canon cannot escape mockery, the cruel fate imposed on him as the result of a bet by his sardonic father.

Resounding laughter, often savage in nature, is heard in the abyss of depravity as well as the heights of solemnity. Conversely, there is lachrymosity in much of the comedy of *La Colmena.* The effect suggests horror. There is a feeling of guilt, self-hatred, on the part of the civilized reader who has learned to distinguish right from wrong. Against his strong moral education, he finds himself "enjoying" morbid humor and burlesque tragedy, as he experiences the drastic lives of the characters of this novel. There is a sense of shame in laughing and crying at what is morally speaking an inopportune time. Yet, there is an inevitable disproportionate alliance of laughter and tears in the reading of this novel. *La Colmena* is basically a grotesque human comedy, which dramatically reflects the malformation of its time, a disfigurement of history.

In perpetuating the scars of the Spanish Civil War, Cela captures in literature the inner life of a period which flounders in irresolute confusion. Its membranes of tradition virtually shattered by the war, the era seems but a fetus in the history of Spain, an undeveloped portion of time which lacks definite form. Only the dormant consciousness of a past and the vague dream of a future prevent its becoming a vacuum. With all its shame and sorrow the epoch survives as a literary object because it is depicted through the creation of characters who are intensely alive. The reality of the misshapen form of life in the early nineteen forties is contained in the characterization of the people. The sympathy which propels the author in forging human existence infiltrates his recreation of the habitat. His discontent with circumstances is tempered with understanding. Madrid of the post-Civil War remains alive because it is painted from within; it is given animation by the people who inhabit it in *La Colmena.*

In the fragmentary vision of man in the early nineteen forties Madrid is recreated only portionally. The description is predominantly introspective. There are hardly any detailed accounts of dwellings or settings in general. Only when their reality relates to people are actual novelistic places considered. In *La Colmena* Madrid is the conglomeration of buzzing lives who relentlessly traverse one another and move nowhere. It is man who gives his contour to his time and place.

At the beginning of the book there is a fierceness about the city that suggests a state of war between the author and his society. Cela seems violently preoccupied with establishing the atmosphere of aimless disproportion. The very first sentence alludes to the loss of a sense of proportion: "no perdamos la perspectiva. . . ." The mood is intensified by the sudden introduction of overwhelming bits of stories and glimpses of people. It is impossible to have a proportioned perspective of clarity. "No perdamos la perspectiva" is an ironical admonition. We already have. The first sight of Madrid is orderless. Only a mass of confusion can be distinguished.

As the book progresses the aura of chaotic existence does not diminish but the author's anger subsides. *La Colmena* begins without charity but it ends on a strong note of pity. The same forbidding Madrid which at first repels, later inspires compassion. Not just a pitiable compassion. Not a mere feeling of gladness proper of sympathizers, who consider themselves superior to the objects of their pity. But a feeling of compassion that includes admiration and even some envy. In the laments of the physical circumstances which surround the capital, there is esteem for the people who in their condemnation strive to transcend or at least struggle blindly with their hopeless existence. Cela's determination to paint the decadent Ma-

drid of 1943 seems not to have taken into account the charm of many of his *madrileños.* They are not dehumanized while they are being crushed by famine and degradation. On the contrary, as the odds against them become unsurmountable, the trivialities of their lives augment in stature. Their fate which at first appeared inconsequential is now tragic; their petty joys attain gigantic proportions. The standard of measure becomes their unique values, not the author's, not the reader's. Twenty two *pesetas* are not translated into piddling cents, but in terms of human sacrifice. The economics of *La Colmena* is human dignity. This is the precious commodity.

Self-respect, a pedestrian possession for the satiated, but a luxury for the hungry, reappears throughout *La Colmena* in strange forms. Pride is not eliminated. It may be no more than a gesture but it is profoundly felt. Petrita takes pride in her sacrifice; Martín Marco spends his fortune to avenge his humiliation in Doña Rosa's *café.* Even the sodomist, the repugnant Pepe, friend of *la fotógrafa,* challenges his detractors to a fight. The esteem of the self is often absurd, but a personal reality nevertheless. If the expression of human dignity does not reach the heights of absolute admiration it is because no such heights exist in Spain of the nineteen forties. The remarkable aspect is that hunger should not have destroyed completely the pride of man. The vision of humanity is not entirely pathetic; but only virtually so. Spain in seen in the process of being overcome but not yet in perfect subjugation. The element of protest though incongruously expressed, is dramatically alive in the evaporating stage setting of *La Colmena.*

In the fractional perspective of *La Colmena* there are novelistic personages who perpetuate through their lives the despair of a nation, the futility of an era. If their existence lacks the traditional well-defined finality of the 19th-century novelistic protagonist it is because the Spanish society of the post-Civil War, devoid of ideals, has no definite form. In their space and time, in the vacuum in which they reside, merely to want to be, encloses novelistic possibilities. In their society the act of conscious survival represents consumation. However feeble, any opposition is heroic, any illusion, a monumental dream. In the world of the "Outer Belt" aimless defiance is lofty.

The three days of the year 1943 with which *La Colmena* is concerned are filled with the anxiety of a world at war and a nation, Spain, in the wake of its own suicidal struggle. In the setting of such a human abyss there no longer exist past criteria of magnanimity for chivalric acts. Survival itself is an accomplishment, cruelty an accepted instrument. Altruistic deviation, however slight, appears gigantic, for man is consumed with the self, that is, with the self of flesh and blood. The attrition of hunger accentuates physical reality. Merely to dream, to hope for the fulfillment of another existence is theatrical; actually to strive for such an achievement is heroic. The appearance of absurdity that the "hero" may assume does not detract from his stature as a protagonist. It just characterizes him as being part of an epoch in which symmetry is not possible. By the circumstances of history, man's own doings, grotesqueness is the national form of human existence in the Spain of the early nineteen forties.

Virtually detached from their heritage, at variance with themselves, faltering indeterminately, the people of *La Colmena* dramatically convey the spiritlessness of an era of disproportion. Outwardly the great war that rages between the Allies and the Axis powers is determining man's fate; inwardly, especially in Spain, man is pitted against himself in a sea of turbulent trivialities. There are no worlds to conquer amidst the trifling realities of living. Hermetically sealed by the despair of material constriction, human existence becomes obsessed with material reality. In the warped preoccupation with self-preservation, there is a tendency to surrender the awareness of being that helps to distinguish man from other animals. It is indeed amazing, a notable testimony of the author's basic faith in man, that this environment should enclose at all, possibilities for human exaltation.

The vision of the novelistic protagonists is quite naturally undeveloped in a literary world which lacks fulfillment. There is no sense of completeness in the art of Cela. It is deliberately unsatisfying. In the evolution of life in *La Colmena* we have before us "missing links" of history in a perspective that lacks totality in time and space. In the diffusion of partial experiences we can hope to capture only glimpses rather than a full view of the actors whose drama we are witnessing. Their growth or regression is swift and intense. There is a brusqueness about their appearance on the stage. Their exit is no more graceful. The reader who is accustomed to the art of the traditional novel is left wanting. Cela thus accomplishes the novelist's mission of transferal. The effect of frustrated reality is implanted upon the audience.

Encompassed in an atmosphere of disintegrating particles, the novelistic entities assert themselves not in the grandiose tradition of Don Quijote, nor in the bourgeois glory of Madame Bovary, but merely by distinguishing themselves from the droning mass of existence that envelops them. By virtue of sheer momentary resistance to commonality they are extraordinary; in their spurts of defiance they loom as august. It is a fleeting impression, but in the evanescent reality of their realm it represents fruition. Eternity is evaluated in terms of the instant, for the whole need not exist. Thus, it is possible for Martín Marco, the central figure of *La Colmena,* to bring about in his tortuous way the intertwining of lives. He serves as the junction for events and in some instances he is the force that incites novelistic action as in the case of Petrita. Whereas Martín's stature as a hero might not fit the pattern of tradition, in the world that is Spain after the Civil War, he wears well the histrionic clothes of the paladin.

Among the women—and it is primarily the female sex which conserves any vestige of traditional vigor in the society of *La Colmena*—, Petrita and Victorita emerge as tragic characters of eminent magnitude. With an unpredictive agonizing resoluteness, untypical of their time and place, they affirm themselves in rebellious defiance against their destiny. Moreover, they strive to forge fate in their own image. Viewed solely from the security of the dollar economy, a most unliterary approach, their trivial conflicts may seem unworthy of human sacrifice. Translated in terms of their own circumstances their personal struggles are monumental. In their tormentive, sporadic attempts to chart the course of their lives they are majestic figures.

Until the moment of decision Petrita bears with placid dignity the impossibility of her dreams. And in her determination to render her illusions liveable, to give form to her fantasy Petrita, the maid, maintains queenly demeanor. It is she who wills her fate. In her defilement she enhances her position of defiance. Her spirit of rebellion becomes more intense. Flauntingly she imperils the security of her betrothal as she clamors her devotion for her idol, symbolically incarnated in the person of Martín Marco. In her submission Petrita has the regal beauty of a lioness.

The driving force that converts Petrita into a novelistic protagonist emanates from within her realm of personal existence. The material state of Spain may shape the form of her conversion, but it is not the determining factor in her growth as a literary character. That is to say, hunger obliges her to debase herself for the paltry sum of 22 *pesetas,* a veritable fortune for her, but it is not hunger that incites her abstract love for Martín Marco. The influence that is exerted on her transcends circumstances of environment. The ideal love which Martín Marco inspires in Petrita recalls the mythical influence of Dulcinea del Toboso on Don Quijote. And just as the unseen Lady of Toboso becomes the knight errant's reason for being, Martín Marco assumes the role of the prime mover in Petrita's existence.

The maid's plane of reality is not romantically unidimensional; she has a multilateral novelistic existence. Her moments of grandeur are dynamically intermingled with her prosaic position as a maid and as the plebeian fiancée of an ordinary simple policeman. Petrita reaches heights of human exaltation and novelistically descends to depths of coarse reality. Like thousands of other maids who steal out of their master's home to join their fiancés after work is done, Petrita makes love with the Galician policeman, Julio García Mazarro, in the wasteplot that is the rendezvous for the poor.

Although the personal predicament of Victorita is embedded in the economic plight of Spain, the shop girl herself shapes her form of confrontation with circumstances. . . . In opposition to her domineering mother, she persists in maintaining her unpromising engagement to her tubercular fiancé, Paco. And from him, who constitutes the impulse for her dazzling dreams but who, himself, is submerged in apathetic decay, she receives no direction. Enmeshed in ubiquitious despair, Victorita almost succumbs to the indigenous deliverances of her society. . . . Beset with the hostility and cruel languor of the world around her, in the turmoil of her solipsistic existence, the eighteen-year old girl musters her will and in agonizing tremor affirms herself as a novelistic character.

In her fall as in her rise, Victorita maintains her dignity. Assailed with doubts about her decision, she retains a consciousness of her migratory planes of reality. Unlike a romantic martyr of nineteenth century literature, Victorita lives the uncertainty of her venture. While wishing to believe herself indomitable in her resoluteness to create a new life for herself and Paco, her trembling body betrays her fears. In striving to attain an abstract ideal of economic security she is intransigent; in the dramatic moment of rendering her dream into concrete reality she is possessed with fearful vacilation. Ultimately she surrenders to the allurement of her dream, but not without incessant struggle. The conflict continues to rage within her when she reaches a verdict and when the moment of imposing sentence upon herself arrives.

The most amazing aspect of Cela's literary achievement, his stroke of genius, is his ability to capture human tragedy and comedy in a desultory style, that is the trademark of *La Colmena.* Within a few photographic pages, their negative form not fully developed, the author succeeds in creating novelistic characters whose livingness gives reality to the portrayal of an era of Hispanic existence. It is by means of creating strikingly real people that the author makes the era come alive. Through the characters a bond of sympathy is established with Madrid in the year 1943.

The microscopic three days of *La Colmena* reveal the core of a singular epoch which is virtually detached from its past. In this speck of time the author dramatizes his own experience of Spain's total historical existence. Out of Cela's vision of Spain, embedded in the disproportion of the present with the past, possibly in terms of personal disillusionment, comes forth the perspective of unsymmetrical fragmentation that constitutes the symphonic theme of the novel. Only the rise of novelistic characters and situations transcends the recurrent melody of dissonance. Cela's vision of Spain constitutes the abstractness of *La Colmena;* his novelistic achievement gives concrete meaning to his artistically distorted perspective. The personal conflicts of Petrita and Victoria, the aimless wanderings of Martín Marco incarnate in a uniquely disjunctive manner the single organic reality of a given time and space.

Although peripherally the recreation of three days of life in Madrid suggests a view of undistinguishable humanity groping for survival, actually there is revealed in this agglomeration of fractional existence the expression of rebellious lives who tower above the natural circumstances of their experiences. Perhaps in a subliminal manner, these characters constitute Cela's "strident voice in the desert." Theirs are the voices that resound perturbably long after the spectacle of arid land evaporates into obliviousness. And the situations that are salvaged from imminent dissolution in *La Colmena* are given perdurable life by the sympathetic creatures who struggle to achieve personal form in opposition to the relentless mass of indistinction that threatens to overwhelm them.

In addition to Petrita, Victorita, and Martín Marco, a gallery of sympathetic characters in their embryonic formation, rise from the depths of mass life to imprint fractions of their personalities in the morass into which they are sinking. One can hardly forget the man who commits suicide because his mouth smells of onions. . . . Nor can one erase from his memory the awkward situation of the man who died in a "third class brothel." His friends wishing to conceal the grotesqueness of his death dress him and bring him home to his wife. Although the suspenders are left behind, doña Juana, the wife of the deceased, in her conjugal devotion, overlooks the detail. She has no doubt of her late husband's ultimate destination. . . . Nor does one find it simple not to recall how Elvirita, the prostitute, puts herself to sleep with prayers over an empty stomach. Then, she is too proud to admit to the gluttonous doña Rosa that unlike the wealthy *café* owner, she need not worry lest overeating interfere with her sleep. In all cases, these and hundreds of others, the quest for dignity, however incongruous the results, gives the episodes a sense of respectability. In their strange ways, many are the people who, if unable to combat, attempt to squirm out of their mire with some degree of dignity.

The horror of human disintegration enclosed within the physical reality of hunger constitutes the outer fabric of *La Colmena,* its facade. Beyond this layer of appearance lies the inner structure of the novel, its foundation. Within the aura of constrictive decay that pervades the novel, life grows and expands. Reminiscent of the Hell of Dante, amidst abjection, the beauty of living is exalted. Already manifest in Cela's earlier novels, the joy for life blooms with fulminating vigor in *La Colmena.* Contained in a receptacle of despair, doomed to evaporation, human existence affirms itself as a sublime experience in its fragmentary moments of vitality.

The first words of *La Colmena* "no perdamos la perspectiva" might serve as an admonition for the discriminating reader.

To be submerged in the panorama of annihilation is to lose our sense of proportion. It is not hunger that sustains the structure of this book. As in some fantastic architecture, the pillars of this book are the living novelistic people who are cemented unto one another with sympathy. (pp. 76-84)

Within the framework of Cela's art, it might be considered impertinent to classify his literary productivity as belonging to one genre or another. Cela's "diabolical" intention has been to explode myths, particularly the one relating to "novels." Next to hunger and possibly the Spanish government, the critic occupies the place of honor in Cela's *Inferno.* He might forgive the innocent audience, but not that body of readers who appoint themselves as judges of art by virtue of academic training. We already know how much he disdains "formal scholarship."

Yet, if Cela has chosen to bring "order by disorder," the critic may be justified in discerning a pattern of literary behavior in artistic expressions which are deliberately disproportionate. Using the broadest possible measures of value one might even categorize the works of Cela quintessentially as novels and books of travels. The rest of his writing, articles, short stories, and collections of inventively grotesque fables, are but fragments, momentary glimpses, of his novels and books of travels.

Cela's preoccupation with Spain constitutes the predominant theme of all his works. His search for Spain is relentless. He seeks to capture the essence of Spanish existence. His quest takes many forms. He cannot exhaust the literary possibilities of recreating life around him. Cela has imposed on himself the fate of Tantalus. But in this sentence the reader shares his agony. The final moment of truth never comes. The experience of living Cela's characters and situations is in itself the aesthetic attainment. The problem of Spain is never solved.

In the novels life is objectivized. Spain is but a stage. Contemporary problems are expressed through the creation of literary characters. Circumstances acquire meaning within the personal dramas of Cela's heroes. Their conflicts—often embryonic—overshadow the plight of society. By means of dreams, illusions and fantasies the protagonists transcend their circumscribed possibilities. The acts of rebellion need not be more fully developed than their fragmentary existence. In the horror of hunger, under the surveillance of guns, a groan becomes a roar. In the Spain of the forties the mere pursuit of human dignity was an act of defiance.

In his travels, Cela, himself, as a literary character, weaves the fabric of human existence. The pattern of life is seen through the eyes of the vagabond. He is the inciting force, the prime mover. He is the character in search of a stage. His compulsion to penetrate the inner recesses of Hispanic life motivates his peregrinations. He must experience all possible forms of reality; he must "drink of Spain." The pilgrimage offers no reward other than the palpation of life. In the world of Cela, the act of living is in itself a joyous fulfillment.

Blended with the specter of horror that pervades the works of Cela is a note of poetic imagery that evokes musical exaltation. Songs are shaped from the most trivial aspects of human existence. Cela, the master of horror, is also the master of delicate sensations. He perceives pathos with the same intensity that he dramatizes cruelty. Even in an atmosphere of human depravity, amidst virtual destruction, there are inextinguishable glimmers of man's love. The art of Cela seems to erupt in unexpected disproportion in form as in content. His composition is deliberately grotesque.

As an artist, Cela finds no symmetry in life and he strives to express that image of his experience. The "order" that he championed as a soldier of Franco never attained reality. It disintegrated into chaos at the end of the Civil War. Its fruition was abortive. It evaporated before it could take shape. For Cela, Spain became a symbol of unfulfilment. His literary career, then, begins on the threshold of a frustrated "Crusade." Disillusionment is his Pierian spring. The possession of genius is inexplicable, but its form of expression is inexorably intertwined with the circumstances into which it is born. Cela creates literature out of the rough variegated fabric of Spanish life.

On the whole there is a marked distinction between the acrimonious Cela of the nineteen forties and the ironical Cela of the nineteen fifties. The inherently rebellious spirit of Cela varies in intensity. Maturity has a noticeable influence on his disposition—and his vision of humanity. He does not relent in his criticism, but his mood becomes more temperate. Only hunger remains as his implacable enemy. He can ridicule most everything, even the absurd excesses of his government, but he cannot retain a sense of humor about starvation. In his writings, the ghost of Cela the man cries out for vengeance. There is no mercy for hunger. (pp. 182-84)

The art of Cela mirrors the inner truth of the Spanish people, as it captures the essence of post-Civil War life. His novels and books of travels probe too deeply, too painfully. Unquestionably, in his new venture, as an academician, he will arouse less hostility. His own life will be more peaceful, even if readers of literature will be the poorer for it.

The course of Cela's career as an artist has been unpredictably diverse. In a sense, his past cannot be taken as an omen for the future. His genius is explosive. It bursts forth in unexpected forms. (p. 184)

[Already] Cela's writings constitute one of the most significant contributions to Spanish literature since the generation of 1898. Almost single handed, Cela resurrected the novel in Spain. To be sure, the genre was not invented by him. There is a bit of the *esperpento* of Valle-Inclán and some vestiges of Baroja's fragmentary style in the prose of Camilo José Cela. Nonetheless, instead of merely reproducing the traditional conflicts of the past, Cela based his novels on his own personal experience of man's agonizing existence. The publication of his first novel, *La Familia de Pascual Duarte,* marked the beginning of a new literary generation. Cela was not afraid to dramatize the plight of his society, living enmeshed in a web of particular circumstances. The protean nature of the novel lent itself to his literary experiment. Out of a degenerate society that groped for survival, Cela forged a new artistic reality. The intense recreation of Spanish life reaches aesthetic heights in the form of characters and situations that reflect the inner truth of man while perpetuating an era of Spanish existence. With intuitive genius Cela molds his art in the image of his society. The explosive shape of his composition conforms to the abortive nature of his times. (pp. 184-85)

> Robert Kirsner, in his The Novels and Travels of
> Camilo José Cela, *The University of North Carolina
> Press, 1964, 187 p.*

THE TIMES LITERARY SUPPLEMENT

For too many years C. J. Cela has been squandering his skills on collections of a distinctive but meatless journalism and novels perversely restricted to a pathology of human decay and loneliness. But in this new novel he has at last got back to a theme which tests his competence rather than simply displays it. *San Camilo, 1936* is an ample and malicious panorama of daily life in Madrid in July, 1936, when . . . a native angst and the political incapacity of Republican Spain suddenly grew into the motives for the Civil War. Cela's novel is certainly not free from the mannerisms of style and attitude or from the *tremendismo* on which he has always been hooked, but it does possess a consistency and range of invention that set it far above any other novel we can expect to get from Spain for some time to come.

The form which Cela has used is punishing but appropriate. *San Camilo, 1936* is the mordant self-inquisition of a young Madrid student who could perfectly well be Cela himself if the novelist had not chosen—typically—to introduce himself additionally into the text in the third person, to create an unnecessary diversion. The narrator's concern with himself and his own sterile psyche merges into and emerges from his presentation of the scene around him without any break, so that the novel makes a single monologue, split, for convenience, into chapters but not into paragraphs.

The technique is a simple development of the earlier *pointillisme* of *La Colmena,* and Cela uses it here with the same fluency and penetration. The narrative circulates hurriedly around considerably cast of *madrileños,* a few of them powerful, a good many mediocre, some downright degraded. Cela does not dwell for more than a few lines at a time on any individual or group because he is interested in the simultaneity of what he is describing. The way is open in fact for some venomous juxtapositions between pretension and squalor which would go down well in a Buñuel film.

The principal juxtaposition naturally has to be between public events and private ones. As the war approaches the balance between them shifts towards the public, but even the occasions big enough to go into history—the twin murders of the left-wing officer José Castillo and the right-wing leader Calvo Sotelo, the storming of the Montaña barracks, the movements of the various Nationalist Generals—are filtered through the popular consciousness as rumour or report, and Cela shows wilful distortion and speculation as crucial factors in the eruption of social antagonisms. He has buried the crises of July 1936 almost gloatingly in the sorry preoccupations of his invented characters and especially of his narrator.

Each chapter starts with the student asking a string of desperate questions of his own image in the mirror. The boy is fearful, solitary, suicidal and lecherous and is seemingly offered as the impersonation of all that is self-destructive in the Spanish temperament. He is in fact a dark and morbid focus for a novel that harps unnervingly on physical and moral inadequacy, until the Civil War comes to look less like a revolt against specific social conditions and more like one against the whole human condition.

San Camilo, 1936 starts with a long and detailed directory to Madrid's brothels, with names and addresses, and all through the book Cela builds up its authenticity by references to precise locations and to the gossip or news items of the week. And he reinforces his horror of bodily decline and contempt for petit-bourgeois credulity by quoting an enormous variety of patent medicine advertisements, making astonishingly free with his sexual and other carnal references—indeed, the language of *San Camilo, 1936* is scabrous far beyond what one would have thought to be the tolerance of the Spanish censorship.

But if Cela has constructed a heavily partial picture of a society scarcely worth saving from the slaughter which begins long before the novel ends, it is a solid picture and not without evidence of positive values. Cela testifies to the decent solidarity of ordinary harassed individuals and, above all, expresses his own sense of the waste of Spanish youth. The novel is dedicated to "the lads called up in 1937 who all lost something: life, freedom, illusion, hope, decency"; it is also dedicated against the foreigners who interfered in a Spanish affair.

Which raises the matter of the book's weird epilogue. In this the narrator is lectured by his wise, disenchanted uncle and asked to extirpate from within himself the malignity that warps every Spanish soul. The uncle's scheme for national regeneration is a good way farther out than one would have expected: love and humility, plus as much sex as you like, a programme he offers as an improvement on those of Buddha and St. Francis—the flames of the *auto-da-fé* are to be quenched finally with semen. But after the 400 icy and often sadistic pages of Cela's novel, this sermon is a bit lightweight. Is Cela being serious, or is he making a sneering obeisance to a notably humourless regime by feigning to detect patriotic virtues in promiscuity?

Whatever the answer, the publication of *San Camilo, 1936* is an encouraging event. It represents a definite recovery of nerve in Spain's most gifted living novelist and it suggests that Cela now believes he has a worthy public in his own country. Lately, he has given the impression of churning out books for readers nowhere near sophisticated enough to appreciate him. The contempt in *San Camilo, 1936* has been reapplied to where, with Cela, it belongs,: to his characters and not his readers.

> *"A Mirror in Madrid," in* The Times Literary Supplement, *No. 3553, April 2, 1970, p. 355.*

JAMES R. STAMM

Camilo José Cela made his reputation on his first novel, *La familia de Pascual Duarte* (*The Family of Pascual Duarte*), published in 1942, and has continued, in a varied and productive literary career, to occupy a major and aggressive position in Spanish letters for more than thirty-five years. *Pascual Duarte* caused a literary sensation with its focus on rural violence and brutality, its almost morbid concentration on the degrading and repulsive aspects of a life devoted to an almost mindless revolt against normal human relationships. The tone of the work was promptly given status as a trend by some critics and was baptized with the name *tremendismo,* signifying a style of realism which dwells on the gruesome detail, which magnifies the monstrous and inhuman aspects of experience.

The novel is presented as the fragmentary personal account of a man sentenced to death for murder. He describes in scenes of great intensity the "family" which makes up the title of the novel: his bullying and drunken father, his nagging and unpleasant mother, his prostitute sister, a cretinous younger brother whose cries go unheeded as his ears and nose

are nibbled off by a passing hog. A climax is reached as Pascual murders his mother, strangling her in her bed in a ferocious struggle. There is no reason or motive for the act; as in Poe's *The Tell-Tale Heart,* which the episode resembles, Pascual simply decides that the time has come to kill her, and so he goes about the task almost without emotion. It is this lack of emotion, this deadness of the spirit, that most defines Cela's *tremendismo.* It differs from the "disengaged" paralysis of feeling which we see in *L'Etranger* of Camus in that it selects the trivial gruesome detail to present a totally brutalized "reality" to the reader. The critics who saw this as an identifiable new direction were somewhat mystified by Cela's next novel.

Pabellón de reposo (*Rest Ward*) bears a superficial resemblance to Mann's *The Magic Mountain* and Maugham's *Sanatorium* in that it concerns the restricted life of victims of tuberculosis in a rest home. The tone here is very calm; nothing of *tremendismo,* of violence and brutality, of the world seen as a place of meaningless and inexplicable ferocity. Rather, under the exterior tranquillity of a way of life that is of necessity without event, we see the internal anguish and suffering of those afflicted with lingering and debilitating illness. It is a world in which hopes and anxieties must necessarily take the place of action. The author writes from experience and the insight gained is reflected in his penetration of the patients' private worlds.

In *Nuevas andanzas y desventuras de Lazarillo de Tormes* (*New Wanderings and Misfortunes of Lazarillo de Tormes*), Cela takes yet another direction. Reviving the long Spanish tradition of the picaresque ambience, he structures a novel which, while modeled on a venerable pattern, is more than an attempt to imitate the genre. In first-person narration, the new Lazarillo tells of his travels and adventures and describes the people he encounters in his life of wandering and beggary. Much of the interest of the book, as is the case with its sixteenth-century prototype, is found in the description of these marginal figures, which Cela creates with impressive artistry. Finally, Lazarillo sums up the lesson of his experience: "I was now a man, and fear, hunger, and calamity had been my only school." He reflects on

> those happy mortals who are born, live, and die without having moved three leagues from the boundaries of their *pueblo,* and I thought, God knows with what anguish, what happiness it would be for me to stop and live out my days in the first houses I ran across. Why Providence would not permit it is something I do not understand; perhaps my flesh was marked with a sign which would not permit it to stop going and going, without sense or reason, from one place to another.

Lazarillo then uses the metaphor of the rolling stone, which must look with nostalgia and envy on the moss-covered rocks that retain the pasture land.

Cela's first extended and really ambitious novel was *La colmena* (*The Hive*), published in 1951. Its setting is post-Civil War Madrid in its poverty and isolation. Cela does not revive the inhuman note of his earlier *tremendismo,* but nonetheless concentrates on a series of lives which are bleak or sordid or pointless, according to their circumstances. The title is perfectly indicative of the character of the work: the author takes the top off the human beehive of Madrid and shows us the swarming mass, involved in day to day activities. He uses a large number of characters—someone has counted 160—to show us the "mass man" of Ortega in action. The novel has no central theme, no plot, no direction, and no heroes. Yet there is movement, the feel of a city, excitement, and a range of emotion as broad as the number of "protagonists," a cross section of the lower middle class in postwar Madrid. Cela has a sharp ear for language and a penetrating eye for detail. The shortcoming of the novel is common to most works of this sub-genre: it tends to disintegrate and to become a series of short stories and vignettes more or less interwoven by chance, proximity, and superficialities. But Cela has given us a true picture—certainly the details are artistically true—of the life of the city at that time, and the lack of structure, the swarming, buzzing confusion, are a necessary part of the presentation of Cela's particular vision.

San Camilo, 1936, published in 1970, returns almost obsessively to the outbreak of the Civil War. The point of view is again panoramic; while *La colmena* has its center of action in a popular café, *San Camilo, 1936* sees events of the earlier period almost exclusively from Madrid's houses of prostitution. The intentional crudity of language and characterization is what one might expect of the chosen environment. This novel, like *La colmena,* is a pastiche of characters and intertwined situations, using clippings from newspapers and the texts of radio broadcasts to give momentum and a sense of immediacy to the narrative.

Cela is among the most prolific and original of contemporary Spanish writers. His work includes two volumes of poetry, the excellent *Viaje a la Alcarria,* among other descriptions of his travels in Spain, four collections of short stories and novelettes, a novel based on his travel to Venezuela, and collected essays and literary criticism. . . . Of the novelists to emerge in the period since the Civil War, he is among the most read, the most discussed, and the most controversial. He is also among the most skilled, varied, and creative of his contemporaries. (pp. 247-51)

> *James R. Stamm, "Spain in the Twentieth Century," in his* A Short History of Spanish Literature, *revised edition, New York University Press, 1979, pp. 201-61.*

JOHN STURROCK

Scientists can get Nobel Prizes in old age for the work that they did when young; so, we now know, can writers. Camilo José Cela, this year's Spanish winner of the Literature prize, has published nothing of more than local note since 1951. There have been a great many book by him in that time . . . but the books which the austere Swedish Academy will have had in mind in Nobelizing Cela are his two most celebrated novels, *La familia de Pascual Duarte* and *La colmena* (*The Hive*), and these go back forty years. *Pascual Duarte* was the book that he started with, in 1942, while *La colmena* first appeared—abroad, in Buenos Aires—in 1951. These are memorably harsh, sardonic novels, much exceeding in their graphic naturalism the other more mannered books that he went on to write. Only once again, in a Civil War novel of 1970, *San Camilo 1936,* did Cela ever seem to take his writing so seriously. His is a small achievement to have gained him a Nobel Prize.

Nor is his fiction of the kind the Swedish academicians are used to voting for. "Compassionate" was the word they gave to it in their citation last week; misanthropic would have been

the truer term. Cela's human beings are not nice. Pascual Duarte is a dim but touchy countryman who murders first his dog, then a villager and finally his mother; *The Hive* is a collective novel, set in Madrid, of urban life at its most desperate and debased. His taste is for the ugly, the malevolent and the stupid, and his novels can be taken as being sour homage in the twentieth century to the picaresque tradition of the sixteenth. He has always got about in Spain and has written at least one remarkable account of it, in his *Viaje a la Alcarria,* but real Spanish life was no sufficient subject-matter for the novelist, who thought it needed more bite and sensationalism if it was to succeed as fiction. In time Cela became concerned less anyway with life and much more with language. Patois and the vernacular were what he sought out, recording their forms and using them himself, until his own writing was often hard or impossible to understand if the only Spanish you knew was Castilian Spanish.

There is another, political reason why Cela is an unlikely Nobel-winner. During the Civil War he fought for the Nationalists: were the Academy in good, social-democratic Stockholm perhaps not told that, or are they forgiving him for it? Later, admittedly, during the intellectual ice-age in Spain that set in with Franco, he wrote with some independence and helped to foster the non-conformist talents of younger Spanish writers by publishing them in his off-shore review, *Papeles de Son Armadans,* during the more than twenty years he lived and wrote in Majorca. But then Cela saw the Civil War not as a political event, but as a pathological one, as an upset in which Spanish, or else just human, nature typically declared itself in all its instinctive viciousness.

> *John Sturrock, "Homage Sweet and Sour," in* The Times Literary Supplement, *No. 4517, October 27- November 2, 1989, p. 1182.*

RAYMOND CARR

Intellectuals enjoy in Spain what must seem, to British eyes, an exaggerated prestige. The award of the Nobel Prize in literature to Camilo José Cela got remorseless coverage in the media. You could not escape him. There he was, column inches long, in the morning paper; in the afternoon on television chat-shows. . . .

Cela presents himself as an austere and solitary genius. But he surely must court the publicity he attracts. . . . Once I asked Malcolm Muggeridge why, after abusing television, he was so often on our screens. 'I think of myself', he replied, 'as a pianist playing "Abide with Me" in a brothel. One of the clients might get the message.' Cela may see himself as the Muggeridge of Madrid, apostle of the purity of the Spanish tongue who must put up with publicity to get his message through. And, given the appalling sociological jargon that has combined with Francoist rhetoric and democratic platitudes to debase the language, he has a mission.

To add to all the fuss, the Minister of Culture, the writer Jorge Semprun, did not turn up in Stockholm for the prize-giving. This raised the ghosts of Cela's past. He had joined Franco's side in the Civil War and afterwards served in the Francoist censorship. Semprun, who had been in Buchenwald and had taken great risks organising the communist clandestine resistance to Franco, no doubt found Cela's political trajectory distasteful and was opposed, it was rumoured, to granting Cela the much coveted Cervantes Prize. . . .

All this should not detract from Cela's virtues as a lexicographer, travel writer, poet and novelist. **The Family of Pascual Duarte** was published in 1942 and it is hard now to recapture the sensation it created at the time. It gave an earthquake shock to the conformist literary landscape of Francoist Spain. Its brutal realism inaugurated the new literary genre of 'tremendousness' (*tremendismo*). Cela is not a political novelist. His later novel, **The Hive,** 'a slice of life drawn without charity', exposes the society which Franco had 'saved' by his victory in the Civil War as corrupt and sordid. It is, as I wrote at the time, not the protest of a radical but of a 'cross-grained man who cannot stomach the society in which he lived'. . . .

[**The Family of Pascual Duarte**] takes the form of Pascual Duarte's account of life written in prison. For a peasant, Pascual Duarte is much given to introspection in an attempt to come to terms with his own violence and the black hatred that consumes him, the evil fate that takes 'special pleasure in dogging him'. He reflects on the writer's difficulties in giving chronological form to the impressions of memory. 'Things are never', he muses, 'as they appear at first glance'; we forget our fancies (eg about the appearance of an un-

known town) 'at the sight of the real thing'. Is this peasant wisdom or the meditations on his craft of an accomplished writer? Is the poetry that flashes out amid the circumambient violence the voice of Pascual Duarte or that of Cela? Is this philosophical assassin a credible person? If he is not, then the novel fails and becomes a mere exercise in the gratuitous violence of *tremendismo.* Against the odds, I think Cela brings it off. Just.

All the media exposure of Cela does reflect a genuine and widespread interest in culture in Spain today and I am glad that Spanish literature has been honoured, even if I think the prize has gone to the wrong man. Master, as he is, of the language he loves, Cela never moves me. I have been much moved by the novels of Miguel Delibes. But Delibes is a private person, not a media man. Nor has he been translated by a member of the Swedish Academy which awards the Nobel Prize.

Raymond Carr, "Cold Comfort Hacienda," in The Spectator, *Vol. 264, No. 8428, January 20, 1990, pp. 27-8.*

Brian Friel

Aristocrats

Award: New York Drama Critics Circle Award for best foreign play.

Friel, an Irish dramatist, short story writer, and scriptwriter, was born in 1929.

One of contemporary Ireland's most respected dramatists, Friel frequently sets his plays in the rural village of Ballybeg, where conflicts and struggles among his characters reflect larger social and cultural issues affecting his homeland. *Aristocrats* is set in a decaying Georgian mansion called Ballybeg Hall, where a Catholic family has gathered for the wedding of the youngest daughter. The characters include a bedridden, domineering father who communicates through a baby-alarm intercom system, four daughters, a son, and a visiting American scholar who is conducting research for a book on the Irish Catholic aristocracy. Their conversations reveal the family's past glories as well as myths, illusions, tragedies, and failures that currently haunt them. The decaying mansion is contrasted with the lush surrounding landscape, further emphasizing the decline of the Irish aristocracy. Like the plays *The Cherry Orchard* and *Three Sisters* by Anton Chekov, whom Friel has acknowledged as an influence, *Aristocrats* emphasizes character studies rather than plot, revealing effects of the father's tyranny, the mother's suicide, the various failures of the children, and the burden of family and social history. Michael Billington noted: "One test of a good play is how much of a society it manages to put onstage: Mr. Friel gives us a comprehensive tour." Billington added: "[The] Chekovian parallel comes to mind in that the most dynamic characters are those with a thwarted hunger for life."

(See also *CLC*, Vols. 5, 42; *Contemporary Authors*, Vols 21-24, rev. ed.; and *Dictionary of Literary Biography*, Vol. 13.)

PRINCIPAL WORKS

PLAYS

Philadelphia, Here I Come! 1964
The Loves of Cass McGuire 1966
Lovers 1967
The Mundy Scheme 1969
The Freedom of the City 1973
Aristocrats 1979
Faith Healer 1979
Translations 1980
The Communication Cord 1983

SHORT FICTION COLLECTIONS

The Saucer of Larks 1962
The Gold in the Sea 1969
The Saucer of Larks: Stories of Ireland 1969

MICHAEL BILLINGTON

[Watching Brian Friel's highly enjoyable *Aristocrats*] you are reminded how Chekhovian Irish life can be.

Mr Friel's family of Catholics from the big house sit in a summer garden smothering resolution in talk, dreaming of the past and impotently confronting the decay of their gaunt, grey Georgian property. And just as Chekhov said of horse thieves, "Let jurors judge them for my business is only to show them as they are," so Mr Friel views his characters with a despairing, non-judicial affection.

The play—first done at the Abbey, Dublin in 1979 . . . —is set in the home of a District Judge overlooking the village of Ballybeg: a standard Friel location that, as Seamus Deane points out in the Faber edition, combines the social depression of Derry with the haunting attraction of rural Donegal.

The O'Donnell clan, representing the local Catholic aristocracy, have gathered for a family wedding; and like the house itself, steeped in questionable literary associations from Yeats to George Moore, they exist in a state of crumbling disrepair.

The old judge himself is now a bedridden tyrant, cocooned in legal fantasy and barking out orders which can be heard over the downstairs baby-alarm. And four of his five children are Chekhovian might-have-beens. Judith, a one-time Bogside protestor, is now his embittered nursemaid; Alice is a childless London-based alkie; lovely Claire is about to marry an aged widower; and Casimir, a failed solicitor, has retreated to Hamburg and a life of consoling illusions. Only Anna, a Zambian missionary, seems fulfilled but even she sends home a taped message full of rose-tinted visions of family life.

One test of a good play is how much of a society it manages to put on stage: Mr Friel gives us a comprehensive tour both of this downmarket Donegal Brideshead and, by implication, of the local community. He does this partly through the family's natural capacity for reminiscence. But he also does this through the astute device of importing a Chicago academic who is studying the impact of the Catholic aristocracy on the ascendancy ruling class and the peasant tradition, and who treats the family as fossilised objects.

The implication is that such groups are socially irrelevant and sustained only by a greed for survival; but ironically that charge is made by a local boy who has married into the family because they represented the myth of 'the quality'.

But Mr Friel is less concerned with class-judgements than with the engrossing spectacle of decline; and, again, the Chekhovian parallel comes to mind in that the most dynamic characters are those with a thwarted hunger for life.

> Michael Billington, in a review of "Aristocrats," in The Guardian, *June 4, 1988.*

PAUL TAYLOR

Once the proud seat of a thriving legal dynasty, Ballybeg Hall, the home of the Irish Catholic O'Donnell clan, is now a crumbling leaky liability. In scarcely better shape psychologically, the current generation of O'Donnells have gathered one hot summer in the mid-Seventies for the marriage of the youngest daughter Claire to a widowed greengrocer twice her age. . . .

[*Aristocrats*] explores with a wry sympathy the plight of these people who are unfairly required to feel guilty for not being able to prop up the tradition of the Irish Catholic gentry—which has outlived whatever relevance it may once have had. Friel aptly symbolises this awkward dilemma with a newly-rigged baby alarm system, through which at disconcerting intervals, we hear the Judge's harsh disembodied croak. The "voice of authority", this makes you realise, has been prolonged parodically and artifically beyond its *raison d'être*. Yet it still has the capacity to make them flinch.

What makes it even worse for the O'Donnells is that their upbringing has given them an unshakeable nostalgia for the myth of the Big House. But they are painfully aware that, even if there were a point to bolstering it, they have singularly little talent to do so. Casimir, the great grandson of a Lord Chief Justice, has failed even to qualify as a solicitor. Working part time now in a food processing factory in Hamburg, he is supported by his German spiritualist wife who is a cashier in a bowling alley.

The girls are little better. Claire is a manic-depressive failed concert pianist; Alice is a childless alcoholic living in a damp London basement and Judity, who once took part in the battle of Bogside, has narrowed her life down to the more mundane struggle of waiting on her incontinent father.

At first, the visiting academic from Chicago, who is researching a book on the Catholic "aristocracy", seems too easy a device for engineering a series of conveniently expository interviews. But the real dramatic value gradually becomes apparent. Interested only in facts and statistics, which he jots in his notebook with the dispassionate scepticism of a doctor recording untoward symptoms, he has the effect of endearing you to the family's myths and illusions about their past—Casimir's wildly anachronistic fantasies, for example, that every stick of furniture in the house has been dented or otherwise marked by some visiting VIP of the arts world.

Recognising a potential stooge in him, the family turn up the irony in their performances of themselves. . . . [Alice] puts quietly insolent quotation marks round her drunken slurring. Attractively, this shows you that, although history may have reduced them to cliches, they are ruefully conscious of being so.

> Paul Taylor, in a review of "Aristocrats," in The Independent, *June 6, 1988. Reprinted in* London Theatre Record, *Vol. VIII, No. 11, May 20-June 2, 1988, p. 739.*

CLIVE BARNES

What would Anton Chekhov have made of contemporary—or near contemporary—Ireland? It is a question that, perhaps quite unconsciously, Irish playwright Brian Friel has set himself to answer in his evocatively crepuscular play *Aristocrats*. . . .

The subject of Friel's play—the decline, fall and conceivable rebirth of a patrician way of life and death—is one that would surely have intrigued the Russian master. And Friel's own treatment of all this petty grandeur and domestic erosion has an agreeably Chekhovian dying fall to it.

The aristocrats of the title are an old Irish Catholic family living in Ballybeg Hall, which overlooks the village of Ballybeg in County Donegal. By chance—well, not really by chance, more by calculated coincidence—the setting is the same as that in Friel's earlier play *Translations*. . . .

In *Translations,* which took place at the beginning of the 19th century, the English were politically annexing Ireland's culture, largely by means of extinguishing its language.

Here, nearly two centuries later, one of the minor results of this can be seen, in these agreeable but decayed gentry, a Catholic family that for some generations had upheld England's Protestant rule with a tradition of lawyers and judges acting as proconsuls for the invaders.

The family is now impoverished, and all but broken up. The father—the last of the old judges—is gaga under death's transom. His talkative and epicene son, home on a visit, has a mysterious wife and family in Hamburg, and of his three sisters (Chekhov, take another bow!) it is only the eldest who tries to keep the home fires burning.

The middle sister lives in London, married to an educated plebeian, low in the Irish diplomatic service, and the young one, the family beauty and pianist, is about to waste her youth on a wealthy, widowed and elderly tradesman.

This is the family Friel gathers for his rituals of death and transfiguration. And just to make sure we make the right sociological connections and political associations, he throws in an American university professor writing a book on Ireland's grand families during English rule.

But as in his earlier **Translations,** Friel, by far the most interesting Irish playwright since O'Casey, never hammers home political issues. These merely help provide the landscape inhabited by Friel's carefully drawn figures.

It is the interplay of characters that illuminates Friel's world and his ornately old-fashioned but usually meaningful plays.

Here Casimir, the brother, a misfit amalgam of two cultures, burbles engagingly about a grand panorama of literary figures and artists long dead, where fact, fancy and family legend are mingled into their own kind of truth.

Then the sisters in various ways long nostalgically for their own odd Hibernian version of Moscow, and it is left to the plebeian patrician-by-marriage (husband of the middle sister and grandson of the house's sometime chambermaid) to have the profoundest regrets of all for a past he only knew second-hand.

Irish writing has learned to transform pain and loss into an ugly kind of beauty, and Friel's sunset glow in County Donegal is no exception.

But there is the promise of a dawn here—Judith, the oldest sister, is to rejoin her daughter, an illegitimate child she acquired during a political foray into the Civil Rights movement in Northern Ireland's nearby Londonderry.

And as this family group meets for what must surely be the last time, to talk of Yeats, listen to Chopin and play imaginary croquet on an almost English lawn, you know that things will never be quite the same for either them or the village of Ballybeg. . . .

It is only when you compare **Aristocrats** with, say, *The Cherry Orchard* or *The Three Sisters,* that you realize it does lack some completeness of vision, some totality of image.

But avoid such comparisons, and you are left with a gently provocative and vastly entertaining play.

> Clive Barnes, *"Rituals of Death & Transfiguration,"* in New York Post, *April 26, 1989.*

FRANK RICH

Audiences arriving at Brian Friel's **Aristocrats** are all but enfolded within a panorama of lush Irish greenery. The setting . . . is a Georgian mansion in provincial County Donegal. Moss and ivy crawl over every wall; a towering tree spills leaves from above; an expanse of bright lawn flows from the house's exposed parlor to the stage's edge. It is summer, the mid-1970's, and the sun is out.

What we see is Ireland at its most ravishing, but Ireland being Ireland, and Mr. Friel being arguably the most penetrating Irish playwright of his generation, the skies cannot remain cloudless for long. **Aristocrats** . . . is Mr. Friel's Chopin-flecked *Cherry Orchard* or *Three Sisters,* in which the ache

of one family becomes a microcosm for the ache of a society. While Mr. Friel's touch in this 1979 work isn't always as subtle as Chekhov's, **Aristocrats** is a lovely play, funny and harrowing. Though the abrupt juxtapositions of the beautiful and the tragic may be any Irish writer's birthright, Mr. Friel makes the Irish condition synonymous with the human one.

To be sure, the house on stage, which belongs to a once-powerful district judge, is haunted by the country's troubles, as well as by the literary ghosts of Yeats and O'Casey, who, we're told, may have visited the mansion in its salad days. But if **Aristocrats** expresses the national political concerns hinted at by its ironic title, the politics follow rather than dictate what is largely the intimate drama of a family reunion prompted by an impending wedding and overtaken by illness. Judge O'Donnell has suffered a stroke, and four of his five adult children have gathered at his deathbed.

The O'Donnells are not a happy clan. The engaged daughter, Claire, is to marry a drab greengrocer twice her age. Her sister Alice is an alcoholic who lives discontentedly in London with her embittered, lapsed activist of a husband, Eamon. Another sister, Judith, has given up an illegitimate child to an orphanage even as she is forced to cope with the second, incontinent childhood of her father. Though the lone brother, Casimir, purports to have a wife and three children in Hamburg, no one in the family has seen them. "It has the authentic ring of phony fiction," Eamon says of Casimir's obsessive boasts of domestic bliss.

What went wrong? We learn of a mother, long dead, who committed suicide. We sense the tyranny of the Lear-like father, who even now, in near delirium, bellows humiliating commands through his sickroom intercom. And in the isolation of each character we see a reflection of the entire household's alienation from Ireland. . . .

Aristocrats has the ring of phony fiction only when Mr. Friel pounds his Chekhovian notes of decay, notably in the neat final-act resolutions and particularly when he brings on a visiting American academic who is studying the local folkways. The rest of the evening offers the blend of psychological ambiguity and crackling theatrical instinct that has been Mr. Friel's signature since **Philadelphia, Here I Come!** more than 20 years ago. Leave it to this writer to inject the esthetics of Beckett into a heartbreak house by creating an elderly uncle in an elegant white-linen suit who remains mute as a matter of principle. Mr. Friel's feel for absurdist black comedy is given even fuller vent when the characters sit obediently in lawn chairs before a boom box to listen to a taped, unwittingly callous message from the one absent sister, an insufferably pious nun who fled to Africa 17 years earlier. . . .

It's typical of Mr. Friel's paradoxical way that he would make his most anti-establishment character—the cynical, working-class Eamon—the most nostalgic upholder of Irish cultural tradition by the final curtain. . . .

All three sisters . . . undergo similar transformations. The initially sunny [Claire], though too gorgeous to pass for the brood's ugly duckling, gradually comes to resemble her departed, depressive mother. [Alice] swings between alcoholic hostility and sweetness, at last to reach an affecting middle ground when she describes how she could reach accommodation with her fearful father only when he could no longer recognize her. [Judith's] moment to dazzle comes when she suddenly tightens her voice and jaw, forsaking her previous maternal lilt, to describe her crippled diurnal existence caring for the dying.

But it is Casimir, the son, most stifled by the father, who is indelible. . . .

Casimir knows he has always been a figure of fun, ridiculed by others as either the village idiot or a homosexual. But with his factory job and presumed family in Germany, he has found a way to feel and give happiness without risking "exposure to too much hurt." . . . Casimir is a jolly life of the party clinging to that role because his own life depends on it.

Only his father, of course, still has the power to send him tumbling back into the terrors of childhood. When the fall comes, as it must, we, too, experience terror, as a grown man collapses into pieces on that beautiful Irish sod and waters it with his tears.

> Frank Rich, "A Family as Symbol of Ireland's Troubles," in The New York Times, April 26, 1989, p. C15.

JOHN BEAUFORT

Brian Friel's poignant comedy [*Aristocrats*] bids a melancholy farewell to a privileged Irish family down on its uppers. The family's reduced state is symbolized by the crumbling Georgian great house that overlooks the village of Ballybeg, in County Donegal.

On a warm summer afternoon in the 1970s, the O'Donnells are preparing to celebrate the marriage of Claire. Irrepressible Casimir has flown in from Germany. Up from London have come alcoholic Alice and husband Eamon, a Ballybeg local who married above himself when he wed an O'Donnell.

The mature and patient Judith runs the household and cares for her senile but still tyrannous Father, a former district judge. Mr. Friel has provided an outsider in the person of Tom Hoffnung, an academic from Chicago doing a cultural survey of contemporary Ireland.

Aristocrats unfolds with a complex Chekhovian mingling of humor, humanity, and psychological insights. Friel's candid view is not without compassion for a family whose self-contained isolationism from the world around them becomes part of their undoing. Although the O'Donnells are Roman Catholics, they have remained aloof from the stirrings of Ireland's latter-day civil rights movement.

Their connections with lower-class fellow Irishmen like Willie Diver, an accommodating handyman, do not include any concern with the world he represents.

With Father's sudden death, a funeral replaces Claire's wedding on the family agenda. The event also leads to the domestic council at which Judith stuns her kinfolk with her response to their well-intended generosity. But not before the playwright has completed his sensitive family portrait. . . .

> John Beaufort, "Comedy About Aristocratic Irish Family's Hard Times Gets Admirable Staging," in The Christian Science Monitor, April 27, 1989.

EDITH OLIVER

[*Aristocrats*] is a faultless production of an ironic, loving,

imaginative, and all but faultless play. Make that a faultless play. Mr. Friel, to refresh your memory, is the Irish author of *Translations,* which lighted up Off Broadway a few seasons back, and *Philadelphia, Here I Come!,* which had a successful Broadway run before that, and *Faith Healer,* which deserved one. *Aristocrats* is set in Donegal in the nineteen-seventies, on the lawn and in the study of Ballybeg Hall, the large manor house of District Judge O'Donnell, and it is about the decline of the O'Donnell family from its eminence at the end of the last century and the beginning of this one. The old judge lies dying in an upstairs bedroom. Four of his five grown children are home to celebrate the marriage of the youngest of them, Claire, who is still in her twenties. The others are Alice, an alcoholic who is married to the son of a former housemaid at Ballybeg Hall; Judith, who is nursing her father in the last stages of senility; and their brother, Casimir, a fascinating, eccentric fellow, rapturous one moment and downcast the next, and never still. . . . Innocently unable to distinguish fact from fancy, he talks about an evening he spent with Yeats, until someone points out that he was born in the year that Yeats died; and his conversation is studded with references to John McCormack, Gerard Manley Hopkins, and Thomas Moore, among others, as if they were old family friends. He lives in Hamburg with a German wife and a couple of sons. Maybe, maybe not—Eamon, Alice's husband, quietly points out that no one has ever seen wife or boys, and Casimir keeps trying to telephone them without success. His delight at being home almost overflows, but at a peremptory bark from his father over the intercom he collapses in tears. What thrills him most is the music of Chopin, played on the piano by his sister Claire. Eamon describes an old woman who plays the harmonium as "the Scott Joplin of Donegal." That kind of joke is at the heart of Mr. Friel's irony; time after time, he punctures the prevailing elegiac or romantic mood with something brisk or factual or modern.

The first scene sets the tone, when we see a townsman named Willie installing the intercom with the help of an all-purpose American—a visiting professor who is writing a dissertation on the great Roman Catholic houses of Ireland, and who is the perfect audience for Casimir's reminiscences. Judith, the very model of a gracious, devoted daughter, recites her grim daily routine of caring for her father and trying to make both ends meet. Casimir plays a tape from the missing sibling, a faraway nun, who is "praying for them," and who sounds particularly smug and fatuous. Claire rushes in, all aglow, and then we learn that she is a depressive, that the groom is a local grocer twice her age, with small children, and that they will all live in her sister-in-law's house.

Although *Aristocrats* does not lack events, the story is in the characters, in all their complexity and richness and sadness—and especially in the members of the family, who seem to be on the brink of collapse at the prospect of leaving Ballybeg Hall, though leave they must. . . . Brian Friel's writing is of a quality we very seldom encounter on or off the stage.

> Edith Oliver, "At Ballybeg Hall," in The New Yorker, Vol. LXV, No. 12, May 8, 1989, p. 104.

MICHAEL FEINGOLD

The clandestine affair between Anton Chekhov and Lady Gregory is never mentioned by their biographers. Yet it must have happened, because Brian Friel's ***Aristocrats*** is unmistakably its offspring: a meld of *Three Sisters* and *The Cherry Orchard* transposed to Donegal in 1970, where, according to Friel, once upper-class families still decay, occupying themselves with trivia and dissipation while their mansions run down, the newly affluent sons of the peasantry take over their lands, and an even newer, educated, technocratic class intermarries with them or, worse, arrives from America to study them as a sociological phenomenon.

All these things happen, in ***Aristocrats,*** to the three daughters and one son of General Prozorov—I mean District Judge O'Donnell, sorry—when they convene for a family wedding which, in the normal Chekhovite course, duly turns into a family funeral, that of the judge himself, leaving his children rudderless, bankrupt, and unhappy. I don't mean that Friel duplicates Chekhov literally. He adds a fourth (offstage) sister, presumably to illustrate Ireland's ongoing commitment to the Catholic tradition of having too many children. Rather than his Irina, a/k/a Claire, his focus of erotic attraction is Olga, a/k/a Judith, who is loved, in the absence of regimental officers, by two locals who split between them the characteristics of Lopakhin, Kulygin, and Yepikhodov. One is married to her sister, and one will not marry her, not wishing to raise the illegitimate child she has had, à la Nina, during a runaway phase.

I don't mean, either, to ridicule Friel's reshuffling of Chekhov's materials; he's proved many times that he can invent his own. Presumably he believes this aspect of Chekhov still applies to Ireland, a point lost on countries where the notion of a landed gentry has long since crumbled. He's made a nice play, a solid, conventional evening's entertainment, not false or stupid. What he can't summon up is the magic pointillism, the numerous tiny unexpected strokes adding up to a complete poetic picture, that makes Chekhov's work apply to everyone, not just decaying landed gentries. Where Chekhov's delicate and precise, Friel is blocky, schematic, overexplanatory: The chat between the brighter of his two Lopakhins and the American sociologist is a heavy nudge. Even the latter's last name—Hoffnung—is translated for us; imagine Chekhov making Trigorin point out that Dorn means "thorn" in German.

Michael Feingold, "The Plough and the Tsars," in The Village Voice, *Vol. XXXIII, No. 18, May 29, 1989, p. 18.*

Donald Hall
The One Day

Award: National Book Critics Circle Award for poetry

Born Donald Andrew Hall, Jr. in 1928. American poet, editor, memoirist, biographer, critic, essayist, dramatist, and author of children's books.

A long poem divided into three sections, *The One Day* presents both a male and a female interpretation of the meaning of life from the onset of old age. In the alternating blank-verse stanzas of ten lines that comprise the first and final segments of the poem, the two narrators relate their lives. "Shrubs Burnt Away," the first section, depicts the despair of each narrator: he is a burnt-out alcoholic, and she is a suicidal sculptor. Their immobilization is in direct contrast to the dynamism of the celebrated middle section, "Four Classic Texts." This part connects the narrative sequences that begin and end the poem, setting the details of the narrators' individual lives in a broader context of defeat, struggle, and eventual reconciliation. In "Prophecy," the first of these "classic texts," the speaker curses unacceptable elements of modern life, from smoked oysters to Acquired Immune Deficiency Syndrome (AIDS). "Pastoral," the second text, is a bitter satire of marriage in which a shepherd and a shepherdess taunt each other with their adultery. "History" juxtaposes ancient and contemporary examples of human destructiveness. In the final section, "Eclogue," the speaker's rage and bitterness are overcome by a visionary acceptance of all living things. This appreciation prepares the way for the nostalgic and joyful attitude found in the final section, "To Build a House." Critics have noted that this arrangement of the poems, moving through despair and paralysis in "Shrubs Burnt Away," aided by the explosive emotional force of the middle section, and ending in the quiet exultation of the final section, forms a continuum of the human condition.

The passionate, dense verse found in *The One Day* collects the work of seventeen years and was published on the occasion of Hall's sixtieth birthday. Commentators noted Hall's highly developed poetic technique, which gives dramatic expression to his essentially meditative or didactic exploration of how individuals find meaning in life. His skillful use of collage—juxtaposing the words of the two narrators—illustrates the interconnectedness of their seemingly disparate lives and draws the reader into what presents itself as a universal experience. In addition, Hall's attention to alliterative and rhythmic effects provide much of the energy and grandeur with which this award-winning poem is credited. Liam Rector remarked: " 'Work, love, build a house, and die,' Hall writes, 'But build a house.' The artistry of *The One Day* is itself evidence of such a triumph of real work, and I suspect those of us who come to poetry for an ultimate spareness of expression—and for even another reason: wisdom—will be pulling this book from our shelves for some time."

(See also *CLC*, Vols. 1, 13, 37; *Contemporary Authors*, Vols.

5-8, rev. ed.; *Contemporary Authors New Revision Series*, Vol. 2; *Contemporary Authors Autobiography Series*, Vol. 7; *Something about the Author*, Vol. 23; and *Dictionary of Literary Biography*, Vol. 5.)

PRINCIPAL WORKS

POETRY

Exiles and Marriages   1955
A Roof of Tiger Lilies   1964
The Alligator Bride: Poems New and Selected   1969
The Yellow Room   1971
A Blue Wing Tilts at the Edge of the Sea: Selected Poems, 1964-1974   1975
The Town of Hill   1975
Kicking the Leaves   1978
Ox Cart Man   1979
The Happy Man   1986
The One Day   1989

OTHER MAJOR WORKS

Andrew the Lion Farmer (children's book) 1959
String Too Short to Be Saved: Childhood Reminiscences
   1961; revised 1979
Writing Well (essays) 1973
Remembering Poets: Reminiscences and Opinions 1978

DAVID LEHMAN

[Donald Hall's *The One Day* is Whitmanic]: loud, sweeping, multitudinous, an act of the imperial imagination. A sustained and unified work in three parts rather than a conventional collection, it is the poet's present to himself for his 60th birthday in September [1988]. I have no hesitation in declaring it a major book—its passion and urgency are rare and remarkable. Basketball players have a word for hot shooting: the man with the hot hand is shooting "unconscious." This seems an apt description of Hall's method and his magic in *The One Day.*

Hall tells us he began writing *The One Day* in fits and bursts, very rapidly, not knowing where he was going; he reports that "it seemed like dictation" at first, like "signals from other lives." Only gradually did he shape the work into a sequence consisting of "ten-line bricks" (stanzas) used to construct a metaphoric house. In the first and third sections of the book, a male voice and a female one (in Roman and italic type, respectively) do the talking. We begin in crisis: "unfit/ to work or love, aureoled with cigarette smoke/ in the unstoried room, I daydream to build/ the house of dying." We end with an assertion of order. This is the poem's climactic line: "Work, love, build a house, and die. But build a house."

The "Four Classic Texts" that form the book's purgatorial middle section are magnificent, particularly **"Prophecy,"** with its rejections and threats ("and the earth [will] split open like a corpse's gassy/ stomach and the sun turn as black as a widow's skirt") and **"History,"** with its violent montage of historical episodes. High on Hall's thematic agenda are age and aging, rage and raging against the dying of the light, but his powerful rhetorical gestures and dazzling juxtapositions communicate a pleasure even beyond the skillful treatment of such themes. (p. 6)

> *David Lehman, "Their Craft or Sullen Art," in* Book World—The Washington Post, *August 28, 1988, pp. 6-7.*

STEPHEN SANDY

[*The excerpt below was also published in* The Day I Was Older *under the title* "An Enlarging Pleasure."]

Donald Hall has written a long poem. Quite possibly *The One Day* is the major accomplishment of his career. Hall's poem is serious, ambitious, graceful. *The One Day* has the force of gravity which a long poem gains in the ear's mind, and an impressive density; a tensile strength resulting from a quilt of narrative shot through with meditation; a startling rhetoric of denunciation; and a judgmental stance which shows Hall at the noontide of his thoughtful powers.

The One Day is a splendid accomplishment, and a demanding one. Great craft informs this poem, the sort of employ-

ment of techniques and devices one scarcely hopes to find in anyone's work anymore. It's as if he's rolled all the Silver Ghosts out of their garages, and we find them well tuned and running, gleaming in the sun, outdoing the rusted Toyotas of our penny-ante poetry. Reading *The One Day* is like experiencing a fast run, with appropriate stops, through the modes, techniques, and manners of Western poetry, from Old Testament invective or Psalmic praise to Theocritan pastoral romance, to Romantic narrative. The presence of Juvenal, Virgil, Dryden, Frost, Whitman, Ginsberg, and Geoffrey Hill as tutelary spirits is detectable; and a feast of echoes and allusions awaits those invited to it by their familiarity with salient poetic texts.

Made up of 110 ten-line stanzas, *The One Day* is the narrative of a life related alternately by an "I" (who, as Hall says in a postscript, "will be taken as the author") and by a woman sculptor, who suffers many travails and, finally, is summoned to The White House to receive a medal. Other voices blend to make a choral consciousness (Hall quotes Picasso, "every human being is a colony"), but the male and female narrators constitute the poet's persona which, so to speak, has undergone mitotic cleavage.

The exposition—with its attendant themes of art holding out against chaos; work holding out against exhaustion; the stigmatizing of a corrupt America—is bisected by an interlude of four movements, **"Prophecy," "Pastoral," "History," "Eclogue,"** each of which joins the indictment afresh, surveying with scorn and wit the decay, apathy, and destructive fatalism of contemporary America.

This central part, each section in a different mode, may be the most compelling piece of the poem. Here there's space only to quote from the first of the "four classic texts," **"Prophecy,"** endearing for the shimmering vibrancy of its Biblical rhetoric. From a viewpoint of privileged awareness, Hall's jeremiad employs techniques of anaphora and cataloguing, denouncing an America whose culture is exhausted and dying:

> I reject Japanese smoked oysters, potted
>   chrysanthemums
> allowed to die, Tupperware parties,
>   Ronald McDonald,
> Kaposi's sarcoma, the Taj Mahal,
>   Holsteins wearing
> electronic necklaces, the Algonquin,
>   Tunisian aqueducts,
> Phi Beta Kappa keys, the Hyatt
>   Embarcadero, carpenters
> jogging on the median. . . .

The tone is briskly serious, convincing; Hall unabashedly engages Old Testament prophecy, even invoking Yahweh: "When priests and policemen / strike my body's match, Jehovah will flame out; / Jehovah will suck air from the vents of bombshelters." Rage flourishes (the luminous closure of **"Prophecy"** is a memorable passage of apocalyptic writing) and is made strong and clean-cutting by an awareness of human failure (exemplified by his own, as the narrator tells us elsewhere in this long text) and by a righteousness made credible by articulate utterance. Condemnation is strengthened as well for being balanced by the theme of the final part, which prescribes while it celebrates a wise prudence in our relations with the earth, its creatures, our desires. "I marry the creation that stays / in place to be worked at, day after day." . . .

[Wallace] Stevens remarked that, "anyone who has read a long poem . . . knows how the poem comes to possess the reader and how it naturalizes him in its own imagination and liberates him there." For those who are up to it, reading Hall's poem will be an enlarging pleasure, and a reminder of how immediate, concrete, and pertinent to our situation a poem can be.

It is a commonplace that a serious poet aspires to write a long poem. Donald Hall's *The One Day* is ambitious in the best sense; it gives us agency, force, intelligence; it is alive with form and figure; it has (in the final part especially) a passional yet thoughtful tone that requires our assent to the whole work. Hall has said that "there is no way to be good except by trying to be great." He has embraced the need the strong poet has to write a long poem and has succeeded impressively. Hall is more than a good poet.

> Stephen Sandy, in a review of "The One Day," in Boston Review, *Vol. XIII, No. 3, October, 1988, p. 22.*

DONALD HALL [INTERVIEW WITH LIAM RECTOR]

[Rector]: *We both grew up spending our summers with our grandparents on farms, you in New Hampshire and I in Virginia. In* **String Too Short to Be Saved** *you wrote of how this shaped your imagination and that residence where imagination and memory comingle. Living now on that same farm where you spent summers, what is your memory, your imagination of the large cities?*

[Hall]: I've never lived in a great city. For me, large cities are excitement, energy, vitality, almost mania. When I go to New York I never sleep. Oh, I've lived for a month or two at a time in London, Paris, Rome. Because Cambridge is virtually Boston, and I went to school there, I suppose I *did* live in a big city—but living in a college isn't the same. I contrast the country not to the city but to the suburbs; Ann Arbor is a suburb without an urb. (Technically it's a city.)

This place is no longer a farm but the rural culture remains amazingly intact, although thirty years ago I thought it was vanishing. I love the landscape more deeply all the time; I am content sitting on the porch and gazing at Kearsarge, or walking in the woods. Carol Bly speaks somewhere of writers who are "mindless nature describers." Touché; I guess I'm a mindless nature lover, but I love also the independence and solitude of the country, which is by no means only a matter of population density. I don't suffer from the deference, mostly ironic, that hangs around writers in universities; I'm the "fellow over there who writes books for a living" and that's a freedom.

Your work has been haunted not only by the grandfather but the father. Did your father encourage your becoming a writer?

My father was soft and volatile, a businessman who hated being a businessman and daydreamed for himself a life in the academy—probably prep school rather than college—where everybody would be *kind* to everybody else. He read books; mostly he read contemporary historical fiction like Hervey Allen and Kenneth Roberts. He was finicky about good prose and suffered from polysyllabic tendencies, especially if he was depressed: "It is necessary to masticate thoroughly." Politically he was conservative and not very thoughtful. He wept frequently and showed feelings which other men would hold

back. He desperately wanted people to like him and many did. He was nervous, continually shaking; quick, alert, sensitive, unintellectual. When he was forty-two he hemorrhaged with a bad bleeding ulcer and remained sickly until he got lung cancer at fifty-one and died at fifty-two. As an adolescent I needed to feel superior to him; when I was about twenty-five, when my son was born, I felt reconciled. I don't think we talked about matters of great substance but we could love each other. He read my things and mostly praised them, but I don't think either of us wanted to talk about them. He tried to encourage me in one direction, constantly, by telling me that my poetry was just fine but my prose was really great. . . . Some of this at least was his desire that I might possibly be able to make a living. When he realized that I was going into teaching, it pleased him because of his imaginary academy.

Your new book, **The One Day,** *is in many ways a departure from* **Kicking the Leaves** *and* **The Happy Man,** *both in its elliptical form, its being a book-length shoring of fragments, and its engagement with the very old and the very new, aside from your personal remembered past which sets much of the tone in the two books before. How do you account for this shift? One section of* **The One Day** *was printed in* **The Happy Man.** *What made you decide to foreshadow the long poem by printing* **"Shrubs Burnt Away"** *there? Had you yet seen the shape that* **The One Day** *would assume?*

If you look at everything from the beginning in 1955, there is lots of moving about and shifting. Surely you're right that the form of *The One Day* is modernist, with its multiple protagonist—but I guess I don't want to. . . . Really, I don't want to talk about the form of it. It's new; I'm still finding out what I did.

The poem began with an onslaught of language back in 1971. Over a period of weeks I kept receiving messages; I filled page after page of notebooks. If I drove to the supermarket, I had to bring the book and pull over three or four times in a few miles to transcribe what was coming. It was inchoate, sloppy, but full of *material:* verbal, imaginative, recollected. And it was frightening. After a while the barrage ceased, but from time to time over the years more would come—with a little label on it, telling me that it belonged to this *thing.* (In my head for a long time I called it *Building the House of Dying.*) The first part was there in inchoate form, much of the first two of "Four Classic Texts," much of the "one day" theme in the third part. Every now and then, over the years, I would look at these notebooks, and feel excitement and fear. In 1980 I began to *work* on it; to try to do something with these words. First I set it out as a series of twenty-five or thirty linked free verse poems: Nothing marched. I worked on it for a year or two; I remember reading it aloud to Jane [Kenyon] one time, and when I finished I was full of *shame!* Shame over what I revealed, shame over bad poetry; after that, I couldn't look at it for a year.

At some point early in the 1980s, Robert Mazzocco suggested casually in a letter that I ought sometime to write a book of linked poems, like Lowell in *Notebook* or Berryman in *Dream Songs.* Thinking of this notion I developed my ten-line stanza, making some into almost-discrete ten-line poems, using others as stanzas. I thought of Keats's *Ode* stanza, developed out of the sonnet and the desire to write the longer ode form. This notion helped me get to work: bricks—cement blocks?— for the house. I worked with these stanzas for a couple of years, then maybe in 1984 developed a three-part idea that somewhat resembles the present version, except that the middle part is totally different. I showed a draft to a few people. I remember [Robert] Bly saying, with his usual diffidence, that the first part was the best thing I had ever done and the second part was the worst thing I had ever done. The second part was a problem until I worked out the notion that turned into "Four Classic Texts"; I stole **"Eclogue"** from Virgil, which always helps. I still thought the third part was my real problem, and sometimes doubted that I would ever finish the whole—because I wouldn't be able to make the third part.

When I put *The Happy Man* together I had **"Shrubs Burnt Away"** more or less finished, "Four Classic Texts" just beginning, and "In the One Day" lying about in pieces. I thought it would be ten years before I would be able to finish the poem as a whole, if I ever did. I had no notion that I might finish it within a couple of years. But I think that printing **"Shrubs"** in *The Happy Man* allowed me to finish the whole poem. Response was encouraging . . . and some reviews helped me understand what I was doing, like David Shapiro's in *Poetry,* with his reference to Freud and the movement from hysterical misery to ordinary unhappiness! (pp. 39-41)

How has Freud affected your view of things? What have the insights of psychology, and psychoanalysis in particular, meant to you and your generation of poets?

I started reading Freud in 1953. Ten years later I started psychotherapy with a Freudian analyst, the only analyst in Ann Arbor who would do therapy. Reading Freud was exciting and gave me ideas; I could have found much the same in Heraclitus: Whenever somebody shows you north, suspect south. Later, the experience of therapy was profound. It touches me every day and it goes *with* the poetry rather than against it. You learn to release, to allow the ants—and the butterflies—to come out from under the rock; but first you have to know the rock's there! The names of the things that run out are up to you. Psychotherapy properly is never a matter of the explanations of feelings, nor of "Eureka!" as in Hollywood. It is a transforming thing. It makes your skin alert; it builds a system of sensors. Jung, on the other hand, seems a mildly interesting literary figure, full of fascinating ideas and disgusting ones mixed together with more regard for color than for truth. Freud is as nasty as the world is, as human life is. Jung is decorative. Freud is the streets and Jung is a Fourth of July parade through the streets, a parade of minor deities escaped from the zoo of polytheism. Freud has the relentlessness of monotheism.

Will you ever write an autobiography of your adult life?

No.

You came to Whitman in your middle age? Some came to him early and take his words as scripture (I think of Ginsberg and Kinnell, particularly, here) and others arrived at him later, such as yourself and Richard Howard. What do you think might account for this?

It was my good fortune that I delayed Whitman, but as so often the provenance of the good fortune was dumb. I grew up reading poems the new critical way, which worked for Donne, and Hart Crane, but didn't work for Whitman. When I tried reading him he looked silly. My inadequacy saved him for me. He was brand new and exciting when I found him in middle age—by which I mean thirty or thirty-two.

Who, aside from writers, have been your most important teachers?

Henry Moore. I spent a good deal of time with him, talking with him, watching him work. He had the most wonderful attitude toward work and his art. He was interested only in being better than Michelangelo, and he knew he never achieved it; so he got up the next morning and tried again. He was a gregarious man who learned to forego companionship for the sake of work. He knew what he had to do. He remained decent to others, although it is difficult; people make it difficult for you when you're that damned famous. He knew the difference between putting in time—you can work sixteen hours a day and remain lazy—and really working as an artist, trying to *break through.*

How would you place your poems among the poems of the past? I'm thinking here of Keats's statement, which you mentioned in **"Poetry and Ambition,"** *that "I would sooner fail, than not be among the greatest." You've also wisely said that we are bad at judging our own work—we either think too much of it or too little of it? But take a crack at it?*

I can't place my poems among the poems of the past and I doubt the sanity or the intelligence of people who say that they can. When Keats said that he would "sooner fail than not be among the greatest," note that he did not tell us that he *was* among the greatest. He *wishes* to be among the English poets when he is dead; he does not tell us that he already *is.* When I was young I had the illusion that at some point or other you would *know* if you were good. I no longer believe that such knowledge is possible. Some days you feel you're terrific; some days you feel you're crap. So what? Get on with it.

The One Day *works with the kind of "multiple protagonist" voice we find in "The Waste Land." Why did you make this choice, rather than staying in the fairly mono-lyrical voice which has before characterized much of your work?*

Picasso said that every human being is a colony. An old friend of mine said that she was not a person but ran a boarding-house. One of the many problems with the "mono-lyrical" is that it pretends that each of us is singular. (pp. 43-4)

> *Donald Hall and Liam Rector, in an interview in* The American Poetry Review, *Vol. 18, No. 1, January-February, 1989, pp. 39-46.*

LIAM RECTOR

Once in a great while a book of poems comes along and one feels that a time has been spoken for. Such is the happy occasion with Donald Hall's *The One Day,* a book that recently, deservedly, received the National Book Critics Circle Award in poetry. A book-length poem in three parts, *The One Day* has about it the wicked satire of a Tom Wolfe, an Old Testament razzmatazz of rant, a prophetic energy akin to Allen Ginsberg's "Howl," and a lyricism which bears Hall's fully developed signature. One thinks of books, among contemporaries, such as Galway Kinnell's *The Book of Nightmares* or A. R. Ammons' *Sphere,* to compare how both ambition and the brickwork of construction might meld themselves into a single structure and presence.

An excerpt from "To Build a House"

Gazing at May's blossoms, imagining bounty of
  McIntosh,
I praise old lilacs rising in woods beside cellarholes;
I praise toads. I predict the telephone call
that reports the friend from childhood cold on a
  staircase.
I praise children, grandchildren, and just-baked
  bread.
I praise fried Spam and onions on slices of Wonder
  Bread;
I praise your skin. I predict the next twenty years,
days of mourning, long walks growing slow and
  painful.
I reject twenty years of mid-life; I reject rejections.
The one day stands unmoving in sun and shadow.

When I rise at eight o'clock my knuckles are stiff.
I sit for an hour wearing my nightgown in a sunny
  chair.
Hot water from the faucet, black coffee, and two as-
  pirin
unstick my fingerjoints, and by these hands I join
the day that will never return. This is the single
day that extends itself, intent as an animal listening
for food, while I chisel at alabaster. All day I know
where the sun is. To seize the hour, I must cast my-
  self
into work that I love, as the keeper hurls
horsemeat to the lion:—I am meat, lion, and keeper.

With Picasso's assertion that "Every human being is a colony" as its credo, *The One Day* is built within an arc of juxtaposed shifts that advance elliptically a multiple protagonist, an almost simultaneous speaking of characters who waft in and out, and the undersong of the book is the choral pitch of so many attempting to do what they want to do. . . .

Hall has long kept his eye and ear upon what is old, what is historical, what seems *behind* us yet is still living with us, and with *The One Day* he moves out into a different terrain from his recent mature books, *Kicking the Leaves* and *The Happy Man.* His ear is still wrapped around the sounds of words and there is a characteristic adherence to the marked rhythms wherein time itself is given form, but the mordant and bloody-minded surge of much of *The One Day* has about it a much surer sense of drama and its through-lines. This is a refinement over his earliest poetry, which was sometimes marred by its own precosity and use of irony, particularly where that irony could not find the means to dramatize itself and find full closure.

Characters and images of stasis and torpor haunt the beginning of the book, lives prevented by the disappointment that was theirs to inherit, lives now grown into an American culture where idleness and entropy are seen to prevent any authentic love or real work. Busyness has become business, and passion is sublimated into distraction and an entertainment unto death. One of the most inspired sections of *The One Day* is the poem **"Pastoral,"** in which a mock-shepherd and shepherdess pipe their song of adultery back and forth to each other—easily some of the funniest and most wincing writing about adultery, and about the suburbs in general, I've ever read. Byron once said, "If fools be my theme, let satire be my song," but as *The One Day* moves toward its climax we know that fools are not here Hall's theme. His writing is invaded

by a sympathy for all that lives, even as satire and rage hover everywhere about what seems, often, only our ridiculous enduring of ourselves.

The final section of the book, **"To Build a House,"** is in fact a coming to terms with the soul's need for repose, based on that "third thing" we look out upon in the mix of our love and building. "Work, love, build a house, and die," Hall writes, "But build a house." The artistry of *The One Day* is itself evidence of such a triumph of real work, and I suspect those of us who come to poetry for an ultimate spareness of expression—and for even another reason: wisdom—will be pulling this book from our shelves for some time. It will even revive those who think they hate poetry, who are convinced they really can't stand The Stuff.

Liam Rector, "The Building of Work and Love," in
Los Angeles Times Book Review, *February 5,*
1989, p. 3.

CHARLES GUENTHER

Donald Hall (born 1928) has written nine books of verse from *Exiles and Marriages* (1955) to *The One Day: A Poem in Three Parts,* which recently won the 1988 National Book Critics Circle Award for Poetry. Yet for nearly 40 years, beginning as poetry editor of *The Harvard Advocate* and the *Paris Review,* Hall has labored in the fields as a poet for poets.

Hall started publishing poetry at age 16, and later studied under John Ciardi, Richard Wilbur, Yvor Winters and others at Harvard and Stanford. Some of his peers at Harvard were Adrienne Rich (whom he twice dated), John Ashbery, Robert Bly, Kenneth Koch and Frank O'Hara. In 1952, as an Oxford undergraduate, he won the coveted Newdigate Prize for poetry, a rare feat for an American, and three years later he won the Lamont Poetry Prize in the U.S. Altogether, since the 1950s he has written dozens of books of poems, stories, essays and biography, and edited scores of others. . . .

Composed during 17 years beginning in 1971, [*The One Day*] consists of 112 ten-line stanzas of roughly formal blank verse—a poem which in 1981, Hall explains, began to fall into three parts. Throughout the poem a variety of voices speak, one resembling the poet's and others being alternates. In the first and third parts two characters speak, the male author and a woman sculptor, and each quotes others. But many of the lines, Hall adds, belong to a general, third-person narrative consciousness.

In the opening section titled **"Shrubs Burnt Away"** a middle-aged, aging man appears (who resembles the old men of W. B. Yeats' poems), whom Hall describes as "an old man hedging and ditching / three hundred years ago in Devon." The old man becomes a figure of the collective consciousness, a figure whose emotions run the gamut from pain and anger to joy:

Night after night I sleep on pills and wake exhausted:
Rage weighs its iron on my chest. I cannot enter
the orchard's farmhouse on the hill, or find the road
vanished under burdock. . . .

and,

I am very happy. I dance supine on my bed laughing
until four in the morning, when the bottle is empty
and the liquor store closed . . . In the morning I lie
waking dozing twisted in the damp workclothes

of lethargy, loathing, and the desire to die.

From that opening part dealing mostly with the past, the poet proceeds to a middle section containing "Four Classic Texts"—**"Prophecy," "Pastoral," "History"** and **"Eclogue."** These are more formal pieces, in the same easy style as the first part, moving among persons, places and events of antiquity. Yet all here, especially in the **"Eclogue,"** seems eternal; it captures a present where:

> swollen grapes turn purple and plump themselves
> into wine, and the oak's acorns fatten for pigs
>   of autumn. . . . Work and love will increase
> as grass enlarges in sun and downpour, emptying
> itself to swell again: summer, autumn, winter, spring.

The third, closing part, titled **"To Build a House,"** resumes with the two characters, male and female. Here is a wondrous present offering "intimations of human possibility" from Hall's many notions of human multiplicity. The author is more intimate, less remote in this largely autobiographical section, laced with fact and imagination. This section provides both the title and the main theme of **The One Day,** and the stanzas alternate from love and joy:

> Here, among the thirty thousand days of a long life,
> a single day stands still. The sun shines, it is raining;
> we sleep, we make love, we plant a tree,
> we walk up and down eating lunch . . .
> The one day extended from that moment, unrolling
> continuous as the broad moon on water, or as
>   motions of rain
> that journey a million times through air to water. . . .

to pain and death:

> The bed is a world of pain and the repeated deaths
> of preparation for death. The awake nightmare
> comforts itself by painting the mourner's portrait:
> As I imagine myself on grief's rack at graveside
> I picture and pity myself. . . .
>   Gradually we recover pulse
> to return to the bed's world and the third thing:
> Still the stretcher forever enters the elevator going
> down, and the telephone lacerates silence.

Donald Hall's own essays, in three of some 30 volumes he edited for the University of Michigan where he worked and taught for 17 years, give broad insights on his background, experience, tastes and attitudes. (In 1975 he settled on a farm in New Hampshire where he is state poet laureate.) Still, nothing but his poetry carries quite the impact of memory and imagination affecting his past and present life. And **The One Day** is a small master-work of that life. With its subtle developments in style, attitude and direction, the poem is roughly comparable to a maturing spirit. While it hasn't the breadth of a vast journey—an *Odyssey* or a *Divine Comedy*— its journey is real and its settings are true. (As a clue to its meaning, we may recall that the poet once began to title the poem, "Building the House of Dying.") Nor is **The One Day** a shuffling, syncopated wasteland. Rather it brings order and sanity and beauty to an age that seems to long for these elements.

In short, it's a marvelous poem.

> *Charles Guenther, "Distillation of a Poet's Labor,"*
> *in* St. Louis Post-Dispatch, *February 5, 1989, p. 5C.*

DANIEL MARK EPSTEIN

It is always a rugged beauty that inspires Donald Hall, and the most perfect and sublime of his poems seems corrugated with the grain of painful reality. **The One Day** is Donald Hall's poem of the midlife crisis, a painful time for men and women alike, and the poet uses midlife as a metaphor that works on several levels—personal, historical and mythic.

This poem is experimental in the best sense, locating itself in the tradition of [Ezra Pound's] *The Cantos,* [Charles Olson's] *Maximus* and [William Carlos Williams's] *Paterson,* modernist efforts to form a bridge from the lyric poem to the narrative. Hall employs a 10-line stanza with variable line length in the three sections of the poem, **"Shrubs Burnt Away,"** "Four Classic Texts" and **"To Build a House."** Most remarkable, he uses two major voices, or *personae,* one male and one female, to tell his stories, creating a mythic counterpoint that reminds one of Jung's theories of *animus* and *anima.*

The male voice is presumed to be the poet's own, as he struggles with demons of midlife—alcoholism, ennui and sexual obsessions: "Now I told my wife: Consider me a wind that lifts / the square white houses up and spins them / into each other; or as a flood loosening houses / from their cellarholes; or as a fire that burns / white wooden houses down. I was content in the dark / livingroom, fixed in the chair with whiskey." The female voice is of a woman sculptor whose problems are more dramatic than the male's since she is mentally ill, suicidal: "I crashed like my daredevil pilots; it was what / I wanted. For two years I moved among institutions, / admitted because of barbiturates—I took pills / to keep from dreaming—alcohol, and depression. / Electroshock blanked me out. If I worked my hands shook; / When I carved, my chisel slipped making errors:— / I contrived art out of errors."

From the struggle of these characters, Hall weaves a remarkable personal narrative. But other voices add layers of meaning to the poem, most notably Senex, an oracle of all times and places who provides a synchronic criticism of history. "For four hundred years and sixteen generations, I kept / my castle while vassals baked flatbread." He observes "how terrorists burn athletes; terrorists dynamite the former ambassador of the executed prime minister" and "my managers fly / to Chicago on Tuesday and divorce in Santo Domingo / on Wednesday. . . ."

As a prosodist, Hall inspired such confidence that we cannot doubt he can write a lovely lyric whenever the spirit moves him; but to make a perfectly beautiful poem in a world so obviously imperfect, Hall's poems would seem to be telling us, is a lie—and Donald Hall is not capable of writing anything but the poetic truth. In this posture, he reminds us of no poet as much as William Carlos Williams. One cannot hope to convey the richness and energy of **The One Day** in a brief review. It must suffice here to say I would have to return to Williams's epic *Paterson* in order to find a long poem with comparable personality and grandeur. (pp. 593-94)

> *Daniel Mark Epstein, in a review of "The One Day,"*
> *in* America, *Vol. 160, No. 23, June 17-24, 1989, pp.*
> *593-94.*

THOM GUNN

[Hall] started, as do most writers, embedded in the idiom of his time. It was the 1950s, and his early, prize-winning poems were about exile and existential estrangement. Holding his new-born child in his arms, he addressed it as "my son, my executioner"; he mourned the decay of rural New Hampshire, where he had spent his school vacations, and he detailed the dull, familiar features of the suburbia in which he had been raised. . . .

But he was looking for something more. Searching for an imagery equivalent to the heartland from which we have been exiled, he entered next upon a different kind of poetry. In **"The Long River"** he rows into a dark, mysterious interior:

> The musk-ox smells
> in his long head
> my boat coming.

The musk-ox is both ominous and vital; his appetites have become forgotten in suburbia. The spondaic phrases give the writing a slowness, a weight, that it has not had before. And its syllabic form—Hall was the inventor of syllabics in our time—make for a more unpredictable verse-movement than in the earlier poetry, with which it has little in common.

It was now the '60s, and he moved into different kinds of free verse. *The Alligator Bride* embodies a kind of jocular surrealism. Such investigations of the irrational, however, led him eventually to the true sources of the rural nostalgia that always had haunted him. He quit teaching at Ann Arbor in 1975, remarried, and moved back to the farmhouse of his maternal grandparents, not as farmer himself but as a writer who wanted to raise poetry on farmland. And he succeeded, writing poems that were less elegies for the past than realizations of it—about the cart horses and the hen yard, the Holsteins and the ox-cart man, their lives thick with things. He lifted the recurrent rhythms of the farming year into the present tense. . . .

The One Day consists of the voices of all of us. The poem is in three parts. The first [,**"Shrubs Burnt Away"**,] opens with an aging man daydreaming and smoking in his yellow chair, "unfit/to work or love." His voice is joined by a woman's but they are the same voice, though they speak of different lives, and we come to understand that they have led the same life, in which the promise of fullness has been answered only by the fact of emptiness. They speak of a self without center, an existence without revelation or joy. . . . The voices weave and alternate, but they speak of the same dead end; of having been herded unwillingly into a present with no real connection to past or future, a present in which they find neither rest nor meaning.

[*The One Day*] is written in a line based on the Old English accentual line as it was loosened and revised by Pound, one of the most useful and flexible technical innovations of the century. The collage and juxtaposition of experience that he uses also is a modified Poundian method, making possible the economical inclusion of a great deal of specific heterogeneous material.

For this poem is all detail and circumstance, the one day made up of many specific days, the one life of many lives, though they lead the speaker into the same narrow place, at the end of which is only fear. At the end of the first part, the female voice tells, with a deadly flatness, how she prepares to give her children pills which will kill them. Then there enters someone whose identity hovers just out of sight, the way a beekeeper's mask darkens a face, who picks up a rag doll

and starts to demonstrate on it the proper ways to dismember a child, as one might a dead fowl, by cutting its limbs carefully into sections.

Though Part One ends thus in nightmare, it has been moderate in tone, that of someone no longer possessing the energy to direct his or her own life. By contrast, Part Two, with the title "Four Classic Texts," starts with rage. **"Prophecy,"** . . . is a curse—against our civilization and against life itself. It is succeeded by the rage of satire, a bitter satire of love and sex and marriage, in **"Pastoral"**. The work is still a bed, in which "we pull off our clothes like opening junk mail." **"History"** follows, rage against the past, and consists of a terrible parody of what already parodies itself, the list of human destructiveness, and Tiberius melts into Stalin. The fourth classic text, though, is not like the others: **"Eclogue"** replaces their destructive rage with its opposite extreme—a visionary certainty, the return to an age of gold through a cyclical process in which we recapture innocence, "the vector of greed withdraws" and there is a "restitution of lost things."

We are to make what we will of this middle section. The "Four Classic Texts" are thrust between Parts One and Three, and we must supply the connection for ourselves. What I think is implied is that his composite protagonist has been moved out of the earlier quiet and rational despair into a full-bodied irrationality, of crazy angers and equally crazy hope, which are at least signs of energy, of not surrendering to the presence with the darkened face.

So that when in [**"To Build a House"**] we return to the original speakers, though they are still old and in the same world, they are changed—*enabled*. The brushes with craziness have released them from their inertia. They still live in the present, but now they live in it fully. No longer "unfit/to work or love," they now find joy in both—

> When my body shook again with the body's passion,
> it was impossible only because I expected nothing.

—and a proposition is reversed, in a kind of echo of John Donne's "The Sun Rising": "A bed is the world," inclusive, and receptive to possibilities. The polysyllabic ironies from earlier in the poem are replaced by praise, not only of blossoms and old lilacs but of "fried Spam and onions on slices of Wonder Bread."

What Hall achieves in this third part is an extraordinarily complex presentation of the grounds for joy, difficult enough to describe at any time, a joy that has nothing in common with complacency, for it is active, intelligent and completely aware that it is to be ended by death, which in fact helps to define it. The rage and satire have been worked off, but the promise of a cyclical return is in its way kept. . . .

There is one day: Past and future are contained in the present of the one day as the whole world is contained in the one bed. Everything is present at the same time:

> The tomcat plays with his mother, sucking and teasing; he cuffs
> his mother's jaw. The tomcat limps home in the bloody
> morning, ear torn. The tomcat sleeps all day
> in a portion of the sun, fur tatty over old scars, pulls
> himself to the saucer of milk, and snores going back
> to sleep, knowing himself the same. The kitten leaps
> in the air, her paws spread like a squirrel's.

The beauty of this writing is not merely in what it says, that the stages of our lives are in some way co-existent, but in the way it so actively *is* what it says, in the specifics of the cat and in the pacing of those specifics. The joy and the acceptance are neither glib nor unexamined.

Among his numerous prose books, Hall has written at least one, **Remembering Poets** (1978), which is of permanent value, not only for its observant memoirs of Dylan Thomas, Frost, Eliot and Pound but also for the brilliant way he moves from them into his reflections about the nature of poetry itself. He says:

> poetry attempts . . . to add old or irrational
> elements to the light of consciousness by
> means of language, which is the instrument of con-
> sciousness.

The poet thus adds unreason to reason, "making a third thing." It seems to me that this describes well what Hall has done in **The One Day:** Mere reason was combined with mere irrationality and the two in combination produce the refined and alert awareness, the late spring, of the third part, a life going through the same processes as a poetry.

And this poem, as a whole, may indeed be seen as the synthesis of a whole life's work. It is one of those books, like Elizabeth Bishop's last collection, which alters the way we look at the jumbled contents of the poetic career preceding it, giving it retrospectively a shape, a pattern, a consistency it didn't seem to have at the time.

> *Thom Gunn, "The Late Spring of Donald Hall," in* Los Angeles Times Book Review, *November 5, 1989, p. 10.*

Kazuo Ishiguro

The Remains of the Day

Award: Booker Prize

A novelist and critic, Ishiguro was born in Japan in 1954 and raised in England.

The Remains of the Day is narrated by Stevens, an elderly butler who has been associated his entire life with an estate named Darlington Hall. Dedicated to such concepts as dignity, service, and loyalty, Stevens believes his proper role in life and work has been to subjugate his personal concerns to those of his master; through such an arrangement, he states, "one can hope to make some small contribution to the creation of a better world." Accordingly, Stevens is emotionally reserved, meticulously attentive to detail, and speaks with impassive formality, qualities considered ideal for his position and mirrored in his narrative. Encouraged by the new owner of Darlington Hall to take a vacation, Stevens uses the opportunity to attempt to procure the services of Miss Kenton, a past housekeeper of the estate. While driving towards a fateful encounter with Miss Kenton, Stevens recollects important incidents in his life and ruminates on his personal values, which are ironically undermined in the course of the novel.

Commentators praised Ishiguro's tonal control in *The Remains of the Day,* particularly as it slowly unfolds Stevens's realization that his life has been characterized by illusions and self-deception. For example, he revered the late Lord Darlington as an influential political figure, yet Darlington had been duped by Nazi sympathisers and was eventually disgraced. Stevens sadly perceives that his habitual emotional restraint rendered him unable to respond to Miss Kenton's love, his father's death, and other significant events in his life. Lawrence Graver described *The Remains of the Day* as "a dream of a book: a beguiling comedy of manners that evolves almost magically into a profound and heart-rending study of personality, class, and culture."

(See also *CLC,* Vols. 27, 56 and *Contemporary Authors,* Vol. 120.)

PRINCIPAL WORKS

A Pale View of Hills 1982
An Artist of the Floating World 1986
The Remains of the Day 1988

ANTHONY THWAITE

There's an Auden sonnet, written in 1938 as part of the "In Time of War" sequence, in which the setting seems to be a country house where great matters are being discussed:

Across the lawns and cultured flowers drifted
The conversation of the highly trained.

The gardeners watched them pass and priced their shoes;
A chauffeur waited, reading in the drive,
For them to finish their exchange of views;
It seemed a picture of the private life.

And then the sestet chillingly spells out what the results of all this are likely to be, as

The armies waited for a verbal error
With all the instruments for causing pain.

Stevens, the elderly butler in Kazuo Ishiguro's third novel, ***The Remains of the Day,*** would never be so vulgar as to price anyone's shoes, but much of his earlier life was discreetly spent in the presence of substantial men exchanging views, at a time of momentous events between the two great wars. In the service of the late Lord Darlington, at Darlington Hall, Stevens was Miltonically aware that they also serve who only stand and wait.

Service, indeed, has been Stevens's guiding principle through

158

a long professional career. He has thought much about 'dignity', as a quality to be striven for by men whose lives are devoted to their employers. Now, in the summer of 1956, generously released for a time to go on holiday while his current employer is away in America, Stevens looks back to his pre-war experience at Darlington Hall. Lord Darlington felt that 'fair play had not been done at Versailles and that it was immoral to go on punishing a nation for a war that was now over'; and, from 1924 on, he set himself the task of organising an 'unofficial' international conference at the hall. Stevens recalls with pride his own preparations for this great event. Summoning the house staff for a preliminary pep-talk, he tells them: 'History could well be made under this roof.'

But gradually it emerges, through the impassive formality of Stevens's reminiscences, that the course of his employer's life was a troubled one. Idealism led to appeasement, to sympathy with the Nazis, even to a period of active anti-semitism. Lord Darlington was in disgrace, during and after the war; his reputation became notorious. Yet Stevens still sees him as 'a gentleman of great moral stature'.

Ishiguro communicates all this with extraordinarily delicate skill, steering Stevens through his solemnities, orotundities, deceptions and self-deceptions, treading with frozen dignity through the corridors of power. The earlier novels, *A Pale View of Hills* and *An Artist of the Floating World,* were wholly or almost wholly set in Japan. This is the first Ishiguro novel to be set wholly in England. But the change is not as marked as one might suppose. In an interview a few years ago, Ishiguro said that he begins by writing his scenes, mainly in dialogue, and then looks for a landscape in which to place them. He has also insisted that he doesn't really write about Japan (which he left for England when he was six years old) but about a country he has invented which merely bears a resemblance to his birthplace. This second point is a little disingenuous, I think, a ploy by which Ishiguro detaches himself from Western Japanophiles who would like to relate him to such 20th-century Japanese novelists as Soseki, Tanizaki and Kawabata: there are distinct Japanese characteristics (such as indirectness) in Ishiguro's work, however much he may disclaim them. But the choice of a loyal elderly senior servant as his English narrator has meant that Ishiguro can use indirectness, obliquity, and indeed the troubling pressures of obligation and indebtedness, in a way that is clearly congenial to him, and in an English context. In a sense, Stevens becomes an English version of that classic Japanese figure, the *ronin,* the masterless retainer who is still tied by firm bands to the master. . . . The stiff formality of Stevens's style, tortuous with circumlocutory negatives and grave protestations, obsessive with obsequiousness and quick to register any slur against whatever may have 'dignity' or be 'distinguished', is an elaborate contrivance. It is a dense hedge against the realisation that he has devoted much of his life to something unworthy, something false, something which had evil consequences.

It is another version of Ono, the artist of *An Artist of the Floating World,* who misjudged his loyalties in pre-war Japan, and who finds that history will not forgive him. Ono, without really knowing it, allowed himself to be made use of; Stevens, seduced into reverence for Lord Darlington, allowed himself to be blind to the direction in which history was going. There follows from this the desire to change things, to rewrite history: so Stevens spends his holiday, long after these events, driving westward towards Miss Kenton, the house-keeper with whom he shared (but also did not share) these experiences, in the hope that she may come back into his life. In his stiff, inhibited fashion, Stevens believes she may redeem the past. But, when at last they meet again, her words 'provoke a certain degree of sorrow' in him: 'After all, there's no turning back the clock now. One can't be forever dwelling on what might have been.'

It's a strange, sad, endearing book, touched with comedy as well as pathos. At times I was reminded of Compton-Burnett, and often of William Trevor. But the lines that kept on coming into my head were from another brooder on things that might have been, on wrong choices, on ruffled dignity:

> no doubt, an easy tool,
> Deferential, glad to be of use,
> Politic, cautious, and meticulous;
> Full of high sentence, but a bit obtuse;
> At times, indeed, almost ridiculous-
> Almost, at times, the Fool.

Ishiguro's Prufrock is a memorable portrait of futility. (p. 17)

Anthony Thwaite, "In Service," in London Review of Books, *Vol. 11, No. 10, May 18, 1989, pp. 17-18.*

GALEN STRAWSON

The Remains of the Day, Kazuo Ishiguro's third novel, has an impressively unpromising opening. Mr Stevens begins to speak in his plonking but catching, sub-Jeevesian, PC Plod Witness Box English. He is a professional butler in his sixties, a very superior subordinate. He has served Lord Darlington (of Darlington Hall, near Oxford) in this capacity for more than thirty years. Today (in July 1956) he is employed by Mr Farraday, the American gentleman who bought the Hall after Lord Darlington's death.

Stevens is running the place with a severely reduced staff of four (once there were twenty-eight). Large areas are dust-sheeted. He is worrying about his staff plan, which is a matter of very great importance ("Indeed, I can say I am in agreement with those who say that the ability to draw up a good staff plan is the cornerstone of any decent butler's skills"). He is slipping; and like his father before him, he fails to see that his errors are a sign of age. Instead he attributes them all to a faulty staff plan: another member of staff is required.

This thought has several causes. Stevens has recently been encouraged to take a holiday by Mr Farraday, and he has received a nostalgic letter from Miss Kenton, the exemplarily professional housekeeper who left Darlington Hall in 1936 to be married. In the letter she announces her separation from her husband, and Stevens proposes to motor down to visit her in Cornwall, principally in order to ascertain whether she might not be induced to return to Darlington Hall.

Such is the motive he admits; the book records his trip west in Farraday's vintage Ford. . . .

His radiator boils dry. He runs out of petrol. He ruminates the past—the great days in the 1920s and 30s when Lord Darlington hosted behind-the-scenes meetings between powerful politicians in the hope of influencing the course of European affairs, motivated at first by his dislike of the way Germany was treated after the First World War, and subsequently exploited by von Ribbentrop and the Nazis, whose accelerating villainy he honourably but regrettably failed to grasp.

Stevens motors through class-obsessed England. He *partakes of refreshments* in *establishments;* he cannot quite control his sequence of tenses; he suffers from "troubled slumber" in strange beds. He is, in his subordinate clauses, a model of moderate and respectful dullness, but his laboriously cautious syntax is not always as respectable as he would hope. . . .

The weather is fine, and he returns repeatedly to a question that has always preoccupied him: "In what does the greatness of a butler consist?" If the best short answer is "Dignity", then what is the essence of dignity? Whatever it is, his greatest desire is to achieve it, and he has no doubt that his butler father possessed it—with his perfect self-control, his "dark, severe presence", his "awesome features" and his preference for being addressed as "Father" even in direct speech, and not only in the vocative. . . .

Examples of dignity are useful, but they are only preliminary to a definition, which Stevens duly attempts. First, it is clearly essential that one should be employed in a "distinguished" household. Second, " 'dignity' has to do crucially with a butler's ability not to abandon the professional being he inhabits. . . . A butler of any quality must be seen to *inhabit* his role, utterly and fully; he cannot be seen as casting it aside one moment simply in order to don it again the next as though it were nothing more than a pantomime costume."

It is to this, then, that Stevens is committed: not just to pomposity under pressure, but to the perfection of what Sartre called *mauvaise foi.* . . .

This is what Stevens has understood, although he is no existentialist. It is the story of his life. But he is so concerned with dignity as a condition one must struggle to achieve that he does not realize that it becomes a condition from which one cannot escape. It precludes close personal relations . . . and it forces blindness when others try to express affection. Stevens occasions a love (Miss Kenton's) which he is unable to acknowledge. And he loves in return, while managing—by sheer force of *mauvaise foi*—to be entirely unaware of this fact. He avoids it by brilliant inconsequentiality, by the perfect inarticulateness of irrelevant wordiness. He is an innocent masterpiece of self-repression. He loses love in the pursuit of an ideal of service. He gives his retentive life to a master whose work turns out to be without value.

This last fact is eventually most painful. For Stevens's generation of butlers holds that "professional prestige [lies] most significantly in the moral worth of one's employer", in whose service one can hope to make some "small contribution to the creation of a better world". So far Stevens has managed to deceive himself about Lord Darlington's efforts. It takes a meeting with Miss Kenton (now for twenty years Mrs Benn), during which he finally understands what he has lost, for the truth about Lord Darlington's failure to break in. He grasps the corollary of his own theory of prestige and dignity: Lord Darlington's failure entails his own: "I trusted I was doing something worthwhile"—but what is the value of working unstintingly in the service of a cause that is without any value? "I can't even say I made my own mistakes. Really—one has to ask—what dignity is there in that?"

There is none. And Mr Stevens gives in to tears on Weymouth Pier, after suffering heartbreak (his term) at the bus stop with Miss Kenton. And there he is, a good man in the sunset, waiting for resignation to bring forth resolution, facing the question of what to do with the remains of the day.

The Remains of the Day is as strong as it is delicate, a very finely nuanced and at times humorous study of repression. It analyses the (by no means entirely unhappy) "false consciousness" of a man disciplined out of existence by an irresistible triunity—his father, his role, and his lovingly imperfect reproduction of his masters' language. It is a strikingly original book, and beautifully made. Reading it, one has an unusual sense of being controlled by the author. Each element is unobtrusively anticipated, then released in its proper place. Stevens's Plod language creates a context which allows Kazuo Ishiguro to put a massive charge of pathos into a single unremarkable phrase. And within its precise confines, the book seems to make no appreciable mistakes. Some of the characters that Stevens meets on his trip to the west are excessively parodical. But there is no reason to think that this is not intended, since we have them, and their words, only in Stevens's report.

The tragedy of failure of communication is arguably the most poignant form of tragedy, and the usual procedure is to win sympathy for one's character or characters, and then distress one's readers by the characters' inability or lack of opportunity to express themselves or declare themselves or otherwise communicate the truth. In this novel the tragedy is more slowly and more interestingly accumulated, because one's sympathy for Stevens is continually inhibited by his apparent lack of full humanity. And yet his humanity and goodness are sufficiently indicated—by the residual honesty of his tear ducts, the fundamental decency of his opinions, and (decisively) by the force of the feelings which he inspires in Miss Kenton.

The Remains of the Day studies this unspoken love, suffered first at close quarters, and then in long remembering. It records the accumulating costs of silence; the way denial spreads its effects, establishing complex diversionary circuitry in the mind. It examines the action of blocked regret—the dangerous loyalty of this emotion as it struggles with the devices of self-deception, and steadily retrieves and corrects the memories that give the truth, whether or not they can be understood.

        Galen Strawson, "Tragically Disciplined and Dignified," in The Times Literary Supplement, *No. 4494, May 19-25, 1989, p. 535.*

SALMAN RUSHDIE

The surface of [*The Remains of the Day*] is almost perfectly still. Stevens, a butler well past his prime, is on a week's motoring holiday in the West Country. He tootles around, taking in the sights, reflecting on his life and encountering a series of green-and-pleasant country folk who seem to have escaped from one of those English films of the 1950s in which the lower orders doff their caps and behave with respect towards a gent with properly creased trousers and flattened vowels.

Nothing much happens. The high point of Mr Stevens's little outing is his visit to Miss Kenton, the former housekeeper at Darlington Hall, the great house to which Stevens is still attached as 'part of the package', even though ownership has passed from Lord Darlington to a jovial American named Farraday who has a disconcerting tendency to banter. Stevens hopes to persuade Miss Kenton to return to the Hall. His hopes come to nothing. He makes his way home. Tiny events; but why, then, is the ageing manservant to be found, near the end of his holiday, weeping before a complete stranger on the pier at Weymouth? Why, when the stranger tells him that he ought to put his feet up and enjoy the evening of his life, is it so hard for Stevens to accept such sensible, if banal, advice? What has blighted the remains of his day?

Just below the understatement of the novel's surface is a turbulence as immense as it is slow; for *The Remains of the Day* is in fact a brilliant subversion of the fictional modes from which it at first seems to descend. Death, change, pain and evil invade the Wodehouse-world; the time-hallowed bonds between master and servant, and the codes by which both live, are no longer dependable absolutes but rather sources of ruinous self-deceptions; even the gallery of happy yokels turns out to stand for the post-war values of democracy and individual and collective rights which have turned Stevens and his kind into tragi-comic anachronisms.

You can't have dignity if you're a slave,' the butler is informed in a Devon cottage; but for Stevens, dignity has always meant the subjugation of the self to the job, and of his destiny to his master's. What, then, is our true relationship to power? Are we its servants or its possessors? It is the rare achievement of Ishiguro's novel to pose Big Questions (what is Englishness? what is greatness? what is dignity?) with a delicacy and humour that do not obscure the tough-mindedness beneath.

The real story here is that of a man destroyed by the ideas upon which he has built his life. . . .

In Stevens's view, greatness in a butler 'has to do crucially with the butler's ability not to abandon the professional being he inhabits'. This is linked to Englishness: Continentals and Celts do not make good butlers because of their tendency to 'run about screaming' at the slightest provocation. Yet it is Stevens's longing for such 'greatness' that wrecked his one chance of finding romantic love; hiding within his role, he long ago drove Miss Kenton away, into the arms of another man. 'Why, why, why do you always have to *pretend?*' she asked in despair. His 'greatness' stood revealed as a mask, a cowardice, a lie.

His greatest defeat was brought about by his most profound conviction—that his master was working for the good of humanity, and that his own glory lay in serving him. But Lord Darlington ended his days in disgrace as a Nazi collaborator and dupe. . . .

But at least Lord Darlington chose his own path. 'I cannot even claim that,' Stevens mourns. 'You see, I *trusted . . .* I can't even say I made my own mistakes. Really—one has to ask oneself—what dignity is there in that?' His whole life has been a foolish mistake; his only defence against the horror of this knowledge is that same facility for self-deception which proved his undoing. It's a cruel and beautiful conclusion to a story both beautiful and cruel.

Salman Rushdie, *"What the Butler Didn't See,"* in The Observer, *May 21, 1989, p. 53.*

GEOFF DYER

[Overall,] *The Remains of the Day* is less impressive than *An Artist of the Floating World* whose scheme and form it repeats almost exactly. There, a retired painter in Japan looks back on his early career as an artist in the pre-war period of imperial expansion. As he returns falteringly to the past, beset all the time by lapses and uncertainties of memory, it emerges that this well-intentioned man had allied himself and his art with the extreme right, even going so far as to betray a pupil to the secret police.

Using again the same vagaries of memory ("having thought further, I believe I may have been a little confused about this matter") Ishiguro [in *The Remains of the Day*] exploits fairly simple ironies of tone, class and history: "As for the British Union of Fascists I can only say that any talk linking his Lordship to such people is quite ridiculous. Sir Oswald Mosley . . . was a visitor to Darlington Hall on, I would say, three occasions at the most." Ishiguro's previous writing has been marked by its delicacy and subtlety; the prose here is as clean and light as ever—the difference is that the subtlety has, as it were, become explicit. Ishiguro's impersonation of the butler is faultless but one is aware that his voice is being not exactly manipulated but *coaxed* in the interests of the larger ironic scheme of the novel.

Since *The Remains of the Day* will be praised for exactly the subtlety and irony that I have taken issue with, it is worth pondering the matter of irony a little further. After a couple of weeks of studying *The Canterbury Tales* at school we became so familiar with Chaucer's treatment of his pilgrims that whenever the teacher asked a question the whole class would happily chant out "Irony" in answer. Later we graduated to Jane Austen, whose elaborately refined ironies still represent, for many people, one of the essential pleasures of fine writing. Reading *The Remains of the Day* makes me wonder if the whole idea of irony as a *narrative strategy* hasn't all but outlived its usefulness. Consider the complexity of conception and execution of a work as intimately stitched into the history that informs it as Gregor von Rezzori's masterly *Memoirs of an Anti-Semite* and you begin to sense how inadequate the notion of irony is, both as an aid to composition and a term of analysis; how the word has come to connote little more than a poised disingenuousness.

Ironically, I suppose, the problem with irony in much contemporary writing is that it is not ironic enough, never calling itself into question, always immune from its own inquiring, exempt from its own attentions. An irony fit for our times should be constantly self-consuming, turning back on itself, dissolving the authorial detachment on which it depends, losing itself, in other words, in the implications of its own unfolding so that it approaches the condition of utter frankness, total intimacy.

Geoff Dyer, *"What the Butler Did,"* in New Statesman & Society, *Vol. 2, No. 51, May 26, 1989, p. 34.*

JOSEPH COATES

Early in *The Remains of the Day,* a perfectionist British butler who is the novel's main character pauses during an auto excursion to look at the rolling English countryside from the top of a hill and reflect on what makes its beauty unique. "I would say that it is the very *lack* of obvious drama or spectacle that sets our land apart," he concludes.

The same might be said about [*The Remains of the Day* and A. G. Mojtabai's *Ordinary Time*], which could be called doughnut novels because they're about people whose lives have a hole in the center—lives whose meaning is defined by events that do *not* occur. In such books, when they work as well as these two, little or nothing happens on the surface, but a great deal happens—and very suspensefully—in the interior spaces where people live. . . .

Kazuo Ishiguro, born in Japan and raised in Britain, has created in the butler Stevens not only the consummate imperial Englishman on the eve of extinction but also a subversive and oddly loving psychological profile of England just past its peak of greatness. We meet Stevens, who is about as old as the century, in July, 1956, when he has been running Darlington House, one of Britain's noble homes, for approximately a generation. Lord Darlington having recently died, the house now belongs to "an American gentleman" who makes the unexpected suggestion that his dedicated servant take a week off for an auto trip in Lord Darlington's splendidly antique Ford.

Stevens literally has no private life, and it takes him a week just to accept the fact of his holiday by reconceiving it as a business trip: the house is short of skilled domestic help owing to reduced circumstances, and a letter from the former housekeeper, Miss Kenton, hints that she might be willing to return now that her marriage has failed. Stevens will make a leisurely motor trip to her distant home and investigate this possibility. The book is his diary of the journey, which we gradually discover—just ahead of Stevens himself—to be really a pilgrimage aimed at reclaiming a lost love.

Rarely has the device of an unreliable narrator worked such character revelation as it does here. Stevens is a thoughtful, intelligent but not introspective man much given to reflecting on the ideals and standards of his profession, and it is only through his expression of these that we realize how completely he has invested his emotional life in his job and in his devotion to Lord Darlington. For example, he first defines the huge hole in the center of his life—his long-ago loss of Miss Kenton and his wish to have her back—as "a defect in the staff plan" of Darlington House. He has turned himself inside out like a glove: he can express his needs only as the needs of the house.

People who turn themselves inside out wear their hearts on their sleeves, visible to everyone but them. So as he gets closer to seeing Miss Kenton again after 20 years, he circles back on his memories of her and of his life in Darlington House, and we hear him tell us things he doesn't know he's letting slip: of his frozen, unwilling rejections of her; of his cold and vengeful treatment of his dying father; of the incompetence and bigotry of his venerated master, who had been an idealistic but influential dabbler in the nation's foreign policy just before the Munich agreement with Hitler.

Only toward the end of the book does his incipient understanding that he's thrown away his life break through the bland, controlled prose.

And only once does he admit to feeling anything at all, when he says that "my heart was breaking" as he recommitted in the present the same inadvertent crime of the heart against Miss Kenton that he had decades before. *The Remains of the Day* (the title puns on "remainder" and "remains," as in corpse) is an ineffably sad and beautiful piece of work—a tragedy in the form of a comedy of manners.

> *Joseph Coates, "Deceptive Calm," in* Chicago Tribune—Books, *October 1, 1989, p. 5.*

LAWRENCE GRAVER

Kazuo Ishiguro's third novel, *The Remains of the Day,* is a dream of a book: a beguiling comedy of manners that evolves almost magically into a profound and heart-rending study of personality, class and culture. At the beginning, though, its narrator, an elderly English butler named Stevens, seems the least forthcoming (let alone enchanting) of companions. Cartoonishly punctilious and reserved, he edges slowly into an account of a brief motoring holiday from Oxfordshire to the West Country that he is taking alone at the insistence of his new employer, a genial American, Mr. Farraday. . . .

In the early part of his story, the strait-laced Stevens plays perfectly the role of model butler as obliging narrator. Attentive to detail, solicitous of others, eager to serve, he primly sketches the history and current state of affairs at the great house and points out the agreeable features of the landscape as he moves slowly from Salisbury to Taunton, Tavistock and Little Compton in Cornwall. Much of this is dryly, deliciously funny, not so much because Stevens is witty or notably perceptive (he is neither) but because in his impassive formality he is so breathtakingly true to type, so very much the familiar product of the suppressive and now anachronistic social system that has produced him and to which he is so intensely loyal.

At different points in his subdued musings on the past, Stevens offers formulations of immemorial English attitudes that are likely to strike many contemporary readers as at once laughably parochial and quaintly endearing. Obsessed with notions of greatness, he proclaims that the English landscape is the most deeply satisfying in the world because of "the very *lack* of obvious drama or spectacle." . . .

Similarly, Stevens provides a long, solemn, yet unwittingly brilliant disquisition on the question of what makes a great butler, a topic that has provoked "much debate in our profession over the years" and continues to obsess him throughout his narrative. The key, he confidently insists, is dignity, which has to do with a butler's ability to "inhabit" his role "to the utmost." . . .

Mr. Ishiguro's command of Stevens' corseted idiom is masterly, and nowhere more tellingly so than in the way he controls the progressive revelation of unintended ironic meaning. Underneath what Stevens says, something else is being said, and the something else eventually turns out to be a moving series of chilly revelations of the butler's buried life—and, by implication, a powerful critique of the social machine in which he is a cog. As we move westward with Stevens in Farraday's vintage Ford, we learn more and more about the price he has paid in striving for his lofty ideal of professional greatness.

The pattern of progressively more ironic revelations begins to take shape on the first morning of the butler's holiday. At Salisbury, we start hearing about the complex fate of the nobleman to whom Stevens had so singularly devoted his long life of service. Lord Darlington was a sincere, well-meaning man, eager to further what he believed to be the common good of humanity. In the years just after World War I, he tried in unofficial meetings to persuade English and European statesmen to amend the Treaty of Versailles because he felt it was too harsh on the Germans. (p. 3)

Much of what Stevens tells us in the middle sections of the novel is about the man he once thought was the epitome of moral worth. Although he is too honest not to provide all the incriminating facts about Darlington, Stevens is still so caught up in his own dream of serving a gentleman of international renown that he keeps trying to paint away the blemishes in his Lordship's portrait. This pattern of simultaneous admission and denial, revelation and concealment, emerges as the defining feature of the butler's personality.

As he pompously (and, for us, humorously) recollects some of his triumphs in service, he also describes incidents that allow us to glimpse layers of guilt and a capacity (not always conscious) for self-questioning. On two occasions he tells anecdotes about recent encounters during which he went so far as to deny that he had worked for Lord Darlington. He also confesses to having made some serious errors in his daily rounds, slips caused by age but also, a reader has to feel, by some subterranean feeling of doubt about the course of his life.

Most troubling are his accounts of the death of his father, the dismissal of the Jewish housemaids and his relationship with the high-spirited Miss Kenton, who tried to get him to respond to her affection. In all these instances, Stevens had suppressed his feelings; he has retreated from the unruly forces of death, politics and love by claiming to be following a principle of order higher than that of narrow individualism.

In the last section of the novel, Stevens does have two very brief and extraordinarily moving moments of self-recognition: one when Miss Kenton confesses that she wishes she had married him, and he speaks for the first time of sorrow and heartbreak; and the other when, in a conversation with a stranger on the pier at Weymouth, he is again stirred to talk about his attachment to Lord Darlington:

> "Lord Darlington wasn't a bad man. He wasn't a
> bad man at all. And at least he had the privilege of
> being able to say at the end of his life that he made
> his own mistakes. . . . He chose a certain path in
> life, it proved to be a misguided one, but there, he
> *chose* it, he can say that at least. As for myself, I
> cannot even claim that. You see, I *trusted*. I trusted
> in his lordship's wisdom. All those years I served
> him, I trusted that I was doing something worth-
> while. I can't even say I made my own mistakes.
> Really—one has to ask oneself—what dignity is
> there in that?" . . .

Yet, even through the shivery pathos of Stevens' recognition of his misguided idealism and barren life, the wry comedy remains. With so long a history of self-deception, the butler can only respond to this impasse by deftly creating still another innocent fiction that will allow him to suppress feeling and knowledge in pursuit of a newly revised ideal of service. At the very close of his narration, thinking of his imminent return to Mr. Farraday and Darlington Hall, Stevens reflects on the jovial American's habit of exchanging playful and teasing remarks, and he decides to sharpen his little-used skills at bantering so that he might better relate to his new, more egalitarian master.

Kazuo Ishiguro's tonal control of Stevens' repressive yet continually reverberating first-person voice is dazzling. So is his ability to present the butler from every point on the compass: with affectionate humor, tart irony, criticism, compassion and full understanding. It is remarkable, too, that as we read along in this strikingly original novel, we continue to think not only about the old butler, but about his country, its politics and its culture. (p. 33)

Lawrence Graver, "What the Butler Saw," in The New York Times Book Review, *October 8, 1989, pp. 3, 33.*

MARK KAMINE

Kazuo Ishiguro takes his time. In his two previous novels, **A Pale View of Hills** and **An Artist of the Floating World,** this Japanese-born, British-educated writer expertly made use of gradual disclosure to build subtly plotted works whose main characters were convincingly complex.

The Remains of the Day has similar qualities. Its narrator is an English butler named Stevens, a kind of troubled Jeeves. He likes to think himself as competent and imperturbable as his celebrated forebears—butlers in the great houses of England's past. . . .

Stevens has the proper attitude and training, and his diction is impeccable—one of Ishiguro's achievements is the way he sustains [a] formal tone . . . (while maintaining our interest) throughout. But when we come upon Stevens he is up against more than a mere tiger. History itself, we eventually learn, is the beast beneath the dining table at Darlington Hall, where he has been employed since he was a young man.

The current owner of the estate, an American businessman, offers Stevens the use of his car and a few days off. The aging butler is at first resistant. Then he decides to tour England with the idea of ultimately contacting a former housekeeper he recently heard from and persuading her to return to Darlington Hall to help him handle its current problems, which he believes are the result of a cutback in staff. It soon becomes apparent, however, that the past, not the present, is what weighs most heavily on Stevens' mind. While driving he begins to reminisce, mull over his regrets, make his apologies and, finally to attempt to justify his life.

The sequence of events shows off Ishiguro's narrative deftness at its best. Slowly and carefully he lays bare the butler's inner thoughts, intertwining past and present, truth and evasion, seeming at times to meander yet inevitably closing in on the series of admissions at the novel's heart.

Although the book is set in the mid-1950s, what Stevens recalls happened 20 years before, when Lord Darlington was still master of Darlington Hall and the guests were aristocratic nabobs in the last years of the British Empire. It is to those days that Stevens' thoughts constantly return as he makes his way through the English countryside to his rendezvous with the housekeeper, Miss Kenton.

A feisty woman, appearing always to be at odds with the more restrained Stevens, Miss Kenton is one of a handful of people prominent in the butler's memory. His father, too, plays an important role. Brought on to the Darlington staff in old age, his presence soon creates an uncomfortable situation. The elder Stevens is senile, which his son refuses to acknowledge but others cannot help noticing. (p. 21)

Lord Darlington, of course, is another vivid figure. In Stevens' initial recollections he is a "shy and modest" man with "a deep sense of moral duty." Like most of the information Ishiguro dispenses early on, though, this turns out to be considerably less than the whole picture.

We already have our suspicions by the time (more than half-way through the book) Stevens gets around to mentioning the visit to Darlington Hall of Joachim von Ribbentrop, Hitler's ambassador to Britain. Lord Darlington, it seems, is an advocate of Neville Chamberlain's policy of appeasement, and thus an unwitting abettor of the Nazi cause as he introduces Ribbentrop to high-ranking British politicians. After he is disgraced, Stevens disavows any connection to his former employer whenever Darlington's name is mentioned to him.

In spite of these denials—made, Stevens explains, for the sake of his career—the butler would like to believe his lordship was not all that bad. The novel is rich with examples of the contortions it is possible to go through to rationalize past errors. Thus Stevens claims Lord Darlington dismissed two Jewish maids not out of anti-Semitism, but because he was manipulated by a strong-willed friend who belonged to Oswald Mosley's British Union of Fascists. Afterward, Darlington asked if it was possible for Stevens to get the girls back. "It is worth pointing out," Stevens argues defensively, "that his lordship had by that time severed all links with the 'blackshirts,' having witnessed the true, ugly nature of that organization." Nevertheless, his lordship continued his efforts to bring the Nazis and the British government together—and Stevens continued to assist.

One of the major issues a reading of *The Remains of the Day* brings to mind again and again concerns the perennial question of personal responsibility for actions carried out at the behest of the state. If a person of consequence like Darlington could commit such folly, how could Stevens be expected to rise to a superior morality? Following orders, after all, is what a butler is supposed to do.

An Artist of the Floating World, Ishiguro's second novel, explored a similar problem by examining the conscience of a painter who had supported Imperial Japan's expansionist policies in the years leading up to World War II. His new work as well exhibits a special ability to create characters who embody the difficulties of ethical situations that occur in the twilight region between right and wrong. In both books, to his further credit, he avoids reaching for simple answers.

Stevens is neither hero nor villain. He has been unprotestingly obedient throughout his life, and he now finds himself full of regret and struggling to give voice to his feelings. His tale is an account of Stevens confronting his moral and his emotional emptiness. A poignant—and economical—example of what he has forfeited is his reaction when Miss Kenton tells him that she might have spent her life with him, instead of marrying and leaving Darlington Hall:

> I do not think I responded immediately, for it took me a moment or two to fully digest these words of Miss Kenton. Moreover, as you might appreciate, their implications were such as to provoke a certain degree of sorrow within me. Indeed—why should I not admit it?—at that moment, my heart was breaking.

It is as big a confession as Stevens makes, and one of the few occasions where he reveals himself. Usually, the butler's feelings are hidden in painfully correct periphrasis, or refracted in dialogue spoken by other characters. In one of the novel's central scenes, Stevens tries to keep the house running smoothly for a score of visitors while his father is dying. He is serving port to the guests when Lord Darlington approaches:

" 'Stevens, are you all right?'

" 'Yes, sir. Perfectly.'

" 'You look as though you're crying.' "

Stevens takes out his handkerchief as if responding to a command and wipes his eyes, making no admission of sadness or loss.

Few writers dare to say so little of what they mean as Ishiguro. His narrators make excuses, keep secrets, tell lies. Stevens labors to construct a wall against his regrets by imagining himself one of the world's greatest butlers—but in the end it is self-deceit he serves more than any proprietor of Darlington Hall. Yet Ishiguro has made Stevens compelling, and his story—not quite farce, not quite tragedy—is often funny, always entertaining, and surprisingly moving. (pp. 21-2)

> *Mark Kamine, "A Servant of Self-Deceit," in* The New Leader, *Vol. LXXII, No. 17, November 13, 1989, pp. 21-2.*

DAVID GUREWICH

The landscape of the modern novel, especially the American one, seems to be full of violence—but not necessarily the kind that comes out of the barrel of a gun; rather, it comes from the writer's effort to subdue and kidnap the reader, forcing him into the writer's world. This turns landscape into a battlefield, and, while it may correctly reflect our *Zeitgeist,* it also sends many readers to seek solace in the calmer tradition of, say, Jane Austen.

Kazuo Ishiguro's remarkable new novel, *The Remains of the Day* . . . opens with a phrase that could hardly sound more traditional: "It seems increasingly likely that I really will undertake the expedition that has been preoccupying my imagination now for some days." The pitch is perfect. It could be 1856 instead of 1956, except that the trip will be made in a Ford, not in a hansom; it will be spread over five or six days, although the distance is about a hundred miles (a character of a typical modern novel goes twice that distance to "take" lunch, or see a Stones concert). A final note to pull this monumental project together: the trip will be undertaken at the suggestion of the hero's *American* employer. The reader has been kidnapped—or should I say lured?

The first-person narrator is an English butler named Stevens, no first name given—that would be improper, and at odds with the tradition. Yet Stevens has little in common with P. G. Wodehouse's lovable caricatures. He is a fully realized character, through whom the author manages the world of his novel as sure-handedly as Stevens himself manages the beloved estate of Darlington Hall. It is the masters who are the supporting characters here. (p. 77)

There is an almost-perfect harmony of style and substance in the book's relationship between the writer and his narrator: Stevens prepares for [a] trip with the meticulousness that is matched only by the way Ishiguro describes it. Like a seasoned general, Stevens plans for every emergency, a facility he developed by planning many an occasion at his master's house. He describes the complicated arrangements that involve valets, maids, and other domestics with the tireless attention to detail that, in the writer's capable hands, is never boring. We realize that Stevens is a perfectionist who demands perfection from others: when he checks into a guest house, he inspects the room with a thoroughness reminiscent of those Leona Helmsley advertisements, minus the latter's snideness—no detail is too trivial to fuss over in doing the job right.

We learn to take this professionalism for granted, and, had Ishiguro left it at that, we would have a readable Arthur Hailey novel—*Estate,* for example. But in the course of his snail's-pace, scrupulously charted progress to Little Compton, Cornwall, on Britain's West Coast, Stevens takes many opportunities to ponder the nature of his *métier.* It is a measure of the author's talent that none of these digressions feels distracting or extraneous; they are introduced in a manner so polite and delicate as to make us feel like guests at the estate of this novel, enjoying the service of its perfect host. So Stevens poses a question: What makes a "great" butler?

After quoting a number of amusing anecdotes, he arrives at the word *dignity.* It transcends mere competence; it "has to do crucially with a butler's ability not to abandon the professional being he inhabits." For example, Stevens's father—who was not merely a butler but a "great" one—once had to serve a guest, an obnoxious general whose military incompetence had caused the death of his son, i.e., Stevens's brother. Not for one moment did his father betray his feelings—and afterward he donated the general's large tip to charity.

The anecdote itself is not very remarkable—the Brits have a long tradition of stiff-upper-lip tales apt to tax a foreigner's patience—but its placement is uncanny. Up until now we had been solidly in Stevens's corner; now there appears to be something disturbing about the *pride* with which he extols his father's obedience.

It is becoming clear that Stevens is not merely contemplating the meaning of butlering, using his father as an example. He is grappling with ways to justify his life, for once you take his professionalism, his *dignity,* out of the picture, not much is left. In describing his service, he implicitly contradicts the truism that no man is a hero to his valet; on the contrary, he says "a 'great' butler can only be, surely, one who can point to his years of service and say that he has applied his talents to serving a great gentleman—and through the latter, to serving humanity." And it is only through his master that Stevens manages to establish his own worth.

Lord Darlington was a powerful statesman who wielded his influence in international affairs. Stevens recalls a behind-the-closed-doors conference taking place at Darlington Hall, one that would re-draw the map of Europe between the wars. Stevens had gone on serving the guests and—he maintains in a voice that throbs with pride—the cause of "justice" (as his master put it). By doing so, he had to ignore his own father, who was in the throes of death. But jumping to conclusions will not take you far. "I know my father would have wished me to carry on just now," Stevens says—and he is likely to be right. What started out as a mild comedy of manners turns into a tragedy, one that never loses its subtlety or power of understatement. (pp. 77-8)

Little by little, with unflagging mastery, Ishiguro unravels the disintegration of the good old world where Stevens and his ideals held value. Miss Kenton gives up on him, gets married, and leaves; following Lord Darlington's death, the house is sold to Mr. Farraday, an American with whose bantering Stevens feels ill at ease; glitches appear in his "staff plans"; and now, in the course of the trip, Stevens's car runs out of gas, and he is forced to seek shelter in a simple village. He recalls a recent incident in which he concealed his years of service under Darlington in response to a visitor's question

(thus invoking his American master's anger: the latter wanted to show Stevens off as a "genuine" English butler!). Now, as the villagers interpret his car, his clothes, and his refined manner as proof of his aristocratic origins, he implicitly encourages them, loath to reveal his true status.

Finally, after twenty years apart, Stevens and Miss Kenton (now Mrs. Benn) meet again. No melodramatics are allowed in the eight pages between "Ah, Mr. Stevens. How nice to see you again," and "It was a great pleasure to see you again, Mrs. Benn"; yet the drama of two middle-aged people whose lives did not quite work out the way they might have is conveyed with exquisite poise. When Miss Kenton confesses that sometimes she gets "to thinking about a life I may have had with you, Mr. Stevens," he is dumbstruck for a moment, but regains his composure quickly and agrees with her that "it is too late to turn back the clock. . . . You really mustn't let any more foolish ideas come between yourself and the happiness you deserve." In an odd way, I was reminded of the ending of Gabriel García Márquez's *Love in the Time of Cholera,* where two old people do get to consummate their passion. The two endings are diametrically opposite, and both work admirably.

If in its description the novel seems a bit calculated—well, it is. A modern reader may feel manipulated by the author's too-convenient timing of the crucial scenes and might argue that it is a TV writer's job to time to the minute the plots of "International Conference Upstairs" and "A Death in the Family Downstairs"; a modern novelist should have more freedom. But such deliberate plotting is strictly in keeping with the nineteenth-century genre that Ishiguro studiously follows. On the other hand, Ishiguro is, perhaps, too eager to cover all bases, as when he exposes Stevens to the populist views of farmers when the butler spends a night in the village. It seems redundant: surely by then the reader has already realized that Stevens's lack of awareness of the world outside his master's estate approaches that of Chauncey Gardiner's, the hero of Jerzy Kosinsky's *Being There.*

But these grievances rear their ugly heads only in post-analysis; such is the author's control over his narrative, so perfect is his command of language, that one simply relishes the story, page after page, suspending the dour reviewer's thoughts. Without Ishiguro's awesome technique this would be just another "little-guy" story, an able Chekhov imitation (Ishiguro has a knack for balancing laughter and tears, too) with no voice of its own; happily, this is not the case.

Ishiguro came to England at the age of six and is the author of two earlier novels; the hero of one of them, ***An Artist of the Floating World,*** is also an old man taking stock of his life. I do not wish to dwell unduly on Ishiguro's background, but when Stevens admires the English landscape for "the very *lack* of obvious drama or spectacle that sets the beauty of our land apart," I cannot help thinking how neatly his description fits some of the Japanese criteria for beauty. Stevens's attention to detail is comparable to that of an origami maker (one might even compare the institution of English high tea with the Japanese tea ceremony). Stevens's insistence on ritual; his stoicism in performing his duties, especially in the face of adversity; his loyalty to his master that conflicts with his humanity—all of these are prominent aspects of the Japanese collective psyche, and Ishiguro imbues his description of Stevens's world with a fine Japanese sensibility. Yet—the proof of his mastery—had he chosen to publish the book under an assumed Anglo name, one would never suspect.

At the end of the novel Stevens sits on the pier at the resort town of Weymouth, waiting for the pier lights to come on. Having just bared his soul to a stranger (who turns out to be a colleague, albeit of lower stature), he muses that

> [perhaps], then, there is something to his advice that I should cease looking back so much, that I should adopt a more positive outlook and try to make the best of what remains of my day. After all, what can we ever gain in forever looking back and blaming ourselves if our lives have not turned out quite as we might have wished? The hard reality is, surely, that for the likes of you and I, there is little choice other than to leave our fate, ultimately, in the hands of those great gentlemen at the hub of this world who employ our services.

At first glance, the "we" comes unexpectedly—you rather thought you were a guest; but the two hundred and fifty pages of narrative have done such a superb job of pulling you into the protagonist's world, of sharing his victories and defeats, however minute they might seem, that for a moment you, too, feel sorry you have to leave. Yet has Stevens caught the virus of American positive thinking from his employer? "Bantering is hardly an unreasonable duty for an employer to expect a professional to perform," he concludes, and resolves to develop this skill and thus to become a perfect butler to his American master. You cannot help wishing him the best of luck. (pp. 78-80)

> David Gurewich, "Upstairs, Downstairs," In The New Criterion, *Vol. VIII, No. 4, December, 1989, pp. 77-80.*

GABRIELE ANNAN

Kazuo Ishiguro was born in Japan thirty-five years ago. He came to England when he was six, and has lived there ever since. . . .

Ishiguro writes in English. His English is perfect, and not just in the obvious sense: it is accurate, unhurried, fastidious, and noiseless. A hush seems to lie over it, compounded of mystery and discretion. The elegant bareness inevitably reminds one of Japanese painting. But at the very start of the first novel, *A Pale View of Hills,* he warns against such a cliché response. A Japanese girl has committed suicide in England:

> Keiko . . . was pure Japanese, and more than one newspaper was quick to pick up on this fact. The English are fond of their idea that our race has an instinct for suicide, as if further explanations are unnecessary.

In a sense, all three of Ishiguro's novels are explanations, even indictments, of Japanese-ness, and that applies equally to the third novel, *The Remains of the Day,* in which no Japanese character appears. He writes about guilt and shame incurred in the service of duty, loyalty, and tradition. Characters who place too high—too Japanese—a price on these values are punished for it.

A Pale View of Hills is eery and tenebrous. It is a ghost story, but the narrator, Etsuko, does not realize that. She is the widow of an Englishman, and lives alone and rather desolate in an English country house. Her elder daughter, Keiko, the child of her Japanese first husband, killed herself some years before. The novel opens during a visit from her younger daughter, Niki, the child of her English second husband. Et-

suko recalls her past, but Niki, a brusque, emancipated Western girl, is not very sympathetic. Her visit is uncomfortable and uncomforting, and she cuts it short: not only because of the lack of rapport with her mother, but because she can't sleep. Keiko's unseen ghost keeps her awake.

Etsuko's reminiscences go back to the days just after the war. She is newly married to a boorish company man, and expecting his child. They live in one of the first blocks to be built in the ruins of Nagasaki. Etsuko is lonely and strikes up an acquaintance with an older woman, an embittered post-1945 Madam Butterfly. Sachiko lives in a derelict cottage among the rubble, and receives visits from an American who is always promising to take her to the States, but never does. She has lost everything in the war except her ten-year-old daughter, Mariko. The child is hostile to people but deeply attached to her cat and kittens. . . .

Etsuko feels guilty about having uprooted Keiko and taken her to England. . . . She knew the child would be unhappy in an English environment, though one can be sure she did not force her to leave Japan with the brutality displayed by Sachiko toward her own daughter. Brutality is not part of Etsuko's docile, self-effacing, well-behaved persona—the traditional persona for a Japanese woman of her generation. Even when she was young it was already so much a part of her that she was unable to see how unhappy she was in her role of Japanese wife, or why she could not get through to Mariko. She wanted very much to help the child, but only to become a well-behaved little Japanese girl; and the only method she could think of was to offer her trivial distractions from her obsessions and her misery.

Ishiguro puts across Etsuko's inadequacy behind her back, as it were, even though he does it in her own quiet, resigned, but very faintly smug voice. Her mask never slips: it faces inward as well as outward, blinding her with self-deception. Masks are what Ishiguro's novels are about, and he himself always chooses the mask of a first-person narrator. All the narrators are sedate and formal people so he never needs to drop into any kind of vulgar slang or colloquialism, and hardly to change gear when he allows them to call up a landscape or an atmosphere. Descriptions are as factual and plain as a Morandi still life, but they exude powerful moods and mostly sad ones: nostalgia, regret, resignation.

Just as Etsuko's disapproval of Sachiko in the past and Niki in the present seeps out from under her mask, so does Ishiguro's disapproval of Etsuko herself. The tension of the novel depends on the gradual revelation, clue by clue, of how misguided her behavior has been throughout her life. Ishiguro uses this detective-fiction format in all his novels and with cunning. The narrator is always blind, a well-intentioned person in good standing with him- or herself when the story begins. The degree of insight and disillusion they attain, the shame and remorse they suffer varies from novel to novel. They never go unpunished, though. Ishiguro is severe, vindictive sometimes; but then he is also very good at compelling the reader's pity, sometimes with positively Dickensian pressure.

A Pale View of Hills is about private guilt, but it has a small subplot about public guilt as well. Etsuko's first father-in-law is a retired teacher, proud of his old pupils and what he did for them. What he did for them was to imbue them with imperialist values and spur them on to die in a patriotic war. In postwar Nagasaki these ideas are discredited. The old man is attacked in print by one of his former pupils, and treated with contempt by his son, and even by Etsuko.

In the second novel, *An Artist of the Floating World,* the teacher of discredited values is the narrator and main character. Mr. Ono is a retired painter and art master, and as in *A Pale View of Hills,* the story bobs about between reminiscences of different periods of the hero's life. Not that Mr. Ono is a hero: in fact, he is the least admirable and sympathetic of Ishiguro's chief characters, an opportunist and timeserver, adapting his views and even his artistic style to the party in power. So it comes that in the Thirties he deserts his first, westernizing master of painting for the strict, old-fashioned style and patriotic content of the imperialist, propaganda art.

An Artist of the Floating World shows the traditional Japanese atelier system of art training in operation. The pupils all work in the master's studio; in this case they even live together in his villa. The arrangement is charming and convivial up to a point: but there is a lot of unkind teasing, ostracizing, and jockeying for position. Still, the students develop a mutual sense of loyalty, especially toward the master, far more intense than loyalties bred on a Western campus. So Ono's breakaway is seen as a betrayal, and causes much pain.

Worse still, he denounces a dissident colleague to the police, but he remains able to persuade himself that all his apparent disloyalties spring from the best of motives—in this case concern for the future of Japan. His own favorite creation is a painting of boys arming for war while politicians debate; he calls it *Complacency.* The title would fit the novel itself: It is a wry and funny novel, with the comedy springing from Ono's impregnable self-regard in the face of every kind of humiliation. (p. 3)

It could be called a comedy—just. Ishiguro's third book, *The Remains of the Day,* is a tragedy in comedy form, both played to the hilt: it is more harrowing than the first book, more broadly funny than the second, but in spite of having recently won the Booker Prize in London, it has more flaws than the others and seems more naive. This time Ishiguro impersonates an aging English butler—one can't help seeing the work as a performance, an act put on with dazzling daring and aplomb. The chronological template is the same as before: from a Fifties present Mr. Stevens recalls the Twenties and Thirties, when he worked for Lord Darlington.

Ishiguro gives a virtuoso performance, telling the story in the old man's pompous, deferential voice. A Japanese soul (or at any rate Ishiguro's critical version of the Japanese soul) could not have chosen a better body to transmigrate into than Stevens's: the butler runs on loyalty, devotion, propriety, and pride in his profession, and after much rumination he decides that the most important quality for a great butler—which his father was and he aspires to be—is dignity. He arrives at this conclusion during a meeting of the Hayes Society, a group of upper-echelon butlers who meet to discuss the finer points of their "profession" with other "professionals."

Sometimes the ghost of P. G. Wodehouse gets into the works. It causes havoc when Stevens tries to carry out instructions to explain the facts of life to Lord Darlington's godson, a young man who has just become engaged to be married. Stevens never gets very far because he keeps being interrupted by the demands of the French foreign secretary, who is staying in the house and wants him to attend to the blisters he got from too much sightseeing. The episode is about as convincing as a country house charade. . . .

While it is going on, Stevens's old father lies dying upstairs. Too frail to go on as head butler in his old post, he has joined Lord Darlington's household as second butler, serving under his own son. Their relations are strictly "professional," without intimacy or warmth. One day the old man falls with a trayful of tea things: he has had his first stroke. His duties are curtailed until all he is allowed to do is push a trolley. The second and final stroke comes on during an important house party: Stevens is too busy with the guests to be with his father when he dies. He just carries on:

> If you consider the pressures contingent on me that night, you may not think I delude myself unduly if I go so far as to suggest that I did perhaps display, in the face of everything, at least in some modest degree a "dignity" worthy of someone like Mr Marshall [a model "great" butler]—or come to that, my father.

Ishiguro specializes in the humiliations and sorrows of old age, and I found old Stevens's end as afflicting as Dickens's readers found the deathbed scene of Jo the crossing-sweeper boy. . . .

Lord Darlington, in Stevens's eyes, is the truly distinguished employer a butler has to have in order to be a truly distinguished butler. He is an *eminence grise* in British politics: his house parties are arranged to further certain causes, and Stevens is convinced that by helping to make the arrangements perfect he is serving not only a great man but his country as well. There is a problem about Lord Darlington though: we watch him develop from a chivalrous critic of the Versailles Treaty into a Nazi sympathizer. Admirers of Hitler gather at Darlington Hall; Herr von Ribbentrop is among the guests; an Anglo-German alliance is being plotted. . . .

After the war Lord Darlington dies, discredited and broken, but Stevens's loyalty to his memory is unshaken. Darlington Hall has been taken over by an American, and Stevens with it, an authentic English butler to go with the authentic Chippendale. Mr. Farraday's genial style is very different from Lord Darlington's hauteur, and the novel opens with Stevens resolving to learn how to banter, since Mr. Farraday seems to expect bantering from him. It is a move in the direction of democracy, and Stevens is proud of his own progressive attitude in making it. When Mr. Farraday takes a holiday he encourages Stevens to do the same. It will be Stevens's first, and Mr. Farraday lends him a car. . . .

Stevens manages to have trouble with his engine, run out of petrol, lose his way. These mishaps may symbolize his incompetence in the face of real life, but they themselves are much less competently handled than the rest of the book. Stevens encounters specimens of ordinary, warm-hearted, decent humanity; each one is an argument for spontaneity, openness, and democracy, and against Japaneseness. They are wooden and implausible, but not as implausible as the sacked maids we read about earlier on: Ishiguro wants us to believe that in the early Thirties there were two Jewish maids on the Darlington Hall staff, and that Lord Darlington instructed Stevens to sack them (he did, of course). I would be prepared to bet that before the arrival of the first German refugees no Jewish maid had ever been seen in an English country house: not for anti-Semitic reasons, but because Jews didn't go in for domestic service. Still, this is Ishiguro's only gross sociological error. . . .

The end is touching, but all the same, *The Remains of the*

Day is too much a *roman à thèse,* and a judgmental one besides. Compared to his astounding narrative sophistication, Ishiguro's message seems quite banal: Be less Japanese, less bent on dignity, less false to yourself and others, less restrained and controlled. The irony is that it is precisely Ishiguro's beautiful restraint and control that one admires, and, in the case of the last novel, his nerve in setting up such a high-wire act for himself. (p. 4)

Gabriele Annan, *"On the High Wire,"* in The New York Review of Books, *Vol. XXXVI, No. 19, December 7, 1989, pp. 3-4.*

IHAB HASSAN

This seamless, comic novel with humdrum title [*The Remains of the Day*] teases us into uneasy thoughts. The questions begin almost casually. Implacably, though, they deepen—such is the novel's preternatural craft. We begin with this fact: A Japanese-born writer, living in England since his childhood, writes a novel about the butler of a great English house. Is the result a Japanese vision of England or, more slyly, an English version of Japan? Or is it both and neither, a vision simply of our condition, our world?

For some readers the suspicion will linger that England and Japan mirror each other at the antipodes. Hierarchic, reserved, aloof—yes, xenophobic—these two insular nations eye the world warily and nurture their respective traditions with a peculiarly moral sense of their purity. Why, then, couldn't life in an English manor illuminate some aspect of Japan? Why couldn't the vices and virtues of one society reflect those of its global shadow? Is there parable and monition in declining Britain for rising Japan?

The Remains of the Day proves such questions, if not pointless, too stark, for its mode is ambiguous, consummately oblique. In it, decency and error are complicit in the best men, and the tribulations of a servant become a subtle allegory of modern history. Thus Kazuo Ishiguro conveys his indefectible sense of current human realities—politics, class, personal suffering, sentimental attachments—through the reticent narrative of Mr. Stevens, chief butler of Darlington Hall.

It is not clear whom Stevens addresses in his memoir, nor why he decides just then to recount certain events. This minor criticism is not altogether technical: In this narrative, point of view is key. The point of view is ironic, gradually disclosing to the reader more than the narrator seems to realize. Call it dramatic irony, the kind Sophocles put to devastating use. Here, though, irony blends gracefully into comedy and brings to the protagonist, Stevens, only slight knowledge. Hence the pathos of the story, once it starts, as the butler's blindness becomes our insight.

The novel, then, depends wholly on its flawless tone, the tone of a distinguished gentleman's gentleman: selfless, fastidious, impassive, prim, professional to a fault. For Stevens considers himself above all a "professional"; not the equal, perhaps, of Mr. Marshall or Mr. Lane—legendary butlers whom Stevens continually invokes—yet a paragon of English service nonetheless. This professionalism shuts out the messiness of life: sex, marriage, personal interests, any choice beyond the ambit of a butler's conduct or ken. It obeys duty and carries the mien of dignity.

Dignity comes in for much dignified discussion in the austere fraternity of butlers. It is, of course, what Mr. Marshall and Mr. Lane possess. It is also what Stevens' father, an imposing butler in his own day, shares with the legends of his profession and—as we see without being told—with his own son. But true dignity emanates from an inner feeling. This is not the feeling of democratic freedom, as some misguided villager argues to the silent disapproval of Stevens; rather, it is one of restraint, self-control, above all, loyalty to the beau ideal of the profession. As Stevens puts it with aplomb: " 'Dignity' has to do crucially with a butler's ability not to abandon the professional being he inhabits."

The subject, we see, invites ideology and caricature; the novel escapes both. . . . [In] serving Lord Darlington, [Stevens] believes that he furthers the cause of world peace. And in serving Darlington's successor, the Bostonian Mr. Farraday, he believes that he preserves a historical legacy, even if his staff must be drastically reduced.

But who, exactly, is this Darlington, this high-minded statesman who repugns the infamous Treaty of Versailles and later hobnobs with Churchill, Eden, Halifax—and Ribbentrop? The dupe of history, just as Stevens seems often his master's dupe? More ominously, Darlington is shown to be a Nazi dupe, and for a time a sympathizer of the English fascist, Sir Oswald Mosley. In every case, though, his lordship acts on principle, whether in dismissing two competent Jewish housemaids—an act, incidentally, that the excellent housekeeper, Miss Kenton, resists more than Stevens—or in helping to pacify Hitler. So, at least, does Stevens assure us, eager to defend his master's probity against the calumnies of history.

Ironically, of course, Ishiguro means Stevens' defense of Lord Darlington to act as an indictment. Still, Ishiguro asks through his loyal butler, was Darlington alone in the thirties in acting as Hitler's or Stalin's dupe? What are the ethics of retrospective judgment? What are the limits of loyalty (in Stevens) and of fecklessness (in Darlington)? And could that shady American senator, Mr. Lewis, be right, after all, when he accuses European leaders of "amateurism"? Or is their version more apt: What he calls amateurism, they call honor? And how can European leaders uphold honor, given the history of colonialism?

Ironies pursue ironies, questions follow questions; the novel shuns dogma with exquisite writerly tact. Thus politics find a habitation in human feelings; public and private motives suffuse one another. (pp. 369-71)

There is an extraneous felicity in all this that beguiles the reader from the start. For who better than a Japanese could savor English restraint? Who more than a Japanese writer could convey silence, the emptiness around things, the very curve of emotions as they move toward oblivion? Indeed, narrative art—form, cadence, voice, symbolic implication—so intimately shapes our sense of Ishiguro's novel that we do well to heed that art. The story is a threefold journey: first, in space, from Darlington Hall, Oxfordshire, to Little Compton, Cornwall, over six days in July 1956 (the reader is tactfully left to recall the bungled Suez invasion in that month, a turning point for the British Empire); second, in time, back to sundry occurrences in the twenties and thirties; and last, in consciousness, as Stevens tries to penetrate the meaning of his life.

The journey in space is adventitious. On his reluctant holiday, hoping to lure Miss Kenton back, after twenty years, to

Darlington Hall, Stevens simply remarks the countryside, having already read Mrs. Jane Symons' *Wonder of England.* Sections entitled "Salisbury" or "Mortimer's Pond," however, are really stages in a time trip, acts of incremental recall, each recursive moment forwarding or *deepening* the story. But the journey, of course, is finally a mental journey, a grudging access to Stevens' past—his life at the hub of great affairs, his neglect of affairs of the heart. The three journeys merge into a painful errand of self-recognition.

What does Stevens recognize? His two signal moments, in 1923 and 1936, entail self-sacrifice, self-transcendence in duty—again, how Japanese! In the first, we have already noted, Stevens attends the eminent guests of Darlington Hall while his father expires. In the second, he stands half-averted before the closed door of Miss Kenton while Ribbentrop secretly confers with the British prime minister upstairs. Miss Kenton, he senses, is crying behind that door; she has despaired of him and accepted a suitor from the village. . . . (pp. 371-73)

In the last section of the novel, in Weymouth, where Stevens spends two nights after seeing Miss Kenton (now Mrs. Benn), he has a chance to reflect upon things. He has discovered that Miss Kenton is reasonably content in her marriage and will not return. She does hint, though, at the life she might have had with him and, most uncharacteristically, he confesses to "a certain degree of sorrow." "Indeed," he adds, "why should I not admit it?—at that moment, my heart was breaking." Later, sitting on a bench next to a stranger and waiting for the lights of the Weymouth pier to go on, he does actually break down and cry. Realizing that he had given his best to Lord Darlington, trusting him wholly, he wonders: "I can't even say I made my own mistakes. Really—one has to ask oneself—what dignity is there in that?"

But *The Remains of the Day* does not end there. As its title blandly indicates, the novel points toward death, framing the interval before it. This is the interval of knowledge, the space of plausible redemption. "Don't keep looking back all the time, you're bound to get depressed," the stranger, a former small-time butler, tells Stevens. "The evening's the best part of the day. You've done your day's work. Now you can put your feet up and enjoy it." This banal advice turns out to be the better part of wisdom when Stevens learns the importance of banter. "Perhaps it is indeed time I began to look at this whole matter of bantering more enthusiastically," he says. "After all, when one thinks about it, it is not such a foolish thing to indulge in—particularly if it is the case that in bantering lies the key to human warmth." And so he resolves earnestly to practice banter with Mr. Farraday who had formerly tried to banter with him in vain.

There is a tradition of English butlers, from the admirable Crichton to the imperturbable Jeeves, that has entertained countless readers with deft irony or farce. In *The Remains of the Day,* Kazuo Ishiguro surpasses that tradition; more precisely, he perfects and subverts it at the same time. He does so with immaculate craft and, less obviously, a compassion as stealthy as the music of time. The past passes again through our minds—everything in this novel, even the future, is made past—and as it passes we come to believe that we understand its melody better. What remains of the day, Stevens' or our own? Ishiguro might answer through his butler's extravagant reticence: the interdebtedness of the human heart. Or he might not answer at all. (p. 374)

Ihab Hassan, "An Extravagant Reticence," in The World and I, *Vol 5, No. 2, February, 1990, pp. 369-74.*

Stuart M. Kaminsky
A Cold Red Sunrise

Award: Edgar Allan Poe Award for best mystery novel.

Born Stuart Melvin Kaminsky in 1934. American novelist, nonfiction writer, and editor.

A Cold Red Sunrise is Kaminsky's fifth novel featuring Inspector Porfiry Rostnikov of the Moscow police force. A free-spirited detective often beset by bureaucratic and political intrigues, Rostnikov uses unorthodox procedures to solve crimes. In *A Cold Red Sunrise,* he is sent to a small Siberian village following the violent murder of a Commissar who had been dispatched there to investigate the death of a dissident's child. Critics praised the richly detailed remote setting and the suspenseful and surprising denouement of *A Cold Red Sunrise.* As with each of his novels in the Rostnikov series, Kaminsky won praise for his intricate plot twists and his introduction of subplots that reveal Rostnikov's conscientiousness and personal interests.

(See also *Contemporary Authors,* Vols 73-76.)

PRINCIPAL WORKS

NOVELS

Death of a Dissident   1981
Black Knight in Red Square   1984
Red Chameleon   1985
A Fine Red Rain   1987
A Cold Red Sunrise   1988

NONFICTION

Don Siegel, Director   1974
Clint Eastwood   1975
John Huston: Maker of Magic   1978

KIRKUS REVIEWS

[In *A Cold Red Sunrise,*] Moscow's middle-aged Inspector Rostnikov . . . [is] dispatched by the powers-that-be to investigate a politically sensitive killing in far-off, desolate Tumsk.

The dead man is one Commissar Rutkin, who was in Tumsk to determine the truth about the death (accidental drowning? murder?) of little Karla, beloved daughter of exiled dissident Lev Samsonov. Was Rutkin killed because of what he had discovered about Karla's demise? Or because he had happened upon some other secret in this "town of exiles"? Rostnikov, already under a cloud in Moscow, must sleuth with kid gloves—especially since his every move is being monitored by a watchdog from the Procurator's Office. (The In-

spector's sidekick, grim Karpo, has also been ordered to inform on his boss.) The suspects include a "retired" general, an ex-priest, a hermit-shaman, and the famous dissident himself . . . who's rumored to be ripe for deportation to the West. And meanwhile, back in Moscow, Rostnikov's beloved Jewish wife Sarah undergoes an operation for a brain-tumor—in the more successful of the novel's two subplots. (The other—a frustrating larceny case for undercover cop Tkach, Rostnikov's young protégé—seems superfluous.)

A quiet, small-scale yet satisfying addition to this impressive series—with a le Carré-ish final twist, chilly Siberian atmosphere, and the wry, somber portrait of much-beleaguered Inspector Rostnikov.

A review of "A Cold Red Sunrise," in Kirkus Reviews, *Vol. LVI, No. 20, October 15, 1988, p. 1494.*

PUBLISHERS WEEKLY

The fifth novel in the Inspector Porfiry Rostnikov series offers another example of Kaminsky's . . . ability to spin a gripping, well-paced narrative peopled with vivid characters. [In *A Cold Red Sunrise,*] the maverick Rostnikov, demoted after numerous battles with the KGB, is assigned to the case of Commissar Illya Rutkin, who was killed in Siberia while investigating the death of dissident Lev Samsonov's daughter, Karla. Inspector Emil Karpo, who accompanies the 54-year-old weightlifting policeman to the small town of Tumsk, has been asked by the KGB to report on his superior. . . . A realist and keen observer of humanity, Rostnikov deals shrewdly with the suspects in Rutkin's slaying. . . . As Rostnikov unravels the baffling crime, the clues point to loyalty and love as the motives for murder. The denouement is stunning and again proves Rostnikov is in a class by himself.

A review of "A Cold Red Sunrise," in Publishers Weekly, Vol. 234, No. 18, October 28, 1988, p. 64.

PETER L. ROBERTSON

[*A Cold Red Sunrise* finds Inspector] Rostnikov's career stuck fast, owing largely to official displeasure at his unorthodox brilliance. His wife is ill, and his son, partly due to bureaucratic revenge on Porfiry, is soldiering somewhere in Afghanistan. The climate and isolation of the murder scene lead to an agreeably short list of suspects for the inspector and his assistant, the robotic, physically daunting Karpo; unexpected interference, however, is encountered from on high. The author has fine-tuned Porfiry and Karpo into a delightful sleuthing team and a fascinating study in odd contrasts. Kaminsky's warm affection for his characters makes for a winning series.

Peter L. Robertson, in a review of "A Cold Red Sunrise," in Booklist, Vol. 85, No. 6, November 15, 1988, p. 542.

JEAN M. WHITE

Has the *glasnost* thaw reached the frozen tundras of Siberia? At least, *glasnost* has not yet changed the life of Porfiry Petrovich Rostnikov, the beleaguered Russian policeman who has enemies in the KGB and a Jewish wife. In *A Cold Red Sunrise,* Rostnikov is sent on a no-win mission to Siberia.

He is to investigate the murder of a commissar who had been dispatched to Tumsk, a "town of exiles," to learn the truth about the drowning death of a prominent dissident's daughter. The authorities obviously don't want any surprises in the politically sensitive case, and a comrade from the Procurator's Office is sent along with Rostnikov to monitor the investigation.

It's a ticklish situation for the conscientious Russian policeman. It also must be a ticklish task for Stuart A. Kaminsky to write Russian police procedurals in the shadow of the best-selling blockbuster *Gorky Park.*

With the fifth entry in the Rostnikov series (*A Fine Red Rain* and *Red Chameleon* are among the others), Kaminsky has staked a claim to a piece of the Russian turf. His stories are laced with fascinating tidbits of Russian history. He captures the Russian scene and character in rich detail.

His hero has an individual identity, surviving precariously within the system without compromising his own moral code. He reads Ed McBain paperbacks while on a stakeout.

He lifts weights to compensate for a game leg from a World War II wound. He loves his Jewish wife and worries about their son, Josef, serving with Soviet troops in Afghanistan.

In *A Cold Red Sunrise,* the murderer does not come in out of the Siberian cold. With a touch of le Carréan moral dilemma, Rostnikov, who realizes an arrest would destroy himself, must allow the murderer to go unpunished, at least for now.

Kaminsky is also the author of the Toby Peters series, a lighthearted, nostalgic romp with a 1940s Hollywood private eye

An excerpt from *A Cold Red Sunrise*

The person responsible for the murder of Illya Rutkin stood in the darkened room near the window. Light came from some windows in Tumsk and the moon helped to brighten the square, but no one was about and no one was likely to be about except those who had no choice. The temperature had dropped again. Even with layer-upon-layer of clothes and the best Evenk-made furs, no one could remain outside tonight without pain. The killer watched, waited, going over the encounter with Rostnikov.

Rutkin had been lucky, had stumbled on a truth, but this one, this quiet block of a man seemed to be working it out. His questions suggested a direction, an understanding, and his suspicion was evident in his watching eyes which belied his stolid, bland peasant face.

There was no point in trying to make his death look like an accident. With two deaths in the small village within a month, it was unlikely that a third death, the death of a man investigating a murder, would be accepted as accidental, regardless of the circumstances. It could be covered up, obscured, but it couldn't be ignored. Perhaps the assumption would be that a madman was at large. It wasn't important. At this point it was simply a matter of slowing things down for five days. In five days or so it would all be over.

The killer poured a drink from the bottle on the table and waited, waited and watched. The secret of success was surprise, patience and anticipation. The killer knew that, had been taught that, had already gone out in the snowy night to take care of the possibility of temporary failure.

And so the waiting continued and was eventually rewarded. Just before midnight a round, bundled figure stepped out of the door of the weather station and limped slowly, even more slowly than he had come up the slope, down toward the square. He was alone.

At his present pace, it would take Rostnikov no more than three or four minutes to get back to the house on the square.

The killer lifted the nearby binoculars and scanned the frost-covered windows of the houses around the small square. No one was visible. It was time for the killer to act.

The rifle was oiled, ready and waiting near the rear door.

and cameo appearances by real film stars. His somber Russian police procedurals are a far more impressive accomplishment.

Jean M. White, "Death Comes to the Commissar," in Book World—The Washington Post, *December 18, 1988, p. 8.*

B. J. RAHN

To celebrate the 44th anniversary of the Mystery Writers of America, 700 writers, editors, publishers, and agents gathered earlier this summer in New York's Sheraton Centre to honor the winners of the Edgar Allan Poe Awards.

Named for the father of the detective story, the Edgars—ceramic statuettes of Poe—are given annually as the Oscars of crime fiction. The books nominated this year reveal a high standard of writing.

The detective novel has come a long way since the early days of the genre.

Until after World War II, the ordinary murder mystery focused on the puzzle plot solved by a sleuth who was an eccentric superman. The other characters were mostly stereotypes, and the setting functioned to limit both the physical area to be searched for clues and the number of suspects to be interviewed. Theme was relegated to a simple demonstration that crime did not pay.

During the past three decades, increased awareness of the rising crime rate has led writers to attempt to portray crime, criminals, and law enforcement more realistically.

Changing attitudes toward antisocial behavior and its punishment caused authors to present victims and villains in a new manner, to explore the circumstances and feelings that produce violent behavior.

Since the 1960s, character has become the main focus of detective fiction; the action of the plot is derived from internal and external conflicts of character. The *who*dunit has become the *why*dunit.

Also employed in a more literary manner, setting is used to create mood, reveal character, influence action, and communicate theme. And themes have become more profound. Some writers began using the form to treat serious social problems and comment on the human condition.

The world view has shifted from one of absolute morality to one of existential values. Detective fiction has drawn closer to mainstream literature by employing its techniques and sharing its goals. The detective novel today has evolved from a fictional crossword puzzle to a fully developed literary art form that explores the causes and consequences of man's inhumanity to man.

Although the five novels nominated for the Edgar in 1989 [*A Cold Red Sunrise,* by Stuart M. Kaminsky; *In the Lake of the Moon,* by David L. Lindsey; *Joey's Case: A Mario Balzic Novel,* by K. C. Constantine; *Sacrificial Ground,* by Thomas H. Cook; and *A Thief of Time,* by Tony Hillerman,] feature

policemen as protagonists, they cannot all be considered police procedurals. Each contains an imaginative, original plot, a story of compelling human interest. Enormous range exists among the heroes; each is a well-defined individual who does not conform to any stereotype. The secondary characters are also well drawn and memorable. Each book is strong in local color, and setting is vivid and evocative. The themes address contemporary political, philosophical, psychological, and social problems of compelling importance.

Stuart M. Kaminsky's *A Cold Red Sunrise,* voted best novel of the year, contains the most exotic setting. In the fifth of his series featuring Inspector Porfiry Petrovich Rostnikov of the Moscow police, his hero travels to Tumsk in Siberia, a small village of about 15 people—wherein winter snow falls every day, dawn is merely a graying of the prevailing darkness, and a temperature of 40 below is normal.

Sent to investigate the bizarre murder of Moscow police Commissar Rutkin, who was stabbed through the eye with an icicle while inquiring into the suspicious death of the young daughter of a famous dissident about to leave for the West, Rostnikov is ordered to concentrate on the death of the commissar, and not to involve himself in the death of the child. He regards this injunction as impossible, because in such a small community the two violent deaths will almost inevitably be linked.

Suspicion falls most heavily on Dr. Samsonov, who discovered the commissar's body and is said to resent Rutkin's bumbling efforts to find his daughter's killer. The suspects also include two voluntary exiles, a former Russian Orthodox priest who spends his time locating and studying such artifacts as a 12th-century Mongol cup, and a retired army general who writes articles discussing alternative strategies for great battles in Russian history, particularly those fought against the Nazis.

Superstitious and pusillanimous, Sergei Marasnikov, the elderly janitor of the People's Hall of Justice, provides suspense and humor. He witnessed Rutkin's murder, but to avoid trouble claims the Evenk shaman, Kurmu, sent a snow demon to kill the commissar for intruding into his domain. After Sergei is shot while defending Rostnikov, his wound is examined and bandaged by Dr. Samsonov. When Kurmu also appears at his bedside, the old man is terrified that the shaman means to kill him for lying about the snow demon.

The shaman, one of the aboriginals who have lived in the forest for thousands of years untouched by the flow of Western history, concocts some medicine from shavings of hot ginseng root and reindeer horn mixed in snow water, which he insists that Sergei drink. He comments, ". . . there has been no need for demons since the whites came across the mountains and brought their own demons within their soul." (pp. 12-13)

B. J. Rahn, "Mysteries: Modern Morality Plays," in The Christian Science Monitor, *August 4, 1989, pp. 12-13.*

Thomas McGrath
Selected Poems: 1938-1988

Award: The Lenore Marshall/*Nation* Poetry Prize

Born in 1916, McGrath is an American poet, critic, scriptwriter, novelist, and short story writer.

Selected Poems: 1938-1988 collects pieces from McGrath's entire career as well as thirty new poems, revealing his political convictions, humor, formal experimentation, and wide range of subject matter. Critics frequently liken his work to that of Walt Whitman, particularly for McGrath's bardic pronouncements, expansive line arrangements, and use of distinctly American diction that includes informal tones and colorful expressions. Often presenting social criticism in his exploration of themes relating to justice, politics, and economic realities, McGrath's work reflects his "unafilliated far Left" inclinations. McGrath was blacklisted as a communist during the early 1950s by the House Committee on Un-American Activities and experienced difficulties in maintaining his professional work as writer and teacher. Concerning the political commentary and playful language in his verse, Terrence Des Pres stated: "McGrath holds high expectations for poetry—he wants to see it change the world by calling us to recovery of our finest dreams—yet he delights in excess and in punning and is, seemingly, hyperbolic by conviction."

The pieces in *Selected Poems: 1938-1988* represent McGrath's diverse interests. Several poems are rendered in a spirited, informal rural voice and are based upon his life in his native North Dakota or his wanderings around the United States. Other poems concern the Depression, World War II, in which McGrath served, the McCarthy era, American involvement in Korea and Vietnam, and the effects of technology. McGrath has also written personal poems on such topics as love, art, and nature. The previously uncollected pieces in *Selected Poems* include a series of brief lyrics on varied topics, observations on the Mediterranean area and numerous large cities, and continuation of poems addressed to his son, Tomasito, as well as the "Praises" series that celebrates aspects of ordinary life. In a review of *Selected Poems,* Ben Howard remarked: "The figure who emerges from this rich miscellany is less the sober Marxist than the romantic visionary and prophetic moralist, who can be, by turns, caustic or lyrical, witty or pious, ribald or religiose."

(See also *CLC,* Vol. 28; *Contemporary Authors,* Vols. 9-12, rev. ed.; and *Contemporary Authors New Revision Series,* Vol. 6.)

PRINCIPAL WORKS

POETRY

To Walk a Crooked Mile   1947
Longshot O'Leary's Garland of Practical Poesie   1949
Figures from a Double World   1955

Letters to an Imaginary Friend, Parts I and II   1970
Movie at the End of the World: Collected Poems   1973
Letters to Tomasito   1977
Trinc: Praises II   1979
Passages Toward the Dark   1982
Echoes Inside the Labyrinth   1983
Letter to an Imaginary Friend, Parts III and IV   1985

OTHER MAJOR WORKS

The Gates of Ivory, The Gates of Horn   1957   (novel)
About Clouds   1959   (juvenile)
The Beautiful Things   1960   (juvenile)

PHILIP LEVINE

[*The tribute excerpted below was first delivered on April 12, 1986 at the Associated Writing Programs Annual Meeting.*]

If you go to an awful school, as I did, you learn to get your teaching where you can, on the run if need be, the way you get psychotherapy from fellow passengers on planes and buses, and investment counseling from cabdrivers. Thus Tom McGrath, who was never a formal teacher of mine, was in fact the most significant teacher in my life as a poet.

I first met Tom McGrath in the late summer of '57. I had heard a great deal about his powers as both teacher and poet from his former student Henri Coulette. There was a certain tension in the air; Henri was about to take McGrath's old job at L. A. State, and perhaps that was responsible. I'd seen some of Tom's poems and had been deeply moved by one in particular, his poem to the American war dead in Korea. It would soon appear in *the* anthology of that time, *New Poets of England and America,* and would be the only poem in the entire book that made mention of that war, which was the war of my generation. (Even now I can only think of one other poem about that war, and I wrote that one.) I had been enormously impressed by his criticism, which was appearing in the most unlikely left-wing journals and called for a poetry of great social and political awareness written in a firm, lyrically sculptured mode, a poetry no one was then writing in America and no one would until Tom did.

The meeting took place at Tom's place. He was disguised as a wood sculptor. He'd recently found such employment after having been canned from L. A. State for refusing to be a mealy-mouthed, apologetic fool; that is, he would neither deny nor beg forgiveness for his radical past nor would he rat on others. I was disguised as an out-of-work poet and graduate-student-to-be at Stanford, where I had a grant to study with Yvor Winters. The first thing Tom said to me was, "Now you've gone and done it." "Gone and done what?" I asked. Tom shook his head sadly and looked at Henri despairingly. "Didn't anyone tell you not to cross the border between the civilized world and Los Angeles? Once you get south of Santa Barbara you start to slide down into the largest sewer in the world." Yet there was such delight in Tom, delight in the companionship of fellow poets and even in that huge jumble of a city he was denigrating, the lights of which spread below his little house in the hills. Nonetheless, I took his advice seriously, and when L. A. State, the same school that fired Tom, offered me a job, I preferred to look elsewhere and wound up in a very different dump, Fresno. (pp. 103-04)

I've also done my best to follow his example and not be afraid to tell the world and the citizens of it I meet what I think they need to be told. Young poets are constantly complaining to me how tough it is to get published, how hard it is to get ahead in academia or the world. I say, "Oh, have you heard about McGrath?" And I tell them about a great poet who did it the hard way and will always be an inspiration for many of us. I suggest that perhaps they do it the hard way, that they take off their hats to no one. Perhaps they'll live with the sort of dignity and inner fire one gets from Tom. When I start feeling too much charity and pity for myself, I look at his example, and I dig in and try to be worthy of my teacher. I try to keep writing in spite of everything, exactly as Tom has. I hope I can someday give this country or the few poetry lovers of this country something as large, soulful, honest and beautiful as McGrath's great and still unappreciated epic of our mad and lyric century, **Letter to an Imaginary Friend,** a book

from which we can draw hope and sustenance for as long as we last. (pp. 104-05)

Philip Levine, "Small Tribute to Tom McGrath," in TriQuarterly 70, *Fall, 1987, pp. 103-05.*

TERRENCE DES PRES

Thomas McGrath has been writing remarkable poems of every size and form for nearly fifty years. In American poetry he is as close to Whitman as anyone since Whitman himself, a claim I make with care. McGrath is master of the long wide line (wide in diction, long in meter), the inclusive six-beat measure of America at large. The scene of his work is the whole of the continent east to west with its midpoint in the high-plains rim of the heartland. His diction, with its vast word-stock and multitude of language layers, is demotic to the core yet spiced with learned terms in Whitman's manner, a voice as richly American as any in our literature. But for all that, McGrath is little known. (p. 158)

If McGrath remains an outsider, his humor might be part of the reason. Apart from Stevens's wispy playfulness and some of Auden's wit, we don't expect an important poet to be broadly comic, especially when the same voice rails in earnest against the time's worst abuses. McGrath holds high expectations for poetry—he wants to see it change the world by calling us to recovery of our finest dreams—yet he delights in excess and in punning and is, seemingly, hyperbolic by conviction. Humor of this kind supports irreverent freedom and a desire to pull things back "down to earth." In his will to dislodge prevailing pieties, McGrath aligns himself as Twain did in *Huckleberry Finn,* with oddity and outcasts:

> —I'm here to bring you
> Into the light of speech, the insurrectionary powwow
> Of the dynamite men and the doomsday spielers, to sing
>   you
> Home from the night.

That is a diction more expansive than the sort now in fashion. McGrath's vigorous vocabulary might therefore be a jolt to genteel readers, who will probably be shaken still further by a bawdy argot of physical frankness informing the whole. McGrath's language is an amalgam of field-hand grit and Oxbridge nicety seasoned by working-class dialect from the 1930's and 1940's. These choices give him an almost fabulous voice, at least on occasion, and a range of lyrical textures uniquely his own. Finally, there is the singular way he manages materialism (Marxist) and sacramentalism (Roman Catholic) side by side as if they composed a doctrinal continuum that surely they don't—except in McGrath's special usage.

We are allowed our hesitations, but the moment of truth comes with McGrath's geography and then his political convictions, both of which enter his art decisively. He identifies himself mainly with the western side of the country and sets much of his best work in the place and rural spirit of the Dakotas, a region by definition graceless and provincial to dominant eastern-urban sensibility, a place and spirit that to many among us is no place and thus a sort of utopian badlands politely forgot. On top of that comes McGrath's politics—an insurrectionary stance that in its Marxist emphasis might have been international but which, nourished by the grainland countryside west of Fargo, is decidedly homegrown, a radicalism that McGrath calls "unaffiliated far Left." (p. 159) Coming to manhood in a time when the land was no way bright nor the poor in a mood to be thankful, McGrath could see that between life and art a no-man's-land of romance was being confected. [An early poem contrasts] "reverence for the land [and] the good life" with the spirit-maiming work of seasons in their "true run," juxtaposing criticism's "gothick Pile / Of talk" with "machine guns down at the docks" where labor organizers, McGrath's friends among them, were getting beat up and murdered.

When McGrath says in **Letter to an Imaginary Friend** that "North Dakota is everywhere," one can fairly hear the strain upon an urbane sensibility that isn't easily able, and may in fact be unwilling, to imagine that the West (outside of California) exists. McGrath says that his own family had to deal with "Indian scare[s]"; that "the past out here was bloody, and full of injustice, though hopeful and heroic." What, after all, is *American* about America if not the frontier experience and how the fate of the Indians questions ours:

> From Indians we learned a toughness and a strength; and
> we gained
> A freedom: by taking theirs: but a real freedom; born
> From the wild and open land our grandfathers heroically
> stole.
> But we took a wound at Indian hands: a part of our soul
> scabbed over

As a boy McGrath saw "the Indian graves / Alive and flickering with the gopher light." In his art the landscape is weighted with the human world. Even when abandoned, the land is not empty. Nature is peopled, strife-ridden and—"where the Dakotas bell and nuzzle at the north coast"—of surpassing beauty. For most of us, however, these early defeats and distant splendors are of little consequence; and in this way geography and politics put McGrath at a disadvantage with prevailing sensibility. Yet he is exactly on target. His untoward and seemingly marginal themes are part of his labor to keep a core of national memory active. The marvel of his poetry is how it persists, how in spite of changing times and timely despair McGrath keeps the vision he inherited, a "minority of one" in Emerson's durable sense.

As a poet who conceives the future as a redemptive dream worth pursuing through a lifetime's work, McGrath is pledged to "the Fifth Season," to a new order beyond the cyclical entrapment of society in its twilight servitude to capital. But while most Americans pretend freedom from history and would go weightless into tomorrow like leaves in a wind, McGrath's practice is to summon the past of his own time and place, the essential history of personal, and then of national, experience insofar as each—the private and the public testaments—bear witness to each other. Like any bard, he keeps the record of his tribe, especially the memory of events in danger of being repressed or forgotten. This is not an easy job, given the trials of recovery. The starting point is acceptance of estrangement, then recognition that much worth recalling is gone for good. Keeping in his mind that McGrath's grandparents homesteaded the farmland that his family worked and his own generation was forced to leave, here (from *Echoes Inside the Labyrinth*) is **"The Old McGrath Place"**:

> The tractor crossed the lawn and disappeared
> Into the last century—
> An old well filled up with forgotten faces.
> So many gone down (bucketsful) to the living, dark
> Water . . .
>
> I would like to plant a willow
> There—waterborne tree to discountenance earth . . .
> But then I remember my grandmother:

Reeling her morning face out of that rainy night.

McGrath plants the poem instead, and his attention turns from cursing to blessing. The outcome is a praise-poem in the manner of elegy, its nostalgia nipped in the bud by "bucketsful." The scene is the dead site of a family farm—of which, in America, there are still sights countless. The aim of the poem is to regenerate the past through memory's witness; or rather, to claim that task as the poet's mission. The "faces" won't be forgotten. The farmyard well is still there, still alive, and becomes an entrance to ancestral sources, a complex emblem of death and rebirth. In its dark water abide the mothering powers of farm and family that McGrath grew up with and from which, as a poet, he draws his strength. (pp. 160-62)

When McGrath began publishing in the early forties, his work was shaped by the strain and agitation of the thirties. For political visionaries it had been a painful but exciting time to come of age. On the disheartening evidence of events, the future was bound to be a glory. After the lament, the exaltation. This doubling—first the bad news, then the good—is the form of the American jeremiad, a type of political-visionary stance that thrives on unfulfillment. It owes much to our founding fathers and little to Marx, but yields an enlarged notion of consensus when recast in Marxist terms. For McGrath, in any case, the jeremiad is a natural vehicle; it allows him to rail and reconfirm, to deplore the failures and backsliding of his tribe without abandoning hope.

In the poems of the forties, McGrath announces and proclaims. His language is abstract and mythic, a style distinct from the kind of line and language in **Letter.** Repeatedly, in these early poems, the poet calls to his tribe and predicts redemptive apocalypse. In **"Blues for Warren,"** a poem of 197 lines with the inscription "killed spring 1942, north sea," the dead man is praised as one "who descended into hell for our sakes; awakener / Of the hanging man, the Man of the Third Millenium." A political prophecy is informed by traditional archetypes, while Marx and the Church are made to join in common cause. Here the hero, a "Scapegoat and Savior," is united—in spirit and in body—with the dispossessed multitudes his death will help redeem:

> Those summers he rode the freights between Boston and
> Frisco
> With the cargoes of derelicts, garlands of misery,
> The human surplus, the interest on dishonor,
> And the raw recruits of a new century.

Much of McGrath's work in his early style—collected in **The Movie at the End of the World**—declares belief, addresses action and actors in the political arena, blesses and blames. Many of these poems are informed by a sense of humor that is tough and playful at once, a manner that reaches a comic highpoint and takes on a new, easy-going confidence with a little volume of poems printed by International Publishers in 1949. Entitled **Longshot O'Leary's Garland of Practical Poesie,** the book is dedicated to the friends of McGrath's waterfront days in New York. Most of these poems express the spirit enacted by the title. The centerpiece is a ballad of nineteen stanzas, **"He's a Real Gone Guy: A Short Requiem for Percival Angleman,"** celebrating the death of a local gangster. Like Brecht, from whom he learned a great deal, McGrath often praises renegades and losers, figures that rebuke the prevailing order as part of capital's bad conscience. **"Short Requiem"** is an exercise, so to say, in jocular realism, a satire that goes to the tune of "The Streets of Laredo." The violence of the west comes east and this is stanza one:

As I walked out in the streets of Chicago,
As I stopped in a bar in Manhattan one day,
I saw a poor weedhead dressed up like a sharpie,
Dressed up like a sharpie all muggled and fey.

The poem portrays a man who was a worker getting nowhere and who turned, therefore, to the profits of crime. (pp. 167-69)

In the uproar and aftermath of the Depression, a poem like this would find its grateful audience. But by the time it appeared in 1949, labor was damping down and in the schools the New Criticism was setting narrower, more cautious standards of literary judgment. McGrath, with his Brechtian huff, was out in the cold, although any reader nursed on Eliot might still appreciate the poem's hollow-man ending:

He turned and went out to the darkness inside him
To the Hollywood world where believers die rich,
Where free enterprise and the lies of his childhood
Were preparing his kingdom in some midnight ditch.

I have cited this poem because I like it, but also because in ways not expected it surpasses its Marxist scene (the world as classes in conflict) with a vision of community (the workers of the world united) that in the last stanza translates a political predicament into spiritual terms. I take it that McGrath, in *Longshot O'Leary,* was after a style at once streetwise and jubilant. He begins to count on slang and local patois more directly to invigorate his diction. A distinctly "Irish" note (nearly always at play in the later poetry) is struck in namings, allusions and parody. Humor becomes a leavening element, and the comedy of wordplay keeps the spirit agile in hard situations. And now McGrath can imagine his audience, lost though it might be. His model derives from the men and women he worked with in New York before the war, tough-minded socialists devoted day by day to the cause, a working commune worth tribal regard. To call this tribe back into action, to witness its past and praise its future, becomes McGrath's poetic task.

In 1954 McGrath took a job at Los Angeles State College, a teaching position that did not last long. The spirit of McCarthy was closing down "the generous wish," and McGrath, after declaring to a HUAC committee that he would "prefer to take [his] stand with Marvell, Blake, Shelley and García Lorca," found himself jobless and without recourse. Being blacklisted was an honor of sorts, but money and prospects were in short supply. So was hope for a better world. It was then that McGrath began his thirty-years' work on *Letters.* It was then, too, that the earlier, more formal style gave way to the lyrical expansiveness, rooted in his Dakota heritage, that marks McGrath's best poetry. (pp. 169-70)

McGrath's importance as a poet resides partly in the political themes to which he bears witness, and partly in the way he deploys language to purge and reconfirm the nation's historical program. He introduces, gradually, a jocular spirit composed of praises and curses together. He envisions the human predicament as an extended Feast of Fools and himself as the "Jester at Court." Drawing on old-world traditions, he turns to the rites of festival and feast day, and takes up a carnival style. And always his choices have political as well as poetic implications. Here is a humor no hierarchy can digest or tolerate. Nor can any imposition stamp it out. When this sort of laughter takes effect, "the great night and its canting monsters turn[s] holy around [us]. / Laughably holy." McGrath possesses a comic charity that precludes *hysterica passio,* but

also a grotesque, expansive laughter turned to the Stevensian notion of imagination as a "violence within" that pushes back against the world intruding. The name for this—the carnivalesque—derives from Mikhail Bakhtin, the Russian theorist for whom laughter, precisely in its most rampant, freely ruthless mood, is "the world's second truth," and whose book [*Rabelais and His World*] is central to my sense of the comic spirit as I find it in McGrath.

In **"Letter to an Imaginary Friend"**, the first sign of carnival comes early, in Section I of Part One, where McGrath turns to the matter of his family. At age five he ran away from home, as children will. He says he has never been back; but says also he "never left." Running from family, he took them along and "had the pleasure of their company":

Took them? They came—
Past the Horn, Cape Wrath, Oxford and Fifth and Main
Laughing and mourning, snug in the two seater buggy,
Jouncing and bouncing on the gumbo roads
Or slogging loblolly in the bottom lands—
My seven tongued family.

Conched in cowcatchers, they rambled at my side.
The seat of the buggy was wider than Texas
And slung to the axles were my rowdy cousins;
Riding the whippletrees: aunts, uncles, brothers,
Second cousins, great aunts, friends and neighbors
All holus-bolus, piss-proud, all sugar-and-shit
A goddamned gallimaufry of ancestors.
The high passes?
Hunter of the hornless deer?

Excess and exaggeration are primary signs of carnival style. As a diction, the lines above might be called the magnified colloquial, a colorful popular idiom found almost anywhere (at one time) in rural America, certainly in the middle south and heartland plains, where people slog over gumbo roads even now. Some of McGrath's diction appears literary, like "gallimaufry," and some, like "loblolly," might be archaic, but who's to say these very words didn't come off the boat with McGrath's grandparents. The point about obscurity is that most *spoken* language, the local speech of a place and its spirit, goes unrecorded. When found in literature it tends to be discounted as regionalism and remains "unofficial." For McGrath, however, the unofficial forces in language are best suited for utopian attack against the press of the established world. Terms for bodily functions, the primary four-letter words, remain off the record despite the fact that they have been the argot of all times and places, the core of nonconsensus (but universal) speech. These are the anchor-words of carnival style, and one or more of them will be operative, setting the earthward pitch of the whole, in any unit (passage, scene, grouping of images) from McGrath's later poetry. Often, as in the example above, an entire batch comes at us holus-bolus, at once in a lump. Language like this is in league with the tall tale (the buggy "wider than Texas") and is decidedly *of the people,* even of the *folk* in the American sense of "just plain folks."

The primary "curse words," as they are often called, can be relied on to upset prevailing taste and established decorum, while at the same time they can *also* convey covert alliance and express goodwill or solidarity. This is an idiom that can be used both to curse and to bless, to reduce and magnify, to pull down and elevate. It is, furthermore, a language independent of scene, wording in no way tied to a specific place or time or class or subject matter, language as available and packed with loamy energies as earth itself. When McGrath calls his family "sugar-and-shit" and "piss-proud," he casts blame while expansively showering praise. This part of McGrath's idiom is, so to say, the spit 'n' image of Mark Twain, the first master of American vernacular. Whitman had that goal as well, but only as a goal; and Twain, of course, had to contend with censorship. With McGrath an American Vulgate comes into its own, a *basso continuo* of the populace at large.

The remarkable thing about this kind of language, slang and curse words especially, is that its status as an agency of symbolic action, in Burke's sense, exceeds any referential or descriptive function it might also have. And being "unofficial," it is invested with powers of the border, wickedly alive. One sees, then, that in the questions at the close of the passage above, McGrath has in mind his piss-proud family, but also the oddity of his linguistic inheritance generally. Of both he asks a crucial question: Is this the stuff of heroes? Was it people like these, with this kind of raucous talk, that set out to take the West and make good the American dream? His answer is "Yes" and *Letter* is his evidence.

To judge from the likes of Whitman, Twain and McGrath, to be an American poet is to speak the language of the hard-pressed but irrepressibly optimistic masses. It's at this linguistic gut level that the "violence within" pushes back at the "violence without." To *speak American* is to combine one's regional idiom with the vernacular at large. It's also to appropriate any other language that seems apt, be it learned, technical, foreign, or just the day's jargon. And to speak American is to exaggerate routinely, to talk in a larger-than-life voice megaphoned by the continent itself. In an interview McGrath has said that "one of the modes of this poem is exaggeration." He is referring to *Letter,* and goes on to say: "exaggeration in terms of language, the exaggeration of certain kinds of actions to the point where they become surreal, fantastic—yes." The element in his style that earlier critics identified as "surreal" is, in the later poetry, the distortive aspect of carnival excess. The result is what Bakhtin calls "grotesque realism"—as in McGrath's bardic image of himself from Book Four of *Letter:*

> And now, out of the fog, comes our genealogizer
> And keeper of begats. A little wizened-up wisp of a man:
> Hair like an out-of-style bird's nest and eyes as wild as a
>   wolf 's!
> Gorbellied, bent out of shape, short and scant of breath—
> A walking chronicle: the very image of the modern poet!

McGrath's combination of excess and vulgarity might puzzle or offend some readers, and we see the excuse it affords to deny him his seriousness. But then we see as well that McGrath's language has earnest, even valiant, purposes. *In the beginning is the word, the curse word; the new world starts by getting down to earth.* That is the logic of carnival. Certainly it's the order that governs McGrath's epic poem. . . . (pp. 182-85)

> Terrence Des Pres, "Thomas McGrath," in TriQuarterly 70, *Fall, 1987, pp. 158-92.*

SAM HAMILL

The poetry and career of the T'ang poet, Tu Fu (712-770AD), are marked by several major events: 1) the An Lu-shan Rebellion in the 750s; 2) poverty so severe that his own young son died of starvation; 3) years of wandering in exile in the north country, writing without an audience (his poems were "forgotten" for nearly three hundred years). Tu Fu honored a commitment to and belief in poetry unmatched by any writer of his time. Kenneth Rexroth has called Tu Fu "the greatest non-epic, non-dramatic poet who ever lived."

Certainly exile, poverty, and anonymity are often the earmarks of a poet's life. We remember that Dante was a prominent member of the city council in Florence from 1295 until his own exile in 1302; he served immediately after a time of crisis, the struggle for power between the "magnates" or wealthy and powerful, and the "popolo" or workingclass traders and shopkeepers. (p. v)

Two examples illustrate the consequences of the search for Justice through poetry; two examples, one from the East and one from the West, frame a few remarks regarding the poetry (there is no "career") and achievement of Thomas McGrath who, in our time, exemplifies both the poet's struggle for Justice through Love, and the importance of commitment and responsibility.

In his earliest full-length book (*First Manifesto* was more a chapbook than a full-blown volume of poetry, and *The Dialectics of Love* was but a third of Alan Swallow's *Three Young Poets*), *To Walk a Crooked Mile* (1947), McGrath opens with **"The Seekers,"** a poem written in Pueblo, Colorado, in 1940. Although a decidedly "new World" poem ("Our grandfathers were strangers . . . "), its thrust, especially in the closing stanza, expresses ideas the classical Chinese poet would readily embrace:

> Every direction has its attendant devil,
> And their safaris weren't conducted on the bosses' time,
> For what they were hunting is certainly never tame
> And, for the poor, is usually illegal.
> Maybe with maps made going would be faster,
> But the maps made for tourists in their private cars
> Have no names for brotherhood or justice, and in any case
> We'll have to walk because we're going farther.

The poem was written a year after McGrath's graduation from the University of North Dakota, a year which would, under normal conditions, have been spent enjoying his Rhodes Scholarship. But he would not visit Oxford until the end of World War II. This war has been to McGrath as the An Lu-shan Rebellion was to Tu Fu: it signalled not only a world in chaos, but a loss of innocence and the lifelong struggle to cling to hope. World War II not only culminated in the invention of the Atomic Bomb, but simultaneously the end of a three-decade struggle for unionization and social organization for the oppressed, and the birth of the Cold War and all its attendant reactionary *realpolitik*. The war against Nazism was father and midwife to the Cold War. Every direction had its attendant devil.

And for the poor, for whom Justice has always been illegal, for the poor whose sons are cannon fodder and whose dreams "are never fancy"? Tu Fu said, "I am happiest among the best people I have found anywhere—poor woodcutters and fishermen." Like Tu Fu, McGrath cannot, by virtue of his erudition, be Common Man, but chooses to be among the common people, to serve as advocate and, when necessary, agent provocateur. In this, he resembles the Bodhisattvas—those who have become "enlightened" but who refuse to enter Nirvana until such time as all sentient beings become enlightened.

"Maybe," McGrath says, "with maps made going would be faster." But there is no map for Justice. The maps are made "for tourists" rather than for those for whom the going itself is everything. We go on foot because "we are going farther," that is, we are going into the realm of ideas, we are entering pure process, the Tao. For McGrath, as for Tu Fu, the means is the end, and the end is a beginning.

It is also useful to note the vast difference in McGrath's use of irony from that of most scholar-poets. McGrath grounds the severe irony of the last line in an idea that is both accessible and useful—it points the way toward a fully-conscious awareness of being. It addresses Dante's notion (and Tu Fu's) of metaphysical "justice" found within one's self. "If thee does not turn to the inner light, where will thee turn?" . . . McGrath begins with a very complex simplicity, one which indeed rimes with that of Tu Fu. Rather than searching his intellect for an ironic closure made entirely of artifice, McGrath seeks limpidity which permits the truth of the poem to find its own resonance—a purely organic irony pointing the way toward the unending journey of the spirit.

Several poems later in the same book, there is a poem called **"The Tourists."** . . . The poet sends a warning about the "dead faces" and "crazy eyes" of the passing populace with its "forlorn" voice. He says they will not stop "for love or for labor, for right or for wrong."

Tu Fu has a poem with a similar warning, albeit quite different circumstances. Visiting the site of the former Ts'ui family estate, he remembers the poet/painter Wang Wei, who accepted a government position only to find the consequences devastating to the family. . . . Just as McGrath, addressing his everyman as "brother," with all its confidentiality of diction, warns against infatuation with superficial travel, Tu Fu recalls the Buddhist/Taoist, Wang Wei, in his home village with its noble working class and implications represented by temple bells and windchimes and cool, clear air. There is calm in the village, and great dignity. There is plenty to eat. Still, Wang Wei wanted power. His government position forced him to leave behind the very source, according to Tu Fu, of his humility, of his greatness. For Tu Fu, as for McGrath, the common workaday experience is the true source of spiritual awakening, the source of the very concept of Justice.

Later, in *To Walk a Crooked Mile,* we come across a **"Postcard"** from Amchitka in the Aleutians where McGrath spent two years during the war. Remembering the midwestern summers and girls, he contrasts those images with the very real images of military movement, the "Nameless figures" which move "over the clamor / The yammer of trucks, in the dark, . . . " The poem reminds a reader of Chinese of Tu Fu's best-known anti-war poem, "Song of the War Wagons," with its opening image of clanging wagons and crying horses in the dust.

Next in McGrath comes a poem, **"Emblems of Exile,"** which is so sturdy, so compassionate, and so truly felt that Tu Fu might have written it. This poem was somehow overlooked during the compilation of McGrath's 1972 collected poems, and so is missing from *The Movie at the End of the World.*

McGrath opens the first stanza with the image of a hunchback "with a halo of pigeons / Expelled from towers by the bells of noon / . . . " and, in the second stanza, to "the beggar in the empty street / On whom the hysteria of midnight falls . . . " This "prince of loneliness" calls "the hours of

conscience" until, in the morning, the "supplicants" bribe him into silence. Calling them "symbols of bereavement," the poet intimates a death much larger than that of a more customary bereavement, and closes his poem with

> And if I assume the beggar's or the hunchback's shape
> It is that I lack your grace which blessed my heart
> Before the war, before the long exile
> Which the beggarman mind accepts but cannot reconcile.

The mind of the poor, of the oppressed, accepts the conditions of exile, but the heart is incapable of reconciling either the injustice of the situation or the absurd logic which creates that situation in the first place. The pointed difference between acceptance of a situation and reconciliation with outrageous social conditions is one of the most recurrent themes in all of Chinese poetry. (pp. vi-ix)

Like Tu Fu, McGrath has spoken often of the (to use Tu Fu's term) "essential goodness" of the poor and the oppressed. Besides the themes I have provided above (and the parallels between the two poets, the shared themes and attitudes, are all but inexhaustible) there are stylistic similarities in abundance. McGrath has written some of the most accomplished formal verses of mid-century, just as Tu Fu revitalized forms during his own time; McGrath and Tu share a common interest in inventing forms and exploring the organic line; each is very much concerned with sound and rhythm and harmony; each writes long poems, short poems, lyrics, polemics, homages, praises, and invective (although Tu Fu wrote very little of the latter). Tu Fu writes praises for flowers, rice, or wine; McGrath writes praises for bread or for beer. McGrath's *Open Songs* and *Letters to Tomasito* are perfect counterparts to Tu Fu's short Taoist poems (or, for that matter, to the *haiku's* predecessor, the *tanka* in Japanese). And McGrath writes new lyrics to an old song (as he did for Cisco Houston to the tune "Matty Grove") just as the *tz'u* poets of the T'ang and Sung wrote new lyrics for their old tunes.

Nearly all poets attempt, at one time or another, to write an *ars poetica.* Most often, the result is self-inflation and/or leaden seriousness. But both McGrath and Tu Fu find enormous good humor in the situation of the poet. McGrath begins his **"You Can Start the Poetry Now, Or: News from Crazy Horse"** with a drunken poet on stage, probably in some tavern, mumbling into a microphone,"—I guess all I'm trying to say is I saw Crazy Horse die for a split level swimming pool in a tree-house owned by a Pawnee—Warner Brothers psychiatrist about three hundred feet above—" when someone in the audience, not knowing whether this unrhymed diatribe is the poem or the introduction to a poem, calls out, first softly, "You can start the poetry now." But the poet continues to mumble along, and the demand to "start the poetry now" grows louder and louder. It is a beautifully funny assessment of a bad poetry reading, and it teaches the young poet a great deal without harangues or insults to poetry itself; it also says a lot about those who have never learned how to listen to a public reading.

And another well-known poem is McGrath's, **"Ars Poetica: Or: Who Lives in the Ivory Tower?"** with its references to roundelays and sestinas, Hedy Lamarr, Gable, Louella Parsons, and the "to hell with the Bard of Avalon and to hell with Eliot Auden." And of course, the poem's famous closing line: "Your feet are muddy, you son-of-a-bitch, get out of our ivory tower."

Tu Fu approaches the poem about writing from another

equally humorous and practical angle, by addressing the necessary arguments of like-minded poets in his "To Li Po on a Spring Day". . . . (pp. ix-x)

Tu is less ironic in his references to past masters, preferring to hold them up as standards which he finds Li Po has met. But the spirit of the poem finds a counterpart in McGrath's drunken mumbler who, no doubt, is as earnest as any poet. And while Tu makes clear that what he really misses is the drinking and arguing—traditional camaraderie among poets of all tongues—he manages to draw a smile from the reader while simultaneously revivifying the need for a dialectic. Tu's homage to Li Po might also recall McGrath's wonderful satire, **"Driving Toward Boston I Run Across One of Robert Bly's Old Poems."** McGrath, like Tu Fu, joins criticism to humor, caustic argument with good cheer.

But neither is a poet whom Plato would admit into the Republic. Plato has Socrates tell Glaucon, "We must remain firm in our conviction that hymns to the gods and praises of famous men are the only poetry which ought to be admitted into our State. For if you go beyond this and allow the honeyed muse to enter, either in epic or lyric verse, not law and the reason of mankind, which by common consent have ever been deemed best, but pleasure and pain will become the rulers in our State. . . . " Socrates goes on to warn Glaucon about the "mob of sages circumventing Zeus," and the "subtle thinkers" who quarrel with philosophy and who are, after all, "mere beggars" in the State. Plato, embarrassed by the emotional truth of the poet who is "drawling out his sorrows in long oration, or weeping, or smiting his breast," admits only the singer of praises for famous men and gods, in short, the platitudinizers of the powerful, into his State. And Plato speaks for every State.

For Tu Fu, the result was a decade and more of wandering through Shensi, Kansu, and Szechuan—the Chinese equivalent of the Badlands—a beggar in a feudal time. He had criticized the ruling class. He had been an advocate, a voice of compassion, a deeply religious poet with no formal religion. He fought a daily war with bitterness, only to write some of the most humane poetry in all history.

Five-hundred-odd years later, Dante, writing in exile, would proclaim, "Let the eyes that weep and the mouths that wail be those of mankind whom it concerns." And still later, in the *Convivio,* states, "I have gone through nearly all the regions to which the tongue [Italian] reaches; a wanderer, a beggar showing against my will the wounds which fortune makes, and which are often unjustly held against the one who bears those wounds. . . . I have appeared to the eyes of many who had perhaps imagined me, through fame, to be otherwise." And, in exile, Dante wrote that masterpiece of precision, thirty-three cantos each, of Hell, Purgatory, and Paradise. In Dante, love and justice become inseparable. We remember, if only by reputation, that Dante survived his Hell and entered Paradise; but we should not forget that Paradise lasts but a day, and Hell is at least seven times longer.

And six-hundred-odd years after that, Thomas McGrath finds himself on the West Coast of North America, in the mid-century, where "things are happening," and the Army-McCarthy Hearings have ended, his old friends can't get themselves into print, Dalton Trumbo and many others are growing famous on the Blacklist, and Eisenhower is giving speeches warning about the "Military-Industrial Complex," and some black folk down South are talking civil rights. The

McCarthy House Subcommittee on Un-American Activities came along when McGrath was in his late twenties and early thirties. It was a daily reality seeing newspaper headlines and photographs of McCarthy, Richard Nixon, and Robert Kennedy as they accused, tried, and sentenced people from all walks of life on the basis of testimony which was itself based upon lies, innuendo, and public fear. It was disillusioning in the same way World War I served to shake the bearings of an older generation.

McGrath sits down one day and writes:

—'From here it is necessary to ship all bodies east.'

It is a line he had carried around for years without finding a way to begin what he hoped would be a poem long enough to invest several years in writing. This time, he wrote it down. And then he wrote:

I am in Los Angeles, at 2714 March Street,
Writing, rolling east with the earth, drifting toward Scorpio,
Hoping toward laughter and indifference.

The rest we know, or ought to know, in the name of poetry and justice. McGrath invests a quarter-century in his poem. He writes his Christmas poem all during the war in Viet Nam. He writes it while the Freedom Riders ride. He writes on through the funerals of the Kennedys and King. He writes while Nixon tells us lies.

And he continues to write little songs, formalist verses, neo-Nerudean polemics, drinking songs, Taoist poems, elegies, and praises—many of his best poems. And because, to quote William Irwin Thompson, "One instinctively suspects people who meet in drawing rooms to praise the peasant over tea and cakes," McGrath returns to the "cold, black North" where he was born, writing in a kind of self-imposed exile, in compassionate, passionate "laughter and indifference."

Poetry and exile—how very often they combine. One remembers Neruda in the Orient, innumerable Chinese sages, the Modernists, the Romantics, Tu Fu, Dante, and McGrath; one recalls Rilke's homelessness, Rexroth's self-exile in Santa Barbara and his teaching for what amounted almost to Teaching Assistant-ship wages at "Surf Board Tech" (University of California, Santa Barbara), the exile of Ritsos and Seferis, and the murder of García Lorca when he refused to leave Spain. One becomes resigned to the circumstances without accepting the injustice; the struggle with the self is greater than the struggle with the State. No poet wants to inhabit Plato's Republic; but neither does one wish for the life of exile and/or poverty. To write is to speak. To speak implies the necessity of audience.

Several years ago, McGrath was questioned by a student about "the writing program" at Moorhead—what would be expected, and what a graduate of the program might look forward to. "The first thing I tell my students," McGrath replied, "is that most of my former students drive right down the road and get a job in the beet-packing plant." His remark says as much about what a poet's responsibilities are as it does about the general situation of poetry in our country. Such is the justice of poetry . . . for McGrath, for Dante, for Tu Fu. . . .

It might have been different. I doubt McGrath ever courted the New York publishing scene. It certainly never courted him. But if it were otherwise, it wouldn't be McGrath. As with Tu Fu, his end lies in his means. The truth of the poem is in the voice, not printed on the paper a "publisher" buys and sells. Poetry contains silence, but is not silent. Nor is Justice. Nor, often, love.

Praise for the achievement of Thomas McGrath is long overdue. And it is only now beginning. But, lest we run headstrong through these parallels with Dante and with Tu Fu, let me close by quoting a quatrain from Senzaki, one which would, I'm sure, please Tu Fu and Dante both, one which serves as epigraph to one of the greatest long poems of our century:

> In the moonlight,
> The shadow of the bamboo
> Is sweeping the great stairs;
> But the dust is not stirred.

(pp. xi-xiv)

McGrath writes some of the finest cadenced poetry of the twentieth century. At his best, he is metrically irregular, the lines lifting and falling with vowel and consonant reverberating through the rhythms of a carefully speaking voice. He also composes in a quantitative line, writes parodies (see **"Driving Toward Boston I Run Across One of Robert Bly's Old Poems"**), variations of haiku, and perfect little Imagist poems. Now Orphic, now extremely personal, there is almost no subject unsuitable for a McGrath poem. His virtuosity is staggering. Some of the poems are, as Kenneth Rexroth said of Lawrence's, "nobly disheveled"; some are semiprecious stones; a few are jewels. . . .

Throughout [*Selected Poems, 1938-1988*] everywhere evident, is Thomas McGrath's great good humor, an astonished observer awed by beauty and sadness and *joie de vivre*—camaraderie found only in the hope for justice and in his fierce commitment to compassion and common good. (p. xiv)

Sam Hamill, in an introduction to Selected Poems: 1938-1988 *by Thomas McGrath, edited by Sam Hamill, Copper Canyon Press, 1988, pp. v—xiv.*

BEN HOWARD

Thomas McGrath has been writing extraordinary poetry for more than fifty years. Now in his seventies, he is the author of the sweeping, autobiographical *Letter to an Imaginary Friend,* one of the important achievements of postwar American verse. Yet he remains outside the mainstream of contemporary American poetry, for reasons that have yet to be explained. A veteran of World War II, a survivor of the Depression years and the McCarthy hearings, McGrath has portrayed himself, not always convincingly, as the North Dakota outcast, the wild Celtic bard, the unregenerate Red. Like the late Basil Bunting in England, he has endured unconscionable neglect and sporadic adulation. He has yet to be accorded what he deserves: a place in the major anthologies and a just assessment of his work.

McGrath has been viewed narrowly as a Marxist polemicist, a political poet of the Thirties, but his *Selected Poems* should lay that easy stereotype to rest. . . . Among its selections are crystalline epigrams, diatribes against the rich, elegies for the poet's brother, laments for the war dead, tender poems for the poet's son, and exuberant hymns of praise for sex, beer, vegetables, and bread. The figure who emerges from this rich miscellany is less the sober Marxist than the romantic visionary

and prophetic moralist, who can be, by turns, caustic or lyrical, witty or pious, ribald or religiose, as he inveighs against the landlords and calls down mercy for the oppressed. Although these pages contain more than their share of sentimentality ("the hunchback weeping among the bankers"), attitudinizing, and windy moralizing, they bring us close to "the eyes of the poor and their terrible judgment," and they leave little doubt that their author is both a master of invective and a man of delicate feeling.

McGrath's compassion is selective—it excludes the "infected banker" and his ilk—but it is deep and affecting. At its weakest, it finds expression as abstract statement ("They are the nameless poor who have been marching / Out of the dark, to that possible moment when history / Crosses the tracks of our time"), but at its strongest, it focuses, in the manner of R. S. Thomas or Patrick Kavanagh, on the hard facts of deprivation. . . . When McGrath does no more than manipulate symbols of good and evil—"the cockroach boss," "the workers"—in the name of social equity, he is less than convincing; and when he dons his literary masks, echoing Yeats, Eliot, Auden, or Donne, he can ring quite false. But often enough, as in the lines above, in such fine lyrics as **"Emblems of Exile"** and **"Beyond the Red River,"** and in his moving wartime poems, he keeps faith with his own poetic credo: "To bring to dance a stony field of fact / And set against terror exile or despair / The rituals of our humanity." (pp. 108-09)

Ben Howard, in a review of "Selected Poems: 1938-1988," in Poetry, *Vol. CLIII, No. 2, November, 1988, pp. 108-09.*

"The Use of Books"

What's there to praise
In that vast library of long gone days
Bound in the failed and fading leather
Of ancient weather?

To free what's trapped or bound
Is my whole law and ground:
Since it's myself I find
Out on the rough roads travelling blind.

Yet, for another's use,
I bind what I let loose
So others may make free
Of those lost finds no longer use to me.

FRANK STEWART

In an early poem, **"The Topography of History,"** Thomas McGrath writes "He shall love at the precipice brink who would love these mountains. / Whom this land loves shall be a holy wanderer." These lines might be the road map through McGrath's best work, which means many of the poems in [*Selected Poems: 1938-1988*].

A large number of the poems are about love and about being a wanderer, a literal and metaphorical voyager, thrown into the world in innocence to wander toward the light, encountering at every turn the dark as well. Such purposeful wandering is not only the subject but, for the most part, the compositional technique of these lyric poems. Often, line by line, they seem to be seeking their form rather than having been composed in patterns. And this is as it should be. When McGrath is at his best, this harmony of subject and technique results in poems that blend controlled inevitability with surprise. McGrath has said, "The poem arises out of something in the back of my head, in the wilderness areas, and it's my problem then to sort of track down its other parts, and you have to do that in large part by waiting."

McGrath has been lauded as one of America's most powerful political poets (Jeffers is another, with similar style and concerns). But the most immediate and enduring poems in this book have less to do with ideology and social statement than with love, and especially in combination with that metaphorical wandering I mentioned earlier. The title **"Love in a Bus"** is a good example of this combination and is the theme McGrath sings of again and again. "Every direction has its attendant devil," he writes in **"The Seekers"**—but what every road seeks is love in both the physical and extended sense. "Bounded by love and by need, my frontiers / Extend to include you," he says in **"A Letter for Marian."**

The expression of the loneliness and suffering in our common lives—assignable often to no other cause than our being human—comes, in these poems, from the voice of a man who participates in the present with us all, and undertakes with us—perhaps even for us—a passage through solitude, loss, and rage. And if some of the early poems favor too much the clichés of class struggle, they avoid the greater fault of retreating into what McGrath has called "the vaporizing of petty bourgeois alienation and solipsism" so common in American mainstream poetry today.

Midway through the book is a poem [**"The Bread of This World; Praises III"**] that shows McGrath at his lyric best, a poem with "a little human music, a little humane music, a little *solidarity*," which, he says, American poetry needs much more of. In it, McGrath defines one of poetry's highest uses at the same time that he expresses the destination of our wandering: what we are traveling toward, on this side of paradise, he says, is home. Recognizing that, and love, poetry perhaps better than any other art, he seems to say, is able to feed us, like the loaves in the poem—and, like the making and communing within the poem's story, poetry makes us capable of praising the mystery and hunger that may transfigure us. (p. 13)

Even without his remarkable long poem, *Letter to an Imaginary Friend*—none of which, for reasons of unity and space, is included in this volume—McGrath would be one of America's most necessary poets, one we would all live more narrow and lonely lives without. (p. 18)

Frank Stewart, "A Wanderer," in The American Book Review, *Vol. 11, No. 1, March-April, 1989, pp. 13, 18.*

CHRISTOPHER BUCKLEY

[The] best poems from fifty years of work by one of America's truly important poets are presented [in *Selected Poems 1938-1988*]. There are poems from all of McGrath's books except the two volumes of *Letter To An Imaginary Friend* which are too long and concentrated to excerpt or condense profitably. (pp. 83-4)

McGrath has been a poet without a "career," one largely uncelebrated, certainly in the sense of New York publishing and honors. Nonetheless, he has made a life's worth of important poems, poems in the "western" tradition in its largest sense of inclusiveness and struggle. His heart and mind have always been with the common working man—his poems have often been political and democratic whether focusing on the politics of nations (**"Ode For The American Dead In Asia"**) or on the politics of poetry (**"Ars Poetica: Or: Who Lives In The Ivory Tower?"**)

McGrath is at the same time a poet of many love poems. The early work sings of basic human love, those moments of passion and compassion in poems such as **"Love in a Bus"** and **"Celebration for June 24."** The final section of new poems also contains some wonderful and sexy love poems—**"Praises IV"** and **"Rediscovery."** Indeed, versatility is one of McGrath's hallmarks, for from early work to late he is a poet of traditional forms as well as organic forms, the short poem as well as the longer one. And always McGrath has poems of great humor and irony and here I think especially of **"You Can Start The Poetry Now"** and **"Driving Toward Boston I Run Across One of Robert Bly's Old Poems."** In all of his work, McGrath's fine lyric voice comes through; he is a poet who knows his music, a poet who can sing of all occasions.

Most importantly, McGrath's earthy and compassionate vision makes clear a spiritual consciousness for us all. He can use mythology or slang in the service of human truth. In **"Fresco: Departure For An Imperialist War"** he brings in a long over-view of history to mitigate any parochial political content or rhetoric—the imagery is specific and yet the voice and diction are objective. McGrath's poems move toward clarity, a vision through which we can enter and see what has become of us, where we should be headed. (p. 84)

Christopher Buckley, in a review of "Selected Poems 1938-1988," in Western American Literature, *Vol. XXIV, No. 1, Spring, 1989, pp. 83-4.*

DALE JACOBSON

Selected Poems includes fifty-two poems from *The Movie at the End of the World,* as well as good portions of two later books, concluding with a section of thirty new poems, altogether drawing from the work of half a century. This book, which represents McGrath's poems throughout his life, provides us with an immense range: every kind of poem can be found here, with all the versatility of McGrath's language, with the exception of work from his long poem *Letter to an Imaginary Friend,* excluded by the dictates of good sense and limited space. Since McGrath received the National Endowment for the Arts Senior Fellowship in 1987 in recognition of his life work, this particular book arrives at an appropriate moment for those who have not come to know his poetry.

In fact, in a recent issue of *TriQuarterly* (Fall 1987) E. P. Thompson, the British historian, in "Homage to Thomas McGrath" makes a perhaps obvious but often neglected comment about U.S. audiences of poetry:

> [The] cultural life of the U.S. is so various, and made up of so many scattered compost heaps, that it is perfectly possible for significant publics to co-exist which do not even know of the existence of each other.

Though Thompson asserts, as is true, that McGrath "has a large and discriminating readership," he also notes that "the

East Coast literary establishment . . . does not know (or does not wish to know) that his work exists." There may be any number of explanations for this neglect, but to my mind two of the most likely reasons are 1) his politics and 2) the pure vigor and vitality of his language. Neither fit well into the dominant esthetic of poetry. His poetry ranges far beyond—and sometimes outright attacks—the existing notions in U.S. poetry of politics (that poetry is or should be *a*political) and language (that poetry should be essentially reductive). Far from being individually moralistic and momentary as most of the protest poetry against the war in Vietnam was, McGrath's politics are collective and revolutionary, while his language is expansive, singing (as he has characterized Brecht) both "high and low." It is therefore likely that the distance *to* McGrath from the poetry establishment E. P. Thompson identifies by geography is not simply an urban prejudice against the agrarian Midwest from which McGrath comes, but rather, the distance of fundamental differences about the direction poetry should take. The fact that his work has survived these differences (which continue to exist and which have meant less serious attention than far lesser poets have often received), gives us some indication not only of the work's excellence but also of the validity of McGrath's direction. The work's persistent renewal at the hands of new readers, the vitality of his poetry against what could have been silencing odds, should tell us that we are involved with the work of a great poet. . . .

I began by noting the range of the *Selected Poems,* not merely in terms of the history it condenses, but also the subjects the poet addresses and the versatility of his language in addressing them. Since we know McGrath *is* political, we know that history is one of the subjects. We also know that since McGrath as a political poet is discontented with history as is, change is another of his subjects. Bringing his readers to consciousness and raising their awareness is another, and all three are linked together to create one of the primary motifs of his work, freedom from political and economic oppression. We also have elegies, statements on poetry itself, the difficulties of loss and survival, many poems of love for his son, political warnings and human lessons, spontaneous zen-like discoveries, poems on other poets, praises of other poets and praises for the gifts of the earth and the harvests of labor, and always, poems for consciousness and awareness, the seeds of potential and possibility. The list can continue but let me say that seen this way, we might notice that McGrath is *political* in the widest possible and most essential manner. He sees what many other U.S. poets seem to forget: at every juncture the existing political realities, with their consequent everyday definitions and limitations, interfere with our experiencing life as we should. McGrath is political to the core, in that he insists that our lives not be diminished. In McGrath we have the accomplishment of a public poetry, when most U.S. poetry is increasingly shrinking into a personal solipsistic world in which society is seen as an amorphous, though threatening, abstraction. It is hardly news that politics govern our century to the degree that the question of our entering the next century has become a serious one. McGrath's poetry has always insisted that *we* insist on our full birthright as members of the social enterprise—and it is at this point that we must understand how the raising of consciousness is also the act of changing our world. . . . In his work it becomes quite clear that action and consciousness cannot exist without each other. One of his most ironical poems ["**Ordonnance**"] illustrates the futility, and near absurdity, of one without the other. . . . (p. 27)

Physics has long known that all matter is a form of energy, down to the "quarks" of the atom, if they exist, and the gluons, if they exist—and energy cannot be other than dynamic. Change, therefore, is built into us. And the recognition of the need for change, and the insistence upon it we find in McGrath's poetry, is also built into his language, which is itself dynamic. Here is an important departure again for McGrath: the solipsistic world is essentially static, dwelling on itself, uncovering itself in layers, interested in discovery but rarely in action, action that would also allow for creation. It may be one thing for poetry to witness—it is another for it to call for action. In a dynamic world, action is a requirement while witness changes nothing. Thus, to connect language to the need for action results in a consciousness capable of creating what it needs—in a metaphorical sense, capable of creating itself, while in an empirical sense, capable of changing the world in which it must live.

Another ground in McGrath's work equally important to his knowledge of the necessity of change (which we must remember is located and rooted in history) is the poet's sense of the dialectical processes, both in nature and in society, by which nothing can exist without its opposite, an inverse marriage that allows for change in the first place. By way of illustration, in ["**Two Songs from 'The Hunted Revolutionaries'**"] we can't but notice how the language circles upon itself, almost demanding by its repetitive power a shift from the absolute authority of the rhyme and rhythm that dominates the first section. This shift occurs in the second song and yet, we must also notice how the second song, by its very opposition, echoes and reflects the first song, as if turning it inside out. . . .

The first song shows power far beyond anyone's control, a mythical power, itself dependent on no one, one that causes always violent change. And yet . . . these same directions hold their opposites that *do* allow us not only to come to some joy, but also to praise the darkness we do not welcome in the first song. "The stars shine clearest in darkest night." An indifferent joy could not be possible without the preceding opposition. Even the rhyme scheme of the second song is a reversal, in the last line of each stanza, from the rhyme scheme of the first song. It is out of the laws of change that we are allowed to discover ourselves. It is interesting as well that there is an impersonal quality to the darkness and light that exist beyond the psyche, out in the four directions of the nation—far beyond where the Romantic or solipsistic mind can by any personal magic take them into possession. We have something objective in McGrath and it is partly this objective discipline that he has that is missing in Whitman. . . .

One message is clear from both these poets, Whitman and McGrath: the solipsistic mind, the "personal" sentiments of the "individual" as supreme worship, the individual as being autonomous and somehow capable of exempting oneself from society (a notion that came into this century by way of the gloomy studies of existentialism), is a dead-end route, which nonetheless is still well traveled today. Certainly the search for community is a prime motivation for McGrath's invoking of change and possibility. And certainly happiness and pleasure, as Whitman defines them, cannot be found in the *absence* of community.

We arrive, then, by way of conclusion, at McGrath's sense of celebration, by which enters into his work the universal subject "we." It is *we* who praise, it is *we* who love, it is *we* who are pleased by what the earth offers and by what we can

offer each other. We are allowed through the praises of Mc-
Grath to see and experience the world as we should, as if in
these poems the communal "we" has been freed.

What is really being celebrated and praised in these poems
is our freedom—inherent in us as *wish* even if unrealized in
the actual world: it is our consciousness as it should be,
knowing ourselves through each other, *through our common
needs*. Needs give rise to praises—the opposites exist even in
celebration, as we see in the poem **"The Bread of This World;
Praises III,"** of which I quote part:

> But we who will eat the bread when we come in
> Out of the cold and dark know it is a deeper mystery
> That brings the bread to rise:
>
> it is the love and faith
> Of large and lonely women, moving like floury clouds
> In farmhouse kitchens, that rounds the loaves and the
>   lives
> Of those around them . . .
>
> just as we know it is hunger—
> Our own and others'—that gives all salt and savor to
>   bread.
>
> But that is a workaday story and this is the end of the
>   week.

The communal "we" is beneath all of McGrath's poetry, as
an acute awareness of its lack or absence, or as wish and
dream for its fulfillment, or as celebration in the praises. His
sense of community is never diminished by the struggle to
discover, invoke, or invent it. McGrath is well aware of the
necessity for community, even in a time when that exchange
between us in this country is less than easy, and from his
awareness of this necessity comes his conviction. Reading his
work, we are given an assertion of community that nourishes
us, insisting upon our connection to one another, through
work, through need, and through struggle, all of which want
to yield freedom, which is the substance, the bread, of communal celebration.

There is clearly much more to say about McGrath's work.
His poetry is deeply rooted in the social realities of our nation, and perhaps no other poetry quite matches it for its spirit and skill of language combined with a content and message
so generous and public and deeply involved in working-class
life. I want to close with the quotation of two appropriate and
brief poems I prize, the second of which is for his son, Tomasito:

"Poem"

You out there, so secret.
What makes you think you're alone?

"Celebration"

How wonderful, Tomasito!
All of us here!
Together . . .
A little while
On the road through . . .

(pp. 27-30)

*Dale Jacobson, "The Journey to Celebration in Mc-
Grath's Poetry," in* The American Poetry Review,
Vol. 18, No. 3, May-June, 1989, pp. 27-30.

AMY CLAMPITT

Thomas McGrath was born in 1916 and grew up on a farm
in North Dakota, where he experienced the stirrings of a
grass-roots left wing at first hand. He graduated from the
state university, won a Rhodes scholarship and became a
member of the Communist Party. This was no passing flirtation. When the House Un-American Activities Committee
caught up with him in 1953, he refused to testify, lost his
teaching job at Los Angeles State College and for the next decade made the marginal living of a blacklisted academic. He
had been writing poetry since his student days, and at some
time in the 1950s he began a long poem, **"Letter to an Imaginary Friend,"** which by 1984—when he pronounced it complete—had grown to epic length. Though his gifts had not
gone unrecognized (he received a number of grants, including
a Guggenheim fellowship), the kind of critical attention that
makes for literary celebrity had not come his way.

Some readers coming upon the ***Selected Poems: 1938-1988***
may indeed wonder why. For a sober and temperate effort to
provide an answer, I am indebted to Frederick Stern's collection of essays, *The Revolutionary Poet in the United States,*
which came to my attention after the judges for this year's
Lenore Marshall / *Nation* Poetry Prize had made their
choice. That choice was unanimous, and was arrived at without prolonged difficulty once we had resigned ourselves to the
agony of having to choose at all among so many works of distinction, freshness or endearingly outright outlandishness, if
not all three.

Such are the vagaries of publishing, reviewing and literary inattention that I had not so much as laid eyes on any part of
the **"Letter to an Imaginary Friend."** Repairing that omission, I found it to be by turns fierce, somber, rollicking and
outrageous—a simmering *olla podrida* of an epic, from which
there is the urge at moments, perhaps, to turn away. Only one
doesn't, much as one can't tear oneself away from a party that
is getting out of hand.

The ***Selected Poems: 1938-1988*** is by comparison sedate,
though it has its extravagances. . . . [A] number of the
poems are perfectly autonomous, and no bigger than a haiku:

> The long wound of the summer—
> Stitched
> by cicadas

is an example. It remains true, as it was true of Wordsworth,
say, or Whitman, that the poems do leave one with the sense
of something single, however large, loose, fragmentary and
indeed at times unruly. Though a fondness for the well-
turned stanza is evident throughout, the poetry seems most
at home in a discursive cadence that settles naturally into a
six-beat line.

If from all this one assumes there is an affinity with Whitman,
or with Sandburg, that assumption is soon confounded: To
begin with, at least, McGrath has said he didn't much care
for either one. Among early likes he has mentioned Conrad
Aiken, Robinson Jeffers and—yes—Hart Crane. When it
comes to outright borrowing—from Eliot, Blake, Keats,
Yeats, Stevens, Marvell, Donne, Rilke, St. Francis—he is unabashed. The strongest unacknowledged influence would
seem to be that of W. H. Auden. The adjectives, the allitera-
tion, the feeling for topography are all at any rate to be found
in an early poem such as **"Up the Dark Valley."** Reticence,
economy and neatness on the page are also to be found in

such later poems as the balladlike **"Remembering the Children of Auschwitz"**:

> And all seemed perfectly proper:
> The little house was covered
> With barbwire and marzipan;
> And the Witch was there; and the Oven.

Imitation conscious or unconscious, pastiche, the trying on of masks, may turn out to be the refuge of whoever grows up alienated. It was true of Eliot, born in St. Louis, and of Pound, born in Hailey, Idaho. Between them they reinvented poetry as a thing of rags and patches. If the *Selected Poems* of Thomas McGrath contains its share of pastiche, of borrowings and unconscious echoes, no one should be surprised. . . . How, it may be asked, can such exuberance consort with the ire of a lifelong Marxist? Uneasily: That much may perhaps be said, though in the end the ire is not merely polemical but is fed by the same deep sources as the poetry itself.

One of those sources, for the poet in question, is the experience of work. No poet since Whitman, I think, has written so obsessively of physical labor as McGrath—though in an altered and more elegiac tone:

> The bunched cooperative labor of poor stiffs in the cold.
> All dead now: that kind of working.
>   Only
> The trees the same: cottonwood,
>   chokeberry; elm; ash;
> Oak and box elder.
>   Every man on his own.
>   It's here
> Someplace
>   all went wrong.
>   For work alone is play
> Or slavery.
>   Went wrong somewhere.

The ire, Marxist or no, that can issue in such sorrow is part of the poet's calling—to brace and bring to its senses what the times have all but narcotized. (pp. 534-35)

Amy Clampitt, "The Lenore Marshall/'Nation' Poetry Prize—1989," in The Nation, *New York, Vol. 249, No. 15, November 6, 1989, pp. 534-35.*

David Adams Richards
Nights below Station Street

Award: Governor General's Award for fiction.

Born in 1950, Richards is a Canadian novelist, short story writer, and poet.

Set in an unnamed milltown in northeastern New Brunswick, *Nights below Station Street* focuses on the Walsh family, their friends, and their acquaintances. At the center of the novel, which is dominated by character studies rather than by events or ideas, is Joe Walsh, an unemployed handyman who has recently joined Alcoholics Anonymous. Rita, his overworked wife, hopes that the violence that accompanied Joe's drunkenness has ended, yet she misses Joe's participation in their limited social life, which he must forego in order to maintain his sobriety. Adele, Rita's daughter from a previous relationship, is a troubled adolescent, and her exaggerated emotions, particularly her animosity towards her younger sister, provide some comic relief in an otherwise bleak, naturalistic tale. Spanning a few weeks, beginning with an unpleasant Christmas scene at the Walsh's and ending with a few surprises after the wedding of family friends, *Nights below Station Street* examines the volatile relationship between Adele and Joe as well as their personal struggles with private demons. Sheldon Currie remarked: "The writing [in *Nights below Station Street*] is clear, efficient, full of comical and sad surprises as well as beautiful characters who affirm the gorgeous complexity and fun of human relationships and defy the inexplicable and the violent."

Nights below Station Street is Richards's fifth novel, the first of a projected trilogy. Set in his native Miramichi River Valley in Canada, this novel continues Richards's focus on working-class life in an economically depressed region. His commitment to examining a small geographic area as a microcosm and his grim portrayal of the human condition have led critics to compare Richards to William Faulkner. Although some fault his simple, straightforward prose style, others note its appropriateness to his subject. Richards has been commended for his ability to convey his characters' inarticulate longing for something more than their straitened circumstances offers them. As in his other works, the beauty and freedom represented by the wilderness just outside of town in *Nights below Station Street* stand in perpetual contrast to the confining and banal lives of Richards's characters.

(See also *Contemporary Authors,* Vols. 93-96; and *Dictionary of Literary Biography,* Vol. 53.)

PRINCIPAL WORKS

NOVELS

The Coming of Winter   1974
Blood Ties   1976
Lives of Short Duration   1981

Road to the Stilt House   1985
SHORT FICTION COLLECTIONS
Dancers at Night   1978

SHELDON CURRIE

Critics who compare David Adams Richards to William Faulkner more often than not imply that Richards is a sort of small-time Faulkner, or a Faulkner for small-time readers, and that Richards should be delighted and flattered by the comparison. In fact the comparison with Faulkner tells us nothing about Richards except that the critic feels the need to aggrandize him. The truth is that Richards resembles Faulker only superficially, and that Richards can be praised without comparison to anybody and without flattery.

Although both Faulkner and Richards at their worst are tedious and annoying, their writing is very different and is tedious and annoying in different ways. At their best they are delightfully different. . . . Faulkner's prose, when he's at his worst or his best, verges on the poetic and philosophic; it is full of images and theories, constantly trying to picture and explain. Metaphors and similes dominate the paragraphs and are the reader's chief source of information about the characters and about Faulkner's vision. . . . Richards' prose, though rich in rhythm and sensuality, is seldom poetic. Metaphors and similies are scarce and when they do occur they tend to be descriptive rather than [philosophic, as in these examples from his *Nights below Station Street*]: "she was thinking like a tourist. This is because she was becoming interested in crafts." "The sun was warm, the sky was pulpy, which always gave Vera a strange feeling, as if the woods would come over her."

If Richards must be compared to another writer Chekov would be useful. Besides getting along quite well without metaphor and other poetic devices, they get along quite well without heroes of epic proportions, without plots of mythic dimensions and political significance, without the grand conflict between the big good guy and the big bad guy. (pp. 65-6)

Richards' writing is as close to pure fiction as you can get, that is, it describes the feelings and behavior of people who live together in society. It tries to be accurate, rather than explanatory, because it takes for granted that life is inexplicable; interesting, comic, sad, tragic, ludicrous, beautiful, but inexplicable. Richards' prose is as good an example of any of [Marshall] McLuhan's dictum, the medium is the message: what you are seeing is what is happening, it means itself. Richards captures people in their most intimate acts of living and reports to the reader on what he observes. Here is a description of Adele and her boyfriend at a movie [in *Nights below Station Street*]:

> At times he would convince Adele to sneak in a bottle for him in her purse, which made them both pretend they were proud and dangerous. And it probably made Adele feel she was fitting in even though she did not drink herself. Adele would often boo the main feature so loudly he would have to put his hand over her mouth. Adele also ate her mitts. She would sit in a movie chewing holes in the thumbs and he couldn't get her to stop doing it, so one day before they went to a movie, he put pepper on the thumbs of her two mitts, and after he did this she said she would never be able to really trust him again.

Adele is the daughter of Joe Walsh. The two of them are the most interesting of a large group of interesting characters. Joe is a man of great size, ability, compassion and energy, but an injury and circumstances keep him from steady work. His wife Rita cares for other people's kids and that helps to keep them going. The humiliation of his position keeps Joe in a constant state of self-examination. His attempt to fight alcohol adds to the pressure. His hardest problem is to help his daughter Adele to grow into a woman and to gain her respect and sympathy. Although Joe understands her frustration, ambitions, and disappointments, he can't find a way to console her and she constantly berates him for his inadequacies. (pp. 66-7)

Fiction is essentially democratic, and *Nights below Station Street* is almost pure fiction. Richards' great achievement is the creation of a point of view whereby the reader sees every

character from the character's own perspective. The characters are always interesting because people always take an interest in themselves and the events of their daily lives. As the reader progresses through the novel he suffers and enjoys the disappointments and triumphs of Joe, Adele and the others. This remarkable identification of reader and character occurs largely because of the author's total respect for his characters. He seems to understand the people of the novel the way we understand people we love. In spite of the fact that accident, circumstance, inexperience and violence cripple and humiliate them, the author sees through the scars and understands their intelligence, sensitivity, and love.

The one instance where Richards' considerable skill fails him is in the character of the doctor. Residents and exiles from the Miramichi will probably recognize Dr. Morrissey, a great character in real life in Newcastle and an interesting and enjoyable one in *Nights below Station Street.* But something is wrong. Here is a sample:

> His biggest concern at this time, and something which if you looked at him you would think he was not capable of being concerned over—because one only had to go back to the volunteer program to see what a misogynist he was, and remember how he told his own sister-in-law Clare to go home and stop bothering the patients by being so nice to them—his one concern was that the nurses who did their work fairly be treated with fairness.

Neither the author nor the character seems to be in control here, as if an invisible bystander stepped in with an inexperienced pencil and started to write, as if to say, here, don't forget about the old doctor; he was quite the character. (pp. 67-8)

Unlike some of Richards' previous work, *Nights below Station Street* is never tedious or annoying. The writing is clear, efficient, full of comical and sad surprises as well as beautiful characters who affirm the gorgeous complexity and fun of human relationships and defy the inexplicable and the violent. (p. 68)

Sheldon Currie, in a review of "Nights below Station Street," in The Antigonish Review, *No. 73, Spring, 1988, pp. 65-8.*

NANCY ROBB

[Richards's] books have been labelled Marxist, compared to William Faulkner's works, and dismissed as bleak. Richards doesn't write about big cities, cosmopolitan life, and yuppie divorces; he works his home ground of northern New Brunswick, the area known as the Miramichi. He's a populist—to add one more label to the list—who concerns himself with the ordinary, the inarticulate, and the poor. His greatest gift as a writer is an ear for common speech. Through the dialect, thoughts, and daily lives of his downtrodden protagonists, he brings dignity and beauty to a segment of society many people don't know and could care less about. . . .

Even as an adolescent, Richards had the calling. He knew he wanted to become a writer when, at age 14, he read *Oliver Twist* ("I swear to God!" he adds, realizing how hokey this might sound). In those early days, Richards wrote "terrible" short stories and "terrible" poems. When he was 16, he wrote a long novel in pen about a drunken husband who beat his wife. "My concerns haven't changed, but my perspective has," he points out. "Now I'm able to have sympathy for the drunk *and* the wife."

That initial attempt, also "terrible", was an inauspicious beginning to what has become a highly respected career. His first publication, in 1972, was a chapbook of poetry entitled *Small Heroics*—"lyrical ballad sort of stuff". But his real entry into Canadian literature came in 1974 when Oberon Press published his novel *The Coming of Winter.* Richards was only 23, an undergraduate English student in Fredericton, but he had already been awarded the Norma Epstein prize for the first six chapters of the book. His talent was confirmed when *Blood Ties* was published in 1976, and in 1981 he took the writing community by storm with a third novel, *Lives of Short Duration.* In between, he wrote a collection of short stories—but "the short-story form is really not my bag," he says—entitled *Dancers at Night. . . .*

Richards kept rolling. In 1985 Oberon published *Road to the Stilt House,* bringing him a nomination for a Governor General's Literary Award. The following year, in a competition sponsored by the Canadian Book Information Centre, he was named one of the 10 best writers in the country under 45. And around the same time he was awarded a silver medal by the Atlantic chapter of the Royal Society of the Arts for his overall contribution to literature in the East. He has also written a stage play, on the life of the 15th-century French poet and criminal François Villon, and two screenplays. . . .

These days, high expectations await any new work by Richards. . . . Richards describes [*Nights below Station Street*] as the first novel in a trilogy that spans a 13-year period. Set beside *Lives of Short Duration* and *Road to the Stilt House,* this book is exceptional for its celebration of family life. But like his other works, it will probably bring more comparisons to Faulkner, as it, too, is set in Richards's universal, fictional world of the Miramichi and deals mostly with the less fortunate. . . .

Richards talks about his favourite writers—Tolstoy, Dostoevsky, Chekhov, Hemingway—and his frequent association with Faulkner. "No, I don't resent it. I just think it's a rather simplistic way of looking at my work. There's really very little connection between how I write and perceive things and how Faulkner does. Faulkner, in most of his work, has a narrator who stands outside quite a bit more than mine does, I believe. His language is also verbose," he says, chuckling at the understatement.

No one could ever accuse Richards, whose prose has a powerful, spare style, of being verbose. Sparse in action, his novels are not so much stories as composite character studies tied together by life's daily minutiae. "I write from the point of view of character," he says. "When I'm writing at my best, I can't be concerned at all about plot, because the characters have to take over." Richards regards his fictional people as extended family and takes their failings personally: "If I don't like some characters' damn polemics or if I have an aversion to the way they treat my favourite characters," he says, "then I have a hard time becoming compassionate towards them."

Nights below Station Street focuses on the Walsh family. The burly father, Joe, is a 43-year-old, unemployed boiler-maker who has just received his one-month chip from Alcoholics Anonymous. Joe has a bad back from lifting a truck motor, and he stutters whenever he feels uncomfortable. Rita, his wife, cleans houses and baby-sits to make ends meet. They have two children: Adele, conceived while Joe was away working in the woods one summer, and young Milly, often the brunt of her sister's selfish teen-age snits.

The novel opens on Christmas day, 1972. Christmas always figures in Richards's books, and it's usually not a happy occasion. "There's always this striving to make it the proper occasion, and so rarely does it live up to that," says Richards, explaining his interest in the holiday setting. "I think it also comes from seeing how Jesus hard my mother worked every god-damn Christmas. She never got a god-damn break from morning, noon, to night."

Christmas is no different in *Nights below Station Street:* "Adele said she never got anything. She went to bed before Midnight Mass, and then on Christmas morning got into a fight with her father and refused to open any of her presents, and instead sat on the stairs in her housecoat complaining about bad nerves and upsetting feelings." Moreover, the holiday serves to set up the relationship between the novel's central characters, Joe and Adele:

> Adele would ignore Joe as she went about the house, and Joe would take out a cigarette and light it as she went by, nodding to her now and then. . . . Joe had always tried to get Adele the best present he could, and yet never seemed to have the money to do it. This year again he was planning to buy her something special, but when it came time to buy it, he only had fifteen dollars on him.

Much later in the novel it's revealed that Adele is actually not Joe's daughter. Joe is constantly feeling remorse for his past, for his drunkenness, for his scrapes with the law, for his lost time with Adele:

> For five or six years he felt uncomfortable with her. And then one day, when he woke up after being drunk, he saw her. She was grumbling to herself, going about with a broom and a dustpan. She had her mother's apron on and was walking around, with a ribbon in her hair, grumbling and complaining about something. From that day forward his feeling changed toward her but it was not until another four years had passed that he began to love her as he did now.

There's no question that love, despite the grim ambiance of hard times, is the undercurrent of this novel. "It's like *Blood Ties* in that way," Richards says. "It's unstated love, love that doesn't have to be questioned." In a particularly touching and beautiful scene towards the end of the book, Adele is sitting on the floor of the men's washroom, pregnant and haemorrhaging: "[Rita] removed Adele's clothing, and the two belts and girdle she was wearing to hide her pregnancy, and kept telling her to lie still. . . . 'Everyone's mad at me now,' Adele managed, 'but I love you all.'"

"I have immediate empathy for characters like Adele, Rita, and Joe," Richards says, "simply because they have gratitude and don't assume any status. Of course, Adele assumes status all the time, but deep in her heart she doesn't. Really, my heart goes out to Adele, because for all this sort of guise of sympathy that certain of her friends can muster, Adele is the one who's really been through everything." It is Adele, after all, who helps little Cindi, the epileptic, when she has a seizure, while her friends go into a restaurant and hide behind a coat-rack. It is Adele who helps clean up Joe's wound—he takes a job as a bouncer at a tavern—even though she passes out at the sight of blood. It is Adele who says "I love you all."

Joe, in spite of Richards's own deep affection for Adele, is the character who immediately evokes empathy in the novel. He "would give away money to people who had more money than he did", yet he is always standing on the outside looking in: he worries that Rita is embarrassed by him; he feels that Gloria Basterashe, one of Rita's chums, doesn't like him; and although he goes with the others to the curling club—the town's symbol of social acceptability—he never participates. He prefers to retreat to the woods, where he feels safe and comfortable. On the other hand, because of his sheer physical strength, his technical skills, and his profuse generosity, he is the one person everyone calls on for favours. "I have a great deal of respect for strength," Richards says, "especially when the people who have it are kind-hearted. It seems to be an added bonus to them." (p. 24)

Humour is abundant in the new novel. Take, for example, Adele piling Kleenex around her plate so Milly can't breathe on it, or Adele putting a bottle of pop in the fridge with a note saying, "MILLY, I SPIT IN THIS." Better still, picture big Joe, working as a welder one winter, lying on the couch at home after being temporarily blinded by a flash. He has tea-bags on his eyes to heal the wound. "When Adele came home from school and saw him lying on the couch, she decided at that instant that she needed to make a cup of tea. Except the only two tea bags in the house were on Joe's eyes. 'I need those bags,' she said. 'Well,' Joe said, 'you can't have them. As you can see I need them and they are on me eyes.' 'For your information Joe, which ya are so stupid about half the time,' Adele screamed, 'I'm having my period. I think for sure ya'd not know that Mom has said I'm to have tea because it stabilizes my system, up and down, so there you go.' With that, Joe lifted a tea bag up and looked at her and she snatched it off of his eye and ran into the kitchen."

There is humour in Richards's other books, even in *Road to the Stilt House,* where the laughs serve to leaven the inescapable, desperate situation of the novel's protagonists. *Stilt House* switches voice frequently from a third-person narrative to the point of view of Arnold, the main character, and then to the voice of Norman, Arnold's cousin. The intense rhythms and recurring images suck you inside the claustrophobic squalor of the house on stilts, where Mabel lives with her two sons, Arnold and Randy, plus her lover and his mother. "There's no doubt this book is a hard bargain," Richards agrees. "I think it's the only time I've truly addressed poverty, real poverty of spirit."

There are "hard bargains" in all of Richards's novels: teenagers who are self-destructive and violent, drunken husbands who beat their wives and vice versa, people who are slovenly and sickly. Some of them are based on actual people: Arnold, for example, is modelled on a guy Richards has seen around town all his life. A few residents of the Miramichi have objected to Richards's characterizations. "Some have accused me of stereotyping and some haven't," he says. "I gave a reading of *Road to the Stilt House* at St Thomas University a couple of years ago, and a guy at the back of the class asked me if I was from the Miramichi. I said 'Yeah', and he said, 'I grew up by guys like Arnold.'" Richards is quick to stress he's writing about the Miramichi in a universal context, much as Hardy did with Wessex County, or Flannery O'Connor with the Deep South, or, of course, Faulkner with Yoknapatawpha County. He's also quick to point out the positive elements in his books. "People might not see the larger human context of love and hope and affirmation," he says.

"If someone somewhere, in any of my novels, loves someone, then that's affirmation. In *Road to the Stilt House,* Norman loves Arnold, and Arnold loves Randy."

It was *Stilt House* that prompted one critic to call Richards a Marxist-Leninist. "I'm about as Marxist-Leninist as my dog," he says, laughing. "The idea of this reviewer was that Richards shows how insufferable liberals can be with their attitudes towards the poor without really doing anything. And I suppose at times Juliet [a social worker] does come across like this. But that doesn't make me a Marxist-Leninist. What I was interested in was Arnold and how he was going to extricate himself from Jerry Bines, a bad mother who is a natural killer and wants to kill him." . . .

The next book [in the trilogy that begins with *Nights below Station Street*] will pick up in 1978 and centre on characters that play a peripheral role in part one; part three will go back to Joe. Like all his other books, they will deal with the underprivileged. "I have trouble dealing with the middle class, and I've never really been able to answer why," he says. "I think my idea of sophistication comes in here. There is a great pretence towards sophistication by the middle class that I don't like. I really think that sophistication relies on one thing only: a lack of nobility in the human soul." That's not to say that better-off people don't crop up in his books, but when they do they are often cast in a negative light, like Vera in *Station Street.* Although Richards claims he respects her "strength", she is a parody: she's a strident feminist who hitches her star to various causes. When it comes right down to it, literature about the middle class irritates Richards. "It bores the arse right off me," he says frankly.

However, Richards is averse to being portrayed as some sort of working-class hero, and "That's exactly what has already happened," he says. "I'm not focusing on the working class so the middle class can have a trip on it. I'm doing it because that's what I do best. Hopefully, the best will come to the surface." (p. 25)

Nancy Robb, "David Adams Richards: Universal Truths from Miramichi Roots," in Quill and Quire, *Vol. 54, No. 4, April, 1988, pp. 24-5.*

DOUGLAS GLOVER

Nights below Station Street is full of the horror, violence, pity, bemused tolerance, and humour that we have come to expect in a David Adams Richards novel. It chronicles the wars of the Walsh family, Joe and Rita and their 15-year-old daughter, Adele, concentrating on Adele and her conflict with Joe, who is an alcoholic trying to reform, trying to atone for the damage he's already done to his family.

Adele is a sweetheart of a girl caught in the Never Never Land of adolescence, confused, rebellious, endearing, and hilarious (unable to decide whether to wear jeans or skirts, spitting in her Coke to keep her little sister from drinking it, screaming at Joe because he won't let her rub his sore back). She exaggerates and embellishes on Joe's mistreatment. She looks for guidance to a character named Vera, the Miramichi's version of the New Person, a university graduate who has spent a year at Oxford and speaks with a mid-Atlantic accent. But the truth of Adele's relationship with Joe is that they love each other deeply.

"It's a book about the conflict for the hearts and souls of the young," says Richards. "There are a lot of people like Vera who have gone away to university and come back to Newcastle with an answer for everything. They wear the right clothes and go to the new malls, the new racketball courts and the new curling clubs, and that's all very well. But the one person who is really trying to be a new human being is Joe, who, with no promises, no guarantees, is giving up his old life, his drinking, his drinking friends."

When Richards talks about his writing, he talks about themes and personalities. He shies from discussions of style. He dislikes being asked about influences. "I don't think of myself in any terms," he says, "except that when I write about Joe Walsh he comes from my fictional world, which is mine and not anybody else's." On one occasion he dealt with the several issues of regionalism, technique, and influence in a single terse sentence: "I think you write like your personality and where you come from."

What animates Dave Richards is the inner life of his characters, their motives, their secrets, their spiritual aspirations and failures. He has a curious way of talking about them, as if you and he were talking about Joe Walsh down the street and not Joe Walsh in a novel. He uses first names, tells you things about them (traits, habits, events in their lives) that aren't written down in any book (Fredericton poet Robert Gibbs calls this "extending the text"), laughs about them, pities them.

Bill Bauer remembers an occasion when Richards came for a visit during the writing of his 1986 novel, *Road to the Stilt House.* "Dave came in and sat down, and our son John was here, and Dave exclaimed sorrowfully, apropos of nothing. 'Oh, jeez, poor little Randy. The poor little bugger—he's just sitting on the porch crying his heart out because he flunked his Scout badge.' After he left, John said, 'I didn't know he had any children. Who's this Randy?'"

When I mentioned this, Richards laughed. He says, "I don't know why I do it. It's something that's on my mind. I try to think continually of what impels people like John and Karen and Leah and Trenda. They are physical presences. When I think of Trenda (like Randy, a character in *Road to the Stilt House*), I can see exactly what she's wearing and how she would walk into this room."

He knows his characters through and through, even the minor ones. Writing *Nights below Station Street,* he became so involved with a set of peripheral characters that he finally realized he had a whole other novel on his hands—the second novel of his trilogy, in fact. Richards's characters populate a huge, continuous imaginative world such that people in one book will show up in another. Kevin and Pamela Dulse from *The Coming of Winter,* for example, show up again in *Lives of Short Duration;* Hudson Kopochus, a secondary character in *Lives,* has a whole story devoted to him in *Dancers at Night.* The effect is one of eerie verisimilitude—as if they were all really alive somewhere.

Richards is a passionate moralist (not moralizer, not social critic) who delights in making precise and minute ethical distinctions. "I am always asking myself," he says, "when presented with a set of difficult choices, how would this character act? What is the proper and correct thing to do, as opposed to the thing that appears proper and correct. . . . A lot of *Nights below Station Street* deals with the difference between the veneer of altruism and real altruism, supposed or assumed generosity and true human generosity."

He distrusts middle-class "sophistication" and "gentility," concepts he sees as pregnant with their own sort of violence. "In all instances where you have to be generous, affected or sophisticated people can be generous; but to be generous when it's not expected or when it causes hardship, when it requires the best part of human nature—my characters can be that more quickly."

This distrust reflects Richards's politics, that combination of antiliberal, antiwelfare, pro-working-class sentiments he shares with fellow Easterners like the late Alden Nowlan, Wayne Johnston, and Eric Trethewey, a Nova Scotia writer now teaching in the U.S. Amazingly, he has been called a Marxist, and his first novel, *The Coming of Winter,* was translated into Russian (though he suspects the Soviets corrupted his text into a socialist-realist indictment of Canadian society). But Richards prefers to call himself a "conservative socialist" and to say things like "To think that politics can solve the problems of the poor is ridiculous. I've always thought politics tended towards the nonsensical."

Sometimes he reminds me of Flannery O'Connor (among other similarities, they're both Catholic). Like O'Connor, Richards expresses himself through characters who live at the bottom of the economic ladder, on the periphery of society, an imaginative territory they both see as inhabited by petty crooks, drunks, suicides, and mystics—for what else is George Terri from *Lives of Short Duration,* dancing drunkenly with a pig's head on a pole in the middle of a burning bridge, but an ancient shaman seeking his vision? And they both get comic mileage out of the clash between the spiritual and the mundane—George's vision turns out to be the DTs.

But where O'Connor is dogmatic (God is a character; grace is a plot device), Richards is romantic. His world, his fictive universe, is Catholic only in a deep sense, in the sense that Catholicism is the most pagan of the Christian sects. Life is nasty, brutish, and short; men and women are ruled by the image of gross flesh, by fantasy, and by social coercion. But beneath the surface they have souls of essential goodness, yearning to be free, to express themselves in decent, loving acts, in generosity.

> Lois had also a tattoo of a tiny rose on her left breast . . . this tiny rose signified something pure and life-giving about her, exuded from her a quality of love, though she said she'd gotten the rose tattoo on a $20 bet with a man, she said, who couldn't hold his own piss.

For Richards, this contrast between the flesh and the spirit, the outer and the inner, is everything. It's the root of both his tragic vision and his comic insight. And this is what most critics miss—it is a theme that is universal, a theme that has generated all great art since the beginning of the Christian era.

Far from being a bland land of desperate poverty and alienation, the Miramichi River area where Richards grew up is a world of almost surreal and operatic contrasts. It is a country of strange, haunting beauty, river and forest and mist-covered estuary, violated by abrupt, smoking mill plants and port towns.

> . . . the quiet light under the snow-covered spruces, the frozen rock where Hudson Kopochus lay with a bear on his journey to kill a man in 1825, and the children catching the bus for school the next day, the dark-faced displaced French, the

stubborn self-destructive Irish, the celtic blood on one of the most violent rivers in the country, "Fuck ya, fuck ya," for "I love you, I love you," or "Help me, help me".

This is Richards's *paysage moralisé,* the country of his imagination.

Richards's grandfather—genes and history tell—was a travelling musician from Wales. The Welsh connection is determinative—music and bombast. Welsh bombast, e.g., Dylan Thomas, fuels Richards's intense hyperrhetoric the way the tradition of Southern bombast fuelled Faulkner. And he sings. When he was younger, Richards would often preface readings with a cappella folk songs. (pp. 10-11)

When he was 14, Richards read what he calls "my first adult book"—it was Dickens's *Oliver Twist.* That was when he decided to become a writer. You can almost see the impulse unfolding. Richards must have recognized in Dickens a symbolic grammar analogous to his own experience: he must have realized all at once that it was really possible to express that experience in beautiful and exciting ways—the subtle dance of wealth, class, and poverty, the contrast between professional do-gooders and the truly good, the manipulation of youth, the drinking, and the violence.

There is a story from David Adams Richards's childhood that is emblematic. When his mother was seven months pregnant, she accidentally tripped and fell while hanging her laundry out to dry. The baby, David, was born prematurely with a brain haemorrhage. His left side appeared somewhat crippled and, as he grew, he was slow to learn to walk—doctors and family feared he might be retarded.

When he was two and a half years old (this is one of Richards's earliest memories), Mrs. Richards took him on the long train journey to Montreal to visit a specialist. The specialist handed the baby a rubber ball and asked him to give it back. The doctor repeated the manoeuvre, urging the child to perform it "Faster, faster!" In frustration, Richards threw the ball, hitting the doctor on the head. The doctor laughed, saying, "This kid is *not* retarded."

This anecdote contains the three hallmarks of a David Adams Richards story: horror, violence, and comedy. Through fate or bad luck, the baby is damaged. Society jumps in with a glib assessment; the word *retarded* is value-loaded, welfare-worker, pseudomedical jargon that dismisses the child, pigeonholes him. It is a type of psychic violence. As Richards says, "It is prior assumption and contempt prior to investigation that destroys people."

The second half of the story, the trip to Montreal, is also exemplary. For it is the pattern of Richards's characters to react to the violence of prior assumption with violence, with drunkenness, or other forms of outrageous behaviour. It is a curious double sign: the violence Richards characters do to correct English, for example, is both an emblem of their debasement, of the place society has put them in, a way of behaving that society expects and allows, and it is also a badge of honour, a symbol of their revolt against "proper" forms of behaviour and speech.

And sometimes the violence is simply causeless and mysterious, at which point it connects with Richards's religious sense, his belief in the fundamental unpredictability, the absolute freedom, of the human spirit.

An excerpt from *Nights below Station Street*

It was boredom that drove Myhrra to become a hospital volunteer this winter. She went there and visited the sick, brought them magazines and read their letters to them. The magazines themselves were two or three months old. Some of the letters had been read before. Some of the people were catheterized, and lay silently under the lights. Some would grow weaker from one visit to the next. And some would look at her suspiciously, and be angry about something.

Dr. Hennessey did not approve of the volunteer program, which was new. He was an old man who looked at her sternly and scared her every time she went there. He'd been in the war, and yet in his manner there was such an overwhelming sense of kindness that she could not be upset with him for long.

His hands shook, and his feet clomped about from one room to the next. He walked about the hospital cursing under his breath, with a nurse following him. People were generally frightened of him. He got into an argument with one old fellow who said he liked it when the volunteers dropped by to see him.

"Well, you shouldn't," Dr. Hennessey said.

"Why not?"

"Just because you shouldn't like them—you should want to be all alone rather than have them coming by."

"You don't like them, doctor?"

"Sure—sure they're the very best, boy—the very best."

And with that, he cut off his conversation and walked down the hall, breathing heavily, smoking in the non-smoking sections.

"Myhrra," he would say to her, "you should go home."

"What do you mean—I'm scheduled to sit with Mr. Salome." And she would haul out a list and show him. He would take the paper, look at it at arm's length and say:

"Well, perhaps—but he's asleep—and mostly dead—and perhaps it's best if you just go home now." Then he would smile and say: "I like your new patent leather shoes." And clumsily she would look up at him in the dark, and clumsily he would walk away.

"Yer sorta religious or what Simon?" Rance said.

"Oh boy—I don't think so—very much."

"Well I just thought all the stories ya told me—about the bears, and running the river—always ended up with 'God bless,'" Rance smiled and looked about.

Simon chuckled.

"I don't know sometimes. Once I bopped a man right over the head for no reason—no-one knows why—I don't know why—but there it is—that's what I'm like."

"Well I'm not going to bother you about it," Rance said.

For Richards's characters are not simply victims. His novels live because they boil with anger, revolt, and humour. His down-and-out working-class types seem always ready to perform the graceful, generous act, or to throw their lives away in some piece of mad, defiant theatre. The best of them have clear ideas of correct behaviour that in many ways are truer than the more sophisticated compromises of middle-class society. "They are doing things, when push comes to shove," says Richards, "that the best part of themselves offers to the world." (p. 12)

Douglas Glover, *"Violent River,"* in Books in Canada, *Vol. 17, No. 4, May, 1988, pp. 9-12.*

DAVID HOMEL

In the first two pages of David Adams Richards's ***Nights below Station Street,*** we are treated to the prospect of a giftless Christmas, a battle with the bottle, falling asleep with a lit cigarette, and a grey mill town divided by a half-frozen river. We know we are in for some good old-time naturalism, as if Emile Zola had come to New Brunswick in the early 1970s. A kind of dismalist view of factory-town life, where if anything can possibly go wrong, it will. In this case, "dismal" is reserved for the characters' lives—not the author's writing.

Richards knows his mill town exceedingly well, and those who inhabit it and the way they speak; he knows too the woods just outside it that, presumably, stand for freedom from it. In this world he has set the Walsh family and their friends, members of the underclass lumpenproletariat. Joe Walsh, the father, is a bear of a man whose past bouts of drinking have ruined his health and ability to work. His harassed wife, Rita, looks after neighbour children and at times her husband too. Her daughter, Adele, the fruit of a rapid union with another man before her marriage to Joe, is an adolescent with a sharp tongue and nowhere to go, continually insecure, as well she might be, about her family's image in town. . . .

Joe's attempts to stay sober form the emotional centre of the book, even if at the beginning we are asked to identify more with Adele's struggles within a family in disarray. Whether the author has intended it or not, Joe Walsh takes over. As he leaves alcohol behind, he discovers that it is the social glue without which his world cannot function. . . .

Joe Walsh is not the hero of ***Nights below Station Street***; if anyone or anything is, it is the neighbourhood, the town, and the wasted nights lived out there. The book develops through juxtaposed portraits: the family, then each of the family members, then the friends and their interactions. That method can become irritating at points: just as we are warming up to Joe's struggles, symbolized by his constant back pain and fight for sobriety, the focus rapidly switches to another figure in the community. Sometimes the juxtapositions are informative: sometimes they are not. At one point a Russian freighter

is stuck in the harbour, and an encounter between Myrrha, a Walsh family friend, and a Russian officer is described, but the effect does not go further than that of a vignette. The same goes for the episode of Joe at Alcoholics Anonymous. The author is treading on potentially significant ground, but the juxtaposition technique he uses means he must quickly abandon it. In the end, Richards is true to his title: he is recounting the nights of a street, one by one.

Richards writes in very simple, spare prose. Applied to Joe's quest to simplify his existence, the style is appropriate. When Richards writes, "This business of not drinking was horrible," the baldness of the statement surprises, then moves us. The scenes of understated jealousy (Rita can partake of a certain alcohol-based social life, whereas Joe cannot) are equally effective. Little by little, the novel shapes up as a story of a man trying to leave behind the only world he knows in a confused sort of fashion, and the people in that world who will not let him do it. And perhaps in the end, Joe triumphs, for the book's last scene is set in a snowstorm, in the woods, which is Joe Walsh's element.

David Homel, *"Forest and Town,"* in Books in Canada, *Vol. 17, No. 4, May, 1988, p. 32.*

MORTON RITTS

Nights below Station Street, Richards's fifth book, again confirms his reputation as a writer of unusual honesty and compassion.

Set in the early 1970s, the novel depicts working-class life in a fictional town patterned after one of northeastern New Brunswick's sombre mill towns on the Miramichi River. Full of finely observed characters, the story centres on the daily struggles of the Walsh family. Joe, the father, is a 43-year-old unemployed ex-alcoholic, strong enough to have once carried a piano on his back up a flight of stairs but now afflicted with a debilitating back problem. His wife, Rita, cleans houses and babysits to make ends meet. Adele, the elder of their two daughters, is a bright, angry and insecure 15-year-old who is derisive of her father and desperate to escape her mother's fate. As the plot progresses, the lives of the Walshes and other townspeople increasingly intersect, allowing Joe and Adele a kind of reconciliation.

While firmly rooted in a physical environment of adversity and deprivation, Richards's characters are ultimately concerned with a search for meaningful values and a sense of self-worth. While that quest is dreary, it is often ironically—even cruelly—humorous: Adele's friend, Cindi, an epileptic, is told disgustedly by a bullying friend, "Try not ta be an epileptic for one night." But if they are unable to articulate the confusion of their lives, the characters of ***Nights below Station Street*** still fight gamely to come to terms with a narrow, fatalistic world. Richards neither patronizes that struggle nor romanticizes it. Rather, he gives it dignity while creating something universal out of the unique fictional territory he has carved from the Miramichi Valley.

Morton Ritts, *"Voices from the Valley,"* in Ma-

clean's Magazine, *Vol. 101, No. 26, June 20, 1988,*
p. 60.

GEORGE WOODCOCK

There is a thinness and a touch of arbitrariness in *Nights below Station Street,* the most recent of the novels that David Adams Richards had set in the small towns of the Miramichi, and as I read it I began to think of the problems of a writer who keeps on going to the same well, and particularly the regional writer whose well has virtually no means of outside renewal. Remembering the dark appeal of Richards' first novel, *The Coming of Winter,* and the complex fictional portrait of a community that he achieved seven years later in *Lives of Short Duration,* I was disappointed by the lack of any really new vision in *Nights below Station Street.* It is a skilful book, making eloquent variations on a plain style, and like the earlier novels it shows Richards' characteristic ability to show lyrical perceptions emerging from the banality of actual living. Yet one has the feeling of a writer marking time, and disappointingly achieving less than in his earlier novels, which had freshness of theme and setting.

Nights below Station Street is a rather slight book, longer and more complex than a novella, but insubstantial for a novel: the French would probably call it a *recit,* particularly as it has that touch of moral criticism which—in the hands of a Gide or a Camus—such a description would imply. (p. 129)

The action of the novel centres around a family and the friends and acquaintances who provide its connections with the general world. Essentially it is a social realist slice of life, open-endedly presented. Joe is a jack-of-all-trades, a man of immense strength who has worked long in the woods and yet has picked up various mechanical skills, as well as a drinking problem which during the few weeks of the novel he is trying to shed. An injury to his back has for the present made him virtually unemployable, so that he has to face the complex strains that come from being deprived of booze and work at the same time. He is a good man of whom people take advantage, and the same can be said of his wife Rita, who not only keeps the house going on precarious means, but also looks cheerfully after the children of her friends and neighbours, so that the house is always crawling with kids.

Joe and Rita are perhaps just a little too good to be true, but their blandness (broken occasionally by the fits of temper in which Joe will destructively show his immense strength) is challenged by the cynical acerbity of their fifteen-year-old daughter Adele (or Delly). Adele's adventures among local teenagers and belated hippies are balanced by the relations of her parents with a variety of small town types, whose life displays an excruciating banality which contrasts with (as in earlier Richards novels) the sombre beauty of the environment to which Joe is attracted and from which he gains—like other Richards characters—an unarticulated inspiration.

Shifting sexual relationships and marriages give the novel a kind of structure, and the climactic point is a wedding at which two of the friends of Joe and Rita get married. At the wedding party Adele suddenly collapses: her carefully concealed pregnancy—which perhaps explains the irrational angers she had displayed through the novel—turns to labour in the men's washroom. After she has been whisked off in an ambulance, the married couple—Myrrha and Vye—leave the

party and take a wrong road into the forest where they get lost in a blizzard. Neither knows much about survival in the woods, and they get separated, to be variously rescued by an old farmer onto whose woodlot Myrrha strays, and by Joe, who—instead of going to the hospital to learn of his daughter's condition—has shown a curious indifference, with neither anger nor anxiety welling up, and has gone off into the woods where he sees and hears the signs of wild animals and is content. (pp. 129-30)

Reading this quite well written but ultimately disappointing novel, one feels that David Adams Richards has reached a critical point in his career as a writer. The well from which he began to draw, the life of common people in the decaying small towns of New Brunswick, seems to be running dry and brackish. If he is to sustain our interest, some new, revivifying current must enter into his work. Otherwise he is in danger of creating his own stereotypes and becoming their prisoner. (p. 131)

George Woodcock, *"Too Often to the Well,"* in Event, *Vol. 18, No. 1, Spring, 1989, pp. 129-31.*

GERALD NOONAN

In *Nights below Station Street,* the territory of David Adams Richards—now emblazoned with this novel's 1989 Governor General's Award for fiction—continues to exert its paradoxical strength. As in his four previous novels, the characters of this one, milltown dwellers by a northern New Brunswick river, succeed in living, without much distinction, distinctive lives.

Almost without exception, these are unknowing people, never fixated upon their own virtues or their errors, who sense nonetheless that their existence unfolds within a wholly known "now irrevocable" process. Richards' achievement is an evocation-from-within of their fluctuating struggles that engenders in the (presumably) more knowing and exterior reader an understanding tinged with poignancy and sympathy. It is an award-winning novel about an award-losing community.

Of all the cast, Joe Walsh, a prodigiously strong and chronically unemployed reformed alcoholic, has—paradox enough—the most distinction. He is an ingenious fixer of things mechanical, an educated woodsman and hunter, a peeler of potatoes for supper, a gentle father for his two daughters, a hyperactive child named Milly, and Adele, a sullen abusive 16-year-old and mindless imitator of her peers. Joe is also afflicted with an ailing back and a stutter—and an incapacity to be as fashionably social as Rita, his hardworking and mostly loyal wife, would like. She would like him to curl, to dress and speak better, dance more, even drink, just a little.

Other characters include Rita's curling club friends, the recently divorced Myhrra, relatives, a local businessman, and Ralphie, Adele's university-educated boyfriend. Apart from the whole complex is the aging and temperamental Dr. Hennessey, one of the local general practitioners, whose secret delight or punishment is to be as contradictory as possible to as many people at one time as possible. "The doctor found himself at an age when he shouldn't have to explain anything of how he thought or felt, of explaining nothing on principle. Much like Joe when it came to reconciling himself with his past."

None of the characters, indeed, do much reconciling with the past, nor with the unknowns of a projected future. The world here is Richards' usual immediate present, at once as real and as transitory as the very smells he evokes so often in his narration: the smell of "darkness," of "iron" and "frost," of "white sheets," "a smell of evening," of "ice," of "late afternoon." (pp. 118-19)

Invariably (perhaps too often) Joe does not know why he has a particular feeling:—"And why 'wife' sounded particularly demeaning at this moment Joe didn't know." Joe, however, like the other adults, does not blame the present, reconciled or not, on the past—as does the insufferable Adele who screeches blame upon her "some foolish" parents "in this here house" that's "As no relation to me," and "I'm not going to do the dishes," plus "And I don't care!" Appropriately, when Adele's better self does emerge it is "without knowing"—"without knowing that she would ever be able to do something like this, she [tears welling in her eyes] took away the face-cloth to look at [Joe's] wound." Whether knowing or unknowing, reconciled or not, Richards' characters tend to be basic human forces in action.

One strand of plot connected to Adele stretches to the limit the willingness of my suspended disbelief. She is such a pouting adolescent, ravaged by recurring idiocy of phrase (who puts signs on the fridge door, "Milly, I spit in this [Coke]!" and on her bedroom door, "To all little creeps—stay out on pain of death") that it is a puzzle why Ralphie, who had some success as a university student, even if he is passively uninspired, could sustain interest in her. Richards adds to my puzzlement by suddenly revealing without explanation, near the end, that "the only person [Joe] loved more than all the others" was Adele.

There are stronger instances of author intrusion in this novel that at best keep the reader aware of the paradoxes in this depicted world and at worst raise the suspicion that Richards is occasionally, after four novels, giving in to the temptation to preach to or about this world he knows so well. For example:

> Because of [Joe's] difficulty, Rita had to start fending for herself at a time when it wasn't as accepted or as natural for women to go out to work. At this time, for a woman to work meant the family had somehow failed. That is, the very women who today were saying that a woman's career was indispensable were quite prepared to stay home then, because staying home was as much commonplace as working now is. (p. 120)

These passages are all the more salient from an author whose style can exude such lean confidence that the sentence, "The winter and then the summer months passed, and fall came" stands alone as the opening paragraph of a chapter. Again, prose sinewy, rhythmic and graphic, such as "On Saturdays, Allain Garrett and he would go partridge hunting, and Joe would walk through the woods on small roads, bathed in cold light, as the partridge fanned themselves in the gravelled dirt" contrasts sharply with the passages of "author speaking."

More oblique is an episode in which the characters play "a game called Risk—a game where everyone had a certain number of armies and tried to take over the world." The rather egregious social evening—there is no reference to another in the whole novel—which includes Ralphie, Joe and Rita, Adele and Milly, Myhrra the divorcée, and the curmudgeonly doctor (would *he* really "come to play" the untried and new-fangled?), helps to set this milltown world into a larger context. The game "depends on aggression" and never quite gets underway satisfactorily. No one wants to start an attack, there is disagreement over what continents are whose territory, and whether the women should go first. The deft disintegration of the "universal" game has multiple significance:

> But Myhrra said if everyone was going to attack her then she may as well not play. The doctor gloomily puffed on his pipe, and everyone listened as the wind rose against the side of the house.
>
> Then Milly crawled upon Rita's knee to watch, and started yelling that she didn't have a chance to play. Then Adele had to go to the bathroom and Ralphie . . .
>
> . . . Ralphie tossed five armies up above his head, and they fell headlong into the Atlantic.

So ends the board game, reverberating, among other places, against the Tolstoy quotation referred to in the epigraph of the novel: "Everyone wants to change the world, but no one will change themselves."

The domestic and regional realities, that is, of Richards' own territory comprise problems that are common to the broad brave world outside. Or, as Joe Walsh thinks (in the process of executing another, and his most dramatic, rescue) as the book comes to an abrupt end:—"he did not feel [the pain] so much—now knowing the processes of how this had all happened, only understanding that it was now irrevocable because it had." (p. 121)

Gerald Noonan, "Understanding Paradox," in The Fiddlehead, *No. 160, Spring, 1989, pp. 118-21.*

James Salter
Dusk and Other Stories

Award: PEN/Faulkner Award: Fiction

American novelist, short story writer, dramatist, and script-writer, Salter was born in 1925.

An author of several respected novels, Salter garnered widespread acclaim for *Dusk and Other Stories,* a collection of new and previously published short fiction from throughout his career. Using varied settings, shifting perspectives, and evocative imagery, Salter centers on such topics as morality, exile, sexuality, and death to examine the despondent lives of characters cut off from cultural tradition and the past by ethical and personal compromises. In "American Express," for example, two lawyers attain wealth as partners in a law firm but gradually succumb to ennui in Italy; in "Foreign Shores," an unhappy upper-class woman is incensed after discovering that the Dutch babysitter whom she fired for associating with a pornographer may have attained status in high society despite her indiscretion. Robert Burke called *Dusk and Other Stories* "the sort of work that should be, as with any masterpiece, approached with wonder and delight," and Michiko Kakutani commented: "[These] stories glimmer with the magic of fiction; they pull us, hungrily, into the mundane drama of their characters's lives."

(See also *CLC,* Vols. 7, 52 and *Contemporary Authors,* Vols. 73-76.)

PRINCIPAL WORKS

NOVELS

The Hunters   1957
The Arm of Flesh   1961
A Sport and a Pastime   1967
Light Years   1975
Solo Faces   1979

SHORT FICTION

Dusk and Other Stories   1988

RHODA KOENIG

[Salter's pieces collected in ***Dusk and Other Stories***] lurk and slink. These are tales of shadows playing across the punitively white, sun-washed wall of a Mediterranean villa, of cruelties greater than any meted out by hunters or nature waiting in the dark heart of the wood. Mrs. Chandler in **"Fields at Dusk"** has lost everything but money—husband, son, and beauty have departed.

> She stood in front of the mirror and looked at her face coldly. Forty-six. It was there in the neck and beneath her eyes. She would never be any younger. . . .

Now she learns that her caretaker, who has lately become her lover, won't be coming back. Thinking of the geese she has seen earlier in the day, and remembering the ones she watched with her child, she imagines,

> Somewhere in the wet grass . . . lay one of them, dark sodden breast, graceful neck still extended, great wings striving to beat, bloody sounds coming from the holes in its beak. . . .

[Salter] writes with a delicate, surgical touch, in a style that is no less powerful for being sly and cool. Most of these stories are set far from America—in Barcelona, Basel, New York—and they are lightly brushed with what we like to think of as Continental perversity. (Though, amusingly, in **"American Express,"** it is the young, hotshot lawyer from the States who corrupts the girl he meets in Italy. "Women fall in love when they get to know you," he tells an importunate girlfriend.

"Men are just the opposite. When they finally know you they're ready to leave.")

Perhaps the most remarkable story in this exquisite collection is **"Akhnilo,"** which concentrates much of what Salter has to say about the mysterious silences and sounds of earth. A former alcoholic wakes before dawn and looks out at the night.

> It seemed he was the only listener to an infinite sea of cries. Its vastness awed him. He thought of all that lay concealed behind it, the desperate acts, the desires, the fatal surprises. . . . In ravenous burrows the blind shrews hunted ceaselessly, the pointed tongues of reptiles were testing the air, there was the crunch of abdomens, the passivity of the trapped, the soft throes of mating. His daughters were asleep down the hall. Nothing is safe except for an hour.

> Rhoda Koenig, "Different Strokes," in New York Magazine, Vol. 21, No. 4, January 25, 1988, p. 63.

JAMES SALTER [INTERVIEW WITH ROBERT BURKE]

[The interview excerpted below was conducted in San Francisco in February, 1988.]

[Burke]: *Your previous publisher of* **Light Years** *made a point on the dust jacket that you were retired military . . .*

[Salter]: Not quite. I *was* in the Air Force.

The reason I ask is that there seems to be something incongruous about the idea of a military person describing your characters in **Dusk** *as well as* **Light Years,** *most of whom are affluent and professional. I guess what I would think of them as East Coast "country club" set.*

Don't be misled by that. I am not a military person. I had some connection with it, but only in the sense that I belong to the generation—and even the locale—of Salinger, Kerouac, and Norman Mailer. The war (World War II) was a big part of life, and I was in the service at the end of the war and for a few years after, but I'm not a career military person. I stayed in because it was thrilling, so I stayed longer than I should have. I would like to have those years back, but in any case, I don't think that it's significant. Getting back to your original question, that "country club" set might have been accurate in O'Hara's time, but I don't think they are significant anymore in New York life, or at least the part of New York life that I know. . . . I agree with you, though, that they (my characters) are people who are educated, able to support themselves, and lead a certain kind of life. What can I say? It's just the kind of life that interests me.

Do you write with a particular audience in mind?

My favorite short story writer is, I think, Babel. He said that he wrote for an ideal audience of one or two people. And his ideal audience was an educated woman, perhaps in her thirties. I like his feeling about that. I write for a few people who I think will like it. Beyond that, you can't imagine who your audience is.

One of the things I noticed in the first story in **Dusk,** *"Am Strande von Tanger,"* is that you seem to have an impulse towards a particular technique where the point of view is refracted. And when you employ that technique, it feels somehow disjointed, that one is following the story but not the characters.*

I wrote that story so long ago—it was the first story that I ever had accepted and published—that I cannot remember my impulses. Let me say that it was the first story of any merit that I had published. I had, in fact, written stories earlier, but they weren't any good. I have had comments about the point of view a number of times, that I'm not being faithful enough to the idea of a single point of view, perhaps a well-defined point of view. That may be true, I really don't know. I don't think of point of view when I'm writing. I don't mean in the act of writing, but when you're looking at a story and working it out and reworking it, the idea of point of view really doesn't enter into my thinking. I'm thinking in more primitive terms: Is this interesting? Is this the way it should be told? Is this what I want, one way or another? That particular story may be more deficient than the others, I don't know. I put **"Am Strande von Tanger"** in there because I liked it, because it was the first successful story I had written, and I put it first because I didn't want to put what I felt was the strongest story first.

You seem to have, especially in **Dusk,** *an incredible empathy for your female characters. There is something very special in that. Do you attribute your empathy for women to anything in particular? There are really so few male writers who write convincingly about women.*

Well, there is Tennessee Williams, of course. In my view, women are my real heroes, and I like to write about them. Whether I know more about them, I don't think I know more than other people. In fact, I'm convinced that men who have never written a word know far more than I do about them. I'm attracted to writing about them, and I admire them greatly. **Light Years** is really more about a woman than anything else, in my view anyway, which is no better than anyone else's. What the writer thinks about the book is often ridiculous compared to what the book turns out to be. Let me say, and I may be way off the mark, that **A Sport and a Pastime** is about a heroic girl. I think of it that way. That's not the only thing that it's about. Since you only have one or two themes in your life—even great writers only have one or two—you keep circling them one way or another, closer and closer. I would say that it seems to be one of the things that interests me, whether consciously or not. It is conscious, but on the other hand it must be something that I really don't understand perfectly.

How do you feel about the idea of classifying writers by region? Do you feel it's valid?

Well, it's valid insofar as it works. I come from the East. All of my associations are with the East, but I'm not a regional writer. Geographical classification is one classification, but it's not the only one. For instance, Dreiser was thought of as the first important American writer who didn't come out of the educated—I don't want to say patrician—he was the first writer from the "gutter," so to speak, from the proletariat. So, before then it would be ridiculous to say that there were these two classes, because nobody from the other class was writing. Now there was Dreiser, and many other writers followed him. You could break it down that way. You could legitimately say that there are "gay" writers whose concerns, whose method of writing, whose stimulus, whose everything is "gay." Or as Gore Vidal put it, who deal in "homosexual matters." But for a long time we've spoken of writers in a regional sense. It's only one of a number of possible classifications. I think that you can do it. The real question, though, is what use do we want to make of these classifications?(pp. 3, 6, 18)

James Salter and Robert Burke, in an interview in
The Bloomsbury Review, *Vol. 8, No. 3, May-June, 1988, pp. 3, 6, 18.*

MICHIKO KAKUTANI

Like the stories of John Cheever, James Salter's tales shine with light—morning light, summer light, the paralyzing light of noon, and the sad, dusty light of early evening. [In ***Dusk and Other Stories,*** he] describes that moment after a shower when the light is "silvery and strange" and those transitory days of Indian summer presided over by a "great, terminal sun." He gives us nights when the sky reveals itself, its "stars shining faintly" and those afternoons when "the sun is white," and the land beneath it is "the color of straw."

There's a painterly quality to Mr. Salter's descriptions, but his impressionism is used in the service of an old-fashioned moral vision. Light, for his characters, is not simply a physical fact, like the weather or the geography of a new town; it's an index of mood, and a state of mind. Perhaps that is why so many of these stories take place at dusk, that "hour of melancholy," when "everything is ended," for most of Mr. Salter's characters find themselves at some kind of turning point that irrevocably divides their lives into a past and future. For some, it's an epiphanic moment that seems to sum up all their previous losses; for others, it's a momentary disappointment that slowly but insidiously swells into something larger and more permanent.

In several of the stories, characters clutch at a shadowy piece of hope, only to see their expectations dwindle and fade away. A traveler in Europe meets the girlfriend of a little known writer and arranges a rendezvous with her; when she fails to show up, he feels "like a man out of work, an invalid," with "no place to go." . . .

In **"Lost Sons,"** a painter named Ed Reemstma goes back to West Point for a reunion, enjoys a brief flirtation with the wife of a former classmate, and in the wake of her abrupt leave-taking, suddenly re-experiences all the feelings of exclusion and oddness he once felt as a student. His awareness of exclusion is not so different, really from what the "minor writer" in **"Via Negativa"** feels. Having spent years becoming "more and more unpromising," he realizes that his girlfriend no longer believes in him, and he proceeds to wreck her apartment, while she goes off with a more successful author.

The conclusion of this story somehow seems too pat; and there are other instances where Mr. Salter's taste for symmetry results in a certain flattening-out of the ambiguities of reality. In **"Am Strande von Tanger,"** a woman's fears about the precariousness of her relationship with her boyfriend are bluntly punctuated by the death of her pet bird; and in **"Foreign Shores,"** a woman, whose own life is unraveling, is horrified to discover that her nice au pair girl has been receiving dirty letters from a pornographer.

In other cases, it's not a sequence of overly ironic events that jars the reader, but a phrase or sentence that insists on assigning a set of emotions to a character or situation. "He walked without direction, he was in search of his dreams," writes Mr. Salter of one hero. Or, of another: "He cared nothing for them, only for the power to disturb. He was bending their love toward him, a stupid love, a love without which he could not breathe."

Such lapses, happily, are rare. As such novels as ***Light Years*** and ***A Sport and a Pastime*** have demonstrated, Mr. Salter is a careful observer of daily life; and this volume attests to his success at pouring those observations into the less capacious form of the short story as well. . . .

The best stories in ***Dusk*** point up the author's gift for condensation. Mr. Salter can delineate a character in a line or two, giving us, in addition to his melancholy heroes, bright, hard cameos of the people they encounter. **"The Cinema,"** for instance, gives us a sense of an entire movie's cast and crew: the leading man who "read his lines as if laying down cards of no particular importance," the leading lady who tries on the screenwriter's lines "like shoes," but never thinks who had made them; the director, who's intent on making "two films a year for 30 years" and the film company executive, who has "a face like a fish, a bass, that had gone bad." We are given hints of the trajectories of each of their lives, the arc of their fortunes.

In fact, when it comes to delineating the passage of time—days, months or decades—Mr. Salter's shorthand is especially persuasive. **"American Express"** traces in some 20 brief pages the lives of two lawyers, from their early days "living in apartments with funny furniture," through their spectacular rise as partners in their own firm; and their gradual drift, abroad, into moral dislocation. Other stories can suggest in a single sentence, an individual's entire history, the complex interplay of longing and fear, hope and need, that has brought about the present. In doing so, these stories glimmer with the magic of fiction; they pull us, hungrily, into the mundane drama of their characters's lives.

Michiko Kakutani, "Epiphanic Moments," in The New York Times, *February 13, 1988, p. 16.*

JON SAARI

Salter writes with a precise and pure style that is usually plain and unadorned, yet contains a subtle emotional power. A careful writer in no hurry to publish, . . . he displays a variety of characters and situations for a writer so firmly rooted in a developed aesthetic and literary sensibility. His stories at first glance appear obvious and familiar, which is really a tribute to his sense of craft. Yet for Salter it is not enough to write well and tell an uncomplicated story. He obviously enjoys exploring an emotional landscape that he shifts from story to story just as he shifts physical location. Salter melds style and substance so the emotional effect may not be as obvious as it is in Joyce Carol Oates, but it is present.

These 11 stories explore life today in places as different as Barcelona, Spain, and Carbondale, Colorado, and in situations both banal and dramatic. Salter can catch a way of life or a moral predicament in a very few words. Scenes are straightforward yet symbolically suggestive of ways of life and portray both individual failure and triumph.

In **"Twenty Minutes"** a woman out horseback riding suffers a fall and knows she will die: she remembers her father's iron will in meeting her own fate. In **"Dusk,"** the volume's best story and a perfect example of Salter's literary intent, a divorced woman named Mrs. Chandler meets at her home a former lover who fears she will expose him to his wife. . . . And in **"Dirt,"** a story of a few pages, Salter captures with poetic power the sense of a working man's whole life right before he dies by retelling a few incidents and anecdotes. These examples are indications of Salter's impressive scope.

Jon Saari, in a review of "Dusk and Other Stories," in The Antioch Review, *Vol. 46, No. 2, Spring, 1988, p. 270.*

An excerpt from **"American Express"**

In the morning the first light was blue on the window glass. There was the sound of rain. It was leaves blowing in the garden, shifting across the gravel. Alan slipped from the bed to fasten the loose shutter. Below, half hidden in the hedges, a statue gleamed white. The few parked cars shone faintly. She was asleep, the soft, heavy pillow beneath her head. He was afraid to wake her. "Eda," he whispered, "Eda."

Her eyes opened a bit and closed. She was young and could stay asleep. He was afraid to touch her. She was unhappy, he knew, her bare neck, her hair, things he could not see. It would be a while before they were used to it. He didn't know what to do. Apart from that, it was perfect. It was the most natural thing in the world. He would buy her something himself, something beautiful.

In the bathroom he lingered at the window. He was thinking of the first day they had come to work at Weyland, Braun—he and Frank. They would become inseparable. Autumn in the gardens of the Veneto. It was barely dawn. He would always remember meeting Frank. He couldn't have done these things himself. A young man in a cap suddenly came out of a doorway below. He crossed the driveway and jumped onto a motorbike. The engine started, a faint blur. The headlight appeared and off he went, delivery basket in back. He was going to get the rolls for breakfast. His life was simple. The air was pure and cool. He was part of that great, unchanging order of those who live by wages, whose world is unlit and who do not realize what is above.

ROBERT BURKE

James Salter is, simply, one of the best writers in this country. He is also one of the most neglected. His novels ***A Sport and a Pastime*** and ***Light Years*** have consistently garnered impressive reviews, yet his work has never excited the popular imagination. Now, with the publication of his first collection of stories, ***Dusk and Other Stories,*** perhaps all of that will change.

Salter is now a short-story writer to be ranked with Alice Adams and somewhere above more popular authors like Raymond Carver and Mark Halpern. Like Adams, with whom he shares certain stylistic similarities, Salter writes with an almost androgynous sensibility which nevertheless maintains a distinctly masculine, as opposed to macho, perspective. Interestingly, Salter's ability to enjoin the psychologies of both sexes is, almost paradoxically, at its most perceptive when he is dealing with female characters. Consider, for

example, the protagonist of the title story [**"Dusk"**]. Vera, middle-aged and newly divorced, lives by herself in the country. Salter is able to give the reader a completely sympathetic portrait in four lines:

> She was a woman who lived a certain life. She knew how to give dinner parties, take care of dogs, enter restaurants. She had her way of answering invitations, of dressing, of being herself. Incomparable habits, you might call them. She was a woman who had read books, played golf, gone to weddings, whose legs were good, who had weathered storms, a fine woman whom no one now wanted.

It is exactly this sort of precision that so many writers aim for and so few attain. Salter has, in this short paragraph, given the reader everything that he or she needs to know about the character, thereby allowing himself the opportunity to develop his most consistent theme: the alienation and disaffection experienced by so many people as they move into early middle-age.

In **"Twenty Minutes,"** the heroine, Jane Vare, could have, in less skillful hands, succumbed to caricature. Wealthy, a member of the "horsey set," separated from a husband who has left her for a younger woman, she is, as a character, an almost temptingly easy mark. Salter is, however, too good a writer to let that happen. Though he certainly displays a keen sense of humor and observation when he describes her room with "ribbons layered like feathers on the walls" or her set as being the sort "where they rode into the dining room on Sunday morning and the host died fallen on the bed in full attire," he is poking fun at the class, not the character. For Jane herself, Salter has the utmost respect. She is a survivor. When she goes out riding at night and is thrown by her horse and seriously injured, she imagines that she has only twenty minutes to be found. And it is in that twenty minutes that she discovers how truly strong and resilient she is. As she struggles to cope with the horse that has thrown her, which she describes as being "big, well formed, but not very smart," Salter wryly allows her to begin associating the recalcitrant horse with the men in her life. The reader ends with a remarkable study of a woman who has endured husbands, fathers, almost lovers, and infidelities, and risen above them all with a strength and character that surpasses them.

Some readers may complain that Salter's stories are, in the final analysis, too completely male oriented. To a certain degree, this is true, but it is also true of the age, class, and character of the women he is describing. These are women who came of age at a time when there were very few options open to women and who, as a result, have been socialized to such a degree that their lives have been constructed primarily around their relationships with men. For these women, there *are* very few options. But what makes them so interesting and believable in Salter's case is that they are, in fact, so self-referential and maintain such clear perspectives on themselves.

But Salter's descriptive talents are by no means limited to his women. In **"American Express,"** his portrait of two middle-aged men who are partners in a successful law firm is just as telling and perhaps even sadder, in that neither of them can identify the real source of their dissatisfaction and ennui, though it is painfully clear to the reader. Alan and Frank begin as clever, young lawyers with a midtown firm who are, in the end, taken in by their own cleverness. Going to work together on a seemingly hopeless patent case, they begin a series of ethical and personal compromises that end with them on vacation in Italy, sharing the company of a young woman with whom they can't even communicate intelligently. This is, in Salter's case, the perfectly honed metaphor for all their relationships. These are two men who see their lives in black and white, oblivious to any subtletles of shading, and therefore cannot identify their sense of lingering unhappiness with any accuracy or precision. . . . The irony, of course, is that for these men, the parts will always be greater than the sums.

There are some failures in *Dusk and Other Stories.* Salter occasionally employs, like Alice Adams, a point of view which is essentially refracted. Such a technique, though interesting, is rarely successful and has been problematic in some of his previous work, such as his novel *Light Years.* The problem is in the distance Salter attempts to maintain from his characters—as in the first story, **"Am Strande von Tanger"**—while at the same time providing the reader with multiple points of view. However, where he falters, Salter at least partially redeems himself with his sly, often wicked sense of humor. . . .

Such minor complaints aren't fundamental to an appreciation of Salter's other stories, which are, to use that almost precious word, exquisite. It is the sort of work that should be, as with any masterpiece, approached with wonder and delight.

Robert Burke, "Life in Mid-Life," in The Bloomsbury Review, *Vol. 8, No. 3, May-June, 1988, pp. 3, 6.*

PETER WILD

Thrown from her horse and badly crushed a lone rider remembers her past lovers. Bored by success, two American lawyers try to expunge their world-weariness on their tour of Italy by picking up a schoolgirl. A well-off divorcée learns to her sadness that a lover has betrayed her. Such are the pangs in James Salter's [*Dusk and Other Stories*]. People fixate on love as life's antidote, only to end up rejected or victorious in the wrong bed.

It's not only that the characters keep "looking for love in in all the wrong places." What troubles here is the steady diet of self-absorption. One feels a bit awkward trying to believe that a lady just crushed by a horse would have little else on her mind than lost love. We may grant two lawyers their fling, but isn't there anything else in Italy to interest them beyond an easy pickup? Can't the divorcée find other matters to dwell on than one more affair gone awry? If not, we are dealing with personalities trivialized into bathos.

One could simply dismiss the book on that basis. One cannot dismiss, however, the technical excellence of the way Salter captures a city in sunset or a day in approaching Fall, or the way he maneuvers a character from one delicate scene to the next. Such abilities make the heart leap. But abilities to what end? The author weds his good writing to hackneyed and unrevealing situations. Mulling over Salter's novels, critics applaud a "pointillist style" unworthy of the choice of protagonists and bemoan Salter's "unearned lyricism that envelops . . . like Muzak." One sees with a disappointed twinge that the flaw has carried over into this latest work.

Peter Wild, in a review of "Dusk," in Western American Literature, *Vol. XXIII, No. 4, Winter, 1989, p. 375.*

Anne Tyler
Breathing Lessons

Award: Pulitzer Prize for fiction.

Born in 1941, Tyler is an American novelist, short story writer, critic, nonfiction writer, and editor.

Critics find Tyler at the height of her powers of observation in *Breathing Lessons* as she defines personality through small details and gestures and emphasizes the influence of a shared history on a marital relationship. Within a day-in-the-life framework augmented by flashbacks, she captures the nuances of compromise, disappointment, and love that make up Ira and Maggie Moran's marriage. The owner of a picture-framing store, Ira is uncommunicative and compulsively neat; Maggie is his warm, clumsy, talkative wife of nearly three decades. Intending to travel to Pennsylvania for a funeral on the Saturday morning of the novel's opening, and to return that afternoon, the couple spend most of the day on the road, making two extended sidetrips caused by Maggie's meddling in the affairs of strangers and relatives. Generously sprinkled with comic set-pieces that reveal her characters' foibles, *Breathing Lessons* has been called Tyler's funniest novel to date.

Breathing Lessons is Tyler's eleventh novel, her second to win a major literary award, following *The Accidental Tourist,* which received the National Book Critics Circle Award for fiction in 1985. Tyler generally organizes her works around a central, unifying metaphor that captures the essence of her idiosyncratic protagonists' means of coping with the world. The impact of the past on the present, the primacy of human relationships, and the ebullience of the human spirit are the mainstays of Tyler's understated fiction. Her dominant theme is the omnipresence of the past, but unlike William Faulkner or Eudora Welty, two outstanding practitioners in the Southern tradition with which she was originally associated, Tyler confines her inquiries to the impact of the personal past on the individual. While the absence of societal or political issues is often faulted by otherwise enthusiastic critics, Tyler's focus on the ebb and flow of relations between spouses, parents and their offspring, and among siblings is considered an important, even fascinating, complement to the body of contemporary literature.

(See also *CLC,* Vols. 7, 11, 18, 28, 44; *Contemporary Authors,* Vols. 9-12, rev. ed.; *Contemporary Authors New Revision Series,* Vol. 11; *Something about the Author,* Vol. 7; *Dictionary of Literary Biography,* Vol. 6; and *Dictionary of Literary Biography Yearbook: 1982.*)

PRINCIPAL WORKS

NOVELS

If Morning Ever Comes   1965
The Tin Can Tree   1966

A Slipping-Down Life   1970
The Clock Winder   1972
Celestial Navigation   1974
Searching for Caleb   1976
Earthly Possessions   1977
Morgan's Passing   1980
Dinner at the Homesick Restaurant   1982
The Accidental Tourist   1985
Breathing Lessons   1988

HILMA WOLITZER

This is Anne Tyler's gentlest and most charming novel and a paean to what is fast becoming a phenomenon—lasting marriage. Maggie and Ira Moran have been married 28 years; *Breathing Lessons* begins with their journey to attend the funeral of an old friend and their corresponding emotional journey toward one another. (p. 1)

Ira and Maggie are driving 90 miles north of Baltimore, to Deer Lick, Pa., to attend the funeral of the husband of Maggie's girlhood friend, Serena. It's hard to believe they'll ever get there in time. On the morning of their departure, Maggie picks up their just-repaired, elderly Dodge at a local body shop. On her way out of the shop, she hears what she believes is her son Jesse's estranged wife, Fiona, announcing on a radio talk show that she's remarrying, this time for security instead of love. In her distress and distraction, Maggie plows into a Pepsi truck and then drives away from the scene of the accident without stopping. She casually imparts this information to Ira as they set out on their trip; he also shortly discovers that she's forgotten to pack the road map and the instructions on how to get where they're going. Intent on all the intricate maneuvers of personal politics, Maggie has little time for the amenities.

The funeral (they *do* manage to arrive in time) turns out to be bizarrely funny and touching. . . . The friends who sang at Serena and Max's wedding years ago are asked to sing the same songs again at the church service for his funeral. With some reluctance—"But this is a funeral! It's not a . . . request program"—and not a little giddiness, they finally acquiesce. Except for Ira, whose sense of occasion and natural reticence keep him from participating. But the rest of them fervently sing "My Prayer," "Born to Be With You," and "Love Is a Many-Splendored Thing."

Maggie is saved from a quavering solo when Durwood Clegg, whom she once rejected in high school, joins her in mid-song. In that moment of rescue, Durwood takes on heroic proportions, and Ira seems like nothing less than a bad sport, a bad choice for a lifetime's partnership.

Ira has belated second thoughts about his life, too. Once he'd wanted to do medical research but was saddled by obligations to his selfish father and disturbed sisters. Now he runs the family's framing shop, supporting everyone. And although he loves Maggie, he can't understand her impetuousness, her impracticality. "She seemed to believe it was a sort of practice life, something she could afford to play around with as if they offered second and third chances to get it right."

There are scenes of wonderful tenderness and humor in **Breathing Lessons.** Max's funeral evokes memories of his wedding to Serena, "a mishmash of popular songs and Kahlil Gibran in an era when everyone else was still clinging to 'O Promise Me.' " As Serena puts on her bridal finery, Maggie asks how she can be certain she's chosen the right man. Serena explains, "It's just *time* to marry, that's all. I'm so tired of dating!" Maggie and Ira's own courtship, orchestrated by Maggie after an hilarious misunderstanding, seems just as arbitrary, rather than some fatal, romantic inevitability.

As always, Tyler's eye for the telling detail is keen—in the Dodge "there were loops of black and red wire sagging beneath the glove compartment; nudge them accidentally as you crossed your legs and you'd disconnect the radio." She captures all the absurd nuances of dieting, mapfolding and the familiar shorthand of married dialogue. But she doesn't ignore the larger issues or dismiss the darker side of things. Ira's eccentric, dependent relatives are seen as the awful burden they really are. And the mystery of who and what we become is examined with appropriate awe. (pp. 1, 9)

Maggie is so truly earnest and morally good that, like Ira, we can't help but accept her idiosyncracies and feel genuine affection for her and wish her well. Her work, after all, is not unlike the novelist's—she must try to make order, somehow, out of chaos. When she fails to do so (at least on a grand scale), when her manipulations of other people's lives don't quite work out, she settles, as we all must, for the evanescent peace or joy of the moment. This is an honest and lovely book. (p. 9)

Hilma Wolitzer, " 'Breathing Lessons': Anne Tyler's Tender Ode to Married Life," in Chicago Tribune—Books, *August 28, 1988, pp. 1, 9.*

RICHARD EDER

No Olympian or high-flying view for Anne Tyler's art and the people it invents. She is a low-flyer, a crop-duster, zooming in at head-height and lifting hats; skimming the ordinary because it provides certain essential kinds of humanity, sometimes catching a wing tip on it or blowing its dust into her engine; and finally, with all the risks, accomplishing a gleeful astonishment.

Her people are arrayed in comic eccentricity. But Tyler waives the preservative chill customary to such a thing. They perform as close as possible to life temperature. They are soft, sometimes too soft.

In almost any Tyler novel there are moments when the reader worries about the low altitude, wonders whether the humor and sentiment are getting perilously close to shtick, suspects that the characters are becoming so comfortable in their quirks as to forfeit movement.

It is Tyler's idiosyncratic form of authority. She gives her people no freedom to be anything but themselves. She never stops imagining them or listening for their possibilities. Sometimes she can't hear them and improvises—we sense a kind of shuffling—but it's not long before they are back in her ken and under orders: Your soil will not change; grow in it. Grow any way you want.

And how they grow. **Breathing Lessons** turns a fraying middle-class household into a mixture of picture palace and puzzle palace; a familiar place made new.

It is set in the 28-year marriage of Maggie and Ira Moran and told in the course of a day trip from their Baltimore home to the funeral of the husband of an old school friend. The marriage is the soil I mentioned, more thin than fertile, and seared by dry spells.

The story is about what grows there: a man and a woman who are two versions of the human condition, two different stories in the same story, like the old tales in which a father sends two children out in opposite directions to seek their fortunes and misfortunes. But Ira and Maggie are never apart. It is their opposite spirits that make their common life a painful, provident slog for the one; and a painful, cloudy passage of dragons and treasures for the other.

We start with what in another author's hands might be two stock figures. Ira is careful and methodical and conceals his warmth beneath a mystique of competence; Maggie is emotional, impulsive, interfering and sloppy.

Each is in a kind of mid-life anguish; Ira, because he gave up his hopes of being a doctor to run the family picture-framing business on behalf of his half-invalid father and two sisters; Maggie, because her two children are grown up and her granddaughter lives with her son's former wife.

Maggie's stock figure is only a starting point. When a friend counsels Maggie to learn to let go, she retorts: "I don't feel I'm letting go. I feel they're taking things from me." In her quixotic and far-fetched efforts to fight life's depredations, and in the repercussions these have on Ira's effortful equanimity, we get not only some of Tyler's most exuberant humor but two of her most moving and penetrating portraits.

The trip to Deer Lick, Pa., begins as it is to continue—in a comedy that, based as it is on a mixture of misadventure, misapprehension and unregenerate originality, is invariably a comedy of character.

Dressed to the nines, but already beginning to come unfastened, Maggie picks up the family car at the auto body shop. Hitting the accelerator instead of the brake, she has her fender mashed by a passing truck. Maggie, and everything she possesses or attempts, will always have dents. . . .

Eventually, [she and Ira] get to the funeral. Serena, the widow, has arranged it to be a replay of her youth and that of her former classmates. Each is assigned to sing one of the pop songs of their day; later, at the reception, a movie of her wedding is shown. The sequence is a remarkable blend of farce and poignancy beneath which we are made to feel the bareness of time and its dwindling choices.

The funeral scenes are intercut with the recollection of Maggie's and Ira's courtship, a phenomenon largely precipitated by another chain of Maggie's misapprehensions and impulses. It was a successful chain, as it happened. . . .

There are moments when Maggie's klutziness seems overloaded, when she is just too funny and inept. But they are minor defects in a portrait that is triumphant because Tyler neither judges Maggie and Ira nor indulges them. Comedy of her sort is the supreme form of kindness; it brings out an extraordinary depth of feeling.

Maggie and Ira—whose portrait is more sparing but equally vivid and compassionate—are not heroes, but they are, in a sense, heroic. It is the heroism of enduring. Each does a number of unforgivable things, but in a marriage that lasts, forgiveness is not the point. Going on to the next day is.

Breathing Lessons may not be Tyler's best book; it is not a comparison I am easy with. The flashbacks sometimes slow down her matchless way with the present tense. The softness is sometimes too noticeable.

On the other hand, it may be her funniest book. Maggie's extraordinary encounter with an old black motorist whose flamboyant disassociations outbid her own is one of the funniest sustained sequences of contemporary writing that I can think of. And there are moments when the struggle among Maggie, Ira, and the melancholy of time passing forms a fiery triangle more powerful and moving, I think, than anything she has done.

        Richard Eder, "*Crazy for Sighing and Crazy for Loving You,*" *in* Los Angeles Times Book Review, *September 11, 1988, p. 3.*

EDWARD HOAGLAND

Anne Tyler, who is blessedly prolific and graced with an effortless-seeming talent at describing whole rafts of intricately individualized people, might be described as a domestic novelist, one of that great line descending from Jane Austen. She is interested not in divorce or infidelity, but in marriage—not very much in isolation, estrangement, alienation and other fashionable concerns, but in courtship, child raising and filial responsibility. It's a hectic, clamorous focus for a writer to choose during the 1980's, and a mark of her competence that in this fractionated era she can write so well about blood links and family funerals, old friendships or the dogged pull of thwarted love, of blunted love affairs or marital mismatches that neither mend nor end. Her eye is kindly, wise and versatile (an eye that you would want on your jury if you ever had to stand trial), and after going at each new set of characters with authorial eagerness and an exuberant tumble of details, she tends to arrive at a set of conclusions about them that is a sort of golden mean.

Her interest is in families—drifters do not intrigue her—and yet it is the crimps and bends in people that appeal to her sympathy. She is touched by their lesions, by the quandaries, dissipated dreams and foundered ambitions that have rendered them pot-bound, because it isn't really the drifters (staples of American fiction since Melville's Ishmael and *Huckleberry Finn*) who break up a family so often as the homebodies who sink into inaction with a broken axle, seldom *saying* that they've lost hope, but dragging through the weekly round.

Thus Ms. Tyler loves meddlers, like Elizabeth in *The Clock Winder* (1972), Muriel in *The Accidental Tourist* (1985) and Maggie Moran in *Breathing Lessons,* her latest novel. If meddlers aren't enough to make things happen, she will throw in a pregnancy or abrupt bad luck or a death in the family, so that the clan must gather and confront one another. (p. 1)

Maggie, surprised by life, which did not live up to her honeymoon, has become an incorrigible prompter. She doesn't hesitate to reach across from the passenger seat and honk while her husband, Ira, is driving. And she has horned in to bring about the birth of her first grandchild by stopping a 17-year-old girl named Fiona at the door of an abortion clinic and steering her into marrying Maggie's son, Jesse, who is the father and, like Fiona, a dropout from high school. Maggie's motives are always mixed. She wants to get that new baby into her now stiflingly lifeless house, and does succeed in installing the young couple in the next room, with the baby and crib being placed in hers. Jesse, in black jeans, aspires to be a rock star to escape the drudging anonymity he sees as his father's fate, in a picture frame store. "I refuse to believe that I will die unknown," he tells Ira (but eight years later is a salesman at Chick's Cycle Shop). Fiona, after the inevitable blowup, soon moves away to the house of *her* mother—the dreadful Mrs. Stuckey—where Maggie follows to spy on the baby.

Maggie is daring, enterprising and indulges her habit of pouring her heart out to every listening stranger, which naturally infuriates Ira, who, uncommunicative to start with, has reached the point where Maggie can divine his moods only from the pop songs of the 1950's that he whistles. Besides whistling, his pleasure is playing solitaire. He had dreamed of working on the frontiers of medicine, but after he graduated from high school his father, complaining of a heart problem, dumped the little family business on him, as well as the duty of supporting two unmarriageable, unemployable sisters.

The sisters and the father still live over the shop, and "for the past several months now," as Ms. Tyler confides,

> Ira had been noticing the human race's wastefulness. People were squandering their lives, it seemed to him. They were splurging their energies on petty jealousies or vain ambitions or long-standing, bitter grudges. . . . He was fifty years old and had never accomplished one single act of consequence.

In reaction, he has become obsessed in his spare time with the efficiency of motors, mechanisms, heaters and appliances, going over and studying them in people's houses where he and Maggie are visiting, or else plunging into one of his solitaire games, which also have at their crux efficiency.

Maggie, by contrast, is working quite happily as an aide at a nursing home, a job she started when high school ended. Her wishful notion that her son would make a good husband and father is based on her memory of him feeding her soup with a spoon once when she was sick. But Ira takes a far more "realistic," severely disappointed view of Jesse, and silently watches Daisy, their daughter—who at 13 months had undertaken her own toilet training and by first grade was setting her alarm an hour early in order to iron and color-coordinate her outfit for school—grow away from them and head off for college. (p. 43)

The book's principal event is a 90-mile trip that Maggie and Ira make from Baltimore, where Ms. Tyler's characters almost always live, to a country town in Pennsylvania where a high school classmate has suddenly scheduled an elaborate funeral for her husband, a radio-ad salesman who has died pathetically soon after discovering that he had a brain tumor. In her grief and confusion Serena, the widow, expects the service to recapitulate their 1956 wedding, with Kahlil Gibran being read and Maggie and Ira singing "Love Is a Many Splendored Thing." The tumult of memories surrounding the funeral works Maggie into such a state that she gets Ira to lay his cards aside and make love to her in Serena's bedroom during the reception, until Serena catches them and kicks them out.

Ms. Tyler, who was born in 1941, has 10 previous books under her belt, which, as one reads through them, get better and better. Deceptively modest in theme, they have a frequent complement of middle-aged solitaire players, anxious grandparents, blocked bachelors, dysfunctional sisters or brothers, urgent snappish teen-agers wanting fame the week after tomorrow, unfortunate small children being raised by parents not quite fit for the project, or parents suffering the ultimate tragedy of the death of a child, and they have progressed from her early sentiment in *Celestial Navigation* (1974) that "sad people are the only real ones. They can tell you the truth about things." Maggie, although exasperating, isn't sad, and like the more passively benevolent Ezra Tull in *Dinner at the Homesick Restaurant* (1982), she is trying to make a difference, to connect or unite people, beat the drum for forgiveness and compromise. As Ira explains: "It's Maggie's weakness: She believes it's all right to alter people's lives. She thinks the people she loves are better than they really are, and so then she starts changing things around to suit her view of them."

In the amplitude of her talent, Ms. Tyler didn't hesitate to

enjoy her apprenticeship by writing novels on subjects like what might really happen if a bank robber seized you as a hostage in a holdup (*Earthly Possessions,*) or the mind of a girl who carves a rock singer's name on her forehead (*A Slipping-Down Life.*) One lark of a book (*Searching for Caleb*) starts out like this: "The fortune teller and her grandfather went to New York City on an Amtrak train, racketing along with their identical, peaky white faces set due north. The grandfather had left his hearing aid at home on the bureau."

But the fun of it all didn't prevent her from learning to stick right with her people, complicating their dilemmas, extracting their sorest memories and most tremulous delusions, not hastily moving on when their thought processes dragged or someone's fragile packet of self-esteem was shattered. In every book the reader is immersed in the frustrating alarums of a family—the Pikes, the Pecks, the Tulls, the Learys—and though Ms. Tyler's spare, stripped writing style resembles that of the so-called minimalists (most of whom are her contemporaries), she is unlike them because of the depth of her affections and the utter absence from her work of a fashionable contempt for life. (pp. 43-4)

It is the amenities of survival that concern her: merciful love, decent behavior in the face of the laming misunderstandings that afflict personal relations. As in *The Accidental Tourist,* she writes of worn, sad streets "where nothing went right for anyone, where the men had dead-end jobs or none at all and the women were running to fat and the children were turning out badly." Nevertheless, she loves the city, with its pearly-tinted sky over such a neighborhood, the whinnying of sound-track horses from the windows of the houses, the women who sweep their stoops even in the midst of a snowstorm and the lilac color of the air while they do so. . . .

The literature of resignation—of wisely settling for less than life had seemed to offer—is exemplified by Henry James among American writers. It is a theme more European than New World by tradition, but with the graying of America into middle age since World War II, it has gradually taken strong root here and become dominant among Ms. Tyler's generation. Macon Leary, the magnificently decent yet "ordinary" man in *The Accidental Tourist,* follows logic to its zany conclusion, and in doing this justifies the jerry-built or catch-as-catch-can nature of much of life, making us realize that we are probably missing people of mild temperament in our own acquaintance who are heroes too, if we had Ms. Tyler's eye for recognizing them. *Breathing Lessons* seems a slightly thinner mixture. It lacks a *Muriel,* for one thing: Muriel, the man-chaser and man-saver of *The Accidental Tourist,* ranks among the more endearing characters of postwar literature. But Maggie Moran's faith that crazy spells do not mean life itself is crazy is an affirmation.

Because Ms. Tyler is at the top of her powers, it's fair to wonder whether she has developed the kind of radiant, doubling dimension to her books that may enable them to outlast the seasons of their publication. Is she unblinking, for example? No, she is not unblinking. Her books contain scarcely a hint of the abscesses of racial friction that eat at the very neighborhoods she is devoting her working life to picturing. Her people are eerily virtuous, Quakerishly tolerant of all strangers, all races. And she touches upon sex so lightly, compared with her graphic realism on other matters, that her total portrait of motivation is tilted out of balance.

Deservedly successful, she has marked her progress by

changing her imprimatur on the copyright pages of her novels from "Anne Modarressi" to "Anne Tyler Modarressi" to "Anne Tyler Modarressi, et al." to "ATM, Inc." That would be fine, except that it strikes me that she has taken to prettifying the final pages of her novels too. And in *Breathing Lessons,* the comedies of Fiona's baby's delivery in the hospital and of Maggie's horrendously inept driving have been caricatured to unfunny slapstick, as if in an effort to corral extra readers. I don't believe Ms. Tyler should think she needs to tinker with her popularity. It is based upon the fact that she is very good at writing about old people, very good on young children, very good on teen-agers, very good on breadwinners and also stay-at-homes: that she is superb at picturing men and portraying women. (p. 44)

Edward Hoagland, *"About Maggie, Who Tried Too Hard,"* in The New York Times Book Review, September 11, 1988, pp. 1, 43-4.

ROBERT McPHILLIPS

In her ten novels, from *If Morning Ever Comes* through *The Accidental Tourist,* Anne Tyler has staked out a comfortable, self-contained fictional landscape recognizably her own. Having grown up in North Carolina and studied with Reynolds Price at Duke University, Tyler initially considered herself a Southern writer. Her first three novels—*Morning* (1964), *The Tin Can Tree* (1965) and *A Slipping-Down Life* (1970)— were set in North Carolina and bear, in their focus on the eccentricities of family life and the strong influence of the past upon the present, a resemblance to the Southern Gothic tradition of William Faulkner, Flannery O'Connor, Eudora Welty and, especially, Carson McCullers.

But Tyler never seemed fully committed to these conventions. If she is concerned with family, history seemingly interests her not at all. She doesn't share Faulkner's obsession with the South's perceived fall from an Edenic state of grace, after the Civil War, perhaps simply because she was born in Minneapolis. Neither is she attracted, like Faulkner and Welty, to the rich allure of Southern dialect or to the potentially garrulous oral tradition so common a staple of Southern narratives. Instead, her style is plain and gently comic. Finally, she avoids the temptation to create the fully grotesque characters we associate with Southern Gothic. Tyler's best characters are, to be sure, socially maladjusted flakes living with their own peculiar set of rules and emotional ticks; but they are, by and large, in their own idiosyncratic ways, approachable and familiar.

And so is Anne Tyler. The most benign of our novelists, she has forged a kind of trust with her readers, who come to her novels expecting to be comforted. And they invariably have been—at least up until now. *Breathing Lessons,* Tyler's eleventh novel, represents a subtle but discernible shift in tone that is likely to surprise her most devoted readers. Having long established a happy marriage with her readers, Tyler now forces them to face the fact that such pacts are founded as much upon compromise as upon romance. This novel's journey presents a vision of marriage as a very rocky road. Even the most faithful of readers may find it a similar trip. (p. 464)

Tyler's central concern with family as a kind of atemporal refuge where, for better or worse, long-lost children, siblings or even parents return for solace, is usually embodied in her

novels by a central organizing metaphor. The most successful of these is the restaurant maintained by Ezra Tull in *Dinner at the Homesick Restaurant* (1982). It serves as a haven "where people come just like a family to dinner," one to which Ezra's father returns after the death of the wife he abandoned thirty-five years earlier. The fact that the Tulls are never able to finish a meal in this homesick restaurant merely serves to underline the complexity of Tyler's vision of family. Tyler's families are invariably not happy, or never precisely so. They nonetheless remain the only dependable unit against which to gauge one's identity. And they usually contain figures, like Elizabeth Abbott [in Tyler's novel *The Clock Winder* (1972)] and Ezra Tull, who combine quixotic with pragmatic qualities, characters who, like Tyler as a novelist, are able to maintain, as if by magic, a sense of order in a universe prone to fragmentation and isolation.

In her best novels, Tyler convincingly expands the definition of family. *Breathing Lessons* shares many of the elements of these novels, though it is finally less sprawling and buoyantly comic, presenting a sourly diminished vision of the resilience of marriage. The action in this novel is limited to one day in the life of Maggie and Ira Moran, a couple in their late 40s, though it is an eventful one that will see both husband and wife re-examine the nature of their union. It is set in motion by the death of Max Gill, the husband of Maggie's closest friend, Serena. (pp. 464-65)

Tyler's strongest card is her ability to orchestrate brilliantly funny set pieces and to create exasperating but sympathetic characters. *Breathing Lessons,* in the first of its three sections, is strong on the former. A number of brief comic scenes—Maggie's accident, a stop at a coffee shop, an argument between husband and wife—build to the novel's strongest scene, Max's funeral and the reception that follows. Love and death are ingeniously juxtaposed when Serena insists that the funeral service re-create her wedding. This proves a mixed success. Ira refuses to sing his half of the duet that initiated their courtship and marriage, "Love Is a Many Splendored Thing," with Maggie. (A hammish old flame of Maggie's fills in for Ira, leaving her momentarily determined to drive back to Baltimore with him instead of her husband.) Similarly, Sugar, one of Serena's more snobbish friends, in the novel's most inspired comic touch, agrees to the scheme only if she can substitute another song for "Born to Be With You." Her choice is the hilariously sappy but apt Doris Day tune "Que Sera Sera."

At the reception afterward, the unexpected revival of Maggie and Ira's erotic life causes a fight with Serena and their dismissal from her house. This leaves a lot of the day left, and a lot of the novel. It also leaves one wondering how Tyler, after building to such an early and successful crescendo, will handle what is essentially a two-hundred-page denouement.

Here the book falters. While the narrative continues to move at a whirlwind pace (Tyler's control of her material as certain as ever), the material itself is less convincing. The novel's second section concerns another side trip instigated by Maggie, which centers around Daniel Otis, an elderly black man whose erratic driving, coupled with Maggie's own interference with her car's horn, causes Ira to swerve off the road. Maggie, determined to avenge this mishap, convinces Ira to pass the driver, whom she then informs that his front wheel is wobbling. Immediately repentant, however, Maggie insists they turn around and tell the driver, who has pulled to the side of the road, that they were mistaken. Nonetheless, the three end up at a garage because he is still convinced the tire is dangerous. Mr. Otis and Maggie exchange anecdotes on modern marriage that advance the novel's anatomization of that topic. But this episode underlines a weakness, inherent in Tyler's preference for the conventions of the romance over those of realism. Although Tyler's handling of this set piece is charming, it fails to confront directly to what extent both Maggie's aggression and guilt are racially motivated, while at the same time Mr. Otis eventually becomes merely a likable stereotype of the self-effacing black who defers to the greater wisdom of his white interlocutors.

Tyler has similar problems in a scene at an abortion clinic in the final section of the novel. Only this late in the book does the significance of its title emerge. It is Maggie, we discover, who took Fiona under her wing during her pregnancy, teaching her how to breathe properly during labor. First, though, she had to convince Fiona, at the ineffectual Jesse's urging, not to go through with a scheduled abortion. Maggie chooses to do so in front of a clinic being picketed by an anti-abortion group. Here, she assumes the role of nurturer. But once again, confronted with a controversial public issue, Tyler seems unsure of herself. While trying to dissuade Fiona from having the abortion, Maggie also spouts liberal platitudes at the antiabortion forces. Her shallow political rhetoric is unconvincing. The failure of this set piece, coupled with Maggie's ultimate failure to reunite the myopically self-centered couple, make "breathing lessons" a far less resonant controlling metaphor than those in her best novels.

Finally, the characters in *Breathing Lessons* disappoint. Ira takes his disillusionment with life out on his family. Given to playing solitaire, communicating with his wife only unconsciously through the songs he hums to himself, Ira lacks any of the redeeming charm we find in Tyler's most engaging male characters like Jeremy Pauling, the reclusive painter of *Celestial Navigation*, or Macon Leary of *The Accidental Tourist*, who writes travel guides for people like himself who would prefer to stay home. Maggie, who haplessly tries to reorganize people's lives with her exaggerations and white lies—which are usually undermined, at crucial points in the novel, by Ira's compulsion to tell the truth, however painful—is at first sympathetic. But her skirmishes with reality outside the claustrophobic confines of her family life make her resilience seem forced and finally insignificant. Tyler, moving outside of the conventions of the romance, fails in her attempt to invest Maggie with a genuine social conscience. This failure ultimately extends to the novel's more atemporal domestic realm as well. The Morans' two children, Jesse and Daisy—the latter remains largely off-stage as she packs to leave home for college the next day—as well as Fiona remain sullen and lifeless. Maggie's unflappable belief in their potential is not, alas, infectious.

Breathing Lessons is far less consoling and emotionally satisfying than any of Anne Tyler's novels since the slight *A Slipping-Down Life,* her weakest. While the reader is dazzled and entertained by the author's skillful manipulation of plot and her ability to continue to conjure up some of the funniest and most incisive scenes in contemporary American fiction, one is ultimately left feeling that Tyler has failed in her attempt to broaden her fictional universe, to combine successfully the conventions of social realism with those of the romance, as Hawthorne himself was able to do in *The Scarlet Letter, The House of the Seven Gables* and, somewhat more tentatively in *The Blithedale Romance*. In the past, Tyler has used her

magic to illuminate seemingly drab lives. Here, she forces one to confront directly lives that even willful magic can't fully alleviate. (pp. 465-66)

Robert McPhillips, "The Baltimore Chop," in The Nation, *New York, Vol. 247, No. 13, November 7, 1988, pp. 464-66.*

ROBERT TOWERS

[In] Anne Tyler's novels, sympathetic recognition of her characters comes almost too easily, even as their expected oddity holds out the promise of small surprises. Like the *Rabbit* novels of John Updike, her books expertly render a familiar world in which our own observations are played back to us, slightly magnified, and with an enhanced clarity. Anne Tyler seems to know all there is to know about the surfaces of contemporary middle-middle- to lower-middle-class life in America, and if she chooses not to explore the abysses, she is nonetheless able to dramatize—often memorably—the ordinary crises of domestic life, of marriage and separation, of young love, parenthood, and even death. Though her style lacks Updike's metaphoric glitter, it has a strength and suppleness of its own. She can also be very funny.

In her recent novels—*Dinner at the Homesick Restaurant* and *The Accidental Tourist*—she has seemed at her best. The latter novel, particularly, is a luminous book. Beginning with the senseless murder of a twelve-year-old boy, it traces, with psychological cunning and humor, the steps of the boy's eccentric and obsessive father as he blunders his way toward a new life. Her eleventh novel, *Breathing Lessons,* strikes me as less substantial, more susceptible to the tendencies to whimsicality and even cuteness that sometimes affect her work. It is nonetheless shrewd in its insights and touching in its tragicomic vision of familial hopes and disappointments.

Breathing Lessons begins in absurdity. A middle-aged housewife, Maggie Moran, goes to a repair shop to pick up their car so that she and her husband Ira can drive from Baltimore to a funeral in Deer Lick, Pennsylvania.

> She was wearing her best dress—blue and white sprigged, with cape sleeves—and crisp black pumps, on account of the funeral. The pumps were only medium-heeled but slowed her down some anyway. . . . Another problem was that the crotch of her panty hose had somehow slipped to about the middle of her thighs, so she had to take shortened, unnaturally level steps like a chunky little wind-up toy wheeling along the sidewalk.

As she is leaving the body shop, Maggie hears on the car radio what she takes to be the voice of Fiona, her ex-daughter-in-law, announcing on a talk show her intention to remarry—this time for security instead of love. Meaning to brake, Maggie accelerates instead and runs in front of a Pepsi truck that smashes into her left-front fender—"the only spot that had never, up till now, had the slightest thing go wrong with it."

Such is the start of what turns out to be a very full day in the lives of the warm-hearted and scatterbrained Maggie and cranky, taciturn Ira. (pp. 40-1)

I can think of no one who captures the flavor of car travel in America today better than Anne Tyler—the attempt to pass an oil truck, disputes over directions, a stop at a roadside grocery-café ("The café lay at the rear—one long counter, with faded color photo of orange scrambled eggs and beige link sausages lining the wall behind it"), where Maggie, who loves to spill out her life's story to strangers, engages in a heartfelt conversation with a sympathetic waitress and in a long flashback recalls an elegant old man whom she had loved in the nursing home where she now works. The couple finally arrives at the church in Deer Lick where they are informed by the widowed Serena that she has invited to the funeral all of the old friends who had attended her wedding and that they are all expected to sing the same 1950s songs that they had sung then. When Maggie and Ira are asked to sing "Love is a Many-Splendored Thing," Ira balks. What follows is a comical set piece, including, after the funeral, the showing of a movie of Serena and Max's wedding years ago, and the attempt, which is interrupted, of Maggie and Ira to have a "quickie" in Serena's bedroom while the funeral reception is going on downstairs.

It was at this point that I felt that Anne Tyler had allowed her novel to slip into whimsy and slapstick. While the unconventional Serena, with her mixed feelings about her husband's illness and death, is carefully drawn, the funeral itself and its aftermath are simply preposterous. I was relieved to get back onto the highway, to see things from Ira's cooler point of view for a change, and to move on to the family drama involving Fiona, Jesse, and Leroy that occupies the final hundred and fifty pages of *Breathing Lessons.* We do not know until nearly the end whether Maggie's irrepressible determination to make everything work out is doomed or not.

Maggie is presented as a meddler in other people's lives but a lovable one. Tyler invites the reader to participate in Maggie's schemes, to laugh at her misadventures and miscalculations, but also to admire her resiliency. And for the most part one goes along. But Maggie sometimes seems too broad in relation to the much subtler handling of the other characters— she is too awkward, too silly, to carry the burden that has been assigned to her. The sentimentality in the conception of her character becomes an irritation.

Ira, on the other hand, displays that firmness of outline and richness of specification that we associate with Anne Tyler's most successful characters—especially her quirky men. Ira is presented as a gruff failure, frustrated in his ambitions, exasperated by his "whifflehead" wife, disappointed in his feckless son, saddened by the humorlessness of his overachieving daughter. He had wanted to be a doctor but has ended up running a framing shop which he had to take over when his father, declaring himself disabled by heart trouble, gave up the attempt to support himself and his two incapacitated daughters. Ira now supports all three of them as well as his immediate family. He makes fun of Maggie's vagaries, plays solitaire, and maintains long silences. Yet he is shown to be capable of complex feelings of tenderness even when most irritated by his family.

> He had a vivid memory of Jesse as he'd looked the night he was arrested, back when he was sixteen. He'd been picked up for public drunkenness with several of his friends—a onetime occurrence, as it turned out, but Ira had wanted to make sure of that and so, intending to be hard on him, he had insisted Maggie stay home while he went down alone to post bail. He had sat on a bench in a public waiting area and finally there came Jesse, walking doubled over between two officers. Evidently his wrists had been handcuffed behind his back and he had at-

tempted, at some point, to step through the circle of his own arms so as to bring his hands in front of him. But he had given up or been interrupted halfway through the maneuver, and so he hobbled out lopsided, twisted like a sideshow freak with his wrists trapped between his legs. Ira had experienced the most complicated mingling of emotions at the sight: anger at his son and anger at the authorities too, for exhibiting Jesse's humiliation, and a wild impulse to laugh and an aching, flooding sense of pity.

It is writing of this authority and delicacy that justifies the admiration accorded to Anne Tyler's work—and redeems *Breathing Lessons* from the excesses of its whimsy. (p. 41)

Robert Towers, "Roughing It," in The New York Review of Books, *Vol. XXXV, No. 17, November 10, 1988, pp. 40-1.*

HOPE HALE DAVIS

Up to now Tyler has given us irresistible "idiosyncratic characters who amble about in Chekhovian fashion," as a reviewer of *The Clock Winder* described them. Fantastic as these endearing oddballs may be, the world they live in is no never-never-land. Unequipped to manage in it, they can sometimes be saved by meeting the right unlikely person. We exult in the happy ending, which seems almost too good to be true. And indeed it may be. An amazingly bountiful one is offered Jeremy, the preoccupied artist who strives to cope with real-life demands in *Celestial Navigation,* but it is taken away again, through simple and unbearable human misunderstanding. In *Dinner at the Homesick Restaurant* Ezra tries time after time to put on a festive family reunion, but concludes in the end, "I really, honestly believe I missed some rule that everyone else takes for granted; I must have been absent from school that day."

The readers who so quickly made *Breathing Lessons* a best seller must have expected some similar memorably loving hero. They had recently read *The Accidental Tourist,* laughing while taking in its message (running like a warm undercurrent through all the earlier works) that nobody can be too offbeat to win some discerning soul. Looking forward to her next novel with such anticipation, have they been a little let down by *Breathing Lessons*? Here the eccentrics are only minor characters acting in small comic set pieces along the way, not moving spirits like James in *Tin Can Tree* or Morgan in *Morgan's Passing,* who spends not only his life but even his pseudo-death impersonating.

For all its incidental flashes of inspiration and comedy, [*Breathing Lessons*] gave me a sense of slackening, even of retreat. It opens, in fact, with a stale, statistically way-off male chauvinist cliché. In a farcical scene where Tyler's humor is surprisingly labored, Maggie retrieves the car from the body shop that has just repaired the latest of her crumplings, and (distracted by a voice on a call-in radio show that she thinks is her daughter-in-law's) promptly heads out into the path of a passing truck.

The sexist slander becomes worse: Maggie makes an irresponsible escape, and then within minutes is pretending to search in her hopeless handbag for a map she doesn't dare admit she has left at home. (This is an almost identical repeat of a scene in *Searching for Caleb.*) A few miles farther on, at a stop for a snack, to the distress of Ira, Maggie confides to the café waitress a detailed family history. Though she sometimes slips out of character and exposes the brain of her author, here Maggie is exactly what her husband calls her, a whiffle-head.

Tyler clearly is no feminist, seeing half of humanity good and the other half villainous. This is mostly a virtue, except that female subjugation is merely one of the monstrous social facts and threats of which Tyler has seemed virtually oblivious throughout her writing. In *Breathing Lessons* Maggie prevents Fiona's abortion at a clinic where patients are harassed by a mob of Right-to-Lifers, whose behavior and dubious propaganda show Tyler as close as she has ever come to taking a social position. Yet Maggie is there for strictly personal reasons, preoccupied by the fibs she must tell to make sure her grandchild will be born. Tyler presents a black in this novel, but only in one of her comic divertissements, and he is a sweetly subservient oldtimer with an IQ of 50.

The lives of Tyler's characters, including the better-educated ones, are affected solely by other individuals. She does know that when they make up a family, the change is qualitative, the family group becomes a force, sometimes malign. She demonstrates this so well that she captures—yes, captivates—us within her smaller world. What she reveals is how rare and precious goodness is, in man or woman, how fragile its carriers. And how someone of either sex can be an exploiter, or a victim, for reasons that are more complex than gender.

Breathing Lessons is mainly Maggie's story, but she is presented as a questionable heroine. Maddening as Ira's withholding can be (it has crushed the development of his son), Tyler shows his life of quiet sacrifice, running his father's framing shop to support his inadequate sisters. For a few brief minutes she takes us into his mind:

> He was fifty years old and had never accomplished one single act of consequence. Once he had planned to find a cure for some major disease and now he was framing petit point.

He is as disappointed in his over-achieving daughter heading toward Ivy-land as in his underachieving son, a failing rock singer much like Drumstrings Casey, the anti-hero of *A Slipping-Down Life.* We see Maggie also from Ira's painful point of view:

> He loved her, but he couldn't stand how she refused to take life seriously. She seemed to believe it was a sort of practice life, something she could afford to play around with as if offered second and third chances to get it right. She was always making clumsy, impetuous rushes toward nowhere in particular—side trips, random detours.

Actually, what Maggie is trying to get right on the day of this story is their current life. With the unwilling Ira she carries out a scheme meant to end the separation of their son from his wife and retrieve the lost relationship with Leroy, the granddaughter. Maggie's campaign is Tyleresque, precipitating unexpected comedy. But it involves a problem that is far from comic, one Tyler's characters have struggled with before: Do you dare to take action that affects the course of other people's lives?

In *Celestial Navigation* a spinster who rooms in hapless Jeremy's house overcomes her inhibition and takes a step that permits the happy turn of events, yet can't bring herself to

intervene again, thus letting it fail. In *Searching for Caleb* Justine tries to get the 17-year-old daughter to ride in the U-Haul truck with her father, whom the girl can't forgive for this restless move that is wrenching her away from her school only months before graduation. Justine castigates her own lack of tact or subtlety: "She never would let a quarrel wind up in its natural way. . . . She always had to be interfering."

Meddling is by no means the ruling theme in Tyler's novels, however. Within the limits she has set herself, watching ordinary people anyone might meet, she has also set a goal—the goal of all great writers—to show that even the most infuriating of humans, closely observed, from within and without, can become important, essential, precious. In *Dinner at the Homesick Restaurant* Ezra is faithfully taking care of his difficult mother who has alienated her other sons and daughters. Blind and lonely, she requires him to read aloud from her old diaries. I can't remember encountering a more poignant scene than the one in which he reads an entry revealing her ecstasy and promise at age 18.

So perceptive is Tyler's ear that within their context inarticulate responses like "I see," "Not at all," or "Huh?" can carry deep foreboding. We feel a sense of irreparable loss from a quiet voice saying, "Oh."

Not all Tyler's effects come from hints and auguries. She allows her characters sudden rare conclusions, direct and sweeping. During one flashback in *Breathing Lessons* Maggie recalls the widow Serena as a highly practical bride, buying a wedding dress that could be dyed purple to wear later, and considering whether she could rent (like a bartender) a man to stand in for her unknown father. When Maggie protests at her lack of romanticism about the groom Serena says calmly, "Of course I love him. But I've loved other people as much. I loved Terry Simpson in our sophomore year—remember him? But it wasn't time to get married then, so Terry is not the one I'm marrying."

Tyler permits a pause for reflection, then continues: "So there again, Serena had managed to color Maggie's view of things. 'We're not in the hands of fate after all,' she seemed to be saying. 'Or if we are, we can wrest ourselves free any time we care to.' "

True or false? This may be Tyler's mischievous game. (pp. 19-21)

Hope Hale Davis, "Watching the Ordinary People," in The New Leader, *Vol. LXXI, No. 20, November 28, 1988, pp. 19-21.*

HERMIONE LEE

Things fall sensationally apart in Anne Tyler's accident-prone lives. 'I feel like we're just flying apart!' cries Maggie Moran, the heroine of her enchantingly peculiar new novel, *Breathing Lessons.* Like all Tyler's people, Maggie knows what this feels like, has plenty to say about it, but can't quite find the words: 'All my friends and relatives just flying off from me like the expanding universe or something!'

The titles of earlier novels—*A Slipping-Down Life, The Accidental Tourist*—tell the same story. Their characters feel 'like things are just petering out all around me'; they can't think of a 'single major act' that didn't just 'befall' them. Errors, mishaps, coincidences and recurrences shape their lives.

But, busily pushing against the entropy of 'happenstance' is their desire to control or change their lives. They can be insatiably curious about other people: 'Dying, you don't get to see how it all turns out,' says Pearl, the organising mother in **Dinner At the Homesick Restaurant.** Like her they all over-arrange. (Tyler is very good at obsessively anal types, like the sister in **The Accidental Tourist** who files the groceries alphabetically: 'E for Elbow Marconi'.) They try frantically to prevent whatever surrounds them from 'dissolving in the outside world'.

Maggie, who has only to see a group of strange women talking in the street to have 'a left-out, covetous feeling', is Tyler's most inept and irrepressible fixer, generating a wonderfully unpredictable comedy of errors by her refusal to accept realities. Her stoical husband Ira (who shows his own neurosis for order by his compulsive games of solitaire) is amazed at Maggie's belief that 'it's all right to alter people's lives.' She seems to him to be living a 'practice life'. But there are no 'breathing lessons' for being alive (as there are for pregnant women). So Maggie's life is, breathlessly, all 'side trips and random detours'.

The narrative, breathless itself with rapid incident, sharp detail and floods of talk, plays havoc with the well-tried formula of a day-in-the-life. Maggie and Ira are setting out for a 90-mile trip from his picture-framer's shop in Baltimore (Tyler's usual stamping-ground) to the funeral of Maggie's best friend's husband, which turns out to be a bizarre and pathetic replay of their 1950s wedding ceremony. . . .

While Ira imagines other couples on their day out 'travelling from Point A to Point B . . . holding civilized discussions about, I don't know, current events. Disarmament. Apartheid,' their own journey, after a marvellously untoward and prolonged encounter with an old man in a wandering Chevy, takes on an increasingly diversionary nature. Maggie's unplanned goal, it transpires, is the reconciliation of her rock-playing son Jesse and his runaway wife. . . .

The whole thing teeters on the edge of being cute, but Tyler's sense of the sadness of things prevents it. All the marriages (including Maggie and Ira's) are painful and melancholy. The old man in the Chevy reveals a lifetime of quarrelling: 'Pretty soon,' his nephew tells him, 'one or the other of you is going to die and the one that's left behind will say, why did I act so ugly?' Bleakest of all is Ira's family, his dependent father and two backward sisters. Their marvellously gruesome outings fill him with suffocating emotions of failure, panic and gloomy love.

In **The Tin Can Tree** a photographer is asked if there is 'such a thing as X-ray cameras. Could you take a picture of our house, like, and have the people show up from inside?' Tyler's novels take that X-ray. She is in the best tradition of a provincial, democratic American fiction by women—Eudora Welty or Flannery O'Connor in the South; and Gertrude Stein, whose *Three Lives* also used Baltimore for idiosyncratic fiction—which takes the lid off ordinary-looking lives and shows how they work. She is remarkable.

> Hermione Lee, "Made in Baltimore," in The Observer, *January 15, 1989, p. 48.*

CAROLE ANGIER

[Anne Tyler's] great quality is minute, true, funny-painful observation. The little tragedies of life are her speciality: the way that people's natural pace seems to be out of step with

---

An excerpt from *Breathing Lessons*

He frowned at the road ahead of him. "Um," he said. "You don't suppose she wants me to be a pallbearer or something, do you?"

"She didn't mention it."

"But she told you she needed our help."

"I think she meant moral support," Maggie said.

"Maybe pallbearing is moral support."

"Wouldn't that be physical support?"

"Well, maybe," Ira said.

They sailed through a small town where groups of little shops broke up the pastures. Several women stood next to a mailbox, talking. Maggie turned her head to watch them. She had a left-out, covetous feeling, as if they were people she knew.

"If she wants me to be a pallbearer I'm not dressed right," Ira said.

"Certainly you're dressed right."

"I'm not wearing a black suit," he said.

"You don't own a black suit."

"I'm in navy."

"Navy's fine."

"Also I've got that trick back."

She glanced at him.

"And it's not as if I was ever very close to him," he said.

Maggie reached over to the steering wheel and laid a hand on his. "Never mind," she told him. "I bet anything she wants us just to be sitting there."

He gave her a rueful grin, really no more than a tuck of the cheek.

How peculiar he was about death! He couldn't handle even minor illness and had found reasons to stay away from the hospital the time she had her appendix out; he claimed he'd caught a cold and might infect her. Whenever one of the children fell sick he'd pretended it wasn't happening. He'd told her she was imagining things. Any hint that he wouldn't live forever—when he had to deal with life insurance, for instance—made him grow set-faced and stubborn and resentful. Maggie, on the other hand, worried she *would* live forever—maybe because of all she'd seen at the home.

And if she were the one who died first, he would probably pretend that that hadn't happened, either. He would probably just go on about his business, whistling a tune the same as always.

What tune would he be whistling?

one another. She's especially good on marriage. On how pride blocks love, making the young couple [in *Breathing Lessons*] hide the one thing that would bring them together; on how opposite natures are both necessary and impossible to each other, making the older couple's marriage "as steady as a tree", and yet one long quarrel.

In part one of *Breathing Lessons,* the older couple go to a friend's funeral, which his widow turns into a replay of their wedding. This is, like much else in the book, high farce; it is also a painfully accurate picture of American tastelessness. But most of all, perhaps, it's an image of the novel's subject, which is marriage, or life: of its circularity and absurdity; of the endless desire to come together, the endless fact of being apart.

The older couple are Maggie and Ira Moran. They're wonderful—aging, absurd, absolutely real. Maggie is emotionally profligate, all over the place with love. She longs for everybody to be happy, and incorrigibly fixes the facts to make them so. She's an arch-female, and arch-mother—wholly attuned to hope and need, deaf and blind to limitations. So she's a klutz, and the novel is a comedy of errors and embarrassments. Ira is the opposite. He is detached and isolated; he never says what he feels—though, in a marvellous touch, he gives it away in the tunes he whistles. Where Maggie accepts too little of reality, he accepts too much. What Maggie doesn't destroy of their son's happiness by pretending, Ira destroys by telling the truth. *He* is the arch-male, the arch-father; I hated and loved him, just as Maggie does.

For me, at least, the young couple—the Morans' son Jesse and his child-wife Fiona—are less successful. They don't just seem young and callow, but plain uninteresting. I don't *think* this is Anne Tyler's fault; I think it's mine. I fear I'm not interested in American youth, with their hedonism, their short attention span, their uncouth language.

That is, in general, my one difficulty with Anne Tyler. She is, like Maggie, prepared to love everyone; I'm more like Ira, an old grump. I just don't find the awful but simple Tulls (*Dinner at the Homesick Restaurant*) as interesting as the awful but complicated Learys (*The Accidental Tourist*); and I don't find Jesse and Fiona a patch on Ira and Maggie. So there's a doubt at the heart of this novel for me; and a sense of decline, not hope, in the march of the generations. Anne Tyler is on Maggie's side, the side of foolish hope. I'd like to agree, when old Mr Otis says: "Spill it! Spill it all, I say! No way *not* to spill it". But Anne Tyler has done too good a job on Serena, who greets menopause with relief, and on sad, dignified, truthful Ira. I hang back with him, and wonder.

Carole Angier, "Small City America," in New Statesman & Society, Vol. 2, No. 33, January 20, 1989, p. 34.

ANITA BROOKNER

Anne Tyler's subject matter, carefully chosen and faithfully adhered to, consists of the domestic life of the under-achiever, usually in Baltimore, sometimes straying into Pennsylvania or South Carolina. In this she resembles the chroniclers of the Dirty Realist school, whose numb, glum narratives evoke a resonant ache for diners, used-car lots, frame houses, and front porches in the mosquito-zinging dusk. The effect of all this is to mine a vein of homesickness for things which were in fact never perfect, in which marriages, casually contracted, drift apart in a welter of broken appliances and against a background of popular music. This music tends to whine, as do most of the characters. Anne Tyler stands apart from other practitioners of the genre because she is cheerfully nostalgic, celebrating a tackiness which she gives every sign of enjoying. She is an affectionate and comedic writer whose best novel, *The Accidental Tourist,* now being made into a film, gave enormous encouragement to those who habitually wear the wrong clothes and whose cars, when driven with less than total care, sound like collapsing beer cans.

She may, however, have done it once too often, or relied too heavily on the indulgence of her readers. *Breathing Lessons* charts a day in the life of Ira and Maggie Moran, who set out one morning for the funeral of Maggie's best friend's husband. Serena, the friend, was always unusual and has remained so: her idea is to run the funeral as a replay of her wedding service, with Maggie singing 'Love is a Many-Splendoured Thing'. . . .

Nostalgia reigns back at Serena's house, but the day is only half way through, and Maggie has other plans. She has heard, on a radio phone-in, the voice of someone whom she recognises as her former daughter-in-law Fiona, announcing that although her first marriage was for love her second will be for security. This alerts Maggie to the fact that she must reclaim Fiona for that first marriage (to her son, Jesse) before the poor girl ends up being secure. No matter that Jesse, in his motorcycle gear, plays in an unsuccessful rock band and has never been able to hold down a job. There is a granddaughter in the case, and all Maggie has to do is to bring the family together again, although this will mean a considerable detour to Cartwheel, Pennsylvania.

Maggie has already smashed the fender of the car getting it out of the garage, and on the way to Cartwheel, taking exception to an elderly Chevy trying to pass her (this novel is probably best read by drivers) shouts at the offender that his front wheel is loose. She then sees that he is an old man, and black. Trying to explain to him that his front wheel is not in fact loose proves impossible; there is nothing for it but to take him to the service station where his nephew works and which happens to be some miles distant. Maggie, one of those slapdash characters who is meant to be lovable, strikes up a friendship with the old man. . . .

From the service station it is but a few more miles to Cartwheel, Pennsylvania, where Fiona and her daughter are reluctantly embarked for a family reunion back in Baltimore. Jesse is hijacked into turning up for dinner. In fact Jesse and Fiona have nothing to say to each other, and the pretexts Maggie has assembled to prove to them that they are still in love predictably collapse. Fiona and her daughter exit into the night and Ira and Maggie are left alone. By this time the reader's sympathies are with Fiona, or with Ira. With everyone but Maggie, in fact.

All this is spun out cheerily over 327 pages and is intermittently very funny. The reader is charmed into indulgence by the skill with which the narrative is played out, although impatience erupts from time to time, along with a feeling of acute physical discomfort (Maggie's dress is sticking to her, she still has to pick up something for dinner, the boot of the old man's car is packed solid with blankets). But Anne Tyler can do all this better and has done so. *Breathing Lessons* relies too much on the supposed charm of the characters, particularly that of the heroine, at whom I wanted to take a swipe. A little more anguish, of which there is a hint, might have grounded it. But for those longing for an easy read, this is just the thing to make the new year feel comfortable.

Anita Brookner, "Things Fall Apart and Cannot Be Glued," in The Spectator, *Vol. 262, No. 8375, January 21, 1989, p. 36.*

ELIZABETH BEVERLY

Walking into the wide but comfortable expanse of an Anne Tyler novel can feel like settling down into a porch swing on a late summer evening. The neighbors on the porch next door begin to talk as the swing easily glides. . . .

Imagine the ease of sitting in a porch swing and hearing not only the neighbors' conversation, but overhearing the minds of the neighbors as they sit in silence, unable or unwilling to speak, yearning to make sense of their particular lot.

The minds we overhear in Tyler's eleventh novel, *Breathing Lessons,* belong to Maggie and Ira Moran on a late summer Saturday, as the middle-aged couple drive out of their ordinary suburban Baltimore life to the funeral of Maggie's best friend's husband in rural Pennsylvania. The trip to the mid-morning service should be easy enough, Ira should even be back in time to open his framing shop for afternoon business, but before departure, on page five, as Maggie drives out of the auto body shop, she hears a voice on the radio that sends her lurching into the street, into a new minor accident that seems to loosen everything: the previously intact fender, the past, hopes for the future, faith in her marriage, longing for the grandchild whom the couple haven't seen in years. Just as the car can't stay fixed, the day's tidy plans crumble, and a quest begins.

Breathing Lessons is the story of that quest, modest by the standards of imaginative literature, but deeply felt. As Maggie and Ira undertake this rather haphazard daylong journey, we realize from their cascading memories and hopes that they are both in search of nothing less than the meaning of family. But even as I write these words, I sense that I am making Tyler's novel sound much more earnest than it really is. In fact, the narrative ambles easily, delightfully, at times preposterously. The sure prose, the wonderful telling details, the concerns of busybody Maggie and silent, kind Ira create a world in which we can remain interested, intrigued perhaps, but undisturbed. . . .

Should this bother us? Does the novelist owe the reader a kick in the pants? Should a reviewer criticize a gifted novelist for seeming to refuse the high moral charge of art? No, no, and no! But what about the characters whose lives we've followed so faithfully? What does the novelist owe them? Should they exist simply for our amusement and then be put cozily to bed at day's end before the novelist has even begun to engage in the heartfelt pain they've expressed?

There are no answers to these questions, but if it occurs to a reader to raise such questions at all, to imagine that characters are trapped by the very form that creates them, then we're in the presence of an oddly skewed work, one which raises expectations it has no intention of meeting. The problem is not that the book veers to whimsy, but more that the easy, whimsical tone creates a false sense of peace and thereby devalues the actual longing which rips through the hearts of the characters for whom we care.

I believe that the skewing begins with the conceptualization of Maggie, in whose mind we ride throughout two of the three major sections of the novel. As soon as we meet her on her unsteady way to the body shop, we suspect we shall like her. As soon as we meet her, we learn to laugh with her and at her. (p. 120)

Chunky little Maggie wheels right through the day; she's more scatterbrained than eccentric, more endearing than downright lovable, more "inventive" than simply dishonest. We stick with her because she's funny, always on the verge of amazement, and takes herself half seriously. But not seriously enough, if we're to believe Ira. And we do believe Ira. By the time we are allowed into Ira's head, we find that "he loved her, but he couldn't stand how she refused to take her own life seriously. She seemed to believe it was sort of a practice life, something she could afford to play around with as if they offered second and third chances to get it right."

Ira's insight evolves from his conviction that human life is full of waste, particularly poignant since Ira's youthful ambition to become a doctor was swallowed years earlier by the obligations he assumed for his family, not only for Maggie and their children, but also for his weak father and two dependent sisters, one developmentally disabled, the other emotionally so. The fact that Ira's section occupies the physical center of the novel seems to be no accident. The more sober of the two main characters, he provides the weight to hold the narrative on course. Or he ought to. But the novel itself is Maggie's own crazily conceived course. She is the one who sees what to do, where to go, proceeds through the day and, we suspect, through life, with the only authority this family knows.

This authority gets her into trouble, makes her appear ridiculous: to Ira, to her children, to us. About her kindly meant deceptions, Ira asserts, "It's Maggie's weakness: She believes it's all right to alter people's lives. She thinks the people she loves are better than they really are, and so then she starts changing things around to suit her view of them."

Certain novelists could be described in the same way as Maggie, but I suspect that Tyler agrees with Ira about the suitability of such imaginative whim. I think she believes that the lives she has invented for Maggie and Ira are simply what they are. There is no changing them. It's as if Maggie, Tyler's creation, has more faith in herself and in the world than Tyler herself does. Tyler's world, full of the wonders of language and the tenacity of hope, is an insistently secular world. During the course of the novel, we sit through a funeral designed to make a widow feel better, a wedding rehearsal, a film of a wedding, some choir practice, a few moments in church. But nothing sacred disturbs the quality of these lives. It's no surprise that Maggie's longing for family union seems at moments almost monstrous. There is no promise of any greater union than that expressed in amicable silence. . . .

And so the novel closes with Ira playing solitaire on his side of the bed, and Maggie settling down on her side of the bed. Perhaps Tyler wants us to believe this cozy separation is happiness, that Maggie's ambition is unrealistic, therefore laughable. Perhaps she wants us to recognize that comfort doesn't depend upon how such a day ultimately turns out, but upon the fact that such a day can happen at all, that past, future, and present can occasionally stream through us all at once, and make life appear full and rich and possible.

If this is the case, then it is a mercy that Maggie can so simply close down and go to sleep. But I feel bad that by the end of Maggie's novel I can take her no more seriously than Ira or even Tyler. For she is a neighbor who would want to make my life better if she could, if only I could let her words reach me, disturb me, wake me from my nightlong, easy swing. (p. 121)

Elizabeth Beverly, "The Tidy Plans That Crumbled," in Commonweal, *Vol. CXVI, No. 4, February 24, 1989, pp. 120-21.*

DEAN FLOWER

There's no doubt about it, Anne Tyler has a gift for barbaric yawp. That's the energy behind her fiction. She does not seem to use a voice of her own, just lets us listen in on her characters' conversations, reveries and internal monologues. Character after character crowds into the action, talking herself into existence. Or himself, except that the males are more often silent types. We have to overhear their thoughts, like Macon's in *The Accidental Tourist* (1985) or Ezra's in *Dinner at the Homesick Restaurant* (1983). Tyler likes to play off these inarticulate men, who know little about themselves—and want to know less—against women who love to talk, blurt out what they feel, and make things happen. *Breathing Lessons,* Tyler's eleventh novel and one of her funniest, depends greatly on this device. Maggie and Ira Moran have been married for twenty-eight years; she is full of good intentions but meddlesome, pawky, curious, scatterbrained, a charming mixture of shrewd and daffy. Ira tries and fails to be patient with her, not surprisingly, for she is the sort of woman who always penetrates his silences. Typically, Maggie will seize upon the words of a song Ira happens to be whistling (e.g., "Crazy") and accuse him of comments he never thought he made.

Tyler sends her couple on a 90-mile car trip from Baltimore to small town Pennsylvania and back, a journey that takes in (a) a fender-bender, (b) several quarrels, (c) a trial separation lasting about 30 minutes, (d) a funeral staged as a high school reunion, (e) coitus interruptus in the widow's bedroom, (f) another near accident on the road, (g) a detour into the life of an old black man, and (h) another detour into the lives of Fiona, Maggie's ex-daughter-in-law, and her granddaughter, Leroy. But that is just what happens in the present tense. Much of the story emerges in the lulls when memories take over—the evening Maggie spent on the phone answering a wrong number, for example, or the day she persuaded Fiona not to have an abortion, or the time Ira took his reclusive father and sisters to their first shopping mall. Since all but fifty pages of the novel are from Maggie's point of view, these vivid memories form a colloquial history of her whole marriage. It's a crowded narrative, rich in episode and supporting cast, but lacking in the sort of suspense that Tyler achieved in *The Accidental Tourist,* where the indecisive hero was bounced around by two very different sorts of women for more than three hundred pages.

The suspense in *Breathing Lessons* concerns Maggie's notion of "patching up the differences" between her son Jesse, a high-school dropout trying to become a rock star, and Fiona, the pale vulnerable kid Maggie cares more about than her own daughter. Jesse and Fiona were divorced several years before, but that doesn't discourage Maggie. She meddles—when has she ever not done that?—and the results are worse than ineffectual. Tyler's ending provides a sharp antithesis to all the comedy and nostalgia that came before. It's a rebuke to Maggie's sentimentality, to her longing for a happy ending—and perhaps to the reader's as well. It's also proof of a kind that Tyler has a serious vision of life, that her novel will not merely entertain and console. The only trouble is that Tyler *does* want to entertain and console. She has a lot of the Norman Rockwell in her, showing us the niceness of ordinary people, their fallible decencies. In the novel's last lines when Maggie determines to try again, we are invited to see her as heroic—the inveterate maternal do-gooder doomed to fail, probably, but undeterred, a species of comic existentialist. So it's not—unfortunately—such a grim ending after all. Tyler's best novel remains *Dinner at the Homesick Restaurant,* where many points of view tell the story of an unhappy family, and the distances between people are not so easily resolved. (pp. 133-34)

Dean Flower, "Barbaric Yawps and Breathing Lessons," in The Hudson Review, *Vol. XLII, No. 1, Spring, 1989, pp. 133-40.*

Marina Warner
The Lost Father

Award: Commonwealth Prize

Born in 1946, Warner is an English novelist, nonfiction writer, and author of children's books.

Skipping back and forth in time, spanning from the early twentieth century to the mid-1980s, *The Lost Father* is a family history as chronicled by Anna Colluathor, a divorced mother and collector of ephemera for the Museum of Albion. Anna reconstructs her family's past through conversations with her mother and by writing passages for a book to be titled *The Duel*. Anna is initially interested in events surrounding a duel in which her grandfather, Davide Pittagora, was wounded while defending the honor of his sister. Davide's health gradually detriorates over the next two decades, and his worsening condition parallels the rise of fascism in Italy. Davide emigrated to the United States with his wife, son, and two sisters following World War I, but after repeated failures and hardships the family returned to Italy in the mid-1920s. Following his death, Davide's family endured dire conditions of war and poverty. The story is enriched through insights on social, cultural, and political pressures in Italy as well as the problems, failures, and tragedies that confront Anna and her relatives. Warner's use of folk tales and operatic motifs provide a mythological subtext, and her self-conscious narrative explores themes relating to legends, reality, memory and loyalty. In addition, Warner won praise for her painstaking descriptions of settings in Italy, Greece, England, and the United States. Hermione Lee described *The Lost Father* as an "idiosyncratic and haunting novel: lush, slow-paced, sensual, metaphorical and, at the same time, worrying over the demands of kinship and the trail of history."

(See also *Contemporary Authors*, Vols. 65-68 and *Contemporary Authors New Revision Series*, Vol. 21.)

PRINCIPAL WORKS

NOVELS

In a Dark Wood   1977
The Skating Party   1983

NONFICTION

The Dragon Empress: Life and Times of Tz'u-hsi, 1835-1908
   1972
Alone of All Her Sex: The Myth and the Cult of the Virgin Mary   1976
Joan of Arc: The Image of Female Heroism   1981
Monuments and Maidens: The Allegory of the Female Form
   1985

SHEILA HALE

Most of Marina Warner's non-fictional writing has been about extraordinary, exemplary women (they include the Virgin Mary and Joan of Arc) whose flesh-and-blood reality has been obscured, in a male-dominated world, by layer upon layer of myth and allegory. Her new novel, ***The Lost Father,*** is about an ordinary, likeable man whose true story is mythologised by the women of his petit bourgeois southern Italian family.

The novel, she says, explores the paradox of the strong matriarchal persona which nonetheless dedicates itself to the worship of the male. You can see it in the Roman wall painting reproduced on the dust jacket—it's in the Villa of the Mysteries in Pompeii: the dedication to conjuring the male; it is exactly right about the way my mother and the women around her were brought up in southern Italy to think about men. It was true then, and it's to some extent true of most societies even today. Feminism hasn't come. The queendom hasn't arrived. . . .

The lost father of the title is inspired by her maternal grandfather, who was a provincial lawyer and amateur opera singer born in Apulia in the 1890s. He died in early middle age of a mysterious illness, leaving his wife to bring up their four daughters in genteel poverty during Mussolini's Fascist regime and the conquest of Ethiopia. These women told the story that his death had been caused by a lead bullet lodged in his head during a duel of honour 20 years earlier.

It is a story which has always fascinated her, because 'it was part of the story that it wasn't true. I've always wanted to write it, ever since I first heard the story as a little girl.' But it was only five years ago, when her own English father died, that it began to seem important to preserve, 'even in fantasy', this fragment of her mother's family's past.

She has been reading and making notes for the novel since then, but, though characteristically careful to get her factual history right, she tried to curb her 'natural tendency to do research, because this is, after all, a work of imagination. I suffer from an impulse—it amounts to a real need—to make life richer than it is. And one way of doing that is to create an imaginative version of it.'

She has moved the Villa of the Mysteries from Pompeii to Apulia, which she brings redolently and confidently to life. It was one of her incidental aims to demonstrate that 'Apulia before the war was not a dump inhabited exclusively by corrupt peasants, as some people seem to think.' But she calls it Ninfania, 'place of women; actually the Greek word also means bride. Making it a fictional region left me free to get things wrong'. And the lost father is rediscovered, rescued from the myth which his womenfolk used both to enrich their lives, and to invoke or, when necessary, to evade his authority. He comes to life, a believable and moving character.

> It can't be the real man, because I never knew him. But in fiction, as Milan Kundera has said, everybody has their own truth. Writing a novel is an odd process, it's a way of thinking that takes longer than thinking, because in a novel you can't pontificate, you can't present what you simply desire to be the case. For me it's also rather cinematic: I see them moving. I don't necessarily write it all down, but I have to know exactly where my characters are at any given moment.

I told her that although it wasn't my job to review the book, I found it by far the most compelling of her three novels, also one that gets more rather than less absorbing as you turn the pages. 'Yes, I do have a terrible time beginning. In this book I wanted to *push* you through the mirror, and it took a while to work out how to do that. If it's an improvement on *The Skating Party,* that may be because I've read much more contemporary fiction in the six years since that was published.'

She cites the Chinese American writer, Maxine Hong Kingston:

> I revere her; and Louise Erdrich, who is part Red Indian: she is terrifically rich in visionary imagination. But it is Virginia Woolf's *The Years* which lit the way; the gaps are so marvellous. She taught me the importance of what you leave out. You pick up a character after years and you are astonished by what has happened to it. And Nabokov's *Pale Fire*—have you read it?—I've always liked stories that reverse themselves.

The Lost Father ends with a deeply satisfying and reverberative twist.

        Sheila Hale, "*Worship the Man,*" in The Observer, *September 11, 1988, p. 35.*

HERMIONE LEE

The trail of *The Lost Father* goes back three generations. In the first part (set in 1913), Davide, the tall sensitive son of an ancient Southern family, an opera-lover, a good singer and a future lawyer, fights a duel to avenge the dishonouring of his sister by his best friend, the predatory, anarchic Tommaso. Then, with his wife and baby son and his two sisters (ugly, sensual Rosalba, who loved Tommaso, and Caterina, their go-between), he takes ship, like so many other 'dagoes', for America. The journey is tragic, the new country hostile. The family returns to their snail shell—'Ninfania', in the heel of Italy, on the Adriatic—in 1923.

The story of the second generation centres on the day of Davide's death in 1931. His composer-brother, his widow and her daughters, horns drawn in, will try to keep their family security under the bullying encroachments of Fascism. In the third story, Anna, our narrator, is tracing the trail back via 'old stories'. The novel she is writing, *The Duel,* is partly a way of cracking her mother's defensive shell, partly a means to understand her own life better. But the more she discovers, the less satisfactory the operatic romance of the duel-story becomes. The truth may have had more to do with political history, less with family feelings: 'Old stories change'.

This is a cultural historian's novel, and the scholarly curiosity that went into Marina Warner's fine books on female myths and iconography makes here for a devotedly careful recreation. At times there is a card-index feel to her handling of the rich mass of material (Duelling, introduction and practice of; Socialism, history of under Fascism), but conscientiousness keeps dissolving into living scenes: the evening *passegieta,* a night-time rendezvous, the disastrous staging of a comic opera to the local Fascist authorities. . . .

Davide, the lost father, is sympathetically imagined; but it is his mother and wife, his sisters and daughters, whose lives we most see into. In a culture where virgins and mothers are idealised and spinsters are scorned, the secret feelings of young girls are intense. The novel gets this beautifully, especially in Rosalba's pent-up sense of sexual power, 'trapped inside her like water under the ground'.

But Rosalba, a promising witch, disappears into America and silence. This points to a tantalising quality in the whole book. While the writing is lavishly specific, saturated with natural and domestic imagery (a baby's pair of buttoned shoes are 'fastened across his soft plump feet like napkins over hot bread rolls'), much is made of the intangibility of the past. Anna's authorial anxieties seem to reflect Marina Warner's dilemma about what should have been written: cultural history, unmediated biography, or self-deconstructing fiction?

The effect is of painstaking, truthful uncertainty. What stay in the mind, with great charm, and a touching wistfulness, are not the deliberations over narration, but the vividly salvaged moments from a few of all those lives that 'receded to infinity in an imagined throng of the dead.'

        Hermione Lee, "*On the Heel of Italy,*" in The Observer, *September 11, 1988, p. 42.*

MICHELENE WANDOR

[*The Lost Father*] begins and ends in the Eighties. Anna, an 'independent' woman (a broken marriage, one son, and a job collecting the ephemera of ordinary people's lives for a museum), is engaged in the task of reconstructing her own family's history. The story is addressed to Fantina, Anna's mother, as the two women sit in London, sewing and reading. The emotional atmosphere created at the start is therefore that of the communion between women of different generations. And this theme is continued as the story unfolds, linking Anna and her mother with their immediate female forebears, in particular Anna's great-aunts, Rosa and Caterina. These sisters are indirectly the cause of the most dramatic event in the book: the death of their brother, Davide, the 'lost father' of the novel's title.

In southern Italy at the turn of the century, machismo in men and modesty in women are the cornerstones of social mores. As Rosa's buxom and burgeoning sexuality focuses its attention on Davide's friend (and class inferior) Tommaso, rumours fly round the village. Davide, a sensitive introvert, is roused to do the proper male thing: he challenges Tommaso to a duel. In a quarry, the two men re-enact the mere ritual shadow of the duel, but the game backfires: Tommaso's bullet enters Davide's skull, to remain there, discharging its leaden poison slowly until, years later, it kills him.

This slow poisoning acts, potentially, as an intense metaphor for Italian society as it moves inexorably through the Twenties, the economic crisis and the rise of Mussolini. However, the novel evades the implications of its own invention at this level. Davide's own sensitivity to history, however, is beautifully caught in the early passages: finding an old coin, he speculates on the history of his village; and on the discovery of an amphora he says it is 'like a living body released from the torpor of an unnatural sleep'.

Where Warner is less successful is in pointing up her central theme. True, Davide has to be re-created—from the memories of relatives and from Anna's own imagination. But where is the tension in his 'lostness'? The tensions of the story come from the lives of the women, and Davide is not problematic in their memories—at least, not as far as the structure of the novel is concerned. In a sense this doesn't matter: the book is rivetingly reconstructive of its Italian environment. And while the dialogue is sometimes awkward (a common problem in contemporary novels), Warner's fine descriptive prose makes the events flow like honey.

> Michelene Wandor, "Falls the Shadow," in The Listener, Vol. 120, No. 3080, September 15, 1988, p. 31.

CAROLE ANGIER

[*The Lost Father*] should have been a good novel. Perhaps it is a good novel; maybe it's just me it misses. But it missed me badly.

It is, I think, very ambitious. Its themes are ambitious: changing lives, especially women's; life and art; the possibility, or impossibility, of memory and truth. Its narrative structure is extremely ambitious. . . . It is ambitious in language, in imagery, in cast of characters. And all these ambitions signal to us noisily. They do not grow naturally out of the novel; they

are the novel. They set up great expectations, which then remain unsatisfied.

There are still some satisfactions to be had. The two characters for whom the narrator, Anna, feels most, her mother Fantina and her "lost" grandfather, Davide, have life and depth. The details of poor women's lives ring true. . . . The sudden doubt at the end is effective: was the key to Davide's life the legendary duel, after all, or was it really the political battle Anna only learns of in the last pages? Is the story of her family the story of love and sex she's written here, or has she missed the point altogether? . . .

There are too many characters—two generations of Italian sisters—who remain too thin, and whose talk is often too similar and too literary. The narrative voice itself is irritatingly selfconscious. . . . Marina Warner tries too hard; and often she misses. Trees don't pass by a walker "like the falling pages of a book"; and you can't say (when someone withdraws) that the "shell door slammed", because shells don't have doors.

Above all, there's something wrong with the rhythm of this book. Digressions (like Franco's opera) bulk as large as Davide's duel; for a long time the story seems to be his sister Rosa's, until we lose her in America and never see her again. Marina Warner's ear is off. Her part three begins: "I borrowed Auntie Lucia's fuschia Porsche". Even if you don't read Porsche the German way that's the worst line I've read for years.

> Carole Angier, "Great Expectations," in New Statesman & Society, Vol. 1, No. 15, September 16, 1988, p. 44.

LORNA SAGE

Marina Warner's fiction has a slow, dreamy quality that is at once pleasurable and slightly sinister—as in those dreams where you're mysteriously tethered to one spot, condemned to wander in circles. Maybe it's an effect that derives from the cultural historian's habits of work; [*The Lost Father*] implies as much by casting its narrator as an archivist who is applying her professional skills ("the last person left in Ephemera") to the reconstruction of her own family romance. We're in a mind-museum where different periods of time unfold in different rooms, in bright, separate dioramas: southern Italy pre-First World War over here; the fascist 1930s to your right; America in the 1920s to your left; present-day California round the corner; and in the basement a collection of bits and pieces dating back to classical antiquity.

The lost father of the title is, it turns out, a grandfather. . . . Grandfather died nineteen years after [a] legendary duel—perhaps, as his daughters believe, of slow poison from the lead bullet, but perhaps of the more insidious workings of disillusion. Like the impoverished Italian south itself, he seems gripped by paralysis, able neither to embrace nor resist the new, harsh options that history offers him. Tracking him down through her mother's memories, his granddaughter discovers or invents a man who tries to live gently, even nobly, an archaic man consumed by a vague ideal.

He grows up, Davide Pittagora (his very name recalls Greek Pythagoras, and the grand ancestry of his decayed people), brooding jealously over his mother and sisters, rejecting the adolescent crudities of his friend Tommaso, shuddering at what the wall-paintings unearthed in a local villa reveal; "his women belonged to the shadowy depths of the shuttered rooms, of a tamed interior . . . not in a smoky scarlet painted chamber, spilling liquid, whirling in a tarantella ecstasy, letting animals suck at them. . . ." His women, however, betray him.

The novel keeps a difficult balance between Davide's gallant pathos and the women's very different strategies for survival. His plain, passionate sister Rosalba, obsessed with clumsy Tommaso, prays for something, even dishonour, rather than old maidhood: "Please please don't let nothing happen to me." Her schemes set in train the rumours that lead to the duel, and confirm Davide in his role as would-be protector. In truth, though, it's a part that's already being written out of the script. Like many thousands of his generation, Davide is driven by poverty to take his family to America, and there he finds that his troublesome sisters are in their element. Their energies are focused on living, struggling, patching, making do—and so, he discovers to his dismay, are those of his modest wife, who has to lie to him about the humiliating shifts that keep him and their children fed and clothed. And when he returns home defeated, it's to a country where honour and decency are daily trampled by the Duce's bully boys. . . .

The women share an underlying, ingrained attitude, however different they are—sensual, stoical, pious or brisk—as personalities. One incident set in 1930s Italy, where as "the American girls" they feel particularly threatened, will suggest something of their style. Imma, pregnant by a soldier-husband she hardly knows, suffers a miscarriage, and in defiance of the priest her young sisters Fantina and Lucia smuggle the tiny, grey corpse into their father's mausoleum in a shoe box, at night: "You ought to know," says Fantina to God, "that in our house we never throw anything away."

It's this bleak tone that makes Davide redundant, and provides the book with its main narrative thread, connecting distant Ninfania with present-day America, and with the narrator's world:

> it still gives me pleasure . . . that (Pythagoras) who
> established the doctrine of migrant souls taught in
> my mother's homeland, where corks and bottle
> tops might renew their lives as children's toys. . . .
> In Ninfania, no one threw away the feather of a
> bird or the peel of a fruit or the seed from a
> melon. . . .

By means of such subtle, sometimes over-systematized connections, Marina Warner pictures the continuities of family history. The dream of the father becomes, for the narrator cataloguing her ephemera, a kind of impossible refuge from ruthlessness (she is a woman of this generation, divorced, bringing up her son on her own, a version not of lost authority, but lost tenderness). This is a moving book, and a very bookish one. . . .

Lorna Sage, "Museums of the Mind," in The Times Literary Supplement, *No. 4459, September 16, 1988, p. 1012.*

PATRICK PARRINDER

Rushdie wrote in *Shame* that 'every story one chooses to tell is a kind of censorship, it prevents the telling of other tales.'

His own profuse and multiply-branching fictions do not give the impression that anything has been prevented from being told. Marina Warner's narrator in ***The Lost Father*** is more painfully aware of the difficulty, and the advisability, of choosing and sticking to one story. When she sets out to break the silences and suppressions surrounding her grandfather's life she does not realise, it seems, that to break the silence is also to multiply silences. Some of these emerge from the family history, some are her own, and some inhere in the relationship between character and author. The title has its own sort of silence, since Warner makes no explicit allusions to anthropology, *Finnegans Wake* or psychoanalysis, nor does she expound a thesis on 20th-century patriarchal decline, though doubtless she could do any of these things if she chose. The autobiographical basis of her novel, which is variously hinted at, is another area of silence. And what are we to make of a narrator called Anna Collouthar, museum curator and (presumably collusive?) author?

At the museum of Albion, Anna is charged with collecting ephemera. She has written about her grandfather in an unfinished novel called 'The Duel', but then her reconstruction of his life is apparently undermined by a newspaper cutting, preserved by one of her American cousins. The grandfather grew up in Ninfania, an Adriatic province of southern Italy, in the early years of the century. The territory was fought over in the Second World War, and Anna's own father is a shadowy Eighth Army officer described only as 'plump and clumsy and mostly bald'. It is her grandfather's life which appeals to her imagination, a life which she considers 'lost' because she is so anxious to recover it.

Is authentic recovery possible, however? This is the doubt which shadows 'The Duel', a marvellously vivid and lucid narrative which may, for all that, be no more than an animated diorama, an expression of the present-day 'heritage-culture' to which Anna owes her (precarious) livelihood. If the Ephemera Collection is to survive it will need sponsorship from the owners of Fun City, the world-famous Californian theme-park. 'The Duel', like-wise, needs the revision and authentication which might come from the memories of Anna's Californian relatives. But do they share Anna's concern for the family history, her all-too-British obsession with hoarding ephemera? Wisely, if teasingly, Marina Warner lets us read 'The Duel' before her heroine sets out.

In ancient times Ninfania was a province of Greece, and Anna's family, the Pittagoras, claim descent from Pythagoras. This is at least as plausible, it would seem, as the rest of the family legend. However, there is a diary left behind by Davide Pittagora, describing his voyage to America with wife and child on an emigrant ship, and his miserable years in New York. He returned to Italy in the Twenties, lived through the early years of Fascist rule, and died in 1931, supposedly of the cumulative effects of lead poisoning from a bullet-wound sustained shortly before he decided to go to America. Anna's mother has always believed that he was wounded in a duel, after overhearing his best friend, Tommaso Talvi, insulting the honour of one (or was it more than one?) of the Pittagora sisters. Tommaso, a military cadet, had won the heart of the elder girl, who may or may not have fallen for his wiles; and he had then been indiscreet enough, or so Anna imagines, to compare the two sisters' charms with those on sale in the back streets of Naples. Davide, of course, has no choice but to issue a challenge.

Honour and chivalry, the law of the *mentita:* these are the foundations on which Anna has constructed her (presumably lying) narrative, with its intensely romantic evocations of youth, sexual hunger and family relationships. Marina Warner is particularly good at evoking her characters' dreams, adolescent fears and erotic imaginings, but of course Anna cannot know about these, she has had to invent them. One of the keys to her approach is Italian opera; the characters are constantly bursting into arias. Davide, a baritone, is made to reflect that 'in opera a knave in disguise is quickly discovered, and is unambiguously a knave, nor is the matter of a song a lie from start to finish'—how much better this is than in his own detested profession, the law! But Anna's characters wear no disguises, and Davide's antagonist in the duel is definitely a knave. Such is the family legend that Anna inherits, but her Californian cousins have access to different versions. We are left only with a series of unanswered questions.

The Lost Father is a subtle, lyrical novel, with the suggestion of an outrageous leg-pull about it. Though there is nothing Shandean about Warner's approach, she is telling a cock-and-bull story of sorts (and an excellent one). At the end we realise that this could, perhaps should have been a political novel—the Davide possibly referred to in the long-kept newspaper cutting is a socialist law student caught in a fight with a band of armed mercenaries—but Anna quite clearly prefers the glamorous and old-fashioned male world of 'The Duel' to a Ninfania torn apart by land struggles and class-conflict. This is the family romance which explains her father's later decline, together with the eventual self-assertion of the bereaved sisters and daughters, who have created an immeasurably different life for themselves. Nevertheless, the present-day Pittagoras, whether in London or in Parnassus, California, are unflatteringly seen; theirs is anything but a heroic world. *The Lost Father* shows a compelling imagination at odds with a sceptical and troubled intelligence: but it also contains more humdrum matter, and some potentially useful digressions. If you have new shoes that are too tight, or a table-top bleached by a hot dish or the wet rim of a glass, you might want to try the Pittagora family's remedies. (p. 12)

Patrick Parrinder, "Let's Get the Hell Out of Here," in London Review of Books, Vol. 10, No. 17, September 29, 1988, pp. 11-13.

KATE SAUNDERS

The Lost Father is the story of an Italian family, as seen through the eyes of its female members. Anna is a young divorcee who works in the "ephemera" department of a museum, logging the march of time through comics and sweet-papers. She is trying to capture the history of her mother's Southern Italian family, weaving a complex tale from scraps of vague and romantic tales. At the centre of the Pittagora family legend is Davide, the lost father, who is supposed to have died as the result of a duel over his sister's honour in the early 1930's. The book's structure is like a patchwork quilt, leaping about in time and gradually building into a symmetrical picture. Marina Warner is a richly poetic writer, and at first, her style seems just a touch precious—in an attempt to convey a foreign idiom, she has made some of her characters sound as if they are speaking in a clumsy translation. This apart, however, her evocation of Southern Italy, where the peasants are descended from Icarus, is absolutely fascinating. Ancient folk tales give the book a timeless quality, and a rich sense of continuity with the past. 'Fate could

not be circumvented,' thinks Davide's wife on the day of his death, 'Not when her scissor-blades were on the string.' This is a novel to read slowly, relishing each perfectly-tuned phrase.

Kate Saunders, "In the Family Way," in Books, London, No. 19, October, 1988, p. 11.

An excerpt from *The Lost Father*

As he blacked out, he would have smiled if his face had not felt as if it had turned to syrup. It was a rush of triumph that he experienced, the ecstasy of the sacrificial, but his features were disobedient and he brought his hand up and touched the warm liquid stuffing coming out of his head. He—Davide Pittagora, tongue-tied, indecisive, and withdrawn—had managed to speak out; he heard singing, and the singing was not only the bloodlet from his skull but a wild chorus, giving voice to his joy.

He'd declared his sisters his own, now; everyone would know they had to reckon with a champion. For that he'd fall and fall again till his last breath. This was the southern land where a woman was worth a dozen fights, no, more—twenty, fifty, a hundred—where the princess in the picture with her hands joined in prayer over the battle was worth her weight in gold, and where, when an indemnity was paid to the victim's relations after a trial by combat, the price of a dead man was fixed at ten times less than the price of a dead woman. Rightly, Davide knew, for you can only measure a man's value by his women, you can only appraise a country through its women. The queasiness in his stomach rose; he was plunged into a blood-pudding world where all was dim. Then there came through the total eclipse splinters of color, humming as they came. He strained to see them, they were approaching in a heat haze, their shapes resolving themselves, tapering, dividing, until at last he recognized them. Their arms were intertwined as they swung lightly over the earth, and Caterina was dancing along alone beside them; their dresses flared transparent like the petals of sweet peas. Or was it their faces, opening like flowers with honey in their throats? Even the advancing tide of blackness could not blot the sweetness of their chorus, greeting him in full voice as he leaned over the balcony; he was singing too, in unison with them, something strong and lyrical, and the doves were fluttering upwards into the dome in the last act—and he was going under, to be admitted to their company in paradise.

ANITA BROOKNER

The hidden agenda in Marina Warner's substantial, impressive and difficult novel is the search not for a father but for a maternal grandfather who will establish and reinforce the female strain in her ancestry. For it is impossible to read the novel as anything else but family history, Marina Warner's own, and she presents herself as interlocutor to her mother and even addends a transparent fictional autobiography of her own: she is Keeper of Ephemera at the Museum of Albion (which we can read any way we like) and she pays a visit to an eery grant-giving body in California to distrain for funds. As Marina Warner acknowledges a grant from the Getty

Centre for the History of Art and the Humanities in her fore-word we are alerted to the fact that all this is not very far from the truth.

The narrator then is central but elusive, obscure but present and in control. Some sections of the book are written in the second person singular, as the feminist historian interviews her mother; some are in the form of a diary kept by her grandfather. Davide Pittagora, who left his farm in the south of Italy to journey to New York and who returned home to die; and some are straight narrative, but introduced from an oblique angle. Gradually, very gradually, the story builds up, but the going, especially at the beginning, is inclined to be tough, and readers should be warned that they will need patience to extract from *The Lost Father* its essential meaning and the full sense of its narrative flow. If they are prepared to devote their complete attention to the text—and it is a text, the sort that will give future employment to scholars—they will be rewarded with something that is both unusual and beguiling.

The publishers have already planted a comparison with Visconti's film of *The Leopard,* and it was perhaps inevitable that they should do so, for this is a panoramic account of a southern Italian family. The family is not princely, far from it, but it has its codes of honour and reticent female behaviour firmly established and widely recognised. The patriarch, Davide Pittagora, said to be descended from Pythagoras, is a lawyer and a musician, both in a modest way: he never finishes his studies, and his business is local and seigneurial rather than official. His sisters, Rosalba and Caterina, give him a certain amount of trouble, since they are both enamoured of the same man, Tommaso Talvi, a boyhood friend of Davide's and a member of the Duce's army of conquest in North Africa. It becomes necessary for Davide to fight a duel with Talvi to protect the honour of his sister Rosalba, and in this duel he receives a bullet in the head which kills him 19 years later, after his return from America. Or does it kill him? The narrator reserves a surprise until the last few pages, when, in America on a quest of her own, she learns new facts from a newspaper cutting sent by a cousin whom she has never met. (pp. 31-2)

But was the father lost? Or is it intended that he should be lost? His presence is mild, shadowy, and not altogether real. He is, in fact, the ancestor one has never known and about whom it is appropriate to speculate. But this is essentially a matriarchy, and if anyone could make this idea seductive it is Marina Warner, whose studies in the field of feminist iconography have made her something of a heroine—an icon, in fact—for the movement. The world of the Pittagora women, which is one of subservience but also of immense resource, will challenge current feminist thinking, for here Marina Warner seems to agree with Germaine Greer, that the cause of women is a lost cause if it does not recover simpler and more archaic patterns of behaviour. There is no reason why this should be impossible, although admittedly it will be harder to achieve in the industrialised West than in the very restricted setting of a small Italian town.

If I have presented *The Lost Father* as a document rather than as a novel the reason may be that the author is scrupulous about declaring her interest, and also because a narrative of this kind raises more questions than it resolves. I found it rebarbative, initially impenetrable, but difficult to lay aside, and I was surprised to look up and see how many hours had passed without my noticing them. I could have done without the fairy stories, the operatic excerpts, and the narrator's own insertion, but I was becalmed by the sense of days gone by, of loving hands at home, and of severe but natural standards of decency. Any one of these ingredients—and certainly all of them together—should guarantee Marina Warner a wide readership. (p. 32)

Anita Brookner, "Gentle Customs of an Italian Matriarchy," in The Spectator, *Vol. 261, No. 8361, October 8, 1988, pp. 31-2.*

CONSTANCE MARKEY

Even at first glance, Marina Warner's *The Lost Father* makes for challenging reading. Unconcerned with chronology, the novel darts around in time to cover several generations in one Italian family, now in England, then in Italy and later in America. But plot sequence and verisimilitude are not issues here. Less important than the story's events themselves are the characters' illusions about them.

A Pirandellian game, perhaps, full of questions and no answers? Not really. Warner is not a skeptic and has few existential axes to grind. Quite the opposite, hers is a novel of consolation. It is a story about the power of history and family ties. Jungian in inspiration, it nurtures the notion that personal growth depends not only on self-knowledge but on the awareness of a collective human spirit as well.

The narrator, Anna, a young Englishwoman, is at a turning point in her life. Recovering from a painful modern divorce, she looks to the past for solace. In her Italian ancestry she hopes to find something of herself and discover either a new life or recuperate an older, better way to live.

Her attentions focus first on her grandfather, Davide Pitagora, a strongly patriarchal image and the lost father of the title. . . . Vulnerable, in need of a defender, she looks to him as the "champion . . . who died of a wound he got defending his sister's honor." By his "princely stature" he personifies the archetypal male, supplanting the faulty images of both her own father and the father of her small son.

Even more meaningful to her personal recovery are the family women and the mythology she invents around them. In their strengths, real or imagined, she hopes to find her own. . . .

At novel's end, nothing seems to have happened to Anna and yet everything has changed. In its eternal circular trajectory, time has rebounded on the present and touched her life. In the cosmic scheme, her individual moment in history has arrived. Or to be more precisely Jungian, it is Anna's chance to become what she always was at an unconscious level.

A weighty philosophy this, and one that explains the novel's circular movement and allegorizing. Scarely a name in the novel is without heady symbolic inference. The family name, for example, refers significantly to Pythagoreanism, or the philosophy of transmigration of the soul. Such places as Ephemera, Ninfania and Parnassus also contain hidden messages for the reader to puzzle out.

Author of two previous novels, *In a Dark Wood* and *The Skating Party,* Marina Warner is a cultural historian who loves to put her work into her fiction. Hence, no mythological stone has been left unturned, no pyschology unexplored, in this metaphysical study of one soul's relationship to its primeval origins.

The result is a novel apparently aimless yet highly systematized, dreamy but intelligent. Echoing Umberto Eco, *The Lost Father* belongs to a genre of storytelling that demands a reader with the heart of a poet and the mind of a scholar.

Constance Markey, in a review of "The Lost Father," in Chicago Tribune—Books, *April 23, 1989, p. 6.*

ANN CORNELISEN

Marina Warner is intrigued by myths. Her classic studies—*Alone of All Her Sex* (about the Virgin Mary and the evolution of the female goddess) and *Monuments and Maidens: The Allegory of Female Form*—have established her as something of a specialist. Now, in *The Lost Father,* she explores the more elusive, domestic myths of one family, its various generations and various worlds, primarily that of southern Italy, itself one of the natural homes of myth and superstition.

The Lost Father is described on the jacket as a novel, but it reads and was intended to read like a family memoir, reconstructed in the imagination of an English granddaughter from stories her Italian mother has told her and from diaries and letters. The effect is curious—of fiction with its peculiar magic, yet with an aura of fact, of both less and more than fiction—which is exaggerated perhaps by Marina Warner's dedication of the book to her own mother and her mother's sisters, "the Terzulli daughters." The temptation is to speculate: could our author be, at least in some small part, our narrator, Anna?

The idea appeals. Anna is a clearheaded, observant young woman, given in her Anglo-Saxon way to self-amusement. She is divorced, the mother of a young son, and is also "the last person left in Ephemera," the department she works in at a museum of social history. Cataloguing ice cream wrappers and junk-food slogans leaves her plenty of time to write of her mother's childhood in "Ninfania, most forgotten province of the Mezzogiorno," which to geographers is clearly the area of Italy known as Puglia. Anna reads the manuscript to her mother, who is Fantina, the youngest of the lost father's four daughters. Their conversations, spoken and unspoken, scattered as breaks in the narrative, give a tonic jolt of mod-

ern perspective to what otherwise would be a Mediterranean fable. . . .

The author shunts back and forth between stories of Davide's family, his youth, his sisters, eventually to the duel and, later, to his nightmare voyage to New York with his wife, Maria Filippa, and their baby son (who dies of fever), through their nine grim years there. In New York, Maria Filippa toils at a sewing machine in a sweat shop, and incidentally has three more children, while Davide is often reduced to being a scribe for five cents a letter—until their return to southern Italy. All too soon, Maria Filippa is a young widow in straitened circumstances with four daughters.

Her scrimping and her struggles to maintain the semblance of respectability that will allow her daughters to marry decently are a saga in themselves. You feel the neighbors watching, almost hear their whispers, and when, small blessed wonder, three of the girls marry Allied soldiers, you can imagine the neighbors' slanders.

This is the art of *The Lost Father:* that you do feel the slow suffocation of the Italian south, the resignation that deadens, the smugness and superstition. Fate. Along the way there are falterings. Occasionally, the zigzags in time and place leave the reader playing literary blindman's buff. Occasionally, descriptions are lightly tinged in purple and phrases stilted—"He would help fructify their holdings"; "The air was still and cool in the cold stone's propinquity." The real Puglia is not the land of perpetual sun and wisteria in bloom. It can be as cold and dank and dreary as any place in the world.

But these are slight flaws that fade from memory in the denouement. Toward the end Anna, her son and her mother make a hilarious visit to Hollywood, complete with "Fun City," a mogul given to poetic seductions by telephone, and a chaotic dinner with Fantina's sisters, their husbands, nieces and nephews. Back in London, Anna and her mother face each other over a letter from a distant cousin, which reveals, at last, the facts about the duel and the lost father's life. They must choose between truth and fantasy. Each does, accepting her own version, as most of us have done in our own lives. Marina Warner has added new dimensions and perspectives to the role of domestic myth in our imaginations.

Ann Cornelisen, "The One Left in Ephemera," in The New York Times Book Review, *May 7, 1989, p. 26.*

Wendy Wasserstein
The Heidi Chronicles

Awards: Pulitzer Prize for Drama, Tony Award, and the New York Critics Circle Award.

Wasserstein is an American dramatist, born in 1950.

The Heidi Chronicles explores the spirited personality of Heidi Holland, a witty, unmarried art historian approaching middle age, who has difficulty coping with the disintegration of social principles that shaped her life. Spanning twenty-three years, the play begins with Heidi's slide lecture on women artists, affirming her strong feminist values, and goes back in time to the 1965 high school dance where she meets several lifelong friends who inspired her interest in the women's movement. Upon entering college, Heidi and her friends evolve into ardent feminists and radicals, and ensuing scenes depict the group at such events as a boisterous rally during Eugene McCarthy's 1968 presidential campaign, a 1970 consciousness-raising session, and a 1974 protest march. Throughout the play, Heidi remains a spectator; her personality is defined through her observations and her reactions towards others.

As the 1980s approach and most of her peers are caught up in the materialism they once denounced, Heidi becomes disillusioned. While the others now consider the feminist movement superfluous, Heidi is victimized because of her enduring commitment to its principles. At her high school alumni luncheon, which many critics consider the climax of the play and a *tour de force* for Wasserstein, Heidi delivers a long, impromptu confession concerning her feelings of abandonment and her disappointment with vacuous contemporary women, explaining, "I thought the point was we were all in this together." However, the play ends on an optimistic note with Heidi finding fulfillment as the single parent of a newly adopted daughter. Although critics commented that this unmotivated conclusion compromised Heidi's antecedent values, many praised Wasserstein's acute social observations and humorous yet controlled characterizations. Linda Winer asserted: "[*The Heidi Chronicles*] is a wonderful and important play. Smart, compassionate, witty, courageous, this one not only dares to ask the hard questions . . . but asks them with humor, exquisite clarity and great fullness of heart."

(See also *CLC*, Vol. 32; *Contemporary Authors*, Vol. 121; and *Contemporary Authors Bibliographical Series*, Vol. 3.

PRINCIPAL WORKS

PLAYS

Uncommon Women and Others   1977
Isn't It Romantic?   1981
The Heidi Chronicles   1988

CLIVE BARNES

The Baby Boomers have boomed, the yuppies have yupped, and our stages are taking note. Few boomer plays are likely to be more nostalgic, and even fewer as witty, as Wendy Wasserstein's *The Heidi Chronicles*. . . .

The Heidi, whose chronicles these are, starts at a high-school dance in 1965, and ends in a new apartment, complete with a newly adopted baby, in 1988. In between she runs the gamut of our times—or such a gamut as might be appropriate to a white, educated, affluent professional, whose friends are fashion's slaves.

It is, you see, a sheltered gamut, but one with which presumably many theatergoers will be able to identify, and in chronicling it Miss Wasserstein has produced an elegantly entertaining play, eloquent on the vacuous perils of the uncommitted and disconnected.

Although Wasserstein's self-absorbed characters take the Me Generation so seriously that every walk across the road becomes a passage in autobiography, the play finds its firm focus in the character of Heidi herself, and Heidi's struggles in the war for women's liberation.

Heidi is an art historian—a specialist on the role, wouldn't you have guessed, of women in art—who, as she explains, is "neither an artist nor a spectator but a highly trained observer." And it is an observer attitude [the] play itself takes to Heidi's saga.

We see 23 years of Heidi and her awakening, we see her friends and the two men in her life—one, Peter, a homosexual pediatrician, and the other, Scoop, a womanizing lawyer/editor—all swimming around like happy piranhas in the yuppie aquarium.

Wasserstein takes her Heidi through the lot—from the women's consciousness-raising group right up to the scourge of AIDS—while all the time Heidi, just a little wiser and smarter than the rest, stands outside triviality, safe and secure in her observer role.

Many of this playwright's set pieces are like revue sketches, but beautifully done. For example, the scene of consciousness-raising is exquisitely funny in the way it catches the lingo of its time, as does a scene of a group of women proceeding to picket the Chicago Art Museum for its lack of representation of women artists.

Then there is a hilarious skewering of morning chat-show TV; a hostess with the leastest, faced with two guests anxious both to shine and to make her look more stupid than even TV intended.

This kind of darting social satire is right on the mark, and perhaps best of all are Heidi's two lectures on painting, models of parody and perception that give us insight into the character as well as making the gentlest and informed fun of art criticism.

The difficulty of the play is the triviality of its issues and its people. Even serious subjects like women's lib and, seemingly thrown in for serious ballast, AIDS, become trivialized, because everything and everyone is reduced to a chic cartoon joke—amusing but essentially light-weight.

The Heidi Chronicles is slickly written and glossily packaged. As Miss Bankhead once so memorably remarked on another occasion: "There is less in this than meets the eye." But what does meet the eye, and mind, is unquestionably diverting.

> Clive Barnes, "Hello, I'm the Me Generation," in New York Post, *December 12, 1988.*

MEL GUSSOW

Deep into *The Heidi Chronicles,* Wendy Wasserstein's enlightening portrait of her generation, the title character makes a speech to her high school alumnae at a "Women, Where Are We Going?" luncheon. In the speech, a tour de force for the author, Heidi vividly describes an aerobics class that proved to be an epiphany. While exercising, she was surrounded by an Inferno of "power women" both young and old. With sudden intuition, she realized that as a child of the 1960's—as a woman subjected to judgment by men and as a humanist trying to position herself among feminists—she is stranded, and no one is about to rescue her.

She simply wants to be Heidi, but the closest she can come to self-definition is ambivalence, empathizing with the Heffalump in *Winnie-the-Pooh*. As chronicled by Ms. Wasserstein, Heidi's search for self is both mirthful and touching.

In *The Heidi Chronicles . . . ,* the author looks beyond feminism and yuppie-ism to individualism and one's need to have pride of accomplishment. We are what we make of ourselves, but we keep looking for systems of support. As Heidi learns, her friends are her family. . . .

In *Uncommon Women and Others* Ms. Wasserstein offered a collage of Seven Sisters school graduates. In *Isn't It Romantic?* she sharpened her focus on a single woman (and her best friend) trying to be grown up. With her ambitious new play, she both broadens and intensifies her beam, to give us a group picture over decades, a picture of women who want it all—motherhood, sisterhood, love and boardroom respect.

The play opens with Heidi as art historian, delivering a lecture on the neglect of female painters from "the dawn of history to the present," and uses that neglect as an artful motif to depict man's exclusionist attitude toward women. During a series of pithy flashbacks, we see Heidi on her own rock-strewn path to liberation. As she moves from high school intellectual to awakening feminist, in the background we hear about political and cultural events. Heidi and her group are emblematic of their time, but the historical references never become intrusive. They form a time line on which Heidi teeters like a tightrope walker.

Around her, women take advantage of opportunity and one man, Scoop Rosenbaum, takes advantage of Heidi. Scoop is an arrogant idealist. Even as he offers Heidi no choice but subjugation to his will, he is becoming a prime mover of his generation, through his high-flying magazine, *Boomer,* the beacon of the baby-boomer crowd. . . . One necessarily wonders why Heidi has such a diehard affection for him. Far more believable is Peter Patrone, a hugely successful pediatrician, who is gay. In all matters except sexuality, he is Heidi's soulmate.

Ms. Wasserstein has always been a clever writer of comedy. This time she has been exceedingly watchful about not settling for easy laughter, and the result is a more penetrating play. This is not to suggest, however, that *The Heidi Chronicles* is ever lacking in humor.

Several of the episodes are paradigmatic comic set pieces—a consciousness-raising session, the aerobics speech and a hilarious television program in which Heidi, Scoop and Peter are brought together as representative spokespersons. The colloquy is misguided by an airhead talk-show hostess. When Scoop becomes characteristically self-serving, the pediatrician steals the spotlight, as is often the case. . . .

Subtly the play parallels aspects of the original *Heidi* novel. As we are reminded, in the first two chapters the heroine travels and then "understands what she knows." At the beginning of her journey, Ms. Wasserstein's Heidi is adamant that she will never be submissive, especially to men. To our pleasure, the endearing character finally finds selfless fulfillment. Following the chronicles of Heidi, theatergoers are left with tantalizing questions about women today and tomorrow.

> Mel Gussow, "A Modern-Day Heffalump in Search of Herself," in The New York Times, *December 12, 1988, p. C13.*

SYLVIANE GOLD

If you were a bright young thing in the late '60s, attending the college of your choice and forging lifelong friendships in this or that crusade, maybe you are Heidi Holland. The heroine of Wendy Wasserstein's penetrating new play, *The Heidi Chronicles,* is the girl who took along a book to read at the high-school dance, who turned up at a Eugene McCarthy mixer because a friend was going, who marched in demonstrations but felt a bit taken aback by their belligerence.

In ordinary times, Heidi would have been the classic outsider, always a bit out of step with the world at large and well aware of it. But through a quirk of chronology, Heidi belongs to the baby-boom generation, which, for a little while, at least, thought it was in to be out. As Ms. Wasserstein's pithy scenes follow Heidi from 1965 to the present, we watch her get swept up in a mass movement, and then we watch as she gets left behind. Heidi buys the rhetoric of the first, heady years of feminism, only to find that in the '80s, she's supposed to be buying $200 running shoes. She never quite catches on as the simple proposition "All people deserve to fulfill their potential" evolves into greedy narcissism. No wonder Heidi says she feels stranded.

To Ms. Wasserstein's credit, she shows as all this with a minimum of hand-wringing or finger-pointing, and with her usual humorous twinkle. As Heidi and her assorted friends and lovers wind their way through the decade—accompanied always, of course, by the appropriate rock music, *The Heidi Chronicles* becomes a mordant comedy of manners. Ms. Wasserstein accurately captures the nervous, jaunty patter of high-schoolers meeting at a dance (I'm not sure she's quite so accurate when she has them recall it line for line some 20 years later). Her 1970 consciousness-raising session recreates the euphoric spirit of the time even as it lampoons its inane, huggy rituals. And a 1984 power lunch, at which the execs neither eat nor listen, is etched in acid. (Clearly, Ms. Wasserstein has taken one or two of those.) . . .

My . . . quibble with *The Heidi Chronicles* concerns the ending, in which Heidi's sense of sadness and betrayal is assuaged by proxy, as it were, Ms. Wasserstein, who has been so cleareyed about her characters' self-deceptions, suddenly allows her heroine to cop out. But these small flaws don't change the fact that this is Ms. Wasserstein's finest, most deeply felt work to date. Yes, Heidi is kin to the sweetly befuddled heroines we know from the author's earlier plays (*Uncommon Women and Others* and *Isn't It Romantic* are the best-known). And yes, it's not exactly news that Ms. Wasserstein is an entertaining writer. But there's a new note of savagery in this play, an almost Shavian exasperation with the way things go. It's what gives *The Heidi Chronicles* its deeper resonance, and moves Ms. Wasserstein from the ranks of the talented wits to those of the serious social critics. I can't wait to see what comes next in the Wendy chronicles.

Sylviane Gold, "Circle Pins to Power Lunches," in
The Wall Street Journal, *December 16, 1988.*

MIMI KRAMER

At the emotional turning point of *The Heidi Chronicles,* Wendy Wasserstein's manless heroine Heidi Holland, an essayist and art-history professor, is supposed to deliver a speech at the Plaza Hotel. The occasion for the speech is an alumnae luncheon, the topic "Women, Where Are We

Going?" We've seen Heidi speak in public before—in the classroom sequences that, prologue-like, begin each act—and we've grown familiar with the mock girls'-school bonhomie she exhibits toward the women painters who constitute her particular area of expertise. Ordinarily, the public Dr. Holland is a model of wry composure. On this occasion, however, instead of giving a speech (she hasn't prepared one) Wasserstein's heroine gets up and extemporizes. She begins by sketching a fictional portrait of herself as an "exemplary" New Woman, whose busy and full life—complete with ideal husband and children—would excuse her showing up speechless at a luncheon where she herself was the featured event. Then, in an apparent non sequitur, she tells a story about going to the health club and being too much affected by the other women in the locker room to go through with the exercise class she had planned to attend. Wasserstein never makes the connection between the two halves of the speech; she leaves it to us to infer that Dr. Holland was "too sad" to produce a speech for the Miss Crain's School luncheon, just as she had been "too sad to exercise" that day. Moreover, the cause of Heidi's depression—her manlessness—is never alluded to. Instead, Wasserstein duplicates that feeling in us by having Heidi describe the women in the locker room: two girls discussing "the reading program at Marymount nursery school;" a woman her mother's age complaining about her daughter-in-law; another older woman "extolling the virtues of brown rice and women's fiction." She imagines the young mothers thinking that women like her "chose the wrong road":

> "A pity they made such a mistake, that empty generation." Well, I really don't want to be feeling this way about all of them. . . . It's just that I feel stranded. And I thought the whole point was that we wouldn't feel stranded, I thought the point was we were all in this together.

(p. 81)

[*The Heidi Chronicles*] is actually a very funny play. The scene at the Plaza is a tour de force: it justifies the whole play, yet nothing in the play has prepared us for it. We have never been told that the heroine is to make a speech; we have never heard of the Miss Crain's School. . . . That we are able to feel, once we're there, that this scene is where Wasserstein's play has been leading all along is a mark of her artistry.

The Heidi Chronicles is probably Wasserstein's best work to date. What distinguishes it from her earlier plays is that it actually says something. It's one thing to be able to record an experience or capture the spirit of a time—to write bittersweet autobiography about the bright, promising people one knew in college (*Uncommon Women and Others*) or how hard it is to grow up and break free of overprotective parents (*Isn't It Romantic?*)—and quite another to send us out of a theatre feeling that we see something in a different light. *The Heidi Chronicles* is autobiographical only in the most interesting way: Wasserstein's heroine is, like Wasserstein herself, a student of other women—particularly women engaged in creating images of womanhood. It's significant that the women we see Heidi lecturing on belong to another time: it suggests that Wasserstein's subjects—the young men and women who came of age in the sixties and dropped out to work on radical newspapers or in women's collectives—stand somehow outside the purview of her own and her heroine's experience. Wasserstein wants Heidi to be not an advocate of the women's movement but one of its victims—a vessel carrying around the ideals and experiences of her time. Throughout the play, Heidi remains mostly mute and passive, aloof from the proceedings. . . . "You're the one whose life this will all change significantly," warns a charismatic pseudo-radical young man Heidi meets at a McCarthy rally in Manchester, New Hampshire, in 1968, and we see his prophecy fulfilled. At a consciousness-raising session in Ann Arbor in 1970, Heidi is an interloper, forced by feelings and circumstances into "sharing" with the other women and surrounded by them, at the end of the scene, in an uncomfortable embrace. We witness Heidi's seduction by the women's movement just as we witnessed her seduction by Scoop, the charismatic young man in the scene before—one of that horde of clever, intense young men who knew how to badger women into profound conversations and shallow beds by making astute personal remarks. It's one of the clevernesses of Wasserstein's play that she makes Scoop a *pseudo*-radical. "You'll be one of those true believers who didn't understand it was just a phase," she has him say. Twenty years later, a routine philanderer and the editor of his own lifestyle magazine, Scoop will be thinking of going into politics, and Heidi will be adopting a baby. We'll never find out exactly what makes Heidi tick, but then we never really find out what makes Isabel Archer tick.

This moving-snapshot style of theatre, in which the progress of a particular character is charted through a succession of years in different towns and cities, is popular among playwrights of Wendy Wasserstein's generation and is most often used to chronicle their disillusionments and disappointments, as Wasserstein uses it here. The danger inherent in such an approach—one that has to go so far afield in space and time in order to make a point—is that what the playwright has to say may turn out to be either trivial, as in the case of Michael Weller's *Loose Ends,* or untrue, as in the case of David Hare's *Plenty.* Freed from the necessity of discerning some *pattern* of truth in human action, one can, after all, say anything.

Like the health-club speech, Wasserstein's entire play is a tour de force: it mimics the faults of her generation's style of theatre yet manages to transcend them. It spans twenty-three years and rockets us back and forth in time and place. And though it tracks the main characters from the sixties to the present there isn't a single scene in which anything that anyone does has consequences in a later scene. That the play manages to seem economical can only be attributed to some alchemical combination of graceful-mindedness and good writing; the Chekhovian fabric of the dialogue—the degree to which characters' ways of talking differ from one another or change over time—creates a Stanislavskian offstage life, so that to witness one conversation between Scoop and Heidi is to know what their subsequent relationship as lovers will be like. Wasserstein never states anything that can be inferred; it's one of the ways she keeps her heroine free of righteousness and self-pity. We aren't shown Heidi's disappointment when her charming, self-effacing friend Peter announces that he is gay, just at the moment when we're wondering why Heidi doesn't settle down with him (the way we keep wondering why Isabel doesn't settle down with one of the nice young men in *Portrait of a Lady*); instead, we feel disappointed ourselves.

There's generosity in the writing, toward the characters, certainly, not one of whom is made to seem ludicrous or dismissible. . . . [Wasserstein] is herself too much a lady to moralize. She condemns these young men and women by simply capturing them in all their charm and complexity, with-

out rhetoric or exaggeration. They are measured and found wanting. Her final comment on the me generation is contained in Heidi's wish for her daughter: that no man should ever make her feel she is worthless unless she demands to have it all. (pp. 81-2)

Mimi Kramer, "Portrait of a Lady," in The New Yorker, *Vol. LXIV, No. 45, December 26, 1988, pp. 81-2.*

JOHN SIMON

The worthy Wendy Wasserstein's latest and maturest play, **The Heidi Chronicles,** is awash in glitzy one-liners coming thick and fast from all directions, alert to all the issues currently concerning us, and ultimately unsatisfying. . . .

The alliteratively named art historian Heidi Holland flaunts her identity with the equally alliteratively named author; the goyish best friend, here called Susan Johnston, is familiar from W. W.'s **Isn't It Romantic?,** and most of the ten other women are her **Uncommon Women and Others** roughly twenty years later. There are, however, men as well: five shadowy ones of small importance and two significant ones. It is with these two (fairly recognizable to those who know the author, though no mere transcripts from life) that the difficulties begin. For in this examination of how women, with or without benefit of feminism, adjust to their emotional-biological needs, men matter—except to Fran, the lesbian. And these two aren't enough to convey the other half of the problem.

Peter Patrone is charming, handsome, sensitive, witty, a good friend—everything Heidi wants from a man, save that he is a homosexual who rejects her as wife or lover. He is, in the play, a pediatrician as well as a—what is the counterpart of womanizer? Manizer?—a gay Lothario (that's it!), both of which afford good opportunities for accosting AIDS in the home stretch (the play spans the period from 1965 to 1988), something that Miss W. does in the same dutiful way she ticks off all the trends and buzzwords of her times. Either less or more would have been more. The other man is Scoop Rosenbaum, desirable, worldly, epigrammatic, cynical, editor of ever bigger magazines, selfish, and sexist. He accepts Heidi as lover but passes her over as wife for a non-liberated, affluent housewife type, and Heidi is out of luck again.

Now, these two men simply do not embody all there is for a smart, talented, attractive young woman to choose from. But, then, oversimplification is rampant where women are concerned, too; even Susan lacks Heidi's dimensions, which isn't fair. The playwright concedes that her alter ego is shy, sometimes sweetly bumbling, and often wryly outspoken; but my God, most people would consider these alleged defects virtues. If Miss W. had the candor of Albert Innaurato in *his* self-portraits, her plays would gain considerably. Heidi's problem as stated—that she is too intellectual, witty, and successful for a mere hausfrau—just won't wash.

I find particularly distressing the glib solution: Heidi adopts a baby even as women artists, her babies, start making it big; a final slide shows us Heidi hugging her infant in front of the Met's Georgia O'Keeffe banner. That is too easy; I'll buy that ending when I hear that Miss Wasserstein has adopted a baby: There are times when life had better imitate art if we are to believe either of them. (p. 49)

John Simon, "Partial Autobiographies," in New York *Magazine, Vol. 22, No. 1, January 2, 1989, pp. 48-9.*

CATHLEEN McGUIGAN

Wendy Wasserstein, pushing 40, has been called a young, up-and-coming playwright long enough. The off-Broadway satirist of contemporary women's angst . . . is finally sitting at the grown-ups' table: her latest play, **The Heidi Chronicles,** opened last week on Broadway, and in it, Wasserstein is working on a bigger canvas than she has before. Tracking the coming of age of a feminist art scholar named Heidi Holland, Wasserstein re-creates key moments in baby-boomer history from the McCarthy campaign and radical feminism to the Me Decade and the rise of the Yuppie. At the heart of the play is bitter disillusionment, particularly with the women's movement. "I feel stranded," says Heidi, single, fortyish and out of step with the eager young women who snap open their alligator Filofaxes in the locker room of her health club. But themes like the co-opting of feminist politics don't sell tickets—and make no mistake, Wasserstein aims to write popular entertainment. Her message comes in a bright comic package, full of gags that skewer everything from consciousness-raising groups to power lunches to TV talk shows.

Heidi's career as an art-history professor makes a neat theatrical device: the play opens with Heidi giving a witty slide lecture on women artists. But like her profession as "neither a painter nor a casual observer," she's detached from the action. She is someone around whom other characters dance, reflecting social change. This is a tricky strategy. Heidi . . . doesn't always succeed in both being removed and making us care about her. Her best friend Susan is merely a foil. Susan leaps from a Supreme Court clerkship to a rural women's collective in Montana to a career in Hollywood as a sitcom producer, and we have no idea why. Other women are simply caricatures, such as the radical lesbian in fatigues or the bubbly young businesswoman in gray suit and running shoes. The men in Heidi's life are more interesting: Scoop Rosenbaum is an impossibly glib, arrogant, philandering lawyer/editor/politician who's got a surprising sentimental soft spot; Peter Patrone is a sensitive gay pediatrician who has a deep streak of cynicism. Wasserstein sometimes can't balance savagery and heart, but her satire is never empty; she has a strong point to make about lost values.

Wasserstein, 38, swears that Heidi is not Wendy—even if both she and her protagonist are named after storybook heroines. "I was trying to write about someone a little separate from me," she says. . . . But she admits that she rang doorbells for McCarthy as a Mount Holyoke undergraduate, and she shares some of Heidi's dashed expectations. The climactic speech in which Heidi tells her girls' school alumnae luncheon that she feels stranded came out of a period when Wasserstein felt sad and disconnected. "Sometimes I write to make order for myself," she says. "It was that whole idea of the We Generation, and then suddenly everyone was going off in their own direction . . . Was the purpose of all this so that 21-year-old girls can get M.B.A.'s?" (pp. 76-7)

Cathleen McGuigan, "The Uncommon Wendy Wasserstein Goes to Broadway," in Newsweek, *Vol. CXIII, No. 12, March 20, 1989, pp. 76-7.*

JOHN SIMON

Having been less enthusiastic than other critics about Wendy Wasserstein's **The Heidi Chronicles** Off Broadway, I hasten to point out that, reversing the pattern, it looks and plays better on. . . . [The] bigger space allows more room for the play's grand ambition to portray two decades of change in our society. A school dance looks more like a school dance, a pediatrics ward is more up to the old pediatrics, etc. And it's nice to bask in oversized slide projections in the hall where Heidi Holland—Wendy Wasserstein transmuted into a feminist art historian—lectures on women in art. . . . (p. 66)

The play chronicles Heidi's progress from a frightened but fast-quipping wall-flower at a 1965 Chicago high-school dance, through becoming a timid onlooker at a New Hampshire Eugene McCarthy rally (1968), to being a Yale grad student in fine arts visiting a friend in Ann Arbor and shyly observing her consciousness-raising group in session (1970), then to a women-in-art protest march on the Chicago Art Institute (1974), and so on through thirteen scenes—all the way to 1988, when Heidi moves into a commodious New York apartment and adopts a baby girl. Cautiously, she does not name her Sofonisba, Artemisia, or even Angelica, after one of her beloved women artists.

Here the first problem surfaces: the inconsistencies in Heidi's character. In contrast to her feminist and postfeminist friends, Heidi remains an almost Candide-like innocent, despite one of the sharpest and fastest tongues this side of the Pecos. When she lectures, however, her humor changes from vertiginous epigrams to patronizing down-home jokiness. Further, she seems to have an ample and diversified offstage sex life with one editor or another, yet is involved on stage with only a couple of unlikely men throughout.

There is Scoop Rosenbaum, a dazzling opportunist who goes from liberal journalism to putting out *Boomer,* the slickest of slickly upward-mobile magazines, and thence (as I understand it) into politics. Heidi has an off-and-on affair with him, but he wenches around and finally marries an intellectual 6 (instead of her 10)—a wealthy young woman who becomes a leading book illustrator, which is not bad for a 6. And there is Peter Patrone, as cynically scintillating at repartee as Scoop; he, however, becomes an earnest and distinguished young pediatrician. We follow him, a homosexual, through a number of liaisons with men; as far as I can tell, he never sleeps with Heidi. But she is, for obscure reasons, enormously important to him as, in the end, we see him bitterly grappling with AIDS among both his special friends and his child patients.

Now, there are in life beautiful women who have weird problems with men, and witty women who are nevertheless shy; but to make them credible on stage takes a heap more than we are accorded here. . . . Equally hard to take are the smart-aleck rapid-fire epigrams from almost everyone; this fits into the unrealistic, stylized milieus of Wilde, Coward, and Orton, but clashes with W. W.'s naturalistic ambience. Finally, the play is a mite too much of a survey course in women's studies; or, to put it bluntly, a check, or even laundry, list. All the same, it is clever and funny and sometimes even wise. . . . (pp. 66, 68)

John Simon, "Jammies Session," in New York *Magazine, Vol. 22, No. 13, March 27, 1989, pp. 66, 68.*

WALTER SHAPIRO

The anger came first, but it is not an easy emotion for play-wright Wendy Wasserstein. Her natural instinct is to charm, to disarm, to retreat from harm. The nervous giggles, the wispy, high-pitched voice, the ingratiating brown eyes and perhaps even the plump figure all seem protective camouflage. For Wasserstein, self-mocking humor has always been the first line of defense against both the judgment of others and her enveloping Jewish family, which cannot understand why a nice girl like Wendy is not married with children at 38. Even her closest friends sometimes find her hard to take entirely seriously. "With that stupid little voice and ratty fur coat," laughs fellow playwright William Finn, "you initially think this lady's a loon, a modern-day Dorothy Parker."

But such surface judgments mask the intensity within Wasserstein, the vision that spawned her new hit Broadway play, *The Heidi Chronicles.* "I wrote this play because I had this image of a woman standing up at a women's meeting saying, 'I've never been so unhappy in my life,' " Wasserstein explains. "Talking to friends, I knew there was this feeling around, in me and in others, and I thought it should be expressed theatrically. But it wasn't. The more angry it made me that these feelings weren't being expressed, the more anger I put into that play."

But Wasserstein is far too deft a satirist, and far too gentle a person, to compose a screed. Instead, with subtlety and humor in *The Heidi Chronicles,* she has written a memorable elegy for her own lost generation. *Heidi* tells the story of a slightly introverted art historian, a fellow traveler in the women's movement, who clings to her values long after her more committed friends switch allegiance from communes to consuming. At the pivotal moment in the play's second act, Heidi stands behind a lectern on a bare stage, giving a luncheon speech to the alumnae of the prep school she once attended. Slowly the successful veneer of Heidi's life is stripped away as she tries to ad-lib a free-form answer to the assigned topic, "Women, Where Are We Going?" Heidi's soliloquy ends with these words: "I don't blame any of us. We're all concerned, intelligent, good women." Pause. "It's just that I feel stranded. And I thought that the whole point was that we wouldn't feel stranded. I thought the point was that we were all in this together."

There has always been a feminist subtext to Wasserstein's plays, even in her earlier work when she relied on Jewish-mother jokes and collegiate sexual confusions for laughs. Her first success, *Uncommon Women and Others,* depicted a reunion of Mount Holyoke College alumnae six years after they have left the campus to make their way in the working world. . . . Her 1983 hit comedy, *Isn't It Romantic?,* which ran for two years off-Broadway, is a thinly veiled tale of Wasserstein's relations with her own larger-than-life mother. But even here, Janie Blumberg, the playwright's alter ego, rejects a suffocating marriage with a very eligible doctor and utters *Heidi*-esque lines like "I made choices based on an idea that doesn't exist anymore." Still, the spirit of the play is more aptly conveyed by Janie's comically maladroit efforts to cook a roast chicken for her boyfriend.

Only in a written playscript does Wasserstein allow herself to be assertive. In conversation, she flees from all self-important declarations of artistic intention. It takes coaxing for Wasserstein just to admit that *Heidi* represents her bid "to demand attention and announce, 'I have something to say, and I want you to listen.' " (p. 90)

Many of the reviews have been a press agent's dream. The New York *Daily News's* critic hailed *Heidi's* recent arrival on Broadway with this pronouncement: "I doubt we'll see a better play this season." The other New York papers, as is the custom, chose to let their off-Broadway reviews stand. An "enlightening portrait of her generation," declared the *Times,* while *Newsday* poured on the laudatory adjectives: "smart, compassionate, witty, courageous." There were some sharp dissents. *Time's* theater critic, William A. Henry III, complained that "Wasserstein has written mostly whiny and self-congratulatory clichés."

The playwright does not deny that bad reviews wound. But these days, there is also a keen pride as Wasserstein views her handiwork on Broadway. "I'm normally a self-deprecating person," she says, putting it mildly. "But when I saw those women on stage in the feminist rap group, I said, 'Good for them, and good for us.' This is a play of ideas. Whether you agree or not doesn't matter." (pp. 90, 92)

Wasserstein's natural medium . . . [is] humor. As she explained in a painfully honest essay called **"Funny Girl"** in *New York Woman* magazine, "I don't think about being funny very much because it's how I get by. For me it's always been a way to be likable but removed." The result is that outsiders can misinterpret her manner and mistakenly belittle her talent. Playwright Terrence McNally complains that "what people often miss about Wendy is the thoughtful, passionate, mature womanly side of her. She is far more interesting as a mature artist than as this giggling, girlish, daughter-person that people want to take care of."

A few days after *Heidi* opened on Broadway, Wendy's parents Lola and Morris Wasserstein were asked about their youngest daughter, the successful playwright. Much of the conversation sounded like a leftover scene from *Isn't It Romantic?* "We're very proud," said Lola, who even in her 70s takes four dance classes a day. "But there's a vacuum," added Morris, a prosperous Manhattan businessman. "Where's the children? Where's the husband?" Here Lola broke in, "Normally, I'm the one to say that. But today I'm on good behavior." A few moments later, the Wassersteins were asked how many grandchildren they have. "Nine," said Lola, "and we're waiting for the tenth." To underline the point, Morris chimed in, "We're waiting for Wendy. Patiently."

Both of these doting parents are Jewish émigrés from central Europe who came to New York City as children in the late 1920s. For years, Lola has been the richest source of her daughter's comic material. "Do you know what my mother said to me on the opening night of *Uncommon Women?*" Wasserstein asks rhetorically. " 'Wendy, where did you get those shoes?' " . . .

[The] other Wasserstein children are such paragons of conventional success they could almost be lifted out of a Judith Krantz novel. . . . Wendy was closest to her brother Bruce, three years her senior. A path-forging mergers-and-acquisitions lawyer, he is a co-founder of the investment-banking house Wasserstein Perella & Co., which the *Wall Street Journal* dubbed "the world's hottest dealmakers." . . .

Even now Wendy remains fascinated by the way she and her brother have come to represent almost twin poles of the age-old dialectic between art and money. Wendy delights in telling the story of how during the off-Broadway previews of *Heidi,* she was locked in an intense artistic discussion with Joan Allen [the actress playing Heidi] when she was handed a message: "Your brother Bruce called. Can't come to the play tonight. Is buying Nabisco." . . .

Early in *Heidi,* the heroine says in exasperation over male self-confidence, "I was wondering what mothers teach their sons that they never bother to tell their daughters." The playwright is inordinately fond of that line, since it springs directly from her own family experience. "God knows," she exclaims, "I'm not going out to merge Nabisco. I stay in my house and write plays." But judging from Wendy Wasserstein's triumph in writing what may be the best play about her generation, there is much to be said for what mothers teach their daughters. (p. 92)

Walter Shapiro, "Chronicler of Frayed Feminism," in Time, New York, Vol. 133, No. 13, March 27, 1989, pp. 90-2.

ROBERT BRUSTEIN

The Heidi Chronicles is not yet the work of a mature playwright, but it is a giant step beyond the cute dating games and Jewish mother jokes of *Isn't It Romantic?* Wasserstein has a wry, self-deprecating humor that helps her avoid self-righteousness without losing her sting. And while her heroine is both more self-conscious and self-aware than the various self-deluded types she encounters on her spiritual journey, she is a charter member of her own generation. The playwright is old enough to have experienced the protest movements of the 1960s along with the disillusionment of the '70s and the cynicism of the '80s. This experience endows her play with themes of nostalgic retrospection. *The Heidi Chronicles* could be considered *The Big Chill* of feminism.

It is also *The Common Pursuit* of failed American dreams. Instead of using the device of a reunion, Wasserstein . . . creates an episodic narrative, beginning in Chicago in 1965 and ending in present-day New York, designed to dramatize the gulf between the ideals and actions of her baby boomer characters. Following a 1988 prologue in which Heidi, a professor of art history, lectures on the neglected art of women, we encounter her as a high school student at her first dance, as a college peace marcher during the Vietnam War, as a graduate student member of a consciousness-raising feminist rap group, as a protester against the exclusion of women artists from museums—which is to say, in most of the radical postures of the passing decades. During these episodes, she meets a variety of militant women and two recurrent male friends—one a homosexual pediatrician, the other a womanizing lawyer—and in virtually every case witnesses the idealist causes she joined, however marginally, being transformed into opportunism, careerism, and compromise, not to mention marriage without love.

In a typical scene, Heidi is approached by two old friends—formerly feminists, now absorbed in media manipulation. They want her as a consultant on a TV sitcom ("all we need is three pages—who these people are and why they're funny"), not because of her intrinsic talents but because "sitcom is big—art is big—and women are big." Later addressing an alumni group, she breaks down, finding it unbearable that her generation made so many mistakes. . . . The growing emptiness of her world is symbolized by her empty, unfurnished apartment. Unable to connect with a man—there is always an unconsummated relationship with some shadowy editor in the background—she becomes the single mother of an adopted child, hoping its generation will grow up better than hers.

Throughout this odyssey, Heidi remains a bemused outsider with one eyebrow raised at the absurdity of her contemporaries. She has no answers—neither does the playwright—except to maintain a degree of grace and style in the face of the general disillusionment. Wasserstein is an acute social observer. She seems to recognize that despite the typically American hunger for total fulfillment, it's just not possible to have it all. She also seems to suggest that the feminist movement, instead of reforming society, has succeeded largely in introducing women to the ravening competitiveness of the '80s, which is to say, adapting women to the worst qualities of men.

This is not a conclusion destined to please the sisterhood, but it is a lot more honest and courageous than the moral of, say, [Mike Nichols's] *Working Girl,* where the heroine's ascent up the Wall Street ladder is cheered on by virtually everyone, no matter whose eye gets pierced by her stiletto heels. Despite her disenchantment, Heidi will no doubt continue to battle on behalf of her sex for equal rights and recognition. And her slide lecture, like Wasserstein's play, makes a convincing case for women artists achieving the same ready acceptance as men. But Heidi's argument for true equality also demands that women be assessed by the same ethical criteria as men, which makes *The Heidi Chronicles* less a celebration of the yuppie standard of values than a subterranean assault on it.

Wasserstein's handling of female character is as deft as her treatment of feminist ideology, and her collective of lesbians, career women, radicals, and professionals is amusingly drawn, especially in the rap session when the militant women end up hugging each other and singing camp songs, as well as in a talk-show sequence featuring a vacuous blond hostess with a coffee cup who keeps repeating, "Boy, I'm impressed." Where I still sense theatrical immaturity is in the playwright's handling of dialogue—not because of a lack of wit but from an excess of it. Wasserstein's characters, all of them educated, are almost ferociously witty. Their weakness for wisecracks makes them seem shallower than intended and undercuts the seriousness of the work. It remains to be seen whether in her next play Wasserstein will manage the infinitely more difficult task of *not* being clever. (pp. 32-4)

Robert Brustein, "Women in Extremis," in The New Republic, Vol. 200, No. 16, April 17, 1989, pp. 32-4.

MOIRA HODGSON

The sorry state of Broadway this year was summed up by the Pulitzer Prize, awarded to Wendy Wasserstein for a successful bad play called *The Heidi Chronicles*. . . . It is hard to write about women, the 1960s, gays, yuppies and single motherhood without slipping into cliché, and Wasserstein can't help it. It's a harmless play, perfect for Broadway since there is nothing in it to offend deeply or shake up the house, but just enough to make the audience feel knowing. (It's also overlong, enough to induce slight boredom so that those in their seats will feel they've been exposed to art.) Despite some good moments and clever ruses the evening drags. . . .

Heidi, whose odyssey we follow, is without interest, except when she is lecturing on women in art (the best part of the play, apart from a predictable but very funny encounter on a TV talk show). The men in her life are a teen-age boyfriend who turns out to be gay and a man who marries someone else because he wants a woman to look after him while he climbs the career ladder. (p. 605)

For the most part the dialogue in *Heidi* is labored and irritating, lacking any real wit. The most moving insight comes when Heidi, who feels betrayed by the women's movement, says, "I was a true believer who didn't understand it was just a phase." Indeed, many women who were part of the movement in the 1960s feel stranded in the 1980s. So what does Heidi do? She adopts a baby. The snatches of 1960s rock—the Rolling Stones, Janis Joplin, Bob Dylan—that bridge the scenes in this play are the best thing about it, but they only briefly rouse the audience from its torpor. (pp. 605-06)

> Moira Hodgson, in a review of "The Heidi Chronicles," in The Nation, New York, Vol. 248, No. 17, May 1, 1989, pp. 605-06.

GERALD WEALES

In the 1950's, Broadway comedy was peopled with fairly affluent, mostly professional, usually suburban characters who faced genuine problems—marital difficulties, generational differences—in a sex-free, politics-free environment which sanitized the situations. The happy endings were dictated not by circumstances nor character development but by the genre itself. . . . [The current comedies] are not Broadway, in origin at least, and the happy endings are muted, ironic. The characters are fairly affluent, mostly professional, usually urban, and they face an even more complex range of problems than the 1950's allowed. Sex is not only possible but almost mandatory, and even politics is permissible as long as it does not upstage the personal. Yet, despite their nodding acquaintance with offstage reality, the characters in Wasserstein's *The Heidi Chronicles* . . . seem less like the people in the next block or at the next table than like the children of the characters in F. Hugh Herbert's *The Moon Is Blue* and George Axelrod's *The Seven Year Itch*. The toughest comedies can be subversive. These are oddly comforting, using laughter or sentiment or cagey rhetoric to rub the cutting edge off pain. (p. 573)

In a series of sketches, . . . [*The Heidi Chronicles*] follows the titular Heidi from 1965 to 1988. A bright young woman, at once comfortable with and slightly witty about her intelligence, she moves through the convolutions of the period—political, social, feminist—ostensibly retaining her sense of self while her chameleon friend creates a new personality to fit the ever-changing scene, each role a new cliché conceived broadly by Wasserstein. Heidi's two visible male friends are a homosexual doctor, who offers understanding, jokes, and finally the expected shock of AIDS, and her sometimes lover, a self-serving, self-deluding journalist who mistakes the main chance for the high road. The Heidi we meet in the present is an art scholar, intent on reasserting the female presence in the history of art. On the surface an established professional with a rich and rewarding life, she is in fact nagged by a sense of emptiness, of the unfulfilled promises in society and her own life. Since the character is largely reactive, a quiet center in often ludicrous scenes, the revelation of her angst (except for one scene in which a speech to her old school turns into

a cry of despair) comes obliquely. The happy ending, if that is what it is, finds Heidi with an adopted child, although why single parenthood should fill the vacuum in her life is never clear in the script. Within the context of the play, which manages to trash most of the idealistic impulses of the 1960's and 1970's, the ending looks like an upscale variation of the macho ditty that soldiers used to sing to the tune of "Pretty Baby" during World War II: "If your husband's in the service / And you're feelin' kind of nervous / Have a baby."

The art lectures that open both acts of Wasserstein's play are symptomatic of a disturbing tone in her work. Even if academic success is not enough to make a complete woman/person of Heidi, surely Wasserstein intends the lectures as a reflection of her heroine's intelligence and their subject as a worthwhile scholarly enterprise. Maybe not. She provides Heidi with professorial mannerisms—little jokes, apologetic giggles—which suggest that the playwright is making fun of academic lectures or of the attempt to correct the female imbalance in art history or of Heidi herself. The ambiguity in these scenes echoes Wasserstein's own statements about her position as an "artist"—a word that would probably set her laughing. Yet, she is serious about her work. In a group interview with four women dramatists in *The New York Times* (7 May 1989), Wasserstein said, "What drives me to write, the urgency, comes from experiences I've actually had as a woman. . . . But I see myself as a playwright." Seriously a woman, then, and seriously a playwright, but she cannot sustain the position without succumbing to comic overstatement. "I went to graduate school at Yale, and I remember all those Jacobean plays we would read about men kissing the skulls of women and then dropping dead. And I thought, I can't identify with this." Were there all that many skull kissings? I suspect that Robert Brustein's 1970 production of *The Revenger's Tragedy,* in which he famously played a dwarf, was still the talk of the school corridors when Wasserstein got there a few years later. What she has here is a nice bizarre image for the male domination of Western drama, but oddly—to my ear at least—it doubles back on itself and the cleverness upstages the point being made. Anyone who has seen Wasserstein on a panel can imagine her speaking those lines through the laughter that regularly bubbles out of her public self (as with Heidi), sensibly rejecting solemnity but somehow losing seriousness in the process. It is as though she could not recognize that funny lines or attempted funny lines give off waves that infect the context. (pp. 574-75)

Wasserstein can be funny and she has a sharp and caricaturing eye for idealistic fads, but her attempt to use laughter in the interest of any kind of significant social or psychological statement dissolves into amiability. (p. 575)

> Gerald Weales, "American Theater Watch: 1988-1989," in The Georgia Review, Vol. XLIII, No. 3, Fall, 1989, pp. 573-85.

LAURIE WINER

The Heidi Chronicles suffers from a severe credibility gap. Its heroine is not the woman she—and others—claim she is.

Just why is Heidi Holland so angry, or sorrowful, as the case may be? According to the play the reasons are these: As a Vassar student in the late 1960s, Heidi attends a college mixer where she met an overbearingly arrogant but charismatic young Eugene McCarthy canvasser with the unlikely name of Scoop Rosenbaum. Scoop immediately assesses his soon-to-be conquest as a "serious good person"—the characters often offer Heidi unsolicited, admiring descriptions of herself; in another prescient moment, Scoop informs Heidi that she will be "interesting, exemplary, even sexy, but basically unhappy." "The ones who open doors usually are," he explains soberly.

While Heidi does try to help open some doors for women in the 1970s, she is hardly the martyred warrior that Ms. Wasserstein . . . would have us believe. It's true, however, that she dutifully attends a women's consciousness-raising group at which she reluctantly confesses to four cloyingly supportive group members her demoralizing secret: she is in love with a man, Scoop, who is ambivalent toward her.

At the same time, this serious good person begins to develop the ungenerous trait of sitting in judgment—always by way of a cleverly bitchy zinger—on any woman who has something she does not: a husband, higher earning power, a more recent birth date. Yet Ms. Wasserstein side-steps the issue of Heidi's need to condemn. The playwright constantly stacks the deck against the characters to whom Heidi feels superior, and, with one exception, she never imagines the play from anyone else's perspective.

When Scoop marries a pampered Southerner named Lisa who illustrates children's books (read: an intellectual lightweight), Heidi attends the wedding with her best friend, a homosexual pediatrician named Peter. . . . Peter is Heidi's equal in acerbity, and he's the only character in the play Ms. Wasserstein seems to regard as Heidi's equal in suffering. He, too, is a serious good person. We know this because Ms. Wasserstein has given him an impeccable cause: he specializes in helping children with AIDS.

But while Peter may be a good-hearted doctor, he's a rude wedding guest. He and Heidi waste no time in trashing the bride—always wittily—whether she's in the room or not. When Lisa dares to refer to her new husband as "sweetie," Heidi and Peter immediately pick up the ball, addressing each other as "sweetie," with just the right mock ironic tone. Not to worry, though: the bride is not hip enough to realize she's being insulted.

It should come as no surprise that Scoop concurs with Heidi's assessment of his wife. And when the band strikes up the bride and groom's favorite song (Sam Cooke's "You Send Me"), Scoop lingers in the anteroom with Heidi rather than return to the wedding. With the connecting door open (read: anyone could walk in), Scoop kisses Heidi and sways her tightly to the music in an intimate embrace.

That this man would risk his minutes-old marriage for the sake of a last kiss from Heidi could only mean that he is absurdly arrogant, psychic or that the playwright is mythologizing her heroine's charms.

John Updike once said of the English writer Henry Greene, "He never asks us to side with him against a character, and he never dramatizes his own prodigious acceptance of human incorrigibility." Ms. Wasserstein, on the other hand, is guilty on both counts. As Heidi gets older, her generosity evaporates toward younger women—those she and her friends see as ungratefully reaping the rewards of their hard-fought battles.

In a scene at a baby shower, a younger woman who "took

women's studies at Brown" is proved, ipso facto, to be a representative bubblehead of the coming generation. When a shower guest describes the young woman with whom Scoop is now illicitly involved, the unfortunate adultress is elevated to a symbol. "She's like that entire generation," confides the guest conspiratorially to her friends. "They have opinions on everything and have done nothing."

While Ms. Wasserstein does not put that sentence in Heidi's mouth, Heidi soon enough reveals her own bias. In a pivotal monologue, Heidi finally examines her own growing unease. She describes a kind of breakdown she had in the locker room at her gym. While stripping for aerobics class, Heidi becomes almost immobilized with depression as she listens to the other women jabbering around her. Her observations about these women center on what they're wearing, how old they are, where they shop and what they own.

One woman has "perfect red nails," another shops at Lord & Taylor, another likes brown rice and women's fiction. Most offensive, however, are "two 27-year-old hotshots," both wearing purple and green leather, who have busy careers, alligator datebooks and who bring their own heavier weights to class.

For once, Heidi's barbed tongue is rendered impotent by these women and their possessions; paradoxically, she feels their own judgments weighing heavily upon her. She imagines that they view her as having chosen "the wrong road." Childless, single and unhappy, Heidi says she feels stranded. She looks for the source of her unhappiness, but doesn't find it. "I don't blame the ladies in the locker room for how I feel," she says, after blaming them all. (pp. C13, C16)

At the play's conclusion, Heidi adopts a baby. Ms. Wasserstein avoids the question of motivation (was the adoption a reaction to the women in the locker room?), and the logistics of exactly how Heidi acquired the child. But Heidi's wish for her daughter, Judy, is simple and universal: that for Judy, "maybe, just maybe, things will be a little better."

Perhaps Ms. Wasserstein believes that in writing this scene, she has finally bestowed upon Heidi that generosity of spirit so lacking before. But if Heidi resents younger women who appear to have it easier than she did, how will she shield her own daughter from that resentment? When she blames the women's movement for leaving her stranded and alone, she chooses to ignore the real culprit. The person who has let Heidi down is none other than Heidi herself. (p. C16)

Laurie Winer, "Christine Lahti as an Angry Heidi in 'Chronicles'," in The New York Times, *October 9, 1989, pp. C13, C16.*

CORINNE ROBINS

It has become harder and harder to put together experiences and make sense out of our private and public lives. Four months ago, in a Broadway theater, slides of women artists flashed on a giant scrim and I saw the paintings and heard the names Artemisia Gentileschi, Sofonisba Anuissola, and Clara Peeters. It was exciting. I felt I was experiencing the breaking of the bounds of a secret, esoteric knowledge that we had mined in the nineteen-seventies. Women art historians I knew all had told me I must see *The Heidi Chronicles,* and in the play's opening moments I understood why: here in a public theater, I thought, I am watching the final dismantling of an art historical closet.

By the end of the play's first flashback, I was surprised and then horrified to discover that **The Heidi Chronicles** had been written with a very different purpose. In the famous children's classic, Heidi is a sickly little Swiss girl who goes to live on a mountaintop with her grandfather. In Wendy Wasserstein's play, heroine Heidi goes to live on the mountaintop of feminist art history, and thereby fails to live a normal life from the years 1965 to 1988. The play is a chronicle of the time, and Heidi Holland is the child/woman heroine the women's movement betrayed by seducing her into believing in an intellectual career for herself. As her lover in the play, Scoop Rosenbaum, publisher of a magazine called *Boomer,* explains (and we are supposed to accept that here he is talking for the author), Heidi has become an A+ and no man wants an A+ as a wife! There is even an implication that he is doing her a favor later on in continuing to visit her as part-time friend. Peter Patrone, the play's only sympathetic character, male or female, in the course of the first act discovers he is gay and takes up the women artists' protest placard and leads the march for Heidi. In the second act, he has become a pediatrician, is the only character to achieve a rewarding one-on-one relationship (besides being given the best lines), and wins nationwide recognition for his crusade for treating children with AIDS.

Indeed, the subtext of **The Heidi Chronicles** as a play is children. It seems the women's movement has condemned Heidi to a life of childless loneliness, and the next generation of women has been made into frantic, soulless careerists intent on having it all—careers, husbands, children—and hysterically unhappy. The play satirizes consciousness-raising groups and is rough on lesbians. All the images of women marching are shown as funny object lessons. And with all its talk about children and baby showers, and with minor characters running around with extended bellies, the question of abortion and of women's rights in any real context is never, never raised. The women's movement is presented as at best a quaint but somewhat dangerous aberration of the recent past, an old style whose power to attract has fallen away and, therefore, a timely subject for a historical overview. At the play's end (happy?), after being, as she says, lonely for so many years, Heidi is shown in a bathrobe taking care of her adopted baby daughter, fulfilled at last. So, of course, in the retro eighties, the play won a Pulitzer Prize.

Sitting listening to the slick Broadway jokes, I found myself becoming very angry. The image of a woman art historian had been carefully chosen because such intellectual distinctions as Heidi manages to achieve are of minor importance and have little or no effect on her or anyone else's life. But then, watching the photomontages of the women picketing, I suddenly felt absurdly happy: there we were, marching, smiling, being heard—the truths of consciousness-raising sessions and the real achievements the play set out to mock and minimize came bounding back. We had done it, I thought. Wasserstein had got it all wrong. I remembered my own past, how like many women of that time I went into the movement because I had a child, specifically a daughter, and was determined she should have a better chance. And it worked. We had done something. Today, there are no more "Help Wanted Male" employment sections. Equal opportunity laws, while under assault, are still in effect. And for sixteen years, women have not had to die under the knife of illegal abortions. We set out to do something and we made a difference.

We did something that, alas, looks like in part it may have to be done over. Even as we must live with the betrayals of the Wendy Wassersteins and Sandra Day O'Connors, who while profiting from the movement have set out to undermine it, women all over the country are gearing up, their bodies and their lives at stake, all of us aware that the war may be even harder the second time around.

Corinne Robins, "Betrayals," in The American Book Review, *Vol. 11, No. 5, November-December, 1989, p. 4.*

Fay Weldon
The Heart of the Country

Award: *Los Angeles Times* Award for fiction.

Weldon, born in 1933, is an English novelist, short story writer, scriptwriter, and dramatist.

In the opening pages of *The Heart of the Country,* real estate broker Harry Harris abandons his wife Natalie and their two children. Before he flees, Harry empties their bank accounts and Natalie's jewelry box, leaving employees and bills unpaid. Natalie, depicted as having the appearance and vitality of a doll, is forced to quickly come to terms with her new circumstances and rid herself of her passivity. In the process, she finds within herself a resilience and a will to survive she had not known she possessed. Narrated by Sonia, another abandoned wife, who shelters Natalie and her children after the loss of their home, *The Heart of the Country* presents Natalie's predicament in an ironic, unsentimental light. Melissa Pritchard commented: "With sure, succinct craft, Weldon melds highly comic fiction with acerbic social outrage. Even Sonia's occasionally over-shrill polemics are rescued by a manic, marvellous wit. With hell-bent, head-on energetic style and skill, *The Heart of the Country* lifts effortlessly above its considerable weight of rightful indignation. It is a provocative, brilliantly controlled performance."

Weldon has written numerous scripts for British television, stage, and film, some of which provide the basis for her popular novels. Her works are known for frequent authorial intrusions in which Weldon speaks to her characters or translates the unspoken meaning of their conversations for the reader, providing comic relief in plots that often concern marital abandonment and the consequent loss of custody of one's children. *The Heart of the Country,* like Weldon's other works, is blackly humorous, featuring unusual accidents and ridiculous incidents. Natalie Harris is a seemingly feminist heroine, beginning the novel in ignorance and apparent helplessness, learning how to call upon heretofore unrecognized inner resources, and eventually achieving some form of a victory out of seeming defeat. Critics noted that Natalie's otherwise bleak circumstances are somewhat brightened by her active sex life. *The Heart of the Country* is not considered a feminist novel, however, because Natalie readily gives up the self-respect to be found in her new, working-class life in order to become a wealthy man's mistress. Rather, the target of Weldon's satire in this novel is big business and bureaucracy in Margaret Thatcher's England. One of the most important lessons Sonia teaches Natalie is how to manipulate the system in order to survive as a single mother. Although some critics found Weldon's characters solely motivated by self-interest and incapable of arousing sympathy, all agreed that Weldon's satiric wit and energetic prose style are well represented in *The Heart of the Country.*

(See also *CLC,* Vols. 6, 9, 11, 19, 36; *Contemporary Authors,*

Vols. 21-24, rev. ed.; *Contemporary Authors New Revision Series,* Vol. 16; and *Dictionary of Literary Biography,* Vol. 14.)

PRINCIPAL WORKS

NOVELS

The Fat Woman's Joke   1967; also published as *And the Wife Ran Away,*   1968
Down Among the Women   1971
Female Friends   1975
Remember Me   1976
Words of Advice   1977; published in England as *Little Sisters,*   1978
Praxis   1979
Puffball   1980
The President's Child   1982
The Life and Loves of a She-Devil   1984
The Shrapnel Academy   1986
The Hearts and Lives of Men   1987
The Rules of Life   1987

Leader of the Band 1988
The Heart of the Country 1988

SHORT FICTION COLLECTIONS

Watching Me, Watching You 1981
Polaris and Other Stories 1985

BRENDA MADDOX

[In *The Heart of the Country,* pretty] Natalie Harris is presented one morning with a feminist's tabula rasa. Husband disappeared; bank account empty, jewelry gone, school fees unpaid—and his office staff too. Children and dog hungry. Surely Harry will return to face his responsibilities? He doesn't. . . .

Natalie is totally unprepared for life in the abyss. She does not even know if there is a mortgage on the house. Let's get you out, Fay Weldon seems to say to her heroine. And Weldon does, in a way that allows her to indulge her wit, her philosophy (all men are shits), and her rage at Mrs. Thatcher's Britain. Weldon also draws upon what may be her deeper faith—in the power of pagan spirits emanating from the ancient landscape.

The West Country where Natalie lives (in a Somerset village between Wells and Glastonbury) is a magical part of England, where a hand once reached from a lake and proffered a sword to the young Arthur. King Arthur is buried in the grounds of Glastonbury Abbey, and Weldon conjures up the image of alpha waves emanating from the dead king's brain as he sleeps, ready to wake in the hour of England's need.

Natalie certainly needs a hero. Weldon, whose greatest marvel is probably not her fast pace nor her brilliant asides but her wit and wisdom about sex, never allows Natalie to lose interest in the two-backed beast. Natalie's first reaction upon desertion is that she is being punished for adultery: "Another man has entered in where no other man has any right to be." Her second is to find another man.

Another "unsupported" mother, Sonia, gives Natalie and her two children a place to live in a cramped council flat. Soon Sonia is in love with Natalie and doing propaganda for the female alternative. But Natalie cannot cooperate, even to please Sonia, and soon goes out and sells herself to fat admiring Angus in exchange for a roof and a good screw. . . .

Weldon's kids are satiric gems: the real test of a writer whose forte is women. Ben, the elder, speaks in his father's voice (and his prime minister's too, Weldon implies). Curling his lip at the squalid front yards of the poor, Ben sneers: " 'It doesn't cost them anything just to tidy up, does it? But they'd rather live off the rest of us than lift a finger . . . ' "

In the end (which comes far too soon) the children and the dog have bettered their lot and ditched Natalie. She finds a more satisfying, if transparently temporary solution—downmarket, but well supplied with the fleshly pleasures. The suspense remains, through to the last page, even after the fiery climax, which suggests that witches will not be defied, nor will the heterosexual itch.

The novel, already a television series on the BBC, owes part of its rollicking pace to Weldon's refusal ever to apologize,

ever to explain. *The Heart of the Country* is very political, a wicked satire of survival in the British 1980s, a world of fatherless families, rapacious auctioneers, greedy property speculators, and snobby children. Weldon might just as easily have titled it *Last Days of the Welfare State.* "King Arthur," she seems to cry out, "Your Country Needs You!"

Brenda Maddox, in a review of "The Heart of the Country," in Ms., Vol. 17, November, 1988, p. 78.

SUSAN ISAACS

Right from the start of [*The Heart of the Country,* a] toughminded, witty novel, the narrator informs us that Natalie Harris's husband has run off with a local carnival queen, leaving Natalie with two children, a dog and cat, a mortgaged-to-the-hilt house and an awesome pile of debts. Natalie is ill-equipped to face adversity, much less the impersonal malignity of the British welfare system.

> Picture Natalie. Round face, blonde-haired, pretty as a girl in an early Charlie Chaplin movie, with that same blank look of sexy idiocy on her face. It was as if she was born to go around with subtitles: *Help me, save me. Poor little me.* It was how she had been brought up to look; not her fault. And, as it turned out, when faced by disaster she was in fact competent enough.

Something funny is going on in *The Heart of the Country,* and it is more than Fay Weldon's celebrated sardonic humor; it is the narrator, clearly no imperturbable, omniscient observer. The voice that tells the story is shrewd, bitchy and emotional: "For his unkindness, for his blindness, Harry Harris deserves to be unhappy with Miss Eddon Gurney 1978, though I don't suppose he will be."

The voice, the reader learns soon enough, belongs to Sonia, welfare mother, feminist, censorious social critic—and inmate of a mental hospital. She relates Natalie's story, starting from the first awful realization that although Harry did leave the family Volvo, it's so low on gas it won't get her two sullen children to school, and continuing through her battles with the private and public sectors: the forced sale of her house, the auction of her property, her victimization by men. . . .

But this is not a comforting feminist fiction where sisterhood is powerful and Natalie, Sonia and their put-upon neighbors emerge with the wisdom of Athena and the iron backbone of the Statue of Liberty. Weldon's women—flighty, unbalanced, vulnerable, angry or naive—are up against the monsters of Big Government and Big Business. The author is taking on modern society; her vision is broader, deeper than the conventional, minutely observed domestic world of "fine" American fiction. Unlike so many female novelists in the United States, she does not indulge in the literary *petit point.* Rather, Weldon the artist is the Abstract Expressionist. She paints with broad, gestural brush strokes, offering the reader mordant visions of people flailing about in a desperate attempt to preserve their own self-interest against forces—sexism, poverty, a poisoned environment, idiot government agencies—they are ultimately powerless to control.

Because all the characters in the novel, even the bad guys, are ultimately victims of these forces, the reader pities them. But the people in *The Heart of the Country* are vehicles for Weldon's satire and political observations rather than flesh-and-blood individuals. The characters are also somewhat less than appealing because they reflect their rapacious culture; their main motivation is self-interest. Sonia, for example, offers personal consciousness-raising assistance to Natalie, but she is not completely altruistic. She wants a sexual relationship with Natalie. And Natalie, for all her awakening, her new-found sensitivity, her willingness to withstand horrendous working conditions (for horrible wages) in a quarry to get off the dole, is ultimately willing to turn over her children to the no-good Harry and live as the mistress of the congenial, bumbling, chauvinistic, manipulative auctioneer who sold her down the river in the first place.

Fay Weldon is an insightful and persuasive social commentator. She is also a very funny writer. Ultimately, however, the novel's power is somewhat diminished by its own stylishness and cleverness. Instead of being moved, the reader is entertained with smart, cool prose. Only God could love these foolish motals; the reader can only like them. *The Heart of the Country,* in other words, lacks heart. But it certainly has an exhilarating mind.

Susan Isaacs, "A Woman Scorned," in Book World—The Washington Post, *November 13, 1988, p. 3.*

MELISSA PRITCHARD

In her latest novel, *The Heart of the Country,* Fay Weldon presents us with a fierce, ironically funny performance where aerialists of fiction and social criticism catch hand-over-hand without a slip or lapse—in fact, work together with dazzling effect.

The aptly satiric title is dual in implication. To dwell in the Elysian heart of the countryside is presumed the ideal existence. Yet the inhabitants of this pastoral refuge wreak economic chaos and sexual mischief among themselves—humanity the chancre at the blissful heart of nature. The heart of Great Britain, Weldon's country of residence, with its political turmoil and stagnant buracracy, also comes in for wry observation. . . .

The Heart of The Country begins when doll-faced, childishly naive Natalie, having been kept in cozy ignorance under the mantle of male privilege, is abruptly deserted—left with children and without funds by her husband Harry, who has bounded off with a local carnival queen. Meanwhile, through the mordant commentary of Sonia, another abandoned wife with children, we are witness to Natalie's plummeting descent and slow, sassy comeback.

Sonia is not like Natalie, numbed by the potent anesthetic of self-interest. Instead, she is motivated by an unquenchable thirst for justice (with an emphasis on sexual inequities) that literally drives her mad. Her narration, the entirety of the book, is addressed to us from the psychiatric hospital. When her psychiatrist, incredibly, proposes marriage, Sonia, cursed with an acute political and social consciousness, declines such illusory happiness, preferring her slightly mad, passionate quest for justice.

Before her hospitalization, Sonia has taken Natalie and her two thoroughly spoiled children into her home, tutoring Natalie in the treacherous ways of the welfare system and its nefarious treatment of abandoned mothers with children. Natalie learns competently enough, yet opts out of feminism and sisterly loyalty the first chance she is offered rescue by

a man—helpless to resist the monetary and emotional consolation that men so often feel compelled to offer her. . . .

With sure, succinct craft, Weldon melds highly comic fiction with acerbic social outrage. Even Sonia's occasionally over-shrill polemics are rescued by a manic, marvellous wit. With hell-bent, head-on energetic style and skill, *The Heart of the*

An excerpt from *The Heart of the Country*

Natalie had sinned badly that morning, taking her children to school (private, of course), driving too close to Sonia, an unsupported mother, who, with Edwina (4), Bess (5) and Teresa (6) filed along the busy road in the rain, as close in to the prickly hedge as they could, for fear of sudden death on their way to a school (not private, of course) which all three children hated, but which the law obliged them to attend. Natalie simply didn't see them: she didn't even notice they were there.

Alice, Natalie's little girl, noticed. Alice said, 'It's raining. Why don't we give them a lift?'

Ben said: 'You're so stupid, Alice. We don't give lifts to people like that.'

But Natalie just said, peering through a misty windscreen, which neither wipers nor demister at full blast would clear: 'Do be quiet, children,' without actually hearing a word they were saying. In her defence it was a nasty morning for driving, but that is not the kind of excuse the Prime Mover likes to hear. He, after all, sends the rain. He worked in his mysterious way, and Sonia helped. She looked after the retreating five-door Volvo Estate. (Of course it was a Volvo. What else?) Jax the Alsatian, the Harris' dog, looked back at Sonia and grinned. Even the dogs of the rich live better than do the new poor. The dogs ride; the poor walk, or go by bus. There are very few buses anymore in the countryside. The rich don't take them. That means buses don't, on the whole, make profits. So they have to be subsidized. But who's going to subsidize them? The rich, who don't need them or use them? Ho, ho!

'God rot her,' said Sonia aloud. 'Rich bitch!' Sonia had been born a nice round pleasant thing. Her life and times had turned her sour, so now she could deliver a curse or two, effectively. God heard. God sent his punishment on Natalie. Or was it the Devil? He forgave her other sins, but got her for this one. Natalie committed the sin of carelessly splashing Sonia. Sonia cursed her. Misfortune fell on Natalie. Cause and effect? Surely not. Let's just say coincidence, and remind ourselves that the trouble at Harrix and in the Harris household long predated this particular event. Except of course God may send his punishments retrospectively. We may all of us be being punished *now* for sins we are about to commit. Time may not be as linear as we suppose.

'What have I done?' asked Natalie, pretty white sinful hand, used to exploring Arthur's chest hairs, to her mouth. She addressed the universe as much as Hilary.

Well, as I say, the wages of sin! There's no telling. The day Natalie Harris splashed Sonia with mud was the day Harry Harris left for work in the morning and did not return home, ever. Some sins are obviously worse than others.

Country lifts effortlessly above its considerable weight of rightful indignation. It is a provocative, brilliantly controlled performance.

Melissa Pritchard, "A Fierce, Manic Wit Fuels Fay Weldon's Vivid, Rural Satire," in Chicago Tribune—Books, *November 20, 1988, p. 6.*

ROSEMARY DANIELL

[Weldon] writes for readers with a taste for irony, and in *The Heart of the Country,* as in many of her other novels, she starts with a situation that could easily become melodrama.

Instead it turns into high comedy, yet comedy with meat, full of pronouncements on society, the plight of women and the relationships between the sexes. Nor do these pronouncements—in this case, issuing mostly from the sometime narrator, Sonia, an English welfare mother who has been hospitalized after committing a murder—sound at all didactic. Ms. Weldon merely verbalizes the kinds of observations we've made ourselves, the kinds of insights we've had but may not have expressed. And she does so with skills that have been honed to the sharpness of an exclamation point (which appears to be her favorite form of punctuation).

When *The Heart of the Country* begins, doll-like Natalie Harris is the sort of woman who, before driving her children to school in the morning, spends "twenty minutes washing, dressing, plucking, preening." ("The rest of us," Sonia dryly notes, "pull on a pair of jeans and yesterday's sweater.") Then suddenly Natalie is left penniless, with two children (one teary, one surly), without enough gas in the car or a few spare pounds to pay her maid. Out of the blue, her husband, Harry, proprietor of a company called Harrix, has absconded to Spain with his secretary, "Miss Eddon Gurney 1978," after first cleaning out the marital and business bank accounts—and even Natalie's jewelry box. Because Harry cheerily waved goodbye to her that morning, promising to be home by 6:30 to greet their dinner guests, Natalie at first resists the alarming evidence.

She next blames herself, since she has rather passionlessly been trysting every Tuesday and Thursday afternoon with Arthur, a local antiques dealer who is also married. Another of the sins of which Natalie is guilty is "the special sin of splashing the poor," which she has committed that very morning while driving her children to school. Heedlessly, even haughtily, she has sped past Sonia, walking in the rain with her three youngsters, further drenching the little group without even thinking of offering a ride.

But very soon Natalie has acknowledged Harry's treachery. And as the unfortunate Sonia and her brood trudge homeward, Natalie—quickly softened by misfortune, or is it expediency?—offers the other woman a lift. Already looking toward her poverty-stricken future, she asks the surprised Sonia where the welfare office is located. (p. 11)

Ms. Weldon is excellent at the telling image: the details of a meal in preparation, the state of a house. (She is especially fond of dinner parties as scenes for revelations of plot, motivation.) And when she describes Natalie's shoes, we know exactly what kind of woman she is: "She owned eighteen pairs, and fifteen of these had high heels, so when the hard times came she had only three for getting about in, and two of those were sandals."

Yet, almost immediately, Natalie begins to draw energy from a source previously unknown to her—that is, her own will to survive. Before long, our formerly well-shod heroine is reduced to accepting the gift of an unplucked, uncleaned chicken from a pharmacist named Angus who, hearing of her distress, determines to become her next lover. . . .

Within weeks, Natalie—once perfectly dressed, sparklingly housed—has lost all the accouterments of her middle-class life: car (repossessed), house (sold for taxes and debts), furnishings (auctioned off by Arthur). Thus reduced, she arrives with her children to bang on Sonia's front door, pleading for sanctuary.

Sonia, expert in the ways of the disenfranchised, at first instructs Natalie. Then—fat, puffed by anger and out of touch with men—she falls in love with her roommate, enjoying their cozy if shabby proximity and Natalie's dependence. When Natalie, by now straggling home each day from a thankless, low-paying job as a gofer in the office of a local quarry, gives in to Angus's entreaties—not to mention his offer of support and a fine flat—Sonia is enraged. Thereafter the plot (which includes several other well-developed female characters) thickens, concluding with the murder that has put Sonia in the mental hospital from which she speaks.

Despite all this, almost everyone ends happy (even Sonia), yet not at all in a predictable manner, bringing home Ms. Weldon's point that a materialistic, conventional "happiness"—in other words, the suburban nuclear family—is not always what it's cracked up to be. . . .

The Heart of the Country also deals with human resilience, the lessons to be learned from hardship, the primacy of the will to survive and the fact that women are never really free without a degree of economic and sexual parity—and that they still so infrequently have either. In some of Ms. Weldon's other novels, her characters' naïveté, her love of the offbeat, occasionally become a test of her readers' credulity. But in this book there's hardly a moment that doesn't ring perfectly true. (p. 12)

Rosemary Daniell, "The Comforts of Downward Mobility," in The New York Times Book Review, *December 11, 1988, pp. 11-12.*

CHRISTINE BENVENUTO

It's the wars at home that Weldon is concerned with, and her novels are laconic eyewitness reports on the modern British housewife. Collaborators in their own and each other's misery, women, says Weldon, snare themselves in familial traps, and just because they are caught, think they are safe as well. But ties to parents, husbands, even children are highly perishable: bowled over by the most predictable of marital disasters, Weldon's characters can't possibly survive the ensuing chaos as they are. So they change, and in the process turn out to be made of less flimsy stuff than they thought. Families may be replaceable but, once shattered, a woman's sense of complacency will never be the same.

The Heart of the Country is narrated by Sonia, a spectator in the story she tells of one affluent housewife's punishment for her sins. Sonia's subject is pretty, stupid Natalie, and the sins in question include Natalie's biweekly assignations with Arthur, one of two local business moguls; her habit of always appearing smartly groomed, even first thing in the morning, while all the other suburban housewives look like . . . suburban housewives; and whizzing through the rain in a soon-to-be-repossessed Volvo, splashing those who must walk and calling down upon herself the curses of the less fortunate, which in Weldon's universe (*Puffball, The Life and Loves of a She-Devil*) can have an awesome destructive power. But Natalie's worst offense is her utter ignorance of family finances and the shaky basis of her own apparent prosperity. When husband Harry Harris permanently declines to come home one day, that luxury is the first to go. Though no emotional blow, Harry's abdication results in the loss of Natalie's car, credit, family dog, home, and comfortable delusions.

With nowhere else to turn, Natalie and her two children appear on Sonia's doorstep. Sonia, who has been abandoned herself, takes them in and gives Natalie a crash course on life with small children in the welfare state. "For the heart of the country," says Sonia, "read the pocket of the country." The underside of Natalie's Somerset is a landscape of public-assistance degradation, Oxfam clothes, and frozen fish fingers for dinner. It's Sonia's view that the most compelling reason for holding on to a husband is economic, and Weldon drives this point home by scattering grim statistics on divorce and unemployment throughout the narrative.

Weldon's scenarios are brutal but not depressing, in part because she's so witty, but also because she allows her characters, no matter how abject, plenty of sex. Natalie ends her affair with Arthur when she is abandoned by Harry, but soon takes up with Angus, the town's other prime mover. (pp. 3-4)

Through Angus, Natalie gets work on a "housewives' float," to be entered in the annual West Country parade as a real-estate advertisement. Ninety feet long, the float is decked out with replicas of houses, effigies of Arthur and Angus, and, dressed in frilly aprons and brandishing feather dusters, Natalie, Sonia, and nearly all the novel's peripheral females. But the women have secretly rigged the float to explode the cozy image Arthur and Angus intend to sell. The miniature town sails through cheering crowds blaring Pete Seeger's "Little Boxes," wreaking havoc and tragedy, and shifting the course of a number of lives.

Weldon has written a pithy, almost epigrammatic *Middlemarch* for the late-20th century. She provides psychosocial commentary on each of the characters, doling out blame, kudos, and an appropriate fate to all. Natalie herself recapitulates, in 200 pages, the progress of the Weldon heroine over the course of a dozen-odd novels from self-deceived victim to clear-sighted survivor. As in any morality tale, her hardships end up being good for her by making her not more virtuous, but more daring. To quote Sonia, "Unlike virtue, courage is not its own reward. It has results." (p. 4)

Christine Benvenuto, in a review of "The Heart of the Country," in VLS, January-February, 1989, pp. 3-4.

VALERIE MINER

The Heart of the Country is set in rural West Somerset, as much a metaphor for Thatcherite England as it is an actual place. . . . Weldon's approach is startlingly agitprop with its statistics about desertion, divorce, sex-differentiated income and welfare subsidies.

Fay Weldon's high irony leaves readers reeling. Just when we think nothing more can happen, just when we're gaining breath between gasps and laughs, something worse does occur. *The Heart of the Country* is a picaresque novel in which the protagonists, being village mums, don't go anywhere, but have more than their share of adventures, thank you very much.

The story opens on an average day in a middle-class home as Natalie Harris is preparing a dinner party for her husband and two other local couples. Until now, Natalie's biggest challenge has been how to keep the chicken entrée from drying out. During the day, she discovers another snag in the forthcoming soirée:

> Harry Harris ran off leaving his wife living in a dream bungalow mortgaged up to the hilt and beyond, no money in the bank and school fees owing. He left her with no job, unqualified and untrained, and with no experience other than as a businessman's wife and mother of two extremely self-centered children, aged eleven and twelve.

At first Natalie takes this in her stride, which is to say she denies what is happening. She manages to make it through the dinner party, pretending Harry has been delayed at work. But the next day dawns with a series of impossible realities. She has to remove the kids from private school, get rid of her housekeeper, put the bungalow on the market, surrender the car and sell her soul to the Department of Health and Social Security. Shortly she moves her family into the crowded flat of her formerly despised neighbor, the ragged welfare mother Sonia.

Who is the protagonist—Natalie, treacherously sliding down the socio-economic scale, or Sonia, already stuck at the bottom? (Sonia, the narrator, is relating this story from a mental hospital where she is serving time for arson and murder—but we are ahead of ourselves here.) Sonia, an insistent, sometimes intrusive and always engaging raconteur, unveils her own life as she describes Natalie's. Another middle-class woman dumped into poverty by her husband, she proves more savvy than Natalie. She is a member of the Claimants' Union and is managing to raise her three daughters by herself. After taking in Natalie's family, she shows her how to negotiate with the DHSS and helps her back on her feet. In the process she falls in love with her, but manages to keep her feelings properly discreet so that they do damage only to herself.

Sonia and Natalie are a study in sympathetic contrasts. As clueless as Natalie is at the outcome, she is a survivor who winds up being taken care of by yet another man. Sonia, with her clear, radical analysis, is judged mad by society. In the end, she too survives, but forgoes the safety of heterosexual coupling to continue shaking up the world and risking a return to the padded clinker. Weldon presents both these options as reasonable and unreasonable and most of all as authentic.

Weldon's broad humor is seamed into the character's allusive names—beginning with Harry Harris, owner of the Harrix firm, who runs off with his secretary, Marian Hopfoot. Natalie has an affair with Arthur, the antique dealer, who is married to Jane. After Arthur, she turns to Angus, the realtor, whose wife is named Jean. The men with the interchangeable spouses also have interchangeable positions in Tory consumerism—one sells houses while the other sells the things that go into the houses. We also meet the failed yuppie couple, Sal and Val, and the romantic bohemian Flora, who blossoms in her life at the town dump with her ever-faithful boyfriend, Bernard, woman's best friend.

One fine Weldonian stroke is the integration of statistics to support sardonic moments. Near the beginning of her story, Sonia alludes to a scene—which we later experience more fully as the climax of the book—where the local women ride on a commercial parade float.

> Who else but men would dress their wives and mistresses, those they torment, abuse and exploit, in the clothes of the fifties, hand them feather dusters, oblige them to smile and parade the streets of Somerset on a ninety-foot float consisting of pretty little estate houses with lace curtains? In a world where something like 40 percent of women are out at work (and 45 percent of men), 25 percent of mothers are on social security, 40 percent (and rising) are over 60 years of age, how can men still cling to the consoling myth of the loving female in the dream house? Husband out to work, two children at school, mother at home looking after them— that's the rarity these days, not the norm, just 23 percent of the total of households.

Weldon applies her seasoned scepticism even-handedly. None of her characters is politically correct or morally righteous. She is not saying that only males "cheat" on their partners, rather that because heterosexual men control the surroundings in which we all have sex, sleep and eat, they usually wind up on safe ground. The narrative tensions build inexorably on a series of internal metaphors. Flagrant adultery within the sanctified homes of West Somerset is paralleled by mindless adulteration of the earth by entrepreneurs like Angus and Arthur, whose investment in British agriculture requires injecting carcinogenic additives into the soil.

The climax in this heartless country is a brilliant montage representing Thatcherite free enterprise. Angus and Arthur have commissioned a carnival float to parade their civic contributions. However, they leave construction of the mobile monument to local women, who create grotesque caricatures of the greedy businessmen. As the float passes through the village advertising Tory avarice, the crowds fall apart laughing at the effigies of Angus and Arthur. Then, in a stroke of Pythonesque headiness which Sonia hopes will be the crowning moment, she sets the float afire. Everyone escapes except Flora, who dies in the blaze. Weldon could have rescued Flora, but that would have resulted in a morality play in which the innocent are saved and the culpable damned, and she is less interested in didactic resolution than in Brechtian provocation.

Weldon's dialogue and sense of theatrical moment are impressive (she has written six stage dramas as well as thirteen previous books of fiction). What stays with me most, however, is the complex development of Sonia's character. As we proceed deeper into *The Heart of the Country,* Sonia gets saner and readers grow wiser. Sonia obviously enjoys telling her story, although parts of it are almost unbearably painful. She is sharp, economical, wry and conscious of the place of feminist instincts in fiction and in real life.

> Not for Sonia, Flora's triumphant puff of smoke, her exaltation; not for Sonia, Natalie's glorious debasement: no, for Sonia comes a proposal of marriage from a good man, who knows her every failing. She can't accept, of course. Happy endings are

not so easy. No. She must get on with changing the world, rescuing the country. There is no time left for frivolity.

(p. 36)

Valerie Miner, "Living through Politics," in The Women's Review of Books, *Vol. VI, Nos. 10-11, July, 1989, pp. 36-7.*

MARIANNE WIGGINS

There is no woman writing in the United States to whose reputation Fay Weldon's place in British letters can be compared. To begin with, for the last 15 years, every novel of hers has been a bestseller in Great Britain. She is singular among her generation here (she is the generation of Margaret Drabble, Penelope Lively and Anita Brookner) in that she frequently adapts her novels for television, or novelizes one of her own teleplays, and so she has a large and loyal following among people who may never read her books. She herself often appears on television. . . .

In a season which has seen the British litcrit furiously swallow its own tail in torment over the "anaemic" state of English fiction, Weldon has retained a robust reputation. Hers are not the cozy parlor novels, nor does she dabble in nostalgia for this country's faded manners. Her views are formed around the front page news: Her topics range from moral aspects of genetic engineering to the effects of fallout from Chernobyl and the breakdown of all forms of social caring under the sheer wear and tear of daily life in Margaret Thatcher's Britain. One can count upon the news appearing as a leitmotif in Weldon's work, but the real abiding passion at the center of her fiction is the mess that men and women seem to make as soon as they begin to think they like each other. Her subject is the war that doesn't need to issue draft cards, dears: the one between the sexes.

In print, she is an ironist. In person, she's a giggler. She delights in life and her enthusiasm for it sparkles through her prose. She likes to lecture readers now and then with stern asides, but the things she lectures on are things as thrillingly arcane as beans and salt, and if and when to add the salt to the beans while cooking them. She is spirited and fun to read and bloody sexy in the way she handles characters and situations, and she's not afraid to detonate the F-word right there on Page 1. Nor is she afraid to quip and, if so moved, equivocate. Asked by an interviewer before an audience of British feminists, "Do you call yourself a feminist writer?" she quickly answered, "That depends on the company."

Technically, hers is a poison pen—apt, but dreggy with a smartchick's murderous intent. She has a killing wit. There is a Weldon style, and it's dependable. There is, especially, a Weldon style of plot. This is generally composed of a) an arch, ironic narrative spiked with b) a lot of sex between c) stereotypically gruesome men and d) neurotically heroic women who are the keepers of e) weird and/or precocious children accustomed to f) scenes of domestic violence in g) a topsy-turvy random world where people suffer all sorts of h) physical grotesqueries. Oh yes, and i) the women pretty nearly always win the war between the sexes and j) the prose is broken on the page by distinctive spaces between episodes, defining brief vignettes as salty and addictive and as easy to consume as individual nibbles in a bag of chips.

The Heart of the Country, the novel for which she's been

awarded [the 1989 *Los Angeles Times* award for fiction], is a classic of her genre. The "country" in question is the England of the recent years, where everything is being privatized except romance. Its "heart" is nominally Somerset, but it could just as well be Chevy Chase, Bethesda and Carmel—anywhere where people live in private homes that aren't attached, own cars and trade in gossip about neighbors. The "country," too, is marriage; and its "heart" is pumping something black.

The women in the novel meet and bond because they need each others' comfort. The men associate for profit and use the women as a sport. There are tips throughout (those little lectures) on how to milk The System, every system, ranging from the dole to public transportation. And there is madness, accidental murder and, too, as the result of madness, a final accidental love.

Accidents, both catastrophic and mundane, occur in Weldon's prose as if they're a part of grammar. Her characters aren't more prone to accidents than any other writer's characters, but it's clear that she believes the world they live in *is*. And the world they live in isn't something she's invented, it's the world she has observed, it's ours as much as theirs and hers. . . .

Frivolous Fay Weldon isn't, nor fainthearted. To read [**The Heart of the Country**] is fun. The kind of fun that can be had when we are deadly serious about sending up the forces of oppression with sophisticated and unholy humor.

Marianne Wiggins, "Unholy Humour from the Heart of the Country," in Los Angeles Times Book Review, *November 5, 1989, p. 9.*

In Memoriam

Edward Abbey
January 29, 1927 - March 14, 1989

American novelist and nonfiction writer.

For an overview of Abbey's life and work see *CLC,* Vol. 36; *Contemporary Authors,* Vols. 45-48, 128 [obituary]; and *Contemporary Authors New Revision Series,* Vol. 2.

BARRY LOPEZ

I first met Ed Abbey in Salt Lake City. We'd each been invited separately to the University of Utah to speak. He was kind enough to ask if I'd like to join him, to merge our dates in a benefit reading for the Utah Wilderness Association. I told him I'd be honored.

The hours before the reading were chaotic. Each of us spoke to separate groups of people. We lunched and then dined with faculty and students. We didn't have a chance to talk for more than a few minutes. But my impression of him hardly changed after that. He seemed both serene and startled in our moments together. There was something vital in him. I liked him immediately.

Writers, of course, are exceedingly diverse, and perhaps more wary around each other on first meeting than most, when they are put together by someone else in a public situation. The public persona each maintains to protect his privacy can make a wall between them, and distort what they might otherwise easily share. Too, one writer might believe the other is simply a drummer of some kind, and no writer. (p. 62)

Readers bring writers together in curious ways. To some extent, writers are the creations of the shorthanded imagery of newspapers, of literary gossip. They are grouped regionally, placed in various "schools," or presumed to be somewhat like each other because they write about similar things. But writers maintain only tenuous friendships on these grounds—or become estranged because someone of note has glibly put them together, or separated them. Writers do not become friends solely because they write about the same things, nor solely because they admire each other's prose. They have to like each other as people, often as the people readers rarely know, because no writer can stand that kind of intimacy with readers and go on writing.

Ed was about to take a bite of his dinner when I said I thought you had to be respectful of vulnerability in readers. He paused with his fork in the air, and said yes, from somewhere far away in himself. The two of us, private men, both somewhat shy, found ourselves looking silently into the same abyss, and acknowledging a similar vulnerability in ourselves. A cynical remark at that moment and we would have forever

gone our separate ways. But there was none. It was a moment of trust. (p. 63)

In those first moments with Ed I was struck by what I admire most in anyone: honesty; unpretentious convictions; a bedrock opposition to what menaces life. I imagined we might share enemies, though I felt no inclination to enumerate or describe them.

We read that evening together. The stories we read, about men and women in unmanipulated Western landscapes, expressed sentiments closely shared with people in the audience. I felt that night, strongly, almost physically, the beliefs I have about language—its power to evoke life and to remove pain—and the obligation writers have to dismantle the false notion of their own prophesies, the unexamined prejudices that can compel a public figure to demagoguery. I spoke that evening of a Spanish concept—*querencia,* a common, defended ground, an emotional landscape shared by listener and storyteller. Its defense implies a threat; without threat, without menace, there is neither literature nor heroism.

Abbey, with his caustic accusations and droll humor, his Western skepticism, was an encouragement to stand up for belief. As I listened to him read, I thought, well, here is a good man, a fine and decent neighbor. He reads before university audiences like this, is misunderstood, misquoted, misappropriated, but he goes on writing—an endless penetration of his own mind, a hunger for greater clarity, precision. How better this than were he to turn to politics, or to take solemnly the notion that he speaks for anyone but himself.

Since that evening I have gotten to know Ed better. The large and slow pleasure he takes in looking over the contours of a landscape, his affinity for music. A characteristic broad, sudden, and uncalculated smile. His ingenuous shyness, so at odds with the public image of a bold iconoclast.

We have specific disagreements, he and I, which we do not pursue, out of courtesy and a simple awareness of the frailty of human life, the gulf between human intent and human act. But nothing much has changed between us since that night, except that we have grown closer out of mutual regard, some unspoken sense of an opposition to a threat, a definition of which we largely agree upon.

You can point to the quirks and miscalculations of any writer exposed to the searing heat of public acclaim. Better to select what is admirable and encouraging, if a man is not a charlatan. Abbey's self-effacing honesty, the ease with which he can admire someone else's work without feeling he diminishes his own—these are qualities wonderful to find in any human. How fortunate for all of us that they are found in a man widely known and well regarded, who persists in writing out his understanding of the world as though it mattered to more than only himself. (pp. 64-5)

> *Barry Lopez, "Meeting Ed Abbey," in* Resist Much, Obey Little: Some Notes on Edward Abbey, *edited by James Hepworth and Gregory McNamee, Harbinger House, 1989, pp. 62-5.*

THE NEW YORK TIMES

Edward Abbey, a naturalist, novelist and one-time forest ranger, died of a circulatory disorder yesterday [March 14, 1989] at his home in Oracle, Ariz. He was 62 years old.

Mr. Abbey was described as "a voice crying in the wilderness, *for* the wilderness," by Edwin Way Teale in *The New York Times Book Review* on Jan. 28, 1968 [see *CLC,* Vol. 36]. Reviewing *Desert Solitaire: A Season in the Wilderness,* Mr. Teale wrote that to "the builders and developers" among park administrators, "his book may well seem like a wild ride on a bucking bronco. It is rough, tough and combative. The author is a rebel, an eloquent loner."

In that work Mr. Abbey offered a prescription on how to save the West's dwindling natural resources and monuments:

> No more cars in national parks. Let the people walk. Or ride horses, bicycles, mules, wild pigs—anything—but keep the automobiles and motorcycles and all their motorized relatives out . . . A civilization which destroys what little remains of the wild, the spare, the original, is cutting itself off from its origins.

Mr. Abbey's most recent novel, *The Fool's Progress,* was published last fall. Among his other titles are *Good News,* a novel on 21st-century life in the United States. *The Journey*

Home, Down the River and *Beyond the Wall,* books of essays; *Abbey's Road, The Hidden Canyon* and *The Monkey Wrench Gang,* a novel about a gang of ecological saboteurs that destroys railroads and bridges in the American Southwest. The book, published in 1976, sold in the hundreds of thousands in paperback, and made Mr. Abbey an underground cult hero throughout the West. A sequel to *The Monkey Wrench Gang* is to be published next winter.

> *An obituary in* The New York Times, *March 15, 1989, p. D19.*

BURT A. FOLKART

Edward Abbey, the irreverent writer and impassioned environmentalist whose popular books perpetuated their author's dream of seeing "the whole American West made into a wilderness," has died in Tucson.

The man dubbed "the Thoreau of the American West" by *Lonesome Dove* author Larry McMurtry died Tuesday at his home at age 62 of internal bleeding caused by a circulatory disorder, said Jack Macrae, a friend who also is editor-in-chief of Henry Holt & Co., Abbey's publisher.

Abbey recently had completed a draft of *Hayduke Lives,* a sequel to his best-known book, *The Monkey Wrench Gang,* which told of a group of environmentalists plotting to blow up Arizona's Glen Canyon Dam.

Hundreds of thousands of paperback copies of *The Monkey Wrench Gang* were sold after its publication in 1976, making Abbey a sort of underground hero to the burgeoning environmental movement.

His writings have been credited by founders of the hard-line environmental group Earth First! with providing the underpinnings of their philosophy.

Hayduke Lives would be the 20th book by the one-time park ranger, firefighter and political radical.

The renegade outdoorsman once said there was nothing wrong with throwing beer cans out car windows, since paved roads were abominations and unworthy of respect. He had grown to hate the survey stakes, aircraft and golf courses that marred his once-pristine desert landscape.

Anthologies refer to him as "irascible," "cantankerous," "iconoclastic" and "crusty."

Abbey himself resisted simple summations, even those calling him environmentalist or naturalist. "If a label is required," he once wrote, "say that I am one who loves the unfenced country."

Despite the fact that he found himself "getting more radical as I get older," as he told *The Times* last year, he was not without a sense of humor.

Two years ago *Outside* magazine asked Abbey for an almanac of the high and low points of the 1975-85 decade.

Under "Low Point" he wrote: "Beef ranchers in Montana and Wyoming harvest 155 'troublesome' grizzlies."

The "High Point" read: "Grizzlies in Montana and Wyoming harvest 22 'troublesome' tourists."

In *One Life at a Time Please* he offered essays guaranteed

to offend everyone he touched. Cattlemen were "nothing more than Western parasites." Recent arrivals to the West were "instant rednecks."

But Abbey represented far more than the wise-cracking, one-time farm boy he was.

In a review of *Desert Solitaire,* Pulitzer Prize-winning author Edwin Way Teale noted that Abbey's work as a park ranger had brought him to the wilderness before the invasion of "the parked trailers, their windows blue tinged at night while the inmates, instead of watching the desert stars, watch TV and listen to the canned laughter of Hollywood."

He called Abbey "a voice crying in the wilderness, for the wilderness." (pp. 3, 34)

Although he became a champion of the outdoors, [Abbey] was not one to rhapsodize its qualities.

He faulted writers "gushing about finding God in every bush."

"I sat on a rock in New Mexico once," he said, "trying to have a vision. The only vision I had was of baked chicken." . . .

Known not at all for his religious beliefs, he wrote what could only be called an invocation in his *Desert Solitaire,* a 1968 book he said was inspired by "two seamless perfect seasons" with the Arches Park Service in Utah:

> "May your trails be crooked, winding, lonesome, dangerous, leading to the most amazing view.
>
> "May your rivers . . . meander through pastoral valleys tinkling with bells, past temples and castles and poets' towers into a dark primeval forest where tigers belch and monkeys howl. . . . "
>
> (p. 34)

> *Burt A. Folkart, " 'Thoreau of the American West,' Edward Abbey, Dies," in* Los Angeles Times, *March 16, 1989, pp. 3, 34.*

THE TIMES, LONDON

Edward Abbey, the American essayist and novelist, has died in Tucson, Arizona, at the age of 62. . . .

He worked for the US National Parks Service in various capacities, but proved—from its point of view—an expensive employee, who (as the novel *The Monkey Wrench Gang,* in which he appears as "George Haycraft", made clear) engaged in an extensive campaign of sabotage aimed at undermining what he, rightly perhaps, thought of as its misguided policies.

The Monkey Wrench Gang is less a work of fiction, in fact, than an incitement to environmentalists to take the law into their own hands, often by means of vandalising whatever they considered to be themselves examples of vandalism and overkill.

The book was influential, and in it Abbey certainly went too far; but, as the sometimes egotistic essays in such collections as *Abbey's Road* demonstrate, he remained unhappily aware of the price paid by those who pursue the truth too relentlessly: his was a worthy ideal, but a strained one.

Where his first book *The Brave Cowboy* (1958) is characte-

rised by aggression, his last completed one of thirty years later, *The Fool's Progress* (*1988*), is redolent of disenchantment and disillusion.

Abbey was essentially an American phenomenon, not only because his ecological concerns were centered on the wild South West—most particularly the parklands of Utah and Arizona—but also because his style, partly modelled on Thoreau (though he lacked Thoreau's genius for imaginative literary expression), was specifically American.

Perhaps the unhappy mood of his last years was brought about by his failure to achieve subtlety and maturity in his writing—even his affirmations too often turned into strings of confused and sentimental cliches.

But friends of nature will be thankful for the quietness at the heart of his turbulence.

> *"Edward Abbey: A Turbulent Environmentalist," in* The Times, *London, March 28, 1989.*

CHARLES BOWDEN

He was an easy guy to know because fortunately there were no big moments. And he wasn't the guy you imagined from reading his books. A while back, we met in this Mexican joint. Marc Gaede, a friend of mine, was in from Los Angeles hoping to entice Ed Abbey into writing a preface for his next picture book, and he'd brought huge prints of the West as the bait. Over the phone, Abbey had been putting Gaede off—no, by God, he didn't want to be photographed. In person, he was, as usual, very soft-spoken and almost shy—except when he laid down his order for a platter of good greasy eggs and some pig meat on the side. Things were creeping along—Marc would set a print on a chair and Ed would mumble uh-huh—until the talk spun off into the technical aspects of monkeywrenching. It seems Gaede in an earlier incarnation had once wielded a righteous chainsaw in his own highway beautification program. Abbey began to drink in all the details, the American novelist busy stealing yet another life. Sure, he said, like he'd discovered a long-lost friend, he'd write the preface.

Then Abbey squared off before a small mountain of his books Marc had brought and autographed them for Gaede's kids. That done, Abbey insisted on showing off his new joy, an old red Cadillac convertible that looked like it had been pre-owned by a pimp. I said, "Christ, Ed, you've got no shame." His face brightened at such a wonderful thought.

I had lunch with him a week or so before he died at an Abbey kind of place—the air rich with the scent of seared red meat, the tables dotted with coeds. As usual, he admonished me to "get out of that silly magazine" (a city rag where I toiled at capturing the *Angst* of the city's overfed and overpaid), and to get back into the desert with a pack on my back. And then he shoved forward a pile of books I must read—he always showed up with books he wanted to share. He spoke softly and with a slight smile on his face. The enemy of every government on Earth, the bogeyman of squads of developers, a man seemingly crazed with saving every scrap of wild ground—well, the same guy laughed a lot, and seemed to coast through the day fascinated and amused by the absurdity of life, including his own. He was 20 years older than I, but whenever I was around him, I was absolutely convinced that he was younger than I ever could be. I'd get almost furous because he seemed to be having more fun than I was. . . .

He was not a simple person to consider. He believed the population had to be drastically reduced, yet fathered five kids. He was a lifetime member of the National Rifle Assn., a one-time Army MP, a man who advocated destroying bulldozers to save land, tossed his beer cans out the truck window, and was addicted to classical music. He never made a lot of money, he gave 10% of his income to environmental causes, and for years and years he scraped along with part-time jobs and kept writing and writing. He hardly seemed to raise his voice but had logical, coherent, fierce opinions. He had an anarchist's contempt for government and was like a distillate of whatever the word *American* means.

And he could write better than any other man or woman I have ever known.

Many have pointed out these traits, and others, as contradictions. They were not. They were Edward Abbey, a bundle of appetites, ideas and delights. . . .

The first time I met him I was out at his house to interview a guest of his for the local paper. I was leery, kind of like I was disturbing a national monument. So I tapped timidly on the door. He opened it up, introduced himself, and instantly thrust a copy of my first book into my hands—a text that had fallen dead from press and taken almost 10 years to sell 2,000 copies. He asked if I would autograph it and went on and on about its wonders. So he may have had pretty bad literary taste, but he was one of the kindest men I have ever known.

We became friends. And what we did was, well, we talked about books and ideas, mainly. I don't think I ever spent 10 minutes kicking around environmental issues with him—I guess they were simply a given. He worked very hard at his writing. An Abbey draft was blitzkrieged with crossed-out words, with clauses and sentences moved, and had the general appearance of a bed of writhing serpents. Of course, it read like he was talking to you, like he had just dashed it off. He wrote so well that a lot of people did not appreciate the craft in his work—you can crack his books open almost anywhere and just start reading out loud. But if you start looking closely, you'll find he makes every word count, every sentence, every paragraph. The stuff's as tight as the head of a drum.

Of course, what stopped people like myself in their tracks was not simply his style, it was his mind. He wasn't just an entertainer, he had ideas to sell, and for decades he explored his ideas, refined them, and forced us to snap awake and pay attention. Ed Abbey invented the Southwest we live in. He made us look at it, and when we looked up again we suddenly saw it through his eyes and sensed what he sensed—we were killing the last good place. His words were driven by a moral energy, a biting tongue, and, thank God, by an abundant sense of humor. It's pretty hard to read him without laughing.

And he was radical. Want to save the National Parks? Get the stinking cars out. Want to keep Arizona beautiful and healthy? Let's make half of it a wilderness. Want to bring the Colorado River back to life? Let's blow up Glen Canyon Dam. There are damn near 20 books. Read them and see. I suppose his reputation will now fall into the claws of the Visigoths of the English departments, and I don't know what they'll make of him. But here's what I think: When I'm dead

and dust, people will still be reading Edward Abbey. Because the stuff he wrote is alive. . . .

The last time I talked to him, he told me how he'd written an essay a year or so ago in which he'd noted that nobody in his family ever died. And then, suddenly, his brother had died from cancer, his mother had been run over and killed by a truck. He looked up at me with a mad twinkle in his eyes.

I said, "Maybe you ought to print a retraction."

God, I'm going to miss him. Who in the hell is going to keep us honest? The guy we counted on, well, he moved on.

Charles Bowden, "Requiem for an Honest Man," in Los Angeles Times Book Review, *April 2, 1989, p. 11.*

PAUL T. BRYANT

When Edward Abbey visited my campus some years ago, I was curious to know what he was like. His public lecture was in the tone one might expect from his writing—a mixture of Jack Burns and George Washington Hayduke. But I was interested in the person behind the public image. At a reception at a colleague's house, after the lecture, I hoped to meet that person.

Before many people had arrived, Abbey was quiet, affable, relaxed. As the number of people increased to a loud, milling mob, he became visibly less comfortable. Finally, he retreated as unobtrusively as possible to the kitchen. I was already there, having made a similar retreat a few minutes earlier. We had a quiet conversation that ended only when others found where he had fled.

From that brief acquaintance, I got the strong sense that Edward Abbey was not the sharp-tongued, outrageous anarchist so many believe him to have been . . . , but rather a quiet, shy, thoughtful man who created a far different persona for public consumption. Confirmation has since come from others. Barry Lopez, for example, writes of Abbey's "ingenuous shyness, so at odds with the public image of a bold iconoclast". (p. 37)

My thesis here is that such a personality, and such a vision, lie at the bottom of the aggregate of Edward Abbey's writing. This idea is hardly new, of course. Other critics, such as Garth McCann, Ann Ronald, and Jerry Herndon, have found a balanced, eminently rational environmental moderate in Abbey's non-fiction nature writing, despite his more extreme statements, and despite popular emphasis on some of his more extreme fictional characters. I would like to demonstrate the soundness of that thesis, and to explore the complex ways this moderation beneath the surface of extremism has been stated outright in Abbey's non-fiction and has evolved as a definitive counterpoint to the more colorful extremism in his fiction. (pp. 37-8)

[Abbey's] position is clearly stated in ***Desert Solitaire.*** Early in that book Abbey observes not, as readers of his fiction might expect, that wilderness is the desirable alternative to civilization, but rather that "wilderness is a necessary part of civilization." No Luddite, he can make use of the genuine benefits of civilization. The refrigerator, for example, is a useful machine for producing ice for his drinks: "Once the drink is mixed, however, I always go *outside,* out in the light and the air and the space and the breeze, to enjoy it. Making the best of both worlds, that's the thing" (**Desert Solitaire**). Despite his often stated enjoyment of solitude, Abbey in **Desert Solitaire** also denies that he is misanthropic. The one thing better than solitude, he says, is society, not of crowds but of friends. What he objects to, he insists, is what he calls anthropocentricity, not science, but science and technology misapplied. "Balance," he concludes, "that's the secret. Moderate extremism. The best of both worlds . . ."

The same theme arises in **The Journey Home.** There Abbey denies that technology and industry are inherently evil, but insists that they must be kept under control, "to prevent them from ever again becoming the self-perpetuating, ever-expanding monsters we have allowed them to become". "Optimum industrialism, neither too much nor too little," a moderate level of technology, is what he urges.

Consistent with this Hellenic moderation is Abbey's praise of objective realism and rationality. Again in **The Journey Home** he says that the poet of our age must begin with the scientific view of the world. There is, he says, "more charm in one 'mere' fact, confirmed by test and observation, linked to other facts through coherent theory into a rational system, than in a whole brainful of fancy and fantasy". In short, Abbey does not display the romanticism or the sentimentality so often associated with extreme environmentalism. His vision is that of the moderate realist. As he says in **Abbey's Road,** he wishes "to stand apart, alone if need be, and hold up the ragged flag of reason. Reason with a capital R—sweet Reason, the newest and rarest thing in human life, the most delicate child of human history".

Thus the Abbey of his non-fiction takes moderate views, yet the colorful extremists of his fiction continue to attract the attention and usually the sympathy of Abbey's readers. Are they the true representative of Abbey's environmentalism? Once his imagination has left the realistic constraints of non-fiction, does it give us Abbey's deepest beliefs? And do these creations of Abbey's imagination contradict or somehow give the lie to his more restrained and rational essays? No, they do not. Examined with care, and as part of the larger pattern of Abbey's work, these characters fit his vision of realistic rationality, not contradicting it but only keeping it open-ended and still available to the idealistic imagination.

To consider this pattern, perhaps it will be useful first to distinguish between two closely related but not identical themes in these works: human freedom, on the one hand, and nature undominated by human activity, on the other. The extreme of human freedom is anarchy, and the extreme of nature without human domination is wilderness. The two are intertwined in Abbey's work because wilderness is the one possible site for anarchic freedom. Wilderness, Abbey says in **Desert Solitaire,** is an assurance of freedom. Urban masses in a technological landscape are more easily controlled.

The anarchists in Abbey's writing begin with Jonathan Troy's father, the one-eyed Wobbly in Abbey's first novel. An ineffectual figure, the father is killed in a bar, shocking the protagonist into fleeing the bonds of his childhood. Thus the pattern for the anarchists in Abbey's fiction begins with monocular vision—seeing things from only one side—and with defeat.

In **The Brave Cowboy,** on the other hand, resistance to the established order takes two forms: the active, atavistic resistance of Jack Burns, the brave cowboy, and the passive, somewhat self-centered resistance of Paul Bondi. Both, with-

in that novel, fail, but in Jack Burns, Abbey has begun to develop a figure that will finally suggest the necessary unquenchability of the spirit of freedom.

In his reversion to nineteenth-century ways of living, and the idealism of the romanticized old West (the solitary stranger fighting always for justice and the underdog), Burns is a quixotic figure in modern Duke City (Albuquerque). To emphasize this quixotic quality, Abbey makes Burns tall, thin, a college man turned cowboy, a clear parallel with Don Quixote, who is tall, very thin, and comes to knight errantry after its time has passed, through reading books. Burns is addressed by the Chicano children as "don charro," another indicator of the parallel. The final quixotic comparison, of course, is that Burns's mission to free Paul Bondi is mistaken because Burns misunderstands Bondi's reasons for draft resistance. And Jack Burns fails.

John Vogelin, in **Fire on the Mountain,** again stands quixotically against all odds—in his case the U.S. Government—and again fails. Abbey does not even allow him a moral victory. Vogelin has to acknowledge that the land he is trying to keep the government from "stealing" from him had come to him through a long line of theft and chicanery back to the time it was taken from the Indians, and perhaps even before that. Again, the anarchist is at least partially in the wrong, and he fails.

At this point in the development of the anarchic idea in Abbey's work, the fiction and the non-fiction cross in an interesting detail. In **Desert Solitaire,** Abbey devotes an entire chapter to the moon-eyed horse, who has broken free from working for humans and fled to a hard and lonely life in an arid Utah canyon. It is a tall, gaunt animal, seventeen hands high, gelded, blind in one eye (monocular vision), and totally alone in a harsh life of the barest subsistence. Abbey pursues it and tries to bring it back to society by talking to it of grain, lush grass, easy living, and the companionship of its own kind, but the horse will have none of it.

The monocular vision of the lonely horse suggests the monocular vision of Nat Troy. Thus having one eye begins to suggest a single, extreme way of seeing the world, the way of completely untrammeled freedom. The fact that the horse is gelded suggests that the anarchic drive for complete freedom, a traditional western theme, is essentially sterile.

This set of images—the anarchist disposition associated with the single good eye, the tall, gaunt, quixotic figures of horse and man, continue in **The Monkey Wrench Gang** in the one-eyed "lone ranger" who befriends Hayduke. By the time Hayduke is resurrected at the end of the novel, he, rather than the one-eyed man, is riding the tall (as before, seventeen hands high) horse. By this time, too, the tall horse is named Rosie, clearly suggesting Don Quixote's tall, thin horse Rozinante. (pp. 38-41)

Offsetting these figures, Abbey provides a suitable set of villains, but the most interesting of these are the sympathetic villains, the men who oppose Don Quixote, but do so with sympathy, and not totally to the death. In **The Brave Cowboy,** there is Sheriff Morlin Johnson, a complex, educated, balanced man who appreciates the wilderness, and understands Jack Burns's desire for freedom well enough to know how to pursue him successfully. In **Fire on the Mountain,** Lee Mackie is not a villian, but he presents again the balanced man who can understand both sides of the dispute.

In *The Monkey Wrench Gang,* the novel in which all the threads of Abbey's interest in wilderness and freedom come together most completely, there is a whole spectrum of figures ranging from George Washington Hayduke, the total anarchist, to Bishop Love, the arch-representative of the Establishment. Seldom Seen Smith loves the wilderness, freedom, and women, but lacks the preoccupation with violence that Hayduke has. Bonnie Abbzug and Dr. Sarvis are environmentalists but not anarchists *per se.* Anarchy merely becomes their hope for saving the habitability of the Southwest. When their freedom is pitted against their social obligation to render medical aid, they choose to honor their social obligation.

Perhaps the most interesting on the villains' side of this spectrum is Bishop Love's younger brother Sam. Again we have the sympathetic, less-than-total villain. He even appears to have guessed Hayduke's final trick on the rocky point, calling into the cleft in the rock, to "Rudolf," that he cannot always fool everyone.

Finally, even the Bishop softens his position, forgiving Seldom Seen Smith the cost of his vehicle. So at last only Hayduke and the one-eyed stranger remain unyielding extremists, defeated but still alive to fight another day. Even Hayduke has an unspoken debt to Sam for not revealing his trick on the rocky point: it is the moderate who allows the anarchist to survive.

Yet another sympathetic villain appears in *Good News,* in the figure of Colonel Charles Barnes. Barnes is made the alienated but partially understanding son of the anarchist. By creating this connection Abbey seems again to be emphasizing the essential relationship, the shared humanity, of the extremists of both camps. Barnes finally conceals from authority the fact that Jack Burns, with his singular vision of freedom, may yet live. Again the moderate allows the anarchist to survive.

What has evolved, then, is an image of a quixotic searcher for freedom and wilderness undisturbed, a figure that is extreme, ironic, always doomed to failure, but nevertheless immortal. The immortality has been added as Abbey's themes have developed. With it, Abbey suggests that extremism cannot succeed, but that perhaps the extreme of anarchy and wilderness is necessary to counterbalance the repressive and environmentally destructive forces of unbridled technology and exploitation. For this reason, it should be allowed to survive. (pp. 41-2)

Paul T. Bryant, "Edward Abbey and Environmental Quixoticism," in Western American Literature, *Vol. XXIV, No. 1, May, 1989, pp. 37-43.*

EDWARD HOAGLAND

Edward Abbey, who died in March at the age of 62, seemed, at his best, the nonpareil "nature writer" of recent decades. It was a term he came to detest, a term used to pigeonhole and marginalize some of the more intriguing American writers who are dealing with matters central to us—yet it can be a ticket to oblivion in the bookstores. Joyce Carol Oates, for instance, in a slapdash though interesting essay called "Against Nature," speaks of nature writers' "painfully limited set of responses . . . REVERENCE, AWE, PIETY, MYSTICAL ONENESS." She must never have read Edward Abbey; yet it was characteristic of him that for an hour or two, he might have agreed.

He wrote with exceptional exactitude and an unusually honest and logical understanding of causes and consequences, but he also loved argument, churlishness and exaggeration. Personally, he was a labyrinth of anger and generosity, shy but arresting because of his mixture of hillbilly and cowboy qualities, and even when silent he appeared bigger than life. He had hitchhiked from Appalachia for the first time at age 17 to what became an immediate love match with the West, and, I'm sure, slept out more nights under the stars than all of his current competitors combined. He was uneven and self-indulgent as a writer and often scanted his talent by working too fast. But he had about him an authenticity that springs from the page and is beloved by a rising generation of readers, who have enabled his early collection of rambles, *Desert Solitaire* (1968), to run through 18 printings in mass-market paperback. His fine comic novel, *The Monkey Wrench Gang* (1975), has sold half a million copies. Both books, indeed, have inspired a new eco-guerrilla environmental organization called Earth First!, whose other patron saint is Ned Ludd (from whom the Luddites took their name), though it's perhaps no more radical than John Muir's Sierra Club appeared to be when that organization was formed in 1892.

Like many good writers, Abbey dreamed of producing "the fat masterpiece," as he called the "nubble" that he had worked on for the past dozen years and that was supposed to boil everything down to a thousand pages or so. When edited in half, it came out last fall as *The Fool's Progress,* an autobiographical yarn that lunges cross-country several times, full of apt descriptions and antic fun—"Ginger Man" stuff—though not with the coherence or poignance he had hoped for. A couple of his other novels hold up fairly well, too: *Black Sun* and *The Brave Cowboy,* which came out in movie form starring Kirk Douglas and Walter Matthau in 1962 (*Lonely Are the Brave*) and brought Abbey a munificent $7,500.

I do think he wrote masterpieces, but they were more slender: the essays in *Desert Solitaire* and an equivalent sampler that you might put together from subsequent collections like *Down the River, Beyond the Wall* and *The Journey Home.* His rarest strength was in being concise, because he really knew what he thought and cared for. He loved the desert— "red mountains like mangled iron"—liked people in smallish clusters, and didn't mince words in saying that industrial rapine, glitz-malls and tract-sprawl were an abomination heralding more devastating events. While writing as handsomely as others do, he never lost sight of the fact that much of Creation is rapidly being destroyed.

"Growth for the sake of growth is the ideology of the cancer cell," he wrote. And he adopted for a motto Walt Whitman's line: "Resist much, obey little." Another motto was Thoreau's summary in *Walden:* "If I repent of anything, it is very likely to be my good behavior. What demon possessed me that I behaved so well?"

Abbey traveled less than some writers, but it is not necessary to go dithering around our suffering planet, visiting the Amazon, Indonesia, Bhutan and East Africa. The crisis is plain in anyone's neck of the woods, and the exoticism of globe-trotting may only blur one's vision. Nor do we need to become mystical Transcendentalists and commune with God. (*One Life at a Time Please* is another of Abbey's titles. On his hundreds of camping trips he tended to observe and enjoy the wilds rather than submerge his soul.) What is needed is honesty, a pair of eyes and a dollop of fortitude to spit the truth out, not genuflecting to Emersonian optimism, or journalistic traditions of staying deadpan, or the saccharine pressures of magazine editors who want their readers to feel good. Emerson would be roaring with heartbreak and Thoreau would be raging with grief in these 1980's. *Where were you when the world burned? Get mad, for a change, for heaven's sake!* I believe they would say to compatriots of Abbey's like Annie Dillard, Barry Lopez and John McPhee.

Abbey didn't sell to the big book clubs or reach bestsellerdom or collect major prizes. When, at 60, he was offered a smallish one by the American Academy of Arts and Letters, he rejected it with a fanfare of rhetoric, probably because it had come too late. So the success, wholly word-of-mouth, of *The Monkey Wrench Gang* in paperback pleased him more than anything else, and he delighted in telling friends who the real-life counterparts were for its characters, Seldom Seen Smith, Bonnie Abbzug and George Washington Hayduke. They too had torn down billboards, yanked up survey stakes, poured sand into bulldozer gas tanks and sabotaged "certain monstrosities" in fragilely scenic regions. (p. 44)

"Let's keep things the way they were," Abbey liked to say. Yet he was a bold, complex man who had five wives and five children by the end of his life; and although he spilled too much energy into feuds with his allies and friends, he was often a jubilant writer, a regular gleeman, not just a threnodist, and he wanted to be remembered as a writer of "that letter which is never finished"—literature—as *Desert Solitaire* is.

We corresponded occasionally for 20 years, wanting to go for a lengthy sail on the Sea of Cortez or go camping somewhere in the hundred-mile Air Force gunnery range that for its isolation eventually became another favorite redoubt of his. I hoped we could drift down the Yukon River together and compile a dual diary. ("Is that dual or *duel* ?" he asked once.) He had lived in Hoboken, N.J., for a couple of years while unhappily married, with the "Vampire State Building" on the skyline—he had also lived in Scotland and Italy—and he responded to Manhattan's incomparably gaudy parade of faces as a cosmopolitan, though he was marked as an outlander by his uncut grayish beard, slow speech, earnest eyes, red-dog-road shuffle, raw height and build, and jean jacket or shabby brown tweed. On his way home to Oracle, Ariz., after conferring in New York with editors, he'd usually stop in the Alleghenies to visit his mother, Mildred, a Woman's Christian Temperance Union veteran, and his father, Paul Revere Abbey, a registered Socialist and old Wobbly organizer, who met Eugene V. Debs in his youth and has toured Cuba and still cuts hickory fence posts in the woods for a living.

Abbey was a writer who liked to play poker with cowboys, while continuing to ridicule the ranch owners who overgraze the West's ravaged grasslands. The memorial picnic for him in Saguaro National Monument outside Tucson, Ariz., went on for 12 hours, and besides the readings performed with rock-bottom affection there was beer-drinking, love-making, gunfire and music, much as he had hoped. The potluck stew was from two "slow elk," as he liked to call beef cattle poached from particularly greedy entrepreneurs on the public's wildlands. He was an egalitarian, he said—by which he meant that he believed all wildlife and the full panoply of natural vegetation have a right to live equal to man's—and these beeves had belonged to a cowman who specialized in hounding Arizona's scarce mountain lions.

Abbey died of internal bleeding from a circulatory disorder, with a few week's notice of how sick he was. Two days before the event he decided to leave the hospital, wishing to die in the desert; at sunup he had himself disconnected from the tubes and machinery. His wife Clarke and three friends drove him as far out of town as his condition allowed. They built a campfire for him to look at, until, feeling death at hand, he crawled into his sleeping bag with Clarke. But by noon, finding he was still alive and possibly better, he asked to be taken home and placed on a mattress on the floor of his writing cabin. There he said his gentle goodbyes.

His written instructions were that he should be "transported in the bed of a pickup truck" deep into the desert and buried anonymously, wrapped in his sleeping bag, in the beautiful spot where his grave would never be found, with "lots of rocks" piled on top to keep the coyotes off. Abbey of course loved coyotes (and, for that matter, buzzards) and had played his flute to answer their howls during the many years he had earned his living watching for fires from Government towers on the Grand Canyon's North Rim, on Aztec Peak in Tonto National Forest and in Glacier National Park, before he finally won tenure as a "fool professor" at the University of Arizona. His friend who was the model for G. W. Hayduke in *The Monkey Wrench Gang* was squatting beside him on the floor as his life ebbed away. "Hayduke" is actually a legend in his own right in parts of the West, a sort of contemporary mountain man who returned to town as to a calving ground several years ago when he wanted to have and raise children. The last smile that crossed Abbey's face was when "Hayduke" told him where he would be put.

The place is, inevitably, a location where mountain lions, antelope, bighorn sheep, deer and javelinas leave tracks, where owls, poor-wills and coyotes hoot and cacomistles scratch, with a range of stiff terrain overhead and greasewood, rabbit-brush, ocotillo and noble old cactuses about. First seven, then ten buzzards gathered while the grave was being dug; as he had wished, it *was* a rocky spot. One man jumped into the hole to be sure it felt O.K. before laying Abbey in, and afterward in a kind of reprise of the antic spirit that animates *The Monkey Wrench Gang,* and that should make anybody but a developer laugh out loud, went around heaping up false rockpiles at ideal gravesites throughout the Southwest, because this last peaceful act of outlawry of Abbey's was the gesture of legend and there will be seekers for years to come. (pp. 44-5)

There's a saying that life gets better once you have outlived the bastards—which would certainly be true except that as you do, you are also outliving your friends. Sitting in silence with him in restaurants as our twinned melancholy groped for expression, or talking with him of hoodoo stone pillars and red rock canyons, I've seldom felt closer to anybody. Honesty is a key to essay-writing: not just "a room of one's own," but a view of one's own. The lack of it sinks more talented people into chatterbox hackwork than anything else. And Abbey aspired to speak for himself in all honesty—*X: His Mark*—and died telling friends he had done what he could and was ready. He didn't buzz off to Antarctica or the Galapagos Islands, yet no one will ever wonder what he really saw as the world burned. He said it; he didn't sweeten it or blink at it or water it down or hope the web of catastrophes might just go away.

He felt homesick for the desert when he went to Alaska, and turned back, yet if you travel much there it is Abbey's words you will see tacked on the wall again and again in remote homestead cabins in the Brooks Range or offices in Juneau, because he had already written of greed, of human brutality and howling despair, better than writers who write books on Alaska have.

Last year a paean to Abbey's work in *National Review* finished with a quote from a passage in Faulkner: *"Oleh, Chief. Grandfather."* To which we can add Amen. But instead let's close with a bit of Ed Abbey, from a minor book called **Appalachian Wilderness** (1970), which foretold why he chose that lost grave where he lies:

> How strange and wonderful is our home, our earth, with its swirling vaporous atmosphere, its flowing and frozen climbing creatures, the croaking things with wings that hang on rocks and soar through fog, the furry grass, the scaly seas . . . how utterly rich and wild. . . . Yet some among us have the nerve, the insolence, the brass, the gall to whine about the limitations of our earthbound fate and yearn for some more perfect world beyond the sky. We are none of us good enough for the world we have.

(p. 45)

Edward Hoagland, "Edward Abbey: Standing Tough in the Desert," in The New York Times Book Review, *May 7, 1989, pp. 44-5.*

BOB SIPCHEN

Edward Abbey died on March 14 at age 62. That evening, friends hauled the author of **The Monkey Wrench Gang** into the desert and buried him under a big pile of black rocks, somewhere out in the middle of nowhere.

Over the weekend, some of those same friends, accompanied by hundreds of others, walked into another part of that vast slick rock and cacti cemetery to celebrate the life of a man, who, more quickly than any writer since Jack Kerouac, has been resurrected as a modern myth.

In **Desert Solitaire,** the 1968 book that incited a generation of environmentalists, Abbey described hauling the bloated carcass of a tourist from a remote canyon in Arches National Park. Then a seasonal ranger, Abbey congratulated the man on his good fortune in dying under the desert sky, away from meddling doctors and priests.

"If we had loved him," he added, "we would sing, dance, drink, build a stupendous bonfire, find women, make love . . . and celebrate his transfiguration from flesh to fantasy in a style proper and fitting, with fun for all at the funeral."

Saturday, folks did just that—presumably all of it. They also talked at length about why, as one speaker said, so many of the disparate people who had arrived at this remote mesa from around the country would recall the moment they heard Abbey had died as vividly as the moment they learned that John Kennedy had been shot.

As the morning sun lifted layers of gray from the surrounding red and black bluffs, poet Wendell Berry told the congregation that Abbey's work gave people courage.

Berry is forbidden to read Abbey at night because his laughter wakes up the house, he said. But concealed in Abbey's humor, he added, is a commitment to a serious vision and an antidote to the despair that sometimes seems integral to modern life.

"I never laid down a book by Edward Abbey that I did not feel more encouraged than when I picked it up," he said.

The tribute was staged a short hike up a dirt road that had been the entrance to the park when Abbey worked there. Soaring Entrada sandstone cliffs framed one side of the setting; in another direction hovered the snow-capped Tukuhnikivats, which Abbey called "the mightiest mountains in the land of Moab."

Someone had set an American flag beside the small podium, from which speakers addressed the several hundred people spread out across a gentle slope of lichen-mottled sandstone.

Larry McMurtry, author of *Lonesome Dove,* has termed Abbey "a modern Thoreau."

John Nichols, the author of *The Milagro Beanfield War* whose bad heart kept him at his Taos, N.M., home this weekend, said of Abbey by telephone: "I think **Desert Solitaire** will stand up as a powerful classic. And **Monkey Wrench Gang** will always be a lot of fun."

Besides Monkey Wrench—the romantic tale of a ragtag band of river rats who rampage through the Southwest ripping up survey stakes, dismantling bulldozers and launching other quixotic attacks on alleged progress—the author wrote eight other novels (the last of which is scheduled for release in the fall); five coffee table photographic collections, and six collections of essays. All reflect his preference for the natural over the man-made world and a strong-headed individualism in combat against technocracy.

Abbey's books, "were burrs under the saddle blanket of complacency," author Wallace Stegner wrote in a letter Berry read to to the gathering. "He was a red-hot moment in the conscience of the country, and I suspect that the half-life of his intransigence will turn out to be comparable to uranium."

George Foreman, who co-founded the radical environmental group Earth First!, raised a beer-can toast to the man who inspired what has been called "red-neck environmentalism."

"Ed said that one brave deed is worth a thousand words. But every novel, every essay, every story Ed wrote has launched a thousand brave deeds," he said. The people cheered. A string quartet played Mozart.

Word about the tribute spread in a way the anarchist Abbey might have approved. Throughout his life, he had fired off fusillades of white postcards to praise, scold and maintain contact with the countless people, who, for whatever reasons, drifted into his field of influence, those who knew him said.

Saturday's affair, announced with a postcard barrage and a few notices in publications of the environmental fringe, drew academic admirers and reverential young Abbey cultists who insist on chucking beer cans out car windows because their iconoclastic hero was known to have done so. A physician who attended said he had worked with Chico Mendes in the Amazon rain forests before that organizer of the rubber-tappers union was murdered. Another man who came said he spent his life exploring for gas and oil throughout the Southwest. He felt no guilt about what might appear to be hypocrisy. Abbey would understand his need to work outdoors, he said. (pp. 1-2)

Nichols, who shared Abbey's environmentalism but denounced aspects of his politics, said that the author's humor defused any true antipathy. "When I think of Ed Abbey, I think of Emma Goldman, who said, 'If I can't dance, I don't want to be part of your revolution,' " he said.

Congress is now considering a bill that would make several million acres along the Utah-Colorado border a wilderness area. A congressional sponsor of the proposal has recommended that the area be named after Abbey.

Other parts of the land he cherished, though, have fallen to his worst fears.

In *Desert Solitaire,* Abbey decried the "industrial tourism" he felt the National Park Service encouraged with its paved campgrounds and flush toilets. Such places disregard the adventurous urbanites who came for a rare taste of "the primitive and remote." Instead they attract "the indolent millions, born on wheels and suckled on gasoline."

In fact, tourists now march into the air-conditioned visitor's center at Arches National Park and ask if there are sights they can see without leaving their motor homes. The winding main roads are now paved and lined with numbered signs pointing out each spectacular mesa and rock formation. . . .

Saturday night, at a guest ranch outside Moab, hundreds of Abbey aficionados danced and drank.

It probably was not as raucous as Abbey had wanted, but someone did let the horses out of the corral, and at least one young woman, wearning only a blouse, staggered across a lawn littered with cars and trucks.

The ranch, complete with a bookstore well-stocked with naturalist writings, poetry, and wildflower guides, is run by Ken Sleight, widely acknowledged to be Abbey's inspiration for the Monkey Wrencher, Seldom Seen Smith.

"I'm meeting all sorts of people I thought were myths tonight," said Sleight's wife, Jane.

Among the myths she knows well is Douglas Peacock, reportedly the man upon whom Abbey based George Washington Hayduke, the Monkey Wrench hero who is gunned down by a government helicopter like an American *mujahedeen* defending God's Country. . . .

"Ed borrowed traits from some of us to wrap the characters around," Sleight, 59, said, his words coming slowly after a full day of toasting a friend. "But they were also very autobiographical.

"I think the Abbey myth is going to get bigger and bigger," he said. "I encourage it, because I believe in what he had to say." . . .

Before he died, Abbey completed the sequel to the Monkey Wrench Gang—*Hayduke Lives.* Long before the sequel was announced, though, "Hayduke Lives!" bumper stickers became ubiquitous throughout the Southwest.

Now there's an addendum.

On the road leading into Sleight's ranch, where a hundred or more cars and trucks with raft frames and kayaks and mountain bikes on top lined up, at least one sticker on one dirty Jeep had been defaced with the words: Abbey Lives!

Bob Sipchen, "In Desert Solitude, Faithful Pay Tribute to the Abbey Myth," in Los Angeles Times, *May 22, 1989.*

FRANK GRAHAM, JR.

Edward Abbey was not a naturalist. Librarians might classify his nonfiction books under "Natural History," and lovers of wild things might hope to enshrine him in a pantheon beside Archie Carr or Jane Goodall, but Abbey would have none of it.

He was, he insisted, a novelist. His avowed heroes lay mostly outside the fields of natural history and conservation, in what more effete souls than Abbey might call "the humanities." And his avowed ambition was to write a very good, very long novel ("the fat masterpiece").

"That accomplished, I shall retire to my hut in the heart of the desert and spend the remainder of my days in meditation, contemplating my novel," he wrote. "I hope to become a rock. I plan to return in future incarnations as a large and lazy soaring bird."

Yet there was no more effective advocate in our time for wilderness preservation. *Desert Solitaire, The Journey Home,* and other books were not novels but descriptions of his own encounters with the American West. They lured thousands of young men and women to the environmental persuasion despite Abbey's contention that the only birds he could identify were turkey vultures and fried chicken, and that he always threw his beer cans out his car window because they weren't as ugly as the highway.

Was he kidding? It doesn't make any difference to his readers, who treasure his outrageous remarks about all the gadgets American consumers generally crave, his incessant bashing of the exploiters roaming loose on wildlands, his "visions and hallucinations." Compromise was no part of Abbey's vocabulary. In *Desert Solitaire* he laid down his law: "No more cars in national parks. Let the people walk. Or ride horses, bicycles, mules, wild pigs—anything—but keep the automobiles and motorcycles and all their motorized relatives out." And in his most notorious novel, *The Monkey Wrench Gang,* he mythologized ecofreaks who roamed the West knocking out dams and the other technological intrusions that he deplored.

A writer's grandiose fantasies? Rather, his essays showed him to be something of a saboteur himself, cutting down billboards, shooting insulators off powerlines, and even making a detour "to doctor up a pair of bulldozers belonging to the U.S. Bureau of Reclamation."

Like any good hater, he fumed in hyperbole. And like any ardent lover, he could murmur the most tender nonsense. But at his best, he cut through to the truth about what was happening to our country by saying things more circumspect commentators would shy away from.

"The idea of wilderness needs no defense," he wrote. "It only needs more defenders."

Unhappily, it now has one less. Edward Abbey died last March at sixty-two, much too soon, and America as he feared goes on cutting itself off from its origins in the wild world. (pp. 14, 16)

Frank Graham, Jr., "Edward Abbey," in Audubon, *Vol. 91, No. 4, July, 1989, pp. 14, 16.*

Donald Barthelme

April 7, 1931 - July 23, 1989

(Also wrote under the pseudonym of Lily McNeil) American short story writer, novelist, essayist, and author of books for children.

For an overview of Barthelme's life and work see *CLC,* Vols. 1, 2, 3, 5, 6, 8, 13, 23, 46; *Short Story Criticism,* Vol. 2; *Contemporary Authors,* Vols. 21-24, rev. ed., Vol. 129 (obituary); *Contemporary Authors New Revision Series,* Vol. 20; *Something about the Author,* Vol. 7; *Dictionary of Literary Biography,* Vol. 2; and *Dictionary of Literary Biography Yearbook: 1980.*

HERBERT MITGANG

Donald Barthelme, a short story writer and novelist whose minimalist style placed him among the leading innovative writers of modern fiction, died of cancer [July 23, 1989] in Houston at the University of Texas M. D. Anderson Cancer Center. He was 58 years old. . . .

Mr. Barthelme's short stories frequently appeared in *The New Yorker* before being collected into books. He won a National Book Award in 1972 for a children's book entitled **The Slightly Irregular Fire Engine** and the PEN/Faulkner Award for fiction in 1982 for his **Sixty Stories.** He was a member of the American Academy and Institute of Arts and Letters, the Authors League of America, the Authors Guild and PEN.

Mr. Barthelme once likened his style to that of collage. "The principle of collage is the central principle of all art in the 20th century," the author said.

Rebutting criticism of himself and of other writers as being too difficult, Mr. Barthelme said:

> Art is not difficult because it wishes to be difficult, rather because it wishes to be art. However much the writer might long to straightforward, these virtues are no longer available to him. He discovers that in being simple, honest, straightforward, nothing much happens.

"Writing is a process of dealing with not-knowing, a forcing of what and how," Mr. Barthelme said. "We have all heard novelists testify to the fact that beginning a new book, they are utterly baffled as to how to proceed, what should be written and how it might be written, even though they've done a dozen. At best there is a slender intuition, not much greater than an itch. The not-knowing is not simple, because it's hedged about with prohibitions, roads that may not be taken. The more serious the artist, the more problems he takes into

account, the more considerations limit his possible initiatives."

In public appearances and in print, Mr. Barthelme often defended what he termed "the alleged post-modernists" in literature. He placed himself in this category and included, among Americans, John Barth, John Hawkes, William Gass, Robert Coover and Thomas Pynchon. Among Europeans, he named Peter Handke, Thomas Bernhard and Italo Calvino. . . .

Mr. Barthelme was born in Philadelphia on April 7, 1931. He had a Roman Catholic upbringing in Houston, where his father was a professor of architectural design at the University of Houston. While studying at the university, he adopted an existentialist philosophy. After serving in the Armed Forces in Korea and Japan, he returned to Houston, where he worked as a reporter for *The Houston Post.* In 1961-62, he became the director of the Contemporary Arts Museum in Houston.

Mr. Barthelme moved to Manhattan in 1963. He lived in

Greenwich Village with his fourth wife, the former Marion Knox, whom he married in 1978. Mr. Barthelme described New York City in the same terms as his own work, "as a collage, as opposed to a tribal village in which all the huts are the same hut, duplicated. The point of collage is that things are stuck together to create a new reality." In 1974-75, he served as a Distinguished Visiting Professor of English at the City College of the City University of New York.

His first novel, *Snow White*, . . . brought him national attention. His interpretation owed more to the Walt Disney film than to the Grimm story. It parodied the fairy tale with erotic touches. Some critics described the story as a surrealistic Snow White. In the story, Snow White shares a shower and an apartment with the seven dwarfs, who become respectable bourgeois entrepreneurs.

His books of stories included: *Come Back, Dr. Caligari* (1964); *Unspeakable Practices, Unnatural Acts* (1968); *City Life* (1970); *Sadness* (1972); *Amateurs* (1976); *Great Days* (1979), which was fashioned into an off-Broadway play in 1983; *Sixty Stories* (1981), and *Overnight to Many Distant Cities* (1983).

His novels, apart from *Snow White,* included: *The Dead Father* (1975), and *Paradise* (1986). In addition to the children's book, he was author of a book of parodies, *Guilty Pleasures* (1974).

The critic Alfred Kazin, in *Bright Book of Life: American Novelists and Storytellers From Hemingway to Mailer,* called Barthelme an "antinovelist who operates by countermeasures only."

"He is outside everything he writes in a way that a humorist like S. J. Perelman could never be," Mr. Kazin continued. "He is under the terrible discipline that the system inflicts on those who are most fascinated with its relentlessness."

Herbert Mitgang, "Donald Barthelme Is Dead at 58: A Short Story Writer and Novelist," in The New York Times, *July 24, 1989.*

THE TIMES, LONDON

[Donald Barthelme] was one of the very few writers of his generation to communicate the peculiarly modern sense of life as absurd and meaningless, without recourse to silliness or exhibitionism. . . .

Donald Barthelme was born in Philadelphia on April 7, 1931. He received a Roman Catholic upbringing and an interest in modern art from his parents; but while attending Houston University he lost his faith, a process in which Sartre's *Being and Nothingness* (and similar books) played a notable part. However, modern art, and French modern art in particular, remained a permanent influence. . . .

Barthelme served in the American forces in Korea, reaching there after hostilities had ceased. On his return to Houston he took a variety of jobs, in journalism and then as a university public relations man. Mainly, however, he devoted himself to work as curator of a gallery of modern art. For a time he edited a magazine, *Location.* He also began to publish, often in *The New Yorker,* the stories he would later collect together in his first book, *Come Back, Dr. Caligari* (1964).

In these stories, which were received by discerning critics in

a mood that blended the despair so well expressed by the author with admiration of his skill, humour and panache, Barthelme exploited some of the methods of the European surrealism of the 1920s in order to present the contemporary world as not only an irrational but also a wicked place.

He was thus—even though never able to discover a mode of existence that would justify the rage for order which lay at the heart of his inspiration—a moralist. In the characteristic **"Me and Miss Mandible"** the hapless 35-year-old narrator is bureaucratically changed into an 11-year-old, and enrolled in Miss Mandible's elementary class; but he is surprised in the cloakroom with his teacher and expelled. Barthelme was demonstrating that reeducation for adults is impossible.

Snow White (1967) took its inspiration from the Disney film, and was replete with bitter ironies and hilarious pastiche-parodies of modernist fiction—but it read well, and much better than most other American fiction which was trying to do the same thing in a more cerebral manner. The book still reads like a fairytale. Other collections, including *City Life* (1971), *Guilty Pleasures* (1974) and *Overnight to Distant Cities* (1984) followed. *The Dead Father* (1975), a grotesque tale of 19 children hauling their father—both living and a huge corpse—across a city, was of novel length.

"Donald Barthelme: Reclusive Teller of Cautionary Tales," in The Times, *London, July 25, 1989.*

RICHARD PEARSON

Donald Barthelme, 58, a critically acclaimed author of novels and short stories who also wrote and illustrated a prize-winning children's book, died of cancer July 23 at a hospital in Houston.

He was best known for his short stories, which appeared in *The Atlantic, Paris Review,* and most often *The New Yorker,* before being collected into volumes that ranged from *Come Back, Dr. Caligari,* published in 1964, to *Sixty Stories,* which won the 1982 PEN/Faulkner Award for fiction. . . .

Although Mr. Barthelme's books won prizes, appeared in the nation's leading literary journals and were hailed by critics, they did not have long runs on best-seller lists. Among the reasons for this may have been his complicated stylistic techniques and the unusual themes of his work.

Snow White, for example, was a parody of the Disney film version of the classic fairy tale. The Barthelme version included a Snow White who became good friends (and shared her shower) with seven oversexed dwarfs. The dwarfs also become successful capitalists, a Grimm Brothers embodiment of small businessmen. Prince Charming is delayed not only by the evil queen but also by a perverse fondness for hot baths.

Mr. Barthelme's short story collections were no less singular. His *Caligari* was composed of 14 seemingly unconnected stories. They ranged from a brief tale of a seemingly defeated Batman whose career is saved by friends to one about an abandoned husband who takes up residence in a radio station where he broadcasts the saga of his marriage while a band plays "The Star-Spangled Banner."

While most critics applauded his work, especially his wry humor and innovative style, some complained of writing they found tedious, repetitive, and above all, depressing. *Harper's* wrote that he and Truman Capote were "depression freaks whose anger is muted in pessimism and discontent. The rage takes the form of despair over the possibilities for life."

Others applauded what they perceived as a surreal, diverse and dizzying writing act. One of his stories consisted of a single sentence, albeit a sentence without a subject. Another is composed of 100 numbered sentences. His writing featured varying rhythms, typographical inventiveness, and even footnotes. It was as convoluted as life itself.

Hailed by the *New York Times* as a worthy successor to Franz Kafka, Mr. Barthelme said he considered himself one of the "alleged postmodernists" whose ranks he said included John Barth, John Hawkes, Thomas Pynchon and Italo Calvino.

> Richard Pearson, "Donald Barthelme Dies at 58; Wrote Short Stories, Novels," in The Washington Post, *July 25, 1989.*

THE NEW YORKER

Donald Barthelme died the other day, at the age of fifty-eight. His departure came much too soon for his readers and stricken friends to attach to him that sense of satisfaction and gratitude one extends almost reflexively to an author who has achieved a longer span, but the brilliance and the dimensions of his work would have honored several lifetimes. He was the author of four novels (one to be published next year), nine collections of stories, and a celebrated book for children. His contributions to this magazine extended across twenty-six years, and included dozens of unsigned Notes and Comment pieces, some film criticism, and a hundred and twenty-eight stories—these last of such a dazzling, special nature that each one was invariably spoken of, here and elsewhere, as "a Barthelme." The tag was almost essential, because a typical Barthelme story was simultaneously rich and elusive, evanescent and nutritious, profound and hilarious, brief and long-term, trifling and heartbreaking, daunting to some readers and to others a snap, a breeze, a draught of life. During his lifetime, Donald Barthelme was variously summarized as an avant-gardist, a collagist, a minimalist, a Dadaist, an existentialist, and a postmodernist, but even a cursory rereading of his work leaves one with the certainty that none of these narrowings are of much use. Categories seemed to accumulate around him of their own accord (the phenomenon must have pleased him, for he loved lists), but a brief rundown of some common ingredients in his fiction only brings back his unique swirl of colors and contexts: songs, museums, headlines, orchestras, bishops and other clerics, jungles, babies, commercials, savants and philosophers, animals (gerbils, bears, porcupines, falling dogs), anomie, whiskey, fathers and grandfathers, explorers, passionate love, ghosts (zombies and others), musicians, filmmakers, recipes, painters, princes, affectations, engravings, domesticity, balloons, battalions, nothingness, politicians, Indians, grief, places (Paraguay, Korea, Copenhagen, Barcelona, Thailand), dreams, young women, architects, angels, and a panoply of names (Goethe, Edward Lear, Klee, Bluebeard, Cortés and Montezuma, Sindbad, Kierkegaard, President Eisenhower, Eugénie Grandet, Snow White, Captain Blood, the Holy Ghost, Perpetua, Daumier, the Phantom of the Opera, St. Augustine, St. Anthony, and Hokie Mokie the King of Jazz).

This explosion of reference, this bottomless etcetera, may account for his brevity—short stories and short novels—and for the beauty of his prose. His names and nouns were set down in a manner that magically carried memories and meanings and overtones, bringing them intact to the page, where they let loose (in the reader) a responding instinctive flood of recognition, irony, and sadness—too many emotions, in fact, to work very well within the formal chambers of a full novel. The Barthelme sentences, which seemed to employ references or omissions in the place of adjectives or metaphors, were sky blue—clear and fresh, and free of all previous weathers of writing. It was this instrument that allowed him to be offhand and complex and lighthearted and poignant all at the same time—often within the space of a line or two. (p. 23)

[Many readers] were put off by Barthelme's crosscutting and by his terrifying absence of explanation, and those who resisted him to the end may have been people who were by nature unable to put their full trust in humor. Barthelme was erudite and culturally rigorous, but he was always terrifically funny as well, and when his despairing characters and jagged scenes and sudden stops and starts had you tumbling wildly, free-falling through a story, it was laughter that kept you afloat and made you feel there would probably be a safe landing. It was all right to laugh: sometimes (he seemed to be saying) that was the only thing we should count on.

All this took some getting used to—readers who encountered his long and ironically twisted **Snow White** in this magazine in 1967 wrote us in great numbers to ask what had happened to them—but if you could give yourself to it (there was no code, no set of symbols, no key) you were all right. One writer here said last week, "Somehow, he taught us how to read him—it's almost the most surprising thing about him—and what had felt strange or surreal in his work came to seem absolutely natural and inevitable. And there were times, particularly in the Nixon years, when his stuff seemed more real—saner and much more coherent—than anything else going on in the world."

Donald Barthelme was tall and quiet, with an air of natural gravity to him—a *light* gravity, if that is possible. He had an Ahab beard and wore Strindbergian eyeglasses; some people thought he looked more postmodernist than he wrote. He was entertaining and sad, and without pretension. He took himself seriously but presented himself quietly. . . . He was a great teacher, unfailingly generous and hopeful in his estimation of beginning writers. He was busy in intellectual and literary circles, here and in Europe. He was a romantic and a family man (as anyone who reads him can see), and an exceptionally gentle and affectionate father. Many people, of all ages, seemed to find a father in him, in fact, and they are missing him now in a painful and personal fashion. One woman on our staff, a writer, said, "When he was writing a lot, you had this sense that there was someone else sort of like you, living in your city, and saying things that meant something about your life. It was like having a companion in the world."

And an older man, also a writer and contributor, said almost the same thing:

> He always seemed to be writing about my trashiest thoughts and my night fears and my darkest secrets, but he understood them better than I did, and he seemed to find them sweeter and classier than I ever could. For a long time, I felt I was going to be all right as long as he was around and writing. Hav-

ing him for a friend was the greatest compliment of my life.

(pp. 23-4)

"The Talk of the Town: Notes and Comment," in The New Yorker, *Vol. LXV, No. 26, August 14, 1989, pp. 23-4.*

JOHN BARTH

"The proper work of the critic is praise, and that which cannot be praised should be surrounded with a tasteful, well-thought-out silence."

This is to praise the excellent American writer Donald Barthelme, who, in a 1981 *Paris Review* interview, cited in passing that arguable proposition (by the music critic Peter Yates).

Donald worked *hard* on that anything-but-spontaneous interview—as wise, articulate and entertaining a specimen as can be found in the *Paris Review's* long, ongoing series of shoptalks. He worked hard on all his printed utterance, to make it worth his and our whiles. His untimely death in July at the age of 58, like the untimely death of Raymond Carver just last summer at 50, leaves our literature—leaves Literature—bereft, wham-bang, of two splendid practitioners at the peak of their powers.

Polar opposites in some obvious respects (Carver's home-grown, blue-collar realism and programmatic unsophistication, Barthelme's urbane and urban semi-Surrealism), they shared an axis of rigorous literary craftsmanship, a preoccupation with the particulars of, shall we say, post-Eisenhower American life, and a late-modern conviction, felt to the bone, that less is more. For Carver, as for Jorge Luis Borges, the step from terse lyric poetry to terse short stories was temerity enough; neither, to my knowledge, ever attempted a novel. Barthelme was among us a bit longer than Carver and published three spare, fine specimens of that genre—all brilliant, affecting, entertaining and more deep than thick—but the short story was his long suit. Without underrating either Carver's intellectuality or Barthelme's emotional range, we nevertheless associate Raymond with reticent viscerality and may consider Donald the thinking man's—and woman's—Minimalist. . . .

His writing is not the only excellent thing that Donald Barthelme leaves those who knew him personally or professionally. He was by all accounts a first-rate literary coach (most recently at the University of Houston), a conscientious literary citizen much involved with such organizations as PEN, and a gracious friend. But his fiction is our longest-lasting souvenir and the one that matters most to those of us who knew him mainly, if not only, as delighted readers.

"We like books that have a lot of *dreck* in them," remarks one of the urban dwarfs in Barthelme's first novel, **Snow White;** and included in that novel's midpoint questionnaire for the reader is the item, "Is there too much *blague* in the narration? Not enough *blague?*" In fact the novel is *blague*-free, like all of Donald Barthelme's writing. Not enough to say that he didn't waste words; neither did extravagant Rabelais or apparently rambling Laurence Sterne. Donald barely *indulged* words—he valued them too much for that—and this rhetorical short leash makes his occasional lyric flights all the more exhilarating. . . .

Bright as is his accomplishment in it, the genre of the novel, even the half-inch novel, must have been basically uncongenial to a narrative imagination not only agoraphobic by disposition but less inclined to dramaturgy than to the tactful elaboration of bravura ground-metaphors, such as those suggested by his novels' titles: **Snow White, The Dead Father, Paradise.** His natural narrative space was the short story, if *story* is the right word for those often plotless marvels of which he published some seven volumes over 20 years, from **Come Back, Dr. Caligari** in 1964 to **Overnight to Many Distant Cities** in 1983. . . . These constitute his major literary accomplishment, and an extraordinary accomplishment it is, in quality and in consistency.

Is there really any "early Donald Barthelme"? Like Mozart and Kafka, he seems to have been born full-grown. One remarks some minor lengthening and shortening of his literary sideburns over the decades: the sportive, more or less Surreal, high-60's graphics, for example, tend to disappear after **City Life** (1970), and while he never forsook what Borges calls "that element of irrealism indispensable to art," there is a slight shift toward the realistic, even the personal, in such later stories as **"Visitors"** and **"Affection"** (in **Overnight to Many Distant Cities**). But a Donald Barthelme story from any of his too-few decades remains recognizable from its opening line:

> "Hubert gave Charles and Irene a nice baby for Christmas."
>
> "The death of God left the angels in a strange position."
>
> "When Captain Blood goes to sea, he locks the doors and windows of his house on Cow Island personally."

I have heard Donald referred to as essentially a writer of the American 1960's. It may be true that his alloy of irrealism and its opposite is more evocative of that fermentatious decade, when European formalism had its belated flowering in North American writing, than of the relatively conservative decades since. But his literary precursors antedate the century, not to mention its 60's, and are mostly non-American. "How come you write the way you do?" a Johns Hopkins apprentice writer once asked him. "Because Samuel Beckett already wrote the way *he* did," Barthelme replied. He then produced for the seminar his "short list": five books he recommended to the attention of aspiring American fiction writers. No doubt the list changed from time to time; just then it consisted of Rabelais's *Gargantua and Pantagruel,* Laurence Sterne's *Tristram Shandy,* the stories of Heinrich von Kleist, Flaubert's *Bouvard and Pécuchet* and Flann O'Brien's *At Swim-Two-Birds*—a fair sample of the kind of nonlinear narration, sportive form and cohabitation of radical fantasy with quotidian detail that mark his own fiction. He readily admired other, more "traditional" writers, but it is from the likes of these that he felt his genealogical descent.

Similarly, though he tsked at the critical tendency to group certain writers against certain others "as if we were football teams"—praising these as the true "post-contemporaries" or whatever, and consigning those to some outer darkness of the passé—he freely acknowledged his admiration for such of his "teammates," in those critics' view, as Robert Coover, Stanley Elkin, William Gaddis, William Gass, John Hawkes, Thomas Pynchon and Kurt Vonnegut, among others. . . .

How different from one another those above-mentioned teammates are! Indeed, other than their nationality and gender, their common inclination to some degree of irrealism and to the foregrounding of form and language, and the circumstance of their having appeared on the literary scene in the 1960's or thereabouts, it is not easy to see why their names should be so frequently linked (or why Grace Paley's, for example, is not regularly included in that all-male lineup). But if they constitute a team, it has no consistently brighter star than the one just lost.

Except for readers who require a new literary movement with each new network television season, the product of Donald Barthelme's imagination and artistry is an ongoing delight that we had looked forward to decades more of. Readers in the century to come (assuming etc.) will surely likewise prize that product—for its wonderful humor and wry pathos, for the cultural-historical interest its rich specificity will duly acquire, and—most of all, I hope and trust—for its superb verbal art.

> *John Barth, "Thinking Man's Minimalist: Honoring Barthelme," in* The New York Times Book Review, *September 3, 1989, p. 9.*

THOMAS E. KENNEDY

The following article, written before Donald Barthelme's death, is perhaps for that very reason an appropriate summation of his career. Not intended as a tribute, it is the best sort of tribute. Free of the elegiac, it measures Barthelme's achievement beyond sentiment and also beyond the fluctuations of literary fashion. Writers such as Donald Barthelme, the late Raymond Carver, and even John Gardner will always have more in common with one another than promoters of trends, schools, and other marketing strategies would like us to believe.—Ronald Sukenick, Publisher [of The American Book Review]

In many ways the continuing survival of Donald Barthelme's fiction in the U.S. is a miracle. That Barthelme should have been nurtured by the *New Yorker* also is amazing, and that he has a sufficient audience to continue to be as prominent as he is, speaks very well, in my opinion, for the literary tastes of the American people at a time when thin brew like *Bright Lights, Big City* is hailed as genius.

Thus, the publication by G. P. Putman's & Sons of Barthelme's *Forty Stories . . .* is cause for celebration—celebration that the fight promoters have not managed to smother this brilliant light under a blanket of dirty realism.

Interestingly, the opening piece in *Forty Stories,* "Chablis"—except for its specific Barthelmisms (e.g., a dog that is a Presbyterian)—has more in common than not with a number of Carver stories. Elements abound here that in Barthelme are dark comic postmodernism but in Carver would be viewed as hyperrealism—such as the one spouse who says to the other, "I feel worse than you feel" (**"Affection"**) or the narrator in **"Chablis"** who sits at five in the morning drinking a chablis on the rocks as he watches the joggers appear on the street below. Some of these pieces seem at times to parody "minimalist-realistic" fiction.

Interesting, too, is that Barthelme titles his book forty "stories"—not tales, fictions, *ficciones,* or factoids, but *stories.* In an interview with Larry McCaffery, however, Barthelme de-

fines a story as "a process of accretion. Barnacles growing on a wreck or a rock. I'd rather have a wreck than a ship that sails. Things attach themselves to wrecks. Strange fish find your wreck or rock to be a good feeding ground."

Indeed, Barthelme's stories abound in strange fish, but their faces often surprise us with disturbingly familiar expressions, odd bits of sentence affixing themselves to other odd bits to create a jarring contrast that makes frighteningly funny sense. The collage effect and the power released from the broken, awkward sentence particularly interest Barthelme. "The point of collage," he told Jerome Klinkowitz, "is that unlike things are stuck together to make at best a new reality. This new reality, in the best case, may be or imply a comment on the other reality from which it came and maybe also much else." **"The Genius,"** included in *Forty Stories* in a version revised from that originally published in *Sadness* in 1972, includes among other snippets the following exchange:

> Q: What do you consider the most important tool
>   of the genius of today?
> A: Rubber cement.

Perhaps Barthelme is making a statement of aesthetic principle here, concealed in his own seemingly offhand methodical madness; perhaps he is also parodying the critics who complain of his methods of collage. One thing is certain, such Barthelmisms provoke reflection on the nature of art and its function in society and convey a battle cry at least as strong as the most directly sociological or "realistic" fictional assault on the way we live now.

The original version of **"Genius"** concludes with the genius smiling as he signs for a delivery of stainless steel tulips given by the city of Houston in tribute to his greatness; the new version leaves him signing for a sword given by the city of Toledo, Spain, signing with one hand and swinging the sword over his head with the other. Not flowers but a sword. Might this be a statement of the innovators' position today? In the seventies, they were given flowers of praise by the administration; today, the administrative powers seem to ignore innovation in favor of the perhaps less spiritually demanding school of realism. Is the answer, then, a sword? . . .

The basic power of Barthelme's work is that his innovations manage to avoid predictable patterns. Just as one thinks one can begin to know what to expect, he takes a new turn: from the essentially realistic, albeit postmodern-chilled **"Concerning the Bodyguard,"** which portrays the dehumanized situation of the functionary whose body is employed to defend a system beyond his ken, to the frighteningly funny, mad logic of **"Baby,"** where the reality is conveyed through the technique of absurdity, or the lime-dry irony of **"January,"** with its subtly parodic interview with a theologian whose self-professed starting point is that he is a fool and an ignoramus who never succeeded in doing anything measurable.

There is something of the meditation about many of Barthelme's pieces, something of the *Pensées,* short pieces that reveal the illogic of the bent principles by which we function or wish to believe that we do. Hence, perhaps, the interest he expressed to McCaffery in the awkward sentence:

> I look for a particular kind of sentence, perhaps more often the awkward than the beautiful. A back broke sentence is interesting. Any sentence that begins with the phrase, "It is not clear that . . ." is clearly clumsy but preparing itself for greatness of

a kind. A way of backing into a story—of getting past the reader's hard-won armor.

Barthelme's fascination with the collage and the broken sentence, and his virtuosity in using them, appear throughout these *Forty Stories.* Here we find artfully dented realism (**"Chablis," "Concerning the Bodyguard," "Jaws," "Affection"**), the truly and wonderfully surreal (**"On the Deck," "The Wound"**), postmodernized fairy tales (**"Sindbad," "The Palace at Four A.M.," "Bluebeard"**), science fiction (**"RIF"**), sociology (**"The New Owner"**), and brilliantly entertaining explorations of the way in which art records the reality being manipulated by and for "higher authorities" (**"Engineer Private Paul Klee Misplaces an Aircraft . . . "**). (p. 3)

I believe that all art by definition, all serious art, deals with reality, with the reality of human existence, or with an attempt to touch that reality or some part of it. Realism works on sociological premises with a more or less conventional reality—the conventions by which, for example, in our daily lives we tacitly agree to ignore that in us which is not congruous with daily "sane" behavior, with an orderly, ordered view of the world. In other words, to achieve a semblance of order, we pretend that the conditions of life are reasonable and just, we edit out our mad dreams and desires and all that is extraneous to the convention of order that we generally refer to when we refer to reality. We pretend to believe that *Time Magazine* or *The New York Times* or *The Washington Post* or even *The New York Post* or *New York Daily News,* not to mention *The National Enquirer* (literalist of the postmodern image), is capable of reporting what we need to know to understand our world, and that mimetic fiction can reflect a coherent picture of a coherent world.

Donald Barthelme, the indefatigable innovator, will not allow us to rest with such beliefs. Barthelme explains to us how "our rhetoric is preserved (for us) by our elected representatives in the fat of their heads" (**"The Explanation"**), the distinctions between a church and a collection plate (**"RIF"**). The realities that Barthelme's broker sentences convey to us can be dark, absurd, and frightening even as they make us laugh with nervous glee, or they can be beautiful as the farewell of the woman in **"Terminus":**

> She comes toward him fresh from the bath, opens
> her robe. Goodbye, she says, goodbye.

Such innovation and invention is required to portray reality in the fullness of its tension and contradiction; realism alone cannot manage the whole job before us in coming to terms with these mad times in this strange condition of existence. (pp. 18, 25)

Thomas E. Kennedy, "Donald Barthelme," in The American Book Review, *Vol. 11, No. 5, November-December, 1989, pp. 3, 18, 25.*

Samuel Beckett

April 13?, 1906 - December 22, 1989

Born Samuel Barclay Beckett. Irish dramatist, novelist, short story writer, scriptwriter, poet, critic, and translator.

For an overview of Beckett's life and work, see *CLC*, Vols. 1, 2, 3, 4, 6, 9, 10, 11, 14, 18, 29, 57; *Contemporary Authors,* Vols. 5-8, rev. ed.; and *Dictionary of Literary Biography,* Vols. 13, 15.

SID SMITH

Samuel Beckett, whose *Waiting for Godot* and other plays revolutionized modern drama and inspired the phrase "theater of the absurd," was buried Tuesday after a small, private service in Paris, his adopted home of many years. He was 83. . . .

He leaves behind a body of theatrical works that are among the most produced and studied of our time. The 1952 *Godot,* about a couple of tramps anxiously biding the hours in a barren landscape, awaiting the mysterious title figure who never comes, epitomized mid-century man—godless and adrift. With *Godot,* and other plays like it, Mr. Beckett gave the theater a unique abstract approach in an era when film had all but co-opted conventional realism.

Instead, Mr. Beckett offered a world of bleak, seemingly nonsensical settings and situations, such as the human duo who live in garbage cans in the 1957 *Endgame.* Especially during the '50s and '60s, Mr. Beckett's works revitalized world drama and, as prime samples of absurdist theater, gave the form a modern day calling card.

But for all their formal experimentalism, Mr. Beckett's works succeed through their contagious compassion for loneliness, despair and drudgery. In *Happy Days* (1961), Mr. Beckett embodied human futility and suffering in a lone woman buried up to her waist in sand for half the play and for the next half buried up to her neck, cooing contentedly as she bravely goes about life's daily mediocrities. In *Krapp's Last Tape,* first performed in 1969, a nearly sightless old man replays a 30-year-old tape of himself and realizes he no longer understands the words of his youth.

Mr. Beckett's plotless, nonlinear world and sparse language have echoes in the works of Edward Albee, Tom Stoppard, David Mamet and Sam Shepard. One of his foremost followers, Britain's Harold Pinter, said Tuesday: "He was totally original and a man of great courage, not only in himself, but in his work. His work knew no bounds."

His life is full of mysteries and contradictions. For someone whose worldwide influence is immeasurable, he shunned the

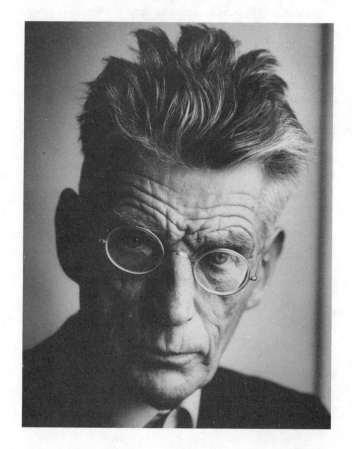

spotlight. When he won the Nobel Prize for literature in 1969, he bypassed the Stockholm ceremonies and fled to Tunisia.

A born-and-bred Dubliner, Mr. Beckett came at the end of a line of Irish literary greats, notably William Butler Yeats, Oscar Wilde and James Joyce, whom Mr. Beckett knew in Paris. But unlike those others, Mr. Beckett made his mark writing important early works, including *Godot,* in French, later translating them into English.

He studied modern languages at Dublin's Trinity College and first came to Paris in 1928 to lecture in English. Later, after his father died and his mother urged Mr. Beckett to drop literature, he settled permanently in Paris, where he worked for the Resistance against the Nazis and won the Croix de Guerre with a gold star. He once said he preferred "France in war to Ireland in peace."

In 1938, he was stabbed during a street brawl and a woman nearby on a bicycle stopped to help him and got him to a hospital. The woman, Suzanne Deschevaux-Dumesnil, became his lifelong companion, and the couple married in 1961. She died in July. They had no children.

In addition to plays, Mr. Beckett wrote novels, including *Murphy* (1938), *Molloy* (1951) and *Watt* (1953); short stories; radio and television scripts; and a screenplay (*Film,* with Buster Keaton, 1965). His last work was an 1,801-word novella published in March, called *Stirrings Still,* a meditation on old age printed in only 200 copies, each selling for $1,720.

> *Sid Smith, in an obituary in* Chicago Tribune, *December 27, 1989.*

MEL GUSSOW

Samuel Beckett, a towering figure in drama and fiction who altered the course of contemporary theater, died in Paris on Friday at the age of 83. He died of respiratory problems in a Paris hospital, where he had been moved from a nursing home. He was buried yesterday at the Montparnasse cemetery after a private funeral.

Explaining the secrecy surrounding his illness, hospitalization and death, Irene Lindon, representing the author's Paris publisher, Editions de Minuit, said it was "what he would have wanted."

Beckett's plays, beginning with *Waiting for Godot,* became the cornerstone of 20th-century theater. In this play, two tramps wait for a salvation that never comes. To pass their time on earth, they exchange vaudeville routines and metaphysical musings—and comedy rises to tragedy.

Before Beckett there was a naturalistic tradition. After him, scores of playwrights were encouraged to experiment with the underlying meaning of their work as well as with an absurdist style. As the Beckett scholar Ruby Cohn wrote, "After *Godot,* plots could be minimal; exposition, expendable; characters, contradictory; settings, unlocalized, and dialogue, unpredictable. Blatant farce could jostle tragedy."

At the same time, his novels, in particular his trilogy, *Molloy, Malone Dies* and *The Unnamable,* inspired by James Joyce, move subliminally into the minds of the characters. The novels are among the most experimental and most profound in Western literature.

For his accomplishments in both drama and fiction, the Irish author, who wrote first in English and later in French, received the Nobel Prize in Literature in 1969.

At the root of his art was a philosophy of the deepest yet most courageous pessimism, exploring man's relationship with his God. With Beckett, one searched for hope amid despair and continued living with a kind of stoicism, as illustrated by the final words of his novel, *The Unnamable:* "You must go on, I can't go on, I'll go on." Or as he wrote in *Worstward Ho,* one of his later works of fiction: "Try again. Fail again. Fail better."

Though his name in the adjectival form, Beckettian, entered the English language as a synonym for bleakness, he was a man of great humor and compassion, in his life as in his work. He was a tragicomic playwright whose art was consistently instilled with mordant wit. As scholars and critics scrutinized his writing for metaphor and ulterior meaning, he refrained from all analysis or even explanation. As he wrote to his favorite director, Alan Schneider: "If people want to have headaches among the overtones, let them. And provide their own aspirin." When Mr. Schneider rashly asked Beckett who Godot was, the playwright answered, "If I knew, I would have said so in the play."

His greatest successes were in his middle years, in the 1950's with *Waiting for Godot* and *Endgame,* and with his trilogy of novels. It was suggested that for an artist of his stature, he had a relatively small body of work—but only if one measures size by number of words. Distilling his art to its essence, he produced scores of eloquent plays and stories, many of those in his later years not strictly defined as full length. But in terms of the intensity of the imagery, plays like *Not I, Footfalls* and *Rockaby* were complete visions.

He wrote six novels, four long plays and dozens of shorter ones, volumes of stories and narrative fragments, some of which were short novels. He wrote poetry and essays on the arts, including an essay about Marcel Proust (one of his particular favorites), radio and television plays and prose pieces he called residua and disjecta.

In his 80's, he became an icon of survival. Even as he vowed that he had nothing more to say, he continued to be tormented and sustained by midnight thoughts and nightmarish images. Having discovered what was for him the non-meaning of life and its brevity (man is, he observed in *Waiting for Godot,* "born astride the grave"), he never stopped looking for ways to express himself. Once in writing about painting he said, "There is nothing to express, nothing from which to express, no power to express, no desire to express, together with the obligation to express." For him, that obligation was ineluctable.

Despite his artistic reputation, his ascension was slow and for many years discouraging. He labored in his own darkness and disillusionment, the equivalent of one of the isolated metaphorical worlds inhabited by his characters. When his work began to be published and produced, he was plagued by philistinism, especially with *Waiting for Godot,* which puzzled and outraged many theatergoers and critics, some of whom regarded it as a travesty if not a hoax.

From the first he had his ardent supporters, who included, notably, Jean Anouilh, the bellwether of French theatrical tradition. He greeted *Godot* at its premiere in Paris as "a masterpiece that will cause despair for men in general and for playwrights in particular." In both respects, Anouilh proved prescient.

Time caught up with *Godot* and with its author. Today the play is generally accepted as a cornerstone of modern theater. (pp. A1, D17)

The name *Godot,* along with that of the author, is part of international mythology. Godot, who may or may not be a savior, never arrives, but man keeps waiting for his possible arrival. Waiting, in Beckett's sense, is not a vacuum but an alternate activity that can be as visceral—or as mindless—as one makes it. For Beckett himself, waiting became a way of living—waiting for inspiration, recognition, understanding or death.

For more than 50 years the writer lived in his adopted city of Paris, for much of that time in a working-class district in Montparnasse—a move that was to have the greatest effect on his life. Though he wrote most of his work in French, he remained definably Irish in his voice, manner and humor.

Even in his final years, when he lived in a nursing home in Paris, he joined friends in a sip of Irish whisky, which seemed to warm his bones and open him to greater conviviality. Throughout his life he was as craggy and as erect as a Giacometti sculpture. When he was healthy, he took long, loping walks on Paris streets.

In no way could he ever be considered an optimist. In an often repeated story, on a glorious sunny day he walked jauntily through a London park with an old friend and exuded a feeling of joy. The friend said it was the kind of day that made one glad to be alive. Beckett responded, "I wouldn't go that far."

Samuel Barclay Beckett was born in Foxrock, a suburb of Dublin, on Good Friday, April 13, 1906 (that date is sometimes disputed; it is said that on his birth certificate the date is May 13). His father, William Beckett Jr., was a surveyor. His mother, Mary Roe Beckett (known as May), was a nurse before her marriage. Samuel and his older brother, Frank, were brought up as Protestants. They went to Earlsfort House School in Dublin. Samuel Beckett then continued his education at Portora Royal School in Enniskillen, County Fermanagh, and at Trinity College, Dublin, where he majored in French and Italian. At school he excelled both in his studies and in sports, playing cricket and rugby. He received his Bachelor of Arts degree in 1927 and his Master of Arts degree in 1931.

In the intervening time, he spent two years in Paris in an exchange program, lecturing on English at the Ecole Normale Supérieure. In Paris, he met James Joyce and other members of the literary and artistic set. He was not, as is commonly thought, Joyce's secretary, but he became a close friend and aide, reading to him when Joyce's eyes began to fail. Beckett's first published work was an essay on Joyce that appeared in the collection **"Our Exagmination Round His Factification for Incamination of Work in Progress,"** the work in progress being Joyce's *Finnegans Wake.* His first poem, **"Whoroscope,"** was printed in 1930, followed one year later by his essay on Proust.

Returning to Ireland, he taught Romance languages at Trinity. He thought briefly about remaining in the academic profession but decided otherwise. He resigned abruptly in 1932 and left Ireland, returning only for annual visits to his mother. (His father died in 1933, his mother in 1950.) He wandered from England to France to Germany before moving to Paris permanently in 1937. . . .

Beckett became a familiar figure at Left Bank cafes, continuing his alliance with Joyce while also becoming friends with artists like Marcel Duchamp (with whom he played chess) and Alberto Giacometti. At this time he became involved with Peggy Guggenheim, who nicknamed him Oblomov after the title character in the Ivan Goncharov novel, a man who Miss Guggenheim said was so overcome by apathy that he "finally did not even have the willpower to get out of bed."

In 1938, while walking with friends on a Paris street, he was stabbed with a knife by a panhandler. A young piano student named Suzanne Deschevaux-Dumesnil came to his rescue and telephoned for an ambulance. One of his lungs was perforated and the knife narrowly missed his heart. Beckett fully recovered from the wound but it left psychological scars. After he recovered, he visited his assailant in prison and asked him the reason for the assault. The man replied, *"Je ne sais pas, Monsieur."* More than ever, Beckett became aware of the ran-

domness of life. The episode had one other long-ranging effect: He began a lifelong relationship with Miss Deschevaux-Dumesnil. . . .

With her, he chose to remain in France during World War II rather than return to the safety of Ireland. Both became active in the French Resistance. Forced to flee Paris, the couple went to Roussillon near the Spanish border. While working as a farm laborer and running messages for the Resistance, Beckett wrote the novel **Watt.** It was often said that his experiences in hiding during the war were an inspiration for **Waiting for Godot** and for the novel **Mercier and Camier.** . . .

After **Watt,** he began writing in French, which allowed him, as the Joyce biographer Richard Ellman observed, "a private liberation from the English tradition." The five years starting in 1947 were his most intense creative period, producing most of his major work. That year he wrote his first play **Eleutheria,** and began the novel **Molloy.** They were followed by **Waiting for Godot,** which he wrote in longhand in a composition book. It took him four months. In a little more than a year he had finished his greatest play as well as the first two parts of his trilogy of novels (**Molloy** and **Malone Dies**).

Though he found a publisher for the trilogy . . . , the plays were more difficult to place. Miss Deschevaux-Dumesnil took them from producer to producer, a thankless route that the playwright once compared to giving the plays to a concierge. Then Roger Blin, the French actor and director, agreed to present one. He chose **Godot** over **Eleutheria** partly because it had fewer characters. At Beckett's behest, **Eleutheria** was never produced in his lifetime. It was only when **Waiting for Godot** was in rehearsal, with Beckett in attendance, that Blin fully realized the excitement of his discovery.

En Attendant Godot, as the play was titled, opened on Jan. 5, 1953, at the Théâtre de Babylone, and, beginning a lifetime practice, the author did not attend. The first review, written by Sylvain Zegel in *La Libération,* said Beckett was "one of today's best playwrights," a fact that was not universally acknowledged. The first London production, using the playwright's English translation and directed by Peter Hall, received generally dismissive daily reviews. It was rescued by Harold Hobson, then the drama critic of *The Sunday Times* in London, who said the play might "securely lodge in a corner of your mind as long as you live."

In January 1956, Michael Myerberg opened the first United States production at the Coconut Grove Playhouse in Miami, with Bert Lahr and Tom Ewell cast in the leading roles as those Beckett tramps, Estragon and Vladimir. Expecting a Bert Lahr comedy, the audience was mystified. As Alan Schneider, the director of that original production, said, doing **Godot** in Miami was like dancing *Giselle* in Roseland.. . . .

That **Waiting for Godot** became a contemporary classic can be attributed to the enthusiasm of its champions and to the profundity of the work itself, which became more apparent with subsequent productions. **Godot** came to be regarded not only as a clown comedy with tragic dimensions but as a play about man coping with the nature of his existence in a world that appeared to be hurtling toward a self-induced apocalypse.

Before **Godot** was produced in London, Beckett completed a second play, **Fin de Partie,** or **Endgame,** as the title was translated. In this dramatic equivalent of chess, Hamm the master oppresses Clov the servant in a bunker looking out on the void of the world. *Endgame* was followed by the radio play *All That Fall* and by the monodrama *Krapp's Last Tape,* written for the actor Patrick Magee. In 1961 after he and Miss Deschevaux-Dumesnil were married, he finished *Happy Days,* about a long and not always happy marriage, in which a woman is buried up to her neck in earth. In 1964 he made his only trip to the United States for the filming of *Film,* the short Beckett movie that Mr. Schneider made with Buster Keaton. . . .

In 1969 he was awarded the Nobel Prize in literature for a body of work that "has transformed the destitution of man into his exaltation." Karl Ragnar Gierow, secretary of the Swedish Academy, said his writing "rises like a Miserere from all mankind, its muffled minor key sounding liberation to the oppressed and comfort to those in need." He was on holiday in Morocco at the time of the Nobel announcement and in characteristic fashion offered no public statement and refused to attend the ceremony. He sent his publisher in his stead. Reportedly he gave his prize money of $72,800 to needy artists.

As undeterred by the acclaim as he had been by his years of obscurity, he continued to write and to maintain his privacy. His plays and prose became shorter and even terser, as in *Not I,* in which the play's principal character is a woman's heavily lipsticked mouth; *That Time,* in which a spotlight shines on a man's head and his corona of white hair, and *Rockaby,* in which an old woman rocks herself to death. In these plays he chose to deal with what he called "the battle of the soliloquy," sifting the past and enduring the continuum of life. . . .

[In 1984], the New York Drama Critics Circle awarded him a special citation in recognition of his body of work and in particular for two evenings of Beckett short plays produced that season in New York. One of those plays was *Catastrophe,* written for Vaclav Havel. It was for Beckett a rare political work about the interrogation of a dissident.

In Beckett's later years, directors staged his radio plays or adapted his prose to the stage. Mabou Mines offered dramatizations of *The Lost Ones, Mercier and Camier* and *Company.* Though Beckett was liberal about allowing adaptations of his prose, he was scrupulous in demanding absolute fidelity to the stage directions as well as to the dialogue in his plays. In 1985, JoAnne Akalaitis, a director with Mabou Mines, changed the setting of *Endgame* from a bare interior to an abandoned subway station. Through representatives, Beckett issued a formal complaint against the production at the American Repertory Theater in Boston, and his objection appeared in the play's program.

On his 80th birthday in 1986, Beckett was celebrated in several cities. In Paris there was a citywide festival of plays and symposiums and in New York there was a week of panels and lectures analyzing his art. As usual, he kept his silence, as in the characteristic note he sent to those who approached him about writing his biography. He said that his life was "devoid of interest."

He steadfastly maintained his routine through his later years. He lived on the Boulevard St. Jacques in an apartment adjoining that of his wife and overlooking the exercise yard of the Sante prison. Periodically he visited his country house, some 60 miles outside Paris. He made daily trips to a neigh-

borhood cafe where he met friends, had a double espresso and smoked several of his thin dark cigarettes. Periodically he wrote brief plays and small prose pieces.

Around him and without his encouragement, his reputation grew unbounded. The Mike Nichols revival of *Waiting for Godot* at Lincoln Center in 1988 was an event of magnitude, drawing together the diverse talents of Steve Martin, Robin Williams and Bill Irwin and selling out for its entire engagement. This year there was a festival of Beckett radio plays on National Public Radio, reminding his audience that this was still another form that he had mastered.

About a year ago, after falling in his apartment, he moved to a nearby nursing home, where he continued to receive visitors. He lived his last year in a small, barely furnished room. He had a television set on which he continued to watch major tennis and soccer events, and several books, including his boyhood copy of Dante's *Divine Comedy* in Italian.

On July 17 this year, his wife died and he left the nursing home to attend the funeral. Late this year, after he became ill, he was moved to a hospital. There are no immediate survivors.

His last work to be printed in his lifetime was *Stirrings Still,* a short prose piece published in a limited edition on his 83d birthday. In it, a character who resembles the author sits alone in a cell-like room until he sees his double appear—and then disappear. Accompanied by "time and grief and self so-called," he finds himself "stirring still" to the end. (p. D17)

Mel Gussow, in an obituary in The New York Times, December 27, 1989, pp. A1, D17.

JOHN PETER

It was said of Tolstoy, in his old age, that while he lived no man needed to feel an orphan. This was not a piece of vague sentimental hero worship, but a recognition that Tolstoy embodied a moral force; that his work issued from a source of pure inner integrity; and that his readers would relate to the moral presence in his writing by recognising something of that presence in themselves. It meant that when you read Tolstoy you were not alone in the world. Art can make no higher claim than that.

Something very like this can be said of Beckett—but with a difference. The aged Tolstoy was a father figure; he was regarded as a living totem of moral authority. In his world you were no orphan because his creative wisdom extended to you the harsh but understanding protection of a spiritual father. Beckett's art, by contrast, expresses the desolation and loneliness of the fatherless condition. In his world you are less of an orphan because you sense that he is an orphan too: he understands the sense of grim, helpless determination in the unprotected, their need to be accountable to someone, and their knowledge that there is nobody to be accountable to. "The bastard!" groans Hamm in *Endgame.* "He doesn't exist!"

That shocking phrase is one of the most religious sentences in modern literature. We could argue, as would Catholics, lapsed Catholics, Freudians and unreconstructed communists, that the very bitterness of the denial speaks of an unconscious acceptance or at least of a need. Beckett would have brushed aside the conclusion but he would have appreciated the paradox. He was one of the most intellectual and cultivated of all great writers, whose range of reading and reference is breathtaking. . . .

His plays are replete with ideas absorbed from pre-Socratic philosophy, the Bible, the Greek and Latin classics, Dante, Descartes, and Heidegger. And yet none of this is ever pretentious, and it never gets in the way of the writing: the drama always earns its way as drama. The texts are laced with ribald jokes, and they pulsate with the steady remorse, the aches and pains of existence. When *Godot* opened in Paris in 1953, Anouilh, in a remark that nobody has yet improved upon, said it was like Pascal's Pensées played by the Fratellini Brothers. The latter were celebrated circus clowns at the time, and Anouilh clearly perceived the unique blending, in Beckett, of spiritual agony and robust laughter.

The curious thing is that Beckett had not originally thought of Vladimir and Estragon as circus clowns: that was the idea of his first director, Roger Blin. Again, it was not Beckett but Peter Hall, who directed *Godot's* London premiere in 1955, who made them into tramps, which is how they have been imprinted on our imaginations. As far as Beckett was concerned they were simply men.

Indeed, one of the most disconcerting things about Beckett's plays is the vacuum in which they are situated. I think it is a mistake to argue, as Jan Kott and Peter Brook have, that Beckett's world has anything in common with King Lear's. In Shakespeare's play, we witness the disintegration of a concrete world, with its political, economic and filial allegiances. In Beckett's plays there is usually nothing to disintegrate. When Lear demands of Edgar "What hast thou been?" he seeks the other man's identity, as do all dispossessed people, by looking for a recognisable past, with its comforting identification tags. The question would be senseless if addressed to Vladimir or Estragon, Hamm or Clov. Beckett's writing really homes in on "the thing itself": the comfortless human creature as he really is, brutish, solitary and dogged.

All Beckett's writing is haunted by the feeling most of us have experienced, but fortunately only rarely and usually not for long: the feeling that we are totally alone in the world, unprotected by higher beings, and not deserted only because we have never really been accompanied; that our past is inexplicable and our future unknowable, and that the dingy body we inhabit is probably all there is. It would be unendurable if it were not so grotesquely laughable, no? To anyone who has ever felt this, a voice that can speak coherently about such things is a consolation and a reassurance: the voice of another orphan.

But Beckett is not in the business of cheering up either himself or other people: his art is too proud, as he once put it, for the farce of giving and receiving. His statement of desolation has its own impersonal dignity and you can derive from it whatever comfort you can: otherwise there is always God, economics, or Ibsen. Unless we recognise the spiritual courage of Beckett's position, the fearlessness with which he contemplates the void, we diminish his stature, and reduce him to the status of an intellectual best seller like Shaw.

Shaw, of course, would have disliked Beckett because he would have been made uneasy and fearful by what he would have thought was a bleak nihilism. . . . Personally, I think Beckett is about as nihilistic as Aeschylus. That old Greek confirmed the immutability of divine justice; Beckett believed in the sad doggedness of human endurance. His art is a realisation and diagnosis of nihilism: he defies nothingness with

the severe objectivity of his gaze and the purity of his observation. There is a sense of mastery in such understanding.

The mistake is to imagine that this makes Beckett a kind of moral tax inspector. No, Beckett's work is essentially amoral, not because it denies the moral validity of things, or because it promotes anything immoral, but because it does not deal in the currency of morality. His world is not a world of right and wrong: you might say that Beckett is too proud for the farce of judging and sentencing. In his world moral values are of little value. Pozzo maltreats Lucky, but is his blindness a punishment for this? We do not know. It would be easier if we did: moral values in literature are like a compass for the sighted or a white stick for the blind. One of the reasons why Beckett's plays can seem either dauntingly stark or childishly simple is that they are not signposted with forbidding "Stop!" or protective "Danger!". This is not the Let's Pretend amorality of Lautréamont or Gide, but the restraint of the compassionate but proud sceptic who knows that teaching is easy but learning is hard. He lets you bring your own values to his world—the generosity of the artist who is truly free and not afraid of judgment.

Those who knew him (I did not) speak of his warm generosity, his humour, and his kindly, reticent charm. He gave unostentatiously and was shy of honours. He retained his lifelong interest in sport, especially cricket, being the only Nobel Prize-winner in literature who is mentioned in Wisden. . . . In one of his last French prose pieces he wrote: *Je n'ai rien contre les cimetières.* This he translated as, "I have no bones to pick with cemeteries." Sweet mother earth.

> John Peter, "Our Fellow Orphan in a Lonely World," in The Sunday Times, *London, December 31, 1989, p. B7.*

CHRISTOPHER RICKS

Samuel Beckett won the Nobel Prize for literature in 1969, for "a body of work that, in new forms of fiction and the theatre, has transmuted the destitution of modern man into his exaltation". But Beckett was a great writer because it was not simply modern man (and woman) for whom he had an unsentimental, comprehensive love, but ancient man.

Beckett had a supreme grasp of the relations between all which changes and all which does not. He had the artist's understanding of civilisation as both everything we have gained and so crave to keep, and everything we have lost and yearn to recover.

He had a ranging religious—blasphemous—consciousness which was matched by a stringent political conscience. He married conscience and consciousness in a style of unimpeachable formal beauty, poignantly sad and piercingly comic. His first novel, *Murphy* (1938), opened with a sentence of death which gave a new turn to the old screw: "The sun shone, having no alternative, on the nothing new."

His late prose-poem, *Ill Seen Ill Said* (1981), contemplated the plight of an "old so dying woman" and defended her with steely dignity against the exasperation which it is self-protectingly human to feel as the bodies of those we love yield to paralysis: "Such helplessness to move she cannot help."

His claims to the Nobel Prize were unignorable. His art is a unique combination of the new and of the old. Of the old, in that his work lives as ever under the aegis of his forefathers

Milton, Swift and Dante. Of the new, in that he was the only great avant-garde writer to flourish after the founding fathers of modernism.

After 1922 the avant-garde mostly lapsed from its high purpose, and sidled its way into "mystification and outrage" (Philip Larkin's words). But Beckett's work never allowed experiment to distort the responses of experience. In an age which had rebounded off a crude empiricism into an airy insistence that everything is imagined and therefore imaginary, Beckett was besieged by these two contraries, the eternal antagonism of "things and imaginings".

He earned the honour of being the only true heir of his canny friend James Joyce and of his wary foe T.S. Eliot. He was a master of words because he was their servant too, and he was a master of technique because he knew, as Eliot put it, that we cannot say at what point "technique" begins or where it ends. From Eliot and from Proust he learned that the writer must see and show not only human feelings but human illusions of feeling.

A novelist and a dramatist, Beckett had a living sense—particularly remarkable for someone so innately and trainedly wonderful with words—that the medium of drama is not words but persons moving about on a stage using words. (The formula is Ezra Pound's.) He valued the English language with all the Irishman's complex understanding of what it is to have not a mother tongue but a stepmother tongue. What should they know of English who only English know? Beckett knew French, and knew it well enough to be able to appreciate all the better what it is to be English or French. Or Irish: asked once if he was English, he replied *"Au contraire"*. What is it, to be the contrary of an Englishman? It is to be an Irishman, or rather a Protestant Irishman from the Republic. Beckett not only created work of high worth in both English and French, he was also his own best translator and indeed set the standards for our time of what translation must be.

A man of letters who was also a great original writer, he was remarkable for the dignity and integrity of his career. In artistic terms, this means his never swerving from the aims which he set himself in 1929 in his essay on Dante and Joyce: the understanding of life neither as heaven nor hell but as purgatory. In personal terms, there is the indeflectible dedication, without either bitterness or elation, with which he lived first through 30 years of the shadow of neglect and then through 30 years of the glare of recognition, manifestly his own man and manifestly, too, a man of supreme loyalty to his art.

He took the most eternal of subjects: death. Then he gave it a fair crack of the whip. Most people most of the time want to live for ever. This is sufficiently acknowledged by literature, not least because it has been in the interests of religion in general and of Christianity in particular to give full weight to this truth. Or rather, this half-truth. For it is true, too, that most people *some* of the time, and some people most of the time, do not want to live for ever. And justice has seldom been done in literature to this truth. Beckett marvelled at "the haze of our smug will to live", at "the crass tenacity of life and its diligent pains". He believed that it was not just some archaic Greek chorus which might be moved to conclude that it is better to be dead than alive, and best of all never to have been born.

Yet if he had an eternal subject, he had too a divination of how our age stands differently even to death, of how modern man has created new possibilities and impossibilities even in the matter of death. He is the great writer of an age which has increased longevity until it has become as much a curse as a blessing, an age which has found one of its most urgent anxieties to be the definition of death.

Death is as definite as it ever was but much less satisfactorily defined. "Fully certified death": that is what Beckett craved to understand, in a world which was constituted for him partly of Dante's cruel immortality and partly of modern technology, here at a moment in human history when men and women—whether as relation and friend, as nurse and doctor, as philosopher, as murderous assailant or insurance company, even as Pope—have been moved to define death as never before.

Beckett realised—that is, he understood in himself and gave reality to it in his art—the longing for oblivion. He imagined the end of all life on the planet, an eventual eventuality for the human race whether or not it blows itself up. "Sky earth the whole kit and boodle. Not another crumb of carrion left. Lick chops and basta." The one thing worse than not living for ever would be living for ever.

May he rest in peace.

Christopher Ricks, "Giving Death a Fair Crack of the Whip," in The Sunday Times, *London, December 31, 1989, p. B7.*

WILLIAM A. HENRY III

The most evident social trend of the 20th century has been consolidation—multinationalized businesses, globalized politics, homogenized cultures. Amid this bustling bigness and togetherness has been heard a persistent cry of smallness and aloneness, a sense that comforting certainties are being stripped away and each individual left isolated with nameless terrors, deterioration and death. Painters and composers, philosophers and poets have struggled to express this sensibility by reducing their art forms to the essential, scaling ambition down from the eternal to the minimal. Where once creators held that truth was beauty, in these despondent works truth is achingly ugly, beauty a mirage of the memory.

Many of the century's most imaginative artists . . . poured their beings into this exploration of nothingness. None did so more persistently and penetratingly than Samuel Beckett, the Irish-born writer whose death was revealed last week in his adopted city, Paris, where for decades he lived in an apartment overlooking the exercise yard of a prison. In such plays as **Waiting for Godot, Endgame** and **Krapp's Last Tape;** in novels, including **Molloy, Malone Dies** and **The Unnamable;** in verse and essays and the script for a wordless Buster Keaton film, Beckett distilled despair.

His works were often funny—the two battered tramps of **Godot** might have been written for Laurel and Hardy and were in fact played by Bert Lahr and Tom Ewell, Robin Williams and Steve Martin—but the humor intensified the sadness. In the play's most vivid and haunting image, one character cries out about all mankind, "They give birth astride of a grave." Beckett regarded himself as a sort of historian, a chronicler of misbegotten times. "I didn't invent this buzzing confusion," he said. "It's all around us, and . . . the only chance of renewal is to open our eyes and see the mess." Yet he had nothing of the reformer, no impulse toward public life. He rarely granted interviews; resolutely declined to discuss his works, rebuffed would-be biographers by saying his life was "devoid of interest." He even refused to show up to collect his 1969 Nobel Prize in literature—an award he had lobbied the Swedish Academy *not* to give him. Characteristically, his death on Dec. 22 was kept secret until after a private funeral four days later.

Born on a disputed date in spring 1906, Beckett claimed to remember being a fetus in the womb, a place he recalled not as a haven but as a dark ocean of agony. The son of a surveyor and a nurse, he had a conventional Dublin Protestant upbringing, studied classics in high school and romance languages at Trinity College. At 21 he went to Paris and fell in with literary expatriates including James Joyce, who became a friend and an inspiration—although, as Beckett noted, Joyce tended toward omniscience and omnipresence in his narrative voice, "whereas I work with impotence and ignorance." Three years later Beckett returned to Dublin, but he soon grew disenchanted with the conservatism of Irish life and, yearning for the Continental avant-garde, emigrated in 1932.

When Paris was invaded by the Nazis, Beckett and his future wife fled to the south of France, hiding by day and journeying by night. That harrowing experience, especially the footsore conversation along the way, probably inspired the futile wandering in *Godot,* according to its first Broadway director, Alan Schneider.

An even deeper real-life influence on Beckett's work, scholars have suggested, came in 1938. As Beckett walked along a Paris street, a panhandler stabbed him in the chest, perforating a lung and narrowly missing his heart. When Beckett later asked why the attack happened, the assailant replied, "I don't know, sir." That glimpse of the random perils of existence may have confirmed Beckett's dark vision but did not initiate it. His novel *Murphy,* published the same year, depicts a destitute Irishman, living in London, who daydreams away his days in a rocking chair until a gas plant explodes and shreds him. At his instruction, his ashes are flushed down the toilet of Dublin's Abbey Theater. . . .

Beckett's images have transfixed countless theatergoers, who watched the tramps in *Godot* wait for a savior who never comes, or heard the old man in *Krapp's Last Tape* review recorded fragments of his life as he murmurs, over and over, "Spool," or shared the haplessness of the elderly couple in *Endgame* as they face the end of the world while encased in trash cans. Beyond his own art, Beckett shaped the vision of countless others. They emulated, if never equaled, his simplicity of means, philosophical daring and ability to engage vast ideas in tiny trickles of closely guarded language. Above all, Beckett's life and work taught others the lesson he said he learned from Joyce: the meaning of artistic integrity. His vision never yielded. Even on a sunny day in London, as he strolled through a park in evident pleasure, when a friend remarked that it was a day that made one glad to be alive, Beckett turned and said, "I wouldn't go that far."

William A. Henry III, "Giving Birth 'Astride of a Grave'," in Time, *New York, Vol. 135, No. 2, January 8, 1990, p. 69.*

MICHAEL FEINGOLD

Unlike his most famous characters, Samuel Beckett has stopped waiting. Given that he bore out his time here with

the ill-concealed impatience of a sage who knows that all time spent in this world of illusions is misspent, the occasion is one to celebrate rather than lament: We may not know where Beckett has gone, or what Godot he has finally met, but we know he would rather be there than here. We know it because he made it his life's work to say so, in incomparably eloquent and original poetic ways, and the poet, as Sir Phillip Sidney said, "nothing affirms, and therefore never lieth." Beckett devoted his art to affirming nothing, both in Sidney's small-n and the Existentialists' capital-N sense of the word. Perhaps his largest achievement was to give an unbelieving century its truest visions of the spiritual life it was creating for itself. Though his theology was a systematic repudiation of his Irish Christian upbringing, Beckett's ongoing artistic project was to map the hell and purgatory that human souls endure on earth, a 20th century Dante circling through endless ruminations, with only a dead dogma for his guide.

To do this, Beckett invented a visionary theater that was like nothing else in the history of the art, though its influence has gone so deep and so wide that its bare, rigid, tight-focused intensity now seems like a comforting old friend. Where the Expressionists had smeared their inner feelings across the stage at random, Beckett boiled his down to essential images, then locked them in the confining spaces and inexorable dramatic logic of Ibsen: He created a Naturalism of the spirit, in which every aspect of our quotidian life found itself mirrored in a harrowing allegory of its own inadequacy.

It was his drive to allegorize, to draw philosophic meaning from the pointlessness of existence, that made critics encountering the early works accuse Beckett of hollowness, aridity, pretension, obfuscation, and even fraudulence. (*Waiting for Godot* is not a real carrot. It is a patently constructed plastic job for the intellectual fruitbowl."—Walter Kerr) Ironically, although the spiritual conditions Beckett explored were arid and hollow, his way of dealing with them was warm, compassionate (albeit unsparing), and funny, with the rich humor of a man for whom the vaudeville stage, and its offshoot the silent film, had been a second study almost as engrossing as Aquinas. . . . Much later in life, when Beckett, now a certifiably immortal Nobel Laureate, took up directing his old plays (while the new ones grew ever tinier in shape and fewer in output, without losing their intensity), he made what were by far the strongest and most bawdily comic productions of them.

In due time—something was taking its course—what actors saw and reviewers failed to see in Beckett became visible to wider and wider audiences, perhaps because, critical cries of "rarefied!" and "pretentious!" notwithstanding ("I am willing to believe the world is a stifling place, but not when my informant is an Egyptian mummy."—Kenneth Tynan), Beckett expressed his most complicated ideas in his simplest words. Far from making pretensions, he ridiculed them, showing his mastery of the techniques pioneered by his admiration James Joyce in his sly selection (and occasional deformation) of six-dollar words for comic effect. (Think of Pozzo's watch, "with genuine deadbeat escapement.")

Nor was his despair, so easily communicated, ever glib: The most stunning fact of Beckett's plays was an audience's ability to recognize in them every human situation, from the individual's daily round to the most ominous large-scale governmental maneuvers, shown for precisely what it was worth. His writing of *Catastrophe* to protest Havel's incarceration was only a superficial sign of the fervent way in which Beckett was a supremely political artist. One instance: When the Free Southern Theatre took **Waiting for Godot** on tour to black communities in the Deep South during the early days of the Civil Rights movement, their audiences had no problem responding to it—the situation of men waiting for an unseen force to liberate them was all too familiar, while some version of the transactions between Lucky and Pozzo could be found in every town square in Mississippi. And from personal experience: When the Watergate scandal broke, the Yale Rep, where I was working as literary manager, created a satirical revue, in which parodies of familiar plays provided various angles on the affair. Somewhat to our surprise, our two most cogent images came from Beckett—Nixon as Krapp, endlessly toiling to fix the tapes that gave evidence of his wrongdoing, and as Lucky, spewing out on cue a babble of desiccated and defrauded ideas mingled with ethnic slurs and abuse of his detractors. The words came from the daily papers, but the meaning from the visions Beckett had created: Nixon, too, lived in his cosmos.

Beckett is gone, but his images will never leave while human beings exist: Hamm sits in his chair, alone. Didi and Gogo wait under their tree. Winnie sinks into the earth as Willie moves to kiss—or kill—her. Krapp spins his tape, a mouth asserts and denies itself to a hooded figure, a woman rocks in her chair and says, "Fuck life." Where he was born it was cool, it was rainy, and they crucified slowly. You're on earth, can't you see, there's no cure for that. And you, he says, what's the meaning of you, what are you meant to mean? Will we ever have done revolving it all in our poor minds.

Michael Feingold, "Samuel Beckett: 1906-89," in The Village Voice, *Vol. XXXV, No. 2, January 9, 1990, p. 95.*

HUGH KENNER

A purveyor of gloom he was not: no, companionable and of unfailing good cheer. His zest at the billiard table . . . one night was something to watch. . . .

I'm told his chess was good too; so good I never ventured to propose a game. In the Twenties he played cricket for Trinity College, Dublin, and is probably the sole Nobel Laureate you'll find mentioned in *Wisden's,* the cricketers' bible. And he once spoke of how, as a youth, he had explored France on a motorbike.

And somehow, in the second half of his life, he found time to retrieve Western drama from the folly of the "well-made play": to restore something Athenians might have understood: a depiction of humans doing what they can, encompassed by the inscrutable, the implacable. "We are waiting for Godot to come, or for night to fall." And what our business with Godot may be we'll not know unless he comes. It instantly got called "Theater of the Absurd," so deep reaches the disease of well-made categories.

Directors, fans of the well-made, went up the wall. It was empty. It needed gimmickry. (The first U.S. gimmick was to cast Bert Lahr.) No. What you do is leave the hollow spaces hollow. (Would you putty up the gaps in Henry Moore?) Yet I've seen productions that had Didi playing hopscotch, or fooling with cat's-cradles of string. *Anything* to relieve the tedium. But the tedium is part of the theme. No one, before Sam, ever saw how to put into art the quantity of our experience that's consumed by nothing in particular.

His greatest play, though—he once concurred in this estimate—is **Endgame,** named for the chess situation when nearly every piece is gone from the board. The Nuclear End? Possibly. We are in a "shelter." We are also in a play with clear connections to the Synge of *The Well of the Saints:* from the two old blind folk in this play, Beckett early learned how much a playwright can do with impairment and nearly no movement. "Who else but John Millington Synge?" was his response to a question about precursors.

And Yeats? Yeats, who set the example of envisaging one's own death? "Now will I make my soul . . ." Our last time together, Sam recited that to the end, clear to "A bird's sleepy cry / Among the deepening shades." His own last work, **Stirring Still** confronts his own impending death. No English prose is more exquisite, more fraught with overtones. He'd just finished, last August, making a French translation. And what will that do with "Stirring"? What with "Still"?

Hugh Kenner, "Samuel Beckett, RIP," in National Review, *New York, Vol. XLII, No. 1, January 22, 1990, p. 19.*

CHRISTOPHER RICKS

Thoughts of Beckett at news of his death. The unforgettable Hardy title has been knocking. "Thoughts of Phena at News of Her Death". It had previously come to mind at news of another death, Philip Larkin's, because of his once pinpointing essentially the birth of his own art: the moment when he stopped condescending to Hardy's. 'As regards his verse I shared Lytton Strachey's verdict that "the gloom is not even relieved by a little elegance of diction." This opinion did not last long; if I were asked to date its disappearance, I should guess it was the morning I first read "Thoughts of Phena at News of Her Death".'

'And age, and then the only end of age': how recent seems Larkin's end, though four years have gone. In my mid-fifties, everything proves to have happened three times longer ago than I first think (a death, a book, a trial), whereas only yesterday it was but twice as long ago.

Thoughts of Beckett. What scenes spread around his last days?

The word had been abroad, a day or two before he died, that he was soon to. A phone-call from a London newspaper broke to me the likelihood, and asked if I would write something. Against his dying. I said no, because I was bespoken, more than bespoken in that I had already set down my say. A couple of years ago the *Sunday Times* had asked me to write, not an obituary, but a tribute, to await the day. [see Christopher Rick's excerpt above]. I remember that it was a discomposing experience, writing it, and new to me, this speaking of someone as if he or she were already dead. I haven't ever written a pickled obituary for the *Times* proper; haven't been asked to. It must require a flexile touch, the plaiting of prospect and retrospect, the unnamable's familiarity.

'Emotion anticipated in tranquillity'. So it was that Geoffrey Madan distilled his obituary-on-phial. 'In the words of an obituary notice, intended for the *Times* but never sent: "A genius for friendship with all and sundry, infectious enthusiasm, selfless devotion to progressive causes, a deep and touching love of animals and of natural beauty"—he would not have claimed for himself any of these so frequent attributes of the lately dead.' These anonymous lapidations always have a Beckett-like *vigor mortis.* I have long collected them, as apt for Beckett's key-cold charity. When not insinuatingly denigratory ('He never married'), the obituaries are informed by a co-operative subconscious, and therefore are rich in the happy infelicities which the Irish employ so adroitly. Verging on the Bull. Philip Larkin had an eye for these; it was he who sent in to the *New Statesman,* for monumental mockery ('This England'), the obituary which said plummily: 'Any sketch of David Glass's work would be incomplete without reference to his *amour propre,* the history of his subject.' Over in America, I miss the *Times* obituaries more than anything else from the English public prints. The USA has no counterpart. The *New York Times* reduces its necrology to a final spasm of public relations, if not by the very deceased, then by what Beckett called the 'nearest if not dearest'.

'I am always glad when one of those fellows dies, for then I know I have the whole of him on my shelf' (Lord Melbourne, speaking of Crabbe).

Beckett and I go back a long way. Not, though, in one another's company. Did I meet him? (Until just now, it was 'have you ever met him?' Students have a way of asking.) Twice. Briefly. Not to be forgotten, not to be memorialised either. 'I live in another world where life and death are memorised.' The reminiscences of Beckett already flourish apace. Best not to join this *cortège* industry.

In the Rue de Seine in Paris there was an English bookshop, 'The English Bookshop' rather. Long gone. Given over now to anthropological art-work. A student, on holiday in Paris in 1954, I flushed out *Watt,* carmine, published the year before in the Collection Merlin of the Olympia Press, the friendly-neighbourhood softish-porn people. A numbered edition of 1,125 copies. I stood there reading the first two pages, I fretted and winced and smiled (I still think them among Beckett's best), and I bought Number 885 for 25 shillings. Also *En attendant Godot,* published in October 1952 but not performed till January 1953. I had heard of Beckett, though not much. He had been sighted and cited by Anthony Hartley—in the *Spectator,* I suppose; Hartley had a great nose and a fine ear for things French, and he let the British in on his finds—I can't think that there is anyone around today who does this work so well.

Waiting for Godot, as the world knows, opened at the Arts Theatre on 3 August 1955. I attended it with impatient young up-and-coming Anthony Howard; he soon came to cease attending to the play, though I can't now remember whether his exasperation moved him to quit, physically. Theatregoers went, during the performance. But then theatregoers are not the only people who go to theatres, and they too much know what they like and want what they know.

Isis, the undergraduate magazine at Oxford, ran a short small series, "Dust-Jacket". Beckett, dust to dust, felt appropriate. The series was mostly bent upon, oh, such as Nigel Balchin. Beckett seemed to me more acutely Mine Own Executioner. So I wrote about him in *Isis,* 16 November 1955. Thirty-four years ago. It is disconcerting to think that he was then appreciably younger than I now am.

Re-reading my youthful cocky piece, I am neither proud nor ashamed of it, or perhaps am equally both. I am glad (slightly different) to have written back then about the novels, *Watt* and *Molloy,* neither yet published in England (1963 and 1960

respectively). 1955 was early days, except for Beckett himself, though he was inured to neglect. My testimony was embarrassingly brash, even then, and yet I am not sorry to have said simply that Beckett is very difficult to understand but that his isn't a small voice. I think, too, that I quoted some very good bits. On love-making:

> What I do know for certain is that I never sought to repeat the experience, having, I suppose, the intuition that it had been unique and perfect, of its kind, achieved and inimitable, and that it behoved me to preserve its memory, pure of all pastiche, in my heart, even if it meant my resorting from time to time to the alleged joys of so-called self-abuse.

And on Godsmiths:

> And I would never do my bees the wrong I had done my God, to whom I had been taught to ascribe my angers, fears, desires, and even my body.

True, in reverting to 1955 I am remembering me, but that doesn't mean I am not remembering Beckett too. Less a diary than a snatch of partial annals.

In 1968 I was mildly thrilled to receive a letter of inquiry from the Nobel Committee of the Swedish Academy. I did not then know that so many such letters get sent out as to make them little more than the thinking man's junk-mail. Though I had no need of weighing whom to nominate, I took pains with how best to do so. My letter of twenty years ago ended in the same terms in which I still wished to praise him in the week of his death: for

> the dignity and integrity of his career, both in artistic terms (his work has never swerved from the aims, at once high and profound, which it set itself in **"Dante . . . Bruno. Vico . . Joyce"**, 1929), and in personal terms: with single-minded dedication and dignity, and without either bitterness or elation, he has lived through forty years of neglect and through twenty years of recognition, manifestly his own man and manifestly, too, a man of supreme loyalty to his art.

About the only change which I had to make to this, in December 1989 as against December 1968, was to match the forty years of neglect with, now, forty years of recognition. In 1969, Beckett won the Nobel Prize. Thanks to me and whose army. He owed it to me? No, I owed it to him.

Over the years I wrote to him from time to time, and he wrote back. This is a less misleading way of putting it than speaking as if we enjoyed a correspondence. I was the one who enjoyed it, and who enjoined it by making an inquiry, never interpretative and almost always textual. Is 'then' a misprint for 'than'? Which wording would he wish to stand by, that of the English or of the US edition? And he would answer the inquiry, on one of those crisp cards with his name, severely elegant, alone at the head. These unmassive missives moved me. From 1972 to 1989.

Often they were deliciously lugubrious. Of the English wording versus the American one in *Company:* 1. 'Yet a certain activity of mind however slight is a necessary complement of company.' 2. 'Yet a certain activity of mind however slight is a necessary adjunct of company.' Beckett: 'I don't know which I dislike more.'

Best was his admission that the cardiac arithmetic in *Company* goes wrong. Ever since people registered that Beckett doesn't tell us what the seventh scarf at the beginning of ***Murphy*** is up to, the critics have been devoted to his numeracy, and in particular to its anomalies. Such anomalies are found more fun if they are believed to be intentional, especially by critics who don't believe in intentionality: an arithmetical anomaly in Beckett is held to intimate to us, surprise, surprise, that Deconstruction rules. I prefer to take Beckett's word for his words, and to see therefore in the heartbeat-count in ***Company*** not a calculated miscalculation but a slip of the calculator. The young man awaits his beloved, his heart beating (as when did it not?).

> You assume a certain heart rate and reckon how many thumps a day. A week. A month. A year. And assuming a certain lifetime a lifetime. Till the last thump. But for the moment with hardly more than seventy American billion behind you you sit in the little summerhouse working out the volume. Seven cubic yards approximately. This strikes you for some reason as improbable and you set about your sum anew.

The precisian's attention—'seventy *American* billion'—has its comedy. But the calculation? As is clear from his card in January 1981, this struck Beckett for some reason as improbable and he set about his sum anew.

> 'Seventy American billion'. Colossal miscalculation. Read 'seventy million': 70 (heart rate) $\times$ 60 $\times$ 24 $\times$ 365 $\times$ 20 (his age then)—735,840,000, unless I have it wrong again and without allowance for leap years.

Well, he both did and did not have it wrong again. 735,840,000 is right, is it not? But it is not 'seventy million'. I pointed this out. He replied. 'Yes of course 700 M. Odd,' he wrote, evenly.

'He was a man of the greatest reticence, but with nothing to conceal; a man of intensely "private life", but wholly transparent'—T. S. Eliot on Spinoza and, incidentally, on himself. Beckett, I suppose, was such another. He was, though, a writer of the greatest reticence but with everything to reveal. Heartfelt. To the last. Not to the last trump (in which he blessedly did not believe), but to the last thump.

Christopher Ricks, "Diary," in London Review of Books, *Vol. 12, No. 2, January 25, 1990, p. 21.*

Sterling Brown

May 1, 1901 - January 13, 1989

Born Sterling Allen Brown. American poet, folklorist, editor, critic, and essayist.

For an overview of Brown's life and work see *CLC,* Vols. 1, 23; *Contemporary Authors,* Vols. 85-88, 127 [obituary]; *Contemporary Authors New Revision Series,* Vol. 26; *Dictionary of Literary Biography,* Vols. 48, 51, 63; and *Black Writers.*

ALAIN LOCKE

[*The essay excerpted below originally appeared in the first edition of* Negro: An Anthology (*1934*).]

Many critics, writing in praise of Sterling Brown's first volume of verse [*Southern Road*], have seen fit to hail him as a significant new Negro poet. The discriminating few go further; they hail a new era in Negro poetry, for such is the deeper significance of this volume. . . . Gauging the main objective of Negro poetry as the poetic portrayal of Negro folk-life true in both letter and spirit to the idiom of the folk's own way of feeling and thinking, we may say that here for the first time is that much-desired and long-awaited acme attained or brought within actual reach.

Almost since the advent of the Negro poet public opinion has expected and demanded folk-poetry of him. And Negro poets have tried hard and voluminously to cater to this popular demand. But on the whole, for very understandable reasons, folk-poetry by Negroes, with notable flash exceptions, has been very unsatisfactory and weak, and despite the intimacy of the race poet's attachments, has been representative in only a limited, superficial sense. First of all, the demand has been too insistent. "They required of us a song in a strange land." "How could we sing of thee, O Zion?" There was the canker of theatricality and exhibitionism planted at the very heart of Negro poetry, unwittingly no doubt, but just as fatally. Other captive nations have suffered the same ordeal. But with the Negro another spiritual handicap was imposed. Robbed of his own tradition, there was no internal compensation to counter the external pressure. Consequently the Negro spirit had a triple plague on its heart and mind—morbid self-consciousness, self-pity and forced exhibitionism. Small wonder that so much poetry by Negroes exhibits in one degree or another the blights of bombast, bathos and artificiality. Much genuine poetic talent has thus been blighted either by these spiritual faults or their equally vicious over-compensations. And so it is epoch-making to have developed a poet whose work, to quote a recent criticism, "has no taint of music-hall convention, is neither arrogant nor servile"— and plays up to neither side of the racial dilemma. For it is as fatal to true poetry to cater to the self-pity or racial vanity

of a persecuted group as to pander to the amusement complex of the overlords and masters.

I do not mean to imply that Sterling Brown's art is perfect, or even completely mature. It is all the more promising that this volume represents the work of a young man just in his early thirties. But a Negro poet with almost complete detachment, yet with a tone of persuasive sincerity, whose muse neither clowns nor shouts, is indeed a promising and a grateful phenomenon.

By some deft touch, independent of dialect, Mr. Brown is able to compose with the freshness and naturalness of folk balladry—**"Maumee Ruth," "Dark O' the Moon," "Sam Smiley," "Slim Green," "Johnny Thomas,"** and **"Memphis Blues"** will convince the most sceptical that modern Negro life can yield real balladry and a Negro poet achieve an authentic folk-touch. (pp. 88-9)

With Mr. Brown the racial touch is quite independent of dialect; it is because in his ballads and lyrics he has caught the deeper idiom of feeling or the peculiar paradox of the racial situation. That gives the genuine earthy folk-touch, and justifies a statement I ventured some years back: "the soul of the Negro will be discovered in a characteristic way of thinking and in a homely philosophy rather than in a jingling and juggling of broken English." As a matter of fact, Negro dialect is extremely local—it changes from place to place, as do white dialects. And what is more, the dialect of Dunbar and the other early Negro poets never was on land or sea as a living peasant speech; but it has had such wide currency, especially on the stage, as to have successfully deceived half the world, including the many Negroes who for one reason or another imitate it.

Sterling Brown's dialect is also local, and frankly an adaptation, but he has localised it carefully, after close observation and study, and varies it according to the brogue of the locality or the characteristic jargon of the *milieu* of which he is writing. But his racial effects, as I have said, are not dependent on dialect. Consider **"Maumee Ruth":**

> Might as well bury her
> And bury her deep,
> Might as well put her
> Where she can sleep. . . .
>
> Boy that she suckled
> How should he know,
> Hiding in city holes
> Sniffing the "snow"?

                                                                            (p. 89)

If we stop to inquire—as unfortunately the critic must—into the magic of these effects, we find the secret, I think, in this fact more than in any other: Sterling Brown has listened long and carefully to the folk in their intimate hours, when they were talking to themselves, not, so to speak, as in Dunbar, but actually as they do when the masks of protective mimicry fall. Not only has he dared to give quiet but bold expression to this private thought and speech, but he has dared to give the Negro peasant credit for thinking. In this way he has recaptured the shrewd Aesopian quality of the Negro folk-thought, which is more profoundly characteristic than their types of metaphors or their mannerisms of speech. They are, as he himself says,

> Illiterate, and somehow very wise,

and it is this wisdom, bitter fruit of their suffering, combined with their characteristic fatalism and irony, which in this book gives a truer soul picture of the Negro than has ever yet been given poetically. The traditional Negro is a clown, a buffoon, an easy laugher, a shallow sobber and a credulous christian; the real Negro underneath is more often an all but cynical fatalist, a shrewd pretender, and a boldly whimsical pagan; or when not, a lusty, realistic religionist who tastes its nectars here and now.

> Mammy
> With deep religion defeating the grief
> Life piled so closely about her

is the key picture to the Negro as christian; Mr. Brown's **"When the Saints Come Marching Home"** is worth half a dozen essays on the Negro's religion. But to return to the question of bold exposure of the intimacies of Negro thinking—read that priceless apologia of kitchen stealing in the **"Ruminations of Luke Johnson,"** reflective husband of Mandy Jane, tromping early to work with a great big basket, and tromping wearily back with it at night laden with the petty spoils of the day's picking. . . . It is not enough to sprinkle "dis's and dat's" to be a Negro folk-poet, or to jingle rhymes and juggle popularised clichés traditional to sentimental minor poetry for generations. One must study the intimate thought of the people who can only state it in an ejaculation, or a metaphor, or at best a proverb, and translate that into an articulate attitude, or a folk philosophy or a daring fable, with Aesopian clarity and simplicity—and above all, with Aesopian candor.

The last is most important; other Negro poets in many ways have been too tender with their own, even though they have learned with the increasing boldness of new Negro thought not to be too gingerly and conciliatory to and about the white man. The Negro muse weaned itself of that in McKay, Fenton Johnson, Toomer, Countee Cullen and Langston Hughes. But in Sterling Brown it has learned to laugh at itself and to chide itself with the same broomstick. (pp. 90-1)

There is a world of psychological distance between this and the rhetorical defiance and the plaintive, furtive sarcasms of even some of our other contemporary poets—even as theirs, it must be said in all justice, was miles better and more representative than the sycophancies and platitudes of the older writers.

In closing it might be well to trace briefly the steps by which Negro poetry has scrambled up the sides of Parnassus from the ditches of minstrelsy and the trenches of race propaganda. In complaining against the narrow compass of dialect poetry (dialect is an organ with only two stops—pathos and humor), Weldon Johnson tried to break the Dunbar mould and shake free of the traditional stereotypes. But significant as it was, this was more a threat than an accomplishment; his own dialect poetry has all of the clichés of Dunbar without Dunbar's lilting lyric charm. Later in the *Negro Sermons* Weldon Johnson discovered a way out—in a rhapsodic form free from the verse shackles of classical minor poetry, and in the attempt to substitute an idiom of racial thought and imagery for a mere dialect of peasant speech. Claude McKay then broke with all the moods conventional in his day in Negro poetry, and presented a Negro who could challenge and hate, who knew resentment, brooded intellectual sarcasm, and felt contemplative irony. In this, so to speak, he pulled the psychological cloak off the Negro and revealed, even to the Negro himself, those facts disguised till then by his shrewd protective mimicry or pressed down under the dramatic mask of living up to what was expected of him. But though McKay sensed a truer Negro, he was at times too indignant at the older sham, and, too, lacked the requisite native touch—as of West Indian birth and training—with the local color of the American Negro. Jean Toomer went deeper still—I should say higher—and saw for the first time the glaring paradoxes and the deeper ironies of the situation, as they affected not only the Negro but the white man. He realised, too, that Negro idiom was anything but trite and derivative, and also that it was in emotional substance pagan—all of which he convincingly demonstrated, alas, all too fugitively, in *Cane*. But Toomer was not enough of a realist, or patient enough as an observer, to reproduce extensively a folk idiom.

Then Langston Hughes came with his revelation of the emotional color of Negro life, and his brilliant discovery of the flow and rhythm of the modern and especially the city Negro, substituting this jazz figure and personality for the older plantation stereotype. But it was essentially a jazz version of Negro life, and that is to say as much American, or more, as

Negro; and though fascinating and true to an epoch this version was surface quality after all.

Sterling Brown, more reflective, a closer student of the folk-life, and above all a bolder and more detached observer, has gone deeper still, and has found certain basic, more sober and more persistent qualities of Negro thought and feeling; and so has reached a sort of common denominator between the old and the new Negro. Underneath the particularities of one generation are hidden universalities which only deeply penetrating genius can fathom and bring to the surface. Too many of the articulate intellects of the Negro group—including sadly enough the younger poets—themselves children of opportunity, have been unaware of these deep resources of the past. But here, if anywhere, in the ancient common wisdom of the folk, is the real treasure trove of the Negro poet; and Sterling Brown's poetic divining-rod has dipped significantly over this position. It is in this sense that I believe **Southern Road** ushers in a new era in Negro folk-expression and brings a new dimension in Negro folk-portraiture. (pp. 91-2)

> *Alain Locke, "Sterling Brown, The New Negro Folk-Poet," in* Negro: An Anthology, *edited by Nancy Cunard and Hugh Ford, revised edition, Frederick Ungar Publishing Co., 1970, pp. 88-92.*

HENRY LOUIS GATES, JR.

[*The essay excerpted below originally appeared in the* New York Times Book Review, *January 11, 1981; a small portion of that review is included in CLC, Vol. 23.*]

By 1932, when Sterling Brown published **Southern Road,** his first book of poems, the use of black vernacular structures in Afro-American poetry was controversial indeed. Of all the arts, it was only through music that blacks had invented and fully defined a tradition both widely regarded and acknowledged to be uniquely their own. Black folktales, while roundly popular, were commonly thought to be the amusing fantasies of a childlike people, whose sagas and anecdotes about rabbits and bears held nothing deeper than the attention span of a child, à la Uncle Remus or even *Green Pastures.* And what was generally called dialect, the unique form of English that Afro-Americans spoke, was thought by whites to reinforce received assumptions about the Negro's mental inferiority.

Dorothy Van Doren simply said out loud what so many other white critics thought privately. "It may be that [the Negro] can express himself only by music and rhythm," she wrote in 1931, "and not by words."

Middle-class blacks, despite the notoriety his dialect verse had garnered for Paul Laurence Dunbar and the Negro, thought that dialect was an embarrassment, the linguistic remnant of an enslavement they all longed to forget. The example of Dunbar's popular and widely reviewed "jingles in a broken tongue," coinciding with the conservatism of Booker T. Washington, was an episode best not repeated. Blacks stood in line to attack dialect poetry. William Stanley Braithwaite, Countee Cullen, and especially James Weldon Johnson argued fervently that dialect stood in the shadow of the plantation tradition of Joel Chandler Harris, James Whitcomb Riley, and Thomas Nelson Page. Dialect poetry, Johnson continued, possessed "but two full stops, humor and pathos." By 1931, Johnson, whose own "Jingles and Croons" (1917) embodied the worst in this tradition, could assert as-

suredly that "the passing of traditional dialect as a medium for Negro poets is complete."

As if these matters of sensibility were not barrier enough, Johnson believed, somehow that until a black person ("full-blooded" at that) created a written masterpiece of art, black Americans would remain substandard citizens.

Johnson here echoed William Dean Howells's sentiments. Howells wrote that Paul Laurence Dunbar's dialect verse "makes a stronger claim for the negro than the negro yet has done. Here in the artistic effect at least is white thinking and white feeling in a black man. . . . Perhaps the proof [of human unity] is to appear in the arts, and our hostilities and prejudices are to vanish in them." Even as late as 1925, Heywood Broun could reiterate this curious idea: "A supremely great negro artist who could catch the imagination of the world, would do more than any other agency to remove the disabilities against which the negro now labors." Broun concluded that this black redeemer with a pen could come at any time, and asked his audience to remain silent for ten seconds to imagine such a miracle! In short, the Black Christ would be a poet. If no one quite knew the precise form this Black Christ would assume, at least they all agreed on three things he could not possibly be: he would not be a woman like feminist Zora Neale Hurston; he would not be gay like Countee Cullen or Alain Locke; and he would most definitely not write dialect poetry. Given all this, it is ironic that Brown used dialect at all. For a "New Negro" generation too conscious of character and class as color (and vice versa), Brown had all the signs of the good life: he was a mulatto with "good hair" whose father was a well-known author, professor at Howard, pastor of the Lincoln Temple Congregational Church, and member of the D.C. Board of Education who had numbered among his closest friends both Frederick Douglass and Paul Laurence Dunbar. Brown, moreover, had received a classically liberated education at Dunbar High School, Williams College, and Harvard, where he took an M.A. in English in 1923. Indeed, perhaps it was just this remarkably secure black aristocratic heritage that motivated Brown to turn to the folk.

Just one year after he had performed the postmortem on dialect poetry, James Weldon Johnson, in the preface to Brown's **Southern Road,** reluctantly admitted that he had been wrong about dialect. Brown's book of poetry, even more profoundly than the market crash of 1929, truly ended the Harlem Renaissance, primarily because it contained a new and distinctly black poetic diction and not merely the vapid and pathetic claim for one.

To the surprise of the Harlem Renaissance's "New Negroes," the reviews were of the sort one imagines Heywood Broun's redeemer-poet was to have gotten. The *New York Times Book Review* said that **Southern Road** is a book whose importance is considerable: "It not only indicates how far the Negro artist has progressed since the years when he began to find his voice, but it proves that the Negro artist is abundantly capable of making an original and genuine contribution to American literature." Brown's work was marked by a "dignity that respects itself. . . . There is everywhere art." Louis Untermeyer agreed: "He does not paint himself blacker than he is." Even Alain Locke, two years later [see excerpt above], called it "a new era in Negro poetry." **Southern Road**'s artistic achievement ended the Harlem Renaissance, for that slim book undermined all of the New Negro's assumptions about the nature of the black tradition and its relation to individual talent. Not only were most of Brown's poems composed in dialect, but they also had as their subjects distinctively black archetypal mythic characters, as well as the black common man whose roots were rural and Southern. Brown called his poetry "portraitures," close and vivid detailings of an action of a carefully delineated subject to suggest a sense of place, in much the same way as Toulouse-Lautrec's works continue to do. These portraitures, drawn "in a manner constant with them," Brown renders in a style that emerged from several forms of folk discourse, a black vernacular matrix that includes the blues and ballads, the spirituals and worksongs. Indeed, Brown's ultimate referents are black music and mythology. His language, densely symbolic, ironical, and naturally indirect, draws upon the idioms, figures, and tones of both the sacred and the profane vernacular traditions, mediating between these in a manner unmatched before or since. Although Langston Hughes had attempted to do roughly the same, Hughes seemed content to transcribe the popular structures he received, rather than to transcend or elaborate upon them, as in "To Midnight Man at LeRoy's": "Hear dat music . . . / Jungle music / Hear dat music . . . / And the moon was white."

But it is not merely the translation of the vernacular that makes Brown's work major, informed by these forms as his best work is; it is rather the deft manner in which he created his own poetic diction by fusing several black traditions with various models provided by Anglo-American poets to form a unified and complex structure of feeling, a sort of song of a racial self. Above all else, Brown is a regionalist whose poems embody William Carlos Williams's notion that the classic is the local, fully realized. Yet Brown's region is not so much the South or Spoon River, Tilbury or Yoknapatawpha as it is "the private Negro mind," as Alain Locke put it, "this private thought and speech," or, as Zora Neale Hurston put it, "how it feels to be colored me," the very textual milieu of blackness itself. Boldly, Brown merged the Afro-American vernacular traditions of dialect and myth with the Anglo-American poetic tradition and, drawing upon the example of Jean Toomer, introduced the Afro-American modernist lyrical mode into black literature. Indeed, Brown, Toomer, and Hurston comprise three cardinal points on a triangle of influence out of which emerged, among others, Ralph Ellison, Toni Morrison, Alice Walker, and Leon Forrest.

Brown's poetic influences are various. From Walt Whitman, Brown took the oracular, demotic voice of the "I" and the racial "eye," as well as his notion that "new words, new potentialities of speech" were to be had in the use of popular forms such as the ballad. From Edward Arlington Robinson, Brown took the use of the dramatic situation and the ballad, as well as what Brown calls the subject of "the undistinguished, the extraordinary in the ordinary." Certainly Brown's poems **"Maumee Ruth," "Southern Cop," "Georgie Grimes,"** and **"Sam Smiley"** suggest the same art that created Miniver Cheevy and Richard Cory. From A. E. Housman, Brown borrowed the dramatic voice and tone, as well as key figures: Housman's blackbird in "When Smoke Stood Up from Ludlow" Brown refigures as a buzzard in **"Old Man Buzzard."** Both Housman's "When I Was One and Twenty" and Brown's **"Telling Fortunes"** use the figure of "women with dark eyes," just as Brown's **"Mill Mountain"** echoes Housman's "Terence, This Is Stupid Stuff." Housman, Heinrich Heine, and Thomas Hardy seem to be Brown's central influence of tone. Robert Burns's Scottish dialect and John Millington Synge's mythical dialect of the Aran Islander in

part inform Brown's use of black dialect, just as Robert Frost's realism, stoicism, and sparseness, as in "Out, Out—," "Death of the Hired Man," "Birches," "Mending Wall," and "In Dives' Dive" inform **"Southern Road," "Memphis Blues,"** and **"Strange Legacies."** Brown's choice of subject matter and everyday speech are fundamentally related to the New Poetry and the work of Amy Lowell, Vachel Lindsay, Edgar Lee Masters, and Carl Sandburg, as well as to the common language emphasis of the Imagists. In lines such as "bits of cloud-filled sky . . . framed in bracken pools" and "vagrant flowers that fleck unkempt meadows," William Wordsworth's *Lyrical Ballads* resound. Brown rejected the "puzzle poetry" of Ezra Pound and T. S. Eliot and severely reviewed the Southern Agrarians' "I'll Take My Stand" as politically dishonest, saccharine nostalgia for a medieval never-neverland that never was. Brown never merely borrows from any of these poets; he transforms their influence by grafting them onto black poetic roots. These transplants are splendid creations indeed.

[In *The Collected Poems of Sterling A. Brown,*] Michael Harper has collected nearly the whole of Brown's body of poetry, including *Southern Road, The Last Ride of Wild Bill* (1975), and the previously unpublished *No Hiding Place,* Brown's second book of poems which was rejected for publication in the late thirties because of its political subjects and which seems to have discouraged Brown from attempting another volume until 1975. Inexplicably, two poems of the five-part "Slim Greer" cycle, **"Slim in Hell"** and **"Slim Hears 'The Call,' "** are missing, as is the major part of **"Cloteel"** and the final stanza of **"Bitter Fruit of the Tree,"** oversights that a second edition should correct. Nevertheless, this splendid collection at last makes it possible to review the whole of Brown's works after years when his work remained out of print or difficult to get. Forty-two years separated the first and second editions of *Southern Road.*

Rereading Brown, I was struck by how consistently he shapes the tone of his poems by the meticulous selection of the right word to suggest succinctly complex images and feelings "stripped to form," in Frost's phrase. Unlike so many of his contemporaries, Brown never lapses into pathos or sentimentality. Brown renders the oppressive relation to self to natural and (black and white) man-made environment in the broadest terms, as does the blues. Yet Brown's characters confront catastrophe with all of the irony and stoicism of the blues and black folklore. Brown's protagonists laugh and cry, fall in and out of love, and muse about death in ways not often explored in black literature. Finally, his great theme seems to be the relation of being to the individual will, rendered always in a sensuous diction, echoing what critic Joanne Gabbin calls "touchstones" of the blues lyric, such as "Don't your bed look lonesome / When your babe packs up to leave," "I'm gonna leave heah dis mawnin' ef I have to ride de blind," "Did you ever wake up in de mo'nin', yo' mind rollin' two different ways— / One mind to leave your baby, and one mind to stay?" or "De quagmire don't hang out no signs." What's more, he is able to realize such splendid results in a variety of forms, including the classic and standard blues, the ballad, a new form that Stephen Henderson calls the blues-ballad, the sonnet, and free verse. For the first time, we can appreciate Brown's full range, his mastery of so many traditions.

In the five-poem ballad cycle **"Slim Greer,"** Brown has created the most memorable character in black literature, the trickster. In **"Slim in Atlanta,"** segregation is so bad that blacks are allowed to laugh only in a phone booth:

> Hope to Gawd I may die
> If I ain't speakin' truth
> Make de niggers do their laughin'
> In a telefoam booth.

In **"Slim Greer,"** the wily Greer in "Arkansaw" "Passed for white, / An' he no lighter / Than a dark midnight / Found a nice white woman / At a dance, / Thought he was from Spain / Or else from France." Finally, it is Slim's uncontainable rhythm that betrays:

> An' he started a-tinklin'
> Some mo'nful blues,
> An' a-pattin' the time
> With No. Fourteen shoes.
>
> The cracker listened
> An' then he spat
> An' said, "No white man
> Could play like that. . . .
>
> Heard Slim's music
> An' then, hot damn!
> Shouted sharp—"Nigger!"
> An' Slim said, "Ma'am?"

Brown balances this sort of humor against a sort of "literate" blues, such as **"Tornado Blues,"** not meant to be sung:

> Destruction was a-drivin' it and close behind was Fear,
> Destruction was a-drivin' it hand in hand with Fear,
> Grinnin' Death and skinny Sorrow was a-bringin' up de
>   Rear.
>
> Dey got some ofays, but dey mostly got de Jews an' us,
> Got some ofays, but mostly got de Jews an' us,
> Many po' boys castle done settled to a heap o'dus'.

Contrast with this stanza the meter of **"Long Track Blues,"** a poem Brown recorded with piano accompaniment:

> Heard a train callin'
> Blowin' long ways down the track;
> Ain't no train due here,
> Baby, what can bring you back?
>
> Dog in the freight room
> Howlin' like he los' his mind;
> Might howl myself,
> If I was the howlin' kind.

In **"Southern Road,"** Brown uses the structure of the work-song, modified by the call-and-response pattern of a traditional blues stanza:

> Doubleshackled—hunh—
> Guard behin';
> Doubleshackled—hunh—
> Guard behin';
> Ball an' chain, bebby,
> On my min'.
>
> White man tells me—hunh—
> Damn yo' soul;
> White man tells me—hunh—
> Damn yo' soul;
> Get no need, bebby,
> To be tole.

Brown is a versatile craftsman, capable of representing even destruction and death in impressively various ways. In **"Sam Smiley,"** for example, he describes a lynching in the most detached manner: "The mob was in fine fettle, yet / The dogs were stupid-nosed; and day / Was far spent when the men drew round / The scrawny wood where Smiley lay. / The oaken leaves drowsed prettily, / The moon shone benignly there; / And big Sam Smiley, King Buckdancer, / Buck-danced on the midnight air." On the other hand, there is a certain irony in **"Children of the Mississippi"**: "De Lord tole Norah / Dat de flood was due / Norah listened to de Lord / An' got his stock on board, / Wish dat de Lord / Had tole us too."

Brown also uses the folk-rhyme form, the sort of chant to which children skip rope: "Women as purty / As Kingdom Come / Ain't got no woman / Cause I'm black and dumb." He also combines sources as unlike as Scott's "Lady of the Lake" and the black folk ballad "Wild Negro Bill" in his most extended ballad, **"The Last Ride of Wild Bill."** Often, he takes lines directly from the classic blues, as in **"Ma Rainey,"** where three lines of Bessie Smith's "Backwater Blues" appear. Perhaps Brown is at his best when he writes of death, a subject he treats with a haunting lyricism, as in **"Odyssey of Big Boy"**:

> Lemme be wid Casey Jones,
> Lemme be wid Stagolee,
> Lemme be wid such like men
> When Death takes hol' on me,
> When Death takes hol' on me. . . .
>
> Done took my livin' as it came,
> Done grabbed my joy, done risked my life;
> Train done caught me on de trestle,
> Man done caught me wid his wife,
> His doggone purty wife.

He achieves a similar effect in **"After Winter,"** with lines such as "He snuggles his fingers / In the blacker loam" and "Ten acres unplanted / To raise dreams on / Butterbeans fo' Clara / Sugar corn fo' Grace / An' fo' de little feller / Runnin' space."

When I asked why he chose the black folk as his subject, Brown replied:

> Where Sandburg said, "The people, yes," and Frost, "The people, yes, maybe," I said, "The people, maybe, I hope!" I didn't want to attack a stereotype by idealizing. I wanted to deepen it. I wanted to understand my people. I wanted to understand what it meant to be a Negro, what the qualities of life were. With their imagination, they combine two great loves: the love of words and the love of life. Poetry results.

Just as Brown's importance as a teacher can be measured through his students (such as LeRoi Jones, Kenneth Clarke, Ossie Davis, and many more), so too can his place as a poet be measured by his influence on other poets, such as Leopold Senghor, Aimé Césaire, Nicolas Guillen, and Michael Harper, to list only a few. Out of Brown's realism, further, came Richard Wright's naturalism; out of his lyricism came Hurston's *Their Eyes Were Watching God;* his implicit notion that "De eye dat sees / Is de I dat be's" forms the underlying structure of *Invisible Man.* In his poetry, several somehow black structures of meaning have converged to form a unified and complex structure of feeling, a poetry as black as it is Brown's. [*The Collected Poems of Sterling A. Brown*], some of which are recorded on two Folkways albums, along with his collected prose (three major books of criticism, dozens of essays, reviews, and a still unsurpassed anthology of black literature) being edited by Robert O'Meally and a splendid literary biography by Joanne Gabbin, all guarantee Brown's place in literary history. Brown's prolific output coupled with a life that spans the Age of Booker T. Washington through the era of Black Power, makes him not only the bridge between nineteenth- and twentieth-century black literature but also the last of the great "race men," the Afro-American men of letters, a tradition best epitomized by W. E. B. Du Bois. . . . A self-styled "Old Negro," Sterling Brown is not only the Afro-American poet laureate; he is a great poet. (pp. 226-34)

Henry Louis Gates, Jr., "Songs of a Racial Self: On Sterling A. Brown," in his Figures in Black: Words, Signs, and the "Racial" Self, *Oxford University Press, Inc., 1987, pp. 225-34.*

JOSEPH D. WHITAKER

Sterling Allen Brown, 87, a poet and retired professor of English at Howard University who was named poet laureate of the District of Columbia in 1984, died of leukemia Jan. 13. . . .

[Brown] saw literature as popular art and framed his own poetry as stories, work songs and strains of the blues that depicted the diversity of black American life.

During his 40 years in Howard's classrooms, he became known as a "red ink man" because he covered his students' papers with critical red marks.

He also learned from his students, collecting from them many of the black folk songs, sayings and local lore that were the basis for some of his writings. His students included actor Ossie Davis and psychologist Kenneth B. Clark.

Mr. Brown may be best remembered for his poetry of the late 1960s and the early 1970s, when black poetry was experiencing a rebirth of spirit and power and many young poets looked to him for influence and guidance.

His poetry, steeped in black folk verse, was especially attractive to writers who wanted to reinforce their blackness. He had the ability to take the simple and emotionally direct language of the poor and make it viable verse for everyone. . . .

During the 1970s, after years of neglect, Mr. Brown's career took an upturn. In 1979 the D. C. Council declared his birthday, May 1, Sterling A. Brown Day. In 1984 he was named the city's poet laureate.

"I've been rediscovered, reinstituted, regenerated and recovered," he said in a 1979 interview with *The Washington Post.*

Mr. Brown graduated from Dunbar High School. He received his undergraduate degree from Williams College and a master's degree in English at Harvard University. He also had received 14 honorary degrees. He became a specialist on blacks in American literature and reigned for many years as America's dean of contemporary Afro-American poetry. . . .

He won the Opportunity Prize Literary Contest in the 1920s and Lenore Marshall Poetry Prize in the early 1980s. His books include **Outline of Poetry by American Negroes,** published in 1931; **The Negro Caravan,** published in 1941, and **Collected Poems,** published in 1980.

Joseph D. Whitaker, "Poet Sterling Allen Brown Dies; Was Howard Professor," in The Washington Post, *January 16, 1989.*

DARRYL PINCKNEY

Sterling A. Brown was one of the few black writers of his generation who did not want to be part of the Harlem Renaissance. He was very proud that he had never shaken hands with Carl Van Vechten, who, he said, had done more than bad liquor to corrupt the Negro. The Harlem Renaissance was a publishers' gimmick, he said. It didn't last long enough to be called a renaissance, and very few Harlemites were in it. Black writers, he said, only went to Harlem for parties. Harlem was "the show-window, the cashier's till." While the young Niggerati were hovering around the tables of white patrons in Small's Paradise, Sterling himself was down in Lynchburg, Virginia, talking to a guitar player, Big Boy Davis, one of the rural characters whose ethos engaged Sterling's melancholy and rebellious sensibility, from which came a folk poetry of lasting originality.

Sterling was born in Washington, DC, in 1901, the youngest of six and the only boy. He died last month in a nursing home near Washington. His father, Dr. Sterling N. Brown, born a slave in Tennessee in 1858, had graduated from Fisk and Oberlin to become pastor of the Lincoln Memorial Temple Congregational Church, a professor of religion at Howard University, and an author of modest Bible studies. He was very much a "race man" in the style of the period. . . .

Whenever Sterling opened his mouth he taught. In 1923 he began teaching at the Virginia Theological Seminary and College, where he met his wife, Daisy, on a tennis court; he taught at Lincoln University in Jefferson City, Missouri, and at Fisk, before he settled in at Howard University in 1929. There he reigned, with some interruptions, until 1975. "I have been hired, fired, rehired, retired, and hired again," he liked to say. Sterling's work is hardly known today, and it has survived mostly through the devotion of generations of black writers, many of whom were his students, or considered themselves such. He spent his life talking—about folklore, stride piano, the shrewdness of the blues, A. E. Housman, Lena Horne, you name it. They used to say that every black in the United States knew every other black, and Sterling was one of those who had stories about everyone, from Jelly Roll Morton to a raconteur barber in Nashville. He was a connoisseur of black history and a guardian of its integrity. Volatile, ironic, and hopelessly genuine, he was in thrall to what he called the "mulch" of black culture. But black culture was also a text that he studied as no other black writer has before or since. He was the last of the New Negroes.

Sterling didn't mind being called a New Negro, though he said he'd been an old Negro for so long it was too late to do anything about it. During the New Negro movement in the early Twenties Sterling's poems began to appear in black magazines and anthologies, but his first collection of poems, **Southern Road,** wasn't published until 1932. The book that made his name came after the parties uptown ended and as the bread lines all over began, and that, as much as his nonconformist temperament, left him to go his own way. . . .

The historian Sterling Stuckey notes in his introduction to [**The Collected Poems of Sterling A. Brown,** see *CLC,* Vol. 23] that part of Sterling's achievement was to reclaim from stereotype such subjects as chain gangs, gamblers, cabarets, and crimes of passion. The itinerant entertainer who sticks his cigarette in his guitar before he sings his mother's favorite spiritual; the "golden, spacious grin" of Jack Johnson taking it like a man; a girl no longer recognizable under her street-walker's paint; a disillusioned veteran who ends up buck-dancing on the midnight air; a woman who steals from the lady she works for "Cause what huh 'dear grandfawthaw' / Took from Mandy Jane's grandpappy— / Ain' no basket in de worl' / What kin tote all date away"—Sterling's poems reveal how in the struggle to exist the historic stands alongside the everyday. Several of his narrative poems involve self-defense, the faith that looks through death, or the fearless, manly man respected in hell. ("He said 'Come and get me' / They came and got him. / And they came by tens.") He had a vision of the folk as a subtle people at the mercy of what could jump out of the ordinary, and who take the tragic with uncommon understatement.

He carefully observed the Joe Meekses, Bessies, Big Jesses, Luther Johnsons, young Freds, Johnnies, and Sams, who abound in his poetry. He paid attention to their walks, their spare-ribbed yard dogs, silk shirts pink as sunsets, bulldog brogans, habits of mind ("Don't be no Chinaman, George"), and to their landscape of locust, flooding rivers, and cotton. He recognized the "folk eloquence" in everyday talk, understood how Ma Rainey could "jes' catch hold of us, somekindaway," but none of the characters in his ballads is treated sentimentally because his first duty was not to his sympathies but to the poem. He already trusted what they stood for, these railroad men highballing through the country, trying to "git de Jack," these lowlifes playing checkers with deacons, and placed the folk tradition of the black firmly within American poetry.

"Laughter is a vengeance," and as a poet Sterling was also a folklorist alive to the humor and paradoxes in his raw material. "Whuh folks, whuh folks; don't wuk muh brown too hahd! / Who's practisin' de Chahlston in yo' big backyahd." He told some tall tales or lies, as they are called, about a rascal, Slim Greer, who passes for white and courts a white woman only to be detected when he plays the piano as only a black can. In another, when "niggers" in Atlanta are forced to do their laughing in a telephone booth, Slim holds up the line because every time he looks at the hundreds of "shines" gripping their sides to keep from breaking the law he can't stop laughing. . . .

In his youth Sterling, like many other black writers of the period, was taken with the muckraking poetry of Carl Sandburg and the dramatic monologues of E. A. Robinson and especially with Frost, the speaking voice in modern poetry. But he has his own remarkable ability to fuse traditional meter with the natural rhythm of the speaker:

> "No need in frettin'
> Case good times go,
> Things as dey happen
> Jes' is so;
> Nothin' las' always
> Farz I know. . . ."

("Old Man Buzzard")

Sometimes he used the meter of the Methodist hymn, which lent a prayerful tone to his folk musing. . . . (p. 14)

Sterling wrote Petrarchan sonnets, free verse in standard En-glish, blank verse, but he achieved his best poetic effects through his reinvention of dialect. He went beyond mimicry of broken English, or transcription of the blues line ("Leave 'is dirty city, take my foot up in my hand") or imitations of folksy metaphor.

James Weldon Johnson once complained that dialect had only two stops, pathos and humor. Though Paul Laurence Dunbar had elevated the medium, young black poets after World War I were in revolt against Negro dialect poetry because of what Johnson saw as the artificiality of its subjects and "exaggerated geniality," which had no relation to "actual Negro life." Johnson believed that black poets had to find racial symbols from within, as Synge had done for the Irish. But *Southern Road* broke with the comic minstrel and plantation traditions. It made use of folk epics and ballads—like "Stagolee," "John Henry," "Casey Jones," and "Long Gone John"—to create what Johnson hailed as "the common, racy, living speech of the Negro in certain parts of real life." Alain Locke pointed out [see excerpt above] that Sterling's portrayal of the Negro folk life succeeded not because it depended on being true to an idiom, but because in his psychological distance "he dared to give the Negro credit for thinking."

Southern Road was widely praised, yet trouble came. Sterling's second book of poems, *No Hiding Place,* was turned down by his publisher, Harcourt Brace, maybe for commercial reasons. Sterling never got over the rejection. He didn't publish another book of poems until 1975 when a black publisher issued **The Last Ride of Wild Bill,** a ballad from the 1930s about a numbers runner. The militant portraits of sharecroppers and "niggrah" clowns of *No Hiding Place* were later included in his **Collected Poems.**

Meanwhile, Sterling continued to produce reviews and essays on black literature, folklore, history, and music. He was a national editor of the Federal Writers Project from 1936 to 1939, and made important contributions to *Washington: City and Capital* (1937) and *The Negro in Virginia* (1940). He developed, with Alain Locke, a series for which he wrote the historical surveys *The Negro in American Fiction* (1937) and *Negro Poetry and Drama* (1937). He published, in the 1940s, unusually cool short stories about the South; traveled throughout the country as a kind of one-man department of black studies; and, of course, taught at Howard and at other universities as a visiting professor.

Sterling's readings were performances; between poems he would tell stories, and managed to be both down-home and as courtly as Duke Ellington. Someone told me he once demonstrated how to dance on a dime. Until I read Sterling's *The Negro Caravan,* dialect, to me, meant Uncle Remus, something to get over, just as stuck-up audiences had looked down their noses fifty years before. Sterling's 1941 anthology is still unsurpassed as a resource, even though black writing from Phyllis Wheatley and the slave narratives doesn't fit between the covers of one book anymore. I had never heard of novelists like J. A. Rogers and William Attaway, or playwrights like Theodore Ward. Spirituals, work songs, tall tales, and the blues became an accessible literature.

Sterling's father and my maternal great-grandfather were brothers. This faded connection mattered more to me than it did to Sterling. I'd heard the usual stories, like the one about Sterling stopping in Opelika, Alabama, on a research trip and being taken to see cotton fields where he caught a boll weevil that got loose in Aunt Clara's house. Some of the after-dinner lore I heard hinted that Sterling was more than just nonconforming: how he had got in trouble for yelling at the dean that he wasn't black, he was yellow; how he got in trouble for yelling that he was indeed black; how he got written up in *Jet* for "flipping out over this black thing."

He seemed to be always ready to set out the gin for visitors. He was famous for his capacity for friendship, his rapport with youth, his eagerness to release into the common air everything he had stored up in his head. I found him as intimidating as the Negro past itself. He had a "hellified" library and record collection. (pp. 14-15)

His vast bibliography trailed off in the 1950s. Occasionally he would mention a new edition of his anthology or a definitive edition of essays, but then nothing happened. Perhaps he was the fence in the way, perhaps having been forgotten for so long had taken its tithe. "It is late and still I am losing, but still I am steady and unaccusing." He said Frost used the second "still" in the Elizabethan sense. He once told me with emotion of the day he, the son of a former slave, and Frost, the son of "an unregenerate confederate," met and embraced. Sterling was crazy about his wife—"Made a man out of me"—and after she died, in 1979, the year his **Collected Poems** was going to press, something aggressive began to spoil the smile of his learning.

Sterling proved to me that nine letters out of ten answer themselves, and he wouldn't give me his telephone number. I had to call his sister, Helen, who lived next door. They shared a garden. He'd call back and tell me things: Machado de Assis wasn't white; I should have been in a black fraternity; Jean Toomer was not, strictly speaking, trying to pass. He sometimes called to announce he was coming to New York and would I please make a reservation at his hotel, but I failed him because I could never find in the phone book the hotel where he liked to stay, and I felt that I had failed, too, whenever I couldn't think of what to say to verdicts like, "When I read *The Waste Land* I thought it was a lie. This is not a wasteland for blacks."

Then came sudden, too-early-for-Saturday-morning calls when I picked up the receiver to hear him in the middle of a sentence about "Yankees who want to be crackers." He'd written about Agrarians, Fugitives—to Robert Penn Warren's "Nigger, your poetry isn't metaphysical," Sterling had answered, "Cracker, your poetry ain't exegitical"—and Southern apologists was a topic he would not let go of. "You need to come down here and get with some black folk. Get away from that Allen Tate." He hung up before I could say that I didn't know Allen Tate. Sometimes he put me in mind of Mark Twain stalking prey with his nineteen rules of literary art, especially when he talked about black characters in fiction, and at other times I didn't know what to think: "Sartre ain't worth a fartre. / Genet is gay. / Imagine a Negro appearing in *The Blacks.*"

One summer afternoon in 1984 I dropped by his house in Washington unannounced. He was bravely holding forth on his side porch. Gin, red wine, and a bucket of what had been ice stood on a table. He was waiting in an old T-shirt for a group from the University of Maryland. Stubble rolled across a face that looked as though it was melting. He seemed to live most of his life on that porch ("I found me a cranny of perpetual dusk"). Records were scattered across the living-room rug and I said it looked as though he needed some help cataloging. The heavens broke. I heard him say in no uncertain

terms that he neither needed nor wanted any help. He stormed off to his basement retreat, returned to tell me that I was not to follow him down there, then blew back upstairs to tell me to get out of his house. I went next door to his sister's. Helen had broken her hip and was confined to a couch. In her time she had been one of those light-skinned, wood-wind-voiced daughters with "good hair." "I know," she said. "I didn't mean to upset him this morning when I told him to take his medicine." She gave me a copy of her father's book, *Bible Mastery,* as a consolation. I heard Sterling calling and I hurried across the yard. He wanted to make sure that I understood that he meant *nevah* come back. He slammed the door so hard my glasses shifted. Some time afterward Helen died and with her my source of intelligence about Sterling.

When I was in Washington last summer August was burning, and Jesse Jackson had just been passed over—"I understand," he told the NAACP. "I wasn't always on television." Because I didn't live in the US anymore, I, clown of God, thought that I would get a soldier's welcome and be forgiven for wanting to take from him more of his anecdotes. Sterling's door was still slammed shut. I knocked at what used to be Helen's. The white guy in jogging shorts who'd bought both houses couldn't tell me where Sterling had been taken, but he offered to let me see the garden again, where I had once watched Sterling feed birds, talk off-color, put on a beret to sing "I'm a bo-diddlie . . . ," and where, stunned by the obtuseness in my lack of response, Sterling had straightened up to a great height: "Son, you ought to know when I'm telling you a tale and learn to appreciate it. That's something we as a people have lost."

> They have forgotten, they have
> never known,
> Long days beneath the torrid Dixie sun
> In miasma'd riceswamps;
> The chopping of dried grass, on the third go round
> In strangling cotton;
> Wintry nights in mud-daubed make-shift huts,
> With these songs, sole comfort.
>
> They have forgotten
> What had to be endured—
>
> (pp. 15-16)

Darryl Pinckney, "The Last New Negro," in The New York Review of Books, *Vol. XXXVI, No. 4, March 16, 1989, pp. 14-16.*

JOHN F. CALLAHAN

Struggling to write about Sterling Brown in commemoration of his passing in January, I failed. Again and again I failed. I could utter only fragments—half-remembered, half-invented phrases from the many conversations we had had in the fifteen years I knew him and was his friend. I tried too hard and, trying, found some lines of Yeats, whom Sterling loved for his music, for his love of Irish folklore, folklife, and folkspeech. These came abruptly into my head, and like uninvited guests lingered on the front porch of my mind: "I sought a theme and sought for it in vain. / I sought it daily for six weeks or so." So Yeats wrote of his travail in "The Circus Animals' Desertion" before he realized that his theme was the heart—not the romantic, sentimental heart of so many metaphors but the funky, down-home heart of his metaphor: "the foul rag-and-bone shop."

I am not a poet like Yeats and Sterling Brown, but I, too, have no theme yet for an *in memoriam* essay of homage to Sterling Brown. It is too early for that; I have too much grieving to do, too much sorting out of what was said and not said, done and not done, or half-done and half-said. Above all, I have too much sorting out of all that I experienced with Sterling Allen Brown and Daisy Turnbull Brown and, after her passing in 1979, with Sterling as he fought a brave and more and more lonely, desolate battle against the physical pain and spiritual losses of old age. For there was little serenity to Sterling's old age; yes, there were some serene times, and they need to be spoken of, to be told. But not too soon, not out of context, and not, as Yeats said in "Easter 1916," "to please a companion / Around the fire at the club." (pp. 91-2)

Sterling Brown was as good a raconteur as I've ever known; he and Gene McCarthy, who thought Sterling's reading of "Strong Men" the high point of Rosalyn Carter's White House gathering of poets in 1980, should have fought it out like gladiators of the word in D.C. dives and Rappahannock general stores. Sure, Sterling told stories on people. I've heard him on Du Bois—"son of a bitch drank my applejack"—on Ralph Bunche, on Mordecai , on Ralph Bunche, on Mordecai Johnson, on Alan Tate, on Zora Neale Hurston, on Leadbelly, and on many others. His stories were lies, his lies stories. They had a bite to them. They had a warmth, too, because he knew a good story, one that lingered and stayed with teller and listener, had to come from some mountain spring of affection—clear, cold, quick-running, and unsentimental—, because those Sterling cared enough about to tell stories on were people of mettle who would have been insulted by the thought that their sensibilities were too tender to have a story told on them. (p. 92)

In his eulogy for Yeats, W. H. Auden said that "the death of the poet was kept from his poems." Well, we couldn't perform that office for Sterling Brown even if we wanted to. His people—Big Boy, Sister Lou, Sporting Beasley, Old Lem, and so many more—know of his passing. They have bowed their heads for an interval—but only for an interval. Their (and our) temporary silence is an act of sympathy for Sterling, who has fallen silent, not by choice, but according to the sway of life and death, according to the rules of the universe. "He has met life's conditions but never accepted them," he said so many times of his heroes.

So let the poet pass, and when he's made his passage we'll speak again. And so will he. We who knew Sterling and his work know this or else should know it. For there is a yet to be revealed body of work written and spoken in his papers and his many hours of autobiography on tape at Howard University. So it is with Sterling Brown's intimate papers, what Hurston's Janie called God's "inside business"—the memories Sterling's friends and colleagues have of him.

For this reason, I believe it is too early to remember Sterling Brown in the manner of formal, *festschrift* remembrance. Our relation to him as poet, critic, and friend who has just passed and maybe is passing still, like the flying African of folk legend, reminds me of the fellow's relation to **"Ma Rainey"** in Sterling's great blues ballad by that name. "She jes catch hold of us somekindaway," the fellow tells the poet *before* he remembers hearing Ma's singing "Backwater Blues." But once memory has taken hold so vividly that Ma Rainey seems to stand before him singing her song, the poet comes in and changes the man's line. Changes especially one word: "She jes gits hold of us *dataway*." So it will be with Sterling Brown.

For now we should accept in his name and ours the wish he gave to Sister Lou: "Den take yo' time . . . . / Honey, take yo' bressed time."

In that silent "bressed time" it will be possible to sort out the poetry, the criticism, the life he lived, and then there will be time to write truly and well our stories and story of Sterling Brown. (pp. 93-4)

John F. Callahan, "Sterling Brown Ain't Dead Nothing. . . . He Ain't Even Passed," in Black American Literature Forum, *Vol. 23, No. 1, Spring, 1989, pp. 91-4.*

JOHN S. WRIGHT

In 1936, the year Sterling Brown and John Lomax joined forces supervising the collection of oral slave narratives for the Federal Writers' Project, Lomax and his son Alan published the first extended study of an American folksinger. That singer, one Walter Boyd, alias Hudie Ledbetter, alias "Leadbelly," had been the self-proclaimed "King of the Twelve String Guitar Players of the World," as well as the number one man in the number one gang on the number one convict farm in Texas. He had fought his way into prison and had sung his way to freedom, to fleeting fame, and to what would be a pauper's death in Bellevue in 1949. A man of prodigious physical strength, emotional volatility, unpredictable violence, and indisputable creativity, unschooled if not unassuming, he was shaped by record, film, and the printed page into the prototypic national image of the "folk Negro." For the recording industry, his songs were a golden hedge against hard times. For the generation of newly professional folklorists that the Lomaxes represented, he was a "find" that helped buttress the assault of the Depression era folklore radical democrats against the old aristocratic folklore scholarship. For the thinkers and artists of the black world-within-a-world from which he came, however, Leadbelly made concrete an old enigma alternately energizing and embarrassing—and one left largely unplumbed by the outspokenly "folk conscious" New Negro movement of the twenties. Lawbreaker, illiterate, brawler, boozer, womanizer, cottonpicker, and vagrant; singer of prison dirges, work songs, cowboy ballads, children's songs, spirituals, lullabies, and barrel-house blues, Leadbelly was a grinning, gold-toothed incongruity. Vernacular tradition's "nachal man" incarnate, he was in one rough frame the bruised and imbruted "man farthest down" for whom Booker T. Washington and the organizations of racial uplift had lowered their proverbial buckets, *and* he was the voice of that transcendent "Negro genius" which W. E. B. Du Bois and the Talented Tenth had exalted as creator of "the most beautiful expressions of human experience born this side of the seas". In the preceding decade Jean Toomer, Claude McKay, Zora Neale Hurston, and Langston Hughes had all directed their imaginative energies to penetrating the layers of abstraction that created incongruity from the folklife Leadbelly nonetheless had to live. But perhaps nowhere had so clear a perspective emerged for seeing such a man whole as in the work of Sterling Brown.

In 1932 Brown had published *Southern Road;* and with a social realism honed to poetic precision, he had struck through the masks with which minstrelsy, local color, the plantation tradition, and Jazz Age primitivism had defaced the folk. (pp. 95-6)

Rejecting the Old Negro and the traditional poetry of folk caricature, James Weldon Johnson had advocated a symbolic rather than a phonetic literary mimesis, and had forecast the doom of dialect poetry. But Sterling Brown perceived that the problem of defining a poetic language for folk portraiture was a problem not so much of materials as of perspective. "Dialect, or the speech of the people," he maintained [quoted in Eugene Redmond's *Drumvoices: The Mission of Afro-American Poetry*], "is capable of expressing whatever the people are. And the folk Negro is a great deal more than a buffoon or a plaintive minstrel. Poets more intent upon learning the ways of the folk, their speech, and their character, that is to say, better poets, could have smashed the mold. But first they would have to believe in what they were doing. And this was difficult in a period of conciliation and middle class striving for recognition and respectability". Brown's less conventional strivings provided critical as well as poetic demonstrations of his own unshakable belief in "the validity, the power, and the beauty of folk culture." His was an aesthetic of reorientation, and its achievement rested no less surely on his poems than on the critical paths he cut through the jungle of theory and interpretation, censorship and commercialization, romanticism and mysticism, that engulfed the study of Afro-American folklore between the 1920s and the 1950s.

The twenties, besides hosting the New Negro movement, fostered another phenomenon not unconnected to the black cultural ferment of the time with its artistic focus on, in Locke's terms, "the revaluation of the Negro": After a war decade remarkable for the *accumulation* of major folklore collections in America, the twenties became a decade remarkable for the *publication* of folklore collections. (pp. 96-7)

When the resurgence of Afro-American folklore collecting appeared early in the twenties, it was with the force of a revitalized national interest in native traditions behind it. John Lomax's publication of *Cowboy Songs and Other Frontier Ballads* in 1910 and Cecil Sharp's *English Folksongs from the Southern Appalachians* in 1917 had pioneered a turnabout in American folklore research by revealing living folksong traditions that were not vanishing but instead surviving and in fact being continually reborn. In 1915, amidst a flurry of regional collecting, music critic Henry Krehbiel had directed attention away from the ongoing "ballad wars" and toward the Afro-American folksongs he sought "to bring into the field of scientific observation". Krehbiel had centered his study around the questions of "whether or not the songs were original creations of these native blacks, whether or not they were entitled to be called American, and whether or not they were worthy of consideration as foundation elements for a school of American composition". Krehbiel had answered all these in the affirmative; and his formulation then of the problems of origins, of methods of composition, and of provenience did much to set the terms of discourse for the new black folklore studies that flowed out into the public arena in the twenties and early thirties.

Those studies revealed a body of Afro-American oral tradition that was massive, vital, and portentous. (p. 98)

In the face of this expanding repository of traditional art and customs, the prevailing notion that no distinctive Afro-American culture existed, or that such culture as did exist was one of either fossilized African survivals or debased imitations of white models, began to give ground. And the folk ideology so central to the New Negro creed formulated by Alain Locke received a concrete foundation of folk myths, legends, symbols, and character types upon which many of the major black literary achievements of the next two decades would build. Prospects for employing the new folklore studies either for aesthetic purposes or in support of the sociopolitical "literature of racial vindication," however, were vitiated by a trio of conceptual problems and controversies that implicated the whole of folklore research and interpretation at the time.

First, American folklorists, who, as Richard Dorson has noted, were rarely trained in folklore and rarely Americanists, subscribed heavily to Eurocentric theories that (a) predicated the existence of folklore on the presence of a traditional peasantry that did not exist in America, (b) treated folklore genres hierarchically, with the Anglo-Saxon ballad first and foremost, and (c) approached American folk forms generally as corrupted, inherently inferior imitations of Old World originals (Dorson). Under the disabling influence of these theories, Fisk professor Thomas Talley, for example, in his pioneering study [*Negro Folk Rhymes*] labored tortuously to force his materials into an elaborate system of ballad classification based on his defensively mystical proposition that "all [Negro] Folk Rhymes are Nature Ballads" with call-and-response structures that somehow "hover ghostlike" over them.

Second, nineteenth-century racist ethnology, though under attack in the anthropological work of Franz Boas and his students, remained a potent force in the new folklore research—reinforced by lingering Social Darwinism and the currents of popular nativism and racism. The mystique of racial "gifts," "temperaments," and "geniuses" helped contort the endless debate over the origins of folk forms waged between diffusionists, who believed in a single origin of folk themes with their subsequent spread, and polygeneticists, who argued for the repeated reinvention of similar materials because of similar psychological or historical conditions. . . . (pp. 99-100)

Third, the new folklore studies were hampered by the absence of any scientific or humanistic theory of American culture and national character capable of comprehending, as a cultural matrix for folklife, this country's modernity, its radical heterogeneity, and its peculiar blend of social fixedness and fluidity. Moreover, the folkloric enterprise was subject to pressures from popularization, commercialization, and the emerging mass media that were plagued with distortions and fabrications of folk culture that produced the "bankrupt treasuries" Stanley Edgar Hyman lambasted in the mid-forties and that led Richard Dorson eventually to coin the distinction between folklore and the rising tide of "fakelore".

Into this fray Sterling Brown brought a keen critical intelligence, his convictions about the cultural integrity and aesthetic significance of folklife, and his instincts as a creative writer. Afro-American folklorists were scarce to say the least, and in the quarter-century of folkloric fervor that spanned the Jazz Age, the Great Depression, and the Second World War, Sterling Brown's essays in *Opportunity* and *Phylon,* and his editorial and scholarly work with the Federal Writers' Project Negro Affairs division, filled the void with a wide-ranging folklore critique fully cognizant of the shifting grounds of folklore scholarship yet fixed unerringly on the perspectives of the folk themselves. Brown had spent the years after the publication of **Southern Road** absorbed in Afro-American literary history and the iconography of racial stereotypy—preoccupations fleshed out in his **The Negro in American Fiction** and **Negro Poetry and Drama.** With his appointment to the Federal Writers' Project in the spring of 1936, he turned toward the sociohistorical study of the black folk and urban experience, immersing himself first in the gathering of ex-slave narratives which was then underway and which would be perhaps the Writers' Project's greatest contribution to the study of Afro-American life.

The collection of slave narratives had been begun in 1934 by the Federal Emergency Relief Administration, at the instigation of black historian Lawrence Reddick, who had voiced the growing historical consensus that the story of slavery and Reconstruction could not be complete "until we get the view as presented through the slave himself" (Mangione [*The Dream and the Deal: The Federal Writers' Project, 1935-1943*]). The Writers' Project had inherited the undertaking; and in 1936, when John Lomax became the Project's first folklore editor, Sterling Brown began guiding the interviewing efforts that would lead finally to the publication of seventeen volumes of manuscripts containing over two thousand slave narratives (Mangione). Under Lomax's supervision, and after 1938 under the leadership of Benjamin Botkin, the Project proceeded to collect folk materials on a scale larger than ever previously attempted.

Under Botkin's influence especially, the Project countered the antiquarian orientation of academic folklorists with an emphasis on oral history and "living lore." Sterling Brown, who had contributed poems and critical reviews to Botkin's four-volume regional miscellany *Folk-Say* between 1929 and 1932, found Botkin's proletarian emphasis congenial to his own. "The folk movement must come from below upward rather than from above downward," Botkin contended; "otherwise it may be dismissed as a patronizing gesture, a nostalgic wish, an elegiac complaint, a sporadic and abortive review—on the part of paternalistic aristocrats going slumming, dilettantish provincials going native, defeated sectionalists going back to the soil, and anybody and everybody who cares to going collecting" (Mangione). Folk imagination more than folk knowledge became the Project's aim, and the outlook and skills of writers such as Sterling Brown became crucial to capturing it.

For Sterling Brown the aim also was, in his words, to "produce an accurate picture of the Negro in American social history," to reveal him as an integral part of American life and to do so in a way that mediated between the competing chauvinisms of both white and black historians (Mangione). The device of correlating folklore with social and ethnic history was the tactic Brown emphasized in his editorial role and in his efforts to have Afro-American materials included in the Project's state guidebooks then being compiled around the country. The publication of *The Negro in Virginia* in 1940 demonstrated the value of this approach. It was produced under the local supervision of black historian Roscoe Lewis, but Brown's role in this field project was considerable. Built upon years of carefully collected oral histories and interviews and on painstaking research that traced neglected materials back to the arrival in Virginia of the first Africans in 1619, *The Negro in Virginia* became a model of documentary research and narrative drama (Mangione).

In a talk before the Conference on the Character and State of Studies in Folklore in 1946, Brown looked back at his years with the Project: "I became interested in folklore," he recalled, "because of my desire to write poetry and prose fiction. I was first attracted by certain qualities I thought the speech of the people had, and I wanted to get for my own writing a flavor, a color, a pungency of speech. Then later I came to something more important—I wanted to get an understanding of people" [see "The Approach of the Creative Artist" in *Journal of American Folklore,* October 1946]. Respectful of the scientific approaches to folklore but untroubled by any definitional or procedural obstacles that might block his access to the "living-people-lore" of, for instance, so fascinating a tribe as urban jazzmen, Sterling Brown had developed a flexible, functionalist approach to folklore. It was an approach that, as Alan Lomax advocated in the same session, rejected views of the folk "as ignorant receptacles for traditions and ideas which they do not themselves understand, and which make very little sense until they are pieced together and explained in historical terms by the comparative scholar." Such an approach instead saw folklore as "equipment for living," saw the folklorist as performing not only an archaeological role but one of recording a vigorous human tradition, and it recognized that "the best interpretations of folklore may be obtained in the end from the folk themselves".

In the early forties, the conviction that the folk may be their own best interpreters became one of the trademarks of Sterling Brown's series of articles on black folk expression. His synoptic essay in The Negro Caravan in 1941, on the sources and genres of black oral literature, stands even today as the single best introduction to the subject because, in threading its way through all the scholarship and interpretative quandaries of the previous decades, it maintains its balance by never falling victim to the disorienting proposition that, as Newman White had myopically insisted, "the Negro never contemplated his low estate."

"Nigger, your breed ain't metaphysical," one of the voices in Robert Penn Warren's poeticized fable "Pondy Woods" had proclaimed, confronting New Negroes with an old stereotype from the crusading New South. "Cracker, *your* breed ain't exegetical," Sterling Brown responded dialectically, as he outlined a critique that treated black forms as distillations of communal *mind* and *ethos.* In his essays on the blues in particular, Brown treated the products of folk imagination as *self-conscious* wisdom—tragic, comic, ironic, shrewd, emotionally elastic and attitudinally complex, capable of supporting a variety of stances toward life, and resistant, as such, to ideological straitjacketing or implications of naïveté. Worldly and self-aware, the spirit of the blues, he submitted, is defined by the songs themselves, in lines which assert that "the blues ain't nothin' but a poor man's heart disease" or "the blues ain't nothin' but a good man way, way down" or, more obliquely, "Woke up this morning, blues walking round my bed / Went in to eat my breakfast, blues was all in my bread." The blues fused stoicism in a concrete, *metaphoric metaphysic:* It was a frank Chaucerian *attitude* toward sex and love that kept even the bawdiest authentic blues from being prurient and pornographic. It was "elemental *honesty,*" "depth of *insight,*" and *sophistication* about human relations that lay behind their appeal across caste lines. It was *imagination* making the love of life and the love of words memorably articulate which turned the best blues into potent lyric poetry.

Brown's reading of the blues tradition did not go uncontested. In a lengthy, two-part essay on the spirit and meaning of black folk expression published in *Phylon* [Autumn 1950], he acknowledged that "the field of folklore in general is known to be a battle area, and the Negro front is one of the hottest sectors". But he needed no new battle pieces, no defensive ethnic chauvinism. Incorporating the insights of Stith Thompson's then definitive study of the folktale, he found, in the newly revealed patterns of interchange and diffusion characteristic of even Old World African folklore, support for his vision of the underlying unity of the world's and the nation's many cultural traditions. After all, he noted, in the cosmology of black folk traditions themselves, "tales about the origin of the races leave little room for chauvinism about a chosen people. The slaves knew at first hand that the black man had a hard road to travel, and they tell of the mistakes of creation with sardonic fatalism". Looking then at the prospects for the future of folklife, he knew that hard road was all too literal. Black folk culture was breaking up, he thought. In migrating to the city "the folk become a submerged proletariat. Leisurely yarn-spinning, slow paced aphoristic conversation become lost arts; jazzed-up gospel hymns provide a different sort of release from the old spirituals; the blues reflect the distortions of the new way of life. Folk arts are no longer by the folk for the folk; smart businessmen now put them up for sale. Gospel songs often become showpieces for radio-slummers, and the blues become the double talk of the dives." And yet, he interjected, "the vigor of the creative impulse has not been snapped, even in the slums," and the folk roots "show a stubborn vitality" [*Phylon* Winter 1953].

Leadbelly was a few years dead then, his pauperized last seasons spent as a resident "living legend" in Greenwich Village coffeehouses. The "blues boom," the "rediscovery" of New Orleans jazz, and the folk revivals of the fifties were taking hold. ***Southern Road,*** though, was out of print and Sterling Brown's poetry largely unremarked since the thirties by the canonizers of American verse. In his various roles as teacher, scholar, poet, husband, mentor, and self-confessed "Teller of Lies," Brown weathered those years, and the years after, sustained by the same lyric loves he found in the blues—the love of words, the love of life, and the love of all things musical,

as he was wont to say, "from Beethoven to the boogie-woogie." And perhaps concluding with this one of Brown's own pointed incongruities makes sense if, blues-like, we "worry" it a bit. Beethoven, save for the tarbrushings that allege him to be quite literally a "soul brother," is a relatively unambiguous reference for defining one aesthetic pole and one kind of hero on the spectrum of "strange legacies" Sterling Brown's work embraces. The boogie-woogie, though, evokes almost as unruly an image as Leadbelly, for the phrase masks onomatopoetically a complex legacy of juxtaposed folk meanings: The boogie-woogie was simultaneously a fast-stepping, Kansas City Jazz-influenced piano blues in which the bass figure comes in double time; it was the knee-flexing jitterbug one danced in accompaniment; it was a racial epithet; it was a wartime moniker for enemy aircraft; it was an intransitive vernacular verb connoting the uninhibited pursuit of pleasure; it was a reference to the devil and all the troubles associated with him; and it was, less openly but no less significantly, a Southern euphemism for a case of secondary syphilis. There was a multilayered joke proffered, in other words, in Brown's wry conflation of Beethoven with the boogie-woogie, an irreverent populist riff that counterpointed democratically the classical with the vernacular, the academy with the Southern road, white icons with black reprobates; and that now, in remembrance, binds Brown the scholar/poet with the many-monikered chaingang songster as nachally as a professing Teller of Lies might be to the legend with the gold-toothed grin. (pp. 100-05)

John S. Wright, "The New Negro Poet and the Nachal Man: Sterling Brown's Folk Odyssey," in Black American Literature Forum, *Vol. 23, No. 1, Spring, 1989, pp. 95-105.*

Bruce Chatwin

May 13, 1940 - January 18, 1989

(Born Charles Bruce Chatwin) English travel writer, novelist, essayist and journalist.

For an overview of Chatwin's life and work see *CLC,* Vols. 28, 57 and *Contemporary Authors,* Vols. 85-88, Vol. 127 [obituary].

THE TIMES, LONDON

Bruce Chatwin, who died on January 18 in Nice of a rare disease of the bone marrow at the tragically early age of 48, had only comparatively recently come to anything like general notice, with the recognition that he was a writer of rare craft and powers of evocation.

He was known as a writer of travel books—albeit travel books of a highly eccentric sort—before his novel *On The Black Hill* appeared, to suggest that what had been thought of merely as an interesting way of looking at geographical and historical facts was, in fact, a genuine creative gift. Chatwin's novels, as his travel books, give pleasure to those who delight in a sense of place, and in that sense the strengths of *On The Black Hill* were of the same order as those of *In Patagonia.*

Chatwin's life bore much resemblance to his written works. It appeared somewhat chaotic, though everything about it had a logic informed by a mind of integrity. He had the talent to have succeeded in many things. Born in wartime Sheffield (May 13, 1940), he spent a dismal childhood in post-war Britain.

[Chatwin] developed an interest in French painting, and learned to speak the language quite tolerably. He joined Sotheby's as a porter, but one day pronounced a Picasso watercolour, which he saw in the saleroom, a fake, and immediately acquired status. He was made a director and seemed settled for life. However there was a mortuary aspect of the saleroom business which repelled him. . . .

Walking out, he took train to Edinburgh where he read Archaeology. Enthused by his idea of the archaeologist's calling he wandered the globe making a living by journalism. . . .

His experience of the nomadic life convinced him that the nomad was the element 'left out' in a conventional view of history, and that perhaps man had 'gone wrong' as soon as Cain had started to found a city. . . .

To the end Chatwin lived the simple, uncluttered life of the nomad, knapsack always at the ready, to be hastily stuffed with the bare essentials, as he embarked on yet another journey. . . . .

[A journey to South America] spawned the book, *In Patagonia* (1977). The bizarreries of the place and its peoples—unlikely communities of Welshmen (still speaking Welsh, though not English), Indians, Russians and Germans, besides those of Spanish stock—were dear to his sense of important things being left on forgotten strands. "Caliban has a good claim to Patagonian ancestry" was a characteristic response.

The Viceroy of Ouidah fictionalized the facts of travels in Dahomey and Brazil, in a story of the slave trade across the Atlantic set in Napoleonic times. Chatwin's sociological research was impressive, while the economy with which he was able to create an exotic atmosphere struck even readers uninterested in his historical exactitude. . . .

On The Black Hill (1982) was again strongly based on place, this time a Welsh hill farm, where twin brothers live out lives rooted in the hard favoured soil which has bred them. The discerning hailed this book, with its strongly evoked sense of the importance of the minutiae which go to make up the life of a small, isolated community, as a major step for Chatwin, marking his "arrival" as a novelist.

The Songlines (1987) disappointed some followers with its twists and turns between various narrative forms and bouts of philosophising. But its brilliance in the unfolding of unusual ideas could never be in question. Not a novel in the conventional sense (any more than, say, *Moby Dick* is merely a novel about the hunting of a whale) it gave itself over to extended passages of meditation on anthropological matters, arising out of a consideration of the nature of nomadic peoples. Commercially, it was his most successful book, and brought him some income, a fact which did not displease him.

Its successor, *Utz* (1988), was slight in physical bulk, but not in quality of matter. Its 150 pages explore, through the oblique medium of a young English historian, the life of a part Jewish Czech, with whose funeral the book opens. The protagonist's gradually revealed obsession with porcelain leads the reader into unexpected corners of human existence. . . .

[Chatwin's] shockingly premature death has, alas, left the unanswered question of whether a very considerable gift could have left us with a corpus of truly major work.

> *"Bruce Chatwin: Nomad into Novelist," in* The Times, *London, January 20, 1989, p. 14f.*

COLIN THUBRON

With the death of Bruce Chatwin a unique man has gone. In his life, as in his books, he was driven by an obsessed intelligence, a fascination with the world's diversity. As a writer he was unclassifiably interesting: lucid, ironic, cool. He seemed to owe nothing to anybody. . . .

[In Chatwin's five books] facts shimmer on the edge of fiction, and fiction reads like fact. They defy category. If he had any literary model, it was perhaps Flaubert, whose cool classicism, and fascination with the bizarre he shared—the Flaubert of Trois Contes. Often Chatwin seemed to understand and define the world by its extravagances, its irrepressible unreason.

On its publication in 1977, *In Patagonia* was recognised at once as an original. It won the Hawthornden Prize and the E M Forster Award of the American Academy of Arts and Letters. Three years later he published *The Viceroy of Ouidah,* based on the life of a Brazilian slave-trader. He first intended this as biography, but a visit to the slaver's grave (and a brief, brutal imprisonment in Benin, after which he was expelled) persuaded him into fiction: a black pendulum between humour and horror. . . .

[In 1987] appeared *The Songlines,* his masterpiece, the culmination of an obsession of more than 20 years. He had gone to Australia originally intending to write a sustained meditation on the desert, but instead he was deflected into a study of the Aboriginal tracks which invisibly criss-cross the continent—tracks laid by "Dreamtime" ancestors who sang the world into existence as they walked. The book became a novel of ideas, an inquest into human restlessness. It merged his original work on the nomads (an unpublished tome called The Nomad Alternative) with anthropological quests in Africa and several journeys into the Outback. He was convinced that man's first and natural condition was mobile. Early men developed speech, he felt, not out of aggression but from the need to co-operate against the sabre-tooth cat which preyed on them. This beast—whose identification brings the book to its eerie climax—continues in the human subconscious (he wrote) as a haunting nightmare: the Prince of Darkness.

Such theories may not survive; but Chatwin's glittering way with a story surely will, and his single-minded passion for a substantial truth. He might have further polished the manuscript, but he was already ill—he laughingly called it "the first draft and the last gasp".

But he lived to write an elegant, quirky novel, *Utz,* based on his acquaintance with a collector of Meissen porcelain in Prague. . . .

It is hard to know how posterity will regard this remarkable writer, but his terse, honed language was built to last. In his lifetime he shed a certain glamour and mysteriousness. The Chilterns home that he shared with his wife resembled an ersatz Norwegian ranch, which might at any moment be abandoned (and often was). He liked to write in other people's houses. His ebullient intellectual appetites, his patrician good looks and his wide friendships among socialites, artists, writers and photographers (he wrote an introduction to a volume of Robert Mapplethorpe's work) combined with his literary achievements to create around him a minor cult. It was impossible to be in his company without feeling that life had grown more exhilarating and extraordinary. He struck people as arrestingly un-English (which pleased him): a mind more Germanic or French in its imaginative intensity and fascination with theory. Yet he was, in the end, *sui generis,* a man whose visual gifts were married most unusually to a questing, abstract reason.

Few people's deaths shrink the world. But Bruce Chatwin's is one.

> *Colin Thubron, "Bruce Chatwin: In Love with Fantastical Tales," in* The Sunday Times, *London, January 22, 1989, p. G9.*

MICHAEL IGNATIEFF

[Bruce Chatwin's] own character was one of his greatest inventions: traveler, adventurer, storyteller, mimic, the most English of eccentrics abroad, and at the same time the most restlessly cosmopolitan English writer of his generation. This multifaceted persona became an essential part of the appeal of his writing. In his books you were addressed not merely by a distinctive voice, but by the fabulous character he had fashioned for himself.

His life could be described as a sequence of escapes—from the English class system and his public school education; from Sotheby's. . . .

He was a master, in his life and in his work, of the art of eluding expectations. When he felt pigeonholed as a travel writer in the English tradition of Patrick Leigh-Fermor and Wilfred Thesiger, he wrote *The Viceroy of Ouidah,* a surreal fable of slavery set in Dahomey, and then when his public began to think of him as a writer of the exotic, he produced *On the Black Hill,* about two Welsh hill farmers who had never left the confines of the Welsh valleys. And when he felt enclosed again by the idea that he was an English realist, he wrote *Songlines,* a metaphysical novel about nomads and wandering, set in the Australian outback, which—like all of his work—was unclassifiable. Was this anthropology, fiction, an essay, disguised autobiography? It was all of these. His best work redrew the borderline between fiction and nonfiction. . . .

No sooner had he finished [*Songlines*] than he began exploring radically different terrain. The result was *Utz,* a strange miniature, in the tradition of Borges, on a porcelain collector in Prague, a pertinacious eccentric who pursued his obsessions in healthy obliviousness to the Iron Curtain across the heart of European culture. As a parable about the human fascination with the beautiful, *Utz* was also Chatwin's oblique commentary on the art of writing. When the book was nominated for the Booker Prize, he said *Utz* was about art and then added, "Art is never enough. Art always lets you down."

Illness began to engulf him in the autumn of 1986 as he struggled to complete *Songlines.* There was then a miraculous period of remission in 1987, when he composed *Utz;* and then illness returned again in 1988.

To the astonishment of those who visited him this past winter, reduced and emaciated, he managed to complete the editing of a collection of his short writing and journalism called *What Am I Doing Here* (to be published later this year). He rediscovered and rewrote these old pieces with pleasure, as if they reminded him of old selves left behind on his travels.

By the autumn of 1988, he was too weak to work, too weak to hold a pen. But the bed was still covered with books. He would still toss odd and unfashionable treasures at you and say, Had you read that? In a weak but excited whisper, he would sketch out scenes from a projected novel. . . .

The novel died with him, and half a lifetime of the work that was in him will not see the light of day. What he did have time to write had a piercing clarity and economy. His books are models of transparency, lightness, and elusiveness in literature; he never mined the same vein of inspiration twice. As a writer, he was a magician of the word; as a man, he lived with a verve that left his friends breathless. He traveled light, and there was nothing—except friendship—he wasn't prepared to leave behind.

On the final page of *Songlines,* composed when he was beginning to die, he wrote: "The mystics believe the ideal man shall walk himself to a 'right death.' He who has arrived 'goes back.' . . . The concept is quite similar to Heraclitus's mysterious dictum, 'Mortals and immortals alive in their death, dead in each other's life.' "

I shall always think of him on a day in the last autumn of his life, lying on the grass outside his house, wrapped in blankets, weak, gray-haired and emaciated, but still incorrigibly stylish in a pair of high-altitude ski sunglasses. He said he had bought them for his next trip to the Himalayas. He lay there and talked in a faint whisper, full of cackles and laughter like some grand and unrepentant monarch in exile, or like one of the fantastic and touching figures of his own fiction, staring up at the bright blue sky, while the white clouds scudded across his black glasses.

> Michael Ignatieff, "On Bruce Chatwin," in The New York Review of Books, *Vol. XXXVI, No. 3, March 2, 1989, p. 4.*

SALMAN RUSHDIE

For a few weeks in 1984, Bruce Chatwin and I drove around Central Australia in a four-wheel-drive station wagon, a vehicle which, we were repeatedly informed, 'must be Toyota's Answer to the Little Subaru'. Bruce puzzled over this curious phrase, trying to invent a mythology that might explain it. The Little Subaru was plainly some sort of Dreamtime Ancestor, but if our car were the 'answer' then what, Bruce (like Gertrude Stein) wanted to know, could possibly have been the question?

To be with Bruce Chatwin was, usually, to be his willing audience. His conversation would soar up Mount Everest (we were half-way up Ayers Rock, and I was half-dead and turning purple, when he mentioned that he'd recently made it to the Everest base camp), and just as swiftly plummet to a discussion of the diseases one might contract from diverse European and African whores. He was a magnificent raconteur of Scheherazadean inexhaustibility, a gilt-edged name-dropper, a voracious reader of esoteric texts, a scholar gypsy, a mimic—his Mrs Gandhi was perfect—and a giggler of international class. He was as talkative as he was curious, and he was curious about everything, from the origins of evil to the question asked by the Little Subaru. His words about the ex-Chamberlain of King Zog of Albania are truer of himself: 'People of his kind will never come again.' What a voice we lost when his fell silent! How much he still had to say!

> Salman Rushdie, "Before the Voice We Lost Fell Silent," in The Observer, *May 14, 1989, p. 48.*

JAMES CHATTO

Caught in a coup in Benin, stripped to his underpants and then marched before a firing squad, Bruce Chatwin "began to count the flecks of milletchaff embedded in the mud-plaster wall . . . " . . . Facing death again, in more poignant circumstances, he retrieved other memories, stories, articles and sketches from his writings of the last fifteen years and gathered them together into a book [*What Am I Doing Here*].

Chatwin was fascinated by collectors and perpetually sought to understand them through their collections. *What Am I Doing Here* is his own collection of the people, places and ideas that he found interesting and as such is revealingly autobiographical, at least about Chatwin the writer. The recurring themes of his previous five books are all present, illuminated as ever by his enthusiasm, erudition and an awe-inspiring eye for detail. The stories can be judged by their dates, he suggests in a brief introduction, and the temptation to rearrange them chronologically is overwhelming. Doing so immediately uncovers the development of his style, the movement from documentary to fiction, from an occasionally pedantic learning to genuine insight, and the fine-tuning of his beautiful, ascetic prose.

What makes his writing so compelling is the use to which he put this precise, disciplined objectivity, tramping the world to discover subjects that glow with flamboyant, exotic colour. Like his friend Donald Evans, who created an imaginary Earth in a series of paintings the size of postage stamps, Chatwin traced yeti, nomad hordes, Patagonian sea-nymphs and Bea Lillie's missing Modigliani with the fine brush of a miniaturist. Perhaps that is what brought such truth to his travel writing. I wasn't the only tourist in Tierra del Fuego last year using Chatwin's *In Patagonia* as a Baedecker. His scrupulous honesty and his heartfelt, almost schoolboy fascination with his surroundings lifts him at once above contemporary American travel writers, who cover the same ground but only in order to explore inner, egocentric horizons. . . .

[An] ability to suspend judgment and to refrain from stating the implicit runs through what is the main body of the book, a group of portraits of notable people, ranging from a leading Hong Kong geomancer to Malraux, Werner Herzog and Mrs Ghandi. Their interest for Chatwin the collector lies in their stubborn individualism and courage, qualities they share with Assunta, the cleaning lady and tea-maker in the hospital where he spent his last, pain-racked months. The two conversational vignettes he devotes to her begin the book and are as powerful and moving as anything he ever wrote.

"My whole life," said Chatwin in 1983, "has been a search for the miraculous." There have been few writers better qualified to seek it, or better able to distinguish the fake from the genuine article.

James Chatto, "Abroad Canvas," in Punch, *Vol. 296, May 26, 1989, p. 44.*

PETE WHITTAKER

[Bruce Chatwin] was a stylish individualist who defied categorisation. His books, whatever it said in the blurb, were an intriguing amalgam of fiction, autobiography and travel writing. It has been said that each of his books was an attempt to escape the previous one. . . . Certainly, from his first book, *In Patagonia,* to *The Songlines, . . .* his concern has been the exploration of ideas rather than literal transcription.

What Am I Doing Here is Chatwin's own selection of his journalism, profiles and shorter travel pieces. As is to be expected with such a wide-ranging collection from such an author, the appeal of the book as a whole is largely a matter of personal taste. There is rather too much on Chatwin's early days at Sotheby's—a seam also mined for his last novel *Utz*—for my liking, and an over-eagerness to seek out the bizarre and the eccentric. However, there is an appealing freshness, almost innocence, about Chatwin's pieces; while this could easily spill over into an amoral numbness (as it does, for instance, in **"Werner Herzog in Ghana"**) he usually manages to balance openness with a critical discrimination. There are several superb evocations of people or places in this collection—Chatwin's account of his trip down the Volga or **"The Very Sad Story of Salah Bourguine",** an inquiry into the roots and reasons of French anti-Arab racism, are alone worth the price of admission. **"Nomad Invasions"** casts an interesting light on the author's obsession with the restlessness of human nature, and could indeed be the key to Chatwin's work; all his writing was informed by his quest to understand the motivation behind actions, both his own and others.

Chatwin has written, in *Songlines,* of his belief in the relationship between travelling and artistic fulfilment. This collection, while flawed, is testament to the fact that Bruce Chatwin never stopped walking in his search for understanding.

Pete Whittaker, "Travelling Man," in Tribune, *Vol. 53, No. 21, May 26, 1989, p. 12.*

MARGARET FORSTER

Last October there appeared on television an interview with Bruce Chatwin during a programme on the Booker Prize. No one who saw it will ever forget it. There was this once beautiful man dying in front of us, his face so emaciated it was hideously distorted and his eyes, though still vital with intelligence, magnified into caricature. His voice was a mere harsh whisper as he gasped out a few words on his shortlisted novel, *Utz.* It was terrible to watch, and naturally there had been much agonising over whether this interview should be transmitted at all, but I gather Bruce Chatwin himself was eager to take part—a measure of his courage and spirit. . . .

[*What Am I Doing Here*] is his own selection of those stories, profiles and travelogues which he wished to have published posthumously (almost all of them having already appeared in magazines and newspapers). But even before I began to read them that television interview got in the way. So did the memory of the many written tributes after his death. It was clear that here was a writer mourned not just for his talent but for his daring and loved not just for himself but for his sense of adventure. What I, who never met Chatwin, picked up most strongly was that this was a man who above all else was not that thing he despised: ordinary.

All the writing in this volume demonstrates Bruce Chatwin's loathing of the humdrum, the dreary, the predictable. What attracted him was the unusual, the weird and wonderful. . . .

There is a great love here of history, resulting in vast amounts of information crammed into too small a space and ending up in potted lectures which lack the abrasiveness displayed elsewhere. In a section on China, for example, an account of the Nomadic Invasions left me desperate to get on to the author's own encounters where he leavens the history with personal perception. Nobody is as good as Chatwin at evoking a whole atmosphere just through putting down exactly what he saw because what he did see was always the telling detail. Swiftly, he could convert it into lines that read like a thriller—"It was another greasy dawn and the wind was blowing hard onshore, buffeting the buzzards and bending the coco-palms . . ."

And yet, as in this piece where he was caught up in a coup in the African State of Benin, Chatwin is also always the intellectual, appropriately reading the story of Mrs Marmeladov in *Crime and Punishment* while incarcerated in the local barracks. His intellectual curiosity is literally never satisfied, nor his love of knowing odd words. Want to know what a dzom is? Want to know what a geomancer does? Read Chatwin.

But at the end the book's title hangs in the air: what was Chatwin doing here? Not confessing—"I don't want to bore anyone with a confession"—he says in a foreword: nor attempting a kind of autobiography (though of course this collection amounts to that). The first section, three simple personal pieces, look as if they will promise something very original but they are over in eleven pages. They are so simple and moving I could have wept with frustration when I realise they were because these revelations of Chatwin's train of thought during his last year was what I wanted.

Yet even here, he gives a warning: these are "stories" and "the word story is intended to alert the reader to the fact that however closely the narrative may fit the facts the fictional process has been at work." Fine—I see it has, but it doesn't prevent me wanting it to have worked much more often to such brilliant effect.

So where does this leave us? Happy with some sparkling prose, sad that we will not have any more, admiring that under sentence of death Bruce Chatwin was not deflected from his declared purpose "never to let anything artistic stand in my way."

Now there's an enigma for you.

         Margaret Forster, "Out of the Ordinary," in Manchester Guardian Weekly, *May 28, 1989, p. 29.*

HANS MAGNUS ENZENSBERGER

Far from withering away, as the veterans of *Kulturkritik* would like us to believe, literature is, in our days, a congested trade. There is too much of it. The writing industry is prone to over-production, rapid turnover and speedy obsolescence. . . . Given this rampant loss of memory, why is it that every now and then somebody is missed, and even mourned? Why, for example, should the disappearance of Bruce Chatwin make such a difference?

It is not enough to say that he died young or that he was full of promise. He never showed the slightest interest in turning himself into a literary giant. Despite his brilliant and early success, he had no patience with the role of the "major novelist", the aspiring Nobel prize winner, or with the countless other inanities of the profession. Far from merely being an endearing trait, this is a mark of his excellence. For the unwillingness—or incapacity—to perform according to the invisible rules of the game has by now become a necessary condition for meaningful writing. In a culture where everybody is talented, you need a peculiar sort of immunity in order to survive. Chatwin never delivered the goods that critics or publishers or the reading public expected. Not fearing to disappoint, he surprised us at every turn of the page. He ignored the mainstream, but neither did he settle for the niche of the anti-novel or bury himself in the chic dead-end of some self-proclaimed avant-garde.

His very first book shows a sublime disregard for the categories of fiction-and non-fiction. *In Patagonia* has been called a "documentary" and a "travelogue", but neither of these odious terms will fit. On the other hand, it showed the hand of a story-teller who did not fall for the illusion of originality. His tales always admit, and even embrace, the voice of others, famous or unknown; this gives them a richness and diversity which the practitioner of a "personal style" cannot hope to achieve. Chatwin's respect for the experience, the mood and the language of other people is borne out by the present posthumous miscellany of short pieces, which shows his range if not his stamina or patience. *What Am I Doing Here* is a title which can do without the question mark, the summary of someone who never found a definite place for himself, a man forever on the move, both in terms of space and of social context, and it is not far-fetched to suppose that a metaphysical query is at the bottom of it.

"Stories", portraits, fragments, "strange encounters": it is a book without a deliberate architecture, a collection so disparate as to border on the hotch-potch. The reader is exposed to the brusquest changes of climate. There is a dinner with Diana Vreeland followed by a visit to the austere *dacha* of Nadezhda Mandelstam. From a poignant memoir of his father, Chatwin turns to an eyewitness account of a military coup in the forlorn West African republic of Benin. Technically speaking, most of the pieces are newspaper or magazine work, and yet Chatwin's meticulous sense of the *métier* made him steer clear of the pitfalls of the commission. Not for him the know-all attitude, the jaded taste and the flashiness of instant reportage. Here is the uncommon spectacle of a writer using the press on his own terms, using the tools and opportunities of journalism to the advantage of literature. This gives a rare freshness even to his most ephemeral pages. . . .

For his constant change of genre, form and perspective there is thus a deeper reason than mere versatility. Chatwin has always shown a passionate interest in migrants and nomads. In his high-minded fashion, he has become one of them, as a matter of temperament and choice. Not for him the comforts of a promising career or of a cherished home; he remained unsettled and unsettling to the end. The rules of his itinerary, like the Songlines he described in his last great book, are nowhere codified. They are a matter of divination. In *What Am I Doing Here,* there is an account of a Chinese geomancer practising his art in Hong Kong. The structure and the position of a new building are determined by the surrounding landscape, invoking not only the physical aspects of the site, but also its "spirits". Much in the same way, Chatwin's prose follows a pattern explored *on the terrain,* a complex landscape both vast and unfamiliar, ranging from a hamlet in the Welsh mountains to the Australian desert and from the labyrinths of Prague to the crumbling cities of West Africa.

To a sedentary reading public most of these places are bound to seem exotic. But Chatwin escapes the lure of the outlandish by not rubbing shoulders, by striking a certain distance, by keeping his unruffled attitude. Though a lot of painstaking research must have gone into his books, their greatest strength is that he trusts his eye and ear. In the evaluation of art, the judgment of the connoisseur is generally more precise than that of the academic historian. In much the same spirit, Chatwin always proudly claimed to be an amateur. He was a man very sure of his own standards, not to be shaken by status, fame, authority, let alone class, race, or money. Not surprisingly, he has been criticized for being too "baroque", too colourful. In fact, his style is far from overblown, and the decisive stroke of his pen is often quite laconic. It is not his fault if the world does not conform to the subdued voices and the minimal hues of the British landscape; and even there, as readers of Chatwin's novel *On the Black Hill* will remember, reality may turn out to be just as extravagant as in Ouidah.

Less fortunate, perhaps, are his occasional sallies into philosophical and theological speculation. There is a certain lack of rigour in these *raisonnements,* and the laconicism so convincing in his story-telling will every now and then degenerate into the merely peremptory *non sequitur.* It is more annoying than illuminating to be told that "Russia's revolution is the outstanding intellectual event of the century". The writer's evocation of Christ and of Rousseau does not amount to much more than a private construct, a metaphysical tent put up in deserts of his own, into which most of us may not be prepared to follow him. He was much attracted by the Thinker and the Sage, embodied by such doubtful figures as Ernst Jünger and André Malraux, both of whom are portrayed in *What Am I Doing Here.* It is possible that in their theoretical flights of fancy Chatwin found an antidote to a certain philistine dread of the intellectual imagination; if so, his penchant for these adventurers of the mind may be an aspect of his flight from Englishness.

But it is surely as a story-teller that Chatwin will be remembered, and missed—a story-teller going far beyond the limits of fiction, and assimilating in his tales elements of reportage, autobiography, ethnology, the Continental tradition of the essay, and even gossip. Yet underneath the brilliance of the text, there is a haunting presence, something sparse and solitary and moving, as in Turgenev's prose. When we return to Bruce Chatwin, we find much in him that he has left unsaid.

Hans Magnus Enzensberger, "Much Left Unsaid,"
in The Times Literary Supplement, *No. 4498, June*
16, 1989, p. 657.

DIANE ACKERMAN

Obsessed with the life of nomads, about which he wrote with insight and tenderness, Bruce Chatwin was himself the essential wanderer, who roamed the world for decades. Although he was forever pitching his tent somewhere new, he was not exactly a "travel writer"; the phrase irritated him because it suggested too insular an attitude toward the planet. Home was everywhere. All countries, in his mind, shared a common frontier. And the people he ran into on his travels were usually eccentric, improbable and exotic. . . .

In **"The Coup,"** Chatwin tells of a visit to the dilapidated former slaving towns on the coast of Benin, where he was arrested as a suspected mercenary, strip-searched and forced to stand against a wall in the raging sun, under a circling of vultures, while an angry crowd chanted "Death to Mercenaries!" Such events prompted him to write a novel, *The Viceroy of Ouidah* which is set in that sort of cinematic locale.

When Werner Herzog decided to film the book, he invited Chatwin to visit the set in Africa. But by now the writer's illness had left him too frail to walk and climb stairs. He needed a wheelchair, but there was no way to haul one through the jungle. Instead, as Chatwin reports in **"Werner Herzog in Ghana,"** the director offered to provide him with "four hammockeers and a sunshade bearer," and the ceremonial suavity of the gesture was impossible to refuse. Chatwin went, and took notes, sketching a wonderfully zany portrait of Mr. Herzog. . . .

The set required many walls of human skulls, and the villagers made hundreds of them out of plaster, which, because it chips, had to be constantly patched and repainted. Bystanders turned the area into a carnival, selling their candies and hot fritters. One surreptitious young man was peddling something illicit-looking in plastic bags that Chatwin took to be marijuana, only to discover that the packets were full of false teeth. A man walking 40 dogs on a leash was busily buying up even more dogs, which, Chatwin learned, he later sold as food in the north of the country. There was a local watering hole called AYATOLLAH DRINKS BAR.

Such vignettes are not uncommon in the unfolding pageant of Chatwin's travels. In China, he accompanies a geomancer, who wears "a blue silk Nina Ricci tie, a gold wristwatch with a crocodile strap, and an immaculate worsted grey suit" to the new Hongkong and Shanghai Bank, whose builders want him to check it for "malign or demonic presences."

Chatwin seemed especially to prefer vibrant, earthy, outspoken, slightly farouche older women. In Russia, for example, he visits the elderly writer Nadezhda Mandelstam, widow of the poet Osip Mandelstam, whose

> hair was coarse, like lichen, and the light from the bedside lamp shone through it. White metal fastenings glittered among the brown stumps of her teeth. A cigarette stuck to her lower lip. Her nose was a weapon. You knew for certain she was one of the most powerful women in the world, and knew she knew it. . . . She waved me to a chair and, as she waved, one of her breasts tumbled out of her nightie. "Tell me," she shoved it back, "are there any grand poets left in your country?" . . .

In India, Chatwin travels with Indira Gandhi and then visits a recently captured wolf-boy. In the Himalayas, he searches for signs of the yeti, accompanied by a young Sherpa named Thunder-Lion, who "had the habit of prefacing his statements with 'I have something to say,' and of closing with 'That is all I have to say.' " The Sherpas remind him that "Man's real home is not a house, but the Road," a theme that reverberates through all of Chatwin's writings. There are also meditations on restlessness itself, and why we are so driven to wander. . . .

In *What Am I Doing Here,* Chatwin comes right out and tells us that five of the pieces are short stories, labeling each of them "A Story" lest there be any confusion. They're the weakest part of this collection, and they read more like outtakes from his other books than self-contained works of fiction. But many of the essays in *What Am I Doing Here* are examples of Chatwin at his best—part observer, part interviewer, part scholar. What brings them alive is his special talent for noticing life's strange, riveting details. He was a born Autolycus, a snapper-up of unconsidered trifles. What comes through in his last book is a life miscellaneous and on the move, traveled on foot, but never pedestrian.

Diane Ackerman, "Home Was Where the Road
Was," in The New York Times Book Review, *September 10, 1989, pp. 9, 11.*

Daphne du Maurier

May 13, 1907 - April 19, 1989

English novelist, dramatist, nonfiction writer, and editor.

For an overview of du Maurier's life and work see *CLC,* Vols. 6, 11; *Contemporary Authors,* Vols. 5-8, rev. ed., 128 [obituary]; *Contemporary Authors New Revision Series,* Vol. 6; and *Something about the Author,* Vol. 27.

JANE S. BAKERMAN

During her long, distinguished career, Daphne du Maurier has tried her hand successfully at both fiction and nonfiction—biography, autobiography, historical romance, short stories and celebrations of place—but her auctorial reputation rests most firmly upon six romantic suspense novels whose plots stem from some crime or crimes. The novels are *Jamaica Inn, Rebecca, Frenchman's Creek, My Cousin Rachel, The Scapegoat,* and *The Flight of the Falcon.* (p. 12)

Central to the du Maurier tradition are sound, exciting, workable plots: an orphan seeks refuge in her aunt's home only to find it the center of a smuggling ring; a young wife lives under the shadow of her predecessor and of her husband's secret; a noblewoman abandons family responsibilities to become lover and cohort of a pirate; a youth falls in love with a distant relative who is not only his beloved cousin's widow but also a suspected poisoner; an Englishman exchanges identities with a Frenchman and lives his double's life for a time; and an aimless young man finds his long-lost brother who is engaged in what may be a diabolical scheme. All of these basic plots are thrilling, all allow for abundant complication and all offer good possibilities for quick pace and great suspense.

Though even so swift a summary of the plots reveals variety, there are elements of commonality shared by all six titles under discussion here. For critics, that commonality has sometimes been dismissed as "formula fiction," and this term (often perceived as demeaning) has contributed to some misapprehension of the skill with which the author combines formulaic elements with experiments in established literary forms, especially variations of the *Bildungsroman,* to create the freshness and innovation which account for so much of her appeal. Indeed, the many, many modern gothics which echo *Rebecca* are good evidence that du Maurier tends to set trends rather than to follow them.

Certainly, it is no disgrace either to establish or to follow a popular, even beloved, literary formula. Du Maurier has done both; she tends to capitalize on some very old, established patterns (some reaching back into folk literature)—the worried, self-conscious second wife, the dangerous dark-haired beauty, the ineffectual male seeking self-definition and

power, the dark, mysterious male—and bend them to her will and to her skill. (pp. 12-13)

The cultural images and symbols du Maurier employs in her romantic adventures are very closely allied with the cultural myths or themes which she explores. *Rebecca,* for instance, opens with one of English fiction's most famous lines, "Last night I dreamt I went to Manderley again." Manderley, the named house which has become so indispensable to modern gothic fiction, is a very important socio-cultural symbol in the novel, for it represents all the pleasures, perquisites, comfort and standing of the powerful upper class to which Maxim de Winter belongs. Manderley is Maxim's heritage both in fact and in symbol and he will do almost anything to protect it.

Similarly yet differently, Jamaica Inn is the central socio-cultural symbol of the novel named after it. Normally, an inn represents a safe harbor for the weary traveler. Jamaica Inn, however, is an ironic symbol: there, plans for theft and bloodshed are laid; there, the spoils of shipwreckers (criminals of the lowest class) are stored. Not only the seat of criminal activity, the inn is also personally dangerous for Mary Yellan, the young woman who seeks refuge there. The emotional impact of both Manderley and Jamaica Inn is very great, for one represents a form of "the good life" any reader can recognize (and many desire) and the other represents all the false hopes and failed refuges most human beings encounter during the short journey between the cradle and the grave.

The cultural materials du Maurier most frequently employs in her romantic crime fiction also indicate elements of social convention. The British class system conflicting with the concept of upward mobility (for females via marriage; for males by assertion of control over lands and money); the idea that outside marriage a young woman has almost no identity; and the importance of retaining one's good name (no matter what reputation one deserves) are all central to these works. In *Rebecca,* for example, Maxim de Winter resorts to extreme violence to preserve his reputation and it is the consensus among those of his peers privy to his secret that he acted properly in doing so. Mrs. de Winter and Mary Yellan desire upward mobility and believe that marriage is their vehicle to security and status. Philip Ashley, the narrator of *My Cousin Rachel,* genuinely mourns Ambrose, the cousin from whom he inherits a vast estate, yet Philip is aware that as the master of the family holding, he enjoys power and position which would have been unattainable in a secondary or even a shared mastery.

Beyond those socio-cultural images and symbols lie others, even more pervasive and more powerful than those based upon class, property and reputation. Du Maurier also explores universal problems which take on the aura of cultural myth. The difficulty of distinguishing between good and evil and the impossibility of purging certain kinds of guilt are important in almost every story. Mary Yellan nearly falls prey to a very wicked man because she mistakes cultural trappings for his real nature. Armino Donati (*The Flight of the Falcon*) wants to trust his brother's charm, poise, and attractiveness, but he suspects that vicious intent lies beneath Aldo's attractive exterior, and John, the protagonist-narrator of *The Scapegoat,* must learn that even the most crass codes of behavior can generate redemptive action.

Maxim de Winter not only hides his crime successfully but also involves his current wife and others in the concealment; he pays with years of misery, the loss of almost everything he sought to protect, yet guilt remains a constant in his life. Philip Ashley weighs the evidence against Rachel, his beloved, judges her—and lives out his years pondering his own guiltiness. Like Maxim de Winter, he has been both judge and jury; like Maxim, he must forever bear the memory and the weight of his actions.

The universal, mythically proportioned problems lying at the heart of du Maurier's most important novels are, indeed, basic. They are also, however, problems with which most human beings are expected to make their peace fairly early in life. One of the most important lessons learned by the very young is the ability to look behind disguise and to discover the essential decency or corruption of others, and very early on, people generally learn to assuage, ignore, or expiate guilt. Though these lessons may well have to be relearned or modified as maturing individuals confront new problems, people and situations, the groundwork, the basic principles of choice and evaluation, ought to be established during adolescence.

Though the du Maurier characters are no longer teenagers, they are, nevertheless, curiously immature for their years.

Preoccupied by hard work and secluded in a small, friendly community, Mary Yellan has missed the experiences she needs to develop her judgment. Carefully protected, Philip Ashley has depended upon his cousin Ambrose for guidance. Both Armino Donati and John, the surnameless hero of *The Scapegoat,* have simply abdicated responsibility; they refuse to act. Maxim de Winter, seemingly an adult in full control of his powers, is caught in the grip of an obsession, Manderley and all it stands for, and is actually the most immature character of the lot. And Dona St. Columb, protagonist of *Frenchman's Creek,* a wife, mother, noblewoman, is frozen into immaturity, for she has substituted social activity and petulant rebellion for awareness and growth. Thus, these important characters are, for all narrative purposes, youngsters, and in her stories, du Maurier exposes them and many of their fellows to the maturation tests and experiences most commonly found in stories about adolescents. This device adds considerably to the novels' suspense, for it is, in a sense, a plot within a plot. Not only do readers wonder when and if the dangers and courtships will be resolved happily, but they also wonder if the characters will be able to come to terms with the worlds in which they must live. Readers are keenly interested in discovering whether or not the characters will ever resolve the question of who they really are.

This question is also linked to another cultural artifact du Maurier exploits widely. She uses one of the oldest of western European tales, the Cinderella story, in various ways throughout these six novels. Almost mythic itself, it becomes the vehicle for the ethical questions (of good and evil, of guilt) upon which the plot complications turn. Various elements of the Cinderella story appear in each of the novels under discussion here and all of them hinge upon the character's discovery of who he or she really is, the discovery at the heart of Cinderella's adventures. (pp. 13-16)

In du Maurier's romantic suspense novels, as in *Cinderella,* the major question is not detection but justice. It is important that Cinderella's triumph include the public humiliation of her wicked relatives because, in the eyes of many people, public punishment is equated with justice. Because the evils which Cinderella confronts, overt cruelty, jealousy and selfishness, are easy to identify and are subject to social disapproval, the wicked are punished; justice, seemingly, is served.

But the evils which the du Maurier protagonists confront are more complex; simple, obvious punishment is not always meted out. Instead, the irony which colors du Maurier's social commentary also affects her portrayal of justice, for while justice is always imposed, it is often served secretly, privately. To du Maurier, the impact of a crime is of far greater interest than the solution of a puzzle and this interest demands sophisticated modes of punishment.

The crime motif in du Maurier's novels is also enriched by another element of the Cinderella story, the disguise pattern. Frequently, the novels' protagonists appear in disguise; Lady Dona St. Columb, for instance, dresses as a boy when committing piracy. To her bitter dismay, Mrs. de Winter unwittingly disguises herself as Rebecca, her predecessor, for she is tricked into duplicating the costume Rebecca once wore to a fancy-dress ball and this scene lays the groundwork for the revelation of Maxim's crime. These disguises are fascinating and useful plot complications, lending action, adventure, or ironic foreshadowing to the stories.

Even more useful, however, are the disguises worn by the

other characters, and these disguises exacerbate the difficulty of separating evil from goodness, one of the mythic themes which pervades these works. In each of the novels, at least one very powerful personality is examined and explored; these characters are charismatic, mysterious, disguised. Several are not what they seem to be and are unmasked. Frances Davey, the Vicar of Altarnum (*Jamaica Inn*), is not really a devout pastor ministering wholeheartedly to his flock but a dangerous criminal. Maxim de Winter is not a man emotionally crippled by the death of his beloved but rather a man tortured by guilt and the refusal to pay for his crime.

Others among these disguised charismatics are better than they first seem. Jean-Benoit Aubéry, the French pirate, *is* actually a criminal, but he is more decent, caring and nurturing than all the nobles among whom Dona St. Columb has lived. Jem Merlyn (*Jamaica Inn*) who makes no attempt to hide his career as petty criminal and horse thief, is far more honest with Mary Yellan than are the other inhabitants of the Bodmin area.

A third group, most notably Rebecca de Winter and Rachel Sangalletti Ashley, are essentially unknowable—one is never sure just which guise is mask, which reality. The world perceived Rebecca as the epitome of feminine grace and beauty, the perfect mistress for Manderley. To Maxim, her husband, she seemed a corrupt monster. To Mrs. Danvers, the housekeeper, and to Jack Favell, Rebecca's lover and cousin, she appeared to be a free spirit, capable of commanding devotion even from beyond the grave. Though most of the characters choose to believe Maxim's interpretation of Rebecca's character, the puzzle is never resolved. Nor is the mystery surrounding Rachel's character dispelled; she may be tragically accused of and punished for a crime she did not commit, a crime which was, indeed, never committed by anyone, or she may be a grasping poisoner who kills for wealth and position. These characters not only drive forward the action, but they also complicate the process of distinguishing between good and evil, sometimes beyond the capacity of the protagonists (and some readers). Unlike the disguises of the Cinderella figures, these enigmatic masks are meant to be impenetrable.

The disguise motif, then, establishes the most difficult tests the Cinderella figures must pass in order to win better lives. Further, because the enigmatic figures may mislead the protagonists, the element of disguise also strengthens the other fictional pattern du Maurier exploits. The education or maturation novel, the *Bildungsroman* (for which *Cinderella* is one of several important prototypes), is deeply embedded in both "serious" and popular fiction throughout western culture. Itself enormously popular, it is prime material for a writer like du Maurier who seeks a very wide audience.

In the traditional *Bildungsroman,* a young person who has great faith in his own power and potential tests his mettle as a means of initiation into maturity. He often takes a journey, acquires mentors of varying levels of reliability and engages in dangerous adventures. Ultimately, he emerges sadder but wiser, ready to take his place in adult society. He has compromised with the ideal and settled for pragmatism. Du Maurier uses this treatment of the *Bildungsroman,* most commonly found in "high culture" novels, very successfully in both *Jamaica Inn* and *Frenchman's Creek.*

In *Jamaica Inn,* Mary Yellan dreams of security and hopes to find peace and opportunity living with her aunt and uncle at the inn. Instead, she finds danger to her life and honor and a host of false mentors. Among them is her criminal uncle, Joss Merlyn, who presents a sexual threat; he finds Mary attractive and to her dismay, she is somewhat drawn to him. For relief, advice and comfort, Mary turns to a local minister, one of du Maurier's masters of disguise, who does, indeed, advise her but who is actually also a false mentor.

Because of his abusive treatment of her aunt and because of his criminal activity, which she slowly comes to recognize, Mary has little trouble recognizing Joss as an evil person; indeed, he represents the worst that life can offer her: sexual excess, constant danger, shared criminal behavior. Dark, mysterious, violent, Joss symbolizes trouble and degeneration. The Reverend Mr. Davey, however, seems to represent redemption until his mask is finally stripped away during a melodramatic series of events that include an abduction and wild chase over the moors.

Not only does the final unmasking of Davey leave Mary without a functioning mentor, it also forces her to question the basic rules of social convention. She has hoped to establish a very normal, secure life on the Cornish coast, and obviously one means of doing so would have been to marry well, preferably, like most of the Cinderellas, to marry *up*. The revelation of Davey as villain and exploiter removes him from the ranks of potential mates and also, importantly, calls into question the viability of Mary's dreams of security and status.

A poor girl with modest dreams, Mary is barred, finally, from upward mobility by the rules of the class system. Tainted by her low birth, her poverty, her association with criminals (she is even an unwilling spectator and thus marginally a participant in one raid), Mary cannot change her status. She shares in the guilt for this last raid because she was there and because willful blindness as well as circumstance have stopped her from preventing it.

Though Mary has learned not to trust outward appearances, her fate lies, finally, in the hands of yet another masquerader. Jem Merlyn, Joss' younger brother, is an enigmatic man who reveals little of his true emotion, a sexually attractive person who prefers liason (when he can get it) to marriage. Nevertheless he loves Mary and is the only individual who acts effectively to save her from rape or murder. Despite the tensions which exist between them in the early days of their acquaintance, Mary "believes" that she loves Jem, that he is her true mate and she rides off with him, " 'Because I want to: because I must; because now and for ever more this is where I belong to be' ".

The real world for which Mary, chastened and tempered, settles is a marginal world in which she will always hover between poverty and security, social acceptance and rejection, love and danger. Ironist that she is, du Maurier gives no guarantees that for this young woman there will be any "happily ever after." Though Mary is a successful *Bildungsroman* protagonist (she has learned, she has matured, she has compromised), she is a failed Cinderella; the class system prevails and Mary Yellan is frozen into the fringes of accepted society. She has love but little else, and du Maurier refuses to promise that that will be enough.

On the surface of her life, Dona St. Columb is, at the opening of *Frenchman's Creek,* Cinderella leading an enchanted life after the glass slipper has slid smoothly onto her foot. Chronologically an adult, Dona is nevertheless a rebellious child. Disgusted with her dull husband, often irritated by the demands of motherhood, and bored with London life, Dona disguises herself and engages in dangerous, illegal pranks, "playing at" highway robbery, until, restless and annoyed with herself as much as with her world, she runs away to Navron House, the family estate, fleeing both her obligations and her escapades.

There, however, she moves even more deeply into disguise and danger, for she comes to love a French pirate who is raiding the Cornish coast. A kind of nautical Robin Hood, Aubéry, the Frenchman of the title, teaches Dona what love and sexual satisfaction really are, and she revels in the relationship. Initially disguised as chic matron, polished noblewoman, Dona believes she has found her true nature when disguised as a thieving boy or sensual lover and she discovers that she is not only a competent thief but also a clever schemer when she undertakes to save her lover from imprisonment and death. During this period, Navron House continues to stand for the positive qualities of whatever is decent in Dona's public life, everything opposed to the corruption symbolized by London. The nearby creek where the Frenchman moors his ship and *La Mouette* itself symbolize freedom, love, the right to break social codes in order to achieve happiness—everything children imagine that adulthood allows.

Eventually, Dona must choose between life with the Frenchman and life as Lady St. Columb and in the end, social convention and family obligation claim her. For her, life as a constrained, post-ball Cinderella *is* reality whereas life on the fringes of society is dream. Except in memory, she will truly become,

> a gracious matron, and smile upon her servants,
> and her tenants, and the village folk, and one day
> she will have grandchildren about her knee, and
> will tell them the story of a pirate who escaped.

Dona will not live happily ever after, but she will live responsibly.

She, too, has been tempered and chastened and like Mary, she responds, however hesitantly, to the lessons she has learned. If Mary Yellan cannot penetrate respectable levels of English society, no more can Dona St. Columb abdicate the upper classes. These young women come to know themselves very well; they find out precisely who they are, but they are, finally, defined by the social roles assigned by birth. Their very traditional *Bildungsroman* journeys, culminating in compromise and pragmatic acceptance, are complete. (pp. 17-21)

In popular fiction, two variations of the traditional *Bildungsroman* occur frequently and du Maurier experiments with these varieties just as she does with the traditional pattern in **Jamaica Inn** and **Frenchman's Creek.** As feminist critics have pointed out, the modern gothic novel is a form of the *Bildungsroman* whose youthful protagonists, usually females, are, either consciously or unconsciously, engaged in a quest for advancement as well as for adulthood. They want power, selfhood, love and maturity and much of the time, they tend to perceive these desirables as interchangeable if not synonymous.

In a sense, they feel that they will be forever unworthy if they are not loved by some greatly desirable person, but also, secretly or even unconsciously, they feel themselves to be the equal—if not the superior—of most of the characters surrounding them. This conflicting sense of self-worth (obvious in *Cinderella*) is often painful and almost always results in the protagonists' maintaining a kind of public guise of meekness

which hides a fiery, judgmental, or even arrogant personality. Cinderellas, they are not only disguised initially by their lowly positions, but also they actively parade a mask of humility.

The second Mrs. de Winter, the protagonist-narrator of **Rebecca,** is precisely this sort of person and because of the confessional nature of the novel, readers are privy to the seemingly meek, the genuinely humble and the bitingly judgmental elements of her nature from the outset. Though she maintains a quiet, obedient exterior, she denounces thoroughly (and with some good cause) Mrs. Van Hopper, an American of abundant financial means and absolutely no taste, whom she serves as companion. She feels distinctly superior to the Van Hopper world but too inexperienced, uninteresting and plain to be a likely helpmeet of Maxim de Winter. Both attitudes cause her considerable trouble. Ironically, she accepts Mrs. Van Hopper's evaluation of her personality and assumes that to Maxim she is merely a toy, a pet, that she can never truly be his equal. Yet, inwardly, she weeps and rages, for she yearns to be his true companion, to move beyond the shadow of Rebecca and into prominence as the mistress of Manderley, with which she has been entranced since childhood.

Maxim, enigmatic, preoccupied with keeping secret the crime he has committed, withholds a large part of himself from his second wife even though he senses and deplores her unhappiness. In turn, Mrs. de Winter, unaware of Maxim's true thoughts, assumes he is still grieving for Rebecca. Both marriage partners maintain disguises, acting out a "happy" married life, refusing to share, pretending before outsiders and one another.

This Cinderella temporarily acquires both her prince and her castle, but she can genuinely enjoy neither, and when truth does finally prevail between the de Winters, it is too late. The prince, the princess and the marriage survive, but the castle, Manderley, symbol of all the perks of upper-class life, is destroyed. Once again, du Maurier's irony intrudes and the class system prevails. Mrs. de Winter deserves her tainted prince *only if* they are exiled from the social circles to which Maxim was born and to which Mrs. de Winter aspires. Cinderella finds that compromise dominates adulthood and the real world; she acquiesces and endures the consequences of fallen pride. Society has preserved its aura of respectability by protecting Maxim from disclosure of his crime, but nevertheless, it has firmly punished the de Winters. Though this *Bildungsroman* hero has learned her lessons all too well, there is nowhere to use her education.

> We can never go back again, that much is certain.
> The past is still too close to us. The things we have
> tried to forget and put behind us would stir again,
> and that sense of fear, of furtive unrest, struggling
> at length to blind unreasoning panic—now merci-
> fully stilled, thank God—might in some manner
> unforseen become a living companion, as it had
> been before.

Instead, the de Winters drift through Europe, maintaining the social façade, marking time until death releases them. (pp. 22-3)

In traditional adventure-suspense fiction, the protagonist takes a slightly different view of himself than do gothic heroes such as Philip Ashley and Mrs. de Winter. They do not perceive themselves as better than others and they do not yearn for status. Usually, these characters have seen something of life, have become aware of its stresses and pitfalls and, as protection, have disguised themselves as "small," inconsequential persons. Each must stretch his capacity, admit his own potential, abandon insignificance, *expand* in order to meet and conquer some criminal threat. Doing so will signify emergence from a willfully chosen, prolonged adolescence into full maturity. Generally, they pass their exacting tests and emerge stronger, more confident, no longer hiding their capabilities from the world.

Du Maurier's experiments with this variant of the *Bildungsroman*, *The Flight of the Falcon* and *The Scapegoat*, allow their protagonists much more promising futures than do her treatments of the traditional *Bildungsroman* or of the modern gothic, even though the events are just as melodramatic, the assessments of human nature just as uncompromising. Furthermore, in these novels, the questions of guilt and evil are expanded considerably, a fact underscored by the use of non-English settings.

Though matters of social class and its privilege remain important in *The Scapegoat* and are echoed by allusions to earlier times in *The Flight of the Falcon,* these novels are allegories and du Maurier uses St. Gilles, the French village dominated by the de Gué family of *The Scapegoat,* and Ruffano, the Italian university city in which *The Flight of the Falcon* is set, as microcosms. In the first novel, she examines the political and economic impact of one man's criminality, selfishness and arrogance. In the second, she explores the effects of a clever, ambitious man's manipulation of oppressive political systems.

Because du Maurier is chiefly a storyteller and not a philosopher, dramatic action dominates theme in these novels; the political implications are not particularly profound and they are certainly not unique. However, these implications intensify the suspense in both books, just as they later intensify her futuristic political study, *Rule Britannia* (1972) and they continue du Maurier's examination of the conflict between personal ambition and one's duty to others which is the subject of such novels as *I'll Never Be Young Again* (1932) and *The Progress of Julius* (1933), novels outside the boundaries of romantic suspense fiction.

Du Maurier complicates the problems of distinguishing between good and evil and of guilt and emphasizes the allegorical nature of *The Flight of the Falcon* and *The Scapegoat* by using Christian symbolism in both. Crucial action in *The Flight of the Falcon* takes place during Easter Week, for instance, and a priest, a character in *The Scapegoat,* states the theme of both books:

> 'There is no end to the evil in ourselves, just as there is no end to the good. It's a matter of choice. We struggle to climb, or we struggle to fall. The thing is to discover which way we're going'.

Both novels also depict Satanic and Christlike figures who are very much alike: in *The Scapegoat,* the men are identical in appearance and in *The Flight of the Falcon,* they are putative brothers. Further, the Donati brothers share a kind of *Doppelgänger,* the spirit of Claudio, a long-dead Duke of Ruffano, who is depicted as both tempted and tempter in an old painting, "The Temptation of Christ." These devices help du Maurier move beyond questions of personal complicity and individual destiny around which *Rebecca, My Cousin Rachel, Frenchman's Creek* and *Jamaica Inn* center and focus

attention, instead, upon the basic duality of human nature. (pp. 24-6)

An examination of her treatments of the Cinderella story and of her experiments with various forms of the *Bildungsroman,* then, indicate that Daphne du Maurier brings a rich imagination, a sound sense of story line and action, and a great willingness to experiment to her fiction. Though individually the novels considered here—*Jamaica Inn, Frenchman's Creek, Rebecca, My Cousin Rachel, The Flight of the Falcon* and *The Scapegoat*—match Cawelti's definition of formula fiction, together, they demonstrate that any formula—or any literary convention—can be reinvented fruitfully. In the hands of a true storyteller, the old is always new and the "du Maurier Tradition" demands bold inventiveness, intelligence and a special awareness of the roots, artifacts, strengths and weaknesses of the culture from which it springs, toward which it is directed. Du Maurier blends all of these requirements into the heady compounds of the expected and the surprising which are so pleasurable to her readers. In achieving these ends, she surpasses her competitors and her imitators. Others may emulate Daphne du Maurier, but she remains dominant. (pp. 28-9)

Jane S. Bakerman, "Daphne du Maurier," in And Then There Were Nine . . . More Women of Mystery, *edited by Jane S. Bakerman, Bowling Green State University Popular Press, 1985, pp. 12-29.*

BURT A. FOLKART

Dame Daphne du Maurier, who once remarked, "I can't say I really like people, perhaps that's why I always preferred to create my own," died Wednesday [April 19, 1989].

[Du Maurier] died in her sleep at her home in the village of Par, in Cornwall, southwest England. . . . (p. 3)

She had moved to that home—a place called Kilmarth—years ago from Menabilly, the legendary old graystone mansion she had immortalized as Manderley in *Rebecca.*

That home, gutted by Oliver Cromwell's troops during England's civil war in the 1600s, typified the historic and adventurous splendor of Miss Du Maurier's writing.

And the opening words of the gothic *Rebecca* ("Last night I dreamt I went to Manderley again") became one of the best loved phrases in modern English literature.

Through the 29 novels and dozens of short stories she penned in her lifetime ran the melded threads of romance and intrigue.

Taking note of some minor shortcomings he found in *Rebecca,* critic V. S. Pritchett still offered this paean to her talent: "Many a better novelist would give his eyes to be able to tell a story as Miss Du Maurier does, to make it move at such a pace and to go with such mastery from surprise to surprise. . . . The melodrama is excellent."

In an art form often distinguished by economic perfidy, Miss Du Maurier, who in 1969 was made a Dame Commander of the Order of the British Empire by the queen, had been a success since publication of her first novel in 1931—*The Loving Spirit.*

Rebecca alone ran to 42 printings with the last edition in 1980. Her books sold well into the millions. (pp. 3, 24)

Several of her works have been adapted for film and television. *Rebecca,* in which Joan Fontaine played the naive second wife of Sir Laurence Olivier, a widower with a funereal secret who is haunted by the image of his glamorous first wife, won an Academy Award as best picture in 1940. . . .

Alfred Hitchcock directed *Jamaica Inn,* a Cornish tale of an orphan entwined with smugglers in 1939. Hitchcock also did *The Birds* in 1963, a stark tale of flocks of birds making wanton attacks on humans. . . .

Miss Du Maurier for most of her life fought an unsuccessful battle to keep her from being branded a Grand Dame of romance. She chose to call her writings "suspense adventures."

But a fairy-tale, real-life romance had sprung from her first book, contributing to that dilemma and eventually bringing her a husband and three children.

Miss Du Maurier was one of three daughters of the renowned actor Sir Gerald du Maurier. She would one day write his biography.

She had been educated by private tutors in Paris and at age 21 published her first articles and short stories. To encourage her, her publisher told her: "Write a novel." Thus evolved *The Loving Spirit* in 1931, a tale of the lives of a boat-building family she had seen in a small English seacoast town.

The novel captivated a young British army major and led to a storied courtship.

The officer, Frederick A. M. Browning, resolved to meet the author. They met in 1932, married a few months later, and in the same year she published her second novel, *I'll Never Be Young Again.* She was just 25.

"It was rather woman's magaziny," she later remarked.

Regardless, she became both a prolific writer and dedicated mother. . . .

She told a long-ago interviewer that her favorite hideaway at Menabilly was a gardener's hut, where, she said, "I'd sit for hours on end, chain-smoking, chewing mints and tapping away at my typewriter." . . .

In 1971 she published *Not After Midnight,* a collection of five novellas containing her special mix of romance and the eerie.

In 1981 she completed her autobiography, *Growing Pains.*

She admitted that she never was

> so much interested in people as in types—types who represent great forces of good or evil. I don't care very much whether John Smith likes Mary Robinson, goes to bed with Jane Brown and then refuses to pay the hotel bill.
>
> But I am passionately interested in human cruelty, human lust and human avarice, and—of course— their counterparts in the scale of virtue.

(p. 24)

> *Burt A. Folkart, in an obituary in* Los Angeles Times, *April 19, 1989, pp. 3, 24.*

HERBERT MITGANG

> Last night I dreamt I went to Manderley again . . .
> I came upon it suddenly; the approach masked by

the unnatural growth of a vast shrub that spread in all directions . . . There was Manderley, our Manderley, secretive and silent as it had always been, the gray stone shining in the moonlight of my dream, the mullioned windows reflecting the green lawns and terrace. Time could not wreck the perfect symmetry of those walls, nor the site itself, a jewel in the hollow of a hand.

With those famous opening lines of *Rebecca,* written by Miss du Maurier when she was 31, she created one of the classic Gothic romances. It is a story about a young woman who marries a widower and becomes the new mistress of a mansion haunted by the image of his first wife. Trying to solve the mystery, she is drawn into a psychological labyrinth. As the model for Manderley, Miss du Maurier used Menabilly, a 70-room manor on the Cornwall coast. Later, fulfilling a childhood dream, she and her husband moved into the mansion that had served as the setting for her novel. . . .

Long after the novel's international success, Miss du Maurier said she could never understand why it had become an instant favorite that eventually sold over a million hardcover copies. "It is true that I immersed myself in the characters, especially in the narrator, but then this has happened throughout my writing career. I lose myself in the plot as it unfolds." . . .

Once, talking about the technique of her writing genre, she said,

> What is a suspense novel? The term is a loose one, covering any story from a whodunit to a frivolity turning on which dark stranger gets the blonde. People in doubt, people mystified, people groping their way from one situation to another, from childhood to middle age, from joy to sorrow—these are the figures in a true suspense novel. They are traveling along a road of uncertainty toward an unseen goal. The suspense novel succeeds if the reader says to himself at the final page, "Yes—it couldn't happen any other way." In its end, to paraphrase Mary, Queen of Scots, is its beginning.

Miss du Maurier spoke of her writing without pretension, according to her friends. Asked if one of her novels was about "boy meets girl," the author replied, "No, it's ghoul meets goon."

> *Herbert Mitgang, in an obituary in* The New York Times, *April 20, 1989, p. B13.*

THE TIMES, LONDON

Dame Daphne du Maurier, DBE, who died yesterday aged 81 at her home at Par, Cornwall, was for many years one of the most popular novelists in the English-speaking world. Her works became best sellers, it seemed, almost automatically both in this country and in the United States.

Within her limits, she was a most skilful story-teller; she had a natural gift both for the evocation of atmosphere and for the maintenance of suspense; she was never afraid either of the purple passage or of the melodramatic situation; and while her novels might lack conviction when considered retrospectively, in the actual course of reading they commanded the assent of her admirers from chapter to chapter. And there was something else, fundamental to these qualities: she trafficked in dreams, dreams of a kind that seem to be inherent in the unconscious minds of many women, indeed of many men. The roots of her success lay in the almost universal appeal of the fairy tale.

Daphne du Maurier was born on May 13, 1907, the second daughter of the actor-manager, Sir Gerald du Maurier and the grand-daughter of George du Maurier, the *Punch* artist and author of *Peter Ibbetson* and *Trilby.* She was, then, the brilliant representative in the third generation of a brilliant Anglo-French family whose undeniable talents were dedicated to the entertainment of perhaps not severely critical audiences. She was educated privately, and the circumstances of her early life may be gathered from the biography of her father, *Gerald: A Portrait.*

She grew up in circumstances that were almost the stereotype in the popular imagination of great theatrical success, life seen as an endless party conducted with champagne and caviar in London, Paris and the Riviera, revolving round the figure of the charming, feckless, prodigal matinée idol irresistible to women. As *Gerald,* which was published in 1934, shows, Miss du Maurier reacted strongly against the values—or lack of values—implicit in her father's mode of life; and though plainly written in honest affection, the book made painful reading as an exposure, written by one so close to him, of the inner emptiness and spiritual bankruptcy of a considerable artist, who, its author felt, had misused his talents.

Perhaps it was part of this reaction against her upbringing that led Daphne du Maurier to shun London and live in Cornwall.

Her first novel, *The Loving Spirit,* appeared in 1931, to be followed in successive years by *I'll Never Be Young Again* and *The Progress of Julian.* But it was with *Jamaica Inn* (1936) and *Rebecca* (1938) that she captured her vast public. These novels represent the two classes into which her fiction falls, the cloak-and-dagger romance on the one hand and the Gothic novel on the other. *Jamaica Inn, Frenchman's Creek* (1941), *Hungry Hill* (1943) and *Mary Anne* (1954) were exercises in what Robert Louis Stevenson called "tushery", a word Miss du Maurier might not necessarily have disowned. She was a devout Stevensonian and Stevenson was one of her acknowledged masters. She wrote stories of smuggling and piracy, violent action, ladies in distress and romantic love in the Cornwall of the seventeenth and eighteenth centuries; and yet a little more than this alone, for at the heart of them lay a small criticism of the human condition.

Thus, in *Frenchman's Creek,* the daring, dazzling Lady St Columb flees in disgust the coarseness and materialism of Restoration London for Cornwall, there to become, for a brief space before returning to her husband and children, the mistress and comrade of a highborn Breton pirate. The novel was at once a protest against and an acceptance of the lot of being a woman. . . .

As she grew older her talents as a story-teller were increasingly recognized: they had appeared conspicuously in *Mary Anne,* which was based on the life of the author's great-great-grandmother, Mary Anne Clarke, the mistress of George III's son, the Duke of York, and *The Glass-Blowers* (1963), a story of the French Revolution, based again on the lives of her glass-blowing du Maurier ancestors.

As early as 1937 she had published a family history, *The Du Mauriers,* and edited *The Young George du Maurier: A Selection of his Letters 1860-1867. The Infernal World of Branwell Brontë* was a serious contribution to Brontë studies, while *Vanishing Cornwall,* illustrated with photographs taken by her son, Christian, was an eloquent elegy on the past of a county she loved so much.

Besides her novels she published a number of volumes of short stories, *Come Wind, Come Weather* (1941); *Kiss Me Again, Stranger* (1952); *The Breaking Point* (1959); *Not After Midnight* (1971); *The Rendezvous and Other Stories* (1980) and two plays, *The Years Between* (1945) and *September Tide* (1948). Her autobiography, *Growing Pains,* appeared in 1977 and *The Rebecca Notebook and Other Memories* in 1981.

An obituary in The Times, London, *April 20, 1989.*

MARGARET FORSTER

Who could blame Daphne Du Maurier for not wanting her novels to be called "romantic" when that once grand term has become so debased? Yet five years ago when the unfairly mocked Betty Trask Prize was inaugurated "for the best novel of a romantic or traditional nature" and it had to be decided what was meant by a romantic novel, the general consensus of opinion was that there were only two real role models: *Jane Eyre* and, in our own time, *Rebecca.*

No other popular novel of our century has ever had quite the emotional impact of Rebecca and no other popular novelist has so triumphantly defied classification as Daphne Du Maurier. She satisfied all the questionable criteria of popular fiction and yet satisfied too the exacting requirements of "real" literature, something very few novelists ever do. . . .

In her fragment of autobiography, *Growing Pains,* published in 1977, she revealed how unexpectedly difficult it was to find the time and privacy to try to write properly. She was the very opposite of the young writer starving in a garret or struggling at the end of a gruelling day's work to become an author; but it is curious how her privileged way of life proved just as much of a hindrance to what she wanted to do. She was always being sent off to holiday with rich friends in Germany or France, sent on delightful skiing or yachting parties, endlessly pampered and cosseted by parents she adored, but who were, in effect, stifling any talent she had. She went along with the kind of life mapped out for her but kept trying in secret to complete short stories. Even then, hers was not the hard road of repeated rejection. Because the family had literary connections, the moment the ink was dry young Daphne's stories were whisked off to be looked at by an established agent, and then a reputable publisher.

But what started Du Maurier on her real career as a novelist was a trip to Cornwall when she was 20. She was one of those writers in whom the right place releases a certain sort of psychic energy. Hampstead, where she had grown up, was alien to her character whereas Cornwall, with its wild seas and rocky coastline, its mists and moors, answered some deep longing inside her. So did the way of life. In Hampstead she had been ill at ease conducting herself according to the ways of her parents and their circle. In Cornwall, she revelled in the sweaters-and-gumboots clothing, the outdoor life and the lack of either pretension or elegance in those around her. It proved to be her natural home, thrilling and exciting her. The wilder the weather, the more sinister the mist sweeping in from the raging sea, the happier she was.

Jamaica Inn, published in 1936 when she was 29, was Du Maurier's fourth novel (her first was *The Loving Spirit,* 1931), but the first in which she captured the atmosphere of the place she had made her home. On the surface it was a tale of smugglers set in a romanticised past but it had elements too of the psychological thriller, which was to occupy a good deal of her future writing life. What most interested her, even then, was not just the old-fashioned virtue of storytelling, but studying strong human emotions. Jealousy, in particular, fascinated her and in her next novel, *Rebecca* (1938), she set out to plumb the depths of the misery it could cause.

It certainly found an immediate response in readers, especially women readers. Who could not feel for the unnamed heroine, so modest and shy and frightened, and who not thrill to Max De Winter's "I am asking you to marry me, you little fool." When Max tells her he has murdered Rebecca, how perfect was the reply: "My heart is like a feather floating in the air. He has never *loved* Rebecca."

There were 14 novels after *Rebecca,* nearly all bestsellers. Several had the same theme—*My Cousin Rachel* (1951) with its male narrator, was the most successful—but none had quite the same sense of timing and menace. After *Rule Britannia,* her least successful novel, Du Maurier turned increasingly to biography. The last book she wrote (not counting the *Rebecca* notebook) was her autobiography *Growing Pains,* subtitled The Shaping of a Writer. This took her up to 1932 when she married Lieutenant General Sir Frederick ("Boy") Browning, then a major in the British army. It was a marriage straight from one of her own novels. They married at Lanteglos Church at Fowey, then loaded stores onto Yggy, their boat, and set off for the harbour mouth and the open sea.

What happened next she never went on to record. There was no second volume of autobiography. But the marriage, from which there were two daughters and a son, seems to have been very happy and fulfilling. . . .

Du Maurier was made a dame in 1969, which would indicate her worth had been recognized; but I doubt that it has. In the encyclopaedic tomes listing 20th century novelists, she receives little attention. Yet *Rebecca* was a seminal work for the post-war generation, just as *Jane Eyre* was for the mid-Victorians, and it has had as many imitators. Even more significant, the films made by Alfred Hitchcock, of Rebecca and later of **"The Birds"**, one of Du Maurier's short stories, showed how scarifying effects could be underpinned by a psychological strength in the text: the written word was not to be despised by film-makers concentrating on visual images.

Nor is Du Maurier to be despised just because she was a repeated bestseller. If all our popular bestsellers were of her excellence then there would be no need to deplore their existence, and the silly snobbery existing between "pulp" fiction and literary fiction would vanish.

> Margaret Forster, *"Queen of Menacing Romance,"* *in* The Sunday Times, *London, April 23, 1989, p. G8.*

SARAH BOOTH CONROY

For half a century or so, Dame *Daphne du Maurier,* who died last week at 81, led enchanted readers into a dream world, endowing them with fantastic abilities to become spectators/spectators in strange lives, and for the space of her tales, to dwell in wonderfully wayward places.

Eagerly, insatiably, hundreds of thousands of us followed her down the drive to Rebecca's Manderley, *Frenchman's Creek, The House on the Strand, Jamaica Inn* and other elusive spaces in 13 bestselling novels, many short stories and seven classic movies.

Not all her novels were ghost stories or dreams told before breakfast. But they all traded on universal fears that good fortune can be too good to be true, and that disaster lurks in the best of luck. She has been called a writer of romance, but she herself preferred to be thought of as the author of suspense and mystery.

Undeniably, she was a storyteller, in the mythic tradition of tales told round the fire that's been set to confound the demons, while outside thunder blasts and lighting strikes. They have the quality of *dejà vu,* legends half remembered, old wives' tales and episodes from epics, with the inevitable but always shocking "Boo" at the end.

I, and many of my ilk, could hardly be prevented from reading her works out loud. Her words have such a rhythm, a singsong, that they echo in your head, coming back in odd moments.

The beginning of *Rebecca* seems to me to be one of the three or four best opening sentences I have read. (pp. F1, F8)

But Dame Daphne wrote rather than spoke her stories, because she herself was painfully shy, almost a recluse, preferring to live in her imagination in stately mansions on the edge of the sea, the abyss, the jumping-off place. She was fortunate in her life as a writer, for her books from the first, *The Loving Spirit,* published when she was 24, enabled her to live as she pleased.

She was a natural daughter to the Brontës, to Poe, to Wilkie Collins. Her characters seemed ectoplasmic, elusive, capable of stepping back into the mist of her beloved Cornwall, just when you thought they were within grasp.

Her women characters often belonged to centuries long past, in fact or temperament. In *Rebecca,* for instance, the narrator, an unnamed "I," is a traditional romantic heroine—a young, naive, self-effacing poor woman of gentle birth. When in my late teens I read *Rebecca,* I could well understand (as other young women before and after me) her feelings of awkward inadequacy, especially in the presence of a more experienced, desirable man; she can hardly believe that her wealthy husband, with his magnificent coastal country house, can love "who, little me?" His dead first wife, Rebecca, is presented as a paragon of sophistication, a worldly hostess, in the '30s prewar manner, everything the young woman is not. . . .

My favorite of her characters, and to me the most real, is Manderley, the house she describes so well in *Rebecca:*

> I can see the great stone hall, the wide doors open to the library, the Peter Lelys and the Vandykes on the walls, the exquisite staircase leading to the minstrels' gallery . . . he bore me off to the library. It was a deep, comfortable room, with books lining the walls to the ceiling, the sort of room a man would move from never, did he live alone; solid chairs behind a great open fireplace, baskets for the dogs in which I felt they never sat, for the hollows

in the chairs had tell-tale marks. The long windows
looked out upon the lawns, and beyond the lawns
to the distant shimmer of the sea.

The fact that Manderley actually exists, a Cornish house really named Menabilly, I find comforting. And it pleases me no
end that if life is so cruel as not to bestow this house of my
dreams on me, Dame Daphne did enjoy its possession (or
more likely it possessed her) for a quarter of a century. She
wrote her books in its gardener's hut, sailed from its beach,
and gardened in its lush flower beds. And after its owners
made her give it back, she rented another fine house, Kilmarth in Par, also in Cornwall.

Her last book, in 1981, was an autobiography, **Growing
Pains.** In recent years, like one of her apparitions, she had
faded slowly from life, or, perhaps, gracefully wafted down
that road into another, from which no traveler returns.

Wednesday, peacefully in her dreams, she passed fully into
that supernatural sphere, which she had glimpsed and given
us glimmers of. I long for her to find ways to send more tales
from the beyond, where I'm sure she lives in more "more
stately mansions, Oh my soul." (p. F8)

> *Sarah Booth Conroy, "Daphne du Maurier's Legacy
> of Dreams," in* The Washington Post, *April 23,
> 1989, pp. F1, F8.*

Mary McCarthy
June 21, 1912 - October 25, 1989

Born Mary Therese McCarthy. American novelist, critic, short story writer, essayist, journalist, and nonfiction writer.

For an overview of McCarthy's life and work see *CLC,* Vols. 1, 3, 5, 14, 24, 39; *Contemporary Authors,* Vols. 5-8, rev. ed.; *Contemporary Authors New Revision Series,* Vol. 16; *Dictionary of Literary Biography,* Vol. 2; and *Dictionary of Literary Biography Yearbook: 1981.*

BURT A. FOLKART

Mary McCarthy, a novelist and essayist who battled the intellectual elite and questioned the value of history and even the worth of the novel itself, died Wednesday.

The author of **The Company She Keeps, Cast a Cold Eye, The Oasis** and **The Group**—probably her best known work—was 77. She died at New York Hospital in New York City. (p. 3)

With a steely pen and sharp tongue, Miss McCarthy touched a multitude of subjects in a career that began shortly after she was a Vassar student in the early 1930s.

There she had hoped to pursue a career in the theater but soon discovered she had no acting talent. She chose to write instead, and began reviewing books for the *Nation* and the *New Republic.*

Even then her willingness to do battle was apparent as she became co-editor of a critical book about book critics.

In a McCarthy biography, Doris Grumbach wrote that the McCarthy signature was to "attack in every direction, without concern for the barriers of established reputation."

Over the years she turned out nine volumes of fiction and two classic books about the art and history of Venice and Florence, compiled reports from Saigon and Hanoi into two books and wrote of the trial of Capt. Ernest Medina, who ordered the destruction of My Lai in Vietnam.

After visiting Vietnam, she opined that "the worst thing that could happen to our country would be to win this war."

She also produced works on Watergate, collected her essays on literature and theatrical criticism into several books and turned out memoirs and autobiographies.

She wrote about subjects as diverse as the pretentious world of academia (**A Charmed Life**) and terrorists (**Cannibals and Missionaries**).

Her acidity touched four generations, including the current

one. When asked in an interview for *Contemporary Authors* whether the women's movement had produced any distinguished writing, she answered simply "no."

Although sometimes critical of Miss McCarthy for not stretching her own creative abilities further, Norman Mailer once called her "our first lady of letters."

Wrote Alfred Kazin, a chronicler of New York's Jazz Age intellectuals, Miss McCarthy had an "unerring ability to spot the hidden weakness or inconsistency in any literary effort and every person. To this weakness she instinctively leaped with cries of pleasure—surprised that her victim, as he lay torn and bleeding, did not applaud her perspicacity."

Although she first made her mark among the brawling New York intellectuals of the 1930s, she managed to reach a wider audience only in 1963 with her novel **The Group.**

The spicy best-selling chronicle of the lives of eight college graduates starting out in the 1930s was made into a movie in 1966 starring Candice Bergen, Joanna Pettet and Hal Holbrook.

More recently she touched a new generation in a celebrated literary feud with Lillian Hellman by declaring, on national television, "Everything she [Hellman] writes is a lie, including 'and' and 'the.' "

Hellman sued for libel, but died in 1984 before the suit reached the trial which Miss McCarthy had eagerly sought.

Most of her writing was autobiographical, beginning with *The Company She Keeps,* published in 1942, a series of inter-connected short stories about the people she knew in New York during the Depression.

Memories of a Catholic Girlhood, published in 1957 and now considered a landmark in autobiographical writing, recount-ed her sordid childhood in Minneapolis, where she was bru-tally mistreated by relatives after her parents died.

Miss McCarthy was born the daughter of Roy Winfield McCarthy and Therese Preston McCarthy, who died within a day of each other during the flu epidemic of 1918.

Mary . . . and three younger brothers were entrusted to the care of Aunt Margaret and Uncle Meyers, whom their ward later described as sadistic and miserly guardians who dressed the children like paupers, fed them a diet of root vegetables, forbade reading and, at night, taped their mouths shut "to prevent mouth breathing."

How I Grew, published in 1987 as a sequel to *Memories,* de-scribed her rescue at 11 by her maternal grandparents, who took her west to Tacoma, Wash., and enrolled her in the fash-ionable Annie Wright Seminary. The seminary, where the contrary student embraced atheism, prepared her for Vassar, where she hobnobbed with the bright, wealthy Eastern soci-ety girls she used as models for her characters in *The Group.* (pp. 3, 36)

Miss McCarthy was often hailed as a feminist before her time. But she always refused that label, saying equality be-tween the sexes was unrealistic.

"Somebody has to give more," she told an interviewer in 1987. Her belief was simple: women should learn to think for themselves and act accordingly.

Among the dozens of awards she won were the prestigious Edward MacDowell Medal and the National Medal for Lit-erature. In May, she was inducted into the American Acade-my of Arts and Letters.

Irving Stock, in *Fiction and Wisdom,* wrote that "though Mary McCarthy's novels are not all equally successful, each has so much life and truth . . . that it becomes a matter for wonder that she is not generally named among the finest American novelists of her period."

Less sanguine was the author herself.

In 1987, at age 74 on the eve of the publication of *How I Grew,* she proved she could be as cold and hard on herself as she was of others.

Asked for a self-assessment, she replied: "Not favorable." (p. 36)

Burt A. Folkart, in an obituary in Los Angeles Times, *October 26, 1989, pp. 3, 36.*

MICHIKO KAKUTANI

Mary McCarthy, one of America's pre-eminent women of letters, died of cancer yesterday [Wednesday, October 25, 1989] at New York Hospital. She was 77 years old and lived in Castine, Me., and Paris.

In her long and prolific career as a novelist, memoirist, jour-nalist and critic, Miss McCarthy earned recognition for her cool, analytic intelligence and her exacting literary voice—a voice capable of moving from the frivolously feminine to the willfully cerebral, from girlish insouciance to bare-knuckled fury.

In 1984, she was awarded both the Edward MacDowell Medal for outstanding contributions to literature and the Na-tional Medal for Literature.

"If there were any real ancestor among American women for Mary McCarthy it might be Margaret Fuller," the critic Eliz-abeth Hardwick, a friend, once observed, referring to the 19th-century American editor, essayist, poet, teacher and translator. "Both women have will power, confidence and a subversive soul sustained by exceptional energy."

Miss McCarthy's accounts of sexual shenanigans in *The Man in the Brooks Brothers Shirt* in 1941 and *The Group* in 1963 created something of an uproar when they first appeared. But her notoriety in literary circles stemmed less from the scandal quotient of her fiction than from her adversarial literary and political stands. She had celebrated public skirmishes with Philip Rahv, Diana Trilling and Lillian Hellman; issued vitri-olic pronouncements on Watergate and the Vietnam War, and became known for the ferocity of her book and theater reviews.

At their worst, those reviews pointed up Miss McCarthy's weakness for catchy one-liners and her taste for willfully per-verse opinions. Of Tennessee Williams's *Streetcar Named De-sire* she wrote, "His work reeks of literary ambition as the apartment reeks of cheap perfume," and of Eugene O'Neill and *The Iceman Cometh* she declared, "He is probably the only man in the world who is still laughing at the Iceman joke or pondering its implications."

Yet at her best (as in *The Stones of Florence*) Miss McCarthy was an erudite cultural historian, using her familiarity with history, politics and the arts—and the application of some plain old-fashioned common sense—to draw surprising con-nections and to make her readers reconsider their preconcep-tions.

"A career of candor and dissent is not an easy one for a woman; the license is jarring and the dare often forbidding." Ms. Hardwick said, "Such a person needs more than confi-dence and indignation. A great measure of personal attrac-tiveness and a high degree of romantic singularity are neces-sary to step free of the mundane, the governessy, the threat of earnestness and dryness. Moderating influences are essen-tial."

In the case of Miss McCarthy, she said, "the purity of style and the liniment of her wit, her gay summoning of the funny facts of everyday life, soften the scandal of the action or the courage of the opinion."

To Robert Lowell, Miss McCarthy was "our Diana, rash to awkwardness, " blurting "ice clear" sentences above the "mundane gossip and still more mundane virtue" of her colleagues. To Alfred Kazin, she was the owner of "a wholly destructive critical mind," a critic with an "unerring ability to spot the hidden weakness or inconsistency in any literary effort and every person." And to Norman Mailer, she was "our First Lady of Letters"—"our saint, our umpire, our lit arbiter, our broadsword, our Barrymore (Ethel), our Dame (dowager), our mistress (Head), our Joan of Arc."

The most tireless mythologizer of her life, however, remained Miss McCarthy herself. There were her memoirs: *Memories of a Catholic Girlhood* (1957), the beautifully observed portrait of her painful youth, and the later, more workmanlike *How I Grew,* published in 1987. In addition, the heroines in Miss McCarthy's fiction form a sort of continuing portrait of the author: Meg in *The Company She Keeps* (1942), the clever Vassar girl, "a princess among the trolls"; Martha, "the bohemian lady" in *A Charmed Life* (1955), whose need to "tell the truth" continually gets her into trouble; Kay, the skeptical iconoclast in *The Group* (1963), and Rosamund, the esthetic mother figure in *Birds of America* (1971).

These novels also included sharp-edged portraits of many of Miss McCarthy's friends and lovers: her second husband, the critic Edmund Wilson, was portrayed as a loud, unappealing intellectual in *A Charmed Life;* and Rahv, her roommate and mentor as editor of *The Partisan Review,* turned up in *The Oasis* (1949).

Yet if Miss McCarthy's novels often read like thinly disguised exercises in autobiography, they also attempted to provide an idiosyncratic chronicle of American life—at least within her own intellectual set—as it changed over some five decades. Sexual freedom in the 1930's, radicalism in the 40's and 50's, Vietnam and the social upheavals of the 60's, Watergate and terrorism in the 70's—these are the larger issues that flicker in the background of the novels.

There is a certain didacticism to these books, a feeling of willed creation, and Miss McCarthy herself acknowledged that she found it considerably more difficult to write fiction than essays or reviews.

Throughout her career, Miss McCarthy seemed preoccupied with two themes: what she called "the idea of justice" and the idea of self-reliance. Both impulses originated in her painful childhood, and both, in a sense, led to her later attempts to invent an identity true to her platonic conception of herself.

Mary Therese McCarthy was born on June 21, 1912, in Seattle, the daughter of Roy Winfield McCarthy, a member of a prominent Roman Catholic family in Minneapolis, and the former Therese Preston, whose father, a transplanted New Englander, was one of Seattle's most successful lawyers. She had three brothers, Kevin, Preston and Sheridan.

The early years of Miss McCarthy's life seem to have been a romantic idyll; she would later portray them as a lovely succession of parties and holidays, with May baskets and valentines.

[Her parents] died in the great flu epidemic of 1918, and the 6-year-old Mary and her three brothers were sent to live with their great-aunt Margaret and her husband in Minneapolis. There, they experienced what she once called "circumstances of almost Dickensian cruelty and squalor." The children were made to stand outdoors for three hours at a time in the snow, and they were regularly thrashed with a razor strop;

Miss McCarthy recalled being beaten in one instance for receiving a school prize, lest she become "stuck up."

When she was 11, Miss McCarthy was rescued from her misery in Minneapolis by her maternal grandfather, Harold Preston, who took her to Seattle and gave her a fine education at the Forest Ridge Convent and the Annie Wright Seminary.

As *Memories of a Catholic Girlhood* and *How I Grew* indicate, the twists and turns of Miss McCarthy's melodramatic childhood would develop two distinct sides to her personality: on one hand, the puritanical student who wants to win prizes for her scholarship and dreams of becoming a nun; on the other, the die-hard romantic who writes moody stories about suicide and prostitution and dreams of becoming an actress. In fact, before she left for college in 1929, Miss McCarthy took some acting classes at the Cornish Drama School in Seattle, where she met the actor Harold Cooper Johnsrud, whom she married a week after her graduation from Vassar. She would divorce him three years later.

By the time Miss McCarthy left Vassar in 1933, she said, she had become "a wayward modern girl," determined, in the words of her colleague William Barrett, "to hold her own with men—both intellectually and sexually." Her finely observed collection of interconnected stories, *The Company She Keeps,* would chronicle—in slightly disguised fashion— many of her adventures in these early post-college years, including the breakup of her first marriage, her desultory love affairs and her dabbling in Trotskyite politics.

Writing of that time, Mr. Barrett described the girlishly pretty writer as "a Valkyrie maiden, riding her steed into the circle, amid thunder and lightning, and out again, bearing the body of some dead hero across her saddle."

Two influential men of letters, Rahv and Wilson, would play important roles in the shaping of Miss McCarthy's career. Rahv, with whom she lived during the 1930's, helped her to get her first literary job—writing theater reviews for the magazine; Wilson, whom she married in 1938, persuaded her to try writing fiction. He put her in a room, she recalled, and told her to stay there until she finished a story. Their tempestuous marriage produced one son, Reuel, and ended in divorce in 1946. Later that year she married Bowden Broadwater, a writer and teacher.

With a clinical eye and an apparently total gift for recall, Miss McCarthy used her satiric wit to illuminate the pretensions and prejudices of her fellow intellectuals. Much of her writing was devoted to exposing what she regarded as the ignorance, bigotry, dishonest sentimentality and affectation that cluttered the intellectual marketplace.

She defended Hannah Arendt and William Burroughs when it was fashionable to assail them, and attacked J. D. Salinger, Kenneth Tynan and Arthur Miller when others were singing their praises.

The litigious Lillian Hellman was so incensed, in 1980, by Miss McCarthy's description of her in a television interview as a "dishonest writer" that she instituted a $2.25 million defamation suit.

Hellman's death in 1984 placed the lawsuit in limbo, making Miss McCarthy feel somewhat put out. "I still feel disgusted by the amount of lying that didn't stop," she said in an interview in 1987. "I wanted it to go to trial, so I was disappointed when she died."

Miss McCarthy married James Raymond West, a former director of information for the Organization for Economic Cooperation and Development, in 1961. They divided their time between an apartment in Paris and their house in Maine.

In recent years, Miss McCarthy had several operations for hydrocephalus (water on the brain), but maintained a hectic schedule, working on another volume of memoirs, contemplating a study of Gothic architecture, teaching literature at Bard College and learning German. She recalled telling a friend some two decades ago that she "never woke up in the morning without a feeling of intense repentance and a resolve to be better."

"I don't do that anymore—or almost never," she said in a recent interview. "But I do have this idea of improvement, if not in one's powers, at least in one's vision, in one's understanding. I suppose it's all tied up with the American belief in progress. Not that I have that as an idea, but I certainly have it in my personal life. I couldn't live without feeling I know more than I did yesterday."

Michiko Kakutani, in an obituary in The New York Times, *October 26, 1989, pp. A1, B10.*

THE NEW YORK TIMES

In the 1930's, New York boasted something very like a European literary subculture. Its house organ was *The Partisan Review;* its luminaries included Philip Rahv, Dwight Macdonald and the two Trillings, Lionel and Diana. But its most vivid presence was Mary McCarthy, who came to be known, half in awe, as the Dark Lady of American letters.

Miss McCarthy, who died Wednesday at 77, wrote unflinchingly about affairs public and private, in a mode captured by one of her book titles, **On the Contrary.** Her value to readers was her refusal to be fazed by tradition and authority. She walked her own path, courting the dismay of friends, officials, Vassar classmates and former spouses, among them Edmund Wilson.

It was this prickliness that gave her writing its savor. She was the privileged relation, with a license to utter unwelcome opinions; her loss is like a death in the family. Anyone who asked her opinion risked getting it, unvarnished, sometimes with litigious results.

When **The Group,** her novel inspired by her classmates, became a best seller in 1963, she was feted, if nervously, by the Vassar Club in Washington. All went smoothly until she was asked what college she would recommend to a bright young daughter. "Radcliffe," said Miss McCarthy, with her disarming, contrarian smile.

"The Contrarian," in The New York Times, *October 27, 1989, p. A34.*

MARTIN SEYMOUR-SMITH

Mary McCarthy, who died in New York on Wednesday at the age of 77, will probably be best remembered in [Great Britain] as the author of **The Group** (1963), a lively, vivid and exceedingly entertaining novel tracing the careers of eight girls, undergraduates together at Vassar, Class of '33, from the time of their graduation until the end of the decade. It was, and deserved to be, a runaway bestseller, in America,

Great Britain and Europe, and was filmed by Sidney Lumet—a little disappointingly—in 1966.

But McCarthy was not taken as seriously, as an American novelist, as she might have wished, or even as her beginnings had promised. At that high level her two best books would probably be reckoned to be the autobiography of her very difficult childhood, **Memoirs of a Catholic Girlhood** (1957), and the long story **The Oasis** (1949), first published in London in book form as **A Source of Embarrassment** (1950).

In this country, the zenith of critical esteem for her work was not in fact reached with **The Group,** but with the devotion of an entire issue of Cyril Connolly's *Horizon* to **The Oasis.** Connolly wrote that she derived "from the world of Congreve and Constant, of Elizabeth Bowen or Compton-Burnett or the Cambridge world of Virginia Woolf". Although this was justifiable praise in terms of the promise she showed, McCarthy was not destined to achieve as much as any of the writers Connolly named.

She was a formidable personality, of ferocious intelligence, who eventually became more a highly professional bitch than a charmer. In the polite 1930s, nervous professors would speak up for her by praising her candour about her sexual exploits.

In **Memoirs of a Catholic Girlhood,** her most serious and deeply felt book, McCarthy describes how both her parents died in the influenza epidemic of 1918, leaving her and three younger brothers in the custody of a "severe great-aunt and her sadistic husband." Some critics felt (and said) that her life thereafter could only be explained by a desire for revenge on both these unpleasant people. But the pungent intelligence of the book partly answers this—and it will always appeal to Catholics and lapsed Catholics as essentially true.

Educated at a convent in her native Seattle and at Vassar, she soon attracted attention: at college, by her participation in the publication, with contemporaries of the calibre of Elizabeth Bishop, of an anonymous magazine, *Con Spirito;* then with articles in the *Nation,* violently attacking reviewing standards of the *New York Times* and other newspapers regarded as above reproach. She became well known as an anti-Stalinist and Trotskyite contributor to *Partisan Review,* then as an opponent of American entry into the second world war. . . .

Mary McCarthy wrote a good deal of criticism and travel journalism, most of it too intelligent to be trivial, although **Venice Observed** (1956) and **The Stones of Florence** (1959), both coffee-table books, came under attack for their gushing pretentiousness—notably from (of all people) Ian Fleming. She was seldom less than readable, and her criticism—**Ideas And the Novel** (1980) is her best example—was stimulating, if never entirely convincing.

Brilliant is the word that comes readily to mind in connection with Mary McCarthy. She could be very funny. But, as was so often charged, she was more interested in ideas than in people; and she displayed little emotional robustness. She had nothing to offer as a substitute for the horrors—of a world of people regarding other people simply as objects—which she so cleverly depicted. But a few of her books will last, if only because they are so brightly observant and shrewd. Her head almost always triumphed over her heart; but it was a deservedly famous victory.

Martin Seymour-Smith, "A Class Chronicler," in The Sunday Times, London, October 29, 1989, p. G7.

CATHLEEN McGUIGAN

Shortly before publishing her notorious best-selling novel about Vassar girls, **The Group,** in 1963, Mary McCarthy told the Paris Review that she'd grown bored with the "quest for the self." "What you feel when you're older is that you really must *make* the self," she said. "You finally begin . . . to make and choose the self you want." When she died of cancer last week at 77, McCarthy had not only written some of the most pungent criticism of her time—as well as journalism, cultural history, fiction and memoirs—she'd also created a legendary persona: moralistic, biting, satiric. As queen of the American literary scene, she was as famous for her feuds—notably with Lillian Hellman—and her love affairs as she was for the piercing intelligence and savage wit of her prose. . . .

Her first novel, **The Company She Keeps** (1942), was scandalous in its day for its description of a seduction aboard a Pullman car. The book was autobiographical, and at moments she skewered the heroine—herself—as mercilessly as she would any enemy, for her pretensions and insecurities. Fiction or not, McCarthy's writings reflected her politics, from her anti-Stalinism in the '30s through her essays about the Vietnam War and Watergate. In a cynical age, she asked moral questions—and she was unforgiving to those who sank below her standards for truth and impeccably reasoned discourse.

No one felt neutral toward her. She possessed "a wholly destructive critical mind," said Alfred Kazin, while Elizabeth Hardwick maintained that "the purity of her style and the liniment of her wit . . . soften the scandal of the action or the courage of the opinion." Lillian Hellman sued her for $2.25 million after McCarthy said on the Dick Cavett show that "every word [Hellman] writes is a lie, including 'and' and 'the'." McCarthy charged that the playwright exaggerated her self-described heroism during McCarthy-era witch hunts. Hellman died before the suit was settled.

Though McCarthy relished a fight, she had a soft side. As a child, she'd dreamed of becoming a nun—or an actress. She'd been a beauty, and the toughmindedness hid a girlish streak of romance. She recalled going to a Trotskyite meeting one February day in the '30s and thinking, "I'm the only person in this room who realizes that it's Valentine's Day!" In her fourth marriage, to ex-diplomat James West, McCarthy found happiness. The couple split their time between Paris and Maine. "Everyone needs the good, hankers for it, as Plato says, because of the lack of it in the self," she wrote. "This greatly craved goodness is meaning, which is . . . incommensurable with reason."

Cathleen McGuigan, "The Company She Kept," in Newsweek, Vol. CXIV, No. 19, November 6, 1989, p. 91.

MARTHA DUFFY

She always thought of herself as old-fashioned. Throughout her enormously industrious 50-year literary career, she plinked away on a manual typewriter, spurned electrical kitchen gadgetry and never took out a credit card. But Mary McCarthy was incorrigibly modern and, in spite of herself, a celebrated pioneer to generations of young women.

She opened the way by ignoring the constraints—and prerogatives—of gender. She emerged from Vassar ('33) a handsome girl with an open Irish face, natural style and a gleeful grin, and she entered the fierce leftist circles in New York City. It was a largely male world, but McCarthy was too smart and too fearless not to make her mark, mostly in articles and criticism in Partisan Review. When challenging the moral underpinnings of political debates—then it was the split between Stalinists and Trotskyites (she was one of the latter); later it would be Viet Nam and Watergate—she could be a scourge. Her wit, like a swift breeze, blew the hats off countless swelled heads, and most of the pedestals she set askew supported men.

When she started writing fiction in 1942, she was equally forthright about sex, especially the consequences of it for a woman. Her novels contain rakingly funny scenes about drunken late-night encounters and the scarlet flush of embarrassment that starts at the nape of the neck the morning after. **A Charmed Life** (1955) traced a wife's exacting moral dilemma over an abortion. McCarthy claimed for serious fiction the terrain of a woman's domestic strategies, her finances, her female friendships, her minute biological concerns. Every syllabus on feminist literature is indebted to her. . . .

Her most eloquent book, **Memories of a Catholic Girlhood** (1957), recounted her own story. Born in Seattle, she spent six idyllic years in a buoyant, prosperous family. But the flu epidemic of 1918 claimed both her parents, and she and her three brothers (including the actor Kevin McCarthy) were shunted off to miserable privation with a grandaunt and granduncle. Eventually, Mary was rescued by grandparents, who educated her in convent schools. She was to have four marriages, including a stormy eight years with critic Edmund Wilson. . . .

Her most autumnal public moment came in a speech at the MacDowell Colony five years ago. "We all live our lives more or less in vain," she said. "The fact of having a small *name* should not make us hope to be exceptions, to count for something or other." For once, this piercing observer and tough social critic was wrong. She was emphatically an exception, and she counted.

Martha Duffy, "She Knew What She Wanted," in Time, New York, Vol. 134, No. 19, November 6, 1989, p. 87.

JENNIFER DUNNING

Friends, relatives and colleagues of Mary McCarthy gathered at the Pierpont Morgan Library yesterday afternoon to celebrate the novelist, critic and essayist, who died of cancer last month in New York at the age of 77.

Inside the wood-paneled library auditorium, about 200 people at the hour-long memorial service listened to recollections of the writer and readings from her work. The historian Arthur Schlesinger Jr. spoke of Miss McCarthy's "absolute fidelity to her own exacting standards," recalling his chagrin at her judging a portentous piece of his early writing as "pre-Raphaelite." She was, he added, "a sublime mix of astringency and tenderness."

"She always made up with her 'sitters,'" recalled the critic

Elizabeth Hardwick, referring to the friends about whom Miss McCarthy wrote in her novels, who would invariably "become the object of Mary's intense friendship" after publication. "Oh," Miss Hardwick said she frequently found herself thinking, "we'll have to have dinner with them for the rest of our lives because Mary made fun of them in her book."

For Miss Hardwick, Miss McCarthy's work was "cheerful, light-hearted and oddly optimistic." Filled with "romantic expectation of persons and the nation," the work recalled "the deflating optimism of Mark Twain," she said.

Jennifer Dunning, in an obituary in The New York Times, *November 9, 1989, p. D27.*

ARTHUR SCHLESINGER, JR.

[*The remarks excerpted below were originally presented at the memorial service for Mary McCarthy, held on November 8, 1989 at the Pierpont Morgan Library in New York City.*]

I first met Mary McCarthy nearly half a century ago—in the winter of 1940 at dinner at Harry Levin's in Cambridge. She was married to Edmund Wilson. I can remember still how transfixed I was by Mary—so beautiful, so intelligent, so witty, so much fun to talk to, her smile so lustrous and penetrating. (p. 14)

I fell in love with Mary on that winter night; and, when I saw her in recent weeks in the intensive care ward at New York Hospital, embraced by the awful technology of modern medicine, she appeared, for all the tangle of tubes and wires, somehow youthful again, almost as beautiful as when we first met so many years ago. But then she never lost her youthfulness—in the sense of endless delight in the oddities of life, endless curiosity about people and ideas and human predicaments, endless interest in the way things worked, endless passion to learn new things, endless anger over hypocrisy and mendacity and cruelty. Mary never grew old.

Memories crowd in—Mary in New York, in Newport, in Wellfleet, in London, in the charming Paris apartment in the Rue de Rennes, in the lovely house in Castine. One summer in the early 1950s in Wellfleet I used every morning to go over to her farmhouse from our cabin in the woods and write *The Crisis of the Old Order* in a room in her barn. Later she read the manuscript and returned it with a series of acute, indeed rather devastating, criticisms. I remember her remark about the prologue, a portentous account of FDR's first inauguration: "almost Pre-Raphaelite," she said. She was absolutely correct. This was shortly after Adlai Stevenson's 1952 campaign, and I was writing history as if I were still writing political speeches. Her comments shifted my whole perspective on the text. I withdrew the manuscript from the publisher and spent a month going over it sentence by sentence and purging it of its flourishes and excesses.

This was typical of Mary—both of her generosity in giving time to her friends and her absolute fidelity to her own exacting standards. As her marvelous essays in autobiography show, she saw her own earlier selves with that same scrupulous objectivity. Of course she changed course from time to time in a vitally engaged life. "Conscience doth make cowards of us all," she once wrote. " . . . If you start an argument with yourself, that makes two people at least, and when you have two people, one of them starts appeasing the other."

There used to be a fine phrase, now banned, I supposed, in this supersensitive age—"man of letters." "Woman of letters" doesn't sound right; "person of letters" is wholly unacceptable. Whatever the contemporary equivalent of the old phrase, it applied vividly to Mary. She wrote with analytical power, startling clarity, keen human insight, silken wit, dispassionate ruthlessness, on an enviable diversity of subjects: the novel, painting, architecture, opera, theater, politics, manners, tastes, religion, language, museums, universities, Vassar, Venice, Florence, France, America, Vietnam. Her novels, stories and essays constitute a brilliant commentary, interpretation, panorama of our disordered age.

From early childhood, Mary had more than her share of troubles in life. She triumphed over them almost to the end by sheer force of an exceedingly strong will, allied to drastic intelligence, boundless courage and a joyous instinct for living. She faced down the various illnesses that harassed her in recent years with a quite extraordinary absence of complaint and self-pity.

Nothing rejoiced her friends more than the singular felicity of her last marriage. In Jim West she found a perfect companion. I can claim some small credit for bringing them together. After I returned from a trip to the Soviet Union and Poland in 1959, the U.S.I.A. asked me which American writers might be usefully sent to Poland. I urged them to send Mary, and she soon met Jim in the Warsaw Embassy. It was one of the best things I have ever done.

Mary was a sublime mixture of astringency and tenderness. For an intensely liberated woman, she luxuriated in housewifely detail. She was a superb cook, kept an immaculate house and loved being Jim's wife; she generally referred to herself as "Mary West" rather than "Mary McCarthy." She may have cast a cold eye, but she had the warmest of hearts. She was the dearest of friends and the best of company. We will all miss her to the end of our days. (pp. 14-15)

Arthur Schlesinger, Jr., "Mary McCarthy: 1912-1989," in Partisan Review, *Vol. LVII, No. 1, 1990, pp. 14-15.*

Robert Penn Warren

April 24, 1905 - September 15, 1989

American novelist, poet, editor, historian, nonfiction writer, essayist, and dramatist.

For an overview of Warren's life and work see *CLC,* Vols. 1, 4, 6, 8, 10, 13, 18, 39, 53; *Contemporary Authors,* Vols. 13-16, rev. ed.; *Contemporary Authors New Revision Series,* Vol. 10; *Dictionary of Literary Biography,* Vols. 2, 48; *Dictionary of Literary Biography Yearbook: 1980;* and *Concise Dictionary of American Literary Biography, 1968-1987.*

STANLEY KUNITZ

[*Reprinted below is a transcript of Stanley Kunitz's introduction to Robert Penn Warren's reading at the Guggenheim Museum on February 7, 1977.*]

These past few weeks, using Robert Penn Warren's new volume of **Selected Poems** as a vehicle, I have been journeying back through more than half a century of his life and art. And what a beautiful, brutal, mind-spinning journey it has been. No writer of our time has been so multi-faceted or myriad-minded. Perhaps his very versatility as novelist, playwright, critic, essayist, editor, teacher, has made it difficult for us to recognize his central achievement as poet. Now, when we contemplate the accumulation of his verse—the many pages of his progress—we can begin to see this achievement in true perspective, as a work truly rare in our time, for its combination of intellect and passion, for its marriage of fierceness and grandeur.

Warren comes out of frontier country, the Kentucky hills. When we first heard of him, he was a Southern Agrarian, associated with John Crowe Ransom, Donald Davidson, Allen Tate, and the others of the Fugitive Group. Of that company, he was the only one successfully to transplant himself in the North. Though he is always reaching back for his Southern memories and roots, though the South gives him themes and poignant occasions for guilt, the true landscape of his imagination can be described in its maturity as American, beyond the regional.

History presents itself to Warren as maelstrom and nightmare, in which he is immersed. The pain of conscience (his phrase) is not to be separated from his awareness of the crimes of a nation, the injustice of Time. The questions that haunt him reflect his moral and philosophical, sometimes his theological, preoccupations. In his *Selected* volume, the opening poem, representative of his newest work, is entitled "A Way to Love God," with its first line reading: "Here is the shadow of truth, for only the shadow is true."

Elsewhere, he tells us that "We must try / To love so well

the world that we may believe, in the end, in God" ["**The Red Mullet**"]. But he does not pretend that the search for the divine principle is easy. In a late poem ["**Loss, of Perhaps Love, in Our World of Contingency**"], he evokes, with a characteristic flick of irony,

. . . the dark little corner under your bed, where God

Huddles tight in the fluff-ball, like a cocoon, that He,
All-knowing, knows the vacuum won't find!

Enormous issues, the great metaphysical riddles, agitate him. Illusion and reality, original sin, the Fall of Man, the idea of good and evil, the meaning of knowledge, the meaning of meaning, the possibility of transcendence, redemption, love. But he brings them down into our world of action and particulars, embodies them, like the Godhead in a fluff-ball under the bed in a dark little corner.

His vision is prevailingly dark and tragic. But the recesses are illuminated by the fires of compassion and the bright will, crying *survive.* If he implies in one of his major poems that every man is brother to the dragon, a sort of monster, he is equally ready to concede under other provocation that every man is a sort of Jesus. And there remains to enchant us that other gift of his, narrative—the blessed motor—propelling his long lines through breathless adventures and inexhaustible transformations. "Tell me a story," ends his astonishing long poem, **"Audubon":**

> In this century, and moment, of mania,
> Tell me a story.
>
> Make it a story of great distances, and starlight.
>
> The name of the story will be Time,
> But you must not pronounce its name.
>
> Tell me a story of deep delight.

(pp. 1-2)

Stanley Kunitz, "On Robert Penn Warren," in Poetry Pilot, *November, 1989, pp. 1-2.*

JAY PARINI

The sun has barely reddened the top of southern Vermont's Mount Stratton before Robert Penn Warren, America's first poet laureate, climbs down the steep slope from his summer house to the pond where he swims for an hour every morning from June through mid-September. At eighty-two, he knows the importance of keeping in shape. "And poems often come to me in the water," he says. "There's something about the rhythm of swimming, or any exercise. I walk a lot, too. Ideas for poems always come when I'm walking." At a time of life when many writers have long since put aside their pens, Warren remains productive. . . .

"I stopped writing novels a few years ago," Warren says. "One day I was beginning work on a new novel, about ten years ago. The novel just wouldn't come. Instead, I found myself scribbling fragments of poetry in the margins of the page. It seemed sensible to give in to the impulse. I've been writing nothing but poetry since." The initial result of this particular burst of creative energy was a volume called **Now and Then,** which brought him a third Pulitzer Prize in 1979, making him the only American to win this prize in two different categories—fiction and poetry. In 1985, he published a new **Selected Poems,** which gathers in one volume all the earlier poems that he "wants to keep in print" and adds nearly a hundred pages of new poetry to the continuously expanding Warren corpus.

He won his first Pulitzer forty years ago for a novel called **All the King's Men,** which was later made into an Academy Award-winning movie with Broderick Crawford in the leading role. The story, concerning Willie Stark, an ambitious southern hick lawyer who makes it to the governor's mansion, is closely modeled on the career of Huey Long, who ruled Louisiana like a dictator in the thirties, when Warren himself was teaching at Louisiana State University. "Huey Long was a huge presence in the state," says Warren. "He poured big money into the university. But the corruption was immense. He was in cahoots with the president of the university, who escaped over the border to Canada just before he was found out. They later caught and jailed him." Long, like the hero of Warren's novel, was assassinated in the state capitol.

Warren spends each summer in a rustic home set deep in the Vermont woods off a gravel drive. It's the sort of place no-

body would ever find without specific directions—a fact that keeps unwanted visitors to a minimum. "This is a place to work," says Warren. The rest of the time, he lives in Connecticut, not far from Yale University, where he taught until his retirement seventeen years ago. His wife is Eleanor Clark, also a celebrated writer. "We both work every morning," she says. "And never break until lunchtime, about 2." Visitors and phone calls are never accepted before that sacred hour. (p. 36)

Warren, who lifts weights as well as swims, is enormously strong for a man his age, though his face is wrinkled like a baked mudflat in late summer. His hair, once red (hence his nickname, "Red" Warren), has turned to white. It is straggly and windblown. He retains the strong southern accent acquired during his boyhood in Kentucky. The South remains an obsession with him. He loves to reminisce about his youth there before the First World War. "Guthrie wasn't a typical southern town," he says. "It was a tobacco market town, thrown down on the map well after the Civil War, at the intersection of two railway lines." He goes on: "My schools were tough. They were the sort of places where the biggest boy might feel it his duty to challenge the new principal with his fists. A tenth-grade classmate of mine was tried for murder, having brained a 'carney hand' after the carnival's evening show with a tent peg. Still, a boy could get a pretty good education there—better than many glistening schools now afford." Warren recalls that Latin was a required subject, and that everyone was forced to read Cicero.

Much of Warren's real education was acquired at home. "We had a whole houseful of books," he remembers. "And both my parents were bookish people." His father read to the family every night from classic texts. "I can still see the gray cover of *A Child's History of Greece*," he says. "It was my father's ambition to be a poet, but he became a banker instead. He never told me about his poetry, but one time, prowling around the bookshelves, I came across a black book containing his poems. It was published—probably by a vanity press—when he was twenty or twenty-one. He refused to say anything about it all."

Born in 1905, Warren grew up the son of a smalltown banker. He was admitted to Vanderbilt University in Nashville at the age of sixteen, but his real ambition was to go to Annapolis. "I wanted to be an admiral. My grandfathers on both sides were Civil War cavalry officers—one a captain, one a colonel, both under General Bedford Forrest." He goes on, "I spent my boyhood summers with my father, Gabriel Penn, on his isolated tobacco farm on the Tennessee border. Those were lovely summers. My grandfather would quote poetry by the yard or discuss the campaigns of Napoleon. We would draw battle diagrams in the dirt with a stick or read aloud from military histories."

This knowledge of history wasn't wasted. Warren's novels and poems are full of southern lore. And he has written straight historical works, too, such as the brilliant book-length essay called **The Legacy of the Civil War** (1961) and a recent essay on Jefferson Davis, who presided over the southern states during the Civil War. In fact, Warren's first published book—long out of print—was a biography of John Brown, **The Making of a Martyr** (1929).

In all of his writings, Warren is the quintessential teacher, conveying information, making judgments, encouraging readers to investigate and think on their own. Not surprisingly, he devoted some of the best years of his life to that profession, beginning in 1930 with a job at a small college in Memphis. He later taught at Vanderbilt, L.S.U., Minnesota, and Yale. "I really loved teaching," Warren says. "As Randall Jarrell once said, 'If I weren't paid to teach, I'd pay for the privilege.' When you've got an idea you want to talk about, the only way you can do that is through teaching. And you meet a certain kind of people in teaching, the real humanists, that you don't meet easily outside of the academy."

In 1938, with his old friend Cleanth Brooks, he co-authored *Understanding Poetry,* a textbook that, nearly half a century later, remains a standard introduction to the art of poetry. It shaped a whole generation of college and high school teachers, preaching the importance of the poem itself, its actual words. Prior to *Understanding Poetry,* teachers often spent more time talking about the poet's failed marriages and mental ups and downs than addressing the words on the page. Warren adds, "That textbook was a sound financial project, too. It made it possible for me to write full-time, whenever I chose to take a break from teaching."

Though his reputation as a novelist came first, Warren has always been a poet at heart. Like his favorite writer, Thomas Hardy, he has devoted the last decades of his writing life to verse. "You see, I began as a poet," Warren says, with a certain urgency in his voice. "Poetry was my first love. I never actually gave it up. *It* gave me up for a few years. In the early fifties, for a while, I couldn't finish a poem to save my life. But that ended with *Promises.* I haven't stopped writing poems since, though I wrote novels, too, until 1975." *Promises* brought Warren his second Pulitzer in 1958. Written in the form of promises to his two young children, the collection ends with a marvelous lullaby to his infant son, Gabriel:

> Till the clang of cock-crow, and dawn's rays,
> Summon your heart and hand to deploy
> Their energies to know, in the excitement of day-blaze,
> How like a wound, and deep,
> Is Time's irremediable joy.
> So, son, now sleep.

Warren sees poetry as "something essential . . . a clarification, a revision of life." He reads very little fiction anymore. "I just don't keep up with it like I used to. I read mostly poetry—the classic poets, and a lot of contemporaries. I recently reread all of T. S. Eliot, for instance." Because his wife is nearly blind, the result of a disease that struck her ten years ago, he often reads aloud in the evenings so she can listen. They recently read the Bible that way. Shakespeare and Dickens have also been read in Warren's crackly, drawling voice. (pp. 36-7)

Whether in Vermont or Connecticut, Warren never misses his morning session with the muse; he often goes back to his desk in the late afternoon or early evening. He generally sits in a desk chair with a clipboard on his knee, "standing in the rain." Inspiration seems to come with almost alarming frequency these days. Old age has brought a certain urgency to his work. It's as if, having come to the top of a high mountain, he feels incredible pressure to say what he can see. The view, in his late poems, is tremendous. The tone of this work is best captured in a poem called **"Heart of Autumn,"** in which the poet-narrator stands watching wild geese cross the northern sky at sunset. The poem ends:

> Path of logic, path of folly, all

> The same—as I stand, my face lifted now
>   skyward,
> Hearing the high beat, my arms outstretched in
>   the tingling
> Process of transformation, and soon tough legs,
> With folded feet, trail in the sounding vacuum
>   of passage,
> And my heart is impacted with a fierce impulse
> To unwordable utterance—
> Toward sunset, at a great height.

(p. 37)

Jay Parini, "Robert Penn Warren," in Horizon: The Magazine of the Arts, *Vol. 30, No. 5, June, 1987, pp. 36-7.*

THE NEW YORK TIMES

Robert Penn Warren, whose complex poetry and novels drawn from Southern life formed an intricate mirror of the human experience, died of cancer yesterday [September 15, 1989] at his summer home in Stratton, Vt. He was 84 years old and lived in Fairfield, Conn.

Mr. Warren, the nation's first Poet Laureate, won the first of three Pulitzer Prizes in 1947 for *All the King's Men,* a richly detailed study of the life and times of a populist politician named Willie Stark, who begins his career as a champion of the people but becomes corrupted by the power they vest on him. The character was inspired by the Louisiana Governor Huey P. Long.

Mr. Warren was also a respected critic and teacher who was on the faculties of Yale, Louisiana State University and the University of Minnesota, among others. Two textbooks he wrote began as pamphlets for his first classes and became widely used in colleges across the country.

After the publication of *All the King's Men* in 1946, Sinclair Lewis hailed Mr. Warren as "the most talented writer of the South and one of the most important writers of the country." In 1949 the novel was made into a movie, which won the Academy Award for best picture of the year.

Mr. Warren's works enjoyed wide popularity, appearing on best-seller lists and as book club selections. . . . (p. 1)

"Everybody knows a thousand stories," Mr. Warren told an interviewer in 1981. "But only one cockleburr catches in your fur and that subject is your question. You live with that question. You may not even know what that question is. It hangs around a long time. I've carried a novel as long as 20 years, and some poems longer than that."

He was a poet of complex works dotted with philosophical reflections—poetry he knew would appeal to a small group of readers. He was awarded the Pulitzer Prize for poetry twice in 1957 and 1979.

His longtime friend, the educator and writer Cleanth Brooks, said yesterday, "He was a gentle and fine spirit, a valiant warrior for the truth, and one of our very finest poets."

Mr. Warren was named Poet Laureate in 1986 and held the post for two years. (pp. 1, 11)

Mr. Warren was an influential figure in the teaching of English literature. His books *Understanding Poetry* and *Understanding Fiction,* which he wrote with Mr. Brooks, taught an entire generation how to read a work of literature and helped make the New Criticism dominant in the decade surrounding World War II. It was an approach to criticism that regarded the work at hand as autonomous, as an artifact whose structure and substance could be analyzed without respect to social, biographical and political details.

In an essay on John Crowe Ransom, who was his most important influence, Mr. Warren wrote, "The problem at the center of Ransom's work is especially modern—but it implies some history." The same sentence could be applied to Mr. Warren himself, for in his fiction, as in a good deal of his poetry, historical elements served as the imaginative springboard for the work.

The current laureate, Howard Nemerov, said yesterday; "*All the King's Men* is certainly one of the great American novels." He also praised Mr. Warren's poetry.

"He was reticent, ironic, reserved and perfectly charming," Mr. Nemerov said, "and I loved and respected him quite apart from his work."

Ransom once pointed out the impoverishment of modern life and the handicap caused to a writer by the destruction of commonly held myths that had been the heritage of the Western world.

Mr. Warren made up for that by searching out and finding historical incidents, folk tales and community anecdotes that he exploited and expanded in his fiction.

Night Rider, an early novel, used the tobacco war of 1906 in his native Kentucky, when farmers fought the tobacco trust. *World Enough and Time* centered on the 19th-century murder trial of Jeremy Beauchamp, whose case Mr. Warren had read about in a penny pamphlet. The heart of *Brother to Dragons,* a lengthy narrative poem, is built around the brutal killing of a slave by the nephews of Thomas Jefferson for what they considered a slight to the family. And for *Audubon, A Vision* he found a threatening and sinister incident that he put to his own use. . . .

All these works, sometimes melodramatic in character, served a larger purpose: Mr. Warren's investigation of the nature of honor and justice, of truth and freedom, responsibility and guilt. But because these inquiries impeded the flow of the story, some readers were critical of the "underdone philosophizing" that they felt marred his books.

Even those who admired him complained of the obduracy of his style. Reviewing *Brother to Dragons,* Randall Jarrell wrote that Mr. Warren's "florid, massive, rather oratorical rhetoric is sometimes miraculous, often effective and sometimes too noticeable to bear."

Arthur Mizener praised him for bringing to the telling of a story "the most penetrating and most beautifully disciplined historical imagination we have." But in reviewing *Band of Angels,* Mr. Mizener wrote that the author's "brilliant and subtle arguments spread speculations . . . over the imaginative life of *Band of Angels* like a blight."

Many critics felt that these characteristics of his work had a more natural place in his poetry. In "**The Ballad of Billie Potts,**" for example, many said that the apostrophes slowed down the story, but that the delays added to the suspense of the poem. . . .

[In 1935, Warren] founded and edited, with Mr. Brooks and Charles W. Pipkin, *The Southern Review,* one of the notewor-

thy and substantive magazines of its time. Though it claimed to express "the regional and sectional piety" of the editors, it was far from a provincial effort and was read eagerly throughout the country. The magazine published stories and poems by Eudora Welty, Mary McCarthy, Ford Madox Ford and W. H. Auden, among others. It was disbanded in 1942, after university officials declared the magazine's success should be defined by whether or not it was self-supporting.

The same year, Mr. Warren accepted a professorship at the University of Minnesota. In 1950 he moved to Yale, where he was named professor of play writing. He left in 1956 to write full time, but returned to Yale as a professor of English in 1961.

Although he never again lived in the South, he remained the essential Southerner, with a keen sense of history and life's webs of tragedy, triumph, upheaval and peace. His attitude toward the region changed over the course of his life. Early in his career he had contributed to *I'll Take My Stand,* a volume that opposed the coming of industrialism to the South and argued for an almost antebellum structure of society.

Mr. Warren's essay, "**The Briar Patch,**" defended segregation as the best hope for blacks to have a decent life. Later, Mr. Warren said he had been wrong. "I remember the jangle and wrangle of writing it, some kind of discomfort, some sense of evasion," he said in a 1968 interview.

But in the 1950's and 60's he published two books, *Segregation* and *Who Speaks for the Negro?* that describe visits he made to the South to interview officials and black leaders about the civil rights movement. And he acknowledged that he could not really return home again. . . .

To his friends he was "Red," from the color of his hair. He was a burly man with a face that seemed carved from stone. It was said he looked like a man who was about to throw you off his land. But his voice, soft with pronounced Southern intonation, belied his fierce demeanor.

As the years passed, Mr. Warren kept on writing. A collection, *New and Selected Poetry,* came out in 1985. New work took up roughly one-fourth of the book's 322 pages, and won particular praise from William H. Pritchard of Amherst College, who wrote in *The New York Times Book Review* that Mr. Warren was "no one-note dweller on remembrance."

Professor Pritchard wrote that his favorite poem in all of Mr. Warren's oeuvre was one of the new ones, "**After the Dinner Party,**" about a couple tarrying at the dinner table after the guests have gone, drinking the last of the wine and holding hands. It ends with these lines:

The last log is black, white ash beneath displays
No last glow. You snuff candles. Soon the old stairs
Will creak with your grave and synchronized tread as each
    mounts
To a briefness of light, then true weight of darkness, and
    then
That heart-dimness in which neither joy nor sorrow
    counts.
Even so, one hand gropes out for another, again.

(p. 11)

An obituary in The New York Times, *September 16, 1989, pp. 1, 11.*

WILLIAM ROBERTSON

When friends die, I go to their funerals. When writers die, I pay my respects in the only way I think that truly matters: by reading their books. So when Robert Penn Warren died . . . , I went to our study and pulled down one of his.

It wasn't *All the King's Men,* the popular and critically acclaimed novel on which Warren's fame rests. Nor was it one of his many volumes of poetry—poetry so radiant that it caused an English professor to remark to a Washington Post reporter that for the last 25 years of his 84, Warren had been "writing his way into heaven."

What I chose was a textbook, *Understanding Poetry,* which Warren wrote in 1938 with his old friend and colleague, Cleanth Brooks. It belongs to my wife, my copy having disappeared long ago, probably during a season of carelessness and neglect. By the time she acquired the book in college, it was into its third edition.

The poems she read are heavily annotated in the pencil of the student. Two comments that particularly caught my interest are written in the margin beside the fourth and fifth stanzas of Thomas Hardy's "Channel Firing": "God uses slang; makes Him more human" and then, more emphatically, "He doesn't threaten them with Hell—just with scrubbing hell's floors." This may explain something of our subsequent life together.

From beginning to end the book is filled with such entries. If they make any point beyond proving that here was one student who read the whole thing, they suggest the influence Robert Penn Warren and Cleanth Brooks had on my wife and me and a whole generation of readers. In a subtle yet profound way, they taught us to read.

Understanding Poetry (now out of print) and a companion volume by Warren and Brooks, *Understanding Fiction* (still hanging on in paperback), were widely used in college English courses during the '40s, '50s and into the '60s.

These books are rooted in a literary movement labeled "New Criticism." Warren, one of its founders and its best-known spokesman, elevated it into belief. In simplified form, "New Criticism" is a way of looking at a work of literature without reference to the author's intentions or biography. It emphasizes close reading and structural analysis. Only what can be found in the work, not outside it, matters. . . .

Warren was no stranger to academia and literary theory. In no small part he was a product of the university. As an undergraduate at Vanderbilt, he changed his course of study from chemical engineering to English when he came under the spell of the teacher and poet John Crowe Ransom. He earned a master's degree from the University of California at Berkeley. He studied another year at Yale before going to Oxford on a Rhodes Scholarship. He taught at Louisiana State University, the University of Minnesota and Yale.

As a teacher and critic, what set Warren apart from his less talented peers was his understanding that literature and attendant ideas on how to read it are not subject to verification by any means except experience. Literary theory isn't theory in the scientific sense. It is governed by common sense, and it is not available to specialists only but to all readers.

You don't have to invoke the canons of "New Criticism" to recognize that its emphasis on the paramount importance of the text and its form is a sensible notion. All you have to do is think about how most people read books. Readers often function in a partial vacuum, knowing little, if anything, about the author or the society he comes from. Frequently they may not have even read his previous work. Yet this lack of information takes none of the pleasure—or, for that matter, the displeasure—from what is on the page.

As he and Brooks make clear in *Understanding Poetry,* Warren believed that poetry in particular and literature in general are not things *out there,* somehow cut off from life.

"By the very nature of the human being," Warren and Brooks tell us, "the ordinary citizen in the ordinary day speaks much of what we might call incipient poetry—he attempts to communicate attitudes, feelings and interpretation, including ideas. And poetry in this sense is not confined to the speech of the ordinary citizen. It appears also in editorials, sermons, political speeches, advertisements and magazine articles—even if it is usually not recognized as poetry."

These extraordinary literary collaborators write from an unyielding and entirely persuasive conviction. Nothing in Warren's long and fulfilling life contradicts his belief that "both the impulse and methods of poetry are rooted very deep in human experience, and that formal poetry itself represents, not a distinction from, but a specialization of, thoroughly universal habits of human thinking and feeling."

William Robertson, "Robert Penn Warren Was a Master at Teaching, Too," in The Miami Herald, *September 24, 1989, p. 7C.*

WALTER CLEMONS

[Robert Penn Warren] was America's first official poet laureate, an ornamental title he accepted in 1986 with gruff humor and a declaration that if it involved writing ceremonial verses he wouldn't accept. "God, no," he said. "I don't expect you'll hear me writing any poems to the greater glory of Ronald and Nancy Reagan."

Over the past half century, he'd already won about every literary honor there was. . . .

In his youth he was a member of the group of Southern agrarians known as the Fugitives, and *All the King's Men* was suggested by the career of the Louisiana populist demagogue Huey Long. The novel will probably remain Warren's most famous book. Yet its narrative power is also an attribute of some of his most memorable poems. In the often anthologized **"The Ballad of Billie Potts,"** he retold, with mesmerizing skill, a Kentucky folk tale of an innkeeper who makes his living by robbing and murdering travelers and mistakenly kills his own son. . . .

He published novels, but his best later work was his poetry, which simply got better and better as he neared 80. In one late poem, he imagined himself a boy seated at his grandfather's feet:

> Eyes, not bleared but blue,
> Of the old man, horizonward gazed—
> As on horizons and years, long lost, but now
> Projected from storage in that capacious skull

The poet laureateship was awarded, not to an extinct volcano, but to a still active master of his craft.

Walter Clemons, " 'Of the Old Man . . . Horizon-
ward Gazed'," in Newsweek, *Vol. CXIV, No. 13,*
September 25, 1989, p. 67.

WALTER SULLIVAN

I first met Red in Iowa City in 1949 when Paul Engle brought him to have lunch with Jane and me. In 1952 I stayed in his apartment in Silliman College at Yale, and after that I saw him frequently or not so frequently, depending on the circumstances of both our lives, but we never lost touch. When he came to Nashville, he usually stayed with Frances and Brainard Cheney. Almost always Fannie gave a party for him, and after dinner she would move her guests into the library and ask Red to read. Sometimes he had brought manuscripts with him, poems still under construction; sometimes he read what was already published. In either event those of us who had listened would go home with his distinctive cadences echoing in our minds.

In terms of personality genius postulates nothing. A talent for writing is only that: sometimes it resides in frail and even perfidious human vessels. Red's virtues were consonant with his gifts. He was the kindest and gentlest of men, a loyal friend, and the best of companions. Though in his later years he seemed to think of himself more as a poet than as a novelist, his instinct for discovering narrative possibilities endured. He told stories about what he had read, what he had seen, what he had done: an old French lady on the Kentucky frontier refusing to die until the priest who had come to give her unction told her the gossip from home; a will that provided transportation and liquor for mourners to travel from eastern Kentucky to a burial in the western part of the state, but made no provision for, as Red put it, "bringing that bunch of drunks back home"; a rich man, eroded by dissipation, who showed Red pictures of his estates and his yacht and declared himself to be "as lonely as God."

As his own time grew short, most of what he heard from Nashville was gloomy. Fannie Cheney had a stroke. Lyle Lanier, friend of his Vanderbilt days and fellow contributor to *I'll Take My Stand,* died. "It may be a feeling not uncommon to the ageing process," Red wrote, "to feel that persons and events of one's youth had special qualities, but, damn it, I know that some of the friends of my youth were extraordinarily impressive, Lyle among them. This not to mention somewhat older people like J. C. R." He was right. They were special. But none was more special than he. (pp. 629-30)

Walter Sullivan, "Robert Penn Warren 1905-
1989," in The Sewanee Review, *Vol. XCVII, No. 4,*
Fall, 1989, pp. 629-30.

NATIONAL REVIEW, NEW YORK

In the autumn of 1921, a thin, red-haired youngster from Kentucky enrolled as a freshman at Vanderbilt University and fell in with a group of instructors and fellow students who would soon constitute one of the most influential literary circles in twentieth-century America. The freshman was Robert Penn Warren, known to his friends as "Red" Warren. The leaders of the group were John Crowe Ransom, a member of the English faculty, and Allen Tate, then a student; they published a short-lived but brilliant journal called *The Fugitive.* (What they were "fugitive" from was "the high-cast Brahmins of the Old South," magnolias and Walter Scottism. They were moderns, of their own sort.)

There at Vanderbilt, Robert Penn Warren began one of the most remarkable careers in the annals of American letters—poet, novelist, critic, editor of *The Southern Review* (with Cleanth Brooks), and teacher, last at Yale. The text he co-authored with Brooks, **Understanding Poetry** (1938), instructed a democratized and raw generation (many of them on the G.I. Bill) how to read. It was the most influential book of its kind ever published. Ironically, Brooks and Warren, working from an essentially aristocratic "New Critical" perspective, had prescribed the how-to manual that made mass higher education plausible after 1965.

As a writer, Penn Warren was not in the very first rank. He wrote no poem as good as the best of his friends Ransom and Tate; one certainly cannot rank him with the greatest of the modernists, Yeats and Eliot. His Huey Long novel, **All the King's Men** (1946), brought him fame and fortune and is both powerful and melodramatic, this last a vice which often tended to displace his tragic muse. His criticism remains useful.

But the whole was much greater than the sum of its extensive parts, and was repeatedly accorded the highest honors. He gave himself for some six decades to serious literature, and for the most serious of reasons. With Ransom as their conceptual mentor, those Fugitives of the 1920s knew an important thing: that while science delivers an "edited" or reductive version of actuality, literature delivers the whole: nuance, concreteness, intuition, moral reflection, religious faith, passion—matters not reducible to formulae.

Robert Penn Warren held to that truth with all of his considerable powers, providing a civilizing example.

"Robert Penn Warren, RIP," in National Review,
New York, Vol. XLI, No. 19, October 13, 1989, p.
21.

LEWIS P. SIMPSON

[The tribute below was originally presented at the Salute to
Southern Authors Dinner, Southern Festival of Books, Nash-
ville, Tennessee, October 15, 1989.]

Any tribute to Robert Penn Warren must recognize the ironic but essential polar aspects of his relationship with the South: one, at the beginning of the most productive phase of his career he left his native world and, save for short visits, never returned; two, he never ceased to be fundamentally engaged with this world. Indeed as James Joyce was a self-declared exile from Ireland, who was always preoccupied with Ireland, Red Warren was a self-conscious exile from the South, who, if not so obsessively or quite so exclusively as Joyce with Ireland, was all his life preoccupied with the South.

I had never quite grasped the complex irony of this preoccupation until one day about a year ago I fulfilled a long-standing intention and in the company of my near neighbor and friend, the writer and editor Charles East, made a little journey to the places where Warren had lived from 1934 to 1942, when he was associated with the Department of English and the *Southern Review* at Louisiana State University.

In our image of Warren's career we tend to think of his arrival on the campus of LSU in 1934 as another event in a connection with the South that had been integral and continuous since his birth in Guthrie, Kentucky, in 1905. On the contrary, according to the implication of his own testimony in interviews and elsewhere, Warren's coming to Baton Rouge marked the beginning of the final phase of a struggle to return to the South that he had carried on since 1930, when, following what he would later refer to as "years of wandering," he had come back to Tennessee. Here he was for one year at Southwestern College in Memphis, and then for three more years on the campus of his undergraduate years, Vanderbilt.

Possibly Warren's reference to his "years of wandering" may be considered somewhat overly dramatic in view of the fact that these years, about six in all, were spent not in bohemian jaunting here and there over the world but mostly in graduate study at Berkeley, Yale, and Oxford (where Warren had the distinction of being a Rhodes Scholar). But nonetheless these were years that had removed Warren well beyond the South he had known as a boy and youth in rural Kentucky, where a significant part of his education had consisted in listening to stories about the War for Southern Independence, particularly as told by his favorite grandfather, Gabriel Thomas Penn, a dedicated soldier of the Confederacy. These were also years that had distanced Warren from the South he had known as a precocious undergraduate at Vanderbilt, where he had been a member of the Fugitive Group and had formed an attachment to John Crowe Ransom, Allen Tate, Andrew Lytle, and Donald Davidson that brought him into the Agrarian Group in the later 1920s. Even as he had participated in the making of the Agrarian manifesto *I'll Take My Stand* (1930) Warren had questioned some of the Agrarian motives—as is evidenced in his contribution to the manifesto, a rationalization of segregation so half-hearted that Donald Davidson did not want to include it, and which Warren later quite explicitly and positively repudiated. Yet at the same time his years away from the South had been a period that had intensified Warren's attachment to other motives of the Agrarians, most profoundly a subtle but pervasive fear on their part of their personal displacement in the South, of their becoming rootless, or placeless, in short, exiles in their own land. When he came back to the South in the year in which *I'll Take My Stand* was published, Warren, to be sure, had been out into a world—the world after World War I—whose poets, novelists, and historians were dominated by a sensibility of deracination and exile that, anticipated even at the very beginning of the modern age in Dante, had by the time of Melville and Flaubert become general in Western literary life and in the century of Conrad, Yeats, Joyce, of Thomas Mann, Stein, Pound, Eliot, Hemingway, and Faulkner had become endemic. In this, our century—which has been not less the century of Ransom, Tate, Lytle, Davidson, and Warren—all writers, whether knowing actual exile or not, have been affected by emotions associated with *depaysement,* or the yearning for a lost homeland; and many have qualified to bear the generic name the Alsatian poet Iwan Goll conferred on the modern author, Jean Sans Terre, John the Landless, or, as we might put it in a very free translation, John the Placeless.

When he came back to Tennessee in 1930, Warren was pursuing what turned out to be only a yearning dream for a place that would allay the fear of placelessness he had experienced in his six years of itinerant existence. "The place I wanted to live," Warren reminisced in the later 1970s, "the place I thought was heaven to me, after my years of wandering, was Middle Tennessee . . . But I couldn't make it work. . . . I was let out of Vanderbilt University, and had to go elsewhere for a job."

The elsewhere, LSU and the country around Baton Rouge, proved to be, as it turned out, the scene of the last effort Warren made to fulfill his yearning quest—a quest he could not effectively disassociate from the South—for a place of permanence, or, to employ the title of his last novel (1977), "a place to come to." I had not quite realized the pathos of Warren's search for this place until—in the knowledgeable company of Charles East—I followed the tangible trail of its final frustration in Baton Rouge and the surrounding countryside. The trail begins with the cottage of a former dairykeeper—located in the suburban outskirts of South Baton Rouge when Warren rented it in 1934—and proceeds to a tiny cabin with a tin roof and an attractive brick chimney in a beautiful forest of red oaks and water oaks—a cabin Warren himself, with the assistance of an "out-of-work carpenter," constructed on a six-acre tract that was well beyond the city limits when he purchased it in 1938 in a liquidation sale. The cabin is still on its original site, preserved on the estate of a Baton Rouge family. From thence the trail of Warren's quest leads down the Jefferson Highway, the old highway to New Orleans, to Prairieville. In this loosely-defined rural community, located some eighteen miles below Baton Rouge in Ascension Parish, Warren discovered a twelve-acre stretch of woods and pasture with a substantial story-and-a-half bungalow located on it. Known when he purchased it in 1942 as the Frank Opedenmeyer Home Place, this rather handsome property remains today in more or less the same state it was in in 1942. The fact that the house is not antebellum—it was in fact built in 1903—is somewhat offset by its placement in a grove of moss-shrouded live oaks growing along a steep bank, below which lies a typical South Louisiana bayou. The gray moss droops over the sluggish dark waters. Standing beneath the trees one cannot fail to remember Warren's poem, one of his favorites, **"Bearded Oaks":** "The oaks, how subtle and marine, / Bearded, and all the layered light / Above them swims." In Prairieville Warren had found the place he had been seeking, his place to come to, the place, as he said later, he "looked forward to enjoying . . . for keeps."

But he had only begun to convert the Opedenmeyer Home Place into the Warren Home Place when, ten months after he had purchased the Prairieville property—embittered by the failure of the LSU administration to continue its support of the *Southern Review* and even more by its unwillingness to meet a salary offer from the University of Minnesota, the sum involved being a mere two hundred dollars—Warren left the place he had thought to come to, this at the very moment when, having begun to establish himself as a novelist as well as a poet and critic, he was obviously on the way to becoming a major figure in the Southern Renascence. In recollection Warren said he felt himself "somehow squeezed out of the South" and so "fled to Yankee land."

It is a little difficult to understand now the depth of the crisis Warren experienced when he abandoned his quest for a place to come to in the South, for we—I refer to white southerners with an antebellum ancestry—have lost, or very nearly lost, the sense of an indissoluble bond between the mystery of one's identity as a person and one's identity as a southerner. I think of an exchange that took place about 1977 between William Styron and Warren on the question of why they are both living in New England instead of the South. Styron said it is simply because he has chosen to do so; but the explanation of simple choice would not, as I have suggested, do at all for Warren. Insisting that he "felt pressured" to leave the South, that it was not a matter of "choice," Warren made an important distinction between the rationale of his departure from the South and Styron's: "Perhaps," he said, "it is 'a generational matter.' " Perhaps in other words, it is a matter of whether or not one has experienced a tangible, living relationship with the mystery of the historical identity of the South of the Confederacy, the defeat, and the Reconstruction as embodied in the mystery of the identity of flesh-and-blood grandfathers and grandmothers, aunts and uncles and cousins. By the time Styron's generation of writers came along the experience of this relationship had either disappeared or had become too attenuated to be fully meaningful. That is, meaningful in the sense of being incarnated in the mystery of the writer and in the art of his or her work. But Warren came along in time to reexperience—to reembody—in the power of his imagination and the skill of his art a distillation of the yet-living experience of memory and history available to a gifted grandchild of the Civil War.

The cost of Warren's art was a self-conscious and painful estrangement from the South, but Warren's estrangement was paradoxically his greatest resource, for it was informed by (to call on the famous phrase from Tate's "Ode to the Confederate Dead") a "knowledge carried to the heart." Under the terms of their history as citizens of a nation invented by history, this is a knowledge that is the heritage of all Americans; but it has never been more plainly manifest than in the experience of the old southerners. I mean the knowledge of the isolation of the individual in history as the irrevocable consequence of the vanquishment of the old society of myth and tradition by the society of science and history. This is the knowledge Jed Tewksbury discovers in *A Place to Come To.* A poor white boy from Alabama who becomes a famous Dante scholar and teaches for a time at Vanderbilt, Jed, who is, along with Jack Burden in *All the King's Men* and Brad Tolliver in *Flood,* one of three novelistic personae of Warren, knows the peculiarly intense quality the American sense of isolation has assumed in the South—a loneliness that is "a bleeding inward of the self, away from all the world around, into an internal infinitude, like a pit." Having been "bred up" to this kind of loneliness, Jed says, he took "full advantage of the opportunities it offered." "I was," he declares, "the original, gold-plated, thirty-third degree loneliness artist, the champion of Alabama."

The smart-assed cynicism of Jed Tewksbury imposes a comic mask on a tragic mask of the persona who, as Warren himself recognized increasingly in his later years, haunts his work: a singularly remarkable body of writings—poetical, fictional, historical, biographical, and critical—that essentially constitutes the "shadowy autobiography" of a man, a southerner, who for all his love of his family and for his legion of friends was at his essential core a "loneliness artist."

The last evocative moment in the story of this artist took place on Sunday, October 8, 1989, when an urn containing the ashes of Robert Penn Warren was buried in a lonely country cemetery not far from his beloved summer home at West Wardsboro, Vermont. I had some account of the last rites for Warren in a telephone conversation with my friend and former student, and Warren's friend and bibliographer, James A. Grimshaw. When, in accordance with his wish, the New England earth was opened for Warren, it was the first time

in one hundred years that this old burying ground had been disturbed. We may fancy that this act expressed the last vision of a place to come to by a poet for whom the mystery of his identity was deeply fused with the mystery of place; for a poet who was an unmovable nonbeliever but who said repeatedly that he yet yearned to believe; for a poet who was southern to the bone—knew that he could never be at home save in the South—and yet knew as deeply that, because of his very nature as a southerner, he was an exile who could never come home again. After listening to Jim Grimshaw's quietly eloquent description of the remembrance for Warren in October—including a graphic detail at the graveside: the poet John Hollander's reading of Warren's Louisiana poem **"Bearded Oaks"** amid the burgeoning color of the New England autumn—I thought about how I have argued at times that between New England and the South there has been a fateful symbiotic relationship, this subsisting in the mystical truth that all southerners are spiritual New Englanders. This is an argument fraught with dark implications but perhaps also some happy ones. I cannot of course return to my argument here. But recalling to mind that a favorite phrase with Warren was "for the record," let me put on the record that at this time I take some consolation in my argument. (pp. 7-12)

Lewis P. Simpson, "Robert Penn Warren and the South," in The Southern Review, *Louisiana State University, Vol. 26, No. 1, Winter, 1990, pp. 7-12.*

CLEANTH BROOKS

[*The tribute below was first delivered on November 14, 1989 in New York City at the memorial service for Robert Penn Warren.*]

I speak first, probably, because of all the little company assembled here on this platform, I knew Robert Penn Warren for the longest period. Indeed, we first met in the fall of 1924 at Vanderbilt University where I, a very faltering freshman, met him, a brilliant senior, already a published poet. But it was typical of his generosity that he remembered that first meeting and that a few years later when I arrived at Oxford I found immediately a note from him on my desk at Exeter College, welcoming me to the old university where he was preparing to spend his final year, and I my first.

I shall not attempt to say much here about my experience of these years with Warren at either Vanderbilt or Oxford. They were important for me, and I enjoyed them very much. But they were not nearly as important or informative to me of my friend's character as were the years that we spent together in the same office at Louisiana State University. When I left Oxford in 1932, in the midst of our great depression, I was fortunate enough to find a job—any job at all—and doubly fortunate in the one I found. I discovered that Louisiana State University was one of the very few universities in the United States that was actually increasing its faculty size, and I was taken on just a few weeks before the 1932 fall semester began. Two years later in 1934, through a series of fortunate circumstances, we were able to hire Robert Penn Warren. At LSU the two of us spent eight years together, actually sharing the same office, and working on many of the same problems.

Those were wonderful years, lived in a very exciting place where almost anything could happen, a place where new ideas could be put in practice but also a place where, in spite of all these advantages, life was rather chancey. Huey Long was still in power and was quite unpredictable in his conduct. He had summarily seen that certain students, who had, he felt, been unfair to him in the college newspaper, were suspended from the university. It was a mistake that he did not repeat, but one could never be certain that it might not happen again.

Yet the university was building, expanding, undertaking new enterprises, and this was all for the good. One of the new enterprises, about which I daresay Long never had any knowledge, was the founding of a university quarterly, the *Southern Review*. The dean of the university, Charles W. Pipkin, young, aggressive, and forward-looking, had already indicated to the president of the university the advantages of having a university quarterly and had got us for a short time involved in bringing back into publication the *Southwest Review*. Thus, soon after Warren arrived at LSU, one Sunday afternoon the president drove up to his door to take him and his wife for a ride and, after having pointed out some of the scenic spots, suddenly put the question to him: "What would it cost to bring out a university quarterly?" Warren rose to the occasion with a specific reply—$10,000. "Could it be done by June 1?" was the president's next question, and Warren replied that it could.

So matters were quickly arranged, and the *Southern Review* did come into being; we didn't quite manage the first number by June 1, but we did by July 1. The magazine occupied a great deal of our attention, even as we were each teaching three courses in addition to our work on the magazine. Moreover, during this period Warren was going ahead with writing and gathering the material for what eventually became his Pulitzer Prize-winning *All the King's Men.* Beyond that, Warren and I did our first two textbooks there in the same period. It was fun working with Warren—he was so bright, so full of energy, so resourceful. Hard work under such circumstances became something like highly intelligent play. I learned a lot in those eight years, about the art of literature, the art of writing, and the art of living.

What did I learn about this remarkable man in those eight years? Too much to tell in any short compass. Let me set down only a few salient features. I learned how generous he was of his time and energy, how helpful to other young writers and students. We had all sorts at Louisiana State University in those days—everyone from graduate students as brilliant as Robert Lowell the poet and Peter Taylor the short story writer to the pleasant old lady in one of Warren's extension classes who was heard mumbling after Warren's lecture on one of the Shakespeare tragedies, "I just don't like reading about bad people. I just can't stand hearing about bad people." But Warren could cope with all kinds of human beings, and cope with them most successfully he did. He had a real gift for friendship and constantly made friends. He did not suffer fools gladly, to be sure, but he even dealt with the dunces in a civilized way and never made fun of them.

I learned, too, about Warren's love of truth. He wanted knowledge but it must be proper knowledge, accurate knowledge, truthful knowledge. "The other side" had to be dealt with fairly and given its proper expression. This concern for truthful knowledge was to come out in many, many ways in his own writings as well as in his lectures. Most of all it comes out in his great poetry where, in more than one poem, he comes to say that real knowledge and real love are almost the same thing, or at least that one leads to the other. One cannot truly love something unless he truly knows it, including its

defects; and to know something thoroughly, completely, becomes a form of love. This wisdom, which few of us attain to, is the strength of the great literature that Warren has shaped for us. He is dead, but his writings will live on to all of us who have the good sense to open our ears and eyes to them. The great writers as human beings die like the rest of us, but they have a voice which continues to speak to our deepest selves. (pp. 2-4)

Cleanth Brooks, "A Tribute to Robert Penn Warren," in The Southern Review, *Louisiana State University, Vol. 26, No. 1, Winter, 1990, pp. 2-4.*

JAMES OLNEY

Writing to Ethel Mannin in a letter of October 1938, only a few months before his death, W. B. Yeats spoke of "an essay on 'the idea of death' in the poetry of Rilke" in which he had found, he said, remarkable consonances with the thought of what he termed his "private philosophy" (as opposed to the "public philosophy" of *A Vision*). "According to Rilke," Yeats explained, "a man's death is born with him and if his life is successful and he escapes mere 'mass death' his nature is completed by his final union with it." In another letter, written within the month of his death, Yeats told Lady Elizabeth Pelham, "I am happy, and I think full of an energy, of an energy I had despaired of. It seems to me that I have found what I wanted. When I try to put all into a phrase I say, 'Man can embody truth but he cannot know it.' I must embody it in the completion of my life." It seems to me peculiarly fitting that these late thoughts that Yeats had about death as the completion of a successful life and the embodiment of the idea of that life should come to mind on the occasion of Robert Penn Warren's death, for in his poetry Warren, like Yeats (and like few other poets besides Yeats), went on improving with age as if his nature were gradually and triumphantly being completed in his last years, as if he were fully embodying his truth, and writing it out in verse, in the completion of his life.

There have been a number of memorial services for Robert Penn Warren around the country these past two or three months, all testifying to this same sense of an almost unbelievably full and productive life, a successful life appropriately concluded—one in a small, disused church in rural Vermont, another in a corner of the vast Cathedral Church of St. John the Divine in New York City, others still at Yale University, Vanderbilt University, and Louisiana State University. In each instance one has the clear impression that the presiding spirit has been much more a spirit of celebration than of mourning, and properly so. This is not, of course, to deny the loss that Warren's death represents: the *Southern Review,* in particular, has lost a great and generous friend with Warren's death; indeed, were it not for Warren and his founding and presiding genius, there would never have been a *Southern Review* at Louisiana State University. The *Southern Review,* however, is but one of many legacies he has left behind, legacies that stand as his achievements in poetry, fiction, and drama, and in critical commentary of every sort, literary, social, cultural, historical.

What we have lost also, and this perhaps most of all, though his example remains as encouragement to live the moral life, is the presence among us of a good and generous man (to put it in unabashedly old-fashioned terms). In a recent telephone conversation, Daniel Hoffman referred to Warren's generosity to other poets, and certainly there are many around the country who could testify to this. Like so many others, I had the occasional opportunity—not as often as I should have liked but often enough to feel that I understood something of his personality—to observe this warm, ready openness and responsiveness in Red Warren's character. It was evident throughout the three or four days he spent at LSU in 1985 when we celebrated the fiftieth anniversary of the founding of the Original Series of the *Southern Review;* it was there again at his inauguration as the first Poet Laureate of the United States (after a luncheon at the Library of Congress as various dignitaries offered up their encomia of Warren's work, he became visibly more restive and finally responded, "I feel like I've been listening to a bunch of hired mourners"—which, due to his accent, I heard at first as "hard mourners," but that seemed alright too); and finally I saw it most clearly when, with my then eleven-year-old son, I visited the Warrens in Fairfield, Connecticut, early in 1987. Never have I known anyone who more perfectly embodied the ideal of the host than Red Warren (though I must say parenthetically that even he could not have been so grand a host had he not had at his side Eleanor Clark). He was unfailingly, exquisitely considerate and thoughtful towards his guests in a way that, in our time, seemed almost anachronistic, as if he had adopted the ideal from the ancient Greeks for whom the gracious reception of guests represented the highest, most solemn obligation. Not that Red was solemn about it, not at all (as was humorously evident when, apropos of some supposed breach of hostly decorum, he feigned horror and ironi-

cally echoed Lady MacBeth's exclamation after the murder of Duncan: "Who alas! / What, in our house?") but he refused to neglect his duties as host even in the tiniest of details: for example, although it was clearly very painful for him to do it because of his physical frailty at the time, he insisted on pulling the corks from wine bottles since, for him, it was unthinkable that he should require a guest to perform this duty of the host.

I think it was this same characteristic—this same generosity of spirit and quick, sensitive responsiveness to the needs of others—that made Red Warren the loving husband and father that he was, for it was not only in his public life as man of letters nor only in his semi-public/private life as host that his life was so perfectly rounded out and beautifully fulfilled; it was also, and especially, in his private existence as husband, as father and grandfather, that we can think of his as a preeminently good life. In such a great poem as **"After the Dinner Party"** (which, not insignificantly, is a very late poem) we can gain a sense of Red Warren in all his public and private roles and in the fullness of his humanity; and while, with that and other achievements in our mind, we must, in one sense, mourn his death, we must, in another sense, celebrate even more his life. (pp. 13-15)

James Olney, "On the Death and Life of Robert Penn Warren," in The Southern Review, *Louisiana State University, Vol. 26, No. 1, Winter, 1990, pp. 13-15.*

Obituaries

In addition to the authors represented in the In Memorium section of this *Yearbook,* several other notable writers passed away during 1989:

Thomas Bernhard
September 11?, 1931—February 12, 1989
Austrian novelist, dramatist, and autobiographer

Renowned in Europe as a major writer, Bernhard expressed in his work a relentlessly bleak, misanthropic view of the human condition. His dense and compulsively repetitive works are dominated by monologues that delineate such concerns as death, decay, and madness. Bernhard's virulent attacks on cultural leaders and anti-Semitism in Austria often sparked controversy. George Steiner called Bernhard "the most original, concentrated novelist writing in German."

Malcolm Cowley
August 24, 1898—March 27, 1989
American critic, historian, editor, poet, and essayist

A leading chronicler of the "Lost Generation," a group of American writers who rose to fame following World War I, Cowley championed the careers of Ernest Hemingway, F. Scott Fitzgerald, and William Faulkner. He served as Literary Editor of *The New Republic* from 1929 to 1944 and subsequently as Literary Advisor to Viking Press. Cowley's best known critical study of the Lost Generation is *Exile's Return: A Narrative of Ideas* (1934), which Lloyd Morris lauded as "an intimate, realistic portrait of the era that produced a renaissance in American fiction and poetry."

Nicolás Guillén
July 9, 1902—July 16, 1989
Cuban poet

Named National Poet of Cuba in 1961 by Premier Fidel Castro, Guillén was recognized by many critics as an important figure in contemporary West Indian literature. He combined the colloquialism and rhythms of Havana's black districts with the formal structure and language of traditional Spanish verse to address the injustices of imperialism, capitalism, and racism while affirming and celebrating the Afro-Cuban experience. Among his many volumes of verse are *West Indies, Ltd.* (1934), *La paloma de vuelo popular: Elegias* (1959), and *Patria o muerte!: The Great Zoo and Other Poems* (1972).

C. L. R. James
January 4, 1901—May 31, 1989
West Indian nonfiction writer, journalist, novelist, and critic.

A noted historian of African, Caribbean, and Soviet revolutionary movements and politics, James was best known as the author of *Beyond a Boundary* (1963), an analysis of cricket and the game's popularity in Great Britain and the West Indies. James's historical studies include *The Black Jacobins: Toussaint L'Ouverture and the San Domingo Revolution* (1938) and *Nkrumah and the Ghana Revolution* (1977).

James Kirkwood
1924?-April 22, 1989
American dramatist and novelist

Kirkwood coauthored the book for *A Chorus Line* (1975), for which he and Nicholas Dante shared a Tony Award and a Pulitzer Prize for drama. This play, which consists of character studies of dancers from all walks of life auditioning for a limited number of chorus roles, was described by Kirkwood as an exposé of "the whole idea of competition." Immensely popular,

A Chorus Line became the longest running Broadway musical ever in 1983, and finally closed in 1990 after over 6,000 performances.

Hans Hellmutt Kirst
December 5, 1914—February 23, 1989
German journalist and novelist

An internationally popular author, Kirst was often described as the novelist of the German soldier class. He served in the German army from 1935 through the end of World War II in Europe, and frequently wrote about his war experiences and how he was "seduced" by Naziism. Many of his works explore means for coming to terms with and atoning for Nazi atrocities.

Danilo Kiš
February 22, 1935—October 15, 1989
Yugoslavian novelist, short story writer, and dramatist

Kiš earned recognition for fiction that concentrates on the persecution of German Jews during World War II and on Stalin's forced-labor camps. In such works as the novel *Basta, pepeo* (1965; *Garden Ashes*) and the short story collection *Grobnica za Borisa Davidovica* (1976; *A Tomb for Boris Davidovich*), Kiš blended factual accounts with lyrical passages, creating a style often termed "documentary" fiction. His highly regarded collection *Enciklopedia mrtvih* (1983; *The Encyclopedia of the Dead*) focuses on the significance of individuals; Josef Škvorecký identified its theme as "the uniqueness, and therefore the equal importance, of every human being."

Norma Klein
May 13, 1938—April 25, 1989
American novelist and short story writer

Author of more than thirty novels for young adults, Klein examined family problems, sexuality, and such social issues as racism, sexism, and contraception. Although her adult fiction similarly centered on these topics, it was her realistic treatment of the presence of these issues in the lives of adolescents that caused controversy and led some authorities to remove her works from libraries.

Scott O'Dell
May 24, 1898—October 15, 1989
American novelist

A leading author of historical fiction for children and young adults, O'Dell is most famous for *Island of the Blue Dolphins* (1960), which won the John Newbery Medal among numerous honors. O'Dell was a recipient of the Hans Christian Andersen Medal, awarded to authors who have made significant contributions to children's literature. The author also created the Scott O'Dell Award for Historical Fiction, a $5000 annual prize for best book of historical fiction for children.

Frederic Prokosch
May 17, 1908—June 2, 1989
American novelist, poet, memoirist, and translator

Prokosch established his literary reputation during the 1930s with *The Asiatics* (1935), his first novel, and *The Assassins* (1936), his first collection of verse, both of which were widely acclaimed. Prokosch's writing featured elements of the heroic adventure and spiritual quest while exhibiting a vision of cultural decay that has been described as vivid and authentic. His memoir, *Voices* (1983), relates his encounters with many of the major literary figures of the twentieth century.

Leonardo Sciascia
January 8, 1921—November 20, 1989
Italian novelist, short story writer, and nonfiction writer

Sciascia is part of the literary tradition exemplified by Luigi Pirandello and Giuseppe di Lampiduso, who explored the peculiarly Sicilian way of life. Best known for his novels about the Mafia, including *Il giorno della civetta* (1961; *Mafia Vendetta*), *A ciascuno il suo* (1966; *A Man's Blessing*), *Il contesto* (1971; *Equal Danger),* and *Todo modo* (1974; *One Way of Another*), Sciascia is usually considered a mystery writer. In all of his works, the history, politics, and interplay of crime and authority in Sicily symbolize greater evils of the modern world.

Georges Simenon
February 13, 1903—September 4, 1989
Belgian novelist, short story writer, and nonfiction writer

An extremely prolific author whose works have been translated into more than forty languages, Simenon, who wrote under many pseudonyms, is best known for his series of detective novels featuring French police inspector Jules Maigret. Central to all of Simenon's work is his view of the inevitablity of destiny, which renders his characters helpless to stop themselves from taking part in criminal actions. He is credited with introducing the psychologically-oriented crime novel, wherein the sleuth relies on intuition rather than deductive reasoning to solve mysteries.

I. F. Stone
December 24, 1907—June 18, 1989
American journalist and nonfiction writer

Best known for his influential, anti-establishment newsletter, *I. F. Stone's Weekly,* Stone was a dogged investigator of political deception and abuse. He was among the first commentators to denounce McCarthyism, American involvement in Vietnam, and vastly increased military spending. Ostracized during the 1950s for his Marxist views, Stone is often described as "a folk hero to the New Left." His notable books include *The Trial of Socrates* (1988), a best-selling, iconoclastic account of the philosopher's death, and *Underground to Palestine* (1979), in which Stone follows the migration of European Jews to Palestine immediately after World War II.

Irving Stone
July 14, 1903—August 26, 1989
American novelist

A prolific and popular author, Stone is often credited with developing the contemporary form of the biographical novel. Among the best known of his meticulously researched works are *Lust for Life* (1934), the story of Vincent Van Gogh; *Love is Eternal* (1954), about Mary Todd Lincoln; and *The Agony and the Ecstasy* (1961), based upon the life of Michelangelo.

May Swenson
May 28, 1919—December 4, 1989
American poet

Swenson was noted for her experiments with poetic form and her celebration of animal life and ordinary human concerns. In reviewing *New and Selected Things Taking Place* (1978), which collects verse from her first six collections, Dave Smith observed that Swenson's poems "are characterized by extreme reticence of personality, an abundant energy, and an extraordinary intercourse between the natural and intellectual worlds."

Barbara Tuchman
January 30, 1912—February 6, 1989
American historian and journalist

A popular and critically acclaimed writer, Tuchman combined prodigious research and a vivid prose style to create dramatic and accessible historical narratives. Among her eleven works are two Pulitzer Prize-winning histories, *The Guns of August* (1962), a study of World War I, and *Stillwell and the American Experience in China, 1911-1945* (1971). *The First Salute* (1989), a history of the American Revolution, was on the *New York Times* bestseller list at the time of her death.

Topics in Literature: 1989

The Fiftieth Anniversary of
John Steinbeck's *The Grapes of Wrath*

An American novelist, short story writer, dramatist, nonfiction writer, journalist, and essayist, **John (Ernst) Steinbeck** was born in 1902 and died in 1968. The following entry presents criticism on Steinbeck's novel *The Grapes of Wrath* (1939). For discussion of Steinbeck's complete career, see *CLC*, Vols. 1, 5, 9, 13, 21, 34, 45.

Considered a major work of American literature, *The Grapes of Wrath* exposed the tragic plight of Southwestern sharecroppers and farmers who lost their land and livelihood during the 1930s. Devastated by adverse economic conditions of the Depression and by a prolonged drought that turned fertile farmland into the "Dust Bowl," thousands of rural families from Oklahoma, Texas, and Arkansas migrated to California in search of employment. Emblematic of these dispossessed farmers are Steinbeck's protagonists, the Joad family, who survive numerous hardships during their journey and encounter hostility and victimization in California as part of an overabundant labor supply. The particular struggles of the family alternate with chapters on general topics that encompass contemporary social events, American ideals and myths, and natural phenomena, extending the implications of the Joads's conflicts into universal significance. Louis Owens observed: "We can and should read *The Grapes of Wrath* as a testament to a historical and sociological phenomenon—the Dust Bowl—perhaps the greatest combined ecological and social catastrophe in American history. . . . Steinbeck brilliantly documents the suffering of a people in flight, the tragic loss of homeland, and the discovery that in the land of plenty there isn't enough to go around." Owens added: "Behind the political and historical message lies the archetypal pattern of American consciousness, the so-called American myth."

The Grapes of Wrath generated heated controversy upon publication. Finding the novel threatening and sensationalistic, associations of farmers in California appealed for a statewide ban that was partially successful. Authorities and librarians in such cities as Kansas City and Buffalo removed the book from circulation, citing vulgar language, casual sexuality, and Steinbeck's graphic portrayal of deplorable living conditions. Several sources, including *Collier's* magazine, treated *The Grapes of Wrath* as communist propaganda. In Congress, Representative Lyle Boren of Oklahoma denounced the book as a "lying, filthy manuscript" that unjustly portrayed Oklahomans as shiftless. Meanwhile, *The Grapes of Wrath* was championed in the press by Eleanor Roosevelt, a spirited public figure during the Depression-era administration of her husband, President Franklin D. Roosevelt. The novel also helped promote social legislation; a commission chaired by Senator Robert M. LaFollette reformed migrant labor practices, and a Supreme Court decision in 1941 overturned migrant labor laws in twenty-seven states. *The Grapes of Wrath* is popularly perceived as having inspired widespread interest and compassion toward an oppressed people, and is often

linked with other powerful works that helped induce social change, including Harriet Beecher Stowe's *Uncle Tom's Cabin,* Victor Hugo's *Les Miserables,* Upton Sinclair's *The Jungle,* and several novels by Charles Dickens.

Steinbeck was born, raised, and lived most of his life in the lush Salinas Valley region of California, where he witnessed conflicts between laborers and owners of large farms. Many of his works are set in that locale, including *In Dubious Battle* (1936), which depicts the efforts of farm workers to unionize and strike for better wages, and *Of Mice and Men* (1937), an immensely popular novel and Broadway play. These works and *The Grapes of Wrath,* which won the Pulitzer Prize for Fiction and was adapted into an acclaimed film by John Ford, secured Steinbeck's reputation as a major American writer and contributed greatly to his winning the Nobel Prize in Literature in 1962.

In autumn of 1936, Steinbeck helped publicize injustices faced by migrant workers in California by contributing an essay to the *Nation* and a series of seven articles under the heading "The Harvest Gypsies" to *The San Francisco News.* These pieces were collected in a pamphlet, *Their Blood Is Strong* (1938), which was expanded and reissued in 1989 as *The Harvest Gypsies: On the Road to 'The Grapes of Wrath.'* Based on Steinbeck's experiences in migrant makeshift settlements and in camps established by the federal government, the articles contain case studies, statistics, and recommendations as well as details of the miserable living conditions endured by migrants and their confrontations with large landowners. Steinbeck met Tom Collins, an official with the Farm Security Administration who managed a clean, well-run government resettlement area that served as the model for the Weedpatch Camp in *The Grapes of Wrath.* The novel is dedicated, in part, to Collins ("For Tom, who lived it"). Deeply moved and angered by the hardships of migrant workers, Steinbeck was determined to dramatize their experiences, particularly after having witnessed death and destruction by flood in a Visalia migrant settlement. This incident is recreated in the final chapter of *The Grapes of Wrath* and exemplifies Steinbeck's artistic embellishment of actual events.

The novel begins with a description of the Dust Bowl, the Southwestern plains area devastated by drought, and the people most severely affected. The second chapter introduces Tom Joad, who is returning home to his family after having served four years of a seven-year term for manslaughter. Tom encounters Jim Casy, a lapsed preacher who, like Jesus Christ, underwent a meditative retreat to the wilderness. During the course of the novel Casy expounds a philosophy, similar to Christ's, that emphasizes the importance of developing from an individualistic to a collective outlook, or "from I to we." Tom and Casy reach the Joad homestead but find it abandoned and ravaged. They meet Muley Graves, a nervous and desperate ex-farmer being hunted by authorities, who informs them that the Joads, like other sharecroppers in the area, have lost their land to banks and are planning to relocate to California.

Tom and Casy meet the Joad clan the next morning at the home of Tom's uncle, John. The family has invested the bulk of their savings on a car that they have converted into a flatbed truck and loaded with most of their possessions for the journey to California. Their decision to leave Oklahoma is prompted by handbills advertising employment opportunities and by their own idyllic visions of California as a land of plenty. The Joad family includes Tom, Sr., or Pa, and his brother, John, both of whom feel humiliated by their loss of livelihood, and Mrs. Joad, or Ma, who gradually emerges as head of the family through her efforts to keep the group together. The offspring comprise Al, an adolescent obsessed with girls and automobiles; Rose of Sharon, or Rosasharn, a pregnant teenaged newlywed; the slow-witted and somewhat mystical Noah; and the children Ruthie and Winfield. Also making the journey are Tom and Casy, Granpa and Granma Joad, and Connie, Rosasharn's husband. Steinbeck's detailing of the family's preparations for the journey and their misfortunes along Route 66, the highway they follow to California, is generally considered the most successful portion of *The Grapes of Wrath.* While on the road, the family descends into more dismal emotional and financial conditions; they hear negative reports from people returning from California, and the elder Joads die. Upon reaching California, Connie and Noah desert the clan to pursue their own interests.

When the Joads finally enter northern California farmland, they are startled by the hostility of residents and authorities before learning that the handbills have lured an overabundant migrant labor supply, allowing landowners to drive down wages. Harassed, forced to live in dire conditions, and unable to save money, the Joads find themselves among thousands of families competing for work and struggling for survival. Casy and Tom become involved in attempts to organize workers, and when Casy is murdered as a labor agitator, Tom becomes a fugitive after striking down the man who killed his friend. In a moving farewell to his mother, Tom asserts his intention to continue Casy's efforts on the part of the deprived. His statement, "[A] fella ain't got a soul of his own, but on'y a piece of a big one," reflects the influence of Casy's collective philosophy. The novel concludes with the family's camp threatened by flooding; while Pa, Al, and Uncle John attempt to build a dike, Rosasharn delivers a stillborn child. In the notorious final scene of *The Grapes of Wrath,* Ma gently persuades Rosasharn to use the milk of her breast to suckle a starving man.

The intercalary chapters that alternate with the story of the Joads underscore and connect their distress to larger social and natural phenomena. Steinbeck's description of a turtle's slow and frustrating journey across a highway, for example, can be likened to the Joads's arduous westward trek, and a description of a dust storm reveals farmers at the mercy of forces beyond their control. Other chapters describe feverish wheeling and dealing at used car lots, a meditation on how the advent of the tractor changed the nature of farming, descriptions of roadside diners, gas stations, and other businesses along Route 66, and contemplations of the California landscape and people. These elements, along with biblical symbolism and principles of American thought, broaden the scope of *The Grapes of Wrath.* Among Christian allusions, the novel's title derives from a biblical phrase, and the migration of the Joads is often compared to that of the Israelites, a homeless, persecuted people who sought the promised land. Numerous critics have traced affinities between Casy and Christ, both of whom took on the sins of others and were sacrificed. Just before he is killed, Casy cries out, "You fellas don' know what you're doin'," which parallels Christ's utterance, "Forgive them Father, they know not what they do." Critics have also noted Steinbeck's allusions to the agrarian values of Thomas Jefferson, the transcendentalism and pantheism of Ralph Waldo Emerson, the nationalist aesthetics promoted by Walt Whitman, and the pragmatist philosophy of William James.

The Grapes of Wrath is generally considered a major American novel, yet many critics express reservations concerning Steinbeck's artistry. Negative commentators usually cite strained poetic prose, simplistic and mystical political observations, melodrama, and awkward symbolism, particularly in the final scene involving Rosasharn and the starving man. Steinbeck's recreation of Southwestern dialect has received mixed response. Many critics, however, believe the various elements in the novel are successfully unified, and *The Grapes of Wrath* endures as a powerful and tragic novel in the tradition of protest literature. Upon rereading the novel on the occasion of the fiftieth anniversary of its publication, William Kennedy observed: "Steinbeck had the power. And if at times he lacked the language and the magic that go with mythic literary achievement and status, he had in their place a mighty conscience and a mighty heart. And just about 51 years ago this time, that man sat down and put pencil to paper; and in five miraculous months he wrote a mighty, mighty book."

Among observances of the novel's fiftieth anniversary, conferences and papers were sponsored by the Steinbeck Research Center at San Jose State University and by the University of Alabama, and an anniversary edition was published with an introduction by Studs Terkel. Diary entries written by Steinbeck during and after the composition process are collected in *Working Days: The Journals of 'The Grapes of Wrath'*. Revealing his daily struggles with the text, his thoughts and observations on scenes and characters, and the interruptions and doubts that plagued Steinbeck as he attempted to complete his work, *Working Days* is considered an invaluable companion to the novel. The diary also reveals the strong support of Steinbeck's second wife, Carol, who suggested the novel's title and to whom *The Grapes of Wrath* is partly dedicated ("To Carol, who willed this book"). The diaries were edited by Robert DeMott, who provided an assessment of *The Grapes of Wrath:* "Wherever human beings dream of a dignified society in which they can harvest the fruits of their own labor, *The Grapes of Wrath*'s radical voice of protest can still be heard. As a tale of dashed illusions, thwarted desires, inhuman suffering, and betrayed promises—all strung on the most fragile thread of hope—*The Grapes of Wrath* not only summed up the Depression era's socially conscious art, but, beyond that, has few peers in American fiction."

(See also *Contemporary Authors,* Vols. 1-4, rev. ed., 29-32, rev. ed. [obituary]; *Contemporary Authors New Revision Series,* Vol. 1; *Something about the Author,* Vol. 9; *Dictionary of Literary Biography,* Vols. 7, 9; *Dictionary of Literary Biography Documentary Series,* Vol. 2; and *Concise Dictionary of American Literary Biography,* 1929-1941.)

JOHN STEINBECK

In sixty years a complete revolution has taken place in California agriculture. Once its principal products were hay and cattle. Today fruits and vegetables are its most profitable crops. With the change in the nature of farming there has come a parallel change in the nature and amount of the labor necessary to carry it on. Truck gardens, while they give a heavy yield per acre, require much more labor and equipment than the raising of hay and livestock. At the same time these crops are seasonal, which means that they are largely handled by migratory workers. Along with the intensification of farming made necessary by truck gardening has come another important development. The number of large-scale farms, involving the investment of thousands of dollars, has increased; so has the number of very small farms of from five to ten acres. But the middle farm, of from 100 to 300 acres is in process of elimination.

There are in California, therefore, two distinct classes of farmers widely separated in standard of living, desires, needs, and sympathies: the very small farmer who more often than not takes the side of the workers in disputes, and the speculative farmer, like A. J. Chandler, publisher of the Los Angeles *Times,* or like Herbert Hoover and William Randolph Hearst, absentee owners who possess huge sections of land. Allied with these large individual growers have been the big

incorporated farms, owned by their stockholders and farmed by instructed managers, and a large number of bank farms, acquired by foreclosure and operated by superintendents whose labor policy is dictated by the bank. For example, the Bank of America is very nearly the largest farm owner and operator in the state of California.

These two classes have little or no common ground; while the small farmer is likely to belong to the grange, the speculative farmer belongs to some such organization as the Associated Farmers of California, which is closely tied to the state Chamber of Commerce. This group has as its major activity resistance to any attempt of farm labor to organize. Its avowed purpose has been the distribution of news reports and leaflets tending to show that every attempt to organize agricultural workers was the work of red agitators and that every organization was Communist inspired.

The completion of the transcontinental railroads left in the country many thousands of Chinese and some Hindus who had been imported for the work. At about the same time the increase of fruit crops, with their heavy seasonal need for pickers, created a demand for this mass of cheap labor. These people, however, did not long remain on the land. They migrated to the cities, rented small plots of land there, and, worst of all, organized in the so-called "tongs," which were able to direct their efforts as a group. Soon the whites were inflamed to race hatred, riots broke out against the Chinese, and repressive activities were undertaken all over the state, until these people, who had been a tractable and cheap source of labor, were driven from the fields.

To take the place of the Chinese, the Japanese were encouraged to come into California; and they, even more than the Chinese, showed an ability not only to obtain land for their subsistence but to organize. The "Yellow Peril" agitation was the result. Then, soon after the turn of the century Mexicans were imported in great numbers. For a while they were industrious workers, until the process of importing twice as many as were needed in order to depress wages made their earnings drop below any conceivable living standard. In such conditions they did what the others had done; they began to organize. The large growers immediately opened fire on them. The newspapers were full of the radicalism of the Mexican unions. Riots became common in the Imperial Valley and in the grape country in and adjacent to Kern County. Another wave of importations was arranged, from the Philippine Islands, and the cycle was repeated—wage depression due to abundant labor, organization, and the inevitable race hatred and riots.

This brings us almost to the present. The drought in the Middle West has very recently made available an enormous amount of cheap labor. Workers have been coming to California in nondescript cars from Oklahoma, Nebraska, Texas, and other states, parts of which have been rendered uninhabitable by drought. Poverty-stricken after the destruction of their farms, their last reserves used up in making the trip, they have arrived so beaten and destitute that they have been willing at first to work under any conditions and for any wages offered. This migration started on a considerable scale about two years ago and is increasing all the time.

For a time it looked as though the present cycle would be identical with the earlier ones, but there are several factors in this influx which differentiate it from the others. In the first place, the migrants are undeniably American and not deportable. In the second place, they were not lured to California by a promise of good wages, but are refugees as surely as though they had fled from destruction by an invader. In the third place, they are not drawn from a peon class, but have either owned small farms or been farm hands in the early American sense, in which the "hand" is a member of the employing family. They have one fixed idea, and that is to acquire land and settle on it. Probably the most important difference is that they are not easily intimidated. They are courageous, intelligent, and resourceful. Having gone through the horrors of the drought and with immense effort having escaped from it, they cannot be herded, attacked, starved, or frightened as all the others were.

Let us see what the emigrants from the dust bowl find when they arrive in California. The ranks of permanent and settled labor are filled. In most cases all resources have been spent in making the trip from the dust bowl. Unlike the Chinese and the Filipinos, the men rarely come alone. They bring wives and children, now and then a few chickens and their pitiful household goods, though in most cases these have been sold to buy gasoline for the trip. It is quite usual for a man, his wife, and from three to eight children to arrive in California with no possessions but the rattletrap car they travel in and the ragged clothes on their bodies. They often lack bedding and cooking utensils.

During the spring, summer, and part of the fall the man may find some kind of agricultural work. The top pay for a successful year will not be over $400, and if he has any trouble or is not agile, strong, and quick it may well be only $150. It will be seen that rent is out of the question. Clothes cannot be bought. Every available cent must go for food and a reserve to move the car from harvest to harvest. The migrant will stop in one of two federal camps, in a state camp, in houses put up by the large or small farmers, or in the notorious squatters' camps. In the state and federal camps he will find sanitary arrangements and a place to pitch his tent. The camps maintained by the large farmers are of two classes—houses which are rented to the workers at what are called nominal prices, $4 to $8 a month, and camp grounds which are little if any better than the squatters' camps. (pp. 302-03)

The small farmers are not able to maintain camps of any comfort or with any sanitary facilities except one or two holes dug for toilets. The final resource is the squatters' camp, usually located on the bank of some watercourse. The people pack into them. They use the watercourse for drinking, bathing, washing their clothes, and to receive their refuse, with the result that epidemics start easily and are difficult to check. Stanislaus County, for example, has a nice culture of hookworm in the mud by its squatters' camp. The people in these camps, because of long-continued privation, are in no shape to fight illness. It is often said that no one starves in the United States, yet in Santa Clara County last year five babies were certified by the local coroner to have died of "malnutrition," the modern word for starvation, and the less shocking word, although in its connotation it is perhaps more horrible since it indicates that the suffering has been long drawn out.

In these squatters' camps the migrant will find squalor beyond anything he has yet had to experience and intimidation almost unchecked. At one camp it is the custom of deputy sheriffs, who are also employees of a great ranch nearby, to drive by the camp for hours at a time, staring into the tents as though trying to memorize faces. The communities in which these camps exist want migratory workers to come for

the month required to pick the harvest, and to move on when it is over. If they do not move on, they are urged to with guns.

These are some of the conditions California offers the refugees from the dust bowl. But the refugees are even less content with the starvation wages and the rural slums than were the Chinese, the Filipinos, and the Mexicans. Having their families with them, they are not so mobile as the earlier immigrants were. If starvation sets in, the whole family starves, instead of just one man. Therefore they have been quick to see that they must organize for their own safety.

Attempts to organize have been met with a savagery from the large growers beyond anything yet attempted. In Kern County a short time ago a group met to organize under the A. F. of L. They made out their form and petition for a charter and put it in the mail for Washington. That night a representative of Associated Farmers wired Washington for information concerning a charter granted to these workers. The Washington office naturally replied that it had no knowledge of such a charter. In the Bakersfield papers the next day appeared a story that the A. F. of L. denied the affiliation; consequently the proposed union must be of Communist origin.

But the use of the term communism as a bugbear has nearly lost its sting. An official of a speculative-farmer group, when asked what he meant by a Communist, replied: "Why, he's the guy that wants twenty-five cents an hour when we're paying twenty." This realistic and cynical definition has finally been understood by the workers, so that the term is no longer the frightening thing it was. And when a county judge said, "California agriculture demands that we create and maintain a peonage," the future of unorganized agricultural labor was made clear to every man in the field.

The usual repressive measures have been used against these migrants: shooting by deputy sheriffs in "self-defense," jailing without charge, refusal of trial by jury, torture and beating by night riders. But even in the short time that these American migrants have been out here there has been a change. It is understood that they are being attacked not because they want higher wages, not because they are Communists, but simply because they want to organize. And to the men, since this defines the thing not to be allowed, it also defines the thing that is completely necessary to the safety of the workers.

This season has seen the beginning of a new form of intimidation not used before. It is the whispering campaign which proved so successful among business rivals. As in business, it is particularly deadly here because its source cannot be traced and because it is easily spread. One of the items of this campaign is the rumor that in the event of labor troubles the deputy sheriffs inducted to break up picket lines will be armed not with tear gas but with poison gas. The second is aimed at the women and marks a new low in tactics. It is to the effect that in the event of labor troubles the water supply used by strikers will be infected with typhoid germs. The fact that these bits of information are current over a good part of the state indicates that they have been widely planted.

The effect has been far from that desired. There is now in California anger instead of fear. . . .

It is fervently to be hoped that the great group of migrant workers so necessary to the harvesting of California's crops may be given the right to live decently, that they may not be so badgered, tormented, and hurt that in the end they become avengers of the hundreds of thousands who have been tortured and starved before them. (p. 304)

John Steinbeck, "Dubious Battle in California," in The Nation, *New York, Vol. 143, No. 11, September 12, 1936, pp. 302-04.*

LOUIS KRONENBERGER

[*The Grapes of Wrath*] is in many ways the most moving and disturbing social novel of our time. What is wrong with it, what is weak in it, what robs it of the stature it clearly attempts, are matters that must presently be pointed out; but not at once. First it should be pointed out that *The Grapes of Wrath* comes at a needed time in a powerful way. It comes, perhaps, as *The Drapier's Letters* or *Uncle Tom's Cabin* or some of the social novels of Zola came. It burns with no pure gemlike flame, but with hot and immediate fire. It is, from any point of view, Steinbeck's best novel, but it does not make one wonder whether, on the basis of it, Steinbeck is now a better novelist than Hemingway or Farrell or Dos Passos; it does not invoke comparisons; it simply makes one feel that Steinbeck is, in some way all his own, a force.

The publishers refer to the book as "perhaps the greatest single creative work that this country has produced." This is a foolish and extravagant statement, but unlike most publishers' statements, it seems the result of honest enthusiasm, and one may hope that the common reader will respond to the book with an enthusiasm of the same sort. And perhaps he will, for *The Grapes of Wrath* has, overwhelmingly, those two qualities most vital to a work of social protest: great indignation and great compassion. Its theme is large and tragic and, on the whole, is largely and tragically felt. No novel of our day has been written out of a more genuine humanity, and none, I think, is better calculated to awaken the humanity of others.

Throughout the Southwest hundreds of thousands of small farmers and share-croppers have been driven, by the banks and the big landowners, from their farms—to move westward, with their families, in a dusty caravan of jalopies, to California. (p. 440)

In the fate of one such family—the Joads of Oklahoma—John Steinbeck has told the fate of all. Their fate is the theme of an angry and aroused propagandist, but the Joads themselves are the product of a lively novelist. A racy, picturesque, somewhat eccentric tribe, with certain resemblances to Erskine Caldwell's Georgia exhibits, . . . the Joads, with their salty, slanting speech, their frank and boisterous opinions, their unrepressed, irrepressible appetites, would, in a stable world, be the stuff of rich folk-comedy. But suddenly uprooted and harassed, they are creatures forced to fight for their very existence. During the first half of Steinbeck's long book the Joads, both as people and as symbols, have tremendous vitality. Steinbeck's account of this one family leaving home and journeying forth in a rickety makeshift truck is like some night-lighted, rude Homeric chronicle of a great migration. It has a vigor, as of half-childlike, half-heroic adventuring, that almost blots out the sense of its desperate origins and painful forebodings.

But after the Joads reach California, something—a kind of inner life—disappears from the book. The economic outrage, the human tragedy are made brutally clear. The chronicle of the Joads remains vivid; the nature of their fate becomes ever

more infuriating. As a tract, the book goes on piling up its indictment, conducting the reader on a sort of grand tour of exploitation and destitution. And all this has, emotionally at least, a very strong effect. But somehow the book ceases to grow, to maintain direction. It is truly enough a story of nomads; but from that it does not follow that the proletarian novel must fall into the loose pattern of the picaresque novel. Artistically speaking, the second half of *The Grapes of Wrath,* though it still has content and suspense, lacks form and intensity. The people simply go on and on, with Steinbeck left improvising and amplifying until—with a touch of new and final horror—he abruptly halts.

The Grapes of Wrath is a superb tract because it exposes something terrible and true with enormous vigor. It is a superb tract, moreover, by virtue of being thoroughly animated fiction, by virtue of living scenes and living characters (like Ma), not by virtue of discursive homilies and dead characters (like the socialistic preacher). One comes away moved, indignant, protesting, pitying. But one comes away dissatisfied, too, aware that *The Grapes of Wrath* is too unevenly weighted, too uneconomically proportioned, the work of a writer who is still self-indulgent, still undisciplined, still not altogether aware of the difference in value of various human emotions. (pp. 440-41)

But one does not take leave of a book like this in a captious spirit. One salutes it as a firey document of protest and compassion, as a story that had to be told, as a book that must be read. It is, I think, one of those books—there are not very many—which really do some good. (p. 441)

Louis Kronenberger, "Hungry Caravan," in The Nation, *New York, Vol. 148, No. 16, April 15, 1939, pp. 440-41.*

CLIFTON FADIMAN

If only a couple of million overcomfortable people can be brought to read it, John Steinbeck's *The Grapes of Wrath* may actually effect something like a revolution in their minds and hearts. It sounds like a crazy notion, I know, but I feel this book may just possibly do for our time what *Les Miserables* did for its, *Uncle Tom's Cabin* for its, *The Jungle* for its. *The Grapes of Wrath* is the kind of art that's poured out of a crucible in which are mingled pity and indignation. It seems advisable to stress this point. A lot of readers and critics are going to abandon themselves to orgies of ohing and ahing over Steinbeck's impressive literary qualities, happy to blink at the simple fact that fundamentally his book is a social novel exposing social injustice and calling, though never explicitly, for social redress. It's going to be a great and deserved best-seller; it'll be read and praised by everyone; it will almost certainly win the Pulitzer Prize; it will be filmed and dramatized and radio-acted—but, gentle reader, amid all the excitement let's try to keep in mind what *The Grapes of Wrath* is about: to wit, the slow murder of half a million innocent and worthy American citizens.

I don't know and in truth I don't much care whether it's the "work of genius" the publishers sincerely believe it to be. What sticks with me is that here is a book, non-political, non-dogmatic, which dramatizes so that you can't forget it the terrible facts of a wholesale injustice committed by society. Here is a book about a people of old American stock, not Reds or rebels of any kind. They are dispossessed of their land, their pitiful little homes are destroyed, they are lured to California by false hopes. When they get there, after incredible hardships, they are exploited, reduced to peonage, then to virtual slavery. If they protest, they are beaten, tortured, or their skulls are smashed in. Even if they do not protest, they are hounded, intimidated, and finally starved into defeat. The industrial and political groups that do these things know quite well what they do. Hence they cannot be forgiven. (p. 81)

Along Highway 66, ribboning from the Mississippi to Bakersfield, California, these disinherited, in their rickety jalopies, have been for the last five years streaming into the Far West. Driven off their farms by the drought, dust, or the juggernaut of the tractor, the small farmers and sharecroppers of half a dozen states, but mainly Oklahoma and Arkansas, have been staking their salvation on the possibility of work in California.

Steinbeck creates a family—the Joads of Oklahoma—and makes them typify a whole culture on the move. At the same time he gives us this migrant culture itself, in all its pathetic hopefulness, its self-reliance, the growing sense of unity it imparts to its people.

If ever The Great American Novel is written, it may very possibly be composed along the lines here laid out by Steinbeck. No one since the advent of Sinclair Lewis has had so exact a feeling for what is uniquely American. This feeling Steinbeck shows not only in his portrayal of the Joads themselves, in his careful notation of their folk speech, folk myths, folk obscenities, but in a thousand minor touches that add up to something major: the description of the used-car market, of the minds of truckdrivers and hash-house waitresses, of Highway 66, of the butchering and salting down of the pigs. It is this large interest in the whole lives of his Oklahoma farmers that makes *The Grapes of Wrath* more than a novel of propaganda, even though its social message is what will stick with any sensitive reader.

The book has faults. It is too detailed, particularly in the latter half. Casy, the ex-preacher, is half real, half "poetic" in the worse sense of the word. Occasionally the folk note is forced a little. And, finally, the ending (a young girl who has only a day or two before given birth to a dead child offers the milk of her breasts to a starving man) is the tawdriest kind of fake symbolism. Just occasionally Steinbeck's dramatic imagination overleaps itself and you get a piece of pure, or impure, theatre like these last pages. One should also add that his political thinking is a little mystical. The sense of unity that his migrants gradually acquire is not necessarily, as he implies, of a progressive character. It is based on an emotion that can just as easily be discharged into the channels of reaction. In other words, are not these simple, tormented Okies good Fascist meat, if the proper misleaders are found for them?

It is unlikely, however, that such misgivings will occur to you in the reading of the book. Its power and importance do not lie in its political insight but in its intense humanity, its grasp of the spirit of an entire people traversing a wilderness, its kindliness, its humor, and its bitter indignation. *The Grapes of Wrath* is the American novel of the season, probably the year, possibly the decade. (pp. 81-2)

Clifton Fadiman, "Highway 66—A Tale of Five Cities," in The New Yorker, *Vol. XV, No. 9, April 15, 1939, pp. 81-2.*

JOSEPH HENRY JACKSON

"You never been called 'Okie' yet? 'Okie' use' ta mean you was from Oklahoma. Now it means you're scum. Don't mean nothin' itself; it's the way they say it. But I can't tell you nothin' You got to go there. I hear there's three hundred thousan' of our people there—an' livin' like hogs, 'cause ever'thing in California is owned. They ain't nothin' left. And them people that owns it is gonna hang on to it if they got ta kill ever'body in the worl' to do it. An' they're scairt, an' that makes 'em mad. You got to see it. You got to hear it. Purtiest goddamn country you ever seen, but they ain't nice to you, them folks. They're so scairt an' worried they ain't even nice to each other."

That was the tale told to the Joad family, tractored out of the red-earth-and-gray-dust country of Oklahoma and headed for California in a groaning jalopy for which they had paid almost their last cent. They had seen fine printed handbills telling them that California needed pickers for fruit, for peas, for cotton. Work for thousands; that was what those notices said. And the Joads, tractored, blown, swept off the land on which they and their family had lived for years, were on their way to find out. They were strong; all they wanted was a job. They were willing to work, every last one of them, even Ma and the children. Surely they would find an opportunity in California. Maybe they could even lay by a little and have a nice house. With four or five men, all working, it wouldn't be so hard to do. . . .

Multiply the Joads by thousands and you have a picture of the great modern migration that is the subject of [*The Grapes of Wrath,*] which is far and away the finest book [Steinbeck] has yet written. Examine the motives and the forces behind what happened to the Joads and you have a picture of the fantastic social and economic situation facing America today. Cure? Steinbeck suggests none. He puts forward no doctrine, no dogma. But he writes "In the souls of the people the grapes of wrath are filling and growing heavy, growing heavy for the vintage." I have no doubt that Steinbeck would not enjoy being called a prophet. But this novel is something very like prophecy.

The Joads were only one family to learn that a bank was not a man. It was made up of men, but it was a bigger thing and it controlled them, even though sometimes they hated to do what the bank-monster said they must. That monster moved out the Joads and other thousands. . . .

So the Joads and the thousands of the dispossessed came to the promised land. And they learned what they had been brought there for. There was work, yes, in the pears, in the almonds, in the prunes and the peaches and the cotton. The handbills were right. But what the handbills hadn't explained was that when there were too many workers then wages could be forced down. Pay five cents a box for peach picking where there were starving men who would work for four, or three or even two and a half? We're paying two and a half cents. Take it or leave it. There's a thousand other men want the work. If you don't want it, then move along. Keep moving. And better not mention "decent wages." That's Red talk. There's deputies with guns and pick-handles for Reds. Keep moving. Take it or leave it. Who cares about a bunch of dirty Okies?

What happened to the Joads is the immediate story of this novel. What happened and is happening to the thousands like them is the story behind the story, the reason Steinbeck wrote *The Grapes of Wrath.* What may happen—must happen, he believes—in the long run is the implication behind the book.

> "Whereas the wants of the Californians were nebulous and undefined, the wants of the Okies were beside the roads, lying there to be seen and coveted; the good fields with water to be dug for, earth to crumble in the hand, grass to smell. . . . And a homeless, hungry man, driving the roads with his wife behind him and his thin children in the back seat, could look at the fallow fields which might produce food but not profit, and that man could know how a fallow field is a sin and the unused land a crime against the thin children."

There is the hint. And here again:

> And the great owners, with eyes to read history, and to know the great fact: when property accumulates in too few hands it is taken away. And that companion fact: when a majority of people are hungry and cold they will take by force what they need. And the little screaming fact that sounds through history: repression works only to strengthen and knit the repressed.

Prophecy perhaps. Certainly a warning.

For the story itself, it is completely authentic. Steinbeck knows. He went back to Oklahoma and then came West with the migrants, lived in their camps, saw their pitiful brave highway communities, the life of the itinerant beside the road. He learned what was behind the handbills. And he came back with an enormous respect for the tenacity of these dispossessed, and with the knowledge that this migration is no less a forerunner of a new way than was that migration of those earlier Americans who took California from another group of landholders who had grown too soft to hold it.

It is a rough book, yes. It is an ineffably tender book too. It is the book for which everything else that Steinbeck has written was an exercise in preparation. You'll find in it reminders of *Pastures of Heaven,* of *In Dubious Battle,* of *The Red Pony,* even of *Tortilla Flat.* But here there is no mere exploration of a field, no tentative experimenting with a theme. This is the full symphony, Steinbeck's declaration of faith. The terrible meek will inherit, he says. They will. They are on their way to their inheritance now, and not far from it. And though they are the common people, sometimes dirty people, starved and suppressed and disappointed people, yet they are good people. Steinbeck believes that too.

It is easy to grow lyrical about *The Grapes of Wrath,* to become excited about it, to be stirred to the shouting-point by it. Perhaps it is too easy to lose balance in the face of such an extraordinarily moving performance. But it is also true that the effect of the book lasts. The author's employment, for example, of occasional chapters in which the undercurrent of the book is announced, spoken as a running accompaniment to the story, with something of the effect of the sound track in Pare Lorentz's *The River*—that lasts also stays with you, beats rhythmically in your mind long after you have put the book down. No, the reader's instant response is more than quick enthusiasm, more than surface emotionalism. This novel of America's new disinherited is a magnificent book. It is, I think for the first time, the whole Steinbeck, the mature novelist saying something he must say and doing it with the sure touch of the great artist.

Joseph Henry Jackson, "The Finest Book John Steinbeck Has Written," in New York Herald Tribune Books, *April 16, 1939, p. 3.*

MALCOLM COWLEY

While keeping our eyes on the cataclysms in Europe and Asia, we have lost sight of a tragedy nearer home. A hundred thousand rural households have been uprooted from the soil, robbed of their possessions—though by strictly legal methods—and turned out on the highways. Friendless, homeless and therefore voteless, with fewer rights than medieval serfs, they have wandered in search of a few days' work at miserable wages—not in Spain or the Yangtze Valley, but among the vineyards and orchards of California, in a setting too commonplace for a color story in the Sunday papers. Their migrations have been described only in a long poem and a novel. The poem is "Land of the Free," by Archibald MacLeish, published last year with terrifying photographs by the Resettlement Administration. The novel, which has just appeared, is John Steinbeck's longest and angriest and most impressive work.

The Grapes of Wrath begins with Tom Joad's homecoming. After being released from the Oklahoma State Penitentiary, where he has served four years of a seven-year sentence for homicide, he sets out for his father's little farm in the bottom lands near Sallisaw. He reaches the house to find that it is empty, the windows broken, the well filled in and even the dooryard planted with cotton. Muley Graves, a neighbor, comes past in the dusk and tells him what has happened. It is a scene that I can't forget: the men sitting back on their haunches, drawing figures with a stick in the dust; a half-starved cat watching from the doorstep; and around them the silence of a milelong cottonfield. Muley says that all the tenant farmers have been evicted from their land—"tractored off" is the term he uses. Groups of twenty and thirty farms are being thrown together and the whole area cultivated by one man with a caterpillar tractor. Most of the families are moving to California, on the rumor that work can be found there. . . .

Next morning Tom rejoins his family—just in time, for the uncle too has been ordered to leave his farm. The whole family of twelve is starting for California. Their last day at home is another fine scene in which you realize, little by little, that not only a family but a whole culture is being uprooted—a primitive culture, it is true, but complete in its fashion, with its history, its legends of Indian fighting, its songs and jokes, its religious practices, its habits of work and courtship; even the killing of two hogs is a ritual.

With the hogs salted down and packed in the broken-down truck among the bedclothes, the Joads start westward on U.S. Highway 66. They are part of an endless caravan—trucks, trailers, battered sedans, touring cars rescued from the junkyard, all of them overloaded with children and household plunder, all wheezing, pounding and screeching toward California. There are deaths on the road—Grampa is the first to go—but there is not much time for mourning. A greater tragedy than death is a burned-out bearing, repaired after efforts that Steinbeck describes as if he were singing the exploits of heroes at the siege of Troy. . . .

The second half of the novel, dealing with their adventures in the Valley of California, is still good but somewhat less impressive. Until that moment the Joads have been moving steadily toward their goal. Now they discover that it is not their goal after all; they must still move on, but no longer in one direction—they are harried by vigilantes, recruited as peach pickers, driven out again by a strike; they don't know where to go. . . . The story begins to suffer a little from their bewilderment and lack of direction.

At this point one begins to notice other faults. Interspersed among the chapters that tell what happened to the Joads, there have been other chapters dealing with the general plight of the migrants. The first half-dozen of these interludes have not only broadened the scope of the novel but have been effective in themselves, sorrowful, bitter, intensely moving. But after the Joads reach California, the interludes are spoken in a shriller voice. The author now has a thesis—that the migrants will unite and overthrow their oppressors—and he wants to argue, as if he weren't quite sure of it himself. His thesis is also embodied in one of the characters: Jim Casy, a preacher who loses his faith but unfortunately for the reader can't stop preaching. In the second half of the novel, Casy becomes a Christlike labor leader and is killed by vigilantes. (p. 382)

Yet one soon forgets the faults of the story. What one remembers most of all is Steinbeck's sympathy for the migrants—not pity, for that would mean he was putting himself above them; not love, for that would blind him to their faults, but rather a deep fellow feeling. It makes him notice everything that sets them apart from the rest of the world and sets one migrant apart from all the others. . . . [*The Grapes of Wrath*] has the force of the headlong anger that drives ahead from the first chapter to the last, as if the whole six hundred pages were written without stopping. The author and the reader are swept along together. I can't agree with those critics who say that *The Grapes of Wrath* is the greatest novel of the last ten years; for example, it doesn't rank with the best of Hemingway or Dos Passos. But it belongs very high in the category of the great angry books like *Uncle Tom's Cabin* that have roused a people to fight against intolerable wrongs. (pp. 382-83)

Malcolm Cowley, "American Tragedy," in The New Republic, *Vol. XCVIII, No. 1274, May 3, 1939, pp. 382-83.*

EARLE BIRNEY

[*The Grapes of Wrath*] is a MUST book. It is not only the novel by which Steinbeck steps from the fashionable second-raters to the front ranks of living American fictionists. It is not only a work of concentrated observation, folk humor, and dramatic imagination playing over the whole American continent. It is, more importantly, what Milton would call a "deed"—the act of a man out of the pity and wrath of his heart.

It is a rebellious protest, tempered but by no means obscured by art, against the gradual murder of a half-million southwest farmers by the human instruments of an inhuman and outworn economy. . . .

The book is not free from Steinbeck's old faults. In the ending especially there is theatricality; pain and cruelty are sometimes sensationalized in the manner of Faulkner and Hemingway. There are overtones of mysticism and sentimental individualism which occasionally confuse the dominant social

philosophy. The feel of dirt in the farmer's fingers seems at times more important than tractors. The central character, Ma Joad, is too infallibly heroic and sybilline, the preacher too shadowy for his important role. The crudities of American folk-speech are perhaps exaggerated. (p. 94)

But the sweep of the book's vision and the controlled passion of its style will carry away all but the most hardened prudes. In one short sentence, Steinbeck can catch the whole human tragedy of an abandoned farmhouse: "The wild cats crept in from the fields at night, but they did not mew at the doorsteps any more."

This is no "proletarian novel." It is rather the only thing a class-conscious artist can write so long as the working people of the earth—of our Canadian prairies too—suffer and die like this under their economic overlords. Steinbeck has no pseudo-Marxist hero from the Daily Worker office organizing the farmers along with their bosses into Leagues for Peace and Democracy. These proletarians of the soil are in the bitter process of learning for themselves in their own terms what wage-labor and capital mean, of creating for themselves fire-hardened leaders and cadres for the coming revolution.

That the end will be revolution is implicit from the title onwards. Self-interest dictates that the Haves will not concede; self-preservation and the ultimately superior power of numbers means that the masses will win, so long as they retain the will to "turn their fear to wrath." The inevitable fruit of the system are the bitter grapes of wrath, and there will one day be a tramping out of the vintage. The book will not, as Clifton Fadiman hopes [see excerpt above], "effect something like a revolution in the minds . . . of overcomfortable people," as he assumes *Les Miserables* and *Uncle Tom's Cabin* did. *Les Miserables* did not prevent the Paris Commune nor *Uncle Tom's Cabin* the Civil War. Steinbeck is not so much warning the rich, whom he sees cannot help themselves, as arousing the poor, who can, to courage, endurance, organization, revolt. (pp. 94-5)

Earle Birney, "A Must Book," in The Canadian Forum, *Vol. XIX, No. 221, June, 1939, pp. 94-5.*

THOMAS W. McMANUS

[*Reprinted below is a report by Thomas W. McManus, Secretary of the California Citizens Association. The report, dated July 1, 1939, was originally published in* Grapes of Gladness *(1939), which was compiled and edited by Marshall V. Hantraft.*]

Despite optimistic announcements of a decline in the number of migrants coming to California principally from Oklahoma, Arkansas, Texas, and Missouri, the burden on the taxpayers of our state has become more acute. It is now that the local and state relief rolls are being filled with artificially created "residents," subsidized by the Farm Security Administration for the year's required eligibility. It is now that we are feeling the financial pressure of building new schools for the migrants' children.

It is *now* that we are paying.

Records of the Kern County Hospital show that 44 per cent of the patients taken care of there during the past year were nonresidents, and the origin of 77 per cent of that number was in the four states mentioned. In this period more than 110,000 cases were treated free.

These migrants are not farmers who have been dispossessed. Even the Farm Security Administration, which once claimed evidence to the contrary, now admits that they were either sharecroppers or laborers in their home states. It is plain that there was no place for them here when there were already five unemployed for every available agricultural job in California.

Even in the potato fields of Kern County there were dozens of people for every job, and that is true also of the other crops. In face of this fact, most of the migrants have been living on public bounty since coming to California.

The reduction in acreage in all branches of agriculture and the necessary proration to keep the industry from disaster are such as to limit labor needs. The migration came at the time when it was utterly impossible to give employment to additional workers without destroying the established farm economic system.

The United States Employment Service is authority for the fact that no effort was made by any California farm group to bring labor here, by advertising or any other means. The farmers neither needed nor wanted additional workers, nor did they want the tax cost of supporting unneeded migrants. (pp. 138-39)

The author, John Steinbeck, in his novel, *Grapes of Wrath,* did great injustice both to Californians and to the migrants themselves. These hapless people are not moral and mental degenerates as he pictures them, but victims of desperate conditions—conditions which can bring to California the same tragedy that drove them from their home states.

The recounting by Steinbeck of incidents in which violence was used upon the transients is based upon nothing more than the envisionings of an over-worked imagination. It is absolutely untrue.

A deep-set prejudice seems to be the only explanation for the involving of the American Legion in a fictionally-created harassment of these people.

The California Citizens Association, made up of various organizations, presented to the Congress petitions signed by hundreds of thousands of people, directing the attention of the government to the fact that no further migration could be endured by the people of California. The record of the California Citizens Association has been one of sympathy for these people, but one that must now be tempered by a deep desire to maintain our standard of living and by the natural law of self-preservation. (p. 139)

> *Thomas W. McManus, "California Citizens Association Report," in* A Companion to 'The Grapes of Wrath,' *edited by Warren French, The Viking Press, 1963, pp. 138-39.*

PUBLISHERS WEEKLY

"A book is no place to put these words." With this dictum, according to a report of the American Civil Liberties Union, Dr. Alexander Galt, librarian of the Buffalo Public Library, recently barred John Steinbeck's *Grapes of Wrath* from the shelves of Buffalo libraries on the ground that "vulgar words" are employed by characters in the book. The National Council on Freedom from Censorship, through a letter from Quincy Howe, has protested, calling the ban an "arbitrary subordination of the verdict of the best literary taste of the nation to personal preference," and declaring that "literature which is deemed not fit for public consumption can be effectively suppressed by court action, and this is the proper procedure to be taken in a democracy."

Grapes of Wrath has been banned in other libraries on similar grounds, the ACLU has learned. Some librarians, instead of announcing an outright ban, have simply ignored the volume, or bought but one copy.

> *" 'Grapes of Wrath': Banned by Buffalo Library," in* Publishers Weekly, *Vol. CXXXVI, No. 7, August 12, 1939, p. 453.*

THE NEW YORK TIMES

BAKERSFIELD, CALIF., AUG. 22.—Mapping a State-wide ban on John Steinbeck's *Grapes of Wrath* in schools and libaries, the Associated Farmers of Kern County urged all organizations in the San Joaquin Valley today to approve an interdiction ordered by the Kern Board of Supervisors.

The appeal was made by W. B. Camp, president of the Kern unit of the agricultural organization.

Other groups indicated that they will join the fight on the book now being led by the farmers, Mr. Camp said.

The farmers of the county are acting to remove the "smear" on the good name of Kern, California and agriculture generally, he explained.

> *"War on Steinbeck Book," in* The New York Times, *August 23, 1939, p. 17.*

COLLIER'S

Some say that John Steinbeck's best-selling novel, *The Grapes of Wrath,* is a twentieth-century *Uncle Tom's Cabin* and then some. Others call it a despicable piece of propaganda. The debate is moving a lot of people to read the book, so we'll tell what we think of it.

For one thing, we think *The Grapes of Wrath* is a very moving book, crammed with human tragedy and comedy (plus considerable dirt), and written in an extremely graphic style. It has to do with poor, broken Southern sharecroppers forced out of Dust Bowl cotton fields into a flight to California by drought and tumbling cotton prices. You can't help feeling sorry for the poor, harassed devils. A social system that can work such hardships on any substantial number of people unquestionably has its rotten spots.

But we also think that *The Grapes of Wrath,* as charged by many critics, is propaganda for the idea that we ought to trade our system for the Russian system. It is Mr. Steinbeck's or anybody else's privilege to publish such propaganda in this country—which fact is one of the glories of America.

But it is also anybody's privilege, of which we here avail ourselves, to point out that a similar novel could be written about Russia.

The locale would be the Ukraine, Russia's best wheat and farm area; time, winter 1931-32. The characters would be salty Russian peasants, in place of Mr. Steinbeck's hymn-roaring, hell-raising sharecroppers. . . .

The score in the end would be between three and four million

Russian peasants actually and literally dead of starvation—as against perhaps 300,000 American share croppers forced out of the Dust Bowl and into a California which, while it didn't welcome them with glad cries, at least didn't let them starve to death.

Responsible for the Russian tragedy would be the government at Moscow—quite a contrast to the government at Washington, which strives endlessly to prevent or alleviate such miseries as *The Grapes of Wrath* depicts. . . .

As we say, we don't defend the flaws in our system that are to blame for the sharecropper tragedies.

But we do suggest that a country where everybody is free to think, talk, write and act (short of violence) against every social ill has a better chance to work out a just economic system eventually than has a country where all power resides in one man, and where you are shot or tortured or exiled or starved to death if you are caught as much as thinking that things might be a little better run.

> *An editorial on "The Grapes of Wrath," in* Collier's, *Vol. 104, No. 10, September 2, 1939, p. 54.*

PUBLISHERS WEEKLY

Continued attempts to suppress *The Grapes of Wrath* are reported in the press and by the American Civil Liberties Union. Of particular significance is the action of California business farmers whose policies were attacked in John Steinbeck's portrayal of social conditions among the western migratory workers and dispossessed farmers [see *New York Times* piece above, dated August 23, 1939]. . . .

Meanwhile the book has been barred from public libraries of Kansas City by the Kansas City Board of Education, on grounds of obscenity. The National Council on Freedom from Censorship has protested, pointing out that alleged obscenity can be challenged in the courts, and citing the widespread critical praise of the book. Similar protests have been made against bans in Buffalo [see *Publishers Weekly* piece above, dated August 12, 1939], and in Oklahoma towns. The California farmers' ban is a somewhat different matter, since it is based not only on grounds of alleged obscenity, but also upon political grounds.

> *An article on "The Grapes of Wrath," in* Publishers Weekly, *Vol. CXXXVI, No. 10, September 2, 1939, p. 777.*

THE TIMES LITERARY SUPPLEMENT

[*The Grapes of Wrath*] is a campaign, and Mammon is the enemy. While lesser American writers complacently recall their country's past, Mr. Steinbeck is anxiously in touch with its present. He, too, describes an exodus to the West, but this is made in ramshackle motor-cars instead of lumbering wagons. Here there are no battles to bring glory, and at the end the land of promise is a bitter disappointment. . . .

From a background that is stated chiefly in short interludes wherein the anger only gives pace to the dramatic rhythms, one group of people stands out. These are the Joads, tenant farmers of Oklahoma, whose land has been mortgaged little by little and forfeited at last to the bank, which controls its own farming corporation. . . . Like all their fellows, the

Joads can only fasten their hopes on the Californian advertisements for labour. The memories of several generations they must leave behind them with the land, but ahead at least is the chance of work and a new home. Their implements and beasts go for nothing to opportunist buyers; for their wagon they get five dollars towards the purchase of a scrapheap car; and into this precarious transport are piled the essential household goods. They have begun to be at the mercy of opportunists of all kinds.

Mr. Steinbeck looks beyond his people and he sees the universal reverence for profits, but he sees his people first. If he despises and derides Mammon, he does so not because he dislikes a theory but because he sees the practical effect in human misery. Are not his Joads the victims of a system for which no man will take the responsibility? The Joads are certainly not the puppets of a theory. Their essential decency and good citizenship are evident beneath their various raffish surfaces, but they are not mere personifications of these qualities. The grandparents whose love for each other shows itself in continual verbal sparring, the mother who can endure anything so long as the family holds together, the son who has been in prison for manslaughter and knows that he would defend himself again, and the young married daughter fussing about the safety of the child she carries: these are individual men and women. When they speak, it is not to fill in an extra paragraph but to express or conceal their thoughts. When they act, their actions are their own. If they do not rebel, it is because money has become a despot against which rebellion is hopeless.

It is not pretended that this passion is sustained unbroken for the whole course of a long book. At their most wretched, these people have the refuge of memory and humour, and in their recollections of past raciness we are enabled to see the superior colour and variety of a society in which the owners lived on their land, worked it themselves and measured their prosperity directly against its prosperity. There is, besides, the tedium inseparable from any long work pledged to a single idea; but here the tedium is at its lowest. Against such falling off as there is may be set those passages in which the author makes still more transparent the barrier between his mind and our own. We know his mind now for an original one. He has passages in this book that restate the idea of the interlude in *To the Lighthouse* in terms of another country; but his just understanding of character, the candour and forcefulness of his dialogue and his mastery of climaxes are all his own and inimitable.

> *"Victims of Mammon," in* The Times Literary Supplement, *No. 1962, September 9, 1939, p. 525.*

SAMUEL SILLEN

A campaign to suppress *The Grapes of Wrath?* Seems a little absurd, on the face of it. How can you suppress a book that has already sold 200,000 copies? Few literate Americans have failed to hear of the book. The justified claim of the publisher that Steinbeck's novel is "the fastest selling, most highly praised, most fervently discussed" book of the year would seem to rule out any possibility of organized censorship. . . .

Bowdler, Mrs. Grundy, and Comstock operated in the horse-and-buggy age of censorship. The enlightened decisions in the *Jurgen* case (New York Court of General Sessions, 1923) and the *Ulysses* case (U.S. District Court, 1933) undermined the censor's reliance on his ancient standby, the courts. At the beginning of the nineteenth century, Lord Eldon refused to protect by injunction Southey's *Wat Tyler* and Byron's *Cain.* The jurist expressed doubts (he hoped they were "reasonable") as to the innocent character of Milton's *Paradise Lost.* A jury held the publication of Shelley's *Queen Mab* to be an indictable offense. But recent American court decisions have challenged the ingenuity of the censors. They respect Hitler for his book-burning efficiency, and they are aping the master.

If they can't very well burn the libraries, they can at least spray them, as the California growers spray "surplus" oranges. Thus, the Kansas City Board of Education, by a four-to-two vote, has ordered all copies of *The Grapes of Wrath* removed from the city libraries. Miss Annette Moore, leader in the censorship forces, objected to the book's "portrayal of women living like cattle in a shed," and particularly to the scene in a boxcar where Rose of Sharon's baby is stillborn. "It portrays life in such a bestial way," laments Miss Moore. And nearly two thousand miles away, in the city of Buffalo, the book has been banned on the ground of "obscenity." According to Alexander Galt, Buffalo librarian, the book contains "vulgar words," and "a book is no place to put these words." (p. 23)

It is a characteristic of all moral guardians that they confuse their own corruptibility with the sound and healthy minds of those they pretend to protect. Commenting on *The Grapes of Wrath* in "My Day," Mrs. Roosevelt pointed out that there are coarse and brutal moments in the book, but that there are also coarse and brutal moments in life. She added that there are fine things in life which outweigh the brutal. These are beautifully portrayed in a book whose effect is to renew our faith in the masses of mankind struggling under the most adverse circumstances. Mrs. Roosevelt's robust attitude toward the book coincides with the reaction of most readers and critics.

But the librarians' charge of "obscenity" is a minor issue. The campaign against *The Grapes of Wrath* is motivated by a fear—justified, of course—that the conditions which it exposes will arouse the resentment of the American people. It is significant that, as I shall show, the attack on *The Grapes of Wrath* has gone hand in hand with an attack on Carey McWilliams' factual study, *Factories in the Field,* which contains no "obscenity" or "vulgar words." And it is noteworthy, above all, that the attack stems from the California growers and their Associated Farmers, Inc., who are directly responsible for the terrible plight of the migratory workers.

John E. Pickett of the *Pacific Rural Press,* organ of the Associated Farmers, also attacks Steinbeck because "He peeks into the privies of life." Commenting on this gem of literary criticism, the San Francisco *People's World* points out: "Now it is a matter of record and common knowledge that many authors have peeked into life's privies. *But what irritates Mr. Pickett is that Steinbeck has peeked into privies and found the Associated Farmers.*" Mr. Pickett, incidentally, in addition to being revolted by privies, coupled the names of Steinbeck and McWilliams with "Communist agitation."

Mr. Pickett writes about books; his playmates burn them. Last June, four thousand delegates of the American Library Association attended a convention in San Francisco. At just about this time, Librarian Robert Rea, who had ordered only one (1) copy of *The Grapes of Wrath* for the central library in the Civic Center, was giving specific instructions to the branch libraries not to catalogue or advertise the book. Here is the text of the note to branch librarians, as revealed by the *People's World* on June 2:

> You are going to receive *one copy* of John Steinbeck's ***The Grapes of Wrath.*** *You will not receive the book jacket or catalogue cards for this book, and it will not appear in the monthly bulletin.*
> Since the book fund for the present year has been exhausted and next year's budget has been greatly cut, you will not receive any additional copies of this book, *regardless of the number of postcards you have.*
> You must use discretion in taking cards, explaining to the patrons that they will have to wait. *This book will not be kept on the open shelf when it is off reserve.* [Sillen's italics.]

Funds? According to the *People's World,* five copies of Kathleen Norris' latest love story were bought for the main library, only one of ***The Grapes of Wrath.*** Funds? Librarians in many California towns are refusing offers of local citizens to donate the book. . . .

The board of supervisors of Kern County, scene of much of the action in ***The Grapes of Wrath,*** has banned the book. Last week the Associated Farmers of Kern County announced the beginning of a campaign to extend the censorship on a statewide scale. I understand that they may change their tune, because of popular pressure. Progressives in Kern County discount the charge of "obscenity" and attribute the suppression to the expose of the lawless methods used by the corporate landowners to crush the exploited agricultural workers. The Oil Workers Union, Local 19, condemned the decision of the supervisors and praised Supervisor Ralph Lavin, who was elected with CIO and AFL support, for opposing the board's action. Dan Harris, editor of the AFL Kern County *Labor Journal,* denounced the decision. The county librarian, Gretchen Kneiff, explained that as an employee she had no choice but to remove forty-odd copies of the book from county circulation, and she hinted that a similar censorship was expected of *Factories in the Field.* Other unions took action: the Butchers Union, the legislative representative of the Brotherhood of Locomotive Engineers, the Hod Carriers Union. Organizer Bill Bonar of the Hod Carriers said: "The attempted suppression of this book of Steinbeck's will only help advertise it more widely, but as far as we are concerned in the labor movement it is the beginning of a fascist regime. This helps to expose the faces of these local fascists." One union official reminded the mass protest meeting that last spring the neighboring city of Oildale refused to allow Marian Anderson to sing. Censorship never rains; it pours.

The following day, August 24, a meeting of a different sort was held in San Francisco. It was attended by members of Pro-America, the Hearst-sponsored association of Republican women. The delegates, reports Sue Barry in the *People's World,* arrived in limousines. Swathed in silver foxes, they assembled to "refute" ***The Grapes of Wrath.*** The literary experts: Harold Pomeroy, executive secretary of Associated Farmers; H. C. Merritt, Jr., owner of the infamous Tagus Ranch; Thomas McManus of the Kern County Citizens Committee; and chairman Ruth Comfort Mitchell, a wee bit of a novelist herself, wife of vigilante leader Col. Sanborn Young. . . .

"There is no doubt," writes Gov. Culbert L. Olson in *Look*

magazine (August 29), "that John Steinbeck's story, *The Grapes of Wrath,* has a factual basis, but it is a national story and by no means confined to California." Certainly it is a *national* story. That is why we must keep our eye on Kansas City and Buffalo as well as on San Francisco and Kern County. That is why *Collier's,* issue of September 2 [see excerpt above], devotes a lead editorial to the novel, charging that it "is propaganda for the idea that we ought to trade our system for the Russian system." What's Steinbeck kicking about, *Collier's* wants to know. Look how much worse off the "starving" Ukrainians are, and so on *ad nauseam.* This is a typical Red-baiting attack which, in the context of the other facts I have cited, underscores the existence of a nationwide movement to discredit and suppress the book. The extent of this movement is indicated by a letter from a sailor reporting that the book has been suppressed on the *U.S.S. Tennessee:* "Although there was a waiting list of over fifty men who wished to read *The Grapes of Wrath,*" he writes, "the chaplain removed it from the shelves of the ship's library."

The federal government camps in California have weekly newspapers printed by the migratory workers. According to Charles L. Todd (New York *Times* magazine, August 27), the Indio camp's *Covered Wagon* boasts: "We write what we say; we say what we think; we think what we darn please." This is the spirit of the American people. And in this spirit we cannot countenance the suppression of *The Grapes of Wrath.* Readers of *New Masses* should investigate the situation in their local communities. Are your libraries making an effort to meet the demand for the book? Is an attempt being made to hinder its circulation? (p. 24)

Samuel Sillen, "Censoring 'The Grapes of Wrath'," in New Masses, *Vol. XXXII, No. 12, September 12, 1939, pp. 23-4.*

KATE O'BRIEN

Some weeks ago the whole British public was counselled emphatically over the air to read a forthcoming American novel called *The Grapes of Wrath.* The gently pontifical tones of Mr. Alexander Woollcott, breaking over our Sunday supper tables, informed us that, along with Franklin D. Roosevelt's, John Steinbeck's is at present *the* American voice, the representative one, through which America should be heard and judged. Here it is, then—immensely ushered in, and accompanied, for the encouragement of reviewers at least, by a whole booklet of acclamation of the man behind the voice, to say nothing of a full-length studio portrait of him.

All this is very nice, but is the booklet necessary, or even advisable? Surely we have heard of John Steinbeck, even in darkest England? Have we not admired *Tortilla Flat* and *The Cup of Gold,* and was not *Of Mice and Men* a Shaftesbury Avenue success until Hitler put out the town's lights? But Mr. Woollcott's claim is that "a young writer who had already written several good books . . . has now written a great one." I do not agree with this. I think that "a young writer, &c.," has now written another good book, but one in which he has had the courage, if you like, to give fuller rein than formerly to a sentimentality which for some of us disfigured his early work.

The theme of *The Grapes of Wrath* is quite magnificent; so is its documentary informativeness; so are its moral and its desolate warning. It is indeed a vivid, generous sermon on modern misery, on the crassness and savagery of some who create it, and the nobility of its victims. Mr. Steinbeck's heart is passionately fixed in the right place, but it would be unfair to the great variety of his talents to suggest that perhaps his trouble, *quâ* writer, is that he is all heart.

The story is of the present-day destruction of the land of the Western States of America, and so of the people who, in both senses of the word, live on it. . . . And in this book we can read about it and see, through the desperate sufferings and adventures of one decent, outcast Oklahoma family, how big business, industrialisation, is destroying the United States.

The Joad family, captained by Tom, the elder son, who is a *parole* man, having done time for manslaughter, have to flee from their long-held forty acres which the inexorable tractor is tearing up. They depart, a large troupe of all ages, in the shakiest of trucks, perilously loaded. They "aim to" start a new life in California. They have read handbills, have heard of the universal trek West, to the peach-pickin', orange-pickin' sun, fertility and fortune in the West. Their journey is heroic, nothing less; and their subsequent slow disillusionment, though immense, actually does not quite use up their common stock of fortitude. When we leave them at the end, somewhat reduced by death and desertion and with their courageous Tom forced on the run again because of another manslaughter, they and their chance friends of the road are more destitute, more weary and directionless than it is easy to convey—but in spirit they are "a fambly" still, their patient hearts still beat, with "Ma," great creature, driving death off, Heaven knows why—saving the starved, dying stranger in the wayside shed with the unneeded milk of her young daughter's breasts.

Mr. Steinbeck gives us an enormous, vivid setting; he fills it with odd and lively characters; he uses an attractive Western States *patois,* and he tells a terrible, moving story of universal and immediate significance. Why, then, am I not enthralled by his book? Simply because, right or wrong, I dislike his manner of writing, which I think epitomises the intolerable sentimentality of American "realism." I think he wrecks a beautiful dialect with false cadences; I think he is frequently uncertain about where to end a sentence; I think his repetitiveness is not justified by emotional result; and whereas the funny, niggling coarseness which he jovially imposes on his pathetic migrants may be true to type, it seemed to me out of tone, and to offend against the general conception. But the book is good, interesting and generous, and its wide popularity would be a beneficial thing.

Kate O'Brien, in a review of "The Grapes of Wrath," in The Spectator, *Vol. 163, No. 5803, September 15, 1939, p. 386.*

ANTHONY WEST

The story of *The Grapes of Wrath* is very simple. Prior to 1820 the smallest acreage which the settler could buy from the United States Government was 320, which had to be paid for at the rate of two dollars an acre and paid for in four years. Subsequent to 1820, however, the Government policy changed, and it became possible to buy lots of as little as eighty acres, and after the Civil War the policy was further modified and settlers were able to take up these small farms for nothing. An eighty-acre farm is uneconomic without highly developed local markets and without very skilful farming; the Middle West never developed any sort of regional economy and even the smallest farmers went in for wheat as a main crop. The result was that the farmers were wholly at the mercy of world prices without local standbys, and the consequence of the unending cropping of wheat was soil exhaustion. After the war a succession of drought years accelerated the slow draining of the fertility of the soil, the top soil began to break up into dust and to blow away. The farmers fell into debt and failed to keep up the payments on their mortgages, the banks took over the farms. This is where [*The Grapes of Wrath*] begins; the Joads, a family of small Oklahoma farmers, have had their notice to quit and have decided to move on westwards in obedience to the lemming-like compulsion which is the vestige of the American pioneer tradition. Like hundreds of thousands of other families, they buy an old car and set off for California; their sufferings on the road and their situation when they arrive at the promised land where they find there is nothing for them but casual labour on an overstocked market make the story of the book. It is a horrible story told with passionate earnestness, distressing and moving, but completely as one is compelled to realise the plight of this human refuse in California the book has great defects as a novel. It is to be compared with Upton Sinclair's novel about the Chicago Stockyards, *The Jungle*. When Sinclair's book first appeared it created the same sort of stir that *The Grapes of Wrath* has made; the working conditions and the brutalised lives it described were as shocking, the case against the meat packers was as strong as the case against the fruit growers, and it was made with the same passion, the same earnestness. People were intensely moved by it. Time has stolen away its force, it is as wholly "1906" as an automobile of that year and as suitable for contemporary use. This old scandal has lost its urgency and cannot horrify one into forgetting that the same thing is being said over and over again and that the book ends when it does because the reader cannot be expected to stand any more. The fact that the sun will look on the puzzled, desperate and utterly defeated people in Mr. Steinbeck's book a few hours after it has looked on us tempts one to overlook similar failings. In form *The Grapes of Wrath* is astonishingly awkward; it combines the novel about the Joads with a generalised account of the experiences of the small farmers of whom the Joads are typical. These two books run concurrently and in such a fashion that a chapter of the generalised account precedes two or three chapters of the novel and forecasts pretty closely what is going to happen. Thus when the Joad family buys its car for the migration first Mr. Steinbeck explains how the Oklahoma farmers who go to California buy bad old cars which use too much oil and go wrong. Then the Joad family buy a car, and they talk about it and decide that they have probably been swindled and that the car is going to use too much oil and that they'll be lucky if it doesn't break down on the road. Then they set out and the car burns up too much oil and breaks down on the road. The Joads, moreover, are slow-thinking people, and they have to hear a thing several times before they believe it, and when they believe it they don't feel easy about it until they've told someone. But they can't bring themselves to say anything straight out; they work up to it by hints and suggestions, by devious back alleys which Mr. Steinbeck follows as enthusiastically and faithfully on page 535 as on page 35. Mr. Steinbeck makes his points with the delicacy of a trip hammer, the book lacks form and ends simply because the characters have reached the ultimate believable degradation and the length has reached the limit which publishers and public can stand. Pity and sympathy tempt

one to suspend purely artistic standards, but this cannot be called a good novel. Its virtue lies in the burning sincerity which has captured the imagination of the American public and awakened them to the human aspect of the dust-bowl disaster. *The Jungle* is dead mutton as literature but it is alive in the American legislation which has amplified the Meat Inspection Bill and the Pure Food Bill of 1906, which the novel called into being within a few months of publication. *The Grapes of Wrath* will take a place beside it in the social history of the United States, but it is its literary fate to lie in that honourable vault which houses the books that have died when their purpose as propaganda has been served. (pp. 404-05)

Anthony West, in a review of "The Grapes of Wrath," in The New Statesman & Nation, *Vol. XVIII, No. 447, September 16, 1939, pp. 404-05.*

FRANK J. TAYLOR

Californians are wrathy over **The Grapes of Wrath,** John Steinbeck's best-selling novel of migrant agricultural workers. Though the book is fiction, many readers accept it as fact.

By implication, it brands California farmers with unbelievable cruelty in their dealings with refugees from the "dust bowl." It charges that they deliberately lured a surplus of workers westward to depress wages, deputized peace officers to hound the migrants ever onward, burned the squatters' shacktowns, stomped down gardens and destroyed surplus foods in a conspiracy to force the refugees to work for starvation wages, allowed children to hunger and mothers to bear babies unattended in squalor. It implies that hatred of the migrants is fostered by the land barons who use the "Bank of the West" (obviously the Bank of America) and the "Farmers Association" (the Associated Farmers) to gobble up the lands of the small farmers and concentrate them in a few large holdings.

These are a few of the sins for which Steinbeck indicts California farmers. It is difficult to rebut fiction, which requires no proof, with facts, which do require proof.

The experiences of the Joad family, whose misfortunes in their trek from Oklahoma to California Steinbeck portrays so graphically, are not typical of those of the real migrants I found in the course of two reportorial tours of the agricultural valleys. I made one inquiry during the winter of 1937-38, following the flood which Steinbeck describes; I made another at the height of the harvest this year [1939].

Along three thousand miles of highways and byways, I was unable to find a single counterpart of the Joad family. Nor have I discovered one during fifteen years of residence in the Santa Clara Valley (the same valley where John Steinbeck now lives), which is crowded each summer with transient workers harvesting the fruit crops. The lot of the "fruit tramp" is admittedly no bed of roses, but neither is it the bitter fate described in **The Grapes of Wrath.**

The Joad Family of nine, created by Steinbeck to typify the "Okie" migrants, is anything but typical. A survey made for the Farm Security Administration revealed that thirty was the average age of migrant adults, that the average family had 2.8 children.

Steinbeck's Joads, once arrived in the "land of promise," earned so little that they faced slow starvation. Actually, no migrant family hungers in California unless it is too proud to accept relief. Few migrants are.

There is no red tape about getting free food or shelter.

The FSA [Farm Security Administration] maintains warehouses in eleven strategically located towns, where the grant officer is authorized to issue 15 days' rations to any migrant who applies, identifies himself by showing his driver's license, and answers a few simple questions about his family, his earnings, and his travels. In emergencies, the grant officer may issue money for clothing, gasoline, or medical supplies. The food includes standard brands of a score of staple products, flour, beans, corn meal, canned milk and tomatoes, dried fruit, and other grocery items. Before the 15 days are up, the grant officer or his assistant visits the migrant family in camp, and, if the need still exists, the ration is renewed repeatedly until the family finds work.

Shelter is provided by the FSA (a unit of the Federal Resettlement Administration) at model camps which Steinbeck himself represents as satisfactory. The one at Shafter is typical. A migrant family is assigned to a wooded platform on which a tent may be pitched; if the family lacks a tent, the camp has some to lend. The rent is a dime a day, and the migrant who wants to save the money can work it out by helping to clean up camp. The dime goes into a community benefit fund, administered by a committee. Camp facilities include toilets, showers and laundry tubs, with hot and cold running water, a community house. These thirteen camps cost around $190,000 apiece, and each accommodates some three hundred families. Last summer there were vacant platforms, though in winter there is a shortage of space.

Various relief organizations divide the responsibility of providing food and shelter for California's migrants. Federal authorities, working through the FSA, assume the burden for the first year. After a migrant family has been in the State a year, it becomes eligible for State relief. After three years, it becomes a county charge. State relief for agricultural workers averages $51 a month in California, as compared with $21 in Oklahoma, less for several neighboring States. The U. S. Farm Placement Service notes that WPA wages in California are $44 per month, in Oklahoma $32. California old-age pensions are $32 per month, Oklahoma's $20. These are U.S. Social Security Board figures. Records of the FSA grant offices indicate that many migrants earned under $200 a year back home—or less than one third the relief allowance in California. Thus thousands of Okies, having discovered this comparative bonanza, urge their kinsfolk to join them in California, where the average migrant family earns $400 during the harvest season and is able, after the first lean year, to draw an equal sum for relief during eight months of enforced idleness.

The advantages of life in California for migrant workers are not limited to the salubrious climate and largess.

When the harvest is on, the base wage for agricultural workers on California farms is $2.10 per day with board, as compared to $1.00 in Oklahoma, $1.35 in Texas, and 65 cents in Arkansas. (pp. 232-33)

Another advantage of life in California is the free medical service. Few of the migrants had ever seen the inside of a hospital or employed a doctor, dentist, or nurse before they came to California. Each FSA camp has a full-time nurse and a part-time doctor to serve the migrant families without charge. Medical supplies, too, are free.

At the Shafter camp, I asked how many babies has been born in camp this year.

"None," the manager replied. "The mothers all go to Kern General Hospital."

At the hospital, supported by Kern County, I learned that, of 727 children born to migrant mothers in the County during the first 5 months of this year, 544 were delivered in the hospital, without charge. In fact, under State law, no general hospital may refuse a mother in labor. Yet in the Steinbeck book a camp manager is obliged to act as midwife.

It is a fortunate break, not only for the migrants but for the Californians as well, that the incoming streams of dilapidated "jalopies," piled high with beds and utensils, converge at Bakersfield, seat of Kern County. As large as Massachusetts (and wealthy, thanks to oil), Kern County maintains a remarkable health service under the direction of Dr. Joe Smith, who believes that an ill person is a menace to others and that it is the County's duty to make him well. (p. 233)

An inference of *The Grapes of Wrath* is that most of the California farmlands are in great holdings, operated by corporations or land "barons." The State has 6,732,390 acres devoted to crops, and the 1935 census shows that 1,738,906 are in farms less than 100 acres in extent, 3,068,742 are in farms of 100 to 1,000 acres, and 1,924,742 are in farms of over 1,000.

An insinuation of *The Grapes of Wrath* is that wages are forced down by the Associated Farmers and the Bank of America, acting in conspiracy. Actually, neither the Association nor the Bank concerns itself with wages. Rates of pay are worked out through the farmer co-operatives in each crop or through local groups, such as the San Joaquin Regional Council, which agrees each spring on a base wage. California farmers pay higher wages than those of any State but Connecticut, according to the U.S. Farm Placement Bureau.

The same federal organization conducted any inquiry into the charge, aired in *The Grapes of Wrath,* that California farmers had distributed handbills through the dust-bowl area, offering jobs to lure a surplus of migrant labor to the State. Only two cases were unearthed, one by a labor contractor in Santa Barbara County, another by an Imperial Valley contractor. The licenses of both have since been revoked. At the Associated Farmers head office in San Francisco, I saw hundreds of clippings from Midwest newspapers—publicity inspired by the Association—advising migrants *not* to come to California. (pp. 237-38)

California's big question—what is going to happen to these people—is still unanswered.

East of Visalia, the FSA is attempting an experiment in co-operative farming. On the 530-acre Mineral King ranch, purchased with federal funds, twenty above-average migrant families were set to work raising cotton, alfalfa, and poultry and running a diary. At the end of the first year, the farm showed a profit of $900 per family, more than twice the average family's earning from following the crops.

At Casa Grande, Arizona, the FSA has another co-operative farm, of 4,000 acres, with sixty families working it.

Co-operative farms, directed by trained men from universities, produce good crops and good livings; but the Okies are rugged individualists. "I'm not going to have any damn government telling me what I'm going to plant," exploded one of the Mineral King farmers, as he packed his family in the car and took to the road again. And so, in spite of the good intentions of the Farm Security Administration, the Governor's Committee on Unemployment, the Simon J. Lubin Society, the John Steinbeck Committee, and other organizations, the highly individualistic newcomers probably will work out their own destiny in their own way.

For a glimpse of how they may do it, visit Salinas, . . . which saw its first invasion eight years ago. The first Okies in the area squatted in squalor outside the town until an enterprising wheat farmer divided his ranch into half-acre lots, which he offered at $250 apiece, $5.00 down, $5.00 a month. The Okies snapped them up and strutted around, proud of their property ownership. Today, in Little Oklahoma City, as the community is called, one can envisage the whole process of assimilation—the ancient trailer resting on its axles, a lean-to or tent alongside it, in the front a wooden shack and, sometimes, a vine-covered cottage. Off to the south, some of the Okies are living in neat little three-to five-room cottages. The Okies of Little Oklahoma City are fortunate. They muscled into the lettuce-packing game and now have virtually a monopoly around Salinas, earning from 50 to 60 cents an hour for eight or nine months of the year. In that one community, three thousand migrants have achieved a respectable standard of living. Their children are intermarrying with the natives. Outwardly, they are Californians.

What they have done can be done by others. Their accomplishment is a challenge to shiftless Okies and an answer to the broad accusations hurled so heedlessly in *The Grapes of Wrath.* (p. 238)

> Frank J. Taylor, "California's 'Grapes of Wrath'," in Forum and Century, *Vol. CII, No. 5, November, 1939, pp. 232-38.*

PUBLISHERS WEEKLY

Most spectacular so far of the local attempts to suppress John Steinbeck's *The Grapes of Wrath* is the order by the Library Board of East St. Louis, Illinois, that three copies of the novel be burned. This symbolic form of attack is characterized by Viking Press as "the first known case of actual burning à La Hitler" as far as the Steinbeck volume is concerned. The burning was condemned in a telegram to the Library Board by the National Council on Freedom from Censorship. The telegram stated that the action "condemns itself as a parallel to recent acts by totalitarian governments." The telegram continues, "Instead of burning the book, more copies should be made available for what your own librarian described as 'the waiting list longer than for any other book in recent history.'"

Interestingly enough, the order for the burning came just as the book had rolled up its biggest week's sales figure in the seven months since publication early last April.

> An article on *"The Grapes of Wrath," in* Publishers Weekly, *Vol. CXXXVI, No. 22, November 25, 1939, p. 1994.*

LYLE H. BOREN

[*The remarks presented below were originally delivered in the United States House of Representatives on January 10, 1940.*]

Mr. Speaker, my colleagues, considerable has been said in the cloakrooms, in the press, and in various reviews about a book entitled *The Grapes of Wrath.* I cannot find it possible to let this dirty, lying, filthy manuscript go heralded before the public without a word of challenge or protest.

I would have my colleagues in Congress who are concerning themselves with the fundamental economic problems of America know that Oklahoma, like other States in the Union, has its economic problems, but that no Oklahoma economic problem has been portrayed in the low and vulgar lines of this publication. As a citizen of Oklahoma, I would have it known that I resent, for the great State of Oklahoma, the implications in that book.

Mr. Speaker, this great American Nation is distinguished from all other countries in the world in that the Government makes no distinction between its people in such a way as to lay any lines of demarcation between classes, whether social, political, or economic, and I want it understood in my subsequent remarks that I use the word "class" in the sense of economic concept and not in application to individuals or groups. I would say that the class of people who make up the farmers of America, and more particularly the tenant farmers, are the most patriotic, most democratic, and finest moral fiber in the Nation. I am 30 years of age and 20 years of my 30 years have been spent on the tenant farms of Texas and Oklahoma.

I stand before you today as an example, in my judgment, of the average son of the tenant farmer of America. If I have in any way done more in the sense of personal accomplishment than the average son of the tenant farmer of Oklahoma, it has been a matter of circumstance, and I know of a surety that the heart and brain and character of the average tenant farmer of Oklahoma cannot be surpassed and probably not equaled by any other group in the world. Today I stand before this body as a son of a tenant farmer, labeled by John Steinbeck as an "Okie." For myself, for my dad and my mother, whose hair is silvery in the service of building the State of Oklahoma, and whose hands are calloused with the toil known by every tenant farmer of Oklahoma, and for every good man and good woman, every fine son and noble daughter of the great, good class of people which this putrid-minded writer labeled as "Okies," I arise to say to you, my colleagues, and to every honest, square-minded reader in America, that the painting Steinbeck made in his book is a lie, a damnable lie, a black, infernal creation of a twisted, distorted mind. Though I regret that there is a mind in America such as his, let it be a matter of record for all the tenant farmers of America that I have denied this lie for them.

Some have blasphemed the name of Charles Dickens by making comparisons between his writing and this. I have no doubt but that Charles Dickens accurately portrayed certain economic conditions in his country and in his time, but this book portrays only John Steinbeck's unfamiliarity with facts and his complete ignorance of his subject. Let me call to your attention the fact that in the first few pages of his manuscript that he had tractors plowing land of the Cookson Hills country where there are not 40 acres practical for tractor cultivation. He had baptisms taking place in the irrigation ditches in country near Sallisaw, Okla., where an irrigation ditch has not run in the history of the world. He took Sallisaw out of the hills of eastern Oklahoma and placed it in the Dust Bowl. His careless disregard for these matters indicates only his complete disregard for the truth. It is certain that he wrote about a country he had never visited and a people with whom he was not acquainted and had never contacted.

Some have said this book exposes a condition and a character of people, but the truth is this book exposes nothing but the total depravity, vulgarity, and degraded mentality of the author.

I am surprised that any preacher in America could find a word of commendation for a book which brings such malicious vulgarity to the door of the church. Let me ask you, and every man of mind and character in America, if there is one of you who would sanction placing this book in the hands of your young daughter?

Let it be to the eternal credit of the Postal Service of the United States that they have banned its obscenity from the mails.

I have worked in the cottonfields, the broomcorn fields, and the wheatfields in almost every area of the State of Oklahoma, yet there is not one thing in the book which would remind me of the thought, the action, or the conditions of the people and the places I have known. I have traveled over the most of the United States and a few foreign countries, and the only places in all America that I ever saw anything which compared in complete negation to this manuscript were the writings on a toilet wall in a dilapidated depot. Take the vulgarity out of this book and it would be blank from cover to cover. It is painful to me to further charge that if you take the obscene language out, its author could not sell a copy.

The grapes of wrath that John Steinbeck would gather in a world of truth and right would press for him only the bitter drink of just condemnation and isolation for his unclean mind.

I would have you know that there is not a tenant farmer in Oklahoma that Oklahoma needs to apologize for. I want to declare to my Nation and to the world that I am proud of my tenant-farmer heritage, and I would to Almighty God that all citizens of America could be as clean and noble and fine as the Oklahomans that Steinbeck labeled "Okies." The only apology that needs to be made is by the State of California for being the parent of such offspring as this author.

Mr. Speaker, let it be a matter of record that the English language does not hold vituperative contents sufficient for me to pronounce completely the just condemnation of this man and his book. The lies that he has written he cannot recall; the words he has put into the mouth of these people will whisper eternally in his ear and haunt his wretched soul as the degraded creations of his hallucinations in filth and mire. (pp. 139-40)

> *Lyle H. Boren, in a commentary on "The Grapes of Wrath," in* United States of America Congressional Record: Proceedings and Debates of the 76th Congress, Third Session Appendix, *Vol. 86, No. 13, January 3, 1940-March 5, 1940, pp. 139-40.*

FREDERIC I. CARPENTER

A popular heresy has it that a novelist should not discuss ideas—especially not abstract ideas. Even the best contemporary reviewers concern themselves with the entertainment value of a book (will it please their readers?), and with the impression of immediate reality which it creates. *The Grapes of Wrath,* for instance, was praised for its swift action and for the moving sincerity of its characters. But its mystical ideas and the moralizing interpretations intruded by the author between the narrative chapters were condemned. Presumably the book became a best seller in spite of these; its art was great enough to overcome its philosophy.

But in the course of time a book is also judged by other standards. Aristotle once argued that poetry should be more "philosophical" than history; and all books are eventually weighed for their content of wisdom. Novels that have become classics do more than tell a story and describe characters; they offer insight into men's motives and point to the springs of action. Together with the moving picture, they offer the criticism of life.

Although this theory of art may seem classical, all important modern novels—especially American novels—have clearly suggested an abstract idea of life. *The Scarlet Letter* symbolized "sin," *Moby Dick* offered an allegory of evil. *Huck Finn* described the revolt of the "natural individual" against "civilization," and *Babbitt* (like Emerson's "Self-reliance") denounced the narrow conventions of "society." Now *The Grapes of Wrath* goes beyond these to preach a positive philosophy of life and to damn that blind conservatism which fears ideas.

I shall take for granted the narrative power of the book and the vivid reality of its characters: modern critics, both professional and popular, have borne witness to these. The novel is a best seller. But it also has ideas. These appear abstractly and obviously in the interpretative interchapters. But more important is Steinbeck's creation of Jim Casy, "the preacher," to interpret and to embody the philosophy of the novel. And consummate is the skill with which Jim Casy's philosophy has been integrated with the action of the story, until it motivates and gives significance to the lives of Tom Joad, and Ma, and Rose of Sharon. It is not too much to say that Jim Casy's ideas determine and direct the Joads's actions.

Beside and beyond their function in the story, the ideas of John Steinbeck and Jim Casy possess a significance of their own. They continue, develop, integrate, and realize the thought of the great writers of American history. Here the mystical transcendentalism of Emerson reappears, and the earthy democracy of Whitman, and the pragmatic instrumentalism of William James and John Dewey. And these old philosophies grow and change in the book until they become new. They coalesce into an organic whole. And, finally, they find embodiment in character and action, so that they seem no longer ideas, but facts. The enduring greatness of *The Grapes of Wrath* consists in its imaginative realization of these old ideas in new and concrete forms. Jim Casy translates American philosophy into words of one syllable, and the Joads translate it into action.

"Ever know a guy that said big words like that?" asks the truck driver in the first narrative chapter of *The Grapes of Wrath.* "Preacher," replies Tom Joad. "Well, it makes you mad to hear a guy use big words. Course with a preacher it's all right because nobody would fool around with a preacher anyway." But soon afterward Tom meets Jim Casy and finds him changed. "I was a preacher," said the man seriously, "but not no more." Because Casy has ceased to be an orthodox minister and no longer uses big words, Tom Joad plays around with him. And the story results.

But although he is no longer a minister, Jim Casy continues to preach. His words have become simple and his ideas unorthodox. "Just Jim Casy now. Ain't got the call no more. Got a lot of sinful idears—but they seem kinda sensible." A century before, this same experience and essentially these same ideas had occurred to another preacher: Ralph Waldo Emerson had given up the ministry because of his unorthodoxy. But Emerson had kept on using big words. Now Casy translates them: "Why do we got to hang it on God or Jesus? Maybe it's all men an' all women we love; maybe that's the Holy Spirit—the human sperit—the whole shebang. Maybe all men got one big soul ever'body's a part of." And so the Emersonian oversoul comes to earth in Oklahoma.

Unorthodox Jim Casy went into the Oklahoma wilderness to save his soul. And in the wilderness he experienced the religious feeling of identity with nature which has always been the heart of transcendental mysticism: "There was the hills, an' there was me, an' we wasn't separate no more. We was one thing. An' that one thing was holy." Like Emerson, Casy came to the conviction that holiness, or goodness, results from this feeling of unity: "I got to thinkin' how we was holy when we was one thing, an' mankin' was holy when it was one thing."

Thus far Jim Casy's transcendentalism has remained vague and apparently insignificant. But the corollary of this mystical philosophy is that any man's self-seeking destroys the unity or "holiness" of nature: "An' it [this one thing] on'y got unholy when one mis'-able little fella got the bit in his teeth, an' run off his own way. . . . Fella like that bust the holiness." Or, as Emerson phrased it, while discussing Nature: "The world lacks unity because man is disunited with himself. . . . Love is its demand." So Jim Casy preaches the religion of love.

He finds that this transcendental religion alters the old standards: "Here's me that used to give all my fight against the devil 'cause I figured the devil was the enemy. But they's somepin worse'n the devil got hold a the country." Now, like Emerson, he almost welcomes "the dear old devil." Now he fears not the lusts of the flesh but rather the lusts of the spirit. For the abstract lust of possession isolates a man from his fellows and destroys the unity of nature and the love of man. As Steinbeck writes: "The quality of owning freezes you forever into 'I,' and cuts you off forever from the 'we.'" Or, as the Concord farmers in Emerson's poem "Hamatreya" had exclaimed: "'Tis mine, my children's and my name's," only to have "their avarice cooled like lust in the chill of the grave." To a preacher of the oversoul, possessive egotism may become the unpardonable sin.

If a society has adopted "the quality of owning" (as typified by absentee ownership) as its social norm, then Protestant nonconformity may become the highest virtue, and even resistance to authority may become justified. (pp. 315-18)

But this American ideal of nonconformity seems negative: how can men be sure that their Protestant rebellion does not come from the devil? To this there has always been but one answer—faith: faith in the instincts of the common man, faith in ultimate social progress, and faith in the direction in which democracy is moving. So Ma Joad counsels the discouraged Tom: "Why, Tom, we're the people that live. They ain't gonna wipe us out. Why, we're the people—we go on." And so Steinbeck himself affirms a final faith in progress: "When theories change and crash, when schools, philosophies. . . . grow and disintegrate, man reaches, stumbles forward. . . . Having stepped forward, he may slip back, but only half a step, never the full step back." Whether this be democratic faith, or mere transcendental optimism, it has always been the motive force of our American life and finds reaffirmation in this novel.

Upon the foundation of this old American idealism Steinbeck has built. But the Emersonian oversoul had seemed very vague and very ineffective—only the individual had been real, and he had been concerned more with his private soul than with other people. *The Grapes of Wrath* develops the old idea in new ways. It traces the transformation of the Protestant individual into the member of a social group—the old "I" becomes "we." And it traces the transformation of the passive individual into the active participant—the idealist becomes pragmatist. The first development continues the poetic thought of Walt Whitman; the second continues the philosophy of William James and John Dewey. (pp. 318-19)

But Steinbeck now emphasizes the group above the individual and from an impersonal point of view. Where formerly American and Protestant thought has been separatist, Steinbeck now faces the problem of social integration. In his novel the "mutually repellent particles" of individualism begin to cohere.

"This is the beginning," he writes, "from 'I' to 'we.'" This is the beginning, that is, of reconstruction. When the old society has been split and the Protestant individuals wander aimlessly about, some new nucleus must be found, or chaos and nihilism will follow. . . . A new social group is forming, based on the word "en masse." But here is no socialism imposed from above; here is a natural grouping of simple separate persons.

By virtue of his wholehearted participation in this new group the individual may become greater than himself. Some men, of course, will remain mere individuals, but in every group there must be leaders, or "representative men." A poet gives expression to the group idea, or a preacher organizes it. After Jim Casy's death, Tom is chosen to lead. Ma explains: "They's some folks that's just theirself, an' nothin' more. There's Al he's jus' a young fella after a girl. You wasn't never like that, Tom." Because he has been an individualist, but through the influence of Casy and of his group idea has become more than himself, Tom becomes "a leader of the people." But his strength derives from his increased sense of participation in the group.

From Jim Casy, and eventually from the thought of Americans like Whitman, Tom Joad has inherited this idea. At the end of the book he sums it up, recalling how Casy "went out in the wilderness to find his own soul, and he found he didn't have no soul that was his'n. Says he foun' he jus' got a little piece of a great big soul. Says a wilderness ain't no good 'cause his little piece of a soul wasn't no good 'less it was with the rest, an' was whole." Unlike Emerson, who had said goodbye to the proud world, these latterday Americans must live in the midst of it. "I know now," concludes Tom, "a fella ain't no good alone."

To repeat: this group idea is American, not Russian; and stems from Walt Whitman, not Karl Marx. But it does include some elements that have usually seemed sinful to orthodox Anglo-Saxons. . . . [The] Joads frankly discuss anatomical details and joke about them. Like most common people, they do not abscond or conceal. Sometimes they seem to go beyond the bounds of literary decency: the unbuttoned antics of Grandpa Joad touch a new low in folk-comedy. (pp. 319-20)

In Whitman's time almost everyone deprecated this physiological realism, and in our own many readers and critics still deprecate it. Nevertheless, it is absolutely necessary—both artistically and logically. In the first place, characters like the Joads do act and talk that way—to describe them as genteel would be to distort the picture. And, in the second place, Whitman himself had suggested the necessity of it: just as the literature of democracy must describe all sorts of people, "en masse," so it must describe all of the life of the people. To exclude the common or "low" elements of individual life would be as false as to exclude the common or low elements of society. Either would destroy the wholeness of life and nature. Therefore, along with the dust-driven Joads, we must have Grandpa's dirty drawers.

But beyond this physiological realism lies the problem of sex. And this problem is not one of realism at all. Throughout this turbulent novel an almost traditional reticence concerning the details of sex is observed. The problem here is rather one of fundamental morality, for sex had always been a symbol of sin. *The Scarlet Letter* reasserted the authority of an orthodox morality. Now Jim Casy questions that orthodoxy. On this first meeting with Tom he describes how, after sessions of preaching, he had often lain with a girl and then felt sinful afterward. This time the movies repeated his confession, because it is central to the motivation of the story. Disbelief in the sinfulness of sex converts Jim Casy from a preacher of the old morality to a practitioner of the new.

But in questioning the old morality Jim Casy does not deny morality. He doubts the strict justice of Hawthorne's code: "Maybe it ain't a sin. Maybe it's just the way folks is. Maybe we been whippin' the hell out of ourselves for nothin'." But he recognizes that love must always remain responsible and purposeful. Al Joad remains just "a boy after a girl." In place of the old, Casy preaches the new morality of Whitman, which uses sex to symbolize the love of man for his fellows. Jim Casy and Tom Joad have become more responsible and more purposeful than Pa Joad and Uncle John ever were: they love people so much that they are ready to die for them. . . . So Casy dies for his people, and Tom is ready to, and Rose of Sharon symbolically transmutes her maternal love to a love of all people. Here is a new realization of "the word democratic, the word enmasse." (pp. 320-21)

Catholic Christianity had always preached humility and passive obedience. Protestantism preached spiritual nonconformity, but kept its disobedience passive. Transcendentalism sought to save the individual but not the group. ("Are they *my* poor?" asked Emerson.) Whitman sympathized more deeply with the common people and loved them abstractly, but trusted that God and democracy would save them. The pragmatic philosophers first sought to implement American idealism by making thought itself instrumental. And now Steinbeck quotes scripture to urge popular action for the realization of the old ideals.

In the course of the book Steinbeck develops and translates the thought of the earlier pragmatists. "Thinking," wrote John Dewey, "is a kind of activity which we perform at specific need." And Steinbeck repeats: "Need is the stimulus to concept, concept to action." The cause of the Okie's migration is their need, and their migration itself becomes a kind of thinking—an unconscious groping for the solution to a half-formulated problem. Their need becomes the stimulus to concept.

In this novel a kind of pragmatic thinking takes place before our eyes: the idea develops from the predicament of the characters, and the resulting action becomes integral with the thought. The evils of absentee ownership produce the mass migration, and the mass migration results in the idea of group action. . . . (pp. 321-22)

Tom Joad is a pluralist—a pragmatist after William James. Tom said, "I'm still layin' my dogs down one at a time." Casy replied: "Yeah, but when a fence comes up at ya, ya gonna climb that fence." "I climb fences when I got fences to climb," said Tom. But Jim Casy believes in looking far ahead and seeing the thing as a whole: "But they's different kinda fences. They's folks like me that climbs fences that ain't even strang up yet." Which is to say that Casy is a kind of transcendental pragmatist. His thought seeks to generalize the problems of the Okies and to integrate them with the larger problem of industrial America. His solution is the principle of group action guided by conceptual thought and functioning within the framework of democratic society and law.

And at the end of the story Tom Joad becomes converted to Jim Casy's pragmatism. It is not important that the particular strike should be won, or that the particular need should be satisfied; but it is important that men should think in terms of action, and that they should think and act in terms of the whole rather than the particular individual. "For every little beaten strike is proof that the step is being taken." The value of an idea lies not in its immediate but in its eventual success. That idea is good which works—in the long run.

But the point of the whole novel is that action is an absolute essential of human life. If need and failure produce only fear, disintegration follows. But if they produce anger, then reconstruction may follow. The grapes of wrath must be trampled to make manifest the glory of the Lord. At the beginning of the story Steinbeck described the incipient wrath of the defeated farmers. At the end he repeats the scene. "And where a number of men gathered together the fear went from their faces, and anger took its place. And the women sighed with relief. . . . the break would never come as long as fear could turn to wrath." Then wrath could turn to action. (pp. 322-23)

Frederic I. Carpenter, "The Philosophical Joads," in College English, *Vol. 2, No. 4, January, 1941, pp. 315-25.*

JOSEPH WARREN BEACH

The Grapes of Wrath is perhaps the finest example we have so far produced in the United States of the proletarian novel. This is a somewhat loose term to designate the type of novel that deals primarily with the life of the working classes or with any social or industrial problem from the point of view of labor. There is likely to be a considerable element of propaganda in any novel with such a theme and such a point of view. And it often happens that the spirit of propaganda does not carry with it the philosophical breadth, the imaginative power, or the mere skill in narrative which are so important for the production of a work of art. Upton Sinclair is an example of a man of earnest feeling and admirable gifts for propaganda who has not the mental reach of a great artist nor

An excerpt from *The Grapes of Wrath*

"Tom," she said. "What you aimin' to do?"

He was quiet for a long time. "I been thinkin' how it was in that gov'ment camp, how our folks took care a theirselves, an' if they was a fight they fixed it theirself; an' they wasn't no cops wagglin' their guns, but they was better order than them cops ever give. I been a-wonderin' why we can't do that all over. Throw out the cops that ain't our people. All work together for our own thing—all farm our own lan'."

"Tom," Ma repeated, "what you gonna do?"

"What Casy done," he said.

"But they killed him."

"Yeah," said Tom. "He didn' duck quick enough. He wasn' doing nothin' against the law, Ma. I been thinkin' a hell of a lot, thinkin' about our people livin' like pigs, an' the good rich lan' layin' fallow, or maybe one fella with a million acres, while a hundred thousan' good farmers is starvin'. An' I been wonderin' if all our folks got together an' yelled, like them fellas yelled, only a few of 'em at the Hooper ranch—"

Ma said, "Tom, they'll drive you, an' cut you down like they done to young Floyd."

"They gonna drive me anyways. They drivin' all our people."

"You don't aim to kill nobody, Tom?"

"No. I been thinkin', long as I'm a outlaw anyways, maybe I could—Hell, I ain't thought it out clear, Ma. Don' worry me now. Don' worry me."

They sat silent in the coal-black cave of vines. Ma said, "How'm I gonna know 'bout you? They might kill ya an' I wouldn' know. They might hurt ya. How'm I gonna know?"

Tom laughed uneasily, "Well, maybe like Casy says, a fella ain't got a soul of his own, but on'y a piece of a big one—an' then—"

"Then what, Tom?"

"Then it don' matter. Then I'll be all aroun' in the dark. I'll be ever'where—wherever you look. Wherever they's a fight so hungry people can eat, I'll be there. Wherever they's a cop beatin' up a guy, I'll be there. If Casy knowed, why, I'll be in the way guys yell when they're mad an'—I'll be in the way kids laugh when they're hungry an' they know supper's ready. An' when our folks eat the stuff they raise an' live in the houses they build—why, I'll be there. See? God, I'm talkin' like Casy. Comes of thinkin' about him so much. Seems like I can see him sometimes."

"I don' un'erstan'," Ma said. "I don' really know."

"Me neither," said Tom. "It's jus' stuff I been thinkin' about. Get thinkin' a lot when you ain't movin' aroun'. You got to get back, Ma."

"You take the money then."

He was silent for a moment. "Awright," he said.

"An', Tom, later—when it's blowed over, you'll come back. You'll find us?"

"Sure," he said. "Now you better go. Here, gimme your han'." He guided her toward the entrance. Her fingers clutched his wrist. He swept the vines aside and followed her out. "Go up to the field till you come to a sycamore on the edge, an' then cut acrost the stream. Good-by."

"Good-by," she said, and she walked quickly away. Her eyes were wet and burning, but she did not cry.

the artist's power of telling a plausible story and creating a world of vivid and convincing people. (p. 327)

With Steinbeck, it is the other way round. He has been interested in people from the beginning, from long before he had any theory to account for their ways. What is more, he is positively fond of people, more obviously drawn to them than any other of our group of writers. More especially he has shown himself fond of men who work for bread in the open air, on a background of fields and mountains. They have always appealed to him as individuals, and for something in them that speaks to his esthetic sense. He sees them large and simple, with a luster round them like the figures in Rockwell Kent's engravings. He likes them strong and lusty, ready to fight and ready to make love. He likes to see the women nursing their babies. He likes to see people enjoying their food, however coarse, and sharing it with others, what there is of it. And when they are in distress. . . .

When people are in distress, you want to help them. If the distress is so widespread that anyone's help is a mere drop in the bucket, you begin to reflect on the causes. You develop theories. The people in distress themselves begin to ponder causes, the rights and wrongs of the case, and they develop theories. Their theories may not be scientific, but they have the merit of growing out of a real experience. The best of social philosophies, so far as fiction is concerned, is that which comes spontaneously to the lips of people trying to figure out a way through life's labyrinth. The best sort of story from the point of view of sociology is one that by the very nature of its incidents sets you pondering the most fundamental human problems. (pp. 327-28)

[The final episode of *The Grapes of Wrath*, in which Rosasharn nurses a starving man with the milk intended for her child,] is symbolic in its way of what is, I should say, the leading theme of the book. It is a type of the life-instinct, the vital persistence of the common people who are represented by the Joads. Their sufferings and humiliations are overwhelming; but these people are never entirely overwhelmed. They have something in them that is more than stoical endurance. It is the will to live, and the faith in life. The one who gives voice to this is Ma. When they are driven out of their Hooverville and Tom is with difficulty restrained from violent words and acts against the deputies, it is Ma who explains to him what we might call the philosophy of the proletariat.

> "Easy," she said. "You got to have patience. Why, Tom—us people will go on livin' when all them people is gone. Why, Tom, we're the people that live. They ain't gonna wipe us out. Why, we're the people—we go on."
>
> "We take a beatin' all the time."
>
> "I know," Ma chuckled. "Maybe that makes us tough. Rich fellas come up an' they die, an' their kids ain't no good, an' they die out. But, Tom, we keep a comin'. Don' you fret none, Tom. A different time's comin'."
>
> "How do you know?"
>
> "I don' know how."

That is, you will recognize, the philosophy of Sandburg in *The People, Yes*—the mystical faith of the poet in the persistence and the final triumph of the plain people. Sandburg knows no better than Ma how he knows. He feels it in his bones. And that feeling is, I suppose, with Ma the very mark of the will to live.

Rosasharn's gesture in the barn is not the only symbol of this will to live. Very early in the book the author devotes a whole chapter—a short one—to the picture of a turtle crossing the highway. It is an act of heroic obstinacy and persistence against heavy odds. This is a gem of minute description, of natural history close-up, such as would delight the reader of Thoreau or John Burroughs. There are things like this in Thomas Hardy's Wessex novels. And as in Hardy, so here—it is not a mere piece of gratuitous realism. It may be enjoyed as such. But it inevitably carries the mind by suggestion to the kindred heroisms of men and women. It sets the note for the story that is to follow.

This chapter is an instance of a technical device by which the author gives his narrative a wider reference and representative character. The story of the Joads is faithfully told as a series of particular incidents in their stirring adventure. We hang with concern and suspense over each turn of their fortunes. But the author is not content with that. He wishes to give us a sense of the hordes of mortals who are involved with the Joads in the epic events of the migration; and along with the material events he wishes us to see the social forces at play and the sure and steady weaving of new social patterns for a people and a nation. And so, to every chapter dealing with the Joads, he adds a shorter, more general, but often not less powerful chapter on the general situation.

There is, to begin with, an account of the dust storm over the gray lands and the red lands of Oklahoma—a formidable example of exact and poetic description matched by few things in fiction. Like Hardy with Egdon Heath, Steinbeck begins with physical nature and comes by slow degrees to humanity. The chapter ends with an account of the reactions of the men, women and children in the face of this catastrophe. The conception is large and noble. Humanity has been stripped of all that is adventitious and accidental, leaving the naked will and thought of man. Under the stress of desperate calamity the children watch their elders to see if they will break. The women watch the men to see if this time they will fail. It is a question of going soft or going hard; and when the men go hard the others know that all is not lost. The corn is lost, but something more important remains. And we are left with the picture of the men on whom they all depend. It is man reduced to the simplest terms—man pitted against the brute forces of nature—man with the enduring will that gives him power to use his brains for the conquering of nature. Man's thinking is an extension of his powers of action—he thinks with his hands. (pp. 332-34)

Most of these intercalary chapters have more particular themes. There is the theme of buying cheap and selling dear—the wonderful chapter of the second-hand automobile dealers. There is the theme of social forms coming into being as occasion requires. In the roadside camps the separate families are quickly assembled into one community; and community spontaneously develops its own laws out of its own obvious needs. There is the theme of large-scale production for economy and profit—the land syndicates in California who ruin the small owners. There is the theme of spring in California—its beauty, the scent of fruit, with the cherries and prunes and pears and grapes rotting on the ground to keep up the price. There are hungry men come for miles to take the superfluous oranges; but men with hoses squirt kerosene on the fruit. "A million people hungry, needing the fruit—and kerosene sprayed over the golden mountains." And there is the theme of the blindness of property in its anonymous forms. . . .

There is the theme of a common interest as opposed to a private and exclusive. "Not my land, but ours." "All work together for our own thing—all farm our own lan'." And finally we have the theme of man who has lost his soul and finds it again in devotion to the common cause.

Some of these themes are expressed in the spontaneous utterance of the Okies; some of them in the more abstract and theoretical language of the author. In general we may say that he is most effective when he puts his views in the mouths of the characters. For this is fiction; and fiction has small tolerance for the abstractions of an author. Still, there are cases where the theme is too broad and too complicated to find adequate expression in the words of a single man on a particular occasion. This is a great challenge to the ingenuity of a writer, and Steinbeck has found a number of ingenious and effective means of dramatizing the thought of a whole group of people faced with a difficult problem in economics. There is one remarkable chapter in which he shows us the debate between the tenant farmers and the agents of the banking syndicates come to put them off the land. It is a debate which recurs over and over again with each unfortunate family; and Steinbeck has presented it in a form that is at the same time generalized and yet not too abstract and theoretical. We are shown the farmers squatting on their heels while the owner men sit in their cars and explain the peculiar nature of the institution which they represent. It is a kind of impersonal monster that does not live on side-meat like men, but on profits. It has to have profits all the time, and ever more profits or it will die. And now that the land is poor, the banks cannot afford to leave it in the hands of men who cannot even pay their taxes. (pp. 334-36)

[In] a kind of parable, with allegorical figures, and with Biblical simplifications, our author has managed to give in summary, in essence, what must have gone on a million times all over the world, when the two groups were confronted—two groups that represent two opposed and natural interests, and both of them caught in an intricate web of forces so great and so automatic in their working that they are helpless to combat them or even to understand them. This is not an individual scene of drama; but many of the remarks must have been made a thousand times in individual cases. It is not an economic treatise; but the substance of many such a treatise is presented in simplified form suited to the apprehensions of the men who speak. There is enough local color to make it appropriate to this story of the Okies; and sufficient differentiation of the manner of the two groups to give it a properly fictional cast. The apologetic tone of the one party, their patience and firmness; the bewilderment and indignation of the other party; the reasonableness on both sides—are admirably rendered. In each case the speaker is like a chorus in ancient tragedy, embodying the collective sentiments of a large group. Anyone who has tried to write will understand the number of difficulties which have been overcome in the application of this literary device. Anyone, at least, who has tried to write fiction, and who has tried in fiction to present a general view of things without cutting loose from the concrete and particular. This is but one of many instances in *The Grapes of Wrath* of Steinbeck's resourcefulness in meeting his main problem—to reconcile the interests of theory with those of imaginative art—to render the abstractions of thought in the concrete terms of fiction. (pp. 337-38)

The narrative method in these chapters is thus an extremely flexible medium, in which many different modes of statement are composed in a consistent whole diversified in coloring as a Persian carpet. What really needs stressing is the virtuosity of the performance, a virtuosity fully as great as—say—Thornton Wilder's, though it is likely to be passed over because of the homeliness of the subject matter, because Steinbeck is supposed to be simply rendering the plain reactions of plain people. And so he is, and much concerned not to introduce any foreign element of preciousness or affectation. But he is rendering them, the reactions of plain people, with tenderness, insight, and artistic detachment, and with the power of modulating freely round the dominant key. He is like an actor capable of doing things with his voice, varying his tone with the changing rôle and emotion. He has more than usual of the storyteller's ventriloquism.

He is one who feels strongly on the subject of man's essential dignity of spirit and his unexhausted possibilities for modification and improvement. It is natural that at times he should slip into a prophetic tone not unlike that of our midwestern poet.

> For man, unlike any other thing organic or inorganic in the universe, grows beyond his work, walks up the stairs of his concepts, emerges ahead of his accomplishments. . . . Having stepped forward, he may slip back, but only half a step, never the full step back. This you may say and know it and know it. . . . And this you can know—fear the time when Manself will not suffer and die for a concept, for this one quality is the foundation of Manself, and this one quality is man, distinctive in the universe.

Here let me lay my cards on the table. About such a passage as this I have a divided feeling, as I do about some of the quietly eloquent sayings of Tom to his mother when he leaves her to take up the cause of labor. These statements of Tom about his mission, these statements of Steinbeck about Manself, do not seem to me among the best things in the book, considered as literary art; and yet I do not see how we could dispense with them. I would not wish them away. For they are important clues to the author's feeling—to his hope and faith in humanity. But they do not seem to me altogether successful as imaginative shapings of the stuff of life in keeping with the most rigorous demands of fictional art.

The passage about Manself and dying for a concept is considerably longer than what I have quoted. It is in substance highly creditable to the author's feeling about man's nature and destiny. But there is something a trifle stiff about it, a trifle abstract, "talky," and magniloquent. It is as if at this point Steinbeck's art, generally so flexible and sure, had weakened—as if he was hurried or tired, and had for the moment allowed mere words to take the place of images or the dramatic evocations which are his most effective medium. In the case of Tom's remarks to his mother when he is setting out on his career as a labor organizer (Chapter Twenty-eight), they are cast, like all the dialogue, in the familiar language of the Okie, the untutored man of the people. Perhaps for that very reason, however, there is something just a bit questionable in the high seriousness, the wistful Christlikeness, of the sentiments he expresses. One does not so much question his harboring these sentiments, along with others less exalted in tone; what one questions is whether he could have brought himself to utter just these sentiments in just this tone. One asks whether the author has not a little too obviously manipulated his material here in order to point the moral of his tale. (pp. 339-41)

If I were asked to say just exactly what are the economic theories of John Steinbeck, and how he proposes to apply them in terms of political action, I should have to answer: I do not know. The book offers no specific answer to these questions. It reminds us of what we all do know: that our system of production and finance involves innumerable instances of cruel hardship and injustice; that it needs constant adjustment and control by the conscience and authority of the sovereign people. This author is concerned with what has been called the forgotten man; it is clear that he holds the community responsible for the man without work, home, or food. He seems to intimate that what cannot be cured by individual effort must needs be met by collective measures. It is highly important that our people should be made aware of the social problems which remain to be solved within the system which is so good to so many of us. And there is no more effective way of bringing this about than to have actual instances presented vividly to our imaginations by means of fiction. For this reason I regard *The Grapes of Wrath* as a social document of great educational value.

Considering it simply as literary art, I would say that it gains greatly by dealing with social problems so urgent that they cannot be ignored. It gains thereby in emotional power. But it is a notable work of fiction by virtue of the fact that all social problems are so effectively dramatized in individual situations and characters—racy, colorful, pitiful, farcical, disorderly, well meaning, shrewd, brave, ignorant, loyal, anxious, obstinate, insuppressible, cockeyed . . . mortals. I have never lived among these Okies nor heard them talk. But I would swear that this is their language, these their thoughts, and these the very hardships and dangers which they encountered. They represent a level, material and social, on which the reader has never existed even for a day. They have lived for generations completely deprived of luxuries and refinements which in the life he has known are taken for granted as primary conditions of civilization.

And yet they are not savages. They are self-respecting men and women with a traditional set of standards and proprieties and rules of conduct which they never think of violating. Beset with innumerable difficulties, cut off from their familiar moorings, they are confronted with situations of great delicacy, with nice problems in ethics and family policy to be resolved. Decisions are taken after informal discussion in the family council organized on ancient tribal lines. Grampa was a rather flighty and childish old fellow. He was still the titular head of the tribe, but his position was honorary and a matter of custom. He had the right of first comment; but actual decision was made by the strong and wise, by Pa and Tom, and above all by Ma. Pa was the representative of practical prudence; Ma the voice of right feeling and generous impulse and the traditional code of decent conduct. It was she who decided that they should take Casy with them although they were already overcrowded. (pp. 345-46)

And so the Joads and the Okies take their place with Don Quixote, with Dr. Faustus, with Galsworthy's Forsytes and Lewis' Babbitt, in the world's gallery of symbolic characters, the representative tapestry of the creative imagination. Will the colors hold? That is a large question, which only time can answer. It depends on whether the dyes are synthetic aniline or the true vegetable product. And who at the present moment can make sure of that?

I will put the question in another way. Is the subject too special for this book to have continuing artistic appeal? Are the issues fundamental enough in human nature to give it what is called universality? Perhaps the best theme is a combination of a particular and local subject with one more general and lasting. The particular subject here is the Oklahoma farmer and an oversupply of labor in the California orchards. The general subject is hunger; the general subject is man pitted against the forces of nature. There is much to remind one of *Robinson Crusoe*. Steinbeck will certainly do well if he can last as long and be as widely read as Daniel Defoe. (p. 347)

Joseph Warren Beach, "John Steinbeck: Art and Propaganda," in his American Fiction: 1920-1940, *The Macmillan Company, 1941, pp. 327-47.*

PHILIP BROOKS

On Nov. 24 [1941] the Supreme Court of the United States handed down a momentous decision in the "Okie" case, that of Fred F. Edwards v. the People of the State of California. A Texan, unemployed and indigent, had been brought to California in violation of the law of that State. The highest court in the land found the law unconstitutional, declaring it an infringement upon interstate commerce as well as national citizenship. At the same time similar laws in twenty-seven other States were invalidated. Figuring prominently in the deliberations was John Steinbeck's *The Grapes of Wrath,* which, apart from its other distinctions, may now be classed with the great social novels that have influenced remedial legislation.

It is some satisfaction to learn that the original typescript of *The Grapes of Wrath* has been placed in the nation's safe-keeping by Frank J. Hogan, the noted lawyer and book collector. Mr. Hogan gave the manuscript to the Library of Congress as a Christmas present. . . .

The typescript, a voluminous document of 751 pages, is filled with revisions and alterations in Steinbeck's hand. Accompanying it is a set of the galley proofs with marginal commentary in the form of a lively debate between the author and one of his publisher's staff. It is invaluable for the way it illuminates his method of work.

Steinbeck did not just toss off his ideas lightly, without intensive preliminary study and a thorough "going over." The interpolated discussions of dialect, for example, offer clues to the subtle variations in style between the Joad and Wilson families and show what care had to be exercised by both editor and author in maintaining consistency in the speech of each character. Steinbeck readily accepted many of the proposed emendations, but rebelled at others. Once he gleefully pounced upon an error that had been passed over by the editor and blasted him with "ha ha ha ha ha."

The importance of the manuscript of a masterpiece like *The Grapes of Wrath* as a record of the contemporary American scene is obvious. In acknowledging the gift Archibald MacLeish, the Librarian of Congress, remarks that it is but one, although a prominent member, of the literary documents of social significance that the Library of Congress is trying to assemble. In this archive are being gathered creative works in prose and poetry that have helped to shape or interpret our civilization or prophesied its future course.

Philip Brooks, in an article on "The Grapes of Wrath," in The New York Times Book Review, *February 1, 1942, p. 22.*

MAXWELL GEISMAR

[The essay below was first published in 1942.]

Success story, '39. In the year 1937 a new Young Lochinvar came writing out of the West with a little fable which dazzled Broadway. So faithful in man's love of man, and so dauntless in war (was it proletarian?), there never was writer like this young John Steinbeck, or so it almost seemed. His career itself was romantic. Ranch hand, carpenter, painter, by his own admission Steinbeck felt himself a loss to the building trades. Newspaper man, then writer of bitter chronicles, caretaker on lonely Lake Tahoe where the silent snows 'melted the hates out of him,' and lastly spectacular young playwright—Steinbeck brought his *Of Mice and Men* into the stony heart of the nation's metropolis. The 'best-laid schemes went a-gley' in a very touching way, and we saw ourselves as authors see us. The poor George of the play, like every man, killed the thing he loved, but few men achieve this at such a handsome profit. 'An' live off the fatta the lan'.' Ironic echo of the outcast's dream, on Lennie's little acre there now was Standing Room Only.

Yet, if *Of Mice and Men* dealt somewhat boyishly with the abnormal, if its effect sometimes reminds us of a pathological fraternity house, here nevertheless was a young writer of unquestioned power creating an exciting show—and not half so good a one as *The Grapes of Wrath* which two years later did for the nation what the little play had done for the metropolis. In the smart set *The Grapes of Wrath* was acclaimed the American novel 'of the season, probably the year, possibly the decade.' Was Mr. Fadiman's sense of symmetry betraying him? [see excerpt above.] The more sober Louis Kronenberger hailed Steinbeck's novel as homeric, breathless, comic, and heartbreaking [see excerpt above]. A chorus of other critics spontaneously recalled *Uncle Tom's Cabin,* 'Leaves of Grass,' and obviously, 'Moby Dick.' Besides, fulfilling the virgin's and the author's desire, *The Grapes of Wrath* appeared to be as popular as it was good. While a score of other books skyrocketed and darkly fell, it stayed. It was not only great literature, it was enjoyable. In ecstasy, the publishers became inarticulate. Burned and banned, borrowed, smuggled, but above all, bought, *The Grapes of Wrath* began to cause a sort of national aesthetic frenzy without parallel in our time; belles-lettres had turned bellicose.

Labeled as 'vile filth' which incidentally frightened tourists away from California, Steinbeck's novel was read by thousands of indignant American families. Articles, surveys, investigations centered around it, and the motion picture rights went for seventy-five thousand dollars. 'Too hot for Hollywood?' demanded the magazine *Look,* while the magazine *Life* was nodding, but never outdone, the entertainment magnates poured a million dollars into this epic of the penniless. Governor Olsen, Walter Winchell, Secretary of Agriculture Wallace, supporting the picture, were opposed by Ruth Comfort Mitchell, President of Pro-America (who could deny her patriotism?), and Emory Hoffman of the Kern County, California, Chamber of Commerce—which was producing a movie itself, rather ominously entitled: 'Plums of Plenty.' *The Grapes of Wrath* was now number one of the best-sellers, and sales were mounting steadily. Was it frightening away tourists from California? The literate nation was visiting Kern County.

Tens of thousands, and then hundreds of thousands of eager Americans thumbed a ride in the engrossing pages of Steinbeck's novel, took a literary hitch on the Joads's jalopy, struggled west along Highway 66, perhaps the most historic route in contemporary literature. Clarksville and Ozark and Van Buren, down from Tulsa and up from McAlester, ten pages of suspense while Al is changing a tire, through Texas, Oklahoma, and there's an end to another chapter. Thunder of tractors plowing under the solid American farming classes, the twisting winds that beat across the Dust Bowl, the whine of dry bearings in the ears of America's millions reading and sharing this tale of their own dispossessed. In Bronx diningrooms and Main Street barbershops, in college study-halls and on Bar Harbor beaches, from the coast of Maine to Louisiana bayous, they are reading the epic of America's disinherited.

A unique modern literary pilgrimage had begun. A twisting draft across a Long Island neo-Tudor reception hall, the heat of middle-western suburbs, the roar of trucks in city streets, and there's an end to chapter twenty of *The Grapes of Wrath.* From Massachusetts, Tennessee, and Virginia the American readers swept onward, from Minneapolis, Minnesota, and Tampa, Florida, and Reading, Pennsylvania, and Oklahoma too they came, their eyes sweeping along the pages of Steinbeck's novel, knocking off the miles along Highway 66. Resting, stopping, stretching, talking to Minnie and Susy and Mae behind the roadside lunch counters of a continent, starting up again on this bitter journey to the modern Promised Land, the Americans read *The Grapes of Wrath.* In frilled boudoirs and in army bivouacs the eyes of America swept along the pages of Highway 66.

Thus, by her own tokens the United States of '39, recalling now the gilded glories of Lardner's '29, had marked John Steinbeck as her favorite literary son—this impassioned radical who exploited the ruling classes, who introduced the proletariat to a multitude of model homes, and brought Marx to Hoover's doorstep. Jerking along to California's shores, the Joads's jalopy had become America's new bandwagon—but the true destination of Steinbeck's novel lay incalculably beyond these geographical boundaries. (pp. 239-41)

A great deal has been said about *The Grapes of Wrath* in the heat of partisanship; it has been defended by radical critics with as little literary feeling as it has been attacked by our conservative and vested interests; we attempt here to view it as a writer's work, and as the present climax of Steinbeck's history.

In this sense, knowing what we do of the earlier Steinbeck, it must become clear how much of Steinbeck's famous novel is borrowed from the past, how many of the characters and themes in *The Grapes of Wrath* are reflections of Steinbeck's younger interests, and of the uneven temperament we have already seen functioning. The inequalities of the American social system are affecting thousands of fine American families. Hence the Joads must be a fine American family. Around them Steinbeck weaves his typical fantasies, so that the Joads emerge as idealized in their own way as those smooth personages who dwell everlastingly in the pages of the *Saturday Evening Post.* Of them, of course, Ma Joad is the guiding spirit, the soul of American motherhood, her home in the kitchen but her spirit in the heavens. . . .

> Her hazel eyes seemed to have experienced all possible tragedy and to have mounted pain and suffering like steps into a high calm and a superhuman understanding. . . . And from her great and humble position in the family she had taken dignity and

clean calm beauty. From her position as healer, her hands had grown sure and cool and quiet; from her position as arbiter she had become as remote and faultless in judgment as a goddess.

Steinbeck's sentimentality has overwhelmed him, his reliance on rhapsody rather than reflection, the violence which characterizes his temperament here turned into idyllic abstraction—these traits which as yet prevent our considering him fully among the writers whose talent he perhaps equals. And if Ma Joad is thus portrayed, what can we say of Rose of Sharon, with her ripe voluptuousness, her drowsing aroma of universal fertility—except that this is again sentimentalized projection. Connie Rivers, in turn, reminds us of Curley's wife and the philosophic witch of the *Cup of Gold* as a symbol of Steinbeck's sexual fascination. . . . And with his 'little bright eyes,' his cantankerous, mischievous little old face, Grampa Joad is too much of a typical Steinbeckian whimsicality for us ever to believe, as, in short, are most of the Joads. As in *Of Mice and Men* we have in *The Grapes of Wrath* the joining of the old and the new Steinbeck, and the older themes are marked with the deterioration which comes when an author retraces without belief the patterns of his past. It is hard to believe that even Steinbeck himself accepts the Joads as people, or that he has thrown in the variety of pagan, weird, earthy, violent concepts for more than their picturesque value. *The Grapes of Wrath,* in short, often represents the dubious nuptials of *Tobacco Road* with the *Ladies' Home Journal.* But the marriage is one of convenience.

For as with *For Whom the Bell Tolls,* we cannot deny the force and sincerity of the novel which break through the moulds of its presentation. The descriptions of the migration, of the highway caravans, of the used-car markets, of truckdrivers and roadside stands, the geographical panorama of the Western States, the evocations of their sociopsychological temper, and those of the strain of industrial conflict, the repeated affirmations of faith and respect in average humanity, the anger at social injustice, and above all the novel's will for life coming in an era of sickness and death—these again and again capture and arouse us. In tone much like Zola's *Germinal* (in our own tradition, the later Steinbeck seems to descend from Frank Norris and Jack London) with very similar Zolaesque flaws, lacks of taste, debatable excesses, ridiculous sensations, *The Grapes of Wrath* has also the same urgency which in Zola's novel holds us some fifty years after its inception, and hence it will be condemned only by those who, in the end, prefer perfection to importance. Before the significance of the book in Steinbeck's own history, and in the history of his society, before the power of it, rough as it may be, we must yield up our reservations to our praise. Lacking the art of *The Pastures of Heaven* and the realism of *In Dubious Battle,* marking, as it also does, a return to Steinbeck's glamor, theatrics, and simplicity of view after the conflicts of his earlier proletarian novel, thus sentimentalized, often distorted, *The Grapes of Wrath* is not at all Steinbeck's best novel. But it is, all in all, his biggest novel.

And in it, what a change has come about in the young author of Morgan's piratical adventures! Urging us, in the *Cup of Gold,* to emulate the individualistic power-drive of the buccaneer, this more glamorous portrayal of the values of '29, Steinbeck is now writing of man's communal good. The blood-thirsty mystic who dwelt among the druidic groves of *To a God Unknown* has settled among the disinherited workers of his land. The advocate of immolation is now protesting the needless sacrifice of human lives. The dazzling playwright of *Of Mice and Men,* busying himself there with theatrical abnormality, is here portraying the drama of the most ordinary lives. The Steinbeck who sought in *The Pastures of Heaven* the causes of human frustration finds its true origin in the social pathology of an economic system both incoherent and inexcusable. The 'Curse' is indeed civilization. But the writer who fled from it in *Tortilla Flat* now argues for social controls! Devoted, as we have noticed, to hobgoblins, Steinbeck at least hasn't treasured the famous one of Emerson's little minds—'consistency.' Having come to realize, however, that our true happiness must derive, not through any mystical and mythical freedom from society, but through making our society genuinely free, Steinbeck's extremes become a virtue, and the grace of his final truth redeems his methodological errors. If indeed Steinbeck suffers throughout much of his work from a sort of belated spiritual adolescence, if his novels are sometimes full of pangs and clichés, spotted with the marks, as it were, of literary puberty, it is also and more significantly true that in the final result he has come of age.

And the importance of this lies not only, of course, with Steinbeck as an individual, but in his relationship with an entire range of American artists and with our culture itself. In the variety of his early 'solutions'—the life of egotistic adventure, and that of bloody daring, the primitive way, the natural and anti-social life, the return to the soil, the dabblings with the abnormal—Steinbeck seems almost to traverse the entire circuit of contemporary artistic escapes. In him are reflected the evasions of his generation. Avoiding the most flagrant of these evasions, and from the first always more American in tone, Steinbeck seems to speak nevertheless for all his fellow individualists, mystics and primitives, symbolists and experimentalists: for all the discontented heirs of Henry James, seeking one or another exit, Kay Boyles, middle-class bohemians gathered in little villages, those who ran from Toklas to Taos. He speaks for all those as well who jumped from 'Transition' to Technocracy, or bold Menckenites scorning the American mob, scholarly humanists from Ohio ignoring the core of humanism, for all those who, in whatever ways, found their souls in Oxford accents, Spanish bullfights, or in red Russia, as well as in the Californian paisanos. In his early evasions Steinbeck is symptomatic of this whole range of American aesthetes whom, as we saw, Thomas Wolfe took off in *The Story of a Novel,* those American refugees to whom a wide world might have cried: Why, why don't you go back where you came from?

And if in his young work Steinbeck reminds us of those who fled what they conceived to be a hostile, narrow, and materialistic environment, in his conversion Steinbeck again illuminates another era of American artistic thought. Through the errors which mark his first attempts at dealing with his own day, his lack of sociological knowledge, the haste with which he dropped a point of view essentially naïve, and in the naïveté which nevertheless accompanies his new views also, here again Steinbeck reflects the American writer in crisis. (pp. 263-67)

The very imperfections, then, of Steinbeck's issue reveal his society, while those of Steinbeck himself make him more effective with this society. The mirror of typical American sentiment that he is, though applying this sentiment to the relatively fresh field of social welfare, Steinbeck is perhaps closer to the American audience than any other comparable writer. The traits in him which fluster the critic are those which endear him to mankind. If angels do rush in where fools fear to tread, they accomplish after all very little, since they are so seldom heeded. The perfection of first-rate art is in one sense sterile, a high peak in itself yet too remote for the majority of us to exist upon, being unable to breathe in the rarefied climate of pure wisdom. But literature of the second order—and we recall *Uncle Tom's Cabin*—may sway continents and for a moment seduce Destiny herself from her chores. If Steinbeck's impact upon his society derives in large measure from his very imperfections, his effect nevertheless can be tremendous. And this is what gives him, and not all our critical carpings can alter it, his final, largest significance. (pp. 267-68)

Maxwell Geismar, "John Steinbeck: Of Wrath or Joy," in his Writers in Crisis: The American Novel, 1925-1940, *195-? Reprint by Hill and Wang, 1961, pp. 237-70.*

JEAN-PAUL SARTRE

There is one American literature for Americans and another for the French. In France the general reader knows *Babbitt* and *Gone With the Wind,* but these books have had no influence on French literature. The greatest literary development in France between 1929 and 1939 was the discovery of Faulkner, Dos Passos, Hemingway, Caldwell, Steinbeck. The choice of these authors, many people have told me, was due to Professor Maurice Coindreau of Princeton, who sent us their works in translation with excellent prefaces.

But a selection by any one man is effective only if he foresees the demands of the collective group to which he addresses himself. With Coindreau as intermediary, the French public selected the works it needed. It is true that these authors have not had in France a popular success comparable to that of Sinclair Lewis. Their influence was far more restricted, but infinitely more profound. We needed them and not your famous Dreiser. To writers of my generation, the publication of *The 42nd Parallel, Light in August, A Farewell to Arms,* evoked a revolution similar to the one produced fifteen years earlier in Europe by the *Ulysses* of James Joyce. Their reception was prepared for by the excellent *Bridge of San Luis Rey* of Thornton Wilder.

It seemed to us suddenly that we had just learned something and that our literature was about to pull itself out of its old ruts. At once, for thousands of young intellectuals, the American novel took its place, together with jazz and the movies, among the best of the importations from the United States. America became for us the country of Faulkner and Dos Passos, just as it had already been the home of Louis Armstrong, King Vidor, the Blues. . . .

What fascinated us all really—petty bourgeois that we were, sons of peasants securely attached to the earth of our farms, intellectuals entrenched in Paris for life—was the constant flow of men across a whole continent, the exodus of an entire village to the orchards of California, the hopeless wandering of the hero in *Light in August,* and of the uprooted people who drifted along at the mercy of the storms in *The 42nd Parallel,* the dark murderous fury which sometimes swept through an entire city, the blind and criminal love in the novels of James Cain. (p. 114)

It is easy to understand my eagerness to see the country of these great writers when I was flying to America in January,

1945. I must confess that in one respect I was disappointed. First, it was impossible to meet any of these men. They were in France, in England, in the Orient—everywhere, indeed, except in the United States. Also, the majority of the cultivated Americans whom I met did not share my enthusiasm for them. An American lady who knew Europe very well asked me one day what American writers I preferred. When I mentioned Faulkner, the other people present started to laugh. The lady, gently amused, said, "Good heavens—that *old* Faulkner!"

Later I met a young liberal writer—the author of some very good historical novels. I told him I had been asked by my publishers to get in touch with literary agents of several writers who were particularly admired in France. He asked me the names of these writers. When I mentioned Caldwell, his friendly smile vanished suddenly; at the name of Steinbeck he raised his eyebrows; and at the mention of Faulkner he cried indignantly, "You French! Can't you ever like anything but filth?" (p. 115)

Because of these experiences I concluded that the American public does not react to its writers in the same way as the French public. This discovery dulled my enthusiasm. Everywhere people told me, "You like Faulkner because you have never read any other novel about the South. We have hundreds of them. Read Dreiser, read Henry James. These are our great writers."

I have also concluded that at the moment there is a very strong reaction against the "pessimistic" literature of the period between the two wars. I must admit that we have the same reaction in France against writers of that period. And finally I observed among many American intellectuals a lively concern about the success in France of certain writers who could not fit into American life. "Between France and us," they told me, "there are today misunderstandings which are inevitable but momentary. We do not attach much importance to them, of course. But is this the time—when all countries must combine their efforts to understand one another better—to present the French with an unjust and black picture of our civilization?"

This is why I feel it necessary to explain to the American readers of this article two essential points. I should like to show them that these unflattering books do not make bad propaganda for the United States. I should also like to make them understand why the French have chosen precisely these books from so many excellent works.

It is true that the Germans tried to use the "pessimistic" works of your authors for propaganda purposes—particularly Steinbeck, because Steinbeck was the most severe critic of the capitalistic form of production in the United States. They permitted the publication of *In Dubious Battle,* although they had previously forbidden all translation of American authors. (pp. 115-16)

Later these same German propagandists tried again by offering Gallimard permission to publish *The Grapes of Wrath.* Gallimard suspected something and refused. This work was later translated and published by a Belgian collaborationist editor, and the offices of the Franco-Germanic Institute were preparing to flood the French market with *The Grapes of Wrath* when the Americans broke through the Nazi line in Normandy. But at the same time, the clandestine Editions de Minuit which had published *Le Silence de la Mer,* began to circulate *The Moon Is Down* by the same Steinbeck—which

seemed to us all like a message from fighting America to the European underground. Thus the most rebellious, perhaps, of your writers held the ambiguous position of being acclaimed at the same time by the collaborationists and by the underground.

In another instance the friends of the Germans miscalculated. When the Vichy newspapers published an extract from the American or English press severely criticizing some Allied military operation, or loyally recognizing some Allied defeat, they thought they would discourage us. They provoked on the contrary among most of us a profound respect for Anglo-Saxon democracy and bitter regret for our own. "Such people," we told ourselves, "have confidence in their rights. They must be both disciplined and stout-hearted to withstand without flinching the announcement of a defeat."

The harsh criticism that your writers made against your social regime we took in the same way. It never disgusted us with America—on the contrary, we saw in it a manifestation of your liberty. We knew that in Germany such a book as *The Grapes of Wrath* could never have been published. Then, need I add, no matter what evils your writers denounced, we have the same faults in our own country. Yes, the Negroes of Chicago are housed in hovels. That is neither just nor democratic. But many of our white workmen live in hovels that are even more miserable.

These injustices have never seemed to us a defect of American society but rather a sign of the imperfections of our time. (p. 116)

Jean-Paul Sartre, "American Novelists in French Eyes," in The Atlantic Monthly, *Vol. 178, No. 2, August, 1946, pp. 114-18.*

WARREN MOTLEY

As the Joad clan disintegrates under the pressure of dispossession and migration, Ma Joad emerges as a central, cohesive force. However, critics exploring the social thinking behind *The Grapes of Wrath* have tended to give her short shrift. Many of them have looked to the articulate Jim Casy rather than to the reticent Joads to explain the family's gradual realization that their survival depends on communal cooperation. I wish to correct that imbalance now. I shall argue that the Joad family shifts from a patriarchal structure to a predominantly matriarchal one. So doing, they dramatize the influence of the anthropologist Robert Briffault on John Steinbeck as he tried to understand the Depression.

Focusing too closely on the ideas of Jim Casy distorts the critical view of Ma Joad. She is too often, and mistakenly, set in opposition to the preacher, as if she shared the social values of her individualistic husband. In fact, she is receptive to Casy from the beginning and is thus marked as a cohesive rather than a fragmenting force. But the preacher does not have to convert Ma Joad. Her communal feelings emerge independently of his pronouncements. Working from Briffault's theories on the matriarchal origin of society, Steinbeck presents Ma Joad's growing power as a source of communal strength sheltering human dignity from the antisocial effects of individualism.

Steinbeck observed the Okies' migration across the Southwest at first hand and could not accept the human wreckage trailed along Route 66 as an instance of the human species sloughing off unsuccessful lower members. Seeking intellectual support, he turned to those scientists and thinkers who believed that cooperation rather than competition was the basis of both evolutionary and social progress. They strove to heal what they saw as the post-Darwinian split between scientific thinking and ethical experience. Steinbeck read Jan Smuts's *Holism and Evolution* and talked of immersing himself in the works of Jan Elif Boodin, author of *The Social Mind* [according to Richard Astro in *John Steinbeck and Edward F. Ricketts: The Shaping of a Novelist*]. In analyzing the shift from patriarchy to matriarchy in the Joad family, Steinbeck's reading in *The Mothers* is particularly important. There, Briffault unfolded a vision of social "solidarity [in the matriarchal clan] almost inconceivable and unintelligible to those who have, like ourselves, developed amid the conditions and ideas created by the strenuously competitive and suspicious individualism of modern societies." As Carol Steinbeck commented to Richard Astro, Ma Joad is "pure Briffault." (pp. 397-98)

Drawing on historical records and contemporary anthropological studies, Briffault argued that society first develops on matriarchal lines and that a matriarchal stage universally precedes the patriarchal structure of more advanced societies. Unfortunately, matriarchy is an awkward term, as Briffault himself understood; to most people it erroneously connotes a topsy-turvy, Amazonian patriarchy in which "women exercise a domination over the men similar or equivalent to that exercised by the men over the women in a patriarchal social order". But to Briffault matriarchy describes a radically different relationship between people based on cooperation rather than power. (pp. 398-99)

Briffault's insistence on the distinctness and precedence of the matriarchal stage reflects his theory that "all familial feeling, all group-sympathy, the essential foundation, therefore, of a social organization, is the direct product of prolonged maternal care, and does not exist apart from it." (p. 399)

Matriarchal cultures, Briffault observed, are "nothing if not equalitarian." The concepts of authority and domination are "entirely foreign to primitive humanity" because the economic advantages on which power rests do not exist. Although labor is divided in matriarchies—men take charge of the hunt and women of the camp—the division is not exploitive. Both men and women work for the community; "the sexes are interdependent, and it is upon that mutual dependence that the association which constitutes society is founded." In fact, if there is a question of advantage, Briffault notes that all the arts and industries of primitive societies—tanning, weaving, potting, home building, and toolmaking—were invented and carried out by women. They then controlled the surplus wealth of the community. Men, on the other hand, had to devote their full energies to providing raw materials for these industries. (p. 400)

According to Briffault, most civilized observers, blinded by their assumptions about femininity, misunderstood the status of women in primitive societies. They took a woman's work as a sign of "slavery and oppression" when, on the contrary, the woman in matriarchal societies "is independent because, not in spite of her labour." "Generally speaking," Briffault concluded, "it is in those societies where women toil most that their status is most independent and their influence greatest."

Patriarchy evolved when primitive economies passed from the hunting and gathering stage to the pastoral and agricultural stages and men gained predominate economic power. The domestication of animals, and the later development of advanced agriculture, gave men economic strength and freed them from hunting and the necessity of supplying raw materials for women-controlled production. As men took over home industries and agriculture, then expanding with the growth of trade, the relationship between the sexes underwent a major realignment. . . . (pp. 400-01)

A definitive shift in values attends the transition to patriarchy. Individualism emerged, Briffault believed, only at the patriarchal stage, not before. The holding of personal and real property separated individuals both economically and psychologically from the group. . . . Briffault could not imagine that the cooperation necessary to the early evolution of man from the animals could have existed if humanity's earliest representatives had been "hordes of jealous and suspicious individualists, in which every member sought his personal advantage only," or if the incipient human social group had been ruled "by the selfishness of a despotic patriarchal male."

Finally, Briffault suggests that since patriarchies are based on masculine economic dominance, society could theoretically return to a matriarchal stage if our "forms of industry and wealth-production [were] to revert to the dimensions of household industry." The return might well be incomplete; Briffault cautions that matriarchal elements remain in societies moving into the patriarchal stage, and it follows that patriarchal elements would survive a reversion toward matriarchy. Still, in an economic catastrophe, one might expect to see "the predominance of women . . . to a large extent . . . automatically restored."

Supplementing his own experience with the migrants, Steinbeck's reading in Briffault offered a theoretical framework on which to measure the changes inflicted on the Joads and their fellow farmers. Steinbeck shows how the shock of dispossession suffered by the Joads undermines the frontier patriarchy and throws the family back to a more primitive economic and social stage. Briffault's belief that individualism could not have motivated the members of pre-patriarchal society reinforces Steinbeck's feeling that the Oklahoma farmers could no longer rely on the values of frontier individualism. As long as they continued to think only in terms of the self-sufficient patriarchal family, their efforts to overcome oppression would be doomed.

The patriarchal structure of the Joad family, although shaken, remains intact through the early chapters of *The Grapes of Wrath.* Gathering to plan their trip to California, they arrange themselves in a hierarchical formation. Evidently habitual, it reflects the traditional authority of the pioneer as clearly as would a legislative chamber. The older men cluster around Grampa Joad, "enthroned on the running board" of the family's truck; the next generation of young men extend the semicircle around the patriarch; and the women and children stand as if in a gallery behind them. (pp. 401-02)

Steinbeck describes the squatting posture of the Joad men in unusual detail, as if, like Briffault, he were recording the symbolic ritual of a primitive tribe. He does so because the gesture embodies the intimate relationship between the frontiersman and his property. In times of adversity, the farmer patriarch draws his strength from his connection with the land, not from his association with society. Thus, the position of greatest authority in the Joad's ceremonial hierarchy is the position closest to the soil. The women and children stand; Grampa Joad, deprived of all but token authority by his age, sits on the truck's running board; the men who make the decisions squat. Their authority is rooted in ownership of the land where Grampa "had to kill the Indians and drive them away" and where Pa "killed weeds and snakes."

However, the Joads' actual, much-reduced circumstances now mock the traditional significance of the squatting posture. Banks and corporate landowners have severed the connection between family and land. The Joads gather around a converted Hudson Super-Six instead of the hearth of the patriarchal homestead. The squatting position, once a symbol of strength, has become instead a mark of their downtrodden status. Confrontation with omnipotent owners transforms the Joads and the other farmers from "squatting tenant men" into "squatters" in the traditional sense of men with no property rights and no power.

Steinbeck signals the Joads' vulnerability by representing their patriarch as senile. Grampa Joad's incontinence and wandering mind epitomize the ineffectiveness of primitive frontier strengths without discipline and direction. His cantankerousness caricatures the inflexibility of the farmers. In defending their independence, they have clung to their fathers' ways without adjusting to the changing economics of farming. They fall prey to the banks, in part, because they do not fully comprehend that placing a mortgage on their farms deprives them of the full rights of ownership. As Grampa Joad's senility gives him the look of a "frantic child," so, following the pioneer tradition inflexibly makes the farmers childlike in their helplessness before oppression.

Above all, the stubborn individualism embodied in the senile patriarch blinds the Joads to the necessity of collective action. When the landowner's tractor cuts across the family homestead, Grampa Joad stands up alone against his enemy with only a gun to guarantee his independence. He levels his rifle steadily at the eyes of the mechanical predator, but the tractor charges forward. The courage and pride Grampa displays mean nothing to the economic forces seizing the farm. The bank puts down the individual family as easily as the tractor caves in the house—as easily as "a dog shakes a rat." United the Oklahoma families might have a chance, but as self-reliant family units, they are defeated one by one.

Steinbeck emphasizes the patriarch's tragically atomistic response by placing another confrontation between tractor and solitary homesteader, similar to Grampa Joad's, in chapter five, the interchapter on the general dispossession of the Oklahoma farmers. According to this classic reading of the relationship between the Joads' saga and the interchapters, the Joad narrative develops on a more intimate level the themes of the interchapters which chronicle the plight of the migrants as a whole. But that relationship can be interpreted more fully. The power of the double narrative depends on the tension between the reader's knowledge that the Joads are representative in their suffering and the failure of the Joad men to recognize their representative status. They act as if their story were unique, when, in fact, it is typical of the tenant farmers' plight.

By establishing parallels between the oppressed and the oppressor throughout *The Grapes of Wrath,* Steinbeck also attributes the external pressures on the Joads, particularly the cruelties of the landowners, to the failure of frontier individu-

alism as a social principle. He argues that both the powerful Californians and the shattered migrants must repudiate those aspects of individualism which deny participation in a larger community. In earlier days, the pioneers of Oklahoma and California had ignored the destructive aspect of their quest because they competed for land with Indians and Mexicans whose humanity they refused to recognize. But now that the frontier has been "closed"—that is, now that the land is owned by other white Americans—American society must confront the antisocial aspects of individualistic competition.

As the older Joad men sink into ineffectiveness and despondency, family authority shifts to Ma Joad. First she aggressively challenges patriarchal decisions that might fragment the family, and by the end of the novel she has taken the initiative. When the men cannot find work at the government camp and have forfeited their patriarchal roles " 'either a-thinkin' or a-workin',' " Ma Joad makes the decision to move on and rouses "her camp" for their early-morning departure. Later she plans Tom's escape from the peach ranch after he avenges Casy's murder. During the final catastrophic chapters Ma Joad controls the family's money, handles Ruthie's betrayal of Tom's hiding place, finds the family work, leads them away from the flooded railroad car, and finally urges Rose of Sharon to suckle the starving man in the ark-like barn at the top of the hill.

On Briffault's anthropological scale this shift to matriarchal authority represents a regression to a more primitive social organization. But Steinbeck offers the step "back" to matriarchy as a promise of hope. In terms of the Joads' predicament, Ma Joad's emergence signals an essential adaptation: under the economic conditions of the migration, survival depends on the collective security of matriarchal society rather than on patriarchal self-reliance. In broader terms, Steinbeck uses Ma Joad's heightened stature to suggest that the communal values Briffault associates with matriarchy might provide an alternative basis for authority in American society as a whole. (pp. 402-05)

Steinbeck's portrait of Ma Joad differs in two critical aspects from classic accounts of the pioneer wife by male writers like Cooper, Mark Twain, Howe, Garland, and Rölvaag. He does not take the diurnal chores and unending childbearing as signs of Ma Joad's oppression, nor is he ill at ease with her physical strength and lack of traditional feminine beauty. Although Cooper, for example, admired at a distance the endurance and self-denial of the pioneer wife, he emphasized her sullen submission to her husband. . . .

Steinbeck, on the other hand, follows Briffault's argument that economically productive labor is a woman's source of power. Ma Joad's work packing away the slaughtered pigs, organizing camp, buying food and cooking it over a succession of improvised stoves represents not submission but the steady shedding of her husband's control. She attains the status of arbiter "as remote and faultless in judgment as a goddess" because, not in spite of her work. The pioneer woman's roughness threatens earlier writers, but to Steinbeck Ma Joad's thickness, her "strong, broad, bare feet," "her thin, steel-gray hair," her "strong, freckled arms" are not signs of femininity laid waste, but rather of "clean, calm beauty." His portrait places Ma Joad with Willa Cather's frontier heroines and Faulkner's black matriarchs, suggesting there may be an unheralded tradition of powerful women in early twentieth-century American literature who come forward in times of crisis and offer alternatives to the values of an individualistic and patriarchal society. (p. 406)

The family's dispossession deprives Pa Joad of his traditional agrarian labor, but Ma Joad's work continues and she remains strong. The tools of her husband's labor—wagons, horses, plows—are sold before the journey, but Ma Joad's kettles and pans are taken along and become, with the truck, the focus of family life. When the Joads make camp the first night, Ma Joad immediately issues an order to find firewood. Because leaving has not diminished her work, her authority is intact. Tom and Al similarly gain stature because their mechanical knowledge gives them work on the journey. But the older men have "the perplexed manner" Briffault finds common among men in primitive matriarchies. Where Ma Joad's eyes convey "superhuman understanding," Steinbeck's initial description of Pa Joad reveals that "his bright dark eyes were failing," and Grampa's eyes move "listlessly" as soon as he leaves the farm.

Because matriarchal strength endures as long as the household industries of camp life can be maintained, it remains available to people cast out of society. Ma Joad is a "citadel," not because she takes action, as Grampa Joad tries to do, but because she can absorb experience and "mount pain and suffering." As the image of an immovable fortress suggests, her strength gives no particular direction to the family. It simply protects the "will to function," to endure, to find some new source of strength for later action. As the family moves west, this citadel replaces the forty-acre farm that sustained the patriarch's individualism. Unlike the farm, Ma Joad's matriarchal citadel is a "strong place that cannot be taken."

Although there are moments of discouragement when Ma Joad reverts to the habits of frontier individualism, from the outset she has a broader understanding of the family's move west than does her husband. She interprets the migration according to the actual experience of the migrants rather than by the inherited and now meaningless patriarchal myth of the frontier. In the West Pa Joad thinks he will find relief from poverty through his individual labor. But his dream depends on land. When he cannot find it, he is crushed. While Ma Joad hopes one day to own a house of her own, a goal of individual fulfillment Steinbeck endorses, she gradually expands her belief that survival until that day depends on keeping the "family unbroke" to include a broader group. Independent of Casy's philosophy, she warns her son not to stand up alone against the landowners. . . . When she first asserts her authority over her husband with the jack handle, she places her family first, but even then she is willing to include Casy and the Wilsons, and earlier she speaks up for Tom and Al's idea of traveling with the Wilsons as a "unit."

Steinbeck suggests that Ma Joad's experience as a woman has made her see the individual as part of a larger whole; when Rose of Sharon grows frightened at her grandmother's illness, Ma Joad soothes her explaining that "dyin' is a piece of all dyin', and bearin' is a piece of all bearin'."As Ma Joad experiences the scorn and savagery of the California deputies, this matriarchal intuition is tempered into political faith. Ma counsels patience: "Why, Tom—us people will go on livin' when all them people is gone. Why, Tom, we're the people that live. They ain't gonna wipe us out. Why, we're the people—we go on."

Ma Joad's matriarchal understanding of unity opens her to the possibility of a new frontier myth founded on the west-ward migration as a process which brings a dispossessed people together. . . . To Pa Joad (Job-road), life on the road seems meaningless. Route 66 is a trial by brutality, inhumanity, and contempt. Stretching to an unknown destination from an irretrievable starting point, the road confronts Pa with an image of time slipping by without the reassuring cyclical pattern of farm life to give him a sense of progress or permanence. Without a farm of his own, Pa Joad feels that "life's over an' done," but Ma Joad contradicts him:

> "No, it ain't," Ma smiled. "It ain't, Pa. An' that's one more thing a woman knows. I noticed that. Man, he lives in jerks—baby born an' a man dies, an' that's a jerk—get a farm an' loses his farm, an' that's a jerk. Woman, it's all one flow, like a stream, little eddies, little waterfalls, but the river, it goes right on. Woman looks at it like that. We ain't gonna die out. People is goin' on."

By the time she offers her husband this reassurance late in the novel, she has extended her belief in the importance of collective strength from the family to the migrants as a people: "Use' ta be the fambly was fust. It ain't so now. It's anybody." Her statement on the end of the family's primacy has been taken to mark her conversion to Jim Casy's transcendental collectivism, but Ma Joad's sense of belonging to the stream of her race has its deepest origins in her own matriarchal nature.

In his account of the government camp at Weedpatch, where the Joads temporarily find sanctuary from the brutalities of the road, Steinbeck offers an image of a society founded on the communal spirit of the matriarchy. Raising themselves from the more primitive life of roadside bivouacs and Hoovervilles, the migrants return to a life as well ordered as they knew on their farms.

In keeping with Briffault's stages of social development, the more complex government of the camp has shifted back toward patriarchal form. But it has done so without sacrificing the matriarchal impulse to keep the "family unbroke." The migrant men are no longer seen as dull and stupid as they were on the road because organizing the camp and its defenses again gives them a sphere of action. But the division of labor in the camp is consistent with the communal economy of the matriarchy in which the people's needs, instead of being supplied by the accumulation of private property, are provided for by communal division of labor between the sexes. Similarly, while the camp is managed by a male government agent, Steinbeck makes clear that his authority is entirely compatible with the egalitarian character of matriarchal society. He is not a chief, but a representative.

Steinbeck uses the meeting between Ma Joad and the camp manager as his principal metaphor for the matriarchal basis of governmental authority. Unlike the sheriffs and deputies Ma Joad confronts along the way, this man greets Ma Joad without condescension or hostility. With a gesture that Steinbeck has carefully prepared, the government agent squats down beside Ma Joad in the traditional posture of the tenant farmer: "He came to the fire and squatted on his hams, and the last of Ma's resistance went down." The emotional impact of this simple act of kindness and decency after so much insult and brutality drives home the symbolic significance of the gesture: the representative of the government meets the representative of the people's collective strength to "go on" at her own level. As the Oklahoma farmer drew strength from his independent plot of soil, this government will draw strength from the people.

Steinbeck proposes the paradox that a stronger communal government would be necessary to protect individual freedom and dignity and anticipates his readers' suspicions. Taking symbols of the red scare, political committees and barbed-wire fences, he transforms them into symbols of a democracy that protects the propertyless and allows them to participate in government. It is not the imposed patriarchal power of a totalitarian regime that protects the camp from the farmers' associations; it is not "that little guy in the office is a-stoppin' 'em," but the community's own collective strength—" 'cause we're all a-workin' together."

However, Steinbeck doubts that his America will adopt Ma Joad's matriarchal sense of community as a governing principle. He knew where power lay, and his experience forbad optimism. The camp presents only a utopian vision; it cannot provide jobs to the migrants, and the Joads are forced back to the road. As in other accounts of westward migration in our literature, Steinbeck correlates the redemption of American values with the rescue of the distressed patriarchal family. For the Joads the outlook is bleak. Ma Joad retards the family's disintegration but cannot prevent it.

At the end of the novel, Steinbeck preserves some hope, however, by insisting that Ma Joad's legacy passes on to Rose of Sharon, to Tom, and, by extension, to a future generation of Americans that might incorporate her values into democratic society. The significance of Ma Joad's bequest differs according to the sex of the two children; traditional male and female roles persist in Steinbeck's working out of matriarchal values. Rose of Sharon inherits her mother's sense of community through her womb; Tom through his mind. When Rose of Sharon offers her breast to a starving man, her smile announces her initiation into a matriarchal mystery: the capacity to nurture life. (pp. 407-11)

Tom Joad carries communal values into a more active mode. From the beginning of the novel, Tom is Ma Joad's chosen child; the core of the Joad family, as of the matriarchal clan, becomes mother and offspring rather than husband and wife. After his years in jail, Tom shares his mother's ability to live day by day on the road. Hunting down Uncle John or calming Al, Tom executes his mother's belief that the family must stay "unbroke." His eventual conversion to the labor cause is convincing in part because his new faith is firmly rooted in his mother's values. When he explains his plans to join the union—"maybe like Casy says, a fella ain't got a soul of his own, but on'y a piece of a big one," his language is not only Casy's. He follows as well his mother's more humble expression of faith—"people is goin' on." In the last days before Tom begins his mission as a labor organizer, Ma Joad claims the task of carrying food to his hiding place among the rushes. When he leaves, he receives the family's meager savings, not from his father but from Ma Joad—not when he takes over as patriarch of the family, but when he leaves the family to work for the people. Tom will tap strength that has come to the migrants by the shared experience of dispossession rather than by the individualism of his frontier heritage.

Tom's chances of staying alive, much less of relieving his people's oppression, are slim. The uncertainty of his future reflects Steinbeck's pessimism not only about the labor movement's prospects, but also about curbing the antisocial effects of individualism. However, the final image of Tom disappear-

ing into the rushes at night has a power independent of his realistic chances of success. In the symbolic drama of the novel, his decision to follow Jim Casy and to act on the matriarchal sense of community represents the potential of the oppressed to take action—of passive endurance to become active resistance. (pp. 411-12)

Warren Motley, "From Patriarchy to Matriarchy: Ma Joad's Role in 'The Grapes of Wrath,'" in American Literature, *Vol. 54, No. 3, October, 1982, pp. 397-412.*

ROBERT DeMOTT

The Grapes of Wrath is a controversial classic because it is at once populist *and* revolutionary. It advances a belief in the essential goodness and forbearance of the "common people," and prophesies a fundamental change to produce equitable social conditions: "There is a crime here that goes beyond denunciation. There is a sorrow here that weeping cannot symbolize. There is a failure here that topples all our success . . . in the eyes of the hungry there is a growing wrath. In the souls of the people the grapes of wrath are filling and growing heavy, growing heavy for the vintage" (Chapter 25). This novel—part naturalistic epic, part dissenting tract, and part romantic gospel—speaks to a multiplicity of human experiences and is squarely located in our varied national consciousness; nearly every literate person knows, or at least claims familiarity with, its impassioned story of the Joad family's brutal migration from Oklahoma's dying Dust Bowl to California's corrupt Promised Land. In their ironic exodus from home to homelessness, from individualism to collective awareness, from selfishness to communal love, "from 'I' to 'we' " (Chapter 14), Steinbeck's cast of unsuspecting characters—Ma Joad, Tom Joad, Jim Casy, Rose of Sharon—have become permanently etched in our sensibility and serve constantly to remind us that heroism is as much a matter of choice as it is of being chosen. Similarly, Steinbeck's rendering of the graphic enticements of Route 66—"the path of a people in flight" (Chapter 12)—from Middle America to the West defined the national urge for mobility, motion, and blind striving. The novel's erotically subversive final scene, in which Rose of Sharon, delivered of a stillborn child, gives her milk-laden breast to a dying stranger, then looks up and smiles "mysteriously" (Chapter 30), simply will not fade from view. Wherever human beings dream of a dignified society in which they can harvest the fruits of their own labor, **The Grapes of Wrath**'s radical voice of protest can still be heard. As a tale of dashed illusions, thwarted desires, inhuman suffering, and betrayed promises—all strung on the most fragile thread of hope—**The Grapes of Wrath** not only summed up the Depression era's socially conscious art, but, beyond that, has few peers in American fiction.

Steinbeck's book has been praised by the left as a triumph of proletarian writing, nominated by critics and reviewers as "The Great American Novel," given historical vindication by Senator Robert M. La Follette's inquiries into California's tyrannical farm labor conditions, and defended by Eleanor Roosevelt for its power ("The horrors of the picture . . . made you dread . . . to begin the next chapter, and yet you cannot lay the book down or even skip a page.") But *The Grapes of Wrath* has also been attacked by academic scholars as sentimental, unconvincing, and inartistic, banned repeatedly by school boards and libraries, and denounced by right-wing ministers, corporate farmers, and politicians as immoral, degrading, and untruthful. (Oklahoma Congressman Lyle Boren, typical of the book's early detractors, called it "a lie, a black, infernal creation of a twisted, distorted mind" [see excerpt above]. In fact, from the moment it was published on April 14, 1939, *The Grapes of Wrath* has been less judged as a novel than as a sociological event, a celebrated political cause, or a factual case study. If the past fifty years have seen little consensus about the exact nature of the novel's achievement, there has been plenty of proof that it elicits widely divergent responses from its audience. Perhaps that is to be expected, considering that Steinbeck intentionally wrote the novel in "five layers," intending to "rip" each reader's nerves "to rags" by making him "participate in the actuality." What each reader "gets" from *The Grapes of Wrath,* he claimed, "will be scaled entirely on his own depth or hollowness." Steinbeck's participatory aesthetic ensured the novel's affective impact on a broad range of readers. By conceiving his novel on simultaneous levels of existence Steinbeck pushed back the accepted boundaries of traditional realistic fiction and redefined the proletarian form. Like most significant American novels, *The Grapes of Wrath* does not offer codified solutions, but instead enacts the process of belief and embodies the shape of faith. (pp. xxii-xxiv)

Like Walt Whitman's *Leaves of Grass,* Steinbeck's novel had a complicated foreground and grew through a similar process of accretion and experimentation. *The Grapes of Wrath* was the product of his increasing immersion in the migrant material, which proved to be a subject of such related intertwining that it required an extended odyssey of his own before he discovered the proper focus and style to do the topic justice. In one way or another, from August 1936, when Steinbeck discovered a subject "like nothing in the world" (Steinbeck and Wallsten, eds., *Steinbeck: A Life in Letters*), through October 1939, when he resolved to put behind him "that part of my life that made the *Grapes*" (Entry # 101 [in *Working Days: The Journals of 'The Grapes of Wrath,' 1938-1941*]), the migrant issue, which had wounded him deeply, remained a central preoccupation.

Between 1936 and 1938 Steinbeck's commitment to his material evolved through at least four major stages of writing: (1) a seven-part series of newspaper articles, "The Harvest Gypsies"; (2) an unfinished novel, "The Oklahomans"; (3) a completed, but destroyed, satire, "L'Affaire Lettuceberg"; and (4) a final fictional version, *The Grapes of Wrath*. Each stage varied in audience, intention, and tone from the one before it. All the versions overlapped, however, because they shared—with differing highlights and resolutions—a fixed core of elements: on one side, the entrenched power, wealth, authority, and consequent tyranny of California's industrialized agricultural system (symbolized by Associated Farmers, Inc.), which produced flagrant violations of the migrants' civil and human rights and ensured their continuing peonage, their loss of dignity, through threats, reprisals, and violence; on the other side, the powerlessness, poverty, victimization, and fear of the nomadic American migrants whose willingness to work, desire to retain their dignity, and enduring wish to settle land of their own were kept alive by their innate resilience and resourcefulness, and by the democratic benefits of the government sanitary camps. From the moment he entered the fray, Steinbeck had no doubt that the presence of the migrants would change the fabric of California life, though he had little foresight about what his own role in that change would be. His overriding concern was humanitarian: he wanted to be an effective advocate, but he did not want to appear presump-

tuous. ("I am actively opposed to any man or group who . . . is able to dominate the lives of workers," he announced later to John Barry.)

Not counting a warm-up essay (in the September 12, 1936, issue of *The Nation* [see excerpt above]), or his editing of Tom Collins' camp reports, Steinbeck's first lengthy excursion into the migrants' problems was published in the San Francisco *News,* a Bay area daily paper. "The Harvest Gypsies" formed the foundation of Steinbeck's concern, raised issues and initiated forces (which reverberate in Part Two of his 1938 journal, and so enter the history of *The Grapes of Wrath*), gave him a working vocabulary with which to understand current events, and furthered his position as a reliable interpreter. (pp. xxxii-xxxiv)

Written mostly in a measured, restrained style (the voice is reasonable, the tone is empirical, the ends to be achieved are understanding and intelligent solutions), Steinbeck's *News* articles are full of case studies, chilling factual statistics, and an unsettling catalogue of human woes (illness, incapacitation, persecution, death) observed from close contact with migratory field workers he had met. But in the best tradition of advocacy journalism, Steinbeck concluded his series with a number of prophetic recommendations for alleviating the conflict with federal aid and local support; this in turn would create subsistence farms, establish a migratory labor board, encourage unionization, and punish terrorism. When they were published in 1936 (and again when they were printed in 1938 as *Their Blood Is Strong*), Steinbeck's articles solidified his credibility—both in and out of the migrant camps—as a serious commentator. "The Harvest Gypsies" (and Tom Collins' continuing reports) provided Steinbeck with a basic repository of precise information and folk values. It would still be more than a year before the subjective intensity of his engagement deepened; however, events were already transpiring in his hometown and elsewhere that would eventually change his attitude from methodical reporter to literary activist.

The last of Steinbeck's San Francisco *News* articles ended with a comment that became the basis for the second stage of his writing: "The new migrants to California from the dust bowl are here to stay. They are of the best American stock, intelligent, resourceful, and, if given a chance, socially responsible." Steinbeck understood that the migrants wouldn't vanish from sight, and couldn't be ignored, though official California tried to do just that. Steinbeck built on his *News* experiences and on at least one more month-long field trip, in October and November 1937, with Tom Collins to plan the writing of a "big" book. They started from Gridley, where Collins was managing a new camp, but then roamed California from Stockton to Needles, wherever migrants were gathered to work. By late in the year, after hitting several "snags," he was working on a "rather long novel" called "The Oklahomans," which, he reported a few weeks later, was "still a long way from finished." Steinbeck, generally guarded with interviewers, revealed enough to journalist Louis Walther [*San Jose Mercury Herald,* January 8, 1938, p. 12] to indicate that the focus of his novel was on the salutary, irrepressible character of the migrants, who, he believed, would profoundly alter the tenor of life in California. "Their coming here now is going to change things almost as much as did the coming of the first American settlers." Furthermore, "The Californian doesn't know what he does want. The Oklahoman knows just exactly what he wants. He wants a piece of land. And he goes after it and gets it."

Quietly, in late January 1938, Steinbeck stopped work on "The Oklahomans" (the manuscript has never been found and it is doubtful that he had actually written a great deal on it). Judging from his comments to Louis Walther, however, it is reasonable to assume that "The Oklahomans' " uncomplicated duality of conception, the untangled lines of its proposed struggle, and the dispassionate tone of its narrative voice (probably a holdover from "The Harvest Gypsies") struck Steinbeck as belonging increasingly to the reductive world of pulp fiction or wish-fulfillment. The truth was the migrant situation had worsened, and along with it, Steinbeck's capacity for pity and his need for direct involvement had grown. (pp. xxxv-xxxvii)

As a novelist, Steinbeck often experienced a delayed reaction to piercing events. He needed time to let them gestate before they rose to the surface of his awareness and began pushing back at him, demanding their transformation to words. From February through May 1938, the third stage of his writing development produced "L'Affaire Lettuceberg." With this abortive—but necessary—venture, Steinbeck's migrant subject matter took its most drastic turn, inspired by an ugly event in Salinas, California, his hometown. Earlier, in September 1936, Steinbeck had encountered the vicious clash between workers and growers in a lettuce strike—"there are riots in Salinas and killings in the streets of that dear little town where I was born," he told George Albee (Steinbeck and Wallsten, eds., *Steinbeck: A Life in Letters*). The strike was smashed with terrorism, and recollections of the workers' defeat festered in Steinbeck for more than a year. Then, in early February 1938, galvanized by reports of the worsening conditions in Visalia and Nipomo, Steinbeck felt the urgent need to do something direct in retaliation. "It seems to be necessary to write things down," he said in [*Working Days*] Entry #1. "Can't stop it." John Steinbeck never became what dyed-in-the-wool activists would consider fully radicalized, but by putting his pen to the service of a political cause, he was stepping as close to being a firebrand as he ever would. He launched into "L'Affaire," a vituperative satire aimed at attacking the leading citizens of Salinas, "the committee of seven," who organize and direct the ignorant army of vigilantes. The cabal of organizers remain aloof, but "work out the methods by which vigilantes are formed and kept steamed up." The vigilantes were assembled from the common populace of Salinas—clerks, service station operators, shopkeepers—all of them "dopes" and "suckers" for creating mayhem. (pp. xxxviii-xxxix)

Within days Steinbeck's critical insight returned. The careful artist triumphed over the ferocious propagandist, and he destroyed "L'Affaire Lettuceberg." Immediately, Steinbeck wrote to Elizabeth Otis, his main literary agent, and to Pascal Covici, who had already announced the publication of "L'Affaire," to inform them that he would not be delivering the manuscript they expected. (pp. xxxix-xl)

The fourth and last stage of Steinbeck's writing culminated in *The Grapes of Wrath.* His conscience squared, Steinbeck stood ready to embark on the longest sustained writing job of his life. From late May 1938, when he struck the first words of the new novel to paper ("To the red country and part of the gray country of Oklahoma, the last rains came gently, and they did not cut the scarred earth"), through the winter of 1939, when the last of the corrections and editorial

details were settled ("I meant, Pat, to print *all all all* the verses of the Battle Hymn. They're all pertinent and they're all exciting. And the music if you can"), *The Grapes of Wrath* was a task which, as the main section of *Working Days* makes clear, fully commanded his energy. Everything he had written earlier—from his 1936 *Nation* article, "Dubious Battle in California," through "Starvation Under the Orange Trees," an April 1938 essay that functioned as the Epilogue to *Their Blood Is Strong*—became grist for his final attempt. From his numerous field travels with Tom Collins, and from countless hours of talking to migrant people, working beside them, listening to them, and sharing their problems, Steinbeck drew all the concrete details of human form, language, and landscape that ensure artistic verisimilitude, as well as the subtler nuances of dialect, idiosyncratic tics, habits, and gestures, which animate fictional characterization. But the choreography of details alone, the dance of his ear and eye, won't fully account for the metamorphosis from "The Harvest Gypsies" to *The Grapes of Wrath.*

Steinbeck's leap from right-minded competency to inspired vision was the result of one linked experience that hit him so hard it called forth every ounce of his moral indignation, social anger, and pity. In late February and early March Steinbeck witnessed the deplorable conditions at Visalia where thousands of human beings, flooded out of their shelters, were starving to death: "the water is a foot deep in the tents and the children are up on the beds and there is no food and no fire, and the county has taken off all the nurses because 'the problem is so great that we can't do anything about it.' So they do nothing" (Steinbeck and Wallsten, eds., *Steinbeck: A Life in Letters,*). In the company of Tom Collins, photographer Horace Bristol, and other Farm Security Administration personnel, Steinbeck worked day and night for nearly two weeks (sometimes dropping to sleep in the mud from exhaustion) to help relieve the misery, though of course no aid seemed adequate. What Steinbeck encountered in that sea of mud and debris was so devastating, so "heartbreaking" he told Elizabeth Otis, that he was utterly transfixed by the "staggering" conditions, and by "suffering" so great that objective reporting would only falsify the moment (Steinbeck and Wallsten, eds., *Steinbeck: A Life in Letters,*).

What Steinbeck witnessed at Visalia had a profound, if temporarily delayed, impact on his novel. From the outset in creating the Joad family to occupy the narrative chapters of *The Grapes of Wrath,* Steinbeck gave his novel a specific human context, a felt emotional quality, and a dramatic dimension all his earlier versions lacked: "Begin the detailed description of the family I am to live with. Must take time in the description, detail, detail, looks, clothes, gestures. . . . We have to know these people. Know their looks and their nature," he reminded himself ([*Working Days*] Entry #17). Steinbeck's symbolic portrayal of this universal human family brought the novel alive for him: "Make the people live. Make them live" (Entry #30). By conceiving the Joads as "an overessence of people" (Entry #30), Steinbeck elevated the entire history of the migrant struggle into the ceremonial realm of art.

Steinbeck's mythology was one of endings as well as of beginnings. Like Ernest Hemingway, whose physical wounding at Fossalta, Italy, in 1918 became the generative event for a string of stories and novels (especially *A Farewell to Arms*), Steinbeck's internal wounding at Visalia marked him deeply, set him apart from his fellow travelers Tom Collins and Horace Bristol. Indeed, a somewhat mystified Tom Collins recalled a conversation with Steinbeck at Visalia in which the latter claimed: " '. . . something hit me and hit me hard for it hurts inside clear to the back of my head. I got pains all over my head, hard pains. Have never had pains like this before. . . .' " (Collins, "Bringing in the Sheaves"). Clearly, Steinbeck's experience opened the floodgates of his attention, created *The Grapes of Wrath*'s compelling justification, provided its haunting spiritual urgency, and rooted it in the deepest wellsprings of democratic fellow-feeling. In the same way that the rain floods the novel's concluding chapters, so the memory of Steinbeck's cataclysmic experience, his recollection of futility and impotency at Visalia, pervades the ending of the book and charges its ominous emotional climate, relieved only by Rose of Sharon's gratuitous act of sharing her breast with a starving man.

Steinbeck's deep participation in the events at Visalia also inspired his creation of Tom Joad, the slowly awakening disciple of Jim Casy, whose final acceptance of the preacher's gospel of social action occurs just as the deluge is about to begin:

> "Wherever they's a fight so hungry people can eat, I'll be there. Wherever they's a cop beatin' up a guy, I'll be there. If Casy knowed, why, I'll be in the way guys yell when they're mad an'—I'll be in the way kids laugh when they're hungry an' they know supper's ready. An' when our folks eat the stuff they raise an' live in the houses they build— why, I'll be there. See? God, I'm talkin' like Casy. Comes of thinkin' about him so much. Seems like I can see him sometimes'."

When the apocalypse occurs, *everything* becomes a fiction, Steinbeck suggests, and *all* gestures become symbolic. Furthermore, in one of those magical transferences artists are heir to in moments of extreme exhaustion or receptivity, Steinbeck believed that Tom Joad, his fictive alter ego, not only floats above *The Grapes of Wrath*'s "last pages . . . like a spirit" (Entry #87), he imagined that Joad actually entered the novelist's work space, the private chamber of his soul: " 'Tom! Tom! Tom!' I know. It wasn't him. Yes, I think I can go on now. In fact, I feel stronger. Much stronger. Funny where the energy comes from. Now to work, only now it isn't work any more" (Entry #97). With that visitation, that benediction, Steinbeck arrived at the intersection of novel and journal, a luminous point where the life of the writer and the creator of life merge. The terms of his complex investment fulfilled, Steinbeck needed only a few more days to finish his novel.

In matters of form, style, and execution Steinbeck was persuaded or emboldened by another host of haunting voices and visions. Especially in *Grapes'* digressive intercalary chapters, Steinbeck drew on the fluid linguistic style of John Hargrave's novel, *Summer Time Ends* (1935), the daring, elastic form of John Dos Passos's *U S A* trilogy (1937), the narrative tempo of Pare Lorentz's radio drama, *Ecce Homo!,* and the sequential quality of Lorentz's films, *The Plow that Broke the Plains* (1936) and *The River* (1937), the stark visual effects of Dorothea Lange's F.S.A photographs of Dust Bowl Oklahoma and California migrant life, the poetic/photographic counterpoint of Archibald MacLeish's *Land of the Free* (1938), the reverberant rhythms of the King James Bible, the inspired mood of classical music, the poignant refrains of American folk music, the elevated timbre of the Greek epics, and the biological impetus of his own phalanx, or group-man, theory. Steinbeck's conscious and unconscious borrowings,

echoes, and reverberations throughout *The Grapes of Wrath* came from a constellation of artistic, social, and intellectual sources so varied no single reckoning can do them justice. All of these elements—and more—entered the crucible of his imagination and allowed Steinbeck to transform the weight of his whole life into the new book. In *The Grapes of Wrath* the multiple streams of subjective experience, ameliorism, graphic realism, and symbolic form gather to create the "truly American book" (Entry #18) Steinbeck had planned.

As a result of shifting political emphases, the enlightened recommendations of the La Follette Committee (that the National Labor Relations Act include farm workers), the effects of loosened labor laws (California's discriminatory "anti-migrant" law, established in 1901, was struck down by the Supreme Court in 1941), the creation of compulsory military service, and the inevitable recruitment of migrant families into defense plant and shipyard jobs caused by the booming economy of World War II (California growers soon complained of an acute shortage of seasonal labor), the particular set of epochal conditions that crystallized Steinbeck's awareness in the first place passed from his view (though not necessarily ours, if we witness the continuing struggles of Mexican-American farm laborers since then). Like other momentous American novels that embody the bitter, often tragic, transition from one way of life to another, *The Grapes of Wrath* possessed, among its other attributes, perfect timing. Its appearance permanently changed the literary landscape of the United States. (pp. xli-xlvi)

> *Robert DeMott, in an introduction to* Working Days: The Journals of "The Grapes of Wrath", 1938-1941 *by John Steinbeck, edited by Robert DeMott, Viking, 1989, pp. xxi-lvii.*

JOHN DITSKY

Before launching into [a] survey of criticism of *The Grapes of Wrath*, . . . I think it instructive to consider a key and often-cited early instance of serious Steinbeck criticism at its best, albeit a somewhat flawed best. In his essay "The Boys in the Back Room" (1940-41) [see *CLC,* Vol. 13], Edmund Wilson decides that Steinbeck's real interests are in "biological realism," and that therefore the inadequacies of Steinbeck's philosophy are to blame for his artistic shortcomings, such as what Wilson perceives to be a failure to create convincingly individualized characters. Wilson describes Steinbeck's "tendency to present human life in animal terms," and claims that the writer "almost always in his fiction is dealing either with the lower animals or with humans so rudimentary that they are almost on the animal level. . . ." But even without the hindsight of almost half a century, one can argue that Wilson, of all people, fails to see the acceptance of the animal in human nature as a precondition for evolution upward on the moral scale or, in other words, that humankind might be a dramatic balancing of the animal aggregate and the choice-making individual. Failing to consider the possibility that there might be a difference between the voices of Tom Joad, Jim Casy, Ma Joad, the narrator of the "intercalary" chapters, or John Steinbeck himself, Edmund Wilson places *The Grapes of Wrath* into a bin called "propaganda novel," where it refuses to be confined. (p. 2)

Steinbeck's familiarity with the California migrant-worker problem was well-known by the time *The Grapes of Wrath* appeared; he had written a series of essays on the situation for a California newspaper in 1936, and these had been published in pamphlet form as **Their Blood Is Strong** in 1938. Mention is made of these accounts in the publisher's promotional booklet the Viking Press issued on the book's initial appearance; entitled *John Steinbeck: Personal and Biographical Notes,* it was written by Lewis Gannett (later to assemble the first Viking **Portable Steinbeck**), and prepares the prospective reviewer for Steinbeck's "biggest and richest and ripest, his toughest book and his tenderest, *The Grapes of Wrath.*" Though Gannett's summation smacks of jacket-blurb writing, his short work is interesting as an index of the state of Steinbeck's reputation in 1939—before the novel appeared. After it had, it was included in Harry Thornton Moore's critical survey *The Novels of John Steinbeck,* the first book-length treatment of the author and also the first extended consideration of the new novel [see *CLC,* Vol. 5]. Though Moore naturally uses extensive plot summary in approaching the recent publication, his assessment is objective throughout; he judges the book's worth initially in terms of its "photographic" qualities, but also notes that Steinbeck has attempted something artistically more complex: an epic dimension that works especially well in the interchapters. Margaret Marshall, writing in the *Nation* [November 25, 1939], attacks Steinbeck's artistry as an example of an unformed, "wilderness" sensibility, while V. F. Calverton took the opposite view, hailing Steinbeck's achievement in the realistic depiction of characters and circumstances in the most positive of terms [*Modern Quarterly,* Fall 1939].

By 1940 Steinbeck's novel began to get the most serious attention it plainly deserved, but not from Lyle H. Boren of Oklahoma, who made a blistering attack upon the book as a "dirty, lying, filthy" besmirchment of the name of the fair state of Oklahoma, and this from the floor of the U.S. House of Representatives [see excerpt above]. Less ludicrously, indeed more accurately, Percy H. Boynton, in *America in Contemporary Fiction,* stresses the fact that in **Grapes,** Steinbeck had discovered his true theme, the unity of mankind in a universal soul. Samuel Levenson's "The Compassion of John Steinbeck" [*Canadian Forum,* September 1940]. effectively removes **The Grapes of Wrath** from consideration as a Marxist call for revolutionary solutions, noting as he does the author's apparent reliance upon "love" as the source of the answer to America's crisis. At a time when the last book reviews were still finding their way into print, Steinbeck's novel was already beginning to be understood in some critical depth.

Early in 1941 one of the most significant of the early articles about **Grapes** was published: Frederic I. Carpenter's "The Philosophical Joads" [see excerpt above]. . . . Yet in the same year Edmund Wilson's classic attack on Steinbeck (previously cited) was published, and in her *The Novel and Society* N. Elizabeth Monroe sniffed her disdain for the characters Steinbeck dared to ask his readers to care about. Finally, though he insists on calling the novel "proletarian," Joseph Warren Beach accords **The Grapes of Wrath** tentative ranking with the accepted classics of world literature [see excerpt above]. (pp. 3-4)

[In *On Native Grounds,* Alfred Kazin presented a] balanced view that Steinbeck had managed to create, in **Grapes,** a kind of realism that avoided the extremes endemic to the thirties [see *CLC,* Vol. 13]. Maxwell Geismar, on the other hand, found himself growing increasingly weary of Steinbeck's artistic escapism, as he saw it, toward the needs of the moment [see excerpt above]. Carey McWilliams, author of the era's

classic *Factories in the Fields,* defended the novel against the charge that its description of the Okies' plight was inaccurate [*Antioch Review,* March 1942]. Other useful articles published during the war years, when scholarship generally declined owing to the pressures of realistic distraction and the shortage of paper, include Barker Fairley's pioneering excursion into John Steinbeck's mode of expression, his use of a refined vernacular [*Sewanee Review,* April 1942]; and Lincoln R. Gibbs's "John Steinbeck: Moralist," which perhaps put the last stake into the heart of objections to Steinbeck's "indecency" of language, and did so, naturally, on grounds of fidelity to realistic presentational needs [*Antioch Review,* June 1942]. Conversely, Floyd Stovall, in *American Idealism,* largely agrees with Frederic Carpenter's assessment of Steinbeck's ideological roots, but seems to be bothered by the writer's acceptance of the "*is*ness" of things. While Martin Shockley [*American Literature* January 1944] finishes the discussion of the Okies begun by Carey McWilliams at the Oklahoma end of U.S. 66, J. Donald Adams, in *The Shape of Books to Come,* appears to be following in Edmund Wilson's narrow path. B. R. McElderry, Jr., wrote "*The Grapes of Wrath:* In the Light of Modern Critical Theory" in 1944 [*College English,* March], and in it vigorously defends the novel against the charge that its "sentimentality" precludes consideration of its greatness. Harry Slochower's *No Voice Is Wholly Lost* (1945) rounds out the war years by reasserting Steinbeck's theme of the group's reformation against the common enemy. (pp. 4-5)

In 1946 James Gray issued *On Second Thought,* the Steinbeck section of which treats the author of **The Grapes of Wrath** as, essentially, a regionalist in whose works the tough and the tender aspects can be seen to clash. W. M. Frohock's "John Steinbeck's Men of Wrath" asserts that the quality of anger is what gives strength to a novel such as **Grapes;** this angry quality is largely missing from the later works Frohock surveys in his 1950 volume *The Novel of Violence in America.* Edwin Berry Burgum's "The Sensibility of John Steinbeck" appeared in *Science and Society* that year (published as part of a book the following year); Burgum argues that Steinbeck's writing is often marred by a "brutality" that only in **Grapes** is redeemed by a "new optimism" that arises out of his characters' educational experience. Finally, Woodburn O. Ross traces the similarities—and differences—of Steinbeck's thinking and that of Auguste Comte, discussing **Grapes** along with the other Steinbeck writings then available [see *The University of Missouri Studies in Honor of A. H. R. Fairchild*]. (p. 5)

[In *The University of Kansas City Review* (Winter 1947), Charles] Eisinger demonstrates how deeply Jefferson's ideas that persons derive their integrity from their relationship with the land permeate Steinbeck's novel, but then observes that agrarianism is, nonetheless, "an anachronism in the midst of the machine-made culture of twentieth-century America." Leo Gurko's survey of the literature of the American thirties, *The Angry Decade,* finds that **Grapes** typifies the era's twin themes of social consciousness and flight from unbearable reality. In "John Steinbeck, Californian" [*Antioch Review,* September 1947], Freeman Champney argues that Steinbeck's strengths and weaknesses alike can be traced to his origins, but acknowledges that **Grapes** overcomes the latter in being "a big book, a great book." . . . Another article by Woodburn Ross, "John Steinbeck: Naturalism's Priest" [*College English,* May 1949], claims that Steinbeck has constructed a curious religion of the acceptance of nature as it is—"holy," as *Grapes*'s Jim Casy put it—while also embracing scientific inquiry into that nature. (pp. 5-6)

The first decade of criticism of *The Grapes of Wrath* ended, and the new decade of the fifties began, with something like a period of apathy toward Steinbeck's major achievement. Michael F. Moloney echoes Woodburn Ross's paralleling of Steinbeck and Comte—and includes some others—in his *Catholic World* piece in [August 1950]. Alexander Cowie [in *The Rise of the American Novel*] briefly praises *Grapes* a year later for its innovative technical features. George F. Whicher indicts Steinbeck for "cleverness" in his chapter on the writer in *The Literature of the American People,* while Frederick Hoffman [in *The Modern Novel in America*] asserts the often-made charge of sentimentality against Steinbeck's works after *In Dubious Battle.* Bernard Bowron rather famously shackles the novel with the appellation " 'wagons west' romance" in the *Colorado Quarterly* [Summer 1954], a journal that a year later [Winter 1955] announced the arrival of Warren French upon the Steinbeck scene . . . with a skillfully argued attack upon Bowron's dismissal of the novel as a variation on a popular-entertainment theme. By the mid-fifties, however, Steinbeck studies, especially those devoted to his most famous work, had entered doldrums that would never find themselves repeated.

In 1956 Charles Child Walcutt's *American Literary Naturalism: A Divided Stream* analyzes Steinbeck's concern with matters of form; Walcutt notes that Steinbeck never lets himself be bound by the patterning of naturalistic theory, whether or not the critic realizes that the novelist may not have been a naturalist at all. . . . Peter Lisca's "The Grapes of Wrath as Fiction," which appeared in *PMLA* [Vol. 72, 1957], satisfies its stated purpose of treating the novel as a serious literary accomplishment rather than as some sort of proletarian document. Lisca concludes that because of its carefully crafted thematic unity, Steinbeck "was able to create a well-made and emotionally compelling novel out of materials which in most other hands have resulted in sentimental propaganda." Lisca expanded his remarks for his pioneering critical study of the bulk of Steinbeck's career output, *The Wide World of John Steinbeck,* published in 1958. (pp. 6-7)

George De Schweinitz contributed a note to an ongoing debate in the pages of *College English* over the "Christian" values of *Grapes,* a debate begun by a key article by Martin S. Shockley . . . and replied to by Eric W. Carlson [Shockley's essay appeared in November 1956 and is excerpted in *CLC,* Vol. 21, Carlson's in January 1958, and De Schweinitz's note appeared in May 1958]. R. W. B. Lewis used a related approach to discuss "The Picaresque Saint," as he referred to Tom Joad in discussing what he saw as Steinbeck's overall failures at character delineation [see *CLC,* Vol. 9]. . . .

[In *Mississippi Quarterly* (Summer 1959), Walter Fuller Taylor] argued that heretofore Steinbeck's critics had been imposing their own readings upon the work instead of assessing it in its own terms; hence, a gap had grown up between the book's substance and the standard responses to it, a gap that the criticism of the future would have to address. Yet the tendency to try to fit a writer into some "stream" or other is an ongoing one, and in 1961 Edwin T. Bowden (in *The Dungeon of the Heart*) found the main theme of *Grapes* to be that traditional American one of the problem of isolation. In 1961 as well, the second important original volume of criticism of Steinbeck appeared: Warren French's *John Steinbeck* [see *CLC,* Vol. 1]. . . . French's chapter on *Grapes,* "The Educa-

tion of the Heart" indicates by its very title the theme he sees as major. French's essay is lucid and—as his later writing proves—well able to adjust to developments in the critic's viewpoint. (p. 7)

College English continued to plumb the biblical depths of *Grapes* by printing pieces by Gerald Cannon, H. Kelly Crockett, and Charles T. Dougherty in its December 1962 issue, with a response from T. F. Dunn following [in April 1963]. . . . A chapter in Edwin M. Moseley's [*Pseudonyms of Christ in the Modern Novel*] is devoted to Steinbeck's depiction of the "increased strength" the people "achieve through Casy's martyrdom." And Arthur Mizener, who had by this time lost all patience with Steinbeck and his works—all of them—asked, tendentiously enough, "Does a Moral Vision of the Thirties Deserve a Nobel Prize?" in the *New York Times Book Review* [December 9, 1962] on the occasion of that award. Mizener, never a man to soften his language, indicted Steinbeck as a writer who, "in his best books, watered down by tenth-rate philosophizing" his "real but limited talent." Seldom have a prize-winning author's public achievements so differed from the assessments of many of his critics than on the occasion of Steinbeck's reception of the Nobel Prize in 1962; he could do nothing right, it seemed, and to critics like Mizener it had become a "melancholy task" to re-read him.

Walter Allen wrote a characteristically balanced appraisal of *Grapes* for his [*Tradition and Dream: The English and American Novel From the Twenties and Our Time*]. . . . Allen's is primarily a consolidation of what has gone before. . . . [In *John Steinbeck: An Introduction and Interpretation* (see *CLC,* Vol. 21), John Fontenrose], professionally a classicist, is especially good at noting the pervasive presence of themes and motifs from classic texts in *Grapes.* Conversely, Robert J. Griffin and William A. Freedman provided a specialized treatment of machine/animal motifs in *Grapes* in [*Journal of English and Germanic Philology* (April 1963)]. J. Paul Hunter defended the novel against those who were beginning to write off Steinbeck's significance entirely by showing how its themes come to an artistically hopeful final focus. [Hunter's essay, "Steinbeck's Wine of Affirmation in *The Grapes of Wrath,*" appears in *Essays in Modern American American Literature,* edited by Richard E. Langford]. Lastly, Warren French's *A Companion to "The Grapes of Wrath"* appeared in the same year, the first collection of original reviews and essays dealing exclusively with this single but acknowledgedly singular effort. (pp. 7-8)

[Robert Detweiler's essay "Christ and the Christ Figure in American Fiction" in *Christian Scholar* Summer 1964] brought together the insights offered by previous articles on the subject. Another specialized view was provided by Walter Rundell, Jr., in his "*The Grapes of Wrath:* Steinbeck's Image of the West" [*American West,* Spring 1964]. James Woodress's "John Steinbeck: Hostage to Fortune" [*South Atlantic Quarterly,* Summer 1964], considers the Nobel Prize winner's career as falling into three "phases," the success of *Grapes* being a crucial factor in this evolution and, as Woodress saw it, decline. *Modern Fiction Studies* [in Spring 1965] published a special Steinbeck issue that included Jules Chametzky's ambivalent reconsideration of Steinbeck's choice of endings for the novel, appropriately entitled "The Ambivalent Endings of *The Grapes of Wrath*"; James W. Tuttleton's survey of Soviet reaction to the publication of *The Grapes of Wrath;* and Peter Lisca's blaming of Steinbeck's "decline" after the war on his abandonment of the biological view of man that animates earlier books like *Grapes*. . . . Warren French's *The Social Novel at the End of an Era* neatly fits *Grapes* into the context of its times. Though *Grapes* criticism was becoming increasingly specialized in nature, some writers were still approaching the work as if for the very first time. (pp. 8-9)

The thirtieth anniversary of the novel's appearance in print led to the reconsideration piece "The Radical Humanism of John Steinbeck" by Daniel Aaron in *Saturday Review* [September 28, 1968]. Finer tuning was provided, also in 1968, by Chris Browning's "Grape Symbolism in *The Grapes of Wrath*" in *Discourse*. Tetsumaro Hayashi, a Japanese-American Shakespeare scholar whose avid interest helped lead to the foundation of the Steinbeck Society, wrote on "The Function of the Joad Clan in *The Grapes of Wrath*" for *Modern Review* [March 1968]. . . . Perhaps the year's biggest event, however, was the appearance of [*A Caseback on 'The Grapes of Wrath'*]. edited by Agnes McNeill Donohue. This enormously useful collection is a landmark in the specialized study of Steinbeck's most attended-to single work. The following year Bryant N. Wyatt surveyed Steinbeck's "protest novels" under the rubric "experimentation as technique" [*Discourse*, Vol. 12]. . . . [In *Thematic Design in the Novels of John Steinbeck*, Lester J. Marks points to] *Grapes*'s characters' arrival at new perceptions, chief among them the one that "the physical unity of all things" can provide "faith in a vast spiritual unity." Marks's book was also the first to attempt an overview of the entire career of the recently deceased novelist.

The 1970s began with something of a second wind being given to *Grapes* criticism. . . . Arnold F. Delisle devoted an entire article [in *Style*, Spring 1970] to the function of the turtle chapter (3) alone. Richard B. Hauck included Jim Casy in yet another survey of Christ figures in modern writing [*College English*, Vol. 31, 1970]. Jack Nimitz [*Hartford Studies in Literature* Vol. 2, 1970] discussed *Grapes* from the standpoint of that then-current buzz-word, "ecology." . . . John Clark Pratt published a monograph [*John Steinbeck: A Critical Essay*, see *CLC*, Vol. 1,] as part of a "Contemporary Writers in Christian Perspective" series. His discussion of *Grapes* is interwoven throughout his essay, but his cogent and open-minded argument praises the novel overall, and points to the final chapter's "syncretic allegory" as a lucid expression of "the paradox that Steinbeck is trying to delineate." (pp. 9-10)

Robert B. Downs returned to the novel's fidelity to documentary fact in a chapter in his *Famous American Books*. And in a section devoted to *Grapes,* Leonard Lutwack included Steinbeck in his critical volume [*Heroic Fiction*]. . . . Pascal Covici, Jr., compiled a revised *Portable Steinbeck* that, though it tended to place new emphasis on the later works, nonetheless included some seven selections from *The Grapes of Wrath.* Another series title, James Gray's [*John Steinbeck*] for the University of Minnesota Pamphlets on American Writers, treats *Grapes*'s centrality in Steinbeck's canon as owing to its being an "admirably modeled work of art having impressive size and just proportion, movement, balance, symmetry, and power," though he faults the book's ending scene for "excessive strain."

Sam Bluefarb, [in *The Escape Motif in the American Novel* (1972), see *CLC*, Vol. 5], treated the Joad family in terms of the "escape" motif, while Peter Lisca discussed "the dynamics of community" in the novel in [an essay published in *From Irving to Steinbeck,* which he edited]. . . . Lisca's festschrift item was followed by [*John Steinbeck; 'The Grapes of Wrath': Text and Criticism*], completely reset and accompanied by critical articles to form an invaluable addition to the Viking Critical Library series. Two of the articles printed for the first time in this collection were delivered at the University of Connecticut's conference on *Grapes* in 1969: that of Pascal Covici, Jr., which emphasized the importance of work in the thinking of Steinbeck and his characters as well; and that of John R. Reed, who defends the novel against those who do not agree that its artistry transforms its rude materials into a spiritually satisfying achievement. Betty Perez, in a chapter appearing for the first time in the Lisca collection, discusses the symbolism of house and home in a deliberately different way than does Paul McCarthy in the aforementioned article. Rather belatedly, Sol Zollman treated the book's polemical dimension in an article in [*Literature and Ideology* Vol. 13, 1972]. . . . (p. 10)

Mary Ellen Caldwell gave us, [in *Markham Review,* May 1973], a fresh look at the functioning of the intercalary chapters, especially the famous chapter 15 "truck stop" incident. . . .

Howard Levant's [*The Novels of John Steinbeck: A Critical Study* see *CLC*, Vol. 45, considered] Steinbeck's total book-length output from a strictly formalist standpoint. Levant rigidly characterizes the book's final quarter as "a hollowed rhetoric, a manipulated affirmation, a soft twist of insistent sentiment." Despite its salient preconceptions, Levant's treatise subjects Steinbeck's works to their most rigorous examinations ever, and *Grapes* largely withstands its own assault. A fascinating illustrated discussion of the likely influence on the novelist of Farm Security Administration-sponsored photographers, especially Dorothea Lange, was contributed by D. G. Kehl to the photography journal *Image* [March 1974]. Because it radically rejects the appropriateness of the "turtle" motif, Stuart L. Burns's piece [in *Western American Literature,* May 1974] on the ending is worth considering. And the indefatigable Warren French added a chapter to Tetsumaro Hayashi's [*A Study Guide to Steinbeck: A Handbook to His Major Works*]. (p. 11)

In 1976 [Jackson J. Benson], then at work on the authorized biography of Steinbeck, issued some of his findings on the background to the writing of the novel [*Journal of Modern Literature,* April 1976]. Horst Groene, giving special focus to the character of Al instead of Tom, discussed Steinbeck's positioning between the poles of agrarianism and technological advancement in an article in *Southern Review* [Vol. 9, 1976], while Lewis Moore Hopfe [*Cresset,* May 1976] returned to the apparently inexhaustible vein of biblical symbolism in the novel. . . . Sylvia Jenkins Cook, in her *From Tobacco Road to Route 66: The Southern Poor White in Fiction,* showed how Steinbeck transformed the poor-white stereotype (while not, strictly speaking, writing about it) by depoliticizing it. Yet another volume of conference proceedings [*Steinbeck's Prophetic Vision of America*], this one cued to the American Bicentennial year, included both Kenneth D. Swan's discussion of *Grapes* as an index to the values Steinbeck searched for in his country, and Warren French's provocative thesis ["John Steinbeck and Modernism"]. . . . that most of the novels following *Grapes* represent "a complete swing of the pendulum from his foreshadowing of Post-Modernism to his embracing of a Pre-Modernist, Victorian compromise with traditional establishments. . . . " But the year's major contribution was British critic Roy S. Simmonds's . . . *Steinbeck's Literary Achievement.* Simmonds's judicious assessment of Steinbeck's standing was both concisely expressed and also free of many of the standing assumptions that weaken some American criticism. (p. 12)

Martha Heasley Cox continued to exploit her knowledge of the *Grapes* journals for a First International Steinbeck Congress (Kyushu University, Fukuoka, Japan) paper on the real and fictional governmental camps Steinbeck knew. [Proceedings from this Congress appear in *John Steinbeck: East and West,* edited by Tetsumaro Hayashi]. Miles Donald discussed the book in his survey *The American Novel in the Twentieth Century.* Finally, Peter Lisca, like Warren French before him, rewrote his original full-length volume of criticism of all of Steinbeck's fiction, calling it *John Steinbeck: Nature and Myth.* While Lisca's new presentation is as strong as ever in support of the novel's greatness, the focus of the new volume necessarily requires pinning that greatness to the exploitation of biblical motifs; however, Lisca's summary of the main themes and devices used in the book is also a model of concision.

The next couple of years, 1979-80, were moderately active ones so far as criticism of *Grapes* went. My recapitulation of the novel's first forty years for *Southern Humanities Review* [Summer 1979] (actually commissioned for a series of *The New Republic* retrospectives) tied the book's enduring power to the great American "road" theme, while calling for new directions in criticism. Mimi Reisel Gladstein, in Hayashi's *Steinbeck's Women,* continued the study of what she calls the "indestructible woman" in Steinbeck. . . . From the following year, Paul McCarthy's [*John Steinbeck,* see *CLC,* Vol. 21] is of interest; its *Grapes* chapter faults the novel whenever "allegorical emphasis . . . dilutes the realism." As if things were going back to their beginnings, this year's studies also included Patrick B. Mullen's consideration of the novel's folkloric aspects [*Journal of American Culture,* Vol. 1, 1978]. (pp. 12-13)

The fifth decade of criticism of *The Grapes of Wrath* hit full stride in 1982, and the pieces published that year nicely index the critical concerns of the eighties. . . . Warren Motley used the standpoint of the eighties to point out the centrality of the progression from patriarchy to matriarchy in the novel [see excerpt above]. Robert Con Davis, in the introduction to [*Twentieth Century Interpretations of 'The Grapes of Wrath'*], makes a balanced appraisal of the major criticism of the novel to date, pointing to the shift from interest in the work's documentary qualities to a concern for its artistic structure, eventually arriving at a realization that the book belongs in the broad tradition of American romantic literature rather than elsewhere. Davis also prints for the first time an essay by Joan Hedrick, whose feminist complaint is that Steinbeck failed to deal realistically with the "myth of the earth mother," and thereby failed to write "a truer, more political, and more humanistic book." Apparently a wave of concerns flowing out of the Modern Language Association conventions of the prior decade had at last washed over *The Grapes of Wrath* by 1982, leaving it none the worse off for its ordeal.

In 1983 F. Odun Balogun compared Steinbeck's work to that of James T. Ngugi (*Petals of Blood*) from the standpoint of supposedly shared proletarian origins and sympathies [*Journal of English,* September 1983]. . . . A volume by Brian St.

Pierre [*John Steinbeck: The California Years*] focuses sharply on the novel's biographical underpinnings. Another study with a regional basis is Stoddard Martin's *California Writers: Jack London, John Steinbeck, The Tough Guys*—uneven but lively. Also in 1983 Mary Allen's *Animals in American Literature* considers the expedient use, generally by killing, to which Steinbeck's characters put the animals in their lives. . . . [Recent] book chapters devoted to Steinbeck continue to develop older notions in greater depth: David Wyatt surveys the Eden myth in Steinbeck's works [in *The Fall into Eden*]; and Carol Shloss faults the writer for not sharing Dorothea Lange's honest photographer's approach to her subject, his adopting a disguise while among the migrants constituting "surveillance" that amounts to "usury" [*In Visible Light*]. Book-length studies of Steinbeck continued to emerge, however, and in 1985 Louis Owens's *John Steinbeck's Re-vision of America* clearly consolidated all that had gone before. *Grapes,* he stated, is "the most thorough evaluation and rejection of the American myth offered by any American writer"; at the same time, the book "both condemns the illusion of Eden in the West and offers a way out of the wasteland created by that illusion." Finally, there is John H. Timmerman confession in 1986 that "A thorough bibliography of articles and book chapters on the novel would cover pages (!)," and again trying to break down the many approaches to the novel in a systematic way; his conclusion might as well serve as this compiler's own: "In terms of thematic complexity and artistic skill, however, the work stands also as one of the masterpieces of American literature." Amen. (pp. 13-15)

John Ditsky, in an introduction to Critical Essays on Steinbeck's 'The Grapes of Wrath,' *edited by John Ditsky, G. K. Hall & Co., 1989, pp. 1-22.*

CHRISTOPHER LEHMANN-HAUPT

The occasion of the 50th Anniversary Edition [of *The Grapes of Wrath*] is a happy one. It gives one a chance to reread the novel after many years and to discover how remarkably well it stands up. Tainted only by Steinbeck's tendency to describe his characters' virtues instead of dramatizing them, his somewhat shallow proselytizing for collective action and the ending in which Rose of Sharon offers the starving stranger her breast, which has always struck this reader as portentous and off-key, the book retains to an impressive degree its power to convey how the plight of the Dust Bowl migrants was the tragedy of an entire social class as well as that of the Joad family.

Working Days: The Journal of 'The Grapes of Wrath' draws our attention to some of the reasons for Steinbeck's success. One of them is his ability subtly to stylize his characters, or, as he puts it in one of his journal entries, to make them "more than people," to capture in them "an overessence of people." As the models for the Joads have faded into the past, Steinbeck's overessential creations have come to stand for reality. . . .

Working Days is less interesting as an explanation of *The Grapes of Wrath* than it is as a portrait of a writer possessed. In his daily entries, which were undertaken as a form of throat-clearing and to take the place of writing letters, Steinbeck has rather little to say about the content of his book beyond, say, expressing his affection for the turtle chapter or warning himself not to overdo Grandpa and Grandma Joad.

What he most insistently conveys is the sense that he is possessed with an idea of which he must prove himself worthy, that to do so he must not only write well but also discipline himself to work on schedule, and that somehow he was failing in both respects. As he was nearing the end of his project, he wrote: "I have very grave doubts sometimes. I don't want this to seem hurried. It must be just as slow and measured as the rest but I am sure of one thing—it isn't the great book I had hoped it would be. It's just a run-of-the-mill book. And the awful thing is that it is absolutely the best I can do. Now to work on it."

From a certain perspective, there's an element of comedy in his attitude. Here Steinbeck was forever bellyaching about his inability to come up to the mark. And then a typical entry would end: "Well, here goes. Got her done and I think it's all right. Feel good about it anyway." . . .

And for all the distractions he complained about—which include visits from friends, letters asking for money or the use of his name, the noisiness of his neighbors, his publisher's bankruptcy, his wife's tonsilectomy, and the purchase of a new ranch to live on—he managed to write the entire 200,000-word manuscript between May 31 and Oct. 26, 1938. And to write it in a single pen-and-ink draft that seems to have required virtually no revision. . . .

[The sense one] gets from reading *Working Days* is of a writer in a heightened state of consciousness taking possession of a gift. The rarity of that experience is only highlighted by what followed the completion of the novel. In the diary that Steinbeck continued to keep for a time, he begins to feel the nemesis of his huge success with *The Grapes of Wrath,* his marriage begins to founder, he senses impending dissolution and he loses his focus on the new work at hand. It no longer matters to him that creative hours are being squandered.

Granted, that particular work, a play called *The God in the Pipes,* came to nothing, and Steinbeck eventually went on to happier times and more successful books, not to speak of an abundance of honors and prizes that included the 1962 Nobel Prize for Literature. Yet nothing he did afterward ever matched the experience of writing *The Grapes of Wrath.* To read the novel now along with the journal he kept with it is to be lifted ever so briefly into the presence of something inexplicable and magic.

Christopher Lehmann-Haupt, "Steinbeck's 'Grapes,' with His Diary of Writing It," in The New York Times, *March 30, 1989, p. C23.*

JAMES D. HOUSTON

John Steinbeck's epic novel, *The Grapes of Wrath,* is about an American legend. The Joads of Oklahoma came to represent the great multitude of displaced families forced to leave farms and lives behind in the Dust Bowl of the 1930s and trek west toward what they hoped would be better times. The book, helped along by the John Ford film, is a legend too, a classic of American fiction. Meanwhile, among Steinbeck buffs, how he wrote his masterpiece has become another kind of legend, a story all its own.

You might say that all three legends are being commemorated this spring when Viking Press releases its fiftieth anniversary edition of the novel. Among the several new books clustering around the birthday celebration, two [*Working Days:*

The Journals of 'The Grapes of Wrath' and *The Harvest Gypsies: On the Road to 'The Grapes of Wrath'*] flesh out the key moments in this most fertile period of the writer's career. Though his life and times have been much written about in recent years, these two books make available to a wider readership materials written by Steinbeck himself that have until now been seen mainly by specialists.

Two years before he started the Joads on their archetypal journey, Steinbeck took an assignment from *The San Francisco News* to do a series of articles on the predicament of the state's migrant farm workers. It was the summer of 1936, and refugees from the South and the Midwest were pouring into California by the thousands.

At the time, Steinbeck and his wife Carol were living near Los Gatos. His first major book on the subject of farm labor, *In Dubious Battle,* had just been published and well received. Certain growers were troubled by his pro-worker point of view, and certain labor radicals did not appreciate his behind-the-scenes account of their Machiavellian organizing strategies. But *News* editor George West, who had met Steinbeck in Carmel a few years earlier, liked what he had read. He arranged to send the thirty-four-year-old novelist on a state-wide tour of the fields and Hoovervilles and the new camps being developed by the Federal Resettlement Administration.

The result of this trip was called "The Harvest Gypsies," seven pieces that appeared in the *News* between October 5 and 12, 1936. They were reprinted in 1938 by San Francisco's labor-oriented Simon J. Lubin Society in a pamphlet titled *Their Blood is Strong.* Steinbeck's potent blend of empathy and moral outrage was perfectly matched by the photographs of Dorothea Lange, who had caught the whole saga with her camera—the tents, the jalopies, the bindlestiffs, the pathos and courage of uprooted mothers and children. . . .

While researching that series, Steinbeck met Tom Collins, the manager of a government Resettlement camp south of Bakersfield, in Kern County. Drawn to each other, the two men were soon traveling companions, as Collins became his migrant-labor mentor, providing raw material—field reports and oral recollections—that would find its way into "The Harvest Gypsies" as well as into the novel. (This camp would also become the model for "Weedpatch Camp," in *The Grapes of Wrath,* and Collins himself would be mentioned on the dedication page as "Tom, Who Lived It.")

In early 1938 the two men were traveling again through the San Joaquin Valley, this time into fields near Visalia and Nipomo, where winter floods had created chaos in the already precarious lives of displaced migrants. Suddenly thousands were without shelter and starving. Steinbeck, who had seen a lot of hardship, had never witnessed anything like it. With Collins he spent two weeks doing round-the-clock rescue work in the mud and rain. At one point Collins heard him say, "Something hit me and hit me hard for it hurts inside clear to the back of my head. I got pains all over my head, hard pains. Have never had pains like this before."

Two months later Steinbeck was sitting down to write an as-yet-untitled novel. At the same time he also began the daily journal that Viking brings out . . . this year. . . . Called *Working Days: The Journals of* The Grapes of Wrath, it covers the period of actual composition, from May to October, 1938, followed by a few post-production entries from the period October 1939 to January 1941. These have been edited, with an admirable commentary—thorough, readable, and generous-spirited—by Robert DeMott, formerly a director of San Jose State University's Steinbeck Research Center. (p. 25)

Judging by the detail in *Working Days,* this was a novel born in pain and sustained by pain. Part of the legend of the making of *The Grapes of Wrath* is the feverish obsession of the writing, at the end of which Steinbeck collapsed from nervous exhaustion. His journal bears this out in sometimes excruciatingly intimate detail. As journals go, this is not the kind of literary speculation we find in *The East of Eden Letters.* It is as if a closed-circuit video camera had been mounted above his desk in the eight-by-eight foot workroom on Greenwood Lane in the foothills outside Los Gatos. These are daily, confessional glimpses of a man who, while giving voice to an American legend, is sweating, brooding, counting words and pages, blacking out, fighting nausea. . . .

During these same five hectic months he is also nursing his wife through a tonsillectomy; buying a ranch; entertaining Charlie Chaplin, Broderick Crawford, and film director Pare Lorentz; worrying over reviews of *The Long Valley,* which came out that summer; and trying to ignore reports that his New York publisher, Pat Covici, was going bankrupt.

What emerges from these rushed entries is the picture of a man whose life is filled to overflowing, whose body is falling apart, while his mind and heart are possessed with a story that will not go untold. . . .

In its first year, 1939, [*The Grapes of Wrath*] sold half a million copies. It has been selling ever since. Why has it endured? There are many reasons, and they are not all literary. Steinbeck's fever, for one thing. It is still in there. His book continues to tell a story that touches the conscience and stirs the blood and cuts close to the bone, with an eerie resonance for the 1980s, as Studs Terkel has observed in his preface to the anniversary edition. The great wheel turns, and once again, while the rich get richer and the poor get poorer, we are confronted with a newly visible and growing underclass of citizens who used to have at least enough to get by but now have fallen through the bottom of the economy.

Though fifty years have passed, this is still not the kind of novel that gives you much distance, historic or aesthetic. It continues to have the holding power of a documentary film. It brings to mind the kind of witnessing that has since been turned over to New Journalism. If Steinbeck had been telling this story thirty or forty years later, he might have tried a non-fiction novel, along the lines of Truman Capote's *In Cold Blood* or Mailer's *The Armies of the Night.* But new journalism and the non-fiction novel had not yet been formulated, so he had to invent a form—part story-telling, part reportage, part sermon, part myth—a form to elevate and make universal the experience that had so appalled and electrified him. (p. 26)

James D. Houston, "Steinbeck's Obsession: A Novel Born in Pain," in San Francisco Review of Books, Spring, 1989, pp. 25-6.

JOHN H. TIMMERMAN

Since its publication 50 years ago this month, John Steinbeck's *Grapes of Wrath* has been considered a great work of literature. Its careful blend of taut drama, studied narration

and soaring lyrical passages marks it as a masterpiece. But it has always been much more than that.

In celebration of this anniversary the Steinbeck Research Center of San Jose State University will sponsor a conference exploring the novel from every conceivable angle—sociological, political, historical and literary. The University of Alabama's prestigious Literary Symposia series will this year focus on "The Steinbeck Question." Dozens of other enterprises have developed, including several new scholarly treatises. Scores of classrooms will turn their attention to the novel.

Such attention to one of America's literary masterpieces is gratifying, but it tends to mask the agony and the ecstasy of the novel. (pp. 341-42)

The seeds of the novel were sown some time before the writing of it. One myth has it that Steinbeck joined the migrants on their long trek from Oklahoma City to Bakersfield. He did not. Returning from a trip to Europe in September 1937, Steinbeck and his wife, Carol, bought a car in Chicago and headed south to pick up Route 66 to California. He traveled enough of the route to provide geographical details, but the firsthand experience with the migrants occurred in the fields of California.

The *San Francisco News* had assigned Steinbeck to do a series of articles on the migrants of California. The migrants' situation had rapidly gone from bad to abysmal. By the hundreds of thousands they arrived in California, driven from the midwestern states by drought and sandstorms that turned the region into a blinding haze of dust. Impoverished and desperate, they looked for homes and a future in the green valleys. . . .

The human drama drew young Steinbeck like a lodestar. He may have been attracted by the potential story, but what he found was a profoundly disturbing revelation of human nature. While traveling through the migrant fields and camps in the winter of 1936, it was Steinbeck's good fortune to meet Tom Collins, a runty, tough Virginia native who at the time directed a migrant camp for the Farm Security Administration. Collins labored long and hard for the people in his care, had a clear mind and administrative acumen, and could spin stories at the drop of a hat. Steinbeck appreciated Collins's stories, and borrowed many of them for *The Grapes of Wrath.* But he particularly admired Collins's willingness to get his hands dirty in the fields of human need.

Collins wrote a work about the migrants called *Bringing in the Sheaves,* under the pseudonym of Windsor Drake. Steinbeck wrote a foreword to it, but the book was never published. The work reveals, however, Collins's sensitivity to the migrants' need, and Steinbeck's deep immersion in the migrants' situation. Collins recalls the cold and mud from the ceaseless rains, the filth and squalor of the tent camps, and the people's sickness and starvation. In one moving passage he relates how he and Steinbeck came upon a starving family and how Steinbeck set out on foot across muddy fields to buy food for them. This came after a night of transporting migrants to drier land that ended with Steinbeck asleep in the mud. Collins described his face as a "mass of mud and slime."

Steinbeck seethed openly about the miserable conditions in a precursor to *The Grapes of Wrath* called "L'Affaire Lettuceberg." Anger was his motivation, the writing a purgation of it. But Steinbeck understood that anger alone was insufficient for a novel. He wanted readers to understand the heart and soul, the hopes and fears of these people, to empathize with them rather than simply witness his outrage. He destroyed the manuscript of "L'Affaire," secluded himself in his cabin at Los Gatos and in June 1938 began methodically rewriting the story from the inside out. This time the experience, in all its pathos and power, would be that of the migrants themselves, as they left the red clay of Oklahoma, crossed the wasteland of the southwest desert in trucks that moved like ancient turtles, and encountered the muddy fields of California. *Grapes* is a travelogue of the human soul, which reaches beyond itself for a glimpse of hope. (p. 342)

Upon publication, *The Grapes of Wrath* attracted immediate attention and stirred tremendous controversy. It soared to the top of the best-seller lists, where it remained for over a year, and it won the Pulitzer Prize in 1940. Its impact upon American affairs was intense. Fierce political backlash broke out on two fronts. California landowners fought desperately to discredit the novel, branding Steinbeck as a communist troublemaker. However unjustified, the label stuck for years. In Oklahoma, political powers organized to censor and ban the novel for allegedly presenting a derogatory view of the migrants.

Also, many people reacted sharply against Steinbeck's faithfully realistic rendering of the migrants' language. The novel has been and still is routinely censored as profane. Oklahoma Congressman Lyle Boren went on record [see excerpt above] in 1940 with this comment: "Take the vulgarity out of this book and it would be a blank from cover to cover." The fact is, the migrants were often a profane people. Referring to another of his novels, Steinbeck commented that he couldn't portray such characters talking like college professors. He aimed for authenticity. The truth of the migrants' plight, he believed, had to be told, and in the power of their own words.

None of these charges, however, can diminish the novel's strength, nor Steinbeck's deep sympathy with a people in terrible need. Why does it move readers today, far removed from the hounding anguish of the Depression, the cruel experience of the dust bowl and the struggle to put a plate of food before a starving family? Perhaps because these conditions, in varying forms, still exist today. Now, too, people wander homeless and helpless in the heart of the promised land. Human need is always with us, and we do well to be mindful of that need. But there are other answers as well.

The novel gives rich testament to a spiritual idea of humanity. In struggling heroically to hold her own family together, Ma Joad nonetheless possesses a vision of the family of all humanity. This idea has not lost an iota of spiritual urgency in our "me-first" age. If the poor are always with us, we are obligated to see them as extensions of ourselves. This is no less a radical and daring concept today than it was in 1939. And no less important.

The novel also establishes a spiritual hope which, while it transcends human hopelessness, is manifested through humans. Rose of Sharon is one of the great heroines of literature. She changes from a naïve little girl whose passion for herself is all-consuming to a woman who can lay down her life and set aside her own need to minister to others. While demonstrating the urgent need for humanity, the novel provides a stirring spiritual response to that need. No wonder the book has made so many so uneasy.

The significance of *The Grapes of Wrath* endures also be-

cause of its literary achievement. For hundreds of pages the reader is spellbound by a story woven with intricate craftsmanship out of the rich fabric of biblical symbolism and the flowing rhythms and patterns of the intercalary chapters. That it was written in so short a time is a wonder.

The Grapes of Wrath earned Steinbeck a Nobel Prize more than 20 years after it appeared. Its greatest commendation, however, lies in the fact that it is still read today. This disquieting drama of a dispossessed people who in 1938 packed their lives aboard dilapidated trucks in search of the promised land is very much a story of America, a story of each of us, which we are constantly rediscovering. (pp. 342-43)

> *John H. Timmerman, "'The Grapes of Wrath':*
> *Fifty Years Later," in* The Christian Century, *Vol.*
> *106, No. 11, April 5, 1989, pp. 341-43.*

WILLIAM KENNEDY

I told a friend of mine, a writer, that I was rereading John Steinbeck's epic novel, *The Grapes of Wrath,* on the occasion of its golden anniversary—it was published April 14, 1939—and my friend said he wouldn't dare reread it. "That was my great book," he explained. "I couldn't bear to find that it doesn't stand up."

John Steinbeck had a similar problem. He was choking with trepidation about the novel as he was writing it. . . . (p. 1)

He wrote the book in five months, beginning in May and ending in late October 1938, writing in longhand and producing 2,000 words a day, the equivalent of seven double-spaced typed pages, an enormous output for any writer, and ultimately a daily tour de force. But he was flagellating himself for this also: "Vacillating and miserable. . . . I'm so lazy, so damned lazy"; "Where has my discipline gone? Have I lost control?"; "My laziness is overwhelming." This novel would be his ninth work of fiction in 10 years, and he would be 37 years old at its publication.

These remarks of his are culled from the diary he kept daily while writing *The Grapes of Wrath,* that diary now published for the first time under the title *Working Days,* with a long, informative commentary and voluminous notes by Robert DeMott, a Steinbeck scholar who teaches English at Ohio University, and some newly discovered Steinbeck letters. It will provide a field day for Steinbeck aficionados, but for its insights into the creative mind it is also a valuable book for writers, aspiring or arrived. The struggle to create an original work is an everlasting one with most writers, and it is well anatomized here. "I've always had these travails," Steinbeck reminds himself halfway through the book. "Never get used to them."

The book also has the fascination of privacy invaded. Steinbeck said he had often been tempted to destroy it, yet he sent it to his editor at the Viking Press, Pat Covici, obviously aware of its worth. He requested first that it not be published in his lifetime and also that it be made available to his sons, so they might "look behind the myth and hearsay and flattery and slander a disappeared man becomes and to know to some extent what manner of man their father was."

The 50th-anniversary edition of *The Grapes of Wrath* itself includes a strong and moving introduction by Studs Terkel, who makes the case for the novel's relevance to the lives of Chicano farm workers in California today and to Midwestern farmers who, in recent years, have lost their farms to the banks.

The novel is also, it seems to me, a vivid 50-year-old parallel to the American homeless: a story of people at the bottom of the world, bereft and drifting outcasts in a hostile society. Here is Ma Joad, the greatest of all the characters in Steinbeck's densely populated story, talking to another Joad family member, Uncle John:

> "We ain't gonna die out. People is goin' on—changin' a little, maybe, but goin' right on."
> "How can you tell?" Uncle John demanded. "What's to keep ever'thing from stoppin'; all the folks from jus' gittin' tired an' layin' down?" . . .
> "Hard to say," she said. "Ever'thing we do—seems to me is aimed right at goin' on. . . . Even gettin' hungry—even bein' sick; some die, but the rest is tougher. Jus' try to live the day, jus' the day."

I can't go on, I'll go on. It's Samuel Beckett's theme before Samuel Beckett. It's the Joads' as well as it is that of thousands now sleeping on heating grates and in cardboard boxes all over America, who somehow survive subzero temperatures and move on to the next ordeal—modern migrants in a nation that has created an urban class abysmally more hopeless than the fruit-picking peon class to which the Joads belonged. That peon class, one soulless corporate farmer said (and Steinbeck noted this), was necessary to the survival of California agriculture. (pp. 1, 44)

The story opens with Tom Joad returning home from prison, where he did time for killing a man who knifed him at a dance; and Tom becomes the catalyst for much of the story's action and movement. He is its intellectual center and, with Ma Joad, carries the principal weight of the book.

Lesser Joads move on and off center stage: Pa, who loses his authority in the family to the wiser and more decisive Ma; Uncle John, summed up in a brilliant paragraph by Steinbeck, but who remains a Johnny-one-note character thereafter; Rose of Sharon, pregnant child bride (who becomes the centerpiece of the unforgettably poignant final scene), and her worthless groom; brother Al, who loves to fool with cars and women; Noah, a simple cipher in the family; Winfield and Ruthie, the children growing wild without a home; Grampa and Granma, the comic elders who fail to survive the family's transplanting; the former preacher Casy, a staunchly moral, honest and godless man; and an assortment of secondary figures like Muley Graves, who loses his farm but won't leave, and lives on, with fugitive, gun-toting hostility toward banks and sheriffs. "I like Muley," Steinbeck wrote in his diary. "He is a fine hater."

When published, the novel became the top best seller of 1939 (430,000 copies sold) and also one of the top 10 best sellers of 1940. It won the Pulitzer Prize in 1940, and to date has sold close to four and a half million copies in the United States, and it still sells 100,000 paperback copies annually. And it has sold more than 14 million copies worldwide.

All well and good for the publisher, but does the book stand up?

It does indeed.

It stands tall.

I read and relished much of the Steinbeck shelf in the 1940's and 50's and yet wasn't impelled to go back to him the way

I go back always to Faulkner and Hemingway, the two writers Steinbeck claimed to admire most. Reading this book, you can see the influence of other peers of his generation: Thomas Wolfe, in the spasms of overblown rhetoric and impersonalized overview of the national life; and John Dos Passos, in the interchapters Steinbeck called "generals," which is to say, general American subject matter that exists outside of, but parallel to, the continuing story of the Joads.

In the generals Steinbeck writes of the dust bowl as phenomenon; the tractor—which plowed the land mechanically and knocked down farm homes—as enemy; the Far Western states as state of mind; the roadside lunchroom; thieving used-car salesmen and much more. These generals get in the way of the story in the same way that the lore of whaling gets in the way of the story of Ahab and Moby Dick. But just as it was Melville's obsession to present the totality of whaling, so was it Steinbeck's obsession with the migrants' plight that led him to excess.

Here's how he saw it at the time: "Better make this scene three pages instead of two. Because there can never be too much of background"; the book "will take every bit of experience and thought and feeling that I have"; "Afraid of repetitiousness. Must watch that."

But he didn't.

He repeated in the generals what he had embodied in the story, an obvious mistrust of minimalism. Even some of the Joad chapters go on past their effectiveness.

Throughout, the Joads personify Steinbeck's ideas of what is and what should be, but he exceeds the dramatic limit at times and forcefeeds the dialogue, as when Muley Graves bemoans the takeover of land and farm by the banks: " 'Cause what'd they take when they tractored the folks off the lan'? What'd they get so their 'margin a profit' was safe?" Maybe Muley always talked about margins of profit, but I doubt it; and so for a moment he lost credibility. But only for a moment. Otherwise I bought him. Whole hog. Whole Muley.

Even Tom Joad's now classic farewell speech, when he's on the run after killing a vigilante, is loaded with Steinbeck's idealism: "Wherever they's a fight so hungry people can eat, I'll be there. Wherever they's a cop beatin' up a guy, I'll be there" and more. Steinbeck's rage pushed Tom beyond seemly boundaries.

Then again, how valuable, really, is the seemly? This novel stood the critics of its day on their ear (with a few exceptions). They saw it had flaws, but they gave it their huzzahs anyway. (pp. 44-5)

Six months after his great novel was published, John Steinbeck wrote in his diary: "That part of my life that made the *Grapes* is over. . . . I have to go to new sources and find new roots." He changed the subject matter and the style of his writing, and also broke with his wife, Carol (a radical who had typed and edited the *Grapes* manuscript, had also chosen its title, a phrase from the "Battle Hymn of the Republic," and to whom Steinbeck dedicated the book).

Steinbeck's second marriage didn't work for long and ended in divorce. Much of his later writing didn't work well either, though there was *Cannery Row* and *East of Eden* (which he undertook after rediscovering this diary of *The Grapes*). Then in 1961 he published *The Winter of Our Discontent*, and the Swedish Academy the following year awarded him the Nobel Prize in Literature. At a press conference the day the prize was announced, a reporter asked Steinbeck if he deserved it. With characteristic self-deprecation he replied: "That's an interesting question. Frankly, no."

Anders Osterling, the secretary of the academy, said the award was based on *Discontent,* adding that it marked a return after more than two decades to the "towering standard" Steinbeck had set with *The Grapes of Wrath.* As reported in *The New York Times,* Osterling described the author as an "independent expounder of the truth with an unbiased instinct for what is genuinely American, be it good or bad."

Not everybody would agree that *The Winter of Our Discontent* and *The Grapes of Wrath* are of equal weight. I am one who would not. But I look back at that long list of John Steinbeck's achievements—*Of Mice and Men, The Long Valley, Tortilla Flat, Cannery Row, East of Eden* and *The Grapes*— and then I look around and try to find other American writers whose work has meant as much to me, and I count them on one hand. Maybe one and a half.

John Steinbeck had the power. And if at times he lacked the language and the magic that go with mythic literary achievement and status, he had in their place a mighty conscience and a mighty heart. And just about 51 years ago this time, that man sat down and put pencil to paper; and in five miraculous months he wrote a mighty, mighty book. (p. 45)

> *William Kennedy, " 'My Work Is No Good',*" in The New York Times Book Review, *April 9, 1989, pp. 1, 44-5.*

JONATHAN YARDLEY

[The] huge popular success of *The Grapes of Wrath* is indisputable but, as a golden anniversary rereading makes plain, its literary reputation is considerably more problematical. . . .

Steinbeck was a writer of limited technical skills but a large, kind heart, and he made his most dramatic expression of his benevolent vision of the human community in this novel, which appeared at just the moment when popular faith in the country's capacity to recover from the Depression was at low ebb; his passionate plea for the displaced Okie farmworkers fell on receptive ears, and readers responded with an ardor not dissimilar to Steinbeck's own.

Indeed, it has become American mythology that enthusiasm for *The Grapes of Wrath* and its message of working-class solidarity was so great that Washington was mobilized on behalf of the migrants—that it became, as the cliché has it, "a book that made a difference." But much though one might wish this to be so, it is not. The book did win a Pulitzer Prize, which gave it a certain establishmentarian imprimatur, but the truth, however little it may appeal to sentimentalists, is that the Okies were saved not by Steinbeck but by the economic recovery brought about by the Second World War; though efforts were made to curb the powers of the California farm cartel, there is evidence enough in the continuing struggle of migrant workers—not Okies, now, but Mexicans—that its back hardly has been broken.

What Steinbeck really accomplished in *The Grapes of Wrath* was not political or literary but cultural: he opened the eyes of the educated middle class to the terrible deprivation and pain being suffered by the migrants, and helped create a cli-

mate of sympathy and concern for them. That the book continues to be read, especially in high schools and colleges, no doubt is evidence that this sympathy has not died over a half-century; too, the book has, as a portrait of a certain time and place, genuine historical value that makes it, like the novels of Sinclair Lewis, immensely useful for teachers and students of 20th-century American history.

But as a work of literature it leaves much to be desired. Its strengths lie in its empathetic portrait of the Joad family— whose name long ago entered American folklore—and in certain of its descriptive passages, notably those involving the Hoovervilles, the government camps, the long train of migrants working their way westward along Route 66 ("It's like a whole country is movin.' "), and the idyllic beauties of California, "where it's rich an' green." But Steinbeck's prose tends to the leaden and his dialogue, heavy as it is with apostrophes and other attempts at folksy authenticity, borders on the embarrassing.

Much the same can be said for the politics with which the book is suffused. *The Grapes of Wrath* is not a political novel in the baser sense of the term; the sorrow and outrage that motivate it are human rather than ideological, and even its watered-down Marxism is incidental to the sense of personal identity that Steinbeck felt with the migrants. But its depiction of "the machine man, driving a dead tractor on land he does not know and love" and its sentimentalization of those "simple agrarian folk who had not changed with industry, who had not formed with machines or known the power and danger of machines in private hands," are almost Luddite in their naiveté.

But like most writers of fiction, Steinbeck had a firmer grasp on the human heart and soul than on the complexities of social and economic institutions. The strange diaries that he kept as he wrote the novel, published for the first time in *Working Days,* underscore the innocent quality of his mind. This is a slight book that can be of little interest to anyone except Steinbeck scholars, but as a portrait of the writer at work it is not without merit or interest. It reveals Steinbeck as a man of strong, and strongly contradictory, impulses: arrogant and unconfident, disciplined and errant, loyal and deceitful. . . .

[*The Grapes of Wrath*] is not a work of literature, at least not as the term is properly understood, but a book of genuine consequence. Like other large, ambitious but artless novels— *Doctor Zhavago* leaps to mind—*The Grapes of Wrath* transcends its limitations. In its clumsy earnestness, its love of the land, its conviction that people are inherently good, it is, as Steinbeck wished it to be, "a truly American book." It is for this rather than for its literary qualities that we still read it, and this is quite enough.

> *Jonathan Yardley, "A New Pressing of 'The Grapes of Wrath',"* in Book World—The Washington Post, *April 16, 1989, p. 3.*

BRAD LEITHAUSER

When seeking a title or an epigraph for one of his many books, John Steinbeck went to his Bible, to his hymnal, to Shakespeare, Milton, Burns, Blake. Grand company, in short—and an initial signal of the grandeur he self-consciously aspired to. Nowhere is this open yearning for magnitude on display more clearly, or more successfully, than in *The Grapes of Wrath*. . . . (p. 90)

Readers like me, induced by the anniversary to examine a writer they haven't looked at in years, will find that *The Grapes of Wrath* contains in profusion the strengths commonly associated with Steinbeck (sympathy for the disenfranchised, moral urgency, narrative propulsion) and also the weaknesses (repetitiveness, simplistic politics, sentimentality). What may prove unexpected is the book's old-fashioned atmosphere—how much further from us it feels than the novels that Hemingway and Faulkner and Fitzgerald were composing at roughly the same time. One could aptly describe *The Grapes of Wrath* as a novel about the homeless, and what subject could have a more current, cutting edge than that? But in its tone, its methods, and the solutions it tenders for the social problems it documents—indeed, in its very willingness to tender solutions for colossal social problems—the book seems miles distant from most contemporary fiction. For better or worse (or, more likely, for better and worse), we have come a long way since.

The Grapes of Wrath is immensely ambitious, and there is nothing old-fashioned about that: our preoccupation with the "big book," the Great American Novel, seems an anchored constant in our floating literary consciousness. What does smack of yesteryear is the piece-by-piece construction and the incremental pacing by which Steinbeck introduces the Joad family and steadily tracks them, mile by plodding mile, from the barren fields of Oklahoma, where dust storms are everywhere tearing farm families from their holdings, to the "promised land" of California, where, amid God's plenty, their misery goes unrelieved because of the greed and chicanery of unseen land barons. Today, the typical stab at a Great American Novel is a much more disjointed affair, revelling in those shifts of style and viewpoint, those metaphysical and metafictional musings which are often called (perhaps with some disservice to the author of *Gravity's Rainbow*) Pynchonesque; in any event, it is far removed in spirit from the sort of family adventure—to which the word "saga" so readily attaches itself—undertaken by Grampa, Granma, Pa, Ma, and various Joad relatives and offspring. Steinbeck builds from the ground up, literally: he commences his novel with a prolonged description of the "red country" and the "gray country" of drought-scarred Oklahoma.

Of *The Grapes of Wrath* you may be tempted to say, "They don't write them like that anymore"—until you lift your gaze from the world of "serious fiction" to that of popular fiction. Maybe they *do* still write them like that, only the books hide themselves on the best-seller lists. Despite his Nobel Prize, Steinbeck seems nearer kin to a "middlebrow" writer like, say, James Michener than to those contemporary novelists apt to be dissected in graduate seminars or the literary quarterlies. And how at home the novel would seem on a current *Times* best-seller list, with a blurb reading something like "Three generations of a dispossessed Oklahoma farm family head west toward hope." Actually, the book remains one of the best-selling American novels of all time, with some fourteen million copies sold worldwide.

In what is one of the novel's last lines of dialogue, and arguably its spiritual summit, Ma says, "Hush. Don't worry. We'll figger somepin out." She has silently resolved that her daughter, Rose of Sharon, who has recently given birth to a stillborn child, will now suckle a middle-aged man—a stranger—who has been found starving in a wet, chilly barn. Dia-

logue of this sort, steeped in cracker-barrel homeyness, would not likely be employed by a modern writer in so pivotal a moment and without the insulation of irony. But Steinbeck plays it straight. And by doing so—by respectfully allowing his Joads for six hundred pages to figger and innerduce and understan', to git a-sayin' and go a-billygoatin'—he succeeds in reaching the tender-hearted and the hard-hearted alike. Indeed, since no partisan is so zealous as the proudly hard-hearted who has experienced a softening, it makes some sense that the normally acidulous Dorothy Parker hailed the book as "the greatest American novel I have ever read."

For all its huge intentions—its weight of symbolism, prognostication, counsel—the novel shows remarkably little strain. . . . (pp. 90-1)

From the outset of composition, evidently, Steinbeck envisioned that climactic moment in which Rose of Sharon takes a stranger to her breast—a scene for which Steinbeck was roundly attacked. Many critics called the book shocking or obscene. Social changes in the last five decades, however, have clearly worked toward Steinbeck's vindication. Given the overload of grotesquerie now required before any author might be labelled shocking or obscene (epithets to which many vainly aspire), and given, as well, what must be called saner attitudes about breast-feeding, the novel's ending is unlikely to rumple any sensibilities today. And, thankfully, now that time has peeled away this distorting veneer of scandal one does not find underneath it what so often lies at the bottom of the formerly shocking: a residue of the merely naughty or smarmy. One senses on Steinbeck's part no spoiling self-congratulation, no hint of the vandal, in having placed Rose of Sharon and the starving man in what is, after all, a sort of manger scene—in having utterly upended the religious and artistic icon of Mother and Child. No, Rose of Sharon's behavior is simply an extension of what the Joads have practiced from the first: in their levelheaded, makeshift fashion, they have always done what was necessary to insure that they, and those around them, survive.

One wishes that the rest of the book had weathered the years so well. For all its layerings of tragedy, *The Grapes of Wrath* is a utopian tale, which is a difficult thing for a realistic novel to be. Steinbeck believed throughout his career in the possibility of earthly redemption, and no doubt this perception of the schism between the "is" and the "might be" was for him a great frustration and a continual creative spur. In his Nobel Prize acceptance speech, delivered in the fall of 1962, he asserted that "a writer who does not passionately believe in the perfectibility of man has no dedication nor any membership in Literature." In *The Grapes of Wrath,* heaven on earth is glimpsed when the Joads settle temporarily at Weedpatch, a government-sponsored but self-policing camp for migrant workers. The family has at last found a place where "folks gits along nice." There is no crime to speak of at Weedpatch, nor any disaffection, lassitude, violence, cruelty, or selfishness. (The camp's greatest moral breach occurs when toilet paper is pilfered; the malefactors turn out to be a trio of little girls, who have cut paper dolls from it.) For obvious reasons, this section is much the flimsiest of the novel, and yet modern readers, even as they deplore Steinbeck's naïveté, may well experience a nostalgia for an era in which an esteemed author might reasonably paint such a picture. Surely no contemporary writer would propose that today's homeless, ravaged by heartbreaking addictions, require of us nothing more than to be put in charge of their own lives.

Which is not to suggest that the utopian novel has vanished altogether from the scene. In my return to *The Grapes of Wrath,* I was frequently reminded of Alice Walker's moving, flawed *The Color Purple*—one of few books of recent times to become, both in sales and in social impact, something of the national phenomenon that Steinbeck's novel was. Both novels dignify the lives of the semi-literate; boldly risk being dismissed as sentimental in an attempt to be life-affirming; indict an insular, racist society; speak, with little authorial intercession, through the voices of the rural poor; and project a vision of terrestrial paradise once certain "ism'"s are recognized and repudiated. (In place of Steinbeck's monopolistic capitalism, Walker's demons are racism and, particularly, sexism; by her novel's close, the latter is sufficiently overcome so that Albert, the former woman-beater and all-around macho man, has become a seamster, contentedly passing his days on the veranda stitching up unisex trousers for a cottage industry called Folkspants, Unlimited.)

In *The Grapes of Wrath,* as in *The Color Purple,* the unlettered are forever pushing toward a poetry of folk wisdom; everybody's always itching to get off a good aphorism. Ma tells Pa, "Man, he lives in jerks—baby born an' a man dies, an' that's a jerk—gets a farm an' loses his farm, an' that's a jerk. Woman, it's all one flow." Pa tells Uncle John, "Sometimes a fella got to sift the law." Tom reassures Casy that the latter hasn't begun "preaching" again: "Preachin's a kinda tone a voice, an' preachin's a way a lookin' at things." Needless to say, the result can be an air of contrivance. There are moments when the characters seem mere mouthpieces; their conversations have the amplitude and reverberation—but also the hollowness—of speech delivered through a microphone. In our own time, any such attempt to put highly poeticized philosophizing in the mouths of the poor and uneducated might be thought foredoomed (or, at least, fore-flawed) if we did not know of a few glittering instances in which it comes off beautifully. A theatregoer doesn't flinch when Linda Loman, in Arthur Miller's *Death of a Salesman,* announces that "a man is not a bird, to come and go with the springtime," and then launches into a little sermon about the innate dignity of the "small man." Nor does a reader feel anything but thrilled when, in Robert Frost's "The Death of the Hired Man," Warren and Mary trade apothegms. "Home is the place where, when you have to go there, they have to take you in," Warren says, and Mary replies, "I should have called it something you somehow haven't to deserve." Admittedly, Miller and Frost have the advantage of working in inherently artificial genres. No one can plausibly demand that stage speech or blank-verse dialogue satisfy all the strictures of naturalism. But things are different in a novel like *The Grapes of Wrath,* where a documentary veracity is expected; one shudders a little as Ma uncorks a line like "They was the time when we was on the lan'," or "Worse off we get, the more we got to do." Here is that old joke-jingle: the *poet* who doesn't *know* it. For Ma's reflections are poetic not just in their compression but in their metre. They are iambic-pentameter lines that could be fitted into "The Death of the Hired Man" without occasioning the faintest metrical tremor.

As is generally the case when diaries or drafts surrounding a famous literary work come to light, *Working Days: The Journals of 'The Grapes of Wrath'* provides more confirmation than revelation. Most of what is here could be intuited from the novel itself. That the book was written rapidly, in a fiercely concentrated five-month out-pouring, comes as no surprise: the writing feels all of a piece. Nor is one surprised to discover that Steinbeck did little revising. If the achievement of his prose is that he everywhere manages to avoid clutter—no small feat—he pulls off few of those bravura touches that arise when, over time, one stylistic refinement unlocks another. His prose is a bit like a cleared, swept, polished ballroom floor on which nobody dances. What *is* surprising about *Working Days* is just how scanty are its collateral pleasures. Precious few nuggets of humor, intelligence, or curiosity glint within it. What one primarily absorbs is Steinbeck's guilt-inspired drive, and one leaves the book hoping forlornly that he learned to like himself better as the years went by. (pp. 91-2)

Perhaps the chief wonder of the novel is that it's as good as it is. Steinbeck was a writer of such variable strengths and such uncertain instincts that any attempt at an epic novel would seem destined for failure. What probably saved *The Grapes of Wrath* was his reservoir of rage. He saw his fellow-Californians responding with fear rather than charity to "the flare of want" in the eyes of the newcomers, and this inhumanity liberated him: it justified his characteristic eagerness to lecture his readers, lent a dignity to his indiscriminate savagings of the affluent (into whose ranks the book would irreversibly propel him), and excused his woolly theorizing about the collective "Manself." The book is a call to arms, and it manages, in the enormity of the iniquity it exposes, to render irrelevant many of the aesthetic qualifications it raises along the way.

It is tempting to construct a mystery around Steinbeck's precipitous decline after *The Grapes of Wrath.* His next novel, *The Moon Is Down,* could be described as an attempt at the second-rate which falls well short of its goal. Although he subsequently published, in 1952, his largest novel, *East of Eden*—a burst footlocker of a book—much of his creative energy after *The Grapes of Wrath* was channelled into nonfiction, a genre for which his talents were strikingly maladapted. Over the years, his politics drifted to the right (although this champion of the downtrodden worker was never the doctrinaire communist that his supporters and his enemies, for their contrary purposes, sometimes made him out to be), and in his last years he was a staunch defender of American involvement in Vietnam. Liberals might wish to view Steinbeck's artistic decline as a concomitant of his growing political benightedness; conservatives might see in his fall from critical esteem the spiteful manipulation of a liberal literary establishment. But it appears, simply, that without the fervor that came from his being a lone artist on a crusade ("The death of children by starvation in our valleys is simply staggering," he wrote to his agent three months before beginning *The Grapes of Wrath*) Steinbeck's own natural deficiencies came to the fore. He lacked the wit and precision necessary for the poised irony so congenial to the conservative (however far to the right he might journey, he was never going to sound like Evelyn Waugh), and his one sizable attempt at political satire, *The Short Reign of Pippin IV,* is an embarrassment. His talent for killing a joke was almost—but unfortunately not quite—laughable. In *Travels with Charley,* an account of some rambles around America with his poodle, he ponders for several pages how his pet may respond to its first glimpse of the redwoods. ("After this experience he might be translated mystically to another plane of existence, to another dimension, just as the redwoods seem to be out of time and out of our ordinary thinking. The experience might even drive him mad. . . . On the other hand, it might make of him a consummate bore.") But when, at last, Charley was let loose among "these ambassadors from another time," he gazed at them with indifference at first. Then he discovered a little willow, and, "after turning this way and that to get range and trajectory, he fired." And I'm afraid that's the punch line.

Most books by Steinbeck leave one unable to shake a regretful sense—in view of his many strengths—of how much better a writer he might have been. With *The Grapes of Wrath,* though, one is cheered to see an artist creating something far better—in view of his weaknesses—than anything one might realistically have expected. If the book offers few surprises the second time around, this in part attests to its merits: even its peripheral incidents linger in the mind. In addition, the book occasionally offers one of the rarest and most gratifying pleasures that literature opens up to us. We behold in it that little miracle of transformation by which, with just a bit of fleshing out, a stick figure becomes an Everyman. (p. 93)

Brad Leithauser, *"The Flare of Want," in* The New Yorker, *Vol. LXV, No. 27, August 21, 1989, pp. 90-3.*

LOUIS OWENS

We can and should read *The Grapes of Wrath* as a testament to a historical and sociological phenomenon—the Dust Bowl—perhaps the greatest combined ecological and social catastrophe in American history. In a letter to his agents, Steinbeck declared, "I am trying to write history while it is happening and I don't want to be wrong." In his attempt to "write history while it is happening," Steinbeck brilliantly documents the suffering of a people in flight, the tragic loss of homeland, and the discovery that in the land of plenty there isn't enough to go around. Simultaneously, *The Grapes of Wrath* offers an education in the dynamics of the laboring class. Unlike the ruthlessly microscopic perspective of *In Dubious Battle,* Steinbeck's previous strike novel, *The Grapes of Wrath* demonstrates how labor organizations, or unions, grow from the desperation of the workers, how capitalism, in its inherent quest for the profit that keeps the machinery going, will oppress and even destroy the laborer. The novel serves as a powerful reminder of the struggle to organize the working class during the twenties and thirties as well as a reminder of the widespread fears of communism that lasted through the McCarthy era of the fifties.

These are historical and political reasons to read this novel, but no great novel can or should be read merely for such reasons. *The Grapes of Wrath* endures. It is taught in high schools and colleges and at the same time it is read throughout the world by men and women with little education. In this book Steinbeck brings together vital threads central to American thought, American history, and American letters. Behind the political and historical message lies the archetypal pattern of American consciousness, the so-called American myth. Behind the preacher Casy's eloquence lies Emersonian

transcendentalism as well as Steinbeck's interest in biology and ecology. Behind the hunger for the land expressed in both the narrator's and the characters' words lies Jeffersonian agrarianism, a quintessential element in the American Dream, but a Jeffersonian agrarianism that is questioned and revised in the course of the novel. Behind the exodus from the Dust Bowl to the Eden of California lies the inevitable human need to believe in a new beginning, a second chance, the possibility of Eden rediscovered.

And containing all of these streams of thought is a superbly crafted work of fiction, a novel that takes impressive risks and succeeds. In this novel Steinbeck's mastery of a complex array of prose styles is apparent, as is his ability to engage the reader's sympathies for characters while consistently undercutting the tendencies toward sentimentality in the creation of such characters.

In American literature only one novel had previously brought together the political, sociological, and aesthetic power found in *The Grapes of Wrath*: Mark Twain's *Adventures of Huckleberry Finn,* with its searing indictment of the South, of the institution of slavery, and of the human conscience, and its unequalled brilliance in the use of a vernacular narrator.

Louis Owens, in his 'The Grapes of Wrath': Trouble in the Promised Land, *Twayne, 1989, 121 p.*

An excerpt from *Working Days: The Journals of 'The Grapes of Wrath', 1938-1941*

Entry #100

[October 26, 1938—10:30, Wednesday]

Today should be a day of joy because I could finish today—just the walk to the barn, the new people and the ending and that's all. But I seem to have contracted an influenza of the stomach or something. Anyway I am so dizzy I can hardly see the page. This makes it difficult to work. On the other hand, it might get worse. I might be in for a siege. Can't afford to take that chance. I must go on. If I can finish today I don't much care what happens afterwards. Wish—if it was inevitable, that it could have held off one more day. My fault really for having muffed on Monday oddly enough. I feel better—sitting here. I wish I were done. Best way is just to get down to the lines. I wonder if this flu could be simple and complete exhaustion. I don't know. But I do know that I'll have to start at it now and, of course, anything I do will be that much nearer the end.

Finished this day—and I hope to God it's good.

Glasnost and Contemporary Soviet Literature

In April, 1985, Soviet Premier Mikhail Gorbachev proposed the adoption of two new policies for governing the Union of Soviet Socialist Republics (USSR): *glasnost,* or "openness," calls for greater freedom of speech than has been customary in the USSR since the 1930s; *perestroika,* or "restructuring," introduces some elements of democracy and capitalism into its previously highly restricted political and economic system. Although aspects of Gorbachev's program have been criticized in both the Soviet Union and in the West, it is widely acknowledged that the re-empowerment of the people of the Soviet Union is an event of great significance.

In *Perestroika: New Thinking for Our Country and the World* (1987), Gorbachev formally extended *glasnost* to artists and writers. He asserted: "Even the most extreme viewpoint contains something valuable and rational, for the person who upholds it honestly and who cares for the common cause in his own way reflects some real aspects of life." Gorbachev's statements and actions have encouraged members of the Soviet print media, as well as those in television, theater, literature, and other venues of creative expression, to exploit this rare opportunity to communicate freely. The Soviet Union's dramatists, poets, and prose writers, as well as its other artists, have been in the vanguard of a nationwide exploration of the limits of dissent now permissible.

Many works by Soviet and foreign authors that had been officially banned have been released by the censors and published in the second half of the 1980s. The enormous volume of previously censored materials includes such examples of literary excellence as Boris Pasternak's *Doctor Zhivago,* Anna Akhmatova's *Requiem,* Vladimir Nabokov's *Lolita,* Yuri Trifonov's *The Disappearance* and *House on the Embankment,* and Yevgeny Zamyatin's *We.* Subscriptions to the country's literary journals have soared, as Soviet citizens attempt to recover what are considered the most influential works produced by their culture. Many commentators remarked that this phenomenon has given rise to complaints that there isn't enough time to read all the important literature now available to the citizens of the Soviet Union.

Correctives to "official" Soviet history in the form of fiction constituted another popular result of *glasnost*. Anatoly Rybakov's *Children of the Arbat* (1988), one of the first explicitly anti-Stalinist works of fiction to be published under *glasnost*, is typical of much of the historical revisionist literature released in the late 1980s. Written in the classic, nineteenth-century style of realism, Rybakov's novel concerns an innocent young man caught in the labyrinthine political machine set in motion by Soviet Premier Joseph Stalin. Arousing great controversy and much acclaim for its author upon publication in the Soviet Union, *Children of the Arbat* received moderate praise from Western critics more accustomed to using aesthetic rather than political criteria for assessing the quality of literature. Deming Brown summarized this phenomenon: "Despite its abundant aesthetic flaws, [*Children of the Arbat*] is enormously popular with Soviet readers, whose hunger for facts about and interpretations of the Stalin era is apparently insatiable."

Outwardly similar in intent, and yet not affected by Gorbachev's reforms, is exiled Russian author Aleksandr Solzhenitsyn's *August 1914: The Red Wheel, Knot I*. This novel differs greatly from official Soviet history in its depiction of pre-revolutionary Russia. First published in the West in 1972, Solzhenitsyn added approximately three hundred pages to the original manuscript after his emigration to the United States allowed him access to historical sources banned in the Soviet Union. Although his best known and most highly acclaimed work, *The Gulag Archipelago,* was published for the first time in the Soviet Union in 1989 due to *glasnost,* Solzhenitsyn, unlike many other exiles, did not have his Russian citizenship returned, and *August 1914* will not, apparently, be published in his homeland. Considering the response of Soviet authorities to this book, it has been surmised that questioning the viability of socialism or the character of Vladimir Ilych Lenin, regarded as the founding father of the Soviet Union, is beyond the present limits of *glasnost*.

The new official openness threatens a common conception of the role of literature and the creative writer in Soviet society. Russian writers have traditionally produced socially responsible works that reflect the truth about life in their country as they know it. Additionally, under Soviet leadership, the creative writer felt obliged to reveal or allude to facts that had been suppressed from newspapers and histories. Since the advent of *glasnost,* however, many Soviet historians and ordinary citizens have taken this responsibility onto themselves, and the official histories are currently being rewritten to include heretofore unmentionable facts regarding the vast system of gulags or prison camps in the Soviet Union and other horrors of Stalin's reign. John Kohan noted: "The essential paradox of *glasnost* is that when cultural leaders raise their voices, they can no longer be heard above the excited babble of an entire nation learning to speak for the first time."

Many prominent writers, particularly those who came of age during the relaxation of regulations that occurred during the era of Premier Nikita Kruschev, use their status to promote *perestroika,* consequently neglecting their creative writing. Some have questioned the appropriateness of writing fiction

in this time of discovering historical facts. Others, particularly the younger generation, have abandoned the writer's traditional social duties; they are more interested in portraying subjective experiences and experimenting with non-realistic narrative techniques associated with modernism and post-modernism. However, since socially responsible literature has long been the norm in Russia, many authors are unsure of their proper subject and role in Soviet society as altered by *glasnost.* William Grimes remarked: "In a dictatorship, literature becomes the opposition, and writers become statesmen. . . . If Gorbachev opens his window to the West, the West of individual liberty and market competition, the Soviet writer will stand on the threshold of a frightening new world, one that offers him every opportunity to become, like his Western counterpart, a superfluous man."

PRINCIPAL WORKS DISCUSSED BELOW

NOVELS

Aitmatov, Chingis
  Plakha (The Execution Block)
Astafiev, Victor
  Sad Detective
Dudintsev, Vladmir
  White Coats
Granin, Daniil Aleksandrovich
  Zubr (The Aurochs; Bison)
Grossman, Vasily
  Life and Fate
Kabakov, Sasha
  The Man Who Would Not Come Back
L'vov, Arkady
  The Courtyard
Pasternak, Boris
  Doctor Zhivago
Rasputin, Valentin
  Pozhar (Fire)
Rybakov, Anatoly
  Children of the Arbat
Sokolov, Sasha
  A School for Fools
Solzhensitsyn, Aleksandr I
  August 1914: The Red Wheel, Knot I
Sorokin, Vladimir Dmitrievich
  The Queue
Trifonov, Yuri
  The Disappearance
  House on the Embankment
Vladimov, Georgii Nikolaevich
  The Faithful Ruslan

PLAYS

Buravsky, Alexandr
  Speak!
Ginzburg, Eugenia
  Journey into the Whirlwind
Kaledin, Sergei
  The Humble Cemetery (A Humble Graveyard)
Misharin, Alexandr
  Silver Wedding
Shatrov, Mikhail
  Tak pobedim! (shest' p'es o Lenine) (That's How We'll Win!
  [Six Plays About Lenin])

Diktatura sovesti (*The Dictatorship of the Conscience*)
  Brestkii mir (*The Brest Peace*)
Dal'she . . . Dal'she . . . Dal'she! (*Further . . . Further
  . . . Further!*)

OTHER MAJOR WORKS

Akhmatova, Anna
  Requiem (poetry)
Goscilo, Helena, ed.
  Balancing Acts: Contemporary Stories by Russian Women
Iskander, Fazil
  Sandro of Chegem (short stories)
Nove, Alec
  Glasnost' in Action: Cultural Renaissance in Russia (non-
    fiction)
Popov, Yevgeny
  Zhdu lyubvi ne verolomnoi (short stories)
Soviet/American Joint Editorial Board of the Quaker
    U.S./U.S.S.R. Committee, eds.
  *The Human Experience: Contemporary American and So-
    viet Fiction and Poetry.*
Tolstaya, Tatyana
  On the Golden Porch (short stories)
Tvardovsky, Alexandr Trifonovich
  By Right of Memory (poetry)
Zalygin, Sergei, comp.
  The New Soviet Fiction: Sixteen Short Stories

INTRODUCTION

MIKHAIL GORBACHEV

The intelligentsia has enthusiastically supported the restructuring [*perestroika*]. I will take the liberty of one digression
here. Dedicated to socialist values, the intelligentsia, an organic part of Soviet society with a deep sense of patriotism,
is our great and, perhaps, unique achievement, our inestimable spiritual capital. Our intelligentsia has had a difficult history. Many intellectuals, including democratically-minded
ones who censured the tsarist regime and even fought against
it, were frightened by the Revolution and were swept away
by the wave of white emigration abroad [those who emigrated
after the 1917 October Revolution and during the Russian
Civil War of 1918-22], where they gave their talent and
knowledge to other peoples. This was a great loss for our
fledgling Soviet society.

The intelligentsia, including intellectuals in the Bolshevik
Party, suffered enormous, at times irretrievable, losses because of violations of socialist legality and the repressions of
the 1930s. This, too, was a formidable blow to the country's
intellectual potential.

Nevertheless, the Soviet intelligentsia continued to form and
grow, mirroring the objective laws governing the development of socialism and its vital needs. The Leninist cultural
revolution ultimately turned our semi-literate and simply illiterate country into one of the most educated countries in the
world.

In the period of stagnation, however, a paradoxical situation
took shape in which our society was unable to adequately use

its enormous cultural and creative potential. Again, the reason was that the development of democracy had been artificially slowed down. All manner of bans, and a fear of new,
creative approaches could not fail to have their effect.

I recall a meeting in June 1986 with the personnel of the ap-
paratus of the CPSU Central Committee. It concerned perestroika. I had to ask them to adopt a new style of working
with the intelligentsia. It is time to stop ordering it about,
since this is harmful and inadmissible. The intelligentsia has
wholeheartedly welcomed the program for the democratic renewal of society.

Congresses of creative unions of film-makers, writers, artists,
composers, architects, theatrical figures and journalists have
been held. They were marked by heated debate. All the congresses sincerely supported perestroika. The participants severely criticized themselves; many former top union officials
were not elected to leading bodies, nor were the loudmouths.
Instead, eminent, authoritative people were elected to head
the unions.

I told those who found the debates too heated that they
should not be surprised or become indignant, that these congresses should be accepted as a normal, albeit new, phenomenon. Democratization is taking place everywhere, acquiring
acute forms at times. Someone objected, claiming that it
would be difficult to work in an environment where each individual is his own philosopher, his own foremost authority,
and believes that only he is right. I replied that it is far worse
to be dealing with a passive intelligentsia, and with indifference and cynicism.

Emotional outbursts are an inevitable part of any complicated endeavor. This has always been the case in revolutionary
times. Today it is as if we are going through a school of democracy again. We are learning. We still lack political culture. We do not even have the patience to hear out our
friends. All this is sure to pass. We will master this science,
too. The thorniest issues have to be discussed with due respect for one another. Even the most extreme viewpoint contains something valuable and rational, for the person who upholds it honestly and who cares for the common cause in his
own way reflects some real aspects of life. For us this is not
an antagonistic, class struggle; it is a quest, a debate on how
we can really get going with the restructuring effort and make
our progress solid and irreversible. So I don't see any drama
in polemics, in comparing viewpoints. This is normal.

Group prejudices and intolerance have indeed surfaced
among writers in view of the new openness. There was a moment when passions were running high in the literary community. We brought home to them the view of the Central
Committee, namely that it would be very sad if the creative
and artistic intelligentsia squabbled instead of consolidating,
and its members started using openness, frankness and de-
mocratism to settle old scores and take vengeance for criticism. The worst thing that can happen is if, in these revolutionary times, the creative intelligentsia allows itself to get
bogged down in trifles, if it gives vent to personal ambitions
and expends its energies on senseless high words rather than
creative endeavor. The Central Committee urged writers to
rise above their emotions, convenient habits and stereotypes.
Elevate yourselves and think of the people and society, we
said. Let the intelligentsia's sense of responsibility also manifest itself in its creative unions, taking care, above all, of society's spiritual development.

The intelligentsia is imbued with a sense of civic responsibility, and it has eagerly shouldered a large share of the restructuring effort. Our intelligentsia has, along with the Party, got down to change. Its public-spirited stand is manifesting itself more and more strongly, and we have a vested interest in this activity; we appreciate everything—the way it joined the effort after April 1985, its enthusiasm and its desire to help the restructuring of society. We hope that this contribution by the intelligentsia will continue to grow. The intelligentsia is rising to a new level of thinking and responsibility. Its guidelines coincide with the political course of the CPSU and the interests of the people. (pp. 80-3)

Mikhail Gorbachev, *"Perestroika Gets Under Way: The First Conclusions,"* in his Perestroika: New Thinking for Our Country and the World, *Harper & Row, Publishers, 1987, pp. 60-134.*

SOVIET THEATER UNDER *GLASNOST*

DAVID JORAVSKY

These nights in Moscow Peter Verkhovensky climbs out of a coffin-shaped trapdoor, comes down to the footlights, a greenish white face glistening against a darkened background, and harshly declaims the message of Dostoevsky's *Devils.* For the intensely silent Soviet audience it is closer to lived experience than to literary fantasy: revolutionary socialism achieves equality for nine tenths of the population by enslaving them to one tenth. Outstanding individual talents destroyed, obedience exalted above all other virtues, guilt shared in the denunciation and removal of suspect people—that is what makes everyone equal, ashamed to have his own belief. Conscience withers away.

The play is defiantly entitled *The Dictatorship of the Conscience.* The author, Mikhail Shatrov, wants to persuade the audience that conscience was sovereign in Lenin's "dictatorship of the proletariat," that it has never been lost in the hearts of good Soviet people, and will win its ultimate triumph over the monstrous values of Verkhovensky that Stalin built into the system. Shatrov has put that message not only in two controversial plays of the glasnost period but also in six earlier plays about Lenin. . . .

Shatrov's personal history taught him that love of Lenin requires denunciation of Stalin. In 1937, when he was five, his Communist father was arrested, secretly condemned, and shot; his uncle, A. I. Rykov, who had been premier of the Republic, was forced to revile himself at a show trial before he was taken back to prison and shot in the back of the head; his mother was arrested when Mikhail was seventeen and beginning to sense his vocation as a playwright. Stalinist mores permitted the offspring of such stock to train for nothing more than engineering, but he persevered and is now, at fifty-six, a major official of the Union of Theatrical Workers as well as the most influential and controversial playwright of the Gorbachev era.

A short, round man, with horn-rimmed glasses usually jammed up into his white hair, Shatrov delights some and alarms others by the increasingly radical bent of his historical

dramas, and by the modernist theatrical devices that point up the link between then and now, between the past reality enacted on stage and the present reality of the audience out front. (p. 34)

In *Further . . . Further . . . Further!* Shatrov's most recent play, . . . shocking speeches abound, delivered from the revolutionary left as well as the right. Rosa Luxemburg recites her 1918 letter from a German prison which hailed the Bolsheviks for overthrowing the old order, and predicted the new one:

Without general elections, without unrestricted freedom of the press and assembly, without a free struggle of opinions, life in every public institution dies out, becomes a mere appearance, and bureaucracy alone remains active. Public life gradually falls asleep; a few dozen extremely energetic and highly idealistic party leaders direct and govern; among them in reality a dozen outstanding leaders rule, and an elite of the working class is summoned to a meeting from time to time to applaud the speeches of the leaders and to adopt unanimously resolutions put to them. In essence this is the rule of a clique, and of course their dictatorship is not the dictatorship of the proletariat but the dictatorship of a handful of politicians. . . . Socialism without political freedom is not socialism. . . . Freedom only for active supporters of the government . . . is not freedom. Freedom is always and uniquely for those who think differently.

To this the stage Lenin of 1988 shouts "Bravo, Rosa!"—quite unlike the state-building Lenin of 1918, who denounced such talk as an opening for counter-revolution, while he assiduously built just such a system as Rosa described. Indeed he added mass terror and, by 1921, a formal ban on "opposition" even within the ruling party.

Each generation creates such pictures of the past as it needs for current purposes. The actual past confines and shapes that creative process, but Shatrov's imagination tries to break free. He claims that he has outgrown his initial fascination with the thought, "That did not happen, but it could have," but the change is in the devices he uses, not the imagination that controls them. He has come to use documents of the actual past to construct "a drama of facts"—so that the corpse in Red Square will rise more vividly from its confining monument to tell Soviet audiences what might have been: their great revolution did not have to generate "barracks socialism," a phrase of Marx's much in vogue these days. A free form of socialism could have emerged if Lenin had not had a stroke, and it will yet emerge if Soviet citizens resume the founding father's earnest quest for a system based upon a sense of moral worth *(chest'),* and on conscience *(sovest').*

"Every one of my plays," Shatrov insists, "*every one* was banned, and broke through [to publication and staging] with enormous difficulty." He made that proud complaint to a recent conference of historians and writers, which asked itself why imaginative writers like Shatrov have been leaders in the critical examination of Soviet history while professional historians have done worse than nothing. They have written whatever the current Party bosses have required. Worst of all: they have heaped evasions and dismissive formulas around the crucial topics that the bosses would rather not hear about, such as the successive waves of mass terror from 1918 to the early Fifties, the brutal realities of collectivization, and the stultification of cultural life. The system that has enforced such servility emerges vividly in a document that Shatrov quoted to the conference, a letter of January 27, 1982, demanding the suppression of his play *That's How We'll Win! (Tak pobedim!)*. The director of the Institute of Marxism-Leninism, A. G. Egorov, urged the chairman of the KGB, Yuri V. Andropov, not only to remove the play from the theater, but also to see to it that "appropriate ministries and offices close off all channels for the possible appearance of similar works." The heresy to be extirpated, Egorov said, was the replacement of "the real problem" that Lenin's revolution faced, how socialism was to be built in our country, by "a different, made-up problem: what kind of socialism should be built."

Evidently Andropov's KGB was willing to tolerate some discussion of alternative socialisms—glasnost did not spring from the brow of Gorbachev—for the play remained in the repertory of the Moscow Art Theater, where it is still put on about twice a month. Shatrov has never been one of those rebellious writers, like Sinyavsky or Solzhenitsyn, who knowingly transgress, most obviously by publishing abroad what Soviet bosses ban at home. He has wriggled out of one ban or another, staying within the official mentality at its left margin, stubbornly exploring the border where Soviet bosses distinguish between constructive criticism and intolerable desecration. He and his kind have been among the few refreshing features of Soviet history, a constantly renewed assortment of almost rebellious writers—or shall we call them licensed critics?—nudging an oppressive system toward reform.

Among them Shatrov made an astonishing choice of genre: the play about Lenin. In 1936 Stalin's Central Committee demanded that such plays be written to promote faith in the existing regime as the continuer of the founder's sacred cause. Displaying to the masses the holiest icon of the state church, plays about Lenin have been not only censored but picked apart and redesigned at the very highest level. Their best-known creator before Shatrov, Nikolai Pogodin, had to do updated versions to suit the bosses' changing moods. So the play about Lenin would seem a hopeless medium for a critic of the system's basic values, yet a potentially powerful medium, if any readiness for critical reflection can be found within official skulls.

To an outsider *That's How We'll Win!* (1981) seems hardly critical at all; it is much closer to a medieval passion play than to a modern drama of ideas. Lenin is shown in the months before his death in 1924, reviewing his incomplete mission, struggling to point his followers along the shining path, away from dark roads to some vaguely sketched perdition. He is painfully isolated among his leading disciples, none of whom comes near the absolute goodness and supreme wisdom that radiate from the great head. Humble members of "the people" appear as anonymous workers and peasants, with factual reports and lamentations that the master transforms into allegorical insights. He is not always gentle with "the people." Those who rose in rebellion against the Soviet state, in Kronshtadt most notably, and in Tambov province, he declares to be unwitting instruments of the reactionary devil, who must be put down with force, but also with rue. Shatrov's 1981 Lenin wrings his hands a bit as he builds the one-party state, but shows none of the liberalism that would appear in the Lenin of 1988. It is the suffering of the people and the inadequacy of his successors that he laments, not the one-party state or the denial of free expression to those who think differently.

One needs an insider's eye, perhaps even a watchdog's nose, to detect in *That's How We'll Win!* the discussion of alternative socialisms that provoked the director of Marxism-Leninism to demand suppression of the play. . . . I feel sure that Soviet audiences carry away from this play far more reverence than doubt about the system that calls itself Leninist. Yet embarrassing questions would occur to a thoughtful viewer. Lenin's chief comrades do not appear on the stage, but they are described, most notably in his notorious "testament," which found fault with each one and therefore, in the context of the play, comes to imply that none was worthy to take the founder's place. However gingerly, the play points to the problem of legitimacy in Soviet history. Most of Lenin's disciples were condemned in the Thirties; the condemners were condemned in the Fifties; and Khrushchev, who tried to "restore Leninist norms," was turned into a "blank spot" by *his* successors, who are now scorned by theirs. How is a thoughtful Soviet citizen to maintain faith in the continuity of Lenin's cause? What *was* his cause, which needs to be continually rescued from a procession of unnameable successors who have distorted and debased it?

Similar unanswered questions hang over *The Brest Peace,* one of Shatrov's oldest plays, yet also one of his newest. He wrote it in 1962, but could not publish or stage it until 1987, when it was one of the first sensations of glasnost. I therefore went to see it with some eagerness, shortly after I arrived in Moscow [in the spring of 1988]—and came away disappointed. What I saw was another exercise in Lenin worship, a celebration of the saintly leader isolated in rectitude among errant disciples. The twenty-five year suppression of the play expressed nothing more momentous than the slothful indecisiveness of Soviet ideological authorities. While they were dithering over the possible rehabilitation of Trotsky and Bukharin, Shatrov dared to show such non-persons as Lenin's comrades in the creation of the Soviet state. He did not, to be sure, present them as worthy comrades, who might deserve "political rehabilitation" as well as "civil." ("Civil rehabilitation" merely overturns the criminal frame-up. "Political rehabilitation" restores Party membership, and therefore involves legitimation of the dead man's political views and activities.) The Trotsky and Bukharin of *Brest Peace* are fools rather than miscreants; they are "caricatures," as Shatrov disconsolately told me in an interview. (pp. 34-5)

The Bukharin of *Brest Peace* is a likeable romantic youth, devoted to the "old man"—in 1918 Bukharin was twenty-nine to Lenin's forty-seven—but so caught up in a fuzzy dream of revolutionary glory that he obstinately opposes Lenin's realistic insistence on the need to sign a shameful surrender to Germany. That is the contested decision on which the drama is supposed to turn. Yet the author never allows the slightest doubt that Lenin was absolutely right, his comrades utterly wrong. The only dramatic tension comes from the obstacles that they foolishly put in his way—when and how will the hero triumph?—and from the anxiety that he still feels as he leaves the stage at the end. They may never prove capable of taking his place.

Shatrov missed an opportunity to dramatize the momentous turn of the Bolshevik mentality that came with the surrender to Germany only a few months after their triumph within Russia—a turn inward, a shift of revolutionary hope to emphasis on magical transformation of a peasant country, away from dreams of magical transformation in the international arena. They had seized power with the hope that the industrial workers of Germany would follow their revolutionary example and help backward Russia. But Germany remained implacably capitalist and imperial, requiring the Bolsheviks not only to admit defeat but to cede a huge amount of territory. Lenin's reasons for accepting the German *Diktat* foreshadowed Stalin's romantic vision of "socialism in a single country," while the stubborn refusal of the majority in the Central Committee—Lenin could get his way only by threatening to resign and cause a public split—anticipated the romantic vision that Trotsky would soon set against Stalin's. Trotsky would argue that socialism in one backward country would prove to be either impossible or monstrous, yet he would reject the logical inference, that the Communists should step down.

Those divisions were inherent in the Leninist strategy of a vanguard party making a socialist revolution in a peasant country. To read them as a contest between the all-knowing leader and his dim-witted disciples is to make a medieval melodrama of the Bolshevik Revolution, to imagine a saint's life in place of the modern nightmare from which revolutionaries in backward countries are trying to awake. Karl Marx used the metaphor of history as nightmare before James Joyce, but Soviet writers are not yet prepared to interpret their history that way.

Stalin supported Lenin in the arguments over the Brest treaty, but Shatrov gives him no credit for that. He pictures Stalin in 1918 as a fanatic of doglike obedience to the leader, whose only original thought is to conceive the Party as a military order, like the Knights of the Sword. . . . I agree with the critic in *Izvestiya* (December 26, 1987), whc thought that the "caricature" quality of Lenin's "comrades-in-arms" was an excusable fault in a play written in 1962. It was, he declared, "a breakthrough to our day," presumably because it broke the ban on mention of Trotsky and Bukharin as Lenin's comrades, and dramatized the need for a deeper understanding of the succession to Lenin. The critic was quite silent on what that understanding might be. Certainly he did not muse about nightmarish dilemmas inherent in Lenin's strategy.

At the beginning of **The Brest Peace** the highest Bolshevik leaders hurtle on stage as a gang, heads down, moving to the beat of loud discordant music. It is a frightening theatrical stroke that fits in with a young widow's bitter denunciation of a proletarian regime for bringing death to peasants and workers, and with laments by Gorky and Blok about the impending destruction of culture. But Shatrov swamps such alarming moments with speeches by Lenin that are reassuringly banal in content—revolutions can be destructive, but ours will be different—and in theatrical style. Indeed, all the political speechifying, which gives the play its bulk, keeps the audience within the conventions that are called realist or "socialist realist." The blanketed bundle in the young widow's basket, to take an especially ham-handed example, stays on stage interminably as a prop for Lenin's expatiations on the infant republic and its needs.

Such soothingly familiar show and tell brings the play to the edge of boredom, from which it is rescued, perhaps, by intermittent moments of modernist discord—by Trotsky's bizarre costumes, by startling montage of characters supposed to be far apart in "real" space and time, most notably by the repeated song-and-dance routine of a pair of *byvshie liudi* (*ci-devants*, former top dogs brought low by revolution). . . . Meaningful uses of clashing theatrical styles can hardly work to portray the Lenin that the Central Committee demanded.

A founding father without flaw, whose revolutionary principles were and remain divinely pure, can be made to seem real only if he consistently appears within the theatrical conventions that signal "reality" to the audience.

When I asked Shatrov why he deifies Lenin, he said he did not; he presented Lenin as a human being with faults. Hadn't I noticed that a love affair with the revolutionary leader Inessa Armand is intimated in **The Brest Peace?** I had, and thought that beside the point. But after all I was an outsider, lacking the long Soviet experience of stage Lenins, the insider's excited sense of divinity possibly compromised by any physical representation. Soviet viewers are startled to see this Lenin performed "without makeup," that is, with the three-piece suit but without the goatee, the mustache, and the fringe about the bald head that made previous Lenins look like the iconic photographs and paintings. Conservatives are further disturbed by this Lenin's violent shouting and vulgar words at moments of exasperation, and they have been revolted by a little stage business that is not called for in the published text. Imploring Trotsky to sign the peace treaty, Lenin falls to his knees—almost. Not even the vainglorious Trotsky can stand such a blasphemy and catches the master before his knees have touched dishonoring ground, promising to sign. (pp. 35-6)

Shatrov's two most recent plays have had an electric effect. They put into print and therefore on stage—on any stage in the Soviet Union where a director and the local bosses are willing to take advantage of the *nihil obstat* stamped on the plays in Moscow—ideas that had previously been locked in forbidden books or ventilated only in private conversations. The earlier of the two, **The Dictatorship of the Conscience** (1986), brings to historical topics the thrill of the moment when restraints are dropping away and it is fun to try out forbidden words in public. Shatrov imagines a newspaper staff at its periodic planning session, with the young people in revolt against the usual banalities and the cautious elders giving way to the demand for something new. A young woman has discovered, in a 1920 issue of *Pravda,* that theatrical groups used to stage a "trial of Lenin" as a way to win support for the revolution. She proposes to publish an updated version. Call to the stand the most serious witnesses against Lenin and his cause, she suggests, then call for cross examination and defense witnesses.

That is the playful context that permits the young journalists to summon Peter Verkhovensky from his Dostoevskian hell to shock a Soviet audience with his harsh sermon on enslavement as the inevitable result of socialist revolution, and then to come back, with reassuring wisecracks, to the "reality" of a goodnatured Soviet collective whose members discuss the moral values they all take for granted but find hard to square with their country's history. Wicked people are shown only in successive plays within the play, distanced from the nice people who are analyzing evil by performing imagined representations of it.

Divinity does not intrude through direct representation of Lenin, so worship interferes with thought much less than in Shatrov's other plays. The challenge that Verkhovensky gives to conventional Leninism, which evades the problem of tyranny following revolution, is reinforced by the French Communist André Marti. Wearing a semimilitary tunic and a mane of black hair that recall Stalin, he gives a chilling matter-of-fact lecture on discipline as the supreme goal of the revolution; arbitrary arrest and punishment are the indispensable way to get such discipline. A janitor comes on mocking at democracy and praising the Soviet state, for he admires officials who win reverence for themselves by showing a total power of life or death over their subjects.

Each skit requires a journalist to transform himself into an imagined witness, so the play becomes a contest in acting skills. The audience especially appreciates a virtuoso representation of an old Bolshevik caught in extortion and bribe-taking back in the Twenties. He gives a private, down-to-earth explanation of his change from a dedicated revolutionary to a venal despot, and then a public speech to the court, confessing the intolerable disgrace he has done to the cause and asking execution, by his own hand, as the only way he can make amends. Shatrov's published text does not suggest how that self-sacrificing vindication of the Leninist cause can be made to fit with the private explanation of the crime: the victory of the Revolution gave the old Bolshevik an irresistible taste for power, which he intensified by taking money that subjects felt obliged to give him.

A stroke of theatrical genius solved the problem of fit. The old Bolshevik gives the private explanation extempore, persuasively, and then reads his public speech from a piece of paper, in the style of Leonid Brezhnev. He puts on the distinctive spectacles and the debilitated pompousness, stumbles over phrases, goes back to get them right, intermittently pauses to cough, roll the phlegm about, and swallow with a little satisfied smack. Of course, after that comic turn it hardly made sense to send him off with a pistol. But the offstage shot was a ludicrous little pop, and the actor came right back to resume his role as a journalist, pausing to acknowledge a happy ovation. Vaudeville had taken the place of tragedy, and why not? Tragic dignity hardly becomes a venal despot, or Leonid Brezhnev, and public confessions of crimes are ripe for mockery. Reformers have been publishing shocking reports of legal officials who routinely assume that their job is to win convictions by forcing confessions from the accused.

The Dictatorship of the Conscience has not provoked a conservative outcry, though the defense of Leninism is much less effective than the prosecution. The play gives Soviet conservatives the formulaic reassurance they require. Verkhovensky is obliged to admit that he is not an authentic socialist but a confidence man *(moshennik),* and no one asks whether the change of label alters the force of his sermon on equality achieved through enslavement. Similarly with André Marti; counsel for the defense of Leninism gets him to admit that he was expelled from the French Communist party, and no one raises questions of when and why and with what relevance to the Leninist use of terror. Those shallow rebuttals are very close to traditional Communist talk of "alien elements" in revolutionary movements, a formula of dismissal that evades the difficult historical question: Why did Lenin's Party, on coming to power, fall so completely and for so long under the control of such "alien elements" as Stalin? *The Dictatorship of the Conscience* avoids that question. It is content with the usual formula of traditional churches: a pure faith is not corrupted by the impure creatures who may profess it. Christ is not tainted by Torquemada.

The purity of the Leninist faith is attested by witnesses for the defense, who simply ignore such characteristically Leninist notions as democratic centralism or the one-party state. They ignore even the dictatorship of the proletariat, which has turned into the dictatorship of the conscience without a word of explanation. Shatrov makes much of a young girl

who wrote a letter to the Communist Youth paper lamenting the cynicism and corruption that prevail in her branch of the organization, and swearing that she will not quietly submit. (pp. 37-8)

For more than thirty years [Shatrov] has been trying to explain how revolutionary action against indignity and oppression could have led to enormously intensified indignity and oppression. In his most recent play he has finally broached the most obvious, yet the most taboo question within such inquiry: Was Lenin to blame? Did his revolution set Russia on the way to Stalin's system?

Without seeing *Further . . . Further . . . Further!* on the stage—it had not yet opened in Moscow when I was obliged to leave—I cannot be sure that I know the play's response. The published text is a sprawling mass of speeches strung along a melodramatic story line. It will undoubtedly be streamlined in close interaction with a director and a company of actors, with keen awareness of the extensive press reaction pro and con, which the play has been getting since its publication in January. I take it for granted that some of the highest Party officials have been or will be involved in the final result, if only by appearing at an early performance, as they did last year to signify approval of *Brest Peace.* Where art leaves off and politics begins in the theatrical representation of Lenin is still hard to say, even for the author no doubt.

The melodramatic story of the new play moves through a single day, October 24, 1917. On the next day, as every Soviet schoolchild knows, the Provisional Government will be overthrown and the Bolsheviks will get the Congress of Soviets to proclaim itself the sovereign power of Russia (with the Bolshevik party as the real sovereign within the Soviets). On October 24 Lenin is still in hiding by order of his Party's Central Committee, because the Provisional Government has ordered his arrest. He is furious at the Committee's other, unspoken reason for keeping him away from Party headquarters at Smolny. His disciples want to put off the insurrection until the Congress of Soviets votes for it. They are timid and legalistic, fearful that a Bolshevik insurrection may fail if it openly tries to preempt the people's will. Lenin knows that delay is "utter idiocy or utter treachery," for a cabal of generals is preparing to seize Petrograd, to crush the armed masses, and thus to start Russia toward a monstrous dictatorship of the right. (The detailed intentions of the generals sound just like Stalin's methods of rule.) By the middle of the night Lenin has become convinced that there is only one way to avoid such a disaster. In violation of the Party's order he sets out for Smolny, to take direct command of the insurrection. It will therefore occur immediately and will succeed. The Bolsheviks will start Russia toward socialism, away from a monstrous dictatorship of the right.

The Western reader who wants to check that story has a variety of histories to consult, with diverse interpretations that draw on a commonly available fund of sources. Soviet readers have been imprisoned for more than fifty years within an official interpretation that requires suppression of crucial sources and vital facts. Shatrov's new play startles such readers by breaking some of the taboos. Trotsky, for example, is permitted to challenge the story that pictures him as trying to avoid the insurrection that, in fact, he was organizing. As head of the Military Revolutionary Committee of the Petrograd Soviet, he was already seizing telegraph offices and train stations when Lenin arrived at Smolny to urge the troops on to the Winter Palace. But Shatrov's Trotsky is not permitted to say that. He is pinned to his public denials, during the days of mounting insurrection, that he was organizing anything more than a defense against the counter-revolution. Those words are used to convict him of being as confused as the Mensheviks by anarchic turmoil, on his way with them to the ashcan of history, when Lenin stepped in to give Communist shape to the Russian Revolution.

So the Soviet reader gets the excitement of previously forbidden debate *and* the reassurance of the standard version, which raises the October Revolution, the founding act of the Soviet state, above messy politics. Lenin, virtually alone, led the people to self-rule. Anything unfortunate in the aftermath can be blamed on the incompetent and unreliable band of disciples who almost obstructed his way in 1917 and really did so after 1922, when a stroke removed him from effective control. (pp. 38-9)

That saint and sinners story of the high command within the revolutionary Party is hardly an advance beyond *Brest Peace* and *That's How We'll Win!* It is still an exercise in Lenin worship (and Stalin loathing) rather than a serious confrontation with the history of the Bolshevik Revolution. What raises [*Further . . . Further . . . Further!*] to a higher level of historical discourse are the frequent interruptions of the one-day melodrama, when everyone pauses to ponder its long-term consequences. Lenin and his disciples, and a variety of critics from outside their Party, step out of their 1917 roles to debate what would actually ensue and why. They know as much as we do of the actual consequences down to the present day, and refuse to be sidetracked by the usual concentration of Soviet histories on the buildup of heavy industry, the victory over the Germans, the transformation of Russia into a superpower. They want most of all to explain why the Stalinist system of rule emerged out of the Leninist revolution.

In this exchange of opinions Lenin is not always the all-knowing deity of old. There seem in fact to be two or three Lenins on stage. In addition to the 1917 Lenin, who is furiously eager to present the Congress of Soviets with the unalterable fact of Bolshevik rule, there is a liberal Lenin of retrospective wisdom, who sees the dangers of one-party rule, the benefit of restraining those in power with rival parties, free discussion, and elections. And there is a self-questioning Lenin, who declares that he shares responsibility for the emergence of Stalinist tyranny, and finally fails to separate himself from Stalin. At the close of the play, as the other historical characters leave the stage one after another, Lenin stands waiting to be alone with the audience, to tell us something of vital importance. But Stalin will not leave, though Lenin shouts that they have nothing more to say to each other. Standing in their separate silences they are both still there as the curtain falls.

A skillful director might conceivably play up the discordant shifts from one Lenin to another, to bring out the multiple possibilities of Leninism for good and ill, but I doubt that will happen. It would be too drastic a break with the traditional faith in Leninism as a pure doctrine of revolutionary goodness, which is the major emphasis of the published text and probably will be so in the actual staging. The excitement that the play has caused rises not so much from Lenin's declaration that he too must be criticized as from the presentation of vigorous critics to do the job. Shatrov has "given the stage to our enemies," as the conservatives say, or presented an array of previously forbidden views of Soviet history, as the reformers say. . . .

[In *Further . . . Further . . . Further!*] Shatrov has presented a Lenin of superficial sentiments, not of deep thought, whether about the sources of the moral feelings that keep people in some semblance of community or about the institutional checks and balances that might minimize the harm people can do to one another regardless of their intentions. When this Lenin is pressed about the despotic consequences of his revolution, he argues that they would not have ensued if his successors had been wiser and more virtuous. (The one specific fault he takes upon himself is his failure to get Stalin out of the post of general secretary.) When pressed harder, he falls back for his ultimate justification on what is yet to come. Past is only prologue. The beneficence of his revolution can be discovered only by getting on with it, by pressing it "further . . . further . . . further!"

The deity that calls Soviet people to that task is definitely not the old-time god of socialist wrath who must be served no matter how sorely he afflicts his worshipers. He may be the god of the sweet by-and-by, who'll give you socialist pie in the sky when you die. But there is another possibility. The Lenin of Shatrov's most recent play may be another prophet of an increasingly commonplace twentieth-century world, where existence precedes essence and the nature of an authentically human state cannot be known in advance of efforts to create it, efforts that are therefore burdened with a terrible risk of doing more harm than good. That is a possible reading of the drama that has Lenin set out for Smolny with foreknowledge of the disaster that may ensue, yet determined to proceed because he knows—or thinks—that inaction will guarantee disaster. A Lenin of that sort might be conducive to deep thinking about the first Communist revolution of our century, but not a Lenin who dwells on purity of heart as the justification of action and the sweet by-and-by as its reward.

It is the saccharine Lenin of the sacred heart who will probably dominate the actual staging of the play. Most of the text points that way, and so does the present climate of opinion in the Soviet Union. Deep thinking about the past would probably be disruptive of present efforts at reform. They require an intellectually shallow consensus, for they must achieve cooperation among highly diverse interest groups and clashing ideological constituencies. "A normal civilized life" is the phrase that echoes in current Soviet talk of reform as the handiest little description of the goal. The Lenin of 1917 would have dropped dead of astonished dismay, I think, if the spirit of the 1988 Lenin had appeared to him on the way to Smolny. But my imagination is that of a bookish outsider, who has not been obliged to live with the consequences of the first Lenin's revolutionary leap from the realm of necessity toward the realm of freedom. (p. 39)

David Joravsky, "Glasnost Theater," in The New York Review of Books, *Vol. XXXV, No. 17, November 10, 1988, pp. 34-9.*

WILLIAM A. HENRY III

In a long-suppressed and now acclaimed production of Dostoyevsky's *Notes from Underground* at Moscow's Theater for Young Spectators, the withdrawn and embittered central character repeatedly pushes with all his might against the immovable proscenium arch at the side of the stage. The gesture is an apt visual metaphor not only for a melancholy nobody's passion to smash the barriers of loneliness but also for the yearning of the whole Moscow drama world to break down the confines of habit and tradition. Everywhere one goes in the theater these days, the same artistic self-criticism is heard: there are almost no vibrant new playwrights or imaginative directors, the basic style and format of productions have not changed in the past quarter-century, beauty and splendor have been forgotten.

In fact the quality of theater in Moscow is very high. Playwriting, if at times too grandiosely spiritual, at least concerns itself with bigger issues than middle-class marriage, the preoccupation of the commercial stage in the West. . . .

Having justified itself for two decades and more as a medium of political expression—obliquely during the Brezhnev years, sometimes rantingly during the current thaw—the Soviet stage sees itself as needing to rediscover its true concern, the human soul. Audiences apparently agree. While theatergoers continue to clap for lines of topical invective, they seem to respond most strongly to intimate glimpses of lost love, betrayal by friends and alcoholic desperation, whether in Chekhov's *Uncle Vanya* at the Moscow Art Theater or in quasi-documentary scripts about prostitutes and gravediggers performed by the city's most impressive acting troupe, the Sovremennik (Contemporary) Theater. Says Konstantin Raikin, artistic director of the Satirikon Theater, where the Russian-language debut of Jean Genet's psychosexual drama *The Maids* is Moscow's hottest show and among the least political: "These days, a measure of a play's appeal is to be able to say that it's not *only* about *perestroika.*"

Relevance is certainly the least of the virtues of *The Maids,* which features men in eye makeup and flamboyant drag playing women. The aggressive gender bending, laced with homoeroticism, brings spectators in for the scandal value but sends them out having seen a world-class display of theatrical wit and invention. Just as Genet speculatively derived his sadomasochistic rituals from an actual news story of a murderous plot by two maids against their mistress, so director Roman Viktyuk subordinates the text to an evocative extravaganza about sex and power, seduction and display. Within the script he finds moments both of striking visual imagery (two chairs and a long red dress abruptly become a casket) and of serene reliance on the words (Raikin, motionless and in shadow, performs a long lament in a hypnotic near monotone). (p. 112)

Austere and philosophical where *The Maids* is lavish and sensual, *Notes from Underground* typifies more conventional Soviet staging at its best. The set looks like a rummage sale in a czarist attic. The dimly lighted action features recurring glimpses of a grinning peasant, a swanking bureaucrat, a howling madman. A virtual monologue in its first half, the piece evokes the wounded vanity and urge toward vengeance of the sort of man who nowadays might become a serial killer. Yet in the mind of director Kama Ginkas, who has been developing his adaptation for some 20 years despite official disapproval, both his version and the Dostoyevsky original comment on "the inevitable alienation resulting from extremes of socialism, the drive to violence underlying the pursuit of universal happiness." Westerners will more likely find the show a poignant portrait of one of life's losers, but every phrase rings true.

At the richly talented Sovremennik, which seems on balance

Moscow's most interesting theater, the men of the company dominate *A Humble Cemetery,* a melodrama about the travails of ordinary workingmen, while the women adorn *Stars in the Morning Sky,* a lament of the cleanup campaign that swept prostitutes, drunks and the deranged off the streets just before visitors arrived for the 1980 Olympics. Both plays combine the hortatory, sentimental style of Stalinist social realism with a topical disregard for those in power. . . .

In Sergei Kaledin's *A Humble Cemetery,* the pressures on the hulking workman Sparrow include a legacy of family violence, a stretch in a work camp, virtual gangsterism in the cemetery where he works as a gravedigger, and a dangerous weakness for vodka. . . .

[The] most memorable scenes show Sparrow alone with his cacophony of fears, climbing arduously up to a bell tower where he can hear the euphony of wind and birds and a distantly remembered lullaby, until a screeching train cuts off his reverie. Emotive yet astringent, these are moments worthy of Charles Laughton in a play sometimes deserving of comparison with Gorky's *The Lower Depths.* If Soviet theater remains for the most part an art in search of significant new voices, in this play and production it has found one. (p. 115)

William A. Henry III, "Voices from the Inner Depths," in Time, *New York, Vol. 133, No. 15, April 10, 1989, pp. 112, 115.*

MIKHAIL SHVIDKOI

One of last year's typical questions among theater critics was, "Perestroika has been going on for almost four years in Soviet society. It is being reinforced by principles of democracy and glasnost. Why, then, does theater remain silent? Why doesn't it respond to events happening today and in the recent past? Why doesn't it try to ride the wave of today's reality, which has never been more dynamic?"

Perhaps this long and therefore clumsy question doesn't include all the complaints that have been lodged against recent theater. But it certainly voices the most relevant ones. The type of thinking expressed here is not new. It stems from a vulgar-bureaucratic approach to art, one which has reigned in our social traditions and ideas about the relationship of art to reality. . . .

Let us try to make sense of this.

Both during the Khrushchev "thaw" and the Brezhnev-era "stagnation," theater existed under the "most favorable conditions" of any art form. The "conditions" were not artificially created by anyone: the general ideological guidelines and limitations applied to theater as much as they did to other art forms. However, due to the nature of this improvisational art which was created "here and now," the libertine spirit was always close at hand. Besides, theater as an art form is sufficiently limited in its access to the public, compared to other mass media forms. Topics prohibited for the general media were permitted theater.

There was no great logic behind this, by the way. A filmmaker might be told "no," yet certain hints about events during the era of the "Stalin personality cult" might still have slipped through, whereas in theater this subject was categorically prohibited. Today it is understood that theater was a type of island of freedom on which, even if things could not be said, they could be stated with such expressive silence that this silence had a great effect on the public. The era of social renewal in the mid-50s after the 20th Congress of the Communist Party of the Soviet Union promoted a number of serious theater personalities, people who had reason to call themselves "children of the 20th Party Congress." (p. 7)

Theater, as befitting ancient Russian traditions, stood at the epicenter of socio-political life in the 50s-70s. Each play became a type of political statement. As a rule, these were the most free expressions that were allowed in theater at that time. But since theatrical expression was far from unconstrained, by the mid-80s playwrights, directors, and actors had stored up many things that they wished to express.

After March-April 1985, when the course for renovation won out in our country (I must emphasize the revolutionary nature of the renewal of our society's existence), theater—by all previous standards—turned out to be fully prepared for the task. Even the press, television, and radio needed some time for their own perestroika. Theater, it seemed, needed no such reconstruction. It is enough to compare the critical stance of such plays as Alexandr Misharin's *Silver Wedding* staged by Oleg Yefremov (the Moscow Art Theater, autumn of 1985), Alexandr Buravsky's *Speak!* (based on Valentin Ovechkin's prose work) staged by Valery Fokin (at the Yermolova Theater in Moscow, December 1986) or Mark Zakharov's stage version of Mikhail Shatrov's *Dictatorship of Conscience* (at the Leninskii Komsomol Theater in Moscow, March 1986) to what was printed on the pages of news publications to see that my statement needs no further evidence. The work and pronouncements of government leaders, above all Mikhail Gorbachev, were marked by ground-breaking concepts that set the tone for perestroika by pointing out the dramatic impossibility of continuing along the same path as before: the country's fate was being decided.

The plays of late 1985-early 1986 were a sort of paraphrases of these speeches. They expressed the pain that had accumulated over decades of silence. They did so hurriedly, sacrificing artistic imagery as a result. Priority was given to the need for speaking directly to the point, unequivocally, discarding the practice of silence, allegory, and metaphor—even going overboard into prophesy. The need for immediate expression, a timely reaction to the events underway in the country in late 1985-early 1986, took precedence over all other needs. Otherwise one could lose the audience's trust. (pp. 7-8)

In the mid-80s, those artists who were most sensitive to current life headed towards the border between art and reality. They were prepared to cross the boundaries dividing life and its artistic incarnation. They did so in the name of life, their fellow countrymen, the direct good and righteousness. "And here art ends; here breathe the soil and fate." Boris Pasternak's lines are like a tuning fork, a criterion of the meaning inherent in this incessant readiness on the part of art to dissolve itself into daily existence, blend in with it while making it richer. The death of art should evoke nothing less out of life than heavy sighs from the soil and fate. Commonplace anger won't suffice.

It is important to note that the above-mentioned plays as well as several others that were staged in various regions throughout the country in the mid-80s were hardly your typical made-to-order productions. None of the new artists tried to please the new leaders. The ideas behind all of these productions were born before March 1985 as part of the natural artistic development of both playwrights and directors who did

not even suspect the kinds of historical events that transformed the entire country's existence. I would like to note that the appearance of *The Silver Wedding, Speak!*, . . . or *Dictatorship of Conscience* occurred in a time that was still brimming with conflict. The opponents of perestroika and new approaches to culture did everything in their power to get in the way of these works being staged before the public. We should therefore not view their appearance as the outcome of a new political line. The best plays tried to understand current events from a historical perspective. By attempting to connect the past to the present, they sought to delve into the future.

But already by late 1986, the theater had begun to exist in a new and unfamiliar context: magazines were full of Russian literary works from the accumulated body of emigré writing and Soviet literature previously unpublished in the USSR. Writers and journalists entered into the literary and social spheres with bold, profound works that began setting the tone in culture and politics. The daily press became something of an anchor for the perestroika forces. It resembled an opposition of sorts, one that tore down the unanimity to which we had become accustomed. By 1985-86 some critics felt as if the theater was discovering another quality in itself. By 1987 it became clear to most that the plays released a year before had in fact gone through a lengthy period of development in the country's theatrical culture that began in the mid-50s. (p. 9)

By the mid-80s the Soviet Union had 640 state theaters representing 54 national cultures. All of these theaters, from those in capitals to the ones in small towns, received constant state subsidies which varied by category (from academic theaters to the Category Three group that was located in towns with 20,000-50,000 inhabitants). These subsidies were lowered throughout the sixties and seventies since funds allocated to culture were not a priority in the state budget. Theaters did not have the right to make independent decisions about either their repertoire or their soio-economic concerns. Every play included in the repertoire required approval from the cultural organ with which the theater was affiliated (ranging from the USSR Ministry of Culture to the cultural departments of cities or regions).

A broad public discussion led to the beginning of an experiment that commenced on January 1, 1987 and included almost 100 theaters around the country. It radically changed the principles guiding the theater's existence. Initially the conditions governing the experiment contained quite a few protective limitations, but in practice these were cast aside. The Union of Theater Workers, a new cultural union, played a significant role in the experiment's radicalization. The Union was voluntarily created by people working in theater in place of the theater societies of each Republic. The oldest of these, the All-Russian Theatrical Society, had been in existence for over a hundred years and played an important role as a charitable organization for theater professionals. Yet it was nevertheless subservient to the Ministry of Culture and did not fight for the most important issue among those for which it was responsible, namely the creative freedom and social independence of theater professionals.

During the All-Union Theater Society congress in the fall of 1986 a decision was made to establish the Union, which was charged with dealing with all matters concerning theater in the country *along and equal with* state cultural organs. It would also have veto power over any unauthorized decisions (from the theater community's perspective) pertaining to the art of drama. After some discussion and debate the USSR Union of Theater Workers was founded in late 1986. Its primary objective was the defense of theater workers' creative and social rights.

The Union's establishment set the tone for the democratization of the country's theater life and stimulated the development of the studio movement. Small professional and semi-professional groups that had led an unofficial and essentially illegal existence until the mid-80s acquired real possibilities for normal artistic work. In Moscow alone there are currently over 100 studio theaters alongside the 35 state theaters. The nationwide figure goes up to 3,000. It is interesting to note—and this is also an indicator of new social tendencies—that no one can give an exact figure for the number of studios existing in the country: they arise and dissolve after staging one play, or else are reborn.

The transition to democracy is not simple. And today we sense the lack of democratic skills and the culture of democracy. Therefore we note how in the work of creative unions "no equals no"—i.e., they employ methods borrowed from ministerial bureaucrats. The positive results, however, are obvious. All of the country's theaters obtained the right to manage their own creative affairs without any interference from the organs of culture as of January 1, 1988. Beginning in 1989, they adopted new business management principles guaranteeing financial independence (while maintaining constant state subsidies).

Theatrical activity has become noticeably more lively: the past four years have seen many new festivals, drama performances and artistic competitions. These include international ones such as the festival of one-act plays, the festival of the best plays based on the work of A.P. Chekhov, and others. The broad studio movement anticipated these competitions, which play such an important role in their artistic practice. (pp. 9-10)

After the launching of a perestroika in theater, certain voices were heard asking, "But where are the masterpieces? Why is it that after four years of unconstrained activity the theater has produced fewer outstanding plays?" It appears as if some of my colleagues are beginning to create a theory about how the quality of theater was better during the stagnation period and, consequently, would it not be better to revert to the administration of art.

Let's not turn back the clock. And along with that we will try to understand the social function of theater today, in 1989.

Our attitude towards culture and art is obviously undergoing a readjustment. Literature and art have always been the arena for political struggle in Russia. This was due to the strict regulation of the population and the lack of civil society, which did not exist in either the 18th or the 19th centuries. Literary groups and factions possessed a definite social character since literary conflicts were most often expressions of social conflict. This created a certain type of artistic thinking. The words of the famous Russian poet Nekrasov—"You need not be a poet, but you are obliged to be a citizen!"—were expressed in various ways in the world of Russian literature, thereby symbolizing one's own approach towards culture. In those rare instances in history like the early 1900s, when the political struggle entered the realm of social life, new artistic currents were born in Russia. These did not, in fact, have anything in common with art for art's sake in the Western sense. Russian art has always been linked with reality and social struggle, even when, during the era of Stalin and Zhdanov's "cultural concepts," it shamelessly engaged in "glossing over reality."

The sharp transformation of social and political realities during the mid-1980s touched a certain nervous chord in our country. Social practice began taking on democratic and legal forms while political life was granted liberties about which one could hardly dream in the past. Literature and art lost their century-old priority. If someone needed to express his world-view, his opinions on society or politics, he did not need to write a play or novel. Instead he could express his opinion like a person in any democratic society through a newspaper article, on a TV program, or by organizing a demonstration. Leading cultural figures have never played the role of commentator as much as they did during the past three years. (pp. 10-11)

It is no coincidence that after 1986 the majority of the leading theatrical maestros, both directors and playwrights, "paused to look around." A number of leading playwrights, namely A. Gelman, I. Drutse, E. Radzinsky, M. Roshchin and several others, did not publish a single new play during the past three years. Writers from the so-called "new wave," people who made their debut in literature during the second half of the 70s (A. Galin, A. Kazantsev, S. Zlotnikov, L. Petrushevskaya, L. Razumovskaya, V. Arro, and others) also lived off of their old reserves. Even directors, who are obliged to stage productions regularly because they are linked to the actors of their troupes, called their own version of a "time out."

It is only during the new 1988-1989 season that they have become active again. The leading directors of the Soviet stage are however staging classics, and more actively than ever before. The plays of A. N. Ostrovsky, and A. P. Chekhov, staged versions of F. M. Dostoevsky's novels, the "minor classics" (Merezhkovskii and Sologub) from the turn of the century, Soviet classics by Platonov and Bulgakov that were banned for many years, emigré literature and drama, an inseparable part of Russian literature—Nabokov, Kuz'mina-Karavaeva, Evreinov and others—these are the things that currently interest directors and theaters wishing to rise above "today's topical issues." They are striving to develop new artistic and philosophical currents, create a new language, and find a new place for themselves in society's cultural life by engaging in a dialogue with the classics. This does not at all mean that Soviet theater has embarked upon a course of breaking with reality, a style of pure form. I am convinced that it is not facing any such threat since art continues to preserve its most important function: pondering the meaning and nature of life.

There is so much that we have not openly considered, that literature and art—dramatic arts included—face unprecedented opportunities. It is quite obvious, however, that as "the poet's imagination" (to employ Osip Mandelstam's term) turns away from the topical issues of the day, it focuses on trying to understand the eternal questions of mankind's existence. It is precisely these things, and not only elements of political consciousness, that served as the impetus for Mark Zakharov when he staged Ostrovsky's comedy, *Plenty of Simplicity for Every Wise Man,* and Garri Chernyakhovsky when he put on his version of Mikhail Bulgakov's *Zoya's Apartment* at the Vakhtangov Theater, Yuri Yeryomin in his work on *The Possessed* by Camus and Dostoevsky, or Valery Fokin's production of Vladimir Nabokov's *Invitation to an Execution.* This does not mean that our country's theater has given up trying to understand contemporary life. But the way in which it is approached has become more complicated and tense in a philosophical sense. This is no guarantee against mistakes and failures. But a new attempt at a dialogue with the classics, of course, is grounds for hope. For it is here that one clearly sees a new courage in comprehending the fundamental problems of human life.

The appearance of a new group of young playwrights seeking out their path in literature also instills hope. They really are young: the youngest, Dmitrii Lipskerov, is under 25, while the eldest, Vladimir Malyagin, is barely 35. At first glance it seems as if they and their work exist outside the current times and that the stormy developments of society's revolutionary renewal have passed them by. But this is not so. They are trying to comprehend the internal dramatic nature of modern life and express the profound intimate processes at work within the spiritual lives of the people who surround them.

Young playwrights have a difficult enough time in theater. Even their peers in the studio youth theaters (not to speak of older directors) prefer to stage classical works today. But I am convinced that these talented playwrights (one ought to mention Alexei Shipenko, Alexandr Seplyarsky, Felix Sarnov and others) will find a way out of this difficult situation. They will do it just as assuredly as Vitaly Pavlov, a contemporary of theirs and one of the most popular young playwrights. He began staging his own plays; his directors' debut was at the New Stage of the Moscow Art Theater, where he presented his play, *I Built a House,* a drama about the relations between different generations.

We often hear the following formula used in reference to literature and art: "Literature and art are lagging behind life." I think it is time to understand that the formula itself is inaccurate. There is no direct competition between life and art. Their links are extremely complex and, more likely than not, quite dramatic. We should be glad that in the mid-80s we did not see the appearance of a large number of neoconjectural works about "perestroika, democratization, and glasnost" like the plays that appeared in the 60s or 70s in line with other types of campaigns. People in theater acutely sense that the current social transformation is not a temporary campaign: what we are talking about is a radical reconstruction of our entire existence. So they're not in a hurry to "reflect" reality and, in this paradoxical manner, preserve the honor of drama and theater.

When the wonderful Soviet writer Yuri Olesha spoke at the 1st Congress of Soviet Writers in 1934, he noted that during a time of revolutionary and unusually dynamic transformations in life, the writer should think slowly. It appears as if today's writers are heeding this wise master's advice. (pp. 11-12)

Mikhail Shvidkoi, "The Effect of Glasnost: Soviet Theater from 1985 to 1989," translated by Vladimir Klimenko, in Theater, *Vol. XX, No. 3, Fall, 1989, pp. 7-12.*

ALEXEI ALTAYEV

[A] new era is fermenting in the blood supply of Soviet theater today. It is a time of acute contradictions, passionate de-

bates, reform and hope. Like some magical crystal ball, the theater reflects the processes that have encompassed our society; the life of the theater becomes a miniature model of society as a whole. Although it spans a smaller terrain, the theatrical world contains a mixture of the most relevant alternatives currently facing society: creative freedom or the exaltation of necessity, democracy or arbitrariness, self-government or orders from above, initiative or bureaucratic regulations, economic methods of management or the administrative chain of command. One can also convincingly argue that the future of Soviet theater will depend to a large degree on the outcome of perestroika.

If we are going to speak about the past, then the theater occupied a role and place of utmost importance in the history of Russian culture. It was hardly limited to its visual and entertainment aspects. In the past, stage art had a very powerful impact on the social consciousness of its contemporaries. It stimulated thought and evoked a social pathos. This was the distant source of a widely-accepted concept in Russia about theater as "a podium from which good can be said to the world," (Gogol) or as a "social work of broad spiritual significance" (Sumbatov-Yuzhin), or as fulfilling "basic spiritual needs" (Shalyapin). One journalist at the end of the last century closely compared the Moscow theater season's effort to the resonance produced by a parliamentary session in a major West European capital.

Such a high level of esteem for theater among the public eventually evolved into a unique ritual of worshipping the stage— the space where the power lines of social interests intersected and the artistic tastes of several generations became crystallized. This tradition to a large degree predetermined the central role of theater in early Soviet culture shortly after the October Revolution. It was no coincidence that one of the new government's first proclamations in the realm of art was Lenin's decree "on the unification of the theatrical business" which resolved to allocate government subsidies to all artistically-qualified theaters. And theatrical art of the 1920s, which gathered the era's best spiritual forces under its banner, still continues to boggle the imagination with its brilliant fireworks of artistic ideas, innovations, and names.

Perhaps that was indeed the essence of the drama in theatrical consciousness during subsequent decades (a drama that still exists today), a consciousness whose ideals of theater-as-church, theater-as-podium, and theater-as-sacred art form coincided less and less with the catastrophically-changing reality. The establishment of Stalin's absolutism brought with it limitations on and, at times, the destruction of free art forms that did not conform with the ideas of "the leader of all nations" and his cronies. A plethora of normative culture praising the society of triumphant socialism and the one man who inspired all of those victories transformed the theatrical landscape into a desert as far as the eye could see, making theater depressing and boring. Only classic plays produced on the Soviet stage—provided they did not infringe upon the official foundations—had a chance of partially withstanding these destructive tendencies.

The interference of officials "from the arts" into all spheres of the theatrical business, from the artistic side all the way to finances and production, became more and more aggressive. The theater repertoire, the company's composition, its income and expenses, salaries, the number of performances and new productions, the company's travel itinerary—all of this was strictly regulated and precisely recorded in a certain sacred document known as the "Plan." Strict implementation of the Plan was thoroughly enforced by these same officials; any deviation resulted in immediate punishment by a deprivation of prizes, verbal reprimands, firings, and—during the worst of times—possibly even arrest. (p. 18)

It is surprising that under such conditions, in which the bureaucratic persecution machine made such a lengthy, concerted effort, new flowers of theatrical creativity somehow miraculously managed to emerge. The famous ten-year period beginning in the mid-50s yielded a particularly rich harvest. The powerful energy of social renewal stemming from that period's thaw gave our culture a significant number of wonderful beginnings in prose, poetry, art, theater and the cinema. Unfortunately, however, this short period didn't contain enough wisdom and willpower to break up artistic policy mechanisms established during the Stalin era. Its basic principle continued to be voluntarism, although at times it sported a liberal-patronizing costume. (p. 19)

The events of April 1985, the historic Party plenum and M. S. Gorbachev's speech acted as a catalyst for the critical mass of contradictions that had accumulated by that time in theater. A chain reaction began. The fundamental problems of the theater—questions pertaining to its management, organization, and financing—that had been buried for a decade in office files and safes finally broke out into the light of day and have become the achievement of widespread publicity (glasnost). The debates about the theater did not calm down for more than a year in the pages of newspapers, magazines, on television, in meeting halls, and small rooms in artists' unions, ministries, and agencies.

The storm of public opinion, the firm demands of the theater community to change the status quo in the ruined economy of theaters finally led to 82 theaters with various repertoires (out of 640 in the country) being given new working conditions and becoming included in an experiment that began on January 1, 1987.

A comprehensive experiment in upgrading management and improving the effectiveness of theater work (the complete official name of this endeavor), it covers a broad range of questions from the purely artistic to the purely economic. Many of its proposals may seem so obvious that it is difficult not to be amazed by them: why then call this an "experiment"? If a healthy, average person comes down with pneumonia or even gets a heart attack, would he call his treatment an experiment? But just try to push a cripple who has been lying in a cast for ten years out onto the running track. Here indeed you would have something of an experiment, one that would probably require crutches in the beginning stages. And since the second case is closer to our own, perhaps we should briefly pause to discuss the basic ideas of the theatrical experiment.

The creative realm of theater requires doing away with any kind of limitations on repertoire (with the exception of material censored for disclosure of state secrets, propaganda advocating war, cruelty, violence, racial hatred and pornography). This also calls for eliminating any control over the repertoire by a higher authority. The theater itself will choose the play, prepare it for production, and present it to the public by passing the previously unavoidable procedure of having the play "approved" by a special commission.

In addition to the artistic director or main director, decisions concerning the theater's creative and organizational matters

are made by the group's artistic council—an elected, collective organ, comprised of highly professional actors, experienced directors, and other competent creative colleagues. Together with the leader-director, the artistic council works out the theater's creative program: the tactics and strategy of its activities. No outside interference into this process from the government agencies is tolerated. In this way, under experimental conditions, the principles of the theater's creative independence and self-government will be realized. (pp. 19-20)

Furthermore, in accordance with the experiment the number of planning indicators set for the theater by higher-level cultural organs is being sharply reduced. Only two of the former eleven remain: the two are the number of theater-goers and the size of state subsidies. The theaters currently involved in the experiment will independently determine the number of premieres and performances, the number of staff employees, the possibility of combining several professions, etc.—in other words, everything that was so strictly regulated before.

Another important mechanism which is stimulating the economic activity of the theater is a more flexible pricing system being allowed by the experiment. This system allows theaters to independently determine ticket price increases or discounts depending on audience demand and the artistic quality of the plays being staged. One could never have dreamed of anything like this in the previous era. Prices were strictly frozen and unchangeable irrespective of whether the play was a success or a failure.

These are some of the most important introductions in the economic aspect of the experiment. But what does this really mean as a whole? Today one can already draw certain preliminary conclusions. Unquestionably the experiment's expansion of the creative, economic, and organizational independence of theaters has played a positive role in rejuvenating theatrical life. The right to freely choose a repertoire resulted in quite a few interesting plays. Theater posters advertise a richer and more diverse set of plays, which has noticeably warmed up the theater-going public's interest. The new system of planning, financing, and stimulating theaters has yielded a certain latitude for more flexible economic maneuvering; theater workers have much more incentive to perform effective and quality work. Thus the situation is gradually becoming normalized. Soon the conditions of the experiment will be incorporated into every theater of the country without exception. Finally our very sick patient is beginning to improve and he is taking his first steps down the runner's path . . .

Nevertheless the experiment is not a panacea. This is only the first step—"reconnaissance through battle"—on the path to a radical perestroika (restructuring) of the theater system. The experiment as it stands today is incapable of untangling the messy knot of contradictions accumulated by Soviet theater during the past half century. The basic problems of the theater have yet to be resolved.

How can one insure the natural birth and death of theaters? What should be done with the half-functioning monster troupes that are living off of someone else's bread? Where can the additional sources be found to finance theater art? How can we stimulate the theater to create masterpieces? What type of conditions must be created so that the most varied theater forms obtain the right to exist? Here is just a partial list of questions which the theater reforms could answer—

questions that are standing on the threshold of our theater house, a house that is already leaning to one side.

The experiment patched up holes in the worn theater dress. It's time that we changed into a new gown. (p. 20)

Alexei Altayev, "The Economic Experiment: Soviet Theater of the Last Decade," translated by Vladimir Klimenko, in Theater, *Vol. XX, No. 3, Fall, 1989, pp. 18-20.*

GLASNOST LITERATURE IN TRANSLATION

WILLIAM GRIMES

The export trade in Soviet literature has always been subject to sudden and dramatic fluctuations of demand. In the '70s, détente meant full employment for Russian translators, as all manner of literary works were rushed into print. At the same time, the burgeoning dissident movement created a land-office business, with Solzhenitsyn constituting an industry unto himself. Then the tanks rolled into Afghanistan, and demand went soft.

Under Gorbachev, things are looking up again. *Glasnost* and *perestroika* have not yet put toilet paper on the shelves, but the new era of good feeling has gotten the translation mills humming. Once again, the publishing houses seem to be betting that renewed political interest in the USSR will add new luster to all things Russian.

Unfortunately, literary commerce between the U.S. and the USSR has operated on a fixed rate of exchange since the advent of the Cold War. With dreary predictability, American publishers have brought out one dissident work after another, gravitating toward writers whose personal struggles with the Soviet state would add an element of pathos, and a hefty PR push, to the marketing effort. In the process, moral courage became confused with literary merit, politics with aesthetics. The writers, persecuted in their own land, ended up as political hostages of the West, their works enlisted as part of a larger propaganda program.

The dissident model of literary production shows signs of collapsing, however, as Gorbachev threatens to alter the adversarial relationship of the writer to the state. If he reconciles them, American publishers will be thrown into deep confusion. State persecution makes for a useful guide to unfamiliar literary terrain: The good writers are the ones in jail. Soviet writers, too, face bewildering days ahead. For centuries, their role has been defined by oppression, their language shaped by censorship. In a dictatorship, literature becomes the opposition, and writers become statesmen. This has been the literary situation in Russia for two centuries. Suddenly, the forces for positive change are to be found within the Kremlin, and the censors are on the defensive. With greater freedom of the press, Soviet citizens will begin looking to journalists and historians for truths that, in the past, only poets and novelists could provide.

Literature, that is, will be forced to make its own way. The Soviet censors succeeded in turning literature into a political game—a dangerous one—in which writers of conscience came to feel a moral obligation to speak, out loud, the forbidden word. The ever-shifting line between permissible and impermissible speech demarcated the literary frontier. As a result, otherwise mediocre work that managed to express a few uncomfortable truths could cause a literary sensation. For the most part, the Western press has been content to play the same game, awarding points where the KGB would take them away but accepting the same nonliterary criteria of literary value. The laws of inertia insure that even profound cultural change under Gorbachev will do little to affect our literary policy toward the USSR. Publishers will continue to seek out The Book They Dared Not Print. Under current rules of competition, that means a blockbuster of critical realism that asks hard questions about the Stalinist period.

Arkady Lvov wrote ***The Courtyard*** before emigrating from the Soviet Union 10 years ago. History has played him a cruel trick, for the novel he smuggled out on a piece of microfilm hidden in a shoeshine kit might very well be publishable today in the USSR. In another 10 years, it could be superfluous, a work of dinosaur realism.

Judged as a work of political provocation, ***The Courtyard*** will disappoint. It's a thick concrete slab that, together with Vasily Grossman's ***Life and Fate*** and Anatoly Rybakov's ***Children of the Arbat,*** forms a kind of Stalin trilogy, weighty enough to snap any bookshelf made. ***The Courtyard*** asks the tough questions; it may not come up with the right answers, though. The Western press, upping the ante, now requires that any work on the period not only condemn Stalin—that's old hat by now—but also finger Lenin as spiritual father of the purges. Lvov will have to sacrifice bonus points there. Nowhere in the book's nearly 700 pages does the name Lenin appear. Nor does Stalin, a remote, God-like figure, bear the blame for 1937. A good Marxist despite himself, Lvov looks for the causes of the Stalin era in the Russian people themselves.

The Courtyard presents, with a wealth of detail that could be regarded either as mesmerizing or numbing, the lives of 10 families living in an Odessa apartment block from 1936 to 1956. These are ordinary Soviet citizens, workers for the most part, with ordinary concerns. The novel's technique might be called renegade socialist realism. Lvov refuses to analyze character or motive, and for the most part avoids physical description. He relies instead on dialogue and everyday events to paint—laboriously, patiently, stroke by tiny stroke—an absolutely convincing picture not only of life under Stalin but of the fundamental Soviet social unit, the collective.

As its title suggests, the novel maintains a narrow focus. Lvov deliberately pushes the great historical events of the period far into the background. The Nazi occupation of Odessa from 1941 to 1944 gets no more than a few paragraphs of dry historical summary, a quick voiceover account that bridges the time gap and allows the narrative to pick up again after the Germans have left.

War, Lvov seems to suggest, is extrinsic; it tells us nothing about Soviet society. His real subject is the climate of political terror that required either the participation or passive assent of an entire nation. It is Lvov's great achievement that he makes the purges, or the conditions that permitted them, seem not only plausible but unexceptionable. When a Black Maria comes to cart off another victim, it's as though an ambulance has arrived to carry away the sick. Too bad, but these things happen. Besides, everyone in the courtyard knows exactly who has made the decisive phone call to the police: "our Degtyar," the local Party representative. . . .

An iron-willed creature of the Party, Degtyar combines the functions of tribal leader, priest, and policeman. He sorts out disputes, pulls strings with the bureaucracy for his constituents, allocates living space, and organizes civic projects, usually involving "voluntary" Saturday labor. Above all, he oversees the political education of his charges, gathering them together for indoctrinations that combine the worst aspects of tent revivals and group therapy. A typical meeting might start with a discussion of such questions as "What changes in Soviet life were carried out in the period between 1924 and 1936? And what is the essence of those changes?" and then proceed to a gripe session in which Degtyar brings the disapproval of the collective to bear on one of its wayward members.

Lvov masterfully reproduces the Bolshevik political idiom, a distinctive mixture of cliché, invective, and pseudoscientific babble, uttered with smug forcefulness or, even better, shrieked. It requires a fist banging on the rostrum or, on the printed page, italics for every fourth word (see the works of Lenin, passim). Under Stalin, overkill was both a rhetorical style and state policy. "When tens of thousands of people are demanding a place to live," Degtyar tells one dismayed housing applicant, "every case should not just be looked into by one commission, but a commission on top of that one and another one on top of that. And still that wouldn't be enough." Degtyar likes the phrase "a hundred times right," which he occasionally bids up to a thousand or even, in the case of Gorky's "he who is not with us is against us," a million. . . .

Disciplined, self-sacrificing, vigilant, and unforgiving, Degtyar makes a dangerous enemy. He is especially ruthless in his efforts to eradicate vestiges of petit bourgeois behavior, which pit him against two harmless courtyard residents who persist in doing odd jobs to earn extra money. One of them earns a free pass to Siberia.

Nothing, not even a casual joke, escapes Degtyar's notice. His fellow citizens, however, regard it as quite natural that he should monitor every aspect of their lives. "What would we do without our Degtyar," they say, and they mean it. When Degtyar says, "People are always correcting each other, there's always someone around, we don't live in a void," he's underlining a positive feature of Soviet life. In a bit of obvious symbolism, he dies on the eve of the 26th Party Congress, when Khrushchev initiated the slow, painful process of de-Stalinization. Our Degtyar. And our Stalin. (p. 19)

Vladimir Sorokin's brief novel *The Queue* offers a genuinely witty picture of a Soviet institution nearly as important as the collective: the line. In snatches of anonymous dialogue, it records the uncertain progress of a mammoth line of Soviet citizens. The goal remains unclear. Desirable imported goods lie just around the bend, although debate rages over whether the country of origin is Yugoslavia, Czechoslovakia, Sweden, or England.

Gradually, the line takes on a life of its own; it coheres socially. From nowhere, enterprising souls start assigning numbers and taking roll. Those in the line, confident that their place is being held, begin running other errands or head off to grab a bite. When a beer wagon parked on a shady street comes into sight, the line, in a mighty movement of the collective will, reroutes itself to take advantage. The line even generates

its own economy, as speculators move in and sell places: a spot in the first hundred goes for 15 rubles.

The line, of course, is the Soviet Union. Those in it live for a better future just over the horizon and in the meantime convince themselves that the pace is picking up, the line really does seem to be moving, just a few more hours to go now. In many ways, standing in line is not so bad. Russians are past masters at making the best of a bad situation, and the line comes to seem a sociable, cozy sort of place to be, ideal for talking over the events of the day or indulging in a bit of philosophizing. Vadim, the closest thing to a character in *The Queue*, strikes up an acquaintance with a certain Lyudmila, and love blooms. They run off to her apartment, get to talking about poetry, and fall into bed. Meanwhile, the line crawls on, its members unaware that all the goods have been packed up and taken back for inventory.

With Sorokin, the wobbly outline of a future Soviet literature becomes visible through the haze. Now in his early thirties, Sorokin has simply declined to recognize literature as practiced under the official rules, not even bothering to seek publication. The time-honored role of novelist as political messiah or national conscience leaves him cold; he prefers to follow a more modern tradition. "At the end of the nineteenth century," he explains, "literature had great social importance. Now this literature has become a monster. The Soviet writer is above all someone serious who must react to social problems. My position is that of one who gives himself over to the playful, the game of literature."

If Sorokin were by temperament inclined to seek company, he might find a fellow refusenik in the émigré writer Sasha Sokolov, some 10 years his senior and already, on the strength of *A School for Fools*, assured of a place in the pantheon of 20th century Russian literature. Sokolov continues a literary tradition that the Soviet Union has never really known how to deal with. It begins with Gogol, passes through Bely and Olesha, and in the '20s takes a sharp turn into exile, eventually producing Nabokov, the model for Sokolov's style and aesthetic views, right down to the love of butterflies. It is a tradition that worships language and locates human liberty in the imagination, specifically the imagination engaged in the act of perception. Hence the obsession, particularly clear in Nabokov, with verbal invention, the mot juste, and the precise rendering of physical detail. (pp. 19-20)

Sokolov will be tough for Soviet critics to get a grip on. He is a prose poet who combines, to a rare degree, linguistic precision, imaginative boldness, and wit in its profounder sense—the intellectual faculty that directs a penetrating, pencil-thin shaft of light on that elusive point where absurdity and sadness meet. His novel does not so much deal with, as flit in and out of, the consciousness of a schizophrenic student at a special school, touching along the way most of the themes: love, loneliness, desire, freedom, injustice, beauty, and the unbearable sadness of being. It is poetry as Nabokov defined it in his book on Gogol: "the mysteries of the irrational as perceived through rational words." . . .

Characters [in *A School for Fools*] tend to polarize along the axis established by the boy's disease, assuming two aspects, real and mythic. The scientist Arcady Acatov, for example, sometimes appears as Leonardo da Vinci (and in that guise assigns his young pupil homework that echoes Sokolov's literary program: "Describe the jaw of a crocodile, the tongue of a hummingbird, the carillon of the Convent of Novodevichy, describe the bird cherry's stem, Lethe's circum-flexion, the tail of any local dog, a night of love . . ."). The kindly Pavel Norvegov appears sometimes as an oppressed geography teacher, at others as the Sender of Wind, symbolic of the unfettered imagination. In a grand rhetorical moment, he threatens to spin a globe and thereby cause rivers to back up and street signs to blow away, ushering in the days of wrath when the "murdered and humiliated" return to wreak vengeance against the powerful. . . .

Sokolov constitutes a test case for *glasnost,* perhaps even more than Solzhenitsyn, who, after all, has worked within the tradition of Tolstoy and dedicated much of his life to ca-taloguing the crimes of the Stalin era, a project that serves Gorbachev's own interests. To embrace Sokolov would be, from a purely literary standpoint, a far more radical step: the recognition of an excommunicated literary tradition, and the values it held sacred—the free play of language and the imag-ination.

Soviet writers may find the air of freedom harsh and thin. Like the pathetic students in Sokolov's special school, they've grown to depend on the familiar system of confinement and control, looking to the state, even in opposition, for valida-tion. Should Gorbachev open his window to the West, the West of individual liberty and market competition, the Soviet writer will stand on the threshold of a frightening new world, one that offers him every opportunity to become, like his Western counterpart, a superfluous man. (p. 20)

William Grimes, "Through a Glasnost Darkly: Nov-elists Face Up to Freedom," in VLS, *No. 70, Decem-ber, 1988, pp. 19-20.*

HENRY GIFFORD

In his introduction to *The New Soviet Fiction* Sergei Zalygin writes:

> I would like to voice the opinion that our litera-ture—at its best, naturally—has, on the whole, al-ways risen to the occasion, even during the period of stagnation.

By "the period of stagnation" he means the lethargic Brezh-nev era, which continued under his faltering successors, An-dropov and Chernenko. After which all was talk about Gor-bachev's perestroika. Zalygin is the editor of *Novy Mir,* which in the 1950s and 1960s kept Russian literature going within Soviet borders. Thereafter, the editor Alexander Tvardovsky having been deposed, *samizdat* largely took over the same task; and one by one Soviet writers of talent and independent mind made their way, or were forced to make it, to the West. Perestroika remains in many respects a promise that it has become more urgent than ever to fulfill; but glasnost—though still with some limitations—is a vivid reality. It would not have advanced so rapidly if the best of Russian literature, "even during the period of stagnation," had failed to carry out its immemorial task: to be, in Zalygin's concluding sen-tence to the introduction, "a witness of its time."

What we may hope to see—but hopes are seldom realized in Russian history—is unimpeded collaboration between the metropolitan and overseas provinces of Russian literature, so that it may derive strength both from the writers in exile and from those who, in Akhmatova's words, can say

> I have been with my people

> Where to its misfortune my people
>   was.

It has not always been a voluntary choice. But for Tatyana Tolstaya, today widely recognized as the brightest star of her generation, to leave Russia in pursuit of such advantages as the West can offer is unthinkable. In an interview with David Remnick of *The Washington Post* she remarked: "But after the good life, what would be next? Here, I feel needed." . . .

On the Golden Porch, containing thirteen [of Tolstaya's sto-ries] in all, appeared in Moscow two years ago. It sold out im-mediately, as good and necessary books do in the USSR; but on this handful of short stories, mostly running to a mere fif-teen or so pages in large print, her reputation was firmly es-tablished. They show an exceptional virtuosity in language which, unlike Nabokov's, makes for itself no ostentatious claims. Their originality can be appreciated best after a glance at the work of other women writers in *Balancing Acts.*

Sergei Zalygin claims that the short story is an indispensable genre in Soviet literature. The main literary journals need to publish at least one in every issue, which would otherwise look "incomplete and unusual" to their readers. Yet he has included only three women in his anthology—the well-known veteran I. Grekova; Lyudmila Petrushevskaya, anec-dotist and also playwright, and Tatyana Tolstaya. In her an-thology of Soviet women writers, [*Balancing Acts: Contem-porary Stories by Russian Women*], Helena Goscilo has, of course, also chosen one story by Tolstaya—"**Peters,**" about a sad boy who is kept away from other children, her first to be published in *Novy Mir* and the one that alerted the public to her significance. A number of the women in Goscilo's col-lection could have contended for a place in Zalygin's. One thinks among others of Viktoria Tokareva, with her cool wit and irony; of Nina Katerli, observant and austere in her ac-count of the impracticalities of passion in middle age; and of the geologist Anna Mass, whose story "**A Business Trip Home**" gave Goscilo the title for her collection. Soviet women too often face the problem of this story's main charac-ter, to "throw a little bridge . . . to cross over from one life to the other," the professional and the domestic.

Traditionally, as Goscilo explains, few Russian women have written novels. In the last century they were confined to what were considered minor genres, and notably memoirs. The im-plications of this Barbara Heldt has explored in *Terrible Per-fection: Women and Russian Literature.* Women, it is contin-ually claimed, enjoy equal rights with men in Soviet society. Goscilo points out that all they have gained is "increased ob-ligations camouflaged as expanded benefits." She quotes a Russian feminist now in the West: "Ideally, a woman is ex-pected to have children, to be an outstanding worker, take re-sponsibility for the home, and, despite everything, still to be beautiful." Grekova speaks for very many others when she tells of the choices that must be made: "It is either work or home," adding in parenthesis "with me it was my home that suffered." This is the all but impossible act of which Anna Mass writes. Her narrator in "**A Business Trip Home**" has "the sensation that two separate people—not doubles, but to-tally dissimilar individuals—really ought to merge into one." . . .

Women in the USSR, as these stories make abundantly clear, are exposed to the manifold inconvenience of daily life in a way that Soviet men have usually avoided, since the husband is not by and large involved either in domestic labor or in raising the children. Goscilo cites a passage from Nina Katerli's story "Between Spring and Summer." The speaker, Vasya, is a husband—Katerli, we learn, "prefers to view events from a male center of consciousness." Vasya reflects that equality between the sexes has left a man "the least important person" in his own home:

> What had happened to men? And where had these women come from who ran everything, whether at home or on the job? . . . War had happened. Not once, but three times. And remember, all three right in a row. . . . The men had been killed off, and the women were left with the kids. Who was the head of the house? The strongest? The smartest? Who was the protector? Who knew how to do everything? The mother.

And when the daughter grows up and marries, she will naturally follow this example.

It is no wonder, Goscilo writes, that "recent women's fiction paints a bleak picture of Russian society, exposes the disintegration of family ties, and communicates all too vividly the debasing indignities with which Russian women contend daily." A woman writer whom she quotes in a footnote to this observation has described "family life Soviet-style" as "a living hell." To judge from the stories in *Balancing Acts,* it has all the rootlessness of Western society with many additional drawbacks. Little is said in them about the incursions of the state, although Grekova's "No Smiles" (in *The New Soviet Fiction*) tells of the isolation endured by a woman scientist when her work is at one point found ideologically unsafe. Family life in the midst of shortages is itself full of shortages. One of the most serious is that children have very few siblings. The only child is often looked after by his or her grandparents, as best they can; the mother in these stories may be a doctor, an engineer, a geologist, who is usually away on expeditions, an actress, or even the chairwoman (there is no equivalent to "chairperson" in Soviet usage) of a collective farm. The father is usually discontented and uneasy at home, discontented and no more comfortable when he strays from it into infidelity. (p. 3)

Russian literature has always recognized the duty of dealing with public issues, a duty, needless to say, in which it was often impeded. Many of the Soviet women writers selected by Goscilo are in a sense sociological field-workers, but the hurt is their own; the stresses imposed by society are realized in deep personal frustration. The complaint is sometimes made that they concentrate too much on what Russians call *byt*—the humdrum, the daily routine, which is really, according to the novelist Yuri Trifonov, "what life consists of," with all its "mutual relations between friends, co-workers, love, arguments, jealousy, envy."

Tatyana Tolstaya has her own position in this matter, and in that way is unrepresentative. The best writers usually are, and only later are they seen to have understood their time in greater complexity and shown it more truly than their contemporaries did. *On the Golden Porch* takes its title from a story of the same name, the first of hers to be published, in the fall of 1983. The phrase, in full "On the golden porch sat: Tsar, tsarevich, king, prince, cobbler, tailor," belongs to a children's counting song. By using it Tolstaya makes tacit acknowledgment of the source from which her art draws sustenance—the child's imagination. Several of the stories deal with the sometimes outrageous fantasy of a child (or an im-

mature or unfulfilled adult). It is that of an exceptionally gifted child, as Tolstaya herself clearly was.

> In the beginning was the garden. Childhood was a garden. Without end or limit, without borders and fences, in noises and rustling, golden in the sun . . .

Let no one suppose from this opening to her story that we are about to enter the frail idyllic scene of Kenneth Grahame's *The Golden Age.* Russian writers too are capable of sentimentalizing memories of their earliest years; but Leo Tolstoy never did this in his first work, *Childhood.* Nor does Tatyana, though it has to be admitted that only in this respect does she resemble her great kinsman. Fantasy was not his strong quality: he ranks among the "literalists of the imagination," and owes little or nothing to the tradition of Gogol. Tatyana's writing has affinities with the riot and color of Gogol's Ukrainian stories especially. Gogol, like her, was always aware of the evil behind the enchantment. But he exults in the play of fantasy, in the rich and overpowering detail of life as he conceives it, in absurdity and in the grotesque.

The child in Tolstaya's fiction moves naturally in the world of Russian fairy tale, with a freedom and responsiveness very difficult for most children to attain today; for they are deprived of the power to visualize for themselves, as the little boy Petya does in **"Date with a Bird,"** those legendary creatures from Russian folk tales: The Sirin, the Finist, the Alkonost. The process that began with Disney seems to have paralyzed that nerve in their imaginations, just as the telling of fairy tales must be endangered in Russia with the disappearance of the old peasant nurse, like Nanny Grusha in "Loves Me, Loves Me Not." The children can always rely on her for a genuine thrill:

> Her gray head holds thousands of stories about talking bears, and blue snakes that cure people with tuberculosis by climbing in through the chimney during the night, about Pushkin and Lermontov.

So Petya, eating his rice porridge, sees the butter floating on top as a doomed Atlantis, and the gorgeous city, with its emerald-roofed white palaces, temples whose doorways are curtained with peacock feathers, "sharp silver obelisks with inscriptions in an unknown tongue," and the presiding statue of a golden god with three eyes in his forehead all "slip, list, into the warm, transparent waves." This capacity for dream persists in many of the adults depicted by Tatyana Tolstaya. The drabber their surroundings, the more disadvantaged and restricted in life they are, the surer will come to their rescue a vision of southern seas and a promised paradise. Even Peters, who had not been allowed to join in children's play, and becomes hopelessly frustrated when he grows up, is granted as an old man sight of "the naked golden spring" that cries "laughing: catch me, catch me!" And so he "smiled gratefully at life—running past, indifferent, ungrateful, treacherous, mocking, meaningless, alien—marvelous, marvelous, marvelous." These are significantly the last words of the book. (pp. 3-4)

A. Mikhailov, who wrote a generally sympathetic afterword to the Russian edition [of *On the Golden Porch*], found some of the Tolstaya stories "rather far-fetched." He cited "Okkervil River," about the long forgotten singer Vera Vasilevna, whom a lonely Leningrader, much addicted to playing her records, seeks out one day to his disillusionment, and "A Clean Sheet," which tells how an unhappy husband, with a care-worn wife, an ailing child, and an unfaithful mistress, visits a doctor for the mysterious operation that will transform him into an elated and appallingly active go-getter. Mikhailov is fairly indulgent to such excesses, as he sees them. But even the most extravagant kites flown by Tolstaya are attached to a tough wire that brings them down to earth.

Her stories must be read with close attention to their economy, the inner coherences that bring out their meaning, and to the oblique but searching light they cast on the daily pressures and restrictions of Soviet life. One of her more recent stories, **"Sweet Dreams, Son"** (1986), yields rather more than is apparent on a cursory reading. I should place it among her very best, and it must be emphasized that such stories of hers call for the attention we normally give to a poem, or at least to the prose fiction of poets—like Pasternak's *The Childhood of Luvers* or Mandelstam's *The Egyptian Stamp,* even though both run to the length of novellas.

"Sweet Dreams, Son" is set in the 1970s, that "period of stagnation" rivaling the "muffled" or "godforsaken" years of torpor in the 1880s. Sergei's mother-in-law, Maria Maximovna, an obvious beneficiary of the system, cannot get over the loss of a very special fur coat, which had a silk lining with a pattern of lilies of the valley. A handsome and comfortable widow, she had been wearing the coat in the flea market, where she went to buy a squirrel fur coat for everyday wear. She handed her treasured coat to Panya the cleaning woman; and it was gone in a flash. After thirty years Maria Maximovna still cannot forget this dreadful episode—the great tragedy of her life. Sergei, newly married to the daughter of the family, unable to "resist her watery charms," is told this story, and it comes to us mostly in his mother-in-law's words. Tolstaya is adept at switching from one register to another, as she views what she has to tell through the consciousness of different actors in the story. . . . Sergei will hear his mother-in-law tell this story many times. With each repetition the nature of the family he has married into becomes clearer to him.

Sergei had his own really tragic loss, when the mother whose name he never knew was killed by a bomb in the war, and he was saved, to enter an orphanage. There they issued him a name and an estimated date of birth. Life in the orphanage is brilliantly evoked: "Long winters, hungry eyes, shaved heads, some adult giving a quick pat on the head as he ran past; the smell of mice in the sheets, the dull light." His motive for marrying the unresponsive Lenochka was to come out of the cold. He "married in fear and delight, hazarding a guess, understanding nothing." Lenochka, whom he cannot make out, is "steady and passionless, a sister instead of a wife. Mother and sister—what more could a lost boy want?"

He could want a father. The obvious candidate is the missing member of the family, that high-ranking military doctor who in 1944 had found the fur coat in Germany and immediately sent it to his young wife. Maria Maximovna describes the long ago deceased Pavel Antonovich with genuine admiration—"a warrior against the plague, . . . complex, quick to judge; terrible in his wrath, and honest in his work." But Lenochka can barely remember him—she thinks of him in his official car, with its chauffeur who had steel teeth, common in those hard times. Lenochka recalls the "angry nape" of her father's neck and her only other memory of him is a scene of his terrible wrath, on some trivial pretext at home. By then her father had been "insulted, abandoned," while his ungrateful students carried "the slightly soiled banner on-

ward." That phrase is surely not Maria Maximovna's. It reveals the first crack in her idol. (pp. 4, 6)

It is hard not to see this story, about homelessness, the utter loss of parents and connection with the past, the iniquities of power, and corruption in high places, as a reading not only of Soviet life, but also of what man can easily do to man in the best-intentioned of societies. (p. 6)

Henry Gifford, "The Real Thing," in The New York Review of Books, *Vol. XXXVL, No. 9, June 1, 1989, pp. 3-4, 6.*

IRVING HOWE

What has happened to Aleksandr Solzhenitsyn? The novelist, now living in the United States, who sketched the gulag with such crisp exactitude in *One Day in the Life of Ivan Denisovich,* who grazed moral sublimity in his beautiful story "Matryona's House" and who created a vibrant exchange of Russian intellectual opinion in *The First Circle* has all but vanished. Replacing him is a shrill and splenetic polemicist who shatters his fictions in behalf of questionable theories, showers adversaries with sarcastic contempt and employs his talents to cudgel readers into submitting to his increasingly authoritarian views.

For at least 20 years Mr. Solzhenitsyn has been working on a vast cycle of novels called **The Red Wheel,** which he envisages as a panorama of modern Russia, but still more as a corrective to what he regards as the distortions of Russian history by writers contaminated with liberal and radical ideas. **August 1914** appeared in an earlier version in 1972; now completely retranslated into serviceable English by H. T. Willetts, it is some 300 pages longer than the first version. The book forms the opening volume of *The Red Wheel,* which is structured as a series of what the author calls "knots," or renderings of crucial historical moments that have determined the course of Russian, perhaps all of modern history.

This is a swollen and misshapen book, a good many of its pages laden with obscure historical detail in small print that, I can testify, causes strain on both eyes and nerves. Mr. Solzhenitsyn writes with the single-mindedness of a man possessed—prophecy being not the least risk of aging. He writes out of the conviction that he has the correct view—the only correct view?—of his country's tragic experience, and it becomes very hard, indeed impossible, to respond to **August 1914** in strictly literary terms. Mr. Solzhenitsyn himself would probably not want that; he is after "bigger" game.

Despite an occasional borrowing from modern literature, such as his use of the "newsreel" device in John Dos Passos' *U.S.A.,* Mr. Solzhenitsyn's novel begins in the customary manner of multilayered 19th-century fiction, with several vignettes of Russian figures and families shortly before World War I. We meet a wealthy merchant, Tomchak, and his daughter Ksenia. We meet an idealistic student, Sanya, who has a brief talk with the venerable Leo Tolstoy (a piquant incident that was, I think, richer in the 1972 version, which contained some Tolstoyan reflections on poetry that Mr. Solzhenitsyn has now cut).

Several strands of action are thus initiated, and readers familiar with the schema of the traditional novel will await the reappearance of these characters, juxtaposed in both amity and conflict. But that seldom happens in these 854 pages, and only at very long intervals. The characters glimpsed at the outset are suspended in limbo while Mr. Solzhenitsyn turns to what really concerns him: an exhaustive account of Russia's military disasters in 1914. By the time he troubles to get back to his fictional characters, mostly at the very end of this very long book, it has become hard even to recall who the characters are or why we should care about them—since Mr. Solzhenitsyn himself doesn't invest much emotional energy in them. The fictional portion of *August 1914* soon comes to seem merely dutiful, and largely without that desire to imagine other people that is the mark of the true novelist. (pp. 1, 17)

There are some good pages in the hundreds that sag under endless battle detail. Especially so are those about the historical General Samsonov, whom Mr. Solzhenitsyn models in part on Tolstoy's Kutuzov in *War and Peace,* but without Kutuzov's intuitive strategic grasp or mysterious good fortune. Also strong are some pages devoted to the fictional Colonel Vorotyntsev, an officer who travels from corps to corps as the witness of defeat and who comes, meanwhile, to serve as Mr. Solzhenitsyn's center of intelligence. Samsonov speaks for traditional patriarchal Russia, blunt and honest but quite lost in modern warfare (as Tolstoy's Kutuzov might also have been), while the nervously intelligent Vorotyntsev speaks as the modernizing voice that Mr. Solzhenitsyn apparently wishes had been commanding in 1914, loyal to czarism but impatient with the feeble Czar and his scraping court.

The pages devoted to battle on the eastern front—pages crammed with dull generals, obscure place names, confusing divisional maneuvers—soon become wearying. It is possible that some Russian readers, at least those leaning, in the days of glasnost, toward a chauvinist nostalgia, may be roused to excitement by the doings of Generals Zhilinsky and Martos, but it is hard to suppose anyone else will. Some fatal lack of proportion is at work here, an indulgence of authorial vanity and ideological obsession.

It will no doubt be said that in *War and Peace* Tolstoy also devoted many pages to battle. Yes, but Tolstoy was Tolstoy, the greatest master of prose narrative we have ever had. Tolstoy was also generous enough to provision his novel with a rich and varied cast, taking the precaution to make most vivid precisely those characters with whose opinions he disagreed. By now Mr. Solzhenitsyn has become too impatient, too irritable for the novelist's job, and one readily surmises the reason: for a writer pulsing with prophetic urgency, mere literature dwindles in importance.

The new material in *August 1914* centers on historical events that took place several years before the war. Pyotr Arkadievich Stolypin, a shrewd politician, was Prime Minister of Russia from 1906 to 1911, when he was assassinated by Dmitri Bogrov, a shady figure who had successively been linked to revolutionary terrorists and the czarist secret police and who had perhaps become a double agent betraying both sides. In fairness, it should be said that Mr. Solzhenitsyn does try to get inside Bogrov to scrutinize his motives, but not with much success; for he cannot control his anger and disgust, and too often he descends to sarcasm, the lowest of rhetorical devices.

It is Mr. Solzhenitsyn's thesis that if Stolypin had been able to complete the reforms he had begun, Russia might have been spared the traumas of Bolshevism, but that a tacit alliance of reactionary officials and revolutionary insurgents thwarted Stolypin's plans. He had proposed to grant the recently emancipated peasants legal right to small allotments of land and thereby to free them from their dependence on the mir, or agricultural commune. Had this happened, Mr. Solzhenitsyn argues, Russia might have become a modern society resting on an independent agrarian class. (p. 17)

Only when writing about Stolypin ("a figure of epic presence") does Mr. Solzhenitsyn relax into ease or rise to something like lyricism. This idealization of a bureaucrat who was hated by Russian democrats and leftists for his severe repressions after the 1905 revolution is not just a whim; it is the thought-out conclusion of the political outlook Mr. Solzhenitsyn has adopted in recent years, one that might be described as modernizing authoritarianism. "The secret ballot," he scoffs, "suited the Russian peasant as a saddle suits a cow"— and since peasants formed the bulk of the Russian population, democracy could have played little or no role. As for the rationale he offers, it is all too familiar: right and left authoritarians proclaim it everywhere, with the same haughty certitude.

Somewhat sprightlier than the long chapter on Stolypin is his 80-page historical excursus about Nicholas II, the last of Russia's hereditary autocrats. Though caustic at times about this royal dunce—some passages here recall Trotsky's more concise and elegant excoriation in his *History of the Russian Revolution*—Mr. Solzhenitsyn seems finally unable to come to a clear judgment about the Czar. At one point he writes that the Czar was a "weak but virtuous man," yet the overwhelming thrust of his own depiction is to show Nicholas as petty, selfish, mindless. When Stolypin lay dying in a hospital, the Czar did not even bother to visit his minister, apparently suspecting him of "liberalism." That hardly seems evidence of virtue, either weak or strong.

Mr. Solzhenitsyn winds up *August 1914* with one of his better scenes, in which Colonel Vorotyntsev reports to the Grand Duke, supreme commander of Russia's armies. The colonel's few honest words acknowledging defeat are scorned, the general staff clings to its deceptions, Russia is doomed.

What, I asked at the outset, has happened to Mr. Solzhenitsyn? The answer is that his zealotry has brought about a hardening of spirit, a loss in those humane feelings and imaginative outreachings that make us value a work of literature, regardless of the writer's political opinions. In *August 1914* Russian radicals are portrayed as rapists, murderers, "mad dogs"; and while, as polemicist, Mr. Solzhenitsyn has every right to attack them, as novelist he has a primary obligation to make them seem plausible versions of men and women. The Russian middle class, sneeringly referred to as "society," is shown to be preparing the way for Lenin by joining in irresponsible attacks on czarism.

A still deeper revelation of Mr. Solzhenitsyn's current state of mind is to be found in this sentence: "An aversion to Russia and the Russian people, and a belief that everyone in Russia was oppressed and that there was no freedom there, had been created by relentless Jewish propaganda" in America.

This is ugly stuff. Could Mr. Solzhenitsyn not have found it in his heart—it would have taken just two more lines—to mention that this "Jewish propaganda" was in response to the Kishinev pogrom of 1903 and a succession of pogroms two years later, during which czarist authorities either gave the killers a free hand or looked the other way? These pogroms "cost the Russian Jews about 1,000 dead [and] 7,000-

8,000 wounded," we read in *The Russian Jew Under Tsars and Soviets* by Salo Baron (a scholarly work that, in view of Mr. Solzhenitsyn's declared interest in history, he might do well to consult).

It is all very sad, this self-immolation of a once major writer who a quarter of a century ago, in *The First Circle* and *Cancer Ward,* won our admiration for his loveliness of feeling. The Russian critic M. M. Bakhtin once remarked that "for the prose artist the world is full of the words of other people." By now, for the prose artist Aleksandr Solzhenitsyn the world resounds with the words of only one person. (pp. 17-18)

Irving Howe, "The Great War and Russian Memory," in The New York Times Book Review, *July 2, 1989, pp. 1, 17-18.*

PAUL GRAY

Laboring nearly twelve hours a day, seven days a week in a three-story building behind his house that serves both as a workplace and library and as a typesetting and proofreading center, [Solzhenitsyn] has produced more than 5,000 printed pages in Russian of an epic called *The Red Wheel.* Using the techniques of fiction but based on exhaustive historical research, this project aims at nothing less than a vast overview of the events leading up to and culminating in the Russian Revolution of 1917.

It will be years before the complete cycle of novels is available in English. But an enormous preview of what lies in store is being published this week as *August 1914.* This novel first appeared in English in 1972; after his banishment from the U.S.S.R., Solzhenitsyn was free to explore new troves of archival material, particularly at Stanford's Hoover Institution, and has now expanded the text by some 300 pages. Much of the additional material concerns the evil (in Solzhenitsyn's view) activities of Lenin during Russia's hasty entrance into World War I, and the heroic (ditto) career of Pyotr Stolypin, the Prime Minister under Czar Nicholas II who was assassinated in 1911 by an anarchist named Dmitri Bogrov. Translated by Harry T. Willetts, this version is essentially a brand-new work.

And it is not, it must be added, a day at the beach. Those who feel guilty, summer after summer, about not reading *War and Peace* can positively grovel at the prospect of the unquestionably difficult and demanding *August 1914.* It offers an encompassing narrative, told from dozens of different perspectives, of Russian life circa 1914 and of the nation's stark unpreparedness for the military offensive launched against Germany in August of that year. With this story Solzhenitsyn mixes snippets from contemporary newspapers, a succession of official documents and a series of "Screens," scenes described as if they were intended for a film script. The overall effect of this avalanche of information is daunting indeed.

But patient readers will be amply rewarded. The maze of detail can be captivating. Characters are introduced and then vanish for hundreds of pages, only to reappear memorably. At the same time, individual identities are forged and melted in the crucible of history. Throughout the panoramic events, a persistent voice points out the folly and tragedy of what is being recorded: a cataclysm that wrecked a nation and changed the modern world.

Late in the 20th century, Solzhenitsyn has produced a 19th century icon, a saga that presupposes a readership intelligent and leisured enough to follow and stick with it. Coming from someone else, this novel—not to mention the looming immensity of *The Red Wheel*—would seem either quixotic or an example of monumental hubris. But the author, 70, has spent his adult life challenging impossible odds, and recent events indicate that he may be winning.

Suddenly, his reputation in the Soviet Union is soaring. The monthly Moscow literary journal *Novy Mir* will soon begin publishing excerpts from *The Gulag Archipelago,* Solzhenitsyn's searing account of political prisoners, himself included, in the extended network of Stalinist labor camps; the entire work will also be published in book form. And the Union of Soviet Writers recently announced the reversal of its 1969 decision to expel the author from its ranks for "antisocial behavior" and called on the Supreme Soviet to give back Solzhenitsyn's citizenship.

Vadim Borisov, the *Novy Mir* editor who is handling Solzhenitsyn's literary affairs in the Soviet Union, has no doubts about the author's importance to his homeland:

If all of Solzhenitsyn's works had been published in their time and not banned, the character of Russian prose today would be different. When his epic historical cycle is read in its entirety, it will have the same significance for Russian literature as Dante's *Divine Comedy* has for European literature.

Paul Gray, "Russia's Prophet in Exile," in Time, New York, Vol. 134, No. 4, July 24, 1989, p. 56.

ALEKSANDR SOLZHENITSYN [INTERVIEW WITH DAVID AIKMAN]

[Aikman]: *The novel* **August 1914** *was first published in 1971 in Russian, and now the English translation of a completely new edition is just being published. Why did you feel it necessary to add some 300 pages to the original manuscript?*

[Solzhenitsyn]: The chapter on Lenin is the first addition. But the greater number of new chapters came from the fact that, with the years, I understood that the movement toward revolution and its causes could not be understood simply in terms of World War I, 1914. My initial conception was one that the majority of those in the West and East today share, namely that the main decisive event was the so-called October Revolution and its consequences. But it became clear to me gradually that the main and decisive event was not the October Revolution, and that it wasn't a revolution at all. What we mean by *revolution* is a massive spontaneous event, and there was nothing of the sort in October. The true revolution was the February Revolution. The October Revolution does not even deserve the name revolution. It was a coup d'état, and all through the 1920s the Bolsheviks themselves called it the "October coup." In the Soviet Union they consciously and artificially replaced the February Revolution with the October one.

Do you think, then, that the February Revolution was more of a break with Russian history than the October Revolution?

Yes, it was much more of a break. The February system—if you can call it that—never even got established before it already started to collapse. It was collapsing from week to week. The October coup only picked up the power that was lying on the ground and that belonged to no one.

Why did you decide to call the entire cycle of novels **The Red Wheel,** *and why do you refer to each different stage in the narrative as a "knot" [uzel in Russian]?*

We are not talking about the wheels of a car, after all. We are talking about a gigantic cosmic wheel, like a spiral galaxy, an enormous wheel that once it starts to turn—then everybody, including those who turn in it, becomes a helpless atom. A gigantic process that you can't stop once it has started. And I used the knots for the following reason: I started to deal with the period 1914-22. If I were to rewrite in detail about the period 1914-22, the volume would be too great, so I reached for episodes where I thought the course of events was being decided. These are the knots, the most decisive moments, where everything is rolled up and tied in a knot.

The one person in this novel whom you obviously admire greatly is [Russian Prime Minister Pyotr] Stolypin. How would you summarize his role in Russian history?

What is characteristic is that during the years he was active, conservative circles considered him the destroyer of Russia. And the Kadets [Constitutional Democrats], who considered themselves liberals but were in fact radicals in the European context, called him a conservative. Actually, he was a liberal. He thought that before creating civil society, we had to create the citizen, and therefore before giving the illiterate peasant all sorts of rights, you had to elevate him economically. This was a very constructive idea. Stolypin was, without doubt, the major political figure in Russian 20th century history. And when the revolution occurred, it was the free democratic regime of February 1917 that abolished all his reforms and went back to square one.

For 70 years, we have been destroying everything in our country, the life of the people, its biological, ecological, moral and economic basis. Naturally, people look to the past for some point of support, some constructive idea. Now people are looking here and there and finally coming across Stolypin's reforms and how he dealt with the peasantry.

How do you see Lenin in the whole complex of Russian culture?

Lenin had little in common with Russian culture. Of course, he graduated from a Russian gymnasium [high school]. He must have read Russian classics. But he was penetrated with the spirit of internationalism. He did not belong to any nation himself. He was "inter" national—between nations. During 1917, he showed himself to be in the extreme left wing of revolutionary democracy. Everything that happened in 1917 was guided by [proponents of] revolutionary democracy, but it all fell out of their hands. They were not sufficiently consistent, not sufficiently merciless, while he was merciless and consistent to the end, and in that sense his appearance in Russian history was inevitable. (pp. 57-8)

Some critics have accused you of anti-Semitism on the basis of your depiction of the terrorist Bogrov in August 1914, and one writer even used the words "a new Protocols of the Learned Elders of Zion" *to describe the book. What is your response to these accusations?*

I described Bogrov in the most realistic way, with every detail of his life, his family, his ideology and his behavior. I recognized his brother's interpretation of him as the most correct and convincing. In no way did I belittle the heroic impulse that moved him. I think that the application of the term anti-Semitic to *August 1914* is an unscrupulous technique. I had earlier thought this was possible only in the Soviet Union. The book was not yet available because I had not released it, but people stated quite loudly that this was a disgusting, imperialist, revolting, loathsome book, etc. It wasn't possible to check what was being said, because people couldn't obtain the book.

But what is really at issue here? The word anti-Semitism is often used thoughtlessly and carelessly, and its actual meaning becomes soft and squishy. I would propose the following definition: anti-Semitism is a prejudiced and unjust attitude toward the Jewish nation as a whole. If one accepts this definition, it becomes clear that not only is there no anti-Semitism in *August 1914* but it would be impossible to have anti-Semitism in any genuinely artistic work. No real artist could be prejudiced and unjust toward any entire nation without destroying the artistic integrity of his entire work. A work of art is always multidimensional, is never made up of empty abstractions.

My novel has no generalizations about the Jewish nation in it. In writing a book one cannot always ask, How will this be interpreted? You have to think, What actually happened? My duty was to describe things as they happened.

Do you believe the completed **Red Wheel** *will be published some day in the Soviet Union?*

I have no doubt about that.

You have said your writings must return to the Soviet Union before you are willing to do so.

Yes. I worked 53 years on *The Red Wheel.* Everything I have thought, discovered and worked over in my mind has gone into it. If I had to return to the Soviet Union prior to *The Red Wheel,* I would be sort of mute. No one would know where I stood. I would have expressed nothing. Once people read it, then we can talk. The book has to be available at every bookstore in the U.S.S.R. (p. 58)

You have said you are a writer in the 19th century Russian tradition. What do you mean by this?

It does not mean following precisely the genres and the artistic techniques of the period. Far from it. My material is entirely unusual and requires its own genres and its own technique. But it does mean maintaining the responsibility toward the reader, toward one's own country and toward oneself, which was found in Russian 19th century literature. They wrote very responsibly. They did not play games.

The American novelist Henry James once described Russian novels as "huge, loose, baggy monsters." Your own **Red Wheel** *epic will result in several thousand pages, many times larger in fact than* War and Peace. *Is there something about the Russian condition and Russian literature that asks for much greater length in the novel than is usual in other countries?*

Mine is indeed very large, I admit. There is an aphorism: He who forgets his own history is condemned to repeat it. If we don't know our own history, we will simply have to endure all the same mistakes, sacrifices and absurdities all over again. This book is not designed to be read through easily, for amusement, but to understand our history. And to understand our history, I feel that my readers definitely need this book.

So then, in your view, literature continues to have a very high, moral, philosophical and political purpose?

Yes, in Russia it's always been that way.

You have been compared with both Tolstoy and Dostoyevsky, both in scope of your subject matter and in your treatment of the psychology and ideas of your characters. What is your relationship to each of these two authors?

I have a very great feeling of respect and kinship to both of them, although in different ways. I am closer to Tolstoy in the form of the narrative, of the delivery of material, the variety of characters and circumstances. But I am closer to Dostoyevsky in my understanding of the spiritual interpretation of history. (p. 59)

Today there are events of enormous significance taking place both in the Soviet Union and throughout the whole Communist world. Why do you choose to be silent about these changes?

If I had started being silent at the onset of these changes, it might have been surprising. But I started in 1983, before there was even any suggestion of these changes. Was I going to interrupt my work and start acting as a political commentator? I didn't want to do that. I had to finish my work. I am over 70 years old, and age is pressing on me. . . .

More than anything else, your reputation in world literature is linked to your searing portrayal of Soviet labor camps. Did your experience of the camps provide you with a dimension of understanding of Soviet life that you could not have had without it?

Yes, because in those circumstances human nature becomes very much more visible. I was very lucky to have been in the camps—and especially to have survived. (p. 60)

> *Aleksandr Solzhenitsyn and David Aikman, in an interview in* Time, *New York, Vol. 134, No. 4, July 24, 1989, pp. 57-60.*

MICHAEL SCAMMELL

One of Aleksandr Solzhenitsyn's more endearing characteristics is his refusal to truckle to received opinion or pander to popular taste. It is now nine years since the publication of his last major work in English (the memoir *The Oak and the Calf*), and he has been almost forgotten, or written off as a has-been, by much of the reading public. After such a long silence, a major new work of fiction would seem the perfect occasion to assert his continuing potency and prove his detractors wrong, yet this "new" book of his turns out to be a rewrite and an expansion of an old one first published no fewer than 17 years ago, under the same title and with essentially the same cast of characters (with one significant exception, which we will come to later). Whatever else he may be trying to achieve, Solzhenitsyn is certainly not courting his audience.

What could be the reasons for this eccentricity? They certainly don't include laziness or writer's block. *August 1914* has already been followed by its thousand-page sequel in Russian, *October 1916,* and by a third work, *March 1917,* that runs to no fewer than four volumes and 2,800 pages. A fourth massive narrative is well on the way to completion, and there will be others before the series is finished. Whatever the final number, many years will go by before American readers can hold the whole series in their hands, and more still before a judgment can be reached on its literary and historical merits. Given these dimensions and such a time scale, questions of audience reception and literary reputation tend to lose their urgency.

The chief explanation for Solzhenitsyn's behavior, however, is to be found in his intentions for this vast epic, to which he has given the overall title of *The Red Wheel.* The "wheel" in question is the wheel of the Russian revolution, and Solzhenitsyn's immense enterprise is designed to re-examine Russian history at the start of the century in order to explain exactly how and why the revolution happened. His interpretation of that history is of course a revisionist one, and anti-Leninist (not to speak of "anti-Soviet") in its basic thrust, and it depends on a close analysis of the events and personalities of the time.

But here we come to the crux of the matter. Solzhenitsyn is utterly convinced that his explanation of Russian history is the correct one, and has staked the remainder of his life and reputation on persuading his fellow countrymen of his correctness. However, the original version of *August 1914* was written while he was still in the Soviet Union and deprived by the censorship of much essential information. Since being deported to the West, he has discovered a lot of important new evidence for his thesis, which he feels obliged to bring to the notice of his readers, and it is this that has driven him to rewrite his book and bring it out in its new form before proceeding to publish the others.

The readers that Solzhenitsyn has foremost in mind, of course, are his Soviet readers, who are still deprived of the information that Solzhenitsyn found in Western libraries. The vast majority of those readers have become thoroughly disoriented in their thinking about the pre-revolutionary Russian past by Soviet propaganda, and Solzhenitsyn has set himself the task of reawakening their historical awareness and forcing them to re-examine old assumptions. From this point of view, American—and Western—readers are irrelevant to Solzhenitsyn. If we like what he writes, all well and good; if not, so much the worse for us.

So what does he write? Like its predecessor, the new *August 1914* is devoted to the years leading up to World War I and the first—disastrous—year of the war itself. At the center of the narrative is an exhaustive account of the Battle of Tannenberg in East Prussia, where a Russian army, led by General Samsonov, was heavily defeated by the Germans and put to flight. In the wake of that debacle, Samsonov committed suicide. Much of this part of the story is told by the author's transparent alter ego, Colonel Georgi Vorotyntsev, an irritatingly self-satisfied know-all who has been sent to the front by the Supreme Command Headquarters on a reconnaissance mission. At the same time, Solzhenitsyn's old-fashioned and leisurely realism allows him to enter the minds of other characters too, and the depiction of Samsonov's inner turmoil and ultimate suicide remains one of the finest things in the novel.

Through a number of flashbacks we get to learn a little of Vorotyntsev's domestic life before the war, and there are other scenes of peacetime glimpsed through the lives of three young conscripts—Sasha Lenartovich, Yaroslav Kharitonov, and Sanya Lazhenitsyn—and of members of a wealthy, self-made family of landowners, the Tomchaks, in the northern

Caucasus. These characters are all based on biographical models drawn from Solzhenitsyn's own family.

Unfortunately, these scenes of peacetime life are mostly confined to the first nine chapters and chapters 75-78 (out of 82 altogether), so that one loses track and forgets about them in the welter of military and historical detail filling the bulk of the book. But they do point to another of Solzhenitsyn's intentions, namely to compete with Tolstoy and write a *War and Peace* for our times. This intention is signalled not only by a scene in which the young Lazhenitsyn visits Tolstoy at Yasnaya Polyana and is disappointed by Tolstoy's answers to his questions, but also by Solzhenitsyn's open polemic against Tolstoy's theory of history that he carries on throughout his book. Indeed, the whole purpose of his book seems to be to offer an alternative theory.

It is in this context that Solzhenitsyn's additions and changes to the novel assume their relevance. Of the 300 or so pages that Solzhenitsyn has added to his original version, some 200 are devoted to the career and activities of the Russian statesman Pyotr Stolypin, who was prime minister of Russia from 1906 until his assassination in 1911, and 100 pages to the tragi-comic figure of Nicholas II, the last tsar of Russia.

Stolypin's claim to fame was that he tried to carry out a kind of revolution of his own from above. Initially appointed to restore order in the Russian empire after the upheavals occasioned by the 1905 revolution, Stolypin made himself feared and hated by his policy of summarily hanging thousands of peasants accused of instigating riots, and exiling or jailing all those suspected of revolutionary activities. However, this fierce repression was accompanied by a determined attempt to transform the structure of peasant society by breaking up the ancient Russian commune system and handing over the land to individual and independent peasant farmers.

It was a bold attempt both to quell peasant unrest caused by land hunger and to create a new class of peasant properties as a basis for social stability, a classically conservative answer to the problems that had been besetting Russia ever since the emancipation of the serfs in 1861. And it looked as if Stolypin would succeed. However, his implacable hostility to all forms of progressive or liberal ideas, his willingness to ignore or overrule the conservative state *duma* (parliament), and his autocratic habit of using emergency decrees to get his way created powerful enemies on all sides, not least at court, where the weak Nicholas resented his power. In 1911 Stolypin was assassinated by Mordko Bogrov, a shadowy Socialist Revolutionary who, in classic Russian fashion, also had connections with the secret police. Official connivance in the murder was suspected but never proven.

It is not difficult to see why Solzhenitsyn sympathizes with Stolypin. He was the very type of authoritarian but far-sighted ruler whom Solzhenitsyn has been urging upon his countrymen ever since his *Letter to the Soviet Leaders* in 1973. In his view, Stolypin was the one man who could have saved Russia from revolution, and there are strong grounds for thinking he may be right. Solzhenitsyn also urges upon his readers the anti-Tolstoyan idea that the course of history depends not on some mighty and impersonal "flow" of events (which Lenin melded with Marx's concept of the inevitability of the dialectical process), but on the actions of strong and powerful individuals like Stolypin, Lenin (who makes a cameo appearance here and plays a bigger role in subsequent

volumes), Bogrov, and Nicholas II—who was powerful, even if not personally strong.

Of course, history is full of "what ifs," and not even Solzhenitsyn can bring back the past, but the writer has repeatedly proved his prescience before, and this seemingly dusty reconstruction of the past turns out to have a surprising relevance to the present. For what is Gorbachev but a Soviet reincarnation of Stolypin, at least in his strength of purpose, steadfastness and authoritarian disposition, if not, so far, in his repressiveness? And is not Gorbachev, in his land reforms, trying belatedly to accomplish a version of that social revolution that Stolypin strove to realize some 80 years ago? After 70 years of development in the opposite direction, during which the Soviet state sought to smash the peasantry once and for all, there is a bitter irony in this latest twist of Soviet policy, especially for Solzhenitsyn. So far he has failed to commit himself publicly to an opinion on Gorbachev's *perestroika* and *glasnost,* but this very silence is eloquent against the background of his denunciations of everything that preceded them.

August 1914, then, has an undeniable relevance for Soviet readers, but what is there to recommend in it for Americans? Unfortunately, not very much. Neither the information it contains nor the interpretation of history is very new. Worse still, this "narrative in discrete periods of time," as Solzhenitsyn calls it (wisely eschewing the word "novel") is turgid and wooden beyond belief. Despite some exciting battle scenes and a sympathetic portrait of Samsonov, its hectoring narrative voice and feebly imagined didactic dialogues make it sound, for long stretches of the book, like an endless series of editorials by a superannuated columnist. . . .

This is a book to be read for selective information about prerevolutionary Russia, presented tendentiously, or for a glimpse of where a great writer has got to in the twilight of his career. It is not, unfortunately, either entertainment or art. The master has lost his way.

> *Michael Scammell, "Rewriting the Russian Revolution," in* Book World—The Washington Post, *August 13, 1989, p. 5.*

CLARENCE BROWN

[*The Human Experience*] is the brainchild of a committee of Philadelphia Quakers, who induced the Soviets to go along with it, and it has the unexceptionable aim of bringing our two peoples closer together by having them read each other's writers. We are in far greater need of it than the Russians, let me hasten to say, since that nation of voracious readers is familiar with Salinger, Styron, Updike, and Alice Walker, not to mention classic American writers. Even literate Americans are, by and large, familiar only with those Soviet writers whose extraliterary activities have landed them on the front page.

But this arriving all swaddled in good intentions should not induce criticism to lay down its arms. It is on balance a valuable collection of good writing, well worth the price of admission. But its program, its upbeat feel-good theme—that we and they are just folks, very similar, and ought to know each other better—admits into its pages that drop of tar in the honey, as the Russian catchphrase has it, that can be highly irritating.

Take two brief works as representatives of the tar. Andrei Voznesensky's **"At Ford's Theater"** conjoins the poet reading his poems "in a quavering voice" with the imagined ghost of Lincoln. It is a silly and inauthentic poem to begin with, and the English translation is so clunkingly inept as to provide a kind of sodden fun, but how it fits the theme! Soviet poet and Great Liberator! That it is a terrific cultural interface seems to have obscured the fact that it is also a waste of paper. John Updike is the author of some fine short fiction, but his contribution here is a weak sketch called "Still of Some Use" (the members of a sundered family rummage, literally, in the attic of their past); its Norman Rockwell quotient is sufficiently high to qualify it. The tendentious impulse behind *The Human Experience,* admirable as it is, means that something other than literary excellence rules the choice of its selections.

Still, *The Human Experience* is fortunately also full of wonderful writing, both Soviet and American. I am personally very grateful to have encountered works of my own compatriots I didn't know before. Bel Kaufman's "Sunday in the Park," for instance, is a jewel of a story. (p. 40)

American readers will encounter here one of the Soviet Union's greatest contemporary writers, Valentin Rasputin, though the story selected (it has been published in an edition for children) lacks the darkness and the moral weight of his finest work. Bulat Okudzhava's powerful **"Girl of My Dreams"** is one of the few fictions that alludes to the Gulág. The title refers poignantly both to the impossibly glamorous heroine of a movie and to the narrator's mother, released in a near-vegetative state from a labor camp the very week when the movie held all Tbilisi in thrall. Anatoly Kim's moving story "Road Stop in August" presents three Red Army soldiers, an officer and two men, one of whom is being taken to court-martial for refusing to fire on an escaping prisoner. Free of any special pleading, it is full of a genuine pathos.

The better collection, *The New Soviet Fiction,* consists of 16 stories, most of them published very recently, and all of them chosen by one man, Sergei Zalygin, editor of the highly influential journal *Novy Mir.* This is not a feel-good anthology, nor has it any ideological ax to grind. His principal criterion for inclusion appears to have been nothing more than literary excellence, though a secondary yen for variety must be held to account for one or two of the lesser things. It is a banquet of good reading—some of it grim, some of it inspired silliness, and one, at least, a mindblowingly complex work of metafiction.

The world presided over by bureaucrats, politicians, and police dogs is for the most part simply irrelevant and goes unmentioned, which will come as quite a surprise to readers familiar only with the work of those Soviet writers who normally manage to excite any attention in foreign translation. There are exceptions to this, and two of them, tellingly enough, were written in the "Period of Stagnation" and only achieved publication under Gorbachev's new arrangement.

One is I. Grekova's **"No Smiles,"** an account of a woman scientist (under her real name, Elena Ventsel, the author is one of the U.S.S.R.'s most distinguished mathematicians) whose unspecified ideological error leads her to be subjected to the standard ritual degradation, a public pillorying by her own colleagues. Written in 1970, this first appeared in 1986. The other is a narrative by Vladimir Soloukhin, **"Stepanida Ivanovna's Funeral,"** in which the narrator describes the harrowing and degrading red tape he must fight his way through

in order to bury his mother in her native village. First the funeral supply store is out of coffins, then he must stand in line to get a quite unsuitable coffin (the only model to arrive), then (but only with some high-level pull from the ministerial level) he manages to get the coffin sealed in lead for the train journey, then he is obliged to trick the village priest into performing the service without the necessary permit, then he must intervene, with imperfect success, to save the priest from the wrath of the bureaucrats . . . and so on. He constantly reflects on how simple and humane this business formerly was, and still is, he supposes, in the West. It was written even earlier in the Brezhnev era, in 1967, and had to wait 20 years to see the light of day.

These two works read more like reports than works of the imagination, but the only other story with any overt political content could never be accused of factuality. It is a burlesque romp by Bulat Okudzhava called **"The Art of Needles and Sins,"** a parody of the whole ethos of Stalinism. The mere fact that the narrator, Okudzhava himself, wears a mustache and comes from Georgia lends him enough kinship with the dictator whose image glowers down from every wall to ease his way slightly; but he is still clapped into jail for sitting in a railway restaurant late at night nursing his drink. A handbook warns citizens that Western spies can be detected by their habit of sitting alone at tables with no food and one drink.

Two of the best works deal with the mysteries of time. S. Yaroslavtsev's "The Details of Nikita Vorontsov's Life" is a work of science fiction (under his real name, Arkady Strugatsky, the author collaborates with his brother Boris on fiction known to SF fans around the world), about a man who lives serial existences, all starting from the same point.

Equally gripping and with much greater philosophical depth is the best story in the collection, Andrei Bitov's **"Pushkin's Photograph (1799-2099)."** It is a meta-fictional narrative, and true to the mode, it is intensely conscious of itself as narrative. The author appears in person and even describes the very circumstances in which he is producing the fiction in hand—the insects around his lamp, the interruptions of his little boy, the scene out the window. It is the summer of 1985. Starting here, he creates a range of time that stretches a century into the future and an equal length into the past. In the future (2099) a cultural congress has returned for its meeting to the Earth, now more or less a museum relic, with the better parts such as Petersburg preserved under glass. On this 300th centenary of Pushkin's birth they lament the skimpiness of the great poet's iconography. A committee selects one Igor Odoevtsev (a descendant of characters in Bitov's best-known novel, *Pushkin House*) to become the first chrononaut and return to the time of Pushkin in order to photograph him and record his voice. (pp. 40-1)

Like most of Bitov's work, this story is full of wit and the electric excitement, the sheer exuberance of creativity—art delighting in the miracle of its own existence. The art of Pushkin, finally, is the true heroine of the work. Igor returns defeated and mad, with no photographs of the person and no recordings of the voice. But the words of Pushkin—they are the genuine, the indelible time-travelers. No such "moral" is spelled out, of course, but that, as I read it, is the implication. It is highly satisfying, and so is the greater part of this valuable collection. (p. 41)

Clarence Brown, "Pen Pals," in The New Republic, *Vol. 201, No. 14, October 2, 1989, pp. 40-1.*

SONYA MICHEL

The Russian Revolution brought with it a flowering of experimental culture that not only captured the optimistic spirit of the new Soviet society but also won for Russian literature, music, and visual arts a prominent place in the modernist movement. By the mid-1920s, however—even before the advent of Stalinism—the government had begun to clamp down on cultural expression, and the brave, bold creations of the Mayakovskys and Briks were displaced by the leaden, dutiful productions of the Gladkovs and Serafimoviches. Until the recent era of *glasnost,* neither Westerners nor Russians had caught more than a brief glimpse of any form of Soviet culture that did not carry the official imprimatur. Smuggled manuscripts, mimeographed *samizdat* texts, the writings of exiles—these have been the vehicles for authentic literary voices. We will never know how many works went unwritten or unpublished during the decades when artistic production was tightly controlled and dissidents risked persecution.

The appearance of three collections of recent Russian short stories not only signifies the far reaching effects of *glasnost,* but also assures us that even during its darkest hours the Soviet government failed to stifle literary production entirely. Writers continued to write, apparently cherishing the hope that someday they would be able to publish. Stories appearing for the first time in [*Balancing Acts: Contemporary Stories by Russian Women,* edited by Helena Goscilo; *The Human Experience: Contemporary American and Soviet Fiction and Poetry,* edited by the Soviet/American Joint Editorial Committee of the Quaker U.S./U.S.S.R. Committee; and *The New Soviet Fiction: Sixteen Short Stories,* edited by Sergei Zalygin] were written years, even decades ago. The writers have witnessed, in their own lifetimes, an abrupt shift in the cultural climate and in their literary fortunes. In the words of S. Yaroslavtev, an author in the Zalygin collection, these authors have all "been wanting to sing for some time now."

The extent of Soviet cultural repression—indeed, of political repression of all sorts—is no secret to Americans. Thus I could not help finding William Styron's foreword to *The Human Experience* disingenuous. . . . Speaking through the persona of a Japanese historian writing in the year 2050 about the United States and the Soviet Union in the twentieth century, he claims, "What strikes the historian most forcibly is how similarly the two countries behaved as powers in the world arena and how, in ideals and ambitions, they so closely resembled each other." Their "greatest common sin . . . lay in not leaving other nations and other people alone, to work out their destinies on their own terms."

In seeking common sins, Styron obscures that which was unique to the Soviet Union: the *gulag.* The United States can surely be faulted for failing to protect the civil and human rights of all its citizens, but its record pales in comparison to that of the U.S.S.R. Styron's equation holds up only as long as one ignores decades of Soviet history, something Daniil Granin, the author of the Soviet foreword to the collection, is unwilling to do. Until recently, he writes, the best Soviet books have appeared "not at the authorities' behest but despite the authorities. . . . *Perestroika,* democracy, and *glasnost* are rapidly freeing minds from fear, mental stupor, and other people's imposed truths." (pp. 23-4)

To bring out what is universal and shared in the lives and literary styles of the Americans and Soviets, the book orders pairs of "matching" stories and poems according to the stages of the life cycle. Yet, like the two forewords, many of the pairs work *against* the intentions of the editors, highlighting contrasts rather than parallels.

Nonetheless, these turn out to be illuminating in their own right, for, like most comparisons, they reveal aspects of both Soviet and American life that might otherwise remain obscured. Take two stories about childhood, Valentin Rasputin's **"French Lessons"** and Joyce Johnson's "The Children's Wing." In the Russian story, a poor young man leaves his village to attend high school in a distant town. Desperately hungry, he gambles with his schoolmates to win money for food. His French teacher, aware of his plight, offers him meals, which he refuses out of pride. To preserve her student's fragile dignity, the teacher herself gambles with him, gets caught, and ends up losing her job.

In Johnson's story, a mother stops at a Chinese takeout restaurant on the way to visiting her son in the hospital. Food is just one of the many things she buys: "With a sick child, you're always trying to bring different pieces of the outside in, as if to say, *That's* the reality, not this." For the American mother, food is merely an interchangeable cultural sign, while for the Russian student it constitutes an element of survival, without which his very pursuit of culture is in jeopardy.

Americans like Johnson's mother and the family in another story in this collection, John Updike's "Still of Some Use," enjoy a level of consumption that would be unthinkable for most of the Russian characters, who live in a world of cramped communal apartments and scarce, shoddy goods. Not surprisingly, the Americans' attitude toward "things" is casual, taken for granted. For all their *materialism*—their acquisitiveness—they are indifferent to *materiality.* Things are valued less for their functions than for the meanings that accrete to them. As Updike's Ted, a divorced father, cleans out the attic of his former home with his ex-wife and teenaged sons, he meditates nostalgically on the detritus of contemporary American childhood—broken games with names like "Mousetrap" and "Drag Race"—which becomes a symbol of his ruined marriage.

One of the starkest stories in the collection, Bulat Okudzhava's **"Girl of My Dreams,"** casts a very different light on the material world. A twenty-two-year-old student makes plans to receive his mother, returning after ten years in a Siberia. He knows she will no longer resemble the young woman of his boyhood memories, but he thinks that after a quiet talk over a good meal they will go to a movie—the popular *Girl of My Dreams*—and she will begin to relax and ease back into normal life.

His neighbor in the communal apartment knows better. A veteran of the gulag himself, Meladze is not surprised when the woman cringes, barely able to speak or respond to her son's attentions, and he gently tells the young man not to expect too much.

> "Buy fruit for her," Meladze said.
> "What kind of fruit?"
> "Cherries. Buy cherries."

Following Meladze's advice, the son asks his mother:

> "Do you like cherries? . . . "
> "What?" She didn't understand.
> "Cherries. Do you like cherries?"
> "I?" she asked.

While Updike's Ted gives meaning to the world around him by saturating it with his own narcissistic, bittersweet memories, Okudzhava presents us with a character who can barely connect with anything outside of herself because her organ of perception—her sentient self—has been virtually obliterated. (p. 24)

Unfettered by specific thematic concerns, Sergei Zalygin, the compiler of *The New Soviet Fiction,* has aimed for—and achieved—an unabashed display of writerly virtuosity. . . .

By arranging his selections alphabetically by author, Zalygin grants himself the last word, and, whether it was deliberate or simply fortuitous, the position allows him to ruminate on the existential status of Soviet authors, including those who precede him in the volume. The narrator of **"Prose,"** one Vladimir Ivanovich Gustov, recounts his painful dealings with opportunistic writers' unions, arbitrary editors, envious literary consultants, and family members who are less than awed by the idea of having a famous author in their midst. . . . Hiding behind Gustov's lamentations, Zalygin, tongue-in-cheek, no doubt thoroughly enjoys skewering the literary establishment to which he himself belongs. But, like many Russian intellectuals before him, he is also concerned that his country not be dismissed as a cultural backwater. Gustov informs his readers that the stuff of modern and postmodern literature is not real events, which are too numerous to be of interest, but myths, legends, parables:

> Laksess—remember his *Nuclear Power Plant?* What is it if not a legend, completely in the spirit of an Icelandic saga, only contemporary? . . .
> The greatest contemporary writer will be the one who creates a *Divine Comedy* for the twentieth century.
> What if Vladimir Ivanovich Gustov were to create this *Comedy!* What if it were he? Well?

Though his story is clearly ironic, Zalygin seems to have followed his own character's advice in selecting the remaining stories for the volume, for few fit the mode of traditional realism. Even the most factual, **"No Smiles"** by I. Grekova (the pseudonym of Elena S. Ventsel, a mathematician as well as writer), uses eponyms referring to personal characteristics, instead of proper names, for its characters, lending the story a kind of depersonalized, Kafkaesque quality. The narrator, a mathematical researcher, is accused of some vaguely defined violations of the "RG" (rules of the game) of her institute. Afraid to call on her friends, Slim, Dark, and Bald, for fear of contaminating them, she goes alone to face her persecutors, Grayhair, Slick, Gnome, and Blowhard. The procedure drags on for months, and she learns that her case has been resolved in her favor only when her colleagues again begin to smile at her as she arrives at the institute one morning.

Grekova and her literary colleagues have no doubt found the devices of postmodernism congenial for working in an uncertain cultural climate. The authorial distancing and disclaimers that have become almost clichés in Western "metafictions" serve a function here that is both practical and poignant. Viktor Konetsky claims to have received the texts that make up "Cat-Strangler Silver" from a "chance reader . . . who had become mentally ill after a car accident." S. Yaroslavtsev (pseudonym of Arkady Strugatsky) tells "The Details of Nikita Vorontsov's Life" through fragments of a diary and transcripts of interviews. Other writers undermine potential claims to (or accusations of) verisimilitude by introducing supernatural or preposterous elements into their narratives. **"Love in Mustamagi"** by Arvo Valton is a romance about a couple whose relationship is conducted entirely by watching one another through the windows of their facing high-rise apartments. Though they never meet in person (Valton refuses to trivialize a state of pure alienation by reducing it to mere sentimentality), the woman becomes pregnant and gives birth to a baby girl, whose paternity the man claims and the woman acknowledges. . . .

In contrast to these highly stylized stories, Vladimir Makanin's **"Antileader"** appears to lack any literary qualities at all. In detached, clinical style, it recounts the demise of Kurenkov, a man wracked by uncontrollable jealousy, which poisons one friendship after another, bringing each to a violent end. Kurenkov's wife and even the administrators of the labor camp where he winds up patiently try to reach him, but he is beyond help. There seems to be no point to this depressing tale—until one begins to read it as an allegory of destruction, of the damage one powerful, relentless individual can wreak on the society around him.

The other "theme" collection, *Balancing Acts,* includes short fiction by women that is less self-consciously literary, more concerned with what the Russians call *byt*—day-to-day life. This is not surprising, for, although Soviet women have long been integrated into the labor force, the domestic division of labor between women and men has been even slower to change there than here. It is women who at the end of the workday must wait in queues for scarce commodities and conduct delicate negotiations over communal living space. The women's fiction reflects this in several ways. Instead of experimenting with aesthetics, the authors here probe more directly the psychology of women and men coping with an impersonal, highly bureaucratic society. Work figures significantly in the lives of female characters, who often reserve their greatest passion for their jobs. Not unlike American women, their "balancing acts" involve careers and family, personal desires and collective goals, momentary satisfactions and long-term emotional stability.

In **"A Business Trip Home,"** Anna Mass explores the feelings of an ambitious scientific researcher returning from an extended field expedition. Her elderly parents fail to dote on her with their usual lavish attention, in part because they are drained from caring for her teenaged son, who also greets her coolly. She reflects,

> "I wanted to comfort [him], but how? He has his secrets, which he has no desire to share with the woman sitting next to him, this so-called mother who lives two parallel lives and knows nothing, nothing about that unique, that most important life which she herself once created and which now has become alien to her.

Though Mass writes with a heavy hand, her portrayal of the tense relationship between this woman and her son will resonate with every working mother.

Career also serves as a source of identity and redemption for Agrippina, the title character in Maia Ganina's **"Stage Actress."** Agrippina's company is playing in a busy vacation town when a cholera epidemic hits. As the evacuation begins, some of the actors want to leave, but Agrippina pleads with the directors to let the company stay: "Art is essential for people at times of disaster; it helps them think, unites them, and gives them faith." After a successful performance, "she thought about how good it was that she would stay through to the end, see how things developed, and experience it just like everyone else." Though Agrippina's attitude of dutiful self-sacrifice would be worthy of any socialist-realist heroine of labor, the story as a whole can be read as a radical statement of the responsibility of the artist in dark times.

In these heady days, it is easy to assume that the writers and artists who, like Agrippina, kept the faith can now breathe free. There are, however, many observers from both East and West, left and right, who express serious reservations about the direction and permanence of *glasnost*. Because the Soviet Union now faces severe economic and ethnic crises, they warn, a reversal may occur at any moment. True enough. But the collections here have drawn on a deep wellspring of writings that will not soon be exhausted and would be difficult (though not impossible) to dam up. (p. 25)

> Sonya Michel, "They Had Been Wanting to Sing for Some Time," in Boston Review, *Vol. XIV, No. 6, December, 1989, pp. 23-5.*

SALLY LAIRD

This November [1989] Glasgow played host to a group of writers, poets and critics from the Soviet Union as part of its excellent *New Beginnings* festival of Soviet arts. . . .

The choice of guests inevitably reflected the tastes of the organizers—particularly that of Katya Young, the chief co-ordinator of the two-weekend event; but the general, laudable, aim was to introduce new names and faces and give prominence to those writers and critics who have only been able to emerge fully (or to re-emerge) in the past two or three years. The list of invitees included veterans such as Vladimir Lakshin, the sympathetic critic of Solzhenitsyn and Bulgakov who had to "bury himself in the classics" all through the Brezhnev years; Vladimir Makanin, a powerful and well-established prose writer who has only recently found a properly appreciative audience; and Vladimir Sorokin, a talented thirty-three-year-old whose original, comic and often obscene prose has yet to be published in the Soviet Union (although it has been widely translated).

For anyone concerned with the progress of *glasnost,* the works of Sergei Kaledin—who was present at the first of the two literary weekends—are of particular interest. Kaledin began writing in the mid-1970s, but it wasn't until 1987 that he was able to publish a volume of short stories. The reason for the long ban on his work is not hard to fathom: he treats a range of unmentionables, from life at the bottom end of the Soviet army to the pleasures of a graveside drink or what happens to a corpse in sandy soil. His reputation was established by two novellas which eventually appeared in the journal *Novy Mir*—*The Humble Cemetery* and *The Construction Battalion.* The latter, however, was published only after a delay of eight months: it was held up when the military censors objected to the depiction of the "low moral and political state" of the battalion in question. . . .

The Humble Cemetery is a bizarre, rambling tale of the life of gravediggers in Moscow, all of them out to make a quick ruble from the "late lamented", sometimes by the hasty recycling of "ownerless" graves. Catriona Kelly has done an impressive job in finding a convincing English strain of gravediggerese to match the Muscovite version. . . .

Another of the participants, Yevgeny Popov, who disappeared from view (and from the Writers' Union) after the "Metropol" scandal of the late 1970s, has now resurfaced in print with a volume of short stories entitled ***Zhdu lyubvi ne verolomnoi*** (literally, "I seek unperfidious love"). The brevity of his stories seems to reflect a kind of stuntedness in his characters' melancholy world-view (though most have fleeting and uncomfortable intimations of greater and lovelier lives). Popov, like Kaledin, uses a vernacular to convey his characters' thoughts, and it is a specifically *Soviet* vernacular, one in which the syntax of thought itself, its logic rather than its vocabulary, has been turned over to cliché. Non-Russian-speakers in the audience had to get by with an English translation piped over the earphones; just about all right for the stories, but they would have to take on trust that poets such as Olga Sedakova, Ivan Zhdanov or Aleksei Parshchikov were really all they are cracked up to be.

> Sally Laird, " 'Glasnost' in Gravediggerese," in The Times Literary Supplement, *No. 4526, December 29, 1989-January 4, 1990, p. 1440.*

SOVIET LITERATURE UNDER *GLASNOST*

CRAIG R. WHITNEY

Imagine the freedom of suddenly being able to write what you think—after years of censorship, of suddenly being able to say the things you want to say instead of only the things the authorities will let you say—and you will have some idea of both the excitement and the difficulty of being a writer in the Soviet Union today.

"In Russia, a poet is more than a poet," Yevgeny Yevtushenko once said, and that may be part of the problem. Hardly a day goes by that he and Andrei Voznesensky, young poets when they stood up to Nikita Khrushchev in the 1950's, are not making speeches defending the frontiers of glasnost, the new openness, against the bureaucrats and blackguards who oppose it. Hardly a week leaves Anatoly Rybakov alone in his study. The man whose novel ***Children of the Arbat*** was the most openly anti-Stalinist work ever published here [in the Soviet Union] when it came out in 1987 is called on instead to write articles and open letters to mainstream newspapers and magazines demanding justice for the innocent victims of Stalin's purges. These writers see their mission as making the country come to terms at last with its terrible past, in the hope that the truth about it can never again be suppressed and freedom stifled, as it was for more than two decades after Khrushchev first tried to lift the lid in the 50's. (p. 1)

[A] poet who is more than a poet is also something less. Writers caught up in a whirlwind of public activity are often too busy to write. Glasnost has not yet led to a new golden age of Russian literature; it has lifted the bans on the last one and restored to Soviet readers the heritage of works long denied them. Vladimir Nabokov, Mikhail Bulgakov and Nikolai Gumilev fill the pages of the literary journals, along with previously forbidden works by recent émigrés—so much so that there's no room for younger writers.

Works by Soviet writers that lay unpublished in their desk drawers for 20 years, and could only be circulated in samizdat in the 60's, can now be printed officially, and the result is an outpouring of books exploring the previously forbidden themes of Stalin's reign of terror in all its horrifying detail and complexity. But these are the preoccupations of an older generation, not of the younger one. And many of the books were written years ago by authors who expended their creative energies in the struggle to get them published, with little strength left to tackle today's problems. And there is the deeper, more troubling question raised by the fact that in the past the penalty for defying the censors was ostracism. Defiant authors either were never admitted to the official Writers' Union and sent to prison for "parasitism" for not holding a recognized job, or were expelled from the union and persecuted. Thus so-called official writers became dissidents, dissidents became émigrés, and the country lost some of its greatest literary talent—Aleksandr I. Solzhenitsyn, Vladimir Voinovich, Joseph Brodsky, Vasily Aksyonov. With some courageous exceptions, "official" writers had to be content with the minor, Aesopian art of sneaking clever allusions past the censor. But today critical writers no longer have to be dissidents to say what they think. Instead, there is a different, equally difficult challenge: to match the high literary standard of the past and to develop a new voice for the present. And they are finding it isn't easy.

As Mikhail S. Gorbachev keeps reminding everybody, change in this society is not a battle won—it's a battle that needs to be fought every day. "You have to read all the time," Mr. Voznesensky said on a rare weekend at home in his dacha in the writers' colony of Peredelkino.

> Every night, on television, in the papers, there's something new. It's impossible to keep up with everything that's happening. So artists aren't spending their time writing—they're reading, and talking. People want us to help them, to speak for them—they have to call on poets to do it, because we have no politicians in our country. But if you spend all your time this way, you don't have time to write a good novel. And if you stop fighting to go off to write a novel, maybe you'll find the freedom has been cut off. (p. 26)

"Journalism has reached such high levels," observed Sergei Zalygin, the editor of the magazine *Novy Mir,* "that writers aren't writing novels and poems—they're writing journalism. Pushkin, Tolstoy, Gogol and Dostoyevsky—they all turned away from literary form to public activity in their day, too."

Sergei Baruzdin, Mr. Zalygin's counterpart at the literary journal *Druzhba Narodov,* agreed: "The journalistic forms—articles, essays, expository prose—may be as good as the classic short story or tale used to be. Maybe we need journalism more just now."

These two monthlies, each with a circulation of 1.6 million, help define the upper contours of Soviet culture and set the agenda for it. Explaining change, calling for it, revealing the evils of the past are higher on their agendas right now than is exploring new art forms. "At its very basis, glasnost is a speaking from the mind, and its primary cultural expression is the document," the American scholars Nancy Condee and Vladimir Padunov wrote recently in *Forum,* the W. Averell Harriman Institute's journal of Soviet studies. Glasnost's aim is "to expose existing shortcomings and to galvanize popular support for social reform."

The most celebrated example of this kind of writing in fiction is Mr. Rybakov's ***Children of the Arbat,*** whose sequel *"1935 and Other Years"* is being published in book form [in 1989]. The two books—written in a simple, popular prose—tell what a group of ordinary people lived through during Stalin's years, revealing how Stalin had all his rivals assassinated or convicted in phony show trials, starved millions of peasants to death in the forced collectivization of agriculture and sent more millions of innocent Communist Party members and their families to their deaths in labor camps. Mr. Rybakov is immensely proud of the enormous success of ***Children of the Arbat*** in the Soviet Union and completely baffled by the less enthusiastic appraisal of the book when it came out last year in the United States, where some critics read it not as a document but as a literary work.

It took great courage for him to write ***Children of the Arbat*** in the 70's, and he went through many difficult years of doubt before *Druzhba Narodov* finally printed it in 1987. But he was not the first Soviet writer to take on Stalin—only the first to be rewarded instead of silenced or exiled for doing it. Mr. Solzhenitsyn, who tackled many of the same themes in *The Gulag Archipelago,* went further, saying that Lenin, whom the Soviet censors still will not permit writers to criticize, really ought to be held responsible for the system Stalin put in place, and for the reason Mr. Solzhenitsyn, who was stripped of his Soviet citizenship and deported in 1974, is still unpublishable [in the Soviet Union] although his work is still circulated privately. His name can't even be mentioned in print most of the time, reportedly on orders from Vadim A. Medvedev, the Politburo member in charge of ideology.

Mr. Solzhenitsyn is one of the few Russian authors living abroad (in Vermont) not competing for space in the Soviet literary journals these days with his former compatriots, who also have to measure up to posthumous works being published in Russia for the first time. Boris Pasternak's ***Doctor Zhivago*** was finally published in *Novy Mir* [in 1988]; Nabokov's *Lolita,* which Soviet customs used to seize as obscene literature, and Yevgeny Zamyatin's anti-Utopian novel *We* were both finally allowed to be printed here years after their publication in the West. ***The Disappearance,*** a previously unpublished novel about the effects of Stalin's terror on the families of high Communist Party officials, also came out last year; its author, Yuri Trifonov, died prematurely at age 55 in 1981. For Soviet readers who hadn't had a chance to read Mr. Brodsky's verse, or Mr. Voinovich's humorous satires about life in the Army, or Georgi Vladimov's brilliant fable about a prison-camp guard dog, ***The Faithful Ruslan,*** these are also feast days. But for contemporary Soviet writers, the competition has never been so tough. (pp. 26-7)

"Readers are now used to such a high literary level that it's simply impossible for most Soviet writers to satisfy their expectations," said Mr. Zalygin, the *Novy Mir* editor. His counterpart at *Druzhba Narodov,* Mr. Baruzdin, agreed:

> "Now we have only one problem: space. There are perhaps 10,000 members of our Writers' Union—probably only 300 of them are really good writers in any sense of the word. Nabokov is no threat to some of those 300—they don't write any worse. But he is a threat to the rest. They wrote what was expected of them in the past—but it wasn't literature. (p. 27)

It was hardest, in the Brezhnev years, to get provocative allusions past the censor and onto the 30 or so mainstream establishment stages in Leningrad and Moscow. One of the most daring in the 70's was the Taganka Theater, directed by Yuri Lyubimov. He was hounded out to the West in the early 80's but lately has been invited back, and the only thing some Moscow intellectuals fear is that it may be too late. This season, and the last one, with a few exceptions, the established Moscow theater has been dead, a judgment the leading Soviet directors don't quarrel with.

What's the problem, you might wonder—now that they can finally put on long-banned plays by Beckett, Ionesco and Cocteau, wouldn't people be flocking to see them? "These plays were written many years ago, and have aged considerably," the critic Irina A. Vasilinina wrote in the monthly journal *Teatr,* "they have little in common with our social context or our whole theatrical tradition."

And modern Soviet plays? There have only been a few of note in the last several seasons. It's as if most contemporary writers for the theater knew only one way to make a point—the theater of allusion—and now that it's no longer necessary, they don't know what to write. "The virtuosity of the art reached dizzying heights," Ms. Vasilinina wrote. "The entire theatrical world—from authors and officials to viewers in the audience—came to expect, in any production, whether classical or contemporary, portentous allusions to the present day." Mr. Lyubimov's productions, whether of Bulgakov's great novel, *The Master and Margarita,* or of Trifonov's **House on the Embankment,** underlined the allusions to evil with gongs, flashing lights and deafening music so obviously that no one could possibly miss them. "The theater was trying to be a tribunal, alluding to the faults of contemporary society and suggesting the way to bring about a better future," Ms. Vasilinina explained.

It seemed like exciting theater in the Brezhnev days when the official line was that nothing was wrong in the best of all possible worlds. But today, as Ms. Vasilinina wrote, "More has been said directly from the very highest tribunals of the country about the tragic facts of the past and the open sores of the present than the most courageous of our theaters could ever hint at." She quoted one director (Yuri N. Pogrebnichko): "If you had asked me 15 to 20 years ago what kept me from putting on good plays, I would have answered, they won't let me. Now I would answer, I don't know."

One answer may be that mainstream Moscow theater may not be the right place to look for the renewal. Experimental, underground theaters—the equivalent of Off Off Broadway in New York—have proliferated in Moscow and Leningrad in the past few years, and there almost anything goes. Sergei Kurginyan's Na Doskakh (On the Boards), a little theater on the third floor of a recreation hall behind the dormitory for Moscow Conservatory students, is one that recently made it to officially recognized status.

After a recent performance of a play on the sensitive theme of the Chernobyl accident, Mr. Kurginyan came out and explained the purpose of the play to the audience. "In the last 25 years," he told them, "there's been a deheroization—not only in literature but in politics and in every other sphere of our life. Society can't deal with real heroism any more. We need to raze everything, and start all over again; we need to build a completely different, parallel structure to the society." He spoke in a torrent of words, passionately, but before the evening ended one man in the audience told him there was only one thing wrong—he didn't think it was art.

Viktor Yerofeyev, one of the champions of the new generation of prose writers—those whose works the editors of the monthly journals haven't had room to print much of yet—thinks the new literature that emerges from glasnost will not be political at all, for the very same reason Mr. Kurginyan says it has to—disillusionment. "The Russian avant-garde, the generation of the 1960's, were all liberal in spirit," Mr. Yerofeyev said.

> They believed in the perfectibility of man. Now, after all the corruption and immobility of the 1970's, the hypocrisy of the Brezhnev years, younger Russian artists are more skeptical. I think it's a healthier attitude, because one of the most dangerous tendencies in our culture is messianism, the point of view that we are superior to everybody else.

As a result of this change, some of the younger poets are renouncing the Yevtushenko-Voznesensky role and abjuring politics altogether, exploring pure form and the play of words instead. One such writer is Aleksei Parshchikov, a bearded, bespectacled young man invited with the well-known poet Bella Akhmadulina to represent the Soviet side at an evening of poetry readings at Spaso House, the United States Ambassador's residence in Moscow, in honor of the visiting American poet Howard Nemerov. Mr. Parshchikov read his **"New Year Verses"** under the magnificent chandeliers of the vast, pastel-blue living room:

> If the origin of time is ringing in your ears
> remember the taming of the beasts,
> how they entered the waters of the flood, yet emerged:
> a sheep brought the alphabet in a skin bag,
> a to z in a fuzzy baalamb;
> a horse as if baked in ice
> more graceful than man
> apostle of motion;
> a cow descended from terrestrial orbit
> but still there in thought;
> a donkey—head in front,
> otherwise—a back on little legs,
> use it!

Whether poems with no political content like these can be published in the big literary journals and what the censors think of them are things that matter little to these new writers. Another one who was present at Spaso House, Tatyana Shcherbina, a poet in her early 30's who writes nonpolitical verse and who has not been admitted to the Writers' Union despite recommendations from Miss Akhmadulina and the well-known writer Fazil Iskander, pointedly told the newspaper *Sovetskaya Kultura,* "The avant-garde expresses everything possible—not anything useful or important." She later heard that Mr. Medvedev, the Politburo ideology chief, had telephoned the editor to say he thought publishing the interview with her was a mistake.

"I write what I have to," she said.

> The question of whether it will be published, or how, doesn't interest me. I won't adapt to their system—they can either print what I've written, or goodbye. That's [Joseph] Brodsky's position, and he got the Nobel Prize. The same people here who are now saying he's a great poet, and that it's our loss that he left, were saying a few years ago that he really was mediocre, and a traitor as well. They changed. Tomorrow the situation will be different,

and they'll change again. I don't put much trust in it, or in them.

"I don't know how you can write intelligibly about today," Mr. Okhudzhava said. "About the past, everybody knows what to say. But about today, even our leaders are telling us they don't know what to do. It's become much more difficult to write. You need to understand the times before you can have something to say about them." (pp. 27-8)

Tankred Golenpolsky, a critic and freelance publisher, said,

It's vitally important that this country regain its past. Trashy writers and dangerous ideas sprang up in the past because we were denied our past, people were simply ignorant about it. But in the future we'll begin to judge writers not by how sharply they criticize Stalin but by whether they show artistic qualities. We're coming to the point where we need new content, and new forms. In literature they have to find a new kind of hero. Critical realism has to come back—the traditional, Russian creative realism of Gogol and Chekhov. The human being against the state, the establishment against the individual—the Kafkaesque corridors of power. Yuri Trifonov died too soon, but then, the most powerful works always have appeared precisely when they were forbidden.

The new freedom came too late for some of the greatest Russian writers who were forced to emigrate in less tolerant times, and the literary scene is poorer without them.

"The situation for our younger writers is very difficult," said Mr. Zalygin.

These are new times, and new times call for a new style. Dostoyevsky and Tolstoy created one appropriate for their day. But only writers of genius, like them, can create a new style. Our writers are looking for one—but they haven't found it yet. If the older generation weren't so much involved in journalism, I think they might find one—maybe Valentin Rasputin would, or Fazil Iskander, or Viktor Astafyev, but they're all too distracted by other things. There are only seven or eight writers of great stature in the last wave of emigration—Solzhenitsyn, Brodsky, [Aleksandr] Galich, Vladimir Voinovich, Vasily Aksyonov. If Aksyonov had stayed here, I think he might have created the new style. . . .

"If Aksyonov had stayed here, I think he might have created the new style," Mr. Zalygin repeated, "but he can't do it abroad. You need to be among your own people, immersed in your own language. We lost a—potentially—very great writer in Aksyonov."

"Last year was the freest year in more than 70 years of Soviet power," Mr. Yerofeyev said. "I think it will also turn out to be a very strong literary year as well." (p. 28)

Craig R. Whitney, "Glasnost Writing: So Where's the Golden Age?" in The New York Times Book Review, March 19, 1989, pp. 1, 26-8.

JOHN KOHAN

A cyclone fence and metal bars encircle the stage. Like a caged animal, a slender young woman in black paces back and forth. Suddenly, she rattles the prison door, her pale fea-

tures exposed by the spotlight. "Three hundred forty-nine days! Three hundred forty-nine days!" she screams. "Bite on your hat, anything to keep from sobbing!" Few in the audience at Moscow's Sovremennik Theater stifle the emotion inspired by such searing scenes from Eugenia Ginzburg's memoirs of the Gulag, *Journey into the Whirlwind.* An innocent victim of the Stalinist purges, the heroine endures humiliating interrogations, strip searches and endless nights during which she covers her ears to block out the cries of the tortured. In a final, chilling tableau, she even welcomes assignment to the labor camps as a liberation. Viewers leave speaking in hushed tones, bludgeoned by the past.

In the colonnaded auditorium of the House of Physicians, other Muscovites listen transfixed to a recording of poet Anna Akhmatova reading her long-banned poem *Requiem* in a deep, rasping voice. When the melancholy cadences end, literary historian Lydia Chukovskaya, 82, recounts how she memorized the verse from scraps of paper that Akhmatova had handed her before the poet burned them in an ashtray.

The lights come up at the House of Composers after a screening of *The Puppy,* director Alexander Grishin's new film about a young defender of *perestroika* who loses his battle to expose corruption. At least one viewer is disturbed by a final scene showing the body of the youth floating in factory waste water. "Why can't the film have a positive ending?" asks the decorated war veteran. "Everything is so negative today." He is interrupted by hoots of protest from the audience.

Forget those quiet Moscow nights of song. There are not enough evenings in the month now to attend all the theater premieres, art exhibitions, poetry readings, film previews and cultural debates taking place in the Soviet capital. Time has to be set aside for watching trend-setting "musical-information shows" such as *View* or the monthly video digest *Before and After Midnight,* or for perusing the thick monthlies like *Novy Mir* and *Znamya,* which Soviets affectionately call the "fat journals." If the short-lived liberalization that followed the death of Joseph Stalin in 1953 was known as "the thaw," the cultural revolution set in motion by Mikhail Gorbachev has proved to be nothing less than a spring flood.

Culture has not remained the exclusive domain of Moscow intellectuals. On the Arbat pedestrian mall, would-be Pushkins and Pasternaks peddle their autographed poetry for a ruble or more a page. Sunday painters in Izmailovo Park display their labored tributes to the Russian futurists, suprematists and constructivists of the early 20th century. More than 200 experimental studio theaters have sprouted in Moscow alone. The cultural explosion has been felt as far away as the Pacific port of Nakhodka, where local artists set up a puppet theater workshop, and in Yaroslavl in the Soviet heartland, scene of a rollicking street festival celebrating the arts.

Artistic exiles and émigré art have been joyously welcomed home. Director Yuri Lyubimov is working again at Moscow's Taganka Theater, with the company he led until he was forced into exile in 1984. Literary journals print works by émigré writers like Georgi Vladimov, whose chilling moral parable of a Gulag guard dog let loose in society, *Faithful Ruslan,* appeared two months ago in *Znamya.* Nobel laureate Alexander Solzhenitsyn remains an exception, awaiting official rehabilitation from his sylvan refuge in Vermont.

Rejected works such as Boris Pasternak's epic novel *Doctor Zhivago* and Vasili Grossman's saga of the Battle of Stalingrad, *Life and Fate,* now occupy their rightful places on Soviet bookshelves. Mikhail Bulgakov, who died in 1940, has been accorded more recognition today than he enjoyed when he was alive; dozens of productions of his plays and prose works have been staged in Moscow since the advent of *glasnost,* including his satiric tale of Soviet social engineering, *The Heart of a Dog.* Says literary critic Vladimir Lakshin: "Even if *perestroika* were to end today, what has already been accomplished in the past three years will go down in the history of Russian literature."

Soviet audiences once delighted in conspiring with performers to find double meanings and nuances in every turn of phrase. Reading between the lines of classic and seemingly innocent plays became a form of art, a weapon against literal-minded censors who failed to perceive the broader message. The loosening of state controls over the press has made such clever stratagems irrelevant. Blunt social criticism can be found in the latest copies of the weeklies *Ogonyok* and *Moscow News.* Says theater critic Vilas Silunas: "When the press can say everything in black and white, why resort to stagings of Shakespeare?" (pp. 108-09)

Yet the new freedoms have not inspired anything approaching a Soviet Renaissance. The two landmark works that represent *glasnost* in the West, Tengiz Abuladze's film *Repentance* and Anatoli Rybakov's novel **Children of the Arbat,** were completed before the new period of liberalization. Says theater critic Igor Shagin: "Our artists now have freedom, more money, the right to travel abroad and meet foreigners here. People want to know where all the masterpieces are."

Poet Bulat Okudzhava, one of a handful of artists whose works captured the spirit of the first post-Stalinist era of reform, wonders about the aftereffects of the long period of stagnation. "The 'thaw' generation is tired and burned out," he says. "But the next generation is simply not prepared to carry on the reforms." Filmmaker Elem Klimov, the head of the Cinema Workers' Union, admits that the transition has been difficult, like "struggling to break down a wall, only to confront yourself on the other side." Says he: "For so long we have said, 'Give us our freedom, and we will show you!' But having freedom is not so simple. Many have discovered they have nothing to say."

Though the country's cultural life is being invigorated by a transfusion of the best of six decades of banned Soviet and émigré art, the competition has exposed the mediocrity of many established artists. The freshly released crop of classics has also set exceedingly high standards for aspiring artists, who were spoon-fed notions of official culture that are now held up to ridicule. Says Sergei Zalygin, editor in chief of *Novy Mir:* "Like Tolstoy and Dostoyevsky in the past century, our artists need to find a new style and a new way of thinking if they hope to create a psychological portrait of society today."

The sense that the artist has a prophetic mission in society has haunted Russian culture since the 19th century. That heavy burden crushed novelist Nikolai Gogol, who was never able to equal his masterpiece *Dead Souls.* It ultimately led other writers, like Leo Tolstoy, away from art and into dogmatic polemics. The weight can be felt today on the Soviet artistic community. But the essential paradox of *glasnost* is that when cultural leaders raise their voices, they can no longer be heard above the excited babble of an entire nation learning to speak for the first time. (p. 109)

John Kohan, "Freedom Waiting for Vision," in

Time, *New York, Vol. 133, No. 15, April 10, 1989, pp. 108-09.*

CELESTINE BOHLEN

As a short-story writer, Tatyana Tolstaya deals in ambiguities. As a Soviet citizen, she knows how to live with them. "Things can be good, while also being bad," said the 38-year-old great-grandniece of the author of *War and Peace.* "We can understand contradictions."

But Miss Tolstaya reached the limit of her tolerance for contradictions last month in Moscow when she learned that the Soviet Union's conservative literary establishment had been involved in organizing a chapter of PEN, an international organization of writers and editors devoted to respect for literary freedom.

"I was just astonished," she said in New York the other day during a tour to promote the English translation of her highly acclaimed collection of stories, **On the Golden Porch.** "It is all false. People who prosecuted writers not so long ago now have chosen to be members of PEN, which is a movement for human rights, not a literary organization. It is an awful situation because the victims are together with those who prosecuted them."

Miss Tolstaya's view—shared by among others, the Soviet émigré poet and Nobel Prize laureate Joseph Brodsky and, in Moscow, a group of about 100 writers—has raised questions within the PEN organization over how to treat a formal Soviet membership application at its 53d international conference, in Masstricht, the Netherlands. (p. C15)

In 1924, PEN turned down the Soviet Union's request to join and since then it has consistently opposed Soviet membership on grounds of persecution of writers and intellectuals.

Miss Tolstaya said the Moscow group had no legitimate standing. It was put together, she said, from two lists—one drawn up by conservative officials, and the other drawn up by more independent-minded writers and editors—that were presented as one. The group's first action was to protest the death threats against Salman Rushdie, whose treatment of Islam in his new novel, *The Satanic Verses,* has provoked the wrath of Ayatollah Ruhollah Khomeini.

"It is very easy to protect Rushdie, it is the easiest thing in the world," Miss Tolstaya said. "But when things happen in your own home, it is different. In our country, if our writers are put into prison, it would be good to have an organization that will use every means to protect us."

Today, with debate freer and the past more exposed, Soviet literary figures have brought old grievances into the open, confronting one another in the pages of literary journals or at writers' forums, seeking, if not retribution, then at least some form of explanation and, perhaps, confession of past misdeeds.

The prosecutors Miss Tolstaya referred to are those writers, editors and officials who in the past have been complicit in rooting out the liberal, the unorthodox or the impolitic from the world of Soviet letters—from the works of writers like Boris Pasternak, Alexander Solzhenitsyn, Vasily Aksyonov and Mr. Brodsky. Most of these—with the major exception of Mr. Solzhenitsyn—have had their reputations restored since the Soviet leader, Mikhail S. Gorbachev, increased official tolerance for open debate, but in the Soviet Union writers have long memories.

"People can change, and people can feel guilty for what they have done years ago," she said. "But I don't see any signs of these people confessing their guilt."

According to Miss Tolstaya, the degree of complicity varied. Sometimes, she said, it meant signing a letter or a petition of criticism or denunciation; sometimes, it meant voting to oust people from the privileged ranks of the Soviet writers' union. In some cases, it may have been simply well-timed silence.

Deciding who among Soviet writers is morally eligible to join PEN is a tricky question, one on which natural allies disagree. Miss Tolstaya parts company with Mr. Brodsky, for instance, in saying that the poet Yevgeni Yevtushenko's quiet efforts on behalf of writers in trouble make him acceptable.

In her view, writers on the initial list who did not deserve to be there included Yuri Bondarev, a leading conservative voice (who actually took himself out of the running soon after the controversy came out into the open in Moscow); Valentin Rasputin, whose Russian nationalism, in Miss Tolstaya's view, should be a disqualifier, and writers and editors—like Daniel Granin, an author, and Sergei P. Zalygin, editor of the literary monthly Novy Mir—who, while now regarded as progressive, she said had joined publicly in the condemnation of fellow writers.

Vladimir V. Karpov, head of the writers' union, she said, should not belong because his official status is simply incompatible with the independence required of a PEN chapter.

In several cases, Miss Tolstaya said, she is more forgiving than some émigré writers—whom she left unnamed—who she feels are out of touch with the world they left years ago. "Now we have glasnost, and they turn out to be far behind, with old ideals, old fears," she said. "And some things they say irritate us. It is like working the trapeze in the circus without a net, and they are below, telling us where to jump."

Miss Tolstaya's grandfather was Aleksei Tolstoy, who is known for his biography of Peter the Great; and her great-granduncle was Leo Tolstoy, the master of Russian prose. Miss Tolstaya—one of seven children of a Leningrad professor, the wife of a Greek-born philologist and mother of two sons—began to write only six years ago, a rare female voice in a predominantly male literary world. (pp. C15, C18)

This spring [1989], an alternative writers' group, April, has started in Moscow. Miss Tolstaya said she would like to see the new, independent writers' organization trade on the moral authority writers enjoy in Russia, and use it to protect their rights.

"April could be a force if, if, if—" she said. "If it develops a strategy, if it is based on common sense, if writers stop quarreling. That is many ifs."

"But Russians always go to extremes," she said. "This is the difficulty of building a democracy out of nothing. It is like a cat becoming a dog. It may be possible, but it will take a long time. And there will be a stage when the cat can no longer catch mice, and when she still can't bark." (p. C18)

> *Celestine Bohlen, "Soviet Author with Strong Feelings about PEN," in* The New York Times, *May 9, 1989, p. C15, C18.*

BETTY ANN KEVLES

The devil, his demons and a talking black cat appear suddenly in Moscow in Mikhail Bulgakov's 1938 masterpiece, *The Master and Margarita*. Suppressed by Stalin, the novel was not published until 1966. Since then, the stairwell to Bulgakov's apartment, the putative site of the extraordinary events he details, has been decorated with graffiti cats by literary pilgrims.

I was advised to visit the site when I stopped in London recently, en route to Moscow. At the Soho office of International PEN, I also picked up a list of writers concerned with *perestroika,* some of whom had represented the Soviet Union in May [1989] at the PEN congress at which six Soviet centers joined the world association of writers.

When I was chair of the Writers in Prison Committee for PEN Center USA West, nearly 150 writers were imprisoned in the U.S.S.R. Today the number is down to three. Not only Bulgakov's novel but Boris Pasternak's works are available in bookstores. So are Vladimir Nabokov's, mention of whose name was virtually forbidden only five years ago. And soon Aleksandr Solzhenitsyn's *The Gulag Archipelago* will be published in both Estonian and Russian.

In my hotel room near Lenin Prospect, I began telephoning the writers—an ordinary enough gesture but one I am advised would have been foolhardy even a year ago—whose telephone numbers I had in hand. (There is no telephone directory in Moscow.) Those I reached were happy to get together to exchange information on what it is like to be a writer today in the Soviet Union and in the United States. . . .

Russians read seriously. Half a century ago Stalin recognized writers as "the engineers of the soul." He understood their status in Russian society and tried simultaneously to placate and control them. Pushkin and Gorky were elevated to Olympian heights. Issac Babel and Osip Mandlestam were murdered. And he established the tenets of Soviet Realism as an artistic straitjacket, removing from the canon satirical fantasies like Bulgakov's. His stick was suppression, or worse. His carrot—membership in the Writer's Union.

Vladimir Stabnikov greeted me in front of a statue of Tolstoy in the garden. The Writer's Union is a large, graceful building in the embassy-row quarter of Moscow, originally the home of a friend of Tolstoy, the Countess Alsufyeva, and the setting for the scene in *War and Peace* where Pierre becomes a mason. Chartered in 1932, the union claims 10,000 members today, although now, as in the past, there are famous writers who have never applied for membership, and others of stature who have been rejected or expelled. But membership brings with it such a host of privileges that few can afford to ignore it. Members enjoy access to special housing, loans, and summers at writers' colonies, as well as the considerable prestige of joining the elite in this most highly stratified society.

Stabnikov, handsome and intense with dark eyes and a dark beard, is a union official, a consultant in the International department, who represented the Writer's Union in the Soviet delegation in Holland. . . .

Stabnikov is optimistic about *glasnost,* but wary about *perestroika.* "A thousand churches have opened in the past year," he noted, "but people still complain about the shortage of soap." Stabnikov's own recent accomplishment is yet one more testimonial to *glasnost:* He translated *The Russia*

House, John le Carré's newest espionage novel, into Russian. And he pointed out, eyes twinkling, that it has become very popular without benefit of advertising, talk shows or bookstore appearances. I cannot tell if the capitalist style of promoting books pleases or offends him.

There doesn't seem to be any need, at the moment, to convince Soviet citizens that they ought to buy certain books. Word of mouth suffices to make hot commodities of the newly released work of once suppressed writers. Not everything is off the censor's list, of course. The authorities recently stopped the distribution of a Russian edition of Freud.

And the Writer's Union? It is more than an elegant club with good food and copying facilities (unavailable generally in the Soviet Union). Along with material perks, Stabnikov explains, each member has the right to hire a secretary, a position sometimes filled in difficult times by non-union writers, like Josef Brodsky, to shelter them from prosecution for the crime of parasitism.

Translators such as himself, Stabnikov explained, are a large portion of the membership. In the multilingual federation that is the Soviet Union, translators not only translate literature from English into Russian as Stabnikov does (he also translates from Portuguese), they also translate literature from Russian into Armenian, Georgian, Estonian and the other official languages of the Soviet Union. . . .

I want to know how a writer initially gets published, joins the Writer's Union, makes contracts and earns a living. Do most writers use pen and paper? Does the paper shortage affect them? Beginning with the last question, he tells me that there is paper to write on although not always enough to publish books. Most writers type or get their manuscript typed by a typist. Word processors are rare, and the programs available lack a spelling check or a dictionary. As for breaking into print, the first step is acceptance by one of the "thick magazines," publications such as *Novy Mir* or *Ogonyok.*

Books usually appear in serial form, and if they are well received, may be published later between hard covers. Getting an editor's attention is a matter of a writer's persistence and connections. There are, of course, no literary agents. Writers represent themselves. But of course friendship helps. The company of other writers is not only creatively stimulating but a practical necessity.

The logistics of publication are unchanged since Tolstoy's day, Stabnikov believes. A writer presents a proposal to one of the dozen or so publishers in Moscow or Leningrad, gets a contract with an advance that is, in fact, his salary. Writers are paid per word, not by sales, and it is anyway impossible to know the sales figures of middle-level books. There are 7 million copies of **Children of the Arbat** in circulation (including the original thick magazine publication), apparently printed to satisfy demand, but the average print run is 15,000 copies, and only with a second printing will the author get more money. There are no royalties, no book market. Libraries are captives of the system, and the number of books printed seems to depend on whim. Moreover, Stabnikov points out, there is no way to know how well a book is selling. There is no mechanism, no computers, no way of gauging inventory and tracing the books.

One measure of success is the black market. If a novelist has only a few thousand books printed that sell for a couple of rubles, the same book may be available within days of distribution on the black market for many times the face price. One way to get rich off your own writing is to buy your own books as they appear and watch them inflate.

In Moscow, there is the Writers' Union way, and then, as ever, there is another way. On a clear evening in daylight that stretches almost to midnight, I stroll along the Arbat, once the intellectual hub of Moscow where about 15 years ago bulldozers destroyed many well-loved buildings and produced Moscow's only pedestrian mall. In this spring of heady freedom, there is the mood of Berkeley in the early '60s. Between poster shops and galleries closed for the night, soapbox orators attract small crowds. I listen to a Christian evangelist and a Hare Krishna. Knots of students drift from speaker to speaker, and when they hear American voices shyly open conversations. They want to know what we think about the Soviet Union, Moscow, *glasnost* and the Arbat. We ask what they think about [the clampdown on the student uprising in] China, the news of the massacre just leaking in via short-wave radio. But they are too caught up with what is happening inside the Kremlin to consider Tian An Men Square, about which there are only brief, official news clips.

Except for Yuri Ivanovich Gubar. He is a middle-aged, middle-sized man whom I notice standing beside a ledge where he is selling hand-typed poems for a ruble each. He tells me he is a plasma physicist on the faculty of Moscow University but also a poet manqué. So he has decided to market his wares the way the new co-op restaurants are selling caviar, a practice for which he was chastised in a recent periodical by a critic appreciative of his poems but irate at him for making poetry a commodity, for "selling poetry, especially in the shadow of the Pushkin Museum."

Gubar translated his poems freely for me, and I bought a few he had written during the first week in June [1989]. . . .

Ironic political verses of questionable quality. Do they reveal anything about the life of a Soviet writer? Though far from the elite in the Writer's Union, Gubar, too, now has the freedom to criticize. The Congress may turn out to be, like the Arbat, a safety valve where the disenfranchised vent pent-up frustrations that, once voiced, will be ignored:

> On the Arbat Street
>   Holler, and wild people will get
>   together.
> Because a fool hears
> Another fool from afar.

Gubar's fools are those who dare to see and tell the truth. Under *glasnost,* even fools and poets such as Gubar feel free to peddle their wares.

Betty Ann Kevles, "Making It in Literary Moscow," in Los Angeles Times Book Review, *August 13, 1989, p. 15.*

MARGARET ZIOLKOWSKI

In a recent issue of *Ogonek,* currently one of the most radical Soviet publications and a magazine to which even a recent and formerly hostile émigré like the writer Vladimir Voinovich now subscribes, there appeared a short poem by Nikolai Panchenko entitled **"Museum of the Year 1937."** The title refers to the worst year of the so-called Great Terror that shook the Soviet Union in the late 1930s. The poem begins with a reference to the Moscow headquarters of the

KGB and ends with a reference to Osip Mandelshtam, one of the most significant twentieth-century Russian poets:

> It will be opened in the building on the Lubianka,
> About which the press will give information,
> An old woman with the head of a monkey
> Will be appointed to greet
> the inquisitive
> And to turn on the light—
> Where there will be a text and a panorama,
> Where a young historian will recite
> In a sing-song voice Mandelshtam's verse
> about the mountaineer
> Over Stalin's moldering head.

This poem epitomizes many of the trends characteristic of the present-day Soviet literary publishing world. Its date of composition is given as 1961, a year that evokes the heyday of cultural liberalism under Khrushchev. Many of the works now being published, Anatolii Rybakov's **Children of the Arbat** doubtless being the best-known example, were initially composed in the 1960s in an atmosphere of what subsequently proved to be unjustified optimism about prospects for literary frankness. Panchenko's poem also conjures up another, very different period of literary activity, with its mention of Mandelshtam's famous poem about Stalin, whom the poet called "the Kremlin mountaineer." The composition and recitation of this poem served as the immediate reason for its author's arrest in 1934. It has now finally been published in the Soviet Union, as have numerous other previously suspect works by members of Mandelshtam's generation, many of whom perished or spent years in labor camps in the 1930s or 1940s. Finally, by its very title, as well as by its mention of Mandelshtam, his poem, the Lubianka, and Stalin, Panchenko's poem points to what is undeniably the major thematic interest of contemporary Soviet literature, the crimes and upheavals of the Stalin era. Important literary works that focus on the present are certainly being written and published, but the past has become an obsessive object of fascination with which the more mundane present cannot compete in the eyes of many readers. (pp. 639-40)

Soviet literature today is engaged in a massive effort to fill in the "blank spots" that exist because of deliberate suppression of specific writers, works, or themes. The older prose writers who now often appear in the tables of contents of the more liberal journals have been called "the passion-sufferers of truth" (*strastoterptsy pravdy*), a designation suggestive of the nearly religious intensity of the desire to recover the past. Those mentioned in these terms include Andrei Platonov, Boris Pasternak, Mikhail Bulgakov, Evgenii Zamiatin, Boris Pil'niak and Varlam Shalamov, all arguably victims of Stalinism. Pasternak's **Doctor Zhivago,** Bulgakov's story "The Heart of a Dog," Platonov's *The Foundation Pit,* several of Shalamov's Kolyma tales, Pil'niak's "Tale of the Unextinguished Moon," and Zamiatin's *We* are among the works recently made available to the Soviet reading public. One might also mention stories by Isaac Babel, another prose writer who could certainly be included in the list of "passion-sufferers." Older poets are also enjoying a renaissance, one aptly symbolized by the publication in 1987 of Anna Akhmatova's well-known and long suppressed **Requiem,** a lament on the imprisonment of her son, by not just one, but two journals, one of which accused the other of unethical preemption. Besides Akhmatova, the publication of poems and other writings by poets like Mandelshtam, Maksimilian Voloshin, Nikolai Kliuev, Nikolai Gumilev, and Marina Tsvetaeva should be mentioned, as should the publication of various of Vladimir Nabokov's works, most notably *The Defense.* Nabokov evokes very mixed reactions in Soviet circles, and there are still those who scorn him as the epitome of decadence, but the shift in official attitudes toward this so very unsocialistic writer has nonetheless been remarkable. In a recent round-table discussion of Nabokov in the prominent weekly *Literary Gazette,* the author Vladimir Soloukhin wryly told of being reprimanded for even speaking positively of the writer in a 1979 interview with the Voice of America and concluded in near amazement: "And now we're sitting here, and we're having a 'round table' on Nabokov. That's splendid."

Another important group of writers that is just beginning to be published are the "third-wave" émigrés, writers who left the Soviet Union in the past two decades. Many of Joseph Brodsky's poems have already been published, as well as an unofficial transcript of his 1964 trial for parasitism. Numerous poems by the playwright and bard Aleksandr Galich have appeared in various journals and there are plans for the creation of a special commission on his creative legacy. Vladimir Voinovich's satire *The Life and Extraordinary Adventures of Private Ivan Chonkin* is now appearing, as well as Sasha Sokolov's **A School for Fools,** a piece of literature unmatched for experimental daring by anything that has appeared in the Soviet Union in past decades. Another work by a third-wave writer soon to be published is Georgii Vladimov's **Faithful Ruslan.** Other third-wave productions that have been mentioned with enthusiasm in the Soviet press include, for example, Vasilii Aksenov's *The Burn,* Vladimir Maksimov's *The Seven Days of Creation,* and various works by Andrei Siniavskii, a writer imprisoned in the 1960s because of his irreverent pseudonymous publications in the West. Siniavskii himself, in an interview with the weekly *Moscow News,* an event which was a milestone in and of itself, expressed the opinion that his writings could easily be included in today's expanded literary spectrum. There is even talk of Alexander Solzhenitsyn in the press, and at a recent evening of readings at a theater in Leningrad, one participant read aloud a chapter about Stalin from *The First Circle.* And on July 12, 1989, in a stunning reversal of the long-lived anathema, Sergei Zalygin, the editor of *Novyi mir,* announced that a Soviet publishing house would issue the complete text of *The Gulag Archipelago.*

The émigré works whose titles are mentioned most often as candidates for publication in the Soviet Union frequently fall into the category of works that has attracted the greatest attention since the inception of *glasnost',* literature concerned with the Stalin era. Like **Children of the Arbat,** many of these works were published in the Soviet Union for the first time anywhere. Examples include Iurii Trifonov's **The Disappearance,** Daniil Granin's **Bison,** Vladimir Dudintsev's **White Robes,** Boris Mozhaev's *Peasant Men and Women,* Sergei Antonov's *Ravines* and *Vas'ka,* Anatolii Genatulin's *Tunnel,* Boris Iampol'skii's *Moscow Street,* Anatolii Pristavkin's *A Golden Cloud Spent the Night,* Anatolii Zhigulin's *Black Stones,* and several stories by Vladimir Tendriakov. The subject matter of these works ranges from the terror and the deportation of nationalities to Lysenkoism and the oppression of the postwar years. Similarly critical portrayals of the Stalin era previously published in the West and only recently officially available in the Soviet Union include, for example, Aleksandr Bek's *The New Assignment,* Iurii Dombrovskii's *The Department of Unnecessary Things,* Vasilii Grossman's **Life and Fate** (soon to be joined by his *Forever Flowing*), certain stories from Fazil' Iskander's cycle **Sandro of Chegem,** Lydia Chukovskaia's *Sof 'ia Petrovna* [*The Deserted House*], and Aleksandr Tvardovskii's poem **"By Right of Memory."** These literary exposés are by no means all equally radical in their implications, and it is possible to identify a progression toward increasing frankness among recent publications. In this connection, Latynina points out that literature has moved from the isolated consideration of the tragedy of 1937 typical of the Thaw to a broader perspective that includes the fate of the peasantry, the deported nationalities, the intelligentsia, the clergy, and religious believers. She also suggests that it is now possible to depict a hero who is not only anti-Stalinist, but alienated from orthodox Communist ideology as well, like the major protagonist of Dombrovskii's *The Department of Unnecessary Things.* (pp. 640-42)

The flood of writings about the Stalin era, fictional, memoiristic, and documentary, is so great that it has aroused fears in some quarters about the possible cheapening of the desire for information about the past. Rybakov summarizes the essence of this potential problem: "Everyone has rushed to criticize Stalin, including those who formerly glorified him, . . . people are writing about Stalin who have absolutely nothing to say about him. . . . All of this devalues, cheapens the subject, makes criticism untrustworthy, and that means unconvincing as well." Others fear that the truth may simply drown in a flood of literary and other discussions. Tat'iana Ivanova, however, takes a radical tack in responding to those who have had enough of literature on the camps, repression, and torture, and asserts that those who are less jaded will not miss a single " 'camp' publication, poem, or page of reminiscences, even if they are written quite awkwardly." Ivanova's assertion reflects an assumption of historical veracity, as well as the sense that this is what gives literature value.

Progressives like Ivanova and Rybakov are not alone in their concerns about current literature and its impact on Soviet readers. A vocal conservative point of view finds constant expression on the pages of congenial journals. "It's such a relief for a weary soul to pick up [the journals] *Our Contemporary* or *Young Guard.* The last stalwarts of Bolshevism!" declares a KGB employee in a humorous sketch by Reuven Piatigorskii. *Literary Gazette* also frequently gives space to diametrically opposed points of view. Conservatives fulminate on a variety of issues—on excessive and prejudiced concern with the past, on the absence of positive models, on the fear that **Children of the Arbat** may become a new *Short Course* (the notoriously biased official history of the party written in 1938), and on the mediocre artistic merits of works like **White Robes.** As progressive critics are quick to point out, conservative aesthetic strictures are often red herrings, introduced in an attempt to undermine the prestige of ideologically inimical productions.

A source of particularly spiteful conservative opprobrium is the growing corpus of works by previously little-known or unknown authors that feature controversial themes and contemporary settings and often represent a radical departure from established literary norms, a deliberate alternative to traditional styles and themes. While the authors of such works are younger than writers like Dudintsev, Granin, and Rybakov, they are generally by no means novices; they have often been active in literature for a decade or more, but may not have been published until now, except perhaps in the West. For example, Venedikt Erofeev's *Moscow to the End of the Line* [*Moskva-Petushki*], a controversial saga with an

alcoholic narrator, has received much attention abroad; it is now appearing in the Soviet Union in both journal and book form. Another novel published in the West is *Pushkin House,* an intricately crafted treatment of urban intellectuals by Andrei Bitov. Stories by, among others, Tat'iana Tolstaia, Liudmila Petrushevskaia, Sergei Kaledin, Viacheslav P'etsukh, and Valeriia Nabrikova, were published in Soviet journals for the first time anywhere. Such writings may offend traditional literary tastes through both their language and their subject matter. Sex, drunkenness, shattered families, domestic violence, the sordid and squalid existence of the economically, culturally, or spiritually deprived—these are the themes of much contemporary literature. The treatment of such topics in a style that often exploits the crudest of substandard colloquialisms, completely unmediated by a highminded authorial voice, is an extraordinarily radical phenomenon in a Soviet context and one that many readers find profoundly disturbing. (pp. 643-45)

Margaret Ziolkowski, " 'Glasnost' in Soviet Literature: An Introduction to Two Stories,' " in Michigan Quarterly Review, *Vol. XXVIII, No. 4, Fall, 1989, pp. 639-47.*

WILLIAM G. ROSENBERG

Few elements of culture are more central to the ways a society understands and defines itself than its representation of its past; and no aesthetic form plays a greater role in exploring the complexities of past experience than literature set in an historical context. For the past 50 years, as V. V. Karpov, the Secretary of the Writers Union reminded his colleagues at a symposium of historians and writers in April 1988, history in Soviet Russia has been a singular description of heroic achievement, a means of assuring that "our people, and especially our youth, could deeply understand the superhuman strength of our grandfathers and the sacred crystal purity of our fathers, the Leninist Guard. . . . " Fiction, drama, and poetry devoted to historical themes, meanwhile, has focused almost exclusively on the ostensible qualities of this heroism, fabricating the less apparent layers of historical "truth" as they were supposedly experienced by ordinary as well as "superhuman" actors. Together, history and literature distorted the past, corrupted an understanding of the present, and deeply affronted the sensibilities of all who knew better.

Perestroika and *glasnost'* have had a truly explosive impact on Soviet historians and writers. The foundation of reconstruction is an honest assessment of current realities, a condition that can only be met by peeling away layers of dissimulation and ignorance and understanding their origins. Few weeks pass without pathbreaking articles or stunning revelations in *Voprosy istorii, Novyi mir, Literaturnaia gazeta, Ogonek, Moscow News,* or even *Pravda,* which has begun regularly to publish "Pages of History." The very need to rebuild is recognition first and foremost of the limitations of Soviet development, not its heroic achievements; and recognizing the urgency of this need is itself to censure strongly the ways historians and writers have practiced their craft. *Glasnost'* has thus involved an agonizing self-evaluation within these professions, but it has also, paradoxically, made new efforts here absolutely central to the ongoing processes of revelation and rethinking that lie at the core of Gorbachev's struggle to rebuild. The task of creating a trustworthy history and of overcoming a broad disdain for the ways the past has been depicted in literature . . . are thus as important an element of *perestroika* as that of overcoming lack of confidence in the Communist party itself. Reconstructing the past is also, as the writer Astaf'ev argues, an act of atonement "for our shame and our guilt." (pp. 549-50)

Among historians there is broad agreement that new archival material should be made available, and that new factual data should be gathered and published about significant past events. Most of this concern is naturally centered around the distortions of the Stalin period. Few will disagree that important periods in Soviet political history, and especially the 1930s, now need to be thoroughly and honestly researched. For those under 40, even such titanic episodes as the Soviet experience in World War II largely remain "blank spaces". As the writer Astaf'ev confesses . . . , his own personal experiences during the "Great Patriotic War" bore absolutely no relationship to what is depicted in the official 12 volume history, nor do the experiences of countless others. "I was fighting in a completely different war," he reports. "Our historiography has never known a more falsified, concocted, invented publication."

Yet attacks on Stalin and efforts to get to the truth of the Stalinist period can also serve as "lightning rods", . . . protecting broader and more consequential myths from being destroyed. What, for example, of the relationship between Stalinism and Leninism, of the possible links between Lenin's conceptions of party organization and the ways in which Stalin and others used and distorted them? And what about the revolution itself? To what extent should the facts of early Soviet history be scrutinized, the myths of Lenin himself debunked? Questions of history serve, of course, not only as a means of understanding the past, but also of legitimizing political and social institutions, of creating and reinforcing the values and principles of political and social life. (p. 550)

These issues are clearly recognized by S. P. Zalygin, a senior editor of what is arguably the most important and progressive literary journal, *Novyi mir* . . . Zalygin, in effect, is arguing with his colleagues for an approach to historical literature that probes far beneath appearances, and urging them to explore the realities of emotion, feeling, fantasy, myth, and other components of experience whose existence can be represented even in objectively unrealistic literary scenarios. Clearly, however, this is still not an easy case to make. While such masters of the nature of man as Bulgakov and Pasternak are revered by millions of intelligent Soviet readers, many literary figures still in positions of authority clearly hope to preserve the forms and outlooks that produced what [has been described] as the "rich and varied socialist literature" created under Soviet rule.

There are, of course, several very different reasons for this conservatism that together suggest both the complexities and difficulties of cultural *perestroika* as well as the remarkable nature of its achievements so far. One is simply the way in which new modes of thinking jeopardize jobs, as those pressing from both above and below for liberalization demand freer thinkers in positions of institutional responsibility. (p. 551)

Cultural reconstruction requires Soviet historians and writers to press the boundaries of their own inhibitions, to think how prepared they are to tailor their "protocols of behavior" according to who says what in which offices. Such self-imposed restraints are hardly unknown elsewhere, however, and even those among us overly satisfied with our own degree of intel-

lectual independence must respect and admire the courageous Soviet struggle now underway. (p. 552)

William G. Rosenberg, "The History-Literature Debate," in Michigan Quarterly Review, Vol. XXVIII, No. 4, Fall, 1989, pp. 549-52.

KENT JOHNSON AND STEPHEN ASHBY

As with much else in the age of *perestroika*, Soviet poetry is undergoing an accelerated process of exploration and change. Indeed, the spirit of linguistic and conceptual experiment that has characterized a new generation of Soviet poets in the 1980s may be seen as approaching a "paradigmatic" moment in Russian literature, analogous with the avant-garde surge of early century and the poetic revival that accompanied the liberalization of the '50s and '60s. It is in this sense that Soviet critics have begun to speak of a "third wave" of literary innovation building at century's end.

A noteworthy feature of this new poetry is that nearly all of its representatives are in their thirties or forties. But more significant than generational criteria is the fact that these writers share a self-consciously oppositional stance toward the established literary culture, publishing almost exclusively, up until the past few years, through the channels of *samizdat*. What is "opposed", it must be pointed out, is not only the straight-jacket legacy of "apparat-art", but the romantic, vatic voice that has typified the dominant mode of "second-wave" verse since the 1950s. As the prominent young Soviet critic Mikhail Epshtein recently wrote to us, the new poetry realizes "(t)he ideal of mystical communism . . . in the sphere of linguistic practicums, as the expropriator of sign-systems from all epochs and styles, the destruction of their value hierarchies . . . the abolition of lyricalness as a relic of ego and humanism."

If there are echoes of Bakhtin and Khlebnikov in the above, it is fitting; for in the degree to which explorations of the material valencies of the text characterize its production, the new poetry stands as a century-end renaissance of the Russian experimental tradition. Parallel to Language writing in the United States, which has extended the avant-garde traditions of modernism into a critical interrogation of discursive codes, there is in the new Soviet poetry a move toward reconstituting writing as dialogical site, where textuality explores linguistic and ideological registers that more traditional and "realist" modes cannot attain. A reconstitution, that is, not merely along the axis of "tone" or "style", but in terms of basic epistemological assumptions underlying poetic practice. In this writing, boundaries of genre and relations between author, text, and reader are often posed, openly, as issues of composition.

This is not to suggest, by any means, that there is a consensus of method or voice among these new poets. To the contrary, the "third wave" might be helpfully represented as a wild carnival of practices: "conceptualism", "post-conceptualism", "metarealism", "Moscow Time", "Medical Hermeneutics" are a few of the "movements" or tendencies (if often amorphous) that have appeared as coordinates in initial mappings of the current scene. (pp. 719-20)

Skeptical of the discursive and institutional underpinnings of the "artistic", Conceptualist texts seek a dispersion of conventional "aesthetic" criteria so as to provide space for new inflections of perception and practice. In some ways, the movement might be seen as a hyper-intellectualized variant of Dada, and were Duchamp living in Moscow today he would probably be somewhere in the circle of these poets. . . .

Though by no means constituting a "school", [writers practicing "metarealism", "presentalism", or "multi-code"]—as distinct from the "analytic" anti-art of conceptualism—may be seen as engaging deconstructive modalities at higher, "synthetic" levels of composition. Futurism, strains of American Language writing, even the more radical instances of Acmeism (Mandelshtam's "The Horseshoe Finder" for example) may be mentioned in the family trees of these writers. In the past few years, all have seen a sudden rise of their reputations in the USSR and abroad. (p. 720)

[The group known as "Medical Hermenentics"] employs "ready-made" literary models (traditional prosodies, plagiarized passages) as springboards for a caustic de-coding of aesthetic auras.

Clearly, the proliferation of poetic discourses cannot be separated from the current cultural and political landscape of the USSR. For in a process where an entrenched structure of metaphors and signs is being shaken, a writing which aims to destabilize the conventions of language itself almost inevitably assumes a partisan role. And it is particularly now, when "the door to the editor's office has been pushed slightly ajar and glaringly unorthodox material has begun to appear on the pages of journals . . ." that such a "literature" holds out, as promise, its subversive charge. As Epshtein puts it, "(p)oetry—the training grounds of the future democracy, if such a thing should come to be in our country—is the possibility of switching from one language to another, perhaps not understanding, but also not interrupting each other. On the ruins of a social utopia there now arises a utopia of language: a Tower of Babel of the word . . . "

In a curious sense, perhaps, the image of the tower evokes Vladimir Tatlin's never-constructed "Monument to the Third International": swirling, de-centered, positing hope in the very precariousness and incompleteness of its form. If these poets do not fully share the dreams that inspired the early avant-garde, they create from the similar conviction that artistic praxis can—by crossing the wires of language at the base—help spark in the new. (p. 721)

Kent Johnson and Stephen Ashby, "Switching Languages: The New Soviet Poetry," in Michigan Quarterly Review, *Vol. XXVIII, No. 4, Fall, 1989, pp. 719-21.*

DEMING BROWN

Unfortunately, readers in the Soviet Union now have neither the time nor the ear to catch Chekhov's subtleties. The newspapers drip with the blood of Stalin's victims; the diamonds Leonid Brezhnev is said to have stolen dazzle their eyes; there are demonstrations in the streets and vehicles rumble past loaded down with the newest Soviet rockets. Who has time for *The Cherry Orchard* when the orchards near Chernobyl are turning black? People here want clear answers, not subtleties. How did crime against the people happen—and without the people's cooperation? Who cares about Chekhov? In the past, if a mention of "pincenez" were heard on the street, people would think of Chekhov and his elegant little spectacles; now

the phrase reminds them of Lavrenti Beria. Stalin's chief of the secret police, who also wore them. (Andrei Voznesensky, review of V.S. Pritchett, *Chekhov: A Spirit Set Free,* in *The New York Times Book Review,* November 27, 1988. p. 35.)

The Soviet monthly magazine *Foreign Literature* (*Inostrannaia literatura*) is now publishing serially the full text of James Joyce's *Ulysses,* a novel that is excruciatingly difficult to translate into Russian—or any other language, for that matter. The magazine is doing this because of its editors' sense of cultural obligation, in the knowledge that the novel's publication in the USSR is overdue by more than half a century. Moreover, *Foreign Literature* is printing *Ulysses* (which will surely never gain mass popularity) in the face of an ominous circulation battle with other monthlies such as *New World* (*Novyi mir*) and *Banner* (*Znamia*), whose readership is now skyrocketing.

It is ironic that *Foreign Literature,* whose commercial success, until recently, has been assured by Russian readers' hunger for writing from the outside world, should now find itself in fierce competition against magazines publishing works mainly of domestic origin. Ironic, but gratifying and promising. We must wish *Foreign Literature* well in its continuing effort to acquaint the Soviet public with world literature; we also cannot help cheering the news that Russian literature has become compellingly interesting to readers at home.

Why so interesting? There is indeed a handful of talented writers (age 40-70) who have been publishing respectable prose for years and continue to do so, and there is a growing cluster of youngsters, more experimental writers who may represent an exciting "new wave." But neither of these groups accounts for the current startling popularity of Russian writing. The source, rather, is an aggregation of authors, most of them dead but some still living, whose works have been brought to light as a result of the cultural policies of Mikhail Gorbachev. This is the so-called "repressed" literature that has been accumulating in archives and desk drawers for many decades, which is now flooding publishing houses, and which is being consumed eagerly by rapidly increasing numbers of Soviet readers.

The newly discovered works include many that have long been known in the West. Examples are Evgenii Zamiatin's dystopian novel *We* (which influenced George Orwell's *1984*), Boris Pasternak's **Doctor Zhivago,** and Anna Akhmatova's **Requiem,** a cycle of poems about the suffering of Russian women under Stalin's Terror. These works, and many other newly-revealed treasures from twentieth-century Russian writing, had been known in varying degrees by the Soviet *literati,* who for years had been reading them in circulated manuscript form or in foreign editions smuggled into the USSR. For the broad reading public, however, such works were a revelation.

Less than five years ago, the above works were all politically and ideologically taboo. So were a great many writings by more contemporary authors, living or recently deceased, whose criticisms of the Stalin era in particular were thought to be too vivid, frank and powerful to bear the light of day, but which have now been published. Such is a cycle of four stories by the late Vladimir Tendriakov, one of which appears in translation in [*Michigan Quarterly Review,* Fall 1989]. The novel in this category that has caused the greatest sensation is Anatolii Rybakov's **Children of the Arbat,** a panoramic depiction of people and events—private and public, fictional and historical—centering on the year 1933. (A major character is Stalin himself; Rybakov records his sinister imagined thoughts and ruthless treatment of his underlings.) Despite its abundant aesthetic flaws, the novel is enormously popular with Soviet readers, whose hunger for facts about and interpretations of the Stalin era is apparently insatiable. Dozens of other novels and stories about the Stalin period continue to come out. Unlike *Children of the Arbat,* few of them will probably be translated into English because the Western reading public has long known details about the Stalin era which Soviet readers are just now discovering.

In a category almost by himself among recent Soviet discoveries is Vladimir Nabokov, who emigrated as a youth and died in self-imposed exile in Switzerland after a distinguished career as a novelist. Anathematized by Soviet commentators until recently as an immoral apostle of decadent art, Nabokov is now in great vogue, the subject of innumerable scholarly symposia and round-table discussions, and a widely-proclaimed influence on current Soviet writing itself. For years the appetite for Nabokov was covert—partially fed by Ann Arbor's Ardis Publishers, whose Russian editions of Nabokov filtered to the USSR in considerable numbers—but now the Soviets have begun to publish Nabokov themselves.

A similar turnabout is taking place with more recent Russian émigrés, such as Joseph Brodsky, Vladimir Voinovich, Sasha Sokolov and several others, who were either expelled from the Soviet Union or left it under intolerable pressure. Their works, at least in part, are now published in Russia and discussed in Soviet criticism, and several of them have been invited to visit the USSR in person. In February 1989 in Moscow I witnessed, in awe, the tumultuous welcome of the poet Naum Korzhavin, who has been living near Boston for the past fifteen years and still does. Korzhavin, a fine poet who had a good but not outstanding following before he went into exile, was greeted as a celebrity, with poetry readings, interviews and TV appearances.

There is, of course, a ceiling on this atmosphere of amnesty. Despite considerable talk, and some published commentary, about the desirability of greatly increased communication between the Soviet and émigré literatures, and despite some insistence that these two literatures really be treated as one, not every émigré is welcome to rejoin the community. Vasilii Aksenov, the gifted novelist who earned a reputation as a dissident and disrupter of the literary establishment and who now thrives in Washington, D.C., seems still to be in bad odor, at least for the time being. And the most famous émigré of all, Alexander Solzhenitsyn, a man of tremendous influence before his expulsion from the Soviet Union, is still under an official pall. (pp. 761-63)

We can be sure that if and when Solzhenitsyn's major works are published in the Soviet Union, they will be widely read. Few if any contemporary writers can match his feel for the trenchant details of Soviet existence, his moral awareness and ideological acuity. His concerns are precisely those of contemporary Soviet readers: what is the essence of the Stalinist heritage under which they labor; how, and to what extent, has this heritage shaped their attitudes and personalities; and how can they best contend with this heritage? (Solzhenitsyn, a Russian nationalist, goes far beyond a condemnation of Stalinism. He now includes Lenin in his indictment—a charge that few members of the Soviet public may be fully prepared to accept.) With or without Solzhenitsyn, however, Soviet literature is intensely and profoundly preoccupied with the Stalinist past.

Changes in the social, political and cultural climate have strongly influenced literary modes over the past three decades. In the late 1950s and 1960s, the leaders in the effort to restore depth and humanity to Soviet literature—following the long Stalinist freeze—were the poets. Love and death, and the whole spectrum of private emotions associated with the term "lyric"—subject matter that had been forcibly muffled in the Stalin era—reappeared mainly through the medium of verse. At the same time, poetry became aggressively political. Andrei Voznesensky, Evgenii Yevtushenko and other members of a discontented and relatively daring young generation began voicing demands for creative freedom, greater openness and diversity of opinion. Nikita Khrushchev had partially revealed the crimes of Stalin and the evils of his regime at the 20th Party Congress in 1956. Colorful, hortatory poetry was the most effective literary means of expressing the nation's shock over these disclosures, and of arousing national awareness of the need and potential for change.

Poetry, like every other form of political protest, became quieter during the period of "stagnation"—the Brezhnev years. It has remained so, thus far, during the Gorbachev years. Yevtushenko and Voznesensky are still very active, but they function mainly as prominent public figures campaigning in articles, speeches and TV appearances for the goals of *perestroika,* and their poetry as such has lost most of its significance. In general, Soviet poetry has consolidated its hard-won gains of the Fifties and Sixties—its right to be intimate, humane, even religious. It has lost, however, its *civic* thrust and importance, and is now in a period which one Soviet literary critic recently characterized as "quiet lyricism."

It might have been expected that after its service as a forum and source of inspiration during the period of the Khrushchev "thaw," poetry might once again become a tribunal in the present time of upheaval. I discussed this question with a number of critics in Moscow in February 1989. All of them agreed that poetry is now relatively insignificant, and that now is a time for prose which, as one of them put it, "makes the present climate." Why should this be? The answer seems to be that what is needed these days is not emotion, not exhortation, not flashes of poetic insight, but *analysis* of what is going on in society and in the lives and souls of its members. The Soviet people, these critics argue, want information and evaluation that will help them to understand the profound changes which, they feel, are taking place about them and which may affect their existence in fundamental ways. A precondition for such an understanding, all agree, is a full and truthful account of the national past, free of the heretofore dominant official formulations, distortions, omissions and pure inventions which, they now increasingly realize, have warped their understanding of their situation. Only the deliberate, thorough exhaustiveness of prose, it is felt, can lead to the kind of evaluation that is urgently needed today.

Currently the most popular Soviet literature is retrospective. Ranging from historical novels set in nineteenth-century Russia to grim accounts of life and death in the *gulag,* Soviet writing is engaged in a massive re-examination of the national experience. A key word at present is *dokumental'nost'* (documentariness), which means the writer's reliance on the display of facts rather than the workings of his imagination. Literary critics these days are inclined to brush aside the question of whether a piece of journalism can be a work of art, or whether the presentation of information is less worthy, aesthetically, than a writer's invention. It is not that literary standards have fallen, or that writers and critics have somehow become coarse, negligent or obtuse about literary matters. Many simply feel that the times so urgently demand a literature of factual disclosure that, for the present, verifiable truth is more important than finesse and fantasy.

In this connection, two features peculiar to the Russian scene are important. First, from its very beginnings, Russian literature has been heavily freighted with extra-literary concerns. Russian readers have looked, for example, to the novels of Tolstoy, Turgenev and Dostoevsky, or the stories of Chekhov, for a treatment of social, political, ideological and moral questions which, in other countries, are the province of books and essays by sociologists, philosophers, political commentators and other specialists. Second, Soviet *historians,* by their own admission, have until very recently been so heavily indoctrinated with official dogma and so intimidated by ideological and political restrictions, that they have often been much less reliable in their testimony than writers of imaginative literature. It was natural, therefore, for literature to assume, at least in part, the burden of chronicling the events and developments that have led up to the turbulence of today.

There is a strong ingredient of *dokumental'nost',* for example, in the novels of Boris Mozhaev and Vasilii Belov about peasant life and collectivization in the Twenties and Thirties and in Daniil Granin's semi-fictional work, **Bison (Zubr),** about a famous Russian geneticist who elected to work in Hitler's Germany rather than Stalin's Russia. Excellent examples of a writer's urge to provide documentary support for works of fiction are the stories of Tendriakov which were printed in *Novyi mir.* These harrowing portrayals of the insanity and cruelty of the collectivization of agriculture are supplemented with appendices quoting facts and statistics as evidence of the artist's veracity. The stories are powerful and stand by themselves; the documentation seems aesthetically gratuitous. But this artistic flaw, if that it be, illustrates the strength of the documentary trend.

Documentary literature includes a significant amount of writing about World War II. Its purpose, as illustrated in the writings of Ales' Adamovich, Elena Rzhevskaia and Svetlana Alekseevich, is to augment and correct the record by providing largely eyewitness accounts of the facts about military events and wartime conditions that have heretofore been kept secret or distorted by official myth. Another prominent documentary genre is that of memoirs. Those of Nadezhda Mandelshtam, widow of the martyred poet Osip Mandelshtam, published abroad nearly two decades ago and recognized in the West as a major document of Russian cultural history, are at last being made available to Soviet readers. The memoirs of the widow of Nikolai Bukharin, one of the major political opponents whom Stalin executed and who has now been posthumously rehabilitated, have recently appeared. Still another kind of documentary work is a recently published "novella in letters" consisting of the desperate correspondence of, and papers concerning, the distinguished satirist Mikhail Zoshchenko, in the years when the Stalin regime hounded him out of literature and to his death.

I have mentioned that this seems to be an era of prose. In the realm of prose *fiction,* however, not all forms enjoy equal prestige at present. Russians have always enjoyed reading big novels, good or bad, and there is plenty of popular material to keep them occupied, such as the detective and spy novels of Julian Semenov and the historical adventure novels of Vladimir Pikul'. Readers who expect fiction to confirm the fixed view of the world which decades of official indoctrination have instilled in them (and there are masses of such readers) continue to subsist on the long, formulaic, primitive and reactionary novels of such "socialist realist" establishment hacks as Aleksandr Chakovskii, Vadim Kozhevnikov, and Georgii Markov. For more discriminating readers, however, the contemporary novel has little to offer. An informal poll I took among literary critics this February [1989] indicates, as I had previously felt, that shorter forms (the short story and the novella—the Russian term is *povest'*), as employed by such authors as Vladimir Makanin, Tat'iana Tolstaia and Vasyl' Bykov, are now being written more successfully than the large novels for which Russians have traditionally been so famous.

The critics vary and sometimes contradict one another in their explanation of this phenomenon. Some argue that the short story is weak these days, as compared to its condition in the 1960s, when such writers as Aksenov and Iurii Kazakov brought it to a very high level. Others insist that in the hands of Liudmila Petrushevskaia, Tolstaia, Viacheslav P'etsukh and others the short story is on the verge of a genuine renaissance. Nearly everyone agrees, however, that the dominant prose genre today is the novella, as written by Makanin, Bykov and the late Iurii Trifonov. The novella, it is argued, is a response to rapidly changing times, when writers cannot confidently see the world as a whole. Puzzled and disturbed by accelerating social developments and cultural instability, and lacking complete and fully-rounded philosophies, writers concentrate on limited segments of human experience, emphasizing the local at the expense of the general, and dramatizing moral or ideological problems without attempting to solve them. A novella is smaller, more fragmentary, less complicated than a novel, but it is not less profound. Rather, at its best, it provides a sharp focus on discrete but important issues.

With one exception, the critics with whom I talked this year agreed that the novel is the weakest Soviet prose form today. At the same time, they insisted that the *need* for good novels is greater than ever. A retrospective genre, the fullscale novel can examine, analyze and interpret the past, give it shape and meaning, and illuminate its significance for the present. There are plenty of novels that do just this, but these novels are entirely lacking in intellectual individuality and merely illustrate the prefabricated, conventional, "official" conception of things. The people, events, attitudes and conflicts of the Stalin era, and the Brezhnev period as well, need to be seen through fresh and independent eyes.

The problem today, critics argue, is that the writing of a really good novel requires an original, full conception of life by an artist who is well-informed and free of crippling inhibitions. The best Soviet writers, they feel, are still too bemused, and aware of their own ignorance, to embark on large novels with the necessary confidence. It is hoped that as fuller and more reliable information about the past, including the recent past, becomes available, and as the atmosphere of creative freedom improves, the "real novels" the critics long for will begin to appear.

Meanwhile, Soviet readers must content themselves with honest, revealing, but aesthetically unimpressive novels such as **Children of the Arbat.** In their laments over the absence of first-class novels, however, the critics make one exception: the late Vasilii Grossman's *Life and Fate.* Completed and rejected for publication in 1960 on the grounds that it was anti-Soviet, the novel's manuscript was confiscated by the KGB, in apparently all of its drafts, in 1961. Grossman died in 1964, but one overlooked manuscript made its way to the West, where it was published for the first time. (The English translation appeared in 1985.) Finally, the novel was published in the Soviet Union in 1988.

A vast, panoramic work centering on the Battle of Stalingrad in 1943, *Life and Fate* is much more than a military novel. Although its battlefield accounts are detailed, vivid and authentic, based on Grossman's own eyewitness experience, what distinguishes it from hundreds of other Soviet war novels is its huge sweep, its social and moral depth. It devotes much more space to life behind both the Russian and German lives than to actual combat. The main focus is on the Soviet population (especially the scientific intelligentsia, although all classes are included), but there are numerous portrayals of Germans, including Hitler. There are scenes of the Nazi gas chambers and poignant characterizations of their victims among Soviet Jews, as well as extensive depictions of the Soviet *gulag* system, in all its brutality, as it operates in wartime.

Life and Fate contests the myth of wartime unity and harmony among the Soviet people. Anti-Semitism is shown to operate at all levels behind the Russian lines. Although the novel includes abundant accounts of Soviet steadfastness and heroism, it also shows sheer brutality, venality, opportunism, and political intrigue among both the military and the civilian populace. There are only glimpses of Stalin, but his unseen presence permeates the novel. Grossman is not an impressive psychologist, but his portrayal of the numerous painful moral tensions, choices and compromises which Soviet citizens are forced to make is powerful. *Life and Fate* is not the Soviet *War and Peace* which the critics keep hoping for, but with its large and varied cast of characters and its depiction of Soviet wartime society as a historically conditioned, complex organism, it is profoundly convincing.

Another work that is universally admired but that can only be called a novel for want of a better term, is Fazil' Iskander's *Sandro of Chegem,* a loose accumulation of novellas set in the Caucasian region of Abkhazia and centering (although not consistently) on Sandro, a local character who embodies many of the most colorful traits of his small, exotic, Muslim ethnic group. Iskander's Abkhazia is a mythical construct that is nevertheless, like William Faulkner's Yoknapatawpha County, authentically rooted in a regional culture. The stories Iskander tells about it extend over nearly the entire twentieth century, although they concentrate on the past fifty years. They are lively, often improbable, full of adventure, arresting characters and local color, and packed with robust humor. Until 1988, when it was finally published in full, the Sandro epos had been printed in the Soviet Union only in fragments; many of its stories—especially those featuring wickedly sly satires on Stalinism—had been rejected by the censors. It is probable that *Sandro of Chegem* (which is available in English translation) will eventually be regarded as a classic of twentieth-century Russian literature.

Beginning with the nineteenth century, Russian literary criticism has traditionally been heavily didactic, laden with ideological, political and moral argumentation. As one critic commented to me, Russia has never had its own "Hyde

Park" and criticism has served as a kind of substitute. These days, criticism operates with particular vehemence as an interpreter of current public issues and problems, and even as a guide to behavior. Writing itself, as we have seen, is heavily involved in civic matters, and criticism uses its commentary on literature as a device for an even stronger involvement.

Critics who have shown in the past that they are capable of sensitive and sophisticated discourse on the purely artistic features of a given literary text now insist that aesthetic judgements are irrelevant for the time being. What is needed, they feel, is elucidation and evaluation of the ideas, the social, political and ethical implications of a novel, play or story. But Soviet criticism seems to want to go even beyond the ideological explication of a literary work; it wants to penetrate to the reader's very soul. An American who is used to reading *The New York Times Book Review* would be startled at the way in which Soviet criticism often takes pains to spell out the lessons, the implications for ordinary human conduct, of a given book. This heavily didactic strain, critics assure me, is welcomed and even demanded by readers. One critic for the weekly *Literary Gazette* told me that she receives up to 100 letters from the public for every article she writes. *Perestroika,* readers feel, involves a profound transformation in everyday attitudes and behavior, a spiritual re-examination with wide, if uncertain, implications, and they look not only to literature, but to criticism as well, for help in understanding the personal changes they are undergoing.

It is well known that *perestroika* involves a massive conflict between the forces of change and the forces of reaction in Soviet society, and that this struggle is carried on both overtly and beneath the surface. Literary criticism has become a major arena in this ideological civil war. Soviet literary magazines are in fact identified as much in terms of their political leanings as they are in terms of their strictly literary interests and values. Much more so than their Western counterparts, Soviet readers see in criticism a medium for political polemics, and they look eagerly to the critics for aid in forming their opinions on fundamental public questions. *Glasnost'*, the Soviet public is learning, involves not only an increase in freedom of expression but also an increase in perplexity. Soviet readers are looking not only to literature but also to literary criticism to help them cope with their confusion. (pp. 763-70)

Deming Brown, "Literature and 'Perestroika'," in
Michigan Quarterly Review, *Vol. XXVIII, No. 4,
Fall, 1989, pp. 761-70.*

MARTIN WALKER

Soviet intellectuals have a taste for the melodramatic, and they have learned that their worst fears have a nasty way of coming true. Anyone who has lived in Moscow knows about the wonderfully depressing conversations around kitchen tables that last through the night. Muscovites have been predicting civil war for years. But the mood now is extraordinary even by Soviet standards—fatalistic and epic and apocalyptic all at once.

The contrast between the evidence of reformist achievement and the degree of public gloom is somewhat surreal. On the TV screens, Gorbachev greets Orthodox Church elders after letting them conduct the first religious service in a Kremlin cathedral in over 70 years. Marvelous, says the visitor. Sure, grunt Russian friends, but did you know there would be food riots this winter, and that there was a secret plan to introduce rationing after New Year's? . . .

When I lived in Moscow, from 1984 until last August [1989], the Hotel Oktyabraskaya was like the forbidden city. Surrounded by fences and brick guard posts, it was the Party hotel, reserved for guests of the Central Committee. We ordinary mortals could but stare and wonder as the vast electric gates purred to seal us out. There were legends about its marble floors and dining rooms where bills were never presented. Last month I finally saw it from within, when a group of journalists, invited to an International Press Institute conference hosted by the Soviets, was put up there.

Our meeting took place in a conference room so grand we should have been signing the Treaty of Versailles. The 60-foot ceiling contained so many crystal chandeliers that the antiquated Soviet TV cameras needed no extra light. My room was slightly more modest. With its dark wood paneling and heavy furniture, it resembled the 1950s Des Moines hotel where Khrushchev had stayed. But the TV and short-wave radio and the refrigerator all worked. There was a separate shower with two water jets, a big bath and thick towels, and curtains that actually met and kept the light out. Same-day laundry and dry cleaning. Free haircuts. And a real treasure trove—courtesy tubes of Soviet shampoo and shaving cream and toothpaste. None of my Russian friends had seen Soviet toothpaste for months. I carried the tube around in my pocket to show people. It was like a religious relic. Touch and believe.

Capitalism has invaded this Party sanctum. Certainly I could stay on here for a couple of days after the conference ended, I was told. But then came a discreet cough—that would be $300 for two nights, cash in advance. This was enough of an incentive to sample the delights of Gorbachev's free market. You can now hire your own room or sublet a Soviet flat, terms strictly cash. No passport, no papers, no names. (You can rent Soviet cars too, and drive around without the telltale licence plates that disclose whether you are a diplomat, a journalist, or a businessman, and which country you come from. Anonymity in Moscow spy fiction will never be the same.) (p. 22)

This was a heady experience for an old Moscow hand. As soon as I arrived, I started asking people about the hot new exhibitions, the plays and films we must see, the articles we had to read. My Russian friends looked at me oddly. I was still living in early *glasnost*. The read-everything craze is over. *Pravda*'s circulation of 11 million will be halved this year, and not simply because it is perceived as a conservative rag. Subscriptions to the radical *Izvestia* have dropped about 25 percent. Even subscriptions to *Argumenti i Fakti* are reportedly down after last year's extraordinary surge to 23 million. The only publications to show a rise in next year's orders are *Semya* (Family), which is cannily serializing the first Soviet sex manual, and *Asia and Africa Today,* which is presenting a teach-yourself kung fu course.

We are into post-modernist *perestroika,* and the one thing that everyone has read is Sasha Kabakov's novella ***The Man Who Would Not Come Back.*** It is a devastating political satire thinly disguised as a sci-fi yarn. Our hero can travel through time, so a nervous KGB bullies him into zooming ahead to 1993 to see how *perestroika* turns out. What he finds makes Beirut look like Club Med. The only remnant of *perestroika* after the civil war of 1991 is the money, called Gor-

batti, but you have to use ration coupons anyway. The new leader is a General Pamayev, who goes everywhere inside a tank (his gasoline-starved escort rides a horse).

Late at night in the Hotel Oktyabraskaya, with the TV set blaring out that day's stirring debates about a new press freedom law in the Supreme Soviet, I read Kabakov's book. Kalashnikov was escorting a woman through the rubble, looking to buy some shoes. Jews were being smoked out of blown-up apartments. The punks were scouring the city for Metallisti, heavy metal rock fans, and the Leveling Committee was raiding the apartments of bureaucrats and black marketeers. It was Mad Max goes to Moscow.

This is all people want to talk about. How did I like that scene where the body of the Metallist is seen hanging from the balcony of the Hotel Pekin? Did I know that Kabakov's point was that the hero was right to stay in the grim future rather than return to Moscow of 1989, where the KGB still ruled? That Kabakov had said this on the trendy TV talk show "Vzglyad" and had been censored? Did I know he was selling the film rights for millions? I had dinner with Kabakov in one of our old haunts, the Chinese co-op restaurant Mei Hua, and asked about his new fame. "I'd only do one thing differently if I wrote it again now," he said. "I'd bring it all forward to 1991. It ain't going to last till '93." (pp. 22, 26)

It is only 25 years since the Soviet Union had a political coup, with the fall of Nikita Khrushchev in October 1964. In the anniversary week, *Moskovskaya Pravda* ran a full-page article asking bluntly whether it could happen again. The author concluded that he thought not, but that a kind of revolution was possible. He went back to Lenin to cite the three connected preconditions: the rising popular discontent, usually focused on a fall in living standards; a crisis of authority at the top of the government machine; and "a significant increase in the activity of the masses, leading to their chance to play an independent role on the stage of history."

The masses are not yet stomping on stage, but we do not need a front-row seat to hear their noises in the wings. For thoughtful Soviets, the most alarming sign of working-class discontent was not the summer miners' strikes, but the autumn slowdown of the railway workers. The government responded to the strikes with some urgent purchases in Western Europe of women's tights and toothpaste and tape cassettes and soap and prepared foods. Most of this stuff has been rotting at the docks for weeks. The railway workers are not striking, because the new law says they may not. But they are working slowly, and obeying every minor safety regulation in order to get the same special treatment that the miners won, and this is proving hugely disruptive.

It is the slowdown that is responsible for the very real threat of fuel shortages this winter. The Soviet transport system is utterly dependent upon its railways. This is not an economy that goes by road. Indeed, the main route between Moscow and Leningrad degenerates in places to a narrow two-track road that passes through tiny villages where chickens and the odd pig may waddle across the highway.

So when the railway workers let the leadership know that they too want extra soap and sausage, the whole economy trembles. And this is the irony of Gorbachev's *perestroika:* it now faces the sullen resistance of the world's last true industrial proletariat, preserved as if in aspic by the inefficiencies of the command economy. On the docks and down in the pits, in the steel plants and on the railways, the horny-handed sons of toil still exist in exploited millions in this museum of an economy, and they are starting to feel their power.

This is what lies behind the current debate in *Literaturnaya Gazeta* between Democracy and Autocracy. The question is whether supreme power should be vested in Gorbachev today, in order that *perestroika* and democratization can be preserved in the future. The argument stipulates that by stressing *glasnost* and political liberalization, and ducking the tough economic reforms, Gorbachev got it backward. He should have dismantled the price controls and dropped the food subsidies and started to make the ruble convertible back in 1986, when the command economy and the traditional political deference were still in place. Today, if he tries to introduce belt-tightening measures, he faces the fast-organizing opposition of the Workers' Fronts. (p. 26)

This is the new populism, and it is doubly dangerous. On the one hand it is becoming a stubborn force of resistance to the economic reform the system so desperately needs. On the other hand it is volatile in its loyalties and its hatreds. When Ivan Ivanovitch on the Kirov Street omnibus talks about the cooperatives and the speculators, he adds the adjective "Jewish." The anti-intellectual tone of populist discussion carries similar overtones. For some years now one popular (and false) nickname for the much-disliked Raisa Gorbachev has been "Yevreyka," the Jewess. And in *Nash Sovremmenik* and *Molodaya Gvardia,* the house magazines of populist Russian nationalism, the anti-Semitism is as naked as the deep suspicion of all these reforms. Indeed, one recent article in *Nash Sovremmenik* suggested that all this upheaval was another phase in the long plot by "the clever nation of little people" to undermine the big people. Titled "Russophobia," the article perfectly caught the aggrieved tone of so many Russians these days as the other peoples of the Soviet empire are finally saying what they think of Moscow rule.

One evening I sat in a cozy Jewish restaurant called U Iosefa (Joseph's Place), enjoying some gefilte fish and listening to the best skat blues I had heard for a long time. Over a glass of Georgian wine, Joseph handed me a copy of a newspaper I never dreamed I'd ever see, the *Soviet-Jewish Cultural Chronicle.* The next day I chatted with its editor, who goes by the magnificent name of Tankred Golenpolski. He showed me an open letter to Gorbachev in the next issue, complaining of the dangerous rise in anti-Semitism. He had sent one of his reporters to infiltrate Pamyat, a rather ridiculous organization of extreme Russian nationalists who affect black shirts and mystic drivel about Moscow as a Third Rome, but who are very serious indeed about the Jews. The new minimum requirement to join, the reporter discovered, was to deliver the addresses of three Jewish families. There was now serious concern about pogroms, Tankred said conversationally. And did I know about the self-defense units Jews were setting up in various cities?

"Now you understand," said a Jewish friend, when I recounted this. Lev is a Party member who has just pillaged his savings to buy a gun on the black market. (The Afgantsi, the war veterans, brought home a lot of souvenirs.) (pp. 26-7)

The sense of doom and gloom goes very high up. The new deputy prime minister in charge of economic reforms, Leonid Abalkin, went back to his old economics institute last month for a long session with his former colleagues. He ran through the familiar list of crises: the food shortages, the miners' strikes and the slowdowns on the railways, the inflation, the lack of fuel for the winter, the threat of nationalism in the republics, the civil war looming between Armenia and Azerbaijan, the troubles in Eastern Europe, Pamyat and the Jews. "No country in history has ever faced as many problems as now beset our poor land," he mourned. A colleague piped up: "I can think of one. What about Weimar Germany, 1932?" Abalkin replied, "I was hoping you wouldn't bring that up." . . .

But the most hair-raising predictions came from friends who are living examples of the biggest consumer boom the country has ever known. In spite of the opinion polls that say most people are worse off under *perestroika,* there is a lot of hot money about. The new cooperatives that produce Western-style clothes and tape cassettes are thriving. The freedom to travel means anyone who can will come back with a Western personal computer, costing $1,500 in New York discount stores; they can easily sell it for up to 40,000 rubles. A $300 video recorder sells for 6,000 rubles. The writers and journalists and academics who find it easy to travel are suddenly finding themselves relatively rich—and rather frightened.

My friend with the gun explained how the soaring crime rate portends the collapse of civilization as we knew it. He and his wife dare not watch the video after Soviet TV stops broadcasting for the night. The hoodlums watch for the telltale flicker on the curtains after 1 a.m., and mark the apartment for a theft. Did I know about the new Mafia, the armed robberies of the co-op restaurants? And had I heard of the taxi hijackings on the airport road, robberies of people coming back from the West with their computers and videos? "I read *Bonfire of the Vanities,* your Western version of Kabakov," Lev went on. "It is very Russian novel, not about New York at all. It is Moscow. All the fear, all those contrasts of rich and poor."

I thought about it. We had been for lunch at the new Finnish-run Savoy hotel, just down the street from the KGB building on Dzerzhinsky Square. It is for foreigners, the aristocrats of hard currency. We had drunk English ale and watched CNN and eaten shrimp sandwiches and paid by credit card. And as we came out I looked across the road at the grim and crowded Pelmenaya, a stand-up canteen where they serve stodgy Siberian dumplings.

And I thought about the Pekin Hotel, where there is now a West German supermarket selling everything from filet steak to health foods. Naturally, it accepts credit cards only, and the Russians on the street silently watch the loaded trolleys being wheeled to the waiting Mercedes. No wonder everyone cited that scene in Kabakov where the Metallist dangles from the Pekin Hotel balcony. My own fantasies turned more to mobs storming the red-brick bastion of the Oktyabraskaya Hotel, symbol of Party privilege and modern-day Winter Palace, where the vast gates and fences guard a large supply of Soviet toothpaste and not much else. (p. 27)

Martin Walker, "Punk Perestroika," in The New Republic, *Vol. 201, No. 23, December 4, 1989, pp. 22, 26-7.*

GALYA DIMENT

In his new book [*Glasnost' in Action: Cultural Renaissance in Russia*], prolific author and pre-eminent British specialist on the Soviet economy Alec Nove sets as his purpose "to give to the nonspecialist reader some notion of what has happened in the Soviet cultural scene in recent years." Needless to say, even five years ago Nove would have shrugged off as terribly naïve any suggestion that during his lifetime he would get a chance to write a book illustrating the dramatic opening up of Soviet society. But here we are, of course, proving once again that in this world an uninformed shot in the dark is often as good or even better than a thoroughly educated guess.

The subtitle of Nove's book—*"Cultural Renaissance in Russia"*—is rather startling. In his preface he further qualifies it as "a real cultural renaissance," as if to make sure that we know he means it. "Renaissance" is, of course, a loaded word, and one would wish Nove were not quite so quick to bestow it on current developments in Soviet culture. Cultural upheaval, maybe, a cultural revival of sorts, even a cultural revolution, but renaissance? Some will argue that Soviet culture was actually in many ways more sophisticated during the years of "stagnation," when authors had to find subtle ways of fooling the authorities and expressing their artistic or political credos, than now, when almost everything is permitted and subtlety has been too frequently replaced by crude bluntness. Nove himself quotes (but evidently dismisses) this view as expressed by actor Sergei Yursky: "[P]reviously everything was forbidden, now everything is allowed. . . . Paradoxically it is a time of self-restriction. . . ." Self-restriction and moderation may come in time, and we may yet witness a "real cultural renaissance" in the Soviet Union, but so far it simply has not happened.

It takes more than just a couple of years for people to free themselves from the shackles of the previous social and cultural dicta and to re-examine and re-evaluate many of their life-long assumptions. What the Soviets are dealing with now are enormous topics—Stalin, the Terror, the Revolution—but they are also obvious topics, and they lie on the surface. In order to achieve a true rebirth of culture, its best representatives have to lead their followers beyond the surface and make them turn their eyes in various directions, not only outward but also in. As of now, the majority of artists and their audiences are still too politicized and polarized either to demand or to create truly sophisticated works that do more than respond to the most debated issues of the day. (p. 31)

Nove's effort to present a comprehensive survey of recently published materials available, for the most part, only in Russian, is both desperately needed and heroic. Needed, because now a wider Western audience can begin to get a feel for the kind of discussions that are occupying the hearts and minds of the Soviets these days; heroic because even citizens of the Soviet Union, starved as they once were for real information, often groan that they cannot stay on top of all the new articles, books and T.V. programs coming their way. Paradoxically, the very "glasnost" which Gorbachev intended to lay at the foundation of his social and economic re-structuring may one day be seen as one of perestroika's impediments: those now so busy watching the live coverage of political debates and reading new accounts of their history may have even less time left than before to concentrate on their professional fields.

As with most surveys, the greatness of Nove's book lies in its breadth rather than its depth. There are issues, however, on which the very expansiveness of its range proves more effective than any thorough discussion would be. A chapter entitled "The Terror," which handles new revelations about the purges of the 1930s, is a superb example of such a case: no in-depth analysis of Stalin's actions and motives could have made more chilling reading than this succinct summary of the reminiscences now being written by former victims, their relatives and their friends. (pp. 31-2)

Equally competent are Nove's survey of different views on the "proper" route for the Soviet economy and his summaries of the published attempts to re-evaluate history and rehabilitate such former unmentionables as Bukharin (a rather convenient new "hero," since in the twenties he strongly supported economic reforms very similar to the ones Gorbachev is trying to implement), Zinoviév, Kamenev and even Trotsky. But when it comes to the arts, Nove, whose expertise does not spread that far, is on much shakier ground. Thus his excursions into literature tend to be overly simplistic; all currently popular and controversial writers are uniformly made to be "great," "fine," and "talented." Ironically, this amounts to but a superficial reversal of the former Soviet practice in which, as Nove himself points out, all politically loyal, obedient Soviet artists were automatically put "into categories which became pedagogically fixed: 'genius,' 'great,' 'outstanding.' " . . .

Nove also appears to find it hard to strike a balance between impartiality—which his preface claims he wants to maintain—and an excitement that frequently bursts through it, resulting in numerous exclamation points ("A very fair point!" or "Stirring stuff!").

But one has to admit that what is happening in the Soviet Union right now is, indeed, politically and culturally thrilling, and we should probably not begrudge Alec Nove his outbursts of excitement too much. In the many long years he has spent working in the field of Soviet studies, thrills have been few and far apart. Nor has he thrown away all his healthy skepticism. "It is too much to expect the transformation of the USSR into a Western-style democracy," Nove writes in his conclusion. . . .

The New York Times recently reported on a new Soviet video intended to soften the image of the KGB, whose reputation has been devastated seemingly beyond repair by numerous recent revelations. In it one official is shown to sample a prison porridge and good-naturedly compliment the chef on his talent in cooking wild oats (talent which the official, of course, finds to be superior to his wife's—some things never change). The attempt is laughable, but it also shows that whereas the medium may get updated—video superseding print—many of the propagandistic ideas do not. While it is tempting to hope that the Soviet Union has indeed sown the last of its own wild oats and is ready to settle down as a more democratic and enlightened society, we may be well advised to do as Nove encourages us at the very end of his book: just "hold our breath and see." (p. 32)

Galya Diment, *"Putting the PR in Perestroika,"* in San Francisco Review of Books, *Winter, 1989-90, pp. 31-2.*

The 1989
Young Playwrights Festival

Sponsored by the Foundation of the Dramatists Guild, the Young Playwrights Festival is an annual event open to American youths aged nineteen and under. Writers meeting this qualification are invited to submit their original plays to the Foundation of the Dramatists Guild following specific guidelines. All entrants receive a detailed evaluation of their work. A commitee chooses several plays each year for professional engagements in New York City, and the productions are reviewed by noted drama critics. The Young Playwrights Festival was established in 1981 through the efforts of noted dramatist and lyricist Stephen Sondheim, Ruth Goetz of the Dramatists Guild, and Gerald Chapman, who administered a similar festival in London during the mid-1970s. Mr. Sondheim stated: "The festival allows young people to use their creative imagination and to see their work done in collaboration with professionals. . . . But never are the playwrights treated as, quote, kids. Like all writers in the Dramatists Guild, they have total control over their material." Sondheim added: "These young playwrights are the theater's future."

802 plays were submitted for consideration in 1989. A team of 35 readers chose sixteen plays for staged readings in May, and the writers of these plays were were transported to New York. The committee then selected four plays for full productions and three for staged readings, all of which were presented during the eighth annual Young Playwrights Festival in early autumn, 1989. The four plays performed on stage include Janet Allard's *Painted Rain*, which is set in an orphan-

(The four dramatists whose plays were performed during the 1989 Young Playwrights Festival were, from left to right: **Alejandro Membreno, Janet Allard, Debra Neff, and Robert Kerr.**)

age and examines the friendship and strains between a crippled white teenager who yearns to be a painter and a more gregarious black teenager; both characters seek companionship and love. Robert Kerr's play, *Finnegan's Funeral Parlor and Ice Cream Shoppe,* is a dark comic farce centering on an eccentric family whose father intends to put the "fun back in funerals." Debra Neff's *Twice Shy* focuses on a recent rape victim's uneasy relationships with her mother, her homosexual roomate and his lover, and a suitor introduced by her mother. *Peter Breaks Through,* by Alejandro Membreno, is a fantasy in which Peter Pan and Tinkerbell enter a whorehouse to help a prostitute hoping to change her life.

Since 1981 the Young Playwrights Festival has staged forty-nine full productions and involved nearly 200 young people in readings, workshops, and presentations. The Young Playwrights Festival has received numerous honors, including two prizes in 1989: the Margo Jones Award, an annual endowment that encourages the productions of new plays by new and established dramatists, and the George Oppenheimer/*Newsday* Playwriting Award, which recognizes outstanding achievement in playwriting, bestowed in memory of Mr. Oppenheimer, who served as drama critic for *Newsday* from 1963 until his death in 1977.

For further information about the Young Playwrights Festival, including guidelines and helpful advice, please write to the following address:

> Young Playwrights Festival
> The Foundation of the Dramatists Guild
> 234 West 44th Street
> Room 1005
> New York, NY 10036

DIANA MAYCHICK

The Stephen Sondheim wanna-be is making the acquaintance of the Wendy Wasserstein wanna-be.

"You're late," chides the uncommon young woman, appropriately dressed in black. The merrily-rolling-along young man offers an explanation: "I never wear a watch," he says. "I hate to be hemmed in by time."

Close your eyes, and the two young people could well be their Pulitzer Prize-winning idols.

Open them, and you'll find two strikingly vibrant teen-agers, Debra Neff and Alejandro Membreno, winners of the 8th annual Young Playwrights Festival. . . .

Seeing their plays turns out to be the best antidote around to the constant barrage of doom and gloom that tends to overtake discussions of the state of contemporary theater. Meet them, and you feel even more hopeful.

Here are two 18-year-olds who read widely, and for whom writers are bigger heroes than baseball players and movie stars. That the young people are also polite and engaged and curious and spunky turns out to be whipped cream, because these kids can really write.

Neff, an undergraduate at Tufts University, has written a realistic drama, **Twice Shy,** about a rape victim's halting attempt to trust men again. The playwright is a veteran of the program; in 1987, her **Children** was given a staged reading. "I almost never know where I'm going when I begin writing," she says with the kind of candor often missing from her older brethren. "I start with a character, a line of dialogue and it just develops. If I try to force a plot line, I usually get so bogged down in the process, that the piece just doesn't work."

Membreno's entry, **Peter Breaks Through,** subtitled "an alleged tragedy in one act," is his first attempt at the form. A lyrical look at a prostitute visited by Peter Pan and influenced by "Charlie Chaplin, J. M. Barrie, Hitchcock's *Vertigo* and God knows what else." The play was written, he says, to "get the tribute over with. I wanted to thank everybody who influenced me the first time out, so I could write the next one totally on my own. But the real reason I wrote it was to win." He smiles impishly. "And I wanted to win so I could meet Mr. Sondheim. And when I finally did, the world could have ended, I felt so good."

The rest of the playwrights and the audiences must thank composer/lyricist Sondheim as well. As a young man, he found a mentor in Oscar Hammerstein II, and Sondheim credits him with demystifying the world of theater.

Then a decade ago, when Sondheim visited the Royal Court's Young Writers Festival in London, he was so impressed with the professional quality of the productions he saw that he returned to the States determined to launch an American counterpart. In essence, it also served as a way for Sondheim to formalize his gratitude to Hammerstein and encourage other established professionals to share tricks of their trade.

Once the Dramatists Guild agreed to sponsor the project in 1981, its mandate was clear: to introduce young people to the profession at the highest level of achievement. . . .

The statistics are impressive. Since its inception, the festival has presented nearly 200 playwrights under the age of 19 with either full productions, staged readings or workshops. Of the 49 playwrights who have received full productions of their works, an astounding 43 have gone on to either write another play and/or see their work produced elsewhere.

"I understand we're getting the royal treatment," Neff says. "I hear more established playwrights get jealous. But I also know we're going to get older, too. We'll have to deal with producers and budgets."

The more romantic Membreno looks disturbed at the thought. But as soon as the young playwrights begin discussing their directors and actors, the writers could be any age.

"The directors give notes to the actors," Neff says, "and I give notes to the director. It's almost a formalized process, which is the way it's done professionally. I guess. But the writer feels a little left out of the excitement of the performance. You don't have a chance to build up the same kind of intimacy that people playing together do."

Membreno, who has acted in high school productions, recalls the sadness at the end of productions when the players dispersed. "But the writer has the power to conjure another set of circumstances, another play if you will, in order to get a group together," he said. "An actor is more passive; he just has to wait." The verb leads him to free-associate a little. "Wait until you see the costumes they gave me," he continues. "I mean, Peter Pan is stupendous."

That thought brings him back to his own youth. "You know,

when I was 12, I won a bicycle and I sold it and used the money to see *Showboat.* I took my aunt. She was pregnant at the time, and she moaned and groaned right through, but I loved it like nothing else."

"I know what you mean," Neff says. Her first show was *Annie.* "And my little sister just sang and danced right in the aisles. The theater just sunk into her bones."

Two other young playwrights, Robert Kerr (*Finnegan's Funeral Parlor and Ice Cream Shoppe*), and Janet Allard (*Painted Rain*) will be featured at this year's festival, now in previews, opening Thursday. In addition, there will be free staged readings of works by other young writers.

Diana Maychick, "Broadway's Best Hope: The Young," in New York Post, September 12, 1989, p. 38.

MEL GUSSOW

The four writers in this season's Young Playwrights Festival are among the most talented to emerge in the eight years of the annual series. Their short plays opened last night at Playwrights Horizons (three by other playwrights will be given staged readings in October). As was also true last year, there are definite signs that the young playwrights—they have to be under the age of 19 when they submit their work to the Drama–tists Guild competition—are exploring ideas that move far beyond the problems of adolescence.

This is certainly the case in Debra Neff's *Twice Shy.* With its sophistication and understanding of the emotional stress within the closest of relationships, the play would stand out in any one-act festival. . . .

[The] scenes between mother and daughter should provoke laughs of recognition among theatergoers with similar tense but loving familial situations.

At the same time, we see [the heroine] relating differently to three men in her life: her best friend and roommate (who is a homosexual); his lover, who invariably causes [her] to be late for class because he is practicing tai chi in her bathroom, and a new man who enters her life courtesy of her mother.

Each of the three is a vivid character. . . . Wisely, Ms. Neff is unafraid to end her play on a note of tentativeness—as in life. *Twice Shy* is a poignant look at a young woman trying to regain her equilibrium in her imbalanced world.

[In Alejandro Membreno's *Peter Breaks Through*] urban decadence collides with airy fantasy. It would be unfair to reveal the twists of the author's exceedingly clever plot, except to say that the ending is a turnabout in which one character receives a most justified comeuppance. . . .

Painted Rain by Janet Allard—at 15 the youngest of the playwrights—is the most traditional of the quartet. This is a sweet, sad vignette about two lonely boys growing up in an orphanage, one of whom dreams about being a painter. There is a gentle poetic quality in the writing and the imagery. . . . [The actors] communicate the empathy that binds the boys in friendship and the strains that constantly threaten to put them at arm's distance.

At last year's festival, Robert Kerr was represented by *And the Air Didn't Answer,* an absurdist comedy about a free-thinking Catholic schoolboy. This season he returns with a macabre cartoon called *Finnegan's Funeral Parlor and Ice Cream Shoppe*. . . . The title character is an undertaker who has decided to put "the fun back in funerals." In addition to his new soda fountain, Finnegan is contemplating "theme funerals."

The funniest moments in this pitchblack comedy do not deal with deadly events, but with family matters concerning Finnegan's sons. One is an insanely disreputable dropout whose favorite pastime is "rioting by himself", the other is a shy homebody who is unable to speak until encouraged by an attractive young woman applying for a job. . . . [The] boy's speech lessons are wryly amusing. In this and other moments, it is evident—as it was in his play last year—that the author has an outrageous sense of humor. This is one Young Playwrights Festival that warrants an extended engagement.

Mel Gussow, "Four One-Acts by Young Playwrights," in The New York Times, September 22, 1989, p. C5.

CLIVE BARNES

Ever since I was old enough to be considered more or less grown up I have hated infant prodigies. Mozart I would certainly have detested, and I probably wouldn't have felt so great about the young Sir Yehudi Menuhin.

Pure envy, of course. But at least people such as Mozart and Menuhin had the grace to be musicians—imagine how envious I feel of youngsters indulging in my own shaky craft of words?

Take for example the four playwrights having their work showcased [during the Eight Annual Young Playwrights Festival]. . . .

They are brilliant—they use words with precisely that gift of the gab that is the one absolute essential for anyone attempting to write a play. Many experienced adult playwrights might covet their skills, and as for this adult critic, I am amazed at how well they write and how young they are.

These one-acters are not really plays—they are to the play what a short-story would be to a novel, and all four are concerned with a sketch, an incident, perhaps even a feeling. All demonstrate a beautiful sensibility for the theater.

Perhaps the most ambitious is Debra Neff's *Twice Shy,* which describes a young woman, Louise, sorting out her life and relationships after the traumatic experience of a rape.

Funny and honest, the writing is as lively as the play's simple construction is solid. Yet perhaps a more imaginative approach to life and theater was shown by the youngest playwright, 15-year-old Janet Allard.

This play, *Painted Rain,* most touchingly explores the relationship between two young boys in an orphanage, one white and crippled and the other black and chirpy.

It is a little obvious and sentimental, but its language rings pure gold, and its modestly conceived characters behave to the life.

Presumably by chance—not by role-playing—while these two women's plays were seriously intended, both of the male playwrights on this festival bill contributed outrageous farces.

Finnegan's Funeral Parlor and Ice Cream Shoppe by Robert Kerr describes a family that would make the wildest imaginings of Charles Addams seem American Gothic.

Madness, sundaes and burial riotously cavort across a scene spun nuttily by two crazed parents and their family, a mute son, a heavy-metal son and a cannibalistic daughter.

Even crazier and funnier was the closing piece, *Peter Breaks Through,* where Alejandro Membreno describes what happens when Peter Pan follows Tinkerbell (who is sadly zapped) into a whorehouse run by an impotent arsonist and tries to rescue Mona from the flames. This was a zippy, zestful *jeu d'esprit.*

> Clive Barnes, *"Hooray for the Young," in* New York Post, *September 28, 1989.*

JOHN BEAUFORT

One of those annual events awaited with eager anticipation by the New York theater community is The Young Playwrights Festival—and thus far in the festival's eight years of existence, playgoers have not been disappointed.

Judged by the four works receiving full productions at Playwrights Horizons, the latest selection of winning works reflects a sophistication that might be considered beyond the years of the entrants (all the authors were under 19 when their scripts were submitted).

Painted Rain, by then 15-year-old Janet Allard is the only work focusing directly on a teenage situation. Miss Allard deals sensitively and perceptively with the tensions and mutual affection between two young orphans awaiting adoption: the rambunctious Teddy and the more withdrawn Dustin, preoccupied with ambitions to be a painter. The play's ending is heartfelt rather than facile.

Finnegan's Funeral Parlor and Ice Cream Shoppe, by Robert Kerr (18), is a wildly black comedy about a family of mad morticians headed by a paterfamilias determined to adjust the funeral business to the age of gimmicky consumerism.

In *Twice Shy,* the most mature of the four playlets, Debra Neff (18) considers the problems of Louise, a remarkably recovered rape victim, as she seeks to sort out a variety of relationships. Immediately involved are her departing young homosexual apartment mate, her domineering mother, and a potential new boyfriend. The cast responds to the writing, which is insightful, complex, and comic.

Peter Breaks Through, by Alejandro Membreno (18), plunges Peter Pan into the lower depths of New York City pimping and prostitution for a vulgarly impudent send-up of Sir James Barrie's childhood fantasy. A recent preview audience found it hilarious rather than offensive.

The productions in the eighth annual festival adhere to the high professional standards that have come to be expected of these yearly events sponsored by the Foundation of the Dramatists Guild.

> John Beaufort, *"Young Playwrights in the Spotlight," in* The Christian Science Monitor, *October 2, 1989.*

JOHN SIMON

The Eighth Annual Young Playwrights Festival yielded, as usual, much promise and some real achievement. Least interesting is the work of the youngest author, Janet Allard (fifteen), *Painted Rain,* about two troubled adolescents in an orphanage. One of them, in a wheelchair, paints frantically and tries to learn to walk with braces. The other, though sighted, likes to pretend he is blind. One gets adopted, the other sinks into deeper isolation. . . . A gallant attack, this, by a fifteen-year-old novice playwright on a tricky subject, but I for one would happily have waited till she was a bit riper.

Robert Kerr (eighteen) gives us an absurdist farce, *Finnegan's Funeral Parlor and Ice Cream Shoppe,* in which Finnegan tries to run the aforesaid clashing businesses on the same premises. His wife, scarcely less weird, faithfully supports him; Kevin, their eldest, refuses to speak and yearns only to be a barber; Anvil, the second son, loudly veers from anarchist leather boy to freaky transvestite; Pamela, the youngest, likes to nibble on the toes and fingers of her father's stiffs. Carol, the counter girl at the shoppe, wants to convert Kevin into an accountant—the paragon of normality; Mrs. Dewey, a client of the parlor, wants her husband decently buried. Both are to be sadly frustrated. . . . There are funny bits here, but Kerr cannot quite sustain his grotesquerie.

The last play, *Peter Breaks Through,* by Alejandro Membreno (eighteen), is a fantasy that brings Tinker Bell and Peter Pan into a modern whorehouse to rather less comic effect than the conceit promises. . . . Much the finest play is the penultimate, *Twice Shy,* by Debra Neff (eighteen), a situation comedy, if you will, about a disturbed college girl's problems with two homosexual apartment mates, an overprotective mother, and an overeager suitor. But it is done with such psychological finesse and such tellingly funny-painful dialogue that it easily hoists itself onto a higher plane. . . . There is a freshness about all these younger playwrights; long may they resist turning into older ones.

> John Simon, *in a review of the Eighth Annual Young Playwrights Festival, in* New York *Magazine, Vol. 22, No. 39, October 2, 1988, p. 84.*

ALISA SOLOMON

The Young Playwrights Festival, which in its time has produced works by 49 writers under the age of 19, is only eight years old. Perhaps that explains why the festival itself has not yet engaged any of the adolescent questions so often found in the plays it presents: Who am I? Why am I here? Why do I care if people like me? And, to quote from two of the plays on this year's bill, "Why doesn't anyone ever ask me what *I* want?"

Of course the festival encourages talented kids to write for the theater and that's terrific. But is anyone asking them whether a professional, Off-Broadway production and its trappings—a four-week rehearsal period, market pressures, agents, critics—is what *they* want? More important, is it what they—and the theater—*need* ?

It's heartbreaking to see, year after year, festival plays that merely demonstrate that teenagers can successfully imitate the formal and thematic clichés of commercial theater. Debra Neff's *Twice Shy* hides its passion and understanding of a young woman's sexual anxiety beneath pop-psych homilies and stereotyped characters. (Once again our hero's problems are the fault of her bossy, brazen Jewish mother.) Janet Allard's *Painted Rain* is a NutraSweet vignette in which two lonely orphan boys learn, through their strained friendship, to face up to their fears.

Why is Debra Neff cramming her insights into such a superficial vehicle? Why is Janet Allard wasting her poetic ear on such a limited form? These writers might have a future in television, but unless someone tells them it's okay to play around onstage, that they can imagine a show without furniture and psychological explanations, the festival is not doing one of its main jobs.

Alejandro Membreno's *Peter Breaks Through* is more encouraging, a frivolous but fantastical sketch in which Peter Pan flies into the sultry world of a two-bit prostitute who is hoping to turn over a new leaf. Any writer who fries Tinkerbell on a light bulb in the opening moments of his play has a promising future.

But it's Robert Kerr's *Finnegan's Funeral Parlor and Ice Cream Shoppe* that most successfully combines imagination with craft, substance with fancy. This silly, macabre portrait of an American family pushes the familiar images of the demanding dad, conciliatory mom, goody-goody daughter, rebellious son, and sensitive son to hilarious extremes. Here, the daughter delights in seeing her loud, anarchistic brother beaten ("Are you gonna smack him, Daddy? Smack him, Daddy!") as she nibbles cannibalistically on toes cut off of bodies brought into the family funeral business.

Alisa Solomon, "Uncreated Consciousness," in The Village Voice, *Vol. XXXIV No. 40 October 3, 1989, p. 108.*

TERRY HELBING

What's most encouraging about the [*Eighth Annual Young Playwrights Festival*] is that these young people are clearly writing for the theater and not turning out sitcoms or movies of the week masquerading as plays. In addition, this year's one-acts compare favorably with one another, an infrequent occurrence in any evening of collected works.

Painted Rain by Janet Allard benefits from being placed first on the bill. A somber, contemplative character study about two adoptee-roommates who have developed a close relationship, the play would not be received as well by the audience if it followed any of the other, more humorous, works. The introspective tone of the piece makes it come across as what adults must think teenagers are typically concerned about emotionally. . . .

Robert Kerr demonstrates such flair for farce in *Finnegan's Funeral Parlor and Ice Cream Shoppe* that you hope he will continue writing, so that producers can turn to him and not have to produce farces by Ray Cooney. A madcap look at a wildly dysfunctional family, the play is swiftly directed by Thomas Babe and well acted by the seven-member cast. Imagine three children, one of whom can't speak, while the other two are a cannibal and an anarchist (who turns up at one point in *Rocky Horror Show* drag) and who either desperately do or do not want to take part in the family businesses

of the play's title, and you get an idea of Kerr's vivid imagination. His last scene doesn't work, and he didn't seem to know how to write himself out of it, but he nevertheless demonstrates great style and potential.

In *Twice Shy,* Debra Neff gets a bit bogged down in the "What-about-my-needs" concerns of her central character, Louise. . . . Neff is certainly aware of the traditions of the commercial theater in her domestic comedy-drama but reflects 1980's sensibilities and nontraditional family relationships within her realistic-sounding dialogue and scenes.

Alejandro Membreno's *Peter Breaks Through* skit . . . provides a delightfully silly topper for the evening, as Peter Pan and Tinkerbelle find themselves in the room of a not-so-happy hooker and her fetishistic pimp.

Terry Helbing, "For Those Who Think Young," in Theater Week, *October 9, 1989, p. 42.*

LESLIE (HOBAN) BLAKE

Four one-act plays in just under two and a half hours, written by one fifteen year old and three eighteen year olds describes the eighth annual Young Playwrights Festival but the emphasis on numbers is quite misleading. These plays must not be judged on the relative youth of their authors. In fact, this year in particular, the caliber is higher than usual.

Last on the bill and my favorite, *Peter Breaks Through,* by Alejandro Membreno, deals with kinky sex, death and vengeance involving Peter Pan and Tinkerbell . . . yes, Peter, Tink and kinky sex in the same short work by an eighteen year old! In a serious vein there's *Painted Rain,* by Janet Allard, directed by Mary B. Robinson; in a seriocomic vein, *Twice Shy* by Debra Neff, directed by Mark Brokaw and finally, a bizarre farce by Robert Kerr, *Finnegan's Funeral Parlor and Ice Cream Shoppe,* directed by Thomas Babe.

Allard's play gives us two orphans, one handicapped and one black both over usual adoption age and both desperately in need of attention and affection. Their journey to closeness ends with, what might be, a veiled double suicide pact. . . .

Another well meaning adult is Cookie, Louise's mother [in *Twice Shy*]. Louise has withdrawn from social life after she was raped at a fraternity party and Cookie attempts to bring her daughter back out by introducing her to straight young man, Steven. The ying and yang of these multiple relationships is neatly done except for the dramatic convenience of Steven's romance with Louise. Playwright Debra Neff's sense of humor and top notch acting from Lauren Klein save Cookie from a stereotypical Jewish mother role and bring her into Wendy Wasserstein land.

In the macabre *Funeral Parlor,* both Finnegan boys, mute Kevin and punk Anvil are isolated from their Charles Addams-variety suburban Yuppie family. Dad and Mom are Grant Wood Americans gone really gothic, while sister Pamela is a bad seed who nibbles the toes and fingers of her undertaker-father's deceased clients.

It takes outsider Carol to help Kevin speak. He does and announces that he wishes to enter neither of the family businesses—not Mortuary nor Ice Cream Shoppe—which share the same premises. He wishes to become a hairdresser.

Thomas Babe directs at a whirlwind pace but the play doesn't prepare us for the family's final solution to the problem of Kevin.

> *Leslie (Hoban) Blake, "The 1989 Young Playwrights Festival," in* Stages, *December, 1989.*

The *Satanic Verses*
Controversy: Part II

The entry below expands and updates coverage provided in *CLC*, Vol. 55: *Yearbook 1988* of international debate and events surrounding Salman Rushdie's novel, *The Satanic Verses* (1988).

CHRONOLOGY OF EVENTS

•1988•

September 26: *The Satanic Verses* is published by Viking Penguin, Inc. in the United Kingdom. Earlier in the year, an auction was organized at which six publishers bid for English-language hardcover and softcover rights to the novel. Although not the highest bidder, Viking Penguin won the rights for $850,000, considered an astonishing sum in the publishing industry since none of Rushdie's three previous novels—*Grimus, Midnight's Children,* and *Shame*—sold more than 10,000 hardcover copies in the vital United States market.

October 7: After protests are lodged in Parliament and by private citizens, the Finance Ministry of India bars distribution of *The Satanic Verses* in that country. Rushdie protests the ban in a letter to Indian Prime Minister Rajiv Gandhi that is published later in the month in several prominent newspapers around the world.

November 2: A group of Muslims in South Africa protest against an upcoming publicity appearance by Rushdie, and *The Satanic Verses* is officially banned in that country.

November 9: *The Satanic Verses* wins Great Britain's prestigious Whitbread Award for best novel of 1988.

November 22: Grand Sheik Gad el-Haq Ali Gad el-Haq of al-Azhar, the 1,000-year-old Islamic institute based in Cairo, Egypt, urges the 46-nation Organization of Islamic Conference (OIC) to ban *The Satanic Verses*. He also calls on all Islamic organizations based in Great Britain to band together and take legal action to prevent continued distribution of the novel.

December 12: Muslims in Bolton, England demonstrate against *The Satanic Verses.*

•1989•

January 13: Newspapers report that the New York offices of Viking Penguin received an anonymous bomb threat and that the firm has received thousands of letters protesting publication and distribution of *The Satanic Verses* in the United States. Official publication is set for mid-February, 1989.

January 14: A large demonstration by Muslims in Bradford, England, at which copies of *The Satanic Verses* are burned is reported in newspapers around the world.

January 22: In an essay published in *The Observer,* Rushdie responds to protests and book burnings of *The Satanic*

Verses. He discusses Mohammad, founder of Islam; censorship by contemporary Islamic authorities; his intention in those passages of *The Satanic Verses* that Muslims find particularly offensive or blasphemous; and the vital importance of freedom of expression.

January 23: Muslim organizations in Great Britain petition the Home Secretary for changes in the state's centuries-old blasphemy laws, which pertain primarily to offenses against Christianity.

January 30: The Islamic Defense Council urges British Prime Minister Margaret Thatcher to extend blasphemy laws to cover Islam.

February 12: A demonstration against *The Satanic Verses* in Islamabad, Pakistan, turns violent, resulting in five deaths and more than fifty injuries. Several thousand Muslims march on the American Cultural Center, demanding the death of the author and banning of the book in the United States.

February 13: One person dies in Kashmir, India during a demonstration against *The Satanic Verses.*

February 14: Iran's Ayatollah Khomeini, head of the Shiite Muslim sect, issues a *fitwa* (edict) declaring that Rushdie and all those involved in publication of *The Satanic Verses* "who were aware of its contents" are sentenced to death. Rushdie learns of the threat shortly before attending a memorial service for recently deceased author Bruce Chatwin. Rushdie goes into hiding under the protection of Scotland Yard following the service. Rushdie's wife, Marianne Wiggins, joins Rushdie in seclusion.

February 15: Thousands demonstrate in Tehran, Iran, in support of Khomeini's edict. // An Iranian cleric offers a $1,000,000 reward to whoever assassinates Rushdie; the amount will eventually reach $5,000,000. // All Viking-Penguin publications banned in Iran. // Rushdie accepts protection from the Special Branch of Scotland Yard. // A planned book tour by Rushdie in the United States is cancelled.

February 16: The British government issues formal protests against Khomeini's edict, including a condemnation by Prime Minister Margaret Thatcher. // Waldenbooks, America's largest book-selling chain, removes copies from the shelves of its 1200 stores, citing the safety of its 8500 employees. // The Dutch Foreign Minister cancels a trip to Iran in protest against the death threat. // A delegation of politicians and religious scholars in Pakistan submits a written outline of their case against publication of *The Satanic Verses* in the United States to American ambassador Robert Oakley.

February 17: Viking Penguin offices close in New York and Athens after numerous bomb threats. // Iranian President Ali Khamenei states the that death threat against Rushdie will be dropped if the author apologizes; Khamenei warns Iranians against storming the British embassy in Tehran. // Several more American book chains halt sales of *The Satanic Verses.* // Canada temporarily halts imports of the novel while officials investigate whether or not the novel constitutes "hate literature" against Islam. // A public reading in support of *The Satanic Verses* by many major American writers is held in New York City, while a large demonstration against the novel occurs in Rawalpindi, Pakistan. // Egyptian Muslim clerics of the Sunni branch declare that there is no Islamic tradition for Ayatollah Khomeini's death decree.

February 18: The twelve-member European Economic Community (EEC) withdraws ambassadors from Iran and freezes high-level diplomatic visits.

February 19: In a statement published in *The Observer,* Rushdie "profoundly regrets the distress" caused by his novel. Ayatollah Khomeini rejects Rushdie's statement of regret and declares that Muslims are still bound by duty to "send Rushdie to hell."

February 20: EEC members publish a declaration protesting the death edict and recall their top diplomats from Iran. // British Foreign Secretary Geoffrey Howe charges that the threats against Rushdie are an affront to international standards of behavior; Britain virtually suspends all diplomatic relations with Iran; Howe warns of stronger measures against Iran if Rushdie is harmed. // The International Salman Rushdie Committee is formed and publishes in periodicals around the world a statement signed by over eight-hundred prominent writers protesting the threats made against Rushdie.

February 21: Marianne Wiggins cancels an American promotional tour supporting her novel, *John Dollar.* // United Nations Secretary General Javier Perez de Cuellar appeals for a lifting of death threats.

February 22: United States President George Bush calls

Khomeini's death threat "deeply offensive" and warns that Iran will "be held accountable for violence against American interests." // Iran recalls top diplomats from Western European countries in response to the actions of the EEC. // Public readings and demonstrations by writers representing such groups as the National Writers Union, the American chapter of PEN, and Article 19, a London-based organization that tracks censorship, occur in New York and other major American cities. // Sheik Abdelaziz Bin Abdallah Bin Baz, the most senior religious authority in Saudi Arabia, recommends that Rushdie be put on trial *in absentia* for heretical conduct; this declaration establishes the general Sunni Muslim line condemning the book but not supporting the death edict by Shiite Muslim leader Ayatollah Khomeini. // French President François Mitterand condemns the death edict. // New Zealand's Prime Minister, apparently unwilling to risk his country exports of sheep-meat to Iran, refuses to back EEC diplomatic reprisals.

February 24: At least twelve people are killed, over forty wounded, and eight-hundred are arrested as police open fire on Muslims rioting in Bombay, India, against *The Satanic Verses.* // The British Home Secretary meets with Muslims at Birmingham's Central Mosque; he receives a hostile reception when he defends the government's position and urges Muslims to stay within the law.

February 26: Over four-thousand Muslims protest in New York against *The Satanic Verses.*

February 27: Nigerian Nobel Laureate Wole Soyinka receives death threats for publicly condemning Ayatollah Khomeini's edict against Rushdie.

February 28: *The London Times* publishes two letters by writers concerning the Rushdie affair. One, signed by twenty-eight members of the British Society of Authors, expresses regret for the offense taken by many Muslims toward *The Satanic Verses* but supports strong measures taken by the British government against Iran and in support of Rushdie. In the other letter, author Roald Dahl, also a member of the Society, denounces Rushdie as "a dangerous opportunist" who was aware that his book would stir violent feelings among devout Muslims. // Two bookstores in Berkeley, California, are firebombed, apparently in relation to selling *The Satanic Verses.*

March 1: The Iranian Charge d'Affaires leaves London as a result of the Rushdie dispute. // More than one-thousand of the world's most prominent writers, publishers, and booksellers appeal for all nations to ensure that Iran withdraws its death threat against Salman Rushdie.

March 3: British Foreign Secretary Geoffrey Howe criticizes Rushdie's book. // Rioting and demonstrations against *The Satanic Verses* reported in India and Bangladesh.

March 4: A demonstration in support of Ayatollah Khomeini's death edict becomes a riot, leading to destruction of property and looting at the airport in Karachi, Pakistan.

March 5: The Vatican condemns *The Satanic Verses* as "offensive to Islamic sensibilities" but also denounces the death threat.

March 6: Libyan leader Muamar Qaddafi endorses the death edict against Rushdie, while the United Arab Emirates support blasphemy charges but not the death threat.

March 7: Iran breaks diplomatic ties with Great Britain. A week earlier, the Iranian government demanded that Britain declare "its opposition to the unprincipled stands against the world of Islam, the Islamic Republic of Iran and the contents of the anti-Islamic book *The Satanic Verses.*" Britain begins to formally sever ties with Iran. Although diplomatic relations remain strained over the next few months, trade between the two nations continues virtually unaffected.

March 11: Viking-Penguin books banned in forty-six Islamic countries.

March 16: Meeting of the forty-six Foreign Ministers of the OIC, which officially condemns *The Satanic Verses* but does not endorse Ayatollah Khomeini's death edict against Rushdie.

March 21: Ministers of the EEC agree that ambassadors recalled from Iran are free to return.

March 28: Bomb explodes near British Cultural Center in Islamabad, Pakistan, hours after British Foreign Secretary Sir Geoffrey Howe arrived to discuss the *Satanic Verses* controversy.

March 30: Abdullah al-Ahdal, spiritual leader of a liberal mosque in Brussels, Belgium, and his assistant are shot and killed in his office. Ahdal had received death threats following his call for moderation in the Rushdie affair and for declaring Khomeini's edict improper under Islamic law.

April 1: Muslim group in Lebanon claims responsibility for shooting death of Abdullah al-Ahdal and his deputy; states that killings are linked to Ahdal's rejection of Rushdie's death sentence.

April 5: Members of the newly-established Soviet chapter of the international PEN organization issue their first official statement—a condemnation of the death mandate against Rushdie.

April 10: Two London bookstores are firebombed, apparently in retaliation for displaying and selling *The Satanic Verses.*

Late April: Debates in various media over whether or not American and British publishers should set up displays at the Tehran Book Fair, scheduled for mid-May. Some argue for a boycott to protest book banning and threats against Rushdie, while others contend that attendance is crucial to ensure continued dissemination of information. A partial boycott of the Tehran Book Fair is reported in May.

May 28: Thousands of Muslims occupy London's Parliament Square to demand a ban on *The Satanic Verses.*

June 4: Ayatollah Khomeini dies; Iranian leaders maintain death edict.

June 8: Director of Great Britain's Muslim Institute calls on Rushdie to withdraw *The Satanic Verses* and donate proceeds from the book to relatives of people who have died in protests.

June 18: Rioting in Bradford during a demonstration against *The Satanic Verses.*

July 20: The French-language edition of *The Satanic Verses* goes on sale. Despite apprehensions of the publisher and French authorities, public reaction is slight.

September: A poem by Rushdie, in which he responds angrily to critics and vows to continue writing despite death threats, is published in *Granta,* a leading British literary journal.

September 4: London bookstore bombed, appearently in relation to the *Satanic Verses* controversy.

September 22: Three members of the Nobel Literature Prize Committee resign over the body's refusal to speak out against death threats.

October: Debate intensifies concerning possible publication and distribution of paperback editions of *The Satanic Verses. Publishers Weekly,* representing one faction, urges Viking Penguin to forego a paperback edition, maintaining that the principle of free expression has been upheld and that the softcover publication would invite further violence. Others argue that *The Satanic Verses* should be treated like other books, which are published in paperback when hardcover sales begin to slacken.

•1990•

February 12: Two pieces by Rushdie are published in *Newsweek,* one concerning events of the past year, the other explaining his intentions in *The Satanic Verses* and answering his detractors. In the first piece, Rushdie argues for publication of a paperback edition of the novel. He maintains that paperbacks are a means for keeping books in print over an extended period. Within a year or two, Rushdie contends, hardcover editions of *The Satanic Verses* will not be distributed or stocked in bookstores, and, therefore, "effectively the book will have been suppressed."

March 9: *Publishers Weekly* reports American sales in 1989 of over 745,000 hardcover copies of *The Satanic Verses.*

April: In *Mother Jones* magazine, husband-and-wife authors Clark Blaise and Bharati Mukherjee present "confidential internal memoranda" from Viking Penguin revealing that CEO Peter Meyer was pressured by parent conglomerate Pearson against publishing a paperback edition of *The Satanic Verses.* The authors also claim that Meyer has been pressured by Rushdie and his literary agents to issue a paperback edition immediately or revert paperback rights to Rushdie.

April 6: As reported in *Publishers Weekly, Harper's* Index for April, quoting as its source "Viking Penguin London," estimates that Viking Penguin, as of February, has spent $3,400,000 on extra security since publishing *The Satanic Verses* and that the book has earned $3,400,000. (It is likely that the figure of $3.4 million is after manufacturing, promotion, royalties and overhead costs have been accounted for.)

GERALD PRIESTLAND

It is just as well the 1988 Booker prize did not go to Salman Rushdie's ***The Satanic Verses***—that is, if we are to believe Hesham El Essawy, chairman of the Islamic Society for the Promotion of Religious Tolerance in the United Kingdom. One might hesitate over the word "tolerance" in that title, and wonder whether "respect" or "privilege" might be more appropriate—an indication that the meaning of English can be modified by the culture of him who uses it.

Mr El Essawy accuses Salman Rushdie's publisher, Viking, of "having declared war unilaterally on Islam and the Muslims" and warns it that unless it puts matters right "the monster that you have so needlessly created" will grow into something uncontrollable worldwide. "We might as well knight muggers and give mass murderers the Nobel prize." The book, in short, is "insulting in the extreme to everything that the Muslims hold sacred".

Mr El Essawy understands, however, that in a non-Muslim country it is not enough to rely on the Muslim magisterium alone. He cites the familiar European doctrine that everyone's freedom is limited by the freedom of others. Thus: "Mr Salman Rushdie is free to hold any belief, or none, as he pleases . . . but he is not free to tamper with mine." Nor has he the moral right, it is claimed, to take the established facts of an historical figure and alter them as he pleases, even if he disguises the result as a novel.

Here the cultural gap looks unbridgeable. Freedom of speculation and interpretation has a long history in Europe and few Europeans would accept that unorthodox belief has limited or tampered with the beliefs of the orthodox. None of us wishes Mr El Essawy to believe other than he does, and it seems unlikely that Salman Rushdie will subvert him. However, Western Christians are accustomed to the manhandling of their scriptures in a way that devotees of the Koran are not. Few doubt the historical existence of Jesus, but even the gospels leave room for conflicting views of him. It may be a criticism of our fidelity, but generally speaking we took the film, *The Last Temptation of Christ,* in our stride.

To my mind **The Satanic Verses** does present a parody of the prophet Muhammad, and it is not surprising that the government of India (with its large and explosive Muslim minority) should have made the gesture of banning it. But should we in Britain follow India's lead on the grounds that we, too, are a multiracial, multi-cultural, multi-faith society?

The fact is we are not, or not yet, and will not be made so by legislation. The current law against blasphemy protects only the Christian religion, and for two reasons once considered good: that blasphemy would call down the wrath of God upon all of us, and that (Anglican) Christianity was part and parcel of the laws of England.

It being hard to maintain either nowadays, a majority of the law commissioners were in favour of abolishing the common-law offence entirely. A minority, with considerable support from the churches, favoured a new law, not confined to Christians alone, protecting the religious against deliberate insult or outrage.

This sounds liberal but could be used most illiberally. One should take care before making a sin a crime. Who can be sure what might offend some sects? There are even a few cults—though Islam is certainly not one of them—which deserve to be exposed rather than respected.

> *Gerald Priestland, "Now Here's an Odd Sort of Tolerance," in* The Sunday Times, *London, November 6, 1988, p. B2.*

CHRISTOPHER WALKER

Salman Rushdie, the distinguished novelist whose prizewinning work, **The Satanic Verses,** has already been declared blasphemous in his native India, faces the prospect of a ban and legal proceedings throughout the Islamic world.

A ruling by Cairo's Al-Azhar, the most venerated Islamic in-

stitute, was delivered yesterday by the Grand Sheikh of Al-Azhar, Gad el-Haq Ali Gad el-Haq.

He called on all Islamic organizations based in Britain to join in taking legal steps to prevent continuing distribution there. . . .

The sheikh, one of the most influential Muslim leaders, described the novel as containing "lies and figments of the imagination" about Islam which were passed off as facts.

He demanded that the 46-nation Islamic Conference Organization should take concerted action against what he described as "a distortion of Islamic history". . . .

Western diplomatic observers [in Cairo] said they could not recall a recent example of a work of fiction provoking such universal fury among Islamic scholars.

According to the Sheikh of Al-Azhar, who claimed that the necessary measures to have it banned in Egypt had already been taken, it referred to the prophet Muhammad, his wives, and his followers offensively.

The 1,000-year-old Al-Azhar institute, a combined mosque and university, is considered the seat of Islamic theology.

The strength of its ruling against **The Satanic Verses,** which is named after the verses the prophet removed from the Koran on the grounds that they were inspired by the Devil, will ensure that heavy international pressure is now aimed against the book.

Mr Rushdie, who won the 1981 Booker Prize with an earlier novel, **Midnight's Children,** has already disclosed that he received death threats from Muslims after the first publication of his latest work in September.

The extreme sensitivity of Muslims arises from their conviction that the Koran contains the direct words of God as relayed to Muhammad.

Mr Rushdie is not the only novelist of international stature to suffer the wrath of the scholars of Al-Azhar.

This week they renewed their rejection of the publication here of *The Children of Gebelawi,* one of the early novels by the 1988 Egyptian winner of the Nobel Prize for literature, Naguib Mahfouz, on the grounds that it contained "grave insults to religious creeds".

Referring to the book, first banned [in Egypt] in 1959, which questioned religious norms in Islamic society, the Al-Azhar institute decreed: "A novel cannot just be permitted into circulation because its author won the Nobel Prize for literature, since that award does not justify the propagation of misguided ideas."

> *Christopher Walker, "Islamic Leaders Urge Muslim World to Ban 'Blasphemous' Rushdie Book," in* The Times, *London, November 22, 1988, p. 13.*

MALISE RUTHVEN

A special action committee has been set up to present a united Islamic front against what its convener, Dr Mughram al-Ghamdi, who is also Director-General of the Islamic Cultural Centre in Regent's Park, calls "the most offensive, filthy and abusive book ever written by any hostile enemy of Islam". (One wonders how many other offensive books Dr al-

Ghamdi has read.) Another Muslim organization, the World Muslim Congress, is reported to have asked the Attorney-General to take criminal proceedings against Rushdie under the blasphemy laws. The Secretary-General of the Islamic Council of Europe has urged the Islamic Conference in Jeddah—a group consisting of the foreign ministers of all countries with Muslim majorities—to have all Muslim States ban [*The Satanic Verses*], to bar its author from entry and to blacklist all Penguin-Viking publications if Viking fails to withdraw and pulp the book. India, South Africa, Saudi Arabia and Egypt have already banned the book and it seems probable that most Muslim States will follow suit: the row seems set to last for months.

Is the book really blasphemous? In one Genet-like scene in the imaginary city of Jahiliaya (the scene which has caused most offence to orthodox Muslims), a fictional Indian film star suffering a schizophrenic breakdown in which he supposes himself to be the Archangel Gabriel, dreams of a brothel where prostitutes take on the roles of the Prophet Mahound's wives. While the scene might seem deliberately offensive to the pious, who revere the Mothers of the Believers almost as much as the Prophet himself, the author could hardly have gone further in distancing it from any pretensions to historical realism. At the same time, Rushdie is familiar enough with the early Muslim annalists to know just where to stick the knife into orthodoxy: another dream episode, in which his character Salman the Persian mistranscribes a portion of the Holy Quran, is based on the historic account by the annalist al Tabari, who records that one of the Prophet Muhammad's scribes, Abdullah ibn Sa'd, lost his faith after a deliberate mistake in his transcription of the divine text went unnoticed by the Prophet. Similar use is made of the famous episode of the "Satanic Verses" from which the novel takes its title (in which Satan is supposed to have introduced verses into the Prophet's mind permitting a modified version of polytheism, in order to placate the citizens of Mecca). The story is recorded by al Tabari and other early sources regarded by Muslims as unimpeachable. Any scholarly-minded Muslim moving from faith towards scepticism is likely to seize on these and similar stories retold by Rushdie, which undermine the orthodox position that the Quran was "dictated" by God without any human editing.

The issue here goes deeper than a row over what is or is not fiction. Many, if not most, of the books by scholars which deal with the Quran and Islamic origins in a scientific manner, using the methods of textual analysis adopted from biblical scholarship, are banned in Muslim countries. Saudi Arabia—where the fundamentalist Wahhabite sect still holds sway in religious matters—even forbids such religious classics as the works of al-Ghazzali and al-Ashari, because even these might lead the faithful to stray off the strict path of literalism. Most of the institutions calling for the banning of Rushdie are recipients of Saudi or other foreign funds: would the Muslims of Britain be so vociferous in demanding the suppression of a book by Britain's most outstanding Muslim writer if they had a genuinely representative organization of their own?

This tendency to ban books at the drop of a hat is the reverse side of an Islam that has apparently degenerated into a Cult of the Text. For centuries Sunni Muslims were taught that the Quran was the perfect "uncreated" Word of God, dictated by the Archangel Gabriel and written down, unaltered, by the Prophet's scribes. Exegetical commentary was limited to

elucidating the meaning of the text, not, as in Higher Criticism, to establishing its authenticity. The same applied, *a fortiori*, to the Messenger: paradoxically, the fact that the Prophet Muhammad was not officially venerated as a Divine Person (at least in the Sunni tradition) protected his personhood from religious scrutiners. There is no "Muhammadology" comparable to the Christology of Western theologians (though for some Shi'ites, who are more inclined to allegory, his word is the Divine Logos made manifest in speech).

In post-Christian literature, the figure of Christ continually occurs and recurs without scandal to the faith. Even American fundamentalists, who, like their Muslim counterparts, reject Higher Criticism and venerate their Bible as a kind of fetish, have learned to live with *Moby Dick, Light in August* and numerous other novels that make allegorical use of Christian symbolism in a manner that challenges religious orthodoxy (although there have been occasional objections to the presence of *The Scarlet Letter* on school reading lists). The Muslims—or rather, those who are claiming to speak on their behalf in Britain—still appear to have an infantile fixation on the figure of the Prophet and the forms of their Text, a fixation that can only diminish both in the eyes of outsiders. Rather than trying to refute those who question the canonized version of Islamic origins on scholarly grounds, which would require sustained intellectual effort, these Muslim leaders seem to go out of their way to make themselves look ridiculous by demanding boycotts and bans.

Rushdie, inevitably, has the last word, since his novel so accurately anticipates the behaviour of his critics: "Burn the books, trust the Book", says Bilal X, the black muezzin. One of the novel's most vociferous critics turns out to be Dr Hesham al-Essawy, chairman of an organization calling itself the Islamic Society for the Promotion of Religious Tolerance in the United Kingdom—a title which Rushdie, with his love of paradox, must be kicking himself for not having thought up first. "To sanction such a work", writes Dr Essawy in a letter addressed to the Managing Director of Viking, is "to invite agonies and disasters from which none of us will be safe, we might as well knight muggers and give mass murderers the Nobel prize." (Stranger things have happened in the real world, though not apparently the one Dr Essawy inhabits . . . .) As Gabreel Farishta, another sub-angelic *alter ego* of Rushdie's, put it: "Something was badly amiss with the spiritual life of the planet. Too many demons inside people claiming to believe in God."

Malise Ruthven, "Islam and the Book," in The Times Literary Supplement, *No. 4469, November 25-December 1, 1988, p. 1312.*

AMIT ROY AND DEIRDRE FERNAND

Last Monday afternoon, when Salman Rushdie was at his terraced Islington home in London preparing for yet another literary party, Ayatollah Ruhollah Khomeini was at his villa in the northern suburbs of Tehran watching the evening television news.

One item enraged the 88-year-old ayatollah, who makes a point of watching the news every night. It was a report from the Pakistani capital of Islamabad about the deaths of five Muslims who had been demonstrating against an apparently blasphemous book by an Indian writer who was now a British subject.

Khomeini, according to his staff, had never heard of Rushdie or the book, *The Satanic Verses.* But he was soon told that the novel insulted Allah and his prophet Muhammad, and worse, that the author was born a Muslim. To write such a work was an act of a apostasy—punishable by death under Islamic law.

Khomeini is not a man renowned for his tolerance or clemency. But despite his great age and declining powers, he saw the chance of striking a blow for Islam and maintaining the delicate balance of power inside the squabbling government.

He promptly summoned a secretary from the special bureau in his villa at the foothills of the Alborz mountains and dictated a note in his distinctive, ponderous manner. This was taken by courier late that night to the headquarters of Radio Tehran, after the station had been alerted that a *fatwa*—a rarely-used religious edict—from the Imam was on its way.

In London, three and a half hours behind, Salman Rushdie was circulating with his American wife, Marianne Wiggins, among the literati in the elegant art-nouveau atrium of Michelin House in Chelsea. The party was to launch her own book, *John Dollar* (itself a controversial novel about religion and cannibalism) and, according to other guests, she was looking "desperately glamorous".

There was nothing to suggest that Salman was about to be condemned to death by a grim-faced apostle of Islam sitting in front of his television set 3,000 miles away.

None the less Rushdie, normally a loquacious figure, was subdued. He already knew about the deaths in Islamabad, and that day news had reached him of more violent protests against the book in the Indian province of Kashmir. One person had been killed and 60 injured. He was obviously disturbed, though unrepentant.

Alan Yentob, the controller of BBC2, who was at the party, said: "He told me that he was not going to take on his shoulders the death of the people in Pakistan—the actions of a few fanatics were not his moral responsibility." But Yentob detected more: "He had been resilient up until that time. Salman and Marianne have had to live with this situation for weeks. But when people started dying it turned into something extremely distressing."

Afterwards, at dinner at La Poisonnerie de l'Avenue in Sloane Avenue, Rushdie told friends that he had no intention of apologising. "I am not giving in," he declared. Within hours his resolve was to be tested and his life changed, perhaps for ever.

Monitoring stations around the world picked up the Iranian broadcast containing Khomeini's edict on Tuesday morning. . . .

This *coup de foudre* stunned Rushdie and the West. The news was broken to him by the BBC World Service, and that lunchtime he appeared on Radio 4's World at One, where he admitted to taking the threat seriously. Even so, he responded in characteristic style: "Frankly, I wish I had written a more critical book."

The head of the Middle East department at the Foreign Office learned from a Reuters news agency report that the religious leader of Iran was inciting his followers to murder British subjects. The news spread rapidly through Whitehall and Western capitals.

After years of Iranian-inspired political assassinations, nobody could take the threat lightly. . . .

This clash of cultures was something that many had feared ever since the fundamentalist revolution swept Iran a decade ago: a militant and unforgiving Islam deep in its counter-reformation could see little in common with the West, bent on defending freedom of thought and expression. Rushdie, born in Bombay to a Muslim family and educated in Christian Britain, bridged both worlds and had become the unlikely agent of an unprecedented crisis.

Khomeini's brief message was unequivocal. Anyone who died in the cause of ridding the world of Rushdie, he said, "will be regarded as a martyr and will go directly to heaven" . . .

[Rushdie's] last appearance in public was at a memorial service on Tuesday for Bruce Chatwin, the travel writer. Paul Theroux, the novelist, was also there. "I was impressed that he came, that he wasn't spooked to be there," he said. "He was slightly tense and watchful."

As they left the church Theroux whispered: "Your turn next. I suppose we'll be back here for you next week. Keep your head down, Salman." Rushdie ducked and laughed before hurrying off in Yentob's car. . . .

The fear of fanatics was not confined to the author. The publisher, Viking Penguin, its staff also under sentence of death, got police protection. In New York and Athens Penguin closed its offices on Friday, after numerous bomb threats and a reward for the murder of the company's American president.

Penguin was told that all its books would be banned in 45 Islamic countries unless *The Satanic Verses* was pulped. Big American bookshop chains quickly withdrew copies of the novel from display, and several European publishing houses abandoned plans to print.

Publishers and bookshops that refused to be cowed were rewarded with an instant best-seller. It was, recalled some American booksellers, just like *Spycatcher* after the British government tried to ban it. They reported last week they had sold out of 50,000 copies even before the official launch date, and publishers predicted it could make Rushdie $1m, an unexpected bonus for an author whose previous books had sold sparingly in the United States.

The ramifications of the death threats, however, went far beyond the publishing world. Western governments were thrown into a dilemma about how to respond. There was though, for once, a remarkable degree of convergence.

The British, anxious to gain leverage in Tehran, froze what had been a gradual improvement in diplomatic relations. The West Germans recalled their chargé d'affaires from Tehran for consultations; and the Dutch cancelled a trip to Iran by their foreign minister. The French postponed the return to Tehran of their ambassador. The Americans said they were "appalled". In Strasbourg, the European parliament demanded "severe sanctions" against Iranian interests and the use of force to bring those responsible to justice if attempts were made to kill Rushdie or his publishers.

But the affair seemed to have acquired a chilling momentum in the Muslim world. (p. A15)

Some British Muslims agreed that Rushdie deserved to be

killed. The Iranian ambassador to the Vatican declared he was willing to murder Rushdie himself and called for the execution of any Italian publisher who printed the book.

Demonstrators gathered outside the British embassy in Tehran, smashing windows. The World Association of Muslim Youth said it would organise protests at British embassies worldwide. More protests flared in Pakistan on Friday, and in Tehran tens of thousands shouted "Death to America and Britain".

The Pakistanis, despite the reluctance of Benazir Bhutto, the prime minister, made the running. They called for the banning of the book in Britain and the United States and for the destruction of all existing copies. They cited the banning in Britain of *Lady Chatterley's Lover* in 1960.

In Bangladesh, protesters chanted "hang Satan Rushdie". In India, police declared a state of alert in Bombay after a threat to bomb British Airways aircraft. Improbable stories emerged of "death squads heading for Britain".

To the West, it seemed as if the world had suddenly reverted to the Middle Ages. Clerics began to mutter about parallels between the intolerance of the Inquisition and the new brand of Islam. It was, said French publishers, echoing the thoughts of more enlightened Muslims, "a return to barbarism".

The germ of the idea for *The Satanic Verses* was probably planted in Cambridge 20 years ago, when Rushdie was at King's College, writing a paper on Muhammad, Islam and the rise of the caliphs. Some of the material eventually found its way into the novel, in a form that Rushdie knew would be controversial for Muslims desperately protective of their faith.

But he could never have anticipated the intensity of the reaction and the way it spilled into the international arena, sparking probably the biggest literary row of all time.

The story that culminated in Khomeini's edict began last summer in India, where Rushdie has been a celebrated writer ever since the publication of *Midnight's Children,* a novel about post-independence India.

A copy of *The Satanic Verses* manuscript was sent to Delhi for Penguin's Indian subsidiary to consider publication. It decided against it and wrote to Penguin in London in July "vaguely suggesting that Muslims in England could cause trouble".

The controversial nature of the book first emerged in public when two of India's leading news magazines, *India Today* and *Sunday,* published interviews with Rushdie in mid-September. [The *India Today* interview is excerpted in *CLC,* Vol. 55.]

Both reports caught the eye of Syed Shahabuddin, an ambitious Muslim MP. As a member of the opposition Janata party, he immediately called on the government to ban the book.

With a general election due within a year, Rajiv Gandhi's increasingly unpopular Congress (I) party was well aware of the electoral importance of India's 100m Muslims. On October 5, soon after the book was published in Britain, the Indian government telexed Penguin in London announcing the ban. Within weeks it was followed by Pakistan, Saudi Arabia, Egypt, Somalia, Bangladesh, Sudan, Malaysia, Indonesia,

Qatar and South Africa, which has a vociferous Muslim minority.

The matter may have ended there, had not Aslam Ejaz, of the Islamic Foundation in Madras, already written to Faiyazuddin Ahmad, a friend in Leicester, telling him about the impending ban in India. A similar campaign, wrote Ejaz, should be mounted in Britain, which still remained largely oblivious to the blasphemous nature of the book.

Ahmad, who came to Britain from India five years ago, is public relations director of the Islamic Foundation in Leicester. His actions, as much as anything, were to spark the row in Britain.

He sent out a secretary to buy the novel for £12.95 at a local bookshop. The offending passages were photocopied and immediately sent on October 3 to the dozen or so leading Islamic organisations in Britain. Four days later copies were dispatched to the 45 embassies in Britain of the member countries of the Organisation of Islamic Conference (OIC), including Iran.

Ahmad then flew to the Saudi Arabian headquarters of the OIC in Jeddah and canvassed the leadership. As a result, telexes were sent to all member countries calling for a ban.

The Saudis, who were to play an important role, were already upset with Penguin. They had been trying to get a revision of *Roget's Thesaurus,* which had lumped together "bedouin, vagabond, bum, waif, stray and street-Arab" as synonyms.

Back in London, one set of photostat copies arrived at the offices of Dr Syed Pasha, secretary of the Union of Muslim Organisations, an umbrella organisation for Islamic groups in Britain.

Pasha, sensing a serious problem for Britain's Muslim community, summoned the union's 19 council members to a crisis meeting on October 15. One of those present was Sher Azam, a representative from Bradford, whose 50,000 Muslims have since become the centre of protest in Britain against the book.

It was decided to start a campaign to get the novel banned. Pasha wrote to Penguin on October 20 but got no reply. At the same time he asked Margaret Thatcher to prosecute Rushdie and Penguin under the Public Order Act (1986) and the Race Relations Act (1976).

Pasha's letter to the prime minister set the tone for the Muslim assault on Rushdie: "Never have we encountered such a ferocious and savage attack on our Holy Prophet, using abominably foul language," he wrote. He added that "the Muslim community is shocked and seething with indignation".

The response from the prime minister on November 11 was detailed. Thatcher made it clear that "there are no grounds on which the government could consider banning" the book. "It is an essential part of our democratic system that people who act within the law should be able to express their opinions freely."

Thatcher's only concession was to refer the matter to Sir Patrick Mayhew, the attorney-general, who decided the book constituted no criminal offence. But Pasha was not prepared to give up. . . . Last week, a frustrated Pasha commented: "People are looking at this issue through Christian eyes. You must look at it through Muslim eyes."

Meanwhile a parallel campaign was being run from the Regent's Park mosque in London, which houses the Islamic Cultural Centre. The mosque's leaders met at the end of November to discuss the book and chose three Muslim ambassadors to convey their doubts to the Home Office. The government promised to give "careful attention to their views".

By this time Bradford's Muslim community, too, was lobbying actively. As long as two months ago a meeting about the book attracted 500 protesters. It was decided then to make a gesture of burning the book publicly.

The highly evocative photograph of *The Satanic Verses* in flames went round the world on January 14, and an uncomprehending Britain woke up to a crisis that had been simmering for months.

It remains hard to see how the affair can be resolved without either side giving way, or Rushdie remaining in indefinite fear of his life.

His measured apology yesterday in which he "profoundly regrets the distress . . . to sincere followers of Islam", may be sufficient to satisfy some in Tehran, who are clearly embarrassed by the affair. But Iranian experts said it seemed unlikely it would lead to a clear-cut "pardon" by Khomeini. Iran's official news agency quickly said the statement fell short of a public repentance.

The apology also does not appear to take into account the internal political undercurrents of the row in Pakistan and Iran. The determination to pursue him and the book has become part of a complex power struggle in Pakistan. The demonstrators who attacked the United States embassy last weekend were followers of extremist mullahs, who resented the election of Bhutto—a "Westernised woman"—to the premiership.

They also saw this as an opportunity to harm America, Pakistan's leading ally. "The USA, Britain and Israel are the agents of Satan on the earth and they are out to eliminate Muslims," said Abdul Rehman, 21, in a typical comment among protesters, that reflected the paranoia about the book which has been evident all week. (pp. A15-A17)

In the meantime, for Rushdie and his wife life will remain a nightmare. He is, according to friends, naturally nervous and sensitive. "He'll jump every time the cat flap bangs," said Redmond O'Hanlon, a friend and fellow writer.

Unless there is a form of pardon from the ayatollah, his existence will now take on an unfamiliar pattern of drawn curtains, armed policemen and confinement. Nobody can predict how any attempt could be made to kill him. Past experience in London—five people have died in acts of terrorism linked to Iran—suggests that car bombs and shootings are favoured methods.

As a result, police sources said that Rushdie had been given "grade one" protection, the highest level. This means round-the-clock guards, with Special Branch officers protecting him during his "moving hours" and uniformed officers guarding him at night. Scotland Yard has not yet decided how long this can be maintained, though nobody doubts it may have to be for a very long time.

From his unwelcome refuge, Rushdie will be able to watch this surreal story unfold. He will at least take some comfort from the knowledge that American publishers are planning to fight back.

This Wednesday, advertisements will appear in *The New York Times* defending the right to publish. "Free people write books," the adverts will say. "Free people publish books. Free people sell books. Free people buy books. Free people read books."

It is a view as firmly endorsed in the West as it is incomprehensible to the new and vengeful world of Islam. (p. A17)

> *Amit Roy and Deirdre Fernand, "Satanic Curses,"*
> *in* The Sunday Times, *London, February 19, 1989,*
> *pp. A15-A18.*

CONOR CRUISE O'BRIEN

After the Indian government banned the importation of *The Satanic Verses* last October, Salman Rushdie, supported by fellow writers and sections of the media, sent an open letter of protest to Rajiv Gandhi. It was published in the *New York Times,* which again ran it last Friday [February 17, 1989]—in full—with an editorial implying that subsequent events had shown the Indian government's decision to be wrong.

In fact, those events have demonstrated that the fears were only too well founded. If they had allowed the book in, Gandhi and his ministers would have been guilty of a dereliction of the most basic responsibility of any government: preventing a major breakdown of public order.

As it is, with the book firmly banned, there have been riots in India—as in Pakistan—against the mere fact that it has been published at all, anywhere, even thousands of miles away.

India today has almost as many Muslims as Pakistan. Most would regard a decision to allow the importation of *The Satanic Verses* as a deliberate outrage perpetrated against them by their predominantly Hindu government. Hindu bigots would see the decision in the same light, but with unholy glee. Any attempt to circulate and sell the book in India would precipitate the worst disorders the subcontinent had seen since partition in 1947, with many thousands dead.

I can see little point in lecturing countries with large Muslim populations on freedom of expression if that freedom, in this specific case, led to general mayhem. But I can see a lot of point in telling Muslim rulers, very clearly, that the promulgation of a death sentence against a person living within the jurisdiction of another state is incompatible with continued diplomatic and economic relations.

Britain and the other EEC [European Economic Community] countries have withdrawn their diplomats now that Ayatollah Khomeini has deliberately repeated his international incitement to murder [see their statement in *CLC,* Vol. 55]. Relations should remain broken until an Iranian government withdraws that incitement, probably after Allah has gathered the Imam unto Himself.

In terms of Islamic theology, I feel reasonably sure that Khomeini is on sound ground. I have read such of his theological writings as are available in English, and I found them impressive, in a scary sort of way. He believes that the Koran is the Word of God, and he takes God literally at His Word. If God says that you ought to cut off the hand of a thief, stone an adulterous pair to death, or kill a blasphemer, then that is exactly what you have to do.

It is precisely against that belief that *The Satanic Verses* is directed. Rushdie has resurrected and embroidered an old Islamic tradition, dating back at least to the 9th century, according to which the Prophet recognized that certain verses, which he had once mistakenly believed to be of divine origin, were, in fact, inspired by Satan.

To make the message more acceptable to the people of Mecca, Muhammad offered certain verses (later repudiated) which diluted monotheism by offering some praise to the idols of the place. Rushdie, in various dream sequences of his surrealist novel, plays around with this notion until it appears that the Prophet's claim to be the Messenger of God is either a delusion or an imposture, or perhaps a bit of each.

It is true that Rushdie, in that open letter to Rajiv Gandhi, for example, claims that "the book isn't actually about Islam". The book isn't *entirely* about Islam, but large parts of it quite clearly and elaborately are, and even contain quotations from the Koran. In the same letter, Rushdie makes the point that the prophet in *The Satanic Verses* "is not called Mohammed".

True, but perhaps just a shade disingenuous. He is called Mahound. And if you look up Mahound in the *OED*, you will find: *"The false prophet Mohammad . . . A false god, an idol . . . A monster, a hideous creature . . . Used as a name for the Devil."* Hardly expressions that would have a sedative effect on those mobs in the bazaars.

Two aspects of this controversy have a number of adherents in the West but both, in different ways, seem to me erroneous. One, dear to the man in the street, is that the Ayatollah's death sentence on Rushdie is "incomprehensible".

But it ought not to be incomprehensible to a Christian, or to a Jew. In the Old Testament, God tells Moses: "And he that blasphemeth the name of the Lord, he shall surely be put to death and all the congregation shall certainly stone him . . ." (Leviticus, 24.14).

Thomas Aquinas, Luther, Calvin and even Erasmus all taught that blasphemy is punishable by death. Muhammad also taught this. Islam still believes in Revelation. Christendom, deeply irradiated by the Enlightenment, mostly no longer really believes in Revelation.

So when we take Muslims to task for continuing to hold that blasphemy should be punishable by death, it is as if we are saying: "How dare you go on beating your wife, now that I have left off beating mine?"

The other erroneous response, that of excessive respectfulness towards Islam, is one to which some Christian clergy are addicted. Thus, Cardinal O'Connor of New York, preaching in St Patrick's Cathedral last Sunday, urged his congregation to manifest their "respect" for Islam by not reading *The Satanic Verses.*

But what the book is saying about Islam is no more than what Christians have always said: that Muhammad is not truly the Messenger of God. Why should Christians have become so respectful of a religion which claims to supersede Christianity, and aims to replace it, preferably by the use of force?

I suspect that part of the explanation may lie in the nostalgia of certain clergymen for a lost theocracy. With this goes a corresponding admiration for the mullahs, who have managed to keep theocracy as a going concern. . . .

The tendency to be obsequious towards Islam is particularly dangerous right now. The more than Western governments and institutions defer to the *diktats* from Tehran and other Islamic centres, the more they will be open to intimidation and blackmail from the same quarter. In that respect, the decision by some US book-distributing chains not to carry *The Satanic Verses,* and the decision by the Canadian government to keep it out of Canada, are both deplorable.

The Canadian decision should be sharply distinguished from the Indian. Canada has only a small Muslim minority, so there would have been little prospect of a cataclysm of violence.

Rushdie himself remains at high personal risk. It may not be possible to ensure his survival without the closure of the Iranian embassy in London—so far the Iranians are not being expelled, although the Foreign Office has indicated firmly that it would like them to leave. The embassy is committed, on the word of its own highest spiritual and political authority, to the destruction of the blasphemer, wherever he might be found. An embassy with such a commitment should have no place in a modern Western capital.

> *Conor Cruise O'Brien, "Banning, Right and Wrong," in* The Times, *London, February 22, 1989, p. 16.*

S. NOMANUL HAQ

Dear Salman Rushdie,

A few years ago, when I read your *Midnight's Children,* I was overwhelmed. It was not the exuberance of your narrative and stylistic craft, nor the threads of your rich imagination, woven with such effortless intellectual control that engulfed me. Rather, it was your formidable grasp of history and through that of the psyche of a complex culture in all its variations that formed the substratum of your tale.

And yet it is this question of your knowledge of history that I shall raise in connection with your seriously and alarmingly controversial *The Satanic Verses.*

Let me say at once that I do hold you as an artist, not as a historian or a psychologist—nor, indeed, as a theologian. But, at the same time you do make use of what are facts of history and psychology, giving them your own distinct treatment.

No writer, you will agree, writes in a historical vacuum. But then, a responsible artist does not, without powerful grounds, mutilate history. Nor, unless there exists a mammoth mystification, does he disregard the sensibilities and sensitivities of his own milieu, especially when it forms both the subject matter and the bulk of his or her audience.

Strangely, what I am saying is something that I learned from none other than yourself. You might recall your telling criticism of Sir Richard Attenborough's celebrated film *Gandhi.* You enraged Sir Richard, but in the controversy I remained your passionate supporter.

You censured the film for disregarding or minimizing certain important historical facts. And you said that in a work of an artistic nature, one cannot say everything, that there has to be a choice—but that there has to be a rationale of choice. One selects not to mislead but to make the story more meaningful. Ironically, this has precisely been your lapse in the *The Satanic Verses.*

Most of your Western audience are unable to gauge the acuteness of your blow to the very core of the Indian subcontinental culture. They cannot estimate the seriousness of the injury because they do not know the history of the aggrieved.

You do know it and therefore one feels that you foresaw, at least to some extent, the consequences.

There is in your book, for example, the phantasmagoria of your own namesake Salman's corruption of the revealed word by his erroneous rendering of the words of Mahound.

Here the veil is too thin to cover the identity of Mahound: he can be understood in no other way than as a caricature of the Muslim Prophet. You do know that Islam is consistently, acutely and uniquely sensitive to its scripture. Ordinarily, Arabic is written without short vowels, but no copy of the Koran today is vowelless. Muslims insist that it should and can be read only in one way. The Muslim view is that even incorrectly reading the Koran is a cardinal sin. The Koran is neither read nor recited in translation for the very reason that translation might introduce alteration.

This matter is deadly serious and to make it a subject of insensitive fantasy is equally serious.

There is a further issue that your Western reader does not sense: that your corrupt Salman is the namesake not only of you in your book but of a historical personage who was a Persian companion of the Prophet, a companion who has been accorded a particularly elevated status by the Shiites. Given the militancy of the Shiites, when you made Salman the polluter of the revelation, you knew that you were planting your hand in the cluster of bees!

Your response to the uproar has been wavering and inconsistent, and your defense has the odor of self-righteousness. You say that people who have not read your book have no right to criticize it. But do you really think that reading the book will drastically alter their opinions?

Then you talk about freedom of expression. Free speech is a tricky issue and cannot be taken too literally. What do you think the response of black Americans would be if you were to mock the Rev. Dr. Martin Luther King Jr.? Or the reaction of the Jewish community if you were to eulogize Hitler? Or the anger of a pious Hindu if you were to present a graphic description of the slaughtering of a cow?

And to say that the Muslim world has demonstrated a total lack of dignity and tolerance is to utter a historical irrelevance. The Muslim nations have not gone through the turmoils of the Enlightenment and they have seen no scientific revolution; their sensibilities are different. Often, a peaceful demonstration is not their way and we cannot change them overnight. The best thing is to avoid hitting their most sensitive chords. And, Mr. Rushdie, you knew that.

As for your waverings, you started out by expressing regret over the fact that you did not write even a more controversial book. You accused the leaders of the angry demonstration in Islamabad of exploiting a religious slogan for secular and political ends. They may have done so, but what about the innocent and ignorant people who died in the violence? You expressed no sympathy for them.

And now you issue a three-sentence statement [see *CLC,* Vol. 55] that, at best, has the semblance of regret. Quite honestly, Mr. Rushdie, your heart does not beat in this statement, your expression is glaringly perfunctory.

I am saddened that a bounty has been placed on your head and that a great writer like you, rather than presenting himself to the public, is in hiding. You have elicited the rage of entire nations. This is a pity. But, Mr. Rushdie, you have cut them and they are bleeding. Do something quickly to heal the wound.

> *S. Nomanul Haq, "Salman Rushdie, Blame Yourself," in* The New York Times, *February 23, 1989, p. A23.*

THE NEW YORK TIMES

To the Editor:

The writings of Salman Rushdie, a Muslim-born Indian, explore the myths of nationhood against the political realities of the modern world. In his most recent work, *The Satanic Verses,* Mr. Rushdie considers the experiences of postcolonial migration by South Asians to the British Isles. Mr. Rushdie offers his view of the "phenomenon of revelation," and the inception and sustenance of Islam, a world religion with a long tradition of tolerance and learning.

The banning in India of *The Satanic Verses* last October, months after its publication, set a dangerous trend. The book was originally banned by the Finance Ministry in response to the petition of four individuals. There was no sign of agitation at the time by the Muslim community, nor was the Government responding to an overwhelming demand for banning by Muslim leaders. It was an issue of electoral politics.

The Indian Government had impending elections on its mind and by catering to "Muslim sensibilities" attempted to win the Muslim vote. The controversy over the Rushdie novel began and has grown out of deceit and opportunism, clear and simple.

Things have gone much beyond the Indian Government's actions, however. Much of the outcry against the novel's alleged blasphemy comes from those who not only haven't read the book but also insist on referring to specific sections entirely out of context. Fundamentalist Islamic operators have quite proved the author's points regarding the misappropriations of the Islamic faith in the modern world.

When we define secularism as a tolerance of all religions, this does not mean the intolerance of dissent and new ideas. The banning of books always gives them more attention: the works go underground, and their circulation is tremendously increased. Not only was the ban on *The Satanic Verses* an unwise decision but also one that now urgently challenges democratic freedoms in the East and in the West.

LISA L. BHANSALI
PRIVA JOSHI
Washington, Feb. 21, 1989

To the Editor:

It strikes me that the writers protesting the withdrawal of **The Satanic Verses** from bookstores are not addressing the real issue. No one is defending the murder-threatening tyrant of Teheran. At the heart of the matter is simply the old question of the bomb scare. At what point do you evacuate a building or cancel a plane flight after receiving that telephone call?

I think the writers believe that the danger, at least for booksellers, is minimal, and that the bookstore chains were initially chicken, and I agree. But who am I or who is Norman Mailer to make that decision for them?

Suppose a bomb went off in a bookstore and killed a dozen or so shoppers and clerks. Would anyone criticize the owner for banning the book that caused it? And what about the liability? A store is supposed to provide safe working conditions, and had there not been worldwide warning? America's most loved sport is litigation, not book reading. Have we not seen a plaintiff awarded a fortune of millions simply for being scared of contracting acquired immune deficiency syndrome and a giant oil company crippled by one capricious jury in Texas?

Let the Government offer to underwrite all damages resulting from selling **The Satanic Verses,** and the problem will walk away, if it hasn't already.

LOUIS AUCHINCLOSS
New York, Feb. 23, 1989

To the Editor:

John Cardinal O'Connor has not read, does not intend to read, but criticized Salman Rushdie's **Satanic Verses,** while he proclaimed his "sympathy for the aggrieved position the Muslim community has taken on this problem" and "deplored any and all acts of terrorism that would be engaged in" in connection with the book [*The New York Times,* February 20, 1989; see *CLC,* Vol. 55].

The undersigned writers, of widely varying Roman Catholic backgrounds, deplore the moral insensitivity to the plight of Mr. Rushdie and an ecumenical zeal that would appear to support repression. We cannot see how the Cardinal's call on Catholics to work with Muslims to achieve mutual understanding and promote peace, freedom and social justice can be implemented by a position that censors the basic freedoms to write, to publish and to read that give life and possibility to such understanding.

A spokesman for the Cardinal reports that Cardinal O'Connor said of the novel that "he trusted the judgment of Catholics as being mature and recognizing the affront it poses to believers in Islam." Mature Catholics do not believe that any dialogue with the non-Christian world can be conducted within a system that prejudges books. Mature Catholics do not believe that a death threat can be met with ambiguity.

DON DELILLO
MARY GORDON
ANDREW GREELEY, JOHN GUARE
MAUREEN HOWARD, GARRY WILLS
New York, Feb. 21, 1989

The letter was also signed by 11 other writers.

Letters to the Editor in The New York Times, *February 26, 1989, p. 22.*

HADIA DAJANI-SHAKEEL

The uproar in the Moslem world created by **The Satanic Verses** is hardly surprising. For the book has been seen—and perhaps not without justice—as an attack on the lifestyle and message of the Prophet Mohammed. It has been severely criticized as ridiculing the Prophet's wives and also Abraham, the archetype of all prophets, and its author has been declared an apostate, deserving execution.

Here in the West, people may wonder, "Why all the fuss?" The answer is that, in the past few centuries, perhaps nobody has written so bluntly, so openly, about Islam and its messenger. And so nobody is prepared to hear it. Also, a strong Islamic identity is now emerging. People in many parts of the Moslem world are identifying with Islam rather than merely with their nation and they consider this book an attack on their religion. In the Western world, many Christians accept attacks on the Bible because it has long been subject to literary criticism; there was an uproar when it was first criticized, but now that is a part of Western tradition. It is not a tradition in Islam. . . .

There is no doubt that the novel portrays the birth of Islam, often referring to names well known in Islamic history and to places connected with the emergence of the Faith. It also deals with the changes that Islam has undergone throughout the centuries—the way it has adapted itself to different cultures, such as the Indian culture that forms the background of the author, and, in modern times, to the English environment in which large numbers of Indian and Pakistani immigrants find themselves. The author's target is not Islam as such, but what he conceives to be the "fundamentalism" that has afflicted many Moslems.

While the novel refers to specific historical periods and locales, it transcends time and space and strives to pursue the long journey of man, who, having fallen from Paradise, continues to seek his roots, questioning his origin, deities and creation. Those philosophical questions are at the core of the novel. However, the author's references to pre-Islamic deities and Islamic beliefs are apt to cause misunderstanding of the novel's central themes. . . .

The notion of the immigrant is pivotal to the novel because it refers to the migration of the Prophet Mohammed—Mahound in the novel—between Mecca and Medina; to the political exile in London of an Imam, who probably symbolizes Ayatollah Ruhollah Khomeini; and to the author himself. All have one thing in common: a yearning for the land of their birth, and their youth. The immigrant and the exile eventually return to their homelands triumphantly.

Gibreel, the novel's main character, also symbolizes Ishmael, the father of the Arabs. Ishmael's place in Islamic history is connected with the Ka'ba, a house of many deities in pre-Islamic Arabia and directly related to the Satanic verses. By Moslem tradition, Mohammed in those verses at first acknowledged three female deities other than God. Their recognition was seen as a compromise with pagans, and the Prophet quickly recanted, declaring that the verses were not inspired by God but by Satan. In retelling that episode, Rushdie seems to twist history for the sake of artistic creativity. He overdramatizes that issue, which is not basic to Islam.

In addition, Moslems are bound to be offended by the use of the name Mahound—a Satanic figure in medieval times—for the Prophet Mohammed, as well as the unsavory portrayal of his wives and the power-hungry character of the exiled Imam. In all fairness, however, the author explains that Mahound is a repulsive name applied in the medieval West to the Prophet of Islam. As Rushdie says, Mahound is only "the demon tag that the farangis [Westerners] hang around his neck."

Those are some of the main reasons why Moslems have felt the book to be offensive, particularly because it was written by a lapsed Moslem. This is not to denigrate the artistic achievement of the novel. It does have literary merits. And, at times, it demonstrates a touching humanity. But that is another matter, one that has been drowned in the uproar.

Hadia Dajani-Shakeel, "A Twisted History," in Maclean's Magazine, Vol. 102, No. 9, February 27, 1989, p. 21.

BHARATI MUKHERJEE

The great writers of our time are apocalyptic farceurs, comic voices unraveling an elaborate tapestry of the sheerest horror: Grass, García Márquez, Appelfeld, Beckett. Of the recent past: Nabokov, Primo Levi, and Flannery O'Connor; on the sidelines, temporarily one trusts, Thomas Pynchon. Fantasists and blasphemers all, carrying their dispute with God to a final, collective grave. I think there is only one other English-language author who belongs in their company, and his name is Salman Rushdie.

Let us call Rushdie's three novels of the 1980s—*Midnight's Children, Shame,* and *The Satanic Verses*—a trilogy, a vast, comic, morbid masterpiece of conceptual and architectural brilliance. About what? About (in no particular hierarchy) Hindu and Islamic myth; the post-Independence political history of India, Pakistan, and Bangladesh; the tarnishing of the bright ideals of Indian independence (*Midnight's Children*) and Pakistani godliness (*Shame*); the origins of Islam, the metamorphoses of the immigrant, and the death of British decency (*The Satanic Verses*). Its time span is roughly 40 years. Its axis is London-Bombay/Karachi. Its style is a fevered fusion of appropriate and appropriated nativisms, Britishisms, puns, and coinages. Its subject is a restless movement: the *vast* movement of people, not just within the historical Raj but outward to Britain, and their subsequent transformations. Secular Bombay Muslims into impious Pakistanis. Muslims into Hindu gods. Indians into Englishmen. Men into djinns. And always, of course, the psychogenetic aftershocks of colonialism. For Rushdie, a fallen culture inhabited by ghosts and grotesques is the proper setting for postcolonial tragicomedy.

Rushdie's novels identify psychodramatic conditions previously undiagnosed: *sperectomy,* or the draining of hope, as India's founding ideals, her claim to the world's higher moral ground, are trampled in Mrs. Gandhi's "Emergency"; *shame,* in Pakistan's murderous nostalgia, the conversion of "Moghul" culture and history into a pawnshop for shabby tyrants. In *The Satanic Verses,* the condition is distortion: the shape-changing djinn-hood of immigration, the literal loss of

one's unique identity in the rush to translate oneself into a properly acceptable Englishman.

Rushdie's is the voice of postcolonial man. He remembers a nearly tribal past that he cannot return to; he mimics and masters the culture of his erstwhile colonizer. His soul is always at risk, from his past and his present, in wondrous ways that only an intricate and outrageous epic can reveal.

Taken together, Rushdie's books tell one vast story: autobiographical, mythic, political. In *Midnight's Children* the consciousness is born in 1947 in Bombay to a well-off, "relaxed Muslim" family and spends a pampered childhood exercising his extraordinary gifts (they are the special historical gifts of being born simultaneously with the country; born, that is, in a moment of idealistic frenzy, and raised in an orgy of blamelessness). The contradictions eventually claim him: a Muslim in a Hindu country; an idealist in a corrupt state. He carries his gifts and hopes reluctantly to the next-door theocracy, Pakistan, there to end up a soldier against his erstwhile country. He is witness to the breakup of Pakistan, the butcheries in Bangladesh, the venality of modern India (personified by "The Widow" as prime minister); he loses his hopes and his talents. The generation of 1947, those born with a dream of casteless secularism, those with special sensitivities to each other's individual gifts, are systematically murdered or disbanded. The setting is a richly conceived modern India, but politically the stage is the entire Third World—all those Chinas, Ghanas, Cubas, Israels, Egypts, Jamaicas, Nigerias, Indonesias where socialist ideals were meant to thrive, where brotherhood would reign, and where bloodshed, corruption, and heartbreaking poverty have created grotesque parodies of free peoples, made coolies, thugs, and criminals out of the children and grandchildren of freedom fighters.

Shame, too, is a meditation on postcolonial consciousness. Shame (and its shadow-self, shamelessness) is the primitive form of self-consciousness, the only freedom left to a people whose souls are whipped by mullahs, and whose bodies were once the property of resident viceroys, now replaced, seamlessly, by a corrupt train of native generalissimos. *Shame* tells a grotesque fairytale of palace intrigues in a "not quite" Pakistan where a "not quite" Zia eventually ousts, and hangs, a "not quite" Bhutto, leaving a "not quite" Benazir, known as "The Virgin Ironpants," to pick up the pieces. As befits a country ruled by 20 families, all intermarried, *Shame* is grand political guignol, statecraft as soap opera.

Shame's structure is quite remarkable, shaped by irony and division. An overtly autobiographical author, all but named Salman Rushdie, resident of London, infrequent visitor to his family in Pakistan, narrates, bullies, and manipulates his political *Arabian Nights* about modern "Peccavistan" from the controlling metaphorical high ground of shame. He sees evidence of this shame all around him in London, in his own family, in newspaper clippings. He reads of a Pakistani father murdering his daughter out of suspicion that she has shamed family honor, of a Pakistan girl (perhaps his own sister) molested in a London subway; she is too ashamed to tell anyone. And he sees, finally, how shame—a principle of submission—erupts into shameless violence, so-called "race riots," how satisfaction grows from the demonstration of raw, crude, self-defeating, unreasoning violence. All of those awarenesses are projected not onto London but back to a fictionalized Pakistan. Rushdie wants to understand origins, not their accidental consequences. Authorial control, ironic distance, direct passion and address coexist here in proportions rarely seen in the modern, post-Jamesian novel. You'd have to go back to the origins of the novel, or outside the Western tradition altogether, to find their equal.

Rushdie's imagination is cyclically Hindu and dualistically Muslim, with an extravagant inventiveness that seems pan-Indian. Certainly the Hindu and Islamic cosmogonies are richer, fictionally speaking, than the Jewish Genesis, and Rushdie uses them both for modern fictional purposes. According to Islam, humanity was brought into a world already seething with dangers, displacing the angels, who remain jealous, yet still subject to corruption by the subhuman, shape-changing djinns. **The Satanic Verses,** in spite of its much-reported brush with Islamic orthodoxy, is a *very* Muslim book.

The novel is a blatant fantasy, a reenactment (as I understand it) of an Islamic myth of creation, fall, and redemption. The focus this time is on London, or "Ellowen Deeowen." There is, again, a split narrative, with two central characters: Gibreel Farishta, a Bombay actor specializing in Hindu religious roles—he impersonates gods—and Saladin Chamcha, "the man of a thousand voices," a successful, transcendentally British immigrant. Both are Bombay natives.

Gibreel and Saladin meet in a cataclysm. Their Air-India jumbo jet is blown out of the skies by Canadian Sikh terrorists at 29,002 feet, the height of Everest. (Speaking as the coauthor of a book on the actual Canadian-Sikh bombing of an Air-India flight in which all 329 passengers were killed, I can't help wondering why, in Rushdie's version of the disaster, the women, children, and Sikhs are allowed to disembark before the plane takes off. In real life, they were not. Real life shouldn't be starker, more horrible, more unflinching than fiction.) Miraculously, the two men float to a snow-covered British beach, without parachutes or oxygen, there to begin altered lives. They have fallen, after the burst of light. Chamcha, during the fall, becomes a goat: hairy legs, horns, veinous balls. He gets Gibreel's famously ghastly mouth odor. Gibreel remains, outwardly, unchanged. Inwardly, he now believes his own press kit: no longer is he the low-born Bombay tiffin-carrier turned superstar. Now he is the actual Archangel Gibreel who delivered the Quran to Mohammed. His bursts of megalomania (eventually controlled with medication) inevitably result in riots and destruction.

In his new-found arrogance, Gibreel makes a fatal mistake. He denies knowing Chamcha, the goat-man, who, lacking identification or a credible story, is herded away by the British police. Thus is born the enmity, as Chamcha struggles to regain his human form and Gibreel is brought down from his unmerited godliness. Djinn and archangel, struggling to become human. (In realistic terms, of course, they had already lost their humanity in the bloated corruptions of Hindi films or in the abject conformity of immigration.) Iago and Othello, Shakespeare's Moor: one a machine of vengeance, the other a repository of suggestiveness.

The "through-line," as they say in scriptwriting, is rather clear: what it means to be a human being. How varied are the distractions from humanity, how rare and simple are its pleasures. Rushdie is a humanist in very familiar Western terms, but the story he delivers is enormously convoluted, a Persian carpet bloated with symbols and subplots, twisted and turned on its head by every manner of splitting and replication. (pp. 9-10)

Like Grass's improbable narrators—Oskar, or his later dogs

and flounders—or like the bewildered citizens of García Márquez's Macondo, like O'Connor's redneck simpletons and Beckett's tramps, Rushdie's Third Worlders are witnesses to the miraculous. The miraculous speaks through them; they are larger than life. The subplots reinforce their stature; the authorial inventions are Scheherazadean, biblical, protean, symphonic. When the clear, fairly simple, "human" story finally emerges—in **The Satanic Verses,** Saladin Chamcha regains his full humanity when he returns to Bombay to nurse his dying father—we feel we have been treated to the full vision of what humanity means. Rushdie puts us through it, squeezes his characters for all the life they're capable of giving.

There is, of course, a downside to Rushdie's narrative exuberance. His designs inevitably get messy; his plots race ahead like a span of ponies under loose control. Even the 547 pages of **The Satanic Verses** are cramped space for the history he has to tell. Subplots scurry for shelter like tropical insects. Undramatized material lies inert on the page—paid-for props that couldn't be filmed. I admire this book, but I didn't always enjoy it. That is, I respect the design without necessarily connecting with all of the contents. Reading it is like touring room after room in the Versailles Palace or the Taj Mahal: one sometimes wants to get out and just *look* at it, from a long way off. (p. 10)

Consider for a moment the unique plight of Salman Rushdie. (Yes, he's a major world author, a very rich man, and universally honored. This automatically makes his uncomfortable situation a plight.) Whatever his legal status at the moment, he is a citizen, a cultural resource and repository, of three countries: his native India (born Bombay, 1947), his family's Pakistan, and his adoptive Britain. His latest novel comes to us precanonized by a hat-trick of bannings in India, South Africa, and the Muslim world. There have even been attempts by some Muslims to flush it from the British Isles. Censorship on religious grounds is cruel to Rushdie not because it denies him an audience but because it trivializes his message. As a satirist he must be doing something right: he faces literary deportation from all three of his homelands.

"Fantasy or Blasphemy?" asked *The New York Times* last October, reporting on the Indian government's predictable but still outrageous ban on its greatest author's latest book. The easy answer is: both. Most great books, by any imaginative definition of "great," are blasphemies ("showing irreverence to anything regarded as sacred"). To change perceptions—the distinction between greatness and mere excellence—some pieties must be destroyed. But the mullahs and the mullah-minded have historically mandated the obliteration of *any* contradictory or competitive image or idea in their path. Though it's really a minor part of his book, Rushdie makes the charge of blasphemy easy to support. Where Islam holds sway, uncomplimentary mention of the Prophet is blasphemy.

Rushdie's Prophet is admittedly something of a mess. He fears, but cannot express it, that his Quran might be a hoax. The Archangel Gibreel, who delivered the words, might really have been his brother angel, Shaitan. That is, in Rushdie's dualistic universe, Gibreel might be both devil and angel. The all-too-human Mahound (whom the mullahs assume to be Rushdie's rendering of the historical Prophet) has founded a successful religion, even though it teaches some dubious truths and behaves in cruel and arbitrary ways. The religion is quite possibly a joke, but it's too late to change it. (Mahound can't believe the faithful will go along with *five* prayers a day. They insist the number can't be altered.) When he rides his camel out to Yathrib (Medina), the camel looks suspiciously like a tiger.

Rushdie's Mahound is Mohammed the same way his Peccavistan is Pakistan and Ellowen Deeowen is London. Rushdie is an allegorist: his Archangel Gibreel becomes a Bombay film actor, playing Hindu religious roles behind elephant masks and using his god-drag to please his girlfriends; Mount Cone, a sacred hill in Mecca, becomes the blond English mountain climber Alleluia Cone (née Cohen). In Rushdie's fiction, it is always 1400 A.H. (After Hegira). A 20th century sensibility with modern and medieval material. A 600-year-old man—no wonder he writes with such range.

Rushdie humanizes Mohammed—whose nondivinity is one of the pillars of the faith—but in decidedly contemporary terms. Rushdie's Mahound patronizes whores, tolerates a few Arabian tribal gods, and splits the territory with the local competition, Jews and Christians, who've been expanding their franchises on Arabian turf. It's not Mohammed who comes out badly; it's his traditional interpreters, the mullahs, those who've institutionalized Mahound's own fear of self-scrutiny into an aggressive, fortressed denial of all criticism.

Orthodox, intolerant Islam is long overdue for a kick in the pants. Ridicule works on fanatics like salt on a leech, and Rushdie is to the mullahs what Philip Roth as Tarnopol/Zuckerman only fantasizes himself being to suburban rabbis. As a great disillusioned hater, Rushdie plays in a different league from anyone in America; he's up there with Joyce and Solzhenitsyn, an educated, implacable, remorseless dissenter from deep inside the family.

Rushdie's novels are allegorical, mythical, allusive, pop, topical, and satirical, but they are also an autobiographical recording—usually highly realistic—of the postcolonial and immigrant experience. And always on tap are the vulgar energy, high parodic comedy, and many of the archetypes of the Bombay film. Rushdie's voice is that of Bombay, India's brashest city. He is still a rarity, a big-city man from the Third World, a Bombay Augie March. He is topically, even parochially, political—British, Pakistani, or Indian. (pp. 10-11)

The late Terrence Des Pres, writing on Milosz, identified a common denominator for those we might wish to term great: they bear the burden of historical consciousness without despair. And he set a collateral requirement: that they create a language equal to the pressures upon us. Complex visions, in other words, generate a density of structure and expression to carry them. *Dog Years* and *Midnight's Children* and *Autumn of the Patriarch* are like superchips, holding more information and conveying it more rapidly than standard language in conventional forms. Only by inventing a style as rich and eccentric as his plotting and characters could Rushdie express the passion of his indictments. Style announces theme: cool, temperate English is subverted by fevered, subtropical India. The result is transformation: of character, of language, of consciousness. (p. 11)

We of the Third World who grew up in the shadow of a retreating colonialism and the emerging light of independence are all, in essence, "midnight's children." We were born, like Rushdie's Saleem Sinai, with certain gifts of mimicry, talents for empathy across borders and genders. Fifteen or more years into our Indian, Caribbean, or African independence, we were still taking our Overseas Cambridge exams, still

writing odes on never-seen nightingales in passable imitation of Shelley and Keats.

Our collective experience is mirrored in the works of two magnificent writers: V. S. Naipaul and Salman Rushdie. Either—following Naipaul—we are less than fully human, pathetic trained monkeys, mimic men; or we are miraculous translations, Lamarckian mutations, single lives that have acquired new characteristics and recapitulated the entire cultural history of our genotype. Naipaul's prose is a model of poise and exclusion, as pure a literary English as can be written, its rhythms and its desiccation as insistent as T. S. Eliot's. Rushdie's is a fusion of master and slave, imported and native: jangly, harsh, punning, allusive, windy, and grandiloquent.

One of Rushdie's more appealing notions (which I hope is not an unfounded flattery) is that immigration, despite losses and confusions, its sheer absurdities, is a net *gain,* a form of levitation, as opposed to Naipaul's loss and mimicry. Of course, the gain is equivocal. Many of us, Rushdie included, traded top-dog status in the homeland for the loss-of-face meltdown of immigration. He dramatizes that pain, that confusion, with a thousand inventions and some very shrewd, dead-on observations. Rushdie's language is a mask, a way of projecting all the forms of Indian speech at once (bombastic, babu, bureaucratic, Vedantic, vehement, servile, and Sellersish, without mocking or condescending) while remaining true to the essentially damaged, ego-deficient, postcolonial psyche.

Look through Rushdie: distortion is everywhere. Saleem's great nose and his built-in radio transmitter in *Midnight's Children;* "rubescent" Sufiya Zinobia of *Shame,* who absorbs the shame of others around her; the ruttish breath and tumescent goat-body of Saladin Chamcha, inverting all the distortions and repressions he'd gone through to marry his Pamela and become a perfect Englishman. (pp. 11-12)

In the modern world of jet travel and multiple rerootings, millions of Chamchas face this problem every day. Immigrants change their clothes, their accents, their ancient ways of seeing and believing. Death and rebirth are natural. Many have multiple parents. Many pay an occult price. Many turn red with invented shame, slinking when they should have fought—or pull a knife when they should have written their member of Parliament.

Antiblasphemy laws assert that history is immutable, that a truism once learned need never be amended. *The Satanic Verses* is precisely what Rushdie says it is: a novel that faces the problem of history. Not isolated problems *in* history, and not "historical" problems. The problem is not in history; the problem *of* history is in ourselves. History remains stationary. We are changing. We will get nowhere (except on *Masterpiece Theatre*) by recreating history in our likeness, by deforming the past to compliment the present. To understand *how* much we change, how distorted *we* are against the backdrop of history requires grotesque imagery. Grass's dogs, dwarfs, and flounders are just a beginning. García Márquez's patriarch, Appelfeld's zombie-Jews of Badenheim—they all are blasphemies, they all change our perceptions.

Excellent books must be perfect; great books can stumble. *The Satanic Verses* has too many tangential subplots, too much undramatized narration, and too many pages where the major characters simply are not present ever to be confused with workshop excellence. Inevitably, the book will be characterized as bloated; I prefer to think of it as swollen with irritated life. This book completes a trilogy that must be swallowed whole, python-style, hair, horns, and hooves intact. (p. 12)

Bharati Mukherjee, "Prophet and Loss: Salman Rushdie's Migration of Souls," in VLS, No. 72, March, 1989, pp. 9-12.

HOMI BHABHA

The tragic events surrounding the publication of *The Satanic Verses* have so polarised public opinion that it seems difficult to produce a political and cultural initiative that will promote responsibility, understanding and reconciliation. But difficult or not, an intervention is urgently needed. Without one we find ourselves in the eye of the storm, at once becalmed and embattled. *We are embattled in the war between the cultural imperatives of Western liberalism, and the fundamentalist interpretations of Islam, both of which seem to claim an abstract and universal authority.* What results is an implacable antagonism that is continually rehearsed in the media, sometimes by journalistic reportage, at other times as informed opinion or intellectual debate. On the one hand there is the liberal opposition to book burning and banning based on the important belief in the freedom of expression and the right to publish and be damned—and emphatically not to be condemned to death. On the other side, there exists what has been identified as a Muslim fundamentalist position. This seems to include everything from the Ayatollah's death edict and the internal politics of Iran, to the more problematic position of British Muslims who may feel that Rushdie has violated the received wisdom of the Koran, but are resolute that this should not lead to illegal acts of incitement and violence. The blind rage through which these positions are increasingly acted out on the international stage has its own agenda, but meanwhile the lives of Rushdie and of others, in India and Pakistan, are further endangered. Some are already dead. The complex vision of *Satanic Verses* is fast losing its reality. Both literature and humanity are being reduced to empty symbols; symbols that the same time are the prisers of a Western liberal conscience and hostages to an Islamic fundamentalist orthodoxy.

For those of us, who, like Salman Rushdie himself, belong to the black communities, and have worked in various ways for the rights of migrants, refugees and ethnic groups, neither of these two perspectives is adequate. They do not represent the social and political values of the multi-racial society that we identify with, either as a political idea or as a social reality. Our experiences in the classroom, in community work and the media, have made us aware of the problems of the liberal democratic state and its sense of cultural supremacy and historical sovereignty. Having experienced forms of racial and cultural discrimination, and having engaged with its social effects, we can only deplore the anti-Muslim statements and anti-third world sentiments that have emerged in the escalation of international tension. Such political positions are profoundly at odds with Salman Rushdie's own beliefs and the causes to which he has dedicated his entire writing life. There can be no accomodation between racist, cultural stereotypes and the narrative of *Satanic Verses,* which attempts to reveal the hidden injuries of social democratic complacency, while unsettling the pieties of Eurocentrism and ethnocentrism. Equally, those of us who have experienced the authoritarian and patriarchial conditions of orthodox communities, of any colour or creed, and have witnessed their attempts to stifle dissent and discussion, can never endorse demands for censorship and unquestioned conformity. Such quiescence serves and preserves the traditional hierarchies of power and knowledge. So where do we turn, we who see the limits of liberalism and fear the absolutist demands of fundamentalism?

It is Rushdie's painful and problematic encounter with the most intractable and intimate area of his imaginative life. What the book uniquely reveals is a life lived precariously on the cultural and political margins of modern society. Where once we could believe in the comforts and continuities of Tradition, today we must face the responsibilities of cultural Translation. In the attempt to mediate between different cultures, languages and societies, there is always the threat of mis-translation, confusion and fear.

The Satanic Verses is a post-colonial work that attempts the onerous duty of unravelling this cultural translation. The book is written in a spirit of questioning, doubt, interrogation and puzzlement which articulates the dilemma of the migrant, the emigre, the minority. It is by turning back to the social and political experience of these communities—multiethnic and minority—whose historical fate requires them to construct their cultural identities from contesting traditions and imperatives, that we shall be able to reevaluate the message of *The Satanic Verses.* If there were no doubt, no confusion or conflict, would religion or literature have any place in our lives? Would *The Satanic Verses* have been written? (pp. 34-5)

Homi Bhabha, "Beyond Fundamentalism and Liberalism," in New Statesman & Society, Vol. 2, No. 39, March 3, 1989, pp. 34-5.

JIMMY CARTER

In preparation for the Middle East negotiations that led up to Camp David and the Israeli-Egyptian peace treaty, I tried to learn as much as possible about the Moslem faith.

Anwar el-Sadat, Menachem Begin and I had several talks about our common religious beliefs, and Sadat emphasized the reverence that Moslems have for Jesus and the Old Testament Prophets. Although Begin rarely commented himself, there is little doubt that these expressions of good will helped us find common ground in political matters.

Later, when American hostages were held in Iran, I learned more about the fundamentalist beliefs that separated many Iranians from most other Moslems.

Although more difficult to comprehend, their seemingly radical statements and actions are obviously sincere. The melding of fervent religious faith and patriotism during the long war with Iraq has created an environment that has contributed to the furor caused by Salman Rushdie's book, *The Satanic Verses.*

A negative response among Christians resulted from Martin Scorsese's film, *The Last Temptation of Christ.* Although most of us were willing to honor First Amendment rights and let the fantasy be shown, the sacreligious scenes were still distressing to me and many others who share my faith. There is little doubt that the movie producers and Scorsese, a professed Christian, anticipated adverse public reactions and capitalized on them.

The Satanic Verses goes much further in villifying the Prophet Mohammed and defaming the Holy Koran. The author, a well-versed analyst of Moslem beliefs, must have anticipated a horrified reaction throughout the Islamic world.

The death sentence proclaimed by Ayatollah Ruhollah Khomeini, however, was an abhorrent response; surely surprising even to Rushdie. It is our duty to condemn the threat of murder, to protect the author's life and to honor Western rights of publication and distribution.

At the same time, we should be sensitive to the concern and anger that prevails even among the more moderate Moslems.

Ayatollah Khomeini's offer of paradise to Rushdie's assassin has caused writers and public officials in Western nations to become almost exclusively preoccupied with the author's rights.

While Rushdie's First Amendment freedoms are important, we have tended to promote him and his book with little acknowledgment that it is a direct insult to those millions of Moslems whose sacred beliefs have been violated and are suffering in restrained silence the added embarrassment of the Ayatollah's irresponsibility. . . .

To sever diplomatic relations with Iran over this altercation is an overreaction that could be quite costly in future years. Tactful public statements and private discussions could still defuse this explosive situation.

We must remember that Iranian and other fundamentalists are not the only Moslems involved. Around the world there are millions of others who are waiting for a thoughtful and constructive response to their concerns.

Jimmy Carter, "Rushdie's Book Is an Insult," in The New York Times, *March 5, 1989, p. E23.*

CLYDE HABERMAN

ROME, MARCH 6—The Vatican newspaper has declared that parts of *The Satanic Verses* could be considered blasphemous, but it denounced the death threats against the book's author, Salman Rushdie.

In comments published Sunday, the newspaper, *L'Osservatore Romano,* said that millions of Muslims had been offended by the Rushdie novel.

"The very attachment to our own faith induces us to deplore that which is irreverent and blasphemous in the book's contents," it said.

But *L'Osservatore Romano* added: "It should not, however, be difficult to understand that the sacredness of the religious conscience of every individual cannot be set apart from the sacredness of the life of other men. The solidarity of those who have felt wounded in their dignity must be accompanied by a pressing vow to abandon attitudes of hate that also sound like offenses to God."

It was the first time that the Vatican had commented publicly on the Rushdie affair, and the measured tones of the article constituted a semi-official position. Pope John Paul II has said nothing on the subject.

L'Osservatore Romano did not specifically mention the death sentence imposed on Mr. Rushdie by Ayatollah Ruhollah Khomeini, the Iranian leader, but the allusions to it were unmistakable.

Criticism of the Indian-born British author was far more explicit, dominating most of the commentary. It was not clear, however, whether the editors had read the novel.

"It is certainly fair to ask what kind of art or liberty we are dealing with when, in their name, people's most profound dimension is attacked and their sensitivity as believers is offended," the newspaper said. . . .

One of the odder spinoffs of the Rushdie affair occurred in Ravenna, where a group calling itself Guardians of the Revolution threatened to blow up the tomb of Dante Alighieri unless the Mayor disavowed Dante's description of the prophet Mohammed. In the *Divine Comedy,* the poet describes Mohammed as condemned to one of the lower circles of hell, split in two, for having promoted schisms.

Mayor Mauro Dragoni said the letter might have been "a poor joke," but he ordered extra security for the tomb.

Clyde Haberman, "Vatican Newspaper Faults Rushdie Book," in The New York Times, *March 7, 1989, p. A3.*

JEREMY WALDRON

It seems a shallow understatement to say that the threat to Salman Rushdie's life is a threat to free speech. Threats to free speech are things like film censorship, the Official Secrets Act, and the withdrawal of programmes from television. The penalties we think of are fines, High Court injunctions, perhaps suspended gaol sentences. Not book burnings, the consignment of an author to hell, and the offer of eternal bliss and a million dollars to anyone who sends him there. Not rioting, with scores already dead, hostages threatened, bookstores bombed and an author in hiding under armed guard for perhaps the rest of what's left of his life.

Khomeini's murderous anathema raises issues that go deeper and wider than free speech, as it is usually understood. They go deeper because they probe beneath the ideal of toleration to ask about the conditions under which people of different religious outlooks can live together peacefully in society. The events of recent weeks remind us that that issue is not as easy as it looks. How can there be peace when people disagree about what is sacred and what is profane, and when what is known to be sacred evokes the most devout respect on the one hand and all the kaleidoscopic irony of modern literature on the other?

There are other aspects too that make it a wider matter than free speech usually is. When we talk about free speech, we are most often talking about a particular constitutional provision (for example, the American First Amendment) or a particular set of laws. But evidently *The Satanic Verses* is not an issue for just one society. Although Salman Rushdie is a British citizen, he lives (or lived until terror confined him to a guarded room) *in the world,* as so many moderns do. Born in Bombay, he makes his home in England and he travels regularly to America, Europe, India and elsewhere. He lives and works in a circle of authors, publishers, critics and commentators that effortlessly transcends national boundaries. The scope and reach of his novels are cosmopolitan. If he contributes to the market-place of ideas, it is a world market. When he offends religious sensibilities, they are those of a world religion. This is not just a British subject being set upon by Iran.

This is Salman Rushdie, citizen of the world, in confrontation with Islam.

Nor is it simply an enlightened West confronting an older, foreign pre-enlightenment tradition. Things are not so easily divided. Every society in which such an author might live is already a microcosm of the world, of East and Middle East and West: Rushdie's book was burned in Bradford and banned in Ottawa weeks before he was damned in Teheran.

Our understanding of free expression has got to be as wide and cosmopolitan as the context in which this problem has arisen. We know that Iran imprisons, tortures and kills its own dissident writers, for example. Should we condemn that, or is that the imperious imposition of our values on a culture we do not understand? A vague respect for national sovereignty and some muddled thoughts about relativism incline us to tread carefully. We know also that countries like Iran try to remain impervious to outside influences. They ban the importation of corrupt and blasphemous material. And again, part of us wants to say that that's a matter for them.

But the relativist approach is of no use in the Rushdie affair. That "their" ways are not our ways is now the problem, not a solution. The question is whether we shall have free expression *in the world* or not—whether some of the inhabitants of the world are to be threatened with death by others for what they write. No doubt, different cultures, different faiths bring their disparate perspectives to that question. But it needs one answer. Liberals cannot say open-mindedly that the killing of Rushdie by a Shi-ite Muslim would be as valid for the Muslim as literary hubris is for Rushdie. We cannot agree or afford to differ on who has the right to live. This is the place where we have to abandon our relativism and stand and fight for what matters.

That it is an issue for the world does not mean it is for the United Nations or some yet-to-be established world government. There was indeed something gratifying about the speed with which the European Community nations responded to the crisis, just as there was something shameful about the late and pusillanimous response of the American administration [see excerpts dated February 21 and February 22, 1989 in *CLC,* Vol. 55]. But respect for rights is ultimately not a matter for government, and respect for freedom in the world does not presuppose an international state. It is a matter of what the people of the world are willing to live with. When John Stuart Mill wrote *On Liberty,* he addressed it to his fellow citizens, not their government, because he was sure the threat to individuality and freedom came from society "executing its own mandates" rather than from the agency of the State. He did not argue for an enforced constitution or a Bill of Rights, but for "a strong barrier of moral conviction" to protect the freedom of thought and debate. It may be a lost cause, but we must do everything we can to make the case for freedom of expression, freedom from this sort of terror, to those with whom we share the world. Without that, legal or international protection for literary freedom is as fragile and as fearful as the police line that is guarding Salman Rushdie at this moment.

The deeper issues are posed when we remind ourselves that Islam did not invent book-burning—or author burning, for that matter. We have been this way before. Those who waded through blood to plead for toleration in the sixteenth and seventeenth centuries knew that it was religion that was special, and that there was nothing self-evident about the idea that

people of different faiths might get along. Faith treats of eternal life and eternal suffering, prospects in comparison with which earthly laws and earthly sanctions pale into insignificance. A church invests the most mundane objects and actions with immense importance, at once furnishing our culture with the richest symbolism and laying it out as the most deadly minefield of offence and misunderstanding. Religion confers a meaning on the otherwise brutish facts of life and death, mind and body, sex and family—a meaning that people long for and embrace. Yet it is those meanings that divide us; if we do not understand life and death in the same way how can we possibly agree on how to share the world?

To appeal to another for toleration is to invoke some value we both share. It is to say that something like knowledge, or freedom, or security, or even the bare possibility of a decent life for all will be imperilled unless we find a *modus vivendi.* But we cannot make that plea if we have no interests in common, or if all our interests are coloured comprehensively by our rival faiths and outlooks. If someone is convinced that life is literally not worth living, truth not worth seeking, or freedom not worth exercizing in the company of the infidel, there is simply no foothold for argument.

Even if we have that foothold of common interest, it gets us only half the way. There is no evading the fact that lives erected on this common basis may differ profoundly in faith, meaning and aspiration. Some are devout Muslims, some are Jews, some are Hindus, some are Catholics, some are Christian fundamentalists, some are fervent atheists, some are just trying to make it through their lives. What respect is due to those differences? How gingerly must we treat one another's religious sensibilities? Rushdie's critics say that he should have dealt more delicately, more seriously with the themes that he raised, or else avoided them altogether. What are we to say about that?

Toleration, mutual respect, live-and-let-live, can be conceived in different ways. On what we might call a one-dimensional account, toleration involves leaving people entirely alone with their faith and sensibilities. We are all to take care not to say anything that criticizes or cuts across the religious convictions of anyone else. (p. 248)

But faith cannot be sealed off in this way. The religions of the world make *rival* claims about the nature and being of God and the meaning of human life. It is not possible for me to avoid criticizing the tenets of your faith without stifling my own. So mutual respect cannot possibly require us to refrain from criticism, if only because criticism of other sects is implicit already in the affirmations of any creed.

A second kind of toleration concedes this, and adds a dimension of debate. Criticism and discussion between rival faiths is fine and unavoidable, but two-dimensional toleration insists that it must be serious, earnest and respectful in its character. If I disagree with you about the existence of God, I may put forward my arguments, but I must do so in a way that is circumspect and inoffensive, taking full account of the fact that your religious beliefs are not just your *views,* but convictions which go to the core or essence of your being. I must be sensitive to the role these beliefs play in your life, and not deal with them lightly, sarcastically or insultingly.

According to this model, *The Satanic Verses* went wrong, not in saying things against Islam, but in the offensive tone that it took. Rushdie spun fantasies, told ribald jokes, rehearsed heresies, used obscene language to make the points he wanted to make. He mocked the sacred, instead of asking us soberly to reconsider some doctrine.

Two-dimensional toleration would seem to combine the values of truth-seeking—which John Stuart Mill made so much of in his essay *On Liberty*—with a principle of respect. It leaves room for debate, but it eschews mockery, offence, and insult. Above all it enables us to understand notions like sacrilege and blasphemy not as ideals internal to any religion, but as principles embodying what we owe to one another as humans, in respect for deeply held convictions.

But as soon as we say that, we begin to see the fallacy of two-dimensional toleration. What is serious and what is offensive, what is sober and what is mockery—these are not neutral ideas. They come as part of the package, and different religions define them in different ways. In some rabbinical traditions, theological debate cannot proceed *except* through the telling of jokes. Some Muslim sects regard it as an unspeakable affront if a woman participates in religious discussion, no matter how sober her tone. And for a long time in the Christian west, it was regarded as a capital mockery of the Almighty if one not in holy orders dared to debate the ways of God with man. This is exactly what we should expect; the demeanour with which religious disputation is to be conducted is itself an issue on which religious views are taken. It is bound up with the fact that faith addresses the deepest issues of truth, value and knowledge. There is nothing necessarily privileged about the norms of civility that we call moral seriousness, and indeed requiring religious controversy to observe the ponderous debating rules of a Midwestern Rotary Club may be the worst, not the best, of both worlds.

By the same token, it is fatuous to think that there is a way of running a multi-cultural society without disturbance or offence. (pp. 248, 260)

We are pushed, then, towards three-dimensional toleration. Persons and peoples must leave one another free to address the deep questions of religion and philosophy the best way they can, with all the resources they have at their disposal. In the modern world, that may mean that the whole kaleidoscope of literary technique—fantasy, irony, poetry, wordplay, and the speculative juggling of ideas—is unleashed on what many regard as the holy, the good, the immaculate and the indubitable.

How could it be otherwise? Either the issues are important or they are not. If they are, we know that they strain our resources of psyche and intellect. They drive us to the limits of linear disputation and beyond, for they address the edgy, the shy, the disturbing, the frightening, the knowable and the unthinkable. The religions of the world make their claims, tell their stories, and consecrate their symbols, and all that goes out into the world too, as public property, as part of the cultural and psychological furniture which we cannot respectfully tiptoe around in our endeavour to make sense of our existence. We have to do what we can with the questions, and make what we can of the answers that have been drummed into us. . . .

[We] all cast about for an understanding of evil in the world. There is disease, there are great crimes, children are killed in their millions, the heavens are silent and there seems no sense in it. We know the great religions address the issue shyly and indirectly, with a cornucopia of images and stories. Satan lays a wager with God that Job, a good and holy man, can be brought by misfortune to curse Him to His face—a story

which, if it were not already in the Bible, might have earned its publisher a firebomb or two. The point is not a cute *tu quoque:* it is that no one even within the religious traditions thinks this can be addressed without the full range of fantastic and poetical technique. Once again, respect for the sensitivities of some cannot in conscience be used to limit the means available to others to come to terms with the problem of evil. It is already too important for that.

Three-dimensional toleration is not an easy ideal to live with. Things that seem sacred to some will in the hands of others be played with, joked about, taken seriously, taken lightly, sworn at, fantasized upon, juggled, dreamed about backwards, sung about, and mixed up with all sorts of stuff. That is what happens in **The Satanic Verses.** It is not a solemn theological disquisition, and it is not to be defended as such. Nor is it to be defended as a work of art that just happens to include some regrettable passages. Like all modern literature, it is a way of trying to make sense of human experience. It touches on some problems that Islam addresses, and it invokes images and narratives with which Islam has coloured Rushdie's world. It does so playfully and kaleidoscopically, but that doesn't mean that the themes matter less to the author than they do to the millions of the faithful.

It may be too late to make a case for Salman Rushdie's freedom from terror and the threat of assassination. But if we make a plea for others like him in the world, it must be on this high ground—that the great themes of religion matter too much to be closeted by the sensitivity of those who are counted as the pious. There is no other way we can live together and respect each other's grappling with life. (p. 260)

Jeremy Waldron, "Too Important for Tact," in The Times Literary Supplement, *No. 4484, March 10-16, 1989, pp. 248, 260.*

JOHN GARVEY

It can be said that the Ayatollah Khomeini lacks the light touch. Salman Rushdie's novel, **The Satanic Verses,** first provoked outrage throughout the Muslim world, as well as a continuing series of riots in which many have been killed; then the ayatollah proclaimed it an Islamic duty to murder Mr. Rushdie, a duty sweetened by offers of a place in paradise if the assassin were to die in the attempt, or a reward of millions in this world if martyrdom should be denied. Mr. Rushdie's response was somewhat inconsistent. While people were dying in the riots he attacked Islamic censors, but showed relatively little compassion for the dead and their families, or understanding for the inflamed sensibilities of devout Muslims. After the ayatollah's death threat he had an understandable attack of sympathy for the dead and for pious Muslims, and made an apology of sorts, but that wasn't good enough for the ayatollah. Even if Rushdie should become the most pious man in the world, he said, he still deserves death for his blasphemy. . . . (p. 166)

The response of the Western world has been interesting. Mrs. Thatcher's Britain, where Rushdie makes his home, was very careful at first to say as little as possible. . . . George Bush said nothing at all for as long as he possibly could. The French made the first somewhat bold move, and brought the Common Market nations into common accord against the Iranian death threats.

Many of Rushdie's fellow writers were quicker to act. They

organized demonstrations in his support, and some writers agreed to withhold their books from distribution in the large bookstore chains who had dropped Rushdie's book out of fear for the lives of their employees. The chains, perhaps as a consequence of this, are carrying the book again.

Most readers are probably tired of the controversy by now— **The Satanic Verses** has been mentioned prominently on almost every newscast since the controversy started, something a book's author would ordinarily welcome, though I am sure the beleaguered Mr. Rushdie does not. I hope the day comes soon when he can walk the streets without fear, but I doubt it. I think this controversy is an even more significant event than its current prominence suggests, and it has revealed a number of interesting things which are not yet receiving the attention they deserve. Let me list three of them.

[1] *The West has almost no appreciation of Islam.* This unsettling demonstration of Islamic fervor is hardly likely to change the situation; death threats in the name of Allah will not make people want to understand Islam, but will further a distance in understanding which is already too great. Nevertheless, there are reasons for worry about this lack of understanding, quite beyond the obvious good of understanding the teachings of the world's great religions for their own sake or for comparative reasons. They include the fact that Islam is a rapidly growing religion—not only in Africa, but in America (where many black Americans continue to join, not the eccentric version propagated by Elijah Muhammed and continued by Louis Farrakhan, but orthodox Sunni Islam), and in the Soviet Union. Muslim leaders have not spoken with a common voice about the death threat against Rushdie, which many have rejected; they do speak with a common sense of grievance when they say that the West has consistently refused to try to understand Islam. Its contribution is too important, even in our own history, to ignore. Western science, theology, and philosophy owe a great debt to Islam. It was not native Western genius, as we now know, but what the Christian world brought back from the Crusades that gave the late medieval West its knowledge of everything from Aristotle to algebra and the teaching of the great Greek philosophers.

[2] *The response to Islamic anger has been almost entirely secular.* And why not? It is such an attack on what we regard as important in secular terms—freedom of speech, the liberty of an author to use his imagination in the exploration of anything which seems a worthy area of exploration, the right to pursue that exploration wherever it leads. I believe that all of these are important, and believe that the crisis in the West which began with the Enlightenment was an essential thing: religion had grown used to an intertwined relationship with power. Secularism forced us (by us I mean people with a religious rather than secular approach to the world, and I think there is and should be such a separation) to know that religion should move by honest persuasion, not by force or even subtle social or family pressure. We are most in the image of God when we are free.

At the same time, believers have allowed religion to be marginalized. (pp. 167-68)

So far we must agree with those who would insist on Rushdie's right even to blaspheme, if the alternative is to give religion a coercive power it does better without. But many of the writers who came to Rushdie's defense argue that this is a clear case of religious benightedness versus enlightened free-

thinking. At the public reading of his work some of the passages most offensive to Muslims were chosen. It is one thing to defend Rushdie's rights and to repudiate the ayatollah's murder threat; it is another to choose to make a public proclamation of passages which Muslims find offensive. This goes beyond a defense of free speech. . . .

[3] *We must question what the death of blasphemy means.* We have lost something when we do not take the death of Christ and the importance of his teaching to the centers of our being, in the same profoundly heartfelt way we react to the death of Dr. King, or to the murder of millions. It is not a strength of ours that we do not understand why others feel such reverence, for the Koran and for the prophet Mohammed, that they are willing to be outraged at what appears to be a mockery. If for us the most important function of a book is to amuse or provoke, and for them the presence of at least one book is a divine mercy, this is not necessarily to our credit.

The controversy is not just one more news story. It is, I am afraid, the beginning of something significant—a deepening alienation between the secular West, which itself has a growing Muslim population, and the Islamic world. The alienation was there in a less coherent way before. Now the symbol of blasphemy has given it a coherence and a symbolic form it did not previously have. Even before Rushdie, it was interesting that the two groups it was possible to make fun of—say, on TV commercials or in cartoons—without dire consequences were Asians (who are beating us economically) and Arabs. Now secular intellectuals can join in what was, before, low-brow fun, and do it just as ignorantly, with the sanction of the defense of liberty. Of course it is an evil thing for the ayatollah to call for someone's death, and of course the censorship even of bad ideas is dangerous to any decent society. But there is more to the controversy over **The Satanic Verses** than those two issues, and it is extremely important for us to be clear about what lies beneath the obvious and most easily answered questions. (p. 168)

John Garvey, "Offensive Defenders: Rushdie's Rights & Wrongs," in Commonweal, *Vol. CXVI, No. 6, March 24, 1989, pp. 166-68.*

AHMAD ASHRAF

Why did the Ayatollah Ruhollah Khomeini issue a death sentence against Salman Rushdie, author of **The Satanic Verses?** Perhaps a better question is, "What took him so long?"

For the Ayatollah, the book was a miracle—a divine vehicle for buttressing Islamic community solidarity against a hostile world.

His edict is best understood in the light of grave internal difficulties and rising factional infighting: the decline in the power of his young militantly radical supporters as a result of Iran's defeat in the war with Iraq and mounting economic problems, the rise in popularity of moderate pragmatic forces and increasing pressures from traditionalist conservative forces of the bazaar-mosque alliance.

The radicals support the impoverished and advocate innovative jurisprudence. They champion statism, support nationalization of foreign trade, redistribution of agricultural land and a progressive labor law. They are permissive on cultural issues—women's participation in social and political activities, for example—while advocating the export of the revolution.

The bazaar-mosque alliance advocates the sanctity of private ownership and economic liberalism, which Islamic jurisprudence emphasizes, takes a reactionary line on cultural issues and urges a low profile in foreign relations.

The pragmatic moderates represent the new middle classes, whose goals are to reconstruct Iran on the basis of a mixed economy and international cooperation. They are permissive on cultural matters and favor normalization of relations with the outside world.

Ayatollah Khomeini loves the militant radicals and has persistently supported their cause in economic, political and cultural policy. He hates traditionalist conservatives and feels ambivalent toward the emerging camp of pragmatic moderates.

He has issued a number of radical edicts against the private sector and in favor of cultural permissiveness, and has adopted the principle of "masleha"—"the best interest of the community"—in supporting ratification of progressive bills that might deviate from Islamic law.

The retreat of Iranian forces from Iraqi territory was a blow to Ayatollah Khomeini and his radicals. Afterward, a new centrist and pragmatist camp emerged with an agenda of peace, normalization of international relations, a mixed economy and reconstruction of the country.

This camp enjoys the leadership of the speaker of the Parliament, Hojatolislam Hashemi Rafsanjani, and Ayatollah Hussein Ali Montazeri, Ayatollah Khomeini's chosen successor. It also enjoys the tactical support of the bazaar-mosque alliance.

The radical camp has been under mounting pressures from all sides. The 10th anniversary of the revolution, on Feb. 11, gave the rising pragmatist camp a chance to launch a propaganda campaign against the radicals. Ayatollah Montazeri urged the authorities to "make up the past mistakes" and to create an "open society." He called for freedom of foreign trade and regretted that "the people of the world thought our only task here in Iran was to kill."

On Feb. 14, two days after Pakistanis protested against *The Satanic Verses,* Ayatollah Khomeini, apparently acting out of mixed motives, issued his edict for the execution of Mr. Rushdie.

The Ayatollah, who has always believed in a messianic mission to launch a holy war against the Christian West, responded to the expectations of many Moslems worldwide that he take serious steps against the "satanic conspiracies" of the West.

While it was essential that the death sentence be condemned, the Western support for *The Satanic Verses* was interpreted in Iran and by Moslems elsewhere as a vindication of the claims made by Ayatollah Khomeini, backed by the radicals, that the book is a plot designed by Western imperialism to launch a new crusade against Islam.

His anti-Rushdie edict was well received by Moslems everywhere, and he emerged as the leader of the world's Islamic community. Heartened by this support, he mobilized the radicals, attacked his domestic foes, and, as a result, today the radicals' fortunes are again flourishing.

Ahmad Ashraf, "Religion? No. Politics," in The New York Times, *March 25, 1989, p. 27.*

SHAHROUGH AKHAVI

Some observers argue that Ayatollah Ruhollah Khomeini's anathematizing of Salman Rushdie was a deliberate and calculated attempt to clip the wings of the "liberal" speaker of the Parliament, Hojatolislam Hashemi Rafsanjani. They also argue that Ayatollah Khomeini used the Rushdie affair to prevent closer relations with the West and restore fading revolutionary zeal in Iran. To the contrary, his motivation was apparently religious.

I believe Ayatollah Khomeini was surprised when told by his son, Ahmed, that an Indian Muslim had written a book considered by some to blaspheme the Prophet and Muslims in Pakistan had stormed the American cultural center in Islamabad. There is no reason to doubt the sincerity of his wrath by imputing purely political motives to his denunciations against Mr. Rushdie.

As for the arguments that imply political motives, first, Mr. Rafsanjani has never been known as a liberal in Iranian politics. The Ayatollah did warn the liberals against thinking they could ascend to power at about the same time he issued his death threat against Mr. Rushdie. But it appears that his target was not Mr. Rafsanjani, but Mehdi Bazargan, the first prime minister of the revolutionary regime.

Mr. Bazargan, who resigned at the onset of the hostage taking of American diplomats in Teheran in November 1979, has been repeatedly berated as a "liberal." Since last fall some discussion has taken place about legalizing political parties. Mr. Bazargan's Freedom Movement has applied for that status—presumably as a preliminary to Mr. Bazargan's candidacy for the presidency this summer.

Ayatollah Khomeini also warned "certain clerics in Qom," the center of Iran's religious establishment, against making "liberal" sounding counter-revolutionary statements. Intriguingly, his target here seems to be Ayatollah Hussein Ali Montazeri, Ayatollah Khomeini's own designated successor.

Westerners know Ayatollah Montazeri as the sponsor of radical Hezbollah activities in Lebanon, yet he for many years has sounded the theme of toleration, legality and understanding in internal politics. And he recently has made some remarkable statements about the need of the regime to account for what he has called its political and economic failures.

Mr. Bazargan has repeatedly appealed to Ayatollah Montazeri to stand up for legality. The prospect of a Montazeri-Bazargan coalition, no matter how fanciful it may seem, has alarmed Ayatollah Khomeini.

That he has moved to nip it in the bud at approximately the same time that he has acted against Mr. Rushdie should not cause us to confuse cause and effect. That is, the cause of Ayatollah Khomeini's action against Mr. Rushdie was not his desire to send a message to the liberals.

Second, to argue, as some have, that Ayatollah Khomeini is opposed to links with the West is wrong. Ayatollah Khomeini does not oppose ties with Western countries (except the United States). He has argued that Iran needs to have relations with the outside world. It is true, of course, that the consequences of his actions in the Rushdie affair initially brought about Iran's isolation from the Western European states. But this is different from arguing that the cause of his action was the desire for isolation.

Finally, it is maintained that Ayatollah Khomeini only acted when he did against Mr. Rushdie because he discovered other Muslims were taking the initiative, and this was his way of reclaiming ideological leadership of the Islamic world.

Yet, if Ayatollah Khomeini needed to make a calculated move of this sort, why did he wait so long to jump into the fray? Should he not have immediately joined the issue last fall, when Mr. Rushdie's book was first published and Muslim agitation against it broke out in India and Southern Africa?

The Rushdie affair has incidentally provided Ayatollah Khomeini with a forum to recrystallize revolutionary militance and admonish those deemed insufficiently revolutionary. But, given his concerns about the liberals and Ayatollah Montazeri's apparently wayward statements, he surely would have criticized them had Salman Rushdie never published *The Satanic Verses.*

> Shahrough Akhavi, "Politics? No. Religion," in The New York Times, *March 25, 1989, p. 27.*

NEW STATESMAN & SOCIETY

In the beginning were the words of **The Satanic Verses.** *Actions in Bradford and elsewhere, Khomeini's words in Tehran, deaths in India and Pakistan, acts of solidarity with Rushdie, all followed. Then, in Britain, came lies and insinuations about the author and his book. The words which follow are no substitute for Salman Rushdie's freedom and safety. Words have never been able to protect people. Rather they enable us to argue over and give shape to the extraordinary variety of our experience. This is simply and memorably what* **The Satanic Verses** *has done.*

MELVYN BRAGG
British novelist and broadcaster

Rushdie has created a global community of authors. It is difficult to think of any writer who has provoked such a closing of ranks. His isolation has triggered our sense of common purpose.

In Britain particularly, it has encouraged and enabled writers at last to break through that barrier which forbade them to be serious in public on public matters.

KATHY ACKER
US novelist, lives in Britain

Of the many issues surrounding *The Satanic Verses* and many Muslims', especially the Ayatollah Khomeini's, reaction to this book, I personally separate out two: the public and the private.

Privately: Salman Rushdie is both a dear friend and one of the finest writers currently living in England. This is also true of his wife, Marianne Wiggins. The fact that two friends and writers whose works I respect are forced to have their privacies interrupted violently, radically, perhaps even irredeemably, makes me both angry and frustrated.

This private issue is not and cannot be the same as the public or the public ones. Many people, many intellectuals have been commenting on the public issues and I am not sure that I am equipped to do so. Not being Muslim, I cannot and will probably never understand if *The Satanic Verses* is blasphemous to all Muslims or only to Muslims who are fundamentalists. And I cannot deeply comprehend how it is blasphemous (if it is), for I am Jewish and the tradition of the Talmud is profoundly one of arriving at knowledge through argument, discussion, controversy, rather than that of acquiring knowledge through decree.

It's interesting, even ironic, that the Jews and Muslims are racially related and that *The Koran* was influenced (I believe I am understanding this case) by the *Old Testament.*

Most of the white western writers who have discussed the issues around *The Satanic Verses* have proclaimed, as writers and artists, their right to "freedom of speech". (A freedom not publicly applauded when the matter in hand isn't anti-Muslim, if that's what *The Satanic Verses* is, but is rather anti-Zionist, and, as in the case of Jean Genet's final book, pornographic, etc.) I and most white western writers live in a society in which most public and private affairs are conducted via discussion, questioning, gathering of all kinds of information, even controversy. If affairs are not conducted as such, as in the case of the recent decisions about the privatisation of water, I feel I have the right to protest. And I want to live in this kind of society; I do not want to live in a world run by decree, by fundamentalism, Christian, Muslim, or Zionist.

Other people in other societies have made other decisions, to be fundamentalist. "Freedom of speech" is not a human right; it is a political, moral, even religious decision. Part of the fight that is now going on over *The Satanic Verses* is a version of one of the major struggles that is defining the history of the 20th century: the struggle between fundamentalists and non-fundamentalists.

In the case of *The Satanic Verses,* the fundamentalists are Muslim and this fact has led to another problem, one of racism. The continuing racism in England against Muslims and the general dislike of Arabs in the white western world has been exacerbated by the inability of many white intellectuals to recognise the positions of the fundamentalists.

I repeat that I want and would fight for a society based on multiplicity, multiple voices, multiple choices, but I will not fight for a society based on racism.

For me, the main issue is the private one. I miss my friends deeply and am angry at those who have hurt them.

HAROLD PINTER
British playwright

The Satanic Verses is a marvellous bloody book; a work that doesn't sit at home keeping out of trouble but rampages over the landscape turning things upside down; fearless, fiercely inquisitive, joyful. I salute the book and the man.

Where we waver in our resolve to defend the crucial freedoms involved in this matter we are ourselves joining the mob.

If we allow the Rushdie boat to go down we should bear in mind that we will go down with it.

COLIN McCABE
British writer

Salman Rushdie has written an amazingly courageous book about migration, translation and metamorphosis. It is both unbelievable and unsurprising that those who wish to ignore these cultural realities have reacted with threats of murder and violence.

TREVOR GRIFFITHS
British playwright

The only question left in the Rushdie affair is how soon, and in what way, Salman will be returned to the fray. Where I live, the football terrace fascists are using his book and name as sticks to beat the Asians with, and demonstrations against the book's publication are being made the ground for a further escalation of racist violence against Asians and their property. Rushdie's important voice, raised for a decade or more now against the deep racism of this society, is sorely missed. Until the British government can once again guarantee not just the safety but the liberties of its subjects, I suppose he must stay in hiding; but on whose advice does he remain so resolutely silent, a virtual non-person in his own country? And why can his life and liberties not be safeguarded without this total (and damaging) isolation? After all, there has been at least one contract out on Thatcher for several years, but the state has made damn sure her liberties haven't been unduly curtailed. Let's hear it, Salman.

RANA KABBANI
Writer, born in Damascus

We in the Muslim east are your closest neighbours, coming from a world just beyond Europe's borders on that same Mediterranean with which you are so culturally familiar. Yet almost nothing is known about us, as though we hailed from a different planet altogether. If it was merely ignorance that separated us then that would be a bridgeable gap, but prejudice, preconception and even hostility have created a huge gulf between us.

Ever since the Crusades, when Europeans left these shores to convert or destroy us, western writers have indulged in an endless rhetoric of abuse which reduced us to caricatures, which falsified our beliefs and denied us our very humanity. In medieval polemic we were portrayed as a monstrous race, as cannibals with dogs' heads. For a thousand years Muhammad was described by a long line of Christian detractors as a lustful and profligate false prophet, an anti-Christ, an idolator, a "Mahound". Thus the description of him in **The Satanic Verses** cannot but perpetuate this unpleasant polemic, all the more surprising for its author's Muslim origins.

When in Ravenna Muslims recently threatened to blow up Dante's tomb and demanded the banning of *The Divine Comedy,* they were protesting at the way this secular literary text relays the slanders against Muhammad of the medieval church. Their actions can be seen as Islamic self-assertion against misrepresentation by the west.

An extremist political Islam has taken root all over the world, fuelled by historical grievance, by poverty, by an overriding sense of powerlessness. The west bears a measure of responsibility in this phenomenon. For by interfering so forcefully in our lives and in our internal affairs, by overthrowing nationalist rulers and setting up puppet monarchs in their place, by milking our resources and fuelling our wars with the sale of endless armaments, by conspiring to keep us economically and culturally and politically enthralled, you have made us what we are: enraged and unforgiving.

Is your conscience not selective? The west feels sympathy for the Afghan Mujahedin, propped up by American intelligence just as the Nicaraguan contras are, but feels no sympathy for militant Muslims who are not fighting its cold war battles. We have heard a great chorus of outrage at Khomeini's death sentence, but writers are killed in Iraq, children are tortured in front of their parents to extract confessions, some 5,000 Kurds were gassed, yet the west saw fit to side with Iraq to defeat Iran in a war it had not initiated.

Palestinians are dying every day in the occupied territories, 10,000 youths are held in detention camps under the most brutal conditions, 20,000 have been wounded, homes are blown up as a routine collective punishment, pregnant women beaten so that they miscarry, and unarmed boys kicked to death by regular soldiers, yet Israel remains a democracy in your eyes, an outpost of western civilisation.

What are we to think of these double standards? Of these different responses to similar issues? We can only hope that in the Rushdie case, it was a principle that was being defended, not just a British passport.

PETER PRESTON
Editor of the Guardian

The Satanic Verses has been on sale for months, was indeed just falling out of the best-seller charts, when Bradford went wild. Rushdie couldn't have calculated the effect of what he wrote, because the effect came almost as an afterthought. To pretend that he is somehow to blame for the telex that set the Ayatollah rolling is potty.

There are, indeed, things that must give him pause in his isolation. We know he regrets the offence he has given, because he said so. We can guess that the stories of deaths in subcontinental riots, lives lost over words written, must be a churning responsibility to bear. The potential fate of men in Iranian jails or in Beirut attics is an imponderable burden. But none of it is Rushdie's fault, and it is absurd to pass the parcel of guilt back to his door.

Rushdie is a brilliant writer. For all the mesh of protest from writers around the world, he is, like all brilliant writers, essentially alone. His novels aren't tracts for some wider movement. They are his observation, his comment, his world. He isn't at the heart of this macabre affair, and has not been since the Ayatollah spoke. He is merely now a symbol of what has to be defended and protected, without question or qualification, by any individual, any community and any country which purports to put freedom of speech on its list of essential human freedoms. That was where the debate began: it would have been better if it had stopped there.

ANTONIA FRASER
Writer, President of English P.E.N.

Contemplating the fate of *The Satanic Verses* in Britain, I find my thoughts going constantly to the fate of Vaclav Havel in Czechoslovakia (and I remember that the Charter 77 signatories, with their usual forthright courage, were among the first to send a message of support to Salman Rushdie). Then there is the distinguished poet Jack Mpanje in Malawi. The nature of their respective "prisons" (Rushdie's and Mpanje's) is obviously totally different; as a British citizen, Rushdie is rightly being protected by his country's police which has not been the experience of Mpanje, held without trial in prison in Malawi, to put it mildly. On the other hand both writers are being condemned for exactly the same offence: giving free vent to their own creative inspiration. This is absolutely not the same as preaching a political (or religious) message, and it appalls me to find *The Satanic Verses,* that brilliant discursive exploratory work of fiction, widely discussed in terms of political tract as though that was the intention of the author. I hope we can maintain in public not only the right of the creative artist, as with all citizens of this country, to freedom of speech within the law, but also the difference between fiction and non-fiction.

MARTIN AMIS
British novelist

Soon after the publication of *The Satanic Verses,* when the author's life still seemed safe enough, when this book was merely being banned and burned, Salman Rushdie joked that worse things can happen to a writer: he can "be reviewed by Hermione Lee". Hermione Lee had written a dissenting notice; and we can all live with dissent. But what happens when you are reviewed by Khomeini Lee—by the *Ayatollah* Hermione?

Various quislings and pharisees have suggested that there is a kind of justice in the Rushdie affair: that Rushdie knew, or

should have known, "what he was doing". He *did* know what he was doing. In the course of his imaginative engagement with Islam, Rushdie's artistic decisions have a balance and clarity quite beyond the understanding of the career clerics and self-ghettoising community leaders who now bay for his blood. Novels do not change the world, except by accident; equally, novelists are not responsible for the runaway phantasmagoria known as current affairs. The life of Salman Rushdie has been pulled out of shape by a convulsion in Islamic fundamentalism, by Iranian palace politics, by the outcome of the Gulf War, by the trigger finger of the Captain of the *Vincennes* . . .

Fact is stranger than fiction—also stupider, also nastier. Contemplate this sample of magical realism: the most talented novelist of his generation, with a face lift, living between Boormann and Mangele in a dismal suburb of Asuncion. So one awaits the August elections in Iran, the eclipse of Khomeini, some distracting redistribution of temperatures in the moronic inferno. Meanwhile I despairingly say to Salman Rushdie that I pity his situation, that I miss his presence and that I admire his work.

FAY WELDON
British novelist

Before we jeer at the Muslims who want Rushdie dead on hearsay *without even having read the book!* we should perhaps bother to read the Koran; "these revelations, supernaturally received in circumstances of a trance-like nature" explain so much. This wildly prophetic, wonderful poem is also a set of rigid rules for living, perceiving and thinking, and the penalties for doubt and disobedience are extreme: that is to say, the fires of Gehenna wait, and burn fiercely and painfully. Chastisement for error is plentiful and extreme. There is a constant nervous refrain, "Allah is all-forgiving, all-compassionate", but what, I ask myself, does he have to *forgive?* What has this dreadful Lord of Vengeance got to be compassionate *about?* He invents the sin if only occasionally to excuse it. It is a circular argument, odd to western ears, giving rise to our bewildered, "oh, they just don't think like us,"—which along with that other weasel phrase, "the deep hurt and anger" felt by a Muslim community confronted by *The Satanic Verses,* so quickly learned to trip from the host community tongue.

But of course we all think alike, feel alike, reason alike, hope alike. The blank and puzzled look on the face of the devout Muslim when you tried to reason with him about the novel, or indeed about anything to do with Islam, comes, if you ask me, from another source. The distress is real enough: but has little to do with *The Satanic Verses.* The Koran, that terrifying book, is beaten (often literally) into the small male child at the mosque, every day after school, and if you ask me it's terror, not unreason, which looks out of even the most sophisticated Muslim eyes when you try and suggest that you can't kill an idea by killing the person who gives voice to it. He is not allowed to listen. We are the unbelievers, and the unbelievers cry lies, and we are as scum, and if he does listen he will be herded along with others with iron hooks and thrust into the fire. The frightened child looks out of adult eyes. Down come the shutters. Slam! If a chink of light is allowed in, a whole belief structure crumbles.

"Deep hurt and anger." Kill, kill, kill! A kamikaze attack! A suicide attempt! Look, the immigrant Muslim population over here has, for the most part, a rotten time. Who wouldn't want to kill, kill, kill? (Rushdie writes about it in *The Satanic Verses:* it is ironic that this novel, which is so indignantly protective of the immigrant, and does so much to explain the Muslim to the unbeliever, the unbeliever to the Muslim, should have been thus received, but there you are. Gratitude was ever in short supply.) Mr Essawi and his friends, good men and true believers from the Islamic Society for the Promotion of Religious Tolerance, see the younger generation of Muslims, those born and reared here, drifting off into the western world, lured by the unbeliever, tempted by its shoddy values, and want to do something about it. I am not surprised.

The coarseness, violence, depression and profanity of the world in which our urban young live is appalling. I do not blame the fundamentalists for making what capital they could when Rushdie's book came along, using it to rally the troops, fortify belief—look, see, we're under attack! . . . Quick, quick, back into the fold of true belief! (The title, of course, played right into their hands. Fortuitous—if anything in a religious framework can be so described—that its title was *The Satanic Verses* which in translation can only seem to be the Devil's version of the Koran, thus suddenly appearing on earth—forget the detail of page this or that within, the title is enough—who needs to, who dares to, *read on.*)

But then it all got out of hand: some rash person passed the matter on to the Ayatollah, the political and the religious fused, and the west sprang to the defence of its own: our own government, unexpectedly, gratifyingly, included (not nice to be spoken of as Mrs Torture, Mrs Murder—to have to grit the teeth and endure it). In all this Rushdie, who can stand on his head and out-write the rest of us, encompassing and controlling with such enormous vigour ideas we can only tremulously grasp for, is obliged to pay in person the consequence of both the corrupt barbarity of the capitalist west, and the anger and terror of the Muslim east, at the moment of change, as the miserable rigour of the old ways begin to crumble and break. Not so much a sacrificial victim, perhaps, as the outcrop (if you like to see it like that) forced up by subterranean forces, round which the sacrificial dance is played. It must be terrifying to be so selected.

Odd that one translator of the holy book, in the midst of his enthusiasm for the Koran, complains of the repetitiveness and apparently random nature of many of its sections: the same criticism is levelled at *The Satanic Verses.* Perhaps it has something to do with the nature of revelation: of the Word Received.

"Words for Salman Rushdie," in New Statesman & Society, *Vol. 2, No. 43, March 31, 1989, pp. 24-30.*

THE NEW YORK TIMES

Nobody can yet say who murdered a Muslim spiritual leader and his aide in Brussels on Wednesday [March 29, 1989], but the chronology is deeply disquieting. The killing of Abdullah al Ahdal took place nearly six weeks after he said on Belgian television that he did not favor murdering Salman Rushdie as punishment for writing *The Satanic Verses.*

Mr. Ahdal suggested that the British author be allowed to appear before an Islamic tribunal. He said further that in democratic societies, "everyone has the right to express his own thoughts."

Mr. Ahdal made his comments on Feb. 20, the day that 12 European Community countries recalled their envoys from Iran to protest Ayatollah Khomeini's decision to put a price on Mr. Rushdie's life. The Ayatollah, obsessed with efforts to strengthen his control inside Iran, contemptuously brushed the protest aside.

Last week, 11 of the 12 European countries approved the return of their ambassadors to Teheran. Only Britain dissented from what appeared a surrender to the unrepentant Ayatollah. Almost immediately, Ayatollah Khomeini began to purge his Government of anyone who could vaguely be called a critic. The most notable victim was Ayatollah Hossein Ali Montazeri, Ayatollah Khomeini's designated heir and, comparatively speaking, a pragmatist in Iranian politics.

In the wake of the purge, gunmen entered a Brussels mosque and murdered Mr. Ahdal, a Saudi Arabian who is the Muslim spiritual leader in the Benelux countries, and an aide. No message claiming responsibility has yet surfaced, but the deed itself sends a grim message to Muslims in Europe.

It also sends a message to European governments. Mr. Ahdal was murdered in the very headquarters of the European Community. And unless its members respond vigorously, they risk further contempt from Teheran—and, more ominously, further killings.

"Satanic Work in Brussels," in The New York Times, *March 31, 1989, p. 34A.*

NEW PERSPECTIVES

Our interview with the author of **The Satanic Verses** *was set for 3 PM on Sunday afternoon at the Westbury Hotel in New York. The code name used to protect the registered guest from angered Muslims was Ved Saghdev. Then, three days before our scheduled meeting the stakes rose dramatically: Iran's Ayatollah Khomeini issued an assassination order against Salman Rushdie for blaspheming the Prophet Mohammed. Rushdie disappeared and went into hiding.*

What follows instead of a talk with Rushdie are comments from around the world, ranging from the former Iranian president to an Islamic jurist, about the Rushdie-Khomeini affair.

NATHAN GARDELS
Editor, New Perspective's Quarterly

The Satanic Verses by Salman Rushdie is really a novel about the metamorphosis of the contemporary world brought about by migration and communication. It is about the conflicts within individuals and between cultures that result from the immediate juxtaposition in time (mass media, telecommunications) and space (migration) of very different worldviews and civilizations. It is a novel about the conflicts and spiritual dislocation of fragmented individuals in a fragmented world wrestling with its plural identities. **The Satanic Verses** is a novel about the frictions of the global collage.

The furor over *The Satanic Verses* caused by Khomeini's death sentence of Rushdie mimics the very theme of the novel. Rushdie's life could only be at risk in the very kind of world his novel describes. Only through the "juxtastructure" of global integration, of a world where Khomeini and Rushdie effectively live side by side, could the blasphemous battle, engaging in a fatal "war of nomenclatures," a clash of faiths and languages. It's the Word against words. Milan Kundera has said that the novel is able to exist in the West because it requires ambiguity and relativity, not a unique Truth that must be conformed to. Rushdie the novelist, like the Western novel itself, blasphemes The Absolute. Khomeini blasphemes the only sacred values of the West: skepticism, relativism, pluralism and tolerance.

Not in his most fertile imaginative moments could Rushdie have dreamed up a scene where the ancient religious rivalries that drive Iran's revolutionary politics are played out on the bookshelves of America's chain stores, nor could he have envisioned a united, usually squabbling Europe rising to the defense of the idea of the novel. How very extraordinary, after decades of hardened balance-of-power-*Realpolitik,* that the world be divided between those who defend the possibility of literature and those who don't.

Now that the Cold War has lost its impetus, it seems that our new preoccupation (along with the environment) will be with the Battle of the Novel, or as Rushdie himself prefers to put it, the War of the Word—a drama of struggle between different civilizations that must live in one interdependent world.

For the moment, Rushdie and Khomeini, the main protagonists of this dramatic tale, are tasting the fate of all actors in the paradox of history. Inadvertently, Rushdie's "sacrilege" has resurrected Khomeini's waning fundamentalist fervor: infidel as evangelist. Inadvertently, Khomeini's death sentence, against Rushdie but really against the idea of the novel, has revived the waning importance of literature in the West: Imam as literary agent. Such are the unexpected twists of plot, the play of contraries, we will learn to expect as this grand drama of the closing years of the last modern century unfolds.

ABDULLAHI AHMED AN-NA'IM
A leading reformist Islamic jurist.

In the current furor over *The Satanic Verses* one thing should be underscored: Salman Rushdie, by following a long tradition of Muslim intellectuals who have pondered their faith, is not exhibiting aberrant behavior. On the contrary, it is the Ayatollah Khomeini who is out of touch with the laws and traditions of Islam.

Khomeini is in clear violation of Islamic law in three respects: First, even assuming that Rushdie's work is heretical, Khomeini has no jurisdiction over him. In the Islamic notion of jurisdiction, the state or the ruler of the state has jurisdiction only over his own subjects.

Secondly, a person who is being charged with heresy must be charged and tried according to the rules of Shari'a (the historic code of Islam). According to Shari'a, no one can be convicted and sentenced *in absentia* for heresy.

Thirdly, repentance is an absolute defense according to Shari'a, even after conviction. If the person repents at any point before the execution of the sentence, they create the basis for a repeal of the sentence. In fact, the notion of repentance is so fundamental in the Koran and in the Sunna that any sin, any offense would be completely forgiven once the person repents.

Islam is not synonymous with Khomeini and has *never* really been a monolithic, concrete entity. In fact, Islam has been adapted and understood, interpreted and lived by Muslims in strikingly different ways around the world.

In the history of Islam, the period in which the Prophet Mohammed was in Mecca set out the fundamentals of the religion: tolerance, equality and freedom of religion and choice. This period constitutes the eternal ethic of Islam. The adaptation of Islam to concrete historical conditions came after Mohammed's migration to Medina, around 622 A.D. It is during this period that one finds the emergence of the 'Satanic verses', the notion of *jihad,* and the justification for inequality between men and women.

The adaptive quality of Islam is recurrent and has operated during different historical periods to both expand and contract the fundamentals set down in Mecca.

Between the 8th and 15th centuries in Spain, for example, Muslims, Jews and Christians coexisted and thrived in a glorious period of liberal tolerance. On the Indian subcontinent, the accepted universals of Islam—articles of faith, rituals of prayer and worship etc.—are integrated with elements of Hinduism regarding manner of dress and social institutions. In parts of Islamic Africa, women are denied the rights given them by Shari'a in terms of inheritance. In other words, the context in which Islam has been interpreted and applied in Africa sometimes modifies Shari'a itself. And the Muslims of that region see no contradiction in that.

The soul-searching and reflection which has led to Salman Rushdie's current dilemma is an exercise many Muslim migrants to Britain, North America and other areas of the "modern" world have engaged in for decades. People may agree or disagree with the manner in which Rushdie tackled the issues or the language he used, but there should be no question about his right to doubt, to reflect and to express himself artistically.

The phenomena of doubt and skepticism about religion has been experienced by Muslim philosophers and writers throughout history. Some were persecuted and some were executed for heresy. Mahmoud Mohammed Taha, author of *The Second Message of Islam,* was publicly hanged for apostasy in 1985 by Sudanese President Numiery. Others survived the persecution and left us the fruits of their work: Al-Ghazali, a scholar of Sufi mysticism writing in the 12th century, experienced profound periods of doubt throughout his life; scholar Abd Al'Razaq, was threatened with death in the 1920s, stripped of his university degree and finally forced to completely withdraw from public life after he wrote *Islam— The Foundation of Government,* a book which argued that the Prophet did not intend to create a religious state; Taha Hussein, the Egyptian writer and educator, was denounced and attacked for his views on Islam, though he later became one of the major figures of Arabic literature and was named Egypt's education minister in 1950. Others, like Egyptian Nobel laureate Najib Mahfuz, have also questioned their Islamic faith.

In the past, the persecution of such figures and even their execution was taken as normal practice under Islamic law. Today, however, in a world unified by advanced communications, transportation and international law, the traditional response is seen by the outside world as untenable.

The rapid global transformation brought about by communication and travel make it imperative that we in the Islamic world alter our institutions and our legal systems accordingly, as long as we remain committed to the fundamentals of the faith set down in Mecca. No one can afford to live in isolation anymore. Even those who claim to maintain a very closed society, like Saudi Arabia or Iran are, in fact, interacting and benefitting from a new and integrated world order. The leaders of these nations are both inconsistent and intellectually dishonest in claiming the benefits of the new order while denying them at another level.

Finally, one must remember that the phenomenon of Islamic insurgence and resentment toward Western domination has been with us for some time. Rushdie's is not the first incident in which we have had this cycle of Islamic insurgence, resentment, and hostility toward the West, East or whoever else is perceived to be threatening Islamic identity and Islamic religion.

We Muslims need to react to outsiders, whether Westerners or otherwise, by asserting our right to be Muslim, not by rejecting everything just because it comes from outside.

ABOLHASSAN BANI-SADR
First president of revolutionary Iran.

The Satanic Verses is a great victory for Islam. The fact that any writer must resort to crude and blasphemous insults against the Prophet Mohammed and Abraham clearly demonstrates the weakness of the West. In other words, in the absence of any valid critique of Islam, the West must settle for crude insults.

Salman Rushdie's book is in no way detrimental to Islam. After 14 centuries, Islam's principles, rights, and values and the Words of the Prophet have endured. Insults can in no way diminish this legacy.

In order to sell books, this author of the West has sought to transform the House of Islam, which is pure, spiritual and solid, into a bordello. He speaks of the love life of the Prophet to gain notoriety and personal profit. This is a sad commentary on Western culture and more of an insult to the West than to Islam.

If I were still head of state in Iran, I would certainly permit **The Satanic Verses** to be translated and published. I would also write a preface for the Iranian edition, which would say to Muslims of my country, "Hold firmly to your faith. After 14 centuries the West, with all its philosophers and social scientists, can only marshall crude insults against Islam. Our faith has been reaffirmed."

Finally, I would pose this question to Americans: If an author sought to speak of the President of the United States and his wife as Rushdie speaks of the Prophet and his spouse,

would he be allowed to publish? Would he not be roundly condemned, even prosecuted?

Let us all agree that the rights of the Prophet should be respected in the same manner as the rights of any man.

"Salman Rushdie: A Collage of Comment," in New Perspectives, *Vol. 6, No. 1, Spring, 1989, pp. 48-55.*

THE NEW YORK TIMES

Salman Rushdie is still alive somewhere in Britain, nine weeks after Iran put a price on his head for the alleged blasphemies in his book **The Satanic Verses.** The affair has slipped from Page One, and famous writers have gone back to their famous writing.

But look on the inside pages:

Two large London bookstores are bombed after receiving warnings about their continued sale of Mr. Rushdie's novel.

Veiled Threat, *a U.S. film critical of Ayatollah Khomeini, is withdrawn from the Los Angeles Film Festival, whose director claims he cannot assure security.*

The spiritual leader of Belgium's Muslims, Abdullah al Ahdal, is killed after opposing threats against Rushdie. Islamic militants call for the death of the Nigerian Nobel prize author Wole Soyinka for defending Mr. Rushdie.

A play in London titled A Mullah's Night Out, *co-authored by Pakistani-born Tariq Alt, is retitled* Iranian Nights *after cast protests.*

A Molotov cocktail is thrown into Cody's Bookstore in Berkeley, Calif. Fire breaks out in a bookshop owned by Mr. Rushdie's Italian publisher. Meanwhile, windows are smashed in four other Italian bookstores.

Pakistan bans Newsweek *issue containing a forbidden picture of the Prophet Mohammed.*

In Israel, Ashkenazi Chief Rabbi Avraham Shapira urges banning of **The Satanic Verses.**

In France, the singer Veronique Sanson withdraws "Allah," *a song opposing religious fanaticism, after death threats.*

This has not been freedom's finest hour. Some Westerners seem to say that free speech is not a universal value but merely a parochial cultural preference.

Not even the political leaders who set an early example of courage have stayed the course in an initial show of defiance, the 12 Common Market countries recalled their ambassadors from Teheran to protest Ayatollah Khomeini's call for the murder of Mr. Rushdie, a British subject. Within three weeks, all but Britain agreed to send the envoys back—though Bonn, for one, has so far not actually done so.

Islam deserves to be treated with respect and its horror of blasphemy needs to be understood. Jimmy Carter and New York's Cardinal O'Connor are right to plead for such understanding. But no amount of understanding can condone a call for murder. This barbarism needs to be denounced over and again until the threat is withdrawn.

Nor should striving to understand another's principles lead to surrendering one's own. Some Americans come close to suggesting that free speech is a complicated Western concept inapplicable to other societies. This is bad logic and worse policy. Should one by this logic remain mute if non-Western societies condone slavery, torture, infanticide and the immolation of widows?

Free speech is a universal good, not a Western idiosyncrasy. It grew out of the struggle for religious toleration, and opens the way to peaceful co-existence of all faiths. The wise remedy whenever someone feels wronged by someone else's free speech is more free speech. To excuse book-burnings, whether in England or India, is to throw reason itself on the pyre.

Free speech is not a self-executing principle. It demands continued defense, and especially when the circumstancess are dangerous—or wearily familiar. Whether Salman Rushdie is a blasphemer or preacher, a pedant or a poet, he is entitled to the world's unwavering support.

> *"The Rushdie Affair Lives,"* in The New York Times, *April 16, 1989, p. E24.*

RANDY COHEN

Welcome to Montana, Mr. Rushdie: You'll be writing westerns now. Your hero's name is Dusty Chaparral. Your new name is Purvis Larue. Oh, by the way, the wig looks great; I'd think about staying blond on a permanent basis even after the hair transplants grow in.

Tonight I just want you to relax, unpack and familiarize yourself with the house. It's a rental, so you'll have to keep up with the yard work. You know much about power mowers?

One of our tailors will come by tomorrow with some swatches of tweed that will stop anything up to .45 caliber. I've got you down for a couple of sport coats and a bulletproof suit. I'm damned if I know where you'll wear them, but that's the standard order on these relocation jobs.

But listen to me go on. You must be worn out from the trip. It's a grueling way to travel, strapped to the undercarriage like that, especially on the two-lane blacktop. Are you hungry? I picked up a bag of croissanwiches down at the Burger Barn. You want the ham or the turkey? While we're on the subject, you get your milk and eggs at the Gas'n'Go up at the junction. There's a *USA Today* box up there, too. Oh yeah, you don't drive, do you? Well, you're going to call attention to yourself taking taxicabs around Missoula, so I'll be giving you lessons. One thing, though—in the morning, let me start the car. Me and Kaiser. He's trained to sniff things out. You know: Boooooom!

Now, now, Salman, don't cry. It just takes getting used to. Steer clear of the magical realism and you'll be O.K. No herd of mustangs galloping into the clouds to race 747s or anything. And remember: One casual reference to Philip Roth, a single vivid metaphor, even a whisper of irony, and you're a dead man. Hey, it's a joke! To break the tension. There aren't a dozen Shiites in the entire country. Although there is that big mosque in Bozeman. I'm kidding!

Anyhow, you won't be here all that long. I hear President Bush is sending you on a cross-country reading tour on Air Force One—full Secret Service protection—to demonstrate his commitment to free expression. And Cardinal O'Connor is giving you an office right in St. Patrick's to work on your next book. Of course I'm still kidding.

You like a can of Hawaiian Punch to wash down that croissanwich? (p. 528)

> *Randy Cohen, "Write in Plain Sight," in* The Nation, *New York, Vol. 248, No. 15, April 17, 1989, pp. 528-29.*

CARLOS FUENTES

Mikhail Bakhtin was probably the greatest theorist of the novel in our century. His life, in a way, is as exemplary as his books. Shunted off to remote areas of the Soviet Union by the minions of Stalinism for his unorthodox ideas, Bakhtin could not profit from rehabilitation when it came under Brezhnev, simply because he had never been accused of anything. A victim of faceless intolerance, his political nemesis was Stalin, but his literary symbol was Kafka.

His case was and is not unique. I have thought a lot about Bakhtin while thinking about Salman Rushdie during these past few weeks. Rushdie's work perfectly fits the Bakhtinian contention that ours is an age of competitive language. The novel is the privileged arena where languages in conflict can meet, bringing together in tension and dialogue not only opposing characters but also different historical ages, social levels, civilization, and other realities of human life. In the novel, realities that are normally separated can meet, establishing a dialogic encounter, a meeting with the other.

This is no gratuitous exercise. It reveals a number of things. The first is that in dialogue no one is absolutely right: neither speaker holds an absolute truth or, indeed, has an absolute hold over history. Myself and the other, as well as the history that both of us are making, are unfinished. The novel, by its very nature, indicates that we are becoming. There is no final solution. There is no last word.

This is what Milan Kundera means when he proposes that the novel is a constant redefinition of men and women as problems, never as sealed, concluded truths. But this is precisely what the ayatollahs of this world cannot suffer. For the ayatollahs, reality is dogmatically defined once and for all in a sacred text. But a sacred text is, by definition, a completed and exclusive text. You can add nothing to it. It does not converse with anyone. It is its own loudspeaker. It offers perfect refuge for the insecure who then, having the protection of a dogmatic text over their heads, proceed to excommunicate those whose security lies in their search for the truth. I remember Luis Buñuel saying: "I would give my life for a man who is looking for the truth. But I would gladly kill a man who thinks that he has found the truth."

This surrealist sally is now being dramatically acted out in reverse. An author who is looking for the truth has been condemned to death by a priestly hierarchy whose deep insecurity is disguised by its pretension to holding the truth.

The ayatollahs, nevertheless, have done a great service to literature, if not to Islam. Though they have debased and caricatured their own faith, they have shifted the wandering attention of the world to the power of words, literature, and the imagination, in ways totally unforeseen by their philosophy. The intolerance of the ayatollahs not only sheds light on Salman Rushdie and his uses of the literary imagination but, by declaring this imagination so dangerous that it deserves capital punishment, the sectarians have made people everywhere wonder what it is that literature can say that is so powerful and, indeed, so dangerous.

I have always conceived of the novel (at least those I try to write) as a crossroads between the individual and the collective destinies of men and women. Both tentative, both unfinished, but both only sayable and minimally understandable if it is first said and understood that in fiction truth is the search for truth, nothing is pre-established, and knowledge is only what both of us—reader and writer—can imagine. There is no other way to freely and fruitfully explore the possibilities of our unfinished humanity. No other way to refuse the death of the past, making it present through memory. No other way of effectively giving life to the future, through the manifestation of our desire.

That these essential activities of the human spirit should be denied in the name of a blind yet omniscient, paralytical yet actively homicidal, dogmatism is both a farce and a crime in itself. Salman Rushdie has done the true religious spirit a service by brilliantly imagining the tensions and complements that it establishes with the secular spirit. Humor, certainly, cannot be absent, since there is no contemporary language that can utter itself without a sense of the diversification of that same language. When we all understood everything, the epic was possible. But not fiction. The novel is born from the very fact that we do not understand one another any longer, because unitary, orthodox language has broken down. Quixote and Sancho, the Shandy brothers, Mr. and Mrs. Karenin: their novels are the comedy (or the drama) of their misunderstandings. Impose a unitary language: you kill the novel, but you also kill the society.

After what has happened to Salman Rushdie and *The Satanic Verses,* I hope that everyone now understands this. Fiction is not a joke. It is but an expression of the cultural, personal, and spiritual diversity of mankind. Fiction is a harbinger of a multipolar and multicultural world, where no single philosophy, no single belief, no single solution, can shunt aside the extreme wealth of mankind's cultural heritage. Our future depends on expanding the freedom of the multiracial and the polycultural to express themselves in a world of shifting, decaying, and emerging power centers.

The defense of Salman Rushdie is a defense of ourselves. It is a matter of pride to say that Rushdie has given us all a better reason to understand and protect the profession of letters at the highest level of creativity, imagination, intelligence, and social responsibility. (pp. 17-18)

> *Carlos Fuentes, "Sacred Truths, Novelistic Truths,"* in Harper's, *Vol. 278, No. 1668, May, 1989, pp. 17-18.*

BRAD LEITHAUSER

The horrors that have grown up around *The Satanic Verses* make it almost impossible to recollect the time when Rushdie's book seemed merely one controversial novel among many new novels. Yet less than four months ago (to Rushdie, it must seem like four lifetimes ago) he felt free to compose a spirited self-defense [see *CLC,* Vol. 55] for the London *Observer,* in which he lashed out at both the "Thought Police" of militant Islam and the Labour Party politicians who stood ready, in his view, to bargain away creative freedom in a pandering to ethnic voters. But that was before the Ayatollah's decree.

If the various counterdemonstrations in support of *The Satanic Verses* have been heartening reassertions of an artist's right to unfettered expression, Rushdie's sympathizers are left, nonetheless, with a sense of ultimate impotence. In the face of the Ayatollah's pronouncement that the "blasphemer" should be sent "to hell," and that every Muslim should "employ everything he's got, his life and wealth" toward that end, who can grant Rushdie the security of mind and movement which he, as both man and artist, requires? At the moment, little can be done except to comply with his repeated request that his novel be considered as a novel—and that, as such, it be evaluated on its literary merits.

The Satanic Verses picks up where Rushdie's last novel, *Shame,* left off: in the clouds. *Shame* concluded with a billow of smoke that gradually rose and coalesced into the torso of a man. *The Satanic Verses* begins with a literal bang—the explosion of a hijacked jet as it cruises 29,002 feet over the English Channel—that sends cascading down through a cloud bank "reclining seats, stereophonic headsets, drinks trolleys, motion discomfort receptacles, disembarkation cards, duty-free video games, braided caps, paper cups, blankets, oxygen masks." Among the wreck's "titbits" are "two brown men"—Gibreel Farishta, who was for fifteen years the leading star of Indian cinema, and Saladin Chamcha, who, as the Man of a Thousand Voices, has made a fortune in the British film industry, chiefly in commercials. ("If you wanted to know how your ketchup bottle should talk in its television commercial, if you were unsure as to the ideal voice for your packet of garlic-flavoured crisps, he was your very man.") The two men, neither of them equipped with a parachute, manage not only to survive the descent (they are the disaster's sole survivors) but to bicker and sing and remonstrate with each other on the way down. With characteristic bravado, Rushdie at one stroke casts off the constraints of realism and rings the note of fabulism that echoes throughout this outflung, ambitious novel: "Let's face it: it was impossible for them to have heard one another, much less conversed and also competed thus in song. Accelerating toward the planet, atmosphere roaring around them, how could they? But let's face this, too: they did."

Gibreel and Saladin are linked, it becomes clear, by more than a miraculous escape, careers in film, and Indian ancestry. Their passage together through five and a half miles of sky initiates a number of complementary, surreal transformations. The first of these seems a purely lighthearted touch. Gibreel has long been notorious for what one of his leading ladies has described as "breath of rotting cockroach dung"; but after the two men find themselves deposited, bones unbroken, on an icy stretch of Sussex coast, it is Saladin whose exhalations suggest "ochre clouds of sulphur." It isn't long before other, queerer changes surface: Saladin begins to grow horns and a tail, while Gibreel's head emits a halolike glow. We have entered the realm of Milton's *Paradise Lost;* the novel's opening detonation, the reader comes to see, was nothing less than a fall of angels.

The nascent halo serves as confirmation to Gibreel, who for many months has suspected that he is an incarnation of his namesake Gabriel, the archangel who was sent to Daniel to explain the vision of the ram and the he-goat, who served as the agent of the Annunciation to Mary, and who—more to the point in this novel—revealed to Muhammad the principles of Islam. Large portions of the book are set in Arabia in the early decades of the seventh century A.D., during those incendiary years when Muhammad—who is here called Mahound—became a prophet, attracted a small cadre of followers, time and again eluded and outwitted his persecutors, and eventually invested himself with sufficient authority, both moral and military, to insure the ongoing life of his new faith. One measure of the book's ambition is that it chronicles the founding of a world religion as a sideline to its primary plot.

I might alternatively say that the whole of the book takes place in the twentieth century, since the sections that depict Muhammad arrive by way of the archangel Gabriel by way of the film star Gibreel. Gabriel's revelations come to Gibreel in dreams. (pp. 124-25)

Dreams of one sort or another suffuse the novel. There are violent dreams, paradisal dreams, daydreams and nightmares and dreams within dreams. They take on a life of their own. This is a world of permeable sensibilities, in which dreams often "leak" from one state of consciousness into another, from one person to another.

Whether one ought to view the Muhammad of *The Satanic Verses* as an impressionistic dream amalgamation or as the solid, historical figure who founded Islam, it is difficult to square Rushdie's portrait with the international turmoil that the book has produced. Although there is much here to offend the faithful—Rushdie's Muhammad is a manipulative, lecherous, and somewhat cynical man, and the novel also depicts a brothel that becomes an "anti-mosque" when its dozen prostitutes adopt the names and mannerisms of Muhammad's wives—the book, when taken in its entirety, is so dense a layering of dreams and hallucinations that any attempt to extract an unalloyed line of argument is false to its intention. Rushdie, who was raised a Muslim but says he now holds no religious beliefs, pointed out in his *Observer* article that Muhammad always discouraged his followers' attempts to apotheosize him, and argued further that the portrait in *The Satanic Verses* is consonant with a man who continually stressed his own humanity.

Most American readers, I suspect, will feel unqualified to sort through the byways of the debate. To take but one example, many Muslims are enraged by Rushdie's practice of referring to Muhammad as Mahound—a name, Rushdie acknowledged in his article, "which, long ago, was indeed used as a derogatory term." He justified himself with a passage from *The Satanic Verses*: "To turn insults into strengths, whigs, tories, Blacks all chose to wear with pride the names they were given in scorn; likewise, our mountain-climbing, prophet-motivated solitary is to be . . . Mahound." Whether Rushdie's analogy is apt or his choice of names is simply, maliciously offensive (that pun on "prophet" does give one pause) remains—for me, anyway—an unresolved issue. But if the American reader is likely to feel removed from the controversy's intricacies he will probably enjoy, by way of compensation, an ability to form artistic judgments the more lucidly for not being embroiled in religious issues—to see, specifically, that the weakest portions of the book are those dealing directly with Muhammad. A bridge of dreams, it turns out, is too flimsy and insubstantial a structure to support heavy traffic between the seventh century and the twentieth; the two worlds never completely fuse. In any final accounting, *The Satanic Verses* must stand or fall according to aesthetic criteria. And when the dust settles (or perhaps one should say, given the book burnings, when the smoke clears) it will be evident that *The Satanic Verses* is a book of splen-

did but segmental components that do not quite cohere into a satisfying whole.

Rushdie is a writer fond of and occasionally besotted with excess. In *The Satanic Verses* he disregards E. M. Forster's distinction between "flat" and "round" characters and seeks to infuse the fullness of life even into peripheral presences. The result is not a sense of enhanced dimensionality so much as of clutter; the propulsion of the tale is forever being retarded by obstructions of its own making. When, for instance, the penmanship of a secondary character is described as "large, looping, back-leaning, left-handed," one can't help thinking that we've been given two, and perhaps three, adjectives too many. A writer blessed with an omnivorous eye, Rushdie at times succumbs to his gift and lets himself be waylaid by any number of things—furniture, faces, advertisements, bibelots, graffiti—that have little bearing on his story.

Still, you must admire the man's titanic energy, proof of which is that his novel, though it runs to more than five hundred pages, often seems too packed but seldom padded. Rushdie has a rare talent for surrealistic invention—an ability to pursue chains of causation and contingency without regard to where they cross or recross the boundary separating the plausible from the fantastic. Curiously, then, the best part of *The Satanic Verses* is a somewhat conventional, thoroughly realistic story. Over the years, Saladin Chamcha, the Man of a Thousand Voices, has grown more English than the English (he weathers his miles of free-fall without losing his bowler), and on one of his trips back to India he is unnerved when a woman named Zeeny Vakil, the first Indian he has ever taken as a lover, speaks of his eventual "reclamation." She prophesies that India is "going to get you back."

Which in some sense it does. After Saladin sheds his satanic horns and tail—his demoniasis (as he thinks of it) departs as mysteriously as it came—he makes another journey to India, to attend to his father, who is dying and from whom he has long been estranged. In the daily business of ministering to a helpless old man—shaving the gaunt cheeks, hauling the atrophied body to the toilet—Saladin discovers a filial love that was lost, seemingly forever, in adolescence, and, what's more, he learns to accept his native country as never before. If the theme of divided loyalties is what might be expected from Rushdie, who was born in Bombay, in 1947, and has spent more than half his life in England, it nonetheless provides the book with the one extended section where the reader's respect and admiration freely give way to something better: empathy.

At times, the punctuation available to writers who work in English looks inadequate to Rushdie's needs. When he composes a novel, the bottom row of his typewriter, where the comma, period, virgule, and question mark are, gets a heavy workout. He's also keen on dashes, hyphens, colons, semicolons, exclamation points, and parentheses. Literary English has undergone a streamlining of punctuation in this century, of course, which can make the reading of fiction written only a hundred years ago seem a slow business—often pleasurably so. Rushdie offers a kindred typographical density. (pp. 125-26)

Rushdie's experiments with punctuation reflect his handling of larger questions of style. He treats the language as though he owned it. At his best, he can wrench syntax to the teasing verge of incomprehensibility without losing his reader, or can burden a sentence with such a weight of clauses that it threatens to collapse and yet stands firm. He is a writer of inspired violence. One feels on every page how much he loves to read and write. His books brim with rapid, glancing allusions. (p. 127)

Shame, which was Rushdie's third novel, was a considerable feat, and **Midnight's Children,** his second novel, was probably better still—but it may be that, so far, his most significant accomplishment lies not in narrative but in language, not in an individual book but in the evolution of a nonesuch style. In borrowing easily from Western and Eastern sources and in experimenting so broadly—with punctuation, sentence construction, abrupt shifts of viewpoint, deliberate incongruities of tone—he has developed a voice we haven't heard before.

As one would suspect, he brings to the English-language novel an invigorating influx of Indian cadences (the Bombay interludes of **The Satanic Verses,** particularly when Zeeny Vakil speaks, have an irresistible bounce and sparkle), but he does far more than that. His prose blends elevated diction, an exclamatory, cartoony collection of words like "zap" and "boom" and "pow," clanging rhymes ("the jouncing and bouncing of youth," "arms wide, feet with the beat"), reportorial flatness, and a jazzy spontaneity. . . . (pp. 127-28)

The effect of this heterogeneous mixture can be a little wearing. As a stylist, Rushdie is continually breathtaking—and a breathless reader is likely to feel winded at times. There are moments, frankly, when one wishes he would get on with it. Now and then, a sentence slips utterly away from him. His parentheses, in particular, have a python's tendency first to engorge whatever wanders into proximity and then to lie there in a digestive slumber. And his naturally arch temperament has a way—as archness naturally does—of becoming cloying. I don't see how anyone could read the following passages without feeling annoyed by them:

> Love, a zone in which nobody desirous of compiling a human (as opposed to robotic, Skinnerian-android) body of experience could afford to shut down operations, did you down, no question about it, and very probably did you in as well.

> Of the fruit of the tree of the knowledge of good and evil they shouldst not eat, and ate. Woman first, and at her suggestion man, acquired the verboten ethical standards, tastily apple-flavoured: the serpent brought them a value system.

Finally, one might wish that Rushdie displayed a greater flair for that variety of beauty whose essence resides in brevity. Although he can produce ravishing imagery, rarely is it of the concentrated type found in those novelists we praise for having a poet's eye. Another novel with an Eastern setting, Forster's *A Passage to India,* offers an instructive contrast. It runs about half the length of **The Satanic Verses,** and yet no single passage in the latter possesses the distilled beauty that Forster commands when, for instance, he ventures into the Marabar Caves. . . . Rushdie, it is true, can enter the mind of either Easterner or Westerner with a conversancy that the more circumspect and wholly English Forster lacked. Still, one sometimes longs, amid the impressive clangor of Rushdie's prose, for the hushed, suspended moment that comes when loveliness is wed to concision.

In the light of such reservations, and of the tragedy and fear that have recently engulfed Rushdie's life, it seems worthwhile to point out that even before this book appeared Rushdie was perhaps the only young novelist in the English-

---

An excerpt from *The Satanic Verses*

The grave. Salahuddin climbs down into it, stands at the head end, the gravedigger at the foot. Changez Chamchawala is lowered down. *The weight of my father's head, lying in my hand. I laid it down; to rest.*

The world, somebody wrote, is the place we prove real by dying in it.

Waiting for [Salahuddin] when he returned from the graveyard: a copper-and-brass lamp, his renewed inheritance. He went into Changez's study and closed the door. There were his old slippers by the bed: he had become, as he'd foretold, 'a pair of emptied shoes'. The bedclothes still bore the imprint of his father's body; the room was full of sickly perfume: sandalwood, camphor, cloves. He took the lamp from its shelf and sat at Changez's desk. Taking a handkerchief from his pocket, he rubbed briskly: once, twice, thrice.

The lights all went on at once.

Zeenat Vakil entered the room.

'O God, I'm sorry, maybe you wanted them off, but with the blinds closed it was just so sad.' Waving her arms, speaking loudly in her beautiful croak of a voice, her hair woven, for once, into a waist-length ponytail, here she was, his very own djinn. 'I feel so bad I didn't come before, I was just trying to hurt you, what a time to choose, so bloody self-indulgent, yaar, it's good to see you, you poor orphaned goose.'

She was the same as ever, immersed in life up to her neck, combining occasional art lectures at the university with her medical practice and her political activities. 'I was at the goddamn hospital when you came, you know? I was right there, but I didn't know about your dad until it was over, and even then I didn't come to give you a hug, what a bitch, if you want to throw me out I will have no complaints.' This was a generous woman, the most generous he'd known. *When you see her, you'll know,* he had promised himself, and it turned out to be true. 'I love you,' he heard himself saying, stopping her in her tracks. 'Okay, I won't hold you to that,' she finally said, looking hugely pleased. 'Balance of your mind is obviously disturbed. Lucky for you you aren't in one of our great public hospitals; they put the loonies next to the heroin addicts, and there's so much drug traffic in the wards that the poor schizos end up with bad habits.—Anyway, if you say it again after forty days, watch out, because maybe then I'll take it seriously. Just now it could be a disease.'

Undefeated (and, it appeared, unattached), Zeeny's re-entry into his life completed the process of renewal, of regeneration, that had been the most surprising and paradoxical product of his father's terminal illness. His old English life, its bizarreries, its evils, now seemed very remote, even irrelevant, like his truncated stage-name. 'About time,' Zeeny approved when he told her of his return to *Salahuddin.* 'Now you can stop acting at last.' Yes, this looked like the start of a new phase, in which the world would be solid and real, and in which there was no longer the broad figure of a parent standing between himself and the inevitability of the grave. An orphaned life, like Muhammad's; like everyone's. A life illuminated by a strangely radiant death, which continued to glow, in his mind's eye, like a sort of magic lamp.

speaking world to have legitimate claims to an international reputation. He is prodigiously gifted. He is especially good on the subject of racism; the reader burns with freshened, re-awakened indignation, as though apprised of prejudice for the first time. And in the meeting of East and West he appears to have sufficient subject matter for a couple of dozen novels. One of the strengths of *The Satanic Verses* is the way in which his "East" encompasses not merely India but—in its range of subplots and allusions—Southeast Asia, the Middle East, even Morocco. Worlds within worlds, dreams within dreams . . . One comes away from *The Satanic Verses,* as from *Shame* and *Midnight's Children,* with an inspiriting sense of multiplicity. (p. 128)

> Brad Leithauser, "Demoniasis," in The New York-er, Vol. LXV, No. 13, May 15, 1989, pp. 124-28.

THE NEW YORK TIMES

LONDON, MAY 27—Thousands of Muslims occupied Parliament Square this afternoon to demand that the novel *The Satanic Verses* be banned.

Some members of the crowd, estimated by the police at between 15,000 and 20,000 people, clashed with the police and each other, and several young demonstrators were arrested by a force of several hundred police officers guarding 10 Downing Street, the residence of Prime Minister Margaret Thatcher.

> "Thousands of Muslims Rally against Rushdie in London," in The New York Times, May 28, 1989, p. 17.

DANIEL PIPES

Twice now in the span of a decade, the Ayatollah Khomeini has challenged some of Western civilization's deepest values. In November 1979, by permitting a seizure of the American embassy, he violated the hallowed laws of Western diplomacy. Then, in February 1989, he struck again, this time against the concept of free speech, by calling for the murder of a British writer, Salman Rushdie, and of the publishers of Rushdie's most recent novel, *The Satanic Verses.*

So far as an outsider can tell, Khomeini issued his edict against Rushdie to strike a blow at what he sees as a threatening, secular West. The chief irony of the affair, therefore, is that Khomeini succeeded in demonstrating how few Western governments are prepared to stand up against him and for their own values. This Western weakness has implications that go far beyond the Rushdie case itself and that may be felt for years to come.

The Iranian press has called Rushdie "a self-confessed apostate," but he is better described as a lapsed Muslim, and he makes no bones about it: "I do not believe in supernatural entities," he has said, "whether Christian, Jewish, Muslim, or Hindu." Though Rushdie is hardly alone in his views, what he stands for perturbs many Muslims. They are especially offended because he has renounced his ancestral country, language, and the Muslim way of life in favor of England, English, and secularism.

Yet while Rushdie has adopted England as his home, he has hardly taken it to his bosom. Thus in *The Satanic Verses,* the British immigration officials who arrest one of his characters behave like the goons of a police state, "thumping and gouging various parts of his anatomy" in such a way that the bruises will not show. As Cheryl Benard of the Baltzman Institute in Vienna concludes in a piece in the *Wall Street Journal,* it is not Muslims who come off the worst in Rushdie's vision: "It is Britons more than Muslims who might have cause to find [*The Satanic Verses*] blasphemous. If Islam is portrayed as somewhat rigid and medieval, then the contemporary West, in his pages, is a nightmare out of [the movie] *Blade Runner.*" New York City he calls "that transatlantic New Rome with its Nazified architectural gigantism, which employs the oppressions of size to make its human occupants feel like worms." In the cruder terms of one of his characters, the West comprises "the motherfucking Americans" and "the sisterfucking British."

This kind of thing notwithstanding, *The Satanic Verses* is an elusive and sophisticated tale, written by an accomplished novelist. Unfortunately, however, to assess its offensiveness in Muslim eyes, it must be looked at through those eyes—which is to say in a literal and anti-literary way. Specifically, to understand the book as many Muslims do, one must take every statement in it as representative of the author's own thinking, even though this is clearly not always the case. (p. 9)

The uproar over *The Satanic Verses* began with the book's official publication date in Britain in late September 1988.

Indian Muslims had learned about the novel in mid-September from *India Today,* a biweekly magazine, which reviewed it, excerpted it, and interviewed the author [see *CLC,* Vol. 55]. Presciently, the reviewer concluded that "*The Satanic Verses* is bound to trigger an avalanche of protests from the ramparts." And, indeed, Syed Shahbuddin, a member of the Indian parliament, not liking what he read in *India Today,* began a campaign to have the novel banned. He met with quick success, as the finance ministry prohibited distribution of the book on October 5, 1988.

Meanwhile, Muslims in Britain also tried to have it banned, but in their case without success; they then resorted to protest in the form of book-burning ceremonies. The first such burning of *The Satanic Verses* took place in Bolton (near Manchester) on December 2, 1988; it attracted a crowd of 7,000 Muslims but scant press attention. A second burning on January 14, 1989, in the heavily Muslim town of Bradford, the so-called capital of Islam in the United Kingdom, did bring out the cameras, which showed the auto-da-fé—the novel attached to a stake and set on fire—in loving, if horrified, detail.

All this proved merely a warmup for the round of violence that began in Islamabad, Pakistan, on February 12. The events of that day are clear, though their causes remain in dispute. A crowd of some 10,000 took to the streets and marched to the American cultural center, where they shouted "American dogs" and "God is great" and set fire to the building. Five demonstrators died at the hands of the police, and about a hundred were injured. A Pakistani guard at the American center was shot by someone in the mob, making him the sixth casualty of the day. The next day, a rioter lost his life in Kashmir, India.

The odd thing about these riots was that *British* property was not attacked, although the novel had been out for months in the United Kingdom, and Rushdie was living in London. This may have had to do with the forthcoming American publication of *The Satanic Verses,* scheduled for February 22. Or the violence may have been directed toward those in the Pakistani opposition who wanted to exploit the opportunity to attack Prime Minister Benazir Bhutto—and the United States makes a better symbol of protest than Great Britain. This, in fact, is the way the Prime Minister herself interpreted the riots. Similarly, Rushdie for his part accused the leaders of the demonstration of exploiting religious slogans for political ends.

In any event, by the middle of February *The Satanic Verses* had occasioned, or excused, substantial disturbances among Muslims in several parts of the world. But although the riots and loss of life attracted great attention, there was still no real political issue for the West to confront. It took the Ayatollah Khomeini, a man who does not play by the usual rules, to mount such a challenge.

Accounts differ as to how Khomeini learned about Rushdie and *The Satanic Verses.* One report says that he was watching a news program on Iranian television, saw the rioting in Pakistan, and was much affected by the scene. Indeed, it is hard to imagine a sight more compelling to Khomeini's sense of solidarity than that of Muslims crying "God is great" before proceeding to die outside an American cultural center. A second account has him hearing about the Pakistan riots from a small transistor radio he takes with him on his constitutionals. A third version has him "shaken utterly" upon reading excerpts from *The Satanic Verses* (presumably in Persian or Arabic translation, as Khomeini knows no English); the name Mahound is said to have been especially enraging to him.

However he may have learned about the book, on February 14 Khomeini took the single most important step of the entire incident when, in an address to "all proud Muslims of the world," he pronounced an Islamic legal judgment (a *fatwa*) against both Rushdie and his publishers:

> The author of *The Satanic Verses* book—which has been compiled, printed, and published in opposition to Islam, the Prophet, and the Qur'an—and all those involved in its publication who were aware of its content, are sentenced to death.

Khomeini called on Muslims to act quickly against Rushdie, and the President of Iran, Seyyed 'Ali Khamene'i, characterized Khomeini's statement as "an irrevocable dictum."

To make the assignment more attractive, the head of an Iranian charity organization offered $1 million to a non-Iranian assassin, and 200 million rials (almost $3 million at the inflated rate of exchange but just $170,000 on the parallel market) to an Iranian. The next day, the religious leader of Rafsanjan (hometown of 'Ali Akbar Hashemi Rafsanjani, speaker of the Iranian parliament) offered another 200 million rials.

Members of the Iranian parliament expressed their support for Khomeini and their "divine anger" at Rushdie. The Iranian ambassador to the Holy See announced that he would "kill Salman Rushdie with his own hands" if he could. In Spain, the representative of the Islamic Revolution News Agency made the same promise (and found himself instantly expelled from the country).

More importantly, a number of groups sponsored by the Iranian government declared their determination to get Rush-

die. Mohsen Reza'i, leader of the Islamic Revolution's Guard Corps, announced the readiness of his forces "to carry out the imam's decree." Interior Minister 'Ali Akbar Mohtashemi called on the terrorists of Hizbullah to carry out the execution, and the leaders of the Lebanese Hizbullah quickly vowed to do "all that's possible to have the honor." So did other Lebanese groups—including Amal, the Islamic Unification Movement, and the Islamic Jihad for the Liberation of Palestine. In addition, Ahmad Jibril's Popular Front for the Liberation of Palestine-General Command announced its intention to join the effort. The Revolutionary Justice Organization, going farther than the others, vowed to attack the British police, if necessary, on the way to an assault on Rushdie. Something of a rivalry soon developed among these groups: who would get to Rushdie first?

Then, on February 17, President Khamene'i of Iran announced that "the people might forgive" Rushdie if he repented. (Khamene'i added ominously: "In that case, the Americans themselves will kill him. They will not allow such a person to remain alive, to reveal their [conspiratorial] policies, and to bring disgrace upon them.") The next day, Rushdie did offer an apology, though a minimal one; it concerned only the effects of his writings, and not the writings themselves [see *CLC,* Vol. 55]. . . . (pp. 11-13)

An Iranian news-agency report suggested that the apology, "though far too short of a repentance, is generally seen as sufficient to warrant his pardon by the masses in Iran and elsewhere in the world." But on February 19 Khomeini himself weighed in with an absolute rejection of Rushdie's statement and, indeed, of any act of contrition on his part. Khomeini also denied foreign reports that Rushdie's repentance would avert the "execution order" against him. . . . (p. 13)

One might have expected the world to dismiss Khomeini's twisted edict as madness, root and branch. But one would have been wrong.

On the official level, to be sure, the Iranians found little support, even in the Muslim countries. The foreign ministers of the 44 states belonging to the Organization of the Islamic Conference, meeting on March 13-16 in Riyadh, adopted not the Iranian position on Rushdie but a more moderate Saudi one, which called for a ban on the book though not the death of its author:

> The conference declares that blasphemy cannot be justified on the basis of freedom of expression and opinion. The conference strongly condemns the book *The Satanic Verses,* whose author is regarded as a heretic. It appeals to all members of society to impose a ban on the book and to take the necessary legislation to ensure the protection of the religious beliefs of others.

Only the Libyan government publicly stood by the Ayatollah and his edict.

On the popular level, by contrast, anti-Rushdie violence by Muslims showed that Khomeini enjoyed a great deal of support. In the Indian subcontinent the violent demonstrations that began on February 12 continued for a month. The largest number of deaths in a single incident occurred on February 24, when rioting in Rushdie's hometown of Bombay turned into a three-hour battle between the police and fundamentalist Muslims. The rioters burned cars, buses, and even a small police station. In response, the police killed twelve persons, detained 500, and arrested 800. On March 4, thousands of Pakistani demonstrators ransacked part of the Karachi airport in protest against the Rushdie novel, smashing doors and looting the VIP lounge; this was their way of welcoming home from Iran the pro-Khomeini Shi'i leader, Sajad 'Ali Naqvi. Naturally, the Iranians gloried in these demonstrations, calling them a "manifestation of Muslim power throughout the world" and "symptoms of this very majesty."

Confronted with such emotion, many leaders in Muslim countries sought to avoid the whole issue. They did not refer to it in public and they instructed their media to cover the controversy without comment. "I don't care to comment about the action of the government of Iran myself," was King Hussein of Jordan's reply to a question on the subject.

From the vantage point of governments wishing to stay out of the picture, the easiest, least worrisome step was to proscribe the book and say no more. Indeed, with the exception of the Philippines, few non-Western governments containing substantial Muslim populations resisted Saudi and Iranian pressure to ban *The Satanic Verses,* and many banned all books put out by Viking Penguin, Rushdie's publisher. Even in Israel, the Ministry of Religious Affairs requested that the Keter publishing house drop its plans for a Hebrew translation.

As for the non-Muslim governments of the West, which after all had both the responsibility and the means for protecting the rights of those threatened by Khomeini, they responded in particularly timorous fashion. In Britain, both Prime Minister Margaret Thatcher and the leader of the opposition, Neil Kinnock, kept silent about the Ayatollah's threat for a full week. The newly-installed American Secretary of State, James A. Baker 3d, could muster no stronger condemnation than to call the death threat "regrettable." The Canadian government temporarily banned imports of *The Satanic Verses;* worse, Ottawa finessed the freedom-of-speech issue by relegating the decision to Revenue Canada, a tax agency. Bonn called the incident a "strain on German-Iranian relations." But it was the Japanese government that produced the most spineless formulation of all: "Mentioning and encouraging murder," it intoned, "is not something to be praised."

Several governments—including the British, French, and Soviet—sought a way out of the diplomatic impasse by noting that Khomeini's edict had been issued not by the Iranian government but by the "spiritual leader" of the Islamic revolution. Yet ten years of experience had shown this distinction to be utterly spurious, and in any case the entire machinery of the Iranian government had rushed to endorse Khomeini's action.

Finally, on February 20, the foreign ministers of the Common Market agreed on a strong statement [see *CLC,* Vol. 55]. . . . (pp. 13-14)

Yet not even the British government—which was the most centrally involved of the twelve—went so far as to break diplomatic relations with Iran, though it did demand that all Iranian representatives leave London, and withdrew all its personnel from Teheran. Observers could recall no precedent for maintaining diplomatic relations without personnel; the British move was understood as a way of expressing strong displeasure and regret simultaneously, and thereby signaling that normal relations could be rebuilt as soon as Khomeini's edict was retracted. But far from retracting, the Iranians passed a bill that stipulated a complete break on March 7 unless the British government declared "its opposition to the

unprincipled stands against the world of Islam, the Islamic Republic of Iran, and the contents of the anti-Islamic book, *The Satanic Verses.*"

Prodded by feelers from Iranian "pragmatists," British leaders did what they could to satisfy Teheran. On March 2, Foreign Secretary Sir Geoffrey Howe went on the BBC World Service to show foreign listeners that his government wished to distance itself from Rushdie:

> We understand that the book itself has been found deeply offensive by people of the Muslim faith. It is a book that is offensive in many other ways as well. We can understand why it could be criticized. The British government, the British people, do not have any affection for the book. The book is extremely critical, rude about us. It compares Britain with Hitler's Germany. (Howe was wrong; the only passage that invokes Nazi Germany comes in reference to New York City, ... Rushdie contested Howe's characterization, challenging the Foreign Secretary to produce the offending sentence.) We do not like that any more than the people of the Muslim faith like the attacks on their faith in the book. So we are not co-sponsoring the book. What we are sponsoring is the right of people to speak freely, to publish freely.

Two days later, Prime Minister Thatcher made similar remarks.

The Iranians acknowledged these gestures but demanded practical measures as well, such as the legal prosecution of Rushdie, confiscation of copies of *The Satanic Verses,* and an injunction against further publication of the book. These steps the British authorities did not even consider undertaking; so, as threatened, Teheran broke relations on March 7, in some of the most unusual language and reasoning to be found anywhere in international diplomacy. The Iranian statement noted that "in the past two centuries Britain has been in the frontline of plots and treachery against Islam and Muslims," and it went on to provide details about the behavior of perfidious Albion in Palestine, Iraq, Pakistan, and elsewhere. It alleged, too, that having suffered severe reverses at the hands of Islamic movements, London was now dropping its old military tactics and resorting to more sophisticated political and cultural weapons—such as sponsoring *The Satanic Verses.* But the Islamic Republic would not tolerate this plot, and was therefore breaking relations with the United Kingdom. A Teheran daily suggested that the break could easily last "at least a decade."

In retaliation, the British government closed down the Iranian consulate in Hong Kong and expelled nine Iranians resident in the United Kingdom. The Foreign Office also urged British nationals to stay away from Lebanon. Further, the Foreign Secretary, using his strongest language since the controversy began, called the Iranian government a "deplorable regime" and (for the first time) condemned its recent "mass exterminations." (Those "exterminations" having taken place up to half a year earlier, many commentators found it unfortunate that the condemnation had to wait until diplomatic relations had been broken.)

For all the animosity between the two states, however, neither side made a move to interfere with existing trade relations. The British continued to purchase Iranian crude oil, the Iranians continued to purchase a wide array of British goods; and such official British services as the Export Credits

Guarantee Department (which provides short-term cover for British exports) witnessed a "fairly busy, regular market." Meanwhile, an official of the Foreign Office, William Waldegrave, went on the BBC's Arabic Service to put

> on record that the British government well recognizes the hurt and distress that this book has caused, and we want to emphasize that because it was published in Britain, the British government had nothing to do with and is not associated with it in any way. . . . What is surely the best way forward is to say that the book is offensive to Islam, that Islam is far stronger than a book by a writer of this kind. (Only the Swedish government, whose ambassador to Teheran called *The Satanic Verses* "blasphemous," went further to satisfy Iranian demands.)

Radio Teheran counted this admission as a major step forward from the Howe and Thatcher statements. But Iran made no concessions in return.

Exactly one month after the decision to withdraw top diplomats of the EEC from Iran, the foreign ministers met again and decided, under Greek, Irish, and Italian pressure, to send them back. Khomeini described the Europeans as returning in "shame, abjectness, and disgrace, regretting their deed." Lamely, the French foreign ministry called this an "exaggeration."

Why did Ayatollah Khomeini make an international incident of *The Satanic Verses?* Curiously, critics and supporters of the Ayatollah offered diametrically opposed explanations.

Critics were nearly unanimous in seeing his act in political terms. Former Iranian President Abolhassan Bani-Sadr saw the *fatwa* as "a political affair and not a religious one," and the leader of the main Iranian opposition group, the Mujahid-in-e Khalq, agreed.

Some emphasized domestic political tensions in Iran. Amir Taheri, author of *Holy Terror: Inside the World of Islamic Terrorism,* saw in *The Satanic Verses* "an issue likely to stir the imagination of the poor and illiterate masses" in Iran. Harvey Morris of the (London) *Independent* interpreted Khomeini's edict as a "revolutionary *coup de théâtre*" intended to replace the Iraq-Iran war as a focus of national unity. Other commentators emphasized foreign-policy aspects. Youssef M. Ibrahim of the New York *Times* explained Khomeini's edict as a bid "to reassert his role as spokesman and protector of Islamic causes." William Waldegrave of the British Foreign Office blamed the incident on "radical elements in Iran, which do not want their country to have normal relations with the West and the Gulf states."

Supporters of the Ayatollah, on the other hand, read his move very differently, and primarily as a religious response. The Iranian chargé d'affaires in London stated unequivocally that to Khomeini the punishment of Rushdie was "much more important than relations between two countries." And the top Iranian diplomat in Cyprus told a local audience that "the verdict issued by the Iranian leaders is a purely religious one and based on religious considerations."

Which side is correct? *Prima facie*, there is strong evidence for the religious interpretation. First, the Muslims in India, Great Britain, and Pakistan who took to the streets before Khomeini spoke had no connection with the internal struggles of Iranian political life, and it was surely their actions that exerted so powerful an effect on the aged leader.

Second, there were and are more direct ways for Khomeini to shut down relations with the West or to exclude those he calls liberals from power in Iran. As an autocratic leader, he rules without rival; had he decided to stop the improving ties, he could simply have so decreed. A politician in his position of authority need not take the extreme step of placing a bounty on a novelist's head.

Third, Khomeini generally means what he says, and says what he means—despite a persistent tendency both in Iran and in the West not to take his assertions at face value. In 1978, as Iranians and others tried to foresee what kind of government the Ayatollah would impose in Iran, the evidence that was plain to see in his writings over many years tended to be ignored in favor of a more conventional interpretation of his goals. Today, the insistence on a political explanation for the Rushdie *fatwa* risks falling into the same error.

Finally, the attack on Rushdie is consistent with other actions by the Ayatollah, two of which deserve mention. He took nearly the same step forty-seven years earlier, when he was still an obscure mullah. In 1942 Khomeini wrote *The Discovery of Secrets,* a polemic directed against Ahmed Kasravi, a prominent writer whose anti-clerical views had gained a significant following in Iran. Khomeini pronounced Kasravi *mahdurr ad-damm* ("forfeit blood"), thus permitting any Muslim to execute him. His book was read by Muhammad Nawab-Safavi, who went on to found a terrorist group, the Fedayin-e Islam, and this group attacked Kasravi with knives, murdering him. Though Khomeini's response to the execution is not on record, his close friend, Shaikh Sadeq Khalkhali, remembers it as "the most beautiful day in my life."

Much more recently, Khomeini inflicted severe punishments on the producers of a Teheran Radio program entitled "Model for the Muslim Woman." On January 28, 1989 they aired what the Ayatollah called "an un-Islamic interview": a woman on the program said that she did not consider Fatima, the daughter of the Prophet Muhammad, to be a suitable model for herself, and claimed to prefer a more up-to-date exemplar—the heroine of a Japanese soap opera. Outraged, the Ayatollah sent a letter to the director of Iranian broadcasting, telling him that if the insult was deliberate, the offending parties would "undoubtedly" be condemned to death. Three days later, a court sentenced one of the producers to five years in jail, and two others to four years each and 50 lashes. And the court made clear that this relative leniency was due to an "absence of malicious intent" on their part; otherwise, all of them would have been sentenced to death. In the end they were pardoned, thanks in part to the intercession of Khomeini's daughter.

Yet granted the offensiveness of Rushdie's (literally interpreted) text, the offensiveness of his (misunderstood) title, and Khomeini's religious extremism, it is still not clear why this book should have been made a top priority of the Iranian government. Here the reason would seem to lie in the strange vision of history held by Khomeini and other fundamentalist Muslims.

Their view is based on a kind of syllogism: strong Muslims live fully by the precepts of their faith; Muslims were once strong, but are now weak; therefore, Muslims are weak because they do not live in strict accordance with the Qur'an and the precepts of Islam. Were they to do so, it follows that they would regain the strength of centuries past. Khomeini's first goal, then, is to get Muslims to live fully by the law of Islam, the Shari'a.

But there is one great obstacle to achieving this: the seductive culture of the West, which for two centuries has been drawing Muslims away from strict adherence to the requirements of their faith. Hence Muslims must engage in battle against Western civilization. And a battle this is, for the West is not a passive purveyor of its own culture, but actively thrusts it on vulnerable Muslims. The West does so because it benefits by weakening Muslims; this allows it to plunder Muslim lands and hire believers as cheap laborers. 'Ali Akbar Hashemi Rafsanjani, speaker of the Iranian parliament, explains the deep historical roots of the effort:

> From the day Western colonialists harbored the intention of colonizing the Islamic countries—or to be more precise, to demolish and create havoc in the Islamic world—they sensed that they must deal with something called Islam. They realized that as long as Islam is in force, their path will be a difficult one, or may be virtually closed off.

> Whoever is familiar with the history of colonialism and the Islamic world knows that whenever they wanted to get a foothold in a place, the first thing they did in order to clear their paths—whether overtly or covertly—was to undermine the people's genuine Islamic morals.

Of course, the imperialists could not entirely do away with Islam, so they did the next best thing, which was to emasculate the religion, reducing the faith to empty ceremonies devoid of real content. By 1978, ceremonial Islam (or "American-style Islam") prevailed at the state level everywhere in the world. But then, Rafsanjani continues, "with the advent of the Islamic revolution, pure Islam entered the scene, and all they had done became undone." The Iranians threatened to lead all Muslims (and other oppressed peoples) against the hegemony of the great powers, the United States and the USSR especially.

Seeing the danger Iran posed, the powers fought back, and continue to fight back. "All the West's plots," declares President Khamene'i, "are aimed at stopping Islam and the revolution from becoming a world model." That is why the Iranians, in turn, have to engage in combat with everything at their command.

According to the Iranian view, the war between Islam and "international blasphemy" has taken two main forms. First, the great powers put their agent, the Iraqi president, Saddam Hussein, up to a war which he obediently carried out against Iran. But this military aggression failed against the hard rock of Islamic fervor. "After ten years," says Interior Minister Mohtashemi, "the world gave up the hope of fighting Islam within Iran through military conflict."

Stumped, the Western governments next "summoned all their devilish experts and mercenaries to draw up anew a strategy against Islam." At the conclusion of all these efforts, "global arrogance" (as the Iranians put it) devised a plan—warfare conducted (again) on the level of culture. This effort, according to a commentary on Radio Teheran, would involve two stages. First, "the aim is to weaken the Islamic faith among Muslims, thereby secularizing Muslim societies; this is then followed by an expansion of [Western] influence and the ultimate plundering of those societies' vital resources."

Not for a minute, then, did Iranian authorities believe that *The Satanic Verses* had been written by a single author pursuing the whimsies of his own imagination. According to Rafsanjani, Muslims reading this book "will not see a mad Indian behind it; they will see Britain, Germany, France, and the United States." In picking Rushdie as the ostensible author, the Western intelligence services chose

> a person who seemingly comes from India and who apparently is separate from the Western world and who has a misleading name [i.e., a Muslim name]. . . . All these advance royalties were given to that person.

> One can see that they appointed guards for him in advance because they knew what they were doing. . . . All this tells of an organized and planned effort. It is not an ordinary work. . . . I believe there has not previously been such a well-planned act as this.

The effort required five years and $1.5 million. British intelligence even managed to have *The Satanic Verses* introduced in Britain as "the book of the year." Had Muslims not protested, it would have been made into a film.

But how, an outsider might ask, can this novel hurt Muslims? The answer is, by dishonoring their faith and their traditions. It hurts to be "ridiculed by world arrogance," and the resultant pain could turn Muslims against Islam. Fortunately for Islam, Muslims understood what was brewing, and showed, "with their rage," that they intended to stymie the plot against them. Their steadfastness stopped the cultural campaign in its tracks.

Thus, in the Iranian view, the Rushdie affair, undertaken by the West as an assault upon Islam, instead became the occasion of a major Islamic reassertion, and therefore a turning point in the fortunes of the faith. Even in Turkey, according to one newspaper editorial, where the government had been taking quiet but effective steps toward "ridding the country of Islam," the shock of *The Satanic Verses* awakened the true Muslims to the dangers in their midst.

Note that Iranian leaders speak always of "the West," or "global arrogance." They do not believe that British intelligence acted alone in putting Rushdie up to the job; as ever, the "little Satan" is seen as working hand-in-glove with the "big Satan," the United States. One Iranian government statement referred to the novel as a "provocative American deed," and called Rushdie "an inferior CIA agent." As Mohtashemi put it, "The book's author is in England, but the real supporter is the United States."

There is, of course, no small irony in identifying Rushdie with the American government. After all, Rushdie is a Muslim of Indian origins who lives in England and holds a British passport. Furthermore, he is widely known as a "man of the Left," who viscerally opposes the policies of the U.S. government. Indeed, he has written a screed against American policy in Central America entitled *The Jaguar Smile.* Yet in the minds of fundamentalist Muslims, anti-Westernism has a way of always turning into anti-Americanism. Britain may once have been the imperial overlord, but now it is nearly defanged; its military potential is all but gone. In contrast, Khomeini saw Americans ruling Iran from 1953 to 1978.

Too, American culture, with its global impact, symbolizes the West. Whether Rushdie lives in London or New York City is a minor detail; the point is that the United States is the leader of the Western world, that lascivious place where attacks on the Prophet and the Qur'an are acceptable, even encouraged.

Demented as this conspiratorial theory may sound to us, when we consider the extent to which Western governments have backed down in the Rushdie affair, it is by no means self-evident that Khomeini was wrong from his point of view in making *The Satanic Verses* the launching pad for his latest battle against the West and its values.

Indeed, Khomeini's edict achieved something remarkable. Throughout the West (and in other regions, too), he instilled an unprecedented fear which affected public figures. Suddenly, such topics as Salman Rushdie, *The Satanic Verses,* Iran, and Islam took on a special delicacy and were subject to an informal censorship. In some cases, offending works of art were repressed; more often, private thoughts were simply not uttered.

In a temporary and partial way, then, Ayatollah Khomeini succeeded in imposing his will on the West. Is the power he achieved an aberration or the beginning of a subtle shift in norms? While it is too early to say, it is clear that the answer depends far more on us than on him. (pp. 14-17)

> *Daniel Pipes, "The Ayatollah, the Novelist, and the West," in* Commentary, *Vol. 87, No. 6, June, 1989, pp. 9-17.*

ALI A. MAZRUI

In the autumn of 1988 a debate started in Britain. It concerned Salman Rushdie's novel *The Satanic Verses.* Muslims in the British city of Bradford exploded in indignation. The novel was declared blasphemous—and copies were ceremonially burnt.

In November 1988 I visited Lahore and Islamabad in Pakistan. Discussions about Rushdie's novel had already started there. One analogy particularly struck me: "It is as if Rushdie had composed a brilliant poem about the private parts of his parents, and then recited the poem in the market place to the cheers and laughter of strangers! These strangers then paid him money for all the jokes about his parents' genitalia." The charge I heard levelled against Rushdie in Pakistan was of pornographic betrayal of ancestry. It was a charge of *treason* in a special sense.

In February 1989 the Ayatollah Ruhollah Khomeini, the spiritual leader of Iran, passed a death sentence on Salman Rushdie. Other leaders in Teheran offered a reward to anybody who killed Rushdie. Before long the reward had risen beyond five million dollars and diplomatic relations between Britain and Iran rapidly deteriorated. Britain was supported by its partners in the European Community, and the President of the United States expressed concern.

At least for a while the debate was a classic case of the dialogue of the deaf between the West and the world of Islam. The West was bewildered by the depth of Muslim anger. The Muslims were bewildered by Western insensitivity. Was this yet another problem of conflict of cultures?

In the debate concerning *The Satanic Verses,* I have had a number of conflicting emotions of my own. I have been torn between being a believer in Islam and a believer in the open society, between being a writer and being a religious worshipper, between being a believer in the *Shari'a* and an opponent of all forms of capital punishment in the modern age. This is not the place to resolve all those issues. If I am wrong in my opposition to capital punishment in the twentieth century, I seek the foregiveness of the Almighty and the tolerance of society and the *Umma.*

I also have strong reservations about censorship. This is partly because I have myself been censored over the years. I have been censored in the Republic of South Africa, in parts of the Muslim world, in my own native Kenya, in Uganda under President Idi Amin, in the United Kingdom and in the United States of America. I have therefore had to argue with my very soul whether the banning of Salman Rushdie's *Satanic Verses* is any more legitimate than the censorship to which I have been subjected in different parts of the world from time to time.

This essay is only partly a response to such questions. Much more pressing is the need for *a translation of values between civilizations*—the need to make some of the emotions of the Muslim world more intelligible to the West, even if still fundamentally different from the dominant paradigms of Western thought.

Central to the crisis of mutual incomprehension is the concept of *treason.* The Western world understands the concept of treason to the state. Indeed, the West understands capital punishment imposed on a traitor to the *state.* What the West does not understand is the idea of treason to what Islam calls the *Umma,* the religious community, treason to the faith.

If Islam does not always distinguish between church and state, English law does not always distinguish between the state and the Royal Family. Treason in England has included violating the King's consort, or raping the monarch's eldest unmarried daughter, as well as the sexual violation of the wife of the eldest son and heir. To the present day treason under English law includes "polluting" the Royal bloodline or obscuring it. In addition, English law does of course regard as treasonable the act of "giving aid and comfort to the King's enemies."

The basic law of the United States defines treason more narrowly in terms of war and military defense. The American founding fathers were aware that the concept of "treason" could be used by tyrants as an excuse for suppressing liberty, stifling dissent, or preventing legitimate rebellion. The founding fathers' own revolt against King George III was "treason" against the English monarch.

And so the American Constitution defined treason to the United States as consisting "only in levying war against them, and in adhering to their enemies, giving them aid and comfort." (pp. 347-49)

In Islam there is no sharp distinction between church and state. The concept of treason is often indistinguishable from apostasy. The supreme penalty of treason to the *Umma,* or the religious community, was often death.

For his novel *The Satanic Verses* Salman Rushdie was perceived by many Muslims as being guilty of *cultural treason.* Rushdie had not merely rejected Islam; nor had he merely disagreed with it. Almost unanimously Muslims who had read the book concluded that Rushdie had *abused* Islam. What is more, he had been lionized, praised, and lavishly rewarded and financed by outright enemies and hostile critics of Islam.

Islam is not unique in regarding attack on religion as a threat to the state. Scottish law until the eighteenth century made blasphemy not only a crime but also a capital offense. The Scottish heritage went back at least to the Mosaic Law on one side and the legacy of Roman Emperor Justinian I on the other. Mosaic law decreed death by stoning as the penalty for the blasphemer. Emperor Justinian—who reigned from 527 to 565 A.D.—reinforced the death penalty for blasphemy.

In Britain today blasphemy is no longer a capital crime—but it is still both a statutory and common law offense. It has been recognized as an offense under the common law from the seventh century. But blasphemy in Britain is only applicable to Christianity. On February 20, 1989, sections of the British press raised the question of whether it was not time that blasphemy in Britain was also defined in reference to Judaism, Hinduism, and Islam, all of which are well represented in the British population. (pp. 349-50)

Perhaps the most fundamental blasphemy in Salman Rushdie's novel concerns the very title, **The Satanic Verses.** To explain the issues to people in the Western world let us first place the Qur'an, the holy book of Islam, in the context of world literature. It is not just Rushdie's book which should concern Western historians or lovers of literature. It is also the Qur'an itself as a work of art—the book which Rushdie virtually abuses by calling it "the Satanic Verses."

The Qur'an is the most widely read book in its original language in human history. The Bible is the most widely read book in translation. The Bible is also a multi-authored work. But the Qur'an is in a class by itself as a book recited by millions of believers, five times every day, in the very language in which it was first written.

If Rushdie had simply said that the Qur'an was the work of the Prophet Muhammad and not the word of God, he would have been repeating the normal interpretation of non-Muslims. Making the Qur'an the work of human genius, rather than divine inspiration, would still put the Prophet Muhammad alongside William Shakespeare as the two most influential literary figures of all time—with one vital difference. The Qur'an is read by a hundred thousand times more people than are the plays of Shakespeare.

Yet, as ordinary human beings, there are similarities between the Prophet and the Bard. Both were of relatively limited formal education, and yet their names are associated with literary works of immense influence. The plays of Shakespeare have greatly enriched the idiomatic heritage of the English language. The Qur'an has had an even greater impact on the Arabic language—stabilizing its pace and change and diversifying its rhythms, images, and power. There is a religious doctrine in Islam to the effect that the Qur'an is impossible to imitate. And yet no book in history has been subjected to more attempts at imitation. (pp. 350-51)

The Qur'an is also a work of immense learning and versatility—obviously sensitized to the legacies of both the Christian Bible and the Jewish Torah. In addition it shows a capacity for direct legislative change, moral reform, refinement of rules of etiquette, and the power of poetry. Could such a book

have been written by a camel herder and traveling salesman? (pp. 351-52)

No other Arab of Muhammad's day has been put forward as the "real" author of the Qur'an. To Muslims, the secret of the miracle is, quite simply, that it is the word of God.

Salman Rushdie's blasphemy does not lie in his saying that the Qur'an is the work of Muhammad. The blasphemy lies more in Rushdie's suggestion that it is the work of the Devil. By the term "Satanic Verses" he refers to more than an alleged incident in the history of Islamic revelation. Rushdie suggests that Muhammad is incapable of distinguishing between inspiration from an angel and inspiration from the devil. Indeed, Rushdie gives the Prophet a name which Rushdie himself describes as "the Devil's synonym: *Mahound.*"

In the English language the second greatest poet after Shakespeare is widely regarded to be John Milton. One thing which Milton's *Paradise Lost* has in common with the Qur'an is that both great works were recited orally before they were written. Milton dictated much of *Paradise Lost* because he was blind; the Prophet Muhammad dictated the Qur'an because he could not himself read or write.

Rushdie suggests that Muhammad was not only incapable of distinguishing between what had been inspired by the Devil and what had come from the Archangel; he could not even distinguish between what he himself had dictated to the scribe and what the inscriber had mischievously substituted. . . . . In the end the scribe carried it too far, and Mahound's suspicion was aroused. But the novelist Rushdie has already done his mischief of creating doubt about the authenticity of the Qur'an even as Muhammad's own work, let alone as the word of God.

But is this any different from suggesting that parts of *Paradise Lost* were not Milton's genius but mischievous substitutions by the person who was taking down the dictation?

One central difference is that *Paradise Lost* is not the equivalent of a constitution of a country, whereas the Qur'an is the ultimate constitution of the community of believers. American political morality expects its citizens to be ready to "uphold, protect and defend the Constitution of the United States." Muslims expect all believers to be ready to defend the Qur'an as their own ultimate fundamental law.

Rushdie not only casts doubt on the authenticity of the source of that fundamental law. He satirizes its rules and attributes fictitious dicta to it:

> . . . rules about every damn thing, if a man farts let him turn his face to the wind, a rule about which hand to use for the purpose of cleaning one's behind . . . sodomy and the missionary position were approved of by the archangel, whereas the forbidden postures included all those in which the female was on top . . .

This is more than suggesting that John Milton did not write *Paradise Lost.* It is worse than alleging that what Americans take to be their Constitution consists of bastardized passages inserted by mischievous scribes still loyal to King George III of England. If American patriotism consists of upholding, protecting and defending the Constitution of the United States, does not undermining and casting doubt on the authenticity of the Constitution come close to being a form of treason?

Americans regard deliberate stepping on their flag, or purposefully urinating on the star-spangled banner, as sacrilege. Each verse of the Qur'an is like a flag to a Muslim. Has Salman Rushdie deliberately urinated on the Holy Book? Has he defiantly defecated on the equivalent of a thousand crescent-spangled banners?

Milton's *Paradise Lost* is partly about Satan as a fallen angel. It is also about the sin of pride and its consequences. In the immortal words of Milton's Lucifer:

> Better to reign in hell than serve in heaven.

Many Muslims believe that Salman Rushdie has shared aspirations with Lucifer in his own "Satanic Novel."

Another issue of the conflict of cultures at the center of the Rushdie debate is the question of comparative defamation. Western laws of libel and slander tend to focus on the *individual,* and seldom on a whole *class* of people. American law is more sensitive to "class action" than British law is, but on the whole it is individuals and institutions rather than groups of people who sue under libel or slander in Western societies.

In Rushdie's novel the question arises whether he has libeled whole classes of Muslims—ranging from Shiite believers (as symbolized by Rushdie's character "the Imam") to the wives of the Prophet Muhammad.

A related difficulty concerns the fact that Western law provides very little protection against libel for those who are dead. If twelve women alive today were portrayed in a novel—under their own names—as the equivalent of prostitutes, they would have some kind of legal recourse. But Rushdie is libeling women who have been dead some fourteen hundred years—the wives of Prophet Muhammad. It is true that Rushdie does not say it was the Prophet's real wives who were prostitutes. He creates prostitutes who adopt the names of the Prophet's wives—whores who play at being the spouses of Mahound. Rushdie uses the trick of a play within a play—like Shakespeare's Hamlet staging a play in order to find out if his uncle killed his father before marrying his mother.

Rushdie suggests that the customers of the prostitutes get additional sexual excitement out of pretending to make love to the Prophet's wives. . . . (pp. 352-55)

Rushdie's game of "a play within a play" is nevertheless a prostitution of the reputations of twelve innocent and respectable women. Had these women been alive Western laws would have protected their reputations. But being deceased for so long, Western law offers no sanctuary.

Is *Satanic Verses* the equivalent of *The Last Temptation of Christ?* In the film Jesus is portrayed as dreaming out his sexual fantasies. The hypothesis is offensive to both Christians and Muslims (since Jesus is a revered Prophet in Islam). But while *The Last Temptation of Christ* is indeed *un-Christian,* it is not *abusive.* Jesus is portrayed as essentially good, even divine. But his goodness is struggling with his humanity as he approaches death. It is almost like the human anguish which made him cry out "Father, why have you forsaken me?" On the whole, therefore, *The Last Temptation of Christ* is far less abusive of Jesus than Rushdie has been of the Prophet Muhammad and his wives.

The real equivalent of comparative blasphemy would be in portraying the Virgin Mary as a prostitute, and Jesus as the son of one of her sexual clients. Also comparable would be any novel based on the thesis that the twelve apostles were Jesus' homosexual lovers, and the Last Supper was their last sexual orgy together. It would be interesting to speculate which of the leading Western writers would march in a procession in defense of the "rights" of such a novelist.

What is clear is that neither the Virgin Mary in the first hypothesis of prostitution nor Jesus and the Twelve Apostles in the second hypothesis of a homosexual orgy would receive much legal protection under Western law of libel, slander or defamation. (pp. 355-56)

I personally have also been censored in Britain and the United States, as well as in South Africa and my own native Kenya. In Program 3, "New Gods" of my BBC/PBS Television series *The Africans: A Triple Heritage,* I start with a bust of Karl Marx. The viewer is supposed to hear my voice saying:

> "Religion is the sigh of the oppressed creature and the soul of soul-less conditions."—So said Karl Marx, the last of the great Jewish Prophets.

The Public Broadcasting System was afraid of offending Jewish viewers. The potentially offending phrase was "the last of the great Jewish prophets"

> Nevertheless, the British viewer heard it.
> Australian viewers heard it.
> Nigerian viewers heard it.
> Viewers in Finland heard it.
> Viewers in Jordan heard it.
> Even viewers in Israel heard it.

But viewers in the United States did not hear me say "the last of the great Jewish prophets". It was censored, in spite of the fact that the deletion made it difficult for me to make the case about "the Semitic impact on Africa" (Jesus, Muhammad and Marx).

But since the series had already been shown in Britain, many American journalists knew about the deletion. I was interviewed nationwide in the United States in 1986 by newspapers and TV programs—including on the issue of "the last of the great Jewish prophets". The President of WETA was attacked at the National Press Club in Washington, D.C., for showing a TV series which had *previously* had the statement "the last of the great Jewish prophets".

No journalist anywhere in the U.S.A. took up the cudgels on my behalf on the issue of my being able to say that Marx was the last of the great Jewish prophets. Originally I expected criticism from my Marxist friends. Marxists might not want to concede that Marx was a "prophet" when he personally saw himself as a "scientist". Marx had repudiated his Jewish heritage—so the Marxists might object to my referring to it. But in America it was not my Marxist friends who were offended—it was my Jewish friends. (pp. 357-58)

Every day of the week something is being censored in the American media. Programs are denied funding for fear of offending advertisers, subscribers, mainstream patriots, mainstream religious zealots, powerful Jews, powerful gentiles. Otherwise reputable publishers turn down manuscripts, edit out ideas, or surgically remove chapters likely to offend powerful groups in the nation. Censorship in the United States is basically *privatized*—as befits a private enterprise system. The state lets the censorship be exercised in the market place by the forces of supply and demand. Freelance censors abound.

What about the Ayatollah Khomeini's death sentence on Salman Rushdie? Surely that is completely outside Western standards of legitimate behavior? What was new about the Ayatollah Khomeini's death sentence was not the idea of murder by remote control—it was the openness with which it was declared. It was worthy of Agatha Christie's famous title *A Murder is Announced.* If Western countries want to kill somebody in some other country, it becomes part of a covert operation. The Central Intelligence Agency or MI5 may take the initiative. The Israelis may fly all the way to Tunis and kill somebody in his bed. Western cinemagoers enjoy James Bond, 007. He is simply an exaggeration of something utterly believable. (pp. 359-60)

As for attempted assassination by bombing, there seems little doubt that the Reagan Administration wanted to kill Muammar Qaddafy from the air in the course of the bombing in Tripoli in 1986. The planes had instructions to bomb what they thought was his residence. In a bid to kill Qaddafy, the Americans killed a lot of other people—and missed their primary target. They did kill Qaddafy's adopted child, though. Was that a consolation prize? In the 1960s the Americans also conspired to kill Fidel Castro. The American attempt to kill Castro may have contributed to the subsequent assassination of John F. Kennedy. Then there was President Reagan's declaration to alleged terrorists "You can run, but you cannot hide." This was a declaration that the sovereignty of other countries was no asylum for enemies of America. The United States skyjacked an Egyptian civilian airplane in international skies because there was a suspect on board. The United States also deliberately violated Italian sovereignty in the course of the same operation.

As for the European Community's collective outrage against the Ayatollah's proclamation of violence by remote control, no such collective outrage was evident when one of the European Community's own members sent agents to blow up *The Rainbow Warrior* in a peaceful New Zealand port. The ship belonged to the environmentalist activist group, Greenpeace, which was protesting France's repeated nuclear tests in the South Pacific. The French authorities decided to teach both New Zealand and the Greenpeace protesters a lesson by sending agents to plant explosives on board the unarmed ship. A Greenpeace member on board was killed as a result of the French sabotage. The whole French exercise was directly intended to silence legitimate protest through an act of state terrorism.

Was the threat of economic sanctions by the European Community ever invoked in connection with the sinking of the *Rainbow Warrior* and the resulting killing of a cameraman? Yes, there was a threat of economic sanctions—but against New Zealand, whose sovereignty had been violated, rather than against France, which had violated it.

New Zealand had caught two of the French agents responsible for the outrage. The agents were tried according to Western concepts of fair trial and due process. The accused were sentenced to long terms of imprisonment. But France secretly threatened economic sanctions against New Zealand if the agents were not handed over for imprisonment under French sovereignty in nearby French colonial islands. And then France blatantly violated the agreement, returned the guilty agents to France and released them. New Zealand's indigna-

tion was kept in check out of fear of losing access to the markets of the European Community as a whole.

The same Community which waxed lyrical in defense of Salman Rushdie and against the Ayatollah's proclaimed "terrorism" stood silently by when one of its own members organized an act of terrorism against a small and friendly country linked to the Western fraternity itself. Nor did the Community show any evidence of outrage when France threatened to deny New Zealand economic access to the Community as a whole if New Zealand refused to bend its own judicial procedures over the convicted French agents.

Four years later the twelve members of the European Community temporarily withdrew their ambassadors from Teheran in the wake of the Ayatollah's threat against Rushdie. Yet they had not threatened even to disgrace France when Paris declared war on a lobbying movement called Greenpeace a little earlier.

When the members of the European Community started returning their ambassadors to Iran in March 1989 after their brief recall, the Ayatollah Khomeini accused the countries concerned of hypocrisy and opportunism. In view of their contrasting attitudes toward the defense of Salman Rushdie's freedom of expression, on one side, and toward the violation of the freedom of Greenpeace to protest, on the other, the European Community did indeed exhibit both hypocrisy and opportunism. The Ayatollah had seen right through their pseudo-moral gestures. (pp. 360-62)

In sentencing Rushdie to death in absentia the Ayatollah Khomeini has understandably been seen as inciting violence against a citizen of another country. And yet Mr. Rushdie is still alive—while twenty other people in the subcontinent in which he was born are dead. Who is inciting whom to violence? Did Mr. Rushdie really fail to see that what he had written was the sort of stuff which could provoke violent demonstrations in the Indian subcontinent? Or did he not care? When India prudently decided to ban the book, Rushdie appealed to Rajiv Gandhi to lift the ban.

But Salman Rushdie and his publishers had been warned about the explosive nature of *The Satanic Verses* by Indian advisors *before* the book was published. Mr. Khushwant Singh, a non-Muslim advisor to Penguin publishers, warned Penguin about the book before publication. He warned that the book could disturb law and order in India. Zamir Ansari, Penguin's representative in India, is reported to have confirmed that such a warning was given. As for Rushdie himself, he was born in India and wrote about the partition of the subcontinent. In a previous book he has shown sensitivity to how easily ordinary people in India can kill each other for religious reasons. Rushdie was probably perfectly aware that a misunderstood article published in *The Deccan Herald,* mistaken as portraying the Prophet Muhammad as an idiot, resulted in riots and the death of 50 people.

Even without being published in India, *The Satanic Verses* has already killed more than a dozen people in Rushdie's country of birth. It has also caused deaths in Pakistan. Had it been actually published in India, casualty numbers would have gone up ten times. Part of the price of having the world transformed into a global village is that incitement can become transterritorial. The West is quite used to destabilization by remote control—incitement to collective violence. The U.S. could destabilize Salvador Allende's Chile—and have the incitement confirmed by President Ford and Secretary of State Henry Kissinger. Iran's nationalist revolution under Muhammad Musaddeq in the 1950s was sabotaged by the Central Intelligence Agency of the U.S.A.—with its own brand of incitement to violence. Moussadeq fell—and the Shah was restored. Both South Africa and Israel incite violence among some of their neighbors.

The Indian Government's ban on *Satanic Verses* has been supported by a large number of distinguished Hindu, Sikh, Christian, as well as Muslim intellectuals of the country. A letter to *The Indian Post* was signed by J. P. Dixit, Nissim Ezekiel, Jean Kalgutker, Vrinda Nabar, Vaskar Nandy, V. Raman, Ashim Roy. Was India's ban of the book a case of building a repressive society? *The Times of India* answers:

> No, dear Rushdie, we do not wish to build a repressive India. On the contrary, we are trying our best to build a liberal India where we can all breathe freely. But in order to build such an India, we have to preserve the India that exists. That may not be a pretty India. But this is the only India we possess.

In Black Africa one could risk publishing *The Satanic Verses* in a country like Senegal—although the country is 80 percent Muslim. But its publication in Nigeria would be a risk—though the country is only about 50 percent Muslim. The serialization of the book in a Christian-owned newspaper in Nigeria could precipitate riots.

The Satanic Verses: Is it the most divisive book in world politics since Hitler's *Mein Kampf*? Of course Hitler's book was *anti-Jewish* while *The Satanic Verses* is *anti-Muslim*. Hitler had political aspirations—while Rushdie's ambitions seem to be basically literary and mercenary. But fundamentally the two books are works of alienation and divisive in intent and in impact.

In protest the Jews of the U.S.A. should have done more to burn *Mein Kampf*. Had I been present and old enough I would have joined them. In the mid-1920s Hitler described himself as a writer. Royalties for his book and fees for newspaper articles were his principle source of income. His tax returns from 1925 to 1929 give figures which approximated closely his income from *Mein Kampf*.

But *Mein Kampf* did not become a political bestseller until after Hitler came to power. Hitler's original title was *Four and a Half Years of Struggle Against Lies, Stupidity and Cowardice*. I am not sure if Rushdie sees himself as engaged in many years of struggle against Muslim "Lies, Stupidity and Cowardice." Amy Max Amann—who was to publish Hitler's book—summarized Hitler's title to *Mein Kampf* (My Struggle). Rushdie and his publishers compressed their title to *The Satanic Verses*.

If Hitler hurt the Jews, and Rushdie hurt the Muslims, did both dislike the *Blacks* as well? There is no doubt about Hitler's Negrophobia. But are there elements of Negrophobia in *The Satanic Verses* as well?

Here we need to define the point of convergence between *religion* and *racism*. In Medieval Europe the ultimate religious symbol of the devil on earth was Muhammad. The ultimate racial symbol of the devil on earth was the Black man. Islam was the ultimate religious distance away from godliness. Blackness was the ultimate racial distance away from humanness.

Much later Rudyard Kipling portrayed the Black colonial subject as "half devil, half child". For a long time Muhammad was regarded as full devil. The white man later had a name of scorn for the Black man. The name was "nigger". The white man in medieval times also had a scornful name for the Prophet of Islam—the word was "Mahound".

Rushdie claims that just as "Blacks all chose to wear with pride the names they were given in scorn, likewise, our mountain-climbing, prophet-motivated solitary is to be the medieval baby-frightener, the Devil's synonym: Mahound". Rushdie adds:

> That's him. Mahound the businessman, climbing his hot mountain in the Hijaz. The mirage of a city shines below him in the sun.

Rushdie also turns his torch-light on Bilal—the first Black Muslim in history. Rushdie reminds us that the Prophet had seen Bilal being punished for believing in one God. It was like Kunta Kinte being whipped to give up his African name, Toby vs. Kunta Kinte.

Bilal was asked outside the pagan Temple of Lat to enumerate the Gods. " 'One' he answered in that huge musical voice. Blasphemy, punishable by death. They stretched him out in the fairground with a boulder on his chest. How many did you say? One, he repeated one. A second boulder was added to the first. One on one. Mahound paid his owner a large price and set him free".

Bilal became the first great *voice* of Islam. The beginning of a Black vocal tradition in world history—from Bilal to Paul Robeson and beyond. *Black Vocal Power in World History began with Sey-yidna Bilal.*

Rushdie seems to give Bilal credit for his uncompromising monotheism—allegedly more uncompromising than even Prophet Mahound himself. After all, according to Rushdie, Mahound temporarily accepted a Pagan Trinity (three pre-Islamic goddesses—below the Supreme God.) Bilal was dismayed. He exclaimed, *"God cannot be four."* Mahound later reneged on this compromise—regarding these verses as Satanic. Rushdie does not give either Bilal or Islam the explicit credit of being a multi-racial religion from so early a stage. Bilal set the grand precedent of Islamic multi-racialism—fourteen centuries before President Jimmy Carter tried to persuade his own church in Georgia to become multi-racial. Rushdie cannot resist certain epithets against the Black man, Bilal. Rushdie makes a character think of the Black man, Bilal, as "scum . . . the slave Bilal, the one Mahound freed, an enormous black monster, this one, with a voice to match his size".

Baal in the novel is the poet and satirist. Probably Rushdie sees himself in the character Baal. And what does the poet Baal say to the Black man Bilal? "If Mahound's ideas were worth anything, do you think they'd be popular with trash like you?" Bilal reacts but the Persian Salman restrains him. Salman says to the Black man, " 'We should be honoured that the mighty Baal has chosen to attack us,' he smiles, and Bilal relaxes, subsides".

Rushdie gives Bilal a reincarnation as a Black American convert to Islam. This time Bilal is called Bilal X—like Malcolm X. Bilal X seems to follow the leadership of a Shiite Imam in rebellion against a reincarnation of the Prophet's wife Ayesha—this time Empress Ayesha. Bilal X has the same old vocal power of the original Bilal. Under the influence of the Imam the Black American wants to rewrite history. He has been taught to rebel against history—to regard it as "the intoxicant, the creation and possession of the Devil, of the great Shaitan, the greatest of the lies—progress, science, right. . . ."

The Black American's beautiful voice is mobilized against history. Bilal X declaims to the listening night [on the radio]:

> We will unmake history, and when it is unravelled,
> we will see Paradise standing there, in all its glory
> and light.

The Imam has taught the Black American that "history is a deviation from the path, knowledge is a delusion . . ." Rushdie tells us: "The Imam chose Bilal for this [propaganda] task on account of the beauty of his voice, which in its previous incarnation succeeded in climbing the Everest of the hit parade, not once but a dozen times, to the very top. The voice is rich and authoritative, a voice of American confidence, a weapon of the West turned against its makers, whose might upholds the Empress and her tyranny". When Bilal X, the Black American, protested such a description of his voice, and insisted that it was unjust to equate him with Yankee imperialism, Rushdie puts the following words in the mouth of the Imam:

> Bilal, your suffering is ours as well. But to be raised
> in the house of power is to learn its ways, to soak
> them up, through that very skin that is the cause
> of your oppression. The habit of power, its timbre,
> its posture, its way of being with others. It is a disease, Bilal, infecting all who come too near it. If the
> powerful trample over you, you are infected by the
> soles of their feet.

Is Rushdie making fun of African-Americans *generally?* Or is he satirizing Afroamerican *Muslims?* Or is he ridiculing the significance of Malcolm X? But since many Afroamerican Muslims regard Islam as one route back towards re-Africanization, and therefore a point of return to Roots, is Rushdie simply continuing his basic contempt for his own roots?

Kunta-Kinte—if Alex Haley is right—was a Muslim. Alex Haley went looking for his own roots. Salman Rushdie turned his back on his own. To the question whether *The Satanic Verses* is as racist as *Mein Kampf* was, the answer is definitely *not.* But there is an undercurrent of Negrophobia in both books. The two books are also both anti-Semitic—but directed at different sections of the Semitic peoples. While Hitler was primarily anti-Jewish, there is an undercurrent of anti-Arabism in Rushdie. Rushdie cannot believe that Muslim Pakistanis can be pro-Palestinian without prostituting themselves to Arab governments.

In his earlier book, *Shame,* Rushdie says:

> . . . about anti-Semitism, an interesting phenomenon, under whose influence people who have never
> met a Jew vilify all Jews for the sake of maintaining
> solidarity with the Arab states which offer Pakistani workers, these days, employment and much-needed foreign exchange . . .

There is a school of thought which says that the case for banning *The Satanic Verses* is implicitly a case for banning the Qur'an also. It is like telling Israelis that if they banned *Mein Kampf* they might as well ban the Bible and the Torah. *Mein Kampf* and *The Satanic Verses* are surely hate literature—the Qur'an and the Torah are not.

In 1971, I published a novel in which I put a dead poet on trial in the Hereafter. The charge was that the poet had subordinated his art to his ethnic loyalties—the accused had decided that he was an Igbo first and a poet second. He gave his life in defense of his ancestry—and Christopher Okigbo's Muse died with him.

If Salman Rushdie were to be killed because of *The Satanic Verses,* the charge in the Hereafter could be exactly the opposite to that against the Igbo poet. If Christopher Okigbo before his death had decided that he was an Igbo first and an artist second, Salman Rushdie decided he was an artist first and an Indian Muslim second. If Okigbo had put ancestry before art in sacredness, Rushdie put art before ancestral society in commitment.

But surely *The Satanic Verses* is not a case of art for art's sake? Surely the novel is a work of social and cultural concern? This novel elevates the pleasure of art above the pain of society. Rushdie subordinates the real anguish of Muslim believers to the titillation of his Western readers.

Salman Rushdie should have known that no great culture can be reformed by abusing it. The best approach toward reform is a reordering of values within the existing paradigm. In order to get Americans to vote for equal rights for their women, it would be counterproductive to tell them that their founding fathers—from Washington to Jefferson and beyond—were just male chauvinist pigs (even if they were). It is better to tell Americans that equal rights for women are the logical conclusion of the wisdom and heritage of the founding fathers ("All *men* are created equal" reinterpreted).

Rushdie says that his novel is not about Islam but about migration. But Islam is partly about migration and asylum. The Muslim calendar does not begin with the birth of Muhammad. It does not begin with the death of Muhammad. It does not begin with the first revelation of the Qur'an—the day he became a Prophet. The Islamic calendar begins with the day Muhammad migrated from Mecca to Medina. The principle of *asylum* is celebrated in the concept of the Hijrah.

Is Islam against writers? Rushdie makes his prophet Mahound say that there is no difference between writers and whores. It is true that some writers prostitute themselves. Rushdie himself has been accused of that, because he enriched himself at the expense of the dignity of others. Could Rushdie have written a novel more respectful of Islam while still critical of that heritage? Of course he could. But it would have amused Westerners less. Rushdie himself says in *Shame,* ". . . every story one chooses to tell is a kind of censorship, it prevents the telling of other tales."

Yet Rushdie makes fun of the Hijrah. He makes his poet Baal compose a valedictory ode after Mahound's departure from Jahiliya (i.e. Mecca).

> *What kind of idea*
> *does "Submission" [Islam] seem today?*
> *One full of fear.*
> *An idea that runs away.*

Of course Rushdie did not know that within a few months of publishing those lines, Rushdie himself would go into hiding—and issue a Satanic verse of apology from his hiding place.

> *"An idea that runs away."*

Westerners have been busy looking for motives behind the reaction of Muslims.

— Was Iran's reaction due to a battle between moderates and hardliners?

— Was Rajiv Gandhi courting the Muslim vote in India?

— Was Benezir Bhutto in Pakistan being undermined through Rushdie?

The motives of Salman Rushdie as a writer hardly interest Western political speculators. On the other hand, Muslims are more mystified by the author's motives than by the motives of the demonstrators in the streets of Dacca or Karachi. Westerners find it hard to understand the anger of the demonstrators and of the governmental bans. Muslims find it hard to understand what they regard as the author's cultural treachery. And yet was it motive enough for cultural treason that the author was reportedly paid advance royalties of over $800,000 to burlesque Islam? Other reports refer to 800,000 *pounds* [sterling] as the real sum, which would raise the advance royalties to 1.5 million American dollars well before the book was sensationalized by the death sentence from Iran.

As for the assertion that one cannot be indignant about a book unless one has read it himself or herself, since when? There are millions of believing Christians who have read only a few pages of the Bible. There are also Muslims who can read the Qur'an without understanding it. There are also believing Jews who know only a few quotes from the Torah. Many of those who have theories about the Ayatollah Khomeini do not speak a word of Farsi. How many know from direct experience that Khomeini has really passed that death sentence on Rushdie? What about those indignant Muslims who *have* read the book? There is the assumption that all Muslim critics of Rushdie must be ignorant of the English language or incapable of understanding great literature.

A religion with the most *sacralized* of all books in history is sensitized to the possibility of *profane* books. Why is the Qur'an the most sacralized of all books?

> (a) It is viewed by a billion human beings as the *direct* word of God: (Not the gospel according to Mark, Matthew, etc.).
>
> (b) It is used five times every day in formal worship—by the bus stop in Indonesia, at the market place in Karachi, in the grain field in Nigeria, at school in Turkey, as well as in the mosque in Syria.
>
> (c) The Qur'an is a miracle of the *non-literate person* articulating the most widely-read book in its original language in history.
>
> (d) The Qur'an has had a stabilizing effect on the Arabic language. It has combined the doctrine of inimitability with the magnet of attempted imitation.

But when all is said and done, Muslims should appeal to the Ayatollah Khomeini to lift the death sentence—and substitute at worst a curse instead. *La-ana-Mal-un. Maghdhub Al-ayhi.* If really necessary, a spiritual sentence of a curse rather than a physical sentence of death would be more appropriate. Better still, leave Salman Rushdie to Heaven! Yes, *ban the hate literature if need be,* but love the author as a fellow human being. After all, the first word of the Qur'an ever revealed was "Read" (Iqra).

Iqra bi-smi rabbika ladhi Khalaq
Khalaqal Insana min alak.
Iqra wa Rabbukal Akkram
Alladhi Allama bil Qalam
Allamal Insana ma lam yaalam

Read in the name of your Lord who creates men from a
   clot
Read, for your Lord is most gracious,
It is He who teaches by means of the pen,
Teaches man what he does not know.
However, man acts as arrogant, for he considers he is self-
   sufficient.
Yet to your Lord will be the return.

Islam is a religion born out of the imperative to read! In the spirit of that first verse, Muslims should respond by celebrating the written word. Amen. (pp. 362-71)

> Ali A. Mazrui, "Is 'The Satanic Verses' a Satanic Novel?: Moral Dilemmas of the Rushdie Affair," in Michigan Quarterly Review, *Vol. XXVIII, No. 3, Summer, 1989, pp. 347-71.*

MICHAEL GORRA

The briefest of the dreams from which the Bombay film actor Gibreel Farishta suffers over the course of **The Satanic Verses** concerns a house in Kensington in which a "bearded and turbaned Imam" in exile plans the overthrow of his country's wine-drinking Empress. To the Imam such blasphemy "is enough to condemn her for all time without hope of redemption." He himself drinks only water, "whose purity . . . communicates itself to the drinker." And he is similarly determined to remain "in complete ignorance" of London, that "Sodom in which he had been obliged to wait; ignorant, and therefore unsullied, unaltered, pure." The Imam relies on an "American filtration machine" to purify his water, on the radio his disciples use to broadcast the words ["Burn the books and trust the Book"]. Nevertheless he stands resolute against the idea of historical process that such technology implies, seeing it as the "greatest of the lies—progress, science, rights—against which . . . [he] has set his face. History is a deviation from the Path, knowledge is a delusion, because the sum of knowledge was complete on the day Al-Lah finished his revelation to Mahound."

But this vision of a Khomeini-like absolutism isn't the only place in which Salman Rushdie's novel seems to prefigure the Islamic world's response to it. In the Jahilia chapters that lie at the heart of what has now gone beyond a controversy, the poet Baal defines the writer's job: " 'To name the unnamable, to point at frauds, to take sides, start arguments, shape the world and stop it from going to sleep.' And if rivers of blood flow from the cuts his verses inflict, then they will nourish him." Rushdie's work has always insisted on what in **Midnight's Children** he called the "metaphorical content" of reality. Yet surely he couldn't have expected, or wanted, the wounds his own satire inflicts to come so grotesquely alive. Nourishment? Riots, bombs, bounties, rumors of death squads—they make Baal's thought too grim for me to enjoy the irony, in a way that reminds me that metaphors aren't finally real.

Or are they? Because that literalization seems to me what the quarrel is about. Is the book blasphemous, as so many Muslims have charged? The prophet Rushdie calls Mahound has no use for Baal's satires, compares writers to whores, and has him beheaded. When I first heard the news of the February 12th riots in Islamabad, which seem to have sparked Khomeini's call for Rushdie's death, I was both moved and troubled by the fact that people had died in a protest about a book. I couldn't imagine anyone here taking any single book so seriously, and recalled the comparison Philip Roth once made between the American writer, for whom "everything goes and nothing matters," and the Eastern European for whom "nothing goes and everything matters." Now I am not so sure. I believe there is such a thing as blasphemy. But I also believe that its definition lies so much in the beholder's eye that the punishment for it belongs to God alone, and not to any man who claims to act for Him. As I write that sentence I'm struck by how Western, and how secular, such a thought is. And by the belief that the freedom to have such thoughts matters profoundly even if nothing else does.

It will be years—if ever—before we can separate *The Satanic Verses* from the storm around it. I was disappointed in the book at first. Its vision of good and evil seemed too cartoonish for what turned out to be a story of personal betrayal; as I read I kept thinking that a Jamesian psychological realism would have yielded a far more complex sense of evil in particular than Rushdie's reliance on fantasy was capable of. More tellingly, the book's thousand and one digressions made it seem not so much a loose and baggy as a bulbous monster. A structural mess, a book of brilliant pages—including those in which a group of prostitutes assume the names of Mahound's wives for business purposes, much as strip joints claim to feature "college girls"—but not a whole. The main line of Rushdie's narrative deals with the fractured personal identities of the immigrants' London, that "city visible but unseen" by most whites, where teenagers may call their parents' homeland "Bungleditch," and yet settle into arranged marriages. But what relation did the Jahilia scenes, did the whole of Gibreel's dreams, have to that narrative? I didn't see much of one at first, but the events of the last ten days have made me think hard about that question. Looking back over the novel I'm now struck more by its thematic consistency than by its heterogeneous structure; one could say, in fact, that that heterogeneity is itself the chief element in that consistency. *The Satanic Verses* is a thematic whole, and that whole does indeed offer a radically different vision of the world than that held by any Imam.

At issue are the two chapters in which Gibreel dreams about the birth of a monotheistic religion in the desert city of Jahilia, chapters that so heavily parody Islamic history and tradition as to puzzle most Western readers. The name "Jahilia," for example—to Muslims it means "darkness" or "ignorance" and is used with particular reference to pre-Islamic times. Here, however, the darkness doesn't vanish when Mahound proclaims the Word of the One God. Such sharp anti-clerical satire has long been familiar in the West, but remains foreign to the Islamic world. Too bad. The joke on "Jahilia" isn't one that most Westerners will have the background to get, but the fact that Rushdie uses it anyway suggests that in some ways his ideal audience, however much the novel wounds them, might be precisely those British Muslims who burned his book in Bradford.

Muslims have found any number of other insults and blasphemies in these chapters. But the most important charge against Rushdie is that he suggests the Quran is not the un-created Word of God, as dictated by the angel through the mouth of the prophet Mohammed, but was instead written by man. In Rushdie's novel the character Salman the Persian, who serves as Mahound's amanuensis—and a figure of that name was one of the actual Mohammed's earliest followers—grows suspicious of the way the revelations Mahound claims to receive from Gibreel accord too neatly with what the Prophet has already decided he wants to do. And so he begins to test Mahound, to change the dictation in subtle ways. . . . Salman hopes that Al-Lah, if there is an Al-Lah and if the Book is really His, will not allow Mahound to preach a mistaken Word; hopes that the Prophet will catch the error, and so confirm his faith. But Mahound doesn't notice and the substitutions remain, implying that the Word is not the only one, that the text of the Quran is not only human but corrupt. Or, as Salman says, "It's his Word against mine."

"Why do I fear Mahound?" the polytheistic merchant Abu Simbel asks himself in the first Jahilia chapter. "For that: one one one, his terrifying singularity. Whereas I am always divided, always two or three or fifteen. I can even see his point of view . . ." One one one truth that sees any concept of pluralism, of conflicting and overlapping truths, of Salman's words rather than the Word, as an assault on its authority. It's of no use to say that Rushdie presents these scenes, which in themselves enact the conflict over *The Satanic Verses,* in the form of Gibreel Farishta's dreams, the dreams of a character who's going mad. For Islam's central belief that the Quran is not just divinely inspired but is itself Divine seems to demand a belief in the absolute integrity of words. It posits a virtual identity of words, belief, and action in a way that denies the Western distinction between the metaphoric and the literal, between character and author. If you accept that distinction, then you are already on the way to seeing Salman the Persian's point—already on the way to a belief in free speech.

But polytheists aren't the only ones who are "always two or three or fifteen." So are immigrants, who unlike the Imam can never remain in "complete ignorance" of their new countries, who are never "unsullied, unaltered, pure." Their identity can never be fixed or singular, but is instead fluid, plural, however much they cling to tradition, or however much they try to shed it. But what's lost in shedding one life, one identity to take up another? And how much of one's old identity remains? "A man who sets out to make himself up," Rushdie writes early in the novel, "is taking on the Creator's role, according to one way of seeing things; he's unnatural, a blasphemer, an abomination of abominations. From another angle, you could see pathos in him, heroism in his struggle, in his willingness to risk: not all mutants survive." The Muslim Gibreel Farishta has built a career out of playing Hindu gods in the "theologicals" cranked out by the Bombay film industry. Yet he rejects that multiplicity in his own life—wants only to remain "*continuous*—that is joined to and arising from his past." But the strain of maintaining that continuity, that oneness, proves too much. He dreams at night of the archangel whose name he bears, and his dreams keep leaking into and overwhelming his "waking self." The novel's other main character, the "unnatural" Salahuddin Chamchawalla, has chosen a different sort of singular identity, doing his best to shed his Indianness and remake himself as an Englishman. (p. 12)

Rushdie's character Zeeny Vakil has written a book attacking India's

> . . . confining myth of authenticity, that folkloristic straitjacket which she sought to replace by an

ethic of historically validated eclecticism, for was not the entire national culture based on the principle of borrowing whatever clothes seemed to fit, Aryan, Mughal, British, take-the-best-and-leave-the-rest?

In *The Satanic Verses* those words stand most obviously as a reproof to Zeeny's friend Saladin, who's sought a different but no less confining "myth of authenticity." But they also describe the eclectic pluralism of Rushdie's vision of Indian identity in *Midnight's Children,* and can serve as well for the bazaar of his style as a whole, in which British diction gets fused with bits of Hindi, with Bombay film slang, with what used to be despised as "babu English." Such prose seems much closer to the inventive energy with which Indians actually speak the language than does the limpid English of an older writer like R. K. Narayan. And perhaps that style can offer a new and liberating model of post-colonial identity. For it encourages us to see that identity as a consciously created pastiche of "whatever clothes [seem] to fit," and in doing so calls into question V. S. Naipaul's concept of the colonial as an essentially unthinking and impotent mimic man, condemned by history to ape the West. But Zeeny's words can also apply to *The Satanic Verses'* vision of what Britain and being British should be, for both native and immigrant. *There Ain't No Black in the Union Jack,* runs the title of the sociologist Paul Gilroy's study of race in England. One of the challenges this novel offers is that it asks us to imagine the ways in which there might be. The sad irony, as Rushdie has noted, is that Muslim protests over his novel will "confirm, in the Western mind, all the worst stereotypes of the Muslim world," and so make that act of imagination a more difficult one for whites and non-whites alike. . . .

What Salman Rushdie has done in *The Satanic Verses* is set fiction against a particularly powerful, absolute, and peremptory myth—a myth that has governed a part of his own life. He has done it as a way of examining a conflict between two mutually exclusive ways of imagining the world: between purity and pluralism, monologue and dialogue, orthodox answers and skeptical questions—the very conflict that *The Satanic Verses* itself has provoked. In Gibreel's dreams, in Jahilia, the conflict takes a religious form; in London, that of examining what, in an interview, Rushdie has called "the discomfort . . . [of having] a plural identity . . . made up of bits and fragments from here, there." One wonders at the obliquity of this, in a writer whose earlier work has been about as subtle as a skyrocket. But it is the same issue throughout, and in fact the different ways in which Rushdie puts that issue serve in the end to underline the novel's essential unity, to emphasize its identity of theme and form.

Salman the Persian's rejection of the Word for words—of the Book for books—has a lesson for us. For it is in his world, and not the Imam's, that Saladin, that we all, must now learn to live. Nothing, paradoxically, demonstrates this better than the "discomfort" with their own inevitably plural identities that *The Satanic Verses* has made so many British Muslims feel. Within the novel, the implicit conflict of values that Rushdie poses between Salman and the Imam is an unequal one. The battle outside will not be so easy. (p. 13)

Michael Gorra, "Burn the Books and Trust the Book" in The Threepenny Review, *No. XXXVIII, Summer, 1989, pp. 12-13.*

DORIS LESSING

[*The statement below is in response to a letter from William Phillips to Doris Lessing about the Rushdie affair.*]

Dear William,

You say you assume I am "stirred" by the Rushdie affair. I hope I am not. Far too many people are "stirred" and vanish into quicksands of hysteria. People I have respected for years as monuments of common sense start emoting in print and on television: there is something in this affair that brings out the worst. . . .

I am an admirer of Salman Rushdie. But when I was sent *The Satanic Verses* I could hardly read it, finding it turgid. I therefore set myself down and reread *Midnight's Children* and *Shame* and found them everything I did before. I decided I would look forward to his next book and forget about *The Satanic Verses.* Then this storm broke.

I have thought Appeals from various bodies emotive and ill-considered, though I signed one of them. The alternative was to frame one of my own, but we who were unhappy with the official Appeals could not do that. One has to support what I suppose we can describe as our trade unions, the Society of Authors, P.E.N., other representative bodies. The main point was, however, made: we support freedom of speech and thought.

This is one of those situations where it is impossible to do right. People who refused to go on television have been accused of cowardice, but they were afraid of the oversimplifications of television. The thousand or so people who signed the big Appeal were described by a distraught Moslem as being "rent-a-signature." If you say you do not admire the book but admire the author, then you are accused of being unsympathetic to his situation. If you say perhaps he should not have written it, then you are against freedom of speech. Salman is reported to have written this book specifically to provoke the fundamentalists, and to air their bigotries. Would he have written it if he had known he would provoke them to this extent? That seems to me a key question, but the answer may have to wait until things have calmed down a bit. If they do. Salman was brought up in a family where the English influence was strong, has been in England since he was a child, at an English public school, and then university. Nothing has been more instructive than to see him on television, and then to see some representative of Islam: two parallel lines, two worlds that don't touch, two sets of assumptions, two civilizations.

The tragedy is that the worst of Islam is being put forward as all of Islam: emotions not felt since the Crusades are surfacing. Yet Khomeini and what he stood for is loathed by most of the Islamic world, which regards his death threats outside Islamic law. Khomeini was, to use old-fashioned language, a wicked man. His rule was marked by mass killings in the prisons, of women and children as well as of men, by mass tortures, by arbitrary arrest—a reign of terror. To say nothing of that terrible war and its cynical brutalities. You could not find a more barbaric regime anywhere in the world. Yet you heard ignorant people talking as if this evil old man and his junta represented Islam, soft-minded people saying that if we believe in freedom of thought we must listen to him. It would help if other Islamic countries would speak out, not only a brave individual here and there. Those of us who have Moslem friends know what they think. This united front of

Islam goes back to the Christian-Saracen Wars, long centuries of them. Surely it is time these frozen attitudes should thaw and new links be made between Christian civilizations and Islamic ones. It is not impossible: the past shows it is not. Once, in Spain, under the Caliphs, in Cordova and Toledo and Seville and other great Islamic cities, Moslem and Christian and Jewish poets and savants lived and worked together, and the civilization they made inspired and influenced all Europe.

Meanwhile, the Rushdie affair rolls on. It has done great damage to this country. People working in the community for better relations with our local Moslems—there are two million of them—say they have been set back ten years, more. It is as if some incomprehensible, alien force has suddenly arisen in our country, and yet it has to be assimilated, accommodated, made part of our culture. I am sure we will do it. When the hysteria has died down. Sometimes it seems as if the whole phenomenon is on some wavelength of unreason, irrationality, that attracts and inflames the like: which does not make it easier to write this letter. . . .

Yours,
Doris Lessing

(pp. 406-08)

Doris Lessing, "On Salman Rushdie: A Communication," in Partisan Review, *Vol. LVI, No. 3, 1989, pp. 406-08.*

BRUCE KING

A striking quotation from Daniel Defoe's *The History of the Devil* prefacing **The Satanic Verses** describes the fallen angel's punishment as exile. In a series of paradoxes he is "confined to a vagabond, wandering, unsettled condition . . . a kind of empire in the liquid waste or air . . . without any fixed place, or space." This epigraph introduces a main concern of the novel—the condition of exile, and such related themes as the problems of living in more than one language and culture, rootlessness, the foreigner's alienation and fear of those with power; the growing awareness that all values are relative, that language and what constitutes history are arbitrary, and that reality itself is unstable. Even the immigrant's process of attempting assimilation is filled with ironies; opposites attract and often change places. The reason that many of our best writers are exiles or immigrants, or have a foot in more than one culture, is that exile and immigration is the condition of the modern world, the condition of radical change we all experience, a reality that seems increasingly speeded up and fantastic. What could be more unlikely and surreal than what has happened to Salman Rushdie since the publication of **The Satanic Verses?**

The most innovative, profound, and amusing of Rushdie's novels to date, **The Satanic Verses** is an almost impossible-to-straighten-out tangle of stories within stories, dreams within dreams, psychotic fantasies, discourses that "leak" into other discourses, parodies, imitations, and ovidian transformations. It is one of the very few metafictional novels written in English to have the punch that comes from the firsthand engagement with politics found in the Magical Realists of Latin America. In places autobiographical, very topical, learned, satiric, journalistic, surreal, outrageous, funny, it is a house of mirrors and a masquerade ball of recurring disguised themes, unexpected allusions, surprising echoes, reincarna-

tions, crazy events, fanatical ideas, unusual parallels. The formalist in me wants to start drawing maps of its structure. How are the Defoe quotations and Rushdie's novel related to *Paradise Lost?* No doubt several doctorates will be earned by tracing the many patterns, annotating allusions, or discussing the intertextuality.

Since Rushdie delights in structural subtleties, it is natural to want to compare Rushdie's novels to those of Nabokov, Borges, and García Marquez. He also has a wry interest in the world of the imagination and the ways imagination may replace or shape reality, and he sketches political allegories within amusing fantasies. Rushdie's **Midnight's Children** created the contemporary English-language Magical Realist novel for commonwealth literature; that national epic revealed both an Indian love for many levels of meaning, as seen by the way events and motifs are repeated in new forms, and also an Anglo-Saxon concern with the immediate real world as empirically known and experienced in terms of matters personal, social, and political. That is part of what got Rushdie in trouble. Among the wild phantasmagoria of tales in **The Satanic Verses** are skeptical parodies of the making of the Koran and of the Prophet Mohammed's idealized rule; there is a brothel scene in which customers fantasize the Prophet's twelve wives. The character who resembles the Prophet is called Mahound (devil). But perhaps more significant among the many exiled characters is an "imam" with "a dream of glorious return . . . a vision of revolution" who thunders "apostate, blasphemer, fraud" about more moderate Muslim leaders and who wants to "make a revolution . . . that is a revolt not only against a tyrant, but against history." For the imam "history is a deviation from the Path, knowledge is a delusion, because the sum of knowledge was complete on the day Al-Lah finished his revelation to Mahound." Most First World metafictions seem to be about writing novels; Rushdie's books are political satires and mirrors of our time. **The Satanic Verses** alludes to and depicts well-known recent events, especially in regard to the immigrant community in Margaret Thatcher's England. The novel is filled with direct and barely disguised references to contemporary writers, politicians, film makers, actors, laws, riots, political protests, police actions, and much else.

Rushdie's novels are usually developed around two apparently contrasting male characters whose lives are intertwined and who represent such opposing polarities as good and evil, cosmopolitan and national, extrovert and introvert. In **The Satanic Verses** Saladin Chamcha, the proper, ethical, upright pseudo-Englishman, literally turns into a devilish fire-snorting goat; Iago-like he maliciously destroys the larger-than-life popular Indian actor Gibreel Farishta by reciting intimate mocking poems (satanic verses) over the telephone, creating jealousy in the foreigner toward his British woman. But it is the injured Gibreel who dreams the scenes that have outraged the Muslims in which the Prophet invents three Koranic verses to placate the powerful religious establishment of his time, and it is Gibreel who imagines the story of Ayesha, a girl (with the name of Mohammed's favorite wife) clothed by butterflies, who, depending upon how you regard it, is an example of faith or of the way new movements demand unquestioning fanatical belief from their followers.

A major theme is that a new belief, a new movement, and even personal revenge requires obsessive single-mindedness. The hijacked airplane blown up by a young fanatical terrorist woman introduces the motif later developed in the Ayesha tale and explored in the Prophet's temptation to compromise (which he rejects realizing that a movement requires purity). Mrs. Thatcher is said to be leading a revolution in which a new class with its ideal of pure capitalism ruthlessly eliminates an older English conservatism. All political and religious movements are ideological, a mixture of good and evil, shaped by the needs of their founders; to succeed they require fanaticism, violence, a rhetoric and discourse that offer hope. How else could the Indian poor go to Mecca if Ayesha cannot make the oceans part to create a pathway?

While analysis in terms of Marxist poststructuralist ideas (Gramsci is certainly an influence) is tempting, the basic story and many tales of *The Satanic Verses* recount a confused, ambiguous conflict between good and evil, which is at the heart of each of Rushdie's novels. Related to that conflict are such themes as how ideas and beliefs are mixed with the desire for power, the way intentions often produce their opposite, how such aspects of life as romantic love are really subjective fantasies, the force of sexual desire, the mutual attraction and repulsion of those of different cultures, and the way basic human emotions (such as jealousy), and prototypical situations (such as losing a wife to a best friend) can be found in various ages and nations. The Indian concept of avatars, in which the same force or god can appear in various manifestations, blends with notions of reincarnation and ovidian metamorphosis; the same characters and events recur in different transformations, times, dreams, imaginings, in films and in the novel's historical and literary parodies. There is both a demythologizing of the past by a secular mind (attempting to understand the Prophet Mohammed in terms of psychology and politics) and a remythologizing since past and present are seen as part of universal recurring patterns. (pp. 144-47)

The notation of many registers of British and Indian usage; the pop, street, radical, even science-fiction vocabulary; the echoes from classic and contemporary literature—all show once more that expatriation and multiculturalism in our time may be more an advantage for a writer than intense familiarity with a locale and participation in a unified tradition or culture. In Rushdie there are multilingual jokes, punning allusions, outrageous Joycean wordplay. The levels keep shifting while words are metaphors existing on several levels of reality and seem to have a life of their own, appearing as patterns without being tied to specific persons or events. *Satanic Verses* descends from James Joyce by way of G. V. Desani's little-known Indian classic, *All About H. Hatterr* (1948; revised 1972), through Foucault, and recent structuralist and poststructuralist theory. But, when Rushdie says that his methods are those of the oral storyteller, he has in mind the way Indian storytellers will recite and vary long complicated cycles of tales in which characters and themes appear, disappear and reappear through countless variations, digressions, and byways while being woven into the pattern. (pp. 147-48)

Since its main characters are two actors, it is appropriate that this is a very visual novel. Many scenes appear written for filming. In the opening pages Gibreel falls through space from the exploded hijacked airliner while posturing and singing as if he were featured in one of those elaborate production numbers common to Bombay musical films. . . . Several of the stories in the novel are, in one of the many puzzling transformations and shifts in levels, later reported as films being made by Gibreel, who (like several contemporary Indian politicians) is famous for playing the parts of gods in those ex-

tremely popular Indian films known as "theologicals." After his supposed death, rediscovery, and return to acting, he appears in "a new type" of theological film which resembles the novel and the controversies that have erupted around it. . . . (p. 148)

Rushdie is correct in saying the passages that Muslims find offensive are the fantasies and dreams of a psychotic character. Gibreel the Indian actor who hallucinates and after falling from a great height into another country is only partly being kept sane by medicine. By the conventions of western literary criticism the views of such a character should not be imputed to the author. But Islamic law forbids *all* representations of Mohammed. The stories within stories are the thoughts of a madman, but the intent is satiric; the passages involved present religious matters of faith seen from a skeptical rationalist point of view. Rushdie has an unusually strong and courageous instinct for conflict with powerful major political figures (Indira Gandhi, the Pakistani government, Ayatollah Khomeini, the British police, even Mrs. Thatcher).

Significant art in modern culture often questions the existing order. While sexuality is no longer a forbidden frontier, two areas still reserved for sacred cows are religion and the Third World. The growth of fundamentalism means that religion has once more become a repressive force in many societies, and therefore it offers the writer a subject to be understood, explored, challenged, satirized. . . . In this novel Rushdie attempts to understand what is wrong, what must be paid, and how the personal too easily becomes confused with the political. Its ethics are not straight-arrow old-fashioned; it meditates on "good" and "power" in a post-Marxist, poststructuralist world in which there are no clear rules. *The Satanic Verses* could be read as an inquiry into praxis. What is the relationship of good and evil to the actuality of making History? What is the difference between excile and being an immigrant? *The Satanic Verses* is not an *Animal Farm* or *1984*, a criticism of the left written from within; but, by including airplane hijackers along with Thatcher and an imam, it opens all political and religious movements to questioning—as can be seen from the antifeminist, radical, black-power demagogue in the novel who is killed by the English police. Us and Them have much in common.

There is an outrageous pun which sums it up. In one of the episodes a Persian scribe called Salman (Rushdie?) tests the divinity of the Prophet by substituting his own words in the Koran. When the Prophet does not comment, Salman loses faith and flees. Asked why he is so certain Mahound will kill him, Salman answers: "It's his Word against mine." A prophecy of our time? The conflict between theocracy and secularization is a struggle over power and freedom. Such conflicts erupt all over the world at present as modernization, which necessarily includes skepticism and relativism, conflicts with the nostalgia that modernization creates for a unified past. The very social, political, and cultural forces that produced Salman Rushdie, a secularized Muslim novelist from India who lives in England and writes in English, have also produced the reaction as represented by the Ayatollah Khomeini. We are all exiles or immigrants. Rushdie is not the only "muslim" writer under sentence of death. Even before the *Satanic Verses* controversy, a letter in a British literary magazine claimed that every new Arab novelist of any stature was banned, living in exile, and mostly dependent on the West for critical appreciation. When Naguib Mahfouz was awarded the Nobel Prize in Literature, his most famous novels were—and remain—banned in Egypt. Those who wish to identify with the Third World by mindlessly repeating "the West versus the rest" slogans ignore that "the rest" is divided and its best writers, rather than being the anticolonial revolutionaries of the past, now criticize the regimes that inherited or seized power. In exploring truth Rushdie criticizes feudalistic and tyrannical Third World regimes along with racism in the West.

The criticism of the Nehru-Gandhi dynasty in *Midnight's Children,* the satire on the Pakistani elite in *Shame* and the skeptical treatment of religious leaders and the Koran in *Satanic Verses* are natural next steps in what might be described as the tradition of the English-language Muslim novel of India and Pakistan. Ahmed Ali's *Twilight in Delhi* (1940) belongs to the preindependence nationalist period when celebrating the lost glories of Moghul Dehli after the Mutiny of 1857 was understood as an act of cultural and political assertion against British colonialism. But it ends with the rise of Hindu nationalism, which in the colonial period was replacing the Muslims as the likely future of India. Ali's *Ocean of Night* (1960) and Attia Hosain's minor classic, *Sunlight on a Broken Column* (1961), recall the rich decadent culture of the Muslim elite of Lucknow and Oudh during the 1930s and 40s. A society had lost its unity of being; unwilling to adapt to modernization, western education, Hindu nationalism, and demands for rights for women, its leaders will flee India for the supposed religious purity of a newly created Pakistan while millions die in the resulting bloody strife over partition. Zulfikar Ghose's *The Murder of Aziz Khan* (1967) reminds us that those who emigrated north imperialized and destroyed the culture of the Punjab by bringing the sophistication of modern politics, planning, industry, and the languages that go with them to what was still a traditional peasant society. Rushdie's *Midnight's Children* and *Shame* followed by noting the increasing impoverishment of a Muslim culture supposedly purified of Hindu, Christian, and other alien elements and by questioning the legitimacy of Pakistan and in recording the worsening difficulties Islam has had in adapting with any consistency to the modern world, especially to demands by women for equality. Besides questioning the authenticity of modern Islamic fundamentalism and politics these novels, taken collectively, show Muslim men treating their women as whores but demanding of them an idealized purity. The scandal over the brothel scenes in *The Satanic Verses* results from Rushdie's literalizing such hypocrisy. Rushdie's point here, as in *Shame,* is that repression raises desire and fantasy and results in violence and tyranny. A poorly written but significant novel by Mehr Nigar Masroor, *Shadows of Time* (1987), attacks Pakistan's Islamic fundamentalism and intolerance from a woman's point of view. What began as a struggle for Muslim liberation concludes: "She became aware that the truth that had supported her all these years had also disappeared."

The Muslim novelist's evolution from nationalist to critic is explained by the tensions within nationalism. Nationalists attempt to expel the colonizer and restore the dignity of the colonized by organizing for political action a variety of people around a "usable past." This past is a modern creation of folk, peasant, pastoral, and linguistic elements brought together for political purposes to show a people and a nation, worthy of self-rule, upon which alien traditions have been imposed. The engaged colonial writer attacks imperialism through cultural assertion and by protesting against foreign rule and injustice. After national independence governments want to continue the protest and cultural assertion of the pre-independence period as a means of energizing, leading, and controlling the populace; but the writer will become a critic of the regime, finding discrepancies between its rhetoric and the reality. Since the government fails to meet mass expectations, it radicalizes its populace in the hope of deflecting criticism; in the name of unity it censors the opposition. Writers, however, are naturally committed to free speech and to personal freedom; they expect justice and equality. Within nationalism there is increasingly a conflict between free thought and political and cultural unity, a conflict between two forms of modernization, the one experimental and open to change, the other looking to the past as a model. Fundamentalism is a radical traditionalism imposing orthodoxy and order on people who feel threatened by rapid change.

The Satanic Verses shows the conflict between modernization and traditionalism within the Islamic and Third World in the contrast between the exiled imam with his eyes continually on the past and the various immigrants, such as Saladin, who live in a multicultural changing world. But it also embodies the conflict by investigating and questioning traditionalism and the past. We live in an age of large movements of population through immigration, rapid international transportation and communication, global politics, and a world economy in which goods and people continually cross borders. Cultural movements or periods represent significant social, demographic, economic, or political changes; the award of the Nobel Prize in Literature to Wole Soyinka (who has received death threats for defending Rushdie) and the international controversy concerning *The Satanic Verses* tell us much about what may be truly significant to our culture and time. (pp. 149-52)

Bruce King, "Satanic Verses and Sacred Cows," in The Sewanee Review, *Vol. XCVIII, No. 1, Winter, 1990, pp. 144-52.*

SALMAN RUSHDIE

It has been a year since I last spoke in defence of my novel *The Satanic Verses.* I have remained silent, though silence is against my nature, because I felt that my voice was simply not loud enough to be heard above the clamour of the voices raised against me.

I hoped that others would speak for me, and many have done so eloquently, among them an admittedly small but growing number of Muslim readers, writers and scholars. Others, including bigots and racists, have tried to exploit my case (using my name to taunt Muslim and non-Muslim Asian children and adults, for example) in a manner I have found repulsive, defiling and humiliating.

At the centre of the storm stands a novel, a work of fiction, one that aspires to the condition of literature. It has often seemed to me that people on all sides of the argument have lost sight of this simple fact. *The Satanic Verses* has been described, and treated, as a work of bad history, as an anti-religious pamphlet, as the product of an international capitalist-Jewish conspiracy, as an act of murder ("he has murdered our hearts"), as the product of a person comparable to Hitler and Attila the Hun. It felt impossible, amid such a hubbub, to insist on the fictionality of fiction.

Let me be clear: I am not trying to say that *The Satanic Verses* is "only a novel" and thus need not to be taken seriously, even disputed with the utmost passion. I do not believe that novels are trivial matters. The ones I care most about are those which attempt radical reformulations of language, form, and ideas, those that attempt to do what the word *novel* seems to insist upon: to see the world anew. I am well aware that this can be a hackle-raising, infuriating attempt.

What I have wished to say, however, is that the point of view from which I have, all my life, attempted this process of literary renewal is the result not of the self-hating, deracinated uncle-Tomism of which some have accused me, but precisely of my determination to create a literary language and literary forms in which the experience of formerly-colonized, still-disadvantaged peoples might find full expression. If *The Satanic Verses* is anything, it is a migrant's-eye view of the world. It is written from the very experience of uprooting, disjuncture and metamorphosis (slow or rapid, painful or pleasurable) that is the migrant condition, and from which, I believe, can be derived a metaphor for all humanity.

Standing at the centre of the novel is a group of characters, most of whom are British Muslims, or not-particularly-religious persons of Muslim background, struggling with just the sort of great problems that have arisen to surround the book, problems of hybridisation and ghettoisation, of reconciling the old and the new. Those who oppose the novel most vociferously today are of the opinion that intermingling with a different culture will inevitably weaken and ruin their own. I am of the opposite opinion. *The Satanic Verses* celebrates hybridity, impurity, intermingling, the transformation that comes of new and unexpected combinations of human beings, cultures, ideas, politics, movies, songs. It rejoices in mongrelisation and fears the absolutism of the Pure. Mélange, hotch-potch, a bit of this and a bit of that is *how newness enters the world.* It is the great possibility that mass migration gives the world, and I have tried to embrace it. *The Satanic Verses* is for change-by-fusion, change-by-conjoining. It is a love-song to our mongrel selves.

Throughout human history, the apostles of purity, those who have claimed to possess a total explanation, have wrought havoc among mere mixed-up human beings. Like many millions of people, I am a bastard child of history. Perhaps we all are, black and brown and white, leaking into one another, as a character of mine once said, *like flavours when you cook.*

The argument between purity and impurity, which is also the argument between primness and impropriety, between the stultifications of excessive respect and the scandals of impropriety, is an old one; I say, let it continue. Human beings understand themselves and shape their futures by arguing and challenging and saying the unsayable; not by bowing the knee, whether to gods or to men.

The Satanic Verses is, I profoundly hope, a work of radical dissent and questioning and re-imagining. It is not, however, the book it has been made out to be, that book containing "nothing but filth and insults and abuse" that has brought people out on to the streets across the world.

That book simply does not exist.

This is what I want to say to the great mass of ordinary, decent, fair-minded Muslims, of the sort I have known all my life, and who have provided much of the inspiration for my work: to be rejected and reviled by, so to speak, one's own characters is a shocking and painful experience for any writer. I recognize that many Muslims have felt shocked and

pained, too. Perhaps a way forward might be found through the mutual recognition of that mutual pain. Let us attempt to believe in each other's good faith.

I am aware that this is asking a good deal. There has been too much name-calling. Muslims have been called savages and barbarians and worse. I, too, have received my share of invective. Yet I still believe—perhaps I must—that understanding remains possible, and can be achieved without the suppression of the principle of free speech.

You see, it's my opinion that if we could only dispose of the "insults and abuse" accusation, then we might be able, at the very least, to agree to differ about the book's real themes, about the relative value of the sacred and the profane, about the merits of purity and those of hotch-potch, and about how human beings really become whole: through the love of God or through the love of their fellow-men and women.

And to dispose of the argument, we must return for a moment to the actually-existing book, not the book described on the various pamphlets that have been circulated to the faithful, not the "unreadable" text of legend, not two chapters dragged out of the whole; not a piece of blubber but the whole wretched whale.

Let me say this first: I have never seen this controversy as a struggle between Western freedoms and Eastern unfreedom. The freedoms of the West are rightly vaunted, but many minorities—racial, sexual, political—also rightly feel excluded from full possession of these liberties; while, in my lifelong experience of the East, from Turkey and Iran to India and Pakistan, I have found people to be every bit as passionate for freedom as any Czech, Rumanian, German, Hungarian, or Pole.

How is freedom gained? It is taken: never given. To be free, you must first assume your right to freedom. In writing *The Satanic Verses,* I wrote from the assumption that I was, and am, a free man.

What is freedom of expression? Without the freedom to offend, it ceases to exist. Without the freedom to challenge, even to satirise all orthodoxies, including religious orthodoxies, it ceases to exist. *The Satanic Verses* is, in part, a secular man's reckoning with the religious spirit. It is by no means always hostile to faith. "If we write in such a way as to pre-judge such belief as in some way deluded or false, then are we not guilty of elitism, of imposing our world-view on the masses?" asks one of its Indian characters. Yet the novel does contain doubts, uncertainties, even shocks that may well not be to the liking of the devout. Such methods have, however, long been a legitimate part even of Islamic literature.

What does the novel dissent from? Certainly not from people's right to faith, though I have none. It dissents most clearly from imposed orthodoxies *of all types,* from the view that the world is quite clearly This and not That. It dissents from the end of debate. Hindu communalist sectarianism, the kind of Sikh terrorism that blows up planes, the fatuousnesses of Christian creationism are dissented from as well as the narrower definitions of Islam. But such dissent is a long way from "insults and abuse." I do not believe that most of the Muslims I know would have any trouble with it.

What they have trouble with are statements like these: "He calls the Prophet Muhammad a homosexual." "He says the Prophet Muhammad asked God for permission to fornicate with every woman in the world." "He says the Prophet's wives are whores." "He calls the Prophet by a devil's name." "He calls the Companions of the Prophet *scums and bums.*" "He says that the whole Quran was the Devil's work." And so forth.

It has been bewildering to watch the proliferation of such statements, and to watch them acquire the authority of truth by virtue of the power of repetition. It has been bewildering to learn that people, millions upon millions of people, have been willing to judge **The Satanic Verses** and its author, without reading it, without finding out what manner of man this fellow might be, on the basis of such allegations as these.

The Satanic Verses is the story of two painfully divided selves. In the case of one, Saladin Chamcha, the division is secular and societal: he is torn, to put it plainly, between Bombay and London, between East and West. In the other, Gibreel Farishta, the division is spiritual, a rift in the soul. He has lost his faith and is strung out between his immense need to believe and his new inability to do so. The novel is "about" their quest for wholeness.

Why "Gibreel Farishta" (*Gabriel Angel*)? Not to "insult and abuse" the "real" Archangel Gabriel. Gibreel is a movie star, and movie stars hang above us in the darkness, larger than life, halfway to the divine. To give Gibreel an angel's name was to give him a secular equivalent of angelic half-divinity. When he loses his faith, however, this name becomes the source of all his torments. His greatest torments have come to him in the form of dreams. His most painful dreams, the ones at the centre of the controversy, depict the birth and growth of a religion something like Islam, in a magical city of sand named Jahilia (that is "ignorance," the name given by Arabs to the period before Islam). Almost all the alleged "insults and abuses" are taken from these sequences.

The first thing to be said about these dreams is that they are *agonizingly painful to the dreamer.* They are "a nocturnal retribution, a punishment" for his loss of faith. This man, desperate to regain belief, is haunted, possessed, by visions of doubt, visions of scepticism and questions and faith-shaking allegations that grow more and more extreme as they go on. He tries in vain to escape them, fighting against sleep; but then the visions cross over the boundary between his waking and sleeping self, they infect his daytimes: that is, they drive him mad. The dream-city is called "Jahilia" not to "insult and abuse" Mecca Sharif, but because the dreamer, Gibreel, has been plunged by his broken faith back into the condition the word describes. The first purpose of these sequences is not to vilify or "disprove" Islam, but to portray a soul in crisis, to show how the loss of God can destroy a man's life.

See the "offensive" chapters through this lens, and many things may seem clearer. The use of the so-called "incident of the satanic verses," the quasi-historical tale of how Muhammad's revelation seemed briefly to flirt with the possibility of admitting three pagan and female deities into the pantheon, is, first of all, a key moment of doubt in dreams which persecute a dreamer by making vivid the doubts he loathes but can no longer escape.

The most extreme passage of doubting in the novel, in which the character "Salman the Persian"—named not to "insult and abuse" Muhammad's companion Salman al-Farisi, but more as an ironic reference to the novel's author—voices his many scepticisms. It is quite true that the language here is forceful, satirical, and strong meat for some tastes, but it

must be remembered that the waking Gibreel is a coarse-mouthed fellow, and it would be surprising if the dream-figures he conjures up did not sometimes speak as rough and even obscene a language as their dreamer.

Let me not be disingenuous, however. The rejection of the three goddesses in the novel's dream-version of the "satanic verses" story is also intended to make other points, for example about the religion's attitude to women. "Shall He (God) have daughters while you have sons? That would be an unjust division," read the verses still to be found in the Quran. I thought it was at least worth pointing out that one of the reasons for rejecting these goddesses was that *they were female.* The rejection has implications that are worth thinking about. I suggest that such highlighting is a proper function of literature.

Or, again, when Salman the Persian, Gibreel's dream-figment, fulminates against the dream-religion's aim of providing "rules for every damn thing," he is not only tormenting the dreamer, but asking the reader to think about the validity of religion's rules. To those who have felt able to justify the most extreme Muslim threats towards me and others by saying I have broken an Islamic rule, I would ask the following question: are all the rules laid down at a religion's origin immutable for ever? How about the penalties for prostitution (stoning to death) or thieving (mutilation)? How about the prohibition of homosexuality? What of the Islamic law of evidence, which makes a woman's testimony worth only half that of a man? Are these, too, to be given unquestioning respect: or may writers and intellectuals ask the awkward questions that are a part of their reason for being what they are?

Let no one suppose that such disputes about rules do not take place daily throughout the Muslim world. Muslim divines may insist that women dress "modestly," according to the Hijab code, covering more of their bodies than men because they possess what one Muslim absurdly described on television as "more adorable parts"; but the Muslim world is full of women who reject such strictures. Islam may teach that women should be confined to the home and to childrearing, but Muslim women everywhere insist on leaving the home to work. If Muslim society questions its own rules daily—and make no mistake, Muslims are as accustomed to satire as anyone else—why must a novel be proscribed for doing the same?

But to return to the text. Certain supposed "insults" need specific rebuttals. For example, the scene in which the Prophet's Companions are called "scum" and "bums" is a depiction of the early persecution of the believers, and the insults quoted are clearly not mine but those hurled at the faithful by the ungodly. How, one wonders, could a book portray persecution without allowing the persecutors to be seen persecuting? (Or again: how could a book portray doubt without allowing the uncertain to articulate their uncertainties?)

As to the matter of the Prophet's wives: what happens in Gibreel's dreams is that the whores of a brothel *take the names* of the wives of the Prophet Mahound in order to arouse their customers. The "real" wives are clearly stated to be living "chastely" in their harem. But why introduce so shocking an image? For this reason: throughout the novel, I sought images that crystallized the opposition between the sacred and profane worlds. The harem and the brothel provide such an opposition. Both are places where women are sequestered, in the harem to keep them from all men except their husband

and close family members, in the brothel for the use of strange males. Harem and brothel are antithetical worlds, and the presence in the harem of the Prophet, the receiver of a sacred text, is likewise contrasted with the presence in the brothel of the clapped-out poet, Baal, the creator of profane texts. The two struggling worlds, pure and impure, chaste and coarse, are juxtaposed by making them echoes of one another; and, finally, the pure eradicates the impure. Whores and writer ("I see no difference here," remarks Mahound) are executed. Whether one finds this a happy or sad conclusion depends on one's point of view.

The purpose of the "brothel sequence," then, was not to "insult and abuse" the Prophet's wives, but to dramatize certain ideas about morality; and sexuality, too, because what happens in the brothel is that the men of "Jahilia" are enabled to act out an ancient dream of power and possession, the dream of possessing the queen. That men should be so aroused by the great ladies' whorish counterfeits says something about *them,* not the great ladies, and about the extent to which sexual relations have to do with possession.

I must have known, my accusers say, that my use of the old devil-name "Mahound," a medieval European demonization of "Muhammad," would cause offence. In fact, this is an instance in which de-contextualization has created a complete reversal of meaning. A part of the relevant context is on page 93 of the novel. "To turn insults into strengths, whigs, tories, Blacks all chose to wear with pride the names they were given in scorn; likewise, our mountain-climbing, prophet-motivated solitary is to be the mediaeval baby-frightener, the Devil's synonym: Mahound." Central to the purposes of *The Satanic Verses* is the process of reclaiming language from one's opponents. *Trotsky* was Trotsky's jailer's name. By taking it for his own, he symbolically conquered his captor and set himself free. Something of the same spirit lay behind my use of the name "Mahound."

The attempt at reclamation goes even further than this. When Saladin Chamcha finds himself transformed into a goatish, horned and hoofy demon, in a bizarre sanatorium full of other monstrous beings, he is told that they are all, like him, aliens and migrants, demonized by the "host culture's" attitude to them. "They have the power of description, and we succumb to the pictures they construct." So the very title, *The Satanic Verses* is an aspect of this attempt at reclamation. You call us devils? it seems to ask. Very well then, here is the devil's version of the world, of "your" world, the version written *from the experience* of those who have been demonized by virtue of their otherness. Just as the Asian kids in the novel wear toy devil-horns proudly, as an assertion of pride in identity, so the novel proudly wears its demonic title. The purpose is not to suggest that the Quran is written by the devil; it is to attempt the sort of act of affirmation that, in the United States, transformed the word Black from the standard term of racist abuse into a "beautiful" expression of cultural pride.

The process of hybridization which is the novel's most crucial dynamic means that its ideas derive from many sources other than Islamic ones. There is, for example, the pre-Christian belief, expressed in the Books of Amos and Deutero-Isaiah and quoted in *The Satanic Verses,* that God and the Devil were one and the same: "it isn't until the Book of Chronicles, merely fourth century B.C., that the word *Satan* is used to mean a being, and not only an attribute of God." It should also be said that the two books that were most influential on

the shape this novel took do not include the Quran. One was William Blake's *The Marriage of Heaven and Hell,* the classic meditation on the interpenetration of good and evil; and *The Master and Margarita* by Mikhail Bulgakov, the great Russian lyrical and comical novel in which the Devil descends upon Moscow and wreaks havoc upon the corrupt, materialist, decadent inhabitants, and turns out, by the end, not to be such a bad chap at all. *The Master and Margarita* and its author were persecuted by Soviet totalitarianism. It is extraordinary to find my novel's life echoing that of one of its greatest models.

Nor are these the only non-Muslim influences at work. I was born an Indian, and not only an Indian, but a Bombayite—Bombay, most cosmopolitan, most hybrid, most hotch-potch of Indian cities. My writing and thought has therefore been as deeply influenced by Hindu myths and attitudes as Muslim ones (and my movie star Gibreel is also a figure of such interreligious tolerance, playing Hindu gods without causing offence, in spite of his Muslim origins). Nor is the West absent from Bombay. I was already a mongrel self, history's bastard, before London aggravated the condition.

To be a Bombayite (and afterwards a Londoner) was also to fall in love with the metropolis. The city as a reality and as metaphor is at the heart of all my work. "The modern city," says a character in *The Satanic Verses,* "is the locus classicus of incompatible realities." Well, *that* turned out to be true. "As long as they pass in the night, it's not so bad. But if they meet! It's uranium and plutonium, each makes the other decompose, boom." It is hard to express how it feels to have attempted to portray an objective reality and then to become its subject . . .

The point is this: Muslim culture has been very important to me, but it is not by any means the only shaping factor. I am a modern, and a modern*ist,* urban man, accepting uncertainty as the only constant, change as the only sure thing. I believe in no god, and have not done so since I was a young adolescent. I have spiritual needs, and my work has, I hope, a moral and spiritual dimension, but I am content to try and satisfy those needs without recourse to any idea of a Prime Mover or ultimate arbiter.

To put it simply as possible: *I am not a Muslim.* It feels bizarre, and wholly inappropriate, to be described as some sort of heretic after having lived my life as a secular, pluralist, eclectic man. I am being enveloped in, and described by, a language that does not fit me. I do not accept the charge of blasphemy, because, as somebody says in *The Satanic Verses,* "where there is no belief, there is no blasphemy." I do not accept the charge of apostasy, because I have never in my adult life affirmed any belief, and what one has not affirmed one cannot be said to have apostasized from. The Islam I know states clearly that "there can be no coercion in matters of religion." The many Muslims I respect would be horrified by the idea that they belong to their faith *purely by virtue of birth,* and that any person so born who freely chose not to be a Muslim could therefore be put to death.

When I am described as an apostate Muslim, I feel as if I have been concealed behind a *false self,* as if a shadow has become substance while I have been relegated to the shadows. Jorge Luis Borges, Graham Greene and other writers have written about their sense of another who goes about the world bearing their name. There are moments when I worry that my Other may succeed in obliterating me.

During 1989 Britain witnessed a brutalization of public debate that seemed hard to believe. Incitement to murder was tolerated on the nation's streets. (In Europe and the United States, swift government action prevented such incitement at a very early stage.) On TV shows, studio audiences were asked for a show of hands on the question of whether I should live or die. A man's murder (mine) became a legitimate subject for a national opinion poll. And slowly, slowly, a point of view grew up, and was given voice by mountebanks and bishops, fundamentalists and Mr. John le Carré, which held that *I knew exactly what I was doing.* I must have known what would happen; therefore, I did it on purpose, to profit by the notoriety that would result. This accusation is, today, in fairly wide circulation, and so I must defend myself against it, too.

I find myself wanting to ask questions: when Osip Mandelstam wrote his poem against Stalin, did he "know what he was doing" and so deserve his death? When the students filled Tiananmen Square to ask for freedom, were they not also, and knowingly, asking for the murderous repression that resulted? When Terry Waite was taken hostage, hadn't he been "asking for it"? I find myself thinking of Jodie Foster in her Oscar-winning role in *The Accused.* Even if I were to concede (and I do not concede it) that what I did in *The Satanic Verses* was the literary equivalent of flaunting oneself shamelessly before the eyes of aroused men, is that really a justification for being, so to speak, gang-banged? Is any provocation a justification for rape?

Threats of violence ought not to coerce us into believing the victims of intimidation to be responsible for the violence threatened. I am aware, however, that rhetoric is an insufficient response. Nor is it enough to point out that nothing on the scale of this controversy has, to my knowledge, ever happened in the history of literature. (pp. 52-4, 56)

I knew that stories of Muhammad's doubts, uncertainties, errors, fondness for women abound in and around Muslim tradition. To me, they seemed to make him more vivid, more human, and therefore more interesting, even more worthy of admiration. The greatest human beings must struggle against themselves as well as the world. I never doubted Muhammad's greatness, nor, I believe, is the "Mahound" of my novel belittled by being portrayed as human.

He did it on purpose is one of the strangest accusations ever levelled at a writer. Of course I did it on purpose. The question is, and it is what I have tried to answer: what is the "it" that I did?

What I did not do was conspire against Islam; or write—after years and years of anti-racist work and writing—a text of incitement to racial hatred; or anything of the sort. My golem, my false Other, may be capable of such deeds, but I am not.

Would I have written differently if I had known what would happen? Truthfully, I don't know. Would I change any of the text now? I would not. It's too late. As Friedrich Dürrenmatt wrote in *The Physicists:* "What has once been thought cannot be unthought."

The controversy over *The Satanic Verses* needs to be looked at as a political event, not purely a theological one. In India, where the trouble started, the Muslim fundamentalist MP Shahabuddin used my novel as a stick with which to threaten the wobbling Rajiv Gandhi government. The demand for the book's banning was a power-play to demonstrate the strength of the Muslim vote, on which Congress has traditionally relied and which it could ill-afford to lose. (In spite of the ban, Congress lost the Muslims and the election anyway. Put not your trust in Shahabuddins.)

In South Africa, the row over the book served the purposes of the regime by driving a wedge between the Muslim and non-Muslim members of the United Democratic Front. In Pakistan, it was a way for the fundamentalists to try and regain the political initiative after their trouncing in the general election. In Iran, too, the incident could only be properly understood when seen in the context of the country's internal political struggles. And in Britain, where secular and religious leaders had been vying for power in the community for over a decade, the "affair" swung the balance of power back towards the mosques. Small wonder, then, that the various councils of mosques are reluctant to bring the protest to an end, even though many Muslims up and down the country find it embarrassing, even shameful, to be associated with such illiberalism and violence.

The responsibility for violence lies with those who perpetrate it. In the past twelve months, bookshop workers have been manhandled, spat upon, verbally abused; bookshop premises have been threatened, and, on several occasions, actually firebombed. Publishing staff have had to face a campaign of hate mail, menacing phone calls, death threats and bomb scares. Demonstrations have, on occasion, turned violent, too. During the big march in London last summer, peaceful counter-demonstrators on behalf of humanism and secularism were knocked to the ground by marchers, and a counter-demo by the courageous (and largely Muslim) Women Against Fundamentalism group was also threatened and abused.

There is no conceivable reason why such behaviour should be privileged because it is done in the name of an affronted religion. If we are to talk about "insults," "abuse," "offence," then the campaign against *The Satanic Verses* has been, very often, as insulting and abusive and offensive as it's possible to be.

I am not the first writer to be persecuted by Islamic fundamentalism in the modern period; among the greatest names so victimized are the Iranian writer Ahmad Kasravi, assassinated by fanatics, and the Egyptian Nobel laureate Naguib Mahfouz, often threatened but still, happily, with us. I am not the first artist to be accused of blasphemy and apostasy; these are, in fact, probably the most common weapons with which fundamentalism has sought to shackle creativity in the modern age. It is sad, then, that so little attention has been paid to this crucial literary context; and the Western critics like John Berger, who once spoke messianically of the need for new ways of seeing, should now express their willingness to privilege one such way over another, to protect a religion boasting one billion believers from the solitary figure of a single writer brandishing an "unreadable" book.

I would like to say this to the Muslim community: life without God seems to believers to be an idiocy, pointless, beneath contempt. It does not seem so to non-believers. To accept that the world, here, is all there is; to go through it, towards and into death, without the consolations of religion seems, well, at least as courageous and rigorous to us as the espousal of faith seems to you. Secularism and its works deserve your respect, not your contempt.

A great wave of freedom has been washing over the world. Those who resist it—in China, in Rumania—find themselves bathed in blood. I should like to ask Muslims—that great mass of ordinary, decent, fair-minded Muslims to whom I have imagined myself to be speaking for most of this piece—to choose to ride the wave; to renounce blood; not to let Muslim leaders make Muslims seem less tolerant than they are. *The Satanic Verses* is a serious work, written from a non-believer's point of view. Let believers accept that, and let it be.

In the meantime, I am asked, how do I feel?

I feel grateful to the British Government for defending me. I hope that such a defence would be made available to any citizen so threatened, but that doesn't lessen my gratitude. I needed it, and it was provided. (I'm still no Tory, but that's democracy.)

I feel grateful, too, to my protectors, who have done such a magnificent job, and who have become my friends.

I feel grateful to everyone who has offered me support. The one real gain for me in this bad time has been the discovery of being cared for by so many people. The only antidote to hatred is love.

Above all, I feel great gratitude towards, solidarity with and pride in all the publishing people and bookstore workers around the world who have held the line against intimidation, and who will, I am sure, continue to do so as long as it remains necessary.

I feel as if I have been plunged, like Alice, into the world beyond the looking glass, where nonsense is the only available sense. And I wonder if I'll ever be able to climb back through the mirror.

Do I feel regret? Of course I do: regret that such offence has been taken against my work when it was not intended—when dispute was intended, and dissent, and even, at times, satire, and criticism of intolerance, and the like, but not the thing of which I'm most often accused, not "filth," not "insult," not "abuse." I regret that so many people who might have taken pleasure in finding their reality given pride of place in a novel will now not read it because of what they believe it to be, or will come to it with their minds already made up.

And I feel sad to be so grievously separated from my community, from India, from everyday life, from the world.

Please understand, however: I make no complaint. I am a writer. I do not accept my condition; I will strive to change it; but I inhabit it, I am trying to learn from it.

Our lives teach us who we are. (pp. 56-7)

Salman Rushdie, "A Pen against the Sword: In Good Faith," in Newsweek, *Vol. CXV, No. 7, February 12, 1990, pp. 52-4, 56-7.*

THE TIMES LITERARY SUPPLEMENT

SALMAN RUSHDIE: TWO STATEMENTS

A year after the death threat issued by the late Ayatollah Khomeini, Salman Rushdie remains in hiding in fear for his life. His publishers continue to be subject to a campaign of intimidation.

By lawfully exercising his right to freedom of expression, Mr Rushdie is committing no crime. However, during the past twelve months, there have been at least a dozen attacks on bookshops. Booksellers in the United Kingdom have reported numerous death threats. Similar threats have been made to Mr Rushdie's publishers and supporters throughout the world. In spite of this, we note a drift in the climate of opinion towards viewing Mr Rushdie's plight with acquiescence and complacency.

We wish to restate that it is the right of all people to express their ideas and beliefs and to discuss them with their critics on the basis of mutual tolerance, free from censorship, intimidation and violence.

On March 2, 1989, over 1,000 of Salman Rushdie's fellow writers around the world signed a statement which appeared on the cover of the *TLS,* and in sixty-one other newspapers and journals in twenty-two countries. The signatories unequivocally supported Mr Rushdie's right to freedom of expression and repudiated the death threat. The principles at stake remain unaltered. Mr Rushdie's fate affects the freedom of us all.

We call upon world leaders and all those in positions of influence to renew their efforts to end the persecution of Salman Rushdie and his publishers.

REZA ALLAMEH-ZADEH (Iran).
ANDREI BITOV (USSR).
BREYTEN BREYTENBACH (South Africa / France).
MARGARET DRABBLE (UK).
AHMAD EBRAHIMI (Iran).
CARLOS FUENTES (Mexico).
NADINE GORDIMER (South Africa).
DAVID GOTTHARD (UK).
GÜNTER GRASS (FRG).
KAZUO ISHIGURO (UK / Japan).
IRAJ JANNATI-ATALE (Iran).
NASSEEM KHAKSAR (Iran).
ESMAIL KHOIE (Iran).
GYÖRGY KONRÁD (Hungary).
HANIF KUREISHI (UK / Pakistan).
JAKOV LIND (Austria).
ARTHUR MILLER (USA).
DANIEL MOYANO (Argentina).
ESMAIL NOORI-AL-LA (Iran).
JUAN CARLOS ONETTI (Uruguay).
PARVIZ OWSIA (Iran).
NASSER PAKDAMAN (Iran).
HAROLD PINTER (UK).
AUGUSTO ROA BASTOS (Paraguay).
ANATOLY RYBAKOV (USSR).
JUAN JOSÉ SAER (Argentina).
AMINA SAÏD (Tunisia).
WOLE SOYINKA (Nigeria).
VÉRONIQUE TADJO (Ivory Coast).
AMIR TAHERI (Iran).
MARTIN VAN AMERONGEN (Netherlands).
PER WASTBERG (Sweden).
ARNOLD WESKER (UK).
YEVGENY YEVTUSHENKO (USSR).

International Committee for the Defence of Salman Rushdie and his Publishers, PO Box 49, London SE1.

We, the President and members of the Council of the Royal Society of Literature, deplore the continuing threats to the life of Salman Rushdie. We join with those who say that it is the right of all people to express their ideas and beliefs and to discuss them with their critics on the basis of mutual tolerance, free from censorship, intimidation and violence.

> JENKINS of HILLHEAD (President).
> JOHN MORTIMER (Chairman).
> FLEUR ADCOCK.
> SYBILLE BEDFORD.
> GEORGE BULL.
> JOHN CAREY.
> WILLIAM COOPER.
> VICTORIA GLENDINNING.
> CHRISTOPHER HAMPTON.
> DAVID HUGHES.
> PENELOPE LIVELY.
> JEREMY TREGLOWN.
> RALEIGH TREVELYAN.
> STEVEN WILLIAMS.

Royal Society of Literature, 1 Hyde Park Gardens, London W2.

> *"Salman Rushdie: Two Statements," in* The Times Literary Supplement, *No. 4532, February 9-15, 1990, p. 145.*

□ Contemporary Literary Criticism

Indexes

Literary Criticism Series
  Cumulative Author Index
Cumulative Nationality Index
Title Index, Volume 59

This Index Includes References to Entries in These Gale Series

Contemporary Literary Criticism

Presents excerpts of criticism on the works of novelists, poets, dramatists, short story writers, scriptwriters, and other creative writers who are now living or who have died since 1960. Cumulative indexes to authors and nationalities are included, as well as an index to titles discussed in the individual volume. Volumes 1-49 are in print.

Twentieth-Century Literary Criticism

Contains critical excerpts by the most significant commentators on poets, novelists, short story writers, dramatists, and philosophers who died between 1900 and 1960. Cumulative indexes to authors, nationalities, and titles discussed are included in each new volume. Volumes 1-29 are in print.

Nineteenth-Century Literature Criticism

Offers significant passages from criticism on authors who died between 1800 and 1899. Cumulative indexes to authors, nationalities, and titles discussed are included in each new volume. Volumes 1-18 are in print.

Literature Criticism from 1400 to 1800

Compiles significant passages from the most noteworthy criticism on authors of the fifteenth through eighteenth centuries. Cumulative indexes to authors, nationalities, and titles discussed are included in each new volume. Volumes 1-8 are in print.

Classical and Medieval Literature Criticism

Offers excerpts of criticism on the works of world authors from classical antiquity through the fourteenth century. Cumulative indexes to authors, titles, and critics are included in each volume. Volumes 1-2 are in print .

Short Story Criticism

Compiles excerpts of criticism on short fiction by writers of all eras and nationalities. Cumulative indexes to authors, nationalities, and titles discussed are included in each new volume. Volume 1 is in print.

Children's Literature Review

Includes excerpts from reviews, criticism, and commentary on works of authors and illustrators who create books for children. Cumulative indexes to authors, nationalities, and titles discussed are included in each new volume. Volumes 1-15 are in print.

Contemporary Authors Series

Encompasses five related series. *Contemporary Authors* provides biographical and bibliographical information on more than 90,000 writers of fiction, nonfiction, poetry, journalism, drama, motion pictures, and other fields. Each new volume contains sketches on authors not previously covered in the series. Volumes 1-124 are in print. *Contemporary Authors New Revision Series* provides completely updated information on active authors covered in previously published volumes of *CA*. Only entries requiring significant change are revised for *CA New Revision Series*. Volumes 1-23 are in print. *Contemporary Authors Permanent Series* consists of updated listings for deceased and inactive authors removed from the original volumes 9-36 when these volumes were revised. Volumes 1-2 are in print. *Contemporary Authors Autobiography Series* presents specially commissioned autobiographies by leading contemporary writers. Volumes 1-6 are in print. *Contemporary Authors Bibliographical Series* contains primary and secondary bibliographies as well as analytical bibliographical essays by authorities on major modern authors. Volumes 1-2 are in print.

Dictionary of Literary Biography

Encompasses three related series. *Dictionary of Literary Biography* furnishes illustrated overviews of authors' lives and works and places them in the larger perspective of literary history. Volumes 1-68 are in print. *Dictionary of Literary Biography Documentary Series* illuminates the careers of major figures through a selection of literary documents, including letters, notebook and diary entries, interviews, book reviews, and photographs. Volumes 1-5 are in print. *Dictionary of Literary Biography Yearbook* summarizes the past year's literary activity with articles on genres, major prizes, conferences, and other timely subjects and includes udpated and new entries on individual authors. Yearbooks for 1980-1987 are in print. A cumulative index to authors and articles is included in each new volume.

Concise Dictionary of American Literary Biography

A six-volume series that collects revised and updated sketches on major American authors that were originally presented in *Dictionary of Literary Biography*. Volumes 1-2 are in print.

Something about the Author Series

Encompasses two related series. *Something about the Author* contains heavily illustrated biographical sketches on juvenile and young adult authors and illustrators from all eras. Volumes 1-51 are in print. *Something about the Author Autobiography Series* presents specially commissioned autobiographies by prominent authors and illustrators of books for children and young adults. Volumes 1-5 are in print.

Yesterday's Authors of Books for Children

Contains heavily illustrated entries on children's writers who died before 1961. Complete in two volumes. Volumes 1-2 are in print.

Literary Criticism Series
Cumulative Author Index

This index lists all author entries in the Gale Literary Criticism Series and includes cross-references to other Gale sources. References in the index are identified as follows:

Buchheim, Lothar-Gunther 1918- .... CLC 6
See also CA 85-88

Buchner, (Karl) Georg
1813-1837 .... NCLC 26

Buchwald, Art(hur) 1925- .... CLC 33
See also CANR 21; CA 5-8R; SATA 10

Buck, Pearl S(ydenstricker)
1892-1973 .... CLC 7, 11, 18
See also CANR 1; CA 1-4R;
obituary CA 41-44R; SATA 1, 25; DLB 9

Buckler, Ernest 1908-1984......... CLC 13
See also CAP 1; CA 11-12;
obituary CA 114; SATA 47

Buckley, Vincent (Thomas)
1925-1988 .... CLC 57
See also CA 101

Buckley, William F(rank), Jr.
1925- .... CLC 7, 18, 37
See also CANR 1, 24; CA 1-4R; DLB-Y 80

Buechner, (Carl) Frederick
1926- .... CLC 2, 4, 6, 9
See also CANR 11; CA 13-16R; DLB-Y 80

Buell, John (Edward) 1927- .... CLC 10
See also CA 1-4R; DLB 53

Buero Vallejo, Antonio 1916- ... CLC 15, 46
See also CANR 24; CA 106

Bukowski, Charles 1920- .... CLC 2, 5, 9, 41
See also CA 17-20R; DLB 5

Bulgakov, Mikhail (Afanas'evich)
1891-1940 .... TCLC 2, 16
See also CA 105

Bullins, Ed 1935- .... CLC 1, 5, 7
See also CANR 24; CA 49-52; DLB 7, 38

Bulwer-Lytton, (Lord) Edward (George Earle
Lytton) 1803-1873 .... NCLC 1
See also Lytton, Edward Bulwer
See also DLB 21

Bunin, Ivan (Alexeyevich)
1870-1953 .... TCLC 6; SSC 5
See also CA 104

Bunting, Basil 1900-1985.... CLC 10, 39, 47
See also CANR 7; CA 53-56;
obituary CA 115; DLB 20

Bunuel, Luis 1900-1983 .... CLC 16
See also CA 101; obituary CA 110

Bunyan, John 1628-1688 .... LC 4
See also DLB 39

Burgess (Wilson, John) Anthony
1917- ..... CLC 1, 2, 4, 5, 8, 10, 13, 15,
22, 40
See also Wilson, John (Anthony) Burgess
See also DLB 14

Burke, Edmund 1729-1797.......... LC 7

Burke, Kenneth (Duva) 1897- .... CLC 2, 24
See also CA 5-8R; DLB 45, 63

Burney, Fanny 1752-1840 .... NCLC 12
See also DLB 39

Burns, Robert 1759-1796........... LC 3

Burns, Tex 1908?-
See L'Amour, Louis (Dearborn)

Burnshaw, Stanley 1906- ..... CLC 3, 13, 44
See also CA 9-12R; DLB 48

Burr, Anne 1937- .... CLC 6
See also CA 25-28R

Burroughs, Edgar Rice
1875-1950 .... TCLC 2, 32
See also CA 104; SATA 41; DLB 8

Burroughs, William S(eward)
1914- .... CLC 1, 2, 5, 15, 22, 42
See also CANR 20; CA 9-12R; DLB 2, 8,
16; DLB-Y 81

Busch, Frederick 1941- ... CLC 7, 10, 18, 47
See also CAAS 1; CA 33-36R; DLB 6

Bush, Ronald 19??- .... CLC 34

Butler, Octavia E(stelle) 1947- ..... CLC 38
See also CANR 12, 24; CA 73-76; DLB 33

Butler, Samuel 1835-1902 ...... TCLC 1, 33
See also CA 104; DLB 18, 57

Butor, Michel (Marie Francois)
1926- .... CLC 1, 3, 8, 11, 15
See also CA 9-12R

Buzzati, Dino 1906-1972 .... CLC 36
See also obituary CA 33-36R

Byars, Betsy 1928- .... CLC 35
See also CLR 1, 16; CANR 18; CA 33-36R;
SAAS 1; SATA 4, 46; DLB 52

Byatt, A(ntonia) S(usan Drabble)
1936- .... CLC 19
See also CANR 13; CA 13-16R; DLB 14

Byrne, David 1953?- .... CLC 26

Byrne, John Keyes 1926-
See Leonard, Hugh
See also CA 102

Byron, George Gordon (Noel), Lord Byron
1788-1824 .... NCLC 2, 12

Caballero, Fernan 1796-1877..... NCLC 10

Cabell, James Branch 1879-1958 ... TCLC 6
See also CA 105; DLB 9

Cable, George Washington
1844-1925 .... TCLC 4; SSC 4
See also CA 104; DLB 12, 74

Cabrera Infante, G(uillermo)
1929- .... CLC 5, 25, 45
See also CA 85-88

Cage, John (Milton, Jr.) 1912- ..... CLC 41
See also CANR 9; CA 13-16R

Cain, G. 1929-
See Cabrera Infante, G(uillermo)

Cain, James M(allahan)
1892-1977 .... CLC 3, 11, 28
See also CANR 8; CA 17-20R;
obituary CA 73-76

Caldwell, Erskine (Preston)
1903-1987 .... CLC 1, 8, 14, 50
See also CAAS 1; CANR 2; CA 1-4R;
obituary CA 121; DLB 9

Caldwell, (Janet Miriam) Taylor (Holland)
1900-1985 .... CLC 2, 28, 39
See also CANR 5; CA 5-8R;
obituary CA 116

Calhoun, John Caldwell
1782-1850 .... NCLC 15
See also DLB 3

Calisher, Hortense 1911-.... CLC 2, 4, 8, 38
See also CANR 1, 22; CA 1-4R; DLB 2

Callaghan, Morley (Edward)
1903- .... CLC 3, 14, 41
See also CA 9-12R; DLB 68

Calvino, Italo
1923-1985 .... CLC 5, 8, 11, 22, 33, 39;
SSC 3
See also CANR 23; CA 85-88;
obituary CA 116

Cameron, Carey 1952- .... CLC 59

Cameron, Peter 1959-............ CLC 44
See also CA 125

Campana, Dino 1885-1932........ TCLC 20
See also CA 117

Campbell, John W(ood), Jr.
1910-1971 .... CLC 32
See also CAP 2; CA 21-22;
obituary CA 29-32R; DLB 8

Campbell, (John) Ramsey 1946- .... CLC 42
See also CANR 7; CA 57-60

Campbell, (Ignatius) Roy (Dunnachie)
1901-1957 .... TCLC 5
See also CA 104; DLB 20

Campbell, Thomas 1777-1844 .... NCLC 19

Campbell, (William) Wilfred
1861-1918 .... TCLC 9
See also CA 106

Camus, Albert
1913-1960 .... CLC 1, 2, 4, 9, 11, 14, 32
See also CA 89-92; DLB 72

Canby, Vincent 1924-............ CLC 13
See also CA 81-84

Canetti, Elias 1905- .... CLC 3, 14, 25
See also CANR 23; CA 21-24R

Canin, Ethan 1960-.............. CLC 55

Cape, Judith 1916-
See Page, P(atricia) K(athleen)

Capek, Karel 1890-1938........ TCLC 6, 37
See also CA 104

Capote, Truman
1924-1984 ..... CLC 1, 3, 8, 13, 19, 34,
38, 58; SSC 2
See also CANR 18; CA 5-8R;
obituary CA 113; DLB 2; DLB-Y 80, 84;
CDALB 1941-1968

Capra, Frank 1897-.............. CLC 16
See also CA 61-64

Caputo, Philip 1941-.............. CLC 32
See also CA 73-76

Card, Orson Scott 1951- .... CLC 44, 47, 50
See also CA 102

Cardenal, Ernesto 1925-........... CLC 31
See also CANR 2; CA 49-52

Carducci, Giosue 1835-1907....... TCLC 32

Carew, Thomas 1595?-1640 .... LC 13

Carey, Ernestine Gilbreth 1908- .... CLC 17
See also CA 5-8R; SATA 2

Carey, Peter 1943-............ CLC 40, 55
See also CA 123, 127

Carleton, William 1794-1869...... NCLC 3

Carlisle, Henry (Coffin) 1926-...... CLC 33
See also CANR 15; CA 13-16R

Carlson, Ron(ald F.) 1947-........ CLC 54
See also CA 105

Carlyle, Thomas 1795-1881 ...... NCLC 22
See also DLB 55

Author Index

Author Index

Author Index

Author Index

Thurman, Wallace 1902-1934 ...... TCLC 6
See also CA 104, 124; DLB 51

Tieck, (Johann) Ludwig
1773-1853 .... NCLC 5

Tillinghast, Richard 1940- .... CLC 29
See also CANR 26; CA 29-32R

Timrod, Henry 1828-1867 .... NCLC 25

Tindall, Gillian 1938- .... CLC 7
See also CANR 11; CA 21-24R

Tiptree, James, Jr. 1915-1987 ... CLC 48, 50
See also Sheldon, Alice (Hastings) B(radley)
See also DLB 8

Tocqueville, Alexis (Charles Henri Maurice
Clerel, Comte) de 1805-1859 .. NCLC 7

Tolkien, J(ohn) R(onald) R(euel)
1892-1973 ...... CLC 1, 2, 3, 8, 12, 38
See also CAP 2; CA 17-18;
obituary CA 45-48; SATA 2, 32;
obituary SATA 24; DLB 15

Toller, Ernst 1893-1939 .... TCLC 10
See also CA 107

Tolson, Melvin B(eaunorus)
1900?-1966 .... CLC 36
See also CA 124; obituary CA 89-92;
DLB 48, 124

Tolstoy, (Count) Alexey Nikolayevich
1883-1945 .... TCLC 18
See also CA 107

Tolstoy, (Count) Leo (Lev Nikolaevich)
1828-1910 .... TCLC 4, 11, 17, 28
See also CA 104, 123; SATA 26

Tomlin, Lily 1939- .... CLC 17

Tomlin, Mary Jean 1939-
See Tomlin, Lily
See also CA 117

Tomlinson, (Alfred) Charles
1927- .... CLC 2, 4, 6, 13, 45
See also CA 5-8R; DLB 40

Toole, John Kennedy 1937-1969 .... CLC 19
See also CA 104; DLB-Y 81

Toomer, Jean
1894-1967 ..... CLC 1, 4, 13, 22; SSC 1
See also CA 85-88; DLB 45, 51

Torrey, E. Fuller 19??- .... CLC 34
See also CA 119

Tournier, Michel 1924- ...... CLC 6, 23, 36
See also CANR 3; CA 49-52; SATA 23

Townshend, Peter (Dennis Blandford)
1945- .... CLC 17, 42
See also CA 107

Tozzi, Federigo 1883-1920 .... TCLC 31

Trakl, Georg 1887-1914 .... TCLC 5
See also CA 104

Transtromer, Tomas (Gosta)
1931- .... CLC 52
See also CA 117

Traven, B. 1890-1969 .... CLC 8, 11
See also CAP 2; CA 19-20;
obituary CA 25-28R; DLB 9, 56

Tremain, Rose 1943- .... CLC 42
See also CA 97-100; DLB 14

Tremblay, Michel 1942- .... CLC 29
See also CA 116; DLB 60

Trevanian 1925- .... CLC 29
See also CA 108

Trevor, William 1928- ..... CLC 7, 9, 14, 25
See also Cox, William Trevor
See also DLB 14

Trifonov, Yuri (Valentinovich)
1925-1981 .... CLC 45
See also obituary CA 103, 126

Trilling, Lionel 1905-1975 .... CLC 9, 11, 24
See also CANR 10; CA 9-12R;
obituary CA 61-64; DLB 28, 63

Trogdon, William 1939-
See Heat Moon, William Least
See also CA 115, 119

Trollope, Anthony 1815-1882 ..... NCLC 6
See also SATA 22; DLB 21, 57

Trotsky, Leon (Davidovich)
1879-1940 .... TCLC 22
See also CA 118

Trotter (Cockburn), Catharine
1679-1749 .... LC 8

Trow, George W. S. 1943- .... CLC 52
See also CA 126

Troyat, Henri 1911- .... CLC 23
See also CANR 2; CA 45-48

Trudeau, G(arretson) B(eekman) 1948-
See Trudeau, Garry
See also CA 81-84; SATA 35

Trudeau, Garry 1948- .... CLC 12
See also Trudeau, G(arretson) B(eekman)

Truffaut, Francois 1932-1984 ...... CLC 20
See also CA 81-84; obituary CA 113

Trumbo, Dalton 1905-1976 .... CLC 19
See also CANR 10; CA 21-24R;
obituary CA 69-72; DLB 26

Tryon, Thomas 1926- .... CLC 3, 11
See also CA 29-32R

Ts'ao Hsueh-ch'in 1715?-1763 .... LC 1

Tsushima Shuji 1909-1948
See Dazai Osamu
See also CA 107

Tsvetaeva (Efron), Marina (Ivanovna)
1892-1941 .... TCLC 7, 35
See also CA 104, 128

Tunis, John R(oberts) 1889-1975 ... CLC 12
See also CA 61-64; SATA 30, 37; DLB 22

Tuohy, Frank 1925- .... CLC 37
See also DLB 14

Tuohy, John Francis 1925-
See Tuohy, Frank
See also CANR 3; CA 5-8R

Turco, Lewis (Putnam) 1934- ...... CLC 11
See also CANR 24; CA 13-16R; DLB-Y 84

Turgenev, Ivan 1818-1883 .... NCLC 21

Turner, Frederick 1943- .... CLC 48
See also CANR 12; CA 73-76; DLB 40

Tutuola, Amos 1920- .... CLC 5, 14, 29
See also CA 9-12R

Twain, Mark
1835-1910 .... TCLC 6, 12, 19, 36
See also Clemens, Samuel Langhorne
See also DLB 11, 12, 23, 64, 74

Tyler, Anne
1941- .... CLC 7, 11, 18, 28, 44, 59
See also CANR 11; CA 9-12R; SATA 7;
DLB 6; DLB-Y 82

Tyler, Royall 1757-1826 .... NCLC 3
See also DLB 37

Tynan (Hinkson), Katharine
1861-1931 .... TCLC 3
See also CA 104

Tytell, John 1939- .... CLC 50
See also CA 29-32R

Tzara, Tristan 1896-1963 .... CLC 47
See also Rosenfeld, Samuel

Uhry, Alfred 1947?- .... CLC 55
See also CA 127

Unamuno (y Jugo), Miguel de
1864-1936 .... TCLC 2, 9
See also CA 104

Underwood, Miles 1909-1981
See Glassco, John

Undset, Sigrid 1882-1949 .... TCLC 3
See also CA 104

Ungaretti, Giuseppe
1888-1970 .... CLC 7, 11, 15
See also CAP 2; CA 19-20;
obituary CA 25-28R

Unger, Douglas 1952- .... CLC 34

Unger, Eva 1932-
See Figes, Eva

Updike, John (Hoyer)
1932- ...... CLC 1, 2, 3, 5, 7, 9, 13, 15,
23, 34, 43
See also CANR 4; CA 1-4R; CABS 2;
DLB 2, 5; DLB-Y 80, 82; DLB-DS 3

Urdang, Constance (Henriette)
1922- .... CLC 47
See also CANR 9, 24; CA 21-24R

Uris, Leon (Marcus) 1924- .... CLC 7, 32
See also CANR 1; CA 1-4R; SATA 49

Ustinov, Peter (Alexander) 1921- .... CLC 1
See also CANR 25; CA 13-16R; DLB 13

Vaculik, Ludvik 1926- .... CLC 7
See also CA 53-56

Valenzuela, Luisa 1938- .... CLC 31
See also CA 101

Valera (y Acala-Galiano), Juan
1824-1905 .... TCLC 10
See also CA 106

Valery, Paul (Ambroise Toussaint Jules)
1871-1945 .... TCLC 4, 15
See also CA 104, 122

Valle-Inclan (y Montenegro), Ramon (Maria)
del 1866-1936 .... TCLC 5
See also CA 106

Vallejo, Cesar (Abraham)
1892-1938 .... TCLC 3
See also CA 105

Van Ash, Cay 1918- .... CLC 34

Vance, Jack 1916?- .... CLC 35
See also DLB 8

Vance, John Holbrook 1916?-
See Vance, Jack
See also CANR 17; CA 29-32R

CLC Cumulative Nationality Index

Nationality Index

Nationality Index

Nationality Index

Nationality Index

Nationality Index

CLC-59 Title Index

Title Index